THE
RISE OF
AMERICAN
CIVILIZATION

THE RISE OF AMERICAN CIVILIZATION

By

CHARLES A. BEARD
& MARY R. BEARD

Decorations by
WILFRED JONES

*New Edition
Two Volumes In One
Revised and Enlarged*

THE MACMILLAN COMPANY·NEW YORK

INTRODUCTION

The history of a civilization, if intelligently conceived, may be an instrument of civilization. Surveying life as a whole, as distinguished from microscopic analysis by departments, it ought to come nearer than any partial history to the requirements of illumination. As long as the various divisions of history are kept separate, each must be incomplete and distorted; for, as Buckle says, the philosophy of any subject (that is, the truth of it) is not at its center but on the periphery where it impinges on all other sciences. Dealing with all the manifestations of the inner powers of a people, as well as the trappings of war and politics, the history of a civilization is essentially dynamic, suggesting capacities yet unexplored and hinting of emancipation from outward necessities. By the sharp questions it raises in every quarter it may give new direction to self-criticism and creative energy, aid in generating a richer "intellectual climate," and help in establishing the sovereignty of high plan, design, or ideal. Besides thus representing an effort at understanding a particular social drama in its many phases, the history of a civilization may symbolize a certain coming to maturity in that civilization itself. What adult with any claim to ripeness of spirit would admit belonging merely to one category of history—as warrior, politician, money-getter, novelist, sportsman, mortician, journalist, husband, wife, father, or mother—and aspiring to nothing more? When the dust of the earth became conscious of the dust, a transformation began to take place in the face of the earth.

This is only another way of repeating Walter Pater's convincing argument that a concentration of interest is the condition precedent to the finest flowering of the arts, sciences, philosophies, and life itself "with all its powers of love and joy and admiration." To make a great age of enlightenment and elevation, "personalities, many-sided and concentrated," are necessary, and as long as artists, thinkers, and directors live in isolation, absorbed in specialties and indifferent to the main stream, they fall short of that universality that gives full stature to genius. If the past of a people is conceived of as a mere string of episodes on the level of village gossip or metropolitan society news, how then can complex and complete personalities be nourished and inspired? On what substance can they thrive? On the abstractions of an absolute philosophy? On borrowings from neighbors presumably superior? On what the Greeks and Romans thought worth while, though remote from the realities of the present age? On cornflakes, electric irons, and "values" verbalized in professorial studies?

Recognizing that even the "fine arts" must have roots in soil of some kind, a writer recently asked in one of our critical magazines whether it was desirable for painters to be intelligent. The question is highly pertinent to the theme under consideration here. And in at least one artistic circle the problem thus posed was discussed with light as well as heat. All the debaters who took part in the argument admitted that the mere copying of models never made an artist, that no copy was ever superior in essence to the work of the original master. All likewise agreed that, while a moron might be ingenious in the handling of brush and color, no moron could be a master painter. He must know "something" and possess some powers of discernment. What "something"? Something about the nature of the people and subjects represented, about the goal to be attained in their portrayal. That much was readily conceded. And the general conclusion seemed to be that, given appreciation of older art forms and personal competence, the more a painter knows about the civilization in which he lives and works, its driving forces, its ruling orders, its ambitions, and its apparent future, the better equipped he is for the kind of artistic achievement that adds to civilization. And how can powers of discernment be sharpened? Scarcely by thrusting them into the fog. If the history of a people is a philosophy of the whole social organism in process of becoming, then it ought to furnish material with which discernment can be whetted. That is what Emerson must have had in mind when he advised Americans, in search of the full life, to stand fast where they are and work out their destiny in the place allotted to them by history for the fulfillment of their capacities.

If it is necessary for artists to know something, what is to be said of the makers of beautiful letters and their critics? Can a great novelist chase heroes, villains, and heroines around the eternal triangle without possessing awareness of anything beyond the number three? Even the stoutest apostle of heredity as the determining factor in genius leaves a loophole for environment and the most cautious speculators in the biologic field suspect that heredity and environment are aspects of the same thing. In any case, separated they are meaningless. How then can the novelist ignore his own heritage and that of his characters and plots, at least if he fain would be great or hopes to be declared great by the verdict of mankind, beyond which there is no appeal? Can he draw with superb skill men and women belonging to a landed aristocracy, a bourgeoisie, or a proletariat without knowing about their origins, about the clashes, types, and modes of living prevalent within these several orders? Take feudalism out of Scott, Victorian poverty out of Dickens, modern urban misery out of Zola, and what would be left? Or at all events, what would be the significance of the vestiges? Is the Russian novelist of today writing in the same vein as the Russian novelist of 1898? Will his successors in 1950 write in the manner of today? If not, why not? We cannot escape the conclusion that with changes in civilization come changes in the nutriment which feeds writers and moralists, and in the materials with which they work. Then it follows that an ideal history of a civilization would help to explain writers to themselves, audiences to audiences, actors to actors while disclosing the reciprocal relations of writers, audiences, and actors. The profounder, wider, and more realistic the history, the greater its services presumably to letters and criticism.

In this relation it is well to emphasize the fact that artists and writers live by patronage. It has always been so. The sculptors who carved the gates for the Pharaohs worked with respect to the desires, whims, ambitions, and concepts of power cherished by their patrons. Medieval artists worked for lords and ladies, merchants, and churchmen. Modern novelists also have to remember the market and literary arbiters. It is hardly thinkable that *Elmer Gantry* is purchased in large quantities by the Daughters of the American Revolution. Who then can and does long pursue that pure, chaste, unworldly thing called art for art's sake? Has the greatest art, plastic or verbal, flowed from its unrealities? By the history of a civilization showing patrons of the arts how they came to be what they are, a new environment might possibly be created for the arts, contributing to the conscious evolution of the civilization described and interpreted.

It must not be thought, however, that the history of a civilization is concerned primarily with arts and letters—the so-called cultural accomplishments—assuming that they could be separated without physical violence from the rest of the organism. It is true, there is a tradition to the effect that the makers of arts and letters must speak scornfully of trade and industry, as "material pursuits" to be distinguished from "spiritual endeavors." And by way of reciprocity practical men are sometimes wont to speak of artists and writers as mere luxuries (frightfully near the lunatic fringe) to be tolerated in the name of respectability. But in plain truth the plastic arts are based on the artisan-ship of practice, while modern trade and industry cannot thrive in an intellectual and artistic desert. In the history of social philosophy there is nothing more interesting than the tardy recognition accorded to the fact that modern business enterprise rests upon the whole heritage of western civilization—its religious disciplines, its laws and morals, its crafts and skills, its sciences and arts, its tastes and aspirations. How, for example, could such enterprise operate without mathematics or design? Let a shrewd capitalist erect a factory in an African jungle and then look around for a competent labor supply and an appreciative market, suppose we say, for electrical appliances!

Business enterprise has been built upon a heritage of civilization, and its directors are likely to be civilized just in proportion as they understand the history of their heritage without which they would be as economic infants. More than that. They are in their turn the makers of civilization as well as patrons of the arts. In some mysterious way thought and the materials of life evolve together.

One classic illustration of this is the invention of gunpowder which, at first blush, seems to have no relation to civilization—at least to civilization considered narrowly in terms of art and mind. But, as Buckle points out, gunpowder, with its accompanying engines, made necessary the development of competent specialists in military affairs and released a large proportion of the population of every country from the responsibility for fighting which fell upon all freemen when pikes and bows and arrows were the weapons of warfare. "In this way immense bodies of men were gradually weaned from their old warlike habits and being, as it were, forced into civil life, their energies became available for the general purposes of society and for the cultivation of those arts of peace which had formerly been neglected. The result was that the European mind, instead of being, as heretofore, solely occupied either with war or theology, now struck out into a middle path, and created those great branches of knowledge to which modern civilization owes its origin." Even if overstressed the point is real. Moreover, gunpowder contributed to the downfall of the be-castled, be-walled, shut-off, and embattled feudal aristocracy and to the rise of modern urbanism with its world outlook and rich exfoliations. If a single matter of gunpowder could make such "contributions to civilization," what may be said of the possibilities of electricity in the hands of modern enterprise? Is it not possible that five centuries from now the beginnings of a new moral and intellectual order may be traced to the first whirling dynamo?

Arising from a complex cultural heritage and being itself a maker of culture, business enterprise cannot survive and develop without civilization. It is sometimes fancied that employers of labor desire only robots to attend their engines and wheels. In a system of very restricted production—such as some writers are fond of praising—production of quality for patricians, no doubt it would be possible for capitalism to succeed in a small way with its workers as cogs—assuming that a cog can follow a master design. But a system of mass production in great variety could never appear in a nation of pure robots; could not endure if perchance it were imported. A human robot needs only food and shelter. Designs, colors, shapes, and diversity of commodities are as naught to a cog. If therefore the modern capitalist is as materialistic, primitive, and indifferent to culture as he is often depicted, then by internal contradictions his order of society is doomed to dissolution. If, as claimed, some form of socialism, based on machine industry, lies beyond the present régime, it will certainly take a civilized people to operate it.

Besides being involved in the whole process of human evolution from top to bottom, in war and in peace, as bearers of the heritage and workers in the arts and sciences, women stand in a peculiar relation to the psychological centrum, the market, around which modern industry revolves, and to the periphery where it affects all culture. Although from Cæsar's day onward, strong men have denounced "those things which tend to effeminacy," as a matter of brutal fact without those very things there would be little more than caves and barracks or bare monastic walls in the wide world. However that may be historically, women are now the chief buyers of goods, including letters and arts, thus within generous limits the directors of business enterprise and taste. According to recent estimates, women in the United States pay taxes on more than three billion dollars of individual income annually, receive seventy per cent of the estates left by men, and sixty-four per cent of the estates left by women. In a burst of prophecy, one statistician tells us that, assuming the continuance of the present rate of transfer, all the property in the country will be in the hands of women by the year 2035!

What then becomes of the feminist dictum that a civilization can rise no higher than the status of its women? Whether this contention is true of societies founded on war and priestcraft, it certainly seems to be true of an industrial order—a system of mass production for diversified popular consumption. Leaving aside for the moment women's relations to arts and letters, it must be admitted that their power as the buyers of goods gives them a strategic position in the unfolding of modern civilization. Hence they too must be drawn into the main stream of history as thought.

So much for the constructive services which might be rendered by the history of a civilization. On the side of negation something also may be claimed. By its very nature this type of history is three dimensional, rather than two. Properly executed, it disposes of the idea that nations are moral personalities which have chosen a way of life out of the loftier wisdom or the lower perversity. It is equally ruinous to the conception of civilization as a kind of garment which willful men and women insist on wearing out of ignorance or conceit, or can put on and off at their pleasure. It offers no tribute to chauvinistic vanities, interests, and intrigues and is a constant warning against the perils of treason to intelligence. Treating a given civilization as a growing organism, it is an antidote to two-dimensional surveys based on sights and sounds of wonderment and bewilderment. It bolsters no political grudges, national or international, in the guise of journalistic portraiture.

But we have attached a condition to all these generalizations—"if intelligently conceived and properly executed." The history of a civilization cannot be written by patching together constitutions, statutes, political speeches, newspaper items, private letters, memoirs, and diplomatic notes. The author of such a work must at the outset accept the theorem that "history is philosophy open at both ends" and in selection and construction must wrestle continually with that baffling proposition. The risks of error are staggering; the danger of folly is greater. But what is the alternative for those who are not content to treat life as an inorganic one-thing-after-another and history as a string of anecdotes? Perhaps those who try to find paths, even where there are none, stimulate path-finding if only by their mistakes. Those who build armatures for artists are not without their uses. To raise some kind of benchmark or point of assertion visible to adepts engrossed in specialties may aid in that process of drawing together, out of which the history of all civilizations may arise, contributing powerfully to the enrichment of civilization.

As early as 1752 Voltaire made a plea for this type of history and sought to exemplify it in his work on France under the Grand Monarch. The very title of his book, "The Age of Louis XIV," was significant. He did not call it "The Marvellous and Miraculous Exploits of Louis XIV drawn from Authentick Accounts of His Life and Deeds" nor did he style it "Louis Quatorze: Ses Amours." In his preface he announced his intention to describe "not the actions of a single man, but the character of society." Military achievements Voltaire summarized; affairs of internal government were given due space; ecclesiastical matters were brought into the picture. But to the staples of old history were added commerce, finance, science, and the progress of the fine arts. In another volume of historical studies Voltaire explained: "I wish to write a history, not of wars, but of society; and to ascertain how people lived in the interior of their families and what were the arts they commonly cultivated. . . . I want to know what were the steps by which mankind passed from barbarism to civilization." Excellent as were the argument and the demonstration, writers attuned to tradition have shrunk from the challenge. When a novice, Henry Thomas Buckle, attempted to meet it, his melancholy failures were more widely celebrated than his notable achievements. Every such wreck added to the discouragements that beset historical explorers.

Yet, conceivably, it might be better to be wrecked on an express train bound to a destination than to moulder in a freight car sidetracked in a well-fenced lumber yard.

Contents

VOLUME I. THE AGRICULTURAL ERA

VOLUME II. THE INDUSTRIAL ERA

VOLUME I

THE
AGRICULTURAL
ERA

THE RISE OF
AMERICAN CIVILIZATION

CHAPTER I

England's Colonial Secret

THE discovery, settlement, and expansion of America form merely one phase in the long and restless movement of mankind on the surface of the earth. When the curtain of authentic history first rose on the human scene, tribes, war bands, and armies had already seared plains and valleys with their trails and roads and launched their boats on the trackless seas. Viewed from a high point in time, the drama of the races seems to be little more than a record of migrations and shifting civilizations, with their far-reaching empires—Babylonian, Egyptian, Persian, Abyssinian, Athenian, Roman, Mongol, Turkish,

3

and Manchu—as fleeting periods of apparent pause and concentration in the universal flow of things.

It was not without some warrant, perhaps, that one of the very earliest Greek philosophers, Anaximander, more than five centuries before the Christian era, reached the startling conclusion that the cosmos which he beheld with penetrating eyes was a limitless flood, ever in motion, throwing up new forms and beings and drawing them again into its devouring immensity according to the law of destiny —whirling worlds, swaying tides, growing crops, wandering herds, puny man, and his little systems erected proudly for a day against eternity being but symbols of an unchanging force, the essence of all reality. Conceived even in terms of modern mathematics, a purely mechanistic philosophy is engaging in its simplicity, but we are warned by one recent historian, Henry Adams, that mere motion cannot account for direction or for the problems of vital energy; and by another, Oswald Spengler, that "there is an organic logic, an instinctive, dream-sure logic of all existence, as opposed to the logic of the inorganic, the logic of understanding and of things understood—a logic of direction as against a logic of extension."

More than two thousand years after Anaximander, in the nineteenth century, the German philosopher, Hegel, seeking the solution to the endless changes of history, came to the conclusion that the evolution of humanity was, in its inmost nature, the progressive revelation of the divine spirit. Assuming, as necessary, God the unconditioned, creator and upholder of all, Hegel saw in the kaleidoscopic time-patterns of civilization, strewn through the ages, mere partial reflections of the grand Idea underlying the universe—"an infinite power realizing its aim in the absolute rational design of the world." Nations rising and declining were to him but pawns in a majestic game, each with its mission to fulfill, with its heroes as servants of their epochs carrying out that aspect of the Idea then fated for realization.

And according to this philosopher, the chosen method of the Absolute was movement by thesis, antithesis, and synthesis: every system, every concept, every situation calling forth from the vasty deep its opposite, its challenge; the conflict of the two finally reaching a reconciling synthesis or solution. Though logic would seem to imply that change must be unbroken in the future as in the past, Hegel in fact announced that the goal of the long process had been reached in Germany and the Prussian monarchy: God had labored through the centuries to produce the ideal situation in which Hegel found himself. But that naïve conviction did not prevent his great hypothesis from affecting deeply the thought of the modern age. If historians, working with concepts less ambitious—with concrete relations rather than with ultimates—have been inclined in recent days to avoid the Hegelian creed, theologians and statesmen have continued to the latest hour to find in it the weight of telling argument.

Near the close of Hegel's century, a German economist, Werner Sombart, seeking the dynamic of imperialism, reduced the process to the terms of an everlasting struggle among human societies over feeding places on the wide surface of the earth and over the distribution of the world's natural resources. While this doctrine is too sweeping in its universality, it is not without illustrations. For three thousand years or more the clash of ancient races and empire builders had, as its goal, possession of the rich valleys of the Nile and the Euphrates, where food for congested populations could be won with ease and ruling classes could be readily founded on servile labor. Every one of the strong empires that rose in those fertile regions and enjoyed a respite of security was in turn overwhelmed by a conquering horde which coveted its land and its accumulated wealth. The spoils of industry were the rewards of valor. When the Athenian empire was at its height, no fewer than a thousand cities paid tribute to its treasury and a lucrative commerce, spread over the Mediterra-

nean, swelled the opulence of its merchants. The age of
Pericles had its price. The Carthaginian empire, embracing in its conquered area Northern Africa, Southern Spain,
Corsica, Sardinia and half of Sicily, was first and foremost
a trading state dominated by the idea of gathering from
its subject provinces every particle of wealth that could be
wrested from them by arms or squeezed out of them by
monopoly.

Before the sword of Rome rich Carthage fell. When
the two powers came face to face on the soil of Sicily, it was
the hope of gain as well as fear of death that carried the
vote for war in the Roman assembly. For this we have the
authority of Polybius: "The military men told the people
that they would get important material benefits from it."
In this simple flash is revealed the powerful passion that
drove the armies of the Republic beyond the borders of
Italy and at length in many centuries of almost ceaseless
aggression extended the empire of Rome to the sands of
Arabia and to the snows of Scotland. Perhaps, as that
modern pro-consul, Lord Curzon, has said by way of justification, the dominant motive was a search for "defensible
frontiers"—something not yet found by any military commander anywhere on the globe. Still the noble lord had to
confess in the same breath that Rome, having conquered
a world, regarded her provinces "solely from the point
of view of revenue." Varus, who was sent out a poor man
to govern Syria, amassed a million in two years.

When Rome had grasped more than she could defend,
her fair cities and fertile fields became spoils of victory
for the German barbarians that had long beaten against
her borders. For two hundred years at least the civilization of the Mediterranean world was at the mercy of
migratory Teutons. Finally there were no more Roman
provinces to seize; then feudal war lords employed their
acquisitive talents for the next thousand years in fighting
one another over manors and towns, pausing occasionally to unite against the Moslem, who threatened them

all with destruction. When, eventually, out of this struggle emerged five states—Spain, Portugal, France, Holland, and England—strong enough in armed might and rich enough in treasure to engage in larger enterprise, fortune opened for them, first, the Atlantic and then the world arena in which to deploy their unresting energies. As the grateful merchants of London long afterward carved on the tomb of William Pitt, that brilliant forerunner of modern imperialism, commerce was again united with war and made to flourish.

It was the age-old lure of substantial things that sent the path-breakers of the seas on their perilous journeys— Columbus across the Atlantic in 1492 and da Gama around the Cape to India six years later. Their adventures were only novel incidents in the continuous search for riches. Centuries before, the Romans had carried on an immense commerce with the gorgeous East; in Oriental markets they gathered spices, silks, perfumes, and jewels for the fashionable shops of the Eternal City, and from their treasure chests poured a golden stream of specie to pay for these luxuries. In vain did the stern Roman moralists—Puritans of that time—cry out against the thoughtless maidens and proud dames who emptied their purses buying gauds and trinkets brought at such cost from the ends of the earth. When the Romans passed, their Teutonic heirs gazed upon the spoils of the East with the same fascination that had gripped the grand ladies of the Via Sacra. All through the middle ages a traffic in the luxuries of the Orient continued with increasing volume, enriching the Mohammedan and Italian merchants who served as brokers for the bazaars of the Indies and the shops of Madrid, Lisbon, Paris, Bruges, and London. If the risks of the overland journeys were great, the gains of the dangerous business were enormous.

Inevitably, therefore, an ardent desire to enlarge their profits by direct operations seized the traders of Europe, driving first the Italians, then the Spanish, Portuguese,

Dutch, English, and French, out upon the wide Atlantic in a search for unbroken water routes to the Far East. It is true that Queen Isabella, on yielding to the importunities of Columbus, stipulated in the bond the conversion of heathens to the true Catholic faith; it is true that Catholic missionaries were pioneers in the economic penetration of unknown lands; but in the main the men who organized and commanded expedition after expedition into Asia, the Americas, and Africa had their hearts set on the profits of trade and the spoils of empire. In fact, Spain followed closely the example of Rome, mother of her civilization, when she sent forth military chieftains to conquer, enslave, rule, and exploit.

Nor were the English less eager to gather riches by this process. Sir Francis Drake, who looted his way around the world during the reign of Queen Elizabeth, swept treasure into his chests with a reckless disregard for the rights of private property that would have delighted the Gothic barbarians who plundered their way through the streets of Rome. Captain John Smith was ordered by his superiors to hunt for gold in Virginia and for a passage to the South Seas, where it was thought more booty awaited new vikings. His men too would have enslaved the Indians and ruled a subject population if the fierce, proud spirit of the natives had not baffled their designs. They tried and failed. Even the voyage of the Pilgrims, who fled to America for their conscience' sake had to be financed; and the capitalists who advanced funds for this hazardous venture expected to reap rewards for their aid.

Nevertheless, the story of human migration cannot all be told in terms of commerce, profits, conquest, and exploitation. A search for trade has not been the sole motive that has led wanderers into distant places, an empire of toiling subjects not the only vision before migratory bands. Unquestionably many of the Greek colonies which adorned the Mediterranean fringe rose on the sites of mere trading posts or were planted to make room for redundant populations at home, but others sprang from domestic unrest and from the ambitions of leaders. Moreover, the Greeks went far beyond mere ruling and exploiting; they often peopled colonies with their own racial stocks, reproducing the culture of their homeland, and sometimes even improving on their inheritance. It was in outlying provinces that two of the greatest Greek philosophers, Thales and Pythagoras, set up their schools and it is on the ruins of tiny cities in lands remote from Athens that some of the noblest monuments of Greek taste are found to-day—mute testimony to a faithful reproduction of Hellenic culture.

Not even the German migrations into the Roman empire were purely economic in origin. They have been attributed by some writers merely to overpopulation; but the records that have come down to us do not bear out that simple thesis. The causes were varied, including the pressure of invaders driving Germans from their own lands, internecine quarrels ending in the flight of the vanquished over the borders into Rome, countless tribal wars springing from lust and ambition, and finally the lure of Roman luxury and peace. It was only in the final stages of the German invasions into Rome that direction of the process was taken by the organized war band rather than by the moving clan with flocks, herds, and household goods—the war band that conquered and settled down upon subject populations. Though the Spanish migrations which later carried Iberic civilization out into a new Latin empire eventually encircling the globe were an extension of the predatory operation, the heroic deeds of Catholic missionaries, daring for religion's sake torture and death, bore witness to a new force in the making of world dominion.

Into the English migration to America also entered other factors besides trade and conquest. Undoubtedly the political motive, though perhaps even it had economic roots, was a potent element in the colonization of the Atlantic seaboard, transferring the dynastic and national rivalries of the Old World to the New. Grudges and ambitions that might have flamed up and burnt out on European battlefields now spread round the earth and precipitated contests for dominion in the four quarters of the globe. The settlement of Virginia under the English flag was, among other things, an act of defiance, directed against the sovereigns of Spain and Portugal to whom Pope Alexander VI had assigned the American continents.

In no relation can the religious motive in English expansion be neglected without doing violence to the record, even though dynastic and economic elements were mingled with the operations of Protestant missionaries as they sought to bring Indians into their own fold and to check the extension of papal authority. The first duty of Virginians, declared Captain Smith, was to "preach, baptise into the Christian religion, and by the propagation of the Gospel to recover out of the arms of the devil, a number of poor and miserable souls wrapt up unto death in almost invincible ignorance." Still more significant in English expansion than the work of preachers in quest of souls to save were the labors of laymen from the religious sects of every variety who fled to the wilderness in search of a haven all their own.

Thus it must be said that as faith in Mahomet inspired the armies that carried forward the scimitar under the crescent, threatening to subdue three continents, so faith in Christ inspired the missionaries who served with the forerunners of expanding Europe and mingled with the hopes and passions of the colonists who subdued the waste places of the New World to the economy and culture of the Old. And to this religious motive must be added the love of adventure, curiosity about the unknown, forced sale into slavery, the spirit of liberty beckoning from the frontiers of civilization, the whip of the law, and the fierce, innate restlessness which seizes uncommon people in rebellion against the monotonous routine of ordered life.

§

Among the movements that have scattered the human race far and wide over the surface of the earth, the English migration to America was in one fundamental respect unique. Spain, like Rome, conquered and exploited, but the English, by force of circumstances, were driven into another line of expansion. They had no less lust for gold than had the Spanish, but the geographical area which fell into their hands at first did not yield the precious treasure. They would have rejoiced to find, overcome, and exploit an ancient American civilization—another Mexico or Peru; their work in India revealed the willingness of the spirit and flesh; and yet in the economy of history this was not to be their fate in the New World.

Instead of natives submissive to servitude, instead of old civilizations ripe for conquest, the English found an immense continent of virgin soil and forest, sparsely settled by primitive peoples who chose death rather than bondage. To this continent the English colonial leaders, like the Greeks in expansion, transported their own people, their own economy, and the culture of the classes from which they sprang, reproducing in a large measure the civilization of the mother country. Unlike the Spaniards and other empire builders, the English succeeded in founding a new state, which became vast in extent, independent in government, and basically European in stock. That achievement is one of the capital facts of world history.

How did it happen that the English, who came late upon the imperial scene, alone among the European powers achieved just this result? It was certainly not because they were first in the arts of exploration, war, and colonization. Far from it; the Italians were the pathfinders of the high sea. Three hundred years before the English ventured from their little island home to plant colonies in Virginia, Italian mariners had sailed out through the Straits of Gibraltar, and down the coast of Africa in search of a water route to the fabled markets of the East. It was an Italian, Christopher Columbus, who unfurled the flag of Spain above a motley crew of many nationalities and made the fateful voyage of 1492 that discovered America. It was a Portuguese, Vasco da Gama, who rounded the Cape of Good Hope with the banner of Portugal flying at his masthead, visited the markets of India, and brought back treasure and tales that filled all Europe with commotions.

Before a single English sea captain dared the wide Atlantic, the impetuous Spaniard held in fee the West Indies, ruled huge empires on two American continents, and laid claims to fair domains in the Orient. More than half a century before Francis Drake bore Queen Elizabeth's pennant round the world, the expedition of the indomitable Portuguese, Magellan, under Spanish patronage, on the most perilous voyage in the annals of the sea, had circumnavigated the globe. When Henry VII, stirring from his insular lethargy for a brief moment, bethought himself in 1497 of high adventure beyond the Atlantic, it was an Italian, John Cabot, who took charge of the king's ships, directed the voyage that skirted the shores of Labrador, and gave England her lawyer's claim to the North American continent.

Three years previous to the planting of the first successful English post in America at Jamestown, the French had established a permanent colony at Port Royal on the banks of the Annapolis. Long before a single English ship had plowed the waters of the Indian Ocean or threaded its way among the spice islands of the golden East, the resolute Dutch had visited a hundred Indian ports, established trading factories, and planted the outposts of empire. Slowly indeed did the idea dawn in the minds of Englishmen that, while other nations might carry goods, religion, culture, and the sword across the ocean, they themselves could found great states, occupied and governed mainly by people of their own stock.

§

The success of the English in this form of colonial enterprise was due to many factors of circumstance and policy.
Their insular position freed them from the expense of maintaining a large army and required them to put their money
into a navy for protection. The ships which protected them,
unlike armies, could sail the seven seas, seize distant territories, and defend broad dominions. Early in the reign of
Queen Elizabeth, English statesmen saw with half an eye
the sign of the sea power. They did not evolve a grand
scheme such as Captain Alfred Mahan, long after the deeds,
formulated in a coherent and cogent theory of words, but
they discovered that lands beyond the seas could be permanently held only by a sovereign who also ruled the waves.

Acting on that understanding they laid the foundations
of the navy which struck down the Spaniards in the battle
of the *Armada* in 1588, the Dutch in a long series of conflicts, the French in two hundred years of warfare, and at
last, in the fullness of time, the Germans who grasped for
the trident. It was through the sea power that England
was able to seize and hold the geographical theaters for her
commercial and colonial empire.

Rivalries and jealousies of the continental states likewise
served England's imperial fortune. Slowly, through their
endless strife with rulers on the other side of the Channel,
English statesmen worked out a flexible system known as
"the balance of power," which made for safety at home and
dominion in America, Asia, and Africa. With a skill that
was a marvel to the seasoned chancelleries of Europe, they
played the Dutch against the French, the French against
the Dutch, the Prussians against the French, and the French
against the Prussians.

By such means the governments of Europe that singly or
in combination might have defied England on the sea were
worn down to wrathful impotence. Dutch soldiers allied
with England sent to their graves thousands of Louis XIV's
best men who, if they had lived, might have built securely
the groundwork of a French state in Canada. The power

of France that might have grasped India was broken by the shock of Frederick the Great's picked Prussian troops on the battlefields of Europe.

The political condition of the Continent, as well as its undying rivalries, was another factor that favored English colonial success.   In the seventeenth century, all eastern Europe was landlocked and slumbering in ancient customs or engaged in local conflicts that had little or no bearing on trade and empire.   Central Europe—the geographical region now occupied by Germany, Austria, Italy, and a number of minor states—was in chaos.   Germany was an aggregation of petty feudal domains from which Prussia was just emerging under Hohenzollern mastery.   Italy was not a nation, merely a "geographical expression"—a collection of warring principalities and jealous cities.

For various reasons, moreover, the Atlantic powers that might have frustrated English colonial designs were not prepared to supply people of their own stock to possess the soil of the New World.   Though the Dutch were full of zeal and enterprise in both hemispheres, they were primarily traders, and the Hudson Valley, which was to be their New Netherland, was wrested from them by the English sea power.   France had a population many times that of England, her people were ardent explorers, skillful traders in distant markets, and shrewd managers in commerce; but French monarchs wasted their substance in interminable wars on the Continent which promised the addition of new principalities or the aggrandizement of their families.   The people, the money, the labor that might have made New France a living reality instead of a mere dream, were destroyed in futile fighting which yielded neither glory nor profit.   Moreover, when in 1685 the French king outlawed all his Protestant subjects, he even denied them a haven in his American dominions.

Spain, whose warriors carried her flag around the world and whose missionaries counted no barrier insurmountable, was also a feudal and clerical power rather than a commercial and manufacturing country; her peasants bound to the land in serfdom could not migrate at will to subdue with plow and hoe the soil won by the sword. Indeed while the English colonies in America were but mewing their infancy, the Spanish empire, majestic in outward appearance, was already racked by administrative incompetence and financial decay. Finally, Spain's resolute neighbor, Portugal, great enough to seize Brazil, was too small to overcome on the sea the might of Britain. So auspicious circumstances on the Continent lent favor to the English cause.

§

Something more than strength at sea, ingenuity in manipulating the balance of power, and weakness among neighbors was, however, necessary to the planting of successful colonies across the Atlantic. Essentially that undertaking was civilian in character. It called for capital to equip expeditions and finance the extension of settlements. It demanded leadership in administration and the spirit of business enterprise. Relying largely upon agriculture for support, at least in the initial stages, colonization also required managers capable of directing that branch of economy. In all its ramifications, it depended upon the labor of strong persons able and eager to work in field, home, and shop at the humbler tasks which give strength and prosperity to society—clearing ground, spinning wool, plowing, sowing, reaping, garnering, and carrying on the other processes that sustain life.

Nor was that all. If the European stock was to preserve its racial strains and not fuse with Indians and Negroes, as was the case in large parts of Spanish-America, colonization could not possibly succeed without capable and energetic women of every class who could endure the hardships of pioneer life. Finally, being a branch of business enterprise, it could not flourish without a fortunate combination of authority and self-government: the one, guaranteeing order and coöperation; the other, individual initiative necessary to cope with strange and protean circumstance.

At the opening of the seventeenth century it was England, of all the powers of Europe, that was best fitted for this great human task. The English people were at that time far ahead of their Continental neighbors on the road from feudal to bourgeois economy, a long and dusty road marked by toil, revolution, and war. In concrete terms, just what did this mean? First of all, it meant the overthrow, or, at least, the social subjugation of the feudal and military class—a class nourished by landed estates and committed to the ideal that fighting was the noblest work of man.

With the decline of the feudal order went the downfall of the monopolistic clergy similarly sustained by landed property. Correlative with this social change was the emancipation of the smaller landed gentry, the yeomanry, and the peasants from the rigid grasp of their overlords—a process of individualization which affected women as well as men, giving to agriculture new forms of ownership and management. Finally through the dissolution of the old order there rose to power in England a class of merchants, traders, and capitalists, dwellers in towns, or "bourgs," from which, for the want of a more comprehensive and accurate term, the word bourgeois has been derived to characterize modern civilization.

With the decay of feudal and clerical authority went political and legal changes of vital significance. For the successful direction of business enterprise, the wayward and irresponsible conduct of absolute monarchs, accustomed to tax, imprison, and harass their subjects at will, was utterly impossible. Regularity in economy called for regularity in government—the standardization of the monarchy by rules of accountancy; hence the development of constitutional law—of political self-government for the classes capable of grasping and retaining it. Being secular in nature,

business enterprise was more concerned with the character
and credit of those with whom it carried on transactions
than with their theological opinions; hence a decline in religious intolerance and the rise of the spirit of practical
accommodation.

Historians have long been at swords' points in trying
to explain England's early transition from a feudal and
clerical civilization to a civilian and bourgeois culture. The
Nordic school of scholars delights in ascribing this development to the peculiar genius of Teutonic peoples for freedom and self-government. Its most eloquent advocate,
John Richard Green, who united racial pride with evangelical enthusiasm, saw in local meetings of rude tribes-
men held in the forests of northern Germany—a moot
more ignorant than an assembly of Russian mujiks—the
origin of the English Parliament, the source of popular
liberty. He looked upon it, he exclaimed, as upon the headwaters of a mighty river.

Though once widely accepted, the interpretation of the
Teutonic school has been sharply challenged in recent times,
French scholars, not to our surprise, advancing to throw
down the gage. Leaders among these doubters seek to
demonstrate with great learning that the bulk of the English people are not Teutonic at all, but Celtic—conquered
first by the Romans, then by the Anglo-Saxons, and finally
by the Normans. English institutions, they tell us, are not
Germanic, but a peculiar mixture of primitive Celtic, ancient Roman, barbaric Nordic, and Gallo-Norman cultures.
If the Teutons had a genius for developing parliamentary
government, trial by jury, liberty of speech and press, a free
peasantry, and a triumphant bourgeoisie, why, such critics
ask, was Germany, the original home of the Teutons, one
of the last nations of western Europe to exhibit these elements of civilization? The question is unanswered and
the battle royal over the true key to English social development goes on.

The sober judgment of those given to research rather

than controversy runs against any single explanation of the peculiarities in the institutions of England in the seventeenth century. Modern scholars are inclined to lay stress upon factors more tangible than innate characteristics of the people, namely, the early establishment of a despotic monarchy and the insularity afforded by the English Channel. The stark William the Conqueror and his powerful successors were able in the main to hold in subjection the feudal lords, lay and clerical, and in time weld warring kingdoms, principalities, and dukedoms into a fairly homogeneous society with one law, one administration, and a single language. Happily for the growing nation, the attempts of the baronage to break the Crown by imposing upon it the anarchic restraints of Magna Carta in the interests of inherited feudal privileges were defeated by the magnificent disregard which King John's successors showed for most of the prohibitions written down in that historic document.

Intimately related to this civilizing process was the English Channel—"The Silver Streak"—which, by cutting England off from her warlike and ambitious neighbors on the Continent, protected her government and her people against invading armies. Not after 1066 did a foreign marauder set foot on English soil; not after the close of the Wars of the Roses in 1485 was there a desperate quarrel of feudal lords to paralyze the fruitful occupations of industry in town and country. The king needed no powerful army and military caste to defend his fields and cities; these agencies atrophied, and as they decayed, the monarch who commanded them and the church that blessed them shared in their decline. To borrow Ruskin's images, the mighty were pulled down from their frowning crags; the bourgeois could sit safely on their money bags; and laborers, in their tattered rags, could search for employment far away.

§

When the feudal nobility was definitely broken as a ruling class, the councils of the king and the ranks of the aristocracy were steadily recruited from the lower orders. All English society moved in the direction of shops and warehouses. Henry VIII's ruthless secular adviser, Thomas Cromwell, was the son of a blacksmith; Cardinal Wolsey, who lamented that he had served his King more faithfully than his God, was the son of a tradesman. After the doughty Henry had quarreled with the Pope over Anne Boleyn, he confiscated the lands of the monasteries, and distributed a large part of it among favorites of lower origins, thus sinking the ancient baronage deeper in a welter of newcomers.

Hard beset for money during his disputes with an obstinate Commons, James I further diluted the military caste by selling honors and titles over the counter at a fixed price to merchants and minor gentry who could command the lucre. By the end of the seventeenth century, therefore, only a handful of noble families could trace their lineage back to proud lords and knights who gathered around the standards of Norman kings. The civil war which raged from 1642 to 1649, with its deaths on the field of battle and sequestrations of estates, almost completed the ruin of the baronage. Henceforward, at least, no iron gates shut the aspiring bourgeois from the fair realm of the titled aristocracy or the councils of state.

This flow of forces which brought disaster to barons of war and lords of church and gave titles to rich merchants was accompanied by prosperity and activity in commerce. The insistent note that runs through the writings of continental travelers who visited England in the sixteenth century is that of surprise at the wealth, comfort, and welfare of the middle classes and artisans of English towns. "The riches of England are greater than those of any other country in Europe!" exclaimed the author of the Italian Relations who knew the land ruled by Elizabeth. Explaining this wonder, he added that the wealth in London "is not due to the inhabitants being noblemen and gentlemen; on the contrary, they are persons of low degree and artificers who have congregated there from all parts of the Island, from Flanders, and from every other place. . . . Still the citizens of London are esteemed quite as highly there as the Venetian gentlemen are in Venice." Artisans became merchants; merchants bought country estates; new landed gentlemen took on the style of old families.

To speak summarily, a passion for bourgeois comfort spread everywhere. The whole domestic life of the mercantile classes was altered: stories were added to their houses; the number of rooms was increased; the use of the entrance hall as a sleeping place was abandoned; servants were more sharply separated from the family; beds took the place of pallets; plate and furniture accumulated; contentment with primitive simplicity in living gave way to the quest for material goods.

Now the comfort so prized by the rising middle class was bought with money and, after the looting of feudal wars was stopped, money was most easily acquired by commerce, especially beyond the seas. It was not uncommon for promoters of trading expeditions to gather in profits running from one hundred to four hundred per cent; indeed some of the early voyages to India netted twelve hundred per cent. In a single year, 1622, a consignment of goods bought in India for £386,000 sold in England for £1,915,000. The gains of peaceful trade were augmented from the spoils gathered by sea dogs, such as Drake and Hawkins, who raided the Spanish towns in America, overhauled galleons laden with gold and silver from Mexico and Peru, and seized Spanish merchant vessels from the East Indies bearing a king's ransom in spices and precious stuffs. From the New World gold and silver poured into Europe in an ever increasing stream, rising, according to Humboldt's estimates, from £52,000 annually at the opening of the sixteenth century to £280,000 annually at its close; and of this influx the manufacturers and merchants of England through various operations gathered in their full share. A frenzy for traffic animated all classes in England; the love of money and the trading spirit "permeated all departments of life and influenced almost every sentiment."

No wonder; as the possession of land gave dignity and power to the older aristocracy, so the possession of houses, factories, and shops gave strength and independence to the new middle class. For the men it opened the way to a position of influence in the affairs of state; to their wives and daughters it gave security, an easier life, an enlarged opportunity to acquire property and enter trade themselves. At the opening of the seventeenth century, the very air was charged with schemes for growing rich in a thousand ventures connected with the commerce and settlements of expanding England.

Living close together in the towns, the mercantile classes early acquired the habit of coöperation whenever capital beyond the reach of a single individual was required. Taking their cue perhaps from old merchant guilds, they learned how to unite their accumulations and their ingenuity in great corporations or companies chartered by the Crown to trade and plant colonies. In the reign of Elizabeth they formed the English Levant Company, which seized a share of the commerce with the East that had been monopolized by the Italians; when, in 1587, the last of the Venetian argosies, as if to celebrate the awful ruin of the Adriatic Queen, foundered in a storm off the Needles on its way to the London market, English capitalists were ready to carry forward the business on their own account. Another corporation, the Muscovy Company, pushed its traffic into Russia, reaching through the river systems of that country far southward into Persia. A third concern, the East India Company, created in 1600, sent its agents over the route opened by Vasco da Gama a hundred years before and founded, on the banks of the Ganges, the trading posts that expanded into the British dominion.

So when the time came to plant permanent settlements in America, the lure of gain had spread throughout English society, capital had been amassed, and the practice of forming corporations for profit had been well established. It was not necessary to beg a pittance from the royal treasury to launch epoch-making expeditions. The middle classes were themselves prepared to furnish both leadership and money. In the London Company, incorporated to develop Virginia, were, besides earls, bishops, knights, and gentlemen, plain commoners, merchant tailors, stationers, shoemakers, haberdashers, grocers, ironmongers, cutlers, leather sellers, saddlers, cordwainers, weavers, carpenters, representatives of all the other important trades, and two women—Katherine West and Millicent Ramsdent, a widow. The great Company that planted the first successful colony represented in fact the dominant elements in English commercial life. Its stock was advertised in the pulpit as well as in the market places and subscriptions were made in the interests of religion, patriotism, and profit.

§

For the agricultural work of colonization, England had two landed classes from which capable leaders could be drawn—country gentlemen and yeomen. The first of these groups consisted of substantial landed proprietors who lived in comfortable manor houses on broad acres, served as local justices of the peace by royal appointment, sat in the House of Commons by election of their neighbors, and thus combined the management of their estates with the functions of a governing class. From this order came the Cromwells, Hampdens, and Pyms, who challenged the rule of the Stuarts and brought Charles I to the scaffold in old England; and the Winthrops, Endicotts, and Eatons, who made the beginnings of a self-governing commonwealth, Massachusetts, in New England.

In the second of these important groups, the yeomanry,

were free and proud owners of small farms, noted for their industry and independence of spirit. They had energy, initiative, character, and property. They knew how to till the soil, rotate and care for crops, manage laborers, and conserve their interests. They, more than the gentry, furnished economic managers to direct the development of colonies in America.

To planting corporations, the very process that transformed England from a feudal into a mercantile state also furnished a mass of laborers detached from the soil and prepared to face the primitive conditions of life and work on the American frontier. It is a fact of deep significance in the history of migration that serfdom practically disappeared in England more than two hundred years before its last legal traces were removed from the Continent. The essential economic characteristic of serfdom was bondage to the soil. A serf was not a chattel; he was not bought and sold in the market place; he was attached to the land, going with the estate whenever it was transferred. As land without his labor was worthless, it was the interest of the lord to hold him fast to it, thus making him virtually a part of real property and depriving him of all initiative for migration.

Against serfdom the drift of economic life in England began to run heavily by the middle of the fifteenth century, but the institution was not abolished by one drastic action, such as Alexander made in Russia in 1861 or Lincoln started in the United States two years later. On the contrary it was by gradual stages extending over two centuries that English serfs commuted their fixed service of labor and produce into the form of a cash payment; it was by becoming renters that they finally broke the tie which bound them to the soil and won their liberty. But that liberty had its disadvantages; for, if the renter could voluntarily leave the soil which nourished him, he could also be driven from it when his lord found more lucrative uses for the land.

As things turned out, the whole rural economy of England was altered with the disappearance of serfdom. Greedy lords now seized the common lands of villages under acts of Parliament, made by their agents, authorizing them to enclose great areas and extinguish the ancient rights of the peasants. When, in the sixteenth century, the woolen industry rose to high prosperity and sheep-raising became more profitable than cropping, thousands of landlords drove off their tenants and turned their fields into pastures, changing prosperous hamlets into deserted villages. At the same time the vast estates of the monasteries, also tilled by peasants, passed into the hands of secular masters bent on profits and the walls of grand old abbeys sank down to ruin to receive their ivy crown. By various procedures, therefore, strong and active peasants, enamored of the soil that nurtured them, were transformed into wageworkers or sturdy beggars; the public poor relief that superseded monastic alms was heavily burdened; city streets were filled with paupers; and political economists were led to cry out: "What shall we do with the surplus population?"

Of all European countries, England alone had an abundance of men and women accustomed to hard labor in the fields and yet cut loose from bondage to the soil. It was a dubious freedom which they enjoyed—so dubious that it prepared them for migration to the New World in spite of all the hazards.

§

Absolutely imperative to the successful development of European civilization in America was the participation of women in every sphere of life and labor. Soldiers could conquer and rule native populations, but colonies could not be founded and maintained without women. And England of the seventeenth century had women of talent and experience, skilled in industrial arts, accustomed to the management of property and employees. On every hand English women took a lively interest in industrial, political, and religious activities. Of this fact indisputable evidence appears in the records of the period—old books on agriculture and the handicrafts, orders and papers of the justices of the peace who tried offenders against the law and who fixed the wages of laborers, documents and entries of craft guilds, archives of the great departments of government, and private memoirs of the day.

Even the women of the landed families were not idly rich. Rather were they responsible managers of large households in which numerous industries, now established in factories, were conducted under their watchful eyes. Nor were their energies confined to domestic pursuits. A granddaughter of Oliver Cromwell was director of a salt works. It is said of her that "she would sometimes, after a day of drudgery, go to the assembly at Yarmouth and appear one of the most brilliant there." Muriel Lyttelton, wife of a condemned Papist, begged her husband's forfeited estate from King James and "with the utmost prudence and economy" retrieved the fortune, educated the children, and discharged the duties of the head of the family. The memoirs of Mrs. Hutchinson, wife of the famous Puritan Colonel, show her maintaining a keen interest in the political controversies of her age and once at least in the lobby of the House of Commons during the absence of her husband, working against the passage of an objectionable measure. Women of her class often acted as executors of estates; they mingled in the throngs at court petitioning for grants of wardships, monopolies, patents, and other royal favors.

In an age when fortunes were relatively small, women of the trading class had not yet joined the leisure order devoted to gaiety and trifles. On the contrary, they were often partners in their husbands' enterprises or, as widows and daughters of merchants, were in business on their own account. In the records of the time they appear with striking frequency as pawnbrokers, money-lenders, stationers, booksellers, shopkeepers of many sorts, shipowners, and clothing contractors for the army and navy. For example, we find Susanna Angell, a widow, and her daughter petitioning the king in 1636 for the right to land a cargo of gunpowder and sell it in the kingdom or transport it to Holland. Court records tell of Ellenor Woodward, an ironmonger, up on a charge of selling short weight. Joan Dant, a Quakeress, widow of a poor weaver, embarked in trade as a pedlar and amassed a fortune of £9,000 in merchandizing, which she devoted to charity. "I got it by the rich," she quaintly said, "and I mean to leave it to the poor."

In industry, no less than in trade, women were active, often combining production with selling. They were bakers and sometimes members of the bakers' companies; the court records of old Manchester tell us of one Martha Wrigley in durance vile for giving her customers short weights. Occasionally they were butchers; of the twenty-three meat dealers in Chester, three were women. They managed flour mills and sold flour. They were in earlier days brewers and innkeepers—brewster being only the feminine of brewer—but when the state made the trade a monopoly their enterprise was confined to the domestic vat. In many of the staple crafts the labor of women was a factor of importance, especially after the guild system commenced to disintegrate. For instance, toward the close of the seventeenth century, when woolen goods formed in value one-third the total export trade of England, there were eight women to every man in the woolen industry, according to one estimate, and on the most conservative reckoning at least three to one.

To a large extent the silk industry, once, almost, if not entirely a feminine monopoly, was still in the hands of women—though it had sunk to the status of a sweated trade in the reign of James I. While men tried their best to control the lucrative broadcloth manufacture for their own benefit, women, especially widows, engaged in it in defiance of local ordinances. In those days the term spinster was not reserved for maidens of uncertain age, but was merely the feminine of spinner—just as webster was the feminine of webber. In fact the textile trade became so attractive to women that they crowded into it from the fields and kitchens, leading Defoe to complain at the opening of the eighteenth century that "wenches wont go to service at 12 pence a week when they can get 7 shillings or 8 shillings a week at spinning," revealing in his lament the existence even then of a servant problem for the English middle classes.

Especially important for colonization were the skill and strength of women in agriculture. Old treatises on farming and schedules of wages fixed by justices of the peace tell impressive stories of their toiling in the fields, raking hay, driving wagons, stowing hay away in mows, guarding flocks in pastures, receiving meager wages—less than the men in those distant days before the demand for equal pay for equal work. For shearing sheep and pulling peas, women earned sixpence a day, against eight for their male competitors. Special wages were paid to women servants "that taketh charge of brewing, baking, ketching, milk house, or malting." Those that helped to thatch roofs were not so favored: "She that draweth thatch hath 3d. a day; and she that serveth the thatcher 4d. a day because she also is to temper the morter and carry it to the top of the house"— runs the entry in one of the books on rural economy. With good reason could a traveler in old England write that "the men and the women themselves toiled like their horses." When, therefore, the various companies and proprietors engaged in colonizing America offered to married men double the quantity of land tendered to single men and made grants to maids as well as bachelors, they knew how valuable were the labors of English women in every branch of husbandry. No doubt the migration of families was determined by domestic council, for the most part, and after the momentous step was taken, the women assumed their share of the hardships and their full burden of responsibilities.

§

The dissolution of the feudal order which was marked by the rise of the middle and laboring classes produced collaterally profound religious and political changes that stimulated colonial expansion. As the rigidity of mediæval economic life was associated with dogmatism and authority in religion and politics, so the break-up of that order was attended by controversy in theology and revolution in government.

On one side the Protestant revolt against the Catholic system was strongly economic in character—a struggle of princes and middle classes to free themselves from the tithes, fees, laws, and jurisdiction of the clergy and at the same time to get possession of the immense estates of the church. Henry VIII's quarrel with the Pope and separation from Rome merely accelerated the inevitable. As far as Henry was concerned, the uprising was to be attended by no vital modifications in religious dogma. During his reign, the church in England was simply made subservient to the Crown; bishops and archbishops became royal appointees and a large part of the confiscated ecclesiastical property was turned over to the king and his favorites— the remainder being dedicated to religious uses under state control.

But having once breached the dike, Henry could not stop the flood of "perverse opinion"; and violent oscillations soon occurred in religious affairs. Under his son, Edward VI, Protestant dogma, tinged with leveling evangelicalism, was made the law of the land; under Mary the country was swung back to Catholicism; under Elizabeth a well-ordered Protestant Church with creed and prayer book was established by act of Parliament.

Each of these changes in the legal religion of the land helped to unsettle the opinions of the people in spite of all official efforts to force conformity upon them. The printing press, the revival of pagan literature, the multiplication of books on travel, commerce, and economy, the translation of the Bible into English so that the multitude could read it and dispute over matters of interpretation, and the corroding insinuations of business and natural science produced a luxuriant variety of religious sectarianism.

On the right were partisans of the Established Church who clung to the lawful order and, more extreme than they, the Catholics who hoped for a return to the vanished past; on the left were Independents, or Separatists, who proposed to abandon the Establishment or to abolish it altogether. In the center were Puritans who merely wished to "purify" the Anglican system by minor changes in creed and ceremony. Scattered along the line at different points stood Baptists, Quakers, Presbyterians, and other sects, each proclaiming its own gospel and its particular path to heaven.

Bewildered at first by the welter of dogmas, the king, the Anglican clergy, and their adherents tried to stem the rushing tides, bringing various engines of oppression to bear upon the dissident elements. In pursuing this policy, they unwittingly aided the work of colonization. It was then that the members of the congregation at Scrooby who afterward found their way to Plymouth "were hunted and persecuted on every side. . . . Some were taken and clapped up in prison; others had their houses beset and watched night and day . . . and the most were fain to fly and leave their houses and habitations."

In the end the advocates of uniformity and suppression failed. Out of the clash of sects, the ferment of opinion, the growth of doubt, and the direction of intellectual energies to practical considerations, finally came a degree of religious toleration which counted more heavily in successful colonization than religious oppression. If the English kings and their advisers hated the heretics, they did not follow the example of the Bourbon monarchs in France by excluding them from the territories lying far away.

Instead of banishing merchants and artisans to enrich
other countries, English statesmen opened the gates of their
American colonies to every kind of religious faith that the
stirring life of the Old World could furnish—to Catholics,
Separatists, Puritans, Quakers, Presbyterians, and Baptists
from the British Isles; to Lutherans, Dunkards, Moravians,
Mennonites, Huguenots, and Salzburgers from the Continent. They looked with favor upon the German Lutherans
who crowded into Pennsylvania, subdued the wilderness,
and produced wheat, corn, bacon, and lumber to exchange
for English manufactures. They even winked at news of
Jews settling here and there in the colonies, especially after
Oliver Cromwell's example in toleration at home. When
the plantations were once started and their significance to
trade and empire disclosed, it was impossible to bring them
into any scheme of religious uniformity. On the contrary
clerical authority waned with the growth of business
enterprise.

§

In the operations that unhorsed the feudal lords and
disintegrated the power of the clergy, the merchants and
landed gentry of England attained a high degree of self-
government and civil liberty. Unlike France and Spain,
England had never discarded the institution of representative government which had sprung up in the middle ages.
Serving as voters and members of the House of Commons
and as justices of the peace in the counties, towns, and
parishes, the gentry and merchants had long taken part in
the administration of public affairs. And in the seventeenth
century they definitely attained supremacy in the state by
the establishment of parliamentary sovereignty. As in
France long afterward, this revolution was accompanied
by violence, the execution of the king, social disorder, the
seizure of property, extreme measures, dictatorship, reaction, and the ultimate triumph of the essential ideas advanced by the leaders in the uprising.

In the age of Elizabeth there were mutterings of discontent; in the reign of her successor, James I, the House of Commons, speaking for the smaller landed gentry and the merchants, set forth the rights of its constituents in language which even a Stuart could understand; Charles I, learning nothing and forgetting nothing, tried a decade of personal government which ended in civil war and his death upon the scaffold in 1649. Then followed experiments in democracy two hundred years ahead of the times, which merely culminated in the Cromwellian dictatorship and, after the death of the stern Oliver, in the restoration of the monarchy. Reaction came as night succeeds the day, but the swelling currents of English commerce steadily recruited the ranks of the middle classes. Accordingly, when James II tried to turn back the tide in 1688, he was overthrown and the supremacy of Parliament was fixed for all time—a House of Lords crowded with newcomers and a House of Commons, both dominated in colonial and foreign affairs by mercantile considerations.

History has attached to this revolution the title "Puritan" as if it were essentially religious in character, but the title is primarily due to the "intellectual climate" of the age. The thought of the times was still deeply tinged with theology and the defense mechanism of men who were engaged in resisting taxes and other exactions was naturally drawn from the literature with which they were most familiar—the Old and the New Testament. "When the monarchy was to be subverted," wrote a shrewd observer of the age, "we knew what was necessary to justify the fact." All that was reasonable enough but the historian need not tarry long with the logical devices of men in action.

In reality, the English Revolution of the seventeenth century was a social transformation almost identical in its essentials with the French Revolution of the next century: a civilian laity emancipated itself from the mastery of Crown, aristocracy, and clergy. The process was long and painful and during its course many preferred the uncertainties of distant colonization to the perils of domestic war.

It was under a government occupied with conflict at home that all the colonies in America, except Georgia, were founded; it was under a Parliament increasingly mercantile in character that they grew into powerful economic and political societies; and it was in the doctrines of John Locke, philosopher of the "Glorious Revolution" of 1688, that they found secular authority for their Declaration of Independence in 1776. Thus the social transformation of England facilitated colonization, gave a practical economic turn to imperial administration, and finally afforded the linguistics of colonial revolution.

In all these things lay the secret of England's expanding power. She had a monarchy, strong but limited—dominated at last by the middle classes rather than by courtiers such as those who disported themselves at Versailles. While Spain and France discarded their representative institutions, England retained her Lords and Commons and made them potent agencies for commercial and industrial promotion. Her Church, shattered by the endless multiplication of sects, was early compelled to grant a certain degree of toleration as the price of peace. The state, racked by two revolutions and subjected to the fire of constant criticism, was forced to give up the censorship of the press and fling wide the floodgates for intellectual interests of a secular cast.

In her social development, as in church and state, England was rapidly moving toward the modern age. She had a large and growing estate of merchants, a body of yeomen ready for adventure, and a supply of free agricultural laborers, men and women, loose from the feudal ties that bound them to the soil. In short, England in the seventeenth and eighteenth centuries was a nation engrossed in applying ever-increasing energies to business enterprise—of which colonization in the New World was one branch for the employment of capital and administrative genius.

CHAPTER II

Laying the Structural Base of the American Colonies

EMPIRE building and colonization, each according to its requirements, call for appropriate leadership. At the forefront of imperial enterprise we see the soldier of courage and martial design: a Genghis Khan sweeping with his hordes over Mongolia and China; an Akbar overcoming India's millions; a Cortez cheering his soldiers to the fray amid the flames of Montezuma's capital. In the vanguard of colonization, essentially a civilian undertaking, we find the administrator with a vision and a mind for business affairs: a Baltimore and a Penn raising capital, calling for tenants, and attempting to build states by the sheer strength of individual resources; a Gates, a Wingfield, and a Winthrop associating themselves with mercantile corporations to accomplish purposes beyond the power of any single promoter; a Carver and a Bradford giving direction and inspiration to a little band of Pilgrims breaking the stubborn soil of Plymouth.

In the nature of things, daring leaders fearing no risk of

fortune had to break the way before judicious merchants would invest their capital in dubious speculations beyond the unknown sea. If among the forerunners who first caught glimpses of England's unique mission and feared not the hazards of adventure, one must be taken by way of illustration, the choice may very well fall upon Walter Raleigh, son of a country gentleman, knighted for service by Queen Elizabeth.

For the great undertaking in colonization, Raleigh's temper and early experience fitted him in a peculiar fashion. Alive to all the important interests of his age, he was fascinated by the multiplying tales of exploration and discovery. Humble geographers were among his friends. The sea dogs, Drake, Hawkins, and Frobisher, had respect for him; he was of their kind. In red scenes of battle, he had showed his daring, helping the Dutch to defy the rule of Spain and England's gallant sailors to send the *Armada* to the bottom of the ocean. Given to brooding upon high enterprise, he pondered upon the destinies of nations, sketching in fact during his later years a grand plan for a philosophic history of the world. Such was the first architect of English colonial fortune who saw in his dreams the American wilderness subdued by the people of his native land.

Unshaken by the fate of his brave half-brother, Sir Humphrey Gilbert, who, returning from one of his voyages of exploration, had perished in a storm, exclaiming as tradition has it, "we are as near to heaven by sea as by land," Sir Walter Raleigh determined to plant under mild skies on southern shores the beginning of a second England. Cautious at first, he sent out at his own expense a scouting expedition under Amadas and Barlowe who brought back reports of a paradise along the Carolina coast. Then Sir Walter sought the help of his sovereign and secured from Elizabeth a wine monopoly yielding him revenues for experimentation, supplementing a grant of land in America that promised to make him a feudal lord over a princely

realm. Twice from his own purse thus recruited and once
with the help of merchant capitalists, he attempted to establish a permanent agricultural settlement in America, not
overlooking the possibility of finding precious metals.

Misfortune of every kind dogged the steps of his adventure, however, and at last, broken in estate, Raleigh
was compelled to accept the verdict of failure. The empire
of which he dreamed was to be built by other hands in
other ways. The treasuries of gold which his captains
sought were not to be found until, in the sweat of their
brow, American colonists had cut and tramped their way
across three thousand miles of forest, plain, desert, and
mountain to the far end of the continent. Instead of
precious metals Raleigh's men discovered a more secure
foundation for a state had they but known it—the lowly
tobacco leaf and the humble potato. The pungent weed
was to furnish a currency no less certain than gold and
afford the staple crop for baronial estates where wealth and
leisure nourished a governing class capable of waging to a
victorious end a dramatic contest with the descendants of
the Raleighs, Leicesters, and Burleighs of the Elizabethan
age. The plain prose of economy in the long run is stranger
than the romance of fiction.

§

Though Raleigh failed, his experiments taught valuable
lessons and his spirit fired contemporaries with emulative
desire. If nothing more, he had proved that successful
colonization was, in the beginning at least, beyond the
strength and resources of any individual. The amount of
capital and the diversity of talent demanded made it of
necessity a coöperative undertaking, at all events until the
first difficulties were resolved and the path was blazed.
Thus it came about that the earliest permanent settlements
were made by commercial corporations.

Four American colonies owed their inception to trading

companies—two of English origin, a third under Dutch-
Walloon patronage, and a fourth under Swedish direction.
It was the London Company chartered in 1606 that led the
way by founding Virginia; it was the Massachusetts Bay
Company incorporated in 1629 that saved the little Plymouth fellowship from destruction and started New England
on its course. In a fierce quest for trade, the Dutch West
India Company, established in 1621, laid in New Netherland the basis of a colony upon which the English forty-
three years later erected the province of New York. Not
to be outdone by Holland and England, the king of Sweden
called into being a West India Company of his own and
commissioned it to break ground for a Swedish state on the
banks of the Delaware.

In a certain sense Georgia may also be included among
the "Company" colonies. If the avowed purpose of its
principal promoter, James Oglethorpe, was philanthropic—
the establishment of an asylum for poor debtors—the legal
instrument for the realization of that design was a charter
granted by George II in 1732, uniting the sponsors of the
enterprise in "one body politic and corporate," known as
the "Trustees for establishing the colony of Georgia in
America." In form of government and in methods of
financing, the Georgia concern did not differ materially from
the trading Company. So it may be said that the corporation of capitalists—the instrument employed in commercial
undertakings—was the agency which planted the first successful colonies and molded their early polity in church and
state and economy.

Now the commercial corporation for colonization,
whether it sprang from the sole motive of profit-making or
from mixed incentives, such as the prosecution of trade and
the spread of religious propaganda, was in reality a kind
of autonomous state. Like the state, it could endure indefinitely—as long as its charter lasted; its members might die
but, by the continuous election of successors, the corporation went on. Like the state, it had a constitution, a

charter issued by the Crown, which formed a superior law binding constituents and officers.

Like the state, it had a territorial basis—a grant of land often greater in area than a score of European principalities. It was a little democracy in itself, for its stockholders admitted new members to the suffrage, elected their own officers, and made by-laws. It exercised many functions of a sovereign government: it could make assessments, coin money, regulate trade, dispose of corporate property, collect taxes, manage a treasury, and provide for defense. Thus every essential element long afterward found in the government of the American state appeared in the chartered corporation that started English civilization in America.

Moreover, that other great arm of the English state, the Church, usually formed an integral part of these corporate enterprises. As a matter of zeal in some instances and of form in others, colonial companies were generally charged with the duty of "propagating the Christian religion to such people as yet live in darkness and miserable ignorance of the true knowledge and worship of God"—to use the language of the first Virginia charter. Either in fact or in theory to conciliate high powers in England, this meant the faith of the Anglican Church established by law. In the Virginia colony, there was no doubt about the injunction: the Company made the creed of that Church the strict rule of the plantation. The first legislature assembled on the soil of America, the Virginia House of Burgesses, enacted that "all persons whatsoever upon the Sabbath days shall frequent divine service and sermons, both forenoon and afternoon."

§

Such was the nature of the agency created by James I in 1606 when he issued the first charter to the London Company commissioning it to establish the colony of Virginia. Among the men whose enthusiasm called the corporation into life were old and seasoned navigators, such as John Smith and Ferdinando Gorges, who had seen America with their own eyes, and industrious students of maritime enterprise, such as Richard Hakluyt, who had been affiliated with Raleigh in his ill-starred experiments. Associated with them were merchants, traders, landed gentlemen, and other persons who knew little or nothing about America and regarded the undertaking as primarily a profit-making venture.

Though the investors insisted on works of piety among the Indians, they wanted a quick return on their capital; their colony was hardly a year old when they demanded a piece of gold and threatened to forsake the settlers as "banished men" if cargoes of goods worth two thousand pounds were not immediately forthcoming. Neither the stockholders nor the majority of the first emigrants had any very definite idea of the labor, land, and administrative systems required for successful colonization.

As a matter of fact the air of England was still charged with vain imaginings awakened by Spanish luck. "Why, man," ran the lines of a play written in 1605 to laud the glories of America, "all their dripping pans are pure golde, and all the chaines with which they chaine up their streets are massive gold; all the prisoners they take are fettered in golde; and for rubies and diamonds, they goes forth in holy dayes and gather 'hem by the sea-shore, to hang on their children's coates and stick in their children's caps, as commonly as our children wear saffron-gilt brooches and groates with holes in 'hem."

With such wild tales afloat to stir the cupidity of the avaricious, it was naturally the soldier of fortune who first grasped at the opportunity of migrating to Virginia. The directors of the Company tried to secure industrious and God-fearing settlers, but, in the first group of one hundred and five emigrants, there were only a few mechanics and twelve laborers; about one-half were set down as "gentlemen" and four as carpenters—bound to a houseless wilderness! The second expedition transported more gentlemen and several goldsmiths, who filled the settlement with clamor about riches until, as John Smith, who was on the spot exclaimed, "there was now no talk, no hope, no work, but dig gold, wash gold, refine gold, load gold." The third and fourth voyages brought more gentlemen, tradesmen, soldiers, and fortune hunters. Finally the exasperated Captain Smith blurted out the bitter truth to the Company: "When you send again, I entreat you rather send but thirty carpenters, husbandmen, gardeners, fishermen, blacksmiths, masons, and diggers up of trees' roots, well provided, than a thousand such as we have."

Indeed, among the early bands of emigrants only one member, this Captain Smith, seems to have grasped the true nature of colonial economy. Though most of his charming tales, including the story of his rescue by Pocahontas, an Indian maid, are now discredited, and though he is set down among the great romancers like Casanova and Sancho Panza, Smith was keenly alive to the realities of the struggle in Virginia. "Nothing," he wrote, "is to be expected thence, but by labor."

Standing on that principle, Smith kept up a constant demand for emigrants not afraid of soiling their hands, and saved the day more than once by enforcing the rule that those who would not work should not eat. Boastful and unpopular as he was, Smith was personally brave in warfare and fertile in practical plans for defending the settlement and producing the means of livelihood. He led in exploring and developing Virginia; when an explosion of gunpowder severely wounded him and sent him back to England for surgical attention, disease and famine almost wiped out the colony. Nothing but the arrival of outside relief saved the survivors from utter ruin. The Company demanded gold of Smith; he gave it something more valuable, a map of the region, a sketch of its resources, and sound advice as to the kind of emigrants suitable for colonization.

In fashioning its land policy, the Virginia Company was

forced to shape its scheme of tenure to the varied character of its emigrants. Having in mind the matter of quick profits, the condition of the free laborers available for transport, and the requirements of independent capitalists desirous of engaging in agriculture on their own account, the Company provided a combination of corporate and individual ownership. In the first place, the directors decided that a part of the land should be held permanently by the Company and tilled by servants sent out at its expense. Under this arrangement, the corporation was to furnish the implements and initial supplies; each able-bodied servant was to work at the task assigned to him; the proceeds were to go into a common store from which allotments were to be made to the laborers according to their needs and profits to the Company according to its investment.

In the second place, a large portion of the land was devoted to individual exploitation, known as "the adventure of the purse." Every contributor who paid a fixed sum of £12.10s. into the corporate treasury was entitled to a warrant for one hundred acres of land and an equal amount in addition as soon as the first lot was under cultivation. To encourage the migration of settlers capable of paying their passage and launching themselves, the Company offered a hundred acres to every adventurer who would risk the hazards of Virginia in person. Any capitalist who transported one laborer to the colony at his own expense was granted one hundred acres and an equal area for each additional laborer so transported—an allowance later reduced to fifty acres—always subject to an annual quit-rent of two shillings per hundred acres payable to the corporation.

Finally great sections of land were set aside to afford incomes for the Company's officers in Virginia with a view to supporting them in a certain degree of style; and huge grants were made from time to time to individuals for "meritorious services," an elastic phrase that covered a multitude of sins. In the main the Company desired to

create a colony of estates moderate in size; but, when the
enterprising spirits who crossed the sea discovered how easy
it was to stake out princely dominions, they managed by
one means or another to engross within a short time all
the lands on the seaboard and transform them into large
plantations, thus forcing the small freeholders up into the
piedmont.

Of these several schemes, that of tillage by servants sent
out at the Company's expense proved to be the most evident
failure. Supervision was difficult, for the colony was far
away. There was little incentive to the laborer to put forth
his best efforts because the results of his toil flowed into the
corporation's warehouse and he gained little for himself
beyond a bare subsistence.

Wretched idleness was the fruit of this program. Some
improvement was made in 1611 when Governor Dale set
apart three acres of land for each company laborer, gave
him one month of free time in which to cultivate his own
plot, and allowed him a small stock of corn from the common store. But even this change could not save the system
of Company tillage. It was too repellent to attract settlers;
it lacked the element of direct and personal supervision;
and at the end of ten years there was only a handful of
laborers, men, women, and children, operating under the
plan. By that time, the experiment had made it clear that
no corporation with its seat in London could successfully
carry on planting in America by ill-requited workers sent
out at its expense and managed by its agents three thousand
miles away. So within a short time the development of
planting in the lowlands of Virginia inevitably fell into the
hands of individual landowners who secured estates by
investment, purchase, or grant, as indicated above, and
obtained by one process or another laborers—freemen,
bond servants, or slaves—to cultivate their acres.

In the sphere of government, as well as economy, the
experience of the Virginia Company was full of profit for
the generations to come. Until near the end of its troubled

life, it suffered from the delusion that Englishmen who had
enjoyed some share in the politics of their native land could
be permanently and happily ruled by governors chosen in
London and sent over with a retinue of servants. None of
the three charters granted to the corporation, 1606, 1609,
and 1612, contemplated any degree of autonomy in the
colony itself. In the contest with the Crown, the rights of
the Company and its stockholders were enlarged, but to
the end the settlers in Virginia remained legally subjected
in all important things to the will of the distant corporation.

Governor after governor was dispatched to manage the
settlement in the name of the Company: Delaware with the
pomp of an Oriental potentate; Dale, harsh, brutal, and
"efficient"; Argall, a petty tyrant who robbed the settlers
and cheated the corporation; Yeardley, a liberal gentleman
who "applied himself for the most part in planting tobacco"; and Wyatt, during whose five years of service the
colony passed from the Company to the Crown. Some of
these governors displayed conspicuous merits, but they all
owed their appointments to politics and intrigues, not to
demonstrated competence in administration.

With quaint irony Captain Smith told the story: "The
multiplicity of Governors is a great damage to any state;
but the uncertain daily changes are burdensome, because
their entertainments are chargeable, and many will make
hay whilst the sun doth shine, however it shall fare with
the generality." Not until the Company became engaged
in a violent quarrel with the Crown did it, with a gesture
of magnanimity, seek an alliance with the colonists and by
the establishment of the House of Burgesses in 1619 grant
them a voice in local government.

While the London Company was feeling its way to
policies that promised success, the colonists in Virginia were
learning their own lessons in days full of trouble. The
first summer for them at Jamestown in 1607 was one long,
drawn-out agony, unbearable heat, unwholesome water,
and spoiling food striking them down with disease and

death. One brief extract from the record of Master George Percy, who looked upon the tragic scene with his own eyes, tells the gruesome story: "The fifteenth day, their died Edward Browne and Stephen Galthorpe. The sixteenth day, their died Thomas Gower Gentleman. The seventeenth day, their died Thomas Mounslie. The eighteenth day their died Robert Pennington, and John Martine, Gentlemen." So the little lives of men were ticked off; when autumn came half the brave and tempestuous band were in their graves.

Those who lived through the awful days quarreled and plotted conspiracies. Governor Dale introduced martial law, hanged, shot, and broke men on the wheel; he chained one malefactor to a tree with a bodkin through his tongue and kept him there till he died; but with all his cruelty the governor was hardly able to suppress disorder. To pestilence and turbulence were added occasional famines. In the "starving time" of 1609 a colony of nearly five hundred persons was reduced in the course of six months to sixty wretched survivors, desperately preparing to leave the scene of their sufferings forever, when relief ships arrived from England. Collisions with the Indians—individual brushes and general conflicts such as the awful massacre of 1622 which swept off three hundred men, women, and children at one dreadful stroke—thinned the ranks of the settlers and held the tiny colony always under the shadow of fear. It is estimated that all in all the Company sent over 5,649 emigrants during its existence from 1606 to 1624, and that of these only 1,095 were in the colony at the end of the period. Some had fled back to England disillusioned; most of them had perished in Virginia.

And yet during these two decades, in spite of every obstacle, the foundations of a prosperous colony were laid as homes were built, the labor supply enlarged, and a profitable crop developed. Early in these years, the fundamental element—European domestic life—which so distinguished the English colonies, was introduced; for two white women came with the second supply ship in 1608, "Mistresse Forest and Anne Buras, her maide."

Recognizing the importance of permanent ties binding the colonists to America, the Company itself undertook to encourage the migration of women; in 1619 it sent at its own risk ninety maidens, "agreeable persons, young and incorrupt," and "sold them with their own consent to settlers as wives at the cost of their transportation." Since this venture yielded a fair profit to the Company besides wielding a moderating influence on the turbulence of the men, other consignments of women were sent from year to year—sometimes with great difficulty, because it was no easy thing to induce comely English maidens "of virtuous education, young, handsome, and well-recommended" to tempt fortune by searching for a good husband among the hustling planters who pressed around the landing stage and offered the purchase money in tobacco. Though the process was rough and ready, it helped to fill Virginia with homes and, as Lord Delaware, the governor, once remarked, with "honest laborers burdened with children." When in the course of time life in the province became reasonably secure, emigrants of every kind took wives and children with them; and so, at the end of thirty years, there rose in Virginia a generation born on the soil, who could not say with their progenitors, "Lord, bless England, our sweet native country."

The second element essential to the prosperity of the landowners, an abundant supply of workers willing to till plantations under the hot sun of Virginia, was even harder to get, but before the close of the Company's career a solution of that problem was found. At the very outset the corporation adopted a practice of sending over on its own account "indentured servants" bound to labor for a term of years, thereby setting an example which was quickly followed by adventurers of the purse and other colonists who bought land from the Company. Some of these laborers, men and women, boys and girls alike, were lured on shipboard by kidnapping "spirits" and borne to sea before they knew their destination and their fate. Others were convicts deported because English judges wanted to get rid of them. Thousands were simply knocked down on the streets of English cities and dragged away by brutal bands which made a regular business of that nefarious traffic. To these bond servants were soon added Negro slaves, the first of whom were brought to Virginia by a Dutch vessel in 1619, but this new class did not become very numerous until the lapse of half a century. For fifty years, indentured white servants from England furnished most of the labor for the fields.

A special impetus was given to the economic life of Virginia by the discovery of a single staple that could be grown easily in large quantities and exchanged readily for cash and goods, namely, "the obnoxious weed," tobacco. Very early the settlers learned that little money was to be made by raising corn or making iron and glass; therefore, they turned almost as one man to the cultivation of tobacco, planting it even in the streets of Jamestown. Great fortunes, equivalent in a few instances to $75,000 a year in present currency, were taken from tobacco crops and the head of every adventurer seems to have been turned by the prospect of sudden riches. One who was on the ground in the early days exclaimed that "tobacco onely was the business and for ought that I could hear every man madded upon that and little thought or looked for anything else."

In addition to bringing quick prosperity, tobacco gave a decided bent to the course of social development in the South; it determined that the land, especially on the seaboard, should be tilled primarily, not by small freeholders such as settled in New England, but rather by servile labor directed by the lords of great estates, with all the implications, legal, moral, and intellectual, thereunto appertaining. So the tobacco plant unfolding its broad leaves in the moist air and hot sun of Virginia gave a direction to economy that was big with fate.

The growing prosperity of Virginia, instead of yielding wealth and security to the Company, only added to its troubles. As the population increased in size difficulties of administration multiplied and these in turn aggravated the dissensions that constantly raged in London. Every part of the social order in England was now being shaken by a conflict between the Crown and the titled aristocracy on one side and merchants and minor gentry on the other, a conflict that was in a few years to break out into civil war and revolution. Each party to this controversy had its spokesmen in the Virginia Company rending its transactions with angry disputes. The mercantile element, prominent both in the corporation and in the House of Commons, steadily opposed all high notions of royal prerogative and all arbitrary schemes of taxation.

Unable to abolish Parliament, the king, James I, resentfully turned his wrath against the Company. Judicial proceedings were instituted calling for the forfeiture of its charter; the case was heard by judges appointed by the king to serve his interests; the conclusion was foregone. In 1624, the charter was annulled and the colony became a royal province administered directly under the king's authority. After sinking £150,000 in an unprofitable speculation but making experiments that pointed the way to successful colonization, the Company thus came to an ignominious end. Yet for the moment no radical changes were made in the economic and political life of Virginia. The last executive sent over by the corporation was continued in office as a royal appointee; the affairs of Virginia were managed by a royal governor aided by a small council designated by the Crown and the House of Burgesses elected by the planters.

Such were the beginnings of the colony which his' are accustomed to contrast with Puritan New Eng' if it were a secular enterprise carried out by free' As a matter of fact, if records are to be taken at f; "neither the desire for treasure nor even the wish to p mote the power of England" was the chief object of the Virginia Company; its heart was set on the glory of God and the propagation of the Christian faith among them that sat in darkness. In their advertisements for colonists the officers of the Company were at pains to indicate that they wished only settlers of correct religious life. "They also made careful provision for the maintenance of the religious habits they prized so highly; churches were built with such elaboration as their means allowed, and the practice of attending the daily services there was carefully enforced. The whole work of colonization was treated as an enterprise in which it was a work of piety to engage and collections were made in parish churches for the college that was planned for the English and the Indians at the Henrico settlement."

Moreover, the House of Burgesses elected by the freeholders of Virginia was in complete accord with the religious professions of the Company and the Crown. It required the church wardens to report for trial "all who led profane and ungodly lives, common swearers and drunkards, adulterers, fornicators, slanderers, tale-bearers; all such as 'do not behave themselves orderly and soberly during divine services,' and all masters and mistresses delinquent in catechising children and 'ignorant persons' placed under their charge."

It is true that the records of Virginia are not sown with Biblical quotations and with references to the wonder-working providence of God, but if statutes, orders, and decrees meant anything at all, then Virginia was as pious as Massachusetts and as devout as Plymouth. Indeed, it must not be forgotten that the Pilgrims originally arranged with the Virginia Company to settle on its soil and that the prospect of securing the accession of this new group of recruits was welcomed by leading members of the corporation. The Pilgrims, in spite of their "perversity" in religious faith, were just the kind of sturdy and sober laborers so eagerly sought by the Company and it was merely an accident in navigation that carried them to land outside the borders of Virginia.

§

Tangible circumstances, rather than a difference in the motives of the London merchants who advanced capital for colonial enterprises, accounted for the contrast between Virginia and Plymouth. The climate and soil of the northern coast, besides being unfit for plantations, afforded no single staple upon which a fortune could be swiftly built; and the bulk of the emigrants for the New England colony was drawn from sources other than those exploited by the Virginia Company. Most of the Pilgrims who settled Plymouth were petty farmers, laborers, and artisans, rather than gentlemen, yeomen, and merchants with pounds to risk in importing servants and slaves.

Even those who came by way of Holland to Cape Cod had seen toilsome days and nights in their alien home. When, as Separatists, they collided with the Church of England and fled across the North Sea, they were forced to learn various trades in their new abode by which to eke out a living. Hence with their sobriety and profound religious faith, the Pilgrims combined a knowledge of agriculture and handicrafts. Moreover, they were accustomed to the severest hardships. As the Dutch craft guilds excluded them from the most remunerative trades, they were able to earn a living while in Holland only by the heaviest manual labor for twelve or fifteen hours a day. Bradford, historian of the little band, recorded that no "newfangledness or other such like giddie humor" inclined them to move to some other land.

In enumerating the "sundrie weightie and solid reasons" for migration, he declared that the Pilgrims found by experience "the hardnes of the place and countrie to be such as few in comparison would come to them and fewer still would bide it out and continew with them. For many that came to them and many more that desired to be with them could not endure that great labor and hard fare with other inconveniences which they underwent and were contented with." Additional reasons for migration given by the chronicler were the oppression of their children who, under heavy duties, became decrepit in early life, and the danger of falling into ungodly ways through contact with those of other faith or no faith at all. Men, women, and youths accustomed to toil long hours at humble crafts in Holland had the will and the strength required to cope with the hardships of colonization in a new country.

But as the Separatists were without sufficient capital to take the great step, it became necessary for them to enter into negotiation with a group of London merchants in order to secure land, ships, supplies, and temporary maintenance. From the London Company they got permission to settle within the boundaries of Virginia and, after much haggling, they came to terms with certain merchant adventurers willing to invest money in their enterprise. A loose stock company was formed in which emigrants and capitalists were united. Every person over sixteen who went out on the expedition automatically became a stockholder and received one share valued at £10; two children between ten and sixteen were regarded as equivalent to the value of one share. The emigrants themselves were also allowed to buy additional stock with money or goods. The remainder of the capital was furnished by regular investors, chiefly Londoners. As a guarantee to the capitalists the whole body of emigrants bound themselves under the terms of an agreement to work for a period of seven years, to put their produce into a common warehouse, and to receive their subsistence out of the common store—all on the understanding that at the end of the period there should be a settlement and a discharge of the obligations.

Having accepted the harsh conditions of their bondage, a little band of Pilgrims set sail in the *Speedwell* from Delftshaven in the summer of 1620, and joined by another party in the *Mayflower* at Southampton, they put to sea.

Finding their first ship unfit for the journey, they soon returned to port, where a few discontented emigrants gave up the voyage, while the others crowded into the *May-flower*. At last, "all being compacte toegeather in one shipe," free and bond, they dropped out of Plymouth harbor in September.

After weathering many cross winds and fierce storms that shook every timber of their little bark and after witnessing "many specialle workes of God's providence," they found themselves on November 6 in sight of land far to the north, out of the limits of the Virginia territory where they had permission to settle. For many days they eagerly searched the coast and finally, on December 21, they made their formal landing at Plymouth harbor.

Before leaving the ship, forty-one adult males in the company—the Pilgrim "fathers," most of whom were' under forty—by a solemn compact bound themselves into a body politic, agreeing to enact and abide by laws and ordinances for the general good. Having chosen John Carver, "a man godly and well approved amongst them," governor for a year, they were ready to confront "the grimme and grislie face of povertie." Soon the cold gray New England winter closed down upon them and before summer came again, out of "100 and odd persons, scarce 50 remained." Yet all through those trying days in the shadow of death they cut trees and built log houses; and when the planting season arrived, they put out twenty acres of corn under the direction of friendly Indians who had visited them during the winter of their adversity, and taught them the arts of forest and field and stream.

From time to time small additions of immigrants were made to the little settlement at Plymouth but it was not destined to grow into a great state like Virginia. It was limited in capital; the number of radical Separatists upon which it could draw for labor was small; and there was no local staple such as tobacco which could be poured into London markets in large quantities. At the end of seven decades, when Plymouth was absorbed into Massachusetts under the charter of 1691, it had only seven thousand inhabitants.

In reality, therefore, the record at Plymouth filled no great page in the history of commonwealths. Like the annals of the poor, it was short and simple. Farming was supplemented by fur trading, fishing, and lumbering, which furnished cargoes for the return voyages. On the lapse of the third year, the system of common tillage which rewarded idleness and penalized industry was given up; and each family was allotted a certain amount of land for cultivation. After chafing three years more under bondage to the London merchants, the old contract was set aside and the colonists bought outright all the claims of the original investors.

Although they thus adopted the idea of individual property in land, the Plymouth settlers maintained a high degree of collective control in the name of the common good. The most minute affairs of private life were subject to the searching scrutiny of the elders; prying, spying, and informing were raised to the height of prime diversions; swift and stern punishment was visited upon all who were guilty of blasphemy, drunkenness, sloth, or irregular conduct. Still the regimen was not without relief. Smoking was permitted; good beer was brewed; "strong waters" were consumed in liberal quantities; and after a while excellent wines were imported from abroad. Within a few years all the Pilgrims had better houses and a more liberal stock of worldly goods than they had been accustomed to in their native land. Beautiful villages rose amid spreading elms and prosperous merchants plumed themselves on lucky voyages. In fact, some of the more fortunate put on airs and set themselves down in the records as "gentlemen," over against the simplemen who had no titles or honors. This was, of course, without prescriptive warrant for few, if any, of them belonged to the gentry in the technical sense, but it gratified an innate passion for "qualitie," and gave a certain artificial diversity to an otherwise plain social order.

§

The tiny religious brotherhood of Plymouth was only ten years old when settlements began to appear in the region to the north under the auspices of a great mercantile corporation chartered in 1629 as the Massachusetts Bay Company. What a strange contrast the two enterprises presented! The humble farmers, laborers, and artisans who, with their families, composed the bulk of the settlers on Cape Cod belonged to an outlawed religious band. In the eyes of the bishop of London, such sectaries were con- temptible trouble-makers, "instructed by guides fit for them, cobblers, tailors, feltmakers, and such-like trash."

On the other hand, the emigrants who founded the Bay Colony belonged to the middle strata of English society. They were not radicals in religion; they wanted moderate reforms in the Church of England but no revolution. They were not dependent for capital upon the good graces of London investors; they were people of substance them- selves. A few of them possessed large landed estates in England; some were wealthy merchants; others came from the professional classes; many were scholars of light and learning from the universities; the majority were at first drawn from the yeomanry and renters of farms in the eastern counties of England. On the roll of this Company were the names of Sir Henry Roswell, Sir John Young, Sir Richard Saltonstall, John Endicott, John Winthrop, and other representatives of the landed gentry and commercial classes—the virile and sturdy stock that, as we have said, gave England its Cromwells, Hampdens, and Pyms.

Unlike the Plymouth band, the Massachusetts Company had a formal charter of incorporation from the king. Its members in the manner of such commercial corporations were authorized to enlarge their number, elect a governor and his assistants, make laws, dispose of the immense domain of land granted to them, and engage in almost every kind of local economic enterprise. In short, it was a corporation knit together by ties of religious sympathy, endowed with abundant capital, and supplied with capable leadership in things economic, legal, and spiritual.

Though it had the general form of the recently extinguished Virginia Company, it differed from that concern in one vital particular; the seat of the corporation, the majority of the stockholders, and the charter of legality were all transferred to America. Instead of trying to plant and govern a colony beyond the sea, the Massachusetts Company came over itself to the scene of action, directed the labors of the planters, and participated immediately in every phase of the enterprise. It was in truth, therefore, an actual self-governing state set up in the New World.

In the spring of 1630, John Winthrop, at the head of a great band of Puritan gentlemen and yeomen, with their families and a goodly body of indentured white servants, sailed with a fleet of ships for the New World, thus beginning a general exodus that lasted for about two decades —the period of turmoil and revolution in England. During the year in which he granted the charter to the new corporation, Charles I began to rule his subjects without Parliament; and for eleven years he laid taxes, imprisoned objectors, and collected forced loans on his own authority. England seemed headed for a despotism.

Deprived of their voice in the House of Commons, the landed gentry of the middle rank, the yeomen, the merchants, and the artisans on whom the burden of the royal exactions fell, were now roused to revolutionary fervor. Those who belonged to the fighting school of the Cromwells and the Hampdens raised the standard of revolt, waged seven years of war, and finally brought the king to the scaffold at Whitehall. Others, despairing of freedom and victory at home, decided to migrate in search of liberty to the New World. They sold their estates, wound up their affairs, assembled their servants and laborers, and transferred their capital and their energy to another sphere—the new settlements springing up at Boston, Charlestown, Salem, and in the neighboring regions.

These Bay colonists carried with them livestock, tools, great stores of supplies, and goods for trading with the Indians, the capital for large economic enterprise. Beyond question, their leaders desired to reproduce in America the stratified society that they had known in England, excepting the titled aristocracy which stood above them in rank and in the affections of the king. If they had not encountered obstacles, they would have made Massachusetts a land of estates tilled by renters and laborers, with yeomen freeholders interspersed and the home of an Established Church directed by a learned clergy according to English forms, though "purified" to suit the taste and temper of the emigrants. "We will not say," exclaimed a Puritan leader in the first great expedition, "as the Separatists were wont to say at their leaving of England, Farewell Babylon, farewell Rome! but we will say, farewell, dear England! farewell the Church of God in England and all the Christian friends there!" Rich in this world's goods, rich in the religious learning of the schools, imbued with a firm belief in the proper subordination of the lower ranks, and endowed with a charter of self-government, the directors of the Massachusetts Company embarked on their great experiment.

As the Massachusetts Bay Colony grew in numbers and prospered, the drift of affairs in the open air of the New World indicated a decided bent in its religious and economic life. Now far removed from the discipline of Anglican bishops and the ambitions of the Anglican clergy, the Puritans floated off into independency, each of the little churches becoming a sovereign congregation before many years had elapsed. Varying likewise from original designs, the course of rural economy ran somewhat contrary to the expectations of those wealthy managers who hoped to see the establishment of large estates tilled by tenants, laborers, or bondmen.

Here, too, circumstances rather than theory proved to be the decisive element: the climate and soil of New England, coupled with an abundance of land and scarcity of labor, made anything like feudalism impossible. It was not because the Puritans had objections to servitude or slavery that they turned from this type of agriculture; they held indentured white servants, tried to enslave the Indians, and used Negro bondmen wherever profitable. It was because they found that in a land of long winters, stony fields, and diversified crops, chattel bondage on a large scale was economically impossible. Controlled by factors beyond their mastery, the Puritans therefore spread over New England under the leadership of freehold farmers; and those who could not endure that arduous career or had no love for a toilsome life among hills and rocks, found an outlet for their capital and energies upon the high seas. From fisheries, the sacred cod and the bulky whale, and from trafficking in ports far and near, the economic directors of New England, whose descendants were to try their mettle with the descendants of Virginia planters in forum and field, accumulated fortunes rivaling in size the riches wrung from the spreading tobacco leaves of the Old Dominion.

These economic factors in turn had a profound effect upon the spirit and procedure of government. Broadly speaking, the political experience of the gentlemen, yeomen, and merchants who came to New England had been no different from that of the dominant classes in Virginia, but their settlement in communities rather than on plantations made the small, compact town, not the county, the unit of political life. As all but church members were for sixty years excluded from the suffrage in Massachusetts, the village church and state became identical—the democratic tendencies of the free congregation accustomed to prayer and exhortation aiding the process of government by discussion.

After the towns had multiplied and meetings of the entire Massachusetts Bay Company at one place became troublesome, a representative system based upon the division into communities was introduced in 1634. Henceforward each town in open meeting, usually with much debate, elected one or two members to speak for it in the general court of the commonwealth. Soon every village had its statesmen prepared to discuss on a moment's notice any question of theology and politics, giving to the whole body corporate the tone of the community and congregation.

§

The niggardly soil, the severe life, and the religious rigor of Massachusetts forced migration, which in time founded the colonies of Rhode Island, Connecticut, and New Hampshire. From religious controversies led by two intransigent radicals, Roger Williams and Anne Hutchinson, sprang the first of these offshoots. Williams, a scholar from Cambridge who came to America in 1631 as a refugee from the autocratic rule of Archbishop Laud, ecclesiastical servant of Charles I, brought with him a theory of life and conduct disturbing to the system of Massachusetts as it had been to old England. He was a pioneer among the bold thinkers of the world in proclaiming religious toleration on principle rather than on expediency.

In Williams' creed were four cardinal points. First was the doctrine that "persecution for cause of conscience is most evidently and lamentably contrary to the doctrine of Christ Jesus." From this simple declaration it followed that "no one should be bound to worship or to maintain a worship against his own consent." Williams' third principle was that church and state should be separated, that to limit the choice of civil magistrates to church members was like choosing pilots and physicians according to their schemes of salvation rather than skill in their professions. Finally, the civil magistrate was not to interfere at all in matters of conscience; "his power extends only to the bodies and goods of men." Thus the ferment which produced Puritanism produced also the inquiring mind that denied the essential doctrine of all dogmatic faiths—universal conformity.

"Like Roger Williams or worse," as the perplexed Winthrop exclaimed, was Anne Hutchinson, who landed three years after the young Cambridge scholar. Mrs. Hutchinson was a woman of high courage, fine character, good family, and undoubted ability—"of ready wit and bold spirit," complained the governor whose supremacy she rejected. According to the faithful she brought over with her "two dangerous errors". She espoused the doctrine of justification by faith and declared that the Holy Ghost dwells in every believer. She also cut at the roots of established Puritanism, for she maintained the sovereignty of private judgment in matters religious against the fulminations of the clergy and the penalties of the civil magistrates. Such sentiments, intolerable enough to the authorities of Massachusetts when avowed by a man, were doubly outrageous in their eyes when disclosed by a woman of "feminist" temperament. It soon became evident that there was no room in Massachusetts for people like Williams and Hutchinson, no more than there would have been under the Established Church of Virginia or under the Holy Inquisition of Spain. So they were both banished from the land of the last word and the final good.

Williams, after spending a terrible winter of privation in the forests, gathered five companions around him and founded in 1636 the settlement of Providence at the head of Narragansett Bay. Two years later, Mrs. Hutchinson, fleeing from the same wrath, planted a colony at Portsmouth. In the path of the pioneers came many sectaries, most of them humble farmers and laborers who chafed under the strict rule of the Massachusetts gentry and clergy as the Puritans had chafed under the dominion of Charles I, Archbishop Laud, and the aristocracy.

Out of this movement, away from the Bay, sprang the colony of Rhode Island—a union of many towns which was granted a royal charter by Charles II in 1663. Soon discontented with the restrictions imposed by forests and rocky hills, enterprising pioneers of the new settlement took to the sea in ships built by their own hands, and many of them waxed rich distilling West Indian molasses into rum and exchanging rum for slaves to be carried to the Southern plantations. "Distillery is the main hinge upon which the trade of the colony turns," averred the Governor and Company on the eve of the American Revolution.

In the settlement of Connecticut, the second offshoot of Massachusetts, religious controversy also formed an element, but it was not the chief factor. As soon as the land around Massachusetts Bay was all taken up, adventurers began searching for better soil, and it was not long before they heard of the wonderful Connecticut River country far to the west. So they went forth to see and to possess. In the winter of 1635-36 an advance guard, driving cattle and carrying their household goods, journeyed overland through the forests to the new Canaan, where, in the coveted valley, they planted the three towns of Hartford, Windsor, and Wethersfield. Under the spiritual guidance of "the son of Thunder," Thomas Hooker, they reproduced in the main the religious policy of the mother colony; and under the indomitable John Mason they fell upon the neighboring Pequods, exterminating them by sword and fire. Inspired by their inherited or acquired talent for communal management, they drew up in 1639 their Fundamental Orders, characterized as "the first written constitution known to history that created a government."

About the same time other Puritans under the leadership of a rich London merchant, Theophilus Eaton, and a famous divine, John Davenport, planted tiny settlements at New Haven and other points along the Sound—self-governing towns which in due course were federated under a written constitution, known as the Fundamental Articles—

a system based on the faith that the Scriptures held forth a perfect rule for the government of all men in church and state and family. In 1662 the two little commonwealths were fused into one colony under a royal charter constituting the "company and society of our colony of Connecticut in America . . . one body corporate and politic in fact and name by the name of Governor and Company of the English Colony of Connecticut in New England, in America."

Other settlements flung off from Massachusetts beyond the Merrimac River grew into a thriving colony which in 1679 was cut away from the parent stem and erected into the royal province of New Hampshire.

§

Among the men of affairs who watched the colonizing experiments in America was a discreet and shrewd Catholic gentleman from Yorkshire, Sir George Calvert, who had risen high in the service of the Crown by the display of talents and complaisance. He was an investor in the stocks of the Virginia Company and when he was driven from the court by the intrigue of another favorite, he consoled himself with elevation to the peerage, as Lord Baltimore, a large sum of money, and adventures in the New World. After some futile tests in Newfoundland, he visited Virginia; and pleased by the milder climate of that region, he obtained from Charles I an immense grant of land in the neighborhood, which he named Maryland in honor of the king's French wife, Henrietta Maria.

By the terms of the charter, Lord Baltimore and his heirs and assigns were made "the true and absolute lords and proprietaries" of the land granted, on the condition of yielding annually to the Crown two Indian arrowheads and one-fifth of the gold and silver ore found in the colony. By the same terms, the proprietor became captain-general of the armed forces, head of the Church, and disposer of all offices, civil and clerical. Besides being authorized to create freehold estates, he was given the express right to establish a mediæval system in the New World by granting manors to vassal lords subject to feudal obligations. These high and extensive powers were, however, tempered by the provision that laws should be made with the consent of the freemen or their representatives. Before this significant document could be signed by the king, the first Lord Baltimore died and the parchment duly sealed passed to his heir, Cecilius Calvert, in June, 1632.

From first to last the Maryland colony was viewed by the Baltimores largely as an economic venture; they invested heavily in it and in time derived an enormous annual revenue from it. At the outset the second Lord Baltimore made provision for various types of immigrants qualified to develop his immense domain on a profitable basis. Heading his program was the allotment of one thousand acres to every gentleman who would transport five able men with supplies and an additional thousand acres for every additional group of five men brought overseas—each such estate to be erected into a manor "with all such royalties and privileges as are usually belonging to manors in England." In the second place, units of fifty and one hundred acres were offered to men and women who came at their own expense, with extra allowances for wives, children, and servants. All lands so granted were to pay a perpetual annual quitrent to the proprietary. With a view to bringing the soil quickly into cultivation, a special form of indenture was drafted for bond servants, and in a short time Negro slavery was introduced. Thus Maryland became a semi-feudal dominion, composed in part of manors owned by great landlords and tilled by white bond servants, tenants, and slaves, and in part of small freeholds cultivated by farmers of the middling order.

In planning his colony, Lord Baltimore adopted the broad principle of religious toleration. Holding a charter from a Protestant king, jealously watched by a nation in which the tide of Puritanism was rising high, he could not possibly hope to erect a purely Catholic community in Maryland. Indeed, his charter, strictly interpreted, contemplated the migration of no Catholics at all, for even their existence in England was without the sanction of law. Yet, being loyal to Rome, Lord Baltimore could hardly close his dominions to his own brethren; on the contrary, his first appeal for emigrants among the gentry seems to have been made mainly to persons of his own creed.

Nevertheless, discretion appears to have been the rule for all the Baltimores; only by the exercise of ingenuity could they expect to hold their property in the midst of the religious disputes that rent the English nation at home and filled with turmoil the colonies in the New World. In the original charter, drawn by the hand of the first Lord Baltimore, it was expressly provided that churches built in the colony were to be consecrated "according to the ecclesiastical laws of England"; thus, in form at least, the Protestant religion of the Established Church was to be the lawful religion of Maryland.

The successors of the original Lord Baltimore were equally circumspect. The son and heir in his instructions to the first governor and commissioners warned them that on the expedition over the sea they should suffer no offense or scandal to be given to any of the Protestants. By way of precaution, he ordered them to "cause all acts of Roman Catholic Religion to be done as privately as may be," and to "instruct all the Roman Catholics to be silent upon all occasions of discourse concerning matters of religion." Sensing troubles ahead, he told them that, in opening their ticklish dealings with Anglican Virginia, they should choose as their messenger "one as is conformable to the Church of England."

When, in 1642, the arbitrary personal government of Charles I had come to an end and England had launched upon the course of revolution, Lord Baltimore was quick to discover a storm blowing in his direction; so he wrote to his governor in Maryland, "that no ecclesiastic in the province ought to expect, nor is Lord Baltimore, nor any of his officers, although they are Roman Catholics, obliged in conscience to allow such ecclesiastics any more, or other, privileges, exemptions, or immunities for their persons, lands, or goods, than is allowed by His Majesty or other officers to like persons in England"—that is, lawfully, none at all. When the second revolution drove the Catholic James II from the throne of England in 1688, the Baltimore family lost its lucrative colony of Maryland. After a lapse of twenty years, Benedict Leonard Calvert, finding recovery on the old terms impossible, abandoned the religious faith of his ancestors and, by this act of apostacy, won back for his heirs and assigns their fruitful heritage.

While thus moving with great discernment amid the factional quarrels of the Protestants, the Baltimores gave careful thought to peopling their estate with planters and laborers. In the first advertisement to prospective emigrants, great stress was laid on the climate and soil of the colony and the possibility of making more than a hundred per cent profit out of each indentured servant transported; but as far as the record runs, the religious creeds of the emigrants were apparently matters of indifference to the proprietor. At all events, there were both Catholics and Protestants on the first expedition, though the exact proportion is a matter of controversy. According to a Jesuit who was on the ground early, the colony was "largely" Catholic; according to the Protestant historian, Henry Cabot Lodge, "it is a fair presumption that a majority of the settlers were Protestants."

Whatever the verdict, it is certain that the Baltimores, if they rendered cautious assistance to priests of their own faith, showed a willingness to sell or rent land to farmers of the Protestant creeds, not overlooking thrifty Puritans in New England. According to an entry in the journal of Governor Winthrop of Massachusetts, "Lord Baltimore being owner of much land near Virginia . . . made tender of land to any of ours that would transport themselves thither, with free liberty of religion and all other privileges which the place afforded, paying such annual rent as should be agreed upon." Though Winthrop added that none of his people had "any temptation that way," as a matter of fact many Puritans from Massachusetts and many Anglicans from Virginia did accept the terms offered to them and settled on the fertile lands of the Chesapeake shore. Indeed, they became so numerous in a few years that they threatened to overturn the original polity of the proprietor. Forgetting their ancient grudges, they made common cause against his mild tolerance, in their effort to get at his Catholic and Quaker subjects. If it had not been for the Toleration Act of 1649, so famous in local history, the Catholics would have been immediately subdued to Protestant dominion.

This measure of religious indulgence has been the subject of so much argument and the basis of such large claims in the name of liberty by both Catholics and Protestants that its history deserves examination in some detail. The practice of toleration, which arose from the principles entertained by Lord Baltimore, from his anomalous position under a Protestant sovereign, and from his eagerness to sell his land to emigrants, brought into Maryland, as we have noted, a decided mixture of religious sects, with the Protestant elements increasing more rapidly than the Catholic. When Charles I in 1648 was engaged in his desperate struggle with the Puritan party at home and was already within the dark shadow of the scaffold, he begged Lord Baltimore to take measures to avoid the charge that his colony was in reality a Catholic stronghold. Complying with this urgent request, Baltimore removed his Catholic governor and council, appointed Protestant substitutes, and sent out to his dominion a draft of a bill for limited religious freedom.

Shortly afterward the great Toleration Act was passed by the Maryland Assembly. At the time the governor and council were Protestants. If, as often claimed, the majority of the lower house was composed of Catholics, the assertion has been stoutly questioned on the other side. The truth is that there are no authentic records upon which to settle the dispute; there are no journals of the legislature showing how the members voted; and in any case, there is no reason why any lover of liberty in the abstract should grow excited over the spectacle. It is exercising restraint to say that a general freedom of conscience had not been up to that time a cardinal principle proclaimed by Catholics, Anglicans, or Puritans wherever they were in a position to coerce.

The terms of the Toleration Act itself reflect the nature of the liberty cherished by the parties which placed it on the statute books. It provided that no person professing to believe in Jesus Christ should be in any way molested in the exercise of his religion; while it imposed the sentence of death, accompanied by confiscation of goods, upon any person who "shall deny our Savior Jesus Christ to be the son of God or shall deny the Holy Trinity, the Father, Son, and Holy Ghost, or the Godhead of any of the said Three Persons of the Trinity, or the Unity of the Godhead, or shall use or utter any reproachful speeches, words, or language concerning the Holy Trinity or any of the said Three Persons thereof."

Other penalties, fines and public whippings, were prescribed for those who spoke reproachfully of the Virgin Mary or any of the several sects and factions—Puritans, Presbyterians, Independents, Catholics, Jesuits, Lutherans, Calvinists, Anabaptists, Brownists, Antinomians, Barrowists, Roundheads, or Separatists. Fines and whippings were laid down for all who "prophane the Sabbath or Lords day called Sunday by frequent swearing, drunkenness, or by any uncivil or disorderly recreation or by working on that day when absolute necessity doth not require." Such are the terms of the Act. Such are the circumstances in which it was passed. Such are the facts in the celebrated case, upon which those who feel called upon to make righteous judgments may base their verdict.

One thing is sure. The respite granted by the Toleration Act was only temporary. In the upheaval that drove James II from his throne forty years later, the pledge of indulgence was grievously wounded. From that time forward Anglicans had the upper hand and, making full use of their opportunity, they established the Church of England in Maryland, authorized the collection of taxes for its support, proscribed the public exercise of Catholic worship, and forbade the admission of Catholic immigrants. Thus they exhibited the symbols of Anglican supremacy in a manner that alienated from the government of England the affections of a powerful and wealthy class. As George III learned to his sorrow, Catholics upon occasion could be as revolutionary as Separatists.

§

The success of the Baltimores, in spite of their tribulations, fired the imagination of other courtiers. When the long night of the Civil War was over and Charles II was secure upon the throne of his fathers, there were many loyal, if not servile, supporters of the old monarchy to be rewarded and many creditors with claims upon the treasury and bounty of the new sovereign. Among the throng that now surged about the throne were eight men of outstanding pretensions: Clarendon, the prime minister whose devotion to the royalist cause had been above suspicion; Monk, the turncoat general of the parliamentary army who had delivered the country to Charles and was rewarded by elevation to the peerage; Lord Ashley Cooper, later the Earl of Shaftesbury, whose facility for changing his opinions in shifting currents won the favor of his ruler; Sir George Carteret, who, as governor of the island of Jersey in the English Channel, had been the last to lower the royal standard before Cromwell's victorious forces; Sir William Berkeley, high Tory governor of Virginia, and his brother, Lord Berkeley, both of whom had sustained the monarchy against the popular party; Lord Craven and Sir John Colleton, with slighter but still considerable claims upon the grace of Charles II. Upon these favorites as proprietors, Charles bestowed a great province, known as Carolina, stretching from the Atlantic to the Pacific, an estate which they were to rule jointly as pleased their fancies, subject to the laws of England and with the consent of a local assembly.

A few years after the charter was sealed, Shaftesbury engaged John Locke, political philosopher and Whig pamphleteer, to frame a constitution for their imperial domain. This task the learned bookman discharged by drafting one of the most fantastic documents now to be found in the moldering archives of disillusionment. He proposed that the eldest proprietor should be palatine and that the others should be admiral, chamberlain, constable, chief justice, high steward, and treasurer, according to lot. The proprietors were to reserve one-fifth of the land as their personal property; another large section was to be laid out into baronies and manors to be held by an aristoc-racy and tilled by hereditary serfs bound to the soil; and the remainder was to be sold to freeholders.

In keeping with this economic structure, an elaborate system of government including a popular assembly was devised, thus reflecting the Whig ideal of a perfect order for the wilderness—an order composed of an aristocracy resting upon servile labor held in check by a body of yeomen —the grand purpose being, as Locke said, to avoid "a numerous democracy," and at the same time to create an administration "most agreeable to the monarchy." This amusing constitution with a high-sounding title was ratified by the proprietors and declared in force, but it could no more be realized in Carolina than in the moon. Its interest to-day lies in the fact that it reveals the type of society which the Whigs, the most liberal of the governing classes in England, would have established in America if they had not been defeated by the irrepressible and stubborn reali-ties of life on the frontier.

Without waiting for the philosopher to complete his scheme, the proprietors raised a fund of £12,000 and fitted out in 1670 a colonizing expedition which planted a settlement called Charleston, removed to the site of the present city ten years later. They also offered inducements to adventurers who would take up land in their concession, turning a current of migration in that direction. Indeed, already in the northern portion of their province were rude settlements made by Quakers who had fled from the rigorous rule of the Established Church in Virginia and by lawless elements that preferred the freedom of the forests to the most respectable offerings of the Old Dominion.

Assured religious toleration by proprietors anxious to sell land, the hunted and discontented from many quarters now poured into the colony: Dutch angered by English supremacy in New York, Puritans weary of the clerical régime, Huguenots fleeing from the dragoons of Louis XIV, Scotch Presbyterians involved in religious and economic disputes at home or in Ireland, Germans seeking land or religious liberty or both, and Swiss who found at New Berne a milder climate and a richer soil than their mountain home afforded. Under skillful management the cultivation of rice and indigo was soon introduced, and the basis of economic prosperity quickly laid, with the aid of a labor supply drawn from Africa. To protect masters against violence, a drastic code was adopted prescribing whipping, branding, ear clipping, castration, and death for various offenses; but the consolations of the Christian faith were not withheld, for the law, while denying the right of manumission, expressly authorized baptism.

It was not long before the proprietors discovered that they had a stiff-necked generation in their miscellaneous collection of subjects attracted to Carolina from many parts of the earth. The governors, whom they sent in turn to the two sections into which the colony was divided—North and South—were always in conflict with the popular assemblies. More than one executive was driven out by the irate people from whom he tried to collect quitrents and other revenues. Again and again, owing to the scarcity of specie, the legislature of South Carolina insisted on issuing large quantities of fiat money, thus enacting early scenes in the controversy between debtors and creditors that was to rage for more than two centuries as the star of American empire moved westward. On one occasion local merchants who protested against paper money were held in jail until they apologized; and when British merchants across the sea induced the proprietors to veto the objectionable currency law, the South Carolina assembly answered by revolution. During the contest, the governor was deposed, a local paper-money man chosen to rule in the king's name, and a protest lodged with the Crown against "the confused, negligent, and helpless government of the proprietaries."

Weary of a fruitless contest that had brought neither profit nor glory, the owners of the Carolinas sold out to the Crown in 1729, each of the territories thus becoming a royal province. With the completion of this sale, the wrath of the colonists that had once raged around the heads of governors selected by the proprietors was transferred to the officers of the king. Freeholders and planters were no more eager to pay quitrents to the royal treasury than to eight English landlords; neither were they willing to tolerate any extensive interference with their vested interests. After nearly half a century of conflict over such issues, the Carolinas were ready for the revolution that put an end to control by the agents of the Crown.

§

Two of the first Carolina proprietors, Lord Berkeley and Sir George Carteret, seeing, at the time the southern project was first launched, a promise of fortune in American land speculation, determined to risk a venture on their own account; and in 1664 they managed to secure from their intimate friend, the Duke of York, a grant of territory between the Hudson and the Delaware to be held on the terms customary in such cases. Giving to their estate the name New Jersey, in honor of Carteret's channel home, the promoters began at once to develop the property by offering small freeholds to emigrants on easy conditions. When the doors were thrown open, settlers came from all parts of the British Isles to join the Dutch who had already built several hamlets on the west bank of the Hudson. The first governor, Philip Carteret, brought with him about thirty adventurers and their servants, who established a community at Elizabeth. Puritans from Connecticut founded the town of Newark; Scotch-Irish Presbyterians poured into the eastern counties; and English Quakers sought their peace and prosperity to the west in the fertile regions of the Delaware.

Before their enterprise had advanced very far, the proprietors found themselves in hot water, even though they sought to govern mildly with the aid of a popular assembly. Some of the Puritan towns, following the custom of Massachusetts, insisted on limiting the local suffrage to church members and in this matter refused to bow before the authority of the common legislature. On one thing, however, they agreed with the Quakers, Presbyterians, and Dutch, namely, on opposition to paying into the proprietary chest quitrents for their lands. When the formal collection began in 1670, all local differences were sunk in a general resistance to the demands of that treasury. The assembly ousted the proprietary governor, installed a pretender, and called for concessions. Sick of the bargain, after haggling for four years, Berkeley sold his interests to certain Quaker adventurers; and somewhat later the Carteret portion passed into other hands too.

But the new proprietors of divided Jersey—East and West—were equally unhappy in their efforts to govern their turbulent tenants and at length, weary of "a very expensive feather," they turned the colony over to the Crown in 1702. Thus New Jersey became a royal province, for a time united with New York, and royal governors fell heir to the troubles of the former proprietors as they also tried to combine administration with the enlargement of their private estates. Undeterred by the past record of the colony, Edward Hyde, eldest son of Lord Clarendon, driven to distraction by his English creditors, secured a place at the head of the combined provinces and in a remarkably short time restored his shattered finances. Incidentally he was aided by an astute chief justice, Roger Mompesson, who had also temporarily "stepped abroad to ease his fortune of some of his father's debts." If the residents of New Jersey were unable to defeat the designs of such adepts in administration, they were at least dexterous enough to block efforts to force upon them the doctrine and discipline of the Church of England. Even when they were later given a separate royal governor of their own, they continued to do battle with the executive over laws and taxes, and so made their way, with more or less tempest, down the stream of time to the crisis of the Revolution.

§

The numerous and varied discouragements under which the Carolina and Jersey proprietors labored did not frighten a young man of large fortune and discreet address who also had a substantial claim upon the attentions of Charles II—a young Quaker, William Penn. As a student at Oxford, Penn had been drawn to the religious life and with utter devotion had cast in his lot with the despised and persecuted sect of Friends, then more frequently called Ranters or Quakers. Neither the harsh régime of the prison to which he was more than once committed nor the heavy blows of his irate father could shake his determination, and after the death of his stern parent in 1670, the young man, finding himself in possession of considerable wealth, became interested in America as a religious haven for his brethren and a place for prudent investment.

Among the parcels of the estate inherited from his father, Penn held a claim against Charles II to the amount of £16,000, then a huge sum. How to extract that debt from the Merry Monarch long perplexed the young creditor; but finally, aided by the gentle arts of the courtier, he managed to obtain in payment a large territorial grant —Pennsylvania, as the king insisted on calling it. In form the charter effecting this transfer was modeled after that of Maryland; by express terms Penn was made the true and absolute lord of his domain and given a wide range of governmental authority, subject to the advice and consent of the freemen, including the power of making war, raising troops, and vanquishing his enemies "by God's assistance."

Finding that the territory covered by this royal charter had no coast line, Penn induced the Duke of York to turn over to him the Delaware region to the south which had been wrested from the Swedes by the Dutch and from the Dutch by the English. Although these lower counties were assigned to Penn on the same terms as his original grant, they were transformed into the separate colony of Delaware in 1702 and remained in that status under the Penn family until the declaration of American independence.

As soon as Penn was in secure possession of his estate, he set to work as a practical man of affairs to develop his territory—already inhabited by about six thousand people, Swedes and Dutch on the Delaware and Quakers who had preceded him in their quest for a refuge. Committed by his faith to the mild and healing principle of toleration, he made it known that all who settled in his colony should enjoy religious liberty. Making the most of this assurance, he collected a band of followers and at their head set sail for America in 1682. On his arrival, in conformity with Quaker pacifism, he made peace with the Indians and paid them for their claims. His title once cleared to the satisfaction of his conscience, Penn created a popular assembly, put into effect a liberal Frame of Government, and laid out

Philadelphia, city of brotherly love, in a fashion calculated to obviate the terrible evils of congestion that cursed the municipalities of the Old World.

Bearing in mind no doubt the methods of Lord Baltimore, Penn offered land to the large investor in five thousand acre lots at £100 each, with fifty acres added for every indentured servant transported, and to every man who would take over and "seat" his family in the colony a five hundred acre holding, all on the basis of an annual quitrent to the proprietor. If climate, soil, and the difficulty of alluring rich settlers had not defeated the plan, Pennsylvania might have become a colony of great estates tilled by tenants and laborers but in the end circumstances made it the home of traders and farmers. Penn's ingenious advertising in England and on the Continent drew merchants, yeomen, and peasants rather than men of wealth with capital to buy estates—English Quakers, Germans of various Protestant faiths, Scotch-Irish Presbyterians, Welsh Baptists, and later some Irish of the old stock, Catholic in religion—seekers after homesteads, not potential landlords of the grand style.

Under the scheme of government established by Penn, toleration was granted to "all who confess and acknowledge one Almighty and eternal God to be the creator, upholder, and ruler of the world and that hold themselves obliged to live peaceably and justly in civil society"; while freeholders and taxpayers professing faith in Jesus Christ were given the right to vote for members of the popular assembly. In practice, however, it appears that neither Catholics nor Jews enjoyed freedom of religious worship, at least in the beginning of the enterprise. Moreover, ungodly revelers were subdued to the law and stage plays, cards, dice, May-games, masques, and excessive hilarity were forbidden. To make easy the burden of taxes on property an excise for the support of the government was imposed on spirits.

Though moderation characterized Penn's theories of state, his days were filled with "hurries and perplexities" until the close of his career. His family's discontent with life on the raw frontier of America, and his interests in England forced him to return to his native land, leaving the administration of his colony in other hands. For some strange reason he chose governors who had little sympathy with his settlers; one, a soldier who ruled with military severity; others, riotous livers who offended his sober and God-fearing subjects.

As if to fill his cup to the brim, the colonists charged Penn with enriching himself from the sale of lands and playing the part of an exacting landlord. Grieved by these strictures, Penn replied that in truth his outlays had been greater than his receipts and that his obstreperous settlers did not pay their quitrents. In fact the dispute became so bitter that Penn was driven by sheer weariness to consider selling out to the Crown—only to be greeted by a declaration from the Pennsylvania legislature to the effect that the very proposition savored "first of fleecing and then of selling." Full of sorrows, Penn died in 1718 at the age of seventy-four.

In the natural course, the proprietorship passed to his three sons, all of whom loved pleasure and good living more than the hard work of efficient administration. So the conflict with the colony went on—quarrels over paper money issued by the legislature in spite of proprietary orders, over attempts of the assembly to tax the property owned by the Penns, over efforts to collect quitrents from recalcitrant settlers, over attempts of the belligerent Scotch-Irish on the frontier to wring from the pacific Quakers assistance in their constant troubles with the Indians.

It was only by trading and huckstering that the Penns managed to hold to their property at all and at best they were playing a losing game. Year by year the party of disaffection grew steadily. Having gained the upper hand in the assembly in 1764, it sent Benjamin Franklin to England to ask for the abolition of the proprietary system and the substitution of royal authority. To such a pass had things come when the restrictive measures of the mother country drove the discontented elements of Pennsylvania to make common cause with the other colonies against all governments deriving their powers from sources beyond the sea.

§

The religious motives that figured so largely in the founding of the English colonies were not especially emphasized by the Dutch West India Company when it raised its flag in the valleys of the Hudson and the Delaware and announced the creation of New Netherland. There was no mistake about the purposes of that corporation when it was established in 1621: its prime object was to earn dividends for its stockholders by trade. It was to carry on large mercantile operations in the Atlantic basin, prey upon Spanish commerce, conquer Brazil, carry slaves to American plantations, reap profits from traffic in furs, and establish settlements. Two years after its charter was duly drawn, the Company took steps looking toward the occupation of the Hudson Valley. Within a short time it built trading posts at Fort Orange, the present site of Albany, and on the Island of Manhattan, purchased from the Indians for sixty guilders, or about twenty-four dollars.

Having obtained two strategic military centers, the Company undertook to develop its estate into a paying property. Appreciating the importance of a freehold peasantry, it offered land in small lots to freemen who would go with their families to the new settlements. By this process it started a tiny trickle of immigrants into the colony, Walloons, or Protestants from the Spanish Netherlands, mingling with sturdy Dutch farmers in laying out homesteads or boweries at favorable points on Long Island and on both sides of the Hudson.

Finding this a slow operation, the corporation in 1629 offered to grant a huge domain to every patroon who would transport fifty persons at least fifteen years old and establish them on the land as laborers bound by servile tenure. In this manner a number of great feudal families was created—some of them so powerful that they survived the storms of factions, wars, and revolutions until near the middle of the nineteenth century. Not yet content with the growth of local industry, the Company, as a regular part of its business, imported slaves from Africa to work in field, shop, and kitchen.

Nevertheless, in spite of these efforts, New Netherland, at the end of forty years, had only about ten thousand inhabitants, of whom approximately one-sixth dwelt in the thriving village of New Amsterdam on the southern end of Manhattan Island. The truth is that the Company found the fur trade with the Indians the most lucrative division of its enterprise; its agents and interlopers exchanged rum and firearms on favorable terms for choice peltries, thus sowing dragons' teeth while earning high dividends. Of all the sickening butcheries that accompanied the conflict of whites and Indians, there was nothing more horrible than the tragedies which occurred on the frontiers of New Netherland.

Still it must not be thought that the Dutch were entirely indifferent to spiritual affairs. On the contrary, their Reformed Church was established in the colony; and the governors sent out by the Company, though usually hardfisted men of affairs, gave no little attention to providing the inhabitants with ministers, teachers, and "comforters of the sick." Their papers were not as full of references to divine interposition as those of English colonial executives, but the doughty old Stuyvesant, on one occasion when very angry at complaints against his rule, referred to God as well as the Dutch West India Company as a source of his authority. Nor were the Dutch entirely indifferent to the spiritual condition of the Indians. Missionaries were sent to the heathen and heroic efforts brought some of the Mohawks to the Christian faith. The harvest, however, was not great and in spite of their efforts, a Frenchman flung at the Dutch the charge that they were lacking in the "constant and laborious zeal for the salvation of unbelievers, the most obvious and distinguishing mark of the true Church of Christ."

From the beginning, the fortunes of the Dutch colony of New Netherland were in jeopardy. The territory on which it was planted was claimed by the English on grounds of prior discovery. On its eastern frontier it was early threatened by advancing pioneers in Connecticut, who offered a direct menace to the farmers and traders of the Hudson Valley. Even the Pilgrims far away at Plymouth, while they remembered the kind treatment they received in Holland, grumbled about the trading cruises of the Dutch along the coast and the transfer of business in peltries to the market at New Amsterdam. Besides this, the English at home, already imperial rivals of the Dutch in two hemispheres, were in a mood to put a term to their competition in the New World at least.

In 1664 the blow fell. King Charles II granted to his brother, the Duke of York, the whole region between the Hudson and the Delaware and, without giving the Dutch any warning, an English fleet descended upon New Amsterdam with a thundering command to surrender. In vain did the testy old governor, Peter Stuyvesant, storm and protest. New Netherland passed under the English flag.

The Duke of York, now in possession of his goodly domain, after assigning a part of it, as we have seen, to Carteret and Berkeley for their colony of New Jersey, gave his name to the rest and ruled it as high proprietor until he ascended the throne in 1685. Fort Orange became Albany; New Amsterdam became New York; and English homesteads began to rise among the Dutch boweries. Under the genial favor of the Duke, English fortune hunters now secured huge grants, running in size from fifty thousand to a million acres, at negligible quitrents, thus adding an English aristocracy, partly absentee, to the Dutch gentry created by the West India Company and retarding the growth of the colony by impediments in the way of freeholders. What was lost, however, in the slow development of agriculture was made up in part by an increase of trade. So in a fashion the society of England was duplicated. Sons of the landed proprietors went in for trade as well as the Church and the army; daughters of rich merchants married sons of landed families; and after New York became a royal province on the coronation of James, in 1685, a little flavor of the court gave tone to the ceremonial life of the upper classes.

§

Among the colonies developed as economic undertakings and religious havens by corporations and proprietors, it is rather difficult to place Georgia, the last of the English settlements in America. It did not spring from the enterprise of a commercial company, the ambitions of a rich adventurer, or the aspirations of seekers after religious liberty. It had its origin in the dream of a philanthropist, James Oglethorpe. That gallant soldier was long oppressed in spirit by the horrible plight of poor wretches languishing in English prisons—often merely unlucky debtors, sometimes unhappy persons unable to accept the prevailing styles in religion, or again the victims of one of the sternest criminal codes to be found in the annals of man's inhumanity.

After pondering long upon the problem thus presented, Oglethorpe came to the conclusion that the solution lay in another American colony. Acting largely on his motion, George II in 1732 vested in the hands of a board of trustees a large dominion below South Carolina, charging them to administer their estate "as one body politic and corporate." At Savannah, during the next year, Oglethorpe made the first settlement in the new colony.

In this undertaking, business and philanthropy were to be combined. Lands were to be granted to emigrants in small lots, none more than five hundred acres in size, and wine and silk were to be produced as staples. To all except Catholics the doors were to be open and the Indians were to be converted to Christianity. Slavery was forbidden because the trustees did not want to create a province "void of white inhabitants, filled with blacks, the precarious property of a few." The sale of rum was prohibited in the interest of industry and good order.

In these circumstances Georgia soon attracted a polyglot population, including Jews from many parts of Europe, Salzburgers from the valleys of the eastern Alps, Moravians led by Count Zinzendorf, Highlanders under John McLeod of Skye, as well as Englishmen of all sorts and conditions. Missionaries came to nourish the spiritual life of the colony: John and Charles Wesley for a time toiled in that curious vineyard; Whitefield and Habersham stormed the sinners with prayers and sermons.

In view of all this diversity, it is not surprising that Georgia early became the scene of domestic strife. Charles Wesley quarreled with Oglethorpe and was sent home, ostensibly as the bearer of dispatches. John Wesley, after betraying a strange indiscretion in an affair of the heart, "shook the dust of Georgia off his feet" in time to escape the consequences of a suit filed by the husband of the lady in the case. The rank and file of colonists also made trouble for the administration by demanding rum and slaves and then more liberty in disposing of their lands.

On the point of rum, the trustees finally had to yield at the end of ten years. In a short time the pressure for slavery also became irresistible. Both Whitefield and Habersham made powerful pleas in favor of the institution on the ground that it would advance the propaganda of the gospel of Jesus. "Many of the poor slaves in America," exclaimed the latter, "have already been made freemen of the heavenly Jerusalem." Seeking advice from their spiritual guides in Germany, the Salzburgers were gratified to hear that "if you take slaves in faith and with the intent of conducting them to Christ, the action will not be sin, but may prove a benediction." Thus encouraged by ministers of the gospel, the merchants of Savannah cried out for "the one thing needful." So the harassed trustees were driven to give their consent, adding slaves to the already mixed population of Georgia.

As a result the lowlands of the colony were laid out into plantations tilled by slaves on their way to the status of freemen in "the heavenly Jerusalem," while the yeomen were driven steadily into the piedmont, giving a sectional flavor to the economics and politics of Georgia that lasted until the age of populism and beyond. When rum and slaves were introduced, the anxieties of the trustees increased rather than diminished until, exhausted by wearisome battles with the local assembly, the corporation gave up the ghost in 1752 and Georgia, like the neighboring Carolinas, became a royal province.

CHAPTER III

The Growth of Economic and Political Power

ONE hundred and seventy years lay between the founding of Jamestown and the Declaration of Independence—a longer period, it is instructive to remember, than the lapse of time since America took her place among the sovereign nations of the earth. To the casual reader of letters, diaries, journals, and other records of the age, those colonial years seem mainly filled with the swirling eddies of purposeless war and politics. There were countless clashes with the Indians, always brutal, often futile. There were wars with the French and Spanish, agonizing phases of the English struggle for the encirclement of the globe that incarnadined the waters of seven seas and the soil of five continents.

There were domestic events that crowded the pages of those who chronicled the passing days: exciting contests in America as the fortunes of contending parties in England flowed and ebbed through revolution, restoration, and revolution; quarrels among the colonies and proprietors over boundaries and commercial regulations; theological disputes, loud and long, as Cotton Mather and Jonathan Edwards lashed sinners or parsons of the Church of England sought to extend their authority over all the king's subjects; flashes of intolerance flaming out against Catholics, Jews, and the holders of novel ideas; dramatic struggles over freedom of the press whenever royal agents laid heavy hands on the engines of public opinion; angry controversies between governors and popular assemblies ending sometimes in the expulsion of the king's officers; epidemics of smallpox sending terror through widespread communities; plagues of popular frenzy such as the execution of witches in New England and massacres of Negroes in New York; patient experiments in agricultural improvements; and the ceaseless pageant of common humanity engrossed in the routine of labor from sun to sun.

And yet from our vantage point we can now see, beneath the apparently driftless whirl of events, deep currents setting in toward independence. Crashing axes and cracking rifles on the Western frontier marked the inexorable advance of the American empire. The ceaseless coming and going of ships meant more hands to labor and more wealth for private chests. Stern old gentlemen, in ruffles and knee breeches, bending over their accounts, were swelling the patrimonies that were to give leisure and power to the Gadsdens, Pinckneys, Morrises, Washingtons, Jeffersons, and Adamses of the American Revolution. Quarrels in colonial assemblies were teaching sons of yeomen and merchants how to draw resolutions, frame declarations, manage finances, make constitutions, and carry on the warfare of the public forum.

In meeting houses, clerical studies, college classrooms, and petty editorial chambers, active minds were gathering the knowledge with which to freight their arguments and give point to their appeals directed to a somnolent, yet potential, nation unfolding into sovereignty. Campaigns against the Indians and the French showed provincials how to organize, supply, and direct that indispensable branch of the state—military force. Colonial privateers, preying on French and Spanish commerce, were learning how to trim their sails and use their guns preparatory to the contest with English seamen. In short, America was acquiring during those colonial years the economic resources, political experience, intellectual acumen, and military arts that were to sweep half a continent into independence and summon into being a governing class capable of sustaining it.

§

In the early stages of colonial development, the stream of migration to America was almost purely English—merchants, yeomen, laborers, artisans, scholars from Oxford and Cambridge, and a few, a very few, scions of noble families usually in quest of materials with which to repair damaged fortunes. This movement was strongest in the century that saw the foundation of the colonies. The Puritan exodus that carried about twenty thousand adventurers to New England was especially large during the years between 1629 and 1640 while Charles I was endeavoring to establish a personal despotism in London; then it dwindled to a thin stream.

Thus it happened that, on the eve of the Revolution, the major portion of the inhabitants in that region were the descendants of original pioneer stock. For different reasons, perhaps, but with similar results the English migration into the Southern colonies also slowed down, after the first spurt of enthusiasm, leaving the older houses in possession of the ancestral heritage.

During the eighteenth century the growth of the English population in America was due to big families among the settlers rather than to increments from the mother country. An abundance of cheap land encouraged early marriages, making a wife and children economic assets, not a drain upon the husbandman's purse. As the records of family Bibles bore witness, the ancient injunction to replenish the earth was literally fulfilled. Maria Hazard, for example, born in Rhode Island, lived to the ripe old age of a hundred years, and "could count five hundred children, grandchildren, great-grandchildren, and great-great-grandchildren. When she died, two hundred and five of them were alive; a grand-daughter of hers had already been a grandmother near fifteen years." Through the fecundity of such families the colonies were in time dominated by generations reared on American soil, who knew not England and whose affections were fixed upon this country as their native land. With few exceptions, the leaders of the nation that waged the war of independence were of the oldest stock. The founder of the Adams family landed in Massachusetts about 1636; the first Washington came to the shores of Virginia in 1656; the original Franklin took up his humble labors on this continent in 1685.

Later additions to the colonial population were, in the main, from peoples who were either hostile to the administration at London or who at least felt no thrill of patriotism when they saw the flag of England waving above their heads. The Scotch-Irish, next in numbers to the English, had, like the Puritans, fled from the regimen of the government of Great Britain. Their ancestors, in the seventeenth century, had moved from Scotland to the north of Ireland—a fertile region vacated by the natives as they were scourged and driven before the sword and torch of Cromwell. There the Scotch kept alive their Presbyterian faith and grew prosperous on the manufacture of linen and woolen cloth until their industry and their religion brought them also into conflict with the authorities of England. On complaints arising from English competition, Parliament forbade the export of their cloth and, in the acts intended to establish the supremacy of the Anglican Church, laid their worship too under the ban. It was in despair of relief from oppression in Ireland that they then turned to America as a refuge.

About the end of the seventeenth century, a tide of

Scotch-Irish migration, augmented by individuals and whole communities direct from Scotland, set in strongly toward the New World and continued unbroken for generations. Finding the coastal region in the possession of the earlier arrivals—English, Dutch, and Swedes—the Scotch were usually forced to the frontier, where their remoteness, their conditions of life and their tense struggle for existence made still weaker the ties that bound them to the Old World. Even less than the Puritans of New England did they have reason to profess loyalty to King George and their number, embracing about one-sixth of the colonial population, made them formidable.

Like the Scotch-Irish immigrants, the Germans, except for a few scattered adventurers, appeared late upon the American scene; not until William Penn opened wide the doors of his colony in the latter part of the seventeenth century did they migrate in large numbers. Most of the Germans were also forced into the interior, where they maintained their separate language, press, religion, and schools, manifesting a serene indifference to all efforts to Anglicize them. If they felt no active hostility toward London, they had no special reason for taking the side of George III against their neighbors and they were not to be ignored for in 1776 they numbered at least two hundred thousand.

The French Huguenots were other late immigrants; the seventeenth century was drawing to a close when Louis XIV revoked their charter of toleration—the Edict of Nantes—and harried them from his land. Having followed commercial pursuits principally at home, most of the Huguenots continued in those vocations on their arrival in the New World. As merchants they were keenly alive to the competition of Englishmen in the American markets. As people of substance and education alien to English traditions, they furnished more than their share of political leadership in the movement that overthrew British dominion.

Perhaps equally numerous in America were the native

Irish, Celtic in race and Catholic in religion, who seem to have come by the hundreds, if not by the thousands, bearing the scars of an age-long conflict with the Anglo-Saxon. Though they met no very cordial reception in the land of their adoption, they flocked to the American army when its standard of revolt was raised. From many lands came the Jews fleeing as of old from economic and religious persecution; like the Huguenots, they turned to merchandising and in a similar fashion were subjected to the pressure of English competition. Thus it happened that, in the peopling of the colonies, the stream of tendency ran against the continuance of political allegiance to the Old World, its powers, governors, and potentates.

Meanwhile intercolonial migrations were breaking down the barriers of purely local circumstance. Puritans, scarcely established in Connecticut, pulled up their roots, moved into Long Island, and then made their way into New Jersey. Quakers from Plymouth, pained by conflicts with their neighbors, passed into Virginia and, meeting little friendliness there, eventually found a home in the western wilderness of North Carolina. A French Huguenot, Faneuil, tried his fortune in New York, transferred his business to Rhode Island, sent his son, Peter, to Boston. In the veins of many colonists of the second generation ran the blood of two or three nations and an English name might well cover a Dutchman, a Swede, or a Scotch covenanter. For instance, Dirck Stoffels Langesstraet sailed from the Netherlands to the New World in 1657; a descendant married a Quakeress in New Jersey; the good old Dutch name became Longstreet; restless offspring took ship for Georgia; finally James Longstreet, trained at West Point, on the river once claimed by Holland, served the Southern Confederacy from Manassas to Appomattox. Benjamin Franklin, nourished in Boston, ripened his talents in the milder atmosphere of Philadelphia, and gave his last years to the service of a continent. It is true that the cross-currents of the population movement were not heavy but the migrations were already mixing many strains, making a new amalgam, known as American.

§

When once a foothold was secured on the coast line, the American colonists with tireless activity carried their enterprise in every direction as they were beckoned by fertile valleys, gaps in somber mountains, and the broad ways of the open sea. Having few mechanical contrivances, their course was largely shaped by the geographical environment in which they found themselves. They followed the roads which nature had laid out. From the seaboard they swept westward into the interior with incredible swiftness in spite of hostile Indian tribes and the vanguard of French imperialism. Fur traders and hunters were on the outer fringe of the combers that rolled onward toward the setting sun; not far behind were men of practical interest lured by curiosity and love of adventure. Then came the land-hungry farmers. On every part of the long line the push continued day and night.

To the north, Puritan pioneers pressed steadily inland until, within less than a century after the founding of Boston, they had their outposts in the Housatonic Valley, on the very edge of Massachusetts and Connecticut. In the neighboring colony of New York the advance on the hinterland was directed mainly up the Hudson River to Albany, the old Dutch center, from which spreading farms soon radiated toward every point of the compass. New Jersey, lying between two prosperous commercial settlements, was quickly filled by migrations from both directions as well as from the Old World; the beginnings of New Brunswick were made in 1681 and of Trenton four years later. For the northward thrust into Pennsylvania the Susquehanna River opened a highway; by 1726 farms were laid out on the present site of Harrisburg; while along the southern frontier a thin line of settlements steadily crept toward the upper waters of the Ohio, reaching the gateway to the Mississippi Valley, before the colony passed from the control of the Penn family.

In the South, the westward march was even swifter. Under the system of extensive and wasteful cultivation by slave labor, the rich coastal plain was quickly occupied, forcing small farmers in search of homes to flock into the upland regions. As soon as settlements were well started in the piedmont, they were fed by streams of migration from the German and Scotch-Irish regions of Pennsylvania. By this process of unremitting penetration, the Blue Ridge country and the Shenandoah Valley were occupied while the English flag still floated over the frontier posts. Even the higher mountain barriers were pierced; as early as 1654 a Virginia colonel was in the Kentucky country, and within forty years trafficking was begun with the Cherokees in the forests of Tennessee.

On the eve of the American Revolution, explorers were zealously searching that segment of the frontier in every nook and cranny—state builders at work. In 1751, Christopher Gist was paddling his canoe on the waters of the Kentucky River; a few years later John Finley was tramping over ground that was soon to be dark and bloody. In 1769, that fearless Nimrod, Daniel Boone, "ordained of God to settle the wilderness," led a band through the Cumberland Gap into the new promised land. Following in the trail of the forerunners went groups of pioneer farmers.

Inspired by their reports, a North Carolina promoter, Richard Henderson, dreaming of profits to be made in western land, organized a company, purchased from the Indians in 1775 an immense domain lying between the Kentucky and Cumberland Rivers, and founded the settlement of Transylvania. Thus, before Washington took command of the revolutionary army at Cambridge a fourteenth English colony was in process of formation far beyond the seaboard line. Speaking of America as a whole, a fertile domain many times the area of England was already staked out, sparsely settled, and brought under rude but productive cultivation. Facts, as Carlyle would say, immense and indubitable!

This inland advance of colonial empire accelerated the tendency toward the predominance of the freehold farmer in the agricultural economy of America. It was the man fired by the passion for owning a plot of ground who led the vanguard of settlers all along the frontier from New Hampshire to Georgia; to him cheap land meant freedom, to his family a rude but sufficient comfort. So the English, German, and Scotch-Irish pioneers who crept out into the narrow valleys, out into the deep forests, and high into the piedmont carried with them the freehold system and the social order inevitably associated with it. They were not peasants, in the European sense of the word, surrounded by agricultural resources already exploited and encircled by ruling orders of landlords and clergy armed with engines of state and church for subduing laborers to social discipline. On the contrary, these marching pioneers were confronted by land teeming with original fertility, by forests and streams alive with game and fish, and they were, under the sun and stars, their own masters.

In these circumstances a new psychology was evoked, making a race of men and women utterly different in spirit from those who dwelt on the great manors of New York and Maryland, on the wide Southern plantations, and in the villages of the Old World. Moreover, these freehold farmers faced the New West, not Europe; their communities were more isolated, more provincial, more independent, more American than those along the Atlantic seaboard. Passing years but strengthened their fiber and their love of liberty, while the ties of memory and affection that bound them to the Old World faded into oblivion.

Inexorably the currents of their life and thought ran in new channels. They would not have been at home in the goodly gatherings of Doctor Johnson's Grub Street friends, nor could they have deported themselves correctly with gentlemen in court dress or lawn sleeves jostling for favor, preferment, and place at a levee of George III. Nothing in their lives made them a part of the system of privilege and class rule that constituted the government of England in the eighteenth century. Nothing in their lives inclined them to look with friendly eyes upon the emissaries of that system—neither the English fur traders who resented every invasion of farmers into the haunts of game nor the English land speculators, often the favorites of royal governors, ever studying colonial maps for magnificent grants with which to enrich themselves and their families. The bonds that united the people of the interior to the English government were as light as gossamer and, when fear of the French and Spanish had been dissipated by war, they were shaken off like dew after the first crack of the rifle at Concord.

From the huge agricultural area already occupied in 1765 flowed annually an immense stream of produce. All the sections save New England raised more provisions than they could consume. The middle colonies sent to the port towns for shipment mountains of corn, flour, salt pork, flax, hemp, furs, and peas, as well as livestock, lumber, shingles, barrel staves, and houses all shaped for immediate erection. Maryland and Virginia furnished the great staple, tobacco, the mainstay of their economic life—an article for which the planters had a steady demand unhampered by competition. It was in tobacco that they paid for imported cloth, tea, coffee, furniture, silver, carpets, and tapestries, and met the bills of their sons studying in Oxford or in Cambridge. Since the crop was sure, those who produced it could easily obtain advances in goods and cash, so easily in fact that from year to year their credits mounted higher and higher until, by the eve of the Revolution, Southern gentlemen were owing English merchants thousands of pounds, the payment of which they were not unhappy to see stayed by the struggle for independence and finally discharged in large part by the government of the United

States under the benign administration of one of their
brethren, Thomas Jefferson. North Carolina offered farm
produce and some tobacco in the market, but paid its London bills mainly in tar, pitch, and turpentine. South Carolina and Georgia furnished rice, shingles, bacon, and salt
beef to the Atlantic and Mediterranean trade, and about
the middle of the eighteenth century, after persistent experiments led by Eliza Pinckney, added indigo to their profitable staples.

§

On the ocean as on the land, American colonists drove
their enterprise until they became no mean competitors of
those hardy mariners who bore the British flag around the
world and into the markets of every known port. The
inhospitable soil of New England early directed the industry
of the Puritans to the sea, to fishing, shipping, trading, and
all the varied interests connected with such undertakings.
Local forests furnished oak for timbers and boards, fir for
masts, pitch for turpentine and tar; fields yielded hemp for
rope; and mines iron for anchors and chains. Why should
man be a serf of the soil when he could ride the bounding
main? All along the northern coast, especially the New
England line, were busy shipyards where, to the music
of hammer and saw, rose splendid sloops and schooners—
swift and beautiful—big enough to sail any sea and sturdy
enough to weather any gale. By the middle of the eighteenth century, New England was launching seventy new
ships every year, New York and Pennsylvania forty-five,
and the states to the south forty. Already London shipbuilders beside the Thames had begun to complain that
their trade was declining, their workmen migrating, their
profits disappearing as a result of American competition.

It was the sea that offered the highest adventure to the
youth of the colonial period. New England boys in their
early years fled from the stony fields, picked up the art of
navigation, saved a little money, and at the age of nineteen

or twenty commanded brigs of their own. The sea permitted them to escape from the terrible sermons of the Mathers, to make a fortune, to rise to a social position, and to wear with dignity the title of gentleman. Sea breezes carried them into distant lands where they saw strange peoples and stranger customs which slowly dissolved in skepticism the faith and usages of their fathers.

When piping times of peace were broken, as often happened, by wars between England and other imperial powers, the losses of regular trade were more than offset by privateering at the expense of the French or Dutch or Spaniards. As soon as a storm burst, the government issued licenses to private shipowners authorizing them to seize the vessels and goods of the enemy wherever found on the high seas. Daring captains, who shared the loot with their sailors, were financed by local merchant princes and let loose in shoals upon the foe. In the journals left by such freebooters, operating under the color of the law with seal and parchment in their cabins, may be read many a tale of exciting adventure. "Brave living with our people," wrote one of them, Captain Benjamin Norton, who sailed for the West Indies in 1741 to singe the Spaniard's beard. "Punch every day, which makes them dream strange things which foretells Great Success in our Cruize. They dream of nothing but mad Bulls, Spaniards and bagg of Gold."

From privateering it was easy to turn to piracy. Thus did the doughty Captain Sawkins, who, with a hardy crew, harried the Panama coasts. When a local Spanish governor asked to see their commission, the Captain replied that they brought "commissions on the muzzles of our guns, at which time he should read them as plain as the flame of gunpowder could make them." Yet Captain Sawkins was not a godless man; finding his pirate crew shaking dice on a Sunday, he threw the shining ivories overboard to express his deep indignation at such profanation of that holy day.

Others equally courageous were more consistently pagan

in their view of life. Captain Bartholomew Roberts, for instance, wearing a "rich crimson Damask Wastcoate, and Breeches, a red Feather in his Hat, and a Gold Chain ten times around his Neck," scorned the polite practices of pulpit, pew, and counting house. His mighty men vowed that they would never be captured and hanged like Captain Kidd's crew, but would rather "put fire with one of their Pistols to their Powder and go all merrily to Hell together." Perhaps they were screwed up to that high resolve by the knowledge that, when imprisoned pirates were being prepared for the gallows, "Sermons were preached in their hearing every day . . . And nothing was left that could be done for their Good."

Ships built by American labor were, of course, mainly employed in the profitable undertakings of peaceful trade. In waters within reach was an abundant supply of whales, cod, salmon, mackerel, and other kinds of fish, which afforded the material for an immense and growing business—catching, curing, and shipping. On this basis rested an important branch of American economy, next in importance, perhaps, to tobacco planting and absolutely essential to the prosperity of the colonies. The best fish were carried to England, Spain, and Italy and the proceeds principally used to pay for manufactures bought of the mother country. Inferior grades were shipped to the West Indies to serve as food for slaves and were there exchanged for sugar and molasses, which were in turn transformed into rum.

In its extent and daring the whaling industry especially aroused the admiration of the Old World. Burke, warning his colleagues in Parliament against treating the Americans as puny children, bade them "look at the manner in which the people of New England have of late carried on the whale fishery. Whilst we follow them among the tumbling mountains of ice and behold them penetrating into the deepest frozen recesses of Hudson's Bay and Davis's Straits, whilst we are looking for them beneath the Arctic circle, we hear that they have pierced the opposite region of polar cold, that they are at the antipodes, and engaged under the frozen serpent of the South. . . . Nor is the equinoctial heat more discouraging to them than the accumulated winter of both poles. We know that whilst some of them draw the line and strike the harpoon on the coast of Africa, others run the longitude and pursue their gigantic game along the coast of Brazil. No sea but what is vexed by their fisheries. No climate that is not a witness to their toils. Neither the perseverance of Holland, nor the activity of France, nor the dexterous and firm sagacity of English enterprise ever carried this most perilous mode of hard industry to the extent to which it has been pushed by this recent people; a people who are still, as it were, but in the gristle and not yet hardened into the bone of manhood."

Out of the oil and candles yielded by this dangerous pursuit flowed a huge business with the mother country and Europe. Under the glow of oil lamps, the cottages of New England farmers were transformed at night from dingy hovels into well-lighted homes where books could be read and games played after the long day's work was done— a novel and appealing scene in the history of agriculture, the beginning of a revolution in culture.

Among the filiated industries of the sea was a formidable traffic in rum which touched many shores and sustained many thriving towns. The sugar and molasses of the West Indies were carried to New England, especially to Rhode Island, where they were transformed by distilleries into a spirit with the qualities of liquid fire. This beverage was then sold in enormous quantities to the fishermen engaged with net and harpoon in biting winds and chilling spray, to stalwart laborers in the dockyards, and to masters of sailing ships, who never failed on the appointed hour to serve grog as named in the bond.

Larger quantities of rum went into the slave trade. It was the staple article in that branch of business enterprise; it passed as currency on the West coast of Africa, where Negroes, to slake their fierce appetite, would sell their enemies, their friends, their mothers, fathers, wives, daughters, and sons for New England's scalding potion. The unhappy victims of this traffic, huddled in the low spaces made vacant by the removal of hogsheads, were taken to the West Indies to raise more sugar or to the plantations of the Southern colonies to toil in the rice and tobacco fields.

From the profits of this exchange came the fortunes of great families and the prosperity of whole communities. When, therefore, the English government sought to favor the plantations of the English West Indies at the expense of the neighboring islands belonging to France, by taxing the sugar of the latter, the action struck deep into the interests of New England manufacturers as well as the business of carriers whose sails were spread under many skies.

Next in importance to the fisheries and the various branches of enterprise connected with them was the general carrying trade, which employed thousands of American ships. First of all, in this relation, was the coastwise traffic —in itself enormous. Since the roads uniting the colonies were few in number and well-nigh impassable for stage-coaches or wagons during a large part of the year, the sea and the rivers had to furnish a substitute. Hence, a regular freight and passenger service sprang up along the shore, permitting the merchants of Boston, Baltimore, Charleston, or New York to set sail for a distant American port almost any day in the week.

Another branch of the sea trade was the transport of the produce of farms and plantations to the West Indies and to Europe and the carriage of manufactures home on the return voyage. As an old writer remarked, the Yankees gave "unremitting attention to the most minute article which could be made to yield a profit" and "obtained for themselves the appellation of the Dutchmen of America." Did the burghers of Holland want sugar for their tea? Americans brought it swiftly from the West Indies and sold it for a bill of exchange on London. Did Spanish

grandees demand choice flour from New York or Pennsylvania? American shipmasters soon had their prows
pointed toward the nearest port of Spain with such cargoes
to be exchanged for precious specie or for old wine to en-
liven good dinners in Boston, Charleston, or Philadelphia.
There was no considerable port of the great Atlantic basin
or the Mediterranean that did not regularly witness the
coming and going of American ship captains seeking to
turn an "honest penny" by trade, sometimes with only
poetic respect for the local revenue laws.

§

Less romantic than the lure of the sea, but no less potent
in the upbuilding of economic strength, was the development
of industries in the colonies. Having at hand all the materials and natural resources for manufacturing, the Americans through necessity and enterprise supplemented their
labors at the bake-oven and the plow with the handicrafts of
loom and forge. From the very beginning, the women of
nearly every home spun and wove and sewed, supplying
serges, linsey-woolseys, and other coarse woolen fabrics
for rough wear. As time went on their skill increased until
they were able to make broadcloth which gentlemen of
fastidious taste could wear without shame at the church
or in the counting house.

Seeing the germs of a lucrative business in this domestic
craft, men also gave their attention to it, building little
mills here and there along the tumbling streams and placing
upon machinery some of the burdens of labor. Under this
double stimulus, production for the use of the family
widened into production for the community, and at length
for a lively export trade to the plantations of the South and
the West Indies. By the opening years of the eighteenth
century the traffic had become so large that the royal governor in New York grew alarmed at the menace of the
competition in textiles; with great foresight he warned the

authorities in London that people who could clothe themselves handsomely without the help of England would soon begin to think of ruling themselves without her supervision. Economically not so important but artistically not a whit behind the woolen industry was the manufacture of fine linens by thrifty housewives; the samples of their work that have come down to us bear witness to their prowess at the wheel and loom.

Into other industrial fields, the enterprising colonials also ventured with signal success. At shops scattered far and wide, hats of no mean style and finish were turned out for local trade and even for export to distant settlements. Skillful weavers at Germantown supplied thread stockings by the thousand dozen at a dollar a pair. Saffron books of colonial merchants tell us of rope, starch, candles, earthenware, leather goods, shirtings, sheeting, duck, glass, refined sugar, and paper made by American labor in increasing quantities, pressing hard upon English imports in many markets and giving promise of indefinite expansion under favorable conditions.

Also in the iron industry—that very basis of modern imperial power—did American enterprise show signs of future greatness. In almost every colony beds of ore were discovered and, as soon as the first days of settlement were over, forges appeared along the rivers of New England, New Jersey, Pennsylvania, and Virginia. The ways of the ironmakers can be illustrated in the progress of Abraham Lincoln's forebears. The third son of the first Lincoln, who came to Massachusetts in 1637, built a forge on the banks of a neighboring brook and prospered; other descendants carried that industry into New Jersey; and a hundred years later Lincolns were engaged in Tubal Cain's art on the Schuylkill in Pennsylvania. With individual initiative, corporate enterprise was combined: a mining company was organized at Simsbury, Connecticut, in 1709.

Whether working for companies or on their own account, most of the masters were content to turn out bar iron for local use, or pig iron for transport to the mills of England; but the more adventurous leaders, especially in the Northern colonies, were not so modest in their ambitions. They set up rolling and slitting mills; they manufactured nails, guns, chains, kettles, hardware, hinges, hoes, spades, and all the coarser articles that could be made of metal. The product of many a colonial foundry survives in the chimneys of Georgian houses and in the museums recently erected by reverent hands.

§

Though, to the statistician of modern trade, the industry of colonial America seems trivial, yet in comparison with the enterprise of England at the time it assumed serious proportions. At all events—and this is the point—in every branch it excited the fears and jealousies of English competitors. Even with the seven seas to command there was hot rivalry in fishing, so hot that, in 1775, an English writer exclaimed: "The Northern colonies have nearly beaten us out of the Newfoundland fisheries, that great nursery of seamen; insomuch that the share of New England alone exceeds that of Britain." Shipbuilders of the Thames, as we have said, protested that the American yards carried off their business, their workmen, and their profits.

Bursting out in anger over the growth of colonial carrying enterprises, a contemporary English observer complained bitterly that "the trading part of the colonies rob this nation of the invaluable treasure of 30,000 seamen and all the profits of their employment; or in other words, the Northern colonies, who contribute nothing to our riches and our power, deprive us of more than twice the amount of all the navigation we enjoy in consequence of the sugar islands, the Southern, continental, and tobacco settlements! The freight of the staples of those sets of colonies brings us in upwards of a million sterling; that is, the navigation of 12,000 seamen: according to which proportion we lose by the rivalry of the Northern colonies in this single article two millions and a half sterling." To emphasize his anguish, the writer put the "Two Millions And A Half" in capital letters. Colonial farmers also drew his wrath for, he declared, "American corn cannot come to an European market without doing mischief to the corn trade of England."

Trivial as it now seems in relative terms, colonial manufacturing set English capitalists by the ears. For example, in 1751, English ironmasters, proprietors of forests that supplied wood for smelting, and tanners who needed cheap bark for their leather industry, all united in protesting against American competition and induced a committee of Parliament to heed their objections. To make a tedious economic story short, in every sphere of economy, American business enterprise aroused the antagonism of rival interests in England and the latter in turn brought to bear on the government at London continuous pressure for legislation and administrative acts favorable to British merchants, shippers, and manufacturers.

Even the lucrative trade in finished commodities which English capitalists managed to hold in spite of the efforts of the colonies to supply themselves had within it the seeds of irritation. For goods bought in English markets, the colonists had no large supply of precious metals with which to pay; they were always heavily in debt for commodities purchased and capital borrowed. Efforts to secure specie, bills of exchange, and acceptable materials by means of which to discharge their obligations in London kept them at their wits' ends.

The people of Rhode Island, by way of illustration, had to find more than a hundred thousand pounds sterling a year to pay for purchases made in England and yet they produced locally only a few articles suitable for European markets, such as flaxseed, lumber, and cheese. Consequently it was necessary for them to compete with English shippers by trading in some roundabout fashion, chiefly through the West Indies, to secure the money and credit required to meet their English debts. Hardly more fortunate in their economy were the Southern planters; although they had in tobacco a marketable staple, its price was fixed in London and they were always hard pressed to keep up with mounting obligations incurred for high living.

On every hand was heard the complaint of the critic that scarcely a penny of specie escaped the vortex which drew money in a torrent to the creditors of the metropolis. In the best of circumstances the exigencies of the colonists in this respect were very pressing; the irritation that arose from them was severe and continuous; from this source came the clamor for "easy money" that led local legislatures to issue paper currency until Parliament by peremptory act put a stop to such measures of relief. Turn and twist as they might, the colonists continually labored under the disabilities of chronic debtors.

§

In connection with a network of trade covering half the world, sprang up along the coast several thriving towns which on the eve of the Revolution compared favorably in wealth and population with such English cities as Liverpool and Bristol. Five stood at the head of the list—Philadelphia, Boston, New York, Charleston, and Newport—the first with about twenty-five thousand inhabitants, counting the suburbs, and the last with seven thousand. Baltimore, Norfolk, Lancaster, and Albany, if not so populous, nevertheless took pride in their growing power.

These urban centers were the homes of three classes destined to play significant rôles in the launching of the Revolution, namely, merchants, artisans, and lawyers. In every city were a few families that led the rest: the Amorys, Hancocks, and Faneuils in Boston; the Whartons, Willings, and Morrises of Philadelphia; the Livingstons, Crugers, and Lows of New York; and the Browns of Providence— "Nicky, Josey, John, and Mosey." Rich, active, and shrewd, they were quick to see points at which their interests clashed with those of English competitors and to file protests against adverse legislation by Parliament; still, conservative at bottom and timid in the presence of violence, they shrank from the thought of actual war.

When the storm broke and they had to choose, many went over to the Tory cause; others vacillated and enlarged their fortunes by selling supplies first to the Patriots and then to the Tories as the tide of battle flowed and ebbed; others threw themselves into the Revolution, helped to finance it, and risked their lives and fortunes in the outcome. John Hancock's name headed the list of signers on the Declaration of Independence; and it was written in letters so large and firm that George III could see it without his glasses. Robert Morris at Philadelphia flung his property into the issue and gave his talents as treasurer to the service of the Continental Congress.

Valuable, but sometimes troublesome, allies were the artisans of the towns who furnished the sinews for stoning English stamp agents, demolishing statues, sacking official residences, and heaving cargoes into harbors. While merchants resolved solemnly and petitioned gravely, artisans shouted hoarsely and rioted vigorously, shocking the timid gentry of store and warehouse who hoped that the business of resisting British measures might be conducted with the decorum of the counting room.

More cautious but especially useful in all verbal contests of economics or politics were the lawyers. Only by gradual stages had they been raised to a high status. In the early days there was no place for them; indeed, they were not viewed with favor by pioneers engaged in the rough work of clearing the wilderness. The authors of the Massachusetts Body of Liberties adopted in 1641, besides expressly permitting every litigant to plead his own cause, were careful to provide that, if unable to help himself and forced to employ an assistant, he was to give his counsel "noe fee or reward for his paines." In the founding years of Maryland a local chronicler rendered thanks that there were no lawyers in that colony and no business to occupy such factious members of a community.

In the course of time, however, conditions changed and old prejudices disappeared. When society became more complex and legal questions more involved, the need of skilled attorneys was recognized and in every colony a class of professional practitioners came into existence, which grew rapidly in numbers and influence during the passing decades of the eighteenth century. The door once opened, lawyers managed to win a higher social position in America than their brethren had ever enjoyed in the mother country. Still true to feudal tradition, the English nobleman and fox-hunting squire looked down on the attorney as a kind of serving man, useful in drawing papers though hardly to be treated as an equal; but there was no such gulf to be bridged in America. Merchants, planters, and farmers of the colonies could erect no insurmountable barriers against the disciples of Coke and Lyttleton.

In politics, similarly—in town meetings and in assemblies —lawyers flourished more abundantly than in England. It was the fashion of English landlords and merchants to elect men of their own order to represent them in Parliament but in America, particularly in the Northern colonies, the voters for various reasons more frequently adopted the practice of choosing lawyers to speak for them in local bodies. In the first colonial conference held in New York in 1690, two of the seven members were lawyers; of the twenty-four men who attended the Albany congress of 1754, thirteen belonged to the legal profession; in the first Continental Congress that launched the Revolution, twenty-four of the forty-five delegates were lawyers; in the second Congress that declared independence, twenty-six of the fifty-six delegates were of that class; and in the convention that framed the federal Constitution, thirty-three of the fifty-five members were lawyers.

With good reason, therefore, did Edmund Burke, in

enumerating the forces that made America dangerous, assign a special place to the legal profession. While warning his parliamentary colleagues against the perils of colonial agitations, he laid particular emphasis on the proclivities of the legal occupation. He told his auditors that the study of the law was more general in America perhaps than in any other country; that the profession there was numerous and powerful; that representatives sent to the congresses were mainly lawyers; that training in law made men "acute, inquisitive, dexterous, prompt in attack, ready in defense, and full of resource." Then he submitted with a broad hint the idea that "when great honors and great emoluments do not win this knowledge to the service of the state, it is a formidable adversary of government."

In rising to social and political power the lawyers gave a peculiar twist to the rhetoric of American statecraft. Before their time, the men who followed intellectual pursuits had been chiefly preachers of the gospel—even the teachers for the grammar schools and colleges had been taken from this class; and while the theologians dominated intellectual interests, weapons for argument, secular as well as religious, were drawn from Biblical lore. The lawyers, on the other hand, consulted and enlarged a body of learning that was secular in nature. Moreover, it was their business to use their learning on any side of any case entrusted to their care, so that they became even more flexible and more adept in dispute than the Hoopers and the Mathers.

Accordingly, the lawyers were well equipped to assume the lead in every public controversy and in fact they did stand in the forefront of the conflict with the mother country. Jefferson, Patrick Henry, John Adams, Madison, Dickinson, Marshall, William Livingston, and many others of light and power in the Revolution were attorneys by training, if not engaged in the active practice of law. Such were the men who furnished most of the arguments and state papers of the struggle. Such were the men who gave to the philosophy and pleas of that great litigation a legal and constitutional garb—one contrasting strangely with the devices of the Puritan revolution more than a hundred years before. In Cromwell's day quotations from the Bible as well as the sonorous words of Coke and Lyttleton gave reason to determination and fed the appetite for justification. In the American Revolution, however, statesmen and soldiers, led and taught by lawyers, resorted mainly to charters, laws, prescriptive rights, parchment, and seals for high sanction, thus giving a peculiar cast of thought and ornament to the linguistic devices of the fray. When these weapons broke in their hands, they turned, not to theology, but to another secular armory—nature and the imprescriptible rights written by sunbeams in the hearts of men.

§

A large part of the labor which underlay the social fabric of the American colonies was furnished by semi-servile whites imported under bond for a term of years and by Negroes sold into chattel slavery. This is one phase of American history which professional writers have usually seen fit to pass over with but a sidelong glance. Bancroft admitted that having "a handful" of data on the subject, he "opened his little finger." In fact, although exhaustive researches have not been made for all the colonies, it seems probable that at least one-half the immigrants into America before the Revolution, certainly outside New England, were either indentured servants or Negro slaves.

The white servants fell into two classes. The first embraced those who voluntarily bound themselves for a term of years to pay their passage. The second class included those who were carried here against their will—hustled on board ships, borne across the sea, and sold into bondage. This gruesome traffic was a regular business darkened by many tragedies and illuminated by few romances. The streets of London were full of kidnappers, "spirits," as they were called; no workingman was safe; the very beggars were afraid to speak with anyone who mentioned the terrifying word "America." Parents were torn from their homes, husbands from their wives, to disappear forever as if swallowed up in death. Children were bought from worthless fathers, orphans from their guardians, dependent or undesirable relatives from families weary of supporting them.

To the great army of involuntary immigrants were added thousands of convicts who were either sent by English judges or who chose deportation in place of fines, prisons, stripes, or the gallows. No doubt many of this class were criminals and incorrigible rascals, but a large portion were the luckless victims of savage laws enacted to protect the property of the ruling classes in England—peasants caught shooting rabbits on some landlord's estate or servant girls charged with purloining a pair of stockings or a pocket handkerchief. Mingled with this motley array of victims were political offenders who had taken part in unsuccessful agitations and uprisings.

The fate of all white servants, whether they voluntarily chose to sell themselves for a term of years to get to America, or were transported against their will, was very much the same. They were bound to serve some master for a period of years ranging from five to seven. They were not tied to the soil, as were the serfs of the middle ages, nor sold like slaves into life-long servitude, but during their term of bondage they were under many disabilities. The penalties imposed upon them for offenses against the law were heavier than those laid upon freemen; if they attempted to escape or committed a crime their term of service could be increased; they could not marry, leave their place of work, or engage in any occupation, without the consent of their masters.

Absolutely at the beck and call of their owners, they could be severely punished for laziness or neglect of duty. They were, in fact, little better off than slaves while their servitude lasted; their fate depended upon the whims of their

masters; and at best it was harsh enough. When the weary
years of indenture were over, the bondmen were set free
to enter any occupation for which they were qualified. The
more fortunate became independent artisans or went into
the interior, where they found liberty as the tillers of small
farms, rising out of bondage into freedom. But others,
weighed down by their heritage, individual and social, sank
into that hopeless body of "poor whites," the proletariat
of the countryside.

Finding it difficult to secure an adequate supply of indentured servants, promoters of settlements turned in the
course of time to Negro slavery. Neither the Puritans nor
the Cavaliers had fixed scruples against the enslavement of
their fellow men, of their own or any other color; it seems
to have been necessity rather than choice that forced them
to resort to Africans. Both sought to reduce Indians to
bondage and to a slight extent were successful; but the
haughty spirit of the red man made him a poor worker
under the lash.

Nor did the Puritans of England show any invincible
repugnance to driving white men and women into perpetual
servitude; Cromwell thought the Irish well adapted to that
career, for he sold as slaves in the Barbadoes all the garrison that was not killed in the Drogheda massacre, and his
agents made a business of combing Ireland for boys and
girls to be auctioned to English planters in the West Indies.
Even Cromwell's own countrymen were sometimes caught
in the dragnet; there is in the archives of London a piteous
petition of seventy Englishmen carried off from Plymouth
and sold in the West Indies "for 1,550 pound weight of
sugar a piece, more or less." Nevertheless, by the latter
part of the seventeenth century, public opinion in England
was running against this form of domestic enterprise and in
favor of seeking slaves abroad.

Though Negro slavery had been common in the Spanish
provinces for more than a hundred years when Virginia was
founded, and though Elizabethan seamen had leaped with

enthusiasm into the slave trade long before English colonization began, the institution spread slowly in the seaboard regions after its introduction at Jamestown in 1619. At the end of three decades there were only about three hundred Africans in the Old Dominion. But before the close of the century the traffic in slaves had grown to immense proportions. Negroes had shown themselves more docile under bondage than their Nordic brethren, and the difficulty of obtaining an adequate supply of white servants had increased. Moreover, English and American capitalists had discovered that enormous profits were to be gathered from the carrying trade, and under that stimulus made the transport of Africans to the New World one of the most lucrative branches of the shipping business. The best families, noblemen, bishops, merchant princes, and politicians invested heavily in it and the English government took good care of their interests. When, for instance, the court of Madrid was humbled in the war of the Spanish Succession, it was forced, in 1713, to grant to English slavers the exclusive right of carrying Negroes to its colonies, saving to Their Majesties, the Kings of England and Spain, each one-fourth of the profits.

Between that year and 1780, it is estimated, twenty thousand slaves were annually carried over the sea; in 1771 nearly two hundred English ships were engaged in the traffic, mainly from Liverpool, London, and Bristol. The first of these cities, in fact, owed much of its prosperity to the trade, and not without reason did a celebrated actor, when hissed by his audience in that commercial metropolis, fling back the taunt: "The stones of your houses are cemented with the blood of African slaves." The same could have been said with equal justice of some New England towns—Newport, Rhode Island, for example—because the Puritans, quick to scent the profits of the business, were not a whit behind the merchants of the mother country in reaching for the harvest.

In the bitter annals of the lowly there is no more ghastly

chapter than the story of this trade in human flesh. The poor wretches snatched from Africa were herded like cattle in the fetid air of low and windowless ship pens. If water ran short, or famine threatened, or plague broke out, whole cargoes, living and dead, were hurled overboard by merciless masters. If a single victim, tortured into frenzy, lifted a finger against his captor, he was liable to be punished by a mutilation that defies description. While Ruskin has attempted to fix the picture of this trade in his immortal etching of Turner's Slave Ship, tossing under a heaven of broken clouds upon a storm-swept sea dotted with the bodies of victims, "girded with condemnation in that fearful hue which signs the sky with horror and mixes its flaming flood with sunlight—and cast far along the sepulchral waves —incarnadines the multitudinous sea," his luminous page sinks down into a dull glow when compared with the lurid leaves in the actual records of the slaving business.

Under the pressure of profitmakers the Southern colonists, always clamoring for cheap labor, were in time abundantly supplied with African bond men and even in the North, slavery spread as widely as economic conditions would permit. After tentative beginnings, the Negro population grew by leaps and bounds; on the eve of the Revolution it was more than half a million. In five colonies, Georgia, the Carolinas, Virginia, and Maryland, it equaled or exceeded the whites in number; even in Delaware and Pennsylvania, one-fifth of the inhabitants were Negroes. In New York one person in six, and in New England one in fifty sprang from African origins.

Though the figures were ominous, not many Englishmen made strenuous protests against slavery. The Quakers, as a rule, did not like it for it offended their religious scruples, and some of them openly declared that Christians could not tolerate it; but no extensive movement for abolition got under way until after Independence. There were, however, frequent outcries against the slave trade itself. An occasional far-seeing economist realized that, owing to the greed of the traffickers, the white population was in danger of being swamped; breeders who raised slaves for the domestic market naturally resented the competition of the importers; and masters already well supplied grew anxious as they saw the value of their property falling with the continued influx of new stock. In response to such considerations, a few of the colonies attempted to prohibit the slave trade, only to be defeated by royal vetoes. The ruling classes of England were in no mood to cut off the princely dividends received from that lucrative branch of English commerce and the volume of business seems to have increased with fair regularity until the crash of the Revolution.

While the owners of manors, plantations, and huge estates found little difficulty in obtaining labor for their fields, those who sought to develop manufacturing had no such good fortune. Various inducements, such as special privileges and bounties, were offered to skilled artisans in England to attract them to America, but with little success. Furthermore, those who did come were seldom content to work long for masters. As soon as a journeyman or apprentice became well acquainted with the trade of the country, he hurried out into a new settlement to establish himself in a small but independent business, or finding that he could buy a farm with a few years' savings, he shook the dust of the towns off his feet and went into the country in search of economic freedom. "So vast is the territory of North America," wrote Franklin, "that it will require many ages to settle it fully; and till it is fully settled, labor will never be cheap here, where no man continues long to labor for others." Accordingly, the merchant capitalist of the colonial era, who engaged a few skilled workmen to manufacture for his trade, was continually handicapped, except in times of business depression, by the lack of an abundant supply of docile labor. Still there was springing up in the chief centers, such as Boston, New York, and Philadelphia, a body of artisans numerous enough to

give no little trouble to the local governing classes when the strong hand of Great Britain was shaken off.

§

As the economic structure of colonial America rose firmly on its foundations there were also erected institutions of self-government which served the ruling orders well in the management of their affairs and in the conflicts with the mother country. For centuries, the upper classes of England had shared in the levying of taxes and the making of laws and, with perfect ease, parliamentary practices were transplanted to the New World. Soon after its inception, every colony could boast of a popular assembly elected by voters who possessed the established property qualifications. Virginia was little more than a decade old when, under the auspices of the London Company, a House of Burgesses chosen by the planters was called into being. Within four years of its first expedition, the Massachusetts Bay Company substituted a representative body for the general meeting of the corporation's members. Knowing full well that they could not attract settlers to their domains if they withheld all political privileges, the proprietors, such as Lord Baltimore and William Penn, early complied with the requirements of their charters by inviting colonists to join in the government of their respective enterprises.

In each colony the representative assembly, by whatever process instituted, was elected by the property owners. The qualifications imposed on voters were often modified but in every change the power of property, in accordance with English traditions, was expressly recognized. In the South, where agriculture was the great economic interest, land was the basis of the suffrage; Virginia, for example, required the elector in town or country to be a freeholder, an owner of land—a farm or a town lot of a stated size. Where agriculture and trade divided the honors, politics reflected the fact; in Massachusetts, for instance, the suffrage was conferred upon all men who owned real estate yielding forty shillings a year income, or possessed other property to the value of £40. Pennsylvania, likewise combining commerce and farming, allowed all men who held personal property worth £50, as well as freeholders, to vote for assemblymen. To the property tests were sometimes added religious provisions: Catholics and Jews were often disfranchised by law and to some extent in practice.

Although property was widely distributed in America and most of the free colonists were Protestants and Gentiles, the various limitations on the suffrage excluded from the polls a large portion of the population—just how large a percentage cannot be ascertained from any records now available. Certainly, in the country districts of Pennsylvania, half the adult males were denied the ballot; in Philadelphia the restrictions disfranchised about nine-tenths of the men, a sore point with a growing class of artisans, and an interesting side light on the concentration of property in that urban area. On the other hand, it is estimated that about four-fifths of the men in Massachusetts were eligible to vote, so numerous were the owners of small farms.

Perhaps more citizens were kept from the polls by indifference than by law. A large share of the population of the colonies, it must be remembered, came from classes in England and in Europe that had never taken part in the governing process. As a rule, English agricultural laborers and artisans had enjoyed no more political rights than French Huguenots or German peasants; and transportation to the New World could not automatically give any of them a political sense. At all events, it seems safe to say that from one-half to two-thirds of the adult males did not vote, even in Massachusetts where interest in political affairs ran unusually high.

The weight of the active property owners in colonial government was further enhanced by qualifications upon members of assemblies. In South Carolina, for illustration, an assemblyman had to be a man of real substance, the owner of five hundred acres of land and ten slaves, or the possessor of land, houses, or other property worth a thousand pounds sterling. In New Jersey only freeholders possessed of a thousand acres of land could sit in the representative chamber. So, by one method or another, control in the popular assemblies of the American colonies was concentrated in the hands of a somewhat compact body of propertied men, freeholders, merchants, and planters, having a common interest in resisting taxation.

These little parliaments enjoyed powers which were nowhere strictly defined in laws, charters, and decrees. From small and obscure beginnings they grew in dignity until they took on some of the pomp and circumstance long associated with the House of Commons. In the course of time they claimed as their own and exercised in fact the right of laying taxes, raising troops, incurring debts, issuing currency, fixing the salaries of royal officers, and appointing agents to represent them in their dealings with the government at London; and, going beyond such functions, they covered by legislation of their own wide domains of civil and criminal law—subject always to the terms of charters, acts of Parliament, and the prerogatives of the Crown.

Endowed with such impressive authority, these assemblies naturally drew to themselves all the local interests which were struggling to realize their demands in law and ordinance. They were the laboratories in which were formulated all the grievances of the colonists against the government of England. They were training schools where lawyers could employ their talents in political declamation, in outwitting royal officers by clever legal devices. In short, in the representative assemblies were brought to a focus the designs and passions of those rising economic groups which gave strength to America and threw her into opposition to the governing classes of the mother country. Serving as the points of contact with royal officers and the English Crown, they received the first impact of battle when laws were vetoed and instructions were handed out by the king's governors or the agents of the proprietors.

§

While the local assemblies, speaking for American farmers, planters, and merchants, were advancing by a steady extension of powers to the position of sovereign legislatures, agencies were developed by the British Crown and Parliament to check and control the swelling authority of colonial democracy. Chief among these agencies was the royal or provincial governor. By a gradual process, beginning with the dissolution of the Virginia Company in 1624 and ending with the extinction of the Georgia corporation in 1752, eight of the thirteen colonies became royal provinces, that is, their executive departments were in the hands of governors appointed by the King of England. In three, Pennsylvania, Delaware, and Maryland, the old proprietary system remained in force until 1776, keeping the governors equally independent of popular assemblies. Only two, Rhode Island and Connecticut, retained the right to elect their own executives through all changes of the colonial period, and they were the objects of suspicion to the British imperialists who feared the "democratical" pretensions of America.

If the friends of "high-toned government" could have had their way, every colony would have been reduced to a single scheme—the province administered by an independent executive and judiciary sustained by permanent revenues collected under parliamentary authority. Events proved, however, that it was only necessary to have eight royal governors to set thirteen communities aflame.

Although there was a wide variety in the types of governors chosen in the course of a century or more to administer colonial affairs, they showed a general tendency toward conformity to pattern. Usually they sprang from ruling classes long accustomed to looking upon government as a system of patronage and emoluments——classes that brought increasing pressure on the Crown and ministers for promotion, places, and pensions as England grew in wealth and population. There were only fifty-nine temporal peers in the last Parliament of Queen Elizabeth; by the opening of the eighteenth century the number had risen to one hundred and sixty-eight; between 1700 and 1760, there were created twenty-six dukes, nineteen marquises, seventy-one earls, fifty-three viscounts, and one hundred and eleven barons, besides numerous baronets, knights, and decorated persons. "Peerages, baronetcies, and other titles of honor, patronage and court favor for the rich!" exclaimed May. "Places, pensions, and bribes for the needy!"

Of such was the stuff of English politics in the eighteenth century. To the spoils of domestic office, the numerous posts in India and America merely added more jobs for dexterous suppliants. No poet had yet coined a phrase like "the white man's burden" or "public service" to give ethical tone to the operations of those who labored at the ends of the empire.

Most of the royal executives for the American provinces were selected from among English politicians, soldiers, and lawyers of an adventurous temper; a few were taken from the more pliant placemen in the colonies. Some of the governors were able administrators of comprehensive views, prepared to live on good terms with the king's subjects committed to their care. Others were martinets with the morals and manners of an English drill sergeant. A few were frankly coarse and brutal; of this tendency was Berkeley of Virginia, who rejoiced in the absence of schools and newspapers and took pleasure in drowning with blood Nathaniel Bacon's uprising. "The old fool," cried Charles II, when he heard of the wholesale executions, "has taken more lives in that naked country, than I for the murder of my father."

On one thing a very large portion of the governors were agreed, namely, the increase of their private fortunes.

William Burnet, almost ruined by the bursting of the South Sea Bubble and sorely taxed to support his large family, was given first the province of New York and then the vineyard of Massachusetts. Robert Hunter, who had fought at Blenheim and commanded the "ready art of procuring money," was allowed to labor in New York and New Jersey. John Montgomerie, after serving in the royal army and then the bedchamber division of the king's household, was sent to the same domain to enlarge his inheritance. Hutchinson, of Massachusetts, though grave and learned, concealed under his cool exterior a passion for money; his sons were deep in the Boston tea business; his private letters teem with references to prices and qualities.

In a paper presented to the board of trade as early as 1715, an observer at the center of things and in a position to know, rendered an opinion to the effect that the colonial offices were "sometimes given as a reward for services done to the crown and with the design that such persons shall thereby make their fortunes. But they are generally obtained by the favor of great men to some of their dependents or relatives and they have sometimes been given to persons who were obliged to divide the profits of them with those by whose means they were procured." To the victors belonged the spoils, and the assembly of New York had authority for declaring that the governors seldom had any regard for the welfare of the people, made it subservient to their own particular interest, and, knowing that their time in office was limited, made haste to employ all the engines calculated "to raise estates to themselves."

It is not necessary to say with Bancroft that America was "the hospital of Great Britain for its decayed members of Parliament and abandoned courtiers," but in seeking for the roots of the controversy that split the British empire we cannot ignore the strife over the profits of office and the symbols of power—a struggle as old as the politics of Rome and as new as the latest election.

In the train of the English executive came a horde of

place hunters; for the governor, except in Massachusetts, appointed his councilors and everywhere filled lucrative posts—administrative, judicial, and military. Some of these places opened the way for peculation in obtaining and confirming grants; the land office in Virginia was a sink of corruption. Others were merely clerical positions attractive to the less ambitious dependents in the governor's official family. Many were sinecures for, following the fashion in England, royal governors created offices with salaries and no duties, to smooth the path for friends in need. In South Carolina and Maryland the sale of political jobs was notorious; in New Jersey an industrious governor, after taking care of many applicants, solicited from the Crown a place for "my son Billy"; and everywhere the disposal of patronage was viewed as a branch of colonial trade. Such practices were by no means deemed reprehensible at the time; they were true to the course of use and wont in contemporary England, where party servants were openly rewarded with honors, places, and titles at the public expense.

While devoting personal attention to the luxuries of office, the more efficient of the royal governors labored hard at devising administrative policies of benefit to the ruling classes of England whose economic interests were at stake in colonial management. Sir Francis Bernard, who saw long service in Massachusetts, was one of the proconsuls given to such mental exercises.

With respect to economics, he evolved a plan that was simplicity itself. "The two great objects of Great Britain in regard to the American trade," he said, "must be to oblige her American subjects to take from Great Britain only, all the manufactures and European goods which she can supply them with: 2. To regulate the foreign trade of the Americans so that the profits thereof may finally center in Great Britain, or be applied to the improvement of her empire. Whenever these two purposes militate against each other, that which is most advantageous to

Great Britain ought to be preferred." That was clear and to the point.

In politics, Governor Bernard was no less explicit, suggesting that the council in each province should resemble as nearly as possible the House of Lords and be composed of persons of wealth enjoying some such title as baron or baronet, all bound to look to the British Crown for honors and appreciation. This happy system was to be perfected by establishing a permanent revenue with which to pay the provincial governors, councilors, judges, and other officers civil and military—a permanent revenue furnished by the colonial legislatures as ordered by act of Parliament. Under this grand design, places and jobs in the imperial government were to become parts of the general royal patronage. Perhaps not many governors saw the goal as clearly as did Bernard, but no doubt the prevailing administrative opinion supported his views. Certainly, as the hour of the American Revolution drew near, British policy was moving in the direction indicated by that indefatigable governor.

§

Naturally, the salaries, emoluments, land grants, and other perquisites of colonial politics, so highly prized by royal governors, were not trifles unconsidered by members of American legislatures. Permanent residents with life estates in the country, the assemblymen could hardly fail to regard the governor from over the ocean as an interloper entitled to small esteem. It cost them no little grief to see lucrative offices filled by henchmen engaged in gainful employments at their expense, and still more anguish to see a royal governor and his train, after a season of suppressed desires in the stuffy atmosphere of the province, depart for the metropolis, laden with spoils, to enjoy a term of pleasing luxury in London.

These observant assemblymen were not, however, without resources. Holding the purse strings, they could be negligent, if not niggardly, in making grants of money to keep up the style of the petty court at the capital; they could darken the days of the colonial governor with bickerings over concessions, appointments, and other favors as the price of money grants. "I have to steer between Scylla and Charybdis," complained Belcher of New Jersey; "to please the king's ministers at home and a touchy people here; to luff for one and bear away for another." He might have added, "and truck and huckster to get my salary from the people's representatives." Governor Dinwiddie of Virginia found his legislature "obstinate, self-opinionated; a stubborn generation." A governor of New York who asked the assembly to vote him a fixed revenue for five years was answered by a demand for the right to appoint every officer deriving emoluments from the grant. Enraged by this boldness, the governor prorogued the assembly and wrote home that the members had taken to themselves "the sole power of rewarding all services and in effect the nomination to all offices, by granting the salary annually, not to the office, but by name to the person in the office." The remedy for such an encroachment on royal authority, in the opinion of the distressed agent of the Crown, was an act of Parliament reducing New York to order. "Till then," he added, "I cannot meet the assembly without danger of exposing the king's authority and myself to contempt."

In this conflict, the fortunes of war were ultimately on the side of the American assembly. Like the English House of Commons, it held the local purse, that powerful engine by which the Crown had been subjected to Parliament. Without legislative grant, there was no money for salaries —a dilemma which could not be avoided by any political legerdemain. Moreover, many governors were as eager to find places for their dependents as to uphold any fine notions of royal prerogative; without appropriation acts, the best of jobs were worthless even to the finest of public servants. In the end, therefore, the popular branch of the colonial legislature became almost sovereign in this sphere.

On the eve of the Revolution, the royal and proprietary governors, beggars at the door of the assemblies, were powerless to enforce by civil process their instructions from England; provincial councils had lost most of their control over law-making; and judges and minor officers had to trim to the legislators to avoid putting their salaries in jeopardy. For practical purposes the colonial assemblies, in their domestic concerns, were their own masters and their strength was increasing. The revolution had actually taken place; nothing but an explosion was necessary to announce it to the world. Such at least is the judgment of those modern scholars who have worked in the dusty records of colonial times rather than in the memoirs of kings, courtiers, and politicians.

§

Thus, possessing a ruling class experienced in the art of government and commanding economic resources of great magnitude, the provinces needed only two things to transform them into an independent nation—a mastery of the art of warfare and the capacity to coöperate on a continental scale. In these branches of statecraft also the eventful years of colonial development gave them some exercise. For self-defense they were compelled to maintain local forces, drilled and disciplined under officers of their own choice, prepared to take part at any moment in desperate fighting with frontier Indians and to test their endurance under fire.

In every one of the violent conflicts in the struggle between England and France over the mastery of North America, the colonists participated, furnishing soldiers and supplies. Four times, between 1689 and 1763, they were called upon to share in this world-wide contest for imperial supremacy—in King William's, Queen Anne's, King George's, and the Seven Years' War. For thirty-one years out of seventy-four they had armed men at the front battling by the side of British regulars against French and Indian warriors skilled in field and forest fighting, ruthless

with bayonet and scalping knife. Not a generation passed
without a baptism of fire—without giving the colonists
experience in the use of that unanswerable argument of sovereignty, military force.

War also taught the colonies, so diverse in their interests
and so hostile to one another in religion and politics, the
art of coöperation. It was the common deadly fear of the
Indians that brought into being the New England Confederation of 1643, uniting Massachusetts, Plymouth, Connecticut, and New Haven for twenty years or more in a
league of offense, defense, and mutual service. It was also
the Indian menace, years afterward, that put the militiamen
of Virginia and the Carolinas under arms in a mutual enterprise. It was to prepare the Americans for general defense
and for the impending struggle with France that the famous
colonial conference was held in Albany in 1754, attended
by representatives of New Hampshire, Massachusetts,
Connecticut, Rhode Island, New York, Pennsylvania, and
Maryland. Although the plan of union there discussed was
never adopted, Franklin, who drew it, lived to serve as a
member of the convention which drafted the Constitution
of the United States. The Albany conference failed, but
the French and Indian war that broke out three years later
drove the colonies into coöperation on a continental scale.

As events proved, that was the last phase in the mighty
contest for the heart of North America. The French, who
had established themselves at Quebec in 1608, one year
after the founding of Jamestown, and at New Orleans
in 1718, fourteen years before the settlement of Georgia,
had planted post after post in the Ohio and Mississippi
Valleys and had served notice that English enterprise was
to be confined to the coast line. When in 1753 the soldiers
of King Louis raised their flag over Fort Duquesne on the
headwaters of the Ohio, they flung out a challenge which
even the most pacific Quaker in Philadelphia had to
heed. And the gesture was quickly answered. George
Washington, a young militia officer of Virginia, was sent

to the frontier to warn the invaders that they were on territory "notoriously known to be the property of the Crown of Great Britain," and he might have added "coveted by the Ohio Land Company recently formed to open up the West."

Thus it happened that the first shot in a war that was to encircle the globe was fired in the wilds of Pennsylvania and the man who was to command the armies of the United States in the struggle for independence heard it echo through the forests. There began a conflict—the Seven Years' War—that spread to Europe, involving England and Prussia on one hand and France, Austria, Spain, and minor powers on the other; that flamed up in India deciding the fate of teeming millions on the other side of the world.

Under the imperial genius of William Pitt, who employed men and treasure without stint in his effort to smash French power on the sea and wreck French empire in three continents, all the energies of England were engaged. Prussia was kept in line under Frederick the Great by princely subsidies; America was fused by the fierce heat of the conflict at her very doors. Though Braddock was defeated in the wilds of Pennsylvania in 1755, Wolfe restored the balance four years later by capturing Quebec and ringing out the doom of French dominion in Canada. When at last peace came formally in 1763, Canada and all the territory east of the Mississippi, except New Orleans, passed under the British flag; while the rest went to Spain, whose empire was already weakening at its extremities. With no powerful neighbors now thundering at their gates, the governing classes of the thirteen American colonies were free to try their strength with the governing classes of England.

Indeed, the very war that set the bells of London ringing in acclaim to the news of victories borne on every breeze opened the way for another explosion. When Pitt fell and the end came, sober accountants had to reckon the cost: the public debt of England stood at one hundred and forty millions and new taxes had to be provided to meet the charges. Who was to pay? In any event, the colonists, having put twenty-five thousand men into the field and sustained them by huge outlays, were in no mood to bear additional burdens. To make matters worse, the swollen war prices collapsed, forcing a liquidation such as usually follows a desperate world conflict, and bringing ruin in its train. There lay the causes of new clashes with the English governing machine.

And America was ready for a trial of strength. The war had developed a body of veterans—officers and men—who were in some measure at least prepared for the test of Revolution when it came. The war had done more. The haughty conduct of the British military officers in America had aroused in the breasts of the colonials a passionate resentment akin to their ill-will for royal governors; while experience in fighting had given confidence to militiamen. In many cases they had done badly themselves but on other occasions they had seen the pomp of British officers and the pride of British regulars pricked like bubbles. The disaster which overwhelmed Braddock, as Franklin said, "gave us Americans the first suspicion that our exalted ideas of the prowess of British regular troops had not been well founded." It was no mere accident that the young officer who had labored to save Braddock's forces from utter ruin in the wilderness of Pennsylvania was called upon twenty years later to draw his sword under the elm at Cambridge in defense of the American Revolution.

CHAPTER IV

Provincial America

THE culture of the colonial period—its social and religious life, its intellectual and æsthetic interests, its apparatus for the diffusion of knowledge and artistic appreciation—was subject to the conditions common to all provincial civilizations. In its origins it was derivative: the whole conventional heritage, from its noblest ideals to its grossest vulgarities, was European, in a strict sense, English. Like the culture of every other age, it was contingent upon the prevailing economic order, the modes of securing a livelihood, the disposition of classes, the accumulation of riches, the development of patronage and leisure, the concentration of population, and the diversification of practical experience. Of necessity also it was bent to the laws of change, affected in every sphere by transformations in the character and weight of economic classes, the growth of secular concerns, and the impact of fresh currents of opinion from abroad.

Materials for the history of colonial culture are rich beyond measure. The spirit of the age shoulders up out of the dead past into the living present in a thousand shapes and forms. In haunting shadows the domestic life hovers around old houses, gray and gabled, crowned by cowls of arching elms and spreading oaks. Counterpanes and rugs seem even now to be taking form under nimble fingers that were moldering in village churchyards when Thomas Jefferson's pen was tracing the Declaration of Independence. Paintings that hang on walls, as they did in the days of Franklin and Washington, call back to power masters and mistresses from classes that ruled and preached and traded and planted in those far-off times. Diaries and letters lift the curtain on gay hours of weddings, fox hunts, and balls and on solemn scenes of worship, tragedy, and death. Quaint towns planned with strong communal purpose, state houses, churches, and college halls, still solid under the weight of years, survive as the visible and outward symbols of vigorous public life. Stagecoaches and models of sailing vessels reveal colonial merchants and wayfarers traveling on land and sea. Narratives and journals throw the light of contemporary opinion on the passing panorama. Books, pamphlets, almanacs, newspapers, and magazines produced on the soil of the New World reflect the depths and shallows of the American intellect; libraries, public and private, collected from the corners of Europe, mark the wide range of colonial research and understanding.

In this treasury of riches diverse minds have been at work; fragments have been selected from it to fit the patterns of many special interests. Enthusiastic makers of family traditions, moved by sentiments as deep as ancestor worship, have disclosed under the radiance of their warm desires progenitors as proud and gracious as the Burleighs and Percys of old England. Simple collectors of curios have gathered up pewter plate, glass, and Windsor chairs. Novelists have discovered plots and preachers have unearthed themes. Hurried critics, feeding the maw of the modern press, have found illustrations to bolster curious creeds and justify varied moods: a Baltimore journalist of remote Teutonic origins has seen reflected in the records the harsh and sour visage of Puritan divines; an Illinois essayist reared in Pilgrim orthodoxy has seen shining from them a great light to guide the weary and godly through all eternity. Searchers for humane traditions have come with joy upon the philosophy of Roger Williams, the journal of John Woolman, the lively wisdom of Benjamin Franklin, the democratic doctrines of John Wise, and the grand plea of Andrew Hamilton in the Zenger battle over the freedom of the press. Trained historians have brought under observation single segments of colonial life—economic, political, social, intellectual, artistic—and have written for specialists huge tomes that never find their way into the main stream of American thought.

By none of these methods apparently can the intimate essence of American culture be grasped. In reality the heritage, economics, politics, culture, and international filiations of any civilization are so closely woven by fate into one fabric that no human eye can discern the beginnings of its warp or woof. And any economic interpretation, any political theory, any literary criticism, any æsthetic appreciation, which ignores this perplexing fact, is of necessity superficial. That a few students recognize the nature of the problem and are beginning the search for a synthesis is a striking sign of the new epoch in American intellectual development.

§

The essential forms of colonial culture, as we have said, were English in their origins. Eminent advocates for the Scotch, Irish, Dutch, Swiss, Welsh, Swedes, and Jews have entered pleas against this ruling in many a portly volume and have placed upon the record facts and arguments worthy of calm review. Some have gone far in their racial claims. One stout partisan has traced the political institutions of America back to Holland through the migrating Pilgrims. Another has given the American Revolution the appearance of a phase in the long contest between Scot and Englishman. An eager Irishman has compiled from crumbling papers and mossy tombstones a mighty roll of O'Rourkes, O'Donahues, and O'Briens that makes colonial history resemble a glorious page in the tale of Erin's sons.

Nevertheless, when the last word is said for all the diverse elements in provincial life, certain indubitable facts obtrude themselves upon the view like giant boulders on a plain. Beyond question, the overwhelming majority of the white people in the colonies were of English descent; the arrangement of classes was English; the law which held together the whole social order was English in essence, modified, of course, but primarily English; the dominant religious institutions and modes of theology were English adaptations of Christianity; the types of formal education, the amusements, furniture, fashions, art, and domestic codes were all fundamentally English too. The language of bench and bar, pulpit and press, was English. Pamphlets and books of the epoch written in Dutch and German no doubt fill a large space on the library shelf; but in truth they are remarkable, not so much for their bulk, as for their relative insignificance when measured against the huge mountain of declamations and arguments in English that have come down from that provincial age. The list of Scotch and Irish soldiers in the revolutionary army is imposing; still more so is the register of Englishmen. Presbyterians of Pennsylvania fought well under Washington; the shot that was heard round the world was fired at Concord by a Puritan. Whether for praise, blame, or merriment, colonial America was basically English; it was governed under the auspices of the English ruling classes; its chief channels of communication with Europe ran along English routes.

§

The prevailing class structure by which the provincial culture of America was so largely conditioned was derived in the main from the mother country. Although it is some-times imagined, on the basis of schoolbook fictions, that the colonies were local democracies formed on the pure principles of a New World philosophy and founded on substantial economic equality, the facts of the case lend little color to that view. In reality, by the colonizing process, the middle orders of England—landed gentry of the minor rank, merchants, and yeomen—with their psychology and social values were reproduced in a new environment.

At home these classes had carried society forward on the long road from feudalism to the modern age; in Amer-ica, freed from the immediate pressure of a titled aris-tocracy and clerical hierarchy, they advanced rapidly ahead of their English contemporaries in the degree of their sovereignty over matters of law, religion, intellect, and æsthetic interest. Every colony had this class heritage developed into a well-articulated scheme of social subordi-nation. It is true that the status of the ruling element was not as plainly marked by legal signs as in the mother country and that the gates of entry were slightly more ajar but its grip upon industry and local politics was no less secure.

In seaboard New England the dominant order was com-posed principally of rich merchants, their dependents, and advocates—a few of them the offspring of English gentry. Though it rested a little lower in the social firmament than the official families of royal governors, distinctions in dress, houses, equipages, and manners separated it widely from the farmers, artisans, and servile elements of the popu-lation. "Most Boston merchants," wrote a scion of later days, "owned slaves as house servants and bought and sold them like other merchandise."

Of course titled persons in old England sniffed as they caught the smell of tar and salt fish on the garments of the mercantile order of the Bay but the sturdy Puritans did not worry about the snub. They even boasted of the smell. "Our ancestors came not here for religion. Their main end was to catch fish," cried a Marblehead sailor when the preacher laid on too hard. As if in defiance, the grandest old families of Boston and Salem decorated their mansions with graven models of the sacred cod and appeared unashamed in the columns of the newspapers as dealers in rum, salt, rope, pitch, grindstones, and fishing tackle. Although bluebloods of ancient lineage might turn up their noses, although the higher strata that pressed about the royal governor might resent the intrusion of "new people," the salt-water merchants managed the politics of New England legislatures with little interference from farmers and mechanics and servants.

Below the Potomac the upper class had another economic foundation—the landed estate kept intact from generation to generation as in England by the rule of entail or primogeniture or both. Cherishing the conventional emotions associated with the soil, Southern planters arrogated to themselves all social prestige, scorning mercantile arts and persons engaged in trade, except, perhaps, in Charleston where occasionally a landed family augmented its fortune by a happy jointure with the master of a counting house.

Like lords and squires in the mother country, slave-owning barons took the lead in politics as they did in social affairs. At elections held in the open air in county towns, they easily cowed all but the bravest freeholding farmers and named their own men for public offices. If a schism among them threatened their dominion, they united again with a swiftness that took the breath of the opposition. Yeomanry from the hinterland often came to the provincial capitals to tilt and charge but all in vain; the landed gentry of the plain could not be unhorsed. Resorting to private tutors or to Oxford and Cambridge for their learning, such as the times yielded, they staved off the growth of popular education in the South and the restive democracy connected with it.

Secure in their economic and political power, the planters of Virginia soon assumed the style of the Cavalier. And their descendants proudly carried on the tradition of Cavalier blood undisputed until a modern historian of scientific temper, T. J. Wertenbaker, made a searching inquiry into the facts of the case and published his findings. By way of preface he pointed out that the title of Cavalier, far from giving a clue to the possessor's rank or lineage, merely indicated membership in a political faction: many a tinker cheered for King Charles.

Then, after a survey of genealogical tables, Wertenbaker came to the conclusion that "a careful collection of the names of the Cavaliers who were prominent enough to find a place in the records shows that their number was insignificant." He could report only three families in all Virginia "derived from English houses of historic note" and three more that sprang from "the minor gentry." So the verdict was rendered that Virginia was settled by merchants, shipping people, yeomen, indentured servants, and slaves. But those who climbed upward into the possession of great plantations quickly assumed the cultural guise of the English aristocracy in that flexible fashion so characteristic of all mankind.

For the social order of the middle colonies a mixture of land and trade gave the economic basis. In Pennsylvania, rich merchants usually carried off the emoluments and the honors, political and cultural. In New York, patroons and mercantile families of Dutch origin retained their high place in society when the English took over their inheritance but in time new houses ruled by the conquerors rose beside Dutch establishments in town and country. Trade and land furnished the military, political, and social leaders of the province. Indeed, the dominant gentry of New York resembled the Whig lords of England who united landed property with fortunes invested in business and they were in some cases connected by ties of marriage with the English nobility. Staats Long Morris, the elder brother of Gouverneur, for example, rose to the post of major in the British army, married the Duchess of Gordon, and

remained loyal to King George to the end of his days.
If the Delanceys were not equal to the Newcastles in
wealth and finesse, they were at least competent to manage
political spoils of no mean proportions.

Even the pocket boroughs of old England had copies on
the banks of the Hudson; some of the lordly masters of
New York manors were represented in the provincial legislature by delegates of their own choosing—with the assent
of their tenants a matter of form. From mansions that
were castles, the Johnsons ruled in the Upper Mohawk
Valley with a sway that was half feudal and half barbaric,
relying on numerous kinsmen, armed negro slaves, trained
bands of Gaelic retainers, and savage allies from the dread
Iroquois to maintain their sovereignty over forest and
plain.

In all the colonies the ruling orders, in English fashion,
demanded from the masses the obedience to which they
considered themselves entitled by wealth, talents, and general preëminence. At Harvard and Yale, authority, houses,
lands, and chattels determined the rank of students in the
academic roll. In churches, Puritan and Anglican alike,
congregations were seated according to age, social position,
and estate. One old Virginia family displayed its regard
for the commoners of the vicinity every Sunday by requiring
them to wait outside the church until the superiors were
duly seated in the large pew especially provided for them.
A member of another proud family of the Old Dominion
kept the vulgar in their place with such severity while she
lived that she felt some atonement necessary in death; so
she ordered her body buried under the pavement in that
section of the church reserved for the poor—as an act of
abasement and reparation. Even the Anglican clergy of
the South were sometimes assigned to a lowly rank.
When, for example, a parson of quality sought the hand
of Governor Spottswood's widow, her family opposed the
marriage with a painstaking argument designed to demonstrate the social inferiority of the position occupied by the

man of God. In New England, of course, no such indig-
nity could be heaped on the head of the preacher. There
he had the choice of the ladies and he could play the rôle
of a pope to powerful merchants; but in Massachusetts
during the later colonial decades his power so waned that
he did not venture to interfere with the serious business of
whaling, trafficking, and slaving.

§

Next in order under the dominant families were the
farmers—yeomen, as they were called in England—owners
of small freeholds as distinguished from the gentry of large
estates. They formed the bulk of the population in New
England and the middle colonies and they peopled the back
country of the Southern provinces. In the North they furnished most of the versatile Yankees, jacks of all trades,
who sailed ships and carried notions to the four quarters
of the world, when they were not working with their wives
and children in the field, at the loom, or in the dye house.
On the Southern seaboard, as we have seen, they founded
many of the landed families who in later days boasted of
Cavalier ancestors. Toward the frontier, especially from
Virginia downward, the yeomanry was recruited to some
extent from the ranks of the more fortunate indentured
servants who found it possible to rise in a land of such
opportunities when their term of service was over.

However diverse its origin, this large body of freeholders
was composed of industrious and ambitious men and
women. They were often illiterate, often housed in
wretched huts, and often spurned by the upper classes but
all through the colonial years they continued to fight their
way upward from poverty in a determined quest for comfort, security, and influence. Aided by abundant natural
resources, they rose higher and faster in the New World
than in the Old, by that process preparing the way for the
revolution in America.

Everywhere the men of this class, enjoying as landowners the right to vote, furnished the numerical majority of the popular party that resisted the pretensions of the English government and its American agents. If the merchants and riotous mechanics of the towns unwittingly started the war which led to independence, it was the farmers who supplied the drive that carried it through and who shed most of the blood spilled in the contest. If a Virginia gentleman of high position commanded the army, it was yeomen fresh from the plow who filled the ranks and carried the muskets. They were to be heard from in the days which followed the overthrow of British dominion in America, protesting against the rule of native merchants, financiers, and planters.

The third layer of the social order was composed of free artisans and laborers. Within the boundaries of each city was a body of independent workmen large enough, as we have seen, to give occasional alarms to timid merchants and to foreshadow troubles ahead, but the growth of this class in numbers and power was slow. Only those who managed to accumulate a little property were allowed to vote; and everywhere the brand of inferiority was stamped upon them. When the son of a Boston bricklayer was elevated to the office of justice of the peace in 1759, his right to the office was attacked on the ground of his low social origins; and his defense was not the dignity of his calling but a reply that the charge was false. "A poor man," lamented a colonial democrat of Philadelphia in the spring of 1776, "has rarely the honor of speaking to a gentleman on any terms and never with any familiarity but for a few weeks before the election. How many poor men, common men, and mechanics have been made happy within this fortnight by a shake of the hand, a pleasing smile, and little familiar chat with gentlemen who have not for these seven years past condescended to look at them. Blessed state which brings all so nearly on a level. . . . Be freemen then and you will be companions for gentlemen annually."

The hope of the laboring classes, thus buoyantly expressed, was generous, but the handicap of their economic status was not to be quickly overcome by any mere effort of the imagination. Even after the declaration of independence their position was not elevated in the eyes of ruling persons by the profession of radical doctrines. "It is of no consequence," coldly remarked John Adams in the Continental Congress in 1777, "by what name you call the people, whether by that of freemen or slaves; in some countries the laboring poor are called freemen, in others they are called slaves; but the difference as to the state is imaginary only. What matters it whether a landlord employing ten laborers on his farm gives them annually as much money as will buy them the necessaries of life or gives them those necessities at short hand? . . . The condition of the laboring poor in most countries—that of the fishermen particularly of the Northern states—is as abject as that of slavery."

§

Below the level of freedom were the indentured servants employed usually in agriculture or menial work. Altogether these temporary bondmen made up a large proportion of the population, especially in the regions south of New York. It is true that, on the expiration of their terms of bondage, such servants passed into the class of freemen and that many acquired property and position in time; but their ranks were constantly recruited by newcomers from England and from the Continent and a large percentage never rose above the level of casual laborers after they served out their indenture. If no legal disability separated them from the main body of the population when their liberty was attained, the badge of their servile experience usually hung heavily around their necks. At all events, in the South, where they were despised by masters and slaves alike, they formed great settlements of "poor whites" that lay like a blight upon the land.

At the bottom of the social scale were the chattel slaves, more than half a million in number when the war for independence commenced. Though manumission was possible in some colonies, the law held most of the slaves in permanent servitude and, whether free or bond, their color marked them off from the other classes of every rank. In economic status, slaves who were fortunate in their masters often had a position superior to that of poor whites and unhappy indentured servants; but under the best of conditions they were silent members of the social order, liable to punishment for the slightest disobedience and to terrible penalties for serious crimes. They served as the foundation of the planting aristocracy in the South and labored as the servants of the mercantile class in all sections. Voiceless themselves, they found but few spokesmen in the white race. It was with extreme caution that John Woolman composed, in 1746, Part I of his pamphlet entitled Considerations on the Keeping of Negroes in which he argued that they were "of the same species with ourselves," endowed with natural rights, and held in bondage on grounds neither righteous nor holy.

§

Like so many elements of the English class structure, the English family system, with its traditions reaching back to the dawn of history and its deep entanglements in property and the struggle for existence, was transported to the American colonies. According to the well-accepted principles of the common law, the husband and father was lord and master of the family establishment, although in practice his sovereignty was often nominal enough. In this arrangement, the wife and mother—the married woman—found her personality merged in that of her husband, her legal existence suspended if not quite extinguished, and numerous disabilities imposed upon her.

On the day of her wedding her lands and houses, in case

she had any such property, passed to the control of her husband unless reserved to her by a solemn pre-nuptial contract. The husband could take and use the rents and profits for his own ends; he could dispose of her interests without her consent; if he committed waste, she had no action against him; if he ran into debt, the estate could be sold for the benefit of his creditors. The woman's personal property—money, notes, bonds, jewels, and movables in general—became also her husband's to hold, use, sell, assign, or consume at his pleasure. "So great a favorite," wrote the learned and genial Blackstone, "is the female sex of the laws of England." So thoroughly were these high doctrines incorporated into American colonial law that two hundred years after the landing of the Pilgrims the American jurist and commentator, James Kent, had only to enumerate them and add a few slight variations to portray the legal rules of domestic relations then in force in the United States. Akin to the command of the husband over his wife was the authority of the father over his children, a strict control over the labor and services of his sons and daughters until they reached maturity, subject to little or no interference from the state.

Coupled with these privileges and preëminences, however, were many duties specified in the law of the family. The head of the house had to discharge his wife's debts incurred either before marriage or during wedded life for the ordinary purchase of goods. He was bound to maintain her by supplying the comforts and necessaries appropriate to his fortune and condition. He was liable for torts and frauds committed by his wife; where imprisonment was the penalty imposed he could be sent to jail for her misdeeds. Moreover, he was required to support his children until they became of age, if the state of his income admitted; and under the laws of some colonies he was ordered to give them the rudiments of education. As a matter of fact, the Massachusetts act establishing a limited compulsory education may be regarded as the entering wedge by which the community finally broke the almost absolute authority of parents.

Another ancient family institution imported into America by the English was the custom of regulating the transmission of landed property with a view to holding wealthy houses intact. To that end, two capital principles were especially adapted: the law of entail made it impossible for the owner of land to sell or give away his estate and the rule of primogeniture provided that, in the absence of a will to the contrary, "where there are two or more males in equal degree, the eldest shall inherit; but the females altogether." The predominance of the eldest male, based upon the economy and government of a feudal society, prevailed in eight of the thirteen colonies.

In the South, from Virginia to Georgia, primogeniture was accepted as a matter of course, for it guaranteed to planting families a certain continuity in the possession of their fortunes; and the practice of entailing estates also extended throughout that region, excepting South Carolina, where the custom had been forbidden by law. With a high degree of consistency, New York and New Jersey, as royal provinces, adhered both to primogeniture and entails, and, for that matter, so did Rhode Island save for a few years in its checkered career. Although the spokesmen of the yeomanry and the merchants often railed against such institutions, they were unable to destroy these vestiges of feudalism. Even in New England, where the leveling spirit of the freeholder was strong and where legislation was enacted favoring equality among children in general, including girls with boys, provision was made for giving the eldest son a double portion of the inheritance.

In accordance with kindred traditions, parents played a large rôle in the negotiation of marriages, especially those endowed with earthly goods—always with a sharp eye to preserving the family status. Landed gentlemen of the South, as in old England, looked for happy matches that might swell their fortunes and elevate their position. Puritans, emphasizing the civil character of marriage rather than religious sanctions, were equally sagacious in effecting jointures; the custom of seeking "good providers" and daughters and widows "well placed" was as firmly fixed in Massachusetts as the common law itself. Among accounts of the high and the low, amusing illustrations of the practice appeared—in Judge Sewall's diary, in advertisements, in Franklin's lampoons, for example. Whenever a lucky bargain was struck, the newspapers caught up the glad refrain. On one occasion a colonial editor announced that a happy groom had wed "a most amiable young lady with £10,000 to her fortune," filling in the details for the public.

The integrity of the family institution was generally protected by laws against carnality. Teachings of the church fathers on the wickedness of human nature, consecrated by centuries of Catholic propaganda and taken literally by Puritan and Anglican, were made, like due process, the law of the land in their new home. Fines, public confessions, brands, or lashings were usually prescribed for the incontinent and the records seem to indicate that, as a rule, it was the woman, not the man, who got the heavier punishment—a practice defended on the ground that her offenses might corrupt the family strain. Originally Connecticut and Massachusetts made adultery a capital crime, but in 1673 the former colony substituted branding for the death penalty and about twenty years afterward the latter adopted in its place a law requiring guilty persons to wear the scarlet letter—a milder rule borrowed from Plymouth. Respecting all the cardinal points of waywardness and all lapses from reputability, the canons of Virginia were as savage as those of Massachusetts.

As is generally the case, the eye of the law was everywhere quickest in discovering the shortcomings of the lowly. The lot of the indentured girl, for instance, was especially hard; if she fell from community grace and brought a child into the world out of wedlock, she was given an extra year or more of bondage, while the father of the child, if the master, usually got off with some trivial penalty imposed by the court of his peers. Even for their frivolities the women of New England were roundly scored in sermons. "At the resurrection of the just," exclaimed a divine, "there will be no such sight to be met as Angels carrying painted ladies in their arms."

In spite of the tenacity of inherited English custom, the relative religious freedom and the economic opportunities of the New World worked radical changes in the spirit of the family institution. The Puritans of Massachusetts were in open revolt against Catholic and Anglican doctrines with respect to matrimony and, in keeping with their professions, they made marriage a civil institution, taking it out of the hands of the clergy, but in 1692 they were compelled by the Crown to accept the ecclesiastical ceremony as of equal validity. Fully aware that the law of England which controlled their charter provided that weddings should be solemnized by ministers, they effected their departure by practice long before they ventured to sanction it by statute in defiance of the mother country.

Putting aside also the Catholic bar against divorce and the Anglican modification which permitted separation only on the ground of adultery, Puritans authorized the dissolution of the matrimonial tie for various reasons, including desertion and cruel treatment. Likewise, among the Quakers marriage became a civil institution requiring for legality merely pledges of loyalty made in the presence of witnesses, while divorce was permitted on scriptural grounds. Moreover, even conduct during marriage was to some extent controlled by law in Massachusetts, where the custom of England which permitted the husband to chastise his wife was abolished and wife-beating forbidden by statute. Thus the Puritan woman was protected against a cruel husband and allowed to escape, if she wished, from his harsh régime. Only in the colonies where the Anglican party was dominant did the strict rules of the English law apply to the making and breaking of marriage bonds—with a tendency, however, even there in the direction of equality in the validity of civil and religious celebrations of wedlock.

The economic conditions of America, as well as religious ideas, gave direction to the evolution of the family. The ease with which youths could enter new occupations, such as merchandising, tavern keeping, fishing, and shipping, tended to break the rigidity of the family's class status, permitting rapid movement up and down the scale. Re-enforcing this process was the abundance of cheap land— the virgin soil of the frontier that was always beckoning sons and daughters away from the parental roof, inviting them to make homesteads of their own in distant places. Furthermore, as we have already indicated, in five of the thirteen colonies, Massachusetts, Connecticut, New Hampshire, Maryland, and Pennsylvania, where the rule of primogeniture did not obtain, inheritances were equally divided among all the children, saving generally to the eldest male a double portion. In the dissolution of estates, the firstborn son was dethroned as head of the family and the ancient pillar of unity thereby destroyed.

Under the pressure of these forces and enlarged opportunities, bonds of kinship were snapped; branches of families and emancipated individuals scattered themselves among settlements all the way from New Hampshire to Georgia; and young men of ability made their way out of poverty with a speed that kept all society in ferment. By no social magic could any institution as secure as the English county family be maintained in America. Even in Virginia, where the most heroic efforts were made to uphold class barriers, pushing yeomen were ever breaking into the older and more seasoned circles; Jefferson, the son of a back-country farmer, could marry the daughter of a Randolph. In this fashion the individual in colonial times began to emerge from the family group, as children commenced to cast off the restraints of class and parents in the choice of mates, occupations, and careers.

§

Among the ruling orders the manners and diversions of the colonial age, so closely affiliated with domestic institutions, were almost identical with those of the middle classes of the same type in Great Britain. Historians for the sake of convenience were wont to speak of Puritan New England, the Cavalier South, and the commercial Middle Colonies as representing distinct schemes of culture but the simplicity of the classification is responsible for many an error. If we look at the statute books, which pretend to universality, it appears that delights of the flesh and skepticism in religion, even the faintest, were condemned with equal severity in Virginia and Massachusetts. Puritan Boston gave to mankind one of the greatest freethinkers of the colonial era, Benjamin Franklin, who was in most matters, including his relations with women, unconventional enough for the gay gentlemen who toasted Prince Charlie; though he fled from Boston to Philadelphia to breathe a freer air, he was the product of Cotton Mather's province.

On the other hand, under genial Southern skies, were reared the families that brought forth in America the two outstanding pietists of the nineteenth century, Robert E. Lee, whose lips were never profaned by an oath, whiskey, or tobacco, and Stonewall Jackson, who opened every battle with a prayer. Rum as hot and wines as rich as any that graced the planter's table were found on the boards of the noblest divines and the strictest merchants of Boston.

Nevertheless, Puritanism threw a dark shadow over many of the amusements deemed harmless in Virginia. The strictness of Cromwell's generation—that excessive reaction to the lewdness and vulgarity of the Elizabethan age—was reproduced with its Biblical sanctions in New England's legal code. Sabbath was made a solemn day, meet only for preaching, praying, and Bible reading; all labor, not strictly vital, and all frivolity were forbidden by law. Theaters and Maypoles—the latter historic symbols of passionate carnality—were frowned upon. Drunkenness, riotous living, and adultery were regarded with horror by the elect and penalized by the lawmakers partly on theological grounds and partly with an eye to industry and thrift.

And yet, far and wide as Puritanism reached, New England was not as deadly uniform as superficial writers imagine. Before Boston was three generations old, alien elements broke the severe regimen of the fathers. In spite of the hostile reception accorded to them Anglicans, Presbyterians, and Huguenots insisted on settling down among the faithful, becoming so strong in numbers and wealth that the English government wrote into the new charter of 1691 a clause making property, instead of church membership, the test for the suffrage. On the eve of the Revolution, more than one-third of the rich merchants of Boston were outside the pale of the Congregational Church, adhering to manners and customs of their own.

In Connecticut, as well as Massachusetts, there were many good Anglicans who winked at the blue laws and thought with King Charles II that God would not punish anyone for taking a few pleasures by the way. Rhode Island too was a thorn in the side of the righteous in Boston because it tolerated from the first a laxity in religious opinion and a personal liberty that violated accepted traditions. In fact, the descendants of the pioneers who followed Roger Williams and Anne Hutchinson into the wilderness were more active in the manufacture and sale of rum than in the enforcement of Sabbatarian discipline. New Hampshire likewise showed strange folkways, especially after the Scotch-Irish began to pour into the province and clear the hills of their crowns. In any event, the law was one thing and its execution another; the clergy and the politicians could get a penal measure through a legislature easier than they could carry it into operation.

Notwithstanding strict laws with respect to Sunday observance and sins of the flesh, there was in the South, above all in Virginia, a joyous, light-hearted, and hilarious mode of life which offered a strong contrast to the more sober hues of New England. Over wide areas the tastes and manners of English landed families were reproduced. Fox hunting, horse racing, circuses, gambling, cock fighting, dancing, and drinking contests were among the frequent and reputable amusements of the time. The economy of the planting South, like its tradition, was on the side of easier and merrier ways among the upper classes. There was more leisure among masters and mistresses of slaves than among the farmers and seafaring merchants of New England who had to depend on sobriety and industry for their daily bread. There were great manor houses equipped with the luxuries that made entertainment a delight: the furnishings, plate, and good wines of the Old World.

As a rule, the planting families were widely separated on huge manors where routine weighed so heavily on their lonely hours that every opportunity for a joyful rebound from the racking tedium of rural life was eagerly seized. Guests and travelers—especially wayfarers bringing news from the outside world—were treated like princes, the revels of gay parties affording an outlet for the pent-up emotions of dull days. Moreover, in the South Sunday was Sunday, not the Sabbath of Puritan holiness; if all persons were supposed to be in their places at the parish church for the appointed services, the ban on solemnity, according to Anglican and Catholic custom, was lifted when devotions were over. The planting section was, therefore, a land of "good living," that is, for the owners of large domains, mansions, and slaves.

From the life of that rich Virginia gentleman, George Washington, abundant illustrations of this statement can be taken. Washington loved the best of clothes, superfine scarlet cloth, gold lace, ruffled shirts, and silver buckles. "Whatever goods you may send me," he wrote to his factor in London, "let them be fashionable." His taste for good wines was known far and wide; though temperate for his day, he usually took four or five glasses of Madeira for dinner and finished off with a draught of beer and a small glass of punch.

A good horseman himself, Washington had a passion for horse races and indulged it by contributing to racing purses, entering his own steeds, attending the contests, and betting cautiously on his favorites. He heartily enjoyed games of chance; in his diary he often records "bad weather, at home all day over cards"; but his bets were never extravagant: the largest winning entered in his account is three pounds and his largest loss nine pounds and fourteen shillings—equivalent to three or four hundred dollars in modern terms. Theaters, circuses, and cock fights had an irresistible appeal for him. He was at the front at country balls in his neighborhood, in moderate drinking bouts at the tavern, and in fox-hunting parties. His own home was the scene of constant merry-making; in two months during the year 1768 he entertained at dinner or had guests for twenty-nine days and dined away from home on seven, with other diversions in the meantime. Between his social obligations and the management of his estate, Washington had little time for literature, even in the days before heavy duties of state fell to his lot. In the journal that tells how he spent his hours, he entered in his youth two notices of works he had read; after that he either found no book worthy of mention or gave up reading entirely.

Though the social life of the South was mainly rural, there were a few towns where the urbanities flourished. Charleston, for example, was a center for pleasure-loving and well-to-do people who came from all directions if only for the season. Music, art, dramatics, and lectures were there added to the customary routine of life; from 1737 to 1822 excellent concerts were given under the auspices of the St. Cecilia Society. No ban was placed upon the theater and English players as well as local talent amused or thrilled the social set—ladies no less than gentlemen. At

Southern ports English men-of-war often lay at anchor for weeks, when the officers from the vessels added color and vivacity to parties and ceremonies on shore.

Pennsylvania evolved a third type of manners and customs. Forbidden by their code to make lavish displays, loyal members of the Quaker sect upheld the ideal of simplicity. Though deeply religious like the Puritans, the Friends believed in perfection more than in sin, in guidance by the inner light rather than in restraints imposed by the authority of the clergy and magistracy. They frowned as darkly upon the joys of the flesh, upon music, drama, and dancing but they did not use as much force in stamping out such diversions among their wealthy neighbors. Their creed of the simple life, though often violated by the rich, notably by the Penns themselves, laid emphasis on equality rather than on distinction, and in that way put most of the sect outside the "society" constructed on the basis of waste and spending power. Leaning in faith toward philosophic anarchy, the Quakers were not absorbed in politics as much as the Puritans of New England or the Anglicans of Virginia. Relying for support on the teachings of Jesus rather than on sectarian dogma, their inclinations were toward tolerance rather than uniformity, inquiry rather than authority, charity rather than damnation.

All these circumstances conspired to make Philadelphia the most tolerant and secular city on the continent. A combination of wealth, philanthropy, and moderation promoted intellectual activity of a humane and realistic character. Long before the Italian Beccaria wrote his treatise on the theory of prison reform, the Quakers had begun the practice. Philadelphia could with justice claim the first circulating library, the first medical school and hospital, the first fire company in America, the earliest municipal improvements, and the first legal journal. It was the scientific center of the colonies for the study of botany, astronomy, mathematics, physics, and natural history. It was the home rightly chosen by Benjamin Franklin when he fled from

New England and selected a seat for his publishing business, the spot from which went forth his call for the foundation of the American Philosophical Society—the scene of continuous meetings of scientific and free speculators until the seizure of the city by the British during the Revolution. At dinners in fine old mansions or at lively parties in taverns, the merchants and scholars of the city assembled to discuss everything under the sun. A serious air, though not Puritan, hung over the place.

Still a fourth type of social life developed in New York, a colony that was neither Puritan like Massachusetts nor Quaker like Pennsylvania. Though its ruling order of merchants and landed gentry was mixed, being composed of English, Dutch, Scotch, and French Huguenots, its social distinctions seem to have been sharper than in New England or the lower Middle colonies. The richest families spent their winters in New York City, where amusements of various kinds from the theater to bull-baiting were furnished for their diversion, and they lived during the summers on their estates up the Hudson or on Long Island. In general, the upper classes of the province were freer from religious inhibitions on pleasure and less given to philosophic speculation than their Puritan neighbors and less scientific in their interests than the intellectuals of Philadelphia. While the Anglican church was established in the colony by law, not one-tenth of the people belonged to that communion or paid any attention to its ministrations. Dissent rather than conformity of any type was the note of the province. So there was a wide liberty of opinion for all except Catholics but it was apparently the liberty of indifference, not of reasoned toleration or skepticism.

Taking colonial America as a whole, therefore, it is evident that, in spite of certain similarities, there was a broad diversity in manners and customs. All the eighteenth century tourists from foreign countries were struck by that fact, by the "strange mingling of the uncouth, the totally wild, and the highly civilized and cultured." They were impressed by the charm of Southern ladies, the number of excellent French books in the libraries of the planters, the elegant plate on the tables of Philadelphia and Boston merchants, the everlasting curiosity and questioning of the rural Yankee, the bustling enterprise of the ports, the forwardness of the laboring people, and the range of the intellectual interests.

If the travelers saw Jonathan Edwards shaking all New England over the roaring flames of hell in 1743, they also heard Benjamin Franklin exclaiming that "the first drudgery of settling new colonies being 'pretty well over,' Americans ought to do their part in scientific and philosophic inquiry." If they discovered any qualities which could be called distinctly American, they likewise found antagonisms of the most pronounced character. "Fire and water," wrote Burnaby, in 1760, after traveling more than a thousand miles in the colonies, "are not more heterogeneous than the different colonies in North America." The comfort of the free masses in contrast with the awful beggary of Europe and the sadness of slavery impressed every voyager. "In the course of 1200 miles," said Burnaby, "I did not see a single object that solicited charity. . . . The condition of the slaves is pitiable; their labor excessively hard, their diet poor and scanty, their treatment cruel and oppressive."

§

The intellectual life of the colonies, like their hierarchy of classes, their social tastes, and their domestic institutions, sprang from the British heritage of the seventeenth century, developed under the influence of local circumstances, and was modified by the currents of new opinion from the Old World that from time to time touched their shores. Inevitably the dominant interest in the beginning was theology. From the break-up of the Roman Empire to the beginning of the colonial era, the clergy had been the leaders in thought and instruction. As a rule they were the makers of books, the teachers in schools and universities, the compilers of laws, the guardians of all things of the spirit.

When John Smith sailed away to Virginia from England, the clergy still ruled intellectual life all over Europe. Secular learning, books on travel, reprints of the classics, and treatises on law were no doubt gaining on theological tomes but the monopoly of the clergy over formal learning was unbroken. The Protestant revolt had come; reformers of the Anglican church—Latimer, Ridley, Hooper, Jewel, and Grindal, some of them martyrs—had assailed the pope, episcopal vestments, high altars, and other symbols of Rome as the trappings of superstition, but with the zeal of the early church fathers they, too, had resorted to the logic and rhetoric of theology for their arguments and kept their minds subdued to that great branch of learning, even when they appealed to reason for support. Puritan divines had attacked the Church of Ridley and Hooper as still savoring too much of things Roman, but they also spoke the language of theology, no matter whether they discussed the salvation of souls or the affairs of the body politic. The Separatists who in turn broke from the Puritans did not depart from religious sources in their search for words and ideas to justify the faith that was in them and the conduct that pleased them. Neither did the clergy who spoke for the Presbyterians, Huguenots, Lutherans, Dutch Reformers, Moravians, and other sects that scattered their congregations from New Hampshire to Georgia. Everywhere, except among the Quakers, who had no clerical estate, preachers, with their passionate interest in dogma, in theology, and in dominion over the minds of laymen, stood at the gates of knowledge with flaming swords.

Following the tradition of sixteen hundred years in the Old World, the Puritan divines of New England took to the printed word with holy fervor, filling yards of shelves with volumes, tracts, and pamphlets. They wrote heavy treatises on The Great Christian Doctrine of Original Sin and brochures on Eternal Damnation and the Punishment of Sinners. Even secular matters, such as wars and shipwrecks, were viewed in the light of divine purpose. In a booklet on troubles with the Indians, a learned author revealed the spirit and method of his craft by adding the subtitle: "Wherein the frequent Conspiracies of the Indians to cut off the English and the wonderful providence of God in disappointing their devices, is declared." The difficult issue of demonology was covered under an ample head: "Cases of Conscience Concerning evil Spirits Personating Men, Witchcrafts, Infallible proofs of Guilt in such as accused with that Crime. All Considered according to the Scriptures, History, Experience and the Judgment of Many Learned Men." Such were the great themes that occupied the most powerful minds of New England in the age of clericalism.

Among the towering theologians of America two stood out as veritable Titans: Cotton Mather, the scholar, and Jonathan Edwards, evangelist and thinker. The first of these, a son of Increase Mather, the thundering clergyman who tried to fasten the church on the state in Massachusetts and then to make the established clergy the masters of the church, was born and reared in Boston. By tireless labor Cotton Mather amassed a prodigious quantity of knowledge mixed with the curious delusions and amazing credulities of his time. He studied Hebrew as well as Greek and Latin, explored the mysteries of theology, dabbled in the secular learning of the ancients, and took an interest in English grammar just separating from the Latin, in missions to the Indians, and in inoculation for smallpox, which was then a burning issue. He wrote huge volumes on religious questions—roads to salvation and ways to hell. He rolled from the press innumerable pamphlets on every conceivable point of theological interest and made pretensions to authority worthy of a Tudor or a Bourbon. His style, like his manner of speaking. as a contemporary remarked, "was very emphatical."

Across the border in Connecticut, Jonathan Edwards, a son of Yale, rose high in the theological firmament just after Cotton Mather's star sank on the horizon. Mather died in 1728; Edwards was born in 1703 and reached the summit of his power as the colonial age was drawing to its close. The Connecticut divine combined a passionate evangelical temper with sober thinking on recondite questions of human destiny. Sinners he scourged with awful fury: "The God that holds you over the pit of hell, much as anyone holds a spider, or some loathsome insect, over the fire, abhors you and is dreadfully provoked; his wrath towards you burns like fire."

With such assurance and violence did Edwards preach this gospel that his labors bore fruit in weeping, wailing, and sudden repentance among his horrified auditors, culminating at length in a tumultuous frenzy, known as the "Great Awakening," that ran over New England like wildfire, spread into the other colonies, and finally expired in a spasm of exhaustion. No excesses alarmed him; no failures damped his ardor. He devoutly believed that the discovery of America was the work of Providence, that the village in which he preached was the special object of God's attention, and that he himself was called from on high to begin the renovation of the earth.

Some of Edwards' ambitions were unfulfilled but his occult writings translated into several foreign tongues excited the enthusiasm and admiration of Protestant theologians in the far corners of the earth; Holland preachers read Edwards in Dutch; in Beirut his volumes appeared in Arabic. John Wesley, the English evangelist who was destined to succeed Edwards as a theological crusader, drew inspiration from his life and sermons. Fichte, the German philosopher, called him "the most original thinker in America." Those in a position to judge tell us that his discussion of free will in his dissertation on the origin of sin is among the great classics of the pre-scientific age. "The only relief I had was to forget it," remarked the droll

Boswell, commenting on Edwardian doctrine in a conversation with Doctor Johnson.

With the spread of printing, the theories of theology, sometimes in curious shapes, ran as current coin among the masses, especially in New England, where even the thundering Mathers could not awe the pews into silence. In fact, the Puritans, men and women alike, went to church with notebook in hand, followed the argument of the preacher with the closest attention, studied it zealously during the week, and discussed it minutely at the regular open forum held for that purpose. They were not monks trying to find out how many angels could stand on the point of a needle; they were plain citizens, whole communities indeed, soberly debating solemn questions of faith and conduct: "Can there be an indwelling of the Holy Ghost in a believer without a personal union? Is it lawful to have dealings with idolators like the French? Should women wear veils?"

To lectures on fine points of personal salvation they were especially devoted. A young lady, whose hand Judge Sewall was seeking, rejected him because she was so engrossed in theological debates that she could not consider matrimony; she would not give up this favorite diversion though he presented her with gifts of books on religious questions and supplemented them with glazed almonds, meers cake, and a quire of paper. In fact, the magistrates of Massachusetts had to reduce the number of religious lectures in order to give laymen more time for business and labor.

In their feverish search for the origin of evil, their continuous output of scholastic literature, their interminable debates on obscure points of theology, and their occasional outbursts of religious frenzy, colonial Americans were merely operating on the mental plane of their European contemporaries. Even the witchcraft hysteria of Massachusetts, one phase of religious experience, was sanctioned by laws and practices already hoary with ten thousand years when the *Mayflower* dropped her anchor off Cape Cod.

The Bible in many passages lent its authority to the idea of witchcraft. "Philosophers and physicians, popes, prelates, divines, statesmen, judges, and monarchs"—the wise, the learned, the high, and the good—had from time immemorial profoundly believed in it, and approved the execution of persons charged with that enormity, often invoking the science of demonology to destroy their enemies.

The very decade that saw the founding of Jamestown also witnessed a new act of the English Parliament laying the penalty of death on persons guilty of witchcraft, sorcery, charm, enchantment, and such "infernal arts"; and nearly a hundred years after the Salem craze the sober Blackstone declared that to deny witchcraft and sorcery was to fly in the face of the Bible and experience. It was in the light of "the wisdom of the ages" that the citizens of Salem made their own adventure in demonology in 1692.

In these circumstances it is not the atrocities committed by the witch hunters but their moderation that surprises descendants of the Puritans: the fit was localized and its term was brief, the killing time lasting only about four months. The number of victims was relatively small: twenty persons were put to death by hanging, fifty who confessed were set free, one hundred and fifty lay in prison when the tempest blew over, and two hundred more were under accusation. Massachusetts judges were no doubt severe but so was Henry VIII; so was Calvin; so was the Spanish Inquisition. The age was cruel in its persecuting spirit everywhere, but it may be said for the witch hunters of New England that most of them became convinced of their error, offered expiation in the form of public mourning, and gave relief to the families of their victims—a degree of abasement and apology for folly not often found in the annals of those who hang and burn the prey of their opinions and delusions.

In reality, therefore, witchcraft in New England was merely one of the scenes in the passing of demonology from the western world. Twenty years after Salem recovered from her spasm, England convicted a witch in solemn trial; sixty years later the Holy Inquisition at Seville ordered a woman burned for practising the black arts; and in 1793 a public execution for that offense was carried out in Germany.

§

Theologians of every sect, school, and persuasion, in struggling to maintain their empire over the intellect of the modern world, were fighting a losing battle against fate. In the colonial age, between the founding of Jamestown and the Declaration of Independence, that is, between 1607 and 1776, there was taking place throughout western civilization a radical upheaval in the affairs and thought of mankind. The discovery and exploitation of the New World, with its luxuriant natural resources, multiplied the numbers and piled higher the riches of the bourgeoisie, a class which was in conduct and interest, whatever its professions of faith, primarily secular.

The same fruitful economic development, that gave thousands of starving European peasants prosperity in America and poured treasures of specie and goods into the markets of the world, opened up before the submerged masses of England and the Continent for the first time in their long history the possibility of attaining for themselves something beyond a bare pittance—some of the certainty, some of the pleasures and luxuries that had been enjoyed only by lords, merchants, and bishops. No philosophy of innate sin, of a baffled life, no promise of transports in heaven could stem the great desire of multitudes for the delights of this life enjoyed by their superiors—and all these strivings were secular in spirit and outcome.

Closely affiliated with this movement were the rise and flowering of natural science, free thought, both as an instrument of inquiry into the nature of mind and matter and as a servant of earthly utility. In 1620, the year in which the Pilgrims began to wrestle with the stubborn soil at

Plymouth, Sir Francis Bacon gave to the world his Novum Organum, the second part of his Advancement of Learning, in which he set forth—not for the first time, but with impressive eloquence—the revolutionary doctrine that man could master nature by observation and experimentation and that the conquest of nature was more important than proficiency in the speculations of the schoolmen. As he said, he cast the light of induction into the obscurity of philosophy, a light that would shine long afterward on the erection of palaces, theaters, and bridges, the construction of roads and canals, the foundation of schools for the education of youth, and the enactment of laws for the improvement of mankind. The tocsin of a new day was rung.

Bacon had hardly passed from the scene when John Milton, in majestic prose, proclaimed freedom of thought and the press as the ideal for all coming ages—emancipation of learning from the clerical censor. "To the pure all things are pure. . . . Knowledge cannot defile, nor consequently the books if the will and conscience be not defiled. . . . All opinions, yea, errors known, read and collated, are of main service and assistance toward speedy attainment of what is truest. . . . To prevent men thinking and acting for themselves, by restraints on the press, is like to the exploits of that gallant man who thought to pound up crows by shutting his park gate. . . . A forbidden writing is thought to be a certain spark of truth that flies up in the face of them that seek to tread it out. . . . Give me the liberty to know, to utter, and to argue freely according to conscience above all other liberties." Such was the novel argument uttered by a Puritan statesman nearly one hundred years before the birth of Thomas Jefferson.

In the spirit of Bacon and Milton, even though usually independent, a score of scientists in England and on the Continent enriched the seventeenth century with intellectual achievements of the first magnitude. Descartes, French iconoclastic philosopher, with amazing effects labored **at**

his chosen task of clearing the mind of scholastic accumulations, breaking the power of authority over reason, and
widening knowledge in mathematics, physics, and psychology. Four years before the death of Descartes in 1650,
there was born, in Germany, Leibnitz, one of the prime
thinkers of all times, who enlarged exact knowledge in
many fields, encouraged original research, and bent natural
science to the service of human welfare. In medicine, startling adventures were announced by indefatigable workers:
in 1628 Harvey, a Cambridge graduate and physician to
the king, published his thesis on the circulation of the
blood; before the end of that century a great Italian doctor,
Malpighi, had laid the foundations of microscopic anatomy.
Even the starry heavens were now being scanned in the
interest of understanding rather than of fortune-telling.
In splendid succession, da Vinci, Copernicus, Kepler, and
Galileo threw their powerful rays further and further into
the limitless spaces of the skies. And then in the very age
when Cotton Mather was composing sermons on sin, death,
and hell, Sir Isaac Newton was expounding a theory of
gravitation for the planets swinging in their orbits, freeing
astronomy from the long-enduring sway of sorcery and
divination.

Among the throngs who witnessed the funeral of Newton in 1727 was a young Frenchman destined to be high
commander in the army of sappers and miners who overthrew the monarchy and clergy of France at the close of
that century. His name was Voltaire. He had been driven
from his own land for an attack on the government and
while in exile he wrote letters on the English, portraying
the religious and political liberty of England, such as it was,
against the dark background of intolerance and despotism
in France. For half a century more he turned out, in a
continuous stream, histories, plays, novels, letters, and articles exalting reason, praising bourgeois comfort, and ridiculing the dogmas and officials of the Catholic church. At
the very end of his days, he greeted Benjamin Franklin,

minister of the American Republic to the Court of Louis XVI, a skeptic from the New World in whom the spirit of liberty likewise fiercely burned. Around Voltaire was grouped an extraordinary body of writers—Diderot, D'Alembert, Condorcet, amid the host—who worked with tireless energy exploring all corners of knowledge and waging war on scholasticism and clerical dominion. Somewhat apart but still one of the great agitators of the eighteenth century was Montesquieu, whose work on the Spirit of the Laws became a text for American political thinkers and writers.

§

The advancement of these new types of secular learning which extended inquiry into the causes of phenomena—from the decay of meat to the composition of the stars—unlike the mastery of theology, could not be effected by a single mind in a monastic cell or a Protestant library. It called for coöperation among numerous workers, for telescopes, laboratories, and mathematical instruments of many kinds. Barely was the need discovered when efforts were made to meet it. In England a center for the promotion of scientific activities was created by the foundation of the Royal Society in 1660; the very next year it appointed a committee to consider "questions to be inquired of in the remotest parts of the earth"; it encouraged research, issued publications, and formed ties among men of scientific temper as far apart as Virginia and Prussia.

Under the patronage of Louis XIV's great minister, Colbert, the new republic of learning was widened by the organization of the French Academy of Sciences. Already Austria had an institution for promoting study of the curiosities of nature, and by the end of the seventeenth century a similar society, inspired by Leibnitz, made its début at Berlin, preparing the way for the Academy of Sciences and Letters later endowed by Frederick the Great. Under royal and private patronage, men of scientific interests were given money and leisure for travel and research, books and instruments were assembled for advanced students, botanical, geological and zoölogical collections were started, and the knowledge attained by inquiry was disseminated among the intelligent and curious of all countries. With the aid of the printing press, the sifted wisdom of the world was made available even to pioneers on the edge of English civilization in America; what it lacked in speed was made up by private correspondence.

Amid this feverish activity in secular learning old branches of knowledge appeared in novel form and new branches emerged from the mass of data as generalizations were made. Mathematics, raised to a high pitch by the Greeks and Arabs, was now pushed still higher by Descartes. The various divisions of natural science known to-day—physics, chemistry, geology, and botany—began to claim the life-long devotion of specialists and before the eighteenth century had drawn to a close each of these branches had at hand a goodly array of materials, discoveries, and hypotheses. In the same movement of intellectual forces, social studies assumed a more scientific or realistic form. History, which since the decline of Rome had been restricted mainly to monastic chronicles of events, began to appear in the guise of long political disquisitions; and finally, under the leadership of the versatile Voltaire, the first of the modern social historians, students of the past commenced to survey the manners and customs of peoples as well as the doings of kings, priests, parliaments, and warriors. Works on economics and politics, usually thrown off in the heat of parliamentary disputes, naturally wore the mask of controversy; and yet in spite of their contentious origin they took on more and more the spirit of science as the eighteenth century advanced.

Echoes of this European development which made inroads upon the theological monopoly, exalted science, and gave increasing significance to secular affairs, including the practical arts, naturally spread out to all continents, beating even upon the shores of Japan through the gate kept open at Deshima by the Dutch. Inevitably the American colonies, as a part of the European system, felt the impact of the new forces, especially after the first crude days of settlement had passed and growing wealth and leisure gave opportunity and time for study and inquiry. Although they contributed no Descartes or Newton or Leibnitz to the world of learning and speculation, the colonies were from the first hospitable to the spirit of science.

Indeed, there is a tradition to the effect that the men who founded the Royal Society in England first contemplated migration to the New World. According to that story, they planned to establish their association "for promoting natural knowledge" in Connecticut, under the presidency of John Winthrop, and only desisted at the request of King Charles. At any rate they made Winthrop, who was in London helping to promote their project, "chief correspondent" of the new academy "in the West." From that time forward Americans were enrolled in the Royal Society as members and contributed specimens, papers, reports, and data for its deliberations and collections. Paul Dudley of Massachusetts prepared noteworthy pages for its philosophical transactions. Even the theologians of New England were stirred by the movement. Increase Mather formed a club of scholars in Boston to pursue studies in natural history. Jared Eliot, "a preacher, physician, naturalist, and farmer," of Connecticut, made researches in agriculture and published in 1748 a significant work on field husbandry.

South as well as North, inquirers now prosecuted scientific studies with zeal and intelligence. In Virginia, John Banister made an exhaustive study of local plant life, which was published in the second volume of a great work by John Ray, the English naturalist, and was preparing a natural history of Virginia when death, in 1693, cut off his useful life. Another Virginian, Mark Catesby, in a comprehensive study of natural objects, covered not only his native province, but the Carolinas, Florida, and the Bahamas, spending sixteen years, between 1710 and 1726, in the self-imposed task. His successors in the field, John Clayton and John Mitchell, both Virginia physicians and botanists, were members of the Royal Society, wrote papers for its transactions, and corresponded with scientists and scientific societies in various parts of the Old World. Clayton was in communication with the great Linnæus of Sweden and sent valuable reports to London colleagues.

The milder theological climate of Pennsylvania and the stimulus of the cosmopolitan center of Philadelphia were especially favorable to the flowering of the scientific spirit. In 1743 Franklin, himself a member of the Royal Society, announced that the time had come to form an American Academy; in a pamphlet on the subject he argued that, notwithstanding the handicaps imposed by the drudgery of settling a new country, something might be done for the advancement of science in America by coöperative efforts. The next year his project—the offspring of a literary and scientific club called the Junto, founded by Franklin in 1727—was started in a modest way; later it was reorganized; and in 1769 as the American Philosophical Society it was launched upon its long and distinguished career.

The purpose of the Society was the promotion of the applied sciences and practical arts and the encouragement of "all philosophical experiments that let light into the nature of things, tend to increase the power of man over matter, and multiply the conveniences and pleasures of life." Its membership included virtually all the leading representatives of secular learning in the colonies and many eminent scientists of the Old World, for example, Buffon, Linnæus, Condorcet, Raynal, and Lavoisier. To make accessible to its members the pertinent researches of scholars, the Society developed, under Franklin's direction and on the basis of his gifts, a library composed of the latest European works of a scientific and practical character, which formed a strange contrast to the theological tomes of the colonial colleges. It began important collections in the various branches of "natural history," held conferences at which learned papers were presented and discussed, inspired the formation of local societies and museums, and has continued its significant career, unbroken, until the present day.

Several members of Franklin's circle won more than local honors as thinkers and investigators. Dr. Benjamin Rush made himself one of the few great mathematicians of his age and wrote important works on medicine besides; in 1773 he presented to the Philosophical Society an "Inquiry into Dreams and Sleep." David Rittenhouse contributed to the development of the thermometer, the compensating pendulum, and several mathematical instruments. When the Revolution broke out and he joined the patriot cause, a Tory poet warned him to stick to his last:

> Meddle not with state affairs;
> Keep acquaintance with the stars;
> Science, David, is thy line;
> Warp not Nature's great design
> If thou to fame wouldst rise.

Of that fellowship a fourth scientist, John Bartram, achieved distinction in botany, traveling far and wide in the colonies studying plant life, founding a botanical garden at Philadelphia in 1739, and earning from Linnæus the high praise of being "the greatest natural botanist in the world."

It is no exaggeration to say that Franklin, who stood head and shoulders above his countrymen in versatility and intelligence, was one of the first men of his epoch in the world and would have been an ornament to any nation. He was an original thinker and a diligent investigator. The range of his interests was boundless. Not only did he master the English tongue by the assiduous study of the best models such as Addison and Steele; he learned to read French, German, and Italian, opening by that labor the door to continental wisdom. He was in regular correspondence with fellow students in the young department of science in England, France, Holland, Italy, and Germany; he knew personally men like Lavoisier, the chemist, and Buffon, the naturalist, and he won by the breadth of his knowledge and his contributions to the new learning the admiration of the leading scientists of his time.

In the practical arts of municipal government, as in natural science, Franklin made many contributions of prime importance. Through his printing establishment he brought the thought of the Old World to the homes of the New; he was the inspiration of the first American scientific society, the moving spirit in the creation of the first college on modern lines, author of significant works in social economy, an inventor, an experimenter and discoverer in the field of electricity, and founder of the first hospital in Philadelphia. Universities honored themselves by giving Franklin degrees; wherever he went the forerunners of the modern age sought him out. He was made a member of all the important scientific associations of Europe and to him were sent opinions and criticisms touching the course of thought throughout the western world. No one can run through the volumes of his published works without being profoundly impressed by the scope of his interests, the shrewdness and freshness of his observations, and the catholicity of his spirit. And to all his intellectual concerns Franklin added heavy business cares, travel, and long public service. It is not too much to say that Benjamin Franklin, in the age of George II, almost divined the drift of the twentieth century.

§

In the field of historical writing more than in natural science the American colonists did work fairly comparable to that of their contemporaries in Europe. By Bradford's amazing story of the Pilgrims, a bridge was built between the narrow work of the monk and the treatise of the scholar. Though Bradford saw the wonders of Providence in the events of every season, he told a tale that makes old Plymouth stand out of the past like a scene at night under the glare of lightning. After a while, historians, becoming less certain about the intimate purpose of God, contented themselves with recording and describing, thus preparing the way for the scientific school. By the opening of the eighteenth century, the spirit of modern critical scholarship appeared in historical writing in America as in Europe. William Stith's account of early Virginia issued in 1747 was based on careful researches in the records which would do credit to a present-day doctor of philosophy; unhappily his first volume was so dull that publication had to be discontinued for want of buyers.

About the same time, Thomas Prince of Boston applied the new methods to the history of New England. "I cite my vouchers to every passage," he remarked, "and I have done my utmost, first to find out the truth and then to relate it in the clearest order." Unfortunately his style was so heavy that he was not encouraged to complete his work. Near the end of the colonial period Thomas Hutchinson brought out the first volume of a history of Massachusetts which combined talent for research with dignity in composition and a certain air of impartiality, even though his loyalty to the British empire shone through every page of his story. Thus, the study of the past with a view to understanding had begun to produce American works at least as severe and detached, if not as pretentious, as the writings of Hume and Robertson in Great Britain. By systematic inquiries into colonial development, intellectual leaders in America were evolving a consciousness of local tendencies and a sense of their own historic mission.

Equally significant was the rise of social science, if in inchoate form. As time passed, the pressing questions of the day— trade, industry, land, paper money, relations with the Indians, western expansion, agriculture, and intercolonial union—were discussed with increasing independence and ability by a host of colonial writers, with Franklin, perhaps, in the lead. All the issues of economics and politics that vexed the provincial age can be traced in detail and generality in the yellow pages of colonial pamphlets, books, papers, and magazines. Indeed, little that was important in current affairs escaped the shrewd writers of the time.

John Woolman, Quaker tailor and itinerant preacher, for example, turned a calm and steady mind upon the very foundations of the social order, the titles of his powerful tracts revealing the catholic spirit of his inquiries: Considerations on the Keeping of Negroes . . . Considerations on Pure Wisdom and Human Policy; on Labor; on Schools; and on the Right Use of the Lord's Outward Gifts . . . Serious Considerations on Trade . . . A Plea for the Poor . . . Considerations on the True Harmony of Mankind—the substance of some conversations betwen a labouring man and a man rich in money . . . The Substance of Some Conversations between a Thrifty Landholder and a Labouring Man. Under such heads Woolman, in the spirit of Jesus and with the caution of a worldly man, condemned slavery, the misuse of wealth, the evils of great accumulations, the miseries of poverty, and the waste of war.

Besides raising some pertinent questions as to the ethics of private property in land, Woolman made a plea for short hours and decent conditions for those who toiled. "The Creator of the earth," he said, "is the owner of it." Convinced that the passion for acquisition was the source of much wickedness and oppression and war, he warned the mighty to use their estates as people holding trusts from Heaven, exciting by his direct language such alarm among the more prosperous brethren in trade that his plea for the poor, though framed in 1764, was not published for thirty years. In the writings of this simple workman born on American soil in the reign of King George II are to be found the roots of American intellectual radicalism.

To the ever-widening group of secular interests, which now embraced science, history, and social economy, was added the law. In mediæval times the clergy had furnished nearly all the lawyers and had tried in their ecclesiastical courts a wide range of important cases. During the Protestant revolt, however, clerical courts were stripped of a large part of their secular business, royal tribunals attended by secular lawyers taking over the development of jurisprudence with its profound economic and social implications. In the late period of colonial history, as we have said, this new profession flourished like the green bay tree, occupying a huge sector in the long battle line of verbal warfare—especially in the division of politics. If the lawyers, unlike the scientists, did not move in the direction of skepticism, they did present a secular front to the claims of the clergy on the empire of mind.

§

The æsthetic interests of the American colonists like those of the intellect were subject to the law of inheritance, the demands of the local environment, the process of change, and impacts from outside. Naturally the passion for beauty, which all save the meanest desire to mingle in some degree at least with their labor, first found expression in objects of utility. None were so poor that they could not command shelter, and when the early stage of log houses passed, American architecture, derivative though it was of necessity, flowered into dignity and grace in many parts of the country. The Dutch clung closely to their own familiar models that were secure in custom. "New Amsterdam," as Lewis Mumford points out, in Sticks and Stones, "was a replica of the Old World port, with its gabled brick houses, and its well banked canals and fine gardens." Masters of baronial estates, in the South, instinctively followed English country-house models, sometimes importing bricks and stones to insure correctness. Thus in Maryland, Virginia, the Carolinas, and Georgia, under semi-feudal influences, rose mansions in the grand style reflecting a classical heritage filtered through Italian and French media and twisted to serve the ends of opulent Georgian merchants in England. These houses revealed taste, precision, and strength but, like the Dutch homes of New Amsterdam, they were copies of traditional designs forced into a new setting. After all, the requirements of the Southern scene called for no essential departures.

It was rather in New England, with its closely-knit democracy and its firm communal life, that domestic architecture betrayed the widest spirit of originality. The subtle influence of use and respect for general interests worked vigorously in the mind of the designer-carpenter-builder; there was a sense of fitness, a grave power, and an engaging serenity in the structures erected by their hands.

All over the colonies, indeed, exigent factors conspired to keep both public and private buildings near to the substance of things. The amount of wealth yet amassed did not permit many designers to expatriate themselves for long years of apprenticeship, thereby cutting themselves loose from affectionate union with the earth of their ancestors. There were riches in colonial America, but few fortunes were great enough to allow that lavish display which separates the arts from the business of living and working. For such reasons as these the noblest examples of colonial architecture revealed the power of restraint and simple beauty, commanding the admiration of succeeding generations, and attracting servile copyists long after the conditions which nourished the models had passed away forever.

Similar influences told, of course, in the manufacture and purchase of colonial furnishings, the English heritage supplying models. The motive of use, as distinguished from sale and profit, gave sincerity to every stick and every fabric in the early days of colonial poverty. Tables and chairs made at Plymouth, like those of mediæval England, were stocky and built to endure for centuries; John Alden's work stands firm after the lapse of three hundred years. In the plain lines and severe forms was reflected a concern for strength and utility, and, perhaps, a spirit of revolt against the ornate designs of clerical establishments, akin to the religious revolt—a disdain of soft things that was not modified until the first battle against the wilderness was won, allowing a certain geniality to creep into the labors of Puritan woodworkers, especially in Connecticut.

There was beauty also in the finest fabrics that came from the looms of colonial women and beginnings of promise in the other arts in the midst of much harsh and formal crudity. Experiments in pottery and glass in New Jersey and Pennsylvania undoubtedly would have flowered into praiseworthy achievements during the eighteenth century, particularly in the German communities, if English restrictions and the influx of cheap Dutch ware had not checked the enterprise of local artisans. Only in the South did economic conditions run severely against the creative arts; rich planters, even more than wealthy merchants of Northern cities, bought their finer goods and wares from England and the Continent; while slave labor bore no fruit of consequence in craftsmanship.

Everywhere, inevitably, the taste of the colonists was affected by the changing styles imported from abroad. When the severity of the Cromwellian age was followed by the luxuriant fancy of the Restoration, weathercock fashions veered anew in the provinces. The age of Queen Anne and the age of the Georges had their counterparts in the New World, introducing more gew-gaws, frippery, and tinsel.

Colonial artists who worked with the brush were truer to English standards than were the people at large to her common law and her patterns of living. Portraiture, being the prevailing form of art in England, naturally became the dominant expression in her colonies. Faces of kings, queens, clerics, nobles, and great bourgeois looked down upon the passing generations in the mother country; so in America faces of eminent divines, prosperous merchants, and rich planters—masters, mistresses, and some of their children—were fixed in oils for posterity. At first these colonial portraits were almost as stiff and awkward as the saints and angels painted by the early Christian artists of Italy, but in time, after wealth brought patronage and leisure and after skill increased, angles were softened and an occasional grace touched with curving line the severity of lips and jaw.

Near the end of the epoch four painters had risen to high distinction and had largely outgrown the provincial setting —Benjamin West, John Singleton Copley, Charles Wilson Peale, and Gilbert Stuart. West, of simplest Quaker parentage, was born in a little village near Philadelphia in 1738. Though self-taught in the beginning, he managed at the age of twenty-two to reach Rome, goal of all aspiring artists, and under the shadows of great traditions his mind took on the form of established modes. Settling finally in London, where a rich market had long offered enticements to the painters of the western world, West was patronized by persons of quality and money. He succeeded Sir Joshua Reynolds as president of the Royal Academy, won the favor of the king, and received royal commissions. A knighthood was conferred upon him and at the close of his prosperous life, he was buried with pomp in St. Paul's. West's painting was "grandiloquent, pompous, pretentious, posed," a strange Quaker product, but his portraits made a strong appeal to the court circles and to the rising bourgeois of his day.

Copley likewise sprang from lowly origins and likewise spent his last years in fashionable London. He was born of Irish parentage in Boston one year before Benjamin West; and, except for some guidance from his father, a painter and mezzotint maker, he too was self-taught. After marrying a rich widow, Copley made the conventional trip to Rome. On the completion of his European studies, he returned to Boston, where he was liberally patronized by the upper classes and where he might have remained had not the Revolution broken in upon his career.

Combining high notions of royal prerogative with skill in portraying ladies and gentlemen of similar political doctrines, Copley, on the outbreak of the War of Independence, threw in his lot with the loyalists, and in the hour of their distress was forced to flee to London. There, like West, he became popular; he exhibited at the Academy, was graciously received in elegant circles, and flourished by painting the portraits of those who could pay. If, as the modern critic, Walter Pach, says, Copley "has the true note of the primitive in the intensity with which he studies his people and must be reckoned with portraitists of almost the highest order," still in none of his work did he break with tradition. It was in the spirit of such a generation that Peale and Stuart received the training which fitted them to become artists of "the republican court" founded after the establishment of independence.

§

Every variety of intellectual interest and all the new streams of tendency were as a matter of course reflected in the colonial institutions for the diffusion of knowledge—schools, libraries, bookshops, and the press. Naturally, organized education, a heritage of the Old World, continued the traditions with which it started, for a mere sea journey of four or five weeks worked no revolution in it. When the period of settlement opened, the idea of free and compulsory education supported by public taxation for the children of all classes had nowhere occupied the thought of statesmen. In Europe education began with the upper ranks of society—in schools and colleges directed by the clergy; and it stopped far short of universality.

England borrowed this education from the Continent. In the Stuart age, when the colonies were founded, her system included the two universities, Oxford and Cambridge, the famous preparatory schools of Winchester and Eton, innumerable private grammar schools in which Greek and Latin ruled the curriculum, and a bewildering variety of elementary schools, including dame schools, where the abecedarians taught the rudiments of learning. All the institutions of the higher range owed their start to private endowments: gifts of monarchs, powerful churchmen, lords, ladies, guilds, and merchants. Some were free to certain classes of students; others combined scholarships with tuition fees. No sign of free, tax-supported education had appeared except in the poor laws which aimed at keeping pauper children off the rates by training them for apprenticeship at public expense. If hungry for learning, the mass of artisans and agricultural laborers had to rely mainly upon the limited elementary instruction supplied by dissenting religious sects to the humbler orders that furnished most of the membership.

The characteristics of this system of education were few and simple. All formal instruction, except the most elementary, was given by the clergy or persons who conformed to the orthodox standards of the Anglican Church. In no seat of learning was religious doubt or heresy stamped out with more zest than at Oxford and Cambridge, where the spirit of Henry VIII's act for abolishing diversity of opinion was deeply cherished. The primary purpose of the higher studies, with Greek and Latin at the center of things, was theological—the preparation of young men for the church; but the religious elements were being rapidly diluted by secular students who sought training in the classics as the key to legal, medical, and other lore. By the seventeenth century, it had become the proper thing for country gentry and rich merchants to send their sons to Oxford or Cambridge as a matter of decorum and reputability. Such being the aims of the higher learning, two other characteristics of the system followed inevitably: the total exclusion of women from collegiate institutions and a marked indifference to the newest learning, especially to the rising subject of natural science.

From top to bottom the English educational system served as a guide to the immigrants who founded colonies in America. It is easy, of course, to point out analogies with Dutch practice and to list important achievements by the Germans, the Scotch, and the Huguenots; indeed, some writers have ingeniously traced the sources of colonial education to Holland; and it must be admitted that there were striking similarities among the early schools of all Protestant countries, similarities which resulted from the fusion of Catholic traditions with sectarian aspirations.

However, the outstanding facts in this phase of colonial history are written plainly in the record. Graduates of Oxford and Cambridge were the educational leaders in the early colonial settlements; nearly two hundred of them came to New England within twenty years after the founding of Plymouth, and they were among the earliest preachers and teachers in Virginia. The first college founded in the colonies was Harvard, authorized by a vote of the General Court of Massachusetts in 1636, endowed by John Harvard two years afterward, and opened under Puritan auspices. The second American college was William and Mary in Virginia, chartered by the Crown in 1693 and launched under Anglican control. The idea of an institution of higher learning had been broached in the Old Dominion as early as 1617, but the governors, as practical men, had frowned upon it. Long afterward when Dr. James Blair, an Anglican of Scotch origin, went to the attorney-general with a request for a collegiate charter and urged that the people of Virginia had souls to be cared for, he was greeted by the explosion: "Damn their souls! Let them make tobacco." But the learned doctor was persistent and the college was founded in 1693. A few years later the third college, a Puritan institution, Yale, was chartered by the legislature of Connecticut to fit youths "for publick employment both in Church and Civil State."

Of the five additional colleges organized near the middle of the eighteenth century, three may be traced mainly to English origins; and all except one arose under religious leadership. Princeton was Presbyterian in inspiration, King's College—now Columbia University—was Anglican,

Brown was Baptist, Rutgers was Dutch Reformed, and Dartmouth, though non-sectarian, was missionary in motive. These institutions, however, had members of various Protestant sects on their boards of control and, unlike Oxford and Cambridge, opened their doors to Christians of many persuasions.

The one departure from the tradition of theological ends was made in the Academy, later known as the College, of Philadelphia. This distinctive institution sprang principally from the labors of Benjamin Franklin, who, in his grip upon realities, was more than a hundred years ahead of the schoolmen of his age. Franklin himself had never been ground through the college mill; he was endowed with a lively imagination and curiosity, a love of knowledge, and an appreciation of the social benefits that might be conferred by education. Soon after his arrival in Philadelphia he gathered around him a coterie of printers, shoemakers, and carpenters who read books and thought things out for themselves—a group known as the Junto, which he called "the best school of philosophy, morality, and politics that then existed in the province." Three questions asked of new members revealed the spirit of this strange academy: "Do you sincerely declare that you love mankind in general of what profession or religion soever? Do you think any person ought to be harmed in his body, name, or goods for mere speculative opinions or his external way of worship? Do you love truth for truth's sake and will you endeavor impartially to find and receive it yourself and communicate it to others?"

With the support of the Junto, Franklin issued a plan for a college, prudently concealing some of his liberal opinions for fear he might alarm the pious. As a result of his appeal for funds, five thousand pounds was raised to start the institution. A board of control was then organized containing the spokesmen of several sects and a Scotch clergyman was chosen as provost; but some of the originality and temper of the founder, as we shall see, was disclosed in the scientific and secular program of instruction offered to those who did not want to concentrate on Greek and Latin.

§

The course of instruction in the early colonial colleges was based essentially on the program of Oxford and Cambridge, which had risen during the Middle Ages under the auspices of the Catholic Church. Since the laws, decrees, services, and literature of the Church were in Latin, that tongue became the original language of learning for all western Europe. In the classical revival of the renaissance, however, the study of Greek began to engross the interest of progressive scholars, and by dint of hard labor champions of that tongue were able to force it into the universities against the protests of the Latinists well content with their monopoly.

The substance of the mediæval university curriculum rested on foundations as old as the academy at Athens. After groping around a long time in their search for a structure of education, the Greeks came to a general agreement upon certain subjects which they deemed appropriate for gentlemen of leisure—"liberal arts," as contrasted with the vulgar arts of trade, industry, and labor. On the basis of the Greek scheme, Catholic scholars, in the early Middle Ages, erected the program of the seven liberal arts— grammar, rhetoric, dialectic, arithmetic, geometry, astronomy, and music—which they bent to theological purposes. When the Protestant clergy of the Established Church took over the universities in England, they turned these studies to the uses of a different creed, but they continued the old tongues and the old methods, to the practical exclusion still of the English language and literature.

On this historic model, with its roots so far back in the past and its purposes so far removed from the ends of trade and agriculture, was fashioned the instruction in the older colonial colleges. In each of them the course was confined mainly to Greek and Latin, drill in Aristotelian logic, a smattering of elementary mathematics, and thin shreds of natural science. For the benefit of the more ambitious theological students, Hebrew was sometimes added. Although the colleges that arose in the later colonial period showed a tendency to widen their program of studies, ancient languages, rhetoric, scholastic philosophy, and logic, shaped primarily for theologians, continued to hold the citadel of the higher learning. Such elements of law, medicine, and science as made their way into the universities of England and America were chiefly fragments in the ancient mosaic.

The vitalizing subjects of English literature, history, geography, and political economy naturally received little attention from the masters of such formal learning. It is true that the age of exploration and settlement produced Shakespeare, Spenser, Ben Jonson, Francis Bacon, Bunyan, Pepys, Dryden, Butler, Swift, Addison, Steele, Pope, and Defoe but in neither the English nor the American colleges did instruction in the great works of English authors receive systematic consideration. In the sight of the schoolmen Latin was more worthy than the language of the sea, the house, the field, and the shop used by the English people in general. As a matter of fact the first grammar of the vernacular tongue, which appeared in 1594, was written in Latin and when, a quarter of a century later, a grammar was issued in English, its author laid stress on the fact that it furnished a groundwork for the study of Latin. Even when the popular tongue was finally disentangled from Latin and a library of noble books had been written in it, the study of English yet found no place in collegiate work.

History and political science also remained among the subjects pursued only by curious gentlemen of leisure or those who turned to the uses of the pamphleteer. Though Oxford had a professorship of ancient history as early as 1622, a century passed before the regius professorships of modern history were founded at the English universities;

and in that respect the colonies lagged behind the mother country. The Revolution was raging when Yale created a professorship of ecclesiastical history—the first chair of history in the colonies—and the nineteenth century was well advanced when Harvard gave Jared Sparks an opportunity to teach the story of America.

With even more neglect at the hands of scholars, geography was left to take form under the direction of travelers, navigators, and collectors of books and maps; as a subject of instruction it found a favorable reception only here and there by some enthusiastic master or astronomer inclined to wander out of his allotted field. Though political economy was added by Franklin to his immense and varied interests and given at least a place in the crowded curriculum of the Philadelphia College, it had no standing as a branch of learning elsewhere. At the other institutions, no professor appears to have given the theme more than a passing glance in the wide sweep of his moral philosophy. In a word, all those grand branches of knowledge pertaining to the material universe and the science of society—branches which are the glory of research and instruction in the modern university—received little more than a fleeting recognition in the colleges of the colonial age either in England or in America. Their very structures were still in the process of formation.

So firmly fixed was the grip of tradition upon learning that Franklin, with all his twisting and turning, could not work a complete revolution in the course of study planned for the College of Philadelphia. In the interest of peace and endowment, a compromise was made. Latin, Greek, and the scholastic subjects of the age were provided for boys who wished to prepare for law, medicine, or divinity. Unto these things were added, for the benefit of those intending to follow other paths, such practical studies as mathematics, surveying, navigation, and accounting; scientific branches—mechanics, physics, chemistry, agriculture, and natural history; instruction in history, civics, ethics, government, trade, commerce, and international law; and finally, for the worldly wise and curious, training in modern languages.

Such was the plan worked out by Franklin in coöperation with the first provost, William Smith, for the college launched in 1755. To suggest that it anticipated the most enlightened program evolved by the liberal university of the late nineteenth century is to speak with caution; in fact, it stands out like a beacon light in the long history of human intelligence. Nor is it without significance that the first liberal institution of higher learning in the western world appeared on the frontier of civilization—in colonial America where an energetic people was wrestling with the realities of an abundant nature and the problems of self-government. Though a Scotch clergyman gave academic form to the course of instruction at Philadelphia, the spirit and concept came from Benjamin Franklin, a self-educated, provincial workman whose mind had never been conquered by the scholastics.

If, on the whole, the colonial college was narrow in its intellectual range, it need not be supposed that the discipline offered was correspondingly thorough in every case or that a deadly uniformity of opinion ruled all classrooms from Cambridge to Williamsburg. Two Dutch travelers who visited Harvard in 1680 found only ten or twenty students in residence and reported somewhat adversely on their attainments: "They could hardly speak a word of Latin so that my comrade could not converse with them. They took us to the library where there was nothing particular. We looked over it a little. They presented us with a glass of wine. . . . The minister of the place goes there morning and evening to make prayer."

Half a century later that impassioned evangelist, George Whitefield, was no more favorably impressed. He thought that Harvard was "not far superior to our Universities in piety and true godliness. Tutors neglect to pray with and examine the hearts of their pupils. Discipline is at too low

an ebb. Bad books are become fashionable among them."
At William and Mary the godly were also shocked by
modernism rampant. William Small, the professor of
mathematics and philosophy, taught from his chair doctrines which almost anticipated the nineteenth century, and
so unsettled the minds of young men like Thomas Jefferson
that fond parents trembled for the morals of their offspring.
It was for this reason that James Madison was sent away to
Princeton where "the fountain of learning was undefiled."

On the whole it would seem that the opportunities for
acquiring knowledge, as distinct from learning, were about
as good in America as in England, if Gibbon, the historian,
is to be accepted as authority. "The Fellows or monks of
my time," he lamented in speaking of Oxford at the middle
of the eighteenth century, "were decent easy men, who
supinely enjoyed the gifts of the founder: their days were
filled by a series of uniform employments—the chapel, the
hall, the coffee-house, and the common room—till they retired weary and well satisfied to a long slumber. From the
toil of reading, writing, or thinking they had absolved
their consciences. Their conversation stagnated in a round
of college business, Tory politics, personal anecdotes, and
private scandal." In any case, collegiate education of the
eighteenth century, both in the mother country and the
provinces, immersed the students in theories and dogmas
that had little or no relation to creative intelligence or
independent thinking.

In this, of course, there was nothing unnatural. The
fundamental purpose in the establishment of all the colleges, except that at Philadelphia, was to train clergymen,
not to foster the inquiring spirit of natural science. Among
the primary motives that inspired the founders of Harvard
was the fear of leaving "an illiterate ministry to the
Churches when our present ministers shall lie in the dust."
Five out of seven of its early graduates became preachers
and, down until the end of the seventeenth century, more
than one half of them turned to that calling. As late as

1753 the legislature of Connecticut, in a resolution referring to Yale, declared that "one principal end proposed in erecting the college was to supply the churches in this colony with a learned, pious, and orthodox ministry." A dearth of learned parsons was also a weighty argument in the plea that led to the foundation of William and Mary, and, indeed, all other colonial colleges save only Franklin's institution.

Still, as time flowed on, young men preparing for law and medicine flocked in increasing numbers to the colleges, even though no radical changes were made in the classical and theological curriculum to meet the requirements of their vocations. As a matter of fact, Greek and Latin, owing to the amount of secular learning locked up in those tongues, were useful to lawyers and doctors. Moreover, much of the dialectic designed to equip preachers for vanquishing sectarian foes and the devil could be turned to good account by lawyer-politicians in the battle of wits that preceded and accompanied the Revolution; for the science of argument and persuasion evolved by the Greeks, adopted by the Romans, and taken over by the theologians was so complete that it seemed hardly necessary to improve on traditional methods. But as in England, so in America, lawyers and physicians had to supplement their collegiate course with apprenticeship to practitioners to secure their professional training; it was 1765 when Philadelphia, in her grand advance all along the line, set even the laggard mother country an example by founding a medical school, the first on the continent of North America.

§

Following similar traditions, the early secondary institutions of America were fashioned after the English grammar school designed to prepare boys for college. When the legislature of Massachusetts in 1647 sanctioned the erection of higher schools in the towns, it indicated that the purpose was the instruction of youths "so farr as they may be fited for ye university." In the Middle and Southern colonies, however, where, with the exception of William and Mary, no college appeared until near the eve of the struggle for independence, the higher schools were shaped to meet the requirements of trade rather than college entrance. For example, the free school or academy of Charleston, South Carolina, established in 1712, taught "writing, arithmetic, and merchants' accounts, and also the art of navigation and surveying and other useful and practical parts of mathematics." The prospectus of a similar institution of the same period in New York advertised "all branches of the mathematics, geometry, algebra, geography, navigation, and merchants' bookkeeping." Practical aims likewise figured in the course of instruction in Franklin's academy, which grew into the College of Philadelphia.

In Virginia the sons of planters who sailed away for Oxford or Cambridge or entered William and Mary nearby were usually prepared for admission by family tutors or at the few private schools kept by clergymen. Jefferson, for instance, was put into a small English school in his neighborhood when he was five years old; at the age of nine he was sent to live as a boarding pupil in the family of a Scotch parson; and he completed his preparation for William and Mary at the private school of James Maury, a Huguenot inclined to skepticism and good living. When at the age of seventeen he set out on horseback for college, he had seen nothing of the world twenty miles beyond the circuit of his home and had never been in a town having more than one hundred inhabitants.

§

The primary schools at the bottom of the system of formal education were, like the colleges, inspired by the religious motive—to which was sometimes joined the material consideration of preparing children of the poor for apprenticeship. The idea of elementary schools supported by taxation, freed from clerical control and offering instruction to children of all classes, found no expression in colonial America. Indeed it was foreign to the experience of the Greeks, Romans, and Europeans of the Middle Ages whose psychology still dominated the West. The slaves of Athens and Rome, the serfs and artisans of the Middle Ages, were not in the mass within the scope of the educational systems of their time, even though bright boys frequently climbed from lowly origins to dizzy heights. Moreover, the Catholic concept of authority did not demand any severe mental drill for the commonalty until the Church was rudely shaken by the Protestant revolt.

It was that cataclysm which marked the beginnings of popular education. Protestant sects, especially the Dissenters in England, having asserted their right to a limited private judgment, found it necessary to resort to the schoolmaster to impose their respective creeds on their children and to defend them against other ideas deemed erroneous. Since they belonged mainly to the mercantile and laboring classes, rather than to the nobility, Dissenters also found it useful to combine with the memorizing of catechisms some additional instruction, in writing, arithmetic, and the practical arts, so useful to the shop and counting house.

Wherever, therefore, a dissenting sect arose in Europe or in Great Britain—Huguenot, Lutheran, Presbyterian, Puritan, Separatist, Baptist, or Quaker—there soon appeared primary schools supported by the contributions of the congregation or by the fees of the parents and dedicated to the instruction of the young in the rudiments of learning. By way of supplement, missionary zeal also entered the field of elementary instruction, providing charity schools for the poor liable to be led astray by the wiles of the wicked. For example, the Anglican Society for the Promotion of Christian Knowledge, founded in 1698, established in many parts of England primary institutions to give the children of the working classes the Anglican view of salvation, together with the elements of reading and writing and the "grounds of Arithmetick to fit them for Service or Apprentices."

To the sectarian, missionary, and charity motives was added another—the relief of the taxes collected for the support of paupers by the training of children likely to become public charges. In response to this practical requirement, the great poor law of 1601, enacted at the close of Elizabeth's reign, ordered the compulsory apprenticeship of all children not provided with an independent living and placed squarely upon property owners the burden of supporting their elementary education. Such were the roots of primary education in America. They were not Dutch or English, Presbyterian or Puritan; they were Protestant and realistic.

Now, the American colonies were peopled largely by dissenting Protestants. Wherever a tiny community of Puritans, Baptists, Presbyterians, Quakers, or Lutherans was formed, some kind of an elementary school for the children of the sect was sure to follow in the course of time. But there were other sections of the populace not as easily supplied with the rudiments. The pioneer districts, with their scattered homesteads, the wide plantation system of the Southern seaboard, and the more densely settled regions with servants poor in worldly goods and often lacking in respect for the religion of their employers, presented special problems that required, as far as they were met at all, special treatment.

In response to such needs several types of educational activities unfolded in the colonies. On the very edge of the advancing frontier ardent missionaries opened log-cabin schools for the members of their sect and any others who would attend. For the children of the poor, the English charity school sprang up here and there in town and country. "Our advice is," declared the Friends of Pennsylvania and New Jersey at their yearly meeting in 1722, "that all Friends' children have so much learning as to read the holy scriptures and other English books and to write and cast

accounts . . . and for that end let the rich help the poor."
In New England the duty of parents to educate their children and masters their apprentices and servants in the ways
of salvation and in the practical arts was early emphasized
by legislative enactment.

The laws of Massachusetts on this point have been so
glossed over with uncritical comment that they have been
hailed as marking the dawn of public education in the
modern and secular form. In reality, seen in their historical
setting, they do no such thing. The act of 1642 required
the chosen men of each town to supervise the children of
the community and "to take account . . . especially of
their ability to read and understand the principles of religion and the capital laws of this country." It likewise
required them—as the overseers of the poor were compelled to do under the legislation of Elizabeth—to put to
apprenticeship the children of all parents "not able and fit
to bring them up." The avowed occasion for the law was
the neglect of masters and parents in training "their children in learning and labor." Five years later came the act
of 1647 which ordered every town of fifty householders to
appoint a teacher for "all such children as shall resort to
him to read and write," and added that every town with a
hundred households should establish a grammar school for
the instruction of youths preparing for college.

These laws, which seem to have been honored in the
breach as well as in the observance, have been greeted by a
modern educator as making for the first time in the English
language "a legally valid assertion of the right of the state
to require of local communities that they establish and
maintain schools of general learning." The unwary are
liable to be misled by this contention. Unquestionably the
first of these acts was conceived partly in the spirit of the
English poor law; while the second flowed from a great
desire to impose on all children the creed of the Puritan
sect. The fact that the education was ordered by "the
state" was of no special significance, for the state and church

were one in Massachusetts at the time; indeed, if the Mathers were to be believed, the church was superior to the state.

At all events no person who was not a member of a Puritan congregation could vote in Massachusetts until the English Crown broke down the barrier in the charter of 1691; and the teachers chosen under the school system established by the law were as orthodox as those selected for sectarian schools supported by the fees and contributions of the faithful or for the charity schools maintained by gifts from the devout. Certainly the New England Primer which "taught millions to read and not one to sin" was not secular in outlook or purpose. Indeed, the Massachusetts law of 1647 was avowedly framed to outwit "that old deluder Satan," by giving the youth a correct knowledge of the Scriptures. And appropriately too the New England Primer was English in origin and purpose and was widely used in the mother country as well as in the provinces.

In any case, whether or not popular education in some form was prescribed by law, as in Massachusetts—and, indeed, in Connecticut, New Hampshire, and Maryland—it was the enthusiasm of the religious denominations, rather than the enlightenment of public officials, that kept the lamp of learning burning in the colonies. No thickly settled community, no sect of any importance, was without its elementary institution at least, supporting teachers by fees and contributions including gifts from England in aid of American missionary efforts. Supplementing the sectarian schools were itinerant pedagogues who collected tuition charges from parents and "boarded around" to eke out a living.

Occasional glimpses into colonial primary schools, afforded by diaries and memoirs, reveal severity in discipline and dogmatism in instruction. Social heritage approved both. Spartans beat their children and cowed them under the rod of war. The Romans seem to have followed their example even with additions: Horace called his teacher "the thrasher." The Middle Ages carried on the vogue; pictures of mediæval teachers represent them with rod in hand as if but seeking an excuse to strike. In this wont and use the Protestants made no change worthy of note; Martin Luther taught that appropriate beatings were good to restrain impudence and advance learning. Rules for the school of colonial Dorchester declared that "the rod of correction is an ordinance of God, sometimes to be dispensed unto children."

Moreover, the school fathers of colonial times, often beset by poverty themselves, could not always be fastidious in the selection of teachers. Sometimes they went down to the docks and bought an indentured servant who professed to know the rudiments and made him schoolmaster for the boys and girls of the community. In fact, interspersed in the columns of the newspapers with advertisements of slaves, rice, boots, lime juice, and crockery were notices of teachers for sale into terms of indenture. "To be disposed of, a likely servant man's time for 4 years who is very well qualified for a clerk or to teach a school, he reads, writes, understands arithmetick, and accompts very well, Enquire of the Printer hereof," runs a notice in the Philadelphia Mercury in 1735. A teacher who could be lawfully beaten by his own master was probably not inclined to spare the rod of authority over little children entrusted to his care.

In this colonial scheme of instruction girls met with the traditional discriminations. They were as a matter of course shut out of the colleges and the grammar schools that prepared for the colleges, for they were not to be preachers, orators, statesmen, doctors, or lawyers. In short, unless a family tutor was provided the avenues to higher learning were automatically closed to them. To the elementary schools, it seems, girls were generally admitted, at least to learn reading, the catechism, and perhaps some arithmetic. For the special use of the middle classes, day and boarding schools were opened in many regions under private patronage, to impart the rudiments deemed essential to the social graces—reading, writing, arithmetic, sewing, music, and dancing. Nowhere, however, was the feminine mind invited by pedagogues to explore curious places. In those days, women, as Governor Winthrop declared, were expected to stick to household matters and to refrain from meddling "in such things as are proper for men whose minds are stronger."

§

If schools confined their students rather closely to the classical and theological routine, shopkeepers provided young and old with the current literature of England and the Continent. From the earliest times it was the common practice for merchants to take orders for books to be imported and to bring over on their own motion stocks for their shelves. Following the custom of the trade, Robert Pringle, in 1744, called the attention of South Carolinians to the fact that he had for sale "very reasonable" a consignment of "sundry goods, particularly a very choice collection of printed Books, Pictures, Maps, and Pickles."

After the newspaper business was fairly launched, printers not only published American books on their own account, but also kept on hand imported works for their customers. Franklin was offering Bacon, Dryden, Locke, Milton, Swift, Seneca, and Ovid to his patrons in the opening days of his career in Philadelphia. So in one fashion or another, the great writings of the times, as well as the classics, were made available to the owners of private libraries, such as Colonel Byrd at Westover, and to enterprising individuals who were trying to educate themselves. Few things of first rate importance in England and France at least seem to have been overlooked. The writings of the French philosophers—Montesquieu, Voltaire, Rousseau, and the Encyclopedists—no less than the heavy theological tomes and the newest scientific books from Great Britain were put into the hands of the colonials with amazing promptness and at moderate prices.

Those who could not afford to buy books were not altogether without resources, especially in the larger towns. By the middle of the eighteenth century, Boston, Newport, New York, Philadelphia, and Charleston had small libraries open to the public. In 1653, Robert Keayne presented the citizens of Boston with a little collection of books; in 1731, Franklin started a subscription library in connection with his Junto; in 1748, seventeen young men in Charleston opened a library for "self-improvement"; in 1754, the Society Library was founded in New York.

For the rising democracy of colonial America, the most noteworthy of these experiments was the subscription library which Franklin established with the aid of a few poor tradesmen and mechanics. It was he who showed how forty or fifty persons could, by pooling meager savings, open gateways hitherto closed to all save the rich. "The institution," as he said, "soon manifested its utility, was imitated by other towns and in other provinces. The libraries were augmented by donations; reading became fashionable; and our people, having no public amusement to divert their attention from study became better acquainted with books; and in a few years were observed by strangers to be better instructed and more intelligent than people of the same rank generally are in other countries. . . . The libraries have improved the general conversation of the Americans, made the common tradesmen and farmers as intelligent as most gentlemen from other countries, and perhaps have contributed in some degree to the stand generally made throughout the colonies in defense of their privileges."

Although no census of literacy was ever taken in the colonial age, there was abundant collateral evidence to support Franklin's contention that a very large proportion of the American people could read and write. It was a fact of no small portent that a hundred thousand copies of Thomas Paine's first pamphlet calling for independence were sold while the issue was fresh from the press. The work of the schools, tutors, libraries, printers, and booksellers was widely supplemented by that of patient fathers and mothers who pored with their children over primers and spelling books. By these routes, little rivulets of opinion were sent streaming down into the torrent that swept the thirteen English colonies into the American republic.

§

That other great institution for the promotion of intellectual interests, the press, rose and flourished as if to emphasize, while distributing, knowledge of worldly affairs. Thus another body of preachers—newspaper editors—could thunder away every week or so and, unlike their brethren of the cloth, cover the whole domain of war, politics, business, current events, and scandal, that is, as long as they avoided collisions with colonial officials. Leaving out of the reckoning the early broadsides and a little sheet, Publick Occurrences, which appeared and died in 1690, the first regular newspaper in the colonies was The Boston News-Letter, a tiny four-page, two-column folder, established in 1704. Fifteen years later, The American Weekly Mercury came from the press of Andrew Bradford in Philadelphia and before long New York, Maryland, South Carolina, Rhode Island, and Virginia could also boast of local papers.

At the middle of the century came a second burst of journalistic enterprise. In 1755, The Gazette was founded in New Haven and within ten years North Carolina, New Hampshire, and Georgia had printers engaged in purveying news, essays, and gossip, domestic and foreign. When the struggle over the Stamp Act began in 1765 every colony, except Delaware and New Jersey, had one or more papers to speak for the contending parties and those two colonies were well served by the printers of New York and Philadelphia. Some of the publishers were sustained by the profits of public printing and held under the thumb of the royal governor; others struggled along under the patronage of the popular party aided by the advertising of friendly merchants.

The political and cultural significance of this early American journalism, crude as it appears to the sophisticated of modern times, can hardly be overestimated. If narrow in its range, it was wider and freer than the pulpit and the classroom and it was an art open to any person, group, faction, or party that could buy a press and exercise enough literary skill to evade the heavy hand of colonial authorities.

By any editor of spirit the note of independence could be struck; indeed, it was sounded early in the eighteenth century by The New England Courant, established in 1721 by Benjamin Franklin's brother and supported by a body of "respectable characters" bearing the audacious title of "The Hell-Fire Club," a little fraternity that wrote rather peppery stuff to give spice to reports of governors' addresses and chronicles of official doings. Essays, done in the style of Addison and Steele—many of them by Franklin, then in his youth—poured ridicule on the great and good. As the authors undoubtedly expected, some of their diatribes got under the skins of the mighty; and on one occasion, the elder Franklin was imprisoned for reflections on the august assembly of the colony. The day foreseen by the rabid governor of Virginia had come. In 1671 he had blurted out his official opinion: "I thank God we have no free schools nor printing; and I hope we shall not have these hundred years. For learning has brought disobedience and heresy and sects into the world; and printing has divulged them and libels against the government. God keep us from both."

Long before the governor's allotted century had vanished, royal agents had come to grips with the unarmed disseminators of dangerous thoughts. In 1734 the first great contest in America over freedom of the press opened in New York with the arrest of Peter Zenger, publisher of

The Journal, for assailing the administration of the provincial governor. The trial which followed proved to be a dramatic episode as well as a defeat for the king's representative. An able attorney, Andrew Hamilton, brought up from Philadelphia to plead for the printer after local lawyers had been cowed into submission, conducted the case with a grand flourish, making the issue "the cause of liberty." Moved by his argument and imbued no doubt with popular sympathies, the jury defied the judge, and amid general rejoicing gave the imprisoned editor his liberty.

When, however, the tables were turned in New Hampshire long afterward by a local editor who attacked the majesty of the colonial legislature and the Continental Congress, the victim did not escape so easily; he was ordered to appear before the provincial assembly, sharply censured there, and solemnly warned not to print more criticisms of the popular party. Thus the twists and turns to be found in the struggle between liberty and authority, so familiar to-day, wound their way into the journalism of the eighteenth century.

Fermenting opinion stirred by mettlesome editors, in the fullness of time, took on a national character. While the circulation of each paper was mainly local, publishers exchanged sheets with one another and reprinted striking articles of continental interest, spreading them all the way from Portsmouth to Savannah. Moreover, citizens of the larger outlook subscribed to journals from distant cities, for in 1758 the colonial post office, which had long carried newspapers without charge, was compelled to fix a rate on the ground that "the News-papers of the several Colonies on this Continent, heretofore permitted to be sent by the Post free of Charge, are of late years so much increased as to become extremely burthensome to the Riders." What seems to be the first cartoon printed in the colonies—Franklin's snake cut into eight pieces, entitled "Join or Die"—an appeal to the provincials to unite against the French and

Indians in 1754, was copied far and wide and became one of the great American symbols of the age. A moving call to arms against the French issued about the same time by the Virginia Gazette was printed again and again by Northern papers in their campaign for solidarity against the common foe. Clearly the institution of the press, operating, at least in a measure, on a national scale, was prepared to serve the lawyers and politicians who were to kindle the flames of revolution.

§

In the newspapers and pamphlets—the latter sometimes printed first in the columns of weekly journals and sometimes issued separately—began to appear the literature of the new politics, swelling in volume as the colonies grew in stature and the controversy with the British government grew in acerbity. It was largely in the form of letters and special articles that the passions of the conflict were first announced outside the halls of assemblies and taverns. Unlike France of the Old Régime, provincial America did not produce, long before the struggle commenced, great treatises such as the Encyclopedia or ringing calls for revolt such as Rousseau's Social Contract.

The reasons were not difficult to find: the colonists already had textbooks of revolution in the writings of Englishmen who defended and justified the proceedings of the seventeenth century—above all, John Locke's writings, wherein was set forth the right of citizens to overthrow governments that took their money or their property without their consent. In such documents arguments for the American Revolution were at hand in clear and authoritative English. All that editors and publicists had to do was to paraphrase, decorate, and repeat. Moreover, the American ruling classes, unlike the French bourgeoisie, had already wrested the government from the royal authorities by 1765; their uprising was designed to preserve what they had, rather than to gain something new and untried.

So when Otis, the Adamses, Dickinson, Hamilton, Jefferson, and other philosophers of revolt set to work on pamphlets, letters, resolutions, proclamations, declarations, and constitutions they found, ready made before them and intelligible to the reading public, all the theories and dogmas which their cause required. They had only to use English rhetoric and precedent in forging their own greater argument; but in actual fact they went beyond the rule of thumb, giving to their noblest writings some of the gravity of Roman orators, some of the rhythm and cadence of Latin poets.

No one can rise from a comparative study of the literature of revolution in all ages without a sense of profound admiration for the ingenuity, the learning, and the mastery of the native tongue revealed in the documents of the American revolt. Lord Chatham pronounced no hollow encomium in saying to his colleagues: "When your lordships look at the papers transmitted to us from America; when you consider their decency, firmness, and wisdom, you cannot but respect their cause and wish to make it your own. For myself, I must declare and avow, that in all my reading and observation—and it has been my favorite study—I have read Thucydides and have studied and admired the master statesmen of the world—that for solidity of reasoning, force of sagacity, and wisdom of conclusion, under such a complication of difficult circumstances, no nation or body of men can stand in preference to the general congress at Philadelphia."

CHAPTER V

The Clash of Metropolis and Colony

CONCERNING the origin of the American Revolution there are as many theories as there are writers of sagas. The oldest hypothesis, born of the conflict on American soil, is the consecrated story of school textbooks: the Revolution was an indignant uprising of a virtuous people, who loved orderly and progressive government, against the cruel, unnatural, and unconstitutional acts of King George III. From the same conflict arose, on the other side, the Tory interpretation: the War for Independence was a violent outcome of lawless efforts on the part of bucolic clowns, led by briefless pettifoggers and smuggling merchants, to evade wise and moderate laws broadly conceived in the interest of the English-speaking empire. Such were the authentic canons of early creeds.

With the flow of time appeared some doubts about the finality of both these verdicts. The rise of democracy in England during the nineteenth century modified the theory long current in that country. In the minds of English Liberals, who hated Tories as much as Lord North and

Dr. Johnson despised Samuel Adams and Patrick Henry, a novel pattern was finally evolved: the contest in America was only the counterpart of the heroic struggle led by Russell, Cobden, Bright, and Gladstone at home to establish the dominion of the English mill owners over Crown, clergy, and landed aristocracy.

Sustained by partisan conflict, this thesis took on the guise of sober history in the writings of May, Green, and Trevelyan and was accepted as the truth at last by the small and select circle in the United States that took pride in being intellectual. Meanwhile there grew up in America a school of so-called scientific historians who looked with hauteur upon all partisan theories—even though well bolstered by documents—and went straight to the original records, papers, memoirs, and other contemporary sources relative to the great epoch. The result of their labors was a number of special studies which somewhat chilled the glowing periods of the orators and slowly broke down under the weight of scholarship the original American articles of faith. Social amenities hastened the disintegration; many descendants of revolutionary heroes, having accumulated or inherited fortunes, found a welcome in the best English society, where they began to look with kindlier eyes upon the offspring of the "minions of George III."

Fury kindled by passions, especially after America entered the World War, fed the stream of tendency. In the fervor of the moment, over-zealous American scholars, rushing from research to propaganda, rewrote their books to show that the American Revolution was more or less of a moral and tactical error on the part of the Patriot Fathers. After all, ran the latest hypothesis, the Revolution was the result of a needless and unfortunate quarrel in which many untrue and unjust things had been said and done; so it seemed best to cover the past with the mantle of oblivion and rejoice that it was the English-speaking people who had from time immemorial led the world in the fight of democracy against autocracy.

But when the economic and ethical reunion of the sun-dered segments of the old British Empire seemed almost effected, the peace of Versailles broke in upon the cele-bration.   Then the voices of the Germans and Irish were heard again in the land and those who had reveled in the sunlight of an Anglo-American alliance suddenly found themselves frosted in the blasts of renewed criticism. History once more registered shifting winds.

On taking up any work dealing with the American Revo-lution it is necessary, therefore, to inquire about the assump-tions upon which the author is operating.   Is he preparing to unite the English-speaking peoples in the next world war?   Does he have in mind some Teutonic or Hibernian concept of American polity?   Or is he desirous of discover-ing how the conflict arose without any reference to the devices of current politicians?   As for this book, the pur-pose is simple, namely, to inquire into the pertinent facts which conditioned the struggle between the men who gov-erned England and those who ruled the thirteen colonies —on the theory that only adolescents allow ancient grudges to affect their judgments in matters international.

§

With respect to the American side, it is hoped, the essen-tial materials assembled in the preceding pages fairly de-scribe the economic activities, political institutions, and cul-tural life which distinguished the American people from those of the mother country.   On the other side, the signifi-cant data can be made to stand out in equally bold relief. England in the eighteenth century was ruled by two power-ful, well-knit classes: landlords and merchants, with little or no restraint from artisans and agricultural laborers.   The fierce contest between the aristocracy and the middle orders that had filled the seventeenth century with revolution had died down into a relatively mild political debate.

Indeed, the ranks of the former were now largely recruited from trading circles; earls did not often object to marrying their sons to the daughters of affluent merchants; dukes were as eager as greengrocers to invest in the stocks of African slavers or American commercial ventures. Both houses of Parliament were controlled by agents of these two branches of English society. The landed proprietors, besides having a permanent stronghold in the House of Lords, commanded many seats in the lower chamber; while the merchants usually found pliant spokesmen in members sent to the Commons from the towns.

By the system of representation the rule of small and active groups in the landed and commercial classes was especially favored. The suffrage was so restricted by property qualifications that not more than one hundred and sixty thousand Englishmen among eight million people enjoyed the right to vote. New cities like Liverpool, Manchester, and Leeds, which had grown up since the origin of Parliament in the middle ages, were without any representatives at all in the House of Commons; on the other hand, petty villages, with very few voters controlled by some neighboring landlord, sent one or two members to Westminster. It would be a conservative estimate to say that ten thousand landlords and merchants ruled the England of George III. Even the Crown was merely one branch of government employed in the realization of their interests. Subjected to Parliament by the Revolution of 1688, it had been further weakened during the reigns of the first Georges who, as long as their purses were filled, were more interested in their German home of Hanover than in quarreling about historic prerogatives with parliamentary leaders. In 1750, therefore, the legislative, executive, and judicial branches of the English political system were dominated by closely knit bodies of landlords and prosperous merchants—with the latter growing in wealth, numbers, and power.

Naturally the policies and acts of the English government reflected the interests and desires of these two estates. Naturally, also, both were affected by the course of economic development in the American plantations. A part of the burden of taxation for empire fell on the landlords; they were likewise concerned about the colonial wool which came into competition with one of their leading staples and about colonial produce in general as it poured in increasing streams into English and Continental markets. Some of them with startling prescience saw that cheap wheat from virgin soil might in time ruin British agriculture. Still more numerous and direct were the points of contact formed by the merchants with colonial affairs. Besides being active in all lines of trade and shipping, they advanced large amounts of capital to promote American enterprises, thus making every branch of provincial economy an object of solicitude on their part.

§

Out of the interests of English landlords and merchants, illuminated no doubt by high visions of empire not foreign to their advantage, flowed acts of Parliament controlling the economic undertakings of American colonists and measures of administration directed to the same end. These laws and decisions were not suddenly sprung upon the world at the accession of George III in 1760. On the contrary, they were spread over more than a century, beginning with the rise of the mercantile party under Cromwell; they crowded the pages of the statute books and the records of the British colonial offices from the coronation of Charles II in 1660 to the outbreak of the American Revolution. Far from being accidents of politics, conceived in the heat of controversy, they were the matured fruits of a mercantile theory of state which regarded colonial trade as the property of the metropolis, to be monopolized by its citizens and made subservient in all things to their interests—a theory which, with modifications here and there, still thrives under the guise of milder phrases and loftier sentiments.

The laws of the British Parliament giving effect to this policy fell into certain broad classes. First were the navigation acts, opening with the famous statute of 1651, which limited the carrying trade to and from the colonies to English-built ships, manned mainly by English sailors. Here was one source of the sea power that defended the empire. American colonists enjoyed the protection of this power, profiting, as Englishmen, by the restriction which excluded alien ships from lucrative business.

A second group of statutes, known as the trade laws, regulated the exports and imports of the dominions and plantations. Under the terms of these measures, colonists had to ship their tobacco, pitch, tar, turpentine, masts, and other enumerated articles to England; with these exceptions they could sell their products wherever they could find buyers. Their importing business was likewise restrained; commodities of European growth and manufacture, as a rule, they could buy only through English factors—the idea being to add to the prosperity of English merchants. A third sheaf of acts put restrictions on colonial manufacturing; for example, woolen goods and hats could not be made for the general trade; mills for slitting and rolling iron and furnaces for making steel were forbidden.

By a fourth group of laws the interests of English creditors were tenderly guarded. With a view to maintaining a sound medium of exchange and preventing the debt-burdened colonials from inflating the currency, Parliament enacted in 1751 a measure prohibiting the issue of paper money in New England—a proscription later extended to other colonies. Equally important for the English creditor was the act of 1752, making the lands, tenements, and slaves of American debtors subject to levy for the obligations of their owners, and placing the affidavit of a resident in England on the same footing with the testimony of a provincial in open court in the colonies. The contest between the bond holder and the debtor had begun in earnest.

The origins of this legislation, or at least the most salient pieces of it, are more or less clearly revealed in the records. Certainly, the restriction on American woolen manufactures flowed from the protests of a competing industry—English landlords and wool-growers, as well as merchants and manufacturers, uniting in the protection of a business which furnished about one-third of England's total export trade when the restrictive act was passed in 1699. Parliamentary legislation against colonial hat and iron industries was likewise the result of specific protests made by interested parties.

Such also was the origin of the prohibition on colonial paper money. According to Franklin's testimony, that irksome ban was devised at the request of a handful of creditors. "On the slight complaint of a few Virginia merchants," he lamented, "nine colonies had been restrained from making paper money, become absolutely necessary to their internal commerce, from the constant remittance of their gold and silver to Britain." Applying the same argument to other statutes, he added: "The hatters of England have prevailed to obtain an act in their own favor restraining that manufacture in America. . . . In the same manner have a few nail makers and a still smaller body of steelmakers (perhaps there are not half a dozen of these in England) prevailed totally to forbid by an act of Parliament the erecting of slitting mills or steel furnaces in America; that Americans may be obliged to take all their nails for their buildings and steel for their tools from these artificers." The measures laying duties on foreign sugar and molasses were passed on the insistence of British planters in the West Indies, of whom, it was alleged at the time, seventy-four were actually sitting in Parliament when the bills were enacted.

There was accordingly some foundation for the complaint published in the Boston Gazette of April 29, 1765: "A colonist cannot make a button, a horseshoe, nor a hobnail, but some sooty ironmonger or respectable buttonmaker of Britain shall bawl and squall that his honor's worship is most egregiously maltreated, injured, cheated, and robbed by the rascally American republicans."

Admitting that British imperial legislation was conceived in the interest of the metropolis, modern mathematicians of colonial politics make a point of the contention that the mother country, while restraining colonial enterprise in some directions, also fostered and stimulated it in others. The facts are indubitable. From the navigation acts, Americans derived distinct advantages; producing lumber and naval stores in huge quantities, they reaped under the cover of the law the rich benefits of a sweeping monopoly. Moreover, many of their products were given preferential treatment in English markets. For instance, the raising of tobacco in England was absolutely forbidden on very practical grounds; the climate and soil were not favorable, the import tax on it was a great source of revenue to the relief of lands and houses, and Southern planters relied largely upon it in discharging their debts to English merchants. Finally, bounties were paid on several colonial articles— hemp, masts, and certain naval stores—materials useful to the sea power by which all British commerce was protected. Though, in the main, the colonial products paid in English ports the same duties levied on identical goods from foreign countries, Adam Smith was right when he said that the imperial policy of Great Britain, broadly considered, had been "less illiberal and oppressive than that of any other European nation."

Magnifying this plea, modern calculators have gone to some pains to show that on the whole American colonists derived benefits from English policy which greatly outweighed their losses from the restraints laid upon them. For the sake of argument the case may be conceded; it is simply irrelevant to the uses of history. The origins of the legislation are clear; and the fact that it restricted American economic enterprise in many respects is indisputable. As usually happens in violent economic collisions, the balance was not turned in 1776 by precise calculations relative to profits and losses appearing in ledgers and registers, but by tempers and theories born of antagonism. The mind of the merchant, or, for that matter, of the most puissant statesman, is seldom able to forecast in pounds, shillings, and pence the exact outcome, near or distant, of any great measure of law or any significant administrative decision. At any rate, whatever may be the verdict of accountancy, there can be no doubt that the landlords and merchants of England, who spread the laws relative to colonial trade upon the statute books, expected benefit, not injury, from them, with the reservation that in some close cases the concerns of one class may have been occasionally bent to serve the advantage of the other.

§

Whatever their source and purpose, these measures did not execute themselves. It was necessary to create or adapt agencies to enforce British law on the one hand and restrain colonial legislatures on the other. Chief among these institutions was a central board of administrative control known by different names at different times. The idea came from two merchants who had large investments in the colonies and in overseas trade. It took definite form in 1660 in the establishment of a committee of the king's council, charged with the duty of meeting twice a week to consider petitions, memorials, and addresses respecting the colonies. Thirty-six years later a regular body, known as the Board of Trade and Plantations, was organized for the purpose of drawing under one high authority every branch of colonial economy and every transaction of consequence effected by His Majesty's governments beyond the sea.

Until the eve of the Revolution, this Board kept all American affairs drawn tightly within its dragnet, holding five meetings a week during most of its career, and, in periods of relaxation, eight or ten sessions a month. If an English merchant or manufacturer had a complaint or suggestion to make about the acts of any colonial assembly, about the doings of any colonial authority, or about methods of controlling American industry, he could find a sympathetic hearing before the Board of Trade. If any person thought his property rights in America jeopardized by local legislation, he could seek relief at the hands of the Board. In fact all acts of the colonial assemblies, with few exceptions, went before it for consideration, and on its recommendation were referred to the Crown for veto or disallowance. If, on the other hand, a colony had a grievance to air, it could instruct its agents in London to appear before the Board to present the case.

Thousands of letters preserved in the English archives bear witness to the range, precision, multiplicity, and minuteness of the Board's grasping activities. From its inception to the accession of George II, it held a tight rein, scrutinizing colonial economy with an eagle eye and recommending with firm insistence the annulment of objectionable bills passed by colonial legislatures. While, under the genial sway of Robert Walpole, whose motto for domestic and foreign statecraft was "let sleeping dogs alone," there was a period of mild administration, it meant no abandonment of established policy. At all events, there opened after the downfall of Walpole an epoch of thoroughness which continued until the stormy prelude of the Revolution was announced. Day after day, year in and year out, this engine of control kept pounding away on colonial affairs. Only to the eye of the superficial observer were the guardians of English imperialism asleep.

If the Board of Trade sometimes let an important matter escape its net, there remained other agencies in England to which aggrieved suitors could appeal. Any person in England or in America could carry to London, under appropriate regulations, cases involving acts of colonial legislatures and decisions of colonial courts. Serving in the capacity of an appellate tribunal, the king in council could, and often did, declare measures passed by local assemblies null and void as violating colonial charters or the laws of England. If the Board of Trade and the appellate courts failed to render satisfaction to complainants, there was always open one more recourse, namely, appeal to the secretary of state in charge of colonial affairs, under different titles from time to time. In this way issues could be carried into politics and, if necessary, made the subject of action in Parliament, where, from time to time, select committees were created to make inquiries or to listen to the demands of English merchants and manufacturers for more stringent restraints on colonial competition. Besides these authorities, treasury and admiralty boards, the attorney-general, the solicitor-general, and the bishop of London exercised supervision over provincial matters.

How far in fact was the British system of restriction and control actually enforced by the agencies used for the purpose? A real answer to that question would call for an exact record of the proportion of exports, imports, and manufactures effected in violation of law. Obviously, no such measurement is possible. How much whisky was consumed in the United States during the year following the adoption of prohibition? In the absence of statistical materials, historians of necessity fall back upon relevant fragments found in colonial papers. On the basis of such evidence one school of writers concludes that breaches of the revenue laws in the colonies were no more numerous or notorious than cases of smuggling in England in the same age. Another picture represents British colonial policy utterly defeated by American intrigue and defiance. Certainly the reports of governors were filled with complaints about violations of law. Even the colonials confessed to many a dereliction. John Adams admitted in 1774 that neither the iron act nor the hat act was obeyed in Massachusetts. By general agreement, the Molasses Act of 1733 was openly flouted.

A cloud of witnesses testified to the flagrant conduct of the Americans in trading with the enemy during the Seven Years' War while England and the colonial governments were engaged in a death grapple with France. When that struggle was at its height, Thomas Penn informed William Pitt that the river at Philadelphia was crowded with "shallops unloading these illegal cargoes, brought at their return and cheating the King of his duties, besides carrying provisions and ready money to the Enemy." Harping upon the same string, Penn's governor on the spot reported that "a very great part of the principal merchants" in Philadelphia were openly trading with the French in the West Indies, making profits while war was raging.

In Rhode Island the traffic with the enemy was even more defiant; exasperated by the conduct of Providence merchants and shipmasters, Governor Bernard, of Massachusetts, wrote home to the Board of Trade: "These practices will never be put an end to till Rhode Island is reduced to the subjection of the British empire, of which it is at present no more a part than the Bahama Islands were when they were inhabited by Buccaneers." Nor did New York appear in any better light. The governor of the province complained that the merchants of the city "consider but their private profit," and made special efforts to uproot their illegal commerce. In fact there is evidence that ships from nearly every American port were trafficking with the enemy. In vain did Pitt cry aloud against "this dangerous and ignominious trade"; in vain did officers of the army and navy inveigh against smugglers, calling them "traitors to their country."

If such was the conduct of the American colonists in time of war when their own safety like that of England was at stake, large inferences can be made with respect to their activities in time of peace. Certainly, the English government had every reason for desiring to tighten its instruments of restraint when George III came to the throne in 1760; and by attempting to enforce the law, it was bound to increase the friction already menacing enough in the ordinary course of events.

§

In the thousands of complaints, appeals, petitions, memorials, rulings, vetoes, decisions, and instructions recorded in the papers of the Crown agencies for controlling American trade and industry are disclosed the continuous conflict of English and American forces which hammered and welded thirteen jealous colonies into a society ready for revolution. The subjects of controversy were definite and mainly economic in character. Colonial laws enacted in the interest of local business enterprises but contrary to English regulations were often set aside by royal disallowance; sometimes blanket orders were issued to colonial governors instructing them not to permit the enactment of any legislation adverse to English commercial undertakings. Colonial populism was struck down by vetoes, warnings, and finally parliamentary action against paper money. To these great sources of economic antagonism was added incessant wrangling between assemblies and governors over salaries and allotments to royal officers, over land titles and land grants, over quitrents due to the Crown or to proprietors, over bankruptcy acts designed to ease the burdens of American debtors at the expense of English creditors, and over efforts of the colonists to promote trade at the cost of their neighbors or of England.

American business and agricultural enterprise was growing, swelling, beating against the frontiers of English imperial control at every point. Colonial assemblies and English royal officials were serving as the political knights errant in a great economic struggle that was to shake a continent.

Considered in the light of the English and provincial statutes spread over more than a hundred years, in the light of the authentic records which tell of the interminable clashes between province and metropolis, the concept of the American Revolution as a quarrel caused by a stubborn, king and obsequious ministers shrinks into a trifling joke. Long before George III came to his throne, long before Grenville took direction of affairs, thousands of Americans had come into collision with British economic imperialism, and by the middle of the eighteenth century, far-seeing men, like Franklin, had discovered the essence of the conflict.

In a letter written in 1754, six years before the accession of George III, the philosopher of Poor Richard set forth the case in terms that admitted of no misinterpretation. With reference to matters of politics, he declared that royal governors often came to the New World merely to make their fortunes; that royal officers in the provinces were frequently men of small estate subservient to the governors who fed them; and that the Americans in reality bore a large share of English taxes in the form of enhanced prices for English goods thrust upon them by monopolistic laws. Turning to questions of commercial economy, Franklin insisted that the acts of Parliament forbidding Americans to make certain commodities forced them to purchase such goods in England, thus pouring more tribute into the English chest; that statutes restraining their trade with foreign countries compelled them to buy dearer commodities in England, adding that golden stream to the same treasury; that, since the Americans were not allowed to stop the importation and consumption of English "superfluities," their "whole wealth centers finally among the Merchants and Inhabitants of Britain." In short, in enumerating grievances that had flourished for many a decade, Franklin gave a clue to the friction which was soon to burst into an agrarian war.

In a larger sense the American Revolution was merely one battle in the long political campaign that has been waged for more than two centuries on this continent. The institutions of metropolis and colony and the issues of their dispute were analogous to the institutions and issues that have figured in every great national crisis from that day to this. On the side of the mother country, a Crown and Parliament sought to govern all America somewhat after the fashion of the President and Congress under the federal Constitution of 1787. The central British government regulated the interstate and foreign commerce of the thirteen colonies in the interest of the manufacturing and commercial classes of England; it directed the disposal of western lands; it struck down paper money and controlled the currency; it provided for a common defense and conducted the diplomacy of the continent. With a view to protecting practical interests, the British Crown and judiciary nullified acts of local legislatures similar in character to those declared void long afterward by Chief Justice Marshall.

On the American side of the colonial conflict, the agent of local power was the popular assembly which aspired to sovereignty and independence, placing all rights of person and property at the disposal of passing majorities. It authorized the issue of paper money; passed bankruptcy acts in the interest of debtors; stayed the collection of overdue obligations; sought to control the sale of western lands, and assumed the power of regulating local trade and industry. The British government brought heavy pressure upon it; an explosion resulted. For a decade the state legislature was sovereign, and it worked its will in matters of finance, currency, debts, trade, and property. Then followed the inevitable reaction in which were restored, under the ægis of the Constitution and under American leadership, agencies of control and economic policies akin to those formerly employed by Great Britain. In a word, the American Revolution was merely one phase of a social process that began long before the founding of Jamestown and is not yet finished.

§

At the close of the French and Indian War in 1763, England found herself in a peculiar state of affairs and under the direction of new men. George II, with his lumbering gait, his German accent, and his passion for Teutonic comfort, had passed away and the Crown had fallen to his young grandson, who gloried in "the name of Briton," spoke English like a native, cherished his mother's motto, "George, be king!" and was prepared for moderate adventures on his own account. No English sovereign for more than a hundred years had been in such a favorable position to uphold royal prerogatives. Unlike the petulant Stuarts, George III was engaged in no quarrel with the Commons; unlike William III, he was not primarily interested in Continental politics; unlike his Hanoverian predecessors, he did not pine for the quiet retreats of his paternal estates. The last of the Jacobite uprisings in favor of the Stuarts had been crushed in blood and Prince Charlie was wasting his life in riotous living on the Continent. The most intransigent of the old opposition had been overcome; Tories, as Macaulay said, always eager to prostrate themselves, paid homage to George III and were favorably received. After the two revolutions, there was no further likelihood of attempts to lay taxes without the consent of Parliament; and the few thousand landlords and merchant capitalists who governed England were fairly content with the best of possible constitutions in the best of possible worlds. There were lingering remembrances of ancient differences among them which classified them as Whigs and Tories, but by the accession of George III, the prime sources of contention were the spoils of office. Though most of the landed gentry, except the newly-made mercantile peers, were in the Tory ranks and the Whigs found their strength mainly in the towns and among the middling orders, no great economic issue now sharply divided them as in the days of the Stuarts.

For nearly half a century the Whigs had held the offices, drawn the pensions, made the bishops, and monopolized the revenues of politics. They had dictated to their sovereigns and treated their opponents with lofty contempt, spitefully proscribing all who would not bow the knee. But the long way had its turning. A host of enemies—some sincere patriots and others disappointed spoilsmen—was raised up, and as soon as George III was safely installed, the Whigs were ousted from power.

Thus a new king and an old party came upon the scene at a critical juncture when a foreign war and its economic effects were in progress. Taking note of these facts, one school of historians has represented the American Revolution which ensued as the bitter fruit of novel measures devised by George III and his Tory supporters. The king himself is put forward to bear most of the blame: "The shame of the darkest hour of England's history," exclaims Green, "lies wholly at his door." But the modern student, on his guard against summary judgments, does well to remember that the chief authors of this creed were themselves either Whigs or Liberals, naturally prone to defend the conduct of their historic party and to shift the blame for the disaster to the shoulders of the king and his Tory adherents.

Their hypothesis does not square with the cardinal facts in the case. No principles essentially new, except that of the stamp tax, were applied to the colonies on the accession of King George, and the stamp tax was quickly abolished with his approval. No new agencies of control were devised to subdue colonial legislatures. Old laws approved by both Whigs and Tories were now enforced with more vigor and old engines of government were worked with more efficiency to carry into effect established rules. Indeed, it was the effort to recover lost ground quite as much as to take new salients that brought on the armed collision.

On none of these things were the Whigs and Tories divided in principle. No fundamental differences with respect to colonial policies separated the one from the other. The domestic fortunes of neither of them—places, patronage, power, honors, and spoils—depended upon the fate of measures for ruling the colonies. If Whig merchants derived benefits from restraints on American trade, Tory landlords found equal advantage in restrictions on American woolen manufactures. To both, imposts on American tobacco brought a pleasing relief in the form of lighter taxes on their houses and lands, and projects for shifting some of the recently acquired war burden to the colonies were greeted by hearty applause from opposing benches.

There was not a single measure designed to tax and control the trade of the American colonies that was not supported by Whigs of some school, including leaders high in that faction. George Grenville, chief author of the forward policy, had long been associated with the Whigs in office; whatever his views, he was hardly a Tory of the old persuasion. Charles Townshend, who helped to complete the ruin, was a Whig—a "Weathercock Whig"—but still a friend of that sect. Lord Rockingham, who, as head of the government, insisted that Parliament in repealing the Stamp Act should proclaim its right to make laws binding the colonies in all matters whatsoever, was a Whig, an outstanding figure in that group, a patron of Edmund Burke. Chatham, who often lifted his voice against coercive measures, was prime minister when Townshend devised and pushed through acts taxing the colonists and making provision for the drastic enforcement of the laws against smuggling. His friends say that at the time the noble lord was distracted with illness; so charity draws the curtain. Yet of all the obsequious men who fawned on George III, none outdid in abasement the Earl of Chatham; according to Burke, a mere glimpse into the royal closet intoxicated him. If he thundered against drastic measures that produced rebellion, he opposed the independence of America to his dying gasp. Of all the great Whigs, Burke alone understood America and pursued a consistent course with respect to American affairs.

It was not the obstinacy of the Tory party, nor the willfulness of George III, that brought on the American war for independence. Grenville, who initiated the specific measures which set fire to the tinder accumulated in America, was no servile tool of the king. On the contrary, George III cordially hated that minister, summing up his opinion in the exclamation: "I would rather see the devil in my closet than Mr. Grenville." Nor was the minister a mere party agent rising to power by the use of spoils and bribery; as Burke truly said, Grenville won his place not through the "pimping politics" of the court, but through conscientious public services, especially in colonial administration.

A methodical and parsimonious bureaucrat—a lawyer who took the parchment view of official duties—Grenville thought more could be accomplished for trade by law than by liberty; and he had the small man's passion for carrying theories to a logical conclusion. Seeing the trade acts violated by American smugglers, he decided to enforce them. Finding the English treasury loaded with a heavy war debt, incurred partly in defending the colonies against the French, he thought it reasonable to transfer to the beneficiaries a share of the burden. But this philosopher of precision was not the sole ruler of England; neither was George III in spite of his pretensions and his bribery of members of Parliament. The Stamp Act passed both houses "with less opposition than a turnpike bill."

§

Under the direction of the laborious and systematic Grenville, aided by Townshend, measures of crucial importance, though by no means wholly novel in principle, emerged from the councils of the British government. On behalf of English creditors, one act of Parliament made the prohibition of paper money binding upon the legislatures of all the colonies. For the benefit of English fur traders and land speculators, a royal proclamation reserved to the Crown the ownership and disposal of all lands in the territory recently wrested from the French and also forbade fur trading without royal license—a stinging blow to squatter settlers and libertine hunters—even if calculated to prevent their bloody clashes with the Indians.

To relieve English taxpayers, elaborate plans for raising money were incorporated in the Sugar Act of 1764, the title of the bill expressly declaring that the object was to obtain revenues in the colonies to be applied toward the expenses of "protecting and securing them" and preventing smuggling. By its terms the old prohibitive rate on molasses was reduced with a view to yielding returns to the treasury; specific duties were levied on a number of imports; the list of enumerated articles which could be sold only in England was enlarged.

Without respect for the feelings of the colonists, every conceivable engine was now brought into play to suppress smuggling. Revenue collectors, officers of the army and navy, and royal governors were brusquely ordered to do their full duty. Naval men, none too enamored of judicial methods at best, were set to work patrolling the coast and overhauling vessels suspected of neglecting legal precautions; shipowners and masters were placed under closer scrutiny; rewards were offered to spies and informers; those who helped to catch smugglers shared in the spoils of the game. Suddenly and almost without warning, the colonists found their easy-going ways proscribed and the minions of the law on their ships, in their warehouses, and even in their homes, armed with general search warrants.

On top of the Sugar Act, and framed with the same reference to English taxpayers, came the Stamp Act, subjecting the colonists to burdens similar to those borne by Englishmen at home. This, too, was a law raising revenues to be devoted toward the expenses of "defending, protecting, and securing" the colonies. It was a long measure of more than sixty sections, dragging within its wide-flung net almost every kind of legal, commercial, and social operation that could be discovered by the skillful draftsmen who drew the bill. Taxes were to be paid on the papers used in legal transactions, such as deeds, mortgages, and inventories, on licenses to practice law or sell liquor, on college diplomas, playing cards, dice, pamphlets, newspapers, calendars, and advertisements. The stamp duties were heavy; penalties were imposed for violations of the law; and governors were ordered to be circumspect in enforcing the Act.

Three features of this Act gave it a revolutionary drive. Unlike most laws relative to trade and shipping, it affected every section and nearly every class in America. The tax on sugar and molasses hit the New England shipper and rum distiller; the impost on tobacco irked the Virginia planter; but the Stamp Act struck at every order in society, making grievances universal. For the first time the thirteen colonies were stung into action by one and the same levy on their purses. In addition to being universal in its application, the Stamp Act was an innovation. "External taxes," that is, customs duties, levied at the ports under parliamentary orders were not new; but laws taking money so directly out of provincial pockets had never been passed before in London. The colonists might well ask whether, if they acquiesced in this beginning, there would ever be an end. Last, but not least, the tax fell heavily upon two classes skilled in controversy, loquacious in expressing themselves, and accustomed to fish in troubled waters—lawyers and editors.

If Grenville and Townshend, laboring under an oil lamp, had searched a lifetime for a plan better calculated to stir rebellion in America, they could not have found it. Yet their colleagues in Parliament were equally innocent; resolutions sanctioning the stamp taxes were carried without a dissenting voice; the bill itself went through the House of Commons without causing a ripple of excitement by a vote of 205 to 49, while in the Lords it was not even necessary to go through the formality of a count. King George, also innocent, was temporarily insane at the time; and the bill was approved by a regency. With similar insouciance Grenville's program was fortified by the Mutiny Act of 1765, which provided for dispatching to America all the troops required to enforce the laws, and by a special Quartering Act, laying down the terms on which the colonists were to house, feed, and supply the army sent overseas to "protect, defend, and secure."

In the eyes of its sponsors, this program seemed nothing more than a reasoned system for maintaining the strength and integrity of the British empire: the American colonies enjoyed the protection of the British army and navy, and it seemed entirely fair to the ministry in London that they should help pay the expenses of that service. It was in the main the logical development of a policy that had been sanctioned by a century of practice. It was not the outcome of Tory principles, for Whigs conceived and voted for it.

Indeed, it was so cleverly designed that Tory landlords and Whig merchants alike rejoiced in the prospects which it opened. The former were delighted at the thought of some reduction in taxes. "I well remember," exclaimed Edmund Burke years afterward, "that Mr. Townshend, in a brilliant harangue on this subject, did dazzle them by playing before their eyes the image of a large revenue to be raised in America." Besides promising a monetary return in relief of taxation, the Sugar Act offered direct gains to the West India planters, of whom there were said to be three score and more in Parliament. On the other side of the economic line, British manufacturers and merchants, whose interests were already well safeguarded in the laws restricting colonial commerce and industry, naturally approved the strict enforcement which the contrivances of Grenville seemed to offer.

If very many people in England, of high or low estate, entertained strong objections on principle to the new schemes, they failed to make their views sufficiently vocal to influence the councils of the government. So the myth that George III conceived this monumental collection of restrictive measures and drove it through Parliament must be dismissed as puerile; the laws were drafted by or for English landlords and merchant capitalists who as a rule looked upon the colonies as provinces to be exploited for the advantage of the metropolis. No doubt, King

George favored these high-toned schemes and was grieved when the American populace broke out in defiance of law and order, but he was not the author and finisher of the policy that shattered the British empire in America.

§

The peculiar state of American affairs made the reception of Grenville's program especially furious. A widespread business depression had just set in. During the seven years of the French and Indian War, American merchants, planters, and farmers had been unusually prosperous; produce of every kind had brought high prices and the specie disbursed by the quartermasters had stimulated economic activity in every field. The estates acquired by war profiteers were numerous and large; many merchants had suddenly risen, complained the lieutenant governor of New York, "from the lowest rank of the people to considerable fortunes and chiefly by illicit trade in the last war." But in the swift reaction that followed inflated prices collapsed, business languished, workmen in the towns were thrown out of employment, farmers and planters, burdened by falling prices, found the difficulties of securing specie steadily growing.

By the new imperial program the evils of depression were aggravated. It struck a blow at the West India trade, that fruitful source of business and specie. It put a stop to colonial paper money, thus sharply contracting the currency. It required the payment of the new taxes in coin into the British treasury, putting another drain on the depleted resources of the colonists. It harassed American merchants by irritating searches and seizures, filling them with uncertainty and dismay, and adding to the confusion of business. Moreover, all the colonies, not merely the commercial North, were now thrown into distress; all classes, too, disfranchised and unemployed workmen of the towns as well as farmers, planters, and merchants. This is significant; it was the workmen of the commercial centers who furnished the muscle and the courage necessary to carry the protests of the merchants into the open violence that astounded the friends of law and order in England and America and threatened to kindle the flames of war.

In fact, the greeting accorded to the Grenville program in America astounded the governing classes on both sides of the water. Before the Sugar Act was passed, Boston merchants, hearing rumors of the impending legislation, had organized a committee, presented a memorial to the legislature, and entered into correspondence with merchants in other colonies. Likewise in New York, commercial men had begun to draw together in anticipation of trouble. When the drastic terms of the Sugar Law and the sweeping provisions of the Stamp Act became known, the wrath of the people knew no bounds. Merchants, lawyers, and publishers held conferences and passed resolutions condemning British measures and policies. Patriotic women flocked to associations, pledged themselves not to drink tea, and, besides refusing to purchase British goods, set to work spinning and weaving with greater energy than ever "from sunrise to dark." The maidens of Providence bound themselves to favor no suitors who approved the Stamp Act.

Artisans and laborers, hundreds of them rendered idle by the business depression, formed themselves into societies known as "Sons of Liberty." Feeling their way toward that political power which was to come in the early nineteenth century, they leaped over the boundaries of polite ceremony. They broke out in rioting in Boston, New York, Philadelphia, and Charleston; they pillaged and razed the offices of stamp agents; they burned stamps in the streets; they assailed the houses of royal officers; in Boston the residence of the lieutenant governor was pried open, his chambers sacked, and his property pitched out into the streets. In fact, the agitation, contrary to the intent of the merchants and lawyers, got quite beyond the bounds of law and order. As Gouverneur Morris remarked, "the heads of the mobility grow dangerous to the gentry, and how to keep them down is the question." Indeed, the conduct of the mechanics and laborers was so lawless that it is difficult to paint a picture of the scene in tones subdued enough for modern Sons and Daughters of the Revolution.

In the colonial assemblies, of course, protests against British policies took on the form of legal arguments and dignified resolutions. The Virginia House of Burgesses declared that attempts to tax the people of the Old Dominion, except through the local legislature, were "illegal, unconstitutional, and unjust"—a declaration supported by a moving speech of Patrick Henry in which he warned George III about the fate of Cæsar and Charles I, silencing dissent by the exclamation, "If this be treason, make the most of it!" Not content with formal protests, the Massachusetts assembly appealed for concerted action, inviting the other legislatures to send delegates to a congress in New York to consult about the circumstances of America and to consider a general plan for obtaining relief.

With surprising alacrity, nine colonies responded to the summons, and in the autumn of 1765 the Stamp Act Congress was duly called to order in New York. After the usual preliminaries, the Congress agreed to a definite profession of faith embodied in a set of solemn resolutions: Englishmen cannot be taxed without their consent; the colonists from the nature of things cannot be represented in Parliament; they can only be taxed by their local legislatures; the Stamp Act tends to subvert their rights and liberties; and other acts imposing duties on the colonists and regulating their trade are grievous and burdensome. This creed was then supplemented by an appeal made to the king and Parliament, begging for the abolition of several objectionable measures. Going beyond "humble supplication," the insurgents gave an effective drive to their demands by a well-timed economic stroke—a general boycott of English goods, which had a deadly effect, within a few months driving the imports rapidly to the lowest point reached in thirty years. With a cry of anguish English merchants set upon Parliament demanding a repeal of the Stamp Act, which yielded no revenue and ruined their business.

§

While stirring events were shaking the colonies from New Hampshire to Georgia, a domestic quarrel arose between George III and his ministry. Far from being a master in his own house, the king was really a servant. He had not formulated and forced through the policy of coercion in America; as far as he understood it, he approved it; but the policy itself came from his ministers. As Macaulay justly says, "the triumph of the ministers was complete. The King was almost as much a prisoner as Charles the First had been when in the Isle of Wight." Angered at length by the haughty insolence of Grenville, George turned to the Whigs for relief, and sanctioned the creation of a ministry under Lord Rockingham.

On the day of his installation the new premier had to face rebellion in America and a political insurrection at home. As Burke said, "the whole trading interest of this empire crowded into your lobbies." The Stamp Act, coupled with the boycott, had ruined its business, and sweeping the statute from the books was the only remedy. Some apostles of high prerogative blustered; but the king, after expressing his personal dislike for the backward step, let it be known that men who opposed the repeal did not speak for him, that he preferred a retreat to the use of force. So the repeal passed amid the cheers of the lobbyists.

And yet, though a victory for the Americans, it was accompanied, on the insistence of Lord Rockingham, by a Declaratory Act which expressly rejected as unfounded the claims of the colonists to the exclusive right of taxing themselves, repudiated as utterly null and void their resolutions, votes, orders, and proceedings denying the authority of

Parliament in such matters, and proclaimed in language that admitted of no double interpretation the power of Parliament to make laws binding the colonies and people of America "in all cases whatsoever."

After repealing the Stamp Act, Parliament proceeded to revise the troublesome molasses and sugar laws. It swept away the wholesale discrimination against the French product and established a uniform moderate duty of one penny a gallon on all molasses, British and foreign, imported into the colonies. While retaining the high rates on foreign sugar, it lowered the cost of British West India sugar by striking off the export tax at the local ports. Thus, in addition to repudiating expressly every claim made by the colonists under the slogan, "no taxation without representation," Parliament actually passed a bill taxing them without their consent: the new Molasses Act, laying a duty on British and foreign molasses, was a tariff project designed to raise revenue.

In reality, therefore, save for the repeal of the Stamp Act, the Americans won a Pyrrhic victory, but the colonial merchants, alarmed by the menace to law and order which their recent protests had let loose, accepted the measures of Parliament with signs of gratitude. Bells were rung, cannon fired, banquets held, toasts to the king drunk from huge bumpers, and professions of profound loyalty made on every hand. Almost in the same breath, however, the merchants in the commercial colonies began to draw up petitions to the House of Commons setting forth the grievances still unheeded. They protested against the duty on molasses; it reduced the profits of New England distillers. They objected to the administrative regulations against smuggling; they were irksome to shippers. They declaimed against the high duty on foreign sugar; it encouraged illicit trading and it was bad for business. They mourned over the prohibition laid on colonial currencies; it brought about deflation and a great scarcity of money. The Stamp Act, that had united all colonists and set the lawyers and publishers in a ferment, had been blotted from the statute books, some concessions had been made to commerce, but in the main the forward policy of the Grenville-Townshend school had not been abandoned.

§

On the contrary, the very next year saw an extension of that policy. In one of the ever-recurring contests among English politicians over power, patronage, and royal favors, the repeal ministry was soon driven from office. After dragging down the Rockingham Whigs by refusing his support, William Pitt, delighted as a child by the flattery of George III, and now elevated to the peerage as the Earl of Chatham, raised himself again to the head of the government, choosing for the position of chancellor of the exchequer Charles Townshend who, as everybody knew, was directly opposed to the old colonial policy of caution and moderation.

It is true, as already remarked, that Chatham was ill during this ministry; Whig historians, his ardent apologists, have always emphasized that indisposition. Still the fact remains that he assumed responsibility for the direction of affairs, thereby preventing the formation of an all-Whig administration, and he put Charles Townshend, "who belonged to every party and cared for none," in a post where he could give effect to the colonial policies which he was known to cherish.

The first problem that confronted Townshend on taking office was a deficiency in revenue, for as a concession to the clamor of the landlords the domestic land tax had been materially reduced. On all sides it was conceded that some kind of revenue from the colonies offered the easiest relief to harassed country gentlemen in England, and Townshend believed in making the most of the opportunity. Having learned from experience that "internal taxes," such as the stamp duties, were out of the question, the eager minister cast thoughtfully about for a form of impost acceptable to the colonists.

One clear way seemed to open, at last. For a long time, under acts of Parliament, duties had been collected at American ports on certain goods; and the recent Sugar Act, which laid a tariff for revenue, had awakened no revolutionary temper in the provinces. Colonial philosophers had not yet proclaimed such "external taxes" to be flat violations of their constitutional and natural rights; neither had they placed these taxes within the mystic category of imposts banned under the principle of "no taxation without representation." Fully aware of this situation, Townshend came to the conclusion that he was taking due account of the sentiments of Americans when, in a revenue law of 1767, he laid duties on lead, glass, tea, and a few other American imports, and dedicated the proceeds to the support of government in the colonies. The taxes were not especially heavy, certainly no more burdensome than the molasses duties which had followed the repeal of the Stamp Act. It was true, colonial merchants had protested against the molasses duties, but their protests had been couched in respectful tones, showing no threat of rebellion. So Townshend and Parliament thought that finally a correct procedure had been found.

If it was constitutional and proper to lay customs duties on goods imported into the American colonies, it appeared to be constitutional and proper to make provision for the collection of the said revenues. So it seemed at least to the English Parliament. Therefore the Townshend program embraced special measures for enforcement. One of these placed the collection of colonial imposts in the hands of British commissioners, appointed by the Crown, resident in the colonies, paid from the British treasury, and independent of local control.

That was ominous enough, but going still further, the new revenue law added "teeth" to the former measures of execution. It expressly legalized writs of assistance, by authorizing the superior courts of the colonies to issue orders empowering customs officers to enter any house, warehouse, shop, cellar, or other place in the British colonies or plantations in America to search for and seize prohibited or smuggled goods. This promise of vigor was accompanied by another monitory gesture. As the assembly of New York had refused to make provision for the king's soldiers sent over to aid in law enforcement, Parliament suspended that legislature until it promised to comply with the obligations laid upon it.

Such was the body of legislation by which Townshend and his colleagues in Parliament hoped to raise a respectable revenue in America and carry into effect the various restrictions on colonial trade and industry prescribed by nearly a hundred statutes spread over the books all the way back to the age of Cromwell. If the chancellor had any inkling of the havoc that his laws would play he gave no sign; he was not fated to live to see the mischief that flowed from his actions.

Among the measures of Townshend's program, none was more odious than the express sanction given to writs of assistance. There was nothing novel, of course, about the summary process of search and seizure, for it had long been used in England, but it made trouble in America, especially in Massachusetts. In fact, the employment of the famous judicial order there in 1755 in connection with illicit trade had raised a strong opposition; and it became a subject of a fierce controversy six years later when an application was made to a Massachusetts court for the writ "as usual."

On that occasion James Otis opposed the project in an impassioned speech of five hours duration. He denounced the practice as an exercise of that arbitrary power which had cost one king his head and another his throne; and condemned it as a tyrant's device which placed the liberty and property of every person in the hands of a petty officer moved by malice as much as zeal for the law. Though Otis had no objection to special writs to search particular places, issued on oath, his wrath against the general writ knew no bounds. "What a scene," he exclaimed, "does this open! Every man, prompted by revenge, ill-humor, or wantonness to inspect the inside of his neighbor's house, may get a writ of assistance. Others will ask it from self-defense; one arbitrary exertion will provoke another until society is involved in tumult and blood." No careful hand made a verbatim record of this eloquent address, but the fragments that survive explain why every man who heard it went away ready to take up arms against writs of assistance. Such was the American attitude toward the hated legal document which Townshend proposed to put in the hands of royal customs officers engaged in executing the provisions of British colonial policy.

Whatever the colonists may have thought of Townshend's program, it was in fact, like the policy of Grenville, a perfect mirror of the mind of the English governing classes. For this we have the high authority of Edmund Burke. In his speech on American taxation, the Irish orator later reviewed the scene to which he had been a witness. He told his auditors that to please universally was the object of Townshend's life. "To render the tax palatable to the partisans of American revenue, he had a preamble stating the necessity of such a revenue. To close with the American distinction, this revenue was *external,* or port duty; but again to soften it to the other party it was a duty of *supply.* To gratify the *colonists,* it was laid on British manufactures; to satisfy the *merchants of Britain* the duty was trivial and (except that on tea which touched only the devoted East India Company) on none of the grand objects of commerce. To counterwork the American contraband, the duty on tea was reduced from a shilling to three pence. But to secure the favor of those who would tax America, the scene of collection was changed and with the rest it was levied in the colonies. . . . The original plan of the duties and the mode of executing that plan, both arose singly and solely from a love of our applause. He was truly the child of the House. He never thought, did, or said anything but with a view to you. He every day adapted himself to your disposition; and adjusted himself before it as at a looking-glass."

§

As soon as the Townshend program took the form of reality in America in the shape of an army of customs officers supported by British regulars and a fleet of revenue cutters, the war of American independence opened, not, of course, with all the panoply of the state, but in the guise of unashamed, flagrant, and determined resistance to law. In a few months a long roll of riotous deeds was registered. An informer who told on Boston smugglers was tarred, feathered, and dragged through the streets of the city; three informers were furnished a dose of the same medicine in New York; the tide waiter at Providence was beaten and given a coat of tar and feathers; a revenue sloop was boarded, smashed, and burnt by a Newport mob because it brought into port two vessels accused of smuggling; when the royal officers in Philadelphia seized fifty pipes of Madeira wine on which duties had not been paid, a mob assaulted them and stole the sequestered goods.

Every few days Boston was filled with alarm over the landing of goods in defiance of law, over forcible seizures by revenue authorities, and over forcible recaptures accompanied by assaults on officers. In June, 1768, when John Hancock's sloop *Liberty* reached Boston with a cargo of wine, temper was high. The collector who went on board to enforce the law was pitched into the cabin of the ship and most of the wine was taken off in spite of his cries. When the customs board ordered the seizure of the vessel, a mob replied by attacking the revenue officers and stoning their houses. When regulars were brought into the city to restore order, the remedy proved to be worse than the disease. Even school children now emulated their elders by jeering soldiers and officers; indeed, one of the first Americans killed in the conflict was a school boy shot by an informer who resented childish ridicule.

This affair was shortly followed by the "Boston Massacre" of March, 1770, starting in comedy as some youths threw snowballs and stones at a small body of British regulars and ending in tragedy with the killing and wounding of several citizens. "The Boston people are run mad," lamented the governor. "The frenzy was not higher when they banished my pious great-grandmother, when they hanged the Quakers, when they afterwards hanged the poor innocent witches." In other colonies the storm also raged. Two years after the "Massacre," John Brown, of Providence, the richest merchant in the town, at the head of an armed mob, boarded the revenue cutter, *Gaspee,* which had run ashore while chasing a smuggler; after seizing the crew, the rioters set the ship on fire.

During these operations in defiance of the law, merchants were organizing non-importation associations and bringing a stringent boycott to bear on the English government. Once more women came to the rescue by denying themselves English goods and by working hard with their wheels and looms to supply the deficiency. "The female spinners kept on spinning six days of the week," caustically remarked a high Tory, "and on the seventh the Parsons took their turns and spun out their prayers and sermons to the long thread of politics." Townshend had aroused passions that were soon to challenge British supremacy on the field of battle.

While radicals were agitating, merchants drawing up resolutions, and women spinning, colonial assemblies were learning the lessons of coöperation. In 1768 the lower house in Massachusetts, under the shrewd direction of Sam Adams, addressed an appeal for union, in the form of a circular letter, to the legislatures of the other colonies. This letter, cautiously phrased, described the state of affairs in

Massachusetts, condemned the British program, expressed the opinion that Parliament could not lay any duties in America for the sole purpose of raising revenue, and declared that the colonies from the nature of things could not be represented in Parliament.

In the rhetoric of humble propriety, the letter submitted to consideration the question whether any people could be free so long as they were subjected to governors and judges appointed by the Crown. Finally notice was taken of the hardships occasioned by the enforcement of the Quartering Act and the conduct of the commissioners of the customs. Displaying a restraint far beyond the wont of Adams, the concluding paragraph expressed a "firm confidence in the King, our common head and father," and confessed the belief that "united and dutiful supplications" would meet with his favor and acceptance. Though the letter was moderate to the point of servility, the governor of Massachusetts ordered the house to rescind it, and on meeting refusal he dissolved the General Court. The appeal had gone forth. The assemblies of Maryland, Georgia, and South Carolina endorsed the sentiments of the circular, and were promptly dissolved for their defiance.

In the same spirit of determination, the Virginia House of Burgesses, aroused by a resolution of Parliament demanding that persons guilty of disorder in the colonies be transported to England for trial, filed its declaration of principles in May, 1769. It announced that the sole right of levying taxes was vested in the legislature of the province and protested against subjecting Americans to English tribunals across the sea. The tone of the resolutions was firm, but the king was assured of "our inviolable attachment to his sacred person and government."

§

While, in the light of later events, the protesting and rioting in America were full of warning, the British government was apparently not alarmed at the time. All through the tempest political maneuvering continued in London on conventional lines; officers were made and unmade with little reference to colonial affairs, and out of the customary intriguing, Lord North, after serving in the treasury and later in the exchequer, rose to the post of prime minister, opening in 1770 a term that was to last for twelve years. Under his leadership, the English ruling classes went on the even tenor of their way unconscious of impending calamity. Although in April, 1770, Parliament repealed all the Townshend duties except the tax on tea, it took this step, if the ministry must be believed, not as a concession to Americans, but because taxes on British manufactures were "preposterous." As a matter of fact, good crops in England and war on the Continent filled the sails of English trade with the winds of prosperity so that the boycott in America, unlike the revolt in the days of the Stamp Act, brought no one to his knees. While admitting that certain vocal grievances existed in the provinces, Lord North went blandly on his course without losing any sleep over the news from the royal governors or the protests of provincial agents in London.

Indeed, North was so little troubled by events in the colonies that he sponsored a law bound to make still more mischief than the Townshend duties or the Stamp Act. At this juncture in commercial affairs, the East India Company had fallen into financial difficulties; famines had decimated its business and rapacious directors had impoverished its treasury by declaring high dividends. In 1772 it was marching swiftly in the direction of bankruptcy, driving a horde of politicians and capitalists to the brink of ruin. On an appeal from the Company, Parliament came to its aid, making it a huge loan at a low rate of interest and transferring many of its high prerogatives in India to the British Crown. During the course of the settlement, the government cast about for a way of unloading a surplus of seventeen million pounds of tea which the corporation had on hand, and naturally America was remembered in this relation.

The result was the Tea Act of 1773. Under this measure the Company was given a refund of the duties paid on any tea imported into England and afterwards transshipped to the colonies. Then an additional favor was conferred on the Company. Hitherto it had sold tea at public auction in England to merchants who exported it to America for sale. Contrary to that practice, the new Tea Act authorized the corporation to go into business on its own account —to export tea in its own ships and to sell tea directly through its own agencies in the colonies. To merchants in America this was a stunning blow—a blow furnishing a precedent to the American Standard Oil Company which, a century later, flung out its branches in every direction to the ruin of independent producers and retailers.

By the Tea Act a path was cut directly from the producer to the consumer. Before it was passed, English tea merchants had purchased their stocks from the Company in England; American importers had bought from the English jobbers; and colonial retailers had been supplied by the local importers, thus compelling the consumers in the provinces to pay four profits. Under the new Tea Act they were to have the privilege of buying tea directly from the Company without the intervention of middlemen. So in spite of small duties levied under the remaining shreds of the Townshend revenue act, tea could now be sold in America lawfully by the Company at a price far below that charged by American merchants who bought their stocks legally in London or even smuggled them through from Holland.

Naturally the news of this Tea Act spread consternation among American business men; for the profits of a lucrative trade were about to be swept away by the stroke of a pen and the agents of a powerful monopoly authorized to operate directly on American soil. The immediate menace was great; if this practice was extended, American enterprise could be utterly destroyed in the interest of British concerns. "Would not the opening of an East-India House in America encourage all the great Companies in Great Britain to do the same?" exclaimed a New York protestant. "If so, have we a single chance of being anything but *Hewers of Wood and Drawers of Water* to them?"

There was the whole colonial case in a nutshell: tea stocks on hand were struck down in value below cost; profits were wiped out; and the prospect was opened of making America a mere tributary to the capitalist system of Great Britain. For a young and energetic people, full of spirit, with the wide sea before them and immense natural resources at their command, such a position of provincial subordination, diverting riches and power to London, was unbearable, impossible.

Swift was the answer of the American merchants in the port towns to the Tea Act. As soon as the first cargoes arrived in the harbor of Boston, a mass meeting, held in the Old South Meeting House, unanimously resolved that the tea should be sent back without being honored by the payment of duty. Hearing of this action, the royal governor ordered the assembly of objectors to disperse, only to have his order greeted with loud and prolonged hissing. For several days negotiations were carried on between the spokesmen of the popular conference and the agents of the government.

At last, on the evening of the twentieth day, the patience of the crowd was at an end; as night fell upon the town, Sam Adams rose in the church and said: "This meeting can do nothing more to save the country." Whether or not this was the signal for direct action remains a mystery, but certainly in a few minutes a huge mob in the disguise of Indians swept down to the docks, boarded the tea ships, and dumped £18,000 worth of property into the water. Words had borne fruit in deeds. Who composed this lawless tea party is not yet settled, but the assiduous searches of A. M. Schlesinger reveal merchants toiling "side by side with carpenters, masons, farmers, blacksmiths, and barbers."

In other cities the tempest over the Tea Act broke out in startling tones. Rioters paraded the streets of Portsmouth, New York, Philadelphia, and Charleston, refraining from open violence only because the customs officers and consignees of tea thought discretion the better part of valor; and Annapolis "out Bostoned Boston." When the *Peggy Stewart* arrived with a cargo of tea, a local mass meeting was held and it was solemnly resolved that the goods should not be landed.

Harder and harder blew the storm until radical elements got possession of the assembly, demanding that ship and cargo be burnt. By a show of force, the owners of the brig, James Dick and his son-in-law, Anthony Stewart, importers already in bad odor with local patriots, were now compelled to consent to the sacrifice of their property—as the price of escaping worse damage, including the destruction of Stewart's home, which was worth more than the ship. So, in the presence of a great throng, the *Peggy Stewart* and the tea were sent up in one grand sky-roaring flame. Evidently affairs in America had passed beyond the realm of parlor patriotism.

As soon as the report of the Boston tea party reached London, the British government resolved upon enforcing respect for law in Massachusetts, where the property of a great trading company had been destroyed. Until that time it had endured with considerable patience the course of disorder. To give a poor customs officer a coat of tar and feathers was one thing; to destroy £18,000 worth of tea belonging to the most powerful corporation operating in the British Empire and in British politics was something quite different. So, at least, it was regarded by the ministry of Lord North.

Accordingly, Parliament by sweeping majorities passed five "intolerable acts" aimed at curing unrest in America. The port of Boston was absolutely sealed to all outside commerce; the old charter granted in 1691 was revoked and town meetings were prohibited except when authorized by the governor; persons accused of murder in connection with law enforcement were to be transferred to England for trial; the quartering of troops in Massachusetts towns was legalized. The fifth measure, which especially incensed the Puritans—the Quebec Act—extended the boundaries of that province to the Ohio River in spite of the claims of Massachusetts, Connecticut, and Virginia, and granted toleration to Catholics in Canada.

Administrative measures supplemented the laws. General Gage, head of the armed forces in the provinces, was appointed governor of Massachusetts; reinforcements were hurried to the point of disaffection; and the majesty of the law was to be vindicated by strong medicine administered to "the rebels," as George III now called his subjects in America. On the part of the British cabinet the task was undertaken with a light heart, for it had been informed by Hutchinson, born and bred in Massachusetts, that a few soldiers would awe the populace into submission and by General Gage that four regiments would be "sufficient to prevent any disturbance." With their usual prescience military authorities and technical experts spoke of the colonials in terms of contempt and prepared to rush into the fray with their customary levity. Since General Wolfe, the hero of Quebec, had declared that "the Americans are in general the dirtiest, most contemptible, cowardly dogs that you can conceive," it seemed reasonable to English officers to suppose that a little cold steel would quickly reduce such persons to order.

CHAPTER VI

Independence and Civil Conflict

O N Monday, May 30, 1774, Nicholas Cresswell, the Tory diarist then traveling in Virginia, entered in his journal: "Dined at Colonel Harrison's. Nothing talked of but the blockade of Boston Harbour. The people seem much exasperated at the proceedings of the Ministry and talk as if they were determined to dispute the matter with the sword." The news of the Intolerable Acts had arrived. It had been made evident that there was to be no repetition of the Stamp Act episode: protest, boycott, and resistance followed by a surrender on the part of Parliament; that the government of Great Britain would meet insurgency with coercion, riots with a demonstration of military force. Up to this point the recent American agitation had been local and fitful, carried on by town and county committees and provincial conventions. Now it took on a national character.

On June 17, the Massachusetts assembly, inspired by Samuel Adams, invited all the other colonies to send delegates to a grand continental convention. The response was impressive. In a hurried and irregular fashion representatives were chosen by colonial assemblies or at mass meetings dominated by fearless leaders, every colony, except Georgia, where the royal governor blocked the selection of delegates, replying promptly to the call from Boston. "The New Englanders," lamented the choleric Cresswell, "by their canting, whining, insinuating tricks have persuaded the rest of the colonies that the Government is going to make absolute slaves of them. This I believe never was intended, but the Presbyterian rascals have had address sufficient to make the other colonies come into their scheme." Such was the Tory's view of things.

When the first Continental Congress assembled in Carpenter's Hall in Philadelphia, it was found that many of the ablest men of America had been sent to speak for the discontented groups in the colonies. Some were bold: Gadsden of South Carolina was for an immediate attack on General Gage in Boston. Others were cautious: Dickinson of Pennsylvania thought that a respectful petition to the king would restore harmony; Washington, like Cromwell long before him, apparently awaited the decree of Providence. "One third Whig; another Tory; the rest mongrel," wrote John Adams. Nevertheless, the delegates agreed upon a declaration of American rights setting forth the grievances and principles of the colonists in clear yet dignified language. This manifesto they supplemented by an address to the king and another to the people of England, disclaiming the idea of independence while vigorously criticizing the policies pursued by the British government.

Advancing beyond the language of declaration and petition, the Congress then approved the action of Massachusetts in resisting British measures and promised the united support of the sister colonies—an ominous gesture but platonic rather than a stroke of power. Aware that something more than rhetoric was required by the occasion, the radicals in the Congress who voted for this resolution demanded coercive measures of action competent to bring the

British ministry to a surrender. After a heated debate, the Congress decided to paralyze British commerce until its demands were conceded; it resolved to stop the importation of British goods into America and to compel obedience to its decree by the establishment of committees of "safety and inspection" elected at the polls.

This was an ultimatum to the wavering masses; a test of allegiance to the American cause. Men who had been silent in the midst of the popular clamor or indifferent to the outcome could no longer avoid making a choice seen of all: they were either for or against the non-importation act; they either bought British goods or they did not; they were either with the radicals or against them. They had to choose whom they would serve, and choose quickly, for no time was allowed for parleys. With breath-taking swiftness local committees were formed to enforce the non-importation agreement and stern measures were employed against those who sold or consumed British goods. Recalcitrant citizens were treated to tar and feathers while the champions of non-importation were hailed as heroes. Subscriptions were taken for the relief of the people of Boston.

Up and down the country companies of militiamen began to drill and mass meetings were held to endorse the actions of the Congress. "The King is openly cursed," recorded Cresswell, "and his authority set at defiance. In short, everything is ripe for rebellion." Having raised the standard of revolt, the Congress took precautions for the future. Before adjourning it provided that a second Congress should meet the following May, if necessary.

If the colonists were firm, the British ministry was firmer. Petitions and declarations by the Congress encountered stony hearts in Westminster. In vain did Chatham and Burke urge the repeal of the laws that had roused the ire of Americans. In vain was a motion pressed and sustained by the eloquence of Chatham in favor of removing the king's troops from Boston. "Every motive of justice and of policy, of dignity and of prudence," warned the orator in his plea before the House of Lords, "urges you to allay the ferment in America, by a removal of your troops from Boston, by a repeal of your acts of Parliament, and by a display of amicable disposition towards your colonies. On the other hand, every danger and every hazard impend to deter you from perseverance in your present ruinous course. Foreign war hanging over your heads by a slight and brittle thread: France and Spain watching your conduct and waiting for the maturity of your errors; with a vigilant eye to America and the temper of your colonies."

But all such advice left Lord North perfectly cold; he would not yield to the demands. The best that he would offer was a set of conciliatory resolutions promising to relieve from parliamentary taxation any colony that would assume its share of imperial defense and make provision for the support of local officers of the Crown. Even this "Olive Branch" he supplemented by a resolution that assured the king of coöperation in suppressing the rebellion and by the Restraining Act of March 30, 1775, which was intended in effect to destroy the entire sea-borne trade of New England.

Tension between the metropolis and the colonies had now reached the danger point. Only a little act of violence was necessary to set the continent on fire; and the way for that fateful event was prepared by General Gage, in command of the British regulars in Boston. His superiors, the British ministers, chafing because the presence of soldiers had not awed the colonists into submission, were inclined to censure him for his inertia. At all events, for some reason, not very clear, Gage resolved upon a show of authority.

Hearing that the colonists had collected military stores at Concord, on April 19, 1775, he dispatched a small force to seize their supplies. News of the movement of troops, carried by Paul Revere and Rufus Dawes, spread like wildfire through the countryside, bringing swarms of minute men to the scene of action. At Lexington, on the road to Concord, the British encountered a small band of militiamen drawn up on the green, and an order to disperse was followed by firing. Whose hand kindled the flame is to this hour one of the mysteries of military romance. The Americans placed the responsibility upon Major Pitcairn commanding the regulars; the British laid the act at the door of the militiamen. The testimony is conflicting and historians still debate the question of the "war guilt." But the fact, stark and fateful, stands out against the fair spring morning at Lexington; the contest was then and there transferred from the forum to the battlefield.

Lord North's ministry now openly accepted the challenge. King George issued a proclamation against the rebels. He declared that the colonists, "misled by dangerous and ill-designing men," were in a state of rebellion; he ordered the civil and military authorities to bring "the traitors" to justice; and he threatened with "condign punishment the authors, perpetrators, and abettors of such traitorous designs." Later in the year, Parliament passed a sweeping act cutting off trade and intercourse with America. Hope of conciliation was not yet dead but it was rapidly fading in the minds of American leaders.

§

The second Continental Congress, which met at Philadelphia in May, 1775, soon took the path that led to revolution. It rejected Lord North's offer of peace on the ground that the right of Parliament to tax was not renounced or offending acts repealed. While it petitioned the king again for a redress of grievances, it turned resolutely to the defense of American claims with all the weapons at hand. Fate decreed that this remarkable assembly should direct the storm for many years, and that all the colonies should afford high talent for its councils. In the long course of its sessions it had among its members nearly every outstanding leader of the Revolution: such as Washington, Jefferson, Wythe, Harrison, the Lees from Virginia; Samuel and John Adams, Gerry and Hancock of Massachusetts; Franklin and Morris of Pennsylvania; Read and Rodney of Delaware; Roger Sherman and Oliver Wolcott of Connecticut.

Its delegates were nearly all citizens of substance and affairs. Of the fifty-six that signed the Declaration of Independence, eight were merchants, six were physicians, five were farmers, and twenty-five were lawyers—members of that learned and contentious profession against which Burke had warned his countrymen. Most of them were tutored in the arts of local politics; many had served in colonial legislatures; a majority had taken an active part in agitations against British policy; nearly all were plain civilians with natural talents for political management. Among them there was no restless son of an ancient family, like Julius Cæsar, eager for adventure in unsettled times; no zealot like Oliver Cromwell, waiting to direct the storm in field and forum; no professional soldier, like Bonaparte, watching for a chance to ride into power; no demagogue, like Danton, marshaling the proletariat against his colleagues.

From beginning to end, the spirit of the Congress was civic rather than martial. Every debate was haunted by a dread of military power, the delegates seeming to fear a triumphant American army almost as much as they did the soldiers of George III. At no time did a dictator attempt to seize the helm of the government. Washington might have made himself master of the scene with ease, but the operation was foreign to the spirit of that Virginia gentleman. When, upon occasion, sovereign powers were conferred upon him by the Congress, he always returned them in due time unsullied by personal ambitions. Even in the most crucial hour there arose in the Congress no tyrannical committee of public safety such as ruled France in the darkest days of her revolution.

Nor were the proceedings of the Congress especially dramatic. Usually there were not more than twenty or thirty members in attendance; and in such an assembly the stormy eloquence of a Marat would have been comic. Although the lawyers present consumed weeks and months in displaying their logical capacities, the Congress was, on the whole, more like a village debating society than the Convention which carried France through the Reign of Terror. Moreover, it met in the little town of Philadelphia, with its twenty thousand inhabitants dominated by Quakers, not in a Paris crowded by half a million people—soldiers, priests, noblemen, merchants, artisans, raging Amazons, and passionate radicals. When, in the sultry days of 1776, it discussed the Declaration of Independence, no throngs pressed into the galleries to intimidate the wavering, no tumultuous mob stormed the doors clamoring for a decision. As a rule its transactions had the air of timidity and negotiation instead of resolution and mastery, disputes, vacillation, and delays marking its operations from session to session.

Its incompetence was not all due, however, as its critics have alleged, to mere perversity of human nature. The members of the Congress labored under the gravest of difficulties. Unlike the party of Cromwell or the national assembly of France, they could not take over an administrative machine that was already organized and working. Exactly the opposite was true; they had to create everything national out of a void—a government, a treasury, an army, even a bookkeeping system, and agencies for buying supplies.

Unlike the English and French revolutionists, they had no centuries of national tradition behind them—no nationwide class informed by a historic solidarity of interests to which they could appeal for support with assurance. Instead, they were largely dependent from the first day to the last upon the good graces of state assemblies and governors for troops, money, supplies, and the enforcement of their resolutions. And in the best of times the states were in arrears on everything; almost on the eve of Yorktown, Washington recorded that hardly one had put one-eighth of its quota of men at the service of the Revolution.

To make matters worse, the Congress itself was beset by the sectional jealousies which divided the states. Everything had to be viewed with an eye to its effect on the commercial or the planting interests. Among the members was no dominant majority invincibly united for a specific end, no single person moved to grasp large powers and enforce by sheer strength of will the acts of the Congress. All business had to be done by committees and on every important committee each state usually had at least one member.

Administration as well as legislation was controlled by commissions: foreign affairs, finance, supplies, and other matters of prime significance were entrusted to boards. Even the treasury was supervised by a committee until near the end of the struggle, when dire necessity forced the appointment of Robert Morris as superintendent of finance. Yet this is the body that gave voice to the national revolutionary movement, directed war, conducted foreign relations, made treaties, won independence, created a government, and nourished the germs of American nationality.

§

In view of the dogged jealousy which plagued the Congress, it was surprising that the members were able to agree upon entrusting the armed forces to the command of a single general. Here, perhaps, the divine winds of fortune favored them. Necessity hurried them into a decision and by one of the strangest ironies of history sectional discords then contributed to unity. When the second Congress met, on May 10, 1775, blows had already been struck at Lexington and Concord and thousands of militiamen had poured into the region around Boston—soldiers without supplies or organization. Confronted by the task of feeding and paying them, the Massachusetts assembly turned to the Congress for help. According to John Adams, every post brought letters from friends "urging in pathetic terms the impossibility of keeping their men together without the assistance of Congress."

But when he asked for help, Adams encountered jealousy at the very outset. More than that, there were some people unkind enough to hint that Massachusetts, having started the war, was trying to share the expenses with her neighbors. At all events, the price of united action was the choice of a Virginia soldier, George Washington, as the Commander-in-chief. Thus the hero of the Revolution, a man beyond question nobly qualified for the task of leadership, owed his selection partly to a political trade. With a certain dry humor, Washington, who was in Congress when the transaction took place, noted that his appointment was due to "the partiality of Congress joined to a political motive."

It was only by exercising the same fine arts of negotiation that the advocates of independence were able to overcome local jealousies and conservative fears and at length bring a majority of the delegates into line for the momentous decision of July 2, 1776. In fact, the idea of breaking definitely with the mother country was slow in taking form and slow in winning its way among the people. Washington and Franklin vowed that before the battle of Lexington no one had thought of revolutionary action. Even Sam Adams, though charged by the Tories with secretly harboring that motive from the beginning, was careful to conceal his opinion if he had the goal of separation always before him.

Months after the first blood was shed, strong men continued to express their affection for England and to hope for a peaceful way out of the prolonged deadlock. "Never let us lose out of sight that our interest lies in a perpetual connection with our mother country," urged a preacher of

Swiss origin in his sermon before the Georgia provincial congress. "Look ye!" roared John Dickinson at John Adams, "if you don't concur with us in our pacific system, I and a number of us will break off from you in New England and will carry on the opposition by ourselves in our own way."

Against this spirit of conciliation, however, opinions and facts made a steady headway in the direction of ultimate independence. The idea was advanced by discussions in newspapers and broadsides, broached in sermons, argued in taverns, covertly mentioned by the extremists in the provincial assemblies. "When one form of government is found by the majority," hinted the President of Harvard in a sermon before the local assembly of Massachusetts, on May 31, 1775, "not to answer the grand purpose in any tolerable degree, they may by common consent put an end to it and set up another." In the highways and byways, this familiar sentiment gathered from the writings of John Locke gradually became the chief topic of conversation and debate. From the thought it was but a step to action, and events were daily, hourly, hastening the movement. War was at hand. Royal governors and their retinues were fleeing from their capitals. Revolutionary committees were taking the places of the old agencies of authority in all the colonies—office holders, who had lived by the British Empire, showing a strange unwillingness to die by it at their posts.

The air was vibrant in the opening days of 1776 when Thomas Paine sent forth from the press the first of his powerful pamphlets, Common sense, calling for absolute independence without fear and without apologies. Casting off the language of loyalty and humility in which the Americans had framed their petitions to the throne, brushing aside the lawyers' pleas for the chartered rights of Englishmen, Paine boldly challenged the king, the British constitution, and the policies of the British government.

In serried array he presented political and economic arguments for separation: the rights of human nature are broad enough and firm enough to support the American cause; the blood of the slain calls for separation; it is not the affair of a city, a county, a province, or a kingdom, but a continent; it is not a concern of the day but of all posterity to the end of time. "O! ye that love mankind! Ye that dare to oppose not only the tyranny but the tyrant, stand forth!" So ran the plea. "Sound doctrine and unanswerable reasons!" exclaimed Washington when he read it. Soon a hundred thousand copies were circulating to the uttermost parts of the colonies, everywhere giving heart to the timid and quickening the intrepid to action.

In the provincial assemblies the cause was also making headway. Early in that year Massachusetts informed her agents at Philadelphia that independence would be welcome. On April 13, North Carolina—the "first," says Allan Nevins, "to give explicit approval"—told her delegates that they might concur with their colleagues in separating from Great Britain. About a month later, Virginia clearly instructed her representatives in the Congress to propose independence and give their assent to that daring act. Although New York had resolved that the people were not ready for revolution, although Maryland still hoped for a happy reunion with Britain, the cords of loyalty were snapping fast. Several colonies had already cast off British authority in fact by setting up new governments of their own; General Gage had been compelled to evacuate Boston; and Washington was moving on New York. The more impatient members of the Congress openly declared that the hour had come for separation. "Is not America already independent? Why not then declare it?" asked Samuel Adams.

On June 7, Richard Henry Lee, in the name of the Virginia delegation, moved that "these united colonies are and of right ought to be free and independent states." In response a committee was chosen to draft the state paper proclaiming the Revolution and stating the reasons for that momentous stroke. Thomas Jefferson, whose facility of expression was known to his colleagues, was made chairman and assigned the delicate task of framing the document. For eighteen days he worked at it, cutting, polishing, and balancing.

When at last the great oration was finished, several suggestions by Benjamin Franklin and John Adams were incorporated and the instrument was laid before the Congress, where a caustic debate followed. While Jefferson twisted and winced, some lines were struck out, others were amended, and a few added. On July 2, the Congress went on record in favor of independence. On July 4, the final draft of Jefferson's paper was formally adopted, merely confirming the fateful step already taken. Contrary to tradition, no drama marked the roll call, no independence bell rang out the news in joyous peals, no far-seeing prophet, looking down the centuries, beheld countless generations celebrating that event with solemn reverence—and firecrackers. Three or four days later the Declaration was read in a public plaza, later known as Independence Square. Copies were spread broadcast and published in city, town, and village from New Hampshire to Georgia. In New York the king's statue was pulled down; in Rhode Island it was provided that anyone guilty of praying for George III, so respectfully addressed a few months before, should be liable to a fine of a thousand pounds.

The Declaration of Independence itself falls into two principal parts. The first, containing the moral ground upon which the Revolutionists rested their cause, takes the form of "self-evident truths": all men are created equal and are endowed by their Creator with certain unalienable rights including life, liberty, and the pursuit of happiness; the purpose of government is to make such rights secure; for these reasons governments are instituted, deriving their just power from the consent of the governed; whenever any form of government becomes destructive of these ends, the people have a right to alter or abolish it and institute a new government in a form most likely to effect their safety and happiness.

These high doctrines, later called "glittering generalities" by a critical orator, were not, as sometimes fancied, French in their origin. As a matter of fact, they were essentially English, being derived, as we have hinted, from the writings of John Locke, the philosopher who supplied the rhetorical defense mechanism for the Whig revolution of 1688 which ended in the expulsion of James II. In Locke's hands the catechism of politics was short indeed: the aim of government is to protect property and when any government invades the privileges of property, the people have a right to alter or abolish the government and establish a new one. The idea was almost a century old when Jefferson artfully applied it in a modified form to the exigencies of the American Revolution. Without effect did the critics assail the creed as borrowed from England and contrary to the facts of life. Jefferson easily countered by saying that he claimed no originality for it. Neither was he oblivious to the historical objections that could be urged against it, but he was appealing to the verdict of the onrushing future, not to the sanction of heavy custom.

The second part of the Declaration contained a summary of colonial grievances launched at George III, making him the scapegoat for the Parliament and ministry of Great Britain. In a long bill of particulars, the king was accused of blocking laws passed by the local legislatures, imposing on the colonies judges independent of their will, sending upon them a swarm of royal officers to eat out their substance, quartering troops upon them, cutting off their commerce, laying taxes upon them without their consent, and sending soldiers to harry their coasts, burn their towns, and murder their people. Against these acts, petitions and warnings had been vain and fruitless. Therefore, no course was open to the colonies except to declare themselves free and independent states and take their place among the sovereign nations of the earth.

§

If the lawyers in the Continental Congress had been as adept in providing money, raising armies, collecting supplies, and directing the course of the Revolution as in drafting state papers, the War of Independence would have been short. But in moving from the sphere of words to the field of material goods and action, they met almost insuperable obstacles. At the beginning they had no national treasury; there had never been such an institution on the American continent. If there was no debt, there was also no national credit. All financial resources had to be raised from the void—and with great discretion.

Since one of the leading grievances against England had been taxation, the Congress itself naturally had to be careful about imposing burdens on the people. So it sought to provide the sinews of war by resorting to paper money, requisitions, and loans. Between 1775 and 1779, the Congress issued about two hundred and forty million dollars in bills to be redeemed by the states on a quota basis, a huge total almost equaled by the emissions of the local legislatures, making in the end over four hundred and fifty millions in such notes. Its paper credits the Congress supplemented by calls upon the states for financial aid, gaining by the operation about fifty-five millions in inflated currency and a small amount of specie.

The next resort was domestic and foreign loans. Certificates, similar to modern bonds, were sold in the home market through loan offices set up in the states; in all, approximately sixty-seven millions in paper was brought into the treasury by this process. To this unstable pyramid was attached a mass of certificates issued by military officers and by supply agents to pay for food, clothing, and other goods impressed for the use of the army. After the conflict was advanced a little way help was obtained from abroad. Small subsidies, in the form of gifts, were secured from France and Spain. These were followed by regular loans: France took more than three-fourths of the total amount; Spain absorbed a portion; Holland risked the remainder in 1782 after victory had been achieved in fact.

Though many attempts have been made to draw up a balance sheet of revolutionary accounts, none is satisfactory; the large variety of bills issued and the wide fluctuations in the value of the money collected from the sale of domestic bonds make all reckonings highly speculative. According to the best estimates, the money obtained from France was nearly equal to the specie value of the paper received from the American purchasers of internal securities. It is difficult to believe that the Congress could have staggered through the Revolution if it had not procured such generous financial assistance from the government at Paris.

The confusion that reigned in the operations of this fiscal system defies description. As paper money was poured out by the Congress it fell rapidly in value: in 1779 one paper dollar was worth only two or three cents in specie. Attempts to stabilize it were futile; it slipped almost steadily downward into the abyss, until at length there was no term of contempt so expressive as "not worth a continental." The paper that flowed from the treasuries of the states suffered a similar fate, sometimes even worse. Virginia finally reached such a low estate that her notes passed at the rate of a thousand to one, most of them expiring in the hands of the holders. In vain did the Congress and the states try to prevent depreciation and fix prices; their most drastic measures produced meager results.

In the end the situation was simply ridiculous. "Barber shops were papered in jest with the bills, and sailors, on returning from their cruises, being paid off in bundles of this worthless paper money, had suits of clothes made of it and with characteristic light-heartedness turned their loss into frolic by parading through the streets in decayed finery." The only people who came out of the orgy with profit were the gamblers who speculated in the currency as it fluctuated on its downward course with good news from the battlefields and rumors of more specie from France. Many doctors of finance, of course, proffered advice but no way was found of overcoming the disease.

In the administration of its funds, the Congress was hardly more successful. Owing to persistent jealousies it refused for six years to erect an independent treasury in charge of a competent executive. For a time it tried to work through two treasurers, both appointed by majority vote; then it created a financial committee of thirteen delegates; in 1776 it appointed a treasury board of five members. Two years later it provided that three of the five should be chosen outside congressional circles. Finally, in desperation, at the opening of 1781, it abolished the board and made Robert Morris, of Philadelphia, superintendent of finance with large powers.

For three years Morris wrestled with the chaos before him, trying to stabilize the currency, collect the arrears from the states, and place the credit of the government on a stable basis. Undoubtedly he achieved great results but his operations involved him in scandals, some of the critics going so far as to accuse him of keeping irregular accounts and speculating in public funds. Indignantly Morris denied these charges and answered each count with a bill of particulars. On weighing the evidence, his friends believed that his vindication was complete and his family biographer has sustained their verdict. However, another historian, Davis R. Dewey, finding it difficult to discover just where the financier's private affairs ended and his public business began, has raised a question as to how Morris was able to escape using in one department the knowledge that he had gained in the other.

To reduce a complicated story to a brief summary, the patriots who controlled the state and continental machinery of government either could not or would not tax their property heavily enough to support the war. In extenuation they could argue that a large part of the movable wealth was in the hands of the Tories who fled from the land and that the farmers who made up the bulk of the population had little money with which to pay taxes. Still the facts stood. The major portion of the war charges, leaving aside the aid rendered by Europe, was met in paper notes, which were practically all repudiated, and by bonds, which were later funded into a national debt sustained chiefly by indirect taxes on consumers. In the process, the heaviest losers were the soldiers who received, in return for their sacrifices, reams of paper currency and paper claims to lands in the wilderness of the West.

§

To win assistance in its tremendous enterprise, the Congress naturally turned to foreign countries. Aware that the colonists had for a long time carried on a lucrative trade with Holland, France, and Spain, lawfully and unlawfully, the Congress hoped to enlarge that business now that the trammels of Great Britain were cast off. Its leading members, men like Franklin, John Adams, and Jefferson, were also thoroughly familiar with the interests, prejudices, and jealousies of Europe which might be bent to good account for the revolutionary cause. Above all, they were acquainted with the prolonged rivalry of the Continental powers with Great Britain in the contest for world empire and world commerce. No acute divination was required to discern that the Congress could use these ancient grudges to serve its pressing needs.

It was well known, for example, that French statesmen were eager to see the colonial quarrel come to an issue of arms. Since the loss of their prize possessions on the American continent in the Seven Years' War, they had impatiently watched for a crisis that might offer an opportunity to repair the damage. When the excitement over the Stamp Act was at its height, Louis XV dispatched agents to America to observe the course of events, to report on the prospects of revolution, and even to aid discreetly the party of discontent. Ten years later, when Franklin was about to leave the post of colonial agent in London, the French ambassador to the British Court paid him a visit and gave him a plain hint that America could count on French assistance. Far-sighted Englishmen, like Chatham, were at the very moment warning their countrymen to take France into the reckoning in dealing with the colonies and to expect her sword to fall into the scales if a war occurred.

Knowing all these things and more, the Congress, soon after it got under way in 1775, created a secret committee to correspond with foreign powers and direct negotiations with them. Early the next year, it sent Silas Deane of Connecticut, often styled the first American diplomat, to Paris to sound the ground. A few months later, after independence had been declared, the Congress associated Franklin and Arthur Lee with Deane as American representatives at the French court. When the Revolution was well advanced John Jay was sent to Spain, John Adams to Holland, and other agents to Vienna, Berlin, and St. Petersburg; but their labors brought scant results compared with the aid won from France. Frederick the Great, King of Prussia, though desirous of building up trade in the United States, had no colonial ambitions and shrank from a collision with the British sea power; so he cleverly declined to give any direct assistance to the American cause. The Empress of Russia, the great Catherine, less cordial, simply ignored the American agent, permitting him to spend his two years of service in humiliating obscurity at her chilly capital. The rivalry of Russia and England over the Straits and India had not yet assumed large proportions in the schemes of diplomats.

It was in Paris alone that the outlook was in any degree favorable, and, of all the men in America available for diplomacy, Franklin was best suited to manage the delicate mission to that strategic city. His fame as a writer, a lover of science, a free thinker, and a wit had preceded him. His more serious works endeared him to the French philosophers; when he and Voltaire kissed each other at the Academy of Sciences, the crowd was in transports and the cry rang through France: "How beautiful it was to see Solon and Sophocles embrace!" Franklin's experiments with electricity were known to French scientists; indeed, with their better equipment they were testing the theories he had advanced. His homely aphorisms recorded in Poor Richard touched the French bourgeois and the thrifty peasant in a tender spot.

Moreover, France was at the moment under the spell of Rousseau's naturalism—a vigorous reaction from the artificiality of court life—and the idea of a simple old man dressed in a plain suit speaking for a republic of merchants and farmers set the kingdom agog. Even the Queen, Marie Antoinette, unwittingly played with fire by encouraging "our dear republican." Though inclined to critical judgments, John Adams, who later joined the American embassy in France, had to admit that Franklin's triumph was complete: "His name was familiar to government and people, to kings and courtiers, nobility, clergy, and philosophers, as well as plebeians, to such a degree that there was scarcely a peasant or a citizen, a valet de chambre, a coachman or a footman, a lady's chambermaid or a scullion in a kitchen, who was not familiar with it and who did not consider him as a friend to human kind." There was a ring of prophecy in Turgot's motto for Franklin: "He has torn the lightning from the sky; soon he will tear their sceptres from the kings." The French Revolution was but a few years off.

Yet Franklin's abilities, great as they were, would have availed little with hard-headed French statesmen in command of royal coffers if the drift of circumstances had not been in his favor—if some of them had not already been convinced that an hour fraught with destiny was at hand.

Indeed, before Deane arrived on the scene, Louis XVI's foreign minister, Count de Vergennes, had showed the King how France could redress her grievances against Great Britain and reduce the power of that haughty empire.

Early in the fray, a dashing Frenchman, Beaumarchais, fired by restless love of adventure and interest in the American uprising, devoted talents and wealth in aiding the revolutionists beyond the sea. In himself he was a host. Author of The Barber of Seville and The Marriage of Figaro, a courtier, musician, publisher, shipowner, manufacturer, and financier, he was widely known among the people and had access to the seats of the mighty. His lightest word in support of the American cause helped to make enthusiasm for it in the streets, at the court, and among business men. Obtaining with comparative ease the sympathy of the French ministry, Beaumarchais organized, in June, 1776, a company under his own direction and commenced at once to ship supplies to the struggling rebels. Until the French government flung off secrecy and made a formal alliance with the United States, he continued to render this service—a service for which he was never paid in full, contributing to history one of its mysteries: "Beaumarchais and the Lost Million."

Though the French were covertly willing to risk money in the American venture, they were very cautious about anything beyond. For more than a year after Franklin's arrival at Paris in November, 1776, the royal government would make him no promise of open assistance. The King naturally did not take to the idea of fomenting revolutions; his own finances were in disorder; and a war with England was not to be entered into lightly. Moreover, the progress of American arms did not give any indication of a final triumph. After Washington had ousted the British from Boston, the course of events on the whole had run against him. He was badly defeated on Long Island in the summer of that year, 1776, driven northward through Harlem to White Plains, forced across the Hudson into New Jersey, and harried on down into Pennsylvania. His brilliant exploit at Trenton on Christmas night and his brush with Cornwallis at Princeton had been followed by disaster at Brandywine, the loss of Philadelphia, a reverse at Germantown, and retreat to Valley Forge. Two strategic ports, New York and Philadelphia, were in British hands; two great rivers, the Hudson and the Delaware, were blocked; and a British general, Burgoyne, was cutting his way into the heart of New York, thus inserting a wedge between New England and the rest of the states.

Every post brought sad news to Franklin but he retained his courage. "Well, doctor," said an Englishman to him with a note of scorn, "Howe has taken Philadelphia." Stunned for a moment, the old wit found a reply: "I beg your pardon, sir; Philadelphia has taken Howe." Had he realized it, the quip was more than wit. The ease and gay life of the city did indeed take possession of Howe and eat into the fiber of his initiative, but the two diplomatic fencers in Paris could not have foreseen that. So, in spite of all linguistic flourishes, the outlook was dark for Franklin. Then suddenly the impossible happened: on October 16, 1777, General Burgoyne surrendered at Saratoga. Early in December a special messenger from America rushed into the courtyard of Franklin's residence at Passy with the news: "Burgoyne and his whole army are prisoners of war."

Beaumarchais, who happened to be dining with Franklin that very moment, grasping the full force of the report, dashed off to Versailles in such haste that he upset his coach and dislocated his arm. The King, also deeply impressed by the news, saw that the time had come to cast off secrecy and join the Americans in their struggle against Great Britain. Treaties of commerce and alliance were therefore framed and, after some haggling over terms, duly signed on February 6, 1778. France recognized the independence of the United States, a defensive alliance was formed, plans for joint military action were drafted, and Louis XVI then openly declared war on England.

In vain did Lord North try to break this union by offering generous terms to the Americans and by proposing peace negotiations. It was then too late—impossible to turn back the flood. Within a few more months races that had fought each other two decades before in the wilderness of Pennsylvania and on the Plains of Abraham were united in battle array against the armies of King George. If Franklin had failed as colonial agent in London, he had been eminently successful at the French court.

Less fortunate, as we have said, were the American ministers in Spain and Holland. John Jay at the court of Madrid, in spite of persistent efforts, was not able to bring the Spanish king into an alliance with the United States. That cautious monarch, besides shrinking from the idea of a democracy on the eastern frontier of his American dominion, was in no mood to open New Orleans to the trade of the Ohio Valley.

Still, he remembered that Britain had destroyed Spain's sea power, had defied her colonial monopoly, and was dominating the Mediterranean from the stronghold of Gibraltar. After much balancing of chances, he made a treaty with France in 1779 which bound his country to enter the war against England, but for the moment he refused to recognize the independence of the United States or become an ally of a revolutionary people. Republics were not to be encouraged; ancient damages only were to be repaired.

Like the Spaniards, the Dutch were not on very good terms with Great Britain. They too had memories of a colonial empire wrecked by the might of England and they also suffered from current irritations. At the opening of the American Revolution, they had rushed to engage in a profitable trade with the rebellious colonies, dispatching cargo after cargo of munitions to their island of St. Eustatius in the West Indies for transshipment to the United States.

Though strictly in accord with the canons of international propriety, this operation was painful for Englishmen to contemplate—old rivals coining money out of American traffic, making powder and shells for Washington's army, and negotiating with the American minister at The Hague. Finding that the business could not be stopped by processes of search and seizure, the British declared war on The Netherlands, seized the island of St. Eustatius, and confiscated military property in a cavalier fashion. With relative ease Adams now won from the Dutch a favorable treaty and managed to induce Dutch bankers, gorged with war profits, to make a loan to the struggling republic in spite of its low standing in the markets of Europe.

§

In military as well as financial and diplomatic affairs the Continental Congress was driven from pillar to post, plagued by its own ineptitude, and lashed by necessity. Hurried by radical pressure into a war for which no real preparation had been made, it was compelled to improvise as it went along. It was well aware that the result depended in final analysis upon the fighting men, but it shrank from the hard test of fact. Its members had read history; they knew how in other times and places armies had dominated civilians, pulled down legislatures, and set up dictators; they recalled the lessons taught by Cæsar and Cromwell; they hoped against hope that the war could be won by militiamen commanded by elected officers and sustained by faith rather than by wages and pensions.

At the outset the congressional statesmen found themselves by chance in control of the raw troops that had rushed to besiege the British in Boston. Under the stress of the hour they transformed that motley array into the Continental Army, supplementing this action later by advising the states to enroll in the militia all able-bodied men between sixteen and fifty. But the Congress was not long in discovering that such an "army" could not be relied upon for severe and protracted campaigns. The men were enlisted for short terms; they lacked discipline; they left in shoals at times when their services were most needed.

Before the war was six months old it was made plain that the volunteer militia system had failed. Washington knew from the beginning that it was bound to fail. "To place any dependence upon militia," he said, "is assuredly resting upon a broken staff." Early in February, 1776, he urged the Congress to take steps toward the creation of a regular army. "To bring men to be well acquainted with the duties of a soldier requires time," he told the august legislature of merchants, doctors, and lawyers. "Three things prompt men to regular discharge of their duty in time of action: natural bravery, hope of reward, and fear of punishment." Accordingly he urged the formation of a national army composed of men enlisted for the war, directed by officers appointed with reference to merits rather than political geography, and guaranteed compensation worthy of the cause.

Only in a hesitant and half-hearted manner did the Congress respond to Washington's demand. In September, 1776, eight months after his emphatic call for help, it ordered the enrollment of eighty-eight battalions enlisted for the duration of the war—a term later changed to three years—and promised, in addition to a small cash bounty, a grant of land at the close of the contest. In December, in an awful fright, the Congress made Washington dictator-general for six months with full power to raise troops, collect supplies, and punish disaffected persons; and a short time after the expiration of this period it renewed the high authority, under closer limitations. Disappointed in these efforts to create an army, the Congress finally "advised" the states to fill their quotas by drafting men for a nine months period. At no time, however, did the central government, such as it was, escape from abject dependence upon the states. Whenever it decreed a new levy, it relied from choice or necessity upon the states to raise the quotas assigned to them. Never, at any time, did it have ready and disciplined for battle more than a fragment of its paper enrollment.

Bitter fruits of this ineptitude were gathered in the bloodshed, agony, and cost of a prolonged war. When the struggle opened, there were approximately ninety thousand American soldiers under arms, against twenty thousand British. At the close the American forces had dwindled to less than one-third the original number and the British had doubled their strength. If the Congress had given Washington a permanent army when he called for it in February, 1776, he might have ended the war in six months. But it could not, or at all events did not, meet his urgent appeal and the conflict dragged on for seven weary years.

In the course of it nearly four hundred thousand Americans were enlisted for some kind of service without ever providing an invincible battle array. Moreover, while the Congress, from the beginning to the end of the contest, complained bitterly about the expenses, the country eventually had to pay heavily for its parsimony. A hundred years after the Declaration of Independence, the Federal Government had disbursed eighty million dollars in pensions to soldiers of the Revolution, and was still remunerating "war widows."

The civilian fear of the army which inspired the military policy of the Congress was even extended to the Commander-in-chief, stimulated by officers who were jealous of Washington or who honestly believed that he was lacking in decision and energy. Some of the critics—men of consequence, such, for instance, as Horatio Gates, Thomas Mifflin, Thomas Conway, and Charles Lee—using their great influence to the limit, worked up in the Congress and in the army a dangerous opposition known as the "Conway Cabal."

Obscurity hung over the early stages of this proceeding

but near the end of 1777 it became evident that there was a strong movement on foot to curtail the General's power and perhaps force him out of the field. Signs of this enterprise were unmistakable. The Congress promoted Conway in spite of Washington's objections, appointed him to the post of inspector-general of the army, created independent commands, and established the worst of all military institutions, a board of control.

Stung by criticism, Washington assured the Congress, with broad irony, that it was "a much easier and less distressing thing to draw remonstrances in a comfortable room by a good fireside than to occupy a cold, bleak hill and sleep under frost and snow, without clothes or blankets." His firmness and good sense rallied his friends and in time he had the pleasure of seeing the cabal fail; but until the victory at Yorktown, his movements were handicapped by detractors in the Congress and his plans were more than once defeated by the failure of that body to furnish the men and supplies necessary for aggressive campaigns.

§

It is hypercritical, perhaps, to magnify the shortcomings of the Continental Congress in fiscal, diplomatic, and military affairs. Certainly a balanced judgment takes into account the fact that it was little more than a glorified debating society speaking for thirteen independent states, each of which claimed to be sovereign and was deeply occupied with its own problems, civil and military. After all, the Congress was only a remote organ of a revolutionary mass movement—an instrument created by the agencies of rebellion in the states. The latter were in reality the prime factors in driving on the conflict with Great Britain. The initiative for independence, as we have seen, came from the advanced colonial assemblies rather than from the delegates at Philadelphia and the support of the war fell mainly on them. State governors, like Trumbull of Connecticut, Clinton of New York, and Rutledge of South Carolina, carried heavier burdens than the president of the Continental Congress.

Among the great engines employed by the Revolutionists in overturning the government of George III were local committees of correspondence and state conventions, irregular in composition and despotic in powers. In the initial stages of the agitation the discontented colonists operated through regular agencies, the town assemblies and local legislatures; but as the contest became more heated the revolutionary leaders began to form independent bodies which finally became the germs of new American governments. Early in November, 1772, there was organized in Boston under the direction of Samuel Adams a committee of correspondence charged with the duty of holding meetings, sending emissaries into other towns, and conducting a campaign of popular education against British policy. Almost in a flash the colonies were covered with a network of local associations of this character.

To and fro among them flew the shuttle of communication, the tireless labors of Adams keeping New England alert and stirring sluggards at the ends of the country. With his trembling hand, he wrote sheaves of letters to the leaders of committees in various towns, encouraging them to stand fast in their resistance to the British Crown. In reply he received reports on the course of public opinion. From the rough scrawl of a fisherman who knew the ocean's rage, he learned about the temperature of local liberties; from a blacksmith who turned from the flaming forge to answer an inquiry, he heard that the popular cause was flourishing.

Upon town and county structures were built the higher agencies of the province. Taking the lead in this operation, the Virginia House of Burgesses, in 1773, or rather its rebellious members, appointed a special committee to enter into communication with the sister colonies and within twelve months all except **one** had such an extra-legal organ of opinion and power. As the struggle advanced apace, colonial assemblies were purged of the loyalists or conventions were organized to take their place, thus providing from the community to the state capital a chain of revolutionary engines. Inspired by a sense of solidarity, informed by a constant exchange of news, the active radicals directed agitation, called periodical conferences of the faithful, seized the reins of government as they fell from the hands of royal officers, laid hold of local treasuries, waged war, and sustained the American cause.

At first the king's officers looked on the petty committee of correspondence as an absurd instrument of factional strife but they soon discovered in it the menacing force of a new state. One high Tory, Daniel Leonard, called it "the foulest, subtlest, and most venomous serpent that ever issued from the egg of sedition." Changing the figure, he continued: "I saw the small seed when it was implanted; it was a grain of mustard. I have watched the plant until it has become a great tree." By this time local committees and conventions had been crowned by state committees and conventions and the entire substructure finished off by the grand convention, the Continental Congress, with its numerous organs for action, functioning in every sphere of sovereignty—legislation, finance, war, and diplomacy. A new political organism had been called into being, feeble at first, but destined to rule a continent and islands in distant seas.

§

In ousting British authorities and their sympathizers from power, the directors of these committees and conventions received only a partial support from the populace. Just what proportion of the people actually favored the Revolution was never ascertained by a referendum and no accurate report on the strength of the patriot party was ever compiled by any official agency. From the fragmentary figures of early elections that have been preserved, however, it seems that a very small per cent of the colonists were politically active in spite of the excitement that often characterized partisan contests.

Consider, for example, the experience of Boston. On the eve of the Revolution, that city had approximately 20,000 inhabitants, of whom about 4,000 were adult males. Roughly speaking, 1,000 of the latter were disfranchised by the existing property qualifications, leaving 3,000 potential voters. From the records of the tempestuous decade between 1765 and 1775 it has been estimated that the highest vote cast in the town during the period was 1,089, while the average vote was only 555, or about one in six of the qualified electors. In the stormy year of 1765 when Boston was shaken from center to circumference over the Stamp Act, an election was held for the colonial assembly, with Sam Adams stirring up furor as a candidate; four hundred and forty-eight votes were cast—two hundred and sixty-five for Adams, awarding victory to him. In other words, the firebrand of revolution elected on that occasion spoke for less than 10 per cent of the eligible voters of Boston. At a Connecticut general election in 1775 when the fray was growing hot, there appeared at the polls 3,477 voters out of a population of nearly 200,000, of whom 40,797 were males over twenty years of age. In the other colonies, the same apathy seems to have prevailed; nothing but an extraordinary contest drew to the polls one-third of the voters.

No doubt there were many voteless mechanics who gave their support to the revolutionary cause. They agitated, rioted, and fought in the army but they were relatively few in number. Moreover, their support was none too welcome; indeed, their demand for the right to take part in the election of committees and conventions was coldly repulsed at first by the enfranchised patriots. Even the choice of local agents to enforce the boycott against British goods, proclaimed by the Continental Congress in 1774, was entrusted only to men who possessed appropriate property or taxpaying qualifications under colonial laws. As a matter of fact, the directors who engineered the Revolution at the top contemplated no drastic alteration in arrangements at the bottom. Taking all these things into account, therefore, it would be conservative to say that, as far as balloting was a measure of popular support, not more than one-third of the adult white males in America ever set the seal of their approval on the Revolution by voting for its committeemen and delegates.

At best the sentiment behind independence was a matter of gradual growth. After the war had been going for a year, an advocate of independence was regarded as a dangerous person, and was likely to be greeted with angry glances in the streets of Philadelphia. As late as that the Continental Congress, though composed of delegates openly opposed to British policy and chosen by groups from which all avowed Tories were excluded, was so divided in opinion that "every important step was opposed and carried by bare majorities." Such at least is the testimony of John Adams. Four months before independence was finally declared there was still in the Congress a powerful group hostile to revolution in any form—a group made up principally of delegates from Pennsylvania, New Jersey, Maryland, Delaware, New York, and South Carolina. Only by the most adroit negotiation were the advocates of independence able to carry the day, and at the bitter end New York abstained from the vote.

In a final reckoning, John Adams decided that two-thirds of the people were at last committed to the Revolution and that not more than one-third opposed it at all stages. On the Tory side, however, this estimate was not accepted. Joseph Galloway, who left official service in Pennsylvania and fled to England when he saw the storm breaking, declared in 1779 before a committee of Parliament that, at the beginning of the conflict, not one-fifth of the people had independence in view and he added that at the moment "many more than four-fifths of the people would prefer a union with Great Britain upon constitutional principles to that of independence."

Obviously both Adams and Galloway were guessing. Doubtless opinion fluctuated with the course of the struggle that raged now in one section, now in another, now accompanied by success, now by failure and discouragement. On the whole, the English historian, Lecky, had some basis for saying that "the American Revolution, like most others, was the work of an energetic minority who succeeded in committing an undecided and fluctuating majority to courses for which they had little love and leading them step by step to a position from which it was impossible to recede." Perhaps after all a nice discussion of the question is only pertinent in an age that lays stress upon mathematical politics.

Whether they formed a majority of the populace or not the revolutionary masses assumed obligations and engineered activities of the first magnitude. Far and wide, through many agencies, they prosecuted with unremitting fervor an agitation in favor of the patriot cause. Independent state constitutions were established. The Tory opposition was suppressed or kept under strict surveillance. All the ordinary functions of government were discharged, at least in a fashion—the administration of justice, the levy of taxes, the maintenance of order, and the enactment of enlightened and humane legislation. To these obligations were joined stern duties connected with the war: raising quotas of men and money, collecting and forwarding supplies, promoting the sale of Continental bonds, and co-operating with the Congress in the restraint of speculators and profiteers. Furthermore, since the fighting spread up and down the coast, most of the states were called upon at one time or another to raise local forces and meet the enemy on their own soil.

§

Intense and wide must have been the agitation carried on by the patriots. Hundreds of pamphlets, bundles of faded letters, files of newspapers, and collections of cartoons, broadsides, and lampoons reveal an intellectual ferment comparable to that which marked the course of the Puritan revolution in England more than a hundred years before. Notices of public meetings held to cheer the leaders in the forum and the armies in the field bear witness to the tumult of opinion that marked the progress of the American cause. Entries in diaries tell of heated debates in taverns where "John Presbyter, Will Democrack, and Nathan Smuggle," to use the Tory gibe, roundly damned the king and his "minions" and put the fear of battle and sudden death into the hearts of royalists and lukewarm subjects. Letters open the doors of private houses, disclosing families and their friends at dinner or seated by fireplaces in lively debate on the fortunes of the day and the tasks ahead. In the familiar correspondence of husbands and wives, such as the letters of John and Abigail Adams or of James and Mercy Warren, are revealed the springs of faith and affection that fed the currents of action.

Ministers of religion in large numbers, especially the dissenters, seem to have turned from the gospel to revolution. Such is the testimony of friend and foe. "Does Mr. Wiberd preach against oppression?" anxiously inquired John Adams of his wife. "The clergy of every denomination, not excepting the Episcopalian, thunder and lighten every Sabbath," replied Abigail. "The few that pretend to preach," snorted the Tory Cresswell, "are mere retailers of politics, sowers of sedition and rebellion, serve to blow the cole of discord and excite the people to arms. The Presbyterian clergy are particularly active in supporting the measures of Congress from the rostrum, gaining proselytes, persecuting the unbelievers, preaching up the righteousness of their cause, and persuading the unthinking populace of the infallibility of success!"

In the sermons that the printing press has preserved, the

philosophy of John Locke is curiously blended with illustrations from the Old Testament. While the right of the people to abolish and institute governments is proclaimed, George III is reminded of the fate of Rehoboam; and states that do not furnish their quotas of men and money to the American cause are told that the people of Meroz were cursed for similar faults. Even the Reverend Oliver Hart, of Charleston, who found time in the very midst of the Revolution to preach a strong sermon on "Dancing Exploded," was so energetic in his support of independence that he did not dare to remain in the city after it was captured by the British.

Among the secular writers, Tom Paine was the most trenchant and influential. His ringing appeal for independence made in Common Sense, printed early in 1776, was followed in December by another shrill cry to the people, rallying them to the patriot side. He had been with Washington's disheartened forces as they retreated from Fort Lee down through New Jersey; he had suffered with them and knew by what frail reeds the Revolution was now supported. "These are the times that try men's souls," he opened in a resounding sentence calculated to muster the wavering. "The summer soldier and the sunshine patriot will, in this crisis, shrink from the service of his country; but he that stands it now deserves the love and thanks of men and women."

In pelting periods, Paine lashed the Tories, accusing them of self-interest, servility, and fear. In shrewd lines of encouragement he made light of the recent reverses strung all the way from Harlem to White Plains, across the Hudson and down into Pennsylvania, assuring the public that this strategic retreat was the promise of victory, not disaster. Coming to the burden of his argument, he warned the patriots that more heroic efforts were needed to save the day, that the militia was unequal to its task, a regular army must be raised, and greater perseverance shown. Drawing in conclusion pictures of victory won by fortitude and of defeat suffered by cowardice, he called upon Americans to choose their fate.

This pamphlet Paine followed by others equally vivid until the goal was at last in sight. Whatever may be said of his shortcomings and his wayward spirit—Theodore Roosevelt, with characteristic impatience and a woeful disregard for exactness, called him "a dirty little atheist"—Paine's services to the Revolution were beyond calculation. For this we have the evidence of men as far apart in their general views as Washington and Jefferson.

§

While one type of patriot was engaged in stirring up revolutionary ardor, in dissolving the intellectual and moral bonds of the old order, and in constructing the ethics of the new day, another was devoted to political action. The rise of revolutionary committees and conventions within the colonial society soon led to the breakdown of the established governments. From royal and proprietary colonies alike, governors, judges, and other high officers usually scurried in haste. Wentworth fled from New Hampshire in the summer of 1775; Martin of North Carolina slipped away from Wilmington to Cape Fear on a dark night in April; Tryon of New York sought safety in July on board a man-of-war in the harbor, laconically announcing: "A committee has assumed the whole powers of government."

Since royal institutions were crumbling, suggestions for new political plans were in order. Anticipating the transition from colony to state, Paine sketched a project in his pamphlet on Commonsense. A short time afterward John Adams brought out Thoughts on Government, in which, with his usual gravity, he argued for a conservative order of things. Meanwhile local assemblies were at work. In January, 1776, New Hampshire drafted an emergency plan of administration, pending reconciliation with England, and in March South Carolina followed her example. This was a gesture toward independence and was so viewed by the critics.

Seeing the drift of events, the Congress, in May, sent out a resolution advising the people of all the colonies to adopt new governments appropriate to their needs. Before the year was over, Virginia, New Jersey, Pennsylvania, Delaware, Maryland, Georgia, and New York had framed constitutions and embarked on careers of self-determination. Connecticut and Rhode Island, already accustomed to electing their own executives and legislatures, replied that in the main their old charters would meet their needs, reference to the king having been deleted. South Carolina in 1778 revised the instrument adopted before independence and two years later Massachusetts, after a heated wrangle, put into effect a constitution that was destined to endure in its broad outlines for more than a century.

Under these new plans, state governments took the place of the revolutionary assemblies that had hitherto directed the fortunes of the thirteen colonies, assuming, with a certain formality, the responsibilities of power. First among their duties, of course, was to aid the Congress in suppressing the opposition and in prosecuting the war. A clear test of allegiance having now been provided, the people of each state were called upon to declare their devotion to the new institutions, while the pressure brought to bear on loyalists by provincial assemblies and irregular combinations of patriots was redoubled. Mobs had tarred and feathered Tories, otherwise cruelly treated them, and wrecked their homes; henceforth the management of dissenters was to proceed more systematically. The most ardent of the known and active opponents of the Revolution were shut up in jail; the prison camp in Connecticut at one time held the former governor of New Jersey and the mayor of New York.

Others less belligerent, after being duly warned, were placed under surveillance. The more timid and skittish, as John Adams characterized the milder Tories, escaped the toils of the law by refraining from irritating conduct. "I might as well be in the infernal regions," groaned Cresswell, "as in this country where my sentiments are known. Every rascal looks on me as an enemy to him and except I could tacitly submit to every insult or divest myself of the faculties of sight, speech and hearing, must be miserable." Thousands who could not endure the new order or feared harsh treatment fled to Canada, England, or some other part of the British Empire.

The property of the Tories, as well as their persons, was now subjected to official control. Early in the course of the Revolution several of the states began to confiscate the goods of the loyalists. Taking the cue from these radical commonwealths, the Congress in November, 1777, advised them all to seize the property of the men who were not entitled to "protection" and apply the proceeds to the purchase of Continental certificates. By the time the armed conflict was over, statutes of condemnation and forfeiture had been enacted everywhere.

This was, of course, delicate business. It was difficult to discover by jury trial or judicial inquiry just what degree of taint warranted the appropriation of property. Moreover, the sale of estates and the administration of funds called for probity of the loftiest order—a kind of Spartan honesty which was not always found in the turmoil of the Revolution. In fact the sequestration of estates was marked by corruption and scandals that shocked all sensitive persons. To the loyalists the revolutionary commissioners were bands of bloodthirsty robbers; to the patriots fighting desperately for independence any moderate treatment of domestic foes seemed to fall short of poetic justice.

In addition to their local labors of administration and patriotism, the state governments furnished most of the men and supplies for the war. Having no direct taxing power, the Congress relied upon them to support its credit. Though its hopes and demands were constantly defeated by weak and negligent legislatures, it managed to wring from their treasuries nearly six million dollars, specie value —an amount almost equal to the sum obtained by Continental bond-sales through the loan offices. It also made requisitions upon them for supplies, corn, pork, beef, rum, and other goods, and all in all it succeeded in securing large quantities by that means.

When Washington's men were freezing and starving at Valley Forge and Pennsylvania farmers were selling their produce to the British in Philadelphia at good prices, Governor Henry of Virginia helped to redress the balance by sending up to the soldiers great loads of food and clothing. It was upon the states also that the Congress had to depend for men to fill the army and, if their short-comings were conspicuous, still it could be said that heroic efforts were often made to comply with the demands. Moreover, some of the state governors were military men and took the field in person against the enemy; and in many theaters local militiamen fought side by side with troops from the Continental Army. If critics deplored their weakness, apologists could make a show of defense by reference to obvious facts.

§

In this mass movement in which preachers, pamphleteers, committees, lawyers, and state governments advanced the revolutionary cause, women in every section played their customary rôle of backing up their fighting men with all the intensity of emotion and loyalty to their kind that war had always inspired in the "gentle" sex, except among a few pacific Quakers. Lysistrata, summoning her sisters to strike against the arbitrament of arms, was a character in fiction created by the mind of man. The revolutionary records seem to indicate patriot valor on the part of women commensurate in fervor with that of men.

Nearly every male leader of the rebellion had a wife, sister, or daughter actively at work in the second line of defense. Propaganda of the pen was waged by Mercy

Warren, sister of James Otis and wife of James Warren, who wrote satires and farces in the elaborate style of the day, scoring loyalists and praising liberty—offering these as replies to the British playwrights and the actors who were delighting New York crowds with their caricatures of the patriots. Women were also to be found among the publishers and editors of newspapers, encouraging the writers of stirring pleas for independence, trying to make the pen as mighty as the sword.

In every branch of economy that kept the social order intact and the army supplied, to the degree that it was, women were industrious laborers and energetic promoters. They had long formed the majority of the workers in the textile industry and throughout the war the whirr of their wheels and the clank of their looms were heard in the land as they spun and wove for soldiers and civilians alike. Letters of the time reveal them sowing, reaping, and managing the affairs of farm as well as kitchen. They gave lead from their windows and pewter from their shelves to be melted into bullets, united in a boycott of English luxuries, combined to extend the use of domestic manufactures, canvassed from door to door when money and provisions for the army were most needed.

As non-combatants it was often women's obligation to face marauding soldiers; Catherine Schuyler, setting the torch to her own crops in her fields near Saratoga before the advancing British troops and watching with composure the roaring flames that devoured her food with theirs, proved how courageously women could fight in their way. In the wake of the British armies, South and North, they labored to restore their ruined homes and hold together the fragments of their family property for the veterans when they should return.

Stern disciplinarians they were too, in their steadfastness to the faith. They formed committees to visit profiteers and warn them against extortion. In one instance they seized a supply of tea in the hands of a stubborn merchant and sold it over the counter at a price fixed by themselves. "Madam," said John Adams to Mrs. Huston at Falmouth, "is it lawful for a weary traveler to refresh himself with a dish of tea, provided it has been honestly smuggled or paid no duties?" The answer was decisive. "No, sir, we have renounced all tea in this place, but I'll make you coffee." There was no redress. "I must be weaned," lamented the wayfarer, "and the sooner the better." The young ladies of Amelia County, Virginia, were reported to have formed an agreement "not to permit the addresses of any person, be his circumstances or situation in life what they will, unless he has served in the American armies long enough to prove by his valor that he is deserving of their love."

§

It would be a mistake, however, in portraying this widespread movement of the people, to represent the patriot masses facing the enemy in solid array. The contrary is the truth. Everywhere the supporters of the Revolution were divided into conservative and radical wings, the former composed mainly of merchants and men of substance and the latter of mechanics and yeomen-farmers, sometimes led by men of the other group. In Massachusetts an insurgent left wing drew up a state constitution pleasing to the politicians but was not strong enough to force its adoption. By a skillful combination, the aristocracy of "wealth and talents" defeated the plan and substituted a system which safeguarded the rights and privileges of property at every bastion. Morison describes the instrument briefly: "The Constitution of 1780 was a lawyers' and merchants' constitution, directed toward something like quarterdeck efficiency in government and the protection of property against democratic pirates."

Pennsylvania was harassed by similar factions—sharply marked in their divisions and violent in their relations—which engaged in long and unseemly wrangles on every issue of the hour. At one time the revolutionary government itself was assailed by a still more revolutionary group and blood was shed. Even after astute management had restored calm among the patriots, local conflicts continued to consume the energies of their leaders until independence was finally won. For this reason, among others, Pennsylvania, though ranking among the largest and richest states, was constantly hampered in complying with the requests of the Continental Congress.

Nor were the Southern states any more fortunate. Throughout the war a desperate struggle was waged in Virginia between planters on the seaboard and small farmers of the interior—"a struggle which involved nothing less than a revolution in the social order of the Old Dominion with its Established Church and its landed aristocracy." As a result many historic families on the coastal plain hated Thomas Jefferson and Patrick Henry far more than they did the Englishmen who served as the king's officers.

A kindred spirit flamed out in South Carolina, where slave-owners of the lowlands and merchants of the towns engaged in almost daily contests with mechanics from the shops and farmers from the back country. On one occasion, the heat of the dispute moved even Gadsden, a leader of the radicals, to inquire "whether there is not a danger amongst us far more dangerous than anything that can arise from the whole herd of Contemptible, exportable Tories." So threatening in fact was the menace—a group of "levelers" bent on overthrowing the aristocracy of "wealth and talents"—that the notables of the state had to exercise considerable skill in saving their privileges and prestige.

Across the border in Georgia the social battle between conservatives and radicals was carried to such a pitch that in a moment of bitter rivalry the patriot party could boast of two legislatures and two executives. While the British were laying waste their state, these factions dissipated their strength in fruitless bickering; on both sides, according to Allan Nevins, historian of the crisis, were many men who preferred defeat at the hands of their common foe to the triumph of their American rivals.

§

These divisions among the patriots were embittered by continuous, vitriolic assaults from the loyalists who stuck by their guns. Before the Revolution had advanced far, Tory partisans—editors, poets, and pamphleteers—had devised a complete scheme of rhetorical offense. Moderates among them admitted that there had been evils in the policies and measures of Great Britain but insisted that, by the process of petition and argument, every wrong could be righted. They all appealed to the verdict of history: the Revolution violated the traditions, the ancient ties, and the ceremonials inherited from a distant past; it was contrary to the divine order expressed in the English régime; the doctrine of equality to which it appealed was "ill-founded and false, both in its premises and conclusions"; the leveling movement fostered by it threatened the world with "a low opinion of government" by treating the state as "a mere human ordinance," and rulers as "mere servants of the public."

The whole revolutionary program, according to this school, was indefensible in the light either of history or reason. "Of all the theories respecting the origin of government," wrote the eloquent Tory divine, Jonathan Boucher, "with which the world has been either puzzled, amused or instructed, that of the Scriptures alone is accompanied by no insuperable difficulties. It was not to be expected from an all-wise and all-merciful Creator, that, having formed creatures capable of order and rule, he should turn them loose into the world under the guidance only of their own unruly wills." No, ran the argument, God had put kings and superior persons in the world to govern it. In short, the Revolution, as the Tories saw it, flew in the face of experience, history, and divine sanction;

hoary and crusted reputability was all on the side of the provincial status.

From this theorem, Tory propagandists proceeded to the next. The Revolution had been stirred up by a few crafty men who had played upon the ignorance and passions of the mob; by a handful of conspirators was the "draught designed to cheat the crowd and fascinate mankind." And these conspirators were "an infernal, dark-designing group of men . . . obscure, pettifogging attorneys, bankrupt shopkeepers, outlawed smugglers . . . wretched banditti . . . the refuse and dregs of mankind." At least in this guise they appeared to the editor of the New York Gazette on May 23, 1778.

> Old Catiline, and Cromwell too,
> Jack Cade and his seditious crew,
> Hail brother-rebel at first view,
> And hope to meet the Congress,

ran a Tory ballad on the patriots who framed and adopted the Declaration of Independence. Individuals partook of the nature of the whole band, General John Sullivan being presented by a poet as a fair type:

> Amidst ten thousand eminently base,
> Thou, Sullivan, assume the highest place!
> Sailor, and farmer, barrister of vogue,
> Each state was thine, and thou in each a rogue.

Nor did the Tory scribes spare the great Washington: at the unconquerable soul of the Revolution Jonathan Odell flung these lines and more:

> Thou hast supported an atrocious cause
> Against thy king, thy country, and the laws;
> Committed perjury, encouraged lies,
> Forced conscience, broken the most sacred ties;
> Myriads of wives and fathers at thy hand
> Their slaughtered husbands, slaughtered sons, demand;
> That pastures hear no more the lowing kine,
> That towns are desolate, all—all is thine.

While such was the Tory view of the revolutionary leaders, outstanding figures in the American cause, the loyalist opinion of the rank and file was even less favorable. Thomas Paine was called "our hireling author . . . true son of Grub Street." The "commissioners of loans, and boards of war, marine committees, commissaries, scribes, assemblies, councils, senatorial tribes" were "wretches whose very acts the French abhor." Washington was "at the head of ragged ranks. Hunger and itch are with him . . . and all the lice of Egypt in his train. . . . Great captain of the western Goths and Huns." The soldiers were "half savages," from "the backwoods." The patriot camp was filled with "priests, tailors, and cobblers, . . . and sailors, insects vile that emerge to light . . . rats who nestle in the lion's den." Their inspiration was "treason . . . ambition . . . hypocrisy . . . fraud . . . bundles of lies . . . calumny . . . zeal . . . riot . . . cruelty . . . cunning . . . malice . . . persecution . . . and superstition."

> Here anarchy before the gaping crowd
> Proclaims the people's majesty aloud. . . .
> The blust'rer, the poltroon, the vile, the weak,
> Who fight for Congress, or in Congress speak.

Having poured the vials of their wrath upon the heads of the revolutionary party, Tory pamphleteers accused the patriots of proclaiming liberty as their goal and then wading through tar and blood and tyranny to attain it.

> For one lawful ruler, many tyrants we've got,
> Who force young and old to their wars, to be shot,

exclaimed one Tory poet.

> Tarr'd, feather'd, and carted for drinking Bohea?—
> And by force and oppression, compell'd to be free?—
> The same men maintaining that all human kind
> Are, have been, and shall be, as free as the wind,
> Yet impaling and burning their slaves for believing
> The truth of the lessons they're constantly giving?

queried another. "You find these pretended enemies of oppression the most unrelenting oppressors," lamented the rector of Trinity Church in New York, "and their little finger heavier than the king's loins. . . . There is more liberty in Turkey than in the dominions of the Congress." And all this had been done, ran the refrain, by self-constituted committees, conventions, and assemblies that had usurped authority and set themselves up as legislators and governors.

§

The weakness of the revolutionary movement, as revealed in controversy, politics, government, and administration, was of course reflected in all phases of the military operations. Improvisation and guesswork marked every stage. When the Revolution assumed the aspect of an organized conflict, there was not available a single army officer experienced in the stratagems of combat on a large scale, as distinguished from local fighting. Washington had been under fire in the French and Indian conflict, showing courage and resourcefulness in the presence of danger and death; but when he took command of the forces at Cambridge in 1775, no one knew the measure of his greatness.

A few of his officers had heard the whistle of bullets: Horatio Gates, Daniel Morgan, and Philip Schuyler had taken some part in the French War, but their knowledge of military science was limited. Most of his immediate subordinates came straight from civilian life. Benedict Arnold, who finally betrayed his countrymen, was a merchant at New Haven when the news of Lexington summoned him to arms; Nathanael Greene, a farmer and blacksmith in Rhode Island; Anthony Wayne, a farmer and surveyor in Pennsylvania; Francis Marion, a South Carolina planter whose military experience was limited to a brush with the Indians; while John Sullivan of New Hampshire was a lawyer more familiar with legal briefs than with the sword. Israel Putnam, a farmer from Connecticut, insisted on riding at the head of his men at Boston in his shirt sleeves with an old hat on his head as if he were still in the cornfield—much to the anguish of spruce young officers from the Middle and Southern states. Though all these men had natural ability and undoubted courage, their genius had not been tried in long campaigns.

Less experienced than their officers were the armed forces usually commanded by untutored captains. The regulars in the Continental line were never very numerous; those who survived the fortunes of the early battles and endured the severity of discipline, flogging and torture, were in the course of time developed into first-rate soldiers able to give a good account of themselves with rifle and bayonet. But even that branch of the army was in constant peril of demoralization. The pay of the men was nearly always sadly in arrears and, when it came, usually in the form of depreciated paper. Their support in materials was deficient. "Our hospital, or rather our House of Carnage, beggars all description," wrote General Wayne to his superior, "and shocks all humanity to visit; there is no medicine or regimen suitable for the sick, no beds or straw to lie on, no covering to keep them warm other than their own thin wretched clothing."

Nor did things seem to improve with time. "Our men are almost naked," declared General Greene in 1782, "for want of overalls and shirts and the greater part of the army barefoot." The plight of the cavalry was no better. Seeing a Virginia regiment ride by, an eyewitness recorded: "Some had one boot, some hoseless with their feet peering out of their shoes, others in breeches that put decency to blush, some in short jackets, others in long coats—all however with dragoon caps." Of course conditions were not always as bad but in the best of circumstances they were bad enough to try the soul of the most devoted patriot. The weaker vessels succumbed, deserting in shoals; neither flogging nor threats of the gallows stayed their flight.

The militiamen, both those associated with the regulars and the independents, gave their officers trouble without end. In more than one test, they proved to be unreliable under fire. At the battle of Long Island whole brigades, as Washington reported, "on the appearance of the enemy . . . ran away in the greatest confusion without firing a shot." After the disaster, he found them "dismayed, intractable, and impatient," angry at "almost every kind of restraint and government," and demoralizing to the rest of the army. "I am obliged to confess my want of confidence in the generality of the troops," he exclaimed in his report to the Congress. When called upon, the militia frequently would not turn out at all or it rallied with such sloth and indifference as to vex the soul of the Commander-in-chief.

At the end of 1776, after more than a year's experience, he complained to Congress that his volunteers "come in, you cannot tell how; go, you cannot tell when, and act, you cannot tell where, consume your provisions, exhaust your stores, and leave you at last at a critical moment." And yet, in the final year of the serious fighting, namely in 1781, more than half the thirty thousand men under arms were outside the ranks of the regulars. There were, of course, many exceptions to the rule but Washington had good reason for his lack of confidence in raw, undisciplined soldiers, often more interested in saving their skins and getting home than in the iron game of war, particularly if the fighting occurred beyond their own locality.

When, long afterward, a United States army officer, General Emory Upton, struck the military balance sheet of the revolutionary army, he had to report a story that shocked those Americans who had supposed that embattled farmers fresh from the plow or hearth overcame the weight of the British Empire. In his laconic record the facts stood out with impressive boldness. When the struggle began a great crowd of patriotic volunteers rushed to the scene of excitement, but as soon as they got a thorough taste of bloodshed and death, masses of them showed a remarkable affection for their homes and safety.

During the remainder of the war, it was only by the most heroic efforts that a force of thirty or forty thousand privates, out of a population of three million people, could be kept in the field. Long before the end, it became necessary to make generous grants of money and land for the purpose of enticing men into the service. One of the Southern states, for example, offered to each volunteer as a bounty "a healthy sound negro between the ages of ten and thirty years, or sixty pounds in gold and silver at the option of the soldier." Put to desperate straits in their search for men, the states enlisted free Negroes in substantial numbers and enrolled slaves who had been freed on condition that they enter the army; in 1778 it was officially estimated that there were on the average fifty-four Negroes in each of Washington's battalions.

Indeed, the states found it so hard in some cases to fill their quotas that they even employed fugitives from the British army to fight for them. "It gives me inexpressible concern," lamented Washington in a letter to Massachusetts, "to have repeated information from the best authority that the committees of the different towns and districts in your state hire deserters from General Burgoyne's army and employ them as substitutes to excuse the personal service of the inhabitants." All in all, it had to be said that the cause of American independence was won in the field by the invincible fortitude and unconquerable devotion of a relatively small body of soldiers and officers who kept the faith to the last hour. When victory crowned their long labors they were given sheaves of paper notes and turned loose upon the tender mercies of a chilly world. Nothing but the most persistent efforts of the soldiers and their friends eventually wrung from the negligent civilians in Congress a tardy recognition of the valorous services that had made a reality out of the paper Declaration of Independence.

§

Against the contentious governments which rose on the ruins of British dominion in America and against the small and badly supported forces of the American army was pitted the might of the greatest empire in the world. Unlike the Continental Congress, the British political system was powerfully organized, the Parliament at Westminster commanding the purses and allegiance of its subjects. The British navy, ruling the sea, could transport men and supplies across the ocean or along the coast with comparative ease. Moreover, King George, besides having at his disposal a substantial body of regular soldiers disciplined in the arts of war, could also summon to his aid a number of high officers who, if they were not supreme masters of strategy, had at least seen more serious fighting than Washington and his subordinates. How then was it possible for the thirteen states, weak and divided in councils, to effect their independence in the test of arms?

In the enumeration of the items that go to make up the answer, all historians agree in assigning first rank to the personality of Washington, commander of the weary and footsore Continental army that clung to the cause to the bitter end. Mythology, politics, and hero-worship did their utmost to make a solemn humbug of that amazing figure but his character finally survived the follies of his admirers and even the thrusts of his detractors made in their reaction to idolatrous adulation. Washington was a giant in stature, a tireless and methodical worker, a firm ruler yet without the ambitions of a Cæsar or a Cromwell, a soldier who faced hardships and death without flinching, a steadfast patriot, a hard-headed and practical director of affairs. Technicians have long disputed the skill of his strategy; some have ascribed the length of the war to his procrastinations; others have found him wanting in energy and decision; but all have agreed that he did the one thing essential to victory—he kept some kind of an army in the field in adversity as well as in prosperity and rallied about it the scattered and uncertain forces of a jealous and individualistic people.

Fortunately for Washington and for the cause of independence there were elements of weakness in the armed might of Great Britain. The English landed gentry and the mercantile classes that shouted for "strong measures in America" did not rush to the standard to fight the battles for which they had called. Long protected against invasion by means of the navy, the British people had not been nourished on the martial spirit. For generations, therefore, the Crown had found it imperative to employ brusque methods in order to secure enough men to fill the ranks of its regular army.

Theoretically it relied mainly on volunteers; practically the statutes and the common law sanctioned a disorderly kind of conscription, two expedients which yielded soldiers of about the same type. The volunteers were drawn chiefly from a miserable proletariat; while the men who were dragooned into the uniform by compulsion, drink, and violence came from what the English historian, Lecky, called "the dregs of the population." The laws pertaining to conscription specifically authorized the snatching of sturdy beggars, fortune tellers, idle, unknown, and suspected fellows, incorrigible rogues, poachers, and convicts. Criminals were pardoned "on condition of their enlistment in His Majesty's army," three British regiments being composed entirely of lawbreakers released from prison.

But all these methods failed to produce enough men for the task of saving America for the landlords and merchants of England. Six months after the battle of Lexington, the British government confessed that its efforts to fill the ranks had failed. Thereupon "the King went into the open market for troops on the continent," and hired from German princes several thousand fighting men—peasants dragged from their fields, mechanics snatched by crimps, and wretches raked up from the highways and byways.

In the wake of the British army followed the usual rear-guard of wastrels. Burgoyne's forces were accompanied by approximately two thousand women, some of them the wives of officers, three hundred "on the strength of the regiments," the remainder "fed and maintained by the soldiers themselves." Although there were good fighting men in the British ranks, although some of the criminal regiments distinguished themselves for valor, the most friendly historian of the British army had to admit that it was not inspired by an intense desire to overwhelm the American rebels at any cost of life and limb.

The British officers, of course, were drawn from a different class but for one reason or another those placed in command in America were lacking in skill or energy or both. Sir William Howe, on whom a large part of the burden fell, though a general of experience and distinction, suffered from many disabilities. He had strenuously opposed the coercive measures which brought on the war and he had publicly declared that he would not fight the Americans if called upon to take up arms. And yet, after making such professions, he had yielded to the appeal of his sovereign and accepted the command. Just why he was chosen for the important post in view of his attitude has never been made clear but it was hinted at the time that he owed the honor to his "grandmother's frailty," that is, to the fact that he was the grandson of George I through an illegitimate connection.

However that may be, Howe was a gay man of the world, loving ease, wine, gambling, and the society of ladies. "In Boston," as the Americans were fond of saying, "this British Anthony found his Cleopatra." Competent critics ascribed his final discomfiture to the "baneful influence" of "this illustrious courtesan." Enamored of indolence, drink, and high living, eager to effect peace by conciliation, Howe shrank from ruthless, swift, persistent, punitive measures. He proceeded on the theory that, by the continued possession of New York and Philadelphia and by the blockade of the coast, he could wear out the patriots. If the French had not intervened with their navy, he might have succeeded in his plan and been hailed as one of the far-seeing statesmen and warriors of his age. But events sank his fortunes beyond recovery. Sir Henry Clinton, who succeeded Howe as Commander-in-chief in 1778, if more active in war, was not much happier in the display of military talents; and of Lord Cornwallis, the less said the better.

Among the other factors favorable to the American cause were advantages due to the geographical situation. The British had to cross three thousand miles of water and then fight on a field that stretched almost a thousand miles north and south merging in the west into a wilderness. With the aid of the navy they could readily seize the ports and strike at the seaboard commerce; although they were definitely forced out of Boston in 1776—in spite of their costly victory at Bunker Hill—they occupied, in the course of the war, New York, Philadelphia, Charleston, and Savannah. All these places, except Philadelphia, they continued to hold until Cornwallis' surrender at Yorktown and their grip on that city was only broken by the menace of the French fleet.

When, however, they ventured far into the interior they met reverses or achieved only temporary victories. Burgoyne was compelled to surrender at Saratoga because he was surrounded, harassed, and cut off from his base of supplies. The British captured Charleston in 1780 and, after beating Gates at Camden, overran most of the state, but whenever they pushed far from their sea support, they were assailed and worried by militiamen. Cornwallis could ravage the coasts of North Carolina and Virginia almost at will; he could even strike far into the interior and give Greene a drubbing at Guilford, but he could not hold the hinterland over which he had raised his flag. As soon as his troops were withdrawn, revolutionary forces took possession of the abandoned territory. In short, the conquest of the American continent by arms called for continuous occupation and for regular government by military process

—a gigantic task to which the British forces dispatched to America were not equal.

In reckoning the elements that brought victory to the United States, the aid afforded by France must be given great weight. Money received from the treasury of Louis XVI paid for supplies that were desperately needed and buoyed up the sinking credit of the young republic. After the fashion of adventurous military men, French officers with the Marquis de la Fayette and Baron de Kalb in the lead joined Baron Steuben of Prussia, Count Pulaski, and Thaddeus Kosciusko of Poland, in helping to furnish inspiration and discipline for the raw recruits from American farms and shops. French regulars dispatched to American camps and fields, besides giving heart to the discouraged forces under Washington's command, rendered a good account of themselves in the business of warfare. At Yorktown, the last scene in the grand enterprise, the French soldiers, almost equal to the Americans in number, stood like a rock against the attempts of Cornwallis to break the cordon of besieging armies. On the sea, as on the land, the power of France, in spite of England's superior strength, counted heavily on the side of victory for America. French captains united with American naval commanders headed by Paul Jones and John Barry in preying upon British commerce, in cutting off ships bearing fresh troops and supplies to Yorktown, and in blockading Cornwallis on the side of the sea. Thus when the final blow was delivered—the blow which brought the British cabinet to terms—the honors were shared by the French and American arms. Once more the balance of power had been utilized, this time in ushering a young republic into the family of nations.

§

In trying to explain the outcome of the war for independence many writers, old and new, have laid great stress on the argument that the English nation showed little zeal for the fighting throughout the long contest. Some have gone so far as to represent the efforts to coerce the colonies by arms as the labors of an arrogant king and subservient ministers who enjoyed little support among the English people at large. Indeed, the Whig historians in England and their copyists in America have laid the main responsibility for the conduct of the war, as well as the measures that led to it, upon George III himself. Sir Thomas Erskine May, a Whig of the Whigs, in his Constitutional History of England issued in 1871, represented the King as managing Parliament during all the contest, distributing patronage, dictating domestic and foreign policies, directing debates, conferring titles and honors, and settling the fate of ministers, in the grand and arbitrary fashion of Louis the Great. "It is not without reason," he concluded, "that this deplorable contest was called the king's war." John Richard Green, describing the North administration in his Short History of the English People, published in 1874, declared that "George was in fact the minister through the twelve years of its existence, from 1770 till the close of the American war."

Many years later another English Liberal, Sir George Trevelyan, a nephew of the great Whig apologist, Macaulay, made a special effort to collect proofs that "the war itself was disliked by the nation." From the evidence assembled he showed that the members of the Commons from London were opposed to the war, that several officers in the British army and navy refused to take part in it, that an open opponent was almost elected to Parliament in Newcastle at a by-election held in 1779 while the conflict was raging, that British consols fell in price, and that there was a great deal of outspoken criticism of the government which would hardly have been tolerated if armed coercion of America had been popular.

Without attempting to traverse that general argument, it is appropriate to recall certain facts equally significant which point to a contrary conclusion. It is true that George

III displayed a lively interest in the proceedings of Parliament, that he indulged in high-flown language about his prerogatives, that he used his power to penalize men who opposed measures on which his heart was set, that he appointed his friends to high offices, and that on one occasion with a somewhat childish gesture he pointed to his sword and threatened to use it if a dissolution of Parliament was forced upon him. But the Whig historians who have raked over every word of the king's correspondence have found no passage showing that George III used his authority to force the enactment of a single coercive law directed against the American colonies.

In reality no such course on his part was necessary for, as the judicious Lecky shows, "all the measures of American coercion that preceded the Declaration of Independence were carried by enormous majorities in Parliament." And he might have added that all the war measures passed after that event were likewise carried by enormous majorities. As a matter of fact the one conspicuous use of royal power over Parliament during the conflict was in the case of Lord North's conciliatory resolution offering "the olive branch" to America in 1775: the proposal was so hotly resisted in the Commons that the king's influence was invoked to push it through. No doubt George III was outspoken in vindicating the course of his government. He once declared that he would accept no minister who favored stopping the war or granting American independence; but a year before he uttered these emphatic words he had actually offered to accept a ministry of peace and independence. So it would seem that the verdict of the Whig historians needs revising; the responsibility for the war, as far as England was concerned, rested mainly on the governing classes, not upon George III alone.

How far the English "nation" approved the prosecution of the war was never determined by anything like a referendum. The general election of 1774, held while the controversy with the colonies was raging, sustained the ministry of Lord North and gave him a thumping majority. Normally, in the course of the conflict, he could muster in the House of Commons about two hundred and sixty votes against the ninety arrayed on the side of the opposition. Beyond all question the landed gentry were solidly entrenched in support of the government and, if Edmund Burke is to be taken as an authority, the industrial and mercantile groups were almost equally stanch in their loyalty. "The mercantile interest," he lamented in January, 1775, "which ought to have supported with efficacy and power the opposition to the fatal cause of all this mischief, was pleaded against us, and we were obliged to stoop under the accumulated weight of all the interests of this kingdom."

Later in the same year Burke made again the same complaint: "The merchants are gone from us and from themselves. . . . The leading men among them are kept full fed with contracts and remittances and jobs of all descriptions and are indefatigable in their endeavours to keep the others quiet. . . . They all, or the greatest number of them, begin to sniff the cadaverous *haut goût* of lucrative war." Burke also found "the generality of the people of England" aligned with the ministers in the prosecution of the war—deluded no doubt by "the misrepresentations and arts of the ministry, the Court, and its abettors," but still loyal to the government in its hour of battle. Long after Burke, Lecky, on reviewing a huge mass of testimony, rendered a similar judgment: "It appears to me evident that in 1775 and 1776 the preponderating opinion, or at least the opinion of the most powerful and most intelligent classes in the community, on the American question was with the King and his ministers."

Certainly the bishops of the Established Church sustained the government and the Universities proclaimed their unquestioning fealty, while the lawyers as a class found historic and constitutional grounds for supporting the proceedings of the ministry. To give verbal expression to official policy, a large group of editors, clergymen, economists, historians, and men of letters devoted their talents, either through conviction or for a consideration, to fanning the temper of those determined to bring the revolutionists to the ground at all costs. Dr. Samuel Johnson, a royal pensioner, hurled against the Americans a weighty diatribe, Taxation no Tyranny; according to the faithful Boswell, "his inflammable corruption" burst into horrid fire whenever the Americans were mentioned; he breathed out threatenings and slaughter, calling them rascals, robbers, pirates, and exclaiming that he would burn and destroy them—this safely in a tavern corner in front of a roast and a pot of ale.

John Wesley, whose varied and dubious career in America had taught him the nature of American emotions, joined the ministerial hosts in condemning the Revolution and attributing colonial resistance to the writings of wicked Englishmen, such as Burke, who were encouraging rebellion and striving to overturn the perfect English constitution. With serene assurance, Wesley informed the Americans that they had no case at all, waving aside the issues of taxation and representation with a short fling: "You are the descendants of men who either had not votes or resigned them by migration. You have therefore exactly what your ancestors left you; not a vote in making laws nor in choosing legislators but the happiness of being protected by laws and the duty of obeying them." The great Edward Gibbon, then at work on his history of the Roman tragedy, though inclined at first to criticize Lord North's policy, after gazing a while upon the contemporary game with a stately amusement, went over to the support of the government, receiving in the going a sinecure of a thousand pounds a year, which helped to eke out his slender income and enabled him to enjoy fine wine while finishing off his immortal pages. Yet he was good natured about the business and, as he said, laughed and blushed at his own inconsequence when he heard himself lashed by Burke for drawing public money in return for nothing but mischief.

On the other side of the controversy in England there was, no doubt, a troublesome opposition that continued to bait the government until the close of the War for Independence. Among the leaders in this group Edmund Burke stood first in discernment, combining an accurate knowledge of American economy and American temper with a profound faith in the healing power of toleration and generosity—a faith that strangely contrasted with the scurrilous dogmatism manifest in his thunderous pamphlets on the French Revolution a little later. Unlike Chatham, who, as his sister often said, "knew nothing accurately except Spenser's Faery Queen," Burke had the statistics of American trade and the history of American progress always on the tip of his tongue. Repeatedly he pointed out in the House of Commons the magnitude of American commerce, the growth of population, the fierce spirit of liberty in the colonies, "the dissidence of dissent" in matters religious, the rise of lawyers "acute, inquisitive, dexterous, prompt in attack, ready in defense, full of resources," the growth of popular government through local assemblies, the feebleness of the Established Church, and the high proud spirit of Southern slaveholders. Having described the power of America, he told his countrymen that coercion would bring nothing but resistance and revolt.

The burden of Burke's grand argument flowed from reason and moderation. The relations of nations, he urged, must be considered in the same fashion as personal relations with respect to sensibilities; generosity will call forth generosity; human affairs cannot be twisted to fit any dogmatic scheme of black and white; great good can come out of liberty unbidden by tyrannical rule and systematic policy; the "unsuspecting confidence of the colonists" is the best hope of prosperous connections; refined, hairsplitting policy is always the parent of confusion; government must be based on barter and compromise; plain, good intention is a great force in the management of mankind; wise governments take into account the nature and circumstance of those who are governed; prudent negotiation is better than force; if force you must have, let it be for some defined object worthy of the sword, not the outcome of foolish arrogance; reverence for black letter learning, for precise constitutional rights, is reverence for a Serbonian bog where whole armies have sunk; "it is not what a lawyer tells me I may do; but what humanity, reason, and justice tell me I ought to do." In such noble words was expressed the serene, friendly, tolerant spirit in which Burke begged the British government to turn back upon its course to the old ways that were followed before Grenville and Townshend started their "systematic imperial policy."

Outside Parliament, Burke had some literary support. David Hume, philosopher and historian, objected to "mauling the poor unfortunate Americans in the other hemisphere." At the beginning of the conflict, Catherine Macaulay, sister of the mayor of London and a historical writer, then the vogue in England and the subject of "flattering attentions" in Paris, lauded the American cause and sent a letter to Washington encouraging him in the course he had chosen. In another quarter, the celebrated Dr. Richard Price, nonconformist clergyman, whose sermon on constitutional reform later called forth Burke's Reflections on the French Revolution, defended the Americans in a powerful tract that quickly passed through eight editions and made a profound impression on the British public, especially on the dissenting elements.

In the houses of Parliament, Burke's attacks on ministerial policies were applauded by a small but distinguished body of Whigs. Whether their contrariety of opinion flowed principally from resentment at exclusion from office or from a confirmed belief in the injustice of war on America, it was impossible to determine. Indeed, there was no unanimity of doctrine among them. Chatham, for example, declared that Parliament had no constitutional right to impose internal taxes on the colonies and favored the repeal of the coercive measures; but he was dead set against granting independence after the armed conflict had begun. Rockingham, on the other hand, upheld with decided vigor the right of Parliament to tax, assailing the measures of Lord North on grounds of expediency.

Great as it was intrinsically, the confusion of the Whigs was increased by the demands of the colonists. Committed by a long tradition to the creed that the power of the Crown should be reduced and the authority of the legislature exalted, the Whigs found themselves invited by American agitators to condemn acts of Parliament in the name of royal prerogative. Not only that, they were called upon by Benjamin Franklin to treat parliamentary interference with America as sheer usurpation—an invasion of the king's undoubted sphere of power—and then they were asked by the authors of the Declaration of Independence to lay the blame for the disaster on George III.

Although a few Whigs made a clean cut through this legal verbiage by discarding the niceties of logic and advocating peace with America on terms of independence, the majority employed it chiefly with reference to the tactics of defeating the ministry and restoring their party to its old control over government and patronage. Of this, there was indisputable proof. In 1778, in the midst of the war, George III was ready to give up; in his name the Whigs were offered "the majority in a new cabinet under Lord Weymouth, on the basis of a withdrawal of the troops from America and a vigorous prosecution of the war with France."

Then and there the Whigs could have ended the armed conflict with America. Fox begged them to do it but they refused, thus taking on their own heads responsibility for the war which they denounced, allowing it to go on to the conclusion so bitter for England. On no simple theory of devotion to American principles, therefore, could the course of Whig politics during the American Revolution be explained, and yet the generous peace of 1783 was in the main their work. In the end it was they who drove Lord North from office, urged George III to yield to necessity, and closed the unhappy quarrel by accepting the United States as one of the free nations of the earth.

§

The negotiation of the treaty of peace, when the moment came, was a delicate task for Franklin and his colleagues at Paris, as well as for the British government. Under instructions from the Congress and the terms of the French alliance, the American agents were bound to consult Louis XVI's ministers at every stage of the transaction. Had nothing intervened, Franklin, easy-going and fond of the French, might have obeyed to the letter the canons of strict propriety, but John Jay, fresh from the intrigues of Madrid, and John Adams, who had learned new tactics at The Hague, were too canny for the diplomacy of Versailles. They knew that France and Spain had not shed blood and spent treasure merely to erect a powerful republic in the western hemisphere. It was no dark mystery that France, still cherishing imperial dreams, hoped to recover the Mississippi Valley and enlarge her fishing rights in western waters. It was no secret that Spain also had irons in the fire. In any event, both powers agreed that the Americans should be satisfied with the seaboard and were prepared to block American designs upon the hinterland.

Called upon to favor the United States, on the one hand, or the French and Spanish, on the other, the British ministry chose to patronize the rebellious provinces. Moreover, the new colonial secretary in London sincerely desired "reconciliation with America on the noblest terms and by the noblest means." Quick to grasp the realities of the problem thus presented, the American commissioners artfully disregarded the decorum of the occasion. Besides holding secret conversations with the British agent, they actually agreed upon the general terms of peace before they told the French foreign minister about their operations. For this furtive conduct, Louis XVI's minister, Vergennes, on hearing the news at last, reproached Franklin, only to receive from the aged gentleman the suave reply that, although the Americans had been guilty of bad manners, they hoped that the great work would not be ruined by "a single indiscretion." Doubtless the French were angry; perhaps, technically, they had a right to be; but those who practiced the arts of diplomacy in those days were usually prepared to accept the rules of the game and the hazards of the combat.

In the end, the shrewd maneuvers of the American commissioners and the liberality of the English cabinet made the general settlement at Paris in 1783 a triumph for the United States. Independence was specifically recognized by the mother country; and the coveted territory west to the Mississippi, north to Canada, and south to the Floridas was acknowledged as the rightful heritage of the young republic. Spain won Minorca and the Floridas but not Gibraltar. For her sacrifices in blood and treasure, France gained practically nothing in territory and commerce, but had the satisfaction of seeing the British Empire dismembered and the balance of power readjusted. In spite of her defeat in America, England retained Canada, Newfoundland, and her islands in the West Indies, made gains in India, and held her supremacy on the sea.

Clear as it was in bold outline, the grand adjustment at Paris left many issues clouded. Not unnaturally, the Tories demanded a return of their sequestered estates and English merchants insisted on the payment of debts owed by American citizens. These were sore points with the patriots and nothing but a compromise was possible. In its final form, the treaty provided that the Congress should advise the states to restore the property they had confiscated and stipulated that no lawful impediment should be placed in the way of collecting just debts—smooth promises difficult to fulfill. In a counter-claim, the Americans demanded a restoration of all goods and slaves seized by the English army during the war, and in the terms of the treaty their exactions were conceded. Here, too, was a pledge easier to make than to discharge; for some of the English were horrified at the idea of sending human beings back to bondage and the recovery of the other property claimed by the patriots proved to be impossible in practice. For good measure, the question of fishing rights off the coast offered irritating problems; issues which vexed the two countries for more than a hundred years.

Many a patriot grumbled when he heard that the treaty promised a return of Tory property and a payment of debts but all such laments were lost in the universal rejoicing that greeted the close of the war. Nothing dampened the ardor of the demonstration. Orators exhausted their forensic powers in portraying the benefits of independence and in framing taunts to the despotisms of the Old World. One preacher, climbing an Alpine peak, summoned his countrymen to look upon the fair opportunity now presented "for converting this immense northern continent into a seat of knowledge and freedom, of agriculture and commerce, of useful arts and manufactures, of Christian piety and virtue; and thus making it an inviting and comfortable abode for many millions of the human species; an asylum for the injured and oppressed in all parts of the globe; the delight of God and good men; the joy and pride of the whole earth; soaring on the wings of literature, wealth, population, religion, virtue, and everything that is excellent and happy to a greater height of perfection and glory than the world has ever yet seen!"

§

The fair prophecy of the preacher, to be fulfilled in a surprising measure in the long reach of time, seemed at the moment to rest on a slender basis. The "America" to which the orator paid tribute was only in the process of making. Politically, it consisted of thirteen independent states, each jealous of its rights, fiercely claiming the loyalty of its citizens, and dominated by ambitious men. The union that bound them together, such as it was, had no guarantee of permanence in the affections of the people. It was new. It had been a product of necessity, long debate, and grudging consent. The idea of an enduring association, raised in the Continental Congress many months before the Declaration of Independence, was not given a concrete form in the Articles of Confederation until more than a year after that event. The autumn of 1777 was far advanced when the Congress, after tedious argument, finally agreed on the document and sent it to the states for ratification. Though all the local legislatures were aware that their common fate seemed to hang upon prompt and united action, a long time passed before the last of them signed and sealed the instrument of federation. The year that saw the surrender of Cornwallis at Yorktown had opened when Maryland, the remaining laggard, gave her approval. It was March 1, 1781, that thundering guns from ships of war in the Delaware announced that the Union "begun by necessity" had been "indissolubly cemented."

The Articles of Confederation, wrung from reluctant delegates in the Congress and from still more reluctant states, in fact made little difference in the system which had been established for revolutionary purposes. It did not materially alter the structure or powers of the continental government created provisionally in 1774. Management of the general interests of the United States was still vested, under the Articles, as before, in a Congress composed of delegates from each state, appointed as the legislature might direct, subject to recall at any time, and paid from the local treasury.

If this system seemed strangely inadequate to the requirements of a potential nation, it corresponded with marked fidelity to the ideas of the radicals who had engineered the Revolution. In their several colonies, they had revolted against the financial, commercial, and political control exercised by the government of Great Britain; by war they had destroyed deliberately that dominion; and they wanted no strong and effective substitute in the form of a central government—even one controlled by Americans. In this sense a fundamental transformation had been wrought in the higher ranges of continental politics.

Within each state, no less than in external relations, the Revolution started a dislocation of authority—a phase of the eventful years which the historians, too long concentrating on spectacular episodes, have just begun to appreciate. The shifts and cracks in the social structure produced by the cataclysm were not all immediately evident; half a century passed before the leveling democracy proclaimed in Jefferson's Declaration of Independence came flooding into power. But still the states of the confederation differed as much from the colonial provinces of Governor Shirley's time as the France of Louis Philippe, hero of the green umbrella, did from the régime of Louis XV. Just as the French Revolution sent émigrés fleeing into Germany and England, so the American Revolution drove out about one hundred thousand high Tories of the old school. By breaking the grip of English economic and political adventurers on the spoils of America, it brought into power new men with new principles and standards of conduct.

It is true that, in the severe and sometimes savage contests between the conservative and radical supporters of the Revolution, the former were generally the victors for the moment and were able to write large their views of economic rights in the first state constitutions. Broadly speaking, only taxpayers or property owners were given the ballot as in colonial times and only men of substantial wealth were made eligible to public office. But in many cases the qualifications were lowered and the structure of the old social system seriously undermined.

Above all, the spirit of domestic politics, especially in the royal provinces, was distinctly altered by the sudden removal of the British ruling class—a class accustomed to a barbarous criminal code, a narrow and intolerant university system, a government conceived as a huge aggregation of jobs and privileges, a contempt for men and women who toiled in field and shop, a denial of education to the masses, an Established religion forced alike on Dissenters and Catholics, a dominion of squire and parson in counties and villages, callous brutality in army and navy, a scheme of primogeniture buttressing the rule of the landed gentry, a swarm of hungry placemen offering sycophancy to the king in exchange for offices, sinecures, and pensions, and a constitution of church and state so ordered as to fasten upon the masses this immense pile of pride and plunder. From the weight of this mountain the American revolutionists delivered the colonial subjects of the British Crown. Within a decade or two after that emancipation they accomplished reforms in law and policy which required a hundred years or more of persistent agitation to effect in the mother country—reforms which gave to the statesmen who led in the agitation their title to immortality in English history.

Naturally the American Revolution, a movement carried to its bitter end by the bayonets of fighting farmers, even though it was started by protesting merchants and rioting mechanics, wrought a far-reaching transformation in the land system that had been developed under British inspiration and control. With engaging conciseness, these changes have been summarized in J. Franklin Jameson's admirable little book on The American Revolution Considered as a Social Movement. First of all, royal limitations on the seizure and enjoyment of vacant lands—notably the prohibition upon the free settlement of regions beyond the Alleghenies contained in the proclamation of 1763—were swept away; and at the same time the "vast domains of the Crown" were vested in the hands of the state legislatures to be dedicated to the uses of their constituents.

Secondly, the quitrents paid to the king and to proprietary families, the Penns and the Baltimores, by farmers and planters according to their acreage were simply abolished, relieving Americans of an annual charge approximating a hundred thousand dollars a year. Thirdly, the rule and the practice of reserving for the royal navy white pine trees suitable for masts were abrogated without ceremony, releasing landowners from an irksome restriction. In the fourth place, there was a smashing confiscation of Tory estates, including Sir William Pepperell's Maine holdings extending thirty miles along the coast, the Phillipse heritage in New York embracing about three hundred square miles, the property of the Penn family worth in round numbers five million dollars, and the Fairfax estate in Virginia stretching out like a province. All in all, the Tories reckoned their losses at no less than forty million dollars and the British Parliament, after scaling their demands to the minimum, granted the claimants fifteen million dollars by way of compensation.

In harmony with their principles, the Revolutionists who made this huge sequestration of property distributed the land by sales in small lots on generous terms to enterprising farmers. The principality of Roger Morris in New York, for example, was divided into no less than two hundred and fifty parcels, while a still larger number of farms was created out of the confiscated holdings of James De Lancey.

Finally, among the effects of the Revolution on agricultural economy, must be reckoned the abolition of the system of entails and primogeniture. Whereas it took a century of debate and then the corroding taxes of a World War to drive a wedge into the concentrated land monopoly of England, the American Revolutionists brought many an ancient structure to earth by swift and telling blows. Three months after he penned the Declaration of Independence, Jefferson opened a war on the entailed estates of the Old Dominion, to the horror of the best people; and before the lapse of a year he pushed through the legislature an act which accomplished his radical design, releasing from entail "at least half, and possibly three-quarters of the entire 'seated' area of Virginia." Within ten years "every state had abolished entails excepting two, and those were two in which entails were rare. In fifteen years every state, without exception, abolished primogeniture"—all save four placing daughters on an equality with sons in the distribution of landed inheritances.

Considered relatively, therefore, the destruction of landed privilege in America by the forces unchained in the War for Independence was perhaps as great and as significant as the change wrought in the economic status of the clergy and nobility during the holocaust of the French Revolution. As in France country lawyers and newly rich merchants swarmed over the seats of the once proud aristocracy, so in the United States during and after the cataclysm a host of groundlings fresh from the plow and counting house surged over the domains of the Jessups, De Lanceys, and Morrises. When members of the best families of France turned to tutoring and translating in London for a livelihood or to teaching dancing and manners in America, in the days of Danton, Marat, and Robespierre, they found ladies and gentlemen who sighed for good old colonial days ready to join them in cursing the rights of man.

The clergy as well as the landed gentry felt the shocks of the American Revolution. When the crisis opened, nine of the thirteen colonies had established churches. In New Hampshire, Massachusetts, and Connecticut it was the Congregationalists that enjoyed this legal privilege, while in Virginia, Maryland, New York, the Carolinas, and Georgia it was the Episcopalians who claimed a monopoly on religion supported by taxes. Before the echoes of Lexington and Concord had died away, an attack on ecclesiastical establishments was launched, and in five of the states where the Anglican clergy possessed privileges and immunities under the law the dissenters, outnumbering their opponents, were quickly victorious. In Virginia, however, where the Anglican party was strong, and in New England, where the Congregationalists enjoyed a supremacy, every clerical redoubt was stubbornly defended.

It took a struggle of more than half a century in the mother country to win political equality for Catholics and Dissenters, and to sweep away tithes for the support of an official religion. The twentieth century opened before France, going beyond England in her evolution, could put asunder Church and State. Only ten years sufficed to carry through the legislature Jefferson's "Statute of Virginia for Religious Freedom," and before the nineteenth century had far advanced, the Congregationalists were finally disestablished—in New Hampshire in 1817, in Connecticut the following year, and in Massachusetts in 1833. So before Jefferson's death Episcopalians could enjoy in Connecticut liberties they had once withheld in Virginia.

In law as in religion the light of reason was being turned on ancient customs. During this stirring period of intellectual and spiritual awakening, the British government was making its penal code more and more savage; when George III came to the throne in 1760 there were about one hundred and sixty offenses for which men, women, and children were put to death; before the end of his reign nearly one hundred new offenses were added to this appalling list.

Although the American colonists had never been so sweeping in their vengeful passions as English lawmakers, they too had adopted penal codes of shocking brutality—codes that loomed black and ominous against the new faith in the common run of mankind. Deeply moved by this incongruity, the impetuous Jefferson, to whom at least his Declaration was no mere mass of glittering generalities, hastened away from Philadelphia soon after independence to start the revolution in the legal system of Virginia. On his arrival he announced that the law must be reformed root and branch "with a single eye to reason and the good of those for whose government it was framed," so alarming the bench and bar by his rashness that it took him twenty years to gain his principal points. In the other states a similar campaign was waged against the barbarities of the statute books, now swiftly, now tardily casting into oblivion great fragments of the cruel heritage. Even at the worst the emancipated colonists were in most matters respecting criminal legislation half a century ahead of the mother country.

Indeed, in nearly every branch of enlightened activity, in every sphere of liberal thought, the American Revolution marked the opening of a new humane epoch. Slavery, of course, afforded a glaring contrast to the grand doctrines of the Revolution, but still it must be noted that Jefferson and his friends were painfully aware of the anachronism; that Virginia prohibited the slave trade in 1778—a measure which the British Crown had vetoed twenty years before; that a movement for the abolition of slavery appeared among the new social forces of the age; and that it was the lofty doctrines of the Revolution which were invoked by Lincoln when in the fullness of time chattel bondage was to be finally broken. If a balance sheet is struck and the rhetoric of the Fourth of July celebrations is discounted, if the externals of the conflict are given a proper perspective in the background, then it is seen that the American Revolution was more than a war on England. It was in truth an economic, social, and intellectual transformation of prime significance—the first of those modern world-shaking reconstructions in which mankind has sought to cut and fashion the tough and stubborn web of fact to fit the pattern of its dreams.

CHAPTER VII

Populism and Reaction

NEARLY nine years after the battle of Lexington, to be exact, on December 4, 1783, General Washington bade farewell to his officers in the great room of Fraunces' Tavern in New York City. When the simple but moving ceremony was over, the Commander marched down the streets through files of soldiers and throngs of civilians to the barge at Whitehall Ferry that was to bear him across the Hudson on his way home to Mount Vernon. Cannon boomed, bells in the church steeples clashed, crowds cheered as the tall Virginia gentleman stood in the boat, bared his gray head, and bowed his final acknowledgments.

When his familiar form faded away on the Jersey shore, the multitudes in the city turned to celebrating the triumph of the Revolution. The last of the British soldiers had disappeared down the bay a few days before and the last symbols of British dominion, except in the distant frontier forts, had passed as in a dream. America was now an independent republic. Those who had assumed leadership in this stirring drama found themselves in a course far beyond all the headlands they had seen in the fateful hours when the quarrel with the mother country was impending. Undoubtedly a few bold thinkers had early envisaged independence as the outcome of revolt but their little designs had not encompassed its full import. Thus do the achievements of people outrun their conscious purposes.

§

In the march of events, profound social and political changes had come to pass. Seven years of war, waged by an improvised Continental Congress without traditions, authority or strength, had thrown all economic functions into confusion and disorganized society in every direction. In colonial times the prosperity of the people depended largely upon the exchange of raw materials for manufactured products in British markets, a traffic that supplied American farmers and artisans with most of the implements and tools used in agriculture and industry, enriched American merchants, brought a steady stream of British capital to these shores, and furnished nearly all the refinements for the homes of the upper classes. This commerce the outbreak of the Revolution ruined—except for the smuggling and trading with the enemy that went on in spite of the war—and the British blockade prevented the opening of new channels sufficient to take its place.

Moreover, the armed struggle itself disrupted over wide areas the ordinary processes of agriculture and industry upon which the people relied for their living, put an intolerable drain upon the slender resources of the backwoods civilization, destroyed by fire and pillage properties of immense value, afforded the occasion for a serious confiscation and transfer of estates, tore cities and communities asunder, introduced varied and fluctuating currencies which made the orderly transaction of business impossible, and delayed the payments of debts while depreciating the medium for discharging them. At the same time it proscribed and drove from the country a large part of the governing class —British executives, judges, merchants, capitalists, and owners of property in general who remained loyal to the Crown.

In many, if not all, respects, the immediate outcome of the Revolution, radical as it was, displayed the deeper purposes of the intransigent leaders who engineered it, especially the dynamic personalities of the second social rank nearest the fighting populace; for they wanted to rid themselves entirely of British political, economic, and judicial interference. When the conflict opened, the thirteen colonies were mere provinces of the British empire under whose dominion they had been forbidden to emit bills of credit, to make paper money legal tender in the payment of debts, and to restrain foreign and intercolonial commerce. Under British authority their industry and trade had been regulated in the interest of British merchants and manufacturers, subduing American agriculture to the rules prescribed by the capitalist process in London. Under the same authority, control over the western lands had been wrested from the grip of American pioneers and politicians and vested in Crown officials. To make secure the economic sovereignty, a highly centralized scheme of judicial and administrative supremacy held the legislatures of the colonies strictly within the bounds of business propriety. In short, while the colonists had been gaining strength in local government, their powers had been limited and the higher functions of diplomacy, defence, and ultimate social control had rested in British hands.

This was the system which the Revolutionists overthrew, pulling down the elaborate superstructure and making the local legislatures, in which farmers had the majorities, supreme over all things. No Crown, no royal governor, no board of trade in London, no superior judge could now defeat the desires of agrarians. They had demanded autonomy; they achieved independence.

Having rid themselves of a great, centralized political

and economic machine, the radical leaders realized their ideal in a loose association of sovereign states; in the Articles of Confederation, their grand ideals were fairly mirrored. The sole organ of government set up by that instrument was a Congress composed of delegates from each state, elected by the legislatures, and paid from the state treasury, if paid at all. Enjoying no independent and inherent powers drawn directly from the people, this government was the creature of the states and the victim of the factional disputes that filled the local theaters of politics. It was in effect little more than a council of diplomatic agents engaged in promoting thirteen separate interests, without authority to interfere with the economic concerns of any. In determining all vital questions, the states were equal: each had one vote; Delaware was as powerful as Virginia, Rhode Island, the peer of Massachusetts.

As if to emphasize the repudiation of the British Crown, no provision was made for a President to symbolize national unity, to concentrate interest and affection, indeed to enforce the laws. It is true the Congress could select an executive to represent the Confederation when it was not in session but that executive was a committee of thirteen— one member from each state—and when an attempt was made to function through this agency, the result was not far from the ludicrous.

In remembrance perhaps of British judicial control, now broken by revolution, the framers of the Articles erected no system of national courts to which the citizens could appeal for the protection of their rights. The structure of the federal government, shaped as it was, managed by committees of the Congress functioning through independent departments, worked for the diffusion of authority among many men jealous of one another, subject to the orders and recall of contending states, restrained by no leadership, and endowed with no power to override the will of state legislatures, governors, and courts after the fashion of British administration in provincial days.

The functions essential to any government of substance—the powers which the colonists had resisted when exercised by the British Crown and Parliament—were, naturally enough, withheld from the Congress which the revolutionists created under the Articles of Confederation. As a matter of course, the solemn duty of defending the country was laid upon it: it could declare war, raise an army, and provide a navy; but it could not draft a single soldier or sailor; it could only ask the states to supply quotas of men according to a system of apportionment. Even if the Congress could have raised the men by this process, it could never have been sure of the materials necessary to support them.

It had power, no doubt, to appropriate money but no authority to levy upon the strong box or economic resources of any citizen. For every penny that went into the common treasury, it had to ask the local legislatures. When it determined the amount of money needed for any fiscal period or for any specific purpose, it apportioned the total among the thirteen states on the basis of the value of the lands and improvements in each, leaving the legislatures free to decide how the quotas assigned were to be met—or not met at all, according to the mood of the party in control at the time. In fact, therefore, the Congress had to assume the rôle of a beggar, hat in hand, at the capitals of the several commonwealths. In practice it experienced what beggars usually do: more rebuffs than pleasant receptions.

If such was the weakness of the Confederation with respect to those prime considerations, military power and money, it is not strange to find the same incompetence in other spheres. Conforming to colonial agrarian traditions, the Congress was given no control over currency and banking, such as the government of Great Britain had exercised in America before independence; on the contrary, these vital economic functions were left to the discretion of the individual states. Nor could the Congress regulate trade among the states or with other countries; England had done too much of that.

Although it could make treaties with foreign countries affecting commercial matters, the Congress had no power to enforce its agreements against the will of recalcitrant states—in fact, no control over the latter in any imporant respect. Almost entirely dependent upon them for the enforcement of its laws and orders, it could not exact obedience from them, punish them by pecuniary penalties, suspend their privileges, or use military force against them. Neither could it intervene in the domestic affairs of a state even if a civil war threatened the overthrow of local government and the dissolution of economic bonds.

To put the case concisely, the states were, for domestic purposes, sovereign, while the Congress presented the "extraordinary spectacle of a government destitute of even a shadow of a constitutional power to enforce the execution of its own laws." The radical leaders of the Revolution had not thrown off British agencies of economic coercion for the mere purpose of substituting another centralized system of legislative, executive, and judicial control.

§

To the eight years of government under these Articles of Confederation, the term "critical period" has been applied and it has become the fashion to draw a doleful picture of the age, to portray the country sweeping toward an abyss from which it was rescued in the nick of time by the heroic framers of the Constitution. Yet an analysis of the data upon which that view is built raises the specter of skepticism. The chief sources of information bearing on this thesis are the assertions and lamentations of but one faction in the great dispute and they must, therefore, be approached with the same spirit of prudence as Whig editorials on Andrew Jackson or Republican essays on Woodrow Wilson.

Undoubtedly the period that followed the close of the Revolutionary War was one of dissolution and reconstruction; that is the story of every great social dislocation. Still there is much evidence to show that the country was in many respects steadily recovering order and prosperity even under the despised Articles of Confederation. If seven of the thirteen states made hazardous experiments with paper money, six clung to more practical methods and two or three of those that had embarked on unlimited inflation showed signs of turning back on their course. While a few states displayed a heartless negligence in paying their revolutionary debts, others gave serious attention to the matter. Though the efforts of the Congress to secure larger powers over taxation and commerce were defeated, an agreement on some control over foreign trade was almost in sight when the constitutional convention was summoned by men impatient with delay. The very fact that the convention could be assembled was in itself evidence of a changing spirit in the country.

On the whole, the economic condition of the country seemed to be improving. No doubt shipping in New England and manufacturing in general suffered from the conflicting tariff policies, domestic and foreign, which followed the war, but, at the opening of 1787, Benjamin Franklin declared that the prosperity of the nation was so great as to call for thanksgiving. According to his judgment, the market reports then showed that the farmers were never better paid for their produce, that farm lands were continually rising in value, and that in no part of Europe were the laboring poor in such a fortunate state. Admitting that there were economic grievances in some quarters, Franklin expressed a conviction that the country at large was in a sound condition.

Nearly a hundred years after Franklin's time a learned, if controversial, historian, Henry B. Dawson, on the basis of minute researches, made out a very good argument to the effect that the "chaos" of the "critical period" was largely a figment of political imagination. Whatever the verdict on this point may be, the difficulty with which the Constitution was "wrung" from a reluctant people and the existence of a large body of voters aggressively opposed to the change will put the prudent inquirer on his guard against the easy assumption that the entire country was seized with a poignant sense of impending calamity.

Nevertheless, when the best possible case is made for the critical period, there remain standing in the record of those years certain impressive facts that cannot be denied or explained away. Beyond all question the financiers had grounds for complaint. Though the principal of the continental debt was slightly reduced under the confederation, the arrears of interest increased nearly fourfold and the unpaid interest on the foreign obligations piled steadily higher. In an equally chaotic condition were the current finances. The Congress in due course made requisitions on the states to pay its bills, but it was fortunate if it received in any year one-fourth of the amount demanded, and during the last fourteen months of its life less than half a million in paper money was paid into the treasury—not enough to meet the interest on the foreign debt alone.

Hence all who held claims against the confederacy had sufficient cause for discontent. Holders of government bonds, both original subscribers who had made sacrifices and speculators who had bought up depreciated paper by the ream, had good reasons for desiring a change in the existing form of government. To them were added the soldiers of the late revolutionary army, especially the officers whose bonus of full pay for five years still remained in the form of paper promises.

Industry and commerce as well as government finances were in a state of depression. When peace came and the pent-up flood of British goods burst in upon the local market, greatly to the joy of the farmers and planters, American manufacturers, who had built up enterprises of no little importance during the suspension of British trade, found their monopoly of domestic business rudely broken. Nothing but a protective tariff, they thought, could save them from ruin. In the same category of the distressed were American shipowners and factors engaged in foreign trade, especially the ubiquitous Yankees who now suffered from discriminations as aliens in the ports of the British empire. In spite of heroic efforts they could not effect a return to prosperity; nor was there any sign of relief in sight as long as the Congress under the Articles of Confederation possessed no power to enact retaliatory measures calculated to bring foreign countries to terms.

In an equally unhappy position were the domestic merchants. They had at hand no national currency uniform in value through the length and breadth of the land—nothing but a curious collection of coins uncertain in weight, shaven by clippers, debased by counterfeiters, and paper notes fluctuating as new issues streamed from the press. Worse than the monetary system were the impediments in the way of interstate commerce. Under local influences legislatures put tariffs on goods coming in from neighboring states just as on foreign imports, waged commercial wars of retaliation on one another, raised and lowered rates as factional disputes oscillated, reaching such a point in New York that duties were levied on firewood from Connecticut and cabbages from New Jersey.

If a merchant surmounted the obstacles placed in his way by anarchy in the currency and confusion in tariff schedules and succeeded in building up an interstate business, he never could be sure of collections, for he was always at the mercy of local courts and juries—agencies that were seldom tender in dealing with the claims and rights of distant creditors as against the clamors of their immediate neighbors. While the Articles of Confederation lasted there was no hope of breaching such invincible barriers to the smooth and easy transaction of interstate business.

Other economic groups likewise had powerful motives for desiring a change in the form of government. Money lenders who held outstanding notes and mortgages objected to receiving in payment paper bills emitted by the treasuries of the agrarian states and demanded a limitation on their right to issue such legal tenders. In a plight no less distressing were the British creditors and Americans to whom British claims had been transferred. Checked by the hostility of state legislatures and local courts, they were usually unable to collect debts solemnly recognized by the treaty of peace and they could hope for no adequate settlement, especially in the South, while the confederation endured. Loyalists who had lost property during the Revolution suffered similar handicaps in the presence of local judges and jurors. Finally, the officers and soldiers, who held land warrants issued to them in return for their war services, and capitalists engaged in western land speculation could count on no realization of their claims until there was a national army strong enough to suppress the hostile Indians on the frontier.

In short, the financial, creditor, commercial, and speculating classes in the new confederate republic were harassed during the critical period just as such classes had been harassed by rebellious patriots on the eve of the Revolution. From every point of view, as they saw the matter, they had valid reasons for wanting to establish under their own auspices on American soil a system of centralized political, judicial, and economic control similar in character to that formerly exercised by Great Britain. They wanted debts paid, a sound currency established, commerce regulated, paper money struck down, and western lands properly distributed; they desired these things quite as much as the governing classes of England had desired them in colonial times. No more than the stoutest Tory of London or Boston did they relish agrarian politics; commerce simply could not thrive in that economic atmosphere. Those who sponsored business enterprise accordingly demanded new central organs of power and control and fresh restraints on the leveling tendencies of local legislatures generally dominated by farmers.

If they objected to the national system of government, they could with equal sanction protest against the administration of the respective states. Indeed, Massachusetts gave them a shock which presaged a swing to the extreme revolutionary left. In that commonwealth a conservative party of merchants, shippers, and money lenders had managed by a hard won battle to secure in 1780 a local constitution which gave their property special defenses in the suffrage, in the composition of the Senate, and in the qualifications of office holders administering the law. Heavy taxes were then levied to pay the revolutionary debt of the state, a large part of which had passed into the hands of speculators. And just when this burden fell on the people, private creditors in their haste to collect outstanding accounts deluged the local courts with lawsuits and foreclosures of farm mortgages.

The answer to this economic pressure was a populist movement led by a former soldier of the Revolution, Daniel Shays. Inflamed by new revolutionary appeals, resurgent agrarians now proposed to scale down the state debt, strike from the constitution the special privileges enjoyed by property, issue paper money, and generally ease the position of debtors and the laboring poor in town and country. Indeed, there were dark hints that the soldiers who had fought for independence would insist that property owners must sacrifice their goods for the cause. In various guises the agitation continued until in 1786 it culminated in an armed uprising known as Shays' Rebellion.

Although the insurrection was crushed, it sent alarms throughout the higher social orders of America. If Jefferson was unmoved because he thought that a little bloodshed was occasionally necessary to keep alive the spirit of agrarian liberty, Washington was thoroughly frightened. On hearing the news, he redoubled his efforts to obtain a stronger constitution—one that would afford national aid in suppressing such local disturbances. There was even talk of a counter-revolution, a military dictatorship supported by funds from merchants.

In foreign relations there were perils as menacing as the difficulties of domestic administration. With respect to Great Britain, many perplexing questions arising out of the treaty of peace remained unsolved and new adjustments of commercial relations had to be made. And not unnaturally the mother country was somewhat ungracious to her wayward child in all such matters. When John Adams, as minister of the United States, appeared at the Court of the King he met a frosty reception, made several degrees chillier by constant reminders that the government he represented was really impotent. If he hinted that British soldiers should be withdrawn from the western part of the United States or that the ports of the British West Indies should be opened once more to American ships on favorable terms, he was reminded that his fellow countrymen had not paid the debts due British merchants and he was shown acts of Parliament which, not without reason, treated Americans as aliens.

Nearer home, foreign relations presented questions calling for more judgment and power in solution than the Congress of the United States showed any inclination to provide. Though nominally isolated in the New World, the confederacy was bounded on the landward side by immense territories belonging to England and Spain, both countries that had been contending for mastery in America for two hundred years. At any moment a new storm might break, involving the weak republic at the very threshold of its career. Even the most case-hardened agrarians could not avoid seeing the possibility of renewed strife among the European powers—which came in 1793—the dangers of foreign intervention in domestic politics, and the perils of disruptive rivalry among the states. If they were indifferent to the demands of public creditors, financiers, and merchants clamoring for relief, they could not ignore the menaces from foreign quarters.

§

Such were the circumstances in which rose and flourished a movement for a drastic revision of the Articles of Confederation. In recognition of the gathering forces, the Congress appealed again and again to the states, asking them to approve an amendment giving it the power to lay and collect certain import duties for the purpose of meeting public obligations. But all such appeals were futile: the approval of every state was necessary to the slightest change and there was always at least one of them unwilling to surrender that "precious jewel of sovereignty," control over its purse.

Finding the efforts of the Congress without avail, leading citizens then called for an economic and political revolution. Indeed, in 1780—even before the adoption of the Articles of Confederation—Alexander Hamilton, impressed by shortcomings of the document, had proposed that a constitutional convention be assembled and a better charter of government framed. Three years afterward, Washington, in his famous Circular Letter to the governors of the states, laid stress upon the need for a supreme central power to regulate the general concerns of the confederation. Already disturbed by the rumblings soon to break out in Shays' Rebellion, the governor of Massachusetts had suggested and the legislature had resolved, in 1785, that the Articles of Confederation be reformed, especially by increasing the powers of the Congress.

The early response to this agitation for a constitutional revision was not impressive. When Virginia turned from rhetoric to action by inviting the states to send delegates to a convention at Annapolis in 1786, only five of the thirteen complied. Had it not been for the consummate skill of Hamilton, the conference would have closed in gloom;

determined never to confess defeat, he induced the Annapolis assembly to pass a resolution advising the states to choose delegates to a second convention to be held in Philadelphia the following year. Taking into full account the well-known opposition to any such project, Hamilton worded his resolution with utmost caution. In form he merely recommended a "revision" of the Articles in order to render them "adequate to the exigencies of the union," and he allayed the suspicions of the local legislatures by adding that any amendments made at Philadelphia should be submitted to the states for their ratification as provided in the Articles.

In due course the proposal of the Annapolis conference was sent both to the state legislatures and to the Congress and in February, 1787, the latter issued a call for the Philadelphia assembly. Exercising Hamiltonian circumspection, it phrased its resolution carefully: the convention was to be held for the sole and express purpose of revising the Articles; proposed amendments were to be submitted to the Congress and to the states for approval; the letter and the spirit of the Articles were to be observed. With an alacrity that must have amazed the leaders in the revisionist movement, all the states, except Rhode Island, acting through their legislatures, now chose delegates as requested—some even anticipating the call. Most of them, however, taking Hamilton's moderation at face value, expressly limited their delegates to a revision of the Articles, saving in all respects the prescribed formalities of the existing constitution.

Among the many historic assemblies which have wrought revolutions in the affairs of mankind, it seems safe to say that there has never been one that commanded more political talent, practical experience, and sound substance than the Philadelphia convention of 1787. In all, sixty-two delegates were formally appointed by the states; fifty-five attended the sessions with more or less regularity; and thirty-nine signed the final draft of the new Constitution. On the list were men trained in war and diplomacy, skilled in legislation and administration, versed in finance and commerce, and learned in the political philosophy of their own and earlier times. Seven had been governors of states and at least twenty-eight had served in the Congress of the union either during the Revolution or under the Articles of Confederation. Eight had been signers of the Declaration of Independence. At the head stood Washington, who, with one voice, was chosen president of the convention. Among those who sat under him were such men as the two Morrises, the two Pinckneys, Madison, Hamilton, Franklin, Rutledge, Gerry, Ellsworth, Wilson, Randolph, Wythe, Dickinson, and Sherman, nearly all of whom represented the conservative wing of the old revolutionary party.

At all events none of the fiery radicals of 1774 was present. Jefferson, then serving as the American minister in Paris, was out of the country; Patrick Henry was elected but refused to attend because, he said, he "smellt a rat"; Samuel Adams was not chosen; Thomas Paine left for Europe that very year to exhibit an iron bridge which he had designed and to wage war on tyranny across the sea. So the Philadelphia assembly, instead of being composed of left-wing theorists, was made up of practical men of affairs—holders of state and continental bonds, money lenders, merchants, lawyers, and speculators in the public land—who could speak with knowledge and feeling about the disabilities they had suffered under the Articles of Confederation. More than half the delegates in attendance were either investors or speculators in the public securities which were to be buoyed up by the new Constitution. All knew by experience the relation of property to government.

When the convention assembled late in May, 1787, there arose at once the question whether the proceedings should be thrown open to the general public or be held behind closed doors. The body was small, oratory was evidently out of place, and none of the members was especially eager to appeal to the gallery. As realistic statesmen, they knew that negotiation and accommodation would be more effective in the attainment of their ends than Ciceronian eloquence and tattered passion. It was well understood that the dissensions bound to arise in the convention would be magnified if irresponsible partisans on the outside learned about them and continually prodded the delegates with popular agitations. It was also known how sharply the country at large was divided over the problems to be solved and how easily timid members might be frightened into voting against their own judgment by the demands of excited constituents.

So, without much argument, the members resolved that the proceedings of the convention should be secret and no one permitted to give out in any form any information respecting its deliberations. In harmony with this decision they likewise agreed that no official record of the debates should be kept, that nothing should be set down in black and white save a bare minute of the propositions before the house and the votes cast for and against them. In their anxiety for security the delegates took every precaution against publicity; they even had a discreet colleague accompany the aged Franklin to his convivial dinners with a view to checking that amiable gentleman whenever, in unguarded moments, he threatened to divulge secrets of state.

If a few members, particularly James Madison, had not made notes of the speeches delivered in the convention, posterity would never have discovered the real spirit that animated the discussions. And it was not until more than half a century later—after Madison, the last surviving member, had died and his private papers were published—that Americans got a clear insight into the proceedings of the great assembly that had drafted their revered Constitution.

Having settled the question of secret sessions, the members of the convention came face to face with a fundamental issue: should they adhere to the letter of their instructions by merely amending the Articles of Confederation or should they make a revolution in the whole political régime by drafting a new constitution founded on entirely different principles? The point was a nice one. The Congress which had called them together and the states that had selected them had simply authorized them to propose amendments to the existing constitutional instrument. Nevertheless such amendments, according to the same instructions, were to make the existing Articles "adequate to the exigencies of government and the preservation of the union."

With good reason an agile mind could take either horn of the dilemma. Paterson of New Jersey, speaking for the small states in danger of losing their equal and swollen authority, argued that "if the confederacy is radically wrong, let us return to our states and obtain larger powers, not assume them ourselves." Randolph of Virginia retorted that he was not "scrupulous on the point of power." Hamilton agreed; to propose any plan not adequate to the exigencies of union because it was not clearly within their instructions, he thought, would be to sacrifice the end to the means.

Having come to accomplish results rather than to chop logic, the majority of the members accepted the liberal view of the matter and refused to be bound by the letter of the existing law. They did not amend the Articles of Confederation; they cast that instrument aside and drafted a fresh plan of government. Nor did they merely send the new document to the Congress and then to the state legislatures for approval; on the contrary they appealed over the heads of these authorities to the voters of the states for a ratification of their revolutionary work. Finally, declining to obey the clause of the Articles which required unanimous approval for every amendment, they frankly proposed that the new system of government should go into effect when sanctioned by nine of the thirteen states, leaving the others out in the cold under the wreck of the existing legal order, in case they refused to ratify.

§

For more than a hundred years it was the custom of historians, in speaking of the work of the delegates, to emphasize their differences of opinion, their impassioned controversies, and their compromises, whereas as a matter of fact they exhibited a striking unanimity of opinion on the great economic objects which they had assembled to attain. For this we have the testimony of a competent modern scholar, R. L. Schuyler, who has put the whole story of the making of the Constitution in a new perspective by showing, on the basis of authentic researches, that the essential agreements of the Philadelphia convention were more significant than its disputes.

In the light of his inquiries, it appears that a safe majority of the members was early mustered on nearly all the fundamental issues before them. If they warmly debated many matters pertaining to means and instrumentalities, they agreed with relative ease that a national government must be erected and endowed with ample power to defend the country on land and sea, to pay the national debt, to protect private property against agrarian legislatures, to secure the return of fugitive servants, and to uphold the public order against domestic insurrection. This basic fact should not be obscured in any consideration of the long and tempestuous arguments that arose over the form of the new government and the representation of the states in it.

On the creation of a great national agency endowed with political power equal to specific tasks of the highest order there was so much solidarity of opinion that the objections of the insurgent few merely emphasized the general concord. A few days after they had formally organized, namely, on May 30, the delegates solemnly adopted in the committee of the whole a momentous resolution "that a national government ought to be established consisting of a supreme legislative, executive, and judiciary." It is true that the vote on this proposition was only six states in favor to one against and one divided and that the alarming word "national" was later struck out, but the debates that accompanied and followed this action clearly indicated the temper of the convention. In commenting on the distinction between a confederacy and a national supreme government, Gouverneur Morris made it evident that the former was "a mere compact resting on the good faith of the parties," while the latter had a complete and compulsive operation. Other members spoke in the same vein; so there could be no doubt as to what was in the minds of the majority; they were determined to establish an efficient national government. One of the protestants, Luther Martin, of Maryland, who later withdrew from the convention in anger, blurted out the plain truth when he said that it was the purpose of the Philadelphia assembly to set up "a national, not a federal government." If somewhat vehement, Martin was remarkably accurate in his judgment.

With reference to other issues of paramount significance there was even more unanimity. It required no heroic measures to bring about an agreement that Congress should have the power to lay and collect taxes, regulate foreign and interstate commerce, and do all things necessary and proper to carry into effect its enumerated functions. No member was in favor of repudiating or sharply scaling down the national debt; the clause sustaining the validity of all outstanding obligations and contracts was carried with but one discordant voice.

Equally general was the conviction that the states should not be allowed to issue bills of credit or impair the obligations of contracts. Almost unanimous was the opinion that democracy was a dangerous thing, to be restrained, not encouraged, by the Constitution, to be given as little voice as possible in the new system, to be hampered by checks and balances. Gerry declared that the evils the country had experienced flowed from "the excess of democracy." Randolph traced the troubles of the past few years to "the turbulence and follies of democracy." Arguing in favor of a life term for Senators, Hamilton exclaimed that "all communities divide themselves into the few and the many. The first are rich and well-born and the other the mass of the people who seldom judge or determine right." Morris wanted a Senate composed of an aristocracy of wealth to "keep down the turbulence of democracy." Madison, discoursing on the perils of majority rule, stated that their object was "to secure the public good and private rights against the danger of such a faction and at the same time preserve the spirit and form of popular government."

§

It was with reference to the form of government capable of attaining their grand objects and the respective weight to be assigned to the leading interests of the country in the balanced machine that the most acute diversity of opinion developed. In that relation the records disclose a strange story. They do not portray a group of inspired individuals convinced in advance that only one project of government could accomplish the general purposes they had clearly in mind. Instead of a disciplined crew under a stern and bright-eyed captain steering the ship of state by the north star, we see a wrangling body of thoughtful, experienced, and capable men, but harassed men, torn by interests, prejudices, and passions, drifting one day in one direction and the next in another, deciding long debated issues, opening them again, altering their previous views, and adopting novel solutions.

It is certainly a startling lesson in the fallibility of statesmen to compare the authentic plans laid before the convention in the opening days with the finished Constitution published at the close. For example, the Virginia scheme presented by Randolph provided for a congress of two houses composed of members apportioned among the states on the basis of wealth or free white population; this congress was to elect the executive—either a single person or a group of men; and to exercise general legislative powers, including that of annulling state laws contrary to the Constitution. The curious cannot help but wonder what would have been the fate of the American union if that plan had been adopted. But such speculation is idle. Randolph's plan had hardly been read when it was condemned by Paterson of New Jersey in the name of the small states calling for a legislature of a single house in which commonwealths, not people, were to be represented and all states given an equal vote. Neither plan was adopted.

In its final form the Constitution, so far as the structure of the government was concerned, was "a bundle of compromises." It was more. It was a mosaic of second choices accepted in the interest of union and the substantial benefits to flow from union.

One of the compromises, fundamental in character, occupies a high place in treatises on the Constitution; that was the adjustment between large and small states. The former, weary of domination by minorities, demanded, as we have just indicated, a congress based on populations instead of political entities. The latter, tenacious in the defense of their interests, insisted with the same emphasis on equality among the commonwealths in the national legislature. And through many exciting sessions the debate over this issue ran on fiercely.

More than once dissolution seemed imminent, the delegates being held together, as one of them remarked, only "by the strength of a hair." Frightened by the spectacle, Franklin, in despair of human devices, proposed that the convention be opened daily with prayer, invoking divine guidance to save it from ruin. Even on this motion, agreement was impossible. The hard-headed Hamilton, according to tradition, thought that they were not in need of "foreign aid," and his colleagues objected on other

318 THE RISE OF AMERICAN CIVILIZATION

grounds, fearing that news of a change in procedure might leak out and give the impression that the convention had come to the end of its earthly resources. Eventually, by the use of extreme tact, they managed to weather the storm without resorting to prayer and to avert the crisis through negotiations and a happy compromise. In the end they agreed upon a national legislature of two houses: in the Senate, with greater powers and dignity, the aspirations of the states were to be satisfied by equal representation; while in the House of Representatives, the interests of the larger states were to be conserved by the apportionment of mem-bers among them on the basis of population, counting three-fifths of the slaves.

No less fundamental than the dispute over the political power to be enjoyed by the large and small states was one which deeply involved the economic interests of sections. Indeed, after listening carefully to the debates for several weeks, Madison noted that the real division in the convention was between the planting interests of the South founded on slave labor and the commercial and industrial interests of the North—startling foresight discerning "the irrepressible conflict" which filled half a century with political controversy and tested the Constitution in the flames of a social revolution.

In all there were only six slave states, counting little Delaware, and they had neither wealth nor population comparable to the resources of the seven commercial states. Climate, soil, tradition, and labor supply seemed destined to make them producers of foodstuffs and raw materials to be exchanged in favorable markets for manufactured goods. Therefore, it was their prime concern to ship at the lowest possible freight rates in vessels sailing under any flag and to buy and sell on the most advantageous terms anywhere on earth. Weaker in number, they feared that the proposed Congress, dominated by a mere numerical majority, might lay an undue burden of customs duties and taxes upon them—the shifting of taxes being one of the grand devices of politics for the transfer of wealth from one class to another. They were also afraid that Congress, under capitalistic influences, would enact tariff legislation and navigation laws injurious to their enterprise.

On the other hand, the trading and industrial interests of the North, languishing under free trade, under financial disorders, and under English discriminations, saw their only hope for prosperity in protective tariffs and favorable commercial legislation. The issue was definite and familiar. It had been made clear in the contest with Great Britain when Parliament sought to restrain colonial legislatures and colonial trade with reference to the profits of British merchants, shippers, and manufacturers. It was to cut athwart the history of centuries to come.

Disputes arising from this inherent conflict of interests ran throughout the proceedings of the convention even when questions apparently remote from the main issue were on the carpet. Especially were they animated on matters of representation and taxation, those sore points in the revolutionary struggle. Anxious to secure a strategic position in the new government through the largest possible strength in the lower house, Southern planters proposed to count slaves as people in distributing Representatives on the population basis. At the same time, aware that their states had fewer inhabitants than the commercial commonwealths of the North, the planters urged that direct taxes be apportioned only on the basis of the free white population. For equally obvious reasons most of the Northern delegates wanted just the opposite of these two propositions. So on this issue a compromise was the last resort. Adopting a well-known expedient the convention agreed on treating three-fifths of the slaves as people for both reckonings, representation and direct taxation.

In framing the provisions relative to the regulation of commerce, the same clash of opinion appeared. If the new government was to have the power to control trade and make treaties with foreign nations. it might prohibit the importation of slaves and enter into commercial agreements detrimental to the planting interest. Here also an accommodation was evidently imperative and it took the form of two provisions: the importation of slaves was not to be forbidden before the lapse of twenty years and a two-thirds vote in the Senate was to be required for the ratification of treaties. An additional concession was made to the South in the clause providing for the return of fugitives bound to servitude—all the more readily because this was highly useful in the North where the restoration of runaway servants was also acceptable to masters.

During the arguments that sprang from the clash of economic interests, the ethics of slavery itself was broached though at no time did it rise to the position of a leading issue. Taking advantage of the occasion several members of the convention denounced chattel bondage in uncompromising language. Gouverneur Morris, of Pennsylvania, condemned it as a nefarious institution and a curse to the states in which it prevailed. Mason, of Virginia, a slave-holder himself, seeing nothing but evil in it, declared that it discouraged the arts and industry, led the poor to despise honest labor, and checked the immigration of whites whose work gave strength and riches to the land.

The voice of defense, raised in reply, came from the Far South. Spokesmen from South Carolina insisted that the whole economic life of their state rested on slavery and that, owing to the appalling death rate in the rice swamps, continuous importation was necessary. With cold optimism Oliver Ellsworth, of Connecticut, advised moderation. "The morality or wisdom of slavery," he said, "are considerations belonging to the states. What enriches a part enriches the whole. . . . As population increases, poor laborers will be so plenty as to render slaves useless."

Technically, Ellsworth was right, for slavery as an institution was not before the convention but some decision had to be made with respect to the importation of Negroes. On this point, too, conciliation was found expedient. Virginia and North Carolina, already overstocked, were prepared to end the traffic in African slaves but South Carolina was adamant. She must have new supplies by importation or she would not federate; hence the clause postponing action at least until 1808. These were the great compromises of the Constitution.

§

By reason of their infinite capacity for practical adjustments and their deep determination to accomplish their fundamental purposes, the members of the convention finally managed to agree upon a great political project. In its form the government which they thus created gave promise of strength and stability. The completed Constitution provided for a single executive chosen indirectly—by electors in their turn selected as the state legislatures might decide—a President of the United States serving for four years (subject to impeachment) and endowed with regal powers in the enforcement of laws and the use of armed might. The possibility of dictatorship in times of stress was foreseen and the issue squarely met. As Hamilton afterward reminded his fellow citizens, often in Roman history it had been necessary to resort to absolute power against social disturbances at home and invasions from abroad. When Lincoln, half a century later, crushed secession by military force, he did but fulfill the prophecy of the Fathers.

Yet in contemplating this outcome, it is interesting to recall that the presidential system was the product of no little guesswork in the convention. The Virginia plan proposed an executive department chosen by a congress but did not specify whether it should be composed of one or many persons. The New Jersey plan, which likewise suggested congressional election, called for a council instead of a single head.

On the various points involved, the convention voted first one way and then another, arriving at the final result as much by accident as by intent. If either the Virginia or the New Jersey scheme had been adopted, parliamentary government would have developed in America and modern publicists would have displayed their enthusiasm and talents in demonstrating the merits of that particular system. Would the history of American politics have been essentially different?

The same consideration for stability and strength marked the adoption of the clauses relative to the legislature. Instead of a single council of ambassadors—for such in effect had been the Congress under the Articles of Confederation—paid by the states and subject to their decisions, the Constitution created an independent bicameral system. If there was a reminder of the old order in the clauses which gave each state two members in the Senate, to be elected by its legislature, the position accorded to the Senators was essentially original. They could vote as individuals, they could not be recalled or bound by instructions, they enjoyed a fixed term of six years, they were to look to the national treasury for compensation.

At the side of the Senate was placed an entirely new body, the House of Representatives, apportioned among the states mainly on the basis of population, elected by popular vote and, like the Senators, paid from the national treasury. In this way, it was believed, the power of any faction or party that dominated a state could be divided at its source and thereby the force of majority rule broken. As Madison pointed out, the mechanism was based on the idea that in actual politics men have to deal with effective powers, not with a mythical entity known as "indivisible sovereignty."

With the idea of creating a central control analogous to that formerly exercised by British courts, a judicial as well as an executive department was added to the government by the Constitution. Under the Articles of Confederation, the state courts had been practically independent of all supervision from above and the Congress had been almost wholly dependent on those frail reeds for any enforcement of laws or treaties which called for judicial process.

A product of the Revolution, that arrangement was no accident, for one of the prime objects of many participants in the uprising had been to break the grip of British agencies on agrarian legislatures and tribunals. Now that the struggle was over, citizens who did not want to pay their debts to British merchants or restore Tory property had additional reasons for clinging to emancipation. But men of affairs, national in their business vision, in their investments, and in their commercial undertakings, took a different view of local judges and jurors.

From any angle, the question was vexatious and had to be handled adroitly by the convention. It was, as Gouverneur Morris said, only by the exercise of extreme caution that the committee in charge of the matter was able to draw up an acceptable clause and reach an agreement on the creation of the Supreme Court and "such other courts" as Congress might authorize, high tribunals endowed with jurisdiction over all cases in law and equity arising under the Constitution, federal laws, and treaties.

In these circumstances much was left to the future, to Providence, as Lamartine once remarked on a similar occasion. It was not expressly stated, for instance, that the federal courts should enjoy the power of declaring acts of Congress null and void on constitutional grounds but the idea that the federal judiciary would use this high prerogative was fully appreciated by adepts in jurisprudence at the time. Measures passed by colonial legislatures had been repeatedly nullified by British courts and a few precedents had been set by American judges during the critical period. Of course, in popular circles the theory and the practice were fiercely attacked but, on the other hand, they were vigorously defended in the Philadelphia convention and outside it by lawyers accustomed to the business of high judicature. Beyond all question veterans admitted to the more esoteric groups of the legal guild understood the issue even if some farmers along the Allegheny ridge failed to grasp its import.

§

The functions of the new government, no less than its structure, presented striking innovations. Authority was conferred upon the President sufficient, as noted, to clothe with legality, should occasion arise, even the exercise of Cæsar's prerogatives. The supremacy of the judiciary, implicit if not expressed, only needed the magic of John Marshall to make it a part of a sacred tradition illuminating the written word. With regard to legislative duties, Congress in its turn received express and general powers adequate to the economic requirements of the classes adversely affected under the Articles.

First of all—recalling the old attempts of Parliament to levy taxes without the consent of provincial assemblies—the necessity of depending upon the state legislatures for federal revenues was entirely eliminated. Congress was authorized to collect taxes, duties, imposts, and excises directly from the people as individuals—by a broad and sweeping clause under which wonders could be worked in the protection, as well as the taxation, of business enterprise. While the prospect of abundant revenues collected with discrimination gave cheer to possessors of depreciated government securities and held out hope to languishing industries, another clause promised succor to those engaged in the arts of trade.

Having clearly in mind foreign discriminations and the commercial anarchy that existed among the states, the framers of the Constitution provided that Congress should have power to regulate foreign and interstate commerce, thus wiping out state tariff lines and creating a national market area behind a federal wall. Moreover, the American estate was to be guarded by effective military defense: Congress was to depend no longer on the good graces of the states for soldiers and sailors; it was given unlimited authority to raise and maintain armed forces for land and sea, besides the privilege of utilizing the state militia in emergencies. Finally the enumerated powers were crowned by a blanket provision in which Congress was given a general mandate to make all laws necessary and proper for carrying into effect the authority expressly conferred. Under the light shed by the expansive imagination of Chief Justice Marshall that clause became a Pandora's box of wonders.

§

While agreeing that these large powers had to be given to the new government, the framers of the Constitution shrank from the very giant they had created. Madison foresaw a time, not far distant, when the great mass of the people would be without landed or any other kind of property, when in spite of all precautions a triumphant majority might get possession of the political machine and make it an engine of their purposes to the detriment of the public good, that is, in the main to the detriment of private property.

Frightened by this specter of democracy, some of the members of the convention proposed to restrain the masses by putting property qualifications on the suffrage and on high federal officers. Though the suggestion was warmly received a number of capital obstacles were pointed out in the course of the debate. If each voter or officer was required to possess a large amount of personal property, such as stocks and bonds, then the existing voters, two-thirds of whom were farmers, would not ratify an instrument that disfranchised them. A landed qualification was, therefore, the only alternative but bitter experience had showed that it was the farmers who sent radicals to the state legislatures and waged the war on money lenders, merchants, and other holders of personal property. After tossing about restlessly for several days, the delegates gave up the idea of entrenching property in the Constitution by specific restrictions on voting and office holding.

Finding that course barred, the delegates chose another way of dissolving the energy of the democratic majority. They broke its strength at the source by providing diverse methods for electing the agencies of the new government and threw special barriers in its path by setting those agencies, with their several ambitions, prerogatives, and insignia, at cross purposes. In short, the Fathers created a system of "checks and balances," dividing the power of government among legislative, executive, and judicial branches with confused and uncertain boundaries. All the world has marveled at their dexterity.

The legislature as they devised it was of intricate structure. Members of the House of Representatives were to be distributed among the states roughly on the basis of population and they were to be elected biennially by those voters authorized by the respective states to take part in the choice of members for the lower house of the local legislature. That, as Hamilton remarked, gave the poorer orders of men a hearing in the government. But the chamber so directly affiliated with the commonalty was by no means to have a clear track in the making of laws. A strong Senate was thrown across its way. Senators were to be chosen by the state legislatures, one degree removed from the multitude; they were to serve for six years instead of two; and only one-third of them were to go out at any time, so that after each fresh election, no matter how tempestuous, a safe majority of the old members were to remain undisturbed in their places. The conservative effect of age was brought into play: Senators were to be at least thirty years old, five years above the minimum set for the lower house.

Opposite the legislature thus divided against itself was set the President elected by yet another process—by a special body of electors chosen as the state legislatures might determine—perhaps two or three degrees removed from the passions of the populace. Thus firmly planted on his own base, the President was to enjoy, in addition to his executive functions, the power of vetoing acts of Congress. To increase the friction of the machine, his term was fixed at four years, not two or six, and it was provided that he could be removed only by a difficult method of impeachment.

Over against the executive and the legislature was placed the Supreme Court composed of judges appointed, not for two, four, or six years, but for life—judges chosen by the President and the Senate, the two federal agencies removed from direct contact with the populace—and in fact, as time proved, endowed with the power of declaring acts of the other departments null and void. As Hamilton explained, the friends of good government thought that "every institution calculated to restrain the excess of law making and to keep things in the same state in which they happen to be at any given period was more likely to do good than harm."

If this doctrine seemed strange to some who had just raised and carried through a revolution, it fell with a grateful sound upon the ears of those to whom it was directed. The problem of accomplishing what they thought good for the public interest and preventing the federal government from doing things evil in their eyes was a perplexing one to the Fathers; but their ingenuity was equal to the occasion.

The recognition of the need for restraining the state governments was also conspicuously present in their deliberations. Under the influence of debt-burdened farmers, as they well knew, several local legislatures had issued paper money and so enabled debtors to discharge their obligations more easily in depreciated currency. Such assaults on vested rights the convention tried to terminate by declaring in the Constitution that no state should emit bills of credit or make anything but gold or silver coin legal tender in the payment of debts. States had been negligent in paying their public debts; they had enacted laws permitting private debtors to pay in land or kind and be rid of their creditors; they had passed laws delaying the collection of matured debts and placing other obstacles in the way of such procedures; one of them had repealed the charter of an incorporated college; and they had done other things injurious to the holders of personal property—as the Fathers reasoned, injurious to the public good. Accordingly the convention, in recognition of private rights, wrote into the Constitution a clause forbidding any state to impair the obligation of contracts.

Nor was it satisfied with that. Dangerous radicals in Massachusetts had raised the standard of revolt against law and order; such a thing might occur again and the flames even spread. Therefore the Fathers provided that the President could, on call from state authorities, send troops to suppress domestic insurrection. In this way, the convention sought to tame the spirits of local statesmen who had run wild after the heavy yoke of the British government had been thrown off. In this way was reëstablished in effect the old British system of politics, economics, and judicial control—this time grounded on American authority created by an American constitution.

§

Fully aware that their plan would be bitter medicine to a large part of the public, the delegates were puzzled about the best method of getting their instrument ratified. The lawful constitution, the Articles of Confederation, and the call under which the convention had been elected decreed that their project should be laid before the existing Congress for approval, transmitted to the states for ratification, and go into effect only after receiving unanimous consent. Now, the state legislatures, the Fathers knew by bitter experience, had been the chief assailants of public credit and private rights; they had repeatedly refused to indorse restraints on their own powers and their unanimous consent was hardly to be expected.

Having regard for realities rather than theories, the Fathers departed from the letter of the existing law in the interest of higher considerations. They did, indeed, provide that the new Constitution should be sent to the old Congress as a matter of form but they advised the Congress merely to pass the instrument along to the states with a recommendation that special conventions be called to decide the issue of ratification. Many citizens of the right sort, they reasoned, who would not take the trouble to serve in a local legislature, would be willing to participate in a ratifying convention; if once the barrier of the populistic state legislatures could be forced, they saw hope of victory.

Still the specter of unanimous ratification remained. After much debate on the point, the convention laid that ghost by an audacious proposal, namely, that the Constitution should go into effect, as between the states concerned, as soon as two-thirds had given their consent. This program, the learned commentator, John W. Burgess, makes plain, was a project for a revolution, a break with the prevailing legal order, a coup d'état, an appeal over the heads of established agencies to the voters, or at least to that part of the electorate prepared to overthrow the Articles of Confederation.

On September 17, after nearly four months of arduous debate, the convention brought its labors to a close. The Constitution was finished and the scheme for ratification formulated. Aggrieved by the decisions of their colleagues, some members had gone home in anger and some who stayed on refused to sign the document, denouncing it openly and opposing its adoption by the people. On the other hand, thirty-nine of the fifty-five members who had attended one or more sessions put their names on the parchment and sent it forth with their benediction, even though they differed widely among themselves in the degree of their enthusiasm for the common handiwork.

Hamilton thought the new government would not be powerful enough and entertained grave doubts about its success. While admitting that they were merely "making experiments in politics," and while expressing his disapproval of many provisions in the document, Franklin declared his faith in divine guidance in the matter. Standing then within the shadow of death, he wrote of the convention's achievement: "I can hardly conceive a transaction of such momentous importance to the welfare of millions now existing and to exist in the posterity of a great nation should be suffered to pass without being in some degree influenced, guided, and governed by that omnipotent, omnipresent, and beneficent Ruler, in whom all inferior spirits live and move and have their being."

With his customary practical view of things, Washington doubtless voiced the general sentiment of his fellow signers when he said: "The Constitution that is submitted is not free from imperfections. But there are as few radical defects in it as could well be expected, considering the heterogeneous mass of which the Convention was composed and the diversity of interests that are to be attended to. As a Constitutional door is opened for future amendments and alterations, I think it would be wise in the people to accept what is offered to them."

On receiving at Paris reports of the proceedings at Philadelphia, Jefferson was at first much troubled. He thought that the proposed House of Representatives would be incompetent to great tasks, that the President, aided by the army, might become a dictator, and that the convention should have been content to add a few sections to the Articles of Confederation, "the good, old and venerable fabric which should have been preserved even as a religious relique." Later, however, he changed his mind and on considering the possibilities of amendment came to the conclusion that the Fathers had done about as well as human circumstances permitted. In the end he came to view the whole operation as a noble triumph for humanity. "The example," he said, "of changing a constitution by assembling the wise men of the state, instead of assembling armies, will be worth as much to the world as the former examples we have given them."

§

Acting on the recommendations of the convention, the Congress submitted the Constitution to the states for their approval or rejection and in turn the local legislatures called upon the voters to choose conventions to pass upon the new project of government. In a trice the country was divided into hostile camps as all the engines of propaganda and political maneuvering were brought into play either to carry or to defeat the plan for a new government. With a bitterness that recalled the factional dispute in the revolutionary party a few years before, both sides resorted to strenuous tactics.

When, for example, certain opponents of the Constitution in the Pennsylvania legislature sought to win time for deliberation by leaving their seats and breaking the quorum, a federalist mob invaded their lodgings, dragged them through the streets, and pushed them back into the assembly room. Applauded by the victors, the vote was then taken and the election of delegates to the state ratifying convention was fixed at a date only five weeks ahead, reducing to the minimum the period allowed for taking "the solemn judgment of the people." Doubtless some gentlemen of the old school entertained regrets that the new law had been ushered in with disorder but the emergency was great.

Again when the New Hampshire convention met and a majority opposed to the Constitution was discovered, the assembly adjourned to prevent an adverse vote and give the friends of the new instrument a chance to work on the objectors. In one case haste, in the other delay, favored ratification.

As the winter of 1787-88 advanced into spring, the conflict was waged at close quarters, with steady gains among the supporters of the new form of government. Promptly and with little tumult, four states, Delaware, Connecticut, New Jersey, and Georgia—among the smallest and least powerful members of the confederation—ratified the Constitution. With similar promptness Pennsylvania added its approval following the events narrated above. Equally emphatic, Maryland and South Carolina, having given the voters ample time for deliberation, decided with a generous gesture in favor of ratification. In Virginia, where the popular verdict was doubtful, the weight of great names, such as Washington, Marshall, Randolph, and Wythe, finally carried the day. In New Hampshire, New York, and Massachusetts, where the election returned avowed majorities opposed to the Constitution, a great deal of clever engineering induced several delegates to depart from their apparent instructions and cast their ballots for ratification. But to the very end, two states, North Carolina and Rhode Island, refused to give their consent, allowing the new government to be erected without their aid and remaining isolated until the pressure of powerful economic forces brought them under the roof.

Intense as it was, the excitement that marked the struggle did not bring out an avalanche of voters to express their opinions at the polls. From the fragmentary figures that are available, it appears that no more than one-fourth of the adult white males in the country voted one way or the other in the elections at which delegates to the state ratifying conventions were chosen. According to a cautious reckoning, probably one-sixth of them—namely, one hundred thousand—favored the ratification of the new form of government. In any case, it is employing a juristic concept, not summarizing statistical returns, to say that "the whole people put restraints on themselves by adopting the Constitution."

Broadly speaking, the division of the voters over the document ran along economic lines. The merchants, manufacturers, private creditors, and holders of public securities loomed large among the advocates of the new system, while the opposition came chiefly from the small farmers behind the seaboard, especially from the men who, in earlier years, had demanded paper money and other apparatus for easing the strain of their debts. In favor of the Constitution, wrote General Knox to Washington from Massachusetts on January 12, 1788, was "the commercial part of the state to which are added all the men of considerable property, the clergy, the lawyers—including all the judges of all the courts, and all the officers of the late army, and also the neighborhood of all great towns. . . . This party are for vigorous government, perhaps many of them would have been still more pleased with the new Constitution had it been more analogous to the British Constitution." In the opposition, General Knox massed the "Insurgents or their favorers, the great majority of whom are for the annihilation of debts public and private."

During the battle over ratification, advocates on both sides produced a large and, in the main, illuminating literature on the science of human government, a literature reminiscent of the grand style of the Revolution. Though time has sunk most of it into oblivion, especially the arguments of the defeated party, the noblest pieces of defense, namely, the letters to the press written by Hamilton, Madison, and Jay in support of the Constitution, were rescued from the dust and given immortality under the name of The Federalist.

In the tenth number of this great series, Madison, who has been justly called the "father of the Constitution" and certainly may be regarded as a spokesman of the men who signed it, made a cogent appeal for ratification on practical grounds: "The first object of government" is the protection of "the diversity in the faculties of men, from which the rights of property originate." After enumerating the chief classes of property holders which spring up inevitably under such protection in modern society, Madison proceeded to show that "the regulation of these various and interfering interests forms the principal task of modern legislation and involves the spirit of party and faction in the ordinary operations of the government."

Then Madison explained how political strife involved economic concerns at every turn: "The most common and durable source of factions has been the various and unequal distribution of property. Those who hold and those who are without property have ever formed distinct interests in society. Those who are creditors and those who are debtors fall under a like discrimination. A landed interest, a manufacturing interest, a mercantile interest, a moneyed interest, with many lesser interests, grow up of necessity in civilized nations and divide them into different classes actuated by different sentiments and views. . . . From the protection of different and unequal faculties of acquiring property, the possession of different degrees and kinds of property immediately results; and from the influence of these on the sentiments and views of the respective proprietors, ensues a division of society into different interests and parties."

Of necessity, according to Madison's logic, legislatures reflect these interests. "What," he asks, "are the different classes of legislators but advocates and parties to the causes which they determine?" For this there is no help. "The causes of factions cannot be removed," and "we know from experience that neither moral nor religious motives can be relied upon as an adequate control." Since that is true, there arises a grave danger, namely, the danger that certain groups, particularly the propertyless masses, may fuse into an overbearing majority and sacrifice to its will the interests of the minority. Given this peril, it followed that a fundamental problem before the Philadelphia convention had been to "secure the public good and private rights against the danger of such a faction and at the same time preserve the spirit and form of popular government." And the solution offered was in the check and balance system which refined and enlarged public views "by passing them through the medium of a chosen body of citizens." This, in the language of a leading Father, was the spirit of the new Constitution—the substance of a powerful appeal to all practical men of affairs.

By argument, by negotiation, and by the weight of personality the friends of the proposed revolution triumphed in the end. On June 21, 1788, the ninth state, New Hampshire, ratified the Constitution and the new system could then go into effect as between the parties that had sealed the contract. Within a few weeks, Virginia and New York, aware that the die had already been cast, gave their reluctant consent. With victory thus doubly assured, the federalists could ignore the smoldering anger of the opposition that had proposed many amendments and could laugh at the solemn resolve of New York calling for another national assembly to modify the Constitution. Leaving North Carolina and Rhode Island still outside the fold unconvinced of its advantages, the old Congress made ready to disband by calling elections for the choice of men to constitute the personnel of the new government.

CHAPTER VIII
The Rise of National Parties

THE controversy over the ratification of the federal Constitution had not died away when the country was summoned to take part in a contest over the election of men to direct the new government. In this struggle the disputants appealed to the passions that had been invoked in the previous battle, but they now encountered among the people an astonishing indifference. Senators and presidential electors were chosen by the state legislators without arousing any popular uproar. There were, it is true, lively skirmishes in a few congressional districts, but, as a rule, Representatives were returned by a handful of voters. In Maryland and Massachusetts, for example, not more than one-sixth of the adult males took part in the balloting for members of the lower house. As many times before in history, an informed and active minority managed the play.

When the results of the poll were all in and the new government was organized, it was patent to everyone that the men who had made the recent constitutional revolution were carrying on the work they had begun in 1787. Washington, the chairman of the constitutional convention, was unanimously chosen President of the United States. Of the twenty-four Senators in the first Congress under the Constitution, eleven had helped to draft "the new charter of liberty." In the House of Representatives was a strong contingent from the body of framers and ratifiers, with the "father of the Constitution," James Madison, in the foreground. The Ark of the Covenant was evidently in the house of its friends; or, to put the matter in another way, the machinery of economic and political power was mainly directed by the men who had conceived and established it. And very soon the executive and judicial departments were filled with leaders who had taken part in framing or ratifying the Constitution.

For the most important post in his administration, namely, that of the Treasury, Washington chose Robert Morris, a member of the convention; when that gentleman declined, he turned to another colleague, Alexander Hamilton, a giant of Federalism. For the office of Attorney General, the President selected the spokesman of the Virginia delegation at the Philadelphia assembly, Edmund Randolph. As Secretary of War, he appointed another ardent advocate of the Constitution, General Knox, of Massachusetts. Only one high administrative command went to a statesman whose views on the new government were, to say the least, uncertain; Thomas Jefferson, who had been in Paris during the formation and adoption of the Constitution, was made Secretary of State in charge of foreign affairs. In the judicial department, there was not a single exception: all the federal judgeships created under the Judiciary Act of 1789, high and low, were given to men who had helped to draft the Constitution or had supported it in state conventions or in the ratifying campaigns. In his appointments to minor places in the government Washington was equally discreet; after attempting to conciliate a few opponents by offering them positions, he flatly declared that he would not give an office to any man who attacked the principles of his administration.

The first government was thus in no sense a coalition. When the paper document of Philadelphia became a reality, it lived on in the reason and will of the men who had constructed and adopted it. It was they who enacted the laws, enforced the decrees, raised the army, and collected the taxes, and so made the new Constitution an instrument of power in the direction of national economy and in the distribution of wealth. In their hands mere words on parchment were transformed into an engine of sovereign compulsion that could not be denied anywhere throughout the length and breadth of the land.

§

Shortly after noon on April 30, 1789, George Washington, escorted by a small guard of cavalry, a committee of Congress, and a cheering throng of citizens, rode from his residence in New York to the new Federal Hall in Wall Street, where, on the balcony of the building facing Broad Street, he took the oath of office as first President of the United States. Immediately afterward, Chancellor Livingston, who had administered the pledge, turned to the crowd below and cried out: "Long live George Washington, President of the United States!" The cry was repeated in the streets and the rest of the day given over to celebrating the great event. Since both houses of Congress were now in session, the new government of America was ready for the heavy tasks ahead—the formulation of laws and policies contemplated by the Constitution.

For guidance these directors of affairs had before them, of course, the customs established under the Articles of Confederation but at best such practices formed a poor sailing chart for a government differently constructed and endowed with more extensive powers, in particular for the executive department. Accordingly Washington had to make precedents of his own, with the advice of his friends. His message to Congress he read with grave dignity before the two houses in joint assembly—giving a touch of the regal manner to American legislative procedure. The practice of calling the chief officers of the administration together in conference was early adopted, marking the origin of the Cabinet, a modified form of that English institution. As far as he deemed it compatible with public interest, Washington rewarded with civil appointments his companions in the war of the Revolution whose sacrifices and financial condition made them "worthy objects of public recognition." In his dealings with the Senate, he sought to establish the custom of consulting that body formally, and in person, about treaties in process of negotiation; but the Senators, feeling constrained by his presence, gave him such stiff and frigid receptions that he finally forsook his plan.

In the sphere of administration it was also necessary to break new ground and after making arrangements for temporary revenue, Congress turned to the pressing task of completing the machinery of government. The management of foreign affairs, finance, and defense on land and sea was committed to appropriate departments: State, Treasury, and War respectively. Anticipating a growth in the legal requirements of the government, Congress instituted the office of Attorney General. Since the post-office was already in operation, it continued the system without much alteration.

The judicial branch of the government was established by the Judiciary Act of 1789, one of the most remarkable pieces of legislation in the history of this continent. With elaborate detail the law provided for a Supreme Court composed of a Chief Justice and five associates and a federal district court for each state with its own attorney, marshal, and appropriate number of deputies. Such were the agencies of power created to make the will of the national government a living force in every community from New Hampshire to Georgia, from the seaboard to the frontier.

In keeping with the spirit of the new order, precautions were taken to bring state courts and state legislatures under federal control. After contriving an ingenious system of appeals for carrying cases up to the federal Supreme Court, the framers of the Judiciary Act devised a process by which the measures of the local governments could be nullified whenever they came into conflict with the federal Constitution. The terms of the law were explicit. If a state court, having final jurisdiction over any matter, declared an act of Congress void, or if it upheld as valid an act of a state legislature, an appeal could be taken to the high tribunal at the national capital, just as to London in colonial times. Every citizen whose personal liberty or property rights under the Constitution were put in jeopardy by neighboring political authorities now had an agency of relief at hand—an agency independent of local authorities, drawing its financial, moral, and physical force from the center. In a word, something like the old British imperial control over provincial legislatures was reëstablished, under judicial bodies chosen indirectly and for life, within the borders of the United States.

While creating the offices of the new government in detail and endowing them with the powers required to give effect to its decisions, Congress was well aware that it was necessary to soften some of the opposition to the new régime with measures of conciliation. The directors of federal affairs knew by what narrow margin the approval of the Constitution had been wrung from a reluctant people. They saw North Carolina and Rhode Island still outside the Union and unrepentant. They had before them a large number of amendments proposed by several of the state conventions and they were assured by any number of the critics that promises to carry some of the demands into immediate effect had been made in winning the votes necessary to ratification. All these amendments, as Congress could not fail to see, showed a fear of the federal government and suggested restraints on its authority. Although some were harmless enough, others betrayed the spirit of Daniel Shays, who, if vanquished, was by no means dead.

To allay, if not remove, the temper expressed in several of the propositions, Madison, therefore, presented in the House of Representatives, and the first Congress adopted, a series of amendments to the Constitution, ten of which were soon ratified and in 1791 became a part of the law of the land. Among other things, these amendments stipulated that Congress should make no law respecting the establishment of religion, abridging freedom of speech or press, or the right of the people to assemble peaceably and petition the government for a redress of grievances. Indictment by grand jury and trial by jury were guaranteed to all persons charged by federal officers with serious crimes. Finally, to soften the wrath of provincial politicians, it was announced in the Tenth Amendment that all powers not delegated to the United States by the Constitution or withheld by it from the states were reserved to the states respectively or to the people.

This overt declaration of the obvious was supplemented seven years later by the Eleventh Amendment, written in the same spirit, forbidding the federal judiciary to hear any case in which a state was sued by a citizen. Assured by the friendly professions of the national government and constrained by economic necessity, North Carolina joined the Union in November, 1789, and Rhode Island in May of the following year.

§

With the machinery of administration in operation and professions respecting natural rights duly made, the directors of the federal government were free to devote themselves to prime questions of financial, commercial, and industrial legislation. In fact, while the philosophers were discussing the constitutional amendments, Hamilton, Secretary of the Treasury, was formulating the great system and the collateral reports forever associated with his name.

First upon his program was the funding of the entire national debt, domestic and foreign, principal and interest, at face value, approximating altogether $50,000,000; in other words, old bonds and certificates were to be called in and new securities issued. A part of this enormous sum was to bear interest at six per cent and a part at three per cent, while the interest on the remainder was to be deferred for ten years.

In the second place, Hamilton proposed that the national government assume at face value the revolutionary obligations of the states, amounting to about $20,000,000, and add them to the debt carried by the general treasury. In this fashion he intended to make secure the financial standing of the United States and force all the public creditors to look to the federal government rather than the states for the payment of the sums due them. To provide a capstone for his financial structure, Hamilton advocated the creation of a national bank in which the government and private investors were to be represented. Three-fourths of the capital stock of this institution was to consist of new six per cent federal bonds and the rest of specie. With a view to assisting the government and the security holders in buoying up the public credit, that is, the prices of federal bonds, provision was to be made for a sinking fund from which the Treasury could buy its securities in the market from time to time.

To sustain this magnificent paper edifice erected on the taxing power of the federal government, duties were to be laid on imports in such a manner as to encourage and protect American industry and commerce. Finally, the public lands in the West, which the Crown of Britain had once sought to wrest from colonial politicians, were to be sold and the securities of the federal government were to be accepted in payment.

It required no very profound economic insight to grasp the import of the Hamiltonian program: holders of the old debt—continental and state—were simply to exchange their depreciated paper at face value for new bonds bearing interest and guaranteed by a government that possessed ample taxing power. Prime public securities, such as were now to be issued, would readily pass as money from hand to hand, augmenting the fluid capital of the country and stimulating commerce, manufacturing, and agriculture. If the government bonds failed to realize all expectations in the line of capital expansion, notes issued by the United States bank were to supply the deficiency. At last American business enterprise, which had suffered from the want of currency and credit, was to be abundantly furnished with both and at the same time protected against foreign competition by favorable commercial legislation. Naturally those who expected to reap the benefits from Hamilton's system were delighted with the prospects. On the other hand, since the whole financial structure rested on taxation, mere owners of land and consumers of goods, on whom most of the burden was to fall, got it into their heads that they were to pay the bills of the new adventure.

As the issues raised by Hamilton's projects came before the people one by one, the tide of political passion rose higher and higher. It was well known that a large part, perhaps the major portion, of the old bonds, state and continental, had passed from the hands of the original purchasers into the coffers of shrewd and enterprising speculators. After the adoption of the Constitution became certain, far-sighted financiers sent agents all over the country, especially into the southern states, with bags of precious specie, bought enormous quantities of depreciated paper at a low figure—sometimes ten or fifteen cents on the dollar—and effected a great concentration of public securities in Philadelphia, New York, and Boston. Inevitably the cupidity of those who had risked their money in this speculation and the anguish of those who had sold their original certificates at merely nominal prices furnished the fuel for an explosion when Hamilton's fiscal plans appeared on the political carpet.

One group in Congress, not very large, immediately proposed to scale down the old debts by buying the obligations at market, instead of face, value. By members of this faction it was contended that very little of the outstanding paper represented specie paid into the continental treasury, that to a marked degree the debt represented goods bought at inflated prices and depreciated notes accepted by the revolutionary government when loans were floated. Although there was much truth in this argument, it was unpalatable to the party bent on funding at face value; and those who advanced it could make no headway against the current of opinion in Congress, where a number of security-holding members united with the friends of public credit in strenuously resisting every proposal that savored of repudiation.

A second congressional group, just as eager as Hamilton to restore public credit, was especially solicitous for the welfare of veterans of the Revolution, original purchasers of bonds, and men who had sold supplies to the revolutionary government. To this party Madison adhered. In a long and careful speech, he analyzed the merits of the controversy. Everyone admitted, he said, that a sacred duty was laid upon the government to pay for value received with lawful interest but it was entirely proper to debate one point, namely, to whom payment should be made. By common concession at the head of the list of creditors were the original investors who still retained their securities; no one could deny their right to have a full discharge of their claims.

Next in order were the original purchasers who had sold their holdings at a low price and the speculators who had purchased paper in the market. The former could rightfully appeal to public faith because they had furnished values and services to the government and, after being treated with neglect and contempt, had been compelled to sell their certificates on ruinous terms. On the other hand, those who had bought securities on speculation had some claims: they had incurred risks, they held the paper bearing a definite promise to pay, they could with reason point to the maxim that the literal fulfillment of obligations is the best foundation of public credit. Yet to pay both the speculative purchasers and the original holders was obviously impossible.

Therefore, urged Madison, let a composition be made; let the former have the highest price that has prevailed on the market and the latter the difference between the face value and the market price. This project, he confessed, would not do perfect justice but would more nearly meet the requirements of honor than any other plan yet proposed. Powerful as was his plea, he could not carry the House of Representatives with him; his proposal was defeated by a vote of thirty-six to thirteen, on February 22, 1790. Having rejected all compromise measures, Congress resolved that the continental debt should be funded at face value.

After carrying the first redoubt, the champions of Hamilton's system turned with confidence to the assumption of state debts. In a way, they reasoned, those debts were likewise national—incurred in a common cause—but they also emphasized the argument that the funding of such floating obligations would increase the fluid capital of the country, attach men by their self-interests to the national government, and stimulate the circulation of money. Whatever weight was in this plea, opponents of assumption, especially from the South, were not impressed thereby. A large part of the state securities, as we have said, was now in the hands of northern speculators and taxes to support the national debt would fall mainly on consumers of taxable imports. Accordingly, in the eyes of the critics, assumption appeared to be a scheme to enrich manipulators principally at the expense of the planters and farmers who imported manufactures and paid taxes. At all events, the argument in this vein was temporarily effective; the faction that accepted it was large and determined: and on April 12, 1790, assumption was defeated in the popular branch of Congress —the House of Representatives.

To the statesmen from the planting South, this result seemed to mark a triumph over the commercial North. In any event, an observant politician, after witnessing the defeat of assumption, immediately wrote to a friend in Virginia, in a vein of good humor: "Last Monday Mr. Sedgwick (of Massachusetts) delivered a funeral oration on the death of Miss Assumption. . . . Her death was much lamented by her parents who were from New England. Mr. Sedgwick being the most celebrated preacher was requested to deliver her funeral eulogium. It was done with puritanic gravity. . . . Sixty-one of the political fathers of the nation were present and a crowded audience of weapers and rejoicers. Mrs. Speculator was the chief mourner and acted her part to admiration; she being the mother of Miss Assumption who was the hope of her family. . . . Mrs. Excise may have cause to rejoice because she will be screened from much drudgery—as she must have been the principal support of Miss Assumption as well as of her mother and all her relations. Mrs. Direct Tax may rest more easy in Virginia as she will not be called into foreign service." Unfortunately for the writer, however, his pæan of rejoicing proved to be premature, for a motion to reconsider was immediately made and, as Senator Maclay, of Pennsylvania, wrote in his diary, "Speculation wiped a tear from either eye."

Given a new hope by this action, Hamilton and his supporters now worked furiously for weeks to convert enough opponents to carry assumption through the House. In the midst of their operations, Jefferson returned from Paris to take up his labors as head of the Department of State, and Hamilton in desperation begged the new Secretary to bring his influence to bear on southern members. For half an hour, he walked Jefferson up and down before President Washington's residence explaining to him that the fate of the Constitution depended upon the passage of the assumption bill, that the creditor states were ready to secede if the project could not be realized.

Impressed by the pathetic anxiety of Hamilton and eager to save the Union, Jefferson arranged a dinner party to be attended by certain interested politicians. The moment the company assembled, he discovered that assumption was indeed a bitter pill to southern congressmen and that something would have to be done to sweeten it. It was only after much argument that a compromise was reached in which it was agreed on the one side that two members should change their minds and vote for assumption while Robert Morris of Pennsylvania should manage certain other Representatives; and on the other side, in exchange, that the national capital should be finally located on the banks of the Potomac after a ten year period in Philadelphia.

"And so," Jefferson wrote long afterward, "the assumption was passed and twenty millions of stock divided among the favored states and thrown in as pabulum to the stock-jobbing herd." On August 4, 1790, the grand bill for funding the national and state debts became a law. Incidentally Congress provided that the bills of credit issued during the Revolution by the Continental Congress should be redeemed at one cent on the dollar, a low figure, practically amounting to the repudiation of two or three hundred millions of paper—which caused deep sorrow among the speculators who had also hoped to reap a rich harvest in that field of business enterprise. In fact the tender was so trivial that only a small part of the currency was ever brought in for redemption; most of it simply perished in the hands of the holders.

After a short recess, Congress took up the third of Hamilton's proposals, the establishment of a United States Bank. On December 14, the Secretary's report dealing with the subject was made public; and five weeks later the Senate passed a bill in conformity with his recommendations. Thereupon an animated debate occurred in the

House, where the passions of the people at large were more accurately reflected. Indeed, the discussion became so acrimonious and Jefferson supported the opposition with such vehemence that Washington became alarmed.

For his own guidance in the storm, he asked the members of his Cabinet for written opinions on the constitutionality of the measure, receiving in response two important state papers: one by Hamilton defending the bill and the other by Jefferson and Randolph opposing it—two great expositions of the Constitution giving the liberal and the strict constructions of that instrument of government.

On reading these opinions, Washington was convinced that the Bank was sound in law and in economy and as soon as the House concurred with the Senate by passing the bill, he signed it, on February 25, 1791. According to its provisions, the charter of the Bank was to run for twenty years; one-fifth of the $10,000,000 stock was to be subscribed by the government; the headquarters of the institution were to be at Philadelphia and branches were to be established in other cities at the discretion of the directors. Besides being empowered to engage in a general banking business, it could issue notes under certain restrictions; and its notes, redeemable in coin, were made legal tenders for all payments due the United States.

Having successfully weathered three great political gales, Hamilton took up the question of protection for American industries. On December 5, 1791, he presented in a voluminous Report on Manufactures a powerful argument for the promotion of business enterprise under the shelter of tariffs and bounties. The benefits of such a system, he said, included a more extensive use of machinery, the employment of classes not otherwise profitably employed—such as women and children "of a tender age"—the encouragement of immigration, the opening of more ample and varied opportunities for talent and skill, and the creation of a steady demand for the surplus produce of the soil. Hamilton then went into detail, specifying the desirable objects of protection, such as iron, copper, lead, coal, wood, skins, grain, hemp, wool, silk, glass, paper, and sugar.

In his proposals there was nothing altogether strange. The first revenue act of 1789, though designed primarily for revenue, had declared in favor of protection as a principle; and Washington had already committed himself to the doctrine that Congress should promote American industries and render the country "independent of others for essential, particularly for military, supplies." But Hamilton raised the tariff to the level of an economic philosophy and forced the country to consider it as an American economic system. In the revenue act of 1792, Congress carried out with modifications the suggestions made by the Secretary of the Treasury, giving particular attention to duties that would afford assistance to American industry.

§

During the prolix and hot-tempered debates that marked the passage of Hamilton's measures through Congress, the country gradually divided into two parties, which grew steadily in coherence of organization and in definiteness of program. To speak more concretely, the antagonism between agriculture and business enterprise that had been so marked in colonial times and had found tense expression during the contest over the Constitution now bore fruit in regular political parties, each with a complete paraphernalia of leaders, caucuses, conventions, names, symbols, and rhetorical defense mechanisms. Candidates were nominated, policies proclaimed, newspapers edited, and spoils distributed with reference to the fortunes of one group or the other. All the passions that go with war were enlisted in contests that eventuated in a counting of heads.

As these two party factions in one form or another have continued to divide the nation, statesmen and theorists have felt called upon to expound the causes of such political antagonisms. Some agree with Macaulay in tracing the origins of party to instinctive differences among people. In every country, that celebrated Whig once declared, there is a party of order and a party of progress; the former, conservative in temper, clings to established things, while the latter, adventurous in spirit, is eager to make experiments. Long afterward a literary critic, Brander Matthews, applied the Macaulay doctrine of innate ideas to American politics; "intuitive Hamiltonians," he said, believe in government by the well-born, while "intuitive Jeffersonians" love and trust the common people. Still another explanation of American parties, one more commonly accepted by Fourth of July orators, is that formulated by James Bryce in The American Commonwealth: our parties originally sprang from differences of opinion concerning the nature and functions of the Union; one exalts federal authority, the other cherishes the rights of the states.

In reality, however, none of these simple explanations does more than skim the surface of politics. None throws any light on the origins of the innate tendencies, for example. With reference to that point all are as cryptic as the statement that God made Federalists and Republicans. Why did one group of politicians take a liberal view of the Constitution and another a narrow view? Whence came the intuitions that divide men? Have they existed since the dawn of history? Why did some trust the people and others fear them? Was it an accident that a New York lawyer stood at the head of the party which despised the masses and a Virginia slave owner led the party which professed democratic faith in the multitude?

The answers to these questions, as far as they are forthcoming at all, lie in the professions of politicians, reported in congressional debates, newspapers, letters, and partisan pamphlets of the Hamiltonian epoch, and if such evidence is to be accepted in court, the causes of the party division were more substantial than matters of temperament or juristic theory. By the time the partisan battle began to rage in full fury, the Federalists had a positive record of achievement to which they could point with pride and assurance. They had restored the public credit by funding the continental and state obligations at face value, incidentally enriching thousands of good Federalists in the process. They had protected American industry and shipping by appropriate economic discriminations against foreign enterprise.

In establishing a national bank and a mint for the coinage of metals, they had provided a uniform national currency for the transaction of business. They had devised a scheme of taxation easily yielding adequate revenues to sustain the huge national debt and all the capitalistic undertakings which rested upon that solid foundation. They had erected a system of national courts in which citizens of one state could effectively collect claims against citizens of other states and they had made it impossible for debtors to outwit their creditors through the medium of paper money and similar methods of impairing the obligation of contracts. They had begun to build an army and a navy, making the American nation so respected abroad that foreign powers no longer dared to treat its ministers with contempt, and giving the flag such substantial significance that the Yankee skipper felt proud and secure under it no matter whether he rode into the waters of European ports, traded rum for Negroes along the African coast, or exchanged notions in Canton for tea and silks. That was an accomplishment measurable in terms of national honor and pride as clearly as in the outward and visible signs of economic prosperity.

Opponents of this general program, taking at first the negative title of Anti-Federalists and later the more euphonious name of Republicans, by no means attacked the idea of exalting American credit and improving the standing of the country among the nations of the earth. In detail, however, they dissented, with varying emphasis, from the propositions contained in the Federalist economic program. They wished to discharge the national debt but not in such a fashion as to enrich speculators or impose a heavy burden of taxation on the masses. Especially were they tender of the people engaged in agriculture. A permanent funded debt and a national bank founded on it, they complained, would tax the farmers and planters to sustain an army of bond holders and stock jobbers.

Speaking on this theme for southern citizens, one Anti-Federalist warned the House of Representatives that his constituents "will feel that continued drain of specie which must take place to satisfy the appetites of basking speculators at the seat of Government. . . . Connecticut manufactures a great deal. Georgia manufactures nothing and imports everything. Therefore, Georgia, although her population is not near so large, contributes more to the public treasury by impost." When the proposal to establish a national bank was before Congress, the same agrarian orator lamented in a similar strain that "this plan of a National Bank is calculated to benefit a small part of the United States, the mercantile interest only; the farmers, the yeomanry, will derive no advantage from it." When the unwrought-steel schedule of the tariff bill was under consideration, Lee, of Virginia, declared that "it would operate as an oppressive though indirect tax upon agriculture, and any tax, whether direct or indirect, upon this interest at this juncture would be unwise and impolitic."

In Five Letters Addressed to the Yeomanry of the United States, a vehement pamphleteer of Philadelphia declared, in 1792, that the laws of the Union were "stained with mercantile regulations impolitic in themselves and highly injurious to the agricultural interests of our country; with funding systems by which the property and rights of poor but meritorious citizens are sacrificed to wealthy gamesters and speculators; with the establishment of Banks authorizing a few men to create fictitious money by which they may acquire rapid fortunes without industry."

Other pamphleteers and partisan editors, writing with a kind of philosophic completeness, denounced the Hamiltonian system root and branch, in the name of the Anti-Federalist faction. Boiled down, their heated arguments amounted to this: the financial interests associated with the funding of the debt, the management of the sinking fund, the control of the Bank, and the protection of industry and commerce by favorable laws have taken possession of the federal government; they operate through the Treasury Department and through the "stock-jobbing" members of Congress; every fiscal and commercial measure adopted at the national capital imposes a burden on agriculture and labor for the benefit of these dominant interests. In a word, the Anti-Federalist leaders saw in Hamilton's policies schemes for exploiting farmers, planters, and laborers for the benefit of capitalists, shipowners, and manufacturers.

Far from being the mere froth of excited politicians, this view represented the matured convictions of leaders given to deliberation and analysis. In several letters addressed confidentially to Washington, Jefferson expounded the economic grievances of his faction. He argued that the national debt had been unnecessarily increased; that the United States Bank had been created as a permanent engine of the moneyed interest for influencing the course of government; and that "the ten or twelve per cent annual profits paid to the lenders of this paper medium are taken out of the pockets of the people who would have had without interest the coin it is banishing; that all capital employed in paper speculation is barren and useless, producing iike that on a gaming-table no accession to itself and is withdrawn from commerce and agriculture where it would have produced addition to the common mass; that it nourishes our citizens in habits of vice and idleness instead of industry and morality; that it has furnished effectual means of corrupting such a portion of the Legislature as turns the balance between the honest voters whichever way it is directed." Of all the mischiefs which Jefferson saw in the Federalist system, "none is so afflicting and fatal to every honest hope as the corruption of the legislature." Of course, Jefferson expressed his alarm over the liberal way in which the Constitution had been construed by the men who formulated and enacted Federalist policies into law, but the gravamen of his complaint was that Hamilton's economic measures exploited one section of society for the benefit of another.

Of the numerous counts in the indictment brought against the Federalists by their opponents, none stung and blistered as much as the charge that members of Congress were enriching themselves by speculating in federal bonds and bank stock. Without any reservations, Jefferson emphatically declared that the grand outlines of Hamilton's system had been carried "by the votes of the very persons who, having swallowed his bait, were laying themselves out to profit by his plans"; and he added that "had these persons withdrawn, as those interested in a question ever should, the vote of the disinterested majority was clearly the reverse of what they had made it."

In two bitter pamphlets, John Taylor, of Virginia, lambasted the "stock-jobbing interest in Congress," even daring to print in thin disguise the names of Senators and Representatives who, according to rumor, held government securities and were interested in the Bank. To this indictment Federalist editors and politicians replied in terse language. Indignantly denouncing Taylor's statements as slanderous and mendacious, they called for demonstrations and insisted that, until substantiated, the allegation "must be regarded as an impotent piece of malice, contemptible alike for its falsehood and its cowardice."

It was, of course, impossible for the Anti-Federalists to prove their charges, for the simple reason that they could not get access to the records of the Treasury Department while the Federalists were in control. When finally, in 1801, the Jeffersonians in their turn were about to take possession of the government, a fire occurred in the Treasury destroying many of the books and papers containing the evidence in the case. By that date the issue had become academic.

More than a hundred years later, however—after the records of the federal loan offices in the several states had been collected in Washington—an examination confirmed the Anti-Federalist indictment. It showed that at least twenty-nine members of the first Congress held federal securities, that some members were extensive operators in public funds during their term of service, and that the list of names given out by John Taylor was astonishingly accurate. Jefferson, therefore, spoke truly when he said that the assumption of state debts could never have been carried if the men who profited by the operation had abstained from voting, on the ground that they were personally interested in it.

Yet it is difficult to see why holders of government bonds were to be denounced for voting in favor of measures affecting their concerns while slave owners were to be pardoned for voting down the Quaker memorials against slavery presented to Congress on March 23, 1790. In fact, Jefferson himself frankly stated that he wanted "the agricultural interest" to govern the country and presumably to pursue policies advantageous to that social group. At bottom, accordingly, the dispute between parties was over economic measures rather than over questions of political propriety.

And the constitutional doctrines and political theories that sprang from this controversy bore a very precise relation to the position taken by the respective parties. The accomplishment of Hamilton's purposes called for a liberal, even an extensive use of the powers conferred upon Congress, and for the imposition of heavy taxes on the masses to sustain the fiscal structure. Wanting above all to gain certain economic ends, the Federalist party naturally came to the conclusion that the Constitution was to be construed freely enough to permit a straight march to the goal. Moreover, since it was the farmers and mechanics rather than the rich and well-born who stood out against Hamilton's system, it was equally natural that its sponsors should fear the triumph of the populace at the polls. On the other side, opponents of that system, forming as they did the party of negation, seized upon every weapon at hand that would help to block the measures they heartily disliked and, by a strict interpretation of the Constitution, discovered legal prohibitions on Federalist proposals.

This was all natural enough in a country so largely dominated by lawyers trained in dialectics, but the intelligent men who made use of such juristic implements were under no delusions about the sources of their thinking. "The judgment is so much influenced by the wishes, the affections, and the general theories of those by whom any political proposition is decided," laconically wrote John Marshall with respect to the Bank, "that a contrariety of opinion on this great constitutional question ought to excite no surprise." On both sides the logicians were equally able and equally sincere; hence it seems reasonable to conclude that neither interpretation of the Constitution, liberal or strict, flowed with the force of exigent mathematics from the language of the instrument itself.

Nevertheless, the politicians and statesmen of the period made much of their appeals to correct views of the Constitution. Leaders of the Federalist party had been largely responsible for the framing and adoption of that document; they understood it; and they demonstrated with a great show of learning that it authorized whatever they wanted it to sanction. The opposition employed the same appeal— for contrary ends. "It is unconstitutional," was the cry that rose daily from the Anti-Federalist ranks as they sought to dethrone Hamiltonism. "Let us return to the Constitution!" exclaimed John Taylor when closing a vitriolic indictment of the Secretary's program and policies. "I scarce know a point," groaned Fisher Ames, "which has not produced this cry, not excepting a motion for adjournment. . . . The fishery bill was unconstitutional; it was unconstitutional to receive plans of finance from the Secretary; to give bounties; to make the militia worth having; order is unconstitutional; credit is ten fold worse." If some of the minor politicians thought their linguistic pattern flowered inexorably from unanswerable premises, there is no doubt that the first thinkers who sat at the loom weaving the texture of American constitutional theory, knew what and how they were designing. It remained for smaller men to treat federal jurisprudence as one of America's Eleusinian mysteries.

In its stark passion the substance of the controversy was brought home to the participants in 1794 when one of Hamilton's measures evoked an explosion. To aid in meeting the increased charges caused by the assumption of state debts, Congress in 1791 after a savage debate passed an excise law laying, among other things, a tax on spirits distilled from grain—an act especially irritating to farmers in the interior already marshaling under opposition banners. Largely owing to the bad roads, which made it hard for them to carry bulky crops to markets, they had adopted the practice of turning their corn and rye into whiskey— a concentrated product that could be taken to town on horseback over the worst trails and through the deepest mud. So extensive was the practice in the western regions of Pennsylvania, Virginia, and North Carolina, that nearly every farmer was manufacturing liquor on a small scale; the first of these states alone according to the reckoning had five thousand distilleries. The excise law, therefore, provided in effect that government officers should enter private homes, measure the produce of the stills, and take taxes for it directly from the pockets of the farmers.

As soon as the news of this excise bill reached the interior, an uprising followed—an outbreak of such proportions that Congress, frightened by the extent of popular dissatisfaction, removed the tax from the smallest stills and quieted the farmers of Virginia and North Carolina. In Pennsylvania, however, the resistance stiffened. Some of the distillers in that state positively refused to pay the tax; while rioters sacked and burned the houses of the collectors just as Revolutionists thirty years earlier had vented their wrath upon King George's agents for trying to sell stamps. When at length a United States marshal attempted to arrest certain offenders in the summer of 1794, a revolt known as the Whiskey Rebellion flared up, resulting in wounds and death.

Stirred by reports of these incidents from the field, Hamilton advised Washington that severe measures were imperative to teach the masses respect for law and order. Though the Secretary's opponents replied that his allegations were unfair, inaccurate, and deliberately planned to strengthen the party in power by a demonstration of authority, the President resolved upon military action. Calling out a strong body of armed men and accompanied by Hamilton, he himself started for the scene of disorder. Before this display of power, the insurgents dispersed and the myth of the rebellion exploded. A few men were arrested and tried; two were convicted only to be pardoned by the President; and an inquiry showed that the gravity of their offense had been exaggerated. Instead of raising the prestige of the administration, the episode added to the strength and pertinacity of the opposition. Jefferson, whose long quarrel with Hamilton had culminated in his resignation from the Department of State, took advantage of the occasion to rally recruits around his agrarian banner.

§

By this time the passions aroused by domestic issues were raised to white heat by dramatic events in the sphere of foreign affairs. A terrible political storm—the French Revolution and the wars let loose by it—was in progress in Europe, leveling kings, princes, aristocracies, and clerical orders, remaking the map of the Old World, and shaking the foundations of all its social systems.

The curtain rose on this scene in the spring of 1789, only a few days after Washington's inauguration, when Louis XVI, the French monarch, on the verge of bankruptcy as a result of royal extravagance and expensive wars, including the costly aid given to the Americans during their struggle for independence, was compelled, after trying many schemes to raise money, to appeal to the people for help. In the hardest of circumstances, he summoned the national parliament, or Estates General, to meet him at Versailles, an action that had not been taken for more than a hundred and fifty years; and amid great excitement, the nobility, clergy, and commoners of France assembled to hear what their king had to say and to say things to him in reply—to ventilate their long-accumulating grievances. Stirred by the thundering eloquence of Mirabeau in the assembly hall, the representatives of the "third estate," the bourgeoisie, brushed aside the nobility and clergy, resolved themselves into a national assembly, and started to exercise sovereign powers in reforming abuses. The ancient dikes once broken, popular floods carried everything before them.

So startling events followed in swift succession. On July 14, the Bastille, a royal prison and symbol of absolutism in Paris, was stormed and destroyed and its prisoners freed. On the night of August 4, the feudal privileges of the nobility, already dissolving in the lurid flames of burning châteaux, were formally surrendered in the national assembly amid tumultuous applause. A few days later the assembly announced the sovereignty of the people, proclaiming the privileges of citizens in a Declaration of the Rights of Man, which immediately took its place beside Jefferson's great charter as one of the imperishable documents in the history of human liberty.

For two long years, one decree after another flowed from the assembly hall, culminating in an elaborate constitution for the kingdom of France which vested the legislative power in a single chamber elected by popular vote. In the autumn of 1791 Louis XVI, frightened by mobs and discovering no avenue of escape, accepted this crowning instrument of revolution. As far as mortal man could see, France had established, largely by peaceable means, a government based on the consent of the governed. The republic of the United States seemed justified in the eyes of the democrats of the Old World.

Nearly all American patriots rejoiced in what seemed to be a fortunate application of the doctrines they had so recently espoused. Thomas Paine indulged in no mere verbal flourish when he declared that "the principles of America opened the Bastille." Certainly the French liberals who had long criticized the evils of their old régime had been encouraged by the American example to undertake this thoroughgoing renovation. French officers and soldiers, after serving in Washington's army, had borne home with them stories of the American experiment that awakened a spirit of emulation. Young philosophers in red-heeled shoes, fresh from the United States, had danced at Louis' court balls and chattered, half in jest and half in earnest, about the superiority of republics over monarchies. The queen, Marie Antoinette, had laughed with them over the foibles of kings and courtiers and, by patronizing Franklin, had given a certain vogue to dangerous republican doctrines.

It was not without reason, therefore, that the citizens of the United States viewed with pride the first stage of the French Revolution as reflecting in some measure their own political wisdom and progressive ideas. "In no part of the globe," wrote John Marshall, "was this revolution hailed with more joy than in America." Those who had misgivings concealed them. "Liberty," exclaimed an overwrought Boston editor, in 1789, "will have another feather in her cap. . . . The ensuing winter will be the commencement of a Golden Age." Washington, to whom La Fayette sent the key of the ruined Bastille, accepted it as a "token of the victory gained by liberty."

Almost at that very moment, however, rumors began to reach the United States that the revolution, so auspiciously opened, was turning into an ominous civil strife. Enraged at the loss of their privileges and at the restraints imposed by the new order, feudal lords and priests fled into Germany, where they plotted to restore the old régime by an invasion of France with German aid. Seeking help in throwing off the shackles imposed on him by the national assembly, Louis XVI, who had sanctioned the recent reforms with vacillating reluctance, now opened negotiations with his brother monarchs across the Rhine. In fact, even before he approved the constitution which it drafted, he attempted to escape from France and was foiled only because some lynx-eyed subject discovered him at Varennes on his way to the border.

While the monarchists were thus preparing a counter-revolution, Paris workmen, denied the ballot by the assembly which had declared the rights of man, held a monster demonstration on the Champs de Mars in the interest of more sweeping reforms, including manhood suffrage. Ordered to disperse, they refused to obey, until they were sent fleeing in every direction by armed forces under La Fayette—a liberal advocate of constitutional government who had no sympathy for leveling democracy. Thus in bloodshed a bitter contest opened between the bourgeois, who had up to this point directed the course of the revolution, and the populace of Paris bent on more radical achievements.

Thereupon life flowed more swiftly and desperately in France, violence rushing to the front of law and argument as the legislative assembly, elected under the constitution recently accepted by Louis XVI, managed by new men, hurried from one action to another in breathless haste. Charging the Austrian Emperor with conspiracy against the reformed régime in France, it declared war on him, adding a foreign conflict to civil discord, mingling the tramp of marching men with the clamor of agitators. As in every electric crisis, dynamic leaders now forged forward to the direction of affairs, while a revolutionary party, known as Jacobins because it held its first session in a monastery of that order, wrested the helm from the feeble hands of the moderates. In June, 1792, the palace of the king was entered by a mob; in July, war was declared on Prussia; in August Louis was deposed; in September, occurred the first of the awful massacres in which counter-revolutionists, innocent and guilty, were put to death. In January, of the following year, Louis XVI was borne to the scaffold. In February, the circle of war was extended to include England and then Spain. Proclaimed first as a bold stroke of defense waged against monarchs determined to destroy democracy, the armed struggle soon developed into a campaign of aggression and conquest that raged for almost twenty-two years with Bonaparte riding the whirlwind to a dictatorship under imperial symbols, meeting at last his nemesis at Waterloo in 1815.

Before this fierce strife was far advanced, a grand national convention was elected and the government of France passed into the hands of a small group of determined radicals, known as the Committee of Public Safety. In every branch, civil and military, extremists took possession of the trappings of power. Resolved to stamp out monarchists, they precipitated a reign of terror in Paris and a civil war in the provinces. Violence answered violence, moving from atrocity to atrocity with the merciless precision of nature. And as the tide of domestic and foreign conflict flowed and ebbed, one factional leader succeeded another in power—Marat, Danton, Robespierre—with increasing passion until the limit of human endurance was reached. Then Bonaparte in 1795 blew away the makers of revolution in "a whiff of grape shot" and gave France twenty years of domestic "order" combined with exhausting foreign wars.

§

The echoes of this shattering conflict—economic, clerical, and political—were heard around the world. Throughout western civilization people were divided into factions according to the nature of their reaction to the course of French events. Across the Channel, in England, Edmund Burke brought up his batteries of thundering oratory to check the spread of French principles; in 1790, even before any serious rioting had lifted its head in Paris, he published his Reflections on the French Revolution, a terrific indictment of the peaceful reconstruction that had been wrought by the national assembly. In this powerful tract he attacked everything that savored of democracy, denouncing the very concept that the English people, for example, had a right to choose their own rulers, frame a government for themselves, or cashier their political authorities for misconduct. The people of England, he said, utterly repudiate the idea; nay, more, "they will resist the practical assertion of it with their lives and fortunes."

Inflamed with wrath at the mere suggestion, Burke could hardly find language hot enough to discharge his emotions against the "frauds, impostures, violences, rapines, murders, confiscations, compulsory paper currencies, and every description of tyranny and cruelty" which marked the drive of the French Revolution. "Learning will be cast into the mire and trodden under the hoofs of a swinish multitude." Dignity, grace, refinement, and all that gives fragrance and beauty to social life, he argued, will be ruined in order that hair-dressers and tallow-chandlers may rule and ruin themselves and then set the world on fire. To stay this process Burke called for war, relentless war, upon the French as monsters and outlaws, demanding the restoration of the genial and benevolent despotism of Louis XVI by English arms. This first assault on French democracy he followed by letters and brochures more and more furious and convulsive until he fairly choked with unquenchable rage.

Though Burke's writings made a furor in England, they might have passed with little notice in America if Thomas

Paine had not undertaken to counteract the campaign of hatred that had been launched against France. But this trenchant pamphleteer, whose appeals had stiffened the backs of American Revolutionists and sent thrills throughout the states in the dark days of the war for independence, now seized his pen again, in order to answer Burke. In a few weeks he flung out to the world the first part of his great apology for democracy—the Rights of Man; and an edition given to the American public with a letter of approval from Jefferson was snapped up with avidity, furnishing the theme of lively debates in taverns, coffee houses, editorial sanctums, and drawing rooms.

"From a small spark," wrote Paine, "kindled in America, a flame has arisen, not to be extinguished." He admitted that disorders had appeared in connection with the French Revolution, but he asked the world to wait on the fullness of time to gather the fruits of the work begun by the national assembly. In any event, Paine argued, man is determined to be free; he will institute his own forms of government; monarchs, aristocracies, and priests cannot stay the tide that rolls in along the shore. "Our people . . . love what you write and read it with delight," wrote Jefferson to Paine. "The printers season every newspaper with extracts from your last, as they did from the first part of your Rights of Man. They have both served here to separate the wheat from the chaff." At a stirring moment in American politics, the pamphleteer had struck a note in perfect tune with the passions of the men then engaged in fighting a bitter campaign against Hamilton's serried ranks of the rich and well-born.

With incredible swiftness the Anti-Federalists organized a network of democratic societies from one end of the United States to the other—using for their model the French political clubs. To Federalists and old Tories it seemed as if new committees of correspondence, such as had engineered the revolution against George III, had sprung into life again, with capacity for infinite mischief.

In all the cities and important towns meetings were held to celebrate the victories of the radical parties in the French Revolution; at a great banquet in Philadelphia hot-headed orators openly exulted in the execution of Louis XVI; everywhere in Anti-Federalist circles the coalition of European monarchs against France—the *cordon sanitaire* against democracy—was denounced as a union of despotism against the principles upon which the American republic was founded.

Applying the lessons to domestic politics, extremists demanded the completion of the leveling process in the United States in accordance with French doctrines. Harmless titles, such as Sir, The Honorable, and His Excellency, were decried as too aristocratic, and in the new language of comradeship, it became the fashion to speak of Citizen Jones, Citizen Judge, Citizeness Smith. In a kindred spirit, excited democrats in Boston insisted on renaming Royal Exchange Alley, Equality Lane; in New York, King Street was rechristened Liberty Street. The President was praised for walking occasionally about the streets like an ordinary person; the Vice-President was criticized for riding in a coach and six. "The rabble that followed on the heels of Jack Cade," exclaimed young John Quincy Adams, "could not have devised greater absurdities than those practiced on America in imitation of the French." Beneath the surface of the popular exuberance, there was a genuine sympathy for the disfranchised artisans in the towns and for the struggling farmers in the country. Poor men contending against adversity saw, or thought they saw, in the success of the French Revolution the final triumph of their faction over "the enemies of the people."

Already deeply moved by domestic agitations, the Federalists became hysterical with fright when the extremists came to the top in the swirling fortunes of Parisian politics. They turned on the democratic societies in America as angrily as Burke turned on English radicals, denouncing them as sappers and miners engaged in destroying the

Constitution. Without restraint, they abused everybody who approved, or who passively refused to condemn with sufficient heat, the proceedings of the French Republic. They applied the term "Jacobin" profusely and indiscriminately to all American citizens who sympathized with France or who attacked the "stock-jobbing squadron" at home. Everything which the "rich and well-born" did not like was damned in respectable circles as "Jacobinical."

Timothy Dwight, president of Yale, stormed and raved. "Shall our sons," he shouted, "become the disciples of Voltaire and the dragoons of Marat; or our daughters the concubines of the Illuminati?" With equal respect for realities, another New England divine declared that Jefferson and his partisans were spreading "the atheistical, anarchical, and in other respects immoral principles of the French revolution." In his anger he read them all out of polite society: "The editors, patrons and abettors of these vehicles of slander ought to be considered and treated as enemies to their country. . . . Of all traitors they are the most aggravatedly criminal; of all villains they are the most infamous and detestable."

A third Puritan clergyman, proposing to go beyond verbiage, called for a war on France so that the Federalist administration could destroy its critics at home—a simple proposal for making traitors out of political opponents. A fourth preacher of the gospel, who lamented the triumph of French principles, thought the course of events especially deplorable because "half a dozen legislators or even scholars bred in New England and dispersed through the different countries of Europe every year" could have changed "the political face of affairs" in the Old World. And now the American radicals had spoiled everything by poisoning the fountains of purity.

§

This pugilistic controversy over revolutionary politics took on a fiercer aspect when American commercial interests became involved in the war between England and France on the high seas; for facts as well as theories now confronted the disputants. English naval commanders seized American produce shipped in French vessels, captured American merchantmen carrying French goods, and searched American ships in a quest for British-born sailors to serve under the Union Jack. On the other side, the French in their way were no gentler; they let loose a flood of privateers, little better than pirates, to prey on American commerce with England; if they did not impress American sailors they often cruelly treated the officers and men who fell into their hands.

When stories of these depredations seeped into the American press, party temper rose accordingly. The Federalists could see every wrong committed by the French; the Anti-Federalists every wrong committed by the English. And things reached a climax when the French Republic called upon the United States for help against England under the old treaty of alliance and friendship made in 1778. Unquestionably the appeal touched a tender spot in America, where the aid rendered to the American Republic in the dark days of her own struggle against England was not forgotten.

But conservative men were at the helm and the times called for discretion. Hamilton, hating French radicalism in every fiber of his being, contended, with more dexterity than logic, that the treaty had been made with the French king and that, on the overthrow of the Bourbon monarchy, the obligations to France were suspended. Also bent on keeping the country out of war at all costs, Washington brushed aside Franklin's famous document and in 1793 proclaimed to the belligerents of Europe the neutrality of the United States. Though Citizen Genêt, the diplomatic representative of the French Republic, was greeted with extravagant acclaim by the Anti-Federalists on his arrival in America, Washington, refusing to be moved by popular clamor, received the emissary with stern formality. When Genêt, angered by this treatment, issued manifestoes, held meetings, attempted to use American ports as bases of operation for French privateers, and, with the aid of American partisans, tried to unhorse Washington's administration, the President bluntly asked the French government to recall the troublesome guest.

With this firm act Washington coupled a policy that augmented the wrath of the opposition. While treating France with frosty propriety, he showed a mild complaisance in dealing with England. British troops still occupied forts in the West; slaves and other property carried off by British soldiers during the American Revolution had not been restored or paid for; and the British navy was playing havoc with American commerce. Against these "wrongs," Jefferson had often protested and on such counts some of his followers, casting off all repressions in their resentment, had repeatedly called for war on England.

On the other side, the Federalist party insisted on peace, its leaders with their usual facility formulating arguments in support of their policy. It was with difficulty, they said, that Washington's administration could raise funds for current outlays and any extraordinary expenditure would bring down in a crash the whole financial structure—the funded debt and the Bank—so recently and so arduously erected by Hamilton. Moreover, American towns were thronged with English merchants; and English investors, besides buying government bonds and bank stock, advanced credit for trade and money for land speculation and industrial enterprise, linking Hamilton's party to the British Empire by a thousand ties of a practical nature. Above and beyond all these things, England was warring on radical France, the detested principles of that republic, on the doctrines of Jeffersonian democracy. Though the Federalists lost heavily from the depredations on their commerce, every consideration of economic interest and political caution commanded them to oppose a second war on King George. In conformity to their wishes, Washington sent the Chief Justice of the Supreme Court, John Jay, to England to negotiate a new treaty disposing of the issues in controversy.

Fully aware of the economic position and military weakness of the United States, the British Government drove a hard bargain with Jay. Its troops were to be withdrawn from the Western forts for that cost no sacrifice and some slight trading concessions were made; but nothing was said about returning the slaves carried off by British soldiers, about the seizure of American ships in the future, or about the impressment of sailors. While England agreed to pay for certain damages done at sea, Jay capitulated on the matter of private debts due British creditors, thereby reopening an old wound.

Many colonial patriots, in joining the revolutionary movement of 1776, had hoped to sponge their accounts with British traders and money lenders—a hope that never died. Even though the treaty of peace which closed the war for independence in 1783 had provided that no barriers should be put in the way of collecting the old bills, a large number of American debtors still managed to postpone the day of judgment and discharge. Never dismayed by delay, British creditors, on their part, continued to prod their representatives at Westminster until finally they had their reward in a clause of the Jay treaty, a clause binding the government of the United States to compensate British claimants for any losses due to impediments placed in the way of collection by judicial process. When the reckoning was made, it was disclosed that three-fourths of the total amount was owed by citizens in the southern states. That was the last straw: the slaves carried away by British soldiers were not to be returned and the hated debts were to be paid—in the last extremity by federal taxation. Planters who regarded with suspicion Jefferson's French ideas were now convinced that the Federalist party at least must be ousted from power and the Jay treaty repudiated.

Jefferson himself denounced the agreement as an infamous alliance between the Anglo-men in the United States and England—a union made in defiance of the people and the legislature. The British minister in Philadelphia, now temporarily the capital of the Republic, was openly insulted by jeering crowds; Hamilton was stoned while attempting to defend the treaty; and Jay was burned in effigy far and wide amid howls of derision from enraged Republicans. For a long time it was found impossible to enlist two-thirds of the Senators in favor of ratification, and the fate of the treaty hung in the balance.

At last, thoroughly alarmed by the peril of defeat, the administration resolved to bring all its influence to bear. Laying down his ledgers, Hamilton wrote a series of powerful papers which he published anonymously. With incisive rhetoric he stung indifferent Federalists to action, warning them that "the horrid principles of Jacobinism" were abroad in the land and that a war with England would throw the direction of affairs into the hands of men professing these terrible doctrines. "The consequences of this," he said, "even in imagination, are such as to make any virtuous man shudder." In the end, by dint of much maneuvering and the use of personal influence, Washington was able to wring from the Senate its approval of the treaty, in June, 1795.

The deed was done but the ill-will aroused by it was not allayed. To display its temper, the opposition in the House of Representatives called upon the President for papers pertaining to the negotiation of the treaty. When it was curtly rebuffed, its wrath deepened, and the populace upon which it relied for support was stirred to renewed opposition. By this time the Anti-Federalists, or Republicans, as they were fond of calling themselves, strengthened by recruits from many quarters, had grown into a fairly coherent party and were evidently resolved upon grasping the powers of the federal government at the coming national election.

§

This state of affairs confirmed Washington in his determination to retire at the end of his second term. He would then be sixty-five years of age and he was weary from his burdensome labors in field and forum. Since the opening of the Revolution, to say nothing of his provincial career, he had spent nearly fifteen years in public service and even while in retirement he had devoted irksome and anxious months to the movement that produced the Constitution. The glory of office had begun to pale. Once he had received respectful homage on all occasions; now near the close of his second administration he was shocked and grieved to find himself spattered with the mud of political criticism. Having definitely aligned himself with the Federalist group and having assumed responsibility for the policies of administration framed by that party, he had voluntarily incurred the risks of partisan attacks. Nevertheless he was distressed beyond measure to hear himself assailed, as he complained, "in such exaggerated and indecent terms as could scarcely be applied to a Nero, a notorious defaulter, or even to a common pickpocket."

These were the circumstances that led him to take advantage of the first opportunity to return to the peace of his Potomac estate. He had accepted reëlection in 1792 only on the urgent solicitation of both Hamilton and Jefferson, who had told him that he alone could save the new fabric of government. But another election was out of the question, not because he regarded the idea of a third term as improper or open to serious objections; he was simply through with the honors and turmoil of politics. Accordingly, in September, 1796, on the eve of the presidential election, he announced his decision in a Farewell Address that is now among the treasured state papers of the American nation.

In this note of affection and warning to his fellow citizens, Washington directed their attention especially to three subjects of vital interest. Having dimly sensed the conflict impending between the North and the South, he gravely cautioned them against sectional jealousies. Having suffered from the excesses of factional strife, he warned them against the extremes of partisanship, saying that in popular governments it is a spirit not to be encouraged. Having observed the turbulent influence of foreign affairs upon domestic politics, he put them on their guard against "permanent alliances with any portion of the foreign world," against artificial entanglements with the vicissitudes of European rivalries, against the insidious wiles of alien intrigues.

Then in simple words of reconciliation he expressed the hope that his country would forgive the mistakes which he had committed during his forty-five years of public life and that he might enjoy, in the midst of his countrymen, "the benign influence of good laws under a free government—the ever favorite object of my heart, and the happy reward, as I trust, of our mutual cares, labors and dangers." Though many Anti-Federalists saw in the Address a veiled attack upon their partisanship and their affection for France, the more moderate elements in both parties regarded it as a message of sound advice from one whose motives were pure and whose devotion to the public good was beyond question.

Hearing that Washington was to retire, the opposition cast off every lingering qualm. Until that moment all save the most brutal critics had curbed somewhat the sweep of their passions, even in denouncing the worst rascals who took shelter behind the great President. At last he was to go from the capital forever and ordinary mortals were to hold the high office which he had filled with such superb decorum. That opened the flood gates. With a show of defiance, Anti-Federalists had branded the Hamiltonians as monarchists and assumed for themselves the name Republican even if it savored of French excesses. Some of them now ventured to call themselves Democrats—a term as malodorous in the polite circles of Washington's day as Bolsheviki in the age of President Harding. Scorning the

Puritan clergy who called Jefferson an atheist and anarchist, all the Anti-Federalists agreed that he was to be their leader and their candidate for President at the coming election.

This challenge the Federalists accepted by nominating a man of opposite opinions, John Adams of Massachusetts. His views on popular government were well known: he had openly declared that he feared the masses as much as he did any monarch and that he favored "government by an aristocracy of talents and wealth." On the main point, therefore, his theories were sound enough for any Federalist; but Adams, even so, was not a strong candidate for a boisterous campaign. While he had spoken contemptuously enough of the crowd, he had poured no libations at the feet of the aristocracy: in an elaborate work he had tried to prove that in every political society there is a perpetual conflict between the rich and the poor, each trying to despoil the other, and that the business of statesmanship is to set bounds for both the contending parties.

Besides being endowed with a somewhat reasoned suspicion of the high and the low, Adams was a student and unfitted for the hustings. He was not an orator or a skillful negotiator; his lightest word smelt of the lamp and his friendliest gesture betrayed a note of irritation. It, therefore, required a desperate campaign to get him into the presidency, with the narrow margin of three votes and, to make the dose more unpalatable, since Jefferson stood second in the poll, Adams found himself yoked for a four-year term with his most redoubtable foe as Vice-President.

Relieved of his burdens, Washington now hurried away from the capital to his haven at Mount Vernon, where praise and affection followed him, yet not without taunts from Republican champions who broke in upon the anthem of gratitude from time to time. In fact, one of the critical editors, a grandson of Benjamin Franklin, flung after the retiring President the burning words: "If ever there was a period for rejoicing, this is the moment—every heart, in unison with the freedom and happiness of the people ought to beat high with exultation that the name of Washington from this day ceases to give a currency to political iniquity and to legalize corruption." If such was the treatment accorded to the great hero of the Revolution, Adams must have been without hope of mercy. And he received none.

Only one measure of the Adams administration won anything like universal approval and that was due mainly to an accident of French politics. Resenting what it regarded as the pro-English policy of President Washington, the Directory at Paris—the executive department established under the constitution of 1795—treated the United States with such lofty contempt that even the hottest defender of France on this side of the Atlantic, as the news was fed to him, felt insulted. Besides bluntly refusing to receive the American minister sent over in the closing days of Washington's administration, it persisted in believing that the President's Proclamation of Neutrality did not represent the real will of the United States. In addition to ordering the confiscation of American vessels bound to and from British ports or engaged in carrying British goods, it permitted French privateers to play havoc with American commerce in the West Indies. Now it was the turn of the Federalists to shed their pacifism and shout for war on "Jacobinical" France. But Adams, refusing to play that game, kept his temper and instead of blustering sent a special commission to France charged with the duty of restoring friendly relations.

When the members of this mission arrived in Paris, they found, so they reported, instead of a decent reception, insolence and effrontery before their faces and intrigue behind their backs. They were denied a formal recognition; but mysterious persons, pretending to speak for the government, visited them after candlelight. Nowhere did they see any signs of good will; on the contrary, according to their accounts, the commissioners were confronted with a demand for an apology from the American government for its past conduct, a large loan, and handsome bribes for

French officials. After haggling for many months in a vain hope for an accommodation, the mission broke off negotiations and sent back dispatches containing a full statement of its difficulties, perhaps not without political embellishments. With a shrewd strategical flair, President Adams immediately laid a report of the transaction before Congress, referring to the Frenchmen who made these demands for tribute and apology as Mr. X, Mr. Y, and Mr. Z.

In the form in which the dose was administered by the President, this was too much even for the stoutest Jacobin in the United States. Some Republicans, it is true, stopped to point out that the American minister sent by Washington and rejected by the French Directory was openly known as a bitter enemy of the French Revolution; others laid stress on the conduct of the British navy toward which the Washington administration had shown so little resentment. But the majority of Jeffersonians, much as they disliked Adams, apparently forgot their French sympathies for the moment and joined the Federalists in shouting: "Millions for defense, not a cent for tribute!" Once more Washington was called upon to take command of the army. Lively preparations for combat were commenced and actual fighting began on the high seas without any formal declaration of war by Congress.

Nevertheless, desiring peace if it could be obtained with decency, Adams renewed negotiations with France amid cries of rage from Federalist fire-eaters. At this juncture, Napoleon Bonaparte, after overthrowing the Directory in Paris by a coup d'état, installed himself as First Consul and indicated willingness to make an accommodation. The following year the two governments succeeded in reaching a kind of agreement that saved their faces, if it did not remove the worst of the irritants. By this time Adams was hopelessly adrift. If he had won some friends among Republicans by declining to plunge into a war against France, he had lost supporters among Federalists, partly by his pacific spirit and partly by his failure to adjust some childish quarrels that arose among officers over precedence in an army that was to fight no battles.

While the Republicans were temporarily weakened by the division of their forces over relations with France, the Federalists resolved in 1798 to destroy the opposition, if possible, with two drastic measures, famous in American history as the Alien and Sedition Acts. The first of these laws authorized the President, in case of war or a predatory incursion, to prescribe the conditions under which alien enemies could be expelled or imprisoned as the public safety might require; thus Adams was given a weapon with which to suppress the activities of the French agents and Irish sympathizers who shared their antipathy for England. The second act was even more severe in its terms; it prescribed fine and imprisonment for persons who combined to oppose any measure of the government, to impede the operation of any law, or to intimidate any officer of the United States in the discharge of his duty; it penalized everyone who uttered or published false, scandalous, and malicious sentiments tending to bring the government of the United States or its officers into disrepute or to excite the hatred of the people.

The Alien Act, although it was not enforced, gave great offense, especially to the many foreigners in danger under its provisions. The Sedition Act was vigorously applied and aroused a tempest. Several editors of Republican papers soon found themselves in jail or broken by heavy fines; bystanders at political meetings who made contemptuous remarks about Adams or his policies were hurried off to court, lectured by irate Federalist judges, and convicted of sedition. In vain did John Marshall urge caution, explaining that the Sedition law was useless and calculated to arouse rather than allay discontent. In vain did Hamilton warn his colleagues: "Let us not establish a tyranny. Energy is a very different thing from violence." The high and mighty directors in the party of "talents and wealth" would be satisfied with nothing short of destroying their opponents.

As Marshall and Hamilton had foreseen, the resentment of the Republicans answered persecution and finally burst all bounds. They denounced the legislation as despotic and its sponsors as tyrants. They invoked the protection of the First Amendment to the Constitution, which expressly forbade Congress to make any law respecting freedom of speech and press. They appealed to the rights of citizens and states.

Not content with the usual verbalism of politics, Jefferson proposed something akin to defiance. He drafted a set of resolutions declaring that the Alien and Sedition Acts violated the Constitution and were therefore null and void —resolutions which were introduced into the Kentucky legislature, passed, signed by the governor, and proclaimed to the country as representing the creed of the state. Simultaneously, Jefferson's competent aide, James Madison, started a similar revolt in Virginia, inducing the legislature to adopt resolutions condemning the obnoxious legislation and advising the states to coöperate in defense of their rights.

Though Kentucky and Virginia discovered that their appeals encountered indifference or even opposition on the part of their neighbors, they were not daunted. The former, hearing from some of the northern states that it was the business of the Supreme Court to decide high questions of law, announced, in reply, the fateful doctrine that a state could review acts of Congress itself and nullify any measure it deemed unconstitutional. While the Virginia legislature shrank from the full logic of this strong doctrine, it did appropriate money for arms and supplies. Fortunately for the Republicans, the fourth presidential election was now at hand and they could call upon the voters to repudiate at the polls the authors of the Alien and Sedition Acts. The issue became a factor, at least a rhetorical factor, in a nation-wide campaign.

§

By unanimous consent leadership among the Republicans went to Jefferson. After some study of Hamilton's system in operation, he had become an irreconcilable opponent of all the leading measures fostered by the Secretary of the Treasury. He had objected to the Bank on economic and constitutional grounds. He had expressed critical opinions about the administrations of Washington and Adams which pleased the most radical among the agrarian faction. Indeed, it was easy for him to satisfy the aspirations of that party for, on matured conviction, Jefferson was primarily a champion of agriculture. He sincerely believed that the only secure basis of a republic was a body of free, land-owning farmers, enjoying the fruits of their own toil, looking to the sun in heaven and the labor of their own hands for their support and their independence.

Like Aristotle two thousand years before and agricultural philosophers through all the succeeding ages, Jefferson distrusted the arts of commerce and industry, the arts of buying in the cheapest market and selling in the dearest. These pursuits led inevitably, he thought, to chicanery, to the accumulation of great wealth by speculation, intrigue, and exploitation. For the artisans and laborers who served the masters of commerce and industry in the crowded towns, he had a great dislike, once going so far as to declare that the mobs of great cities were sores on the body politic, panders to vice, makers of revolution. As a corollary, he was convinced that the American system of liberty would come to an end when the people were congested in cities and dependent for a livelihood upon the caprices of trade. Such was his deliberate judgment formulated long before the Constitution was framed or the fortunes of politics had opened the presidency to him. This opinion was but hardened by his experience at the national capital and the ferocious treatment he had received from "the paper men" whom he had so severely denounced.

Jefferson, however, was more than an avowed opponent of Hamilton's fiscal system and more than a convinced champion of agriculture. He held views concerning human nature and human progress which were abhorrent to those who loved tranquillity in an established social system sustained by dogmatic religious sanctions. In an age when the masses of Europe were without education and were regarded as an inferior order of human beings, Jefferson declared his belief that "man was a rational animal, endowed by nature with rights and with an innate sense of justice; and that he could be restrained from wrong and protected in right by moderate powers confided to persons of his own choice and held to their duties by dependence on his own will." While seasoned politicians of the Federalist school were expressing contempt for theories of popular rule, Jefferson was contending that men "habituated to think for themselves and to follow reason as their guide" could be more easily and safely governed than people "debased by ignorance, indigence, and oppression." With him this was more than a formal faith. "I have sworn upon the altar of God," he wrote to a friend in 1800, "eternal hostility against every form of tyranny over the mind of man."

The same spirit characterized his theories of education. While a New England college president was proudly assuring the public that Gibbon's godless Decline and Fall of Rome was not allowed in his institution of learning, Jefferson was dreaming of a system of universal secular education. In later life he realized a part of this lofty ideal in the University of Virginia, founded under his leadership, where he provided for a democratic scheme of self-government by the professors, rejected all religious tests for teachers and pupils, exalted science, agriculture, and modern languages to a position of equality with the classics, and relied for discipline on student honor. "The institution," he said at the time, "will be based on the illimitable freedom of the human mind. For here we are not afraid to follow the truth wherever it may lead or to tolerate any error so long as reason is left free to combat it."

For his religious ideas as for his political and educational theories, Jefferson was hateful to the orthodox of every sect. In common with so many philosophers of his age he was a deist who regarded Jesus as a great teacher and a good man. He applied higher criticism to the Bible, tested its science in the light of reason, and expressed grave doubts about the authenticity of its statements respecting creation, the flood, and other points relative to the system of nature. Though roundly denounced by theologians as an "atheist," an epithet lacking both in accuracy and fairness, Jefferson made no effort to conceal his liberality of opinion.

If reason was to be the guide in politics, religion, and education it followed that freedom of press and speech must be an essential element in the human scheme of things. This theory Jefferson also carried to its logical conclusion; utterly rejecting the tyrant's plea that liberty can be best protected by "beating down licentiousness," he went the whole length in asserting that the government should not interfere with the expression of opinion until it merged into an overt act. Even open resistance to government, which logic forced him to face, was not so dreadful in his eyes; when he heard of Shays' uprising in Massachusetts, he exclaimed: "God forbid that we should ever be for twenty years without such a rebellion."

§

In view of Jefferson's doctrines it is not surprising that consternation ran swiftly through the circles of wealth and refinement in the middle and northern states when the news of his election to the presidency was sent broadcast in the autumn of 1800. Federalist ladies shook their wise heads over teacups and shuddered with horror as they spoke of the "atheist and leveler from Virginia." Federalist politicians and conservative gentlemen stood aghast:

all the grace and dignity of life, everything founded on knowledge and morals seemed destroyed in a flash. "Reason, common sense, talents, and virtue," wrote one essayist, "cannot stand before democracy. Like a resistless flood, it sweeps all away." The end of all good things had come. "Old Gates used to tell me in 1776," wrote one of John Jay's friends, "that if the bantling Independence lived one year, it would last to the age of Methuselah. Yet we have lived to see it in its dotage, with all the maladies and imbecilities of extreme old age." A journalist who had passed happily through the Revolutionary War bemoaned "the spirit of innovation which has lately gained strength in our borders, and now counteracts the best tendency of regular habits."

The depth of Federalist consternation was exhibited in an astounding proposal of Hamilton to prevent the triumph of Jefferson by a measure of doubtful legality and still more doubtful decency. In New York, where the presidential electors were still chosen by the state legislature, the election of the two houses in May, 1800, indicated that Jefferson would be victorious in the autumn. Therefore, Hamilton proposed that the governor, John Jay, call the old legislature in a special session to change the law and provide for the choice of presidential electors by popular vote in districts so arranged as to assure a majority for the Federalist candidate. In making this suggestion, Hamilton added that "scruples of delicacy and propriety" ought to give way when one was faced with the task of preventing "an atheist in religion and a fanatic in politics from getting possession of the helm of state." This extraordinary step Hamilton thought justified by "unequivocal reasons of public safety," but Governor Jay was unmoved. With simple directness, he wrote on the back of Hamilton's letter these words: "Proposing a measure for party purposes, which it would not become me to adopt." By letting affairs take their normal course, the honest governor assured the victory of a man whose views he heartily disliked.

When the returns were all in after the autumn storm, it was found that the Republican candidates, Jefferson and Burr, had fairly defeated Adams and Pinckney, their Federalist rivals, but were themselves tied; each had received the same number of electoral votes. Of course, everyone understood that the Republicans wanted Jefferson for President but, under the Constitution, the choice had to be determined by the House of Representatives. Consequently a momentary ray of hope gleamed through the murky darkness of Federalist defeat. In making the decision, the delegation of each state represented in the House had just one vote and, under this provision of the law, Federalists commanded a majority. They could choose either Jefferson or Burr for President or they could postpone the choice indefinitely.

As soon as word of the tie was confirmed, there opened a fierce and sordid battle in the House over the selection of the President. Finding that Burr's sense of propriety did not impel him to withdraw from the race, the Federalists began negotiations with him and also with Jefferson for the purpose of gaining from the candidate of their final choice a promise to uphold, when elected, all the essential points in the Hamiltonian program. At first many of them were decidedly inclined toward Burr on general principles—toward that wayward, spectacular, and mysterious grandson of Jonathan Edwards. For some strange reason one of the Federalist leaders thought Burr "a matter-of-fact" man who held "no pernicious theories" and justly appreciated "the benefits resulting from our commercial and national systems." Accordingly, Burr was duly sounded but he would not give the requisite pledges.

In the meantime his deadly enemy, Hamilton, laying aside his bitter hostility to Jefferson, threw himself into the fray on the side of the Virginian candidate. While rumor ascribes Hamilton's hatred for Burr to rivalry for the affections of a woman, it was not necessary to add that hypothesis to the incidents of political strife. Hamilton simply did not share the views of his Federalist brothers; on the contrary he baldly branded Burr as a "Cataline." He thought that Jefferson was fanatical, unscrupulous, not very mindful of the truth and indeed a contemptible hypocrite, but even so more likely to temporize, bargain, and pursue a moderate course than his colleague on the Republican ticket.

So Hamilton suggested that the rival, Jefferson, be invited to give assurances with regard to the preservation of "the actual fiscal system," adherence to neutrality, and the continuance of the Federalists in all save the highest administrative positions. In the end, Jefferson was seen, made known his views, and was chosen by the House over Burr. By his action in the case, Hamilton added fuel to the fire of enmity which culminated in his death three years later at the hands of Burr in one of the most sensational duels ever fought on American soil.

§

On account of his commitments and the strength of the Federalists in Congress, Jefferson had to proceed cautiously after his inauguration; and yet he and his followers moved steadily in the direction which they had mapped out during the campaign of 1800. They had laughed at Adams' coach and six and at attempts of Americans to ape the ceremonials of European courts. In keeping with their agrarian sentiments, Jefferson's inauguration on March 4, 1801, the first at the new capital in Washington, was marked by studied simplicity. Republicans had thought that Washington's custom of reading his messages to Congress smacked of the speech from the throne. Jefferson was no orator; so he adopted the practice of sending his recommendations to Congress by a clerk—a rule that was maintained unbroken until 1913, when President Wilson returned to the example set by Washington.

As if to emphasize his objections to official ritual, Jefferson received the British Ambassador in untidy dress and slippers worn at the heel. He did not, as is sometimes averred, ride to the capitol on horseback, tie his horse to a post, and walk up to take the oath of office; but this apocryphal story illustrated the spirit of the new reign, "the great revolution of 1800," as Jefferson was fond of calling it.

In the business of government, the Republicans, if not intransigent, kept their thesis well in mind. They had denounced the funded debt as a means of creating a "money power"; they did not repudiate any part of it but they paid it off as rapidly as they could. They had objected to the excise tax, especially on whisky, and they quickly abolished it amid the general rejoicing of the back-country farmers. They had protested against the high cost of the federal establishment and they reduced expenses by eliminating many civil offices. They had held commerce in low esteem and viewed the navy as a Federalist device for defending it; in line with this theory they cut down the naval program.

In dealing with the distribution of federal offices, however, the Republicans proceeded with care even though they found all good berths occupied by Federalist politicians. During the negotiations that preceded his election Jefferson had, according to reports, agreed to deal gently with the minor employees of the government; he had also enunciated the noble sentiment that offices should be open to all on the principle of merit alone. Consequently he made no wholesale removals, but as vacancies occurred from time to time he was careful to fill them with trusted partisans as a matter of course. Believing that Hamilton's party had used the branches of the United States Bank in building up its machine, Jefferson expressed himself "decidedly in favor of making all the banks Republican by sharing deposits among them in proportion to the dispositions they show." In actual operation, therefore, he discovered, as he remarked, that "what is practicable must often control what is pure theory."

In keeping with Republican criticism of the sedition law,

Jefferson first proposed to declare it null and void in a message to Congress but finally he just decided not to enforce it against offenders arrested before the expiration of the act on March 3, 1801, and to pardon prisoners then in jail for violation of its provisions. Ultimately Congress repaid most, if not all, the fines that had been collected under the statute. The Republicans had been deeply offended by the stump speeches delivered by Federalist judges when instructing juries; and they promptly voted to impeach Samuel Chase, a justice of the Supreme Court, who had been especially severe in denouncing democratic doctrines from the bench. If they failed to convict him, it was due to no lack of zeal in his prosecution; the Federalists were simply too strong in the Senate where the trial was held.

Though defeated in their effort to oust Chase from office, the Republicans were able to get rid of the new district judges appointed during the "midnight hours" of Adams' administration; this they accomplished by the heroic process of repealing the law creating the judgeships. In vain did the Federalist Senators rave against this "assault upon the judiciary," declare that judges were entitled to a life tenure, and cry out that the repeal of the law would bring the Constitution down as a total wreck about them. The Republicans had suffered much at the hands of Federalist judges and they were in no mood to tolerate a single one who could be ejected from power.

In expelling, reducing, abolishing, and repealing, the Republicans were incidentally following the line of strict construction but they made no particular point of the issue at this time. They were willing to vote federal funds to build a national highway into the West where Jefferson's free farmers were in need of help and were flocking to the Republican standard. They were willing to buy the Louisiana Territory, even though Jefferson believed the purchase without constitutional warrant; for that expansion of the Constitution and the country brought more land on which to rear sturdy agrarians. Jefferson, a practical man as well as a theorist, steered the ship of state by the headlands, not by distant and fixed stars.

§

In their navigation, however, the Republicans, particularly the local politicians of that school, had to reckon with the Federalist interpretation of the Constitution by John Marshall, who, as Chief Justice of the Supreme Court of the United States, from 1801 to 1835, never failed to exalt the doctrines of Hamilton above the claims of the states. No difference of opinion about his political views has ever led even his warmest opponents to deny his superb abilities or his sincere devotion to the national concept. All have likewise agreed that for talents, native and acquired, he was an ornament to the humble democracy which brought him forth. His whole career was American. Born on the frontier of Virginia, reared in a log cabin, granted only the barest rudiments of formal education supplemented by a few months of law at William and Mary, inured to hardship and rough surroundings, Marshall rose by masterly efforts to the highest judicial honor America could bestow.

On him the bitter experience of the Revolution and of later days made a lasting impression. He was no "summer patriot." He had been a soldier in the revolutionary army. He had suffered with Washington at Valley Forge. He had seen his comrades in arms starving and freezing because the Continental Congress had neither the power nor the inclination to force the states to do their full duty. To him the Articles of Confederation had been from the first a symbol of futility. Into the struggle over the formation of the Constitution and its ratification in Virginia, he had thrown himself with the ardor of a soldier. Later, as a member of Congress, an envoy to France, and Secretary of State, he had aided the Federalists in applying their principles of government. When at length they were driven from the executive and legislative branches of the government, he was chosen for their last stronghold, the Supreme Court. By historic irony, he administered the oath of office to his bitterest enemy, Thomas Jefferson; and for a quarter of a century after the author of the Declaration of Independence retired to private life, the stern Chief Justice continued to announce old Federalist rulings from the Supreme Bench.

Marshall had been in his high post only two years when he laid down for the first time in the name of the entire Court the doctrine that the judges have the power to declare an act of Congress null and void when in their opinion it violates the Constitution. This power was not expressly conferred on the Court. Though many able men had held that the judicial branch of the government enjoyed it, the principle was not positively established until 1803 when the case of Marbury *vs.* Madison, involving a section of a federal statute, was decided.

In rendering the opinion of the Court, Marshall cited no precedents, laid no foundations for his argument in ancient lore. Rather did he rest it on the general character of the American system. The Constitution, ran his premise, is the supreme law of the land; it controls and binds all who act in the name of the United States; it limits the powers of Congress and defines the rights of citizens. If Congress could ignore its limitations and trespass upon the privileges of citizens, Marshall argued, then the Constitution would disappear and Congress would become sovereign. Since the Constitution must be and is from the nature of things supreme over Congress, it is the duty of judges, under their oath of office, to sustain it against measures which violate it. Therefore, reasoning from the inherent structure of the American constitutional system, the courts must declare null and void all acts which are not authorized. "A law repugnant to the Constitution," he closed, "is void and the courts as well as other departments are bound by that instrument." From that day to this the practice of federal and state courts in passing upon the constitutionality of laws has remained unshaken.

Yet at the moment this doctrine was received by Jefferson and many of his followers with consternation. If the idea was sound, he exclaimed, "then indeed is our Constitution a complete *felo de se* [legally, a suicide]. For, intending to establish three departments, coördinate and independent, that they might check and balance one another, it has given, according to this opinion, to one of them alone the right to prescribe rules for the government of the others, and to that one, too, which is unelected by and independent of the nation. . . . The Constitution, on this hypothesis, is a mere thing of wax in the hands of the judiciary which they may twist and shape into any form they please. It should be remembered, as an axiom of eternal truth in politics, that whatever power in any government is independent, is absolute also. . . . A judiciary independent of a king or executive alone is a good thing; but independent of the will of the nation is a solecism, at least in a republican government." But Marshall was mighty and his view prevailed, though from time to time other men, clinging to Jefferson's opinion, likewise opposed judicial exercise of the high power proclaimed in Marbury *vs.* Madison.

Had Marshall stopped with declaring unconstitutional an act of Congress, he would have heard less criticism from Republican quarters; but, with the same firmness, he set aside important acts of state legislatures as well, whenever, in his opinion, they violated the federal Constitution. In 1810, in the case of Fletcher *vs.* Peck, he annulled a law of the Georgia legislature, informing the state that it was not sovereign, but "a part of a large empire . . . a member of the American union; and that union has a Constitution . . . which imposes limits to the legislatures of the several states." In the case of McCulloch *vs.* Maryland, decided in 1819, the Chief Justice declared void an act of the Maryland legislature designed to paralyze the branches of the United States Bank established in that state. In the

same year, in the still more memorable Dartmouth College
case, he abrogated an act of the New Hampshire legislature which infringed upon the charter received by the
College from King George long before. That charter, he
asserted, was a contract between the state and the College,
which under the federal Constitution no legislature could
impair. Two years later Marshall stirred the wrath of
Virginia by summoning her to the bar of the Supreme Court
to answer in a case involving the validity of one of her laws
and then justified his action in a powerful opinion rendered
in the case of Cohens *vs.* Virginia.

All these decisions aroused the legislatures of the states,
especially those in Republican control. They passed sheaves
of resolutions protesting and condemning; but Marshall
never turned and never stayed. The Constitution of the
United States, he fairly thundered at them, is the supreme
law of the land; the Supreme Court is the proper tribunal
to pass finally upon the validity of the laws of the states;
and "those sovereignties," far from possessing the right
of review and nullification, are irrevocably bound by the
decisions of the Court. This was strong medicine for the
authors of the Kentucky and Virginia Resolutions and for
the members of the Hartford convention; but they had
to swallow it.

While restricting Congress in the Marbury case and the
state legislatures in a score of cases, Marshall also laid
the judicial foundation for a broad and liberal view of
the Constitution as opposed to narrow and strict construction. In McCulloch *vs.* Maryland he construed generously the words "necessary and proper" in such a way
as to confer upon Congress a wide range of "implied powers" in addition to its express powers. Since the case
involved, among other things, the question whether the act
establishing the second United States Bank was authorized
by the Constitution, Marshall felt impelled to settle the
issue by a sweeping and affirmative opinion. Congress, he
argued, has large powers over taxation and the currency;

a bank is of appropriate use in the exercise of its enumerated powers; and therefore, though not absolutely necessary, a bank is entirely proper and constitutional. "With respect to the means by which the powers that the Constitution confers are to be carried into execution," he said, Congress must be allowed the discretion which "will enable that body to perform the high duties assigned to it, in the manner most beneficial to the people." In short, the Constitution of the United States is not a strait-jacket but a flexible instrument vesting in the national legislature full authority to meet national problems as they arise. In delivering this opinion Marshall used language almost identical with that employed by Lincoln when, standing on the battlefield of Gettysburg, he declared that "government of the people, by the people, for the people, shall not perish from the earth."

CHAPTER IX

Agricultural Imperialism and the Balance of Power

IF the philosophical Jefferson and his official family thought that they could settle down in political power to the enjoyment of peace, light taxes, and arcadian pleasures, they were soon disillusioned. The agricultural interest, which they so proudly represented, was no provincial estate sufficient unto itself. On the contrary, it depended for its prosperity upon the sale of its produce in the markets of the Old World while its advance guard on the frontier cherished imperial designs upon the neighboring dominions of England and Spain.

Therefore American agriculture vibrated in its fortunes with every turn in the European balance of power, never more precisely than in the third year of Jefferson's administration when the fury of the Napoleonic tempest was again unleashed across the sea. No theory of isolation could protect it from the shock of a struggle for empire that extended from London to Ceylon, from Moscow to Mexico City, from Copenhagen to Cape Town, encircling the globe

391

with fire. America as well as Europe was set afloat. Within a few years the Republicans in control of the federal government, buffeted by gales from abroad and by passions at home, were exercising powers greater than any ever claimed by Hamilton and defending the constitutionality of laws which they had once rejected. And in this swift whirl of fact and philosophy, their opponents, the Federalists, were forced into a narrow and crabbed provincialism that made Jefferson's juristic argument against the United States Bank seem broad and generous in comparison.

It has long been the fashion of historians to cite this reversal of fortunes in demonstrating the mutability of human affairs and the hollowness of political professions. Do not the items stand written clearly in the bond? The Republicans had proclaimed their unshakable faith in a narrow interpretation of the Constitution; in 1803 they purchased Louisiana—an act which Jefferson himself called a violation of the supreme law; a few years later they invoked the power of regulating commerce to justify a measure abolishing it and a "force bill" carrying that embargo into effect. Celebrating the virtues of agriculture, they had scorned the arts of trade; yet they vowed that their war on Great Britain was made with a view to upholding American commercial rights upon the high seas. They had opposed a national Bank and a protective tariff; but, at the close of their experiment in war, they resorted to both expedients in spite of their legal scruples.

And on the other side was the record of the Federalists. They had proclaimed their steadfast faith in a liberal view of the Constitution; but they could find no warrant in the parchment for the Louisiana purchase or the embargo. They had taken pride in cherishing the arts of trade; yet they voted against the war on England which was supposed to sustain the inviolability of American commerce. The reversal of politics, considered in terms of political rhetoric, seemed to be absolute.

Considered, however, in economic terms, it was a reversal of means not ends. If the purchase of Louisiana was unconstitutional, it at least added millions of acres of rich farming lands to be developed by Jefferson's beloved "agricultural interest." In the sphere of politics it also meant, as the Federalists said, the overbalancing of "the commercial states" by agricultural commonwealths. If in form the war on England was declared for commercial motives, it was in reality conceived primarily in the interests of agriculture.

This fact the scholarly researches of Julius W. Pratt have demonstrated in a convincing fashion. Agriculture just as shipping suffered from British depredations, for American exports were, in the main, not manufactures but the produce of farms and plantations. The men who voted in 1812 for the declaration of war on England represented the agrarian constituencies of the interior and their prime object was the annexation of Florida and Canada. Hence the opposition of the commercial sections to an armed conflict waged for the purpose of adding more farmers and planters to the overbalancing majority was at bottom no deep mystery.

Nor was the reversal of the Republican position on finance shrouded in obscurity. The second United States Bank, established by that party, did not grow out of a desire to draw the banking fraternity to the support of the government as in Hamilton's time but in truth sprang from a struggle to free the federal treasury from abject dependence on eastern financial interests and rescue the currency from the chaos created by the war. And finally, the protective tariff adopted by the Republicans in 1816 was defended by the spokesman of the planting interest, John C. Calhoun, on the ground that tariff schedules, when properly made, would provide a home market for cotton, corn, and bacon. At that time New England banks, strong enough to stand alone, welcomed no new rival in the hands of Jeffersonian politicians; and New England capitalists, largely engrossed in the carrying trade, did not look with favor on customs duties that promised to cut it down. If reference be had, therefore, to the substance of things desired, some of the ambiguity of jurisprudence seems to be removed and the continuity of economic forces once more demonstrated.

§

The first great stroke of Republican policy in the sphere of foreign relations, namely, westward expansion by the purchase of the Louisiana territory in 1803, was no bolt out of the blue either for the planters and farmers of the West or for Jefferson, who professed to cherish their interests. A decade before that event there were hundreds of American pioneers in the Spanish territory beyond the Mississippi; near the close of the eighteenth century the bishop of Louisiana reported that "the Americans had scattered themselves over the country almost as far as Texas and corrupted the Indians and Creoles by the example of their own restless and ambitious temper." Already promoters in the West had their eyes fixed on Mexico and were blowing up colorful dreams of imperial annexations to be realized in that direction.

Already the war in Europe had forced the fate of the West upon the attention of the federal government. The first phase of that struggle had opened, as we have seen, in 1793, while Thomas Jefferson was still serving as Secretary of State under President Washington, in a strategic post of observation from which he discovered many things. Especially did he grasp the meaning of the fact that, in the general scramble for spoils among the powers of the Old World, England might wrest Louisiana from the feeble grasp of the Spanish monarch—a menace to the United States to be avoided at all costs. Though he retired from the State Department in 1793, Jefferson retained his keen interest in the advancing frontier and continued to appreciate its importance.

During the intervening years until his inauguration as

President, events flowed swiftly in the regions beyond the Alleghenies as a steady stream of settlers moved westward with the sun. Kentucky was admitted to the Union as a state in 1792 and Tennessee in 1796, both of them good agricultural communities that gave electoral votes to Jefferson in 1800. Ohio, then rapidly filling up, was to have a voice in the next presidential election. The whole West was vibrant with prospects of great agricultural enterprise and the leaders who directed affairs in the Mississippi Valley knew what they wanted. They were unanimous in their resolve that the Mississippi must be kept open to American trade all the way to the Gulf of Mexico; and those with the largest imagination, as we have just said, were prepared for imperial undertakings beyond the mighty river. If Jefferson was inclined to hold back and deal timidly with foreign powers, he could not escape the firm pressure of his frontier constituents. In fact the very existence of the western farmers and planters, to say nothing of handsome earnings, depended upon the navigation of the Mississippi without let or hindrance.

Down the river to New Orleans they floated their tobacco, corn, hemp, wheat, pork, and lumber for shipment to the towns on the eastern seaboard or the markets of the Old World. To them this outlet to the sea was as important as the harbor of Boston to the merchants of that metropolis. For their bulky produce, transportation over muddy roads across the mountain barrier was almost prohibitive in its cost. Tea, coffee, cloth, and nails might come to them that way but, before the age of steamboats and improved roads, farm produce had to find a less expensive and more practical route. Therefore, in their search for a livelihood, in their quest for profitable enterprise, the men on the frontier were compelled to keep open the port of New Orleans. Moreover, if their restless spirit of migration was not to be quenched forever on the east bank of the Mississippi, then their next march would carry them beyond the borders of the existing American dominion. By 1800 Kentucky had grown too civilized for Daniel Boone; and signs of the onward surge were clearly evident.

Accordingly, the frontiersmen watched with eagle eyes the fortunes of the King of Spain to whom at the close of the Seven Years' War in 1763 had fallen the prize of Louisiana. While he controlled New Orleans, there was little to fear. No doubt he resented the constant activity of Americans on the banks of the Mississippi; no doubt he grew angry when he read in the reports of his governors that these aggressive aliens looked greedily upon his untilled lands; but he was powerless to hold them in check.

While the outward signs of his immense empire were still imposing, a frightful palsy afflicted it from the center to the circumference. The valor, the energy, the capacity for great undertakings, which in the sixteenth century had made the name of Spain feared throughout Europe and around the world, had departed, leaving infirmity and incompetence supreme at Madrid and in the provinces. So in 1795 when Washington pressed the Spanish sovereign for a treaty granting Americans the right of trade through New Orleans, he won that privilege with relative ease. When five years later Napoleon covertly demanded the return of Louisiana to France, there was no alternative but secret compliance.

In the summer of 1802 a crisis was precipitated: a royal order from Spain in July closed the port of New Orleans to American produce. Hard on the heels of this news came a confirmation of the rumor that Napoleon had really wrested Louisiana from Spain. At any time, therefore, the French flag might be raised on the American border; for a temporary lull in the European War—effected by the treaty of Amiens signed in the spring of that year— promised the Corsican an opportunity to tempt fortune next in the New World. In a few months "the scalers of the Alps and the conquerors of Venice" might appear in

New Orleans, Natchez, and St. Louis. Their capacity for action was notorious.

Immediately the West was ablaze with excitement and alarm. Immediately a turbulent call to arms resounded along the frontier; expeditions were organized to prevent the landing of French troops; the legislators of Kentucky passed resolutions of protest against "invasion," pledging their lives and fortunes to sustain their rights; petitions for immediate aid flooded in upon the philosopher in the White House. Whatever his inclination, Jefferson was thus made aware that willful and irascible leaders in the West would open New Orleans by force if the federal government could not open it by negotiation.

If Jefferson's natural love of tranquillity and his affection for a strict construction of the Constitution had been ten times as great, the clamor of the West would have compelled him to act. He knew a political storm when he saw it on the horizon; so he urged his ebullient frontier constituents to restrain their ardor until he could try the resources of diplomacy.

Then he set the machinery in motion at Paris, thinking all the time of the produce dammed up at New Orleans rather than of the expansion of America in the abstract. The crisis, he evidently thought, was to be considered in terms of corn, tobacco, and bacon. "The cession of Louisiana and the Floridas by Spain to France," he wrote to Livingston, the American minister in Paris, "works sorely in the United States. It completely reverses all the political relations of the United States and will form a new epoch in our political course. . . . There is on the globe one single spot the possessor of which is our natural and habitual enemy. It is New Orleans through which the produce of three-eighths of our territory must pass to market." Spain might have retained it in her weakening hands for years, he went on to say, but the occupation of New Orleans by France would be a menace that could not be ignored. Thus driven by realities Jefferson instructed Livingston to sound Napoleon on the possibility of buying New Orleans and also the Florida territory east of the Mississippi—on the assumption that the latter had gone to France with the Louisiana region.

To fortify Livingston and emphasize the urgency of action, Jefferson sent James Monroe to France with instructions to help make a treaty that would enlarge and secure American rights and interests on the Mississippi and "the territories eastward thereof." But before Monroe arrived in Paris, events had already begun to move with high speed. A French expedition to subjugate rebellious Santo Domingo had met disaster, warning Napoleon against adventures in the New World. Moreover, he had decided to renew the European war and needed to husband all his resources. Fully conscious that he had no fleet capable of coping with England, he knew that the loss of Louisiana in the impending conflict was as certain as fate.

With characteristic abruptness, Napoleon decided to sell to the United States every inch of the territory so recently wrung from Spain and instructed his minister of foreign affairs to open negotiations for that purpose. A few hours later Livingston was suddenly confronted by the astounding offer of the whole Louisiana domain. For a moment he was bewildered because he had no orders authorizing him to buy an empire; but his courage being equal to the occasion, he accepted the proposal. Monroe, who appeared on the scene at this moment, added his approval; and on April 30, 1803, the treaty of cession was signed by the negotiators. According to its terms, the Louisiana Territory, as received from Spain, was to be transferred to the United States in return for $11,250,000 in six per cent bonds plus the discharge of certain claims held by American citizens against France—a purchase price amounting to $15,000,-000 in all. When the deed was done Livingston exclaimed that the action would in time transform vast solitudes into flourishing communities, reduce England from her still dominant position in American affairs, and give the United States a position of first rank among the great powers of the earth.

Spain protested passionately and the French newspapers stormed. Napoleon's brothers, Lucien and Joseph, called on him to remonstrate. According to one story, they found him in his bath but insisted on seeing him at once to present their objections to the sale. Angered by their intrusion, Napoleon rose in haste, berated them for their insolence, and drenched them with water as he plunged back into his tub. When Lucien, not yet subdued, lingered to voice his opposition to the disposal of so fair a province, the First Consul, with an impatient gesture, flung his snuff box to the floor, declaring he would break his own brother in the same fashion if his opposition continued. In France the issue was closed.

When the news crossed the Atlantic the people of the United States were aroused in their turn—no one more astounded than Jefferson. He had thought of buying New Orleans and West Florida for a small sum but an empire had been dumped at his feet at a staggering price. He had cried aloud against the immense national debt amassed by Hamilton and had instructed Gallatin, his own Secretary of the Treasury, to bend every effort to reduce it; now he was asked to add fifteen million dollars to the burden himself at one stroke. He had pledged himself to abide by the letter of the Constitution and he could find no word in it expressly authorizing the government of the United States to buy a square foot of land.

His first thought being for ceremonial correctness, Jefferson prepared an amendment to the Constitution which would authorize the purchase. But delay was dangerous and changing the fundamental law of the land was a slow process. So under the stress of necessity Jefferson abandoned that project and simply called upon the Senate to ratify the treaty of cession. Exercising a keener vision than they had shown a few years before, his friends now discovered authority for that action in the treaty-making clause and in other corners of the nation's supreme law.

Delighted to receive a legal sanction, Jefferson acquiesced on the point of theory, saying that "the good sense of our country will correct the evil of construction when it shall produce evil effects." Thus from slavish adherence to the letter of the covenant, he passed to dependence upon the nebulous "good sense" of his fellow citizens at large. Apparently troubled in conscience, however, he wrote to a friend that the government was like an agent who had exceeded his authority and must throw itself on the mercy of the country knowing that the people would have taken the step if they had been given a chance to do it. In other words, the government could alter the Constitution in a pinch when convinced that the people would have it so. John Marshall doubtless felt competent to amend it himself but he never committed any such doctrine to black and white.

Now it was the turn of the Federalists to appear in the rôle of pinchbeck lawyers and economists. They could find no constitutional warrant for the purchase, no need for such a vast territory, no money with which to pay for it. Manufacturers of Pennsylvania and merchants of New England could see no reason for their being excited about the plight of Ohio, Kentucky, and Tennessee. In fact they feared the growth of the West for they did not want to be outvoted in Congress by farmers from the frontier; they were also offended by rough voices and deficiencies in table etiquette at White House functions. The better educated the Federalists were, it seems, the less they understood the destiny of America. Sons of Federalist fathers at Williams College, after a solemn debate, voted fifteen to one that the purchase of Louisiana was undesirable. Like their sires, they faced the sea. The streets of London, the quays of Lisbon, and the Hong of Canton were more familiar sights to the merchants of the coast than were the somber forests and stump-studded clearings of western America.

Wheeling up all their batteries of argument, the Federalists in the Senate raged against the ratification of the treaty of purchase. Men who had easily found Hamilton's Bank constitutional could not discover in the fundamental law of the land any vestige of warrant for acquiring more territory. Men who thought that the "broad back of America" could bear Hamilton's consolidated debt at six per cent interest now went into agonies over a new bond issue of less than one-fifth the sum at the same rate of interest. They drew doleful pictures as they counted the mass of gold and silver which would be wrung from the people to pay for a wilderness. They pointed out by way of contrast the low price which William Penn had paid for his princely domain. Finally and more directly to the point, they complained that the purchase of Louisiana would break the authority enjoyed by the old and conservative eastern states, shift the balance of political power to the West, and transfer the government of the Union to horny-handed farmers of leveling tendencies. They almost visualized the coming invasion of Andrew Jackson's hordes.

Yet the eloquence of the Federalists could not defeat the treaty. Jefferson commanded the votes and it was ratified. "The grand old republic is lost," mourned the die-hards, as they turned to their journals and ledgers. In December, 1803, the Stars and Stripes were raised over the government buildings in New Orleans; the land of Coronado, de Soto, Marquette, and La Salle passed under the sovereignty of the United States.

How large was the acquisition no one knew, for the boundaries had never been actually defined. When Livingston asked the French minister a question on that point, he received an evasive answer; neither the minister nor anyone else could furnish an accurate map. It is safe to say, however, that Louisiana embraced all the territory at present within the borders of Arkansas, Missouri, Iowa, Oklahoma, Kansas, Nebraska, and South Dakota, besides large portions of what is now Louisiana, Minnesota, North Dakota, Colorado, Montana, and Wyoming. The farm lands which the "little-America" party on the seacoast called "a worthless wilderness" were well settled within less than a century and valued at seven billion dollars—five hundred times the price paid to Napoleon for them.

§

The same fateful course of events in Europe, beyond the will and the purpose of Jefferson, that lifted him from his narrow view of the Constitution to the wide nationalism of the Louisiana Purchase, drew him and his immediate followers into domestic policies more autocratic and sweeping than Hamilton's boldest enterprise; hurried them, pacific as they were in intention, into a struggle not of their own deliberate making; compelled them to resort to hated measures of revenue and finance; and, to cap the climax, thrust their opponents, the Federalists, out into utter darkness, far beyond the confines described in the Kentucky Resolutions and near to the border of secession and rebellion. Those who had set sail to the North Pole suddenly found themselves below the Antarctic circle. All this flowed inexorably from the reopening of the Napoleonic wars in 1803 and the steady advance of the American frontier south and west.

The world-encircling conflict, begun in 1793, now entered upon its last phase, as England and France plunged into a death struggle for supremacy in two hemispheres. The true nature of the armed contest had at last become apparent. The French Revolution had run its course from moderate reform to radicalism; from Marat's radicalism to Bonaparte's despotism. After grasping the scepter of power, Napoleon—who was infinitely more efficient than any of the Bourbons that ever ruled France—undertook to recover from the ancient foe some of the commerce and territory lost in previous wars and make himself arbiter of Europe.

In the accomplishment of his purposes, he annexed Belgium and Holland, assumed the imperial crown, placed his brother, Joseph, on the throne of Spain, brought Italy under his heel, broke the Prussian sword which Frederick the Great had wielded with such effect at Rossbach and Leuthen, created a Rhine Confederation of German states under his own hegemony, humiliated the Pope, and brought the Tsar of all the Russias to his feet. While trampling on Europe, Napoleon attempted to paralyze the lucrative trade of Great Britain and strike a mortal blow at her Indian empire; but it was this undertaking that proved his ruin. Naturally the ruling classes of England were frightened into desperation. Besides fearing that the leaven of Jacobin doctrines would sooner or later produce a revolution in London, they were in mortal terror lest the victorious arms of Napoleon should wrest from them the fairest parts of their overseas dominion.

So the law of the jungle prevailed; and in the frightful contest that followed, the rights of neutrals were as chaff before a hurricane. Unable to form a coalition strong enough to beat Napoleon on land, England undertook to starve him and his allies into submission by the control of the sea. In May, 1806, she declared the coast of Europe blockaded from Brest to the mouth of the Elbe. In November of that year, Napoleon retaliated with his Berlin decree proclaiming a blockade against the British Isles, although he had no navy to enforce it. Within a twelvemonth England countered with a stiffer ukase—Orders in Council requiring American ships bound for the barred zone to stop first at a British port, secure a license, and pay a tax. This, exclaimed Napoleon, was the height of insolence and he replied with his Milan decree announcing that he would seize and confiscate any ship whose master obeyed the recent commands of Great Britain.

The predicament of American commercial interests was now extreme. A ship that sailed directly for the Continent was liable to seizure by the British; a ship that cleared for Great Britain might fall into the hands of the French. An American captain, who sought safety by entering a British port and paying the license fee, lost his cargo and his vessel if Napoleon's watchful officers found him out. And yet, though the risks were great, the rewards of escape were commensurate with the hazards. If one ship out of three wriggled through the net, the profits of the lucky stroke paid the losses and good dividends besides. So American merchants and seamen, who counted as nothing a trip around the Horn to China by way of San Francisco and Honolulu, crowded the little Atlantic with their boats. Steadily their tonnage engaged in foreign trade rose in spite of the appalling ravages wrought by the European belligerents, the violations of neutral rights, and the terrible insults to American pride.

In matters of principle there was slight difference between England and France; if the former seized more American ships, it was due to main strength, not to any tenderness on the part of Napoleon's watchmen. There was one respect, however, in which England was the greater offender and that, too, was due to circumstance rather than discrimination. She was in dire need of sailors for her navy. Her sea captains gave their men filthy food, flogged them half to death for trivial causes, and herded them into quarters unfit for human beings, the mutiny of the Nore, in 1797, bearing testimony to such gruesome practices. Consequently, droves of British sailors fled to American ships in search of better treatment, to earn higher wages and escape the war.

Thus it often happened that an American vessel carried among its crew men whose service could be lawfully claimed by England. But in many cases, it was difficult to tell whether a sailor was an Englishman or an American, especially since the citizens of both countries spoke the same tongue. In fact nothing except official records could determine the nationality of a seaman and frequently that rover on the wide ocean had no authentic document showing the land of his rightful allegiance. Moreover, American naturalization papers were not accepted by England. Adhering to the ancient rule, "Once an Englishman always an Englishman," she steadily refused to recognize the principle of expatriation.

Evidently there were in these conditions good and sufficient grounds for wordy quarrels and acts of hostility. The government of the United States denied the right of British captains to hold up and search American ships at their sweet will. Even if carried out with all possible courtesy, the process itself was distressing beyond endurance. The operation required an American ship, whenever ordered, to "heave to," and remain submissive under British guns while the searching party pried into records, grilled the captain and his crew, seized, handcuffed, and carried off expostulating sailors. In making inquisitions English captains were not always nice in their judgment; in some instances they dragged away, in irons, men born under the American flag. Saints could not have done this work without arousing anger and saints could not have undergone the humiliation without reaching the limits of forbearance.

In point of fact, seamen of that age were not noted for the suavity of their manners; while searching and seizing they did not always observe the amenities of the drawing room. When, for example, in the summer of 1807 the American frigate, *Chesapeake,* refused to surrender some sailors alleged to be deserters from King George's navy, the British warship, *Leopard,* opened fire, killing three men and wounding eighteen—a high-handed act which even the British ministry did not have the hardihood to defend. Besides doing as they pleased on the high seas, the belligerents were none too fastidious in American waters. Both British and French ships patrolled the coasts of the United States and pursued their prey within the three-mile limit. If the French did less damage and inflicted fewer insults, it was due to lack of power and opportunity, not to any high regard for jurisprudence and æsthetics, as their dictatorial conduct in other respects well proved.

The campaign of violence on the seas was accompanied by an angry exchange of notes and opinions among the powers involved. In this sphere neither the English nor the French government was over-refined in its methods. The former paid little attention to American protests and, when it deigned to reply at all, often used the language of irony conceived in contempt. Napoleon, on his part, accused Jefferson of accepting without a blow subjection to the British Empire, issued false statements, and made promises which he did not intend to fulfill. To add to the complexity of the endless diplomatic parley, American congressmen entered into curious relations with British and French representatives—relations that were wanting in taste if not in loyalty.

Stories of these transactions, coupled with reports of atrocities on the high seas, spread controversy and alarm throughout the United States, causing the partisan spirit to flame high. Some citizens wanted to fight England; some wanted to fight France; others wanted peace at any price. True to political forms, Federalist Senators and Representatives, goaded by constituents who had lost ships and cargoes at sea and at the same time bent on political advantages for themselves, resorted to every measure which intrigue and ingenuity could invent to embarrass and discomfit Jefferson in his baffling search for a way out of the dilemma.

Whatever could be said of the President's diplomacy amid these perplexities, one thing was certain: he was eager to keep his nation out of the European quarrel and he managed to do it for six years—as long as he was in power. In maintaining this resolute stand against war, Jefferson coolly followed a policy which he had matured on the basis of long experience and wide study. Peace was with him not only a "passion," as he said; it was a system.

Although by no means a universal pacifist, he was fully convinced that peace was the best policy for the United States, given its geographical position, its democratic institutions, and its agricultural character, insisting with Washington that the age-old battles of Europe were no concern of America. He was not afraid of bloodshed or inherent evils of war; it was the social results of armed conflicts he dreaded. War, he exclaimed, had transformed the kings of Europe into maniacs and the countries of Europe into madhouses while peace had "saved to the world the only plant of free and rational government now existing in it!" Corruption and tyranny, in his opinion, flowed from armed conflicts, whereas "peace, prosperity, liberty and morals have an intimate connection." Therefore, he reasoned, all but "pepper-pot politicians" would hold him in high esteem for keeping the country aloof from a brutal struggle "which prostrated the honor, power, independence, laws, and property of every country on the other side of the Atlantic." In spite of all criticism, it was thus a reasoned and deep-seated conviction—not impulse or caprice—that led Jefferson to keep ever before him the goal of peace during the negotiations and agitations that made his administration so tumultuous.

Seeking with all his talents a solution of the problem in measures short of war, the President resorted at the outset to diplomatic negotiations. Finding that requests and pleas had no material effect on the belligerents, he undertook to bring them to terms by restraining their commerce and cutting off their supplies. When Great Britain blockaded the Continent in 1806, the immediate answer of Jefferson and his party was the Non-importation Act closing American ports to certain British goods—an instrument intended to serve, figuratively speaking, as a club over the head of King George's ministry.

But this law proved to be an idle gesture; British and

French restrictions on American trade became more onerous. Therefore Congress passed in December, 1807, the
Embargo Act, which forbade all American vessels to leave
these shores for European ports. In this fashion a clause
of the Constitution authorizing the regulation of foreign
commerce was stretched to sanction a measure abolishing
it. Though a caustic remedy, this act was equally without
avail in bringing European powers to terms; and, after
applying it for two disastrous years, Congress, in the closing days of Jefferson's administration, repealed the futile
and irksome measure, substituting for it the Non-inter-
course Act, which prohibited trade with England and France
while permitting it again with the rest of Europe—another
arbitrary law which, like the others, brought no relief from
the exactions of the belligerents.

Indeed, the Embargo Act was more destructive to business and agriculture than the English and French depredations on sea-going ships. Before the passage of that law,
bold seamen, lured by high profits, took the risks involved
and carried cargo after cargo safely into foreign ports.
There were sport and speculation as well as danger and loss
in the adventure. Men who cursed Jefferson for failing to
break the Orders in Council and the Napoleonic decrees
could work off some of their frenzy in the excitement of
blockade-running.

But when the Embargo bill was passed, the brave were
tied up in port with the timid. Ships then swung idly at
the docks. Goods decayed in warehouses. Merchants
were driven into bankruptcy; bookkeepers, shipbuilders,
longshoremen, and sailors were thrown out of employment.
Farmers and planters of the South and West found the
export market for their cotton, rice, tobacco, corn, and pork
paralyzed, while the prices of manufactures doubled.

In short, those who obeyed the law were impoverished;
those who violated it by slipping out of the harbors or by
smuggling goods into Canada or Florida for shipment
abroad were liable to be ruined by encountering the agents

of the federal government at any moment. The country at large, angry and impotent, broke into furious wrangling, with editors raging and Federalist politicians fuming. Jefferson himself was heartily sick of the whole business. "Never," he groaned, on the expiration of his last term, "did a prisoner released from his chains feel such relief as I shall on shaking off the shackles of power. Nature intended me for the more tranquil pursuits of science by rendering them my supreme delight."

§

When Jefferson declined reëlection and thus made the third-term doctrine a part of the unwritten Constitution, the presidency devolved upon James Madison, also a man of peace. As the Secretary of State, Madison had for eight years consistently sustained the Jeffersonian policies as a matter of loyalty and conviction. In fact, his whole career had been pacific. Though active in public affairs during the Revolution, he had served in legislative halls and council chambers, not on the field of battle. Small in stature, studious in habits, sensitive in feeling, he was in the bottom of his heart a lover of peace and, if he had been master of his party after the fashion of Jefferson, Congress might not have taken up arms in 1812. But Madison was not a commanding personality and the drift toward war became steadily more marked as the months of his administration rolled on.

Searches, seizures, captures, impressments, and collisions continued to agitate the country and deepen resentment. In the spring of 1811, a British frigate held up an American ship near the harbor of New York and "took from her John Diggio, an apprentice to the master of the brig and a native of Maine." While cruising under orders from the Secretary of the Navy to prevent such outrages, Commodore John Rodgers, commanding the frigate, *President,* came to blows with the British sloop *Little Belt,* smashed her upper works, and killed several of her seamen. If the country had been hunting a pretext for taking up arms against England in defense of commercial rights, it could easily have found one.

As a matter of fact, the rising tide of opinion which bore Congress along in the direction of war did not flow primarily from the commercial sections of the country. It is true that one branch of American mythology represents the second war with England as springing inevitably from her depredations on American trade and her impressment of American seamen, but the evidence in the case does not exactly support that view. Northern shipowners, upon whom the losses fell with special weight, did not ask for armed intervention. On the contrary, they took great pains to prove that the federal government's report listing thousands of impressment outrages was false and they were almost unanimous in their opposition to drawing the sword against England. Moreover, it must be remembered that two days after the United States declared war—before news of the event reached London—the British government withdrew its obnoxious Orders in Council, leaving only the impressment issue unsettled by parleys and diplomacy. If, as had been said, that alone was sufficient cause for war, the fact remained that the communities which suffered most from it did not so regard the matter.

It was in other quarters, as Pratt has conclusively shown in his Expansionists of 1812, that the war fever was rising. All along the frontier from Vermont to Kentucky, advancing pioneers were ready for a new onward surge. Western New York and the Ohio country were filling up with settlers and the call for more virgin soil was being heard in the land. Fully understanding the significance of this demand the Indians, with unerring instinct, turned to the British for help—and received it. Since Canada was still sparsely settled and the western region practically given up to the fur-trading interests, the Indians and British could, without any difficulty, make a common cause against

Americans, both being eager to preserve against the on-coming pioneer the hunting grounds that were the haunts of fur-bearing animals.

In these circumstances, whole tribes of Indians on both sides of the boundary between the United States and Canada—one estimate placing the number at sixty thousand—came under British influence and were ready at any signal to fall upon American outposts with fire and tomahawk. It was to this factor in the diplomatic game that Henry Clay referred when he called for the acquisition of Canada in a war on England, exclaiming: "Is it nothing to us to extinguish the torch that lights up savage warfare? Is it nothing to acquire the entire fur trade connected with that country and to destroy the temptation and opportunity of violating your revenue and other laws?"

Besides getting rid of the Indian barrier to the advance of the agricultural frontier, besides gathering in the rich fur trade enjoyed by the British, the American war party also hoped to acquire the farming lands of Canada. When in 1811 the delicate matter of relations with England was being debated in the House of Representatives, the chair-man of the select committee to which the issue was referred frankly exposed substantial reasons for taking up arms against that country. "We could deprive her," he said, "of her extensive provinces lying along our borders to the North. These provinces are not only immensely valuable in themselves, but almost indispensable to the existence of Great Britain. . . . By carrying on such a war . . . we should be able in a short time to remunerate ourselves ten fold for all the spoliations she has committed on our commerce."

Geographical destiny seemed also to indicate the way. "The waters of the St. Lawrence and the Mississippi," asserted another member of the House, "interlock in a number of places; and the great Disposer of Human Events intended those two rivers should belong to the same people."

If farmers of the Northwest were to get their portion

from a war on England, planters of the South were also to have a reward. For a long time leaders in that section, especially in Georgia and Tennessee, had looked upon the two Floridas as a part of their economic empire. That broad belt of land cut off the gulf on a long coast line; it was inhabited by Indians who sometimes made expeditions into the United States; and in its hospitable swamps and everglades runaway slaves found a refuge. Here were strategic reasons for extending the "natural frontiers" of the United States.

Moreover, there were questions of legality to be considered. Since the terms of the Louisiana Purchase were vague, the American war party could advance a claim, however dubious, to West Florida, and since Spain owed American citizens a large bill for damages done to their trade, the same ambitious faction felt justified in seizing East Florida by way of compensation.

Finally there were contingencies. As the Spanish monarchy was allied with England in the European war, its Florida territory might serve as an English base if hostilities arose between the United States and the mother country. So West Florida was declared to be American soil and to complete the operation, Congress, early in 1811, authorized the President to take possession of East Florida and hold it pending negotiations. It was abundantly evident by 1812 that a war with England might bring about the consummation so devoutly wished.

In the grand sweep of their imagination, "the expansionists of 1812" also brought Mexico within their range. In 1804, John Adair, a valiant soldier who later served under Jackson at the battle of New Orleans, wrote to James Wilkinson, the ambitious freebooter: "The Kentuckyans are full of enterprise and although not poor, as greedy after plunder as ever the old Romans were; Mexico glitters in our eyes—the word is all we wait for." Two years afterward Aaron Burr launched his expedition to realize among other things the hope of the southwest, namely wresting Mexico from Spain and bringing a new empire under Anglo-Saxon hegemony.

Burr failed but his project was not forgotten. "Citizens of the West," exulted a writer of Nashville in the spring of 1812, "a destiny still more splendid is reserved for you. Behold the empire of Mexico. . . . Here it is that the statesmen shall see an accession of Territory sufficient to double the extent of the republic." If the whole program could be carried into effect, the "new United States" of which Clay spoke would include the continent of North America. At all events within a few years Stephen Austin was occupying Texas.

It was the men of the agricultural frontier who cherished these ambitions and at last brought about the declaration of hostilities against England in 1812. There is no doubt on that point. Professor Pratt has plotted on a map the constituencies of the congressmen who voted for the war resolution and has shown that their districts stretched from New Hampshire to Georgia in the form of a great crescent bending westward. "From end to end," he says, "the crescent traversed frontier territory, bordering foreign soil, British or Spanish, or confronting dangerous Indian tribes among whom foreign influence was suspected and feared. . . . Nothing could better demonstrate the frontier character of the war spirit than to observe its progressive decline as we pass from the rim of the crescent to its center at the national capital. Expansionist enthusiasm declined even more rapidly."

Equally rooted in practical considerations was the opposition to the war. "The Federalist party," continues Professor Pratt, "grounded chiefly in the mercantile and financial interests of the coast towns, the college-bred professional men, the more solid and 'respectable' elements in society, was fairly homogeneous in its creeds of both foreign and domestic politics. Abroad it looked upon Napoleon as Anti-Christ and endorsed Pickering's famous toast, 'The world's last hope—Britain's fast-anchored isle.' In home affairs, it was convinced, not without cause, that the Republican administration had deliberately resolved to ruin its commerce and dissipate its prosperity. Holding these views, it could see no worse national crime than a war against England which would render indirect aid to Napoleon, and no worse disaster to its interests than a form of expansion which would mean new states to increase the Republican strength in Congress." There was the alignment of the forces for and against the second war with England.

§

Although the war party was united in overbearing the Federalists and their allies, it was sharply divided against itself over aims and methods, and displayed in that schism a fatal weakness which in the end balked the purposes of both factions. The southern planters who wanted the Floridas looked with deep misgivings upon the project for adding Canada to the growing power of the North; while northern farmers who wanted Canada did not actually wish to see the planting wing strengthened by new estates on the Gulf of Mexico.

This division in opinion appeared in 1811, even before war was declared. When a provisional scheme authorizing the President to raise forces competent to conquer Canada was presented in Congress, "an almost solid South joined with Federalist New England to defeat it." The same discord was manifest a few days after the declaration of war, when the House of Representatives passed a bill empowering the President to occupy East and West Florida. This was, of course, pleasing to the southern contingent, but as soon as an amendment was offered in the Senate looking toward the possession of Canada also, it was voted down by a combination of Federalists and southern Republicans. Once more the issue was presented in 1813 in the form of a bill providing for the occupation of East Florida, which was demolished by a bloc of Senators drawn mainly from the region north of the Potomac. "We consent that you may conquer Canada; permit us to conquer Florida!" exclaimed a Federalist statesman taunting the war faction; but if this was the exact language of the bargain, the parties to the contract could not on any terms unite in an efficient effort to realize their conflicting aims.

The truth seems to be that President Madison's administration—"the Virginia dynasty"—although it was ready enough to annex the Floridas, was lukewarm on the conquest of Canada. At least it was fully aware of the dangers inhering in that operation. Time and again John Randolph of Roanoke, bitter foe of the war, had informed the public that the seizure of Canada would assure northern supremacy over the planting interest and had openly warned his brethren against it. In one of his outbreaks against the expansionists of the Northwest, he declared: "Canada seems tempting in their sight. That rich vein of Genesee land which is said to be even better on the other side of the lake than on this. Agrarian cupidity, not maritime right, urges the war. . . . It is to acquire a preponderating northern influence that you are to launch into war."

Beyond all question, James Monroe, who served first as Madison's Secretary of State and then as head of the War Department, shared Randolph's dislike of the Canadian adventure, going so far as to say bluntly that the invasion of Canada was to be viewed "not as an object of the war but as a means to bring it to a satisfactory conclusion." Indeed, if we may believe General Armstrong, who was forced out of the War Department by Madison, Monroe actually instructed the southern generals on the northern front "not to do too much," explaining to them "that this was secretly the wish of the President."

Although there was some spleen in the General's statement, there can be no doubt about three facts pertinent to the controversy: the northern wing of the war party was rather indifferent about the seizure of the Floridas; the southern wing did not look upon the conquest of Canada with enthusiasm; and the direction of the war was in the hands of the southern contingent.

§

Such was the background for the great decision made by the federal government in 1812 and of the armed conflict it waged. Such were the primary causes of the "second war for independence," as it is often called. Such were the ambitions that inspired the belligerent party which took possession of the House of Representatives in 1811—the party headed by leaders known in history as "war hawks."

Lest there be some doubt as to the real goal ahead, its views were fairly voiced by two young members destined to be mighty figures in the nation: Henry Clay of Kentucky and John C. Calhoun of South Carolina. Both were passionate in their demand for war. Both spoke for the expansionists. Clay, in a blaze of enthusiasm, announced that "the militia of Kentucky alone are competent to place Montreal and Upper Canada at your feet." Calhoun with equal confidence exclaimed: "So far from being unprepared, Sir, I believe that in four weeks from the time a declaration of war is heard on our frontier, the whole of upper Canada and a part of lower Canada will be in our power." With leaders capable of making such forecasts, the rank and file behind the "war hawks" were even more impatient to fling the burden of fire and sword on the army and the navy.

So in June, 1812, the resolution breaking with Great Britain passed the House of Representatives by a vote of seventy-nine to forty-nine and the Senate by nineteen to thirteen—with the spokesmen of the South and West aligned against the members from the commercial Northeast. In this light manner planters and farmers precipitated a struggle on land and sea for which they had made no effective preparation.

At the moment the standing army had about seven thousand men in the field and it was necessary to enlarge the land forces immediately. Instead of profiting from the experiences of the Revolution, Congress resorted to the old devices which had proved so costly then: it supplemented the regulars by a volunteer force and appealed to the state militia. It even made one mistake which had been avoided in the war for independence: refusing to create a unified command under a single general, it committed the grave task of directing the war to many hands. Moreover, it entrusted the business of furnishing supplies and munitions to political contractors later characterized by General Upton as a "swarm of parasites who fattened upon every reverse to our arms."

As a result of these measures and policies, the only offensive stroke of power which the government could really make, namely, an invasion of Canada, failed to accomplish its objective. There was the usual display of valor on the part of officers, regulars, and the best of the militia but their achievements were all out of proportion to their sacrifices.

When the war commenced there were about five thousand British regulars in Canada. Instead of making one consolidated drive upon them and destroying them in a single campaign, the Madison government, divided in counsels and hampered by the anti-war party, made one half-hearted attempt after another, dragged out the war for nearly three years, summoned innumerable bodies of militiamen to the colors, lost more than five thousand soldiers, killed and wounded, and in the end did not destroy the British and take Canada.

Again and again raw recruits failed to meet the iron test. On one occasion four thousand mounted men from a section that had cheered for the war abandoned their commander before they came within a hundred miles of the enemy and rushed back in haste to their homes. On another occasion a body of militia refused to cross into Canada to support their American brethren engaged in a desperate and unequal contest a short distance away—because, the officers alleged, the men were not lawfully bound to serve outside the country.

In the course of this strange contest, the United States called out about fifty thousand regulars, ten thousand volunteers, and four hundred and fifty thousand militiamen to cope with British forces which at the moment of greatest strength did not exceed seventeen thousand disciplined soldiers. On one side of the ledger Madison's administration could show some minor victories in the North and Andrew Jackson's triumph at New Orleans; on the other side it had to place the capture of Detroit by the British, an invasion of New York, and the destruction of the federal buildings in Washington.

The navy within the limits of its equipment was in a better condition than the army. It was not hampered by state interference or by the necessity of handling raw militiamen but it had neither the tonnage nor the guns required for a contest with the greatest sea power on earth. Called upon to defend a long coast line and protect an extensive commerce, it rendered a good account of itself. Perry's victory on Lake Erie, Macdonough's stroke at Plattsburg, and the stirring deeds of Lawrence, Rodgers, and a score of commanders bore testimony to the valor of American seamen. Aided by a swarm of privateers the navy for many months worked havoc on British commerce, repaying the patriots for some of the depredations committed by captains of King George under the guise of "international law."

All this was heroic and afforded new pages for romance but it was not war and the government of the United States was in no position to wage one efficiently. When the British ministry finally awoke to the gravity of the situation, it brought its superior sea power to bear on America with awful effect. It blockaded the Atlantic coast, paralyzed American commerce, foreign and domestic, and held the whole seaboard in a vise-like grip.

§

After a few months of war it became obvious that neither of the contending powers was able to deliver a mortal thrust. Indeed they had hardly begun it when they wished themselves out of it. Less than a year after the first gun was fired, President Madison accepted a tender of mediation from Russia. In reply to the same proposition, Great Britain, not adverse herself, expressed a preference for direct negotiations, offering an olive branch which was eagerly grasped by the President. In July, 1814, authorized delegates of the warring nations met at Ghent and after prolonged negotiations reached an agreement on Christmas eve,—a few days before General Jackson's victory over the British at New Orleans.

It is true that neither party was altogether happy with the outcome but both had good reasons for desiring peace. Great Britain, still fearing another storm in France—which soon came with the return of Napoleon from Elba—was ready for a settlement demanding no sacrifices of goods or principles. The government at Washington, on its side, was careening toward bankruptcy; it was issuing treasury notes in large amounts and steadily swinging in the direction of the paper money policies of the Revolutionary War. Its war loan of 1814 was a disastrous failure; the bonds of that issue were sold at a twenty per cent discount, while state banknotes worth only sixty-five cents on the dollar in specie were accepted as cash. And the financiers who gave their support to the loan, limited as it was, insisted, as the price of their aid, that the war should stop. Thus peace was the only alternative to economic collapse, if not the disruption of the Union. Planters and farmers were taught some lessons in finance and patriotism.

So the peace came. When the treaty reached the United States, the people were surprised to find in it no clause forbidding Great Britain to seize American sailors, destroy American commerce on the high seas, search American ships, or support Indians on the frontier. It was a bitter experience for President Madison to compare his proclamation announcing the objects of the war with the treaty which gathered the fruits of the contest.

Nevertheless we are told when news of the settlement arrived, the people "passed from gloom to glory." Bells pealed in the church steeples; restive school children were released for a holiday; flags were flung out; and the taverns were crowded with patriots drinking toasts to the triumph of a great cause. The victory of General Jackson at New Orleans seemed a grand climax for the celebration.

§

Throughout this controversy over foreign affairs extending from the inauguration of Jefferson to the end of the second war with England in 1815, the division between the commercial and the agricultural interests, to use the language of the day, was clearly discernible. "This war, the measures which preceded it, and the mode of carrying it on," exclaimed Josiah Quincy, the outstanding Federalist champion from Massachusetts, in 1813, "are all undeniably southern and western policy, not the policy of the commercial states." The debates over the Embargo, over measures of national defense, and over taxes to support the government, all betrayed the deep economic cleavage that separated the Northeast from the South and West. When at length war was declared by Congress, the vote, as we have seen, ran true to the line of cleavage, cutting across party ranks and traditional associations.

From the beginning to the end it was the merchants and shipowners who took the lead in opposing the policies and measures of the Republican administration. Though the seamen impressed by the British navy belonged as a rule to their vessels, they apparently did not feel the wound to national honor as deeply as did the planters from the South or the farmers from the West. Though it was their trade that was preyed upon by British and French sea rovers, they were willing to take the bitter with the sweet, losses accompanied by profits, rather than endure the irksome restraints of the Embargo. When the federal government failed to provide a navy strong enough to protect their commerce and coast fortifications adequate to the defense of their towns, they accused the farmers and planters of being the responsible parties.

To them a flag that did not stand for security on the sea as well as on the land was no flag at all. "The term flag," said Josiah Quincy, "is talked about as though there was something mystical in its very nature—as though a rag with certain stars and stripes upon it tied to a stick and called a flag was a wizard wand and entailed security on everything under it or within its sphere. There is nothing like all this in the nature of the thing. A flag is the evidence of power. A land flag is the evidence of land power. A maritime flag is the evidence of maritime power. You may have a piece of bunting upon a staff, and call it a flag, but if you have no maritime power to maintain it, you have a name and no reality; you have the shadow without the substance; you have the sign of a flag, but in truth you have no flag."

After the Republicans had declared war, spokesmen of the commercial interests continued their opposition. They began by filing a minority report in Congress which condemned the administration in severe language and, until peace was finally effected, they worked hard to thwart and prostrate the financial and military measures of the administration. No doubt, they offered coöperation on condition that the invasion of Canada be abandoned, that the land forces he confined to defending existing territory, and that the war on the sea be pressed with vigor. But failing to get their own way, they poured the vials of their wrath on the government, denouncing the invasion of Canada and seeking to hamper it. Voicing their sentiments, Josiah Quincy cried out in Congress that the attack on northern neighbors was less defensible than the conduct of Captain Kidd, the pirate, and the West Indian buccaneers.

In the same strain opponents of the war railed at every one of the administration's bills for raising troops. When, in the hour of distress, the government was driven to the last resort, the draft, Federalist orators exhausted their eloquence in resisting it. In this affray they summoned to their aid the powerful intellect of Daniel Webster, then a young member of the House of Representatives, who responded to the call in a vehement speech—one so furious that it was deemed expedient to suppress its publication for nearly a hundred years.

Without mincing words, Webster accused the majority of trying to demonstrate "that the government possesses over us a power more tyrannical, more arbitrary, more dangerous, more allied to blood and murder, more full of every form of mischief, more productive of every sort and degree of misery than has been exercised by any civilized government, with a single exception, in modern times." He protested because the battles which the conscript was made to fight were "battles of invasion," warned his hearers that "the nation is not yet in a temper to submit to conscription," and vaguely hinted that the pursuit of such policies might end in throwing away the government and dissolving the Union.

In a similar vein the Federalists and a few Republican allies tried to defeat the loan bills and the tax projects devised by the administration for the support of the army and navy. Finally northern critics attacked slavery itself as the basis of the planters' power in a government that forced them to endure and sustain a war they hated.

During this contest of orators, the contending Federalists and Republicans reversed their theories of the Constitution, thereby revealing again the intimate essence of high juristic doctrines. In the earlier years when the representatives of the commercial states, spokesmen of trade, finance, and industry, earnestly wished to fund the continental debt at face value, transfer the burden of state debts to the national treasury, found a bank that would serve business enterprise and enhance the value of federal bonds, enact tariff laws protecting industry, pass statutes encouraging shipping by bounties and preferences, and stifle criticism by sedition bills, the Federalists were hardly able to find language strong enough in which to express their feelings about maintaining national supremacy, repressing states' rights, and upholding the broad view of the Constitution. Being in possession of the government, they easily assumed that Congress could lawfully do anything which they thought "necessary and proper."

On the other hand, the Jeffersonians, then out of power and opposed to most of the economic measures sponsored by the Federalists, took the opposite tack. Everything they did not like was unconstitutional and the United States was to them little more than a league of independent commonwealths.

But as soon as the tables were turned, philosophy turned a somersault too. Republicans now displayed as much agility in expounding the constitutionality of their own measures as they had once showed in opposing Hamilton's measures. When Jefferson was troubled with constitutional scruples in connection with the Louisiana Purchase, as we have seen, he did not press the point; on the contrary, he wrote that "the less that is said about any Constitutional difficulty, the better. Congress should do what is necessary in silence." When Josiah Quincy, angry over the admission of the state of Louisiana, invoked the right of secession, it was a southern member of Congress who called him to order. When pacific resistance to the Embargo appeared in New England, ten years after Kentucky's defiance and twenty years before South Carolina's nullification, it was a congressman from North Carolina who spoke boldly of enforcing federal authority. "What!" he exclaimed. "Shall not our laws be executed? Shall their authority be defied? I am for enforcing them at every hazard." When the minority in Congress protested against the war, President Madison pronounced the act akin to treason.

With the same facility the Federalists now took the narrow view of the Constitution and defended the sovereignty of the state, playing their new rôle with as much astuteness as they had played the old. In keeping with changed circumstances, everything they opposed they declared unconstitutional: the Louisiana Purchase was unconstitutional; the Embargo was unconstitutional; the admission of Louisiana as a state was unconstitutional. It was a rare war measure that did not violate the law of the land. "The issue of paper money receivable in taxes," complained Quincy, "was unconstitutional because it was a violation of faith previously pledged."

In fighting the conscription act, Webster also took refuge in the Constitution. The principles of the bill, he said, "are not warranted by any provision of the Constitution . . . not connected with any power which the Constitution has conferred on Congress. . . . The Constitution is libelled, foully libelled. . . . Where is it written in the Constitution, in what article or section is it contained that you may take children from their parents and parents from their children and compel them to fight the battles of any war in which the folly or the wickedness of Government may engage it? . . . An attempt to maintain this doctrine upon the provisions of the Constitution is an exercise of perverse ingenuity to extract slavery from the substance of a free Government."

And if the federal government insisted on enforcing unconstitutional laws, then, shouted Josiah Quincy, speaking for Massachusetts, in the language of Kentucky, "the people of each of the associated states are competent not only to discuss but to decide." Higher than this line of argument it was not possible for them to go.

Such criticisms were by no means confined to Congress. While the national government was waging its desperate contest, first by diplomacy and then by arms on land and sea, against a formidable antagonist, even while the capitol of the United States was being sacked and burned by the enemy, whole sections of the commercial states were in open and active opposition to what they contemptuously called "Mr. Madison's war."

By formal resolutions official bodies in New England roundly condemned it. A Boston town meeting saw in "the calamities of the present unjust and ruinous war" and the disturbances connected with it, nothing but a prelude "to the dissolution of all free government and the establishment of a reign of terror." The lower house of the Massachusetts legislature called upon the people to organize a "peace party" throughout the country. "Express your sentiments without fear," ran the clarion appeal, "and let the sound of your disapprobation of this war be loud and deep. . . . If your sons must be torn from you by conscriptions, consign them to the care of God; but let there be no volunteers except for a defensive war."

Individuals went beyond official bodies in expressing their emotions. Some members of the Massachusetts legislature were for an open break with the administration at Washington, one of them venturing to declare that he would rather have the British constitution, "Monarchy and all," than the American Constitution with embargoes. Another exclaimed that "the sooner we come at issue with the general government the better." In the same spirit of aggression the Boston Daily Advertiser proposed that New England withdraw from the war, proclaim her neutrality, and make a separate treaty with George III. Taking another tack, the Boston Gazette suggested that the peace party should follow "the example of the convention of which the revered Washington was president," and call a national assembly for the purpose of framing a new constitution to be binding on two, three, four, five, or any number of states ratifying it.

In a philosophical vein, the leading Federalist paper of

Boston, the Columbian Centinel, declared that the allegiance of citizens to the federal government was secondary and qualified while their allegiance to their respective state governments was natural, inalienable, and founded on the will of God "as collected from expediency." More material to the outcome, the financial interests of New York and Boston—still Federalist in politics and opposed to a war forced upon them by planters and farmers—failed to come whole-heartedly to the aid of the administration. In fact, the sale of government bonds in northern cities was deliberately subjected to capitalistic sabotage and the sinews of war withheld from a government fighting for its life.

Resistance to federal authority was by no means limited to paper declarations and private agreements. When, on the authority of the President of the United States, General Dearborn appealed to the governor of Massachusetts for certain militia detachments to protect the country against the foe, the latter, with the approval of his council, bluntly refused to accede to the request. Instead of rushing to arms in defense of the flag, he proclaimed a fast day as an atonement for waging war "against the nation from which we are descended and which for many generations has been the bulwark of the religion which we profess." Equally recalcitrant, the governor and the legislature of Connecticut refused to supply their quota of militiamen and let the President know that "the state of Connecticut is a free, sovereign, and independent state; that the United States are a confederacy of states."

To speak summarily, all the New England governors, except the chief executive of New Hampshire, took the position that they could comply with demands for militiamen or reject them, as their judgment dictated. In practice, they did not oppose recruiting for the United States army by "lawful" process within their states, or attempt to block volunteering; indeed, Massachusetts furnished more soldiers to the regular army than any other state save New York. But they held that the Constitution did not authorize the use of the militia except to execute the laws of the Union, suppress insurrection, and repel invasion, and they were no doubt happy to have legal warrant for declining to aid in the prosecution of the war.

Determined to make resistance to "Mr. Madison's war" more effective, the Massachusetts legislature in October, 1814, issued a call to the other states to send delegates to a general convention "for the purpose of devising proper measures to procure the united efforts of the commercial states, to obtain such amendments and explanations of the Constitution as will secure them from further evils." Connecticut and Rhode Island responded favorably; local conventions in New Hampshire and Vermont promptly chose representatives; and the assembly met at Hartford on December 15, 1814.

In theory and in fact, the Hartford convention was a congress representing commercial interests—appealing to the trading states as against the agricultural sections of the South and West. It set forth, without redundant verbiage, the proposition that the Union was a balance of economic powers and that the commercial states were in mortal danger of being dominated and ruined by a combination of southern planters and western farmers.

Distinctly avowing its purpose to be the protection of the trading interests against agrarian majorities in the Congress of the United States, the Hartford convention offered a series of amendments to the federal Constitution. One clause provided that the power of the planting section be reduced by the complete exclusion of slaves from the count in assigning to the states their Representatives in Congress on the basis of population. Other clauses proposed that a two-thirds vote be required in Congress to admit new states, to impose an embargo on foreign commerce, or to declare war, except in case of actual invasion. The language of the Hartford resolutions, though temperate, was firm, the concluding passages warning the country that if the application for amendments was not successful and the war continued to rage, it would be expedient to hold another assembly armed "with such powers and instructions as the exigency of a crisis so momentous may require."

In answer to the defiant policy of New England, the federal government resorted to no caustic measures. In preparing his message of November, 1812, President Madison felt "constrained to advert to the refusal of the governors of Massachusetts and Connecticut to furnish their required detachments of militia," but Congress passed no alien and sedition acts, created no system for spying upon citizens, made no provision for hunting down those who could see neither justice nor wisdom in the war. Crabbed old John Randolph of Roanoke laughed loud and long when he read that the New England Federalists were standing forth in shining armor as apostles of nullification and the champions of states' rights. The Richmond Enquirer, as if forgetting the Kentucky and Virginia resolutions, broke out in moral indignation: "No man, no association of men, no state or set of states has a right to withdraw itself from this union of its own accord. . . . The majority of states which form the union must consent to the withdrawal of any one branch of it. Until that consent has been obtained, any attempt to dissolve the union or to obstruct the efficacy of its constitutional laws, is Treason—Treason to all intents and purposes."

But the federal government enacted no such sentiments into law, and fortunately for the country, the arrival of news of peace, early in 1815, made it unnecessary for the New England Federalists to hold another convention at Hartford, or anywhere else. Nearly half a century beyond the portals of the hour lay Fort Sumter.

§

The close of the second war with England and the fiscal policies pursued by the government in settling its troubled estate completed the discomfiture of the Federalist party as an organization. With respect to the old issue of the tariff, the revenue act of 1816, made necessary by the requirements of war finance, afforded a degree of protection to American industries that would have delighted Alexander Hamilton. A warm champion of the measure, Clay saw in it the beginning of an American system. Calhoun declared that it guaranteed a domestic market to farmers and planters and made them independent of the vicissitudes of European wars. After protesting mildly in the name of her shipping interests at the moment engaged in a prosperous carrying trade, New England turned to industries fostered by a benevolent shelter. Everywhere the manufacturers—who had flourished while English competition had been cut down by the war—rejoiced in the conversion of the Jeffersonians to "sound national doctrines."

In reforming their disordered finances just as in framing tariff schedules, the Republicans felt compelled to resort to Federalist policies, by establishing a second United States Bank. During the war, the management of the treasury had been unhappy, to say the least. The government had been seriously embarrassed by the refusal of the banking interests to give their loyal support; and the incapacity of the Republican fiscal system to bear extraordinary strain had been amply demonstrated.

Indeed, it could hardly be said that there was any system. On the expiration of its charter in 1811, Hamilton's Bank had been allowed to lapse; and the banking business of the country had passed into the hands of numerous state corporations and concerns of varying strength and soundness. In five years the number of these institutions had increased from eighty-eight to two hundred and forty-six and their note issues had risen from about fifty million to approximately one hundred million dollars—an inflation so magnificent that all but the New England houses suspended specie payment when the city of Washington was captured by the British.

The effect of this chaos on the Madison administration was disastrous. An agricultural government, without the support of a national banking institution, without the generous assistance of the strongest northern banks, it had to finance its operations on the basis of its dubious credit—with baleful results. For its bonds floated between 1812 and 1816 totaling over $80,000,000, the treasury received only about $34,000,000 measured in specie; and in the process the government increased its obligations from $45,200,000 to the appalling sum of $127,334,000, the increment alone amounting to more than the domestic debt incurred during the Revolutionary War and funded by Hamilton.

Accordingly, the economic position of the Republicans in 1816 was very delicate. Their bills were pressing and, in meeting their debts, they had only two alternatives: they could make terms with the bankers of the Northeast or they could create a new national bank under their own political auspices—an insistent dilemma in which they adopted the latter expedient. If this choice compelled them to reverse their position on the legality of the Bank, at least they could say that it spared them a greater humiliation, a Republican surrender to private finance. Even Madison could bring himself to accept the unavoidable. Years before he had declared Hamilton's Bank unconstitutional; the Constitution remained unchanged, but he approved the new bank bill when presented by Congress. So it became a law and by a single stroke an energetic body of men associated with the public debt and the national banking system was temporarily attracted to the Republican interest—Jefferson's agricultural interest—just as in former times a similar group had been affiliated with the Federalists. Although a few old radicals like John Taylor who had thundered against the "corrupt squadron" in Washington's administration protested against "the surrender to the money power," their outcries were in vain. The new Bank was duly chartered in 1816.

Encouraged by the turn in national politics, cautious and wise Federalists, who had a keen sense for the substance of things, gradually shifted to the Republican side. A faithful "rear guard" put up a candidate at the presidential election of 1816, but, after a thorough drubbing at the hands of James Monroe, even it withdrew from the national field and confined its actions, steadily diminishing, to state elections. Harmony then became the keynote. When President Monroe made a grand tour of New England in 1817, the hard-boiled Boston Centinel burst forth in generous words of praise, under the caption: "The Era of Good Feeling"—a phrase that was echoed by the populace and with some reason applied to the eight years of Monroe's service in the White House.

§

This process of conciliation was aided by the temporary drift in the affairs of Europe. While the restoration of the Bourbons in France, after the overthrow of Napoleon at Waterloo in 1815, had allayed the fears of the most incorrigible Federalist, the course of the French Revolution through Jacobinism, dictatorship, empire, and restoration had dashed the high hopes of the most loyal Democrat. Gains had been won for liberty—France was at last a constitutional monarchy—but disillusionment was for more than a decade the dominant note among the Jeffersonian radicals. A great experiment in human rights had been made in Europe but at great cost and with results that fell far short of the aspirations cherished by the idealists of 1793. It seemed, therefore, as if both Federalists and Republicans had heard enough of European politics and were ready to turn their backs resolutely on the quarrels of the Old World.

It was not possible, however, for the stoutest apostle of isolation to avoid altogether the politics of international contacts. Indeed, a short time after the collapse of

Napoleon at Waterloo, the government at Washington was engaged in a serious negotiation with Spain over the fate of the two Floridas, a fate left unsettled by the War of 1812. All the reasons that had led the expansionists of that year to covet the two provinces were still operating. All the grievances that had then afforded grounds of irritation—smuggling across the border, Indian raids, and the escape of slaves into the everglades—were still unredressed. At the same time, Spain, weakened by domestic disturbances and engaged in a contest with her rebellious colonies in South America, was in no position to govern the troublesome Floridas or remove the causes of American discontent. Thus, the seal of propriety was given to punitive expeditions.

In 1818 another Indian outbreak snapped the tension. General Andrew Jackson, acting on vague orders from Washington, led his impetuous men across the border into Spanish territory and commenced a diligent search for offenders against American security and peace. He took possession of St. Marks and Pensacola, summarily hanged two British subjects engaged in dubious undertakings along the coast, and in effect established American sovereignty over the entire region. In these circumstances, there was nothing for the King of Spain to do but make the most of the inevitable, and accordingly, on Washington's birthday in 1819, his minister in Washington signed a treaty yielding the Floridas to the possessor. In exchange the United States agreed to pay five million dollars to its own citizens, discharging claims for damages to American commerce committed by Spanish authorities during the recent European war. As a part of the general adjustment the Secretary of State also accepted the Sabine River and a line drawn to the northwest as the boundary of the Louisiana Territory, in this way disposing of a long-standing uncertainty. Though, in the acquisition of the Floridas, more territory was secured, it did not appear that President Monroe was worried by constitutional scruples. His friend and adviser, Jefferson, still lived but doubts on the point had been laid by tradition.

Hard upon the heels of the Florida purchase came another incident in foreign relations which brought the transactions of Europe forcibly into the purview of American politics. Once more the unsettled state of Spain was the cause of trepidation. During the Napoleonic upheaval and the dissolution which followed, Spanish colonies on the American mainland declared their independence, precipitating a costly and desultory war between the metropolis and the former provinces. In her enfeebled state Spain could not subdue the rebels; in her pride she could not yield to them. And while the struggle was in course, another revolution broke out in Madrid and spread to Italy, threatening the security of the recently pacified Europe. In his dilemma, King Ferdinand frantically appealed to friendly monarchs for assistance.

His brethren of the purple, eager to suppress revolution in the Old World, naturally sympathized with projects for putting down similar disturbances in the New World. On opposition to republics and representative government, the sovereigns of the Continent were all strongly united. Indeed, three of the great autocracies—Austria, Prussia, and Russia—were already formally bound, under the Holy Alliance of 1815 and collateral agreements, to coöperate in maintaining the status quo and in preserving the purity of the monarchical principle. Given a pretext for common action by alarming events in Spain and Italy and moved by appeals for help against popular uprisings, the leading powers sent delegates to a conference at Verona in 1822 to see what could be done to stabilize Europe. It is true that on due deliberation the diplomats shrank from promising direct support to King Ferdinand, but their sympathies were unmistakable. The Tsar of Russia, who in virtue of his extensive claims along the west coast of North America had interests in both hemispheres, was more than platonic: he proposed that military aid be rendered to Spain in her domestic difficulties, paving the way for a possible restoration of Spanish sovereignty over the former provinces, now pluming themselves as republics.

To these plans England refused to become a party. The rising flood of British democracy that was soon to carry the reform bill of 1832 was even then breaking over the bulwarks of established institutions, warning the Tories in office against reactionary adventures abroad. Furthermore, British statesmen, deriving their powers from Parliament, could not consistently approve the doctrines of Verona or give aid to the Spanish monarch in a war on representative government. Still more potent, perhaps, in restraining the London cabinet was the opposition of British merchants to any indorsement of Spain's projects for recovering her American resources. Having built up a lucrative traffic with her colonies after the monopoly of Madrid was broken by revolt, traders on the banks of the Thames were in no mood to see their business destroyed by a restoration of Spanish authority. Thrown thus by political and economic interests on the side of non-intervention in behalf of Spain, the British secretary for foreign affairs, Canning, suggested to the American minister in London coöperation between the United States and England in resolving the Spanish-American crisis.

At the same time, the government at Washington, with John Quincy Adams as Secretary of State in the lead, was taking its bearings. Fully appreciating the importance of the news that Great Britain would not assist the despotic continental powers, President Monroe consulted Madison and Jefferson, receiving from them advice to join forces with England in opposing the restoration of Spain's dominion in the New World. In all other official circles the issue likewise became a subject of animated discussion—so many men expressing similar views on the crisis that the authorship of the policy later known as the Monroe Doctrine was obscured by a cloud of witnesses. With good authority it has been accorded to Adams; with equal sanction the honor has been conferred upon Monroe; a few English writers have put in the claims of Canning.

Undoubtedly the influence of Adams was very great but the idea was in general circulation. The logic of the situation was manifest and Monroe understood it as well as any member of his administration. A fair judgment, therefore, seems to be that the historic Doctrine was the fruit of collaboration by the President, the Secretary of State, and their close political counselors.

The result of their deliberations was embodied in Monroe's message to Congress on December 2, 1823, in which he served notice forcefully and definitely on the autocrats of Europe that he would regard "any attempt on their part to extend their system to any portion of this hemisphere as dangerous to our peace and safety." With the same precision, he declared that, while the United States would not interfere with the colonies in the Western Hemisphere still possessed by European powers, it would range itself on the side of those that had declared their independence. Any attempt by a European country to oppress or control them, he declared in a voice of warning, would be viewed here as "the manifestation of an unfriendly disposition toward the United States."

Besides disposing of that matter, the President also referred to the claims of Russia on the northwest coast. With respect to such pretensions, he admonished all and sundry that "the American continents, by the free and independent condition which they have assumed and maintained," are not henceforth to be considered "as subjects for future colonization by any European power."

Happily formulated, favored by the times, and backed in effect by the British navy, the Monroe Doctrine at once gained a potency in world affairs that went far beyond the military strength of the rising American republic. In the circumstances, neither Spain nor any of her continental associates was in a position to make an effective answer to the ultimatum; so the President's triumph was complete. Fortunately for him, too, the Doctrine pleased all factions in the United States. Democrats saw in it a vindication of revolutionary principles in the spirit of Thomas Jefferson and agricultural imperialists read between the lines the promise of a free hand in the Southwest. Federalists, discovering in the Doctrine a guarantee that Latin-American ports would be open to their enterprise, added their joyful praise to the general pæan. When his term came to an end, Monroe could retire amid the plaudits of his countrymen. It was gratifying to "the bantling America," if somewhat ironical, that a member of the old régime who opposed the adoption of the Constitution could strike a note of such sweeping nationalism.

CHAPTER X

The Young Republic

T HE launching of the new republic produced a ferment of ideas that touched all shores of thought and challenged all the creative energies of the American people. In the profound economic and political movements of the period were effected deep changes in the whole cultural life of the country—its class arrangements, intellectual concerns, æsthetic interests, provisions for the promotion of knowledge and encouragement of the arts.

From foreign sources came impacts scarcely less disturbing to the culture handed down from colonial times. When the provincial status under an insular Britain was cast off, closer affiliations were formed with other centers than London, from Paris round the world to Canton. The gates were widened for a freer inpouring of French, German, and Italian science and opinion, invigorating every branch of life. The colonies had been essentially British, theological, conservative; the new states born of the Revolution were swept into a national current, made a part of the world system of powers, shaken by the multiplication of secular

437

interests, and quickened with the dynamic of the progressive philosophy.

§

By the requirements of the war and the economic exigencies that followed it, the ablest and noblest minds of the United States were forced to think in common terms of national affairs. While the British government and the British navy defended and controlled the thirteen colonies, that intellectual and moral operation had not been necessary. Now it could not be denied or eluded. The continuing requirements of defense, the funding of the continental debt, the assumption of state debts, the creation of a common currency and banking system, the erection of a customs union, and the enactment of protective legislation for shipping and industry nourished classes that looked to the national government as the center of power, stability, and affection.

Moreover, the establishment of the federal capital— first in New York, then in Philadelphia, and finally in the District of Columbia—provided a metropolis where the representatives of all sections and all interests assembled for negotiation, compromise, and adjustment. Beyond question the social and intellectual effects of a common center were positive and constructive. Farmers and planters, as well as merchants, financiers, and manufacturers, turned to it for aid and comfort in the advancement of their projects, and few were so small in mind that they did not now grasp some concept of national destiny associated with the federal union. Those who henceforth appealed to the American people whether in economic and political argument, in drama, in poetry, in fiction, or in the arts had to reckon with national ideas and national emotions.

The development of a central government—one of the emergencies sprung upon the isolated provincials by independence—was of necessity a secular process, thus falling into line with the whole movement so eloquently described by Lecky in his history of rationalism. Puritans might lord it over Anglicans in New England, Anglicans might display their pretensions before Catholics and Quakers in Maryland and Virginia, Catholics might long for an establishment of papal authority over all, and Presbyterians might rule with an iron hand their communities on the frontier, but under Providence none of them was strong enough to get a mastery over the federal government, even if the Deists who wielded high powers in the drafting of the Constitution had been willing to bow before the winds of sectarian passion.

Inexorably, therefore, the national government was secular from top to bottom. Religious qualifications for voting and office-holding, which appeared in the contemporary state constitutions with such profusion, found no place whatever in the federal Constitution. Its preamble did not invoke the blessings of Almighty God or announce any interest in promoting the propaganda of religion. Instead, it declared purposes that were earthly and in keeping with the progressive trend of the age—"to form a more perfect union, establish justice, insure domestic tranquillity, provide for the common defense, promote the general welfare, and secure the blessings of liberty to ourselves and our posterity." And the First Amendment, added by the radicals in 1791, declared that "Congress shall make no law respecting an establishment of religion, or prohibiting the free exercise thereof." In dealing with Tripoli, President Washington allowed it to be squarely stated that "the government of the United States is not in any sense founded upon the Christian religion."

Besides rearing a national government on a secular basis, the Revolution and the forces set in motion by it made many modifications in the arrangement and weight of the social classes. Slavery, at the bottom of the scale, was attacked by abolition in northern states and by an extensive voluntary emancipation in the South. Although the system of indentured servitude remained in the full protection of law and custom, the opening of the western frontier facilitated the rise of freedom in the economic scale and within a generation the immigration of European laborers reduced the practice of indenture to the vanishing point.

At the top of the social order inherited from England and nourished in colonial times dislocations were numerous and significant. In the concrete, the "wealth and talents" of colonial America were decimated by the overthrow of English protectors and defenders. The expulsion and flight of the English official classes—governors, army officers, judges, and retainers of every type—raised to a prouder estate the second stratum of American society—merchants, yeomen, planters, and farmers; and in the general upward heave mechanics soon found their way higher in the scale of things. George Washington could not get an important post in the British army but he became Commander-in-chief of the continental army. John Adams, who in his youth had hoed corn in Massachusetts and in his manhood been snubbed by the superior persons of the British official entourage at Boston, became minister to the Court of King George. Thomas Jefferson, the son of an obscure yeoman of Virginia, was lifted to the post of governor, served as minister to France, directed the nation for eight years as chief executive, and became a leader of defiant democracy, known around the world for his intellectual acumen.

At the very moment when by revolution each stratum of the free society was being raised a notch in the scale, heavy responsibilities for the maintenance of social order and the direction of social destiny were laid upon those who gathered political sovereignty into their hands. They had long been accustomed to a high degree of self-government and that experience was immensely valuable; but their powers had been exercised under the close supervision of British authority—an authority that could be invoked at any moment in the interest of property. Never had they tasted the heady wine of republican freedom to rule or ruin themselves.

So when the protecting walls of the British Empire were shaken down, as the unexpected end of a local outbreak, all the burdens connected with the support of law and order fell upon newly-emancipated governing classes. Inexorably they were invited to consider all questions of religion, ethics, natural science, politics, economics, education, literature, and humanism in a novel relation—in relation to concepts of national destiny. It was in these circumstances that the narrow, stuffy, provincial thinking of the thirteen English colonies flowered into the renaissance of the modern age. If one faction, aided by the old Tories, conceived their task as that of holding slaves, indentured servants, and disfranchised mechanics down to their historic levels, another party rose valiantly above that materialist project and conceived their mission in terms of the larger humanism then sweeping through the western world.

§

In the formation of new and vitalizing connections with the Continent were strengthened the slight bonds that had been forged in the realm of culture during the colonial age. Legations were now established in European capitals and diplomatic representatives of the great powers in due time also appeared at the political center of the United States. Naturally the new relations were closest with the French, who had recently been such welcome allies against the English foe. Indeed, several French officers, attracted by the extraordinary opportunities of the New World, remained in America after the war, casting in their lot with the republic. Among them were artists, scientists, and engineers, including Major L'Enfant who, under the direction of Washington and Jefferson, planned the new capital for the United States. Moreover, statesmen and philosophers in France maintained a lively interest in the American experiment. In 1784, Louis XVI offered Harvard a botanical garden filled with plants from his own collection, in order that American science might receive the stimulus of European experience. French travelers visited the United States and wrote illuminating books on the nature and prospects of the republic.

Simultaneously a French vogue flourished in America. In Puritan Massachusetts arose the American Academy of Arts and Sciences, which deliberately attempted to reproduce "the air of France rather than of England and to follow the Academy rather than the Royal Society." Down in Virginia a French officer, supported by the lieutenant-governor of the commonwealth, organized an Academy of Arts and Sciences and a number of southern gentlemen subscribed heavily to a grand scheme for promoting advanced researches in connection with the institution. If the outbreak of the French Revolution had not placed unexpected obstacles in the way, the project would no doubt have been realized in an impressive style.

Among the many forces which beat upon the new republic through contacts with the Old World, four were of special significance to the development of American culture; namely, the accumulating triumphs of natural science to which all European countries contributed, the achievements of the English inventors who started the technical upheaval known as the Industrial Revolution, the dynamic impulse given to social thinking by the French formulation of the concept of progress, and the intellectual reverberations of the French Revolution in the sphere of politics.

All the scientific forces which had commenced a revolution in the age of Bacon and Descartes multiplied and spread in every direction during the eighteenth century. Joseph Black, a Scotch physician, Bergman, a Swedish investigator, Cavendish, Rutherford, and Priestley, English experimenters, made striking additions to man's knowledge of the material universe. Lavoisier crowned their labors by establishing quantitative chemistry on a sure basis. In electricity Galvani and Volta were making discoveries which broke the way for the work of Morse and Edison.

Physics, botany, zoölogy, comparative anatomy, and physiology were advanced by epoch-making researches which swept into the discard innumerable inherited traditions, superstitions, and vagaries. In 1785, three years before the adoption of the Constitution of the United States, James Hutton of Edinburgh published a new theory of the earth, throwing out a cosmic interpretation that contributed in the decades to come to the series of explosions set off by Lyell and Darwin in England.

Entangled with the researches of the scientists was the work of the inventors, Watt, Arkwright, Crompton, and a host of skillful mechanics, who harnessed power to the engine, fashioned steel fingers capable of spinning spidery threads, and started the emancipation of mankind from the limitations of its material form and physical strength. While American patriots were setting in motion a political avalanche, James Watt was starting a technological drive which destroyed the economic heritage of the centuries.

As fast as scientists and inventors piled up the new knowledge, organizers and publishers distributed it far and wide among the people. While Samuel Adams and Patrick Henry were hammering out their weapons for a social battle in America, Voltaire, Diderot, D'Alembert, Helvetius, and their never-resting colleagues in France were fashioning their vast Encyclopædia—the focus for generations of scientific labors and the starting point for still more expansive efforts. Though associated in the common mind with attacks on religion, its real import was the meager space which it gave to that ancient monopoly as compared with the pages and tomes dedicated to man's understanding of the material universe, his place in it, and the society of which he was a part.

In the midst of the intellectual activities which surged up with increasing power as the eighteenth century advanced was formulated the most dynamic social theory ever shaped in the history of thought—the idea of progress or the continual improvement in the lot of mankind on this earth by the attainment of knowledge and the subjugation of the material world to the requirements of human welfare. This philosophic attitude, as J. B. Bury demonstrates in his excellent history of the subject, was unknown to the ancients, the Greeks and the Romans, and it was also foreign to the spirit and doctrines of early Christianity. If Plato and Aristotle dreamed of an ideal society in which gentlemen of leisure and taste could enjoy "the good life," they did not imagine the possible realization of their hope by progressive efforts over a long period of years; neither did they stumble upon a thesis of social evolution embracing all classes and representing an infinite series of adaptations to human needs, projected through the endless future.

Equally remote from the mind of the mediæval theologian, with his theory of man's degeneration in this life and dream of bliss in a life to come, was the notion of constant change directed to the material benefit of humanity. Indeed, not until the modern age could philosophy throw off the creed of the baffled earthly life, with its resignation to the brutal yoke of untamed nature.

As Bury points out, certain conditions, appearing only in modern times, were essential to the development of the idea of progress. First of all, there had to be a respect for and interest in the common business of labor and industry —a respect which neither the slave owners of Athens and Rome nor the feudal lords of mediæval Europe could acquire. In the next place, there was necessary a climate for secular thought; the renaissance and the commercial revolution effected in the age of discovery and colonial exploitation brought that factor into play. In the third place, there had to be a liberation from slavish adherence to written books handed down from antiquity and the church fathers; natural science by its emphasis on experimentation and observation wrought that revolution in the realm of mind. Finally, the doctrine of the "invariability of nature" was needed to free human affairs from the shadow of an angry and interfering Providence—a mysterious force acknowledging no laws and obeying no decrees save those of caprice; Descartes and the philosophic mathematicians of the seventeenth century gave a well-rounded form to that view, so devastating to those who professed an intimate familiarity with the ways and wishes of Almighty God.

By the opening of the eighteenth century the intellectual climate was all set for the idea of progress and in 1737 it was proclaimed by that curious French philosopher, Abbé de Saint-Pierre, in a work entitled, Observations on the Continuous Progress of Universal Reason. "Here," as Bury says, "we have for the first time, expressed in definite terms, the vista of an immensely long progressive life in front of humanity. Civilization is only in its infancy. Bacon, like Pascal, had conceived it to be in its old age. . . . The Abbé was the first to fix his eyes on the remote destinies of the race and name immense periods of time." At last, wrote Saint-Pierre in effect, by shaking off its inertia and taking thought, mankind can do more to improve its condition in a hundred years than it has done in two thousand years of traditional complacency.

Once announced in France, the thesis worked irresistibly among the thinkers who were preparing the way for the Revolution in that country. The Encyclopædists were more or less swayed by it. Abbé Morellet dallied with it. In 1770, Sebastien Mercier gave it popular currency in Germany and England as well as France, by his futurist novel, L'An 2240.

Two years later Chevalier de Chastellux, who was in a short time to serve in the war of American independence and write a remarkable work on American society, advertised the creed in his book, On Public Felicity, portraying as the goal of progressive endeavor a happiness which consisted "in external and domestic peace, abundance and liberty, the liberty of tranquil enjoyment of one's own." The extraordinary signs of it he proclaimed to be "flourishing agriculture, large populations, and the growth of trade and industry." Then, in the year that Jefferson wrote the Declaration of Independence asserting as nature's gift the right to life, liberty, and the pursuit of happiness, Adam Smith published the Wealth of Nations, a powerful support for the doctrine of progress in which were celebrated opulence and comfort as the great aim of statecraft.

Already well sanctioned by thinkers, the new theory of earthly progress, which in its application included the promotion of science and invention, received an immense impetus during the French Revolution. That cataclysm was more than an economic and political transformation; it was an intellectual upheaval which had relevancies for all the philosophies and institutions of humanity. Even while the Reign of Terror was at its height, committees were at work brushing away the barbarities of the criminal code, trying to reduce civil law to a reasoned system, devising schemes of universal education, and projecting new institutes of science. As the tide of radicalism moved forward, traditional religion was challenged from every side and the concept of continuous development on earth placed beside the ancient promise of bliss in heaven. In creative art and literature as well, new tendencies accompanied the attempt to reconstruct the social order.

All this was known in America. Translations of French works poured from American presses during the early republican age. And on top of appeals from Gallic writers came out of France explosive tracts from Thomas Paine, whose services to the American Revolution won for him a wider hearing in the United States than Condorcet and Voltaire could attain.

In keeping with the spirit of his party, Paine was more than a politician, the wide scope of his interests embracing, besides the whole struggle of humanity against misery, the application of science to tradition. The concluding chapters of his Rights of Man, written, as we have seen, in answer to Edmund Burke's Reflections on the French

Revolution, contained an outline of political economy that embraced universal education, the abolition of poverty, a reform of the criminal law, pensions for the aged, the reduction of armaments and international peace. His Age of Reason which assailed the historic accuracy and the validity of Biblical lore exalted science and reason as the searchlights of truth. If the effects of these flaming thrusts into the fabric of inherited authority were countered by the reaction of Napoleon's imperialism and the Catholic restoration, they were not wholly lost in the Old World or the New. Through England also, Americans drew French doctrines, revamped by the various reformers who were trying to reconstruct George III's system in the spirit of Mirabeau if not of Danton. Moreover, America gave an asylum and an audience to English radicals, such as Priestley and Cooper, who fled from conservative mobs and the operation of penal sedition acts.

§

Under the impact of new forces—political and economic revolution, the advance of science and invention, the accumulation of knowledge, and the blasts of foreign influence—the intellectual climate of the American republic presented to the rising generation features essentially different from those of high significance in the colonial era. By the secularizing political process and the march of scientific skepticism, still deeper inroads were made into the sovereignty of theology and mysticism, especially among the educated classes.

In many circles of America, the trinitarian doctrine of Christianity crumbled under two fires. On the part of the theologians, particularly in New England, there went on during the eighteenth century a continuous debate over the traditional forms of Christian faith which eventuated in a return to one of the primitive creeds, a widespread acceptance of the unitarian view of Christ's teachings and mission.

After the outbreak of the American Revolution, the disintegration of customary worship proceeded rapidly. In 1782, King's Chapel in Boston formally and officially declared in favor of unitarianism. About the same time an English tourist reported believers of that faith in all the cities he visited, even in the village of Pittsburgh on the frontier. At the opening of the nineteenth century, nearly every Puritan preacher in Boston had deserted the trinitarian views of his fathers. In 1803, William Ellery Channing, on taking up his work in the Federal Street Church, definitely inaugurated the unitarian movement which finally split the Congregational churches into two opposing camps.

From another quarter also, less theological in its interest, criticism was poured upon the great structure of theology bequeathed by the ancients and revised by the Lutherans, Calvinists, Anglicans, and Puritans. While the theologians themselves were being perplexed by dialectic difficulties, men of science and laymen who undertook to defend and advance that discipline were drifting steadily in the direction of Deism, a faith in one God derived not from a reading of Christian creeds and professions but largely from a study of nature and pagan literature.

Although the roots of this belief lay deep in the wisdom of antiquity, it did not come into prominence in England until early in the seventeenth century. By 1648, however, the year in which death carried off Lord Herbert of Cherbury, "father of Deism," the Deist movement was well under way. After the profounder meaning of the Copernican concept of the infinite universe had foliated in the minds of students—especially after Newton crowned it with his mechanistic view of the stellar system—a powerful group of English thinkers entirely discarded from their thought the God of the Old Testament and the cosmogony described in the Book of Genesis and elaborated by John Milton.

Out of England Deism was borne to France by Voltaire, where it became the creed of nearly all the skeptics who labored at the Encyclopædia and at the new philosophy of naturalism and humanity. From various directions the doctrine came into America, spreading widely among the intellectual leaders of the American Revolution and making them doubly dangerous characters in the eyes of Anglican Tories. When the crisis came, Jefferson, Paine, John Adams, Washington, Franklin, Madison, and many lesser lights were to be reckoned among either the Unitarians or the Deists. It was not Cotton Mather's God to whom the authors of the Declaration of Independence appealed; it was to "Nature's God." From whatever source derived, the effect of both Unitarianism and Deism was to hasten the retirement of historic theology from its empire over the intellect of American leaders and to clear the atmosphere for secular interests.

Nevertheless at the very moment when Deism was playing havoc with theological sovereignty there arrived from England yet another religious movement more akin to Edwards' Great Awakening than to the spirit of Franklin, Washington, and Jefferson. The new faith was known as Methodism and its founder, John Wesley, on his own confession, was in some respects a disciple of Edwards. Under another guise this movement represented the dissidence of dissent, the leveling fervor which, as Burke remarked, had sharpened the antagonism between America and the mother country, and was in the course of time to furnish the inspiration for a nonconformist upheaval in England.

By proposing to reduce somewhat the Anglican hierarchy and to elevate the laity, Methodism added to the democracy of the pew. In religion, it emphasized the salvation of the individual by prayer and conversion. In morals, it waged a Puritan-like war on dancing and frivolity in general while it specifically exalted the virtues of industry and sobriety. If the sermons and hymns of Methodism jarred on Jefferson's skeptical ears, its emphasis on self-expression as against authority and its appeal to the humble as against the mighty contributed to the swelling stream of mass consciousness that made republicanism secure, beyond the possibility of reaction.

The Peter the Hermit of this new gospel was Francis Asbury, sent over in 1771 by Wesley to take charge of three hundred brethren then in the New World. For forty-four years this tireless missionary labored in the American vineyard, traveling more than two hundred and fifty thousand miles through villages and towns, through thickly settled country districts and dark frontier forests, claiming finally three hundred thousand converts and four thousand ordained clergymen. Though not a learned man, by constant reading of the Bible, Asbury made himself master of all its images, figures, and arguments that stir the emotions. After the fashion of Jonathan Edwards, who set an awful example, Asbury one moment frightened his flock by lurid pictures of hell and the next thrilled it by visions of joy in heaven.

Like Catholic missionaries, Methodists went straight to the frontier, but unlike the Catholics they did not work especially with the Indians or carry to them industrial and decorative arts. On the contrary, they labored mainly with people of their own race, to restrain the harshness and brutality of the backwoods, to tame the hot passions of men quick with the rifle and the dirk, to introduce sobriety into communities terrified by drunken bullies. They built no cathedrals or beautiful missions; they preached on stumps and in barns.

When they found the Sermon on the Mount unavailing, Methodists resorted to the horrors of hell and damnation, shocking with their excesses that finicky English tourist, Mrs. Trollope, who compared in loathing the noisy gospel of the American frontier with the quiet decorum of village churches in England where the vulgar never questioned the dominion of squire and parson or ventured to dabble in theological mysteries—forgetting in her critical attitude toward the American democratic spirit that Methodism was an English importation which, by whipping up the emotions, happened to appeal to the untutored axmen of the backwoods with the same appalling force as to the neglected and despised miners and potters of Lancashire and Staffordshire. If it lacked in the æsthetic appreciation that adorns supported and contented leisure, it appealed intensely to the dawning consciousness of the hewers of wood and drawers of water who were to count heavily in the conquest and government of this continent. Though English in origin, the Methodist organization became more rooted in American soil than the Episcopalian Church; Methodists had brethren and sisters in England but they had no lingering traditions binding them to the primate at Canterbury.

§

While Methodism swept thousands of converts into its fold and defied advancing Deism, it did not turn back the irresistible current of natural science that had been gathering momentum since the age of Bacon and Descartes. Indeed, next to the great political experiment, the growth of scientific interest was perhaps the outstanding feature of cultural life in the early republic.

Some of the men who had contributed to the development of that subject in colonial times lived on into the new epoch to enlarge their discipline under novel conditions. Franklin, full of years and great in honors, saw Washington's administration inaugurated before he passed from the scene. His colleague, Benjamin Rush, continued his work for nearly four decades after the Declaration of Independence, winning from the King of Prussia and the Tsar of Russia official recognition for his contributions to medical knowledge.

From England came two ardent apostles of science, whose labors in America strengthened the cause so dear to Franklin's heart. Joseph Priestley, discoverer of oxygen, who shared honors in chemistry with Lavoisier, found shelter in Pennsylvania from persecutions at home and carried on his researches there until his death in 1804. The other refugee from oppressive laws, Thomas Cooper, arrived in 1795 and for forty-five years labored at chemistry, mineralogy, geology, and political economy, combining disputes with the theologians over "the authenticity of the Pentateuch" and equally bitter controversies with Federalist politicians over policies of government. Arrested and fined under the Sedition Act of a New World after he had fled from one in the Old, driven out of Virginia University by religious critics, he preached science in South Carolina College until he was finally forced into retirement by his clerical foes.

In the meantime a new generation of men was carrying forward the scientific inheritance and adding to its data and theories. Nathaniel Bowditch, Massachusetts mathematician, brought out in 1802 the American Practical Navigator and a few years later undertook the task of translating Laplace's *Mécanique céleste* into English. At Yale, in 1805, Benjamin Silliman gave his first regular course on chemistry, opening a career that was rich in achievement and distinction. Seven years afterward, far away on the banks of the Ohio, John James Audubon, a native of New Orleans, began the labors that were to make him the premier ornithologist of his age. In 1815, Constantine Rafinesque, of Franco-German parentage, published at Philadelphia the first part of his extensive work on botany —early fruits of inquiries by a curious genius who was in his later days to startle his contemporaries by declaring that "new species and new genera are continually produced by derivation from existing forms," foreshadowing the epoch-making proclamation of Charles Darwin in the next generation.

All over the country in fact, in colleges, libraries, and amateur laboratories, a restless searching for the secrets of nature was being prosecuted with energy and intelligence. The great Lewis and Clark expedition from St. Louis to the Oregon coast in 1803-06 was more than a path-breaking enterprise; it was a scientific undertaking of high importance. If none of the American scientists approached in magnitude the giants of the Old World, they at least made a profound impression on the intellectual life of America.

Moreover, the practical men among them—Whitney, Fulton, Stevens, and Fitch, for example—were true sons of the age that gave Watt, Arkwright, and Crompton to the western world. Two revolutionary inventions belong to the early republic: the cotton gin patented under Washington's administration and the steamboat launched as a commercial success during the presidency of Jefferson.

By coöperative effort the inventive genius of isolated individuals was stimulated and supplemented. The American Philosophical Society, founded in colonial times, as we have seen, took on new life after the Revolution. Gathering into its fold members from all parts of America and indeed of western civilization, it began to issue publications to disseminate the results of research; and, since its program included almost everything from mechanical inventions to experiments that "let light into the nature of things," its range was wide enough to embrace the many scientific interests of the day from archæology to aeronautics. Practically all the distinguished Frenchmen who came to America as ministers, travelers, or exiles during the early republican era were admitted to the Society and the custom of enrolling the leaders of European science was continued, several of the Americans in turn being honored by membership in European academies. At the sessions of the American Philosophical Society, all the scientific questions which occupied the thought of the Old World and the New were seriously debated. It could be truly said that no modern speculation or problem discussed by the savants of Europe escaped the scrutiny of the Academy at Philadelphia —that lively center which inspired the formation of similar bodies and special associations in every part of the United States.

Meanwhile, the industrial arts were advanced in another quarter by associations of merchants and mechanics who formed institutes, founded libraries, and promoted research for new ideas and designs. Among these unions of citizens, for example, was the Pennsylvania Society for the Encouragement of Manufactures and Useful Arts, which in 1792 began to stimulate talent in America by offering premiums for the best pottery, china, and other articles of utility. Bonuses were held out as prizes to English craftsmen who would bring over, in defiance of the official orders, drawings and models of the new machines which were making their country the workshop of the world. The spirit of the age was unmistakable: master nature, make her subserve human comfort, and accumulate wealth from the process.

§

In the humanistic sciences, the great note of the age was the idea of progress which now secured a widening empire over the minds of those who reflected on the destiny and duty of mankind. That concept, especially as it flowered in the speculations of Chastellux and Condorcet, had a close relation to, and a deep significance for, the republic in America. Owing to the absence of a priestly monopoly over learning, the relative fluidity of classes, and the existence of immense material resources, conditions in the United States were peculiarly favorable to the application of the theory. In America at least it seemed possible to lift the dream from the realm of speculation and give it effect in the common life of the masses.

This hope inspired Condorcet when, in the shadow of death cast by the tyranny of the French extremists, he wrote, in 1793, the immortal *Esquisse d'un tableau historique des progrès de l'esprit humain,* an outline of the history of progress and a forecast of its impetuous sway over the illimitable future. Into this gigantic pattern Condorcet fitted the American Revolution as the great event of the modern world which was to set in train the dynamic of a new epoch. "In consequence of America declaring herself independent of the British government," he said, "a war ensued between the two enlightened nations, in which one contended for the natural rights of mankind, the other for the impious doctrine that subjects these rights to prescription, to political interests, and written constitutions. The great cause at issue was tried, during the war, in the tribunal of opinion, and as it were before the assembled nations of mankind. The rights of men were freely investigated and strenuously supported in the writings which circulated from the banks of the Neva to those of the Guadalquivir. . . . These discussions penetrated into the most distant and retired hamlets. . . . In this state of things, it could not be long before the trans-Atlantic revolution must find its imitators in the European quarter of the world."

The very next year after Condorcet's sketch of progress was printed, namely, in 1796, a beautiful translation was issued in Philadelphia, rapidly spreading the fame and philosophy of the author through the intellectual circles of America. Coming as it did swiftly upon the publication of Chastellux's observations on American civilization and its probable destiny, Condorcet's volume gave wide currency to the notion that America might realize a grand ideal for the subjugation of the material world to human welfare.

Beyond all question Franklin, who knew the Encyclopædists and Condorcet, early saw the import for America of natural science and the concept of progress. Indeed, fifteen years before Condorcet's sketch of universal prosperity was published, Franklin wrote from the American legation in France to Priestley, the English chemist: "It is impossible to imagine the height to which may be carried, in a thousand years, the power of man over matter. We may perhaps learn to deprive large masses of their gravity and give them absolute levity, for the sake of easy transport. Agriculture may diminish its labor and double its produce; all diseases may by sure means be prevented or cured, not excepting that of old age, and our lives lengthened at pleasure even beyond the antediluvian standard. O that moral science were in a fair way of improvement, that men would cease to be wolves to one another, and that human beings would at length learn what they now improperly call humanity!" Sir Humphrey Davy spoke with full knowledge when he said that Franklin "has in no instance exhibited that false dignity, by which philosophy is kept aloof from common applications; and he has sought rather to make her a useful inmate and servant in the common habitations of man, than to preserve her merely as an object of adoration in temples and palaces."

When Franklin died, the mantle of intellectual leadership fell upon Jefferson. As his letters and his great library showed, he too was thoroughly conversant with the latest advances of natural science and with the idea of progress overriding philosophies of apathetic or stoical resignation to fate; he was constantly meditating upon their meaning for the order of society just established in republican America. On surveying the ground after he laid down public office, he expressed to John Adams his conviction that "one of the questions . . . on which our parties took different sides, was on the improvability of the human mind in science, in ethics, in government, &c. Those who advocated a reformation of institutions, pari passu with the progress of science, maintained that no definite limits could be assigned to progress. The enemies of reform on the other hand denied improvement and advocated steady adherence to the principles, practices, and institutions of our fathers which they represented as the consummation of wisdom and the acme of excellence beyond which the human mind could never advance." There was the key to Jefferson's concept of social evolution.

Appealing especially to the third and fourth economic strata of the American social order, namely, the yeomanry and mechanics, Jefferson was the natural leader of a humanistic democracy. Though himself a planter, he was of yeoman origin. Cutting loose from English patterns of reputability, he came to the conclusion that public felicity was the goal of statecraft. Reviving Roman doctrines, he held that the idea of a republic was something dignified and grand in itself, a noble expression of human nature, and he grew still more democratic as the years went by. As we have seen, Jefferson started early on his program for realizing an individualistic society: destroying primogeniture as the bulwark of the Virginia aristocracy, disestablishing the church in Virginia, promoting freedom of the press and religious worship, eliminating cruelties and superstitions from the laws, advancing free schools and institutions of higher learning, forwarding the study of theoretical and applied science, and extending the knowledge of modern languages as the key to modern wisdom.

In the course of time Jefferson worked out a fairly comprehensive scheme of social science: agriculture should be the economic basis of society; a mild and inexpensive government given to toleration and justice could easily maintain order; an equal division of inheritances and easy acquisition of land would make for a practical equality in status; universal education would afford talents for leadership and give all the people an equal opportunity to get at the wisdom of the ages; immigration should be limited to assimilable stocks and overpopulation avoided; slavery should be abolished and the slaves transported to a land of their own. Thus could America realize in some measure at least the dream of a golden age and move to better things with the advance of knowledge. Whatever criticism might be brought against Jefferson's creed, it had the merit of concreteness and humanism; and, contrasted with the colonial order, was certainly revolutionary from beginning to end.

Against such social theories, as well as against Jefferson's political leadership, was aligned, as he said himself, a party that denied the doctrine of human improvement, clung to theological authority, and sought safety in traditional customs. As a matter of fact there was enough left of the old arrangement of classes and their psychology to give a specious appeal to the prospect of retaining most of the colonial heritage. When the grave consequences of the Revolution, both actual and impending, were fairly grasped, a party of cultural propriety was formed. Its nucleus was made up of the wealthier families from the second colonial stratum which had come to the top in the upheaval. Grouped around this core were the new families enriched during the war by speculation, privateering, confiscations, expropriations, and various forms of legitimate business enterprise. Closely associated with these orders were the old loyalists who had never accepted the Revolution but, while hating it in their hearts, had remained in America and weathered the storm.

Although, in promoting capitalistic undertakings, this party, by one of the twists of fortune, was more revolutionary in the realm of fact than Jefferson himself, in ideas and manners it strove with almost pathetic anguish to gather up the floating timbers of colonial wreckage. Remembering with regret the pomp and circumstance of the provincial capitals, it tried to make the republic socially respectable, surround the President with glitter and ceremony, maintain the powdered wigs, silken hose, and servile livery of the grand style. Without much difficulty this party persuaded Washington to assume some signs of royal dignity, thereby offending those who professed leveling principles. When he went about the capital city on official business, he rode in a fine coach drawn by four horses, making quite a regal appearance. When he and Mrs. Washington gave a ball, the social set tried to envelop them with the style of a royal couple. Perhaps recalling snubs received from the English set in Boston, John Adams now thought that the head of the nation should have an impressive title such as "His Majesty, the President"; while ladies with claims to heraldic devices similarly dubious would have addressed his consort at the Republican Court as "Lady Washington."

After all, this was natural enough, for Washington was indeed a majestic figure compared with the lumbering "Farmer George" who ruled England, and titles of some kind had been cherished by every type of human society since the first primitive chief rose above his fellows. Moreover, if we leave out of account some bucolic members of Congress, the executive, legislative, and judicial authorities of the first government were gentlemen born and bred; so the installation of royal ceremony would not have been as incongruous as it seems at this distance. Furthermore, polished ministers and their ladies from European courts and distinguished visitors, such as Talleyrand, Duc de la Rochefoucauld-Liancourt, and Louis Philippe, future King of France, bringing an atmosphere of reputable custom to the American scene, stimulated by their very presence a desire for emulation.

Although the Jeffersonians laughed heartily at the airs of the daughter of a Philadelphia speculator who married into the English aristocracy and learned to swear and tell malodorous stories with the *savoir faire* of a duchess, there was no doubt about the rigidity of the class lines which separated the party of wealth and talents from the party of farmers and mechanics. During the last days of Jefferson's service as Secretary of State, only three of the "best" families of Philadelphia, then the national capital, deigned to invite to their homes that delightful raconteur, musician, and critic of the fine arts. Once when Mrs. Washington discovered a spot on her immaculate drawing room wall just above a sofa, she reproached her niece with entertaining "a filthy democrat."

In a similar spirit, Federalist Boston read out of polite society Republican leaders, such as Elbridge Gerry, and later even John Quincy Adams when he went over to the Jeffersonian party. In the city of Samuel Adams, regarded by the English as a low demagogue, it became impossible for a member of the strict political sect to dance or drink wine with a "Jacobin." In fact it was as difficult for a reputable Federalist to associate with a Jeffersonian Democrat of the early republican age as for a denizen of Fifth Avenue in the era of William McKinley to drink tea with a disciple of John P. Altgeld or Eugene V. Debs.

If, as most modern historians agree, there was no large monarchist contingent in this party of propriety, it certainly contained a very considerable proportion of people who felt that the strength of their order and its culture depended on close relations with England and that the outcome of the whole republican experiment was at least doubtful. In the year of the peace with England—that is, in 1783—the London Chronicle published a letter from Charleston setting forth the prevailing note in the circle of conventional hopes: "The wise and moderate part of the inhabitants here look back upon their late situation, when connected with Great Britain, with infinite regret and consider the peace, the security, the brotherly regard, and the state of visible improvement which they enjoyed under the protection of the mother country as the true Golden Age of America." Just after the adoption of the Constitution in 1788, another Chronicle correspondent, this time from the center of things, in Philadelphia, while reporting some economic improvement, recorded with pleasure that John Adams had "demonstrated the absurdity of democracy" and abated much of the aversion to monarchy, adding that "it would not surprise many were the United States a monarchy early in the next century."

This sentiment was shortly confirmed by Jonathan Boucher, the celebrated Anglican clergyman, a refugee from the American Revolution, who in 1797 brought out a volume of his sermons prefaced by a note on the lamentable result of the recent uprising in America. With the dialectic artistry of his craft, he argued that the United States was founded on false democratic principles; that it had started the horrible French Revolution and would be shaken down by it; that it would finally become a great empire under a monarch. Culturally, Boucher declared the experiment a complete failure since it owed all the arts, sciences, and other good things to England. Quoting a writer of his school, he exclaimed: "What has America to boast of? What are the graces or the virtues that distinguish its inhabitants? What are their triumphs in war or their inventions in peace? Inglorious soldiers, yet seditious citizens! Sordid merchants and indolent usurers." In the circumstances, the only remedy that the disturbed clergyman could concoct was a permanent alliance of the United States with Great Britain. Though this party of historic propriety, eager to beat back the rising tide of Jefferson's humanistic democracy, was destined to be outvoted at the polls, it possessed enough wealth and power to furnish solid substance for a social development along conventional lines.

§

The shock of the Revolution, the struggles to uphold the independent republic that had been forced upon the people by the accidents of fortune, and the contests of parties over the possession and direction of the national government awakened unexpected creative forces in imaginative literature and art. As in every age of intellectual activity, the operation and flowering of those energies were contingent in a large measure upon the character of their patronage —itself now a complex of economic factors—the nature of the conflicts within the social order, and the dominant features of the spiritual climate in general. Thus conditioned, the product of American vitalism during this era was rich and varied. In its highest forms it was marked by power and distinction. If much of the writing was stilted and bombastic, those faults could be attributed in no small measure to reverence for English and classical models.

Letters and art, as in any other order, had to be sustained under the republic by dollars and cents. Traditionally the support for literature had come mainly from royal, princely, and ecclesiastical sources, supplemented later by subscriptions from members of the landed and mercantile classes; while art and architecture had been fostered by kings, lords, prelates, gentlemen, and merchants who bought the products of the painters and the designers. The theater which Goethe directed at Weimar, like most of the great theaters on the Continent, depended largely upon princely bounty. If the Crown in England did not underwrite the stage or provide a royal opera house, it did patronize artists, actors, musicians, and authors by means of commissions, grants, and pensions. Voltaire's Henriade, which appeared in England in 1728, was subsidized by three hundred and forty-four subscribers, headed by the king, the queen, and noblemen of the court, and it was dedicated in a grand style to Queen Caroline, who gave him a goodly purse.

In republican America there were no kings, princes, queens, or prelates to maintain letters and the arts. Here the makers of imaginative literature were supported by plain civilians who bought books, magazines, and theater tickets. Although the question of government subvention for the theater was raised in a debate in the Pennsylvania legislature and a few persons advocated official subsidy and control in republican interests, the idea bore no fruit. The drama like the novel and poetry had, therefore, to rest upon popular enthusiasm and purchasing power. Art and architecture bowed to the decrees of merchants and landed proprietors who had surplus incomes to spend. Dairy maids and hired men, as a contemporary remarked, could buy the hair-raising stories of the novelists, but they could not buy oil paintings, town houses, or mansions in the country. Neither were they holders of front pews in the congregations that built new churches or voters for legislatures that ordered the state capitols. But each group—the high and the low—found its servants; each was soon offered wares to fit its tastes.

Since there were then few Americans who combined riches with æsthetic talents and hence could withdraw from the world of reality to indulge in their dreams, the literature and art of the republican era inevitably bore the impress of the social and political struggles that went on among the patrons. Writers and artists, living in the world of fact, could not escape the "Sturm und Drang" that raged about them. And the war for independence had left a legacy of emotions. Basically a certain dislike of Britain and things British was unavoidable among the patriots, especially as the clash with the mother country continued long after the treaty of peace was signed. Of kindred necessity a consciousness of national independence and of the challenge which responsibility carried with it forced upward feelings of belligerence and pride. By analogous processes, interest and affection were turned in the direction of France, the great ally in the war for liberty.

At the same time within American society, as we have already indicated, was being waged a spirited battle between capitalistic forces on the one hand and agrarians led by planters on the other—a contest in which the Federalist party, drawing its sustenance mainly from the commercial orders, was thrown back upon traditional ideas in meeting the attacks of Jeffersonian hordes. Since it also included in its ranks most of the old Tories who looked with tearful eyes upon the past that lay buried under the ruins of the Revolution, English writers, classical and contemporary, and English actors and artists could satisfy nearly all the desires of those who longed poignantly for order, for calm, and for prostration. In the circumstances, therefore, most of the creative writers in the realm of imaginative letters, during the early republican period, showed a tendency to drift to the Jeffersonian left.

The immediate environment in which these writers and artists worked presented striking features that could not escape the attention of any observer—features essentially rationalistic, practical, scientific, and humane, with far-reaching implications that touched all elements of the social fabric and its functions. In concrete terms the historic rights of Englishmen, of which colonial America had boasted, meant privileges for merchants and freeholders; whereas the rights of man accorded by nature, in logical requirement at least, embraced privileges for disfranchised mechanics, subject women, indentured servants, and even slaves. At all events, the volcanic awakening of the masses which accompanied the Revolution and the fierce partisan battles that followed it were patent facts standing out vividly in the American scene.

Less ponderable, but undeniable, was a new social spirit, calling for prison reform and the abolition of slavery, which was making advances in the land: it was being discussed in the closets of philosophers; it was destined to rewrite, in blood, as time proved, whole chapters of the law. And as radical interpreters would have it, the rights of man really included rights of women too. Mary Wollstonecraft's startling challenge to masculine supremacy, published in 1792 was as portentous in one sphere as Rousseau's social contract in another. Finally, the intellectual climate of the new age was secular and earthly.

No one could read the current books that flowed from the press in England, France, Germany, Italy, and the United States—and the intellectual life of the republican age embraced all those countries as parts of a common civilization—without discovering waves of reform beating against the traditional headlands. If writers in America could agree on the necessity of sustaining the republican idea, they displayed on other matters shades of opinion that lay far to the left of the "high toned" doctrines espoused by Hamilton and John Adams. In any case they bore the striations of the social drift.

§

It was natural that the republican writers should seek to make the drama an instrument to express their interests and philosophy. In the confusion of the war for independence, of course, the theater, which had grown up in a desultory fashion after its initial appearance at the opening of the eighteenth century, had suffered a serious setback except in New York, where the British used it for their own purposes, during their occupation of the city. Indeed, the Continental Congress, much to the satisfaction of the Puritans, had in 1774 advised all the states to "discountenance and discourage all horse racing, and all kinds of gaming, cock fighting, exhibitions of shows, plays and other expensive diversions and entertainments." It seems that the request was granted with more enthusiasm than calls for money and troops.

But as soon as peace came, the strain was relaxed. Even in Boston the ice then began to crack; throughout Massachusetts, where stage plays had been forbidden by an act of the General Court in 1750, the Revolution and the new secularism had set opinions afloat. By 1791, things had reached such a point that a number of respectable citizens, horrifying Samuel Adams and some of the saints, petitioned for a repeal of the law. The proposal was defeated but, undismayed by the stern aspect of jurisprudence, a troop of comedians visited Boston the very next year, rented a stable, erected a platform, and announced, as a disguise, a series of "moral lectures."

Unhappily for the players, the news was too good to keep and early in December the sheriff swooped down upon a "moral" performance of The School for Scandal. In the foray, one of the actors was arrested and a test case was made while the town rocked with excitement. Since crowds wanted to see and hear the Thespians, the trial was held in that citadel of liberty, Faneuil Hall. Then, to the consternation of the good, a clever trick of the defending counsel forced the acquittal of the wicked one amid a storm of applause. From that time forward theatrical performances were freely advertised and given in the stronghold of Cotton Mather.

While the rising generation was reading and reciting comedies and tragedies, while even the children of Puritans were attending the "Devil's Chapel," as stern old Doctor Tillotson called the play house, American writers were arguing that the theater could be made to serve the cause of the young republic. Indeed, one of the most effective replies to Tory dramatic propaganda was made by Mrs. Mercy Warren in the form of a satirical play, entitled *The Group*, written in 1775. Whether her product was actually put on the boards is not known but the publisher claimed that it had been "lately acted" and was to be "reacted to the Wonder of all Superior Intelligences Nigh Headquarters at Amboyne." If there were some shortcomings in Mrs. Warren's style, there was no weakness in the patriotism which inspired her answers to the attacks of General Burgoyne and other "military Thespians" from England. With a similar confidence in American destiny, William Dunlap, who may justly be called the "father of the American theater," championed the drama on the ground that it could be made an engine for the support of the republic and the improvement of the social order.

On this point, however, there was much difference of opinion. In the debate on the subject, in 1785, in the Pennsylvania legislature, the contestants divided rather sharply according to their political views, the party of "the rich and well-born" lending support to the theater and the party of leveling agrarian democracy taking the other side of the question. Robert Morris declared himself a friend of the theater as offering a rational, instructive amusement—an institution that had improved public manners, given opportunity to genius, afforded lessons to vice and folly—and expressed the hope that in due time American poets would be writing dramas adapted to the circumstances of American life. George Clymer, one of the richest men in Philadelphia and, like Morris, a member of the constitutional convention of 1787, after declaring that no civilized state was without a theater, inquired: "Are we forever to be indebted to other nations for genius, wit, and refinement?"

Against these apostles of Hamilton's Federalism were arrayed two farmers from the frontier who were to vote against the ratification of the Constitution in the Pennsylvania convention. One, John Smiley, thought that the drama would divert the people from their political duties, that Cardinal Mazarin had established the French Academy for that sinister purpose, and that the fine arts "only flourished when states were on the decline." The other, William Findley, likewise a vigorous opponent of the Hamiltonian liturgy, was equally doctrinaire; in his opinion a government-regulated theater would be a dangerous tool, while a free theater would vitiate arcadian taste. Although in the end the project for a theater supported and censored by the state was defeated, it did not mean that in Pennsylvania or anywhere else the drama escaped the impacts of contemporary politics.

On the contrary, the writers of American plays, in keeping with their political professions, deliberately sought to strike the republican note; and after the battle began to rage between Hamilton and Jefferson, they breathed into their lines the animus of the partisan conflict. The second American play given on a regular stage by professional actors, it seems, Royall Tyler's comedy, The Contrast, produced in New York in 1787, represented a yeoman's reaction to the manners and customs of a selfish and luxurious urban society. In this satire, a patriot soldier, Colonel Manly, embodied pride in American independence; a Yankee servant stood for contentment with "twenty acres of rock, the Bible, the cow, Tabitha, and a little peaceable bundling"; while the offspring of profiteering families from the city represented the foibles and outlook of the smart set contemptuous of arcadian democracy.

To the drift of the argument the prologue gives the cue:

Exult, each patriot heart!—This night is shewn
A piece, which we may fairly call our own;
Where the proud titles of "My Lord! Your Grace!"
To humble Mr. and plain Sir give place.
Our Author pictures not from foreign climes
The fashions or the follies of the times;
But has confin'd the subject of his work
To the gay scenes—the circles of New York.
On native themes his Muse displays her pow'rs;
If ours the faults, the virtues too are ours.
Why should our thoughts to distant countries roam,
When each refinement may be found at home?
Who travels now to ape the rich or great,
To deck an equipage and roll in state;
To court the graces, or to dance with ease,
Or by hypocrisy to strive to please?
Our free-born ancestors such arts despis'd;
Genuine sincerity alone they priz'd;
Their minds with honest emulation fir'd,
To solid good—not ornament—aspir'd;
Or, if ambition rous'd a bolder flame,
Stern virtue throve, where indolence was shame.

But modern youths, with imitative sense
Deem taste in dress the proof of excellence;
And spurn the meanness of your homespun arts,
Since homespun habits would obscure their parts;
Whilst all, which aims at splendour and parade,
Must come from Europe and be ready made.

Should rigid critics reprobate our play,
At least the patriotic heart will say,
"Glorious our fall, since in a noble cause.
The bold attempt alone demands applause."

Thus does our Author to your candour trust;
Conscious, the free are generous, as just!

In the course of the play the hero celebrated republican simplicity, decried luxury, praised the glories of Greece in her early career when her people knew "no other tool than the ax and the saw." Expressing doctrines akin to those of Daniel Shays, the Yankee Jonathan boasted that "we don't make any great matter of distinction in our state between quality and other folks." In contrast the gay young lady—the flapper of New York in the century that was passing—laughed at the old-fashioned morals thus revived, declaring that money was one of the chief objects of matrimony, that she could bring more beaux to her feet by "one flirt of this hoop" than by sighing any fine sentiments.

In the end, however, republican virtue triumphed. The "snob" of the play took his leave with a remark about the superiority of his imported Chesterfieldian finish while the hero exclaimed: "I have learned that probity, virtue, honor, though they should not have received the polish of Europe will secure to an honest American the good graces of his fair countrywoman, and I hope the applause of The Public."

Two years after Tyler's comedy appeared in New York, William Dunlap's play, The Father, was produced, opening his career as the dominant figure in republican dramatics. Born in New Jersey, Dunlap was a native American. Nevertheless he was catholic in his interests and tastes, broad in his knowledge of foreign tongues and literatures, and deeply appreciative of older civilizations. He was a prodigious worker, writing in all about fifty plays, ranging from tragedy to comedy and from interlude to opera. More than half of these were original productions; the remainder were translations or adaptations from French and German works.

Besides this, Dunlap studied painting with Benjamin West and brought the sister art to work in close alliance with the drama. So extravagant, indeed, was his taste for great spectacles that he seems to be the originator of that conspicuously American type of production—the gorgeous show making a lavish display of wealth and material goods. His versatile labors Dunlap crowned by writing a history of the American theater.

In the American themes handled in his plays, Dunlap consciously mirrored the aspirations of the idealists around him—"liberty, science, peace, plenty, my country," as he expressed it. The Father presented in 1789 caught up the refrain of The Contrast, which had captivated the people. Especially did his drama, André, enter into the spirit of the Revolution and of the optimists who believed that the republic was about to fulfill the age-long hope of mankind for utopia.

While unfolding the story, Dunlap made one of his characters, M'Donald, a soldier in the field, give an efficient cause for the Revolution:

> As to ourselves, in truth, I nothing see,
> In all the wondrous deeds which we perform,
> But plain effects from causes full as plain.
> Rises not man forever 'gainst oppression?
> It is the law of life; he can't avoid it.
> But when the love of property unites
> With sense of injuries past, and dread of future,
> Is it then wonderful, that he should brave
> A lesser evil to avoid a greater?

Yet when a companion in arms, Seward, asked him: "Hast thou no nobler motives for thy arms than love of property and thirst for vengeance?" M'Donald replied:

> Yes, my good Seward, and yet nothing wondrous.
> I love this country for the sake of man.
> My parents, and I thank them, cross'd the seas,
> And made me native of fair Nature's world,
> With room to grow and thrive in. I have thriven;
> And feel my mind unshackled, free, expanding,
> Grasping, with ken unbounded, mighty thoughts,
> At which, if chance my mother had, good dame,
> In Scotia, our revered parent soil,
> Given me to see the day, I should have shrunk
> Affrighted. Now I see in this new world
> A resting spot for man, if he can stand
> Firm in his place, while Europe howls around him.

Moved by the nobler strain Seward exclaimed:

> Then might, perhaps, one land on earth be found,
> Free from th' extremes of poverty and riches;
> Where ne'er a scepter'd tyrant should be known,
> Or tyrant lordling. curses of creation.

To the land thus blessed with liberty, peace, and plenty were to be added, however, the finest products of European civilization.

> From Europe shall enriching commerce flow,
> And many an ill attendant; but from thence
> Shall likewise flow blest Science; Europe's knowledge,
> By sharp experience bought, we should appropriate;
> Striving thus to leap from that simplicity,
> With ignorance curst, to that simplicity
> By knowledge blest; unknown the gulf between.

When his companion who had listened patiently to this outburst cried, "Dreams, Dreams!" M'Donald brought the vision to an end with the words:

> I'll to my bed, for I have watch'd all night;
> And may my sleep give pleasing repetition
> Of these my waking dreams! Virtue's incentives.

In such themes and in such lines did Dunlap seek to realize his project for using the stage as an instrument to disseminate the ideals of the young republic, improve taste, and elevate morals.

Among Dunlap's contemporaries were two dramatists who went completely over to the Jeffersonian left, boasted of the name Democrat, participated in politics, and openly expressed their judgment on the merits of the contending parties. The first of these, James N. Barker, combined office-holding under Republican auspices with his literary labors and tried to express, in terms of Jeffersonian philosophy, "the genius of America, science, liberty, and attendant spirits."

The second, Mordecai Noah, while discovering the limitations of his art in American conditions, with similar vision freely accepted the restraints imposed upon him by the society in which he worked. "My line, as you well know," he said in a letter to Dunlap, "has been in the more rugged paths of politics, a line in which there is more fact than poetry, more feeling than fiction; in which to be sure, there are 'exits' and 'entrances'—where the 'prompter's whistle' is constantly heard in the voice of the people; but which in our popular government, almost disqualifies us for the more soft and agreeable translation to the lofty conceptions of tragedy, the pure diction of genteel comedy, or the wit, gaiety, and humor of broad farce."

It was indeed those very irksome trammels that drove Noah's distinguished countryman, John Howard Payne, to develop his dramatic art abroad in more traditional themes, such as Brutus and Charles II. If his song, Home Sweet Home, by which he is remembered, recalled the land of his birth, Americans took note of the fact that it was sung for the first time in London, in 1823, after Payne had lived in England for many years.

§

Like the dramatists, the novelists of the early republic also worked in the realism of existing facts and conditions. They too arranged themselves according to their sympathies with the tendencies of their age. On the right, although a champion of republican simplicity, was Royall Tyler, a son of Boston, a graduate of Harvard, a soldier in the army that suppressed Shays' agrarian rebellion, a producer of fiction as well as a writer of plays. In a novel called The Algerian Captive, published in 1797, he gently surveyed and satirized all American society, displaying in the operation both skill and insight.

While Tyler laughed a little at that "certain staple of New England . . . called conscience," at the hard theology of his ancestors, the ingenuities of spinsters, and the quackeries of doctors, he bore down heaviest on points that irked the party of Thomas Jefferson. He laughed loudest at the itinerant doctors who were "especially good at mending a kettle and a constitution." He obviously enjoyed taking a shot at paper money, at Voltaire, d'Alembert, and Diderot, at "light anti-federal sermons," and at the hard-drinking and fox-hunting Jeffersonian gentry of the South. He grew positively exuberant in describing a Virginia parson who came late into his pulpit, red in the face from beating a Negro boy who had delayed his arrival by negligence, and then preached "an animated discourse of eleven minutes on the practical duties of religion." In a parting volley, Tyler remarked that the clergyman was "as much respected upon the turf as upon the hassock."

If many a hearty Federalist laughed over Tyler's thrusts at foibles on the opposite side of the political fence, the spiritual heirs of Cotton Mather and Jonathan Edwards in New England must have wept over the secular note of his novel. It was too strong in its wit to be missed. Lest it be overlooked, however, by the careless, Tyler explained in his preface that he was contributing a native product to satisfy the growing interest of the masses in tales of fancy.

By way of reinforcement, he made his hero describe at length the change in popular taste that had taken place during a few years of his absence from home: "When he left New England, books of Biography, Travels, Novels, and Modern Romances were confined to our seaports; or, if known in the country, were read only in the families of Clergymen, Physicians, and Lawyers; while certain funeral discourses, the last words and dying speeches of Bryan Shaheen, and Levi Ames, and some dreary somebody's Day of Doom formed the most diverting part of the farmer's library. On his return from captivity he found a surprising alteration in the public taste. In our inland towns of consequence social libraries had been instituted, composed of books designed to amuse rather than to instruct. . . . All orders of country life, with one accord, forsook the sober sermons and Practical Pieties of their fathers for the gay stories and splendid impieties of the Traveller and the Novelist. The worthy farmer no longer fatigued himself with Bunyan's Pilgrim up 'the hill of difficulty' or through the 'slough of despond' but quaffed wine with Brydone in the hermitage of Vesuvius, or sported with Bruce on the fairy land of Abyssinia: while Dolly, the Dairy maid, and Jonathan, the hired man, threw aside the ballad of the cruel stepmother, over which they had so often wept in concert and now amused themselves into so agreeable a terrour, with the haunted houses and hobgobblins of Mrs. Ratcliffe, that they were both afraid to sleep alone."

A few degrees to the left of Tyler, but yet no leveling democrat, was a disciple of Jefferson from western Pennsylvania, Hugh Brackenridge, whose novel, Model Chivalry, laid bare the anatomy of American politics in an imitation of Cervantes. Brackenridge was a lawyer who had developed a large practice among the farmers of the Pittsburgh region and shared some of the frontiersman's antipathy for Hamilton's high-toned government. In a satirical vein he belittled the Society of the Cincinnati, that powerful aid of the Federalist faction.

In a true agrarian spirit, lawyers were made the enemies of the people. "They have so much jargon," said the hero of the tale, "that the devil himself cannot understand them. Their whole object is to get money; and, provided they can pick the pocket of half a joe, they care little about the person that consults them. . . . This thing of the law has been well said to be a bottomless pit." The business of education, Brackenridge thought, was "to form the heart to a republican government." A gentle irony was turned on the American Philosophical Society, whose members were made to mistake an Irish whiskey tax collector tarred and feathered by an anti-tax mob for an "Anthroposornis or manbird."

With moderation Brackenridge treated the great reforms of the French Revolution as deserving the applause of all good citizens, though the excesses were to be deplored; but the leveling procedure must not be carried too far. To talk about "vox populi" was to play the demagogue; to speak of "serving" the people or the "majesty" of the people smacked of monarchy. Tailors and laborers were simply silly if they cherished aspirations for public office; they should stick like the cobbler to the last. It was enough that an Irish mechanic should have the "right" to be President, without thinking of exercising that high privilege reserved for his betters. In short, Brackenridge's novel approved good, sound Republican government by gentlemen of the Jefferson type. The "monocrats" and the "democrats" equally deserved to be cast into outer darkness.

Far more radical than Brackenridge, though in practice less concerned with the actual business of politics, was Charles Brockden Brown, the outstanding novelist of the time, forerunner of Cooper and Hawthorne. In Brown's intellect all the eddying currents of the age were reflected. His religion betrayed the drift of the time: though he was born of Quaker parents and continued to regard himself to the end as a Christian, he was first attracted by Rousseau and the German sentimentalists and then drawn to Voltaire and the rationalists. His politics admitted of no doubt for his anti-Federalism was ingrained: he opposed the adoption of the Constitution and was especially aggrieved because that document did not include the Declaration of Independence.

Enabled by his knowledge of modern languages to keep in touch with Continental thought and work, he came to believe profoundly, with the French reformers, that the cruelties and follies of superstition could be cleared away by science and reason. Though he never rejected Christianity, he was clear-cut in denouncing the doctrines of total depravity and infant damnation. "Human beings," he said in approved scientific temper, "are molded by the circumstances in which they are placed. In this they are all alike. The differences that flow from the sexual distinction are as nothing in the balance." Cherishing such notions, Brown seized with avidity upon the writings of the English radicals, especially of William Godwin, philosophic anarchist, and of Mary Wollstonecraft, whose book, A

Vindication of the Rights of Women, appeared in 1792, and was republished in Philadelphia in 1794—just a hundred years after Mary Astell's Defense of the Female Sex and Defoe's advocacy of equal education.

Indeed, Brown was so affected by the prevailing discriminations against women and the discussion of their status, already agitating "advanced" minds, that he wrote a brochure, Alcuin, in which he anticipated twentieth century ideas of feminism with respect to economic independence, political rights, and legal equality. In this dialogue a highly intelligent woman pleaded her own case: "I think we have the highest reason to complain of our exclusion from many professions which might afford us, in common with men, the means of subsistence and independence." In a broad sweep, she objected to the bars against so many pursuits, to the denial of college education and the subjection of married women to the discipline of the common law. "Are you a Federalist?" her questioner asked. "What have I as a woman to do with politics?" she answered. "Even the government of our country, which is said to be the freest in the world, passes over women as if they were not. We are excluded from all political rights without the least ceremony. Law-makers thought as little of comprehending us in their code of liberty as if we were pigs or sheep."

The novels of Brown were also modern and didactic; they all revealed the spirit of the left wing politics. His first work of fiction, Wieland, was a plea for rationalism as a cure for the evils induced by superstition and credulity. Even when he entered the turgid realm of mystery, rationalism entered with him. In Clara Howard, he sang the praise of the yeoman, objected to the poison of servility that had lingered in society from colonial times, and portrayed a new woman thinking and acting for herself. Through his pages walked sociological enthusiasts discoursing on law, marriage, riches, and reform. Scott, Godwin, and Shelley read Brown's books and English reviews commended them but time did not deal gently with his long homilies.

As a matter of fact, if Brown was the most creative novelist of the early republic, women writers were the best sellers and enjoyed the more enduring appreciation by the populace. Pioneers in the field of fiction though they were, their work outlasted the stories of all their male contemporaries. In the year of Washington's first inauguration, Sarah Wentworth Morton published the Power of Sympathy, which critics agree was our first regular novel. A few years later Susannah Haswell Rowson, though English by birth, issued in America a story called Charlotte Temple in which she claimed that "vice however prosperous in the beginning, in the end leads only to misery and shame." It was the old triangle. "A pellucid drop had stolen from her eyes and fallen upon a rose she was painting," ran the refrain; but the Americans bought it by the thousands and it lived in edition after edition for generations. In 1797 Hannah Webster Foster published The Coquette, a novel based upon an American episode, which so charmed the general public that before the death of the author in 1840 it had passed through thirteen editions. Thus did the successors of Anne Hutchinson and Mary Dyer at least invite their generation to consider other themes than salvation and damnation, for many things had happened since the landing of the Pilgrims.

§

In poetry as in imaginative prose the political and intellectual conflicts of the republican age found their expression. The struggle for independence during the American Revolution was mirrored in John Trumbull's McFingal, a long political satire portraying the patriots victorious over the Tories in argument and arms. When the Revolutionary contest was ended and the American social cleavage appeared, a group of verse makers, known as the

Hartford Wits, assailed in the Anarchiad of 1787 the leveling tendencies of the agrarian party with a virulence that forecast Republican editorials on William Jennings Bryan a hundred years later.

Bowing to a kindred passion, Thomas Green Fessenden, in Democracy Unveiled or Tyranny Stripped of the Garb of Patriotism, roundly abused Jefferson, Jacobinism, atheism, and democracy. In fact, no novelties in the intellectual world were allowed to pass unscathed. Voltaire and rationalism were bombarded by Timothy Dwight in the Triumph of Infidelity—a long ode saturated with Biblical lore. Nor must it be forgotten that William Cullen Bryant, dutiful son of a Federalist father, started his career as a poet by a scurrilous attack on Jefferson and his policies which was published in 1808 under the head of The Embargo; that six years later, in a Fourth of July ode, praising England, "Queen of the Isles," he accused his own government of waging a useless war.

On the other side of the line that divided the age into warring camps were poets equally prolific and as fascinated by the art of making verse. Philip Freneau, after rendering effective services to the patriot cause in the days of the war, threw himself enthusiastically into the popular movement led by Jefferson. Indeed as the editor of the National Gazette—partly supported by his salary as translator in Jefferson's Department of State—Freneau employed his biting sarcasm in analyzing the policies and measures of Hamilton. If it is correct to call him "the poet of the American revolution," it is equally proper to say that he was the bard of Jeffersonian Democracy and of the rationalist age.

Into Freneau's party finally drifted the New England poet, Joel Barlow, whose Vision of Columbus, published in 1787, was hailed in England and France no less than at home as a work giving promise of genius. One of the Hartford Wits, Barlow took part in writing the Anarchiad but later, while in France, he espoused the popular cause, was granted French citizenship, and enjoyed the honor of being attacked by Edmund Burke. After he finally settled down in his native land, he brought out, in 1807, the Columbiad, a pretentious poem affecting the grand style but in fact a "geographical, historical, political, and philosophical disquisition" rather than a work of art. President Madison made him minister to France and the rising democracy claimed him as a bright star in its firmament but time was ruthless to his poetry.

If William Cullen Bryant, in an essay on American poetry, written soon after Barlow's death, could with justice lightly dispose of all such efforts as The Columbiad on the ground that they lacked in native instinct and simplicity of style, he could not himself escape the impact of the scientific rationalism which was so highly prized by the democratic philosophers of his country. Federalist though he was in origin, he later became a Democrat and even in his youth he was so steeped in the new skepticism that his great poem, Thanatopsis, written in 1811, was in essence pagan, as his critics said, "because there is no mention of the Deity in it nor recognition of the Christian doctrine of resurrection and immortality."

To this charge his biographer could only reply that the poem "takes the idea of Death out of its theological aspects and sophistications and the perversions of conscience with which they are connected and restores it to its proper place in the vast scheme of things." The apology was itself a confession that Thanatopsis fitted the mind of Jefferson rather than that of Timothy Dwight.

§

The soul of the artist no less than the mind of the poet was in some measure subdued during the early republic to the interests, passions, and conflicts of the period. Workers in the realm of the imagination were then, as always, kindred spirits. The painter, as Charles Caffin points out in his study of American art, is limited by his canvas, while the orator, the poet, or the dramatist can crowd his pages with scenes and characters; but the sentiments behind their work and the influences of their environment are almost identical. No doubt, the emotions expressed by Barlow's Columbiad and by Trumbull's portrayal of Bunker Hill were keyed to the same vibration.

Moreover, the artist, like the writer, had to be sustained. William Dunlap, the sturdy democrat, might scorn the word "patronage" but John Trumbull was near the truth when he said that American artists could not look to the Church or to the legislatures for support and were "necessarily dependent upon the protection of the rich and great"—the strong bulwark of Hamilton's party. That fact, so clearly recognized by a leading painter of the time, meant that art, from the nature of things, could not swing as far to the left as imaginative letters which could be maintained, in part at least, by the pennies of the multitude. If painters sometimes received commissions from city councils and state legislatures or from Congress, they were forced to rely in the main upon the pleasure of those who could pay for oils and miniatures, and to endure the criticisms of the radical democrats who, on account of its historic position, associated art with monarchies and aristocracies as a symbol of servility.

By the cataclysm of the Revolution, the painters of provincial America were divided into factions: one, devoted to the old and conventional society with its aristocratic pretensions; the other, to the simplicity of the republican ideal. For example, as we have noted, Copley adhered to the party of unbending Tories, leaving the turmoil of the New World for the security and milder atmosphere of Georgian London where he could serve landed gentry and merchants of more seasoned fortune than the planters of Virginia or the traders of Philadelphia and Boston. On the other hand, as if to offset this defection, Charles Wilson Peale of Maryland, who was studying in England when the storm broke, hurried home to share the fortunes of his native land, taking a lively interest in the war for independence and the political contests that followed.

Between battles and campaigns, Peale painted portraits of the hero, Washington, fourteen in all, divining as it were the place which the leader was to hold in the affections of the nation which he was so largely instrumental in calling into being. Besides giving form and color to numerous themes chosen from the life of the republic, Peale, without breaking from the classical tradition, took upon himself the task of spurring among his people an interest in art and in the training of artists. He organized the first exhibition of painting in America, tried to persuade New York City to establish a museum of the arts and sciences, and finally induced Philadelphia to raise the money for such an institution in 1805 when New York betrayed indifference.

In founding the Pennsylvania Art Academy, its promoters announced in brave, if quaint, language, "the high and stalwart purpose of the times, a consciousness of the limited conditions of the start, a conviction of the harvest of the future." They proposed "to promote the cultivation of the Fine Arts in the United States of America by introducing current and elegant copies from works of the first masters in Sculpture and Painting and by thus facilitating the access to such standards and also by conferring moderate but honorable premiums and otherwise assisting studies and exciting the efforts of artists, gradually to unfold, enlighten, and invigorate the talents of our countrymen." That was a courageous move; for when John Pine, coming but a few years before to paint revolutionary scenes, brought with him a cast of Venus de Medici, the people of Philadelphia suffered a shock of fright. Even after they recovered a bit, the model could only be shown to a select few; devoted to Doric columns though it was, the city shuddered at the very suggestion of the statues originally housed behind them. Nevertheless the home city of

Franklin survived the ordeal and the young Academy gained strength as the years passed by.

Among his colleagues from New England, Peale had a friendly rival in John Trumbull, of Connecticut, who shared his affection for the republican experiment. Trumbull was nineteen years old when the Revolution came down upon his country but without hesitation he threw himself into the patriot cause, laying aside book and brush for rifle and sword and rising through distinguished service to the rank of colonel, then to deputy adjutant-general. When the triumph finally came at Yorktown, Trumbull went to England to study under West and later to see the work of the old masters on the Continent. Returning to America, he started on his long career as a painter in New York in 1804.

A veteran of the war, imbued with the spirit of the Napoleonic age, and a Federalist of the old school, Trumbull's mind was unresponsive to the naturalism of Rousseau which was stirring poets to ecstasies. Above all a patriot, nothing was more appropriate, therefore, than that he should choose American subjects and seek to immortalize the heroes and scenes of the struggle for independence. With something akin to military rigidity, he made portraits of Washington, Jefferson, and Adams, and painted the battle of Bunker Hill, the signing of the Declaration of Independence, the surrender of Cornwallis, the resignation of Washington, and other phases of the drama, in the imposing style made famous at Versailles. Not a figure was loved into immortality by soft caresses; the same note of starched Roman formalism ran through his painting of Washington that gave structure to Lee's oration on the man "first in the hearts of his countrymen." It was, consequently, with a certain degree of fitness that Trumbull associated himself with a number of rich New Yorkers in 1808 to float the American Academy of Fine Arts as a chartered corporation governed, not by a counting of heads, but by an enumeration of the twenty-five dollar shares held by the several stockholders who financed the venture.

This intimate relation between the psychic affiliations of the artist and the nature of his work was also well illustrated in the paintings of Trumbull's distinguished contemporary, Gilbert Stuart. Though born in Rhode Island, Stuart early forsook provincial America for a life in London, studying with Benjamin West. When, at length, the break with the mother country rent his native land, instead of rushing home like Peale to throw himself into the fray, he remained in England, aloof from the tempestuous passions of the hour, until the safe days of peace returned; indeed, until Washington was reëlected President for a second term. But from 1793 to his death in 1828, he labored with prolific industry in preserving to posterity with ceremonial correctness the faces of great Americans— among them Washington, Adams, Jefferson, Madison, and then John Jacob Astor.

Whatever his subject, Stuart placed on its lights and shadows the stamp of his inner feelings, betraying in the lines of his brush a chill remoteness from the crash of the patriot battles and the fervent strivings of the new republic. "Stuart," justly remarks Caffin, "did not share in the life spirit of the nation," was a bit too elegant and cosmopolitan. "On the other hand, before the grimly intellectual or austerely visionary faces of Smibert's New England divines, the precise elegance and proud self-sufficiency of Copley's men and women of the world, or Peale's bald masculine records of the man upon whom devolved the leadership of a new nation, we can recognize a series of types and in our imagination reconstruct their environment. . . . We may transport ourselves beyond the then present, as the founders of the nation did, 'and feel the future in the instant.' "

It is not a cause for wonder that Washington, the Virginia planter, indomitable leader of a revolutionary cause, and great political pacificator, was subdued by Stuart to the varnish of an old English man-of-arms. Unquestionably the painter was deeply drawn to Washington, confessing that he lost his self-possession in the presence of that illustrious man but he failed to induce the General to part the curtain and reveal his secret self. Although the full length portrait may have satisfied Lord Lansdowne, to whom it was presented, neither that picture nor the Athenæum portrait painted at Mrs. Washington's request gave to posterity a luminous conception of the living personality disclosed by his own diaries, letters, and papers. It may be said, of course, that, whereas Peale painted Washington in the full tide of manhood, Stuart saw him only in later life after responsibility and suffering had given their wonted gravity to his face but this fact alone will not account for the frigid, if correct, solemnity that directs Stuart's every stroke.

In sculpture and architecture, the young republic with all its aspirations could do little more than borrow. The former was yet an alien art among Anglo-Saxons and the Americans consequently had no English heritage on which to build. Apparently American interest in sculpture was manifest at first in the South and shyly, even where Puritan fear of satanic alliances was weakest in its grip. But native talent was wanting. The years were far off when a Celtic genius, Saint Gaudens, born in Dublin but reared in America, could carve a Diana in lines comparable to Houdon's and at the same time catch the unconquerable spirit of a Puritan father.

So the patronage of European artists was the only resort. When Virginia decided to immortalize La Fayette and Washington, it was forced to turn to Houdon, who had already delighted France with his Morphée, if he had shocked the Salon with his nude Diana. It was to his fortunate acceptance that Richmond owed its heroic statue of the great revolutionary leader. In some of the richer southern homes, the love of the plastic arts also found expression in beautiful importations. For instance, from an English admirer, Samuel Vaughan, Washington received an Italian mantel, exclaiming when he first saw it, "I greatly fear that it is too elegant and costly for my room and republican style of living"; but its charm melted his scruples and to the end he cherished it with keen delight.

Through the architecture of the republican age, the political note rang with startling intonations. In casting off monarchy and established church, the patriot Fathers, like their emulative contemporaries, the leaders of the French republic, returned in their dreams, their oratory, and their architecture to the glories of republican Greece and Rome—to the simple columns, roofs, porticoes, and straight lines of early Mediterranean structures. Nothing seemed to them more appropriate. The ornate elaboration of renaissance Gothic appeared out of place in a country that was republican in politics, practical in its interests, and tinged, at least, with democracy. There was of course no strict uniformity of thought but the stamp of the classics was heavy on the official buildings and private mansions of the period.

It was with a mind fixed upon the imposing designs of ancient city planners that Major L'Enfant conceived his elaborate scheme for the city of Washington—a scheme for which he received shabby treatment at the time and trivial recognition in a military funeral nearly one hundred years after he was laid a pauper in a quickly forgotten grave. When, in 1808, the adopted son of Washington built his mansion at Arlington, Virginia, he seemed convinced that the final triumph of art lay in the achievements of the Greeks two thousand years in their tombs. It was to the simplicity, solemnity, and power of Rome, despoiler of Greece, that Jefferson turned for the design of his University of Virginia. In the same reverence for classical antiquity, the colonial Georgian style was now pushed aside by architects who built mansions for southern planters, banks, offices for the federal government, and the capitol to house the Congress of the United States. Those who fashioned material structures and those who drafted orations drew their inspiration from the same source.

§

The moment independence was assured, articles, pamphlets, and books on the function of education in the new social order poured from the presses, the anxiety of private individuals for the future of the republic being supplemented by the stimulus of a prize offered by the American Philosophical Society for "the best system of liberal education and literary instruction, adapted to the genius of the government of the United States; comprehending also a plan for instituting and conducting public schools in this country, on the principles of the most extensive utility." So important did the subject seem to the founders of the republic that the outstanding men of the time bent their minds to it—Washington, Jefferson, Benjamin Rush, Noah Webster, and James Sullivan, as well as writers less known to general history, such as Robert Coram, Nathaniel Chipman, Samuel Knox, and Samuel Harrison Smith. Though most of the tracts and pamphlets lie buried in the dust of libraries, their influence still lives in American educational theory; and a recent scholar, Allen Oscar Hansen, has paid generous tribute to the services of the republican pioneers in his volume on Liberalism and American Education in the Eighteenth Century.

In the wide range of speculation, nothing human or pertinent to the coming centuries seems to have been overlooked by the thinkers who pondered on the rôle of education in civilization. A composite view of their ideas shows that, in their enthusiasm for new and revolutionary concepts, they far outran the commonalty, anticipating in almost every phase projects a hundred years ahead of their day. In the first place, they recognized the deplorable state of the education received from colonial times—miserable schoolhouses, meager equipment, and poorly-trained teachers. On the constructive side they nearly all insisted that there should be a nation-wide system of popular education, universal, sometimes including girls, supported by general taxation, running from the elementary school to the university. "It is a shame, a scandal to civilized society, that part only of the citizens should be sent to colleges and universities to learn to cheat the rest of their liberties," exclaimed Robert Coram.

Turning to the purpose and content of education, the eighteenth century critics were equally explicit. In their view the prime end of education was to help realize the ideal of progress, raise the general level of well-being, bring all citizens within the range of the coöperative life, apply science to the service of mankind, prepare pupils for economic independence, instruct them in the duties of citizenship, instill in them republican principles, strengthen and enrich American nationality. As an instrument for the realization of such theories freedom of thought—the foe of bigotry—was to be encouraged. "A perfect freedom of debate is essential to a free government," urged Noah Webster in his Sketches of American Policy. "A vigorous spirit of research" was to be promoted, according to the creed in Samuel H. Smith's Remarks on Education. "I wish," said James Sullivan, "to excite some of my younger countrymen . . . to bend their attention and endeavor to make deep researches into what constitutes man's happiness individually and in society." Some writers naturally laid stress on one phase to the neglect of others, but broadly speaking the whole structural foundation for modern theory and practice was sketched with wonderful foresight, considering that feminism was then confined to esoteric circles and that the revolution wrought by technology lay hidden in the future.

A resolute nationalist of the Hamilton school, Washington looked upon higher education as the servant of the new constitutional system which had been erected with such labor and required for its maintenance support on every side. In his first message to Congress he dwelt solemnly upon the matter of promoting science and letters and raising up an educated nation competent to the great task of self-government. Though he did not venture to decide the best method of attaining the object, he hinted at aid for existing institutions and the foundation of a national university.

As to Washington's personal views there was no doubt. Having learned from practical experience in the Continental army the advantages to be derived from the mingling of youths from every section, he wished to establish an American University so high in its standing that the necessity of going to Europe would be eliminated and students from every corner of the United States would be attracted to its halls. As an evidence of his interest, he left in his will a sum of money to be devoted to the endowment of such an institution, if Congress should ever be inclined to extend "a fostering hand to it."

Unfortunately the fine vision was not caught by his countrymen. Military and naval academies were, indeed, founded at West Point and Annapolis but the dream of a national university to unite the minds and hearts of those who were to guide America in the coming years was not realized, jealousies among existing colleges and the triumph of the state's rights party defeating the project.

The second great educational proposal of the early period, likewise blighted by indifference, united the nationalism of Washington with the democratic humanism of Jefferson. Appropriately enough, it came from Philadelphia and from Benjamin Rush, one of the Franklin circle. In framing his educational ideal, Rush brought the whole country within his purview, conceiving of its spiritual development as a national unity. The university with which he proposed to crown the hierarchy of schools, serving the cause of human progress as an American institution, was to be a post-graduate college preparing youths for public life.

Its curriculum, worked out in detail by the meticulous author, was to include among the subjects for instruction: the principles and forms of government—everything relating to peace, war, treaties, and general administration; ancient and modern history; agriculture, in all its branches; history, principles, objects, and channels of commerce; principles and practices of manufactures; applied mathematics; the parts of natural philosophy and chemistry relating to agriculture, manufacture, commerce, and war (for war is apt to continue, however un-Christian, he said); natural history; philology, rhetoric, and criticism; modern languages opening the gates to knowledge relative to national improvements of all kinds; athletics and manly exercises.

Thus Rush proposed to explore and teach the new learning, and to teach it in the compelling terms of utility. "The present age," he said, "is the age of simplicity of style in American writings. The turgid style of Johnson—the purple glare of Gibbon—and the studious and thick set metaphors of Junius—are equally unnatural and should not be admitted to our country." Citing the examples of Russia and Denmark, Rush suggested that two specialists be assigned for advanced research in natural science and that four be sent abroad in the quest for new knowledge; not overlooking the fact that northern Europe and England had borrowed heavily from Mediterranean peoples.

"While the business of education in Europe," Rush declared, "consists in lectures upon the ruins of Palmyra and the antiquities of Herculaneum or in disputes about Hebrew points, Greek particles or the accent and quantity of the Roman languages, the youth of America will be employed in acquiring those branches of knowledge which increase the conveniences of life, lessen human misery, improve our country, promote population, exalt the human understanding, and establish domestic and political happiness." To make the teachings of his great school effective Rush proposed that after the lapse of thirty years all civil officers be chosen exclusively from its graduates with a view to eliminating quacks from politics as from law and medicine! The president of this university, he urged, should be a man of extensive education as well as of liberal manners and dignity.

But Washington's project and Rush's plan were too nationalistic in spirit and purpose to secure the cordial support of a country that had begun its career by exalting the sovereignty of the states and had swung back to that creed in 1800 after a temporary period of high centralization. So in keeping with the drift of political opinion it happened that Jefferson, the theorist, became the practical builder in the field of education. No one on the American continent had more enthusiasm for the subject; no one had more confidence in education as the instrument for the preservation and development of democracy. As his political affection centered on the state, so his educational efforts were mainly confined to that sphere, even though he did indorse the idea of a national university.

Remembering, perhaps, the size of Athens and her achievements, Jefferson preferred to devote his talents to Virginia rather than to wear himself out trying to induce Congress to establish a continental system. But in the field he did choose and the work he attempted, the spirit of the modern age shone forth abundantly. Seeing the youth of the land casting off the old learning for "intuition and self-sufficiency," he proposed to hold their intellectual enthusiasm by offering the new learning of the laboratory and research. For the theological and scholastic system so dominant in the colonial régime, he proposed to substitute one that was scientific, modern, and practical in character. He did not, of course, ignore the wisdom of the ancients, far from it, but his emphasis was different. "I am for encouraging the progress of science in all its branches," he wrote to a friend in 1799.

At first Jefferson lavished his affections on his alma mater, William and Mary, which had suffered heavily from the loss of its English revenues during the Revolution. As a member of the board of trustees, he helped to bring about the adoption of his leading ideas and to work a transformation in that college by the introduction of modern languages and the establishment of chairs in law, history, and political economy. Not long after Blackstone began his lectures on jurisprudence at Oxford, Wythe was expounding great principles of the law at William and Mary. In the enthusiasm for innovations, Greek and Latin were for a time dropped from the regular program and could be studied only privately with one of the professors. As if to emphasize the democracy of the age, the status of the students was raised by granting to them a larger freedom in selecting subjects and by adopting the honor system for their examinations. Thus, even in the midst of revolution, Jefferson made to prevail in an Anglican college much of the liberal thesis which he was to apply on a grand scale in the University of Virginia founded by him more than a quarter of a century later.

In the northern colleges, on the other hand, scientific and social studies made slower headway. It is true that Williams College, chartered by the Massachusetts legislature of 1793 and opened under the guidance of Yale alumni, made some novel departures; it immediately permitted the offering of French instead of Greek as an entrance subject and soon established a program of French language and literature, followed by special courses in law, civil polity, mathematics, and natural philosophy. It is true also that Bowdoin College, organized in 1802 under a charter of the Massachusetts legislature, offered a milder brand of Calvinist theology to the boys of the Maine woods who were not rich enough to go to Harvard; and boasted of having on its faculty Parker Cleaveland, who won distinction both at home and in Europe for his contributions to chemistry and mineralogy.

In the main, however, the colleges of the North, excepting Franklin's institution at Philadelphia, escaped the influence of French science, skepticism, and humanism. When Ezra Stiles, on his inauguration as president of Yale in 1778, sketched his scheme of higher education, he left to the classics their wonted authority, relegated geography, mathematics, history, and belles lettres to a secondary place, and bent higher mathematics, natural philosophy, and astronomy to the purposes of theology. In the history of American intellectual development there is nothing more illuminating than the contrast presented by a Yale commencement address of the late eighteenth century and one a hundred years afterward.

Harvard, in the age of Jefferson, likewise clung rather closely to established academic customs. A distinguished, if ungrateful, son, Harrison Gray Otis, flung at his alma mater the charge that she was dominated by pedantry and logic. "May Father Time," he said in 1782, "ameliorate his pace and hasten the desired period when I shall bid adieu to the sophisticated Jargon of a superstitious synod of pensioned bigots and ramble in the field of liberal science." In the bitter exaggeration of the undergraduate was revealed the continued supremacy of ancient ideals in the old institutions of the North—institutions which had passed through the political and economic revolution without breaking the sway of the theological regimen.

§

It was in the theory and practice of secondary education rather than in the higher learning that the most thoroughgoing innovations were made at the turn of the century. The movement of democratic opinion, naturally in favor of popular education, was accelerated by the influence of doctrines from Europe. Out of the philosophy of Rousseau, the fiery French radical, interpreted by German and Swiss experimenters, flowered a varied and luxuriant literature on the training of the young and their relations to society— a literature so rich that, according to estimates, twice as many books on the subject were printed during the last quarter of the eighteenth century as during the preceding three quarters. Certainly no phase of the question was untouched. Education in agriculture and the manual arts, social discipline, gymnastics, moral and religious culture, the secularization of the curricula by emphasis on modern languages, geography, history, and science, and even the complete elimination of theological motives from the class room were now advocated in proposals for reform.

Underlying the new concepts were Rousseau's sentiments: repugnance to tradition and devotion to nature, observation, and the cultivation of social sympathies. Reflecting the political ideals of the age, the child's right to happiness was placed beside the current emphasis on the adult's right to liberty and opposed at every point to the formalism and discipline of governing classes bent upon making artisans, peasants, and soldiers only—humanity against class dominion, democracy against authority. This was the dream which Basedow sought to realize at Dessau in Germany and Pestalozzi at Yverdon in Switzerland. "All the beneficent powers of men are due neither to art nor chance, but to nature," exclaimed the Swiss pedagogue. From that premise it logically followed that "education must pursue the course laid down by nature."

In America, this philosophy and the practice based upon it were strongly advocated by William Maclure of Philadelphia, a retired merchant and amateur in science who visited Yverdon and in 1805 published a book on the school. The next year, Maclure imported from Switzerland an apostle of Pestalozzi to lecture on the new education and give demonstrations. Within a short time Pestalozzian schools were founded at Philadelphia and at various places in Kentucky and the West, planting the germs of a humane and democratic system of education for foliation when the funds with which to nurture them could be provided.

Nothing could have been more acceptable to the disciples

of Jefferson than the revolutionary concept of life embodied in these plans of education for it exactly squared with his philosophy of politics. The conservative system of Europe, he contended, was founded on the doctrine that "men in numerous associations cannot be restrained within the limits of order and justice but by forces physical and moral, wielded over them by authorities independent of their will. . . . We believed that man was a rational animal, endowed by nature with rights and an innate sense of justice." One relied upon formalism and artifices to hold the lower orders of society in check; the other proposed to cut loose from the past, trust in the beneficent powers given to man by nature, and develop them by a simple process into social harmony. So the revolutionary gospel of the European experimentalists fitted neatly into the pattern of the Republican statesman of Virginia.

§

Since the colleges were beyond the reach of the American masses stirred by novel aspirations in the ferment of the revolutionary movement and since the ruling orders in the states were not prepared to tax themselves for the support of public schools, the immediate answer to the new demands was the academy, usually founded under private and local auspices, though in many cases with state aid and support. Unhampered by the traditional curricula of the colleges, and controlled by enterprising individuals rather than by clerical boards of trustees, the academies began to break paths toward a liberal education more precisely adapted to American life.

Unlike the old classical grammar schools, academies escaped the whip of the college entrance requirements, for a time, at least. Bidding for the patronage of sons and daughters of merchants and farmers who could not hope to attend institutions of higher learning, they reached a hitherto untouched middle stratum of the population. In the circumstances greater flexibility of curriculum was possible: the classics and theology were reduced when not omitted entirely, while French, art, history, and literature for the first time found favor in the scheme of secondary education. If, as correctly charged, the academies later became vested interests which opposed the rise of the public school system, still they helped in their day to weaken the grip of scholasticism on the higher learning and prepare the way for the humanities.

Yet at best the academies left unsolved the problem that puzzled radical leaders of the revolutionary age; namely, how to lift the mass of the people from illiteracy into the world of culture, out of subserviency and apathy into coöperative and energetic citizenship. Many a philosopher, with Jefferson in the van, dreamed of the day and sketched plans for universal education, for boys, at least. State constitutions and legislatures made grand declarations of principles on the subject but it was one thing to put a project on paper and another thing to convert the governing classes to the notion of taxing themselves for it or to overcome the age-old inertia of the populace. So in these conditions the sectarian and charity schools of colonial times continued to hold the general field of elementary education, although like the colleges they lost the support of funds from England when the break with the mother country was made.

They were supplemented and extended, however, by two new and important agencies, both imported from England. The first of these was the Sunday school, especially designed to reach the children of the poor on a day when they were not employed. While generally associated with religious sects and always emphasizing instruction in the Scriptures, the Sunday school movement in the beginning was broader than any mere sectarian intent and was supported, especially in England where it originated, by interdenominational societies founded for that object. Though regarded as perilously democratic by conservative Anglicans, the Sunday school was promoted by dissenters with so much fervor that interest in the institution spread to the United States.

In 1791, "The First-Day or Sunday School Society" was organized at Philadelphia for the purpose of extending elementary instruction to the poor. The experiment was true to form but American tendencies gave a peculiar direction to later developments. There was no large submerged mass of paupers in the United States, such as existed in England, and the little schools established here and there by the various sects were already reaching deep down into the social order. So the Sunday schools assumed a more theological tone in America than in England, becoming as a rule mere adjuncts to the churches that sustained them, leaving other than religious training to the ordinary day schools. Nevertheless before the age of compulsory, secular education, they gave elementary instruction in reading to thousands who were not within the fold of the other sectarian institutions.

The second English scheme for reaching the masses with elementary instruction was the monitorial school in which the older pupils transmitted to the younger information they had themselves learned by rote from the teachers. The idea was an ancient one. A Portuguese traveler saw it in operation in India in the early part of the seventeenth century. Jesuits had made extensive use of it, and at various places in Europe it had been developed long before the end of the eighteenth century when England and the United States resorted to the project. Yet, in common opinion, it was with the name of Joseph Lancaster, an English Quaker philanthropist, that the formal beginning of a great movement in 1798 was associated—although Andrew Bell, perhaps with a better show of justice, claimed to have inaugurated the system by an experiment started previously under the auspices of the Established Church. Indeed, in England two schemes of monitorial instruction, one nonconformist and the other Anglican, ran side by side, later with state financial assistance, until the adoption of the board school program in 1870.

Whatever its origin, in the United States the monitorial project soon attracted the interest of educational theorists. In 1809 the Public School Society of New York introduced it into its schools and a few years later Lancaster himself came to America to apply his scheme in person. Although he proved to be a stubborn and intolerant teacher and finally sank into poverty and distress, his method for educating the masses spread into every state in the Union. It was taken up by some of the academies; it was adopted by the schools later instituted for training teachers; and when state education finally entered the field, it was employed at first by Indiana and Maryland. Crude as it was and destined to vanish before the freer systems and practices of Pestalozzi and Froebel, the monitorial plan afforded the only solution to the problem of mass training in an age that had little money or would not impose taxes to pay for anything better. It was cheap, it was practical, it was one step nearer universal, free education.

That ideal—schools for all free children supported by taxation—made slow headway through the years that followed independence. In the midst of the Revolution, 1779, Jefferson brought before the legislature of Virginia a bill proposing to lay the commonwealth out into districts and provide each with a school maintained by public revenues, open to the children of all citizens, free of tuition for the first three years. Though the bill failed to pass, the plan persisted.

While Jefferson's contemporaries did not like imposts and excises any better after the Revolution than before, they had at their disposal a rich treasury of undeveloped natural resources which could be dedicated in part to the uses of education. If they did not dare to tax their constituents for the support of common schools, they could at least reserve wild lands for that purpose. In that relation they had before them a high example set by the Congress under the Articles of Confederation when, in the Ordinance of 1785, it dedicated one section of land in each township of the Ohio Territory to the maintenance of public schools. Moreover, many state constitutions declared, with big flourishes, that schools should be established in the public interest though they provided no means for their support. Rhode Island, Maryland, and the Carolinas, for instance, made grand gestures that came to little or nothing.

There was in America no Prussian monarch to impose a compulsory system on the people for reasons of state. Consequently the project of universal free education had to be evolved gradually in a democratic fashion, under the leadership of men and women with vision, who realized that they could move only as fast as knowledge of the ideal could be disseminated and practical interests enlisted for its support. When at last the task was seriously undertaken, at the middle of the nineteenth century, the stamp of American nationality was clear upon it.

§

During the transition from province to nation, that strange process, so closely described by Carlyle, in which literature "emerged out of the cloisters into the open Market-place and endeavoured to make itself room and gain a subsistence there," worked a revolution in American journalism. The challenge of novel facts, impetuous aspirations, and social controversies enlarged the power of the press and gave substance to writers who fed its capacious maw. Every phase of the dramatic story from the mustering of the Stamp Act Congress to the battle of New Orleans, every hope and every theory of the fermenting age can be traced in the news stories, the editorials, and the fugitive articles that filled the columns of weeklies, monthlies, and eventually dailies.

Throughout the period, magazines bloomed like roses in

summer time, dying with the same regularity. From Boston, Massachusetts, to Lexington, Kentucky, enterprising editors flung out their tiny sheets with wistful patriotism, the titles of their little journals betraying their hearts' desire: The American Magazine, The Columbian Magazine, The American Universal Magazine, and finally the North American Review—the last, founded in 1815, being the only one of a great crowd that survived the rush of time. Leaving the rage of party faction to the newspapers, editors of weekly and monthly periodicals devoted themselves to literature, morals, science, and the arts. Their catholicity of interest was well illustrated by the descriptive note attached to a typical magazine of the time: "A monthly Museum of Knowledge and Rational Entertainment containing Poetry, Musick, Biography, History, Physics, Geography, Morality, Criticism, Philosophy, Mathematics, Agriculture, Architecture, Chemistry, Novels, Tales, Romances, Translations, News, Marriages, and Deaths, Meteorological Observations, etc., etc."

Venturing beyond the written word, some of the more audacious editors included in their pages a few simple engravings which evidently added to the appeal of their journals, for when one of them afterward substituted type for pictures "the admirers of this polite art earnestly called for their re-assumption." Encyclopædic in their range, these early magazines popularized literature, science, and art in an age before public libraries were general and before education was wide and comprehensive. They furnished "subsistence" for a school of writers who broke a path for Cooper, Irving, Prescott, Poe, and Lowell. Their pomposity and ridiculous chauvinism will, no doubt, be pardoned by those acquainted with Old World magazines of the same period.

As if to soften the stresses of life in the New World, the periodicals of the young republic made much of poetry, each having its "Pegasus, its Cabinet of Apollo, its Seat of the Muses. its Parnassiad; even the most prosaic its

Poetical Essays or its Poetical Provisions." They could all boast of narrative verse "both serious and jocose" apparently on the theory that poetry like music could soothe the savage breast. One of them printed An Elegant Ode on the Mechanism of Man; another published some lines To a Lady on Striking a Fly with Her Fan. In any event there was a thirsty craving for "good taste" which led editors to specialize in tabloid culture responding, perhaps, to the taunts of English writers that, bereft of their leadership and authority, the Americans would become "literary ourang-outangs."

With positive poignancy did the Christian's, Scholar's and Farmer's Magazine feel a call to labor among the heathen, receiving from a watchful contributor, who welcomed its efforts, suggestions as to one neglected field that needed cultivation. "A deficiency of learning," he lamented, "hath often been very sensibly regretted by many worthy characters in these states when elevated to public and important offices; and frequently ignorance hath not only exposed them to ridicule but been injurious to the interests of the public."

The writer then illustrated with a case that must have been peculiarly embarrassing to young republicans who had just tossed off British supremacy: "We mention particularly a circumstance that exposed a very popular patriot in London a few years past to contempt and occasioned him to become a subject of ridicule in the public papers of the metropolis. In an oration he made at Guildhall, instead of speaking in the superlative degree, which he wished to have done, through ignorance, he made use of the double comparative—more better." Dreadful error and before a London audience at that! From such grief sprang the first of the American "Mentors" to give to the untutored an education in the superlatives of dining, dancing, and dallying, in addition to proprieties of speech.

From this cultural anguish the ladies were by no means exempt. On the contrary they were early discovered as the very bulwark of correct taste. Independence was hardly declared when one rash editor introduced the "elegant polish of the female pen" and, as the years passed, the ladies won an ever larger share in the pages of the magazines. Their virtues were extolled, love stories were printed for their idle hours, poetical enigmas and rebuses were provided to stretch their tender minds, examples of refined correspondence between the sexes were furnished as guides to ready letter writers, and stray fragments were printed to arouse "desultory thoughts upon the utility of encouraging a degree of self-complacency especially in the female bosoms"—all with a fervent desire to "please rather than wound woman, the noblest work of God." In 1792 came the climax with the appearance of an all-lady repository designed to circulate primarily in the boarding schools, it seems.

The venture was daring, yet discreet; for the ladies' magazines of the young republic, like their successors to the days of Edward Bok, refrained from encouraging any froward feminism. "The female patronesses of literature," insinuated the gracious editor, "while they discover an understanding in the fairest part of intelligent creation to distinguish works of real merit from the false glare of empty professions, at the same time also shed a luster on the amiable qualities which adorn the minds of the fair. It is theirs to ease the weary traveler in the rugged paths of science and soften the rigors of intense study; it is theirs to chase the diffidence of bashful merit and give dignity to the boldest thought. . . . Every lover of the ladies will stand forth as a champion in defense of a work peculiarly calculated for the instruction and amusement of the lovely."

Of all the great flock of magazines that sued for patronage two or three managed to live long enough to attain distinction. First among these was Matthew Carey's Columbian Magazine, founded in Philadelphia in 1786, a staple in intellectual circles for more than half a century. His American Museum, founded the next year, commanded for its pages articles from Franklin, Rush, Freneau, Hopkinson, and Trumbull that were solid in substance, dignified in style and appropriate to the age, emphasizing science and economics rather than theology and polite letters. Somewhat lighter and yet marked by critical discernment was the Literary Magazine and American Register, which ran through a brief career in the same city under the direction of Charles Brockden Brown, already famous as a novelist, the author of Arthur Mervyn.

Not to be eclipsed by Philadelphia, some intellectual Brahmins of Boston—the Anthology Club, composed of several "gentlemen of literary interests"—launched, in 1803, The Monthly Anthology and Magazine of Polite Literature, a work of love edited, as well as sustained, by its sponsors. Convinced that the traffic was now blocked by the mob, by too many writers producing "worthless weeds prematurely," the directors insisted that articles and book reviews for the journal should be characterized by expertness and quality.

Indeed, so excellent was their work that the promoters of the North American Review, when establishing their magazine in 1815, selected William Tudor from the Anthology Club to serve as their editor. Thus favorably inaugurated, this Review continued to be issued in Boston for more than sixty years, marshaling to its aid the most eminent minds of New England and acting as the arbiter of conservative taste in letters and politics in that section —until its removal to New York in 1878. Only when The Atlantic Monthly came into the arena in 1857 did it have a serious competitor for northern patronage.

True to the traditions of emancipated provinces, the poignant persons who edited the magazines of the young republic were vexed with longings to win above all the favor of the Old World. When a French traveler declared that the arts, except that of navigation, received little attention in America and that the "Bostonians think of the useful before procuring to themselves the agreeable," it gave great sorrow to his American readers. "It has been suggested," said the promoters of the Nightingale or Mélange of Literature, in 1796, "that the inhabitants of Boston prefer viewing the manifest of a ship's cargo to a lounge in the library. Let it not be said that in the pursuit of gain, Literature and the Muses are left at a distance, and that a sordid lust for gold has banished every noble sentiment, every mental delight from the bosoms of the avaricious Bostonians. God forbid that any foe to our country shall ever have reason to say that our native town is the residence of Ignorance, though it should be the emporium of Plutus."

While couched in the moving style of the period, this plea was apparently not heeded, for Emerson, looking back upon the history of Massachusetts during the period that lay between 1790 and 1820, felt moved to exclaim that "there was not a book, a speech, a conversation, or a thought in the state." Nevertheless it could be said that those rough sea captains who preferred viewing a ship's manifest to scanning a library shelf, who had never heard of Arius or Gainsborough, were changing the world to which the Philosophers of the Brook Farm school long afterward appealed. From the fabled East, Boston navigators brought tea and silks, fragments of a fragile art, accounts of strange traditions and religions, awakening a spirit of adventure that went far in dissolving the theological monopoly of thought and other Puritan legacies. Quite as much as the dialecticians, they made unitarianism and transcendentalism popular. And if lowly, but indispensable, services were not to be despised, it had to be recorded that they amassed the fortunes which enabled the Ticknors, Brookses, Adamses, Prescotts, Parkmans, Lowells, and Jameses to cut loose from the smell of salt and tar, to dream dreams in the milder atmosphere of the Old World where the sea captains and accumulators of an earlier time had already done their work of preparation for the softer generations to come.

Relieved of literary burdens by magazines, the newspapers sprang full armed into the political arena. During the stormy days of the Stamp Act, they were transformed from colorless bulletins into flaming sheets of sedition, kindling passions that never died away. Throughout the war for independence a battle royal was waged between the Tory and the Patriot press, and when that issue was settled, local disputes of the triumphant Americans still furnished an abundance of fuel for editorial fires. Into the fight over the Constitution publishers plunged with relish, and later, as Hamilton's measures came up one by one before Congress, they secured endless and lively themes for news and comment. When at length the alignment between the Federalists and the Republicans was clearly defined, every newspaper of importance became a party organ, exchanging advocacy for patronage and praise.

As the factional struggle waxed hotter and hotter and the population increased, new papers appeared until at last every city and every village of any size had its press. Forty-three colonial sheets, it is reckoned, survived the Revolution; thirty years later an assiduous counter estimated that the United States had three hundred and sixty-six newspapers.

Of the new journals that entered the fray two of the most powerful were personal organs of the great party leaders, Hamilton and Jefferson. Scarcely was the former installed in office, when he induced John Fenno to bring out in New York in April, 1789, The Gazette of the United States, to defend the administration of Washington, that is, his own economic policies. Jefferson replied in kind about two years later, taking the cue from his rival, by supporting Freneau, the poet, in the publication of the National Gazette at Philadelphia, to which the capital had then been removed.

The age of the daily had now opened; by the close of Jefferson's administration in 1809 there were at least twenty-seven dailies scattered from Boston to New Orleans

—nearly all partisan, sustaining or attacking the administration in power or serving some personal or factional cause. When the capital was transferred to Washington, this city became the center of political journalism, holding that strategic position until the telegraph broke its monopoly and brought every editorial room near to the seat of national sovereignty.

As party organs, these newspapers vividly exhibited the passions of the combatants in the political field, the scurrilities to which both sides resorted passing modern belief, though they were not peculiarly American at the time. With withering scorn and contempt, Hamilton's organ treated the opposition as low-born demagogues. Though his party boasted of commanding the talents as well as the wealth of the country and felt limited—somewhat—by the requirements of gentility, the reader of to-day, when turning over the yellow leaves of the Federalist organs, will have difficulty in discerning the fruits of that restraint. Not without a touch of retribution, perhaps, Jefferson was daily smeared with charges of being an atheist, a leveler, an agrarian, an anarchist, a democrat, a demagogue—all synonyms for criminality in the Federalist camp.

On the other side, Jefferson's party spoke frankly for the people and the editorials of its press savored of the soil. The "corrupt squadron" of speculators in Congress and outside was assailed with every weapon of vituperation known to men, and the secret sessions of the Senate were fiercely attacked until that august body was forced to throw open its doors, at least during the transaction of ordinary business. Nor was Washington, the father of his country, spared; his personal integrity was not laid under suspicion but he got much of the "mud" aimed at Hamilton and felt that "a common criminal" could fare no worse.

To the continuous flow of political rhetoric, the steadily growing proportion of space devoted to domestic and foreign news afforded little relief for the news was all colored by politics. Nothing but a few "features" really relaxed the tension. In 1793 an original columnist, the first perhaps in the New World, Royall Tyler, novelist and dramatist, began to supply readers of the New Hampshire Journal with witty comment on current events, while "A Lay Preacher," a forerunner of Dr. Frank Crane, gave vent to moralizings on things in general. At last "wordless journalism" definitely put in its appearance when in 1811 Benjamin Russell, a New England editor, brought out the "gerrymander" cartoon destined to endure for more than a century—long after many a contemporary editorial on the subject had been buried in the dust of decades. Americans were beginning to laugh at themselves; by quip and picture they could ease a bit the fierce strain of politics and soften the terrors of hell.

CHAPTER XI

New Agricultural States

DURING the years between the inauguration of George Washington and the retirement of James Monroe, the "agricultural interest" was enlarging its area, multiplying its adherents, and increasing its wealth. When the first President of the United States took the oath of office in Wall Street, there were thirteen states in the Union; within a little more than three decades nine new commonwealths had been erected in the Valley of the Mississippi—Kentucky, Tennessee, Ohio, Louisiana, Indiana, Mississippi, Illinois, Alabama, and Missouri—and two on the outskirts of New England—Vermont and Maine. In the same eventful period the population of the country multiplied nearly three times; at its close there were more inhabitants in Kentucky and Tennessee than in Massachusetts, Rhode Island, Connecticut, and Vermont combined. With the movement of peoples and the rise of new communities went of course a westward shift in the center of political gravity.

At the end of Monroe's administration Virginia, mother

507

of Presidents, had to yield the scepter. Four years afterward Massachusetts was also forced to abdicate when her conservative son, John Quincy Adams, who had won the palm by an accident in the grand scramble of 1824, was swept from the White House before the flood of western Democrats headed by Andrew Jackson of Tennessee. The political forces of agriculture which had driven from power Hamilton's party of finance, commerce, and industry in 1800 had now been made apparently invincible by recruits from the frontier.

No wonder the statesmen of "wealth and talents" were in despair as they read the handwriting on the wall. At the Hartford convention a decade before, the assembled Federalists had prophesied that the admission of new western states would destroy the delicate balance between the planting and the commercial sections, that the planting interest allied with the western farmers would for a time govern the country, and that finally the western states, multiplied in number and augmented in population, would control the interests of the whole. To ward off this disaster the soothsayers of calamity had then offered ingenious paper projects in the form of constitutional amendments but words could not stifle the earth hunger of the multitudes nor bar the gates to them.

Through the years the tide of migration rolled westward, leaving in its wake widespreading farms and plantations whose owners, organized in political communities, worked hard at getting and using their full share of political power in the government of the nation. And their labors were not without reward. Of the fourteen Presidents of the United States elected between the passing of John Quincy Adams and the coming of Theodore Roosevelt, all except four, were either born in the Mississippi Valley or were, as residents, from early life identified with its people and its interests.

§

This westward migration—far greater in volume than the invasion that peopled the hills of New England and the lowlands of Virginia—was in one respect distinguished from other significant movements of colonizing races. The English settlements of the Atlantic seaboard were established under the patronage of powerful companies or semi-feudal proprietors encompassed by the protecting arm of a strong and watchful government. In striking contrast, the movement that carried American civilization beyond the Appalachians was essentially individualistic. No doubt, land companies helped to blaze the westward way, but they were few in number and their rôle in the process of occupation was relatively unimportant, especially after the initial steps were taken. It must be conceded also that little associa- tions of neighbors from time to time detached themselves from the older Atlantic communities and went in groups over the mountains, but their adventures, like the under- takings of corporations, were mere eddies in the swarming migration that filled the continental empire. In the main, the great West was conquered by individuals or, to speak more accurately, by families.

When pioneers from English communities on the coast first began to open paths toward the Mississippi, the west- ern region was a wilderness in which several seaboard colonies had conflicting legal rights under charters and grants from kings of England. Though the claimants, for many reasons, including the royal proclamation of 1763 closing the frontier to easy settlement, did little to develop their estate, its value was appreciated, if not by the commonalty, at least by statesmen and by investors with an eye to fortunate land speculations.

By no accident, accordingly, on the outbreak of the Revo- lution, George Rogers Clark, at the head of an armed expe- dition, was dispatched into the West for the purpose of wresting from the Ohio country the grip of England. As contemplated, the stroke was effective. While negotiating the treaty of peace with Great Britain at the close of the war for independence, the American delegation was able to clinch the achievement by fixing the western boundary of the United States at the Mississippi River.

Meanwhile, a lively contest arose in America over the fruits of victory. The politicians in control of the states that had claims, good and bad, naturally wanted to direct the disposal of the western lands and to recoup from that source at least some of the expenses of the struggle against Britain. But the politicians in other states, bitterly resenting this monopoly, declared that the Northwest had been won by common sacrifices and demanded equal shares in the fruits of victory. Finally, after much wrangling the principle of national ownership was adopted and the several claimants, sometimes with specific reservations, ceded their holdings to the United States.

The government to which this huge domain was transferred, namely, the Congress created by the Articles of Confederation, though too feeble to execute any grand plan of colonization, prepared the way for individual and corporate action by creating some of the conditions necessary to effective occupation. By two remarkable ordinances enacted in 1784 and 1785 it set momentous precedents for the Northwest Territory.

In the first of these decrees the Congress enunciated the fateful principle that the territories to be organized in the West should be ultimately admitted to the Union as states enjoying all the rights and privileges of the older commonwealths—not kept in the position of provinces in another Roman Empire ruled by pro-consuls from the capital. The second ordinance made provision for the official surveys which were to carve out farms, towns, counties, and states on a rectangular, or checker-board, pattern. With respect to actual settlement the Congress also arranged for the sale of lands so that pioneers and speculators could acquire holdings by lawful procedure and acquire titles of unimpeachable validity. These measures, excellent as they were, left out of account, however, one important factor, namely, an efficient government for the Northwest Territory—one which could hold Indians, squatters, and outlaws in check and assure investors and farmers the peaceful possession of their property. Until this crowning measure of preparation was passed, successful colonization on a large scale could not be undertaken.

At last under the sharp pressure of private enterprise the missing factor was supplied. In March, 1786, a number of New England citizens, many of them veterans of the Revolutionary War, met in Boston and organized an Ohio land company for the purpose of buying a huge tract in the Northwest. After perfecting their plans, they sent spokesmen, led by the Reverend Manasseh Cutler, to New York to make the necessary arrangements with the Congress of the United States, arrangements which included, besides a cession of land, the creation of an efficient territorial government.

To their amazement these far-seeing promoters met neglect and indifference in Congress until they secretly agreed that several of its influential members should share in the profits of the transaction. With more precision than was customary with the authors of Puritan sermons, the Rev. Mr. Cutler entered a description of the operation upon the pages of his personal journal: "We obtained the grant of near five millions of acres . . . one million and a half for the Ohio company and the remainder for a private speculation, in which many of the principal characters of America are concerned. Without connecting this speculation, similar terms and advantages could not have been obtained for the Ohio company." The price to be paid for the land was fixed at a figure that promised to net the government about eight or nine cents an acre in specie. The scheme of administration was provided by the Congress in the now famous "Ordinance for the Government of the Territory of the United States Northwest of the Ohio."

This memorable document provided for the temporary control of the Northwest by a governor, a secretary, and judges fully empowered to make laws and enforce them. Incidentally members of the Congress and managers of the Ohio land company who had engineered the project became the official rulers of the whole domain. General Arthur St. Clair, president of the Congress, who, after much persuasion, had helped to get the requisite measures through the legislative body over which he wielded the gavel, received as a reward, besides stock in the enterprise, the salaried post of governor in the Northwest Territory. Two of the company's directors were appointed judges to serve with St. Clair, the three constituting in effect the consolidated legislative, executive, and judicial departments of the western province.

Besides making these provisional arrangements, the Ordinance also prepared for the long future. It stipulated that as soon as there were five thousand free males in the territory a popular assembly should be established, male citizens owning fifty acres of land to enjoy the right of suffrage. Religious freedom was guaranteed, the historic safeguards of jury trial, approved judicial procedure, and the writ of habeas corpus were assured to all the people, and the establishment of schools and the promotion of education encouraged. In the spirit of the new humanism slavery and involuntary servitude were solemnly forbidden. Echoing the recent reforms made by Jefferson in Virginia, the accumulation of fortunes under the ancient law of primogeniture was blocked by a provision that estates should be divided among the children of deceased persons in equal parts, saving the rights of widows. Finally, the territories to be formed in the region were in due time to be admitted to the Union on the same footing as the old states.

Such were the broad principles formulated to govern the development of political communities in the West. They were confirmed in 1789 by the Congress which assembled under the Constitution of the United States. Except for the ban on slavery, they were applied the following year to the territory south of the Ohio ceded to the Union by

North Carolina and again in 1798 to the Mississippi domain surrendered by Georgia.

With the question of government out of the way, the next problem was the adoption of methods for selling western land to settlers and speculators. And it was a thorny problem, involving Federalist and Republican theories of state. It had long vexed the advisers of the British Crown and it was to torment American politicians for more than a century. With the refrain of 1776 still ringing in their ears, the members of the Congress in their act of 1785, already cited, had provided for selling western lands in lots of 640 acres at a minimum fixed rate of one dollar per acre in addition to certain administrative charges. But in 1796, after the ardor of early populism had cooled a bit, Congress raised the price to two dollars and authorized the sale by auction.

A part of Hamilton's plan for raising revenues from the public domain, this measure, by favoring the speculator, or at all events the purchaser of large estates, and failing to satisfy the demands of the farmer in search of a little homestead, inevitably raised a tempest of criticism from the followers of Jefferson. After four years of agitation, Congress made concessions by opening land offices in the West for the convenience of buyers on the spot. Still the cry of the poor man was heard, growing louder and louder, until at length in 1820 Congress was compelled to provide for the sale of land in blocks as small as eighty acres at not less than $1.25 an acre. That reform won, the advocates of free homesteads now made their voices heard above the din of Washington politics, again and again, until they were finally silenced by the coveted act of Congress. Thus the drift of public policy—in accord with Jeffersonian political economy—was against the establishment of immense estates tilled by tenants. Even the speculators and companies that bought in large quantities could not develop their holdings by servile labor or retain their purchases for long periods. They were in fact forced to sell in small lots on reasonable terms to actual settlers, contributing in this way to the process by which the small freehold of sixty, eighty, or one hundred and sixty acres, tilled by the farmer and his family, became the typical unit of agriculture in the Northwest.

§

It was a marvelous empire of virgin country that awaited the next great wave of migration at the close of the eighteenth century. As the waters of the Tigris, the Euphrates, and the Nile had invited mankind to build its civilizations along their banks, in remote antiquity, so the valley of the Mississippi now summoned the peoples of the earth to make a new experiment in social economy in the full light of modern times. And what a valley it was! The Mississippi River and its tributaries carried a volume of water greater than that of all the rivers of Europe combined, excluding the Volga.

In the widespreading basin was a climate for every mood and temper, from the freezing winters of the lake country to the semi-tropical summers of Alabama and Mississippi. There were soils and seasons for almost every fruit, vegetable, and cereal that man or woman could demand. There were forests of hard and soft woods adapted to every kind of structure—homes, barns, factories, boats, and barges. From the lakes to the gulf were scattered rich beds of coal, iron, copper, and lead—prime materials for those giant industries on which modern empires are built. And what a theater for action! The nine states created between the old colonies and the Mississippi River contained a dominion greater than the combined area of Great Britain, Germany, and Italy with the Netherlands and Belgium added for good measure. In the Northwest Territory alone, either France or Germany could be comfortably fitted with room to spare.

Into this new arena for enterprise four routes created by nature led from the older states. To the South one ran from Alexandria to Richmond and from Richmond through the Cumberland Gap into the Kentucky country; along this trail Daniel Boone had blazed the way as early as 1769 and in the course of time it had been widened into a wagon road. A second route lay westward from Alexandria over the mountains and across the Great Kanawha to Boonesboro. In the middle region, three roads, starting from Philadelphia, Baltimore, and Alexandria respectively, converged on Pittsburgh, where the wide waters of the Ohio River offered the emigrant an easy journey on into the far country. To the north the Genesee road, beginning at Albany, ran almost due west through level country to Buffalo, on Lake Erie, the principal gateway into the upper reaches of the Northwest Territory.

Each of these natural routes to the West had its own history. For a time the Cumberland road held the primacy. The region into which it led was at the beginning under the governments of Virginia and North Carolina—states that offered lands to settlers on easy terms and gave them a precarious protection against the Indians. The road itself was very near the back doors of the upland farmers in those states and it beckoned them on to a more fertile soil than their plowshares had so far broken. Moreover, the advance of slave-owning planters from the coast exerted a steady pressure on them, driving them to escape by the Cumberland route from that invasion.

When the planting advance got into full swing and the Northwest Territory was opened during the closing years of the eighteenth century, the Ohio River route began to gather an ever-larger portion of the emigrants. Although the journey from the coast to Pittsburgh was beset by difficulties, the rest of the way was easy, for as soon as the immigrant family arrived at the headwaters of the Ohio, it could buy almost any kind of boat for the remainder of the trip—a light canoe for two or three or a ten-ton barge that would carry a score of passengers with household goods, wagons, plows, and cattle down the river to the landing point nearest the chosen destination. And yet before long the Ohio route was rivaled by competing lines to the north, especially by the National Road, begun in 1806, and the Erie Canal, opened in 1825.

The story of the migration into the Mississippi Valley by these various routes is an epic which has found no Homer; but a hundred historians, professional and amateur, have assembled the materials for use when the immortal bard shall appear. Indian trails have been retraced, portage paths uncovered, and old wagon tracks marked on the maps. Archer Hulbert has plotted the first roads over which the empire builders moved to the scenes of their new labors. Local historical associations, crowned by the Mississippi Valley Historical Society, have rescued from old chests and lumber rooms yellow newspapers, faded letters, and saffron diaries that tell of the marching pioneers who wrought for themselves and their children's children. Roosevelt with his usual gusto wrote a long chapter of the story in six volumes, bearing the somewhat misleading title of The Winning of the West. Turner and his school of meticulous workers have analyzed the influence of the advancing frontier on the life and politics of the United States. If, in their enthusiasm for a long-neglected subject, they have pressed their argument too far, at all events they have forced the historians of Puritans and Cavaliers to take note of something more realistic than Sunday sermons and armorial scrolls.

§

The rolling tide of migration that swept across the mountains and down the valleys, spreading out through the forests and over the prairies, advanced in successive waves. In the vanguard was the man with the rifle—grim, silent, and fearless. He loved the pathless forest, dense and solitary, carpeted by the fallen leaves of a thousand years and fretted by the sunlight that poured through the Gothic arches of the trees, where the wild beast slunk through the shadows, where the occasional crash of a falling branch boomed like thunder, and where the camp fire at night flared up into the darkness of knitted boughs as the flaming candles on the altar of a cathedral cast their rays high into the traceries of the vaulted roof.

As he paddled his canoe along the winding rivers or crept through the forest and canebrake, the hunter's nerves kept taut with watchfulness. His clear eye was quick to discern the signs of his foe or prey and to find the rifle range with deadly accuracy. The practiced muscles of his sinewy arm could direct his long dirk with unfailing skill to the vital spot whenever he came to close quarters with an assailant. As alert as the deer he stalked and as silent as the coiling snake that slid across his path, the hunter carried on a dangerous craft against every kind of stratagem known to man or beast. If he heard what seemed to be the call of a harmless bird or the hoot of an owl, he dropped to earth and lay still as death, listening intently until he could be sure that there were no false notes betraying the voice of an Indian poised in the forks of a tree for a shot at him; for, in the long contest with the red hunter for the spoils of the wilderness, he had learned the terrible penalty that awaited the white man who neglected the ways of the forest.

Unsocial as the rifleman was in his hunting habits, he generally had a family on or near the frontier. With the aid of his wife and children, he threw up a rude shelter, often open on one side like the cabin in which Lincoln's mother died. He girdled and killed a few trees near by and laid a rail fence around his lot. There the family planted a "truck patch" of corn, beans, turnips, cabbage, and potatoes. While the hunter was searching for game in the forests or fishing in some neighboring stream, the wife and children vigorously hoed among the tangled roots and tough grasses of the garden. When autumn came the crops were harvested; the corn was stored in a rough crib; the cabbages, turnips, and potatoes, bedded in straw, were buried in great mounds from which the winter's supply could be taken. Wood for the big fireplace of sticks and clay came from the forest's edge. In all its phases the mode of living was crude but it was far removed even so from the depths of primitive culture.

If, amid these rough surroundings, the hunter himself was content, it could not often be said that his wife was equally satisfied with her share in the contest. Nearly always she was a reluctant fugitive from a civilization of a higher order and could not help pining for the softer things of older societies. Usually she was a pathetic figure in her coarse dress of linsey-woolsey and deep sunbonnet, performing in terrifying loneliness the humble duties of her household. Unlike the Indian woman, who was a part of the nature in which she worked and had never known the smoother paths of settled communities, the hunter's wife could seldom sink as quickly as her husband into the ways and temper of the wilderness. But her lot was fixed and she marched resolutely through the encircling shadows of the frontier, taking fate as it came.

When by the immigration of settlers her forest home began to take on some of the elements of civilization, her hunter husband, finding his game supply diminishing, was sure to grow restless and begin to talk of "going West." After much discussion, sometimes interspersed with lamentation, he would induce or command his family "to pull up stakes and strike for the tall timber." After all, for him, the migration was no great effort. Frequently he was a mere squatter on land to which he had no title. If, under the liberal preëmption plan of the government, he had valid claims, they were not worth much and he could readily sell them to a newcomer on the scene. So with a light heart he disposed of his cabin and clearing and with his household turned his face toward the setting sun.

In the wake of the man with a rifle came the seekers of permanent homes. In the Northwest, and usually in the Southwest, the leader in this next phase of occupation was the man with a plow, or, to speak more correctly, the family with established habits of domestic economy—the farming group who understood and loved the steady and sober industry of the field, the housewife who was a mistress of the thousand arts that created comfort, security, and refinement, and the rollicking children who made the frontier ring with merriment and who helped to enrich their parents as they grew in years. Immigrants of this type soon built a fourth side to their abode and set in glass windows; within a short time they substituted well-constructed frame or brick dwellings for their first log cabins. They cleared broad acres for tilling and combined with their neighbors to open roads through the woods, fling rude bridges across streams, and build churches and schoolhouses.

As the settlements of the county expanded into compact farms they made provision for local government, erecting a courthouse and log jail and choosing officers to administer rough and ready justice in civil and criminal cases. Before the first generation was ready to surrender to the children, the county seat had usually grown into a thriving village where, as a traveler through the Ohio country in 1836 declared, "broadcloths, silks, leghorns, crapes, and all the refinements, luxuries, elegancies, frivolities, and fashions are in vogue." A few of the more ingenious men developed into manufacturers and millers on a small scale; business enterprise with all its implications commenced.

Sometimes the family of this class remained rooted for at least two or three generations in its first settlement; but often it was quickly struck with the western fever and moved on like the hunter in search of a new Eldorado. In the far country it was not uncommon to find homesteaders who had camped five or six times on their westward march. Indeed, as the renewal of exhausted soil called for more scientific knowledge than many a farmer could command, migration to virgin country was the easiest way out of poverty for the unskilled.

To the south of the Ohio River, the settlers who followed the hunters were generally white farmers, akin in spirit and purpose to those who peopled the Northwest Territory. If the climate in some sections invited planters to bring their slaves, the task of cutting forests, clearing land, and making the beginnings of civilization usually offered obstacles which they were not well fitted to surmount. So the first drive into the southern wilderness was made also by industrious white families and in the upland regions of Kentucky and Tennessee they remained in permanent possession of the soil. But close behind these home builders, especially into the wider valleys and broader plains, came masters with their slaves, buying up, uniting, and enlarging the holdings of their forerunners. In this way one of the distinctions that marked the old South from the Northwest was widely carried into the lower Mississippi Valley. Though, as southern observers were wont to say, western masters were shrewder and less punctilious than the grand gentlemen of the Virginia and Carolina lowlands, they were all united by ties of common interest, particularly on points touching their "peculiar institution."

§

Considered in chronological order the history of the westward movement presents two distinct phases: one relative to the occupation of the Kentucky and Tennessee region, the other to the settlement of the Northwest Territory. The first advance on the wilderness was made into the district south of the Ohio at a date somewhere in colonial times not fixed in the chronicle of the West. Roosevelt records that as early as 1654 "a certain Colonel Wood was in Kentucky," and that in 1750 Dr. Thomas Walker of Virginia, "a genuine explorer and surveyor," made his way to the headwaters of the Kentucky, writing on his return an entertaining journal of his trip now available in printed form. In a few years more two Pittsburgh hunters,

Stoner and Harrod, were shooting buffaloes on the bend of the Cumberland, near the site of Nashville.

In any case the path had been broken when in 1769 Daniel Boone, with five companions, set out from his home on the Yadkin and pushed resolutely westward until he passed through the mountain fastness and out into the blue grass region. Discovering there an abundance of game that filled him with delight, round-horned elk, bears, and buffaloes, Boone bore home such a tale as had never been told in the hills of North Carolina. Inspired by his stories, other hunters rushed to the West along the trail he had blazed, pressing onward in their operations until they reached the Mississippi and established connections with the French trading posts on the river.

Immediately behind the forerunners came pioneers and their families from Virginia, North Carolina, and Georgia, the major portion of them Scotch-Irish farmers seeking an escape from the clay hills of their native states. In the very year that Boone made his first trip over the mountains, farmers from western Virginia planted a settlement on the banks of the Watauga in eastern Tennessee, then a part of North Carolina. Around blockhouses built along the river, they grouped farms and log cabins, thus giving to their contemporaries a demonstration in the difficult art of combining dispersed agriculture with effective provisions against hostile Indians.

In the middle of the next decade, Boone himself, in cooperation with Henderson, a colossal speculator of North Carolina, led a band of pioneers into Kentucky and founded the post of Boonesboro. Even in the stormy days of the Revolution the migration continued, and, after peace came, it broke all precedents. By 1790 Tennessee had a population of 35,000—while Kentucky reported twice as many, a census return larger than that of Delaware or Rhode Island, then more than a century old. The next year, William Blount, federal governor of Tennessee, built his capital on the banks of the Tennessee River and christened it Knoxville in honor of Washington's Secretary of War, a good Federalist.

The second phase of the westward movement, namely, the great migration into the Northwest Territory, opened under more fortunate auspices. Settlers in the region south of the Ohio had been compelled to do their work under the protection of two rather indifferent parent states, whereas the pioneers of the Northwest, coming later on the scene, were able to invoke the armed might of the new federal government established under the Constitution. Not long after his inauguration President Washington, himself a large holder of western lands who appreciated the future of the Ohio country, took vigorous measures to organize military expeditions against the Indians on the frontier. His commander, General Anthony Wayne, in many clashes with these redoubtable foes of the white invasion, finally brought the leading chieftains to their knees, forcing them in 1795 to sign a treaty which cleared the eastern and southern portions of the Territory for white settlements. Then, by a process of steady pressure accompanied by some fighting, section after section was wrested from the aborigines and thrown open for occupation by farmers. Of course the white rifleman in the vanguard long continued to come into collision with the red man whose hunting ground he was despoiling but after Wayne's treaty there occurred in the Northwest relatively few of those dreadful scenes which had made Kentucky and Tennessee "a dark and bloody ground."

It was sheltered by the strong arm of the national government that promoters of Manasseh Cutler's land company drove upward into the midlands of Ohio from their base, Marietta, founded on the banks of the Muskingum under the guns of Fort Harmar in 1788. It was with less danger from the Indians than their ancestors had encountered at the hands of the Pequods that pioneers from Connecticut commenced to the north the settlement of Western Reserve, an immense domain which the state had retained on surrendering to the Union its historic claims. Without fear, Moses Cleaveland, blazing a path to the shores of Lake Erie, established in 1796 a post that was destined to grow into a great city. From these beginnings two prosperous colonies, both offshoots of New England, rose and flourished.

With faithful precision the town meeting, the Congregational Church, steady-going habits, and Massachusetts thrift were reproduced beyond the mountains, as land-hungry sons and daughters of the Puritans advanced rapidly on the Mississippi, dispersing widely in northern Ohio, Indiana, and Illinois, upward into southern Michigan and Wisconsin and westward toward the great plains. So with accuracy could Webster declare in his magnificent oration delivered on the two hundredth anniversary of the Pilgrims' landing: "New England farms, houses, villages, and churches spread over and adorn the immense extent from the Ohio to Lake Erie and stretch along from the Alleghany onwards, beyond the Miamis, and towards the Falls of St. Anthony. Two thousand miles westward from the rock where their fathers landed, may now be seen the sons of Pilgrims, cultivating smiling fields, rearing towns and villages, and cherishing, we trust, the patrimonial blessings of wise institutions, of liberty, and religion. . . . Ere long the sons of the Pilgrims will be on the shores of the Pacific."

Not a whit behind New England, the middle and southern states furnished their quotas for the conquest of the northwest wilderness. In a huge tract acquired by the mighty speculator, J. C. Symmes, New Jersey folk established a colony at Cincinnati, so named in honor of the many soldiers who took part in the early settlement. Having merely to open their back doors to reach the frontier, Pennsylvania and New York sent settlers into nearly every community beyond the mountains.

From the South, especially the piedmont of North Carolina and Virginia, poured a stream of families already inured to the hardships of pioneer life. Some were Quakers from upper counties of the old North State recoiling before the overbearing power of the slavocracy. Others were nomadic prospectors, such as Lincoln's father and mother, who, growing weary of ill-requited labors on impoverished soil in the East, rolled onward with the tide. Indeed, the southern part of Indiana and Illinois was largely peopled by men and women from Kentucky, Virginia, and North Carolina, who placed their stamp indelibly upon the economy, culture, and politics of that region. Under their coon-skin caps, the principles of Jeffersonian Democracy were to be found with the same regularity as the doctrines of Federalism among the dyed-in-the-wool Puritans from Massachusetts and Connecticut who laid out their prim townships to the north. There were many exceptions of course, but astute politicians knew how to handle them.

By the Old World, as well as the seaboard states of the New, contributions were made to the development of the West. English travelers and capitalists, looking for larger opportunities, visited every important section of the Mississippi Valley during the years at the turn of the century, many of them casting in their lot with the makers of the young society on the frontier. The English book market was soon well stocked with pamphlets, handy guides, and pretentious volumes giving accounts of the journey from "the old country" to "the log cabin in the clearing" and every ship bore English immigrants bound for the western valleys. From the Continent came an ever-increasing host of Germans who scattered widely over the Northwest Territory and across the Mississippi into Missouri. A band of Swiss founded the town of Vevay on the Ohio River while some French settlers were induced by land speculators to try their fortunes in the fertile region which Marquette and La Salle had explored more than a century before.

The rapidity with which these immigrants from all quarters subdued the wilderness almost passes belief. In 1775 there were not more than five thousand whites in the Mississippi Valley, outside New Orleans, and they were mainly French families clinging to their old posts. In 1790 there were about 110,000 white people in that region; within another decade the number rose to 377,000. The national census of 1830 gave 937,000 to Ohio, 348,000 to Indiana, 157,000 to Illinois, 687,000 to Kentucky, and 681,000 to Tennessee. In short, within the forty years after the heavy migration began, the western territory acquired more inhabitants than the original thirteen colonies in a century of development under the stimulus and patronage of governments, companies, and proprietors; more than Canada in the hundred years following the British conquest of that great dominion. Nothing like it had yet occurred in the stirring annals of American settlement.

It was in fact a momentous mass movement. Beginning in 1787 a steady surge of pioneers for the West passed through Pittsburgh; in that year, it is recorded, "more than nine hundred boats floated down the Ohio carrying eighteen thousand men, women, and children and twelve thousand horses, sheep, and cattle, and six hundred and fifty wagons." Travelers tell us that the roads were crowded with immigrants on foot and in wagons, marching west in high hope or with grim determination to win or die. Whole communities in the East were stripped of their inhabitants, as the nomadic fever spread.

While the nineteenth century was still a bantling, the Yankee missionary, Timothy Flint, was lamenting, in the vein of Goldsmith's Deserted Village, that New England, forsaken in the westward rush, was destined to decay. "Our dwellings, our schoolhouses, and churches will have mouldered to ruins," he exclaimed, "our graveyards will be overrun with shrub oak; and but here and there a wretched hermit, true to his paternal soil, to tell the tale of other times." If the prophecy was a bit strained, it breathed the fears of the age.

By 1830 the banks of the Ohio River were strewn with flourishing villages and aspiring cities while the country to the south and north was dotted over with prosperous communities. Wheeling, Marietta, Newport, Cincinnati, Madison, and Louisville, alive with tourists and traders, were dreaming of greater days to come. Cincinnati had 26,000 inhabitants. Dayton, the other terminus of the Miami Canal, was a booming town of 2900. Sandusky, one of the chief points of distribution for the migration of the East by way of Buffalo, was growing like a reed. Cleveland was a lively village expecting to become a metropolis as soon as the canal under construction between Lake Erie and the Ohio could be opened for traffic.

In Indiana the most populous town, Madison, with 2000 inhabitants, was even then noted "for the quantity of pork barrelled there." On the central border not far from the Ohio line, Quakers from Pennsylvania and North Carolina had built the stable settlement of Richmond. Indianapolis, with 1200 residents, was already determined to become the capital of the state. On the banks of the Wabash, Vincennes, "the oldest place in the western world after Kaskaskia," was assuming an air of antiquity. Logansport, Terre Haute, Crawfordsville, and Lafayette were rising in the forests. Robert Owen's communistic colony, "New Harmony," having made the great experiment, had turned back to the ways of individualism. Throughout Ohio, Indiana, Illinois, and Kentucky wild animals had practically disappeared from the regions around the settlements; wolves sometimes swept down to carry off a sheep or a hog and a big bear occasionally was discovered in the family larder seeking honey; but very few dangerous beasts remained to beset the unwary traveler, at least on his way along the roads and blazed trails.

§

As may be imagined from this sketch of its origins, the civilization of the new West was a checkered pattern full of surprises and contradictions. The many contemporaries who tried to describe it found colors, shades, and tints to please their varied fancies. Timothy Dwight, president of Yale and a rabid opponent of Jefferson, crisply declared that most of the pioneers who went from his region into the Ohio country were little better than anarchists; perhaps having in mind the leveling tendencies of small farmers.

"They are," he said, "not fit to live in regular society. They are too idle; too talkative; too passionate; too prodigal, and too shiftless to acquire either property or character. They are impatient at the restraints of law, religion, or morality; grumble about the taxes by which Rulers, Ministers and School-masters are supported and complain incessantly, as well as bitterly, of the extortions of mechanics, farmers, merchants and physicians, to whom they are always indebted. At the same time they are usually possessed, in their own view, of uncommon wisdom; understand medical science, politics, and religion better than those who have studied them through life; and although they manage their own concerns worse than other men, feel perfectly satisfied that they could manage those of the nation far better than the agents to whom they are committed by the public. . . . After censuring the weakness, and wickedness of their superiours; after exposing the injustice of the community in neglecting to invest persons of such merit with public offices; in many an eloquent harangue, uttered by many a kitchen fire, in every blacksmith's shop, and in every corner of the streets; and finding all their efforts vain; they become at length discouraged; and under the pressure of poverty, the fear of a gaol, and the consciousness of public contempt, leave their native places, and betake themselves to the wilderness." In this fashion, thought the good college president, the sober and respectable people of the East, rid of village Gracchi, could enjoy peace and quiet—and they did until at last the terrible earthquake of Jeffersonian Democracy shook down the Federalist temple about their ears.

On the opposite side of the ledger could be placed the

verdict of another New England clergyman, Timothy Flint —that veteran missionary who lived for many years on the frontier and traveled it from end to end. Knowing the pioneers personally in their new homes, he felt moved to repel the imputations of the "learned and virtuous Dr. Dwight." Though he admitted that there were worthless people in the West—"and the most so, it must be confessed, are from New England"—he drew a picture of the frontier which was sympathetic and on the whole favorable. "It is true there are gamblers, and gougers, and outlaws; but there are fewer of them, than from the nature of things and the character of the age and the world, we ought to expect. . . . The backwoodsman of the West, as I have seen him, is generally an amiable and virtuous man. His general motive for coming here is to be a freeholder, to have plenty of rich land, and to be able to settle with his children about him. It is a most virtuous motive. And notwithstanding all that Dr. Dwight and Talleyrand have said to the contrary, I fully believe that nine in ten of the emigrants have come here with no other motive."

Having rendered this opinion in general, Flint explained that the man who had wrestled with bears and panthers and had passed his days in constant dread of Indians was of necessity accustomed to carry a dirk and rifle, to stalk about with a pack of dogs at his heels, and wear the rough garments of the woods. But everywhere, continued the missionary, the stranger was greeted with rude hospitality, springing from an innate gentleness of manner. The somewhat ungracious "Yes, I reckon you can stay all night" was merely a laconic way of putting the best at the disposal of the wayfaring man. While the housewife was "timid, silent and reserved" and declined to sit at the table, she gave unstinted attention to the slightest wish of the visitor. Money in payment for food and shelter was spurned by the host and hostess; even the children that gathered at the door to speed the parting guest turned away from the proffered coin. If the people who fled from the ministrations of the good and wise were originally the wretches portrayed by Dr. Dwight, then the wilderness must have had a redemptive influence on their natures.

In religion the western regions were naturally as diverse as the people who settled them. The Scotch-Irish who moved over the mountains into the Holston and Tennessee Valleys were, of course, still Presbyterians in creed; as soon as a frontier settlement was well-established, a committee was chosen to build a church, select a preacher, and manage the finances of the enterprise. In a similar fashion, the emigrants from New England who went into the Ohio country erected a Congregational church in every township they occupied; while the Quakers made their plain meeting house the center of their community life on the frontier. At the old French posts that stood out occasionally like hulks of sunken ships in the midst of the British flood, Catholic priests continued to baptize, marry, confess, warn, absolve, and bury according to the rites of their historic Church. Wherever the Germans settled, the Lutheran faith flourished; while here and there Episcopalian clergymen undertook the care of souls in a climate none too favorable for their colder ceremonials.

Beside the pastors of established congregations were devoted missionaries of every sect. The girdled trees of the advancing frontier were hardly dead when wandering preachers appeared to save men and women from the danger of relapsing into barbarism. Especially numerous and powerful were Methodist and Baptist itinerants who proclaimed a passionate gospel of hell-fire and salvation that moved the hardest drinkers, boldest fighters, and meanest sinners of the hinterland to repentance, periodically at any rate. Into the most remote spots they penetrated, laying out regular circuits from community to community so that the seed once planted might be carefully cultivated. To fortify the faithful and gather recruits into the fold they held great "camp meetings" to which settlers flocked from near and far for a season of singing, preaching, and testifying—ceremonials that often flowed over into shouting, dancing, screaming, fainting, and other excesses, as religious ecstasy seized the more exuberant of the assembled hosts.

In spite of theological differences a strong note of Puritanism characterized the preaching of all denominations. Methodists denounced dancing, card-playing, and jewelry almost as fiercely as they did drunkenness and profanity. The Congregational missionary, Timothy Flint, though somewhat more liberal in his views, complained that every German farmer had a distillery and that "the pernicious poison, whiskey, dribbles from the corn." But when he remonstrated with them, the Germans always replied, that, "while they wanted religion and their children baptized and a minister as exemplary as possible, he must allow the honest Dutch, as they call themselves, to partake of the native beverage." The Quakers—even those who liked a "night-cap" of good whiskey—would have no "godless" musical instruments in their meeting-houses and their solemn garb marked them as censors of the wicked world in which they had no part.

Even laymen joined in the Puritan crusade. Mrs. Trollope, under the head of literature and prudery, declared that a scholarly gentleman in Cincinnati once exclaimed to her: "Shakespeare, Madam, is obscene, and thank God we are sufficiently advanced to have found it out." At all events, in that city, billiards and card-playing were then unlawful and dancing was viewed with much disfavor. A young German of good breeding gravely offended one of the best families by speaking of "corsets" in the presence of ladies and the manager of a public garden who put up a signboard bearing the figure of a Swiss maiden in short skirts was forced by the outraged women of the community to have a flounce painted on her ankles. Such was the delicacy to be found in a country where boisterous profanity and hard drinking were as common as sunshine—profanity and drinking so shocking that Flint was once moved to distribute among the teamsters of his wagon train copies of "that impressive tract, the 'Swearer's Prayer.'"

Harsh and grinding as life was on the frontier and puritanical as were the devout, there were signs of intellectual interest and craving even in the early days. The very first band of hunters who went through the Cumberland Gap into Kentucky in 1769 carried with them two volumes of Jonathan Swift's Works and whiled away long nights around the camp fire reading the diverting Gulliver's Travels. In August, 1787, when Lexington was but a few years old, an editor, bearing the goodly English name of John Bradford, brought out the first newspaper beyond the mountains, The Kentucky Gazette; and four years later The Knoxville Gazette, under the patronage of the governor of Tennessee, issued a ringing Federalist challenge to all Jacobins and Democrats.

In fact as soon as any village could boast of a few hundred inhabitants and give promise of a future, some enterprising printer appeared with press and type to establish his sanctum in a log cabin. In little weekly sheets, the spleen of the politicians was vented, sermons were reported, and budding poets were allowed to address the muses. With the clergymen and the editors went the lawyers. In every county seat attorneys did a thriving business defending criminals and settling disputes over land titles. Their professional labors they supplemented by delivering to order turgid and high-sounding orations on the Constitution, the genius of Washington, or the spirit of American institutions.

Nor was the training of the young wholly neglected in the tough battle for a livelihood. Those wise statesmen of the East who foresaw the future of the West had early given thought to the education of the people. The ordinance of 1785 set aside in the Northwest Territory a great reservation of land for the support of elementary and higher education. Supplementing this act, the Northwest Ordinance two years later declared that "religion, morality and knowledge being necessary to good government and the happiness of mankind, schools and the means of education shall be forever encouraged."

In the same spirit the territories and states erected in the region set aside land for educational purposes; the constitution of Indiana, for instance, proclaiming in 1816 that the funds derived from the sale of public land dedicated to education "shall be and remain a fund for the exclusive purpose of promoting the interest of literature and the sciences and for the support of seminaries and public schools." But fine declarations such as these, while they expressed excellent intentions, were difficult to realize. Much of the land set aside for education was sold at low figures by corrupt or careless officials and no small part of the money was lost through inefficiency and maladministration. It was not until the middle of the century that the public school system of the middle west was placed on a solid foundation.

More prosaic and complicated than public documents would lead us to believe was the real story of frontier education. As on the seaboard, it opened with a record of private and sectarian effort. The Presbyterian preachers who went into the early communities of Kentucky or Tennessee generally played the triple rôle of farmer, parson, and schoolmaster; emigrant bands from New England into the Ohio country usually took teachers with them; but many a frontier settlement was long without a school of any kind until some of the more energetic citizens took up subscriptions, built a log house, and engaged a master.

Here and there "seminaries" of higher learning arose to keep the lamp burning after the example of the Fathers on the Atlantic coast. At Lexington, Kentucky, in 1807, Cuming, an English traveler, found in Transylvania University a flourishing institution deserving commendation. The president, Rev. James Blythe, according to the report, taught natural philosophy, mathematics, geography, and English grammar; another clergyman was professor of moral philosophy, belles lettres, logic, and history; there was also a professor of languages, one of medicine, and one of law. Enthusiasm was great but salaries low. The professor who taught French would have starved to death if he had not supplemented his "university" stipend by fees from a dancing class. "And here," the tourist adds in an aside, "it may not be impertinent to remark that in most parts of the United States teachers of dancing meet with more encouragement than professors of any species of literary science." Not far from this university, the English wayfarer found an academy where young ladies were taught reading, writing, spelling, arithmetic, grammar, elocution, rhetoric, ancient and modern history, natural history, moral philosophy, music, drawing, painting, fancy work, plain sewing, and other appealing subjects.

Before the nineteenth century was far advanced, Timothy Flint, with a pride worthy of John Harvard, could record that there were six colleges in Ohio: Miami at Oxford, Ohio University at Athens, Kenyon at Gambier, Western Reserve at Hudson, Franklin at New Athens, and Lane Theological Seminary for the Presbyterians at Cincinnati. In addition, the missionary continued, there were fifteen or twenty academies and each session of the legislature was incorporating a new one. On a journey farther west, Flint visited Indiana College, opened in 1829 at Bloomington, where, he said, "a thorough classical education is imparted at an expense as moderate as any similar seminary in the Union."

In backward regions, out of the range of organized instruction, women of breeding often taught untutored husbands and stalwart children their letters and sent them rejoicing through the gateway that led to books and papers. For example, Andrew Johnson, the Tennessee tailor, who was fated to become President of the United States on the death of Lincoln, learned the rudiments from his wife and under her instruction unconsciously prepared for the career marked out for him by destiny. Thus knowledge advanced slowly but steadily upon the ignorance of the hinterland—advanced because there was something more substantial in the fiber of the emigrants from the East than the qualities listed by the excellent tutor, Dr. Dwight, or the excesses of evangelistic revivals would seem to indicate.

§

The economy of the new West, essentially agricultural, rested mainly upon a system of freehold farms. In the lower Mississippi Valley and in the Missouri country, it is true, the planters with their slaves early pushed out toward the frontier; but in large sections of Alabama, Tennessee, and Kentucky, and all through the Northwest Territory, where slavery was forbidden, the small farmer reigned supreme. In this immense domain sprang up a social order without marked class or caste, a society of people substantially equal in worldly goods, deriving their livelihood from one prime source—labor with their own hands on the soil. For a long time there were in that vast region no merchant princes such as governed Philadelphia and Boston, no powerful land-owning class comparable to the masters of Hudson Valley manors. Even the slave owners of the gulf states, though sometimes richer than their brethren on the seaboard, were many years in acquiring the magnificent pretensions that characterized the gentry of Virginia and South Carolina. Sugar makers and cotton growers of the Southwest gave their section no Washingtons, Randolphs, Madisons, and Monroes. Jefferson Davis belonged to the second generation of Mississippi planters and by the time he grew to manhood his class was marching swiftly to its doom.

For many decades, an overwhelming majority of the white men in the West were land-owning farmers. The unit of their society was the family on the isolated holding engaged in an unremitting battle with nature for its living. No benevolent government surrounded it with safeguards; no army of officials inspected its processes of life and labor.

In a thousand emergencies it was thrown upon its own resources; it produced its own foodstuffs, manufactured most of its own clothing, warded off diseases with home-made remedies inherited from primitive women, and often walked in the valley of the shadow of death without priestly ministrations.

In its folkways and mores there was a rugged freedom—the freedom of hardy men and women, taut of muscle and bronzed by sun and rain and wind, working with their hands in abundant materials, shaping oak from their own forests and flax from their own fields to the plain uses of a plain life, content with little and rejoicing in it, rearing in unaffected naturalness many children to face also a career of hard labor offering no goal in great riches or happiness in a multitude of things—none servants of the machine with their energies pinched by steel into fragile finery and their days turned into night by the soot of chimneys—all satisfied by the unadorned epic of Christianity inherited from their fathers, with heaven not far away and a benign Providence taking thought lest some sparrow might fall unnoticed. Although travelers into the pioneer West disagreed on many points they were almost unanimous in enumerating the outstanding characteristics of the frontier people: independence in action; directness in manner, want of deference for ceremony, willingness to make acquaintance with all sorts and conditions of mankind, a rough and ready license of speech with a corresponding touchiness of temper in the presence of real or fancied insults.

Nevertheless the men of the frontier were quick to associate themselves in bodies politic, for besides bearing with them from the older states traditions of self-government, they were eager to safeguard their own interests against the machinations of statesmen in the East. Above all things they were keen to wrest control over the public lands from the politicians at Washington who were as a rule either engaged in speculation on a large scale or indifferent to the needs and claims of the West. For these cogent reasons the pioneers early resolved to have local autonomy, even if it meant snapping the slender ties that bound them to the Union.

Within fifteen years after Boone led his path-breaking party to the West the question of separation became acute in Kentucky. In 1785 a convention was held and a resolution was passed declaring that Kentucky must separate from Virginia and enter the Union as a state. During the brief period of delay that ensued, some of the hot-heads directed by James Wilkinson, a picturesque adventurer of dubious morals, proposed to take matters into their own hands and proclaim Kentucky independent in spite of Virginia or Congress. But calmer counsels prevailed. In 1792 after a season of agitation and in spite of the lamentations of eastern Federalists, Kentucky found a seat in the Union beside Vermont, admitted a year before.

Meanwhile a parallel movement was in full swing to the south. In 1784 the frontier communities of Tennessee elected a constitutional convention which met at Jonesboro in midsummer and without a dissenting voice declared its independence of North Carolina. A constitution was drawn up, a legislature of two houses elected, and the new state of Franklin, as it was called, announced to the public. Immediate provision was made, by the establishment of an academy, for "the promotion of learning." As in the case of Kentucky, a long controversy with the mother state now followed.

At the close of the dispute the infant commonwealth gave up the ghost but its fierce spirit of independence continued to live until at last North Carolina, unable to manage the tempestuous frontier, ceded the territory to the United States. Though subjected by this act to the strong arm of the national government, the pioneers in their passion for self-government refused to be balked. They called another convention, framed a second constitution, elected a governor, chose two federal Senators, and sent Andrew Jackson, with his hair done up in an eelskin, to speak for the new state on the floor of the House of Representatives at Philadelphia, still the capital of the nation. Their constitution was duly laid before Congress and after a brief tussle between the Federalists and the Republicans, Tennessee was admitted to the Union, in 1796.

Across the Ohio in the Northwest Territory, the appetite for self-government was also keen. As a matter of fact, two years before the Congress enacted the Ordinance of 1787 for the district, one John Emerson issued on his own imperial authority a call to the squatters of the region to assemble in convention and draft a government for themselves. In assuming this prerogative the true son of New England declared that men "have an undoubted right to pass into every vacant country and there to form their constitution and that from the confederation of the whole United States, Congress is not empowered to forbid them." But the doctrine was too strong for the times and the assembly was never convened.

For nearly twenty years the district was held under national supervision until the population reached a figure more appropriate to the position of a commonwealth. It was in 1803 that Ohio was admitted to the American federation under a constitution framed with the consent of Congress. A decade more passed and Indiana asked for a place in the Union. In 1816 her constitution was drafted, the approval of Congress obtained, and her government inaugurated at Corydon. Illinois was next in the political arena and could not be denied recognition. Under the spirited leadership of a man born in New York and reared in Tennessee, a plan of government was drawn up; in 1818 Congress admitted the backwoods commonwealth to the privilege of statehood.

Before this time the appeal of the Far South had been heard. By 1810 lower Louisiana claimed a population of more than 75,000 and the people of the metropolis of New Orleans, a center of trade and old Latin culture, thought themselves not unworthy of a place beside Baltimore and Boston. On the cession of the territory to the

United States seven years earlier a promise had been made that the inhabitants should enjoy all the rights of American citizens and in due course be taken into the Union as a body politic equal in all respects to the elder members of the national association.

The idea was naturally pleasing enough to the Republicans at Washington, happy to be reinforced by new Senators and Representatives from the Southwest, but the Federalists, on their part, could hardly find words strong enough to express their horror. When at length the bill to admit Louisiana came before the House of Representatives in 1811, Josiah Quincy of Massachusetts declared that the passage of the measure would be a virtual dissolution of the Union, a death blow to the Constitution, and the signal for some of the states "to prepare definitely for a separation, amicably if they can, violently if they must."

Reinforcing his protest, a committee of the legislature of Massachusetts complained that "if the President and Senate may purchase land and Congress may plant states in Louisiana, they may with equal right establish them on the North-West Coast or in South America." However faultless the logic may have been, it did not soften the hearts of the Republicans. In 1812 Louisiana became the peer of Massachusetts in spite of the latter's dread. Before another decade elapsed, Mississippi and Alabama "poured their wild men," as the Federalists dubbed them, upon the floor of the national Congress.

Far to the north in the Louisiana Purchase, another commonwealth was rising to power on the banks of the Missouri. Into the fertile lands of that region streamed hardy farmers from Kentucky and Virginia, planters with their slaves, land-hungry Yankees from New England, thrifty Germans from Pennsylvania and straight from the Old World—freemen and bondmen mingling in one effervescent community. Though differing in interests, in religion, and sometimes in language, all the white men were agreed on one thing: winning independence as a state.

Pressing their claim upon Congress, they precipitated an angry dispute over slavery, the first of the mighty debates that finally culminated in an appeal to arms. On this occasion a compromise staved off the storm; in 1820 Maine was admitted into the Union as a free state and Missouri was accepted with slavery, while through the remainder of the Louisiana Territory the line of 36° 30′ was adopted to mark the division between freedom and bondage. Before the new legislature across the Mississippi had barely tried its wings, some wag painted on the wall behind the speaker's chair: "Missouri, forgive them. They know not what they do." So the new government was launched with humor as well as with determination.

In fashioning their constitutions, the backwoods draftsmen followed rather closely examples furnished by the older states from which they had emigrated. Sometimes their documents were almost exact copies of admired models. Again they were mosaics; the leader in the Illinois convention, for instance, welded the constitutions of Kentucky, Ohio, and Indiana into a composite law. In every case there were included with mechanical regularity a bill of rights and articles dealing with the executive, legislative, and judicial departments. As a rule, however, the frontier lawmakers stipulated that the governor should be elected by popular vote and not by the legislature, as required by the first constitutions in the majority of the original states; and in several other respects the new commonwealths were also more "democratic" in their politics.

Rejecting the doctrines of the Old Dominion, Kentucky provided that all free male citizens who had resided in the state for two years should enjoy the right of suffrage and that any lawful elector should be deemed eligible for the office of governor or membership in the legislature. Thus was realized on the frontier the political equality of freemen, in an age when property or taxpaying qualifications were still retained by the commonwealths of the Atlantic seaboard. Indeed the departure was too radical for some of

Kentucky's own neighbors. Tennessee, for example, insisted on restricting important offices to freeholders, counting no man eligible to the general assembly unless he owned two hundred acres of land in the county which he represented or worthy to be elected governor unless he possessed a freehold of five hundred acres. Furthermore, across the Ohio River, Indiana, while giving the ballot to all white male citizens, declined to allow any one who was not a taxpayer to serve as a legislator or chief executive.

Yet, in spite of the property qualifications, even the highest, all the new western states were, broadly speaking, democracies of free and equal white men. It was indeed a poor and shiftless pioneer who could not acquire a freehold or become a taxpayer; in fact it was not very difficult to secure the five hundred acres fixed as the economic qualification for governor of Tennessee. So the politics of the frontier was the politics of backwoodsmen, and if a type of the age is needed for illustration, it may well be David Crockett, whose autobiography is one of the prime human documents for the American epic yet to be written.

In early manhood, without any formal education and barely able to write his own name, Crockett was made a local magistrate. Confessing at the time that he had never read a page of a law book in his life, he gave his decisions on "the principles of common justice and honesty between man and man, and relied on natural born sense and not on law learning" as a guide to his judgments. From this petty office Crockett advanced to the state legislature. When the new honor fell upon him, according to his own admissions, he had never read a newspaper, and was under the impression that General Jackson himself was the whole government of the United States. In his campaign for election, Crockett told stories that amused the crowd; usually ending his speech with the remark that he was "dry as a powder horn" and extending a general invitation for the auditors to join him at the nearest liquor store.

On arriving at the capital of the state in the rôle of a

Solon, Crockett was so ignorant of constitutional law that he did not know the meaning of the word "judiciary." Undeterred, however, by a lack of training in books, he widened his information, improved his handwriting, and kept his wits burnished. In due time he was sent to Congress where, for reasons difficult to fathom, he finally turned against General Jackson and ruined his own political career. Stung by defeat at the polls, Crockett now made off for the southwest where he died dramatically at the Alamo, helping to wrest an empire from the hands of the Mexicans. No doubt other politicians from the West were more learned and could make speeches in grammar more elegant but on the whole Crockett was fairly typical of a great horde of hunters and farmers who pushed into the rude chambers of western capitals during the opening decades of the nineteenth century and sent their spokesmen to Washington to instruct the federal government in the politics of frontier agriculture.

CHAPTER XII

Jacksonian Democracy—A Triumphant Farmer-Labor Party

THE creation of nine states beyond the mountains, accelerating the steady movement of political power toward the West, was synchronous with profound social changes on the seaboard—changes equally disturbing to eastern gentlemen of the old school in wigs, ruffles, knee breeches, and silver buckles. While the widening agricultural area was sending an ever-increasing number of representatives to speak for farmers upon the floor of Congress, state after state on the Atlantic coast was putting ballots into the hands of laborers and mechanics whom the Fathers of the Republic had feared as Cicero feared the proletariat and desperate debtors of ancient Rome. Even Jefferson, fiery apostle of equality in the abstract, shrank at first from the grueling test of his own logic; not until long after the Declaration of Independence did he commit himself to the dangerous doctrine of manhood suffrage.

Expressing their anxieties in law, the framers of the first

542

state constitutions, as we have noted, placed taxpaying or property qualifications on the right to vote. The more timid excluded from public office all except the possessors of substantial property; and those who stood aghast at the march of secularism applied religious tests that excluded from places of political trust Catholics, Jews, Unitarians, and scoffers who denied belief in hell. All people thus laid under the ban of the law they regarded as socially unsafe. "The tumultuous populace of large cities," ran the warning words of Washington, "are ever to be dreaded." In Jefferson's opinion also, "the mobs of the great cities" were "sores on the body politic."

Such was the prevailing view among the ruling classes of the time and it was founded on no mere theories of state. The conduct of the rioters in the days of the Stamp Act agitation, the fierce treatment meted out to Tories in the years of the Revolution, and the mass meetings of workingmen in New York and Philadelphia when the first state constitutions were being framed, all indicated that social forces of unknown power were stirring beneath the surface of society.

There was a brief period of peace and reaction while the Constitution was being launched but that was the calm before the storm. Washington had been safely installed only a few weeks when the alarm bell of the French Revolution gave the signal for an uprising of the sansculottes of the western world. Before long, in all the cities of the American seaboard, a movement for white manhood suffrage was in full swing. Indeed, the mechanics of Pennsylvania had already set an example in 1776 by forcing the adoption of a low taxpaying franchise which gave a broad popular base to the government and paved the way for a Jacobinical democracy. During Washington's first administration, in 1791, to be exact, Vermont came into the Union without property restrictions, and Delaware gave the ballot to all white men who paid taxes. Though reckoned among the conservative states, Maryland "shot Niagara" in 1809 by adopting manhood suffrage; and nine years later Connecticut, even less devoted to the quest for novelties, decided that all males who contributed a trivial sum to the support of the government could be trusted with the ballot.

The fire spread to Massachusetts. Into the state constitutional convention of 1820 strode radicals ready to strike down all the political privileges expressly accorded to property, raising anew the specter of Daniel Shays. Frightened at their demands, Daniel Webster, then in the prime of his manhood, and John Adams, at the close of his memorable career, joined in protesting against innovations. With his customary eloquence, Webster warned the convention that all the revolutions of history which had shaken society to its foundations had been revolts against property; that equal suffrage was incompatible with inequality in property; and that if adopted it would either end in assaults on wealth or new restraints upon democracy—a reaction of the notables. In spite of the fact that the argument was cogent, it did not rally the delegates as one man to the established bulwarks. The privileges of riches in the state senate were indeed retained but the straight property test for the suffrage was abandoned and a small taxpaying restriction adopted, merely to be swept away itself within a few years.

A similar contest took place in New York in 1821 when a band of Federalists in the constitutional convention argued, threatened, and raged to save the political rights of property, only to go down in defeat after gaining some petty concessions which were abolished within five years in favor of white manhood suffrage. From this struggle echoes were heard in Rhode Island where the mechanics of Providence, learning of Tammany's victory in New York, called for a similar unhorsing of the freeholders who ruled their own state. Unawed by their hue and cry, the conservatives stood firm while the tiny commonwealth founded by apostles of liberty was shaken by a long and stormy agitation over the rights of man. For nearly twenty years the tempest blew hard, provoking an armed uprising, known as Dorr's Rebellion, and culminating in the substitution of a taxpaying for the freehold qualification on the suffrage.

Equally obdurate were Virginia and North Carolina, notwithstanding the power of Jefferson's great name; the former would not let anybody but landowners vote until 1830; the latter did not surrender that restriction for twenty-six years. But the delay was not so significant, for the growth of the western counties in those two states gave them each a population of small farmers who had no more love for the planters on the coast than the Irish mechanics of New York City had for the stockholders in the United States Bank. Thus it may be said that when the nineteenth century turned its first quarter, political power was slipping from the hands of seaboard freeholders, capitalists, and planters into the grip of frontier farmers—usually heavily in debt to the East for capital and credit—and into the hands of the working class of the industrial towns, already tinged with leveling doctrines from fermenting Europe.

§

As the cohorts of the new democracy marched in serried ranks upon the government, they inevitably modified the spirit and practice of American politics. First of all, they criticized the method of electing the President. Shrinking from the hubbub of popular agitations, the Fathers had sought to remove the choice of the chief magistrate as far as possible from the passions of the multitude; though impressed by the difficulties of the task they hoped to introduce a quiet, dignified procedure about as decorous as the selection of a college rector by a board of clerical trustees. To attain their end, they provided that the President of the United States and also the Vice-President should be carefully chosen by a small body of electors selected as the legislatures of the states might decide.

Given this choice, the legislatures, naturally greedy for

power, proceeded to exercise the right themselves; but before long the new democracy was thundering at their doors, demanding the transfer of that sovereign prerogative to the voters at the polls. Slowly but surely the managers of politics yielded to the cry for the popular choice of the President; in 1824 only six states still allowed the legislatures to choose the presidential electors and eight years later but a single state, South Carolina, clung to the original mode. One of the great safeguards against the tyranny of majorities was now submerged in the tossing waves of democracy.

Yet the all-devouring populace was by no means satisfied with this gain, for the nomination of party candidates for President was still in the control of a small body of politicians known as the "congressional caucus." After the country divided into two parties, it became necessary for each of them to select its candidate in advance of the election; but of course the rank and file of its personnel could not assemble for that purpose in one forum, travel being tedious and expensive even for exalted officers. Accordingly the party members in Congress simply took upon themselves the high function. When the season for choosing the presidential candidate approached, the congressmen of each party met in caucus behind closed doors and agreed upon the dignitary to be put before the people. While the election of President and Vice-President was passing into popular control, the choice of candidates thus remained in the grip of a few managers in Washington.

To the new democracy this situation was intolerable and a roar of protest went up against it. In 1824, on the refusal of "old King Caucus" to nominate General Andrew Jackson, such a clatter was raised that never again did members of Congress dare officially to select the people's candidates for them. When the campaign of 1832 came around, there was substituted for the caucus an institution known as the nominating convention, an extra-legal party conference composed of faithful delegates chosen by local assemblies of loyal partisans. To be sure, Senators and

Representatives were always prominent in the convention but they were now faced by hundreds of party agents "fresh from the people," as Jackson was wont to say.

In fact, the grand convention was mainly ruled by office-holders and aspirants for office. While the election of the President was vested in the people legally, the choice of candidates, in fact, passed from the congressional monopoly to professional politicians at large. This transfer was noted by many eminent observers, especially by those who failed to win a nomination; and soon the convention was denounced in the vivid terms formerly applied to the caucus. Nevertheless, the new party institution took root and flourished; by 1840 it seemed as rigidly fixed as the Constitution itself. It also became at the same time the accepted organ of party operation in the lower ranges of state and county politics. Men who refused to abide by its decisions were anathematized and treated like social pariahs.

The profits as well as the powers of public office now became objects of interest to the new democracy. "To the victors belong the spoils," a slogan of New York politicians, was elevated to the dignity of a national principle in the age of Andrew Jackson. And yet it would be a mistake to assume that the doctrine was a product of the period. To the statesmen of ancient Rome the emoluments of office and the plunder of the provinces were matters of prime concern; the hands of the righteous Cicero were far from spotless. The government of England in the era of the Georges was an immense aggregation of sinecures and profitable positions, the impeccable Pitt having his Newcastle to distribute pelf among the beggars of the better sort that swarmed around Parliament.

In colonial America, contests over lucrative posts filled official circles with petty rackets; the thrifty Franklin made the most of his opportunity as royal postmaster-general of America. Once independence was established, there were problems of statecraft to be considered. Even the virtuous Washington, placed by a sense of honor and private fortune above jobbery in public offices, could not ignore its function in party management. In making his first appointments, he was careful to choose friends rather than enemies of the new Constitution, although he occasionally tried to clip the wings of especially dangerous critics by giving them places in the administration; and, taught by experience the perils of doubters in his own household, he finally vowed that he would henceforth select only well-disposed persons for office, on the highly defensible theory that no government can rely on its foes for success. Jefferson was equally careful, when removals, resignations, and deaths occurred, to make selections with reference to party loyalty.

This practice the labor and agrarian democracy which later swept into power merely amplified by ousting a larger proportion of office-holders and by avowing more frankly that the sweets of place were among the joys of victory. To this doctrine, they added another, namely, rotation in office, demanding that terms be short so that more party workers could share in the delights of conquest. The bucolic openly admitted the purpose; while the sophisticated argued that long tenure made officers lazy, bureaucratic, and tyrannical.

In either form the new gospel weighed heavily with farmers who seldom saw as much as a hundred dollars cash in the course of a whole year and with mechanics who labored at the bench or forge for seventy-five cents a day. To them a chance at the public "trough," as the phrase ran in gross colloquialism, was to be welcomed gratefully on any axiom of ethics. Indeed, it was often difficult to distinguish, except in mathematical terms, between those who suffered from the taint of vulgarity in office-seeking and those who united public emoluments and private retainers in the higher ranges of the public service. Whatever the niceties of the occasion required, it was clear to all that the advent of the farmer-labor democracy was

bound to work changes in the more decorous proceedings
handed down from the Fathers.

§

The flow of time in which occurred these modifications
in American political life carried off the heroic figures of
the Revolution and left the race to the fleet men of a
new generation. Washington died in 1799, still "first in
the hearts of his countrymen," as Light Horse Harry Lee
said in the funeral oration. Patrick Henry had already
gone to his long home; Samuel Adams was soon to follow.
In 1804, Alexander Hamilton, in the prime of life, was
shot in a duel by Aaron Burr. John Adams and Thomas
Jefferson, old and bent under the weight of years, trudged
on in the dusty way until 1826, when they died within a few
hours of each other on July 4, reconciled and at peace.
Charles Carroll, last surviving signer of the Declaration of
Independence, lived to turn the first sod for the Baltimore
and Ohio Railway on July 4, 1828, and to see with dimmed
eyes the outlines of a progressive future; but in four years
he too was no more. James Madison, philosopher of the
Constitution, kept up the good fight long enough to write
a ringing protest against nullification in South Carolina;
then death carried him off at the ripe old age of eighty-five.

When the election of 1824 arrived, there was no Father
of the republic, in the vigor of manhood and crowned with
the halo of a romantic age, able to take up the office laid
down by Colonel Monroe. Time as ever was ruthless.
The Virginia succession had come to an end. Even the
Federalist party, founded by Hamilton and Washington,
was out of the field—or rather incorporated as a disturbing
factor in the all-embracing Republican party of Jefferson.
The "era of good feeling" was closing; buried or concealed
hatreds were reviving. New men, looking to the future
rather than to the past, were jostling one another for
place and power in the forum, but none stood out head

and shoulders above the others as the inevitable successor to Monroe.

Puzzled by this state of affairs, the congressional caucus nominated for the presidency W. H. Crawford of Georgia, a man of ability but not a commanding personality. Its decree was in regular form but it could not be enforced because, forsooth, three other candidates insisted on entering the lists. John Quincy Adams, son of the second President, regarded himself as heir apparent in virtue of his services as Secretary of State; while the frontier brought its hard fist down on the political table with emphasis, announcing the rights of Henry Clay of Kentucky and Andrew Jackson of Tennessee. "The wild men of the Mississippi region" could not be ignored but fortune postponed their mastery.

So divided were the returns from the polls that no one of the four had a majority of the presidential electors as required by the Constitution; Jackson stood at the top, Clay at the bottom. From this it followed that the election was thrown into the House of Representatives, where each state could cast only one vote—the vote of its delegation—and men elected in calmer days held the floor under the leadership of Clay as Speaker. Upon the trained ears of the old political dynasty, the cries of Jackson's hordes swarming into the lobbies sounded like the voices of willful fanatics. Bent on defeating them at all costs, Clay, whose small number of votes left him outside the pale, threw his strength heavily to the right and by skillful management won the presidency for Adams with the office of Secretary of State for himself, perhaps, as alleged, quite accidentally.

Though the roaring flood of the new democracy was now foaming perilously near the crest, the great dike of proscriptive rights still held, for Adams could no doubt give to the government the tone of the old régime. He called himself a Republican in politics, having turned against the Federalists and affiliated with the Jeffersonians in the days when the latter were regarded by the New England aristocracy as "a Jacobinical rabble." Nevertheless, he was no horny-handed farmer, aproned mechanic, or bold Indian fighter, dear to the rising electorate of the age. Educated at Harvard and in the politest circles of Europe, Adams viewed public service as a kind of *noblesse oblige* to be kept untainted by the vulgar odors of loot and spoils—a service capable of protecting democracy by efficient administration against the inroads of the plutocracy.

Besides being out of lockstep in matter of political patronage, he was opposed to flinging western land out to impecunious members of Congress, avid speculators, and gambling farmers. Looking to the long future, he believed in preserving the public domain as a great national treasury of resources to be wisely and honestly managed with a view to revenues for roads, canals, and education in letters, arts, and sciences. Besides anticipating by nearly a hundred years some of the most enlightened measures of conservation, Adams foresaw in a livid flash the doom of slavery in a social war.

By no possible effort could he become a Jacksonian "mixer"; like his illustrious descendant, Henry Adams, he was destined to wander in space without finding rest or peace. From the beginning to the end of his administration, misfortune dogged his steps. When he appointed Clay head of the State Department, the resentment of Jackson's party broke all bounds, worshipers of "Old Hickory," seeing in the appointment conclusive proof that a "corrupt bargain" had defeated their Hero. With a feeling of righteous indignation, they began to prepare for the next election, filling Adams' four years with torment by abuse and with chagrin by gathering in his friends as they fled from the sinking ship. In a tidal wave the country repudiated Adams at the next election.

The campaign of 1828 was marked by extreme rancor—a bitterness akin to that of 1800 when the Jeffersonian hordes drove the elder Adams from power. Metropolitan newspapers, the clergy, federal office-holders, manufacturers, and bankers were in general hotly in favor of re electing Adams; the richest planters of the Old South preferred him to Jackson, even if they had little love for a New England Puritan himself. Against this combination were aligned the farmers, particularly those burdened with poverty and debts, and the mechanics of the towns who shouted their "Hurrah for Jackson!" with a gusto.

Passions of rank and place, rather than definite issues, divided the two factions and in the mad scramble for power both resorted to billingsgate of the most finished quality. Though garbed in the mantle of respectability, the Adams faction pictured Jackson, to use the terse summary of a recent historian, Claude Bowers, "as a usurper, an adulterer, a gambler, a cock-fighter, a brawler, a drunkard, and a murderer." It also turned on his wife, its national campaign committee even sinking so low as to send out bales of pamphlets attacking the moral character of his "dear Rachel" who, although she did smoke a pipe, was a woman of exemplary life. In this unsavory game, Jackson's faction, determined not to be outdone, portrayed Adams as a stingy Puritan, an aristocrat who hated the people, a corruptionist who had bought his own election, and a waster of the people's money on White House decorations; and accused Clay of managing Adams' campaign "like a shyster, pettifogging in a bastard suit before a country squire."

When the smoke of the fray had lifted, it was found that Adams had won nothing but the electoral votes of New England and not even all those; whereas Jackson had carried the rest of the Union, making an absolutely clean sweep in the South and West. The collapse of the Adams party was complete. Gentlemen and grand dames of the old order, like the immigrant nobles and ladies of France fleeing from the sansculottes of Paris, could discover no consolation in their grief.

On March 4, 1829, a son of the soil rode into Washington to take the oath of office. All the Presidents before Andrew Jackson had come from families that possessed property and its cultural accompaniments. None had been compelled to work with his hands for a livelihood; all except Washington had received a college education. Jackson, on the other hand, born of poverty-stricken parents in the uplands of South Carolina, was of the earth earthy. It is not even known just how or when he got the barest rudiments of learning but it is certain that to the end of his life his language, if forceful and direct, was characterized by grammar strangely and wonderfully constructed.

In his youth Jackson had gone to the Tennessee frontier where, as a land speculator, horse trader, politician, and rural genius in general, he managed to amass a large estate and a goodly number of slaves. Tall and sinewy, he loved wrestling matches, fist fights, and personal quarrels. By way of settling one dispute, he killed a man in a duel and ever afterward treasured the pistol that performed the deed as a trophy to show his visitors. In an awful brawl with the Benton brothers, he himself received a bullet which remained imbedded in his flesh for many years as evidence of his hardihood. Whenever an Indian fight occurred in his neighborhood, he rushed to the front.

Elevated to the leadership of the local militia by his undoubted courage, Jackson won the passionate devotion of his men by sharing their hardships and perils. Already a local hero, he had leaped into national fame in 1815 by defeating a blundering and incompetent British general at the battle of New Orleans. Finally, he had added more laurels by wresting Florida from Spain, summarily hanging two English subjects, and stamping out warlike Indians on the border.

This son of the soil, transformed in the eyes of his devotees into a military figure comparable to Napoleon the Great, furnished excellent presidential timber for the new democracy. That his views on the tariff, internal improvements, and other current issues were nebulous in no way detracted from his immense and irresistible availability. He was from the West. He was a farmer—a slave owner, no doubt, but still a farmer. He had none of the unction that marked the politicians of the seaboard school and the mechanics could think of him as one of themselves.

Jackson's opponents, of course, sneered because he was rough in manner, smoked an old pipe, chewed tobacco profusely, told stories that could not be printed, loafed around with a week's bristles on his face, and wore soiled clothes. John Quincy Adams, who knew Jackson well, could hardly suppress his anguish when Harvard gave "the brawler from Tennessee" the degree of doctor of laws. It was not a pure accident that Jackson's chief regret at the end of his presidential course was "that he had never had an opportunity to shoot Clay or hang Calhoun." But the contempt of his enemies only endeared him the more to the masses, especially as all charges were discreetly counterbalanced by news that he regularly read the Bible, recited countless lines of Watts' doleful hymns, and asked the blessing at the table. Moreover, those who saw him dressed in his best, with his pipe and plug laid aside, bowing in his courtliest manner, concluded that the discreditable tales about him were partisan falsehoods.

When the day of Jackson's inauguration came, the city of Washington was jammed with crowds. From near and far thousands of his devoted followers had come to witness the spectacle—and in many cases to get jobs in the new administration. All the decorum of former days was rudely broken. Bowing right and left to cheering throngs, Jackson and his party walked from his hotel to the inaugural ceremonies. After taking the oath of office, he rode in his best military style down the Avenue to the White House, followed by a surging sea of worshippers.

On his arrival at the presidential residence the doors were thrown open to everybody and, if Webster is to be accepted as authority, the pushing idolators behaved like hoodlums, upsetting the punch bowls, breaking glasses, and standing in muddy boots on damask chairs to catch a glimpse of the people's Napoleon. "The reign of King Mob seemed triumphant," groaned Justice Story of the Supreme Court. Recalling the refinements of Jefferson, Mrs. Margaret Bayard Smith, a leader in the local social set, held her nose and wrote: "The noisy and disorderly rabble . . . brought to my mind descriptions I have read of the mobs in the Tuileries and at Versailles."

With utmost dispatch the business of government—and dividing the spoils—was begun. To aid him in the operation, Jackson chose two cabinets. The first, composed of the heads of departments, was filled with men of fair talent and some distinction; many a worse ministry has been assembled since. The second, known as the "Kitchen Cabinet," was made up of Isaac Hill, Amos Kendall, and other private advisers, who served as a collective agency to keep the king informed about the gossip of the capital and to keep the masses in good humor with news meet for their understanding.

As soon as the chiefs were installed, a survey of the gentlemen in federal berths commenced. "No damn rascal who made use of an office or its profits for the purpose of keeping Mr. Adams in or General Jackson out of power is entitled to the least leniency save that of hanging," wrote one of the President's applicants. "You may say to all our anxious Adamsites that the Barnacles will be scraped clean off the Ship of State," declared a member of the kitchen sanhedrin. "Most of them have grown so large and stick so tight that the scraping process will doubtless be fatal to them."

Though the threats were terrifying, in fact the slaughter of the innocents was not as great as the opposition alleged. Indeed, many got only their just deserts; some of the tenants were found to be scoundrels, prosecuted, and convicted for fraudulent transactions while public servants, one of the "martyrs," a personal friend of Adams, being sent to prison for stealing from the Treasury. No doubt hundreds of old and faithful officers were ousted; but on the other hand hundreds were allowed to retain their places in spite of the severe pressure from the Jackson followers, begging for jobs.

It is therefore due to the memory of the President to say that, like Clive in India, he had reason to be proud of his moderation. To this judgment must be quickly joined the statement that Jackson started the custom of making wholesale removals in favor of party workers, giving high national sanction to the practice of bestowing the spoils upon the victors. A few intellectuals, such as James Russell Lowell, soon poured ridicule upon the system; many statesmen, especially those who had never had occasion to make use of it, denounced it; yet as time passed that form of political etiquette became more and more prevalent, hardening into prescription.

In addition to scraping barnacles from the Ship of State, Jackson gave energetic consideration to the political issues of the hour: the tariff, nullification, the Bank, internal improvements, and the disposal of western lands. All these questions were economic in character, presenting new phases of the struggle that had produced the colonial revolt against Great Britain, the reaction under Hamilton, and the swing to Jefferson. And their management involved the fortunes of the three marked sections into which the country was divided—the capitalistic Northeast, the planting South, and the farming regions beyond the seaboard—with the mechanics of the towns coming into the play whenever the aristocracy of wealth and talents was to be pommeled.

Each section had an outstanding champion who sought to make congressional combinations of power in the interest of his constituents. Daniel Webster, as Fisher, his biographer, tells us, was "the hope and reliance of the moneyed and conservative classes, the merchants, manufacturers, capitalists, and bankers." John C. Calhoun acted frankly as the mouthpiece of the planting aristocracy; he acknowledged it and was proud of it. Thomas Hart Benton of Missouri was the shouting spokesman of the western farmers and land speculators who were struggling to wrench the public domain from the grip of the government. Happily placed between extremes, North and South, Henry Clay labored to construct a platform that would command the support of the eastern capitalists and the western farmers, unite hearts and make him President; but he failed to accomplish his design.

Into the lists Jackson entered as gladiator-at-large for the masses against the moneyed classes, declaring that the agricultural interest was "superior in importance" to all others and placing himself, as he said, at the head of "the humbler members of society—the farmers, mechanics, and laborers who have neither the time nor the means" of securing special favors for themselves. They heard him gladly and thought him their Sir Galahad.

§

During Jackson's first administration the oldest of domestic questions, the tariff, became so acute -that, in 1832, it raised a revolt among the South Carolina planters. Between the opening of the century and that date signal changes had been made in the economic condition of the country. The Embargo and the War of 1812, by cutting off the stream of English manufactures, produced an immense growth in American industries, a growth that was further enhanced by the tariff of 1816, enacted, ostensibly at least, to provide a continuous home market for agricultural produce. In this process the economic climate of several regions was radically altered.

Although the leaders of New England—the home of American shipping interests engaged in a lively carrying trade—had opposed the tariff of 1816, they accepted the unavoidable and turned their best energies, together with their capital, to the promotion of manufactures favored by protection. Iron masters of Connecticut, New Jersey, and Pennsylvania, having reaped high profits under the gracious shade of the tariff wall, naturally thought of increasing their earnings by raising the bulwark. Even the wool, hemp, and flax growers of Ohio, Kentucky, and Tennessee, and the sugar planters of Louisiana discovered that, while free trade was good for agriculturists as a general theory, advantageous exceptions could be made in practice. Other economic interests of various kinds veered in the new direction.

And as the number of protected groups increased and their capital augmented, the pressure on Congress for additional safeguards became heavier and heavier. Then political weathervanes veered. Webster, who had fought the tariff of 1816, taking note of drifting flaw, became an ardent champion of protection. If Calhoun, finding the sea lanes to industrial England open once more, turned back upon his course to free trade, his colleague, Clay, developed the idea of "discriminating" customs duties into a perfect national system. "Dame Commerce," he exclaimed, "is a flirting, flippant, noisy Jade and if we are governed by her fantasies, we shall never put off the muslins of India and the cloths of Europe." So he appealed to "the yeomanry of the country, the true and genuine landlords of this tenement, called the United States," to emancipate the nation from dependence on foreign capitalists.

Under the drive of combined economic powers, the tariff was forced up in 1824 and in 1828; and made more logical in 1832. The second of these revisions, known as the "tariff of abominations" among its enemies, was carried through Congress by such a determined union of factions that the planting statesmen who now wanted to trade their produce freely for the manufactures of England were thrown into an unwonted political fear. Badly defeated in the forum at Washington, they began to build a backfire at home. Speaking through the legislatures of Virginia, North Carolina, South Carolina, Georgia, and Alabama, they solemnly denounced the tariff of abominations.

Then, finding such denunciations to be mere rhetoric flung against triumphant fact, South Carolina, weary of sheer verbalism, made ready for open resistance. In the autumn of 1832, the state legislature ordered an election of delegates to a convention, with a view of preparing for the worst. The elections were duly held, the assembly was convened, and an Ordinance of Nullification tossed defiantly in the face of the protected interests. This Ordinance named the battleground and the weapons. It declared that the tariff gave "bounties to classes and individuals . . . at the expense and to the injury and oppression of other classes and individuals." Running true to American political phraseology, it proclaimed the tariff a violation of the Constitution—therefore null and void and without force in the state of South Carolina. It closed with a solemn warning that, if the federal government attempted to coerce the people of the state, they would assert their independence and take their place as a sovereign power among the nations of the earth.

While the issue thus joined was fraught with peril to the republic, it was not absolutely intractable. No doubt, South Carolina's challenge of nullification coupled with secession, like the gesture of New England during the War of 1812, was defiant, but the planting forces were not yet welded into an unyielding cohesion. On the contrary, the cotton states to which South Carolina appealed for support —as she did again in 1860—after condemning the tariff as abominable, refused point blank to approve nullification as a remedy. On the other side, the protected interests, assailed in the rear by Jacksonian farmers, were not strong enough to hold in an open affray sectors they had taken by congressional negotiation nor yet prepared to attempt a suppression of nullification by arms. Capitalism and cotton had many leagues to cover before they could be joined in a death grapple. Evidently an accommodation was both necessary and possible.

To the settlement, President Jackson contributed something, though what and how much it is hard to say. Beyond question his devotion to the Union was deep and sincere. Although he came from a region that had once been ready to "fly off" when the closure of the Mississippi was threatened, his state was now well content with the common roof the Fathers had built. While there were slave owners in Tennessee, and Jackson was one of them, the political community, largely dominated by small farmers, was by no means assimilated completely to the planting system. Cotton was not king there and Jackson's sympathies, as he was wont to say, were with the humble people, rather than with the planters or with capitalists. Moreover, he had a tiger's hatred for Calhoun, apostle of nullification—a personal hatred which grew out of a well-authenticated report that the South Carolina statesman, when a member of Monroe's Cabinet, had proposed the arrest of Jackson for his cavalier conduct during the Seminole War in Florida. Smarting with resentment, the General, at a Jefferson dinner in 1830, had snapped out his warning to Calhoun in a toast: "Our Federal Union—It must and shall be preserved." Besides this, Jackson was President of the United States and he regarded resistance to authority in the light of a personal insult as well as a violation of law.

When he heard the news of South Carolina's action, Jackson therefore declared himself ready to "hang every leader . . . of that infatuated people, sir, by martial law, irrespective of his name or political or social position." Regarding nullification at bottom as a species of sedition, he vowed that he would meet it "at the threshold and have the leaders arrested and arraigned for treason." Still he was careful to confine such heated expressions to private letters and conversations. With a strong feeling for realities, he sent a shrewd politician to South Carolina to sound the earth at the very moment that he was preparing to order out additional troops.

In his public utterances Jackson spoke more softly, using the phrases of law and order rather than the language of the battlefield. Taking refuge in a long and eloquent proclamation, the President announced his firm belief in the sacredness and perpetuity of the Union and his intention to uphold it by the exercise of all the powers vested in him by the Constitution. This document was put in final form, it seems, by his Secretary of State, Edward Livingston, one of the most remarkable figures in American history; but the central idea of the paper was Jackson's own. Though emphatic, it contained no bluster, no threats of executions, no menace of martial law. It was firm, yet conciliatory toward the South Carolinians, appealing, as did Lincoln's inaugural address long afterward, to their love of Union rather than their fear of force. Employing also the tactics of moderation in his messages to Congress on the crisis, Jackson proposed that the tariff against which the nullifiers protested be lowered—that was just what they wanted—and called for new legislation granting the President larger powers in the enforcement of the laws—which they did not mind much if the laws pleased them.

Here was a case for compromise and Henry Clay, past master of that fine art, rose to the occasion, laying before the Senate in February, 1833, a plan which offered consolations to both parties. Turning courteously to the planters, he proposed that the tariff to which they objected be reduced to the level fixed in 1816, which Calhoun himself had then approved. Bowing tactfully to the other side, he suggested that nothing drastic be done immediately, that the proposed reduction should extend over a period of ten years, taking the form of curtailment by easy stages. Remembering the affection which all men professed for the Union, he also accepted a bill making provision for upholding its supremacy by armed force, if necessary. After a warm debate, both propositions—the one lowering the tariff and the other exalting the Union—passed both houses of Congress and were signed by the President on the same day, March 2.

Hailing the outcome as a glorious victory, South Carolina rescinded the Ordinance nullifying the tariff and satisfied her honor by declaring the force bill null and void.

Everywhere planters regarded the triumph of open resistance as complete. According to all outward signs, at least, they had every reason to rejoice, for whatever might be said about the flowers of speech that decorated the contest, they had actually checked the progress of the Hamilton-Webster system—checked it so thoroughly that a few years later, when the manufacturing interests succeeded in pushing the tariff up again, they were able to bring it down by easier means.

On the other hand, Jackson could point with pride to the fact that the Union had been duly preserved, and the protected industries could take pleasure in escaping a single swift blow of repudiation. It was not until his last days that Clay, on reviewing his career of strife and disappointment, found in his mind grave doubts about the wisdom of his course. Would it have been better if he had let Jackson and the nullifiers come to blows in 1833, settling then and there, by force of arms, the mighty economic question that divided the sections? Who, working under the eye of eternity, could make answer?

§

Interwoven with the tariff controversy was the public land question which had worried George III's ministers, plagued Hamilton, and continued to evoke heated dispute. Besides inspiring Senator Benton of Missouri to flights of eloquence, it called forth the celebrated Webster-Hayne debate in 1830, the greatest among the many verbal battles of the Jacksonian era. Although constitutional glosses have almost buried the substance of that disputation, its kernel was essentially economic. It arose over a proposal of a Connecticut Senator, Samuel A. Foote, to inquire into the expediency of limiting the sale of the public lands—a matter of moment both to protected manufacturers and slave-owning planters. The former, as eager to secure an abundance of cheap labor as to find shelter behind a tariff barrier, viewed with grave concern the westward rush to land in the public domain. Working people who forsook flaming forges and whirling spindles to till the soil in the Ohio Valley were lost to the mills; while those who remained behind could raise their wages by threatening to follow in the footsteps of the pioneers. On the other hand, southern planters, not yet aware that a valley of free farmers might in time contest their own sway, saw a possible addition to their strength in the growing agricultural population beyond the Alleghenies. Farmers and planters acting together, the latter reasoned, might overcome the manufacturing capitalists in politics at Washington.

There was nothing occult in this philosophy. Every statesman of the time knew the relation of the land question to the tariff issue and to the balance of power in the American Union, none better than Webster of Massachusetts and Hayne of South Carolina. In fact, Hayne in throwing down the gage was merely supporting a fiery Jacksonian Democrat, Senator Benton, who frankly spoke for the western farmers and kept his heart fixed on their concerns. Webster, taking up the gage, simply made a clever stroke by choosing the champion of slavery rather than the Gracchus of Missouri as the object of his attack. If he had opposed Benton, instead of the South Carolina lawyer, his plea for the Union might have been heard with less pleasure beyond the mountains and the formation of the Republican homestead-tariff bloc at Chicago in 1860 might have been still more difficult.

That problems in accountancy lay solidly beneath the cloud of constitutional argument was made manifest in the course of the debate, especially by the orator from South Carolina. Referring to the War of 1812, Hayne advanced passionately upon Webster, lashing out: "At this dark period of our National affairs, where was the Senator from Massachusetts? How were his political associates employed? 'Calculating the value of the union.'" More than that, he exclaimed, when the nation, in a perilous moment, was fighting for its life against a powerful foe, New England had resisted the enforcement of the law and prepared for a division of the country—all because her commercial interests were impaired.

With generality Hayne included some particulars. "Nothing was left undone," he said, "to embarrass the financial operations of the government, to prevent the enlistment of troops, to keep back the men and money of New England from the service of the Union, to force the President from his seat. . . . With what justice or propriety can the South be accused of disloyalty from that quarter?" In the heat of the fray, Hayne possibly overlooked the fact that his sword cut both ways. If South Carolina was right in 1830, why was New England wrong in 1814? If Massachusetts was disloyal in Madison's administration, what could be said of South Carolina in Jackson's administration? Legally, nothing; ethically, perhaps, nullification was less defensible in war than in peace. The core of the matter lay in the reversed economic situation; but perhaps beyond economics lay something transcendent—national destiny.

In an oration which has by general consent taken its place among the masterpieces of all time, Webster made the most of the opportunity presented by Hayne. He had been taunted with inconsistency; he answered in kind by showing the reversal of South Carolina's opinion on the tariff after 1816. New England had been charged with disloyalty to the Union; Webster faced the issue squarely by saying that, if anything savoring of treason was to be found in the records of New England, he offered not defense but rebuke. To Hayne's itemized bill of indictment against Massachusetts, Webster replied by throwing a blaze of glorious encomium on the record of the state in the Revolution and by adroitly covering the more recent pages of history with the mantle of evasion and oblivion.

The philosophy of nullification had been defended by Hayne; Webster, who had been perilously near it himself but a short time before, now marched upon it with sonorous rhetoric.   Using historical allusions, many of them clouded by doubtful authenticity, employing logical inferences often more adroit than conclusive, he underwrote the doctrine of perpetual union—a union made by the people, not by the states, an object of love and admiration forever.   In his peroration, Webster, the artist and prophetic man of letters, broke through the entanglements of the politician; in an almost superhuman effort he shot the white light of his poetic vision down the shadowed avenue of the future to dark and bloody places where men inspired by his ideal and reciting his moving periods were to die for the cause he had so magnificently celebrated.

In piling Ossa on Pelion, Webster did not overlook mundane considerations—the economic and political substance of the pending issue, the sale of those annoying western lands.   New England had been accused of enmity toward the West, of cherishing a hard and selfish policy; he answered by showing how New England had favored those internal improvements so dear to the West—roads that opened markets to produce and raised the values of land. Then he turned upon Hayne and warned him that the southern statesmen who, like the enemies of Banquo, had killed friendship between the farming and the commercial states would gain nothing in the end because they could never drag the West with them to nullification and secession, another flare of prophecy that was fulfilled in 1861. But Webster was more than an orator.   He was a practical man; when he came from the sky to earth, he moved to postpone indefinitely the resolution of Senator Foote which offended the West, burying it under the mountain of papers on the table.

The South Carolinian thus won a futile victory; and in the process New England also lost.   If eastern members of Congress had in fact approved Benton's long-pending bill for giving away the public lands to farmers, if they had then and there effected a union with the West by yielding on the land question, as they were finally forced to do in

1860, they might have spared themselves a thirty years' struggle with the low tariff party. More than that, they would have made the forces of the Union a combination of power so formidable that secession would have scarcely dared to face it. But they failed to seize this grand occasion for the not unnatural reason that politicians must apparently work in the fear that rises from the instant need of things.

§

If the tariff and land questions had stood alone, the Northeast and the West might have found it easier to draw together in 1830, but the old banking and currency issue that had plagued America since the days of George III was once more to the front in a virulent form. The second United States Bank, chartered for twenty years in 1816 to enable the Jeffersonians to finance their war, was becoming in the minds of western farmers and eastern mechanics the very citadel of tyrannical money power.

Radical Democrats had denounced it on principle from the beginning and their attacks steadily increased in animosity. Others acquired their views from practice. The notes of the Bank, sound throughout the Union, drove from circulation the paper currency of shaky institutions chartered by state politicians, thus inflaming village statesmen with anger against the "rich and well-born." Its managers were accused of showing favoritism to friendly politicians and of discriminating against the followers of Jackson in making loans; indeed a "psychic injury" of this character, alleged to have been inflicted on one of the President's friends, seems to have been the original source of his special rage against the Bank. The managers were likewise charged with using their power to contract the currency for the purpose of punishing their enemies, with giving retainers to some of their orators in Congress, and with spending corporate funds for campaign purposes. So the natural hostility of the masses to the plutocracy was intensified by dark and sinister rumors about a new "corrupt squadron."

That many of the charges against the Bank were groundless was later revealed by historical research. If some of Jackson's men were denied loans for business reasons, it was never proved that discriminations were made against Democratic politicians merely on account of their doctrinal views. If the Bank refused to be used by the brokers in spoils, its motive was economic rather than partisan. In the beginning at least, its president, Nicholas Biddle, it seems, tried to steer his way "on sound business lines" through the maze of politics.

After the war on the Bank commenced, however, both he and his colleagues laid hold of the various weapons at hand. From that time forward, the allegation that members of Congress received retainers from the Bank certainly rested on a substantial basis. In any case its mightiest spokesman in the Senate, Daniel Webster, was on the payroll of the corporation, a fact made clear in distant days by the publication of Biddle's letters and papers. In those documents it is recorded that, two weeks after the opening of a congressional session in which a legal battle was to be fought over its charter, Webster wrote to Biddle, shrewdly conveying the information that he had declined to take a case against the Bank and adding with charming frankness: "I believe my retainer has not been renewed or refreshed as usual. If it be wished that my relation to the bank should be continued, it may be well to send me the usual retainers."

Equally well established now is the charge that the Bank contracted its loans for the purpose of producing distress and breaking the back of the political opposition. Beyond all question, in the midst of the contest a term of financial stringency was deliberately inflicted on the country; Biddle, sure of his ground, declaring to the head of the Boston branch that "nothing but the evidence of suffering abroad will produce any effect in Congress." Webster himself, convinced that pressure on the populace would be useful, wrote to Biddle that "this discipline, it appears to me, must have very great effects on the general question of rechartering the Bank."

In fact, the private correspondence of the period now open to the student shows that the supporters and beneficiaries of the Bank had effected a strong union of forces for the purpose of controlling a large section of the press, dictating to politicians, frightening indifferent business men, and defying Jackson and his masses. "This worthy President," laughed Biddle, "thinks that because he has scalped Indians and imprisoned Judges, he is to have his way with the Bank. He is mistaken."

Pride was, nevertheless, riding for a fall. Jackson's anger, once aroused, was terrible to behold; it was the anger of the warrior rushing on his foe heedless of wounds and death, not the cold and calculating wrath of the counting house. Moreover, he had behind him the accumulating discontent of the agrarian and labor elements in the new democracy—an unrest which he steadily fanned into flame by very clever tactics. In his first message to Congress, Jackson attacked the Bank openly but not with might and main. In his second and third messages, he deftly referred to the subject, warily leaving the decision to "an enlightened people and their representatives."

If the opposition had maintained a discreet silence, a clash might have been avoided; but, boasting of its wisdom, it chose another course. The Bank was uneasy about the future; and Clay, sniffing the presidential air in 1832, decided to make an issue of it then and there. Though its charter had four more years to run, the Bank applied for a renewal and Congress, under the leadership of Clay, passed the bill granting the petition.

Jackson's reply to this defiance was a veto and a ringing message calling on the masses to support his position. Paying his respects to high sentiments, he took his stand by the Ark of the Covenant, declaring the Bank unconstitutional. Knowing full well that the Supreme Court had held otherwise a few years before, Jackson countered this uncomfortable verdict with the bald statement that each officer took the oath to support the Constitution as he understood it, not as it was understood by others—a doctrine that probably set all aged gentlemen in horsehair and robes trembling for the future of their country, while pleasing Old Hickory's followers immensely.

Having paid his homage to the auspices, Jackson got down to the meat of the matter: the alignment of economic forces. He called attention to the fact that the people of the western and southwestern states held only $140,000 worth of the twenty-eight millions of capital stock outstanding in private hands, whereas the capitalists of the middle and eastern states held more than thirteen millions. He pointed out that, of the annual profits of the Bank, $1,640,000 came from nine western states where little or none of the stock was held.

The moral lesson was obvious. It was an economic conflict that happened to take a sectional form: the people of the agricultural West had to pay tribute to eastern and foreign capitalists on the money they had borrowed to buy land, make improvements, and engage in speculation. Jackson did not shrink from naming the contestants. "The rich and powerful" were bending the acts of the government to their selfish purposes; the rich were growing richer under special privilege; "many of our rich men . . . have besought us to make them richer by acts of Congress. By attempting to gratify their desires, we have in the results of our legislation arrayed section against section, interest against interest, and man against man, in a fearful commotion which threatens to shake the foundations of our Union."

That was indeed a call to arms. The head of the Bank, Biddle, declared himself delighted with it. "It has all the fury of the unchained panther, biting the bars of his cage. It is really a manifesto of anarchy, such as Marat and

Robespierre might have issued to the mob." The President's cheer leaders threw up their hats with sheer joy at the spectacle. Western farmers had been charged with seeking to avoid their honest debts; they had replied by asserting that the money they borrowed had been made by the printing presses of the Bank under government authority. Now Jackson embodied their theories and vehemence in a message. If there was any frosty philosopher present, looking serenely upon the battle, he has left us no memoirs.

In the election of 1832, after a campaign of unrestrained emotions, Jackson completely discomfited his opponent, Clay, and returned to the White House like a Roman conqueror with his victims at his chariot. The Bank had fought him; thinking in terms of war, the President proceeded to fight back. Its charter had four years of legal life remaining; the law could not be repealed by military decree; so other means of attack were found. Acting as head of the administration, Jackson ordered the Secretary of the Treasury to deposit no more federal revenues in the Bank or any of its branches and to withdraw in the payment of bills the government's cash already in its vaults. Besides this he distributed the national funds among state banks, remembering to reward those which had correct political affiliations—institutions which became known as "pet banks." As the treasury surplus happened to be mounting, Congress, now in Democratic hands, got rid of it by spreading the money among the state governments, nominally in the form of loans, practically in the shape of gifts.

In 1836 the second United States Bank automatically came to the end of its checkered career and the country under the inspiration of the new democracy entered an epoch of "wild cat" finance. The very next year, a terrible business depression fell like a blight upon the land, bringing as usual more suffering to farmers and mechanics than to the "rich and well-born"; but this calamity was likewise attributed by the masses to the machinations of the money power rather than to the conduct of their hero, President Jackson. Nothing would induce them to retrace their steps. For three decades a union of the South and West prevented a restoration of the centralized banking system. Not until the planting statesmen withdrew from Congress and the storm of the Civil War swept minor gusts before it were the ravages wrought by Jackson repaired by the directors of affairs in Washington.

§

The economic policies and personal conduct of Jackson split wide the Republican party of Jefferson and put a sudden term to the era of good feeling. No President had ever exercised such high perogatives as Jackson or shown so little consideration for the feelings of those who came under executive displeasure. Besides keeping the entire body of minor civil servants in constant terror of reprimand and dismissal, he treated his own Cabinet with scant courtesy, while deciding vital questions himself or with the advice of his backstairs coterie. When one Secretary of the Treasury refused to remove the deposits from the Bank on executive order, Jackson summarily appointed another; when the second also declined to be a mere tool, he chose a third, who finally did his bidding with the alacrity of an errand boy. Angered by a protest lodged by the Senate against his arbitrary conduct, Jackson made his followers force through a measure expunging the hated resolution, one of the lieutenants in flushed exultation blotting the censure from the records. Unawed by the majesty of the Supreme Court, Jackson treated the decisions of Chief Justice Marshall with little respect; and when death eventually removed that distinguished judge from the bench, the President put in Marshall's place Roger B. Taney, an able and astute politician who was known to favor state banking.

In faithful accord with the law of antithesis, the personality and measures of Jackson summoned into being an angry, if motley, opposition. His assault on the Bank aroused the undying hatred of high finance. His approval of a tariff that meant ultimately a material reduction in the protective features set most of the manufacturers fiercely against him. His efforts to stir up "the humble members of society—farmers, mechanics, and laborers," to repeat his phrase—against the "rich and powerful" had worried thousands of prosperous people in the South, especially cautious planters who thought they had as much to fear from the leveling passions of small farmers in the back country as from the tariffs of New England mill owners. In South Carolina they had an additional reason for opposing Jackson for he had talked in a high and mighty fashion of suppressing "insurrection" and hanging "traitors."

Here then were the elements for a powerful political combination if some process of welding could be discovered. Doubtless Jackson's enemies owned the major portion of the working capital of the country. Certainly they commanded oratory and ingenuity; but, as yet united merely by common antipathy to the President and his party—by the timidity of property in the presence of unfathomable dangers—they presented no solid array for a political contest. Only statecraft of the highest order could amalgamate nullifiers and nationalists, protectionists and free traders, planters and manufacturers into a working association. Only skill in appealing to popular imagination could convince the mass of voters that the great hope could be realized at last.

Nevertheless the task was worth while for many reasons and Henry Clay of Kentucky seemed fated for leadership in the undertaking. All things considered, Clay had several kinds of availability: he was from the West and so could invade Jackson's home province; he was favorably known among the manufacturers and financiers of the East but, unlike Webster, was not charged with being the pet and pensioner of capitalists. Though a facile speaker, he had not hopelessly committed himself in his school days to the ponderous periods of Cicero; while he could at times soar to the empyrean, he was always able to talk to the public in the vernacular.

Taking the title abandoned by Jackson, opponents of that popular hero called themselves "National Republicans" and later "Whigs," for short, after the manner of the English adversaries of royal prerogative. In 1832, with Clay at their head, they tried to oust the President by employing all the approved methods of politics, including propaganda and social terrorism.

In an imposing phalanx, they marshaled most of the middle classes—friends of the national bank, advocates of sound money, lawyers, merchants, manufacturers, businessmen of the higher ranges, and college professors. Managers of the Bank subsidized the press by large payments for advertising. Mill owners threatened workmen with dismissal in case Jackson was elected. A packer in Cincinnnati told the farmers that he would pay $2.50 a hundred for pork if Clay was victorious and a dollar less if his opponent, the Democratic President, was returned to power in Washington.

And purists attacked Jackson in their especial field. Since his system of theology was about as nebulous as his politics, they charged him with irreligion. They accused him of beginning a long journey from the Hermitage on a Sabbath and he only escaped the serious censure of the virtuous by showing that he really started on Monday. When he declined to proclaim a day of prayer for relief from the cholera, suggesting instead that under the Constitution it was a matter for the states to decide, Clay pounced upon him for his impiety and moved a resolution in the Senate to name the day for the appeal to God. During the campaign the voters were not allowed to forget that impiety and unsound finance went hand in hand. And still all the legions and all the artillery could not defeat the hero of New Orleans.

§

After ruling the country with an iron hand for eight years, supported by the acclaim of the masses, Jackson naturally regarded the choice of his successor as a part of his sovereign prerogative. Indeed at the opening of his first administration, he had made it known discreetly that he wanted his Secretary of State, Martin Van Buren of New York, to take his place when he left the White House. Obedient to his lightest wish, his kitchen companions bent their efforts to the task of securing the throne for the "crown prince" and their labors were successful.

In a well-selected convention, "fresh from the people," they nominated Van Buren as the party candidate for the presidential election of 1836. By this time the Jacksonians had discarded the safe old title of Republican, chosen by Jefferson, and had taken instead the flaunting label, "Democrat"—a word that once had grated as harshly on urbane ears as its constant companion, "anarchist." Subject to the law of familiarity, the insignia that had frightened grand gentlemen and fine ladies of the heroic days had become a household emblem; men who shrank from it with horror two decades before now wore it proudly on their shields.

Though they had in Van Buren a less formidable candidate to face, the Whigs, failing to unite on a single leader, went down to defeat. But just when everything seemed hopeless, the tide turned. The victorious President fell into a series of misfortunes that gave heart to his enemies. On the threshold of his administration, he encountered a disastrous business panic, the wild tumult of speculation and inflation ending in an explosion. While Jackson's war on high finance had doubtless hastened the inexorable, it was not the sole cause of the crash.

The fact was that one of the periodic cycles of capitalism was at hand and the party in power at Washington could offer no effective remedies, if any there were. On the contrary, it accelerated the ruinous process by repealing the law which provided for the distribution of surplus federal revenues among the state treasuries and by issuing the specie circular which directed federal officers to accept only gold and silver, save in certain cases, in payment for public lands. Having taken these precautions in the interest of its credit, the government simply allowed the winds to blow. Hundreds of banks failed; mills were shut down; work on canals and railways was stopped; thousands of laboring people were turned into the streets; federal revenues fell until a deficit supplanted a surplus; land sales dropped off; and speculation came to a standstill.

Throughout this panic President Van Buren maintained a kind of academic composure. As the leader of Jacksonian Democracy, he could do nothing that would please business men and financiers anyway; and his party had no constructive plan of its own. He, therefore, contented himself with urging the establishment of an independent treasury to receive and guard the funds of the federal government—a simple project of doubtful merit which Congress, after three years of discussion, finally adopted in 1840.

§

At that moment another presidential campaign was at hand. Whigs were making ready to restore Hamilton's system of economy; and Democrats to destroy the last vestiges of the "money power." Astute Whig leaders, counting heads, saw that they would have to be clever if they were to overcome the multitudinous Jacksonian host made up of farmers and mechanics with some of the planters in the vanguard. Accordingly they exercised the wisdom of serpents. They cast aside Clay, whose views on the Bank, tariff, and other economic questions were too well known and beat the Democrats at their own game, by themselves nominating a western farmer and military hero, General William Henry Harrison.

This man of Mars was, of course, no Napoleon comparable to the great Jackson of New Orleans, but he had beaten some Indians at the battle of Tippecanoe and had served with honor in the War of 1812. More than that, at the close of his military career, he had pleased western agrarians by settling down in a modest home in Ohio, To make his appeal perfect in the eyes of Whig managers, Harrison's political opinions were so hazy that no one could be alienated by them.

It was with an eye to such qualifications for the presidency that the shrewd Biddle, tutored by his experience with Jackson, gave sound direction to party managers in this style: "If Genl. Harrison is taken up as a candidate, it will be on account of the past. . . . Let him say not one single word about his principles, or his creed—let him say nothing—promise nothing. Let no Committee, no convention —no town meeting ever extract from him a single word about what he thinks now or will do hereafter. Let the use of pen and ink be wholly forbidden."

Conjuring with this spirit, the Whigs of 1840 refused to frame any platform of principles, and simply offered General Harrison to the country as a man of the people while they attacked Van Buren as an eastern aristocrat. In this fashion the tables were reversed: the old party of Tiberius Gracchus was trying to elect a patrician from New York, whereas the party of the rich and well-born was trying to elevate a Cincinnatus straight from the furrow.

Given these factors, the campaign of 1840 was naturally exuberant. Sobered by the possession of power and led by a man who loved good wine and old silver, symbols of aristocracy, Democrats softened their former raucous campaign cries. But the Whigs, made desperate by two defeats, took up the discarded tactics of their opponents. As a party they adopted no policies, avowed no doctrines. Carlyle's "magnificent" Webster assumed the fustian of the demagogue, announcing that he was ready to engage in a fist-fight with anyone who dubbed him an aristocrat, expressing deep regret that he too had not been born in a log cabin, and rejoicing that his older brothers and sisters had begun their lives in such a humble abode. "If I am ever ashamed of it," he boasted, "may my name and the name of my posterity be blotted from the memory of mankind!" That fastidious New York lawyer, William H. Seward, rode ostentatiously about in an old green farm wagon making speeches at crossroads villages on the superlative merits of the hero of Tippecanoe. The rank and file erected in every town of importance log cabins from which hard cider was served in copious draughts to stimulate the enthusiasm of the voters.

Before gaping crowds, Whig orators berated Van Buren as a man addicted to high living and lordly manners, alleging that he even put cologne on his whiskers and was liable to die of the gout before the end of his term, if elected. They accused him of eating from gold plate and declared that he "laced up in corsets such as women in town wear and if possible tighter than the best of them."

Having summarily disposed of Van Buren, the showmen then presented to the enfranchised their own candidate, General Harrison, as a noble old Roman of the West who lived in a hut, worked with his own hands in field and barn, and left his latchstring out hospitably for the wayfaring man. "We've tried your purse-proud lords who love in palaces to shine," they sang. " But we'll have a ploughman President of the Cincinnatus line."

Probably this buffoonery was distasteful to the staid and respectable Whigs of the East. In any event, since it was not as unpalatable as a low tariff and an unsound currency, they swallowed the medicine of the campaign in the hope of better times after the election. What else could they do? Whatever their pains, the returns from the polls afforded them abundant consolation. Harrison won 234 electoral votes while Van Buren limped in with sixty.

§

After carrying the country in a dust storm, the Whig leaders soon revealed their inmost desires. If Harrison had not died shortly after his inauguration leaving his high office to the Vice President, John Tyler, they might have gone far on the way toward a restoration of the Hamilton system. At any rate, with the aid of protectionist Democrats speaking for special constituencies, they were able to push through the tariff act of 1842 raising the customs duties and destroying the compromise measure enacted nine years before. And, had no factional disputes intervened, they might have established a third United States Bank then and there.

Unfortunately for all designs veering in that direction, their two high captains, Tyler in the White House and Clay in the Senate, were looking beyond immediate results to their own possibilities in the coming election. The President, a Virginia man originally taken up by the Whigs to catch southern votes, knew very well how unpalatable were Hamilton's doctrines below the Potomac and he would only approve a national bank of restricted powers. On the other hand, Clay, long associated with financial interests in a practical way, deluded himself into believing that the country was ready for something more thorough. Neither one of the contestants, therefore, did his best to bring about an accommodation; a fight seemed better to them than a truce. So Tyler vetoed two bank bills in succession and Clay, turning back to the tactics of 1832, proposed to submit the issue to the voters at the polls.

As in the first instance, the solemn referendum of 1844 ended in the discomfiture of those who proposed it. Once more the shout of the Democratic masses rose to heaven against "the money power." Its machinations, they alleged, were more tyrannical than ever, citing for proof the increase in tariff duties and the effort to revive the hated Bank. In addition they drew attention to an attempt made in Congress in 1843 to force upon the federal government the assumption of bonds repudiated by a number of states in the late general panic. Though this scheme was not successful, as everybody knew, it furnished to the rural mind conclusive evidence that eastern capitalists and English creditors were trying to make the whole nation pay debts which it had not contracted.

Furthermore, the Whigs were compelled to bear the brunt of a damaging attack on the score that their English sympathies were as strong as those of the Federalists half a century earlier. In 1842 Webster, as Secretary of State, they were reminded, had negotiated with Lord Ashburton, representing England, an agreement relative to the long-disputed boundary of Maine in which he surrendered to Great Britain a large section of land that, under the treaty of 1783 closing the war for independence, appeared to belong to the United States. In spite of the fact that this concession seemed to be the only alternative to war or continual quarreling, the American public was not at all happy with the outcome and Webster felt it necessary to sweeten the pill by spending some money out of the secret service funds of his department to carry on a favorable propaganda through the religious press of Maine. Though the treaty was eventually ratified, it was roundly condemned by discontented Democrats, and especially by the doughty old warrior, Benton, who called it "a shame and an injury"—"a solemn bamboozlement." When the use of public money in creating opinion for the support of the treaty became known through a congressional investigation, the wrath of the Democrats burst all bounds.

An accumulation of forces was certainly menacing the Whigs when the campaign of 1844 approached. Yet, determined to face the economic issues more firmly than in the previous contest, they nominated Clay—a threat which the Democrats answered by choosing as their candidate a friend and neighbor of Jackson, James K. Polk of Tennessee. In the referendum so clearly put the verdict of the voters was emphatic. The party of the Bank, sound money, and high protection was thoroughly routed, in a sweep as decisive as that of 1800 which ousted the Federalists from the national capital. Spokesmen of the planting aristocracy, now alarmed by slavery agitation and deeply concerned over the fate of Texas, were beginning to comprehend that they had more to hope from leadership in a democracy of farmers, mechanics, and laborers in general, than from coöperation with the elements that composed the Whig party in the North.

On the other hand, the Whigs themselves were made dimly aware that the balance of power was shifting into western hands; but it took more defeats to convince them that they could not destroy their foes with Hamilton's weapons alone. Not until 1860 were they able to make an effective union with the western farmers under the traditional name of Republican—the name which Jefferson had chosen in the early days of his party's history and Clay had approved when in 1832 he had christened the Federalist faction anew.

CHAPTER XIII

Westward to the Pacific

BEFORE the western outposts of Jacksonian Democracy, Louisiana and Missouri, had settled down comfortably in the Union a movement was in full swing to carry the Stars and Stripes through the neighboring territory of Mexico to the Pacific. Nothing could check its momentum; neither the protests of New England abolitionists nor the resistance of the Mexicans; neither the torrid heat of the desert nor the ice-bound passes of the mountains. Within a generation it came to a climax in the annexation of Texas, a war with Mexico, the conquest of California, and the adjustment of the Oregon boundary. In the eyes of abolitionists, the drive on Mexico was a slave-owners' plot, a conspiracy against a friendly country, the seizure of "more pens to cram slaves in."

Many incidents lent color to this thesis but the tough web of facts could not be stretched to cover it. There were other economic forces equally potent: the passion of farmers for more land, the lure of continental trade, and the profits of New England traffic in the Pacific Ocean. Besides all that there was an active body of unknown citizens who held several million dollars worth of the debt and land scrip of Texas and looked to the United States for security—a sum which exceeded in value all the slaves in the Lone Star State in 1845.

Neither slavery nor profit explains, however, the whole westward movement. There was Manifest Destiny which covered a multitude of things and was tinged with mystery by the imagination of the esoteric. According to the version of the seers a virile people turned their resolute faces toward the setting sun. Some of them acquired by fair negotiation lawful possessions in Texas; others pierced the desert and crossed the mountains to gather peltries and engage in honest trade. Their rights were scorned and their flag was insulted by incompetent and dishonest Mexican officials. Innocent persons were imprisoned and some were murdered by barbarians. In such circumstances silence was dishonorable, peace a folly, annexation a virtue. Such was the case submitted in the name of Manifest Destiny.

But this shining shield had a reverse side. The nationalist historians of Mexico present a different version of Manifest Destiny. A ruthless and overbearing race of men, greedy for land and trade, respecting no rights or laws which barred their way, deliberately set themselves to the work of despoiling their neighbor. They violated contracts; they intruded themselves into Mexican territory without passports or permits. Their official representatives at the Mexican capital fomented domestic intrigues, attempted to buy for a song what they intended to take by violence, and shrank not from corruption in gaining their ends. American citizens took part in revolutionary movements to overthrow a friendly government; American naval officers seized Mexican ports in time of peace, pulled down the Mexican flag, and hoisted the Stars and Stripes. Finally, Americans raised a revolution in Texas, tore that province away from a peaceful republic, and then made war to get more territory. Such was the Mexican view of the drama.

§

Although in this bitter controversy a judgment satisfactory to both parties can hardly be rendered, a number of pertinent facts force themselves upon the moralist who feels compelled to hold a court of justice and mercy. Above all it is necessary to take account of the state of Mexico during the first half of the nineteenth century. It is the fashion to speak of the "Mexican government," the "Mexican people," and "Mexican policies." Nothing could be more misleading. Such terms, with some show of propriety, may be used in referring to a settled country with a stable government capable of representing the masses; but even in such nations there are wild oscillations—like that which occurred when the United States, repudiating Wilson and the League of Nations, swung abruptly to Harding and isolation. What seems to be perfidy is sometimes a perfectly legitimate change of opinion.

In the case of Mexico during the period of American pressure, the situation was extremely confused. Between 1800 and 1850, Mexico was not an orderly nation with an authoritative government. At the opening of the century it was a province of Spain. In 1810, it became the scene of a war for independence which broke out with volcanic force, raged for seven years through fluctuating fortunes, and ended in suppression. After three years of peace came a renewed uprising which culminated in 1821 in separation from Spain and the establishment of a provisional government.

The next year, a military adventurer, Iturbide, aping the pomp and ceremony of Cæsar, was crowned emperor with the title of Augustus I. In a few turbulent months, he was overthrown and exiled; when he returned he was shot by his former subjects. In 1824, a federal constitution, fashioned on the American model and marked by certain democratic features, was established, followed by five years of comparative peace. But underground went on a lively political intrigue, with the American minister, Joel Poinsett, aiding the liberal faction, until a revolt put a term to his operations.

In 1829, another military leader, Bustamante, rode into power on the shoulders of a conservative clique, only to be ousted, after three years of tenure, by a more efficient disciple of Machiavelli, Santa Anna, an extraordinary person whose adventures for a quarter of a century rivaled the exploits of a Don Quixote. In 1836, a clerical and highly centralized constitution supplanted the fundamental law erected twelve years before, nullifying all the sundry "plans" which had been concocted in the meantime. Within a few months Bustamante was back in the saddle and Santa Anna in revolt.

In four years, the tables were again turned: Santa Anna was on top for another brief hour; and then driven from the country in 1844. But nothing daunted him, neither his defeat by the Texans at San Jacinto in 1836 nor banishment by his countrymen. Returning to Mexico in 1845, with the help of the American government, he put himself in a trice at the head of the army and led it in the war against the country which had so recently befriended him. He even survived the humiliation of disaster at the hands of the American army; driven from Mexico once more, he came back again, set up a dictatorship, and in 1853 assumed the title of "Most Serene Highness." After a short respite he was expelled, only to reappear and live to a ripe old age. Not until 1876 did he pass from the scene.

Whenever there was a stable government in Mexico during these troubled decades, it was usually a tyranny. Whenever popular elements were in power, political and personal disputes distracted the country. The year 1847, which marked the triumph of American arms in Mexico City, saw three presidents in that capital.

To the superficial observer, therefore, the history of Mexico between 1810 and 1850 seemed like a series of disconnected military adventures without rhyme or reason;

but in reality this was not the whole story. There were important elements running through it all with a fair degree of consistency. A province was struggling desperately to shake off the grip of Spain and to find itself. Indian peons, serfs bound to the soil, were waging a peasants' war against feudal lords, lay and clerical, most of whom were of Spanish origin; a clergy and aristocracy were playing their historic rôles; a small but active middle class, dallying with incendiary doctrines of liberty, democracy, and self-government, had taken up arms against feudal and ecclesiastical privileges; military adventurers, akin to those who filled Europe with tumult for a thousand years after the dissolution of the Pax Romana, were making the most of a crumbling order. Yet in the midst of the discord, there were demonstrations of national pride; domestic quarrels were hushed in the presence of the Northern Eagle.

The theater in which this drama was staged was vast in extent. Reaching from the boundaries of Guatemala on the south, it spread out like a great fan to the borders of Louisiana on the northeast and to the Pacific and the towering mountains of Upper California on the northwest. In 1810 it was inhabited by about six million Indians, pure and mixed in blood, and sixty thousand people of Spanish origin, nearly all concentrated in the region now embraced within the republic of Mexico. A quarter of a century later when the American drive really began, there were approximately only three thousand Mexicans of Spanish origin in Texas and four thousand in California, a mere handful of people composed mainly of priests and monks congregated at the missions, soldiers nominally engaged in keeping order among the subject Indians, and large landowners and cattle raisers.

As may be imagined, the government of these widely scattered settlers between 1810 and 1845 was feeble, erratic, and fitful—presidents and dictators and congresses appearing and disappearing in agitations that shook Mexico from center to circumference. A policy adopted by one government was repudiated by the next; reforms well conceived in spirit could not be executed for lack of power. Without capital and without stability, harassed by revolutions and debts, Mexico could not develop the resources and trade of the northern empire to which she possessed the title of parchment and seals. More than that, she could not occupy it for the simple reason that she did not have the emigrants for that enterprise.

§

Peering over the borders of this almost empty realm was a restless, hardy, conquering people that had carried the American empire westward with a rush and a roar. Almost from the day when independence was declared, the frontier sentinels of the United States had looked upon all the territory from the Mississippi to the Pacific as their property, at least in the process of becoming; as the Germans would say, *im Begriff zu werden*. The happy purchase of Louisiana, in their opinion, only confirmed the inevitable.

When in the Florida-purchase treaty of 1819 John Q. Adams, as Secretary of State, accepted the Sabine River, instead of the Rio Grande, as the western boundary of Louisiana, they thought that their interests had been betrayed by a narrow-minded aristocrat of the New England seaboard. "I will never accept it," blurted out Senator Benton, the agricultural imperialist of Missouri. Clay likewise denounced the surrender of Texas and Jackson favored action on it as soon as eastern opinion could be reconciled to "further change." We must "get the Texas country back" whenever it can be done "with peace and honor"—this was the statesman's way of saying "at the inexorable moment."

While the ink was still wet on the Florida treaty fixing the boundary of Louisiana at the Sabine River, the first phase of the westward movement opened. In 1821 Moses Austin, a Connecticut Yankee, who had made and lost a fortune in Benton's state, secured through the governor of

Texas, then a province of New Spain, a huge grant of land on which to establish three hundred families—"honest, industrious farmers and mechanics," Catholic in religion, and willing to take the oath of allegiance to the Spanish monarch. Before he could execute his contract, however, death blocked his project and the task fell to the lot of his high-spirited heir, Stephen F. Austin. After surveying the ground, the enterprising son chose a spot for his colony not far from San Antonio and there founded a thriving American settlement composed of people drawn mainly from Tennessee, Mississippi, and Louisiana. To make sure of his property rights, Austin obtained a confirmation from the government of Mexico, which had now declared its independence from Spain.

Austin's grant was followed by similar concessions to other impresarios, Mexican, American, English, Scotch, and Irish, until substantially all of Texas was parceled out among adventurers who promised to bring in colonists of good character and Catholic faith, willing to swear allegiance to the Mexican republic. Americans, many of them slave-owners, now streamed over the border, some to develop grants, others without titles or claims, in search of land and fortune. Although a few lawless individuals from the frontier joined in the rush, most of the immigrants were industrious, energetic, and God-fearing men and women bent on establishing communities of the American type. Within ten years there were about twenty thousand people in Texas; a decade under American direction had brought more settlers than three hundred years of Spanish administration. To the rulers at Mexico City that was an alarming fact and when it was too late they tried to close the floodgates at the Texas border.

Far away on the Pacific coast another American invasion had begun without the formality of land grants and official permits. In 1796, a merchantman from New England, with the American ensign snapping at the masthead, careened around the Horn, up along the coast, and into Monterey.

In the wake of this pioneer ship, other vessels quickly followed, establishing at favorable ports lively markets for eastern manufactures. Beads, knives, gunpowder, cotton goods, pottery, and rum were traded for furs; the furs were carried to Canton; and Chinese merchandise received in return was taken back to Boston, New York, and Philadelphia. On a single expedition sometimes huge fortunes were made. One captain in a few hours collected 560 otter skins in exchange for goods that cost him less than two dollars and sold the lot in Canton for $22,400. Another Yankee bartered six hundred yards of cheap cotton cloth for a bale of peltries worth nearly seven thousand dollars in China.

Though Spanish law, and later, Mexican law, forbade foreigners to trade along the Pacific coast, American business enterprise, stimulated by reports of such alluring profits, could not be stayed. Both the theory and the fact of the local trade-monopoly, it is just to say, varied widely with the fortunes of the government in the distant city of Mexico and neither the Californians nor the visiting American merchants paid much attention to the nice technicalities of the situation. At all events commerce flourished in spite of exclusive laws and blustering officials, linking by the mystic cords of interest the Atlantic seaboard with far places on the Pacific. All the visible benefits of Manifest Destiny were not in Texas.

As long, however, as this traffic was limited to the sea, there seemed to be no hidden eventualities in it, at least to the Mexican officials in California; for when they thought of the long voyage around the Horn, they acquired a false sense of security. But just as they were about to settle down to an enjoyment of their domain, they heard a lusty knock at their eastern portals; intrepid American traders shrinking from the perils of the stormy sea had braved the dangers of parched deserts, frosty mountains, and hostile Indians to reach them in another way. While Stephen Austin was busy with projects in Texas, in November, 1826,

Jedidiah Smith, a fur trader of Yankee extraction, appeared at the door of the San Gabriel mission in southern California with a party of trappers. Without asking the permission of the Mexican governor or paying any heed to passport formalities, he had come overland from St. Louis in search of precious peltries. Indifferent to the curt reception accorded him, this dauntless Smith defiantly tramped the West for a decade or more, exploring the San Joaquin and Sacramento Valleys, cutting a way from California to Oregon, and advertising the virtues of the country to his fellow citizens "back East."

The dike being breached, the trickle stole in, followed by the flood. In 1829, Ewing Young opened a trade route from Santa Fé. Twelve years later an organized expedition of American settlers, under the leadership of John Bidwell, literally staggered across desert and mountain, dogged by thirst and hunger, into the fertile San Joaquin Valley. By this time the word had gone forth: Richard H. Dana's Two Years Before the Mast, articles by Hall Kelley, and letters by innumerable travelers were advertising the Pacific coast to the East. The land was good and fair to look upon; American editors said the United States must possess it; and the federal government became much interested. Under official auspices, John C. Frémont made two expeditions overland to California in 1842-5, explaining when questioned by the Mexican governor that his interest was purely scientific; yet it happened that an American army officer was opportunely on the ground to give assistance in the conquest of California when destiny struck the hour.

§

In fact, while American farmers and planters were rushing into Texas, while New England sea captains were garnering the trade of California, while pioneers were breaking the land routes to the Pacific, the State Department at Washington was very much on the alert—watching for an occasion to follow economic penetration by political dominion. A few weeks after Adams was inaugurated President in 1825, his Secretary of State, Clay, wrote to the American minister in Mexico, Poinsett, instructing him to begin negotiation for the purchase of Texas, a commission which Poinsett would have gladly fulfilled if he had been able to make headway against the suspicious government to which he was accredited.

When, to his surprise, Poinsett was recalled for interfering in the domestic politics of Mexico, President Jackson, then at the American helm, selected as his successor a hardy land speculator of the southwest, Anthony Butler, and instructed him to open operations with a view to acquiring first Texas and then California. Now Butler was scarcely the man to carry out such an undertaking with tact and taste. In more respects than one, his character was deficient, Jackson himself being finally forced to confess that Butler was a "liar" and a "scamp," and Sam Houston writing him down a "swindler and gambler." In a final verdict on the point, a modern historian, Justin H. Smith, after flaying with a good deal of justice the Mexicans with whom Butler negotiated, remarks calmly of the American minister: "He was a national disgrace . . . personally a bully and a swashbuckler, ignorant at first of the Spanish language and even the forms of diplomacy, shamefully careless about legation affairs, wholly unprincipled as to methods, and by the open testimony of two American consuls openly scandalous in conduct."

Shortly after Butler's arrival in Mexico City, the local press announced that he had come to buy Texas, spreading alarm among the politicians and patriots of Mexico. Beyond question, the rumor was well founded—an American "trial balloon"; for, as a matter of fact, Jackson had instructed Butler to purchase Texas, after coolly warning the Mexican government that the Americans on the spot "will declare themselves independent of Mexico the moment they acquire sufficient numbers." Since suavity was not a strong point with Butler, this threat tied to an offer to buy failed to land the prize. But, determined not to be balked by any superficial propriety, Butler turned to bribery, proposing to Jackson that several hundred thousand dollars be spent in inducing Mexican officials to sell Texas to the Americans.

When Jackson received this astounding suggestion, he expressed surprise that Butler had not sent it in cipher and declared that bribery was far from his intention of course. In guarded diplomatic language the President then informed the expectant minister that the United States would not undertake to control the distribution of the purchase money among persons in Mexico who had held land grants in Texas, warning him in the same breath to give "these shrewd fellows no ground to charge you with any tampering with officers to obtain the cession through corruption."

Undismayed by the bribery hint, Jackson, after allowing Butler to come to Washington to discuss the matter in person, sent him back to Mexico City with orders to buy California as well as Texas. Failing in this mission, the high-handed minister then baldly advised the President to seize some of the coveted territory by force. That was too much for Old Hickory and, writing on the back of the letter, "What a scamp!" he called Butler home to final obscurity. Whatever may be said about the character of the Mexican officials, humor, if not respect for diplomacy, suggested drawing the veil over the American minister.

§

What negotiation failed to accomplish, the march of events consummated. While countless notes were being exchanged by the governments of the United States and Mexico, the state of Texas was slipping away from the Mexican republic as rumors of Austin's colonizing scheme flew far and wide, even crossing the Atlantic, and arousing the cupidity of English, Irish, and Scotch adventurers. During all the diplomatic wrangling, the offices of administration in Mexico City were jammed with promoters begging and wringing huge grants of land from men none too scrupulous. Few, it seems, were turned away. Within little more than a decade practically the whole of Texas had been distributed among land contractors, the names of Austin, Beale, Williams, Cameron, McMullin, McGloine, Whelin, Zavalla, and Felisola being mingled with strange profusion in the land records of the Mexican capital and written large on the map of Texas.

All these contractors, regardless of their real motive, undertook to import a given number of families in return for a certain acreage. Under official seal, they bound themselves to bring in people of good repute—Catholic in religion and prepared to profess allegiance to the Mexican republic. Having secured their grants and made their pledges, the promoters then issued notes or scrip representing claims to holdings of various amounts, hoping by advertisements and the sale of paper rights to secure immigrants or at least to make a profit out of the "deal."

In this fashion the news of activities in Texas spread all the way from New Orleans to Boston, as Texas scrip flooded the country. In the "fabulous forties" ancestors of people who were long afterwards to buy oil stocks with savage avidity bought up land notes at a few cents on the dollar in the firm conviction that the federal government would aid in realizing on the risks. Their fever penetrated other countries; stories of the New El Dorado flew over the sea to Dublin, London, and Edinburgh, attracting to Texas streams of immigrants from all quarters. By 1835 there were more than twenty thousand invaders in that flourishing province—hardy farmers, lordly planters, droves of slaves, hunters, adventurers, and outlaws. Great events were impending.

Frightened by the diplomacy of Jackson and alarmed at the swarms of aliens crossing the border, the officials at Mexico City drew back in dismay. When it was too late they tried to recover their passing dominion with laws and proclamations which only advanced "the day" by arousing more opposition among the American settlers in Texas and among the holders of scrip everywhere. In 1829, a decree of the Mexican government abolished slavery; but a vigorous protest from American settlers compelled it to exempt Texas from the operation of the order.

About the same time a reactionary revolution put Bustamante in the saddle, swept away the liberal constitution of 1824, and forcibly united the two states of Texas and Coahuila, evoking from the Americans on the spot an angry outcry. Not yet submissive to events, the Mexican government then forbade the importation of slaves, required immigrants to present passports, ordered the expulsion of squatters who could not show lawful titles to their lands, and tentatively abrogated all the land contracts which had not been fulfiled by the promoters, thereby bringing distress to the hearts of land speculators scattered from the banks of the Brazos to the banks of the Thames.

On top of this combustible material was thrown a quarrel over taxation—always a sore point with the Anglo-Saxon. In 1831, on the expiration of an agreement exempting colonists from duties on certain imports for a period of seven years, Mexican officials proceeded in due form to collect taxes according to schedule—in a peremptory and irregular manner, the Americans alleged—stirring wrath from Natchidoches to San Antonio. Finally, as if defying fate, Santa Anna, acting in his capacity as dictator, denied the petition of Texas for separate statehood. Immediately, the Sam Adamses and the Patrick Henrys of the southwest went into caucus. Nothing but a match was needed again to fire the powder train and spring the mine.

This little spark was furnished by Colonel William B. Travis, an impetuous American, who, against the wishes of the more conservative elements in Texas, organized a small force, made an attack on the hated customs office, and expelled the Mexican revenue collector, bag and baggage. Following this ominous action, a number of Americans took the side of a Mexican adventurer in a revolutionary assault on Tampico with the object of unhorsing Santa Anna. From this it was but a step to open resistance. By the advocates of self-government, an appeal was made to friends in the United States for money and men; a declaration of local autonomy was issued in November, 1835; before two months had passed the last Mexican soldier had been driven across the border; and early the next year the independence of Texas was formally proclaimed.

Though torn by internal dissensions, the government of Mexico could not overlook these acts of defiance. Placing himself at the head of experienced troops, Santa Anna swept northward "to restore order." For a time fortune seemed to be with him, for the first clashes resulted in victories, such as they were. In March, 1836, a small band of Texans, embattled under Colonel Travis in the Alamo at San Antonio, was utterly destroyed in one of the most desperate struggles ever waged on the American continent. A few days later another group of Texans, three hundred and fifty in number, was overwhelmed by a superior force and shot in cold blood, an act of cruelty which the Mexicans tried to defend as "justice meted out to traitors."

This deed proved to be their undoing, for the Texans were now thoroughly aroused and strongly united. Under General Sam Houston, their little army of independence fell upon Santa Anna on the banks of the San Jacinto River. With the shout "Remember the Alamo!" and in a tumultuous rush, they carried everything by storm, killing nearly half the Mexican army and capturing most of the foemen who escaped the sword, including Santa Anna himself. In their fury the avenging Texans demanded the life of the Mexican commander but in the end Houston saved him from the firing squad, wrung from him an official recognition of Texan independence, and then sent him under escort into the United States.

Having cleared their soil of Mexican soldiers and taken their place "among the independent nations of the earth," the Texans turned with eager expectancy to the United States, hoping for admission to the Union. Among the statesmen of the South they met cordial sympathy. They had assured the planting interest by writing in their constitution one clause forbidding the legislature to prohibit the importation of slaves by immigrants from the United States and another clause forbidding it ever to proclaim a general liberation of bondmen. So the answer to the Texan overture was emphatic in the South: Mississippi, Alabama, and Tennessee by solemn resolution called upon Congress to admit the Lone Star State to the Union.

The Texans also had a sympathizer in Jackson, the trusted friend of their own president, General Sam Houston; but Jackson, though personally willing, acted cautiously. A national campaign was on in 1836, the Whig opposition in the Senate was too formidable to be flouted, and mustering a two-thirds vote in favor of a treaty of annexation was clearly impossible. Consequently Jackson left the White House without adding Texas to his beloved Union.

For years after Jackson's retirement, the country was agitated over the question of annexation. Mild critics of slavery protested against it. Abolitionists raged with all their might. "I trust, indeed," exclaimed William E. Channing, "that Providence will beat back and humble our cupidity and ambition. I now ask whether as a people we are prepared to seize on a neighboring territory to the end of extending slavery? I ask whether as a people we can stand forth in the sight of God, in the sight of nations, and adopt this atrocious policy? Sooner perish! Sooner our name be blotted out from the record of nations!" With a shout of defiance, William Lloyd Garrison called for the secession of the northern states if Texas came into the Union with her slaves. Recalling his classical studies, John Quincy Adams prophesied the fate of imperial Rome as the just doom of imperial America. Even conservative men who did not condemn slavery trembled at the thought of reopening the bitter dispute that had been closed, they thought, by the Missouri Compromise of 1820.

Amid this tempest of opposition, southern champions of annexation pursued their course with fixed resolution. To them it at last offered security for their peculiar institution against the overwhelming predominance of the free states. Texas was an empire in itself; four or five large commonwealths could be carved out of its generous expanse and given eight or ten United States Senators to balance the representatives from Michigan, Wisconsin, Iowa, and other free states as they arrived one after another upon the floor of the upper chamber. If that project could be realized, the North might have the House of Representatives, it could not enact into law any economic policies detrimental to the planting interest as long as the South possessed equality in the Senate.

To the watchful Calhoun annexation, carrying with it these implications, promised the only guarantee for the perpetuity of the Constitution. Little did he dream that the action which he fondly imagined could save the Union and slavery would in reality reopen the sectional controversy, precipitate a civil conflict, and end in the destruction of chattel bondage itself. So dim is the vision of the wisest of statesmen! So far astray do the calculations of the learned and the great lead them! That which the planting interest thought would save slavery helped to destroy it. That which ardent abolitionists fancied would fasten slavery upon the country forever hastened emancipation.

Though the planters were easily won by the delusive argument that proved to be their destruction, they were not strong enough in Congress to carry the annexation of Texas. It was necessary to win votes above the Potomac where abolitionists were thundering against it day and night, where there seemed to be no powerful economic support for the addition of distant territory, nothing to appeal to save the showy doctrine of Manifest Destiny. But appearances were deceptive. In reality there were also in the North substantial forces working in favor of annexation—forces having in view more immediate, direct, and tangible gains than those offered to the planting interests of the South.

In the financial sections of every large community, quantities of Texas scrip were afloat, as we have seen. In New York City, for example, three land companies, organized to buy claims of doubtful validity, had issued stocks to a gullible public. With these stocks ran current a deep suspicion that the authorities of Mexico would never accept the claims as lawful and that a revolution ending in the establishment of a stable government in Texas under American auspices would be necessary to put profits into the pockets of those who purchased such wild-cat paper. This was likewise true with respect to many other forms of speculative land securities which passed from hand to hand in the North. In a word, the independence of Texas, the admission of Texas to the Union, and the confirmation of acquired land rights were essential to realizing the inflated hopes founded on an immense volume of paper scattered around through the United States.

Even more important in this momentous contest perhaps was the huge quantity of bonds and notes floated by the republic of Texas after its declaration of independence. Like the United States at the beginning of the American Revolution, it had been started on paper. On paper it tried to survive, its finances growing steadily worse from year to year. In 1838, its secretary of the treasury reported an outstanding debt of $1,886,425; in 1841 he dolefully admitted that the expenditures for the year had been $1,176,288 and the receipts only $442,604; by 1845 the treasury was in complete chaos, the debt being then variously reckoned from $7,000,000 to $12,000,000. Every day the paper sank lower, to the dismay of those who held it; bonds and notes drawing eight per cent interest were selling on the streets of the capital at a price as low as three cents on the dollar.

Suddenly these securities appeared in many parts of the United States. Having subscribed to the first loans floated to finance the Texas revolution, Americans bought blocks of subsequent issues emitted to sustain it. Speculators in Texas acquired a large quantity at ridiculous figures and sent it flying across the border in all directions, into the Mississippi valley and to New York by steamer. There was no enigma in this. It was obvious to everybody who held any of the vagrant paper or knew anything about the failing security behind it that the annexation of Texas and the stabilization of its finances could alone prevent its bonds and notes from becoming worthless, destroying real values as well as potential profits for the holders.

How widespread was the influence of the speculators in Texas paper cannot be estimated with any degree of exactness, for the distribution of the bonds and notes is not known. We have, however, the testimony of Jay Cooke, the financier of the Civil War, on this point. He was associated, during the Texan controversy, with a Philadelphia banking house that later handled the government's fiscal business during the Mexican War, and, therefore, in a position to speak with no little authority. And according to his careful biographer, E. P. Oberholtzer, who had access to the family papers, "Mr. Cooke always believed that the northern opposition in Congress to the addition of this large slave territory to the national domain was overcome through the selfish exertions in their own interest of the holders of the Texas debt certificates, many of whom were influential northern men."

That this economic pressure was far-reaching became signally evident in 1850 during the congressional debate on the bill adjusting the boundary between Texas and New Mexico —a measure carrying an indemnity to Texas of $10,000,000 to be applied in part on her debt. The very introduction of the indemnity project swept the price of Texas bonds upward from four or five cents on the dollar to fifty cents. Amid great excitement the Senate passed the bill with alacrity and all was going smoothly when suddenly, to the agony of interested parties, the House of Representatives defeated it.

Then came a motion for reconsideration which, after many days of hard work, was carried with a "loud cry of exultation." On the day the vote was finally taken on the bill, lobbyists pressed around the desks of the Representatives in such force that one of the members asked for their removal from the floor, remarking drily that Texas bondholders could see and hear as well from the galleries. According to Joshua R. Giddings, a congressman from Ohio, three million dollars worth of the paper was afloat in Washington at the time and members were offered as much as fifty thousand dollars apiece for their votes. Though this was possibly a mere surmise, there was no doubt that the depreciated bonds and scrip played an important part in the movement for annexation of Texas from her declaration of independence in 1836 to her admission to the Union.

§

In the decade which followed the independence of Texas, while the planting interest, the speculative interest, the land interest, and Manifest Destiny were preparing the way for annexation, both diplomacy and immigration were swinging California into the American orbit. By 1840 Mexican occupation of that vast province was merely a shadow on the land. The entire army in control did not exceed five hundred regular soldiers, scattered among half a dozen presidios; while no serious pretensions were made at ruling the region north of San Francisco Bay. The weak and changing government at Mexico City, far removed from the scene and confining its activities mainly to passing messages to and fro once or twice a year, could not possibly administer the province efficiently or restrain the foreign invaders who came from every direction. It could issue decrees but it could not enforce them. It could awaken opposition and revolt but could not crush them. At no time could it count on much local support.

As a matter of fact there was little available, for the country, besides being far away, was sparsely settled. Within its borders were only a few tiny towns—San Diego, Los Angeles, Monterey, and Yerba Buena on the site of present-day San Francisco—and the trade in their markets was almost entirely in the hands of Americans. Sprawling over the intervening stretches were the estates of Spanish grandees, vast, uncultivated, and unprofitable dominions. Here and there were old Spanish missions which once had been the seats of prosperous economic life under the direction of shrewd and competent managers, but even they had now sunk into decay because the lands had been secularized in 1834 and bought up by Mexican adventurers and American merchants. In short, California was a wide-open province awaiting the drive of a virile, active, organizing people while all over the United States were restless persons reading about the distant El Dorado in innumerable pamphlets, books, and inspired newspaper articles.

So the great American migration commenced. In May, 1841, a party of men, women, and children, under the leadership of John Bidwell, "the prince of California pioneers," set out from Missouri to the promised land. Compared to the trials and sufferings endured by this party on its tedious journey of six months, the hardships of the voyagers in the *Mayflower* seem positively slight. The colonial Pilgrims were in the hands of good sailors who knew the sea and the stars and were at home on the wide ocean paths. The Bidwell adventurers, on the contrary, crossed an almost uncharted continent, their wisest guides knowing little about the route save that it lay in a westerly direction.

For days they toiled through the horrors of the alkaline desert where thirst consumed them and where mirages lured them to agonizing delusions. After terrible experiences they arrived at the mountain wall where, compelled to cast off and abandon their heavy baggage, they soon came face to face with starvation; before they got over the barrier they were so tormented by hunger that a bit of broiled fat from the windpipe of a coyote seemed a rare delicacy. Certainly the events of this path-breaking expedition recorded in the journal left to posterity by Bidwell, though not as celebrated in annals of history as the doings of the Pilgrims immortalized by Bradford, deserve their vivid chapter in the great American epic.

And yet the Bidwell pioneers fared happily as compared with the Donner party that followed them five years later. Starting merrily in the early spring of 1846 also from Missouri, the second band of emigrants crossed the plains and desert without serious mishap; but while they were on their way over the mountains the members of one division were caught in the icy grip of an early winter. Seeing that they could neither go forward nor retrace their steps, they hastily threw up huts of wood and turf against the cutting blasts and towering snow drifts.

In these wretched shanties, men, women, and children huddled for months; all food failed them except oxhide soup and pounded bones; some of them were driven in their indescribable misery to eat the flesh of their dead. Recoiling from this abyss of madness, nine men and six women made a desperate dash across the snow-bound mountains. Two men and five women, overcoming the perils of the journey, at last carried the tale of horror to the settlements of California. Immediately volunteers sprang to the rescue, scaled the mountains and brought the survivors at the camp on to safety. Of the seventy-nine who wintered in the huts of death, forty-five endured the terrible ordeal—among whom were women with children at their breasts. In the middle of a cabin the rescue party found only one living inhabitant, a breathing skeleton, surrounded by nameless horror, disordered in mind, and evidently guilty of awful deeds that made him an outcast in Sacramento Valley to the end of his days.

If anyone had doubts about the latent powers of civilized women, their fierce will to live, their resolution in the presence of the jungle's law, their heroism when faced by seemingly impossible choices, and their capacity to bring from the unfathomed deeps of their nature resources for unexpected trial, he found a new version of humanity in the story of the Donner migration. Manifest Destiny was in the hands of people with unbreakable will and an unyielding courage.

§

While events were bringing California into the American sphere, diplomacy was searching for sanction. The records do not disclose the name of the statesman who first thought of the maneuvre, but it is certain that President Jackson fully appreciated it. He knew the West and was imperial in temper. As we have said, he instructed the American minister in Mexico City to secure California in connection with the purchase of Texas. At a later date, he also encouraged the agent of Texas in Washington to hope for stronger support from the United States in case California could be added by some procedure to the empire of the Lone Star State, thinking no doubt that this would make annexation more palatable to the shipowners and merchants of Philadelphia, New York, and Boston. It would assure them trading bases and good harbors on the western coast, helping to unite capitalists and planters in a common enterprise. Though the idea had force, Jackson was compelled by circumstances to leave the White House without executing his expansion program. For the moment enthusiasm waned. Jackson's successor, Van Buren, was lukewarm on the project; at heart he was an opponent of slavery, and he could plead domestic financial troubles as a good reason for inaction in foreign affairs. So four years slipped by without a decision. But when Tyler of Virginia came to the presidency, the tide began to turn. He knew what he wanted, yet, like Jackson, he too had to be cautious in making public gestures; for he had been elected with a Whig candidate to enlist planting support and was compelled to coöperate, nominally at least, with the Whigs. In dealing with Congress, Tyler accordingly chose discretion as the better part of valor.

In the sphere of diplomatic action, however, where the veil of secrecy hid all things, Tyler moved with swiftness and resolution, supported by his efficient Secretary of State, Webster, who was as eager to secure points of support for whaling and the China trade in the Pacific as Calhoun was to get Texas for the planters. Working in perfect harmony, the President and Webster tried to get hold of California. They bombarded the Mexican government with claims, notes, demands, and proposals until the atmosphere was charged with the mysterious electricity of rumor.

The American navy was put on the watch. In fact, one of its officers, Commodore Jones, allowed his wishes to overcome prudence, when, in 1842, in command of a frigate and a sloop, he sailed into Monterey Bay, seized the town, and ran up the Stars and Stripes on the strength of a vague report that war had broken out between Mexico and the United States and that California might be handed over to England. Though Jones pulled down the flag as gracefully as possible when he found his information baseless, the incident had lasting effects. It helped to confirm the Mexicans in their opposition to surrendering California to the United States without a blow. So after Commodore Jones had displayed the mailed fist, diplomacy was more powerless than ever to achieve a peaceful annexation of California.

It was thus made evident that nothing but a crisis could bring down the fruit, and deeds did finally take matters out of the control of the diplomats—a turn in events favored by the drift of affairs on the Coast. As time passed, the military grip of Mexico on California, which had always been weak, steadily relaxed; of the army of occupation now numbering about six hundred, one-half were Mexicans and one-half natives of California, an unpaid, undisciplined, and poorly equipped rabble. On more than one occasion, when a foreign vessel fired a salute of honor in a California harbor, the local Mexican officer had to borrow powder from his visitor to return the greeting. Even more absurd was the Mexican navy in the Pacific, consisting as it did of one weatherbeaten ship, so crazed with age and hard wear that the captain could not sail her against the wind.

While Mexican defenses were collapsing, Americans in California were growing in numbers and influence. They were not long in discovering that a very slight rebellion might cut the thread which bound the province to Mexico and they often took part in factional disputes among the Californians in the hope that good fortune would finally perch on their standards. All they needed was a little encouragement from Washington and shortly after the inauguration of Polk in 1845 they received it.

The new President was scarcely installed when he coolly told his Cabinet that California was to be annexed. To give effect to his plans, he informed the American consul on the Coast that the government of the United States would protect the people of California if they cut loose from Mexico and he authorized that official to use his own discretion in handling local affairs. This suggestion was a keen anticipation of history; the very next year, before the news of the outbreak of war between Mexico and the United States reached the Pacific shore, a handful of adventurous Americans, aided by Captain Frémont, nominally engaged in scientific exploration, raised the standard of revolution—the Bear Flag—and proclaimed the Republic of California. The moment so impatiently awaited by the administration at Washington was at hand.

§

Not long after the Bear Flag was flung to the breeze war began between Mexico and the United States. The crisis had at last been precipitated by the annexation of

Texas. As the sponsors of that project in Washington had never been able to muster the two-thirds majority necessary to carry their treaty through the Senate, they finally grew desperate and resorted to a joint resolution of both houses which called for a mere majority. The conclusion was foregone. In February, 1845, during the closing days of Tyler's administration, Texas was made a part of the American Union by act of Congress. A spark was applied to tinder. Since Mexico had never recognized or accepted the independence of Texas, annexation, as everybody knew, was a signal for the rupture of relations—a step which led the Mexican minister promptly to gather up his papers and go home.

It was at this point that Tyler was succeeded by Polk, of Tennessee, who, we have seen, was bent on adding California to the Texan prize, without war if possible. While Polk was really pacific in temper and hoped to accomplish much without shedding blood, he did not confine his efforts to diplomatic notes. Rather, on coming into office, he made preparations to defend Texas, now a part of the United States, and, as already noted too, told the American consul in California, in effect, that he would be supported if he stirred up a local revolution.

As if to expedite matters, an argument arose with Mexico over a boundary question—out of Texan claims to all the land west and south as far as the Rio Grande and Mexican insistence on fixing the border at the Nueces River and a line drawn in a northerly direction. President Polk felt constrained to accept the Texan view and, not unnaturally, having made his decision, ordered General Zachary Taylor, in command of American forces, forward into the disputed zone. This movement, regarded as an act of defense by Americans, was denounced by Mexicans as a clear invasion of their country. In the spring of 1846, a clash of arms took place, staining the sands of Texas red with blood.

"War exists by act of Mexico!" cried Polk, and his cry was echoed among his followers with interest, Congress quickly responding by declaring its confidence with a vote of men and money for the prosecution of American rights by arms. And yet there was no little opposition among the northern Whigs, some of it sincere and some of it partisan. Abraham Lincoln, then serving his single term in the House of Representatives, lifted his voice against the war, apparently with no other result than to throw away his chances for reëlection. Senator Corwin of Ohio flung out to the presidential party his famous defiance that haunted him until the end of his political career: "If I were a Mexican I would tell you: 'Have you not room in your own country? . . . If you come into mine, we will greet you with bloody hands and welcome you to hospitable graves.' "

On the floor of the House, Corwin's colleague, Joshua R. Giddings, condemned the proceedings as "a war against an unoffending people, without adequate or just cause, for the purpose of conquest; with the design of extending slavery; in violation of the Constitution, against the dictates of justice, humanity, the sentiments of the age in which we live, and the precepts of the religion which we profess. I will lend it no aid, no support whatever. I will not bathe my hands in the blood of the people of Mexico, nor will I participate in the guilt of those murders which have been and will hereafter be committed by our army there. For these reasons I shall vote against the bill under consideration and all others calculated to support the war." Through New England also flowed a strong current of feeling against Polk's policies and measures, the legislature of Massachusetts, for example, overwhelming by a negative vote a proposal to appropriate funds in aid of a regiment raised by Caleb Cushing; while meetings of protest against the war were held in Faneuil Hall.

Angered by action which they deemed seditious, defenders of the administration spared no invective in flaying its critics. Speaking for his Illinois constituents, Stephen A. Douglas declared in the Senate: "America wants no friends, acknowledges the fidelity of no citizen who, after war is declared, condemns the justice of her cause or sympathizes with the enemy. All such are traitors in their hearts; and would to God that they would commit such overt act for which they could be dealt with according to their deserts." A close student of the Constitution, Douglas, even so, had either forgotten his history or could not divine the limitless possibilities of sedition laws. If "the Little Giant of Illinois" had been ingenious enough, James Russell Lowell's Biglow Papers would have landed the author in jail and the men and women who could not see the justice of the American cause would have been given ten or fifteen years behind prison bars in which to meditate upon the mutability of human affairs.

The war thus precipitated by "act of Mexico" was prosecuted with vigor by the United States. General Taylor, already on the frontier with a large body of troops, drove southward into Mexico, winning before the lapse of a year four victories, at Palo Alto, Resaca de la Palma, Monterey, and Buena Vista. Indeed he might have delivered the fatal thrust if politics had not intervened. But Taylor was a Whig and Polk, knowing full well American love for military heroes, was anxious to avoid raising up another victorious commander for the opposition to nominate for the presidency. Besides, good strategy was in harmony with politics—the line held by General Taylor was long and as he marched into the interior he left his base of supplies far in the rear.

So the administration at Washington, deciding to divide the honors, sent a second army under General Scott, also a Whig, by sea to Vera Cruz for the purpose of striking directly at Mexico City. In August, 1847, the project was accomplished: the American army was at the gates of the capital of Mexico. If the government of that republic had possessed any strength, peace would have been quickly concluded, but to yield to humiliating terms was beyond the power of any Mexican authority. Not until battles were fought in the suburbs of the city and the American army marched triumphantly into the Plaza de la Constitución—not until the American general offered protection to the defeated government, threatened by rival factions, could a treaty of peace be signed.

Far away on the California Coast military and naval operations on a smaller scale were completing the work of Manifest Destiny. In June, 1845, months before the conflict with Mexico started, the Secretary of the Navy instructed Commodore Sloat, commander of the American forces in the Pacific, to seize the harbors of California immediately on receipt of news that war had begun. Accordingly, as soon as the instructions arrived in July of the following year, Sloat occupied Monterey without resistance and hoisted the American flag. Coming on the scene a few days later, his successor, Commodore Stockton, took charge of affairs, enrolled the men of Frémont's young republic in the American army, and started the conquest of California, assisted in the operation by a small body of regular soldiers, under General S. W. Kearny, who reached California in December after a toilsome overland journey from Fort Leavenworth by way of Santa Fé. A few sharp clashes, hardly to be characterized as battles, sealed the inevitable. The whalers, the China traders, the Bidwells, and the Donners had done their work. California became American soil.

On February 2, 1848, a formal treaty with Mexico closed this chapter in American history, sealing the annexation of Texas and ceding to the United States California, Arizona, New Mexico, and other large fragments—a domain greater in area than Germany and France combined. Thus Mexico lost, if Texas is counted, more than one-half the territory she possessed when she made the first contract with Moses Austin for American colonization, receiving as a balm nothing except the cancellation of certain American claims for damages and fifteen million dollars in cash. In 1853, through the negotiations of James Gadsden, the United States secured another cession of land along the southern border of Arizona and New Mexico in return for a payment of ten million dollars.

Thus a collision which a modern historian, Herbert Ingram Priestley, characterizes as "a biological phenomenon" was brought to a conclusion fortunate for the victor. The Americans who favored annexing the whole of Mexico or at least holding all the territory in the north conquered by General Taylor, after some grumbling, accepted the gains of the settlement as the best that could be accomplished in the circumstances.

§

On top of this victory came an astounding piece of sheer luck. In January, 1848, while the commissioners were still haggling in Mexico City over the terms of peace, James W. Marshall, a laborer employed by John A. Sutter in his saw mill on the American River, discovered in the tail race something that glittered and was gold. This was not, of course, the first time that the precious metal had been found in the soil of California for the Mexicans had previously unearthed deposits; but for some strange reason the spiritual heirs of Cortez and Pizarro who had searched with feverish eagerness the valleys and mountains of Mexico had not swarmed with pick and pan into promising fields of the Coast. By a strange fatality which an Anglo-Saxon might call "Providential," the great discovery was delayed until American occupation arrived.

At first Sutter was not overjoyed with his fortune. Knowing that it would upset the normal course of agriculture and industry, he tried to keep silence, but, as that was a strain too severe for human nature, the news slowly leaked out. By May it was passing current as a rumor in the streets of Monterey—a bit of vague gossip that was turned into truth by an investigator sent to the spot to inquire. Immediately a spasm of frenzied lust burst out in every California community. Artisans dropped their tools, farmers left their cattle to die and their crops to rot, lawyers fled from clients, teachers threw aside their books, preachers cast off their cloth, sailors deserted their ships in the harbors, and women left their kitchens—all in one overwhelming rush for the gold-bearing district. Business ceased in the towns; real estate slumped; deserted houses and shops sank into decay. From every direction fortune-hunters swept down like locusts on the region around Sutter's mill, with dishpans and skillets for washing gold and plowshares beaten into picks and shovels.

From day to day, the acquisitive instincts of the miners were aggravated by tales that floated on every breeze. In the course of a week, it was said, two men found $17,000 worth of gold on a single spot containing only a few hundred square feet; a poor journalist armed with a pick, a shovel, and a pan gathered in a hundred dollars in a few hours; a workingman washed out two pounds and a half of gold in fifteen minutes. Even when all discounts were made, reports showed that in less than six months more than half a million dollars worth of precious metal had been wrested from the river drift and the hills.

Before winter came, the news in authentic form had reached the East, President Polk commenting on it officially in his message of December, 1848. In a flash the pages of the newspapers were packed with rumors, letters, and tales referring to the gold rush, and companies were formed to make expeditions to the scene of buried treasure. With their wonted enterprise merchants advertised goods suited to the needs of men bound for the gold fields—guide books, camping outfits, miners' tools and canned sauerkraut "warranted for twenty-one years." A hustling promoter organized a band of women, "none under twenty-five," to go out and marry the successful miners. Photographers urged departing fortune-hunters to leave behind daguerreotypes for their loved ones. Druggists announced specifics for all the ills that afflict the flesh of mortals, and fakers patent devices for locating rich gold-bearing soils.

From eastern cities the sensation spread to Great Britain and Ireland and then to the distant villages of the Continent, arousing so much cupidity that every vessel sailing from Europe was immediately furnished with a full quota of prospectors bent on reaching the Pacific Coast at the earliest possible moment. Along the docks, in the shops and hotels, at wayside taverns, in the stage coaches and canal-boat cabins, all conversation was devoted to the one absorbing theme—gold in California. The chantie of the Argonaut ran through the country:

> Oh! California, that's the land for me!
> I'm bound for Sacramento
> With the washbowl on my knee.

Before the adventurers, booked for the gold fields, lay a choice of many routes, three involving journeys by water. An all-sea voyage carried them around the Horn in a long and tedious trip that occupied from six to nine months. A more popular route lay through Panama and in a short time that narrow strip, where dull monotony had reigned almost uninterruptedly since Balboa's day, became the scene of stirring events, as thousands of Americans and Europeans swarmed in and out dreaming of riches in California. A third route, also including two sea trips, was by way of Mexico. On the score of safety there was little to choose. Since every kind of crazy craft strong enough to move out of an eastern harbor was employed in the business of transporting prospectors, the risks of all the voyages by water were extremely high. Many a ship that sailed away with singing fortune-hunters disappeared without leaving a sign, a rumor, or an echo to hint at the fate of crew and passengers. Those who tried to go by way of Panama or Mexico usually encountered, besides the dangers of the sea, cholera, scurvy, and Chagres fever. Scores who escaped disease were stripped of their money and murdered by robbers.

Though presumably more safe, the continental routes to

California offered hazards of their own. On the two north ern roads, one by way of Salt Lake and the Truckee River and the other the Oregon Trail, emigrants had to run the long gantlet of barren plains and mountain passes. Even worse was the southern trail through Santa Fé—worse for the torrid heat of parched deserts often sent the thermometer up to 140°, driving prospectors hopelessly insane and then to a wretched death on the sands. Along all the lines, thirst, starvation, storms, Indians, and disease dogged the steps of the wayfarer. From the frontier to the coast, wrecks of wagons, bones of oxen, and graves of dead emigrants marked the paths of the venturesome gold-seeker, fifteen hundred silent mounds, we are told, dotting the road from Salt Lake to Sacramento.

But none of these things turned the gold hunters from their purpose. Before the first quarter of 1849 had expired, at least seventeen thousand sailed away from the eastern shores. In less than one month, during the spring that followed, eighteen thousand people crossed the Missouri River en route to California. How many started, how many perished on the journey, how many arrived safely is nowhere accurately recorded. But the census of 1850 gave California 92,000 inhabitants, and within ten years the number had grown to 380,000. When it is recalled that the colonizing movement of the seventeenth century did not carry more than thirty or forty thousand Puritans to New England in the course of a hundred years, the magnitude of the famous gold rush of 1849 assumes its true proportions.

But how different the two migrations! It was the lure of a quick and easy fortune that swept most of the gold-rush immigrants into California—reckless adventurers fond of hard drinking, gambling, and fighting, offering a curious contrast to the godly men who sought a humble livelihood by hard work under the leadership of Winthrop and Carver. Not many took families along. Indeed, relatively few women went out in the first days of roaring luck and some of those who did were, to say the least, not Puritans either. In the names of the mining towns were reflected the tastes of the occupants; in place of the Providences, Goshens, Salems, and Bethels of New England, there rose Slumgullions, You-Bets, and Jackass-Gulches. When the miner burst into song, he chose "Highland Mary," camp doggerel, or a drinking chant, rather than the Psalms of David. Even some "good citizens" were not ashamed to walk down the main street of Poverty Flat with women who would have had to wear the Scarlet Letter in queer old Salem.

For years the exuberance and tempestuous life of the mining camps affected the character of the whole territory, not excepting the districts in the south devoted to cattle raising, grain fields, and vineyards. Even the distant and relatively peaceful city of Los Angeles could report in 1854 a murder a day on the average. "The Queen of the Cow Counties," wrote a vivacious editor of that town, "bangs all creation in her productions. Whether it be shocking murders, or big beets, jail demolishers, expert horse thieves, lynch justices, fat beeves, swimming horses, expounders of new religions, tall corn, mammoth potatoes, ponderous cabbages, defunct Indians, secret societies, bright skies, mammoth pumpkins, Shanghai chickens, grizzlies, coyotes, dogs, smart men, office seekers, coal holers, scrip, or fights . . . she stands out in bold relief challenging competition."

If such was the state of that sedate settlement so far from the gold regions, what must have been San Francisco, where a fever for speculation raged, as the millions from mines and gulches poured in there for export? Quickly overcoming the slump that followed the first exodus to the mines, real estate dealers, hotel keepers, tapsters, and outfitters waxed fat at their trades. Riotous living racked the town and shooting frays made life precarious.

In the tumult, matters went from bad to worse until the more sober elements were driven to form extra-legal associations, known as Vigilance Committees, rough and ready agencies which dealt out summary justice to the most incorrigible and brazen disturbers of the public peace, hanging murderers and banishing ballot box stuffers. Under the press of business, mistakes were sometimes made but, on the whole, the work of the Committees was salutary—at least until the organized police force was strong enough and decent enough to function in a normal fashion.

The anarchy of the gold rush made still more imperative the necessity, already appreciated by far-seeing citizens, for a settled system of government; but when the problem was presented to Congress, a vexatious delay ensued. At the moment a bitter quarrel over slavery was occupying both houses, the planters wanting their peculiar institution legalized in California and their opponents insisting on freedom; the two factions were gripped in a political deadlock.

Seeing no immediate relief in the offing, the people of California, with characteristic western initiative, took matters into their own hands. Without any authority from Washington, the territorial governor called for a state convention, which was duly elected and met at Monterey in 1849. Provided with a copy of the constitution of Iowa by one of the delegates, the members at once entered upon grave and decorous deliberations, offering to the people at the close a fundamental law forbidding slavery and involuntary servitude of any kind. In a burst of enthusiasm the proposed constitution was ratified by a huge majority and California, with her document in hand, knocked at the door of the Union, just in time to become involved in the great debate which culminated in the Compromise of 1850 and to receive her statehood as a part of that important settlement.

§

During the eventful years which sealed the fate of California, a long conflict with Great Britain over the boundary of the far northwest was brought to an end. In reality this contest was merely the closing phase of a struggle which had opened in colonial times. From the beginning British merchants had relied upon the fur trade as an unfailing source of profits; and in the protection of that interest they had again and again brought influence to bear on the policy of their government. They had been instrumental in securing the momentous decree of 1763 which shut the gates of the hinterland to American squatters.

Defeated by the Revolution, they moved the seat of their empire westward and, in the War of 1812, made the fur trade once more an issue. On one thing both the English and the Indians agreed: the fur-bearing animals of the wilderness must be protected against the soil-tilling pioneers of the United States. But they were banded together in a fight against fate. Though the second war for American independence culminated in a peace that promised a respite, it merely transferred to diplomacy the old battle between resolute farmers and the British fur traders supported by Indian allies, and as the American frontier advanced, exterminating the fur-bearing animals, the clash of these contending forces was pushed onward until it reached the Pacific northwest. There at the water's edge, in the valley of the Columbia River where the British Hudson's Bay Company had its outpost, the long struggle was fought to a finish.

For more than half a century that territory had been a subject of negotiation among the powers of Europe. Spain, Russia, and Great Britain all had historic pretensions to ownership. Many an intrepid Spanish explorer had skirted the coast line and reported discoveries. In their wake the Russians had plowed the seas: the brave Vitus Behring, acting under orders given by Peter the Great, had, in 1741, sailed the cold and stormy waters that washed the Alaskan shores and for nearly a hundred years afterward Russian fur traders had steadily pushed their activities down along the seaboard, taking their flag with them.

Still more formidable were the claims of Great Britain. In 1777, Captain Cook, on the ill-fated voyage that finally bore him to his death in the Sandwich Islands, had rounded the Horn, sailed up the coast of North America, mapped the shore line, and set precedents for those English geographers who wrote "New Albion" on their sketches of the Columbia River Valley. Fifteen years later, Captain Vancouver crept along where Cook had swiftly skirted and outlined the contour of the coast with such care that his charts served for many a decade as safe guides to the mariner. Stirred by reports of the forerunners, British fur traders from Canada, by sea and by land, now descended upon the wilderness, planting posts far and wide as they gathered up the rich peltries by traffic with the Indians.

Not far behind was the ubiquitous Yankee. Indeed, among Captain Cook's men was a versatile and courageous son of Connecticut, John Ledyard, who took his bearings as he sailed along under the British flag and on his return to Hartford brought out in 1783 a fascinating story of his expedition, which was widely read in New England. The Revolution had then come to a formal close; and American merchants, emancipated from British dominance, were ready to make the most of their freedom.

Lured by rumors of the profits reaped from the China trade, Boston capitalists sent two ships to open up enterprise in the Far Pacific, receiving their reward, after three anxious years of waiting, when their vessels, having completed a momentous voyage around the world, dropped anchor safely in Massachusetts Bay. Emboldened by this venture they dispatched other expeditions—one of which, under Robert Gray, made extensive explorations on the northwest coast in 1792, crossed the bar and sailed up the mysterious "River of the West" to which he gave the name of his ship, Columbia. "This river, in my opinion," wrote the captain's mate, "would be a fine place for to set up a factory."

Sea paths being broken, the Americans then began to explore the northwest by land, President Jefferson setting a

bold precedent in 1803 by sending out the memorable
Lewis and Clark expedition, which made a perilous but triumphant journey from St. Louis to the mouth of the Columbia River and home again, bringing authentic descriptions
of the rivers, trails, climate, soil, products, flora, and fauna
of the intervening country and the distant coast. From
St. Louis American fur traders then began to press into the
new territory, exploring as they went and sending back
first-hand accounts of the most inaccessible regions until at
last the geography of the whole continent was outlined.
With an ever-watchful eye for new business, John Jacob
Astor of New York organized the American Fur Company,
built up a lucrative trade by land and sea, and in 1811
planted Fort Astoria near the mouth of the Columbia River.
By strong-willed initiative, therefore, British possession was
thus defied and a fine diplomatic issue raised. Unable to settle the boundary question easily, the United States
and England made a treaty in 1818 providing for joint
occupation of the contested territory during a period of ten
years—an arrangement later renewed for an indefinite term.

For a time it seemed as if the British had the better of
the bargain. Through the powerful Hudson's Bay Company they gained most of the fur trade and pushed out their
operations in every direction. But appearances were deceptive. Before long the American settler with his plow was
pressing hard upon the wilderness exploited by the profit-
seeking trader, a development in which missionaries played
a leading rôle as pioneers. According to tradition four
Indians from the mountains made the long journey to St.
Louis to ask that preachers be sent to western tribes to
proclaim the gospel of Christ, giving a Macedonian call
which the Methodist Church answered by raising funds and
dispatching two ministers, Jason and Daniel Lee, with one
teacher, Cyrus Shepherd, to the Far West.

When they arrived on the coast, they received a cordial
welcome from Dr. McLoughlin, the generous chief of the
British trading post at Fort Vancouver, and on his excel-

lent advice went into the Willamette Valley. In that garden spot they built their first mission house, choosing as the site a "broad, rich bottom, many miles in length, well-watered, and supplied with timber, oak, fir, cottonwood, white maple, and white ash scattered along the borders of its grassy plains where hundreds of acres were ready for the plough." Before many years elapsed the whole region was penetrated by missionaries, both Catholic and Protestant, among them the indefatigable Marcus Whitman and his indomitable wife, Narcissa, whose names are indelibly written in the records of Oregon.

Though the preachers of the gospel met many discouragements in the task of converting and "civilizing" the natives, they waxed prosperous in the cultivation of the fertile soil about their settlements, gradually diverting their zeal, it seems, to the arts of colonization. In any event, on discovering the economic advantages of the rich country in which they found themselves, they began to advertise far and wide the merits of their new home, by means of letters, circulars, books, and lectures. Aided by two clever Massachusetts propagandists, Hall J. Kelley and Nathaniel Wyeth, who had visited the northwest and grown wildly enthusiastic about its "matchless climate" and fertile soil, the missionaries stirred the East by stories of great opportunities in Oregon.

In response, migratory persons, from the Atlantic seaboard to the Mississippi Valley, veered toward the new colony of the Willamette country. In 1839 a shipload of settlers went out by the way of Cape Horn; four years later the first large company made the overland journey from Missouri; in a little while other pilgrims combined a land and sea trip through Panama. "Did you come the Plains over, the Isthmus across, or the Horn around?" ran the query which greeted the new arrivals. Fed by three streams of immigration, the tiny mission posts expanded into prosperous farming settlements—communities of hardy and industrious American citizens.

With unerring instinct the pioneers soon turned to a social compact for self-government and self-protection, solemnly drafting, in 1843, at a mass meeting held in a barn belonging to the Methodist mission at Champoeg, a plan of provisional government, modelled after the constitution of Iowa. Rousseau had thus crossed the Rockies, or rather, perhaps, the spirit of the Pilgrim Fathers had descended upon the distant community. "We, the people of the Oregon territory," ran the preamble to the compact, "for the purposes of mutual protection and to secure peace and prosperity among ourselves agree to adopt the following laws and regulations until such time as the United States of America extend their jurisdiction over us."

It was now clear that the affairs of Oregon were approaching a crisis. On their part, the British in the Far West, observing the trend toward agricultural economy, realized that the fur trade was doomed and that they could only hold the Columbia Valley by following the American example. Their leading representative, Dr. McLoughlin, the statesmanlike agent of the Hudson's Bay Company, though he had been cordial in his treatment of the American settlers, quickly grasped the inexorable, and made the long journey to London to urge upon the British government the adoption of a colonizing policy, but the aid which he sought was not forthcoming. Defeated in his hopes and plans, he resigned the leadership he had so honorably held, letting the drift of western life pursue its own course.

Sniffing battle in the air, Britons and Americans in the Oregon country opened the fray with skirmishes. Since there was no established authority to make land grants and keep order, they engaged in bitter contests over titles and breaches of the peace, each side accusing the other of making fraudulent entries, of selling firearms and whiskey to the Indians, and undercutting in the fur market. Chafing under the monopoly enjoyed by the Hudson's Bay Company and desirous of bringing the whole region under their control, Englishmen on the ground begged their home government in London to unite the Oregon country with Canada and give it local autonomy. With equal force the pioneer Americans in Oregon, numbering over ten thousand by 1846, urged the administration at Washington to settle their troubled estate, give them self-government, and assure them protection.

In the halls of Congress, echoes of the distant Oregon controversy assumed many forms. There were, of course, some members of far vision who could see with the eye of the imagination the rising empire of the West. For example, in 1820, two years after the treaty of British-American occupation, a Senator from Virginia introduced a resolution calling for an inquiry into the expediency of occupying the Columbia River Valley, buttressing his plea with a powerful argument furnished by that unquenchable Oregon enthusiast, Hall J. Kelley. No tangible results flowed from this effort. Again when the joint occupation term was renewed indefinitely in 1828 the issue was once more raised in Congress, where Senator Benton, that stalwart and picturesque representative of Missouri, who had seen Asia from the banks of the Mississippi, opposed the continuance of the arrangement with all the strength he could command—and that was tremendous—and insisted on a sweeping assertion of American rights, including the definite establishment of American sovereignty.

Though, as time passed, Benton's advocacy kindled the interest of an ever-wider circle, there were to the very end men of little faith who confined their affections to their own states and in some cases could hardly see beyond their neighboring counties. Of this school, Senator McDuffie of South Carolina was the leading exponent. "What do we want with this territory?" he asked in the Senate in 1843. With the assurance of an imperious wiseman, he declared that a state as far away as Oregon could not possibly live under the government of the Union. "To talk about constructing a railroad to the western shore of this continent," he exclaimed, "manifests a wild spirit of adventure which I never expected to hear broached in the Senate of the United States." The wealth of the Indies, he asserted, would not suffice to build it and for his climax he drew a terrifying picture of almost insurmountable physical barriers of desert and mountain, clinching his argument with the impossible.

When at last, in spite of the pessimists, enough politicians were rallied to the Oregon cause by the insistent call for action, extremists sprang to the front and partisan frenzy confounded deliberations. "We will have all the territory up to the line of 54° 40′!" shouted the intransigent Democrats, making "Fifty-four forty or fight!" their popular slogan. By a clever stratagem they united the Oregon and Texas issue in the campaign of 1844—declaring the occupation of Oregon and the reannexation of Texas "the burning issues" of the hour. In all seriousness, they seemed prepared to carry out the pledge of their slogan to the letter if necessary. "It is not to be supposed that we shall get out of this scrape," roared Benton in the Senate, "without seeing the match applied to the priming or having the cup of dishonor held to our lips until we drink it to the dregs."

In a whirlwind campaign the Democrats carried the country while the alarmists held their breath. Was there to be a war on two fronts, one against Great Britain and the other against Mexico? The direful question was soon answered by the triumphant Polk. Though, as we have seen, he pursued with Mexico a policy which culminated in an armed conflict, he became as mild as a cooing dove in his negotiations with Great Britain over Oregon. When he was offered a compromise, a boundary line at the forty-ninth parallel, he promptly consulted his party colleagues in the Senate and closed the bargain in 1846. The thundering of cannon was already reverberating along the Rio Grande. While Texas and California were being won by the sword, the great Oregon claim was reduced by diplomacy. War with Mexico being one thing and war with

England another, discretion conquered audacity, especially as the southern planters had no vital interest in the extension of free soil.

Naturally the administration did not escape from this adjustment without taunts from critics. "Texas and Oregon were born the same instant," snapped Senator Hennegan of Indiana, "nursed and cradled in the same cradle, and they were at the same instant adopted by the democracy throughout the land. There was not a moment's hesitation until Texas was admitted, but the moment she was admitted, the peculiar friends of Texas turned and were doing all they could to strangle Oregon! . . . We were told that we must be careful not to involve ourselves in a war with England on a question of disputed boundary. There was a question of disputed boundary between us and Mexico; but did we hear, from the same quarter, any warnings about a collision with Mexico when we were about to consummate the annexation of Texas?" Senator Benton, though a loyal Democrat of the Jackson school, agreed. "Oh! mountain that was delivered of a mouse," he sneered, "thy name shall be fifty-four forty."

The best reply that could be made was framed by Calhoun, who, as Secretary of State, had pressed the annexation of Texas to a successful issue. Boldness in that direction, he said, was necessary to victory while caution was wise in the case of Oregon. "I believe," he argued, "that precipitancy will lose you Oregon forever, no, not forever, but it will lose you Oregon in the first struggle and it will require another struggle hereafter when we become stronger to regain it." Thus the philosophy of the Oregon question was formulated by the master logician of the planting interest. In the end the English offer became the law of the land, for the Senate, under southern leadership, ratified the treaty of compromise. In 1859 a part of the Pacific Northwest was admitted to the Union as the state of Oregon.

On the long trail to Oregon and California was founded in 1847, just after the conclusion of the irritating boundary dispute, the Mormon colony at Salt Lake—in some respects unique among the many strange settlements planted on this continent. The religious sect which made this excursion into the barren and forbidding wastes of the Utah country had been established about fifteen years before, springing, according to legend, from heavenly revelations made to Joseph Smith, of New York, discoverer and translator of the "Book of Mormon."

For a time its adherents wandered to and fro in the Mississippi Valley, suffering severely from the buffets of fate. After stopping a while in Ohio, they journeyed far into Missouri, where they met a hostility that turned them back for a brief period on their westward march. Notwithstanding their professions of peace, they were soon charged with "outrages" and accused of trying to erect a sectarian "dominion."

At any rate, the Mormons were set upon by their critics, beaten and compelled to move across the Mississippi into Illinois. There misfortune continued to pursue them, the New Canaan proving to be no more tranquil than the Old. Their leader, Smith, was shot by a mob and they were all threatened with extermination if they did not leave the state. Now suspected of being committed to the theory and practice of polygamy, they could see little possibility of coming to terms with their Illinois neighbors. Consequently many hailed with joy a proposal of the second prophet-leader, Brigham Young, to migrate far beyond the reach of civilization into the valleys of the Far West where they hoped, as they read in the Bible, that the weary could be at rest.

In the spring of 1847 Young and a picked band of the faithful went forth in search of the promised land. By midsummer they reached the Salt Lake country, where they pitched their tents and within two hours began to break the tough soil with their plows. Soon they were joined by a host that had been left behind, in all fifteen hundred strong, men, women, and children. Convinced that they had found their final haven, the elders of the church dispatched missionaries to the eastern states, to England, Scotland, and the Continent of Europe to win converts and bring back immigrants.

By way of support for this work a perpetual fund was created and an economic argument was adroitly mingled with the religious appeal. To poverty-stricken peasants and struggling artisans of the Old World they offered security and prosperity as well as the consolations of a new faith. To polygamous men they promised wives in abundance; to forlorn maids at least a share in a husband.

Within three years after the soil of the valley was first turned, eleven thousand people were in the Salt Lake district and the community which they called Deseret was large enough to attract the attention of the federal government. In 1850, it was erected into the territory of Utah under Clay's last great compromise. Though the movement which produced such quick results was rightly characterized by the historian, Katherine Coman, as "all in all, the most successful example of regulated immigration in American history," it was accompanied by terrible hardships and an appalling loss of life from hunger, drought, disease, and snowstorms, among other calamities.

In no small measure the amazing outcome of the adventure was due to the economic system directed by Brigham Young. Tested by the widespread prosperity which it eventually produced, in spite of all the difficulties, that system was in most respects superior in results to the methods adopted in any other American settlement organized on communal principles. In the early days of the experiment, speculators and the commercial profiteers were both restrained with an iron hand. Land was not sold at first to settlers outright; but each family was allotted a share—proportioned to its needs—to till for private profit as long as it was thrifty and industrious. None was al-

owed to accumulate a large estate and the industrious poor
were given advantages in competition with their richer
neighbors. The purchase of supplies and the sale of
produce were carried on through a common store, while
irrigation works to provide water for the arid soil were
built by community action and service rights granted to
all families on equitable terms. Iron, woolen, printing
and mining industries were managed also on the coöperative principle, fair wages being paid and the profits going
into the common chest for the promotion of fresh undertakings.

Although the whole system of economy was directed by
the Church fathers, apostles and elders, in theocratic
style under the severe regimen of President Young, although many leaders managed to acquire goodly estates, the
central idea was general comfort, not the enrichment of
individuals—an idea pursued with keen discrimination, as
Young steered a steady course between the perils of communism and the menace of disruptive individualism. While
the faithful were bound to strict obedience, there were no
wretched outcasts such as were to be found in every other
part of the civilized world. On one thing, all travelers
who visited the colony agreed, even when they denounced
"plural marriages" in unmeasured terms, namely, that the
ancient and persistent enemy of mankind, undeserved poverty, was nowhere to be seen.

Among the Mormons, temperance was proclaimed a virtue, and before the Gentile invasion of Salt Lake, there were
no saloons, gambling houses, or brothels. Although
whiskey and beer were made in moderate quantities, there
was no drunkenness and little crime; strictly speaking, the
life of the community was marked by sobriety, frugality, and
industry; idlers who would not till the land allotted to them
were expelled from the colony without mercy, and the
same summary treatment was meted out to brawlers, topers,
and "godless persons" in general. Those who walked in
the paths of labor and piety, according to Mormon tenets,

were commended publicly in Church; those who lapsed from
grace were warned, blacklisted, and, if necessary, banished
In fact, a discipline of Puritan-like rigor held the entire
colony down to the hard and unremitting toil required to
win the victory over a barren and forbidding soil in an un
favorable climate.

Whether internal dissensions would have finally broken
the economic unity of the Utah settlement is idle specula
tion, for the Mormons had scarcely founded their settle
ment when alien forces appeared to disturb their harmony
The discovery of gold in California and the migration to
Oregon made Salt Lake a haven of rest and refuge for
the thousands of adventurers, travelers, and homeseeker
who moved east and west over the long trail. If the sale
of foodstuffs and manufactured goods to these visitor
brought astounding profits to the Mormons, affording them
an immense capital for the extension of their economi
operations, the gains in riches were offset by losses in com
munal solidarity. Lawless elements were introduced an
tares were sowed among the faithful. In the face of loca
protests, Gentiles insisted on settling down in Utah to en
gage in agriculture, merchandising, and industry, bringing
with them their customs and religious beliefs.

Then came federal intervention. On the organization
of Deseret into a regular territory in 1850 the supervision
of the national government followed as a matter of cours
and in a very few months eventuated in an armed conflict
spreading echoes of strange events in Utah all over the
continent. Charges of outlawry and murder, not alway
groundless, were brought against the Mormons; Presiden
Young himself was accused of instigating assassination
polygamy, in its best light revolting enough to the nationa
mind, was portrayed in the most vivid language, horrifying
the public. Unavoidably, therefore, the Mormons and thei
plural marriage became a national issue.

Taking account of the rising tide of opinion, the young
Republican party in its platform of 1856 called upon Con

gress to prohibit in the territories "those twin relics of barbarism, polygamy and slavery." And in the fulfillment of their pledge, the Republicans included in the Morrill bill of 1862 a provision designed to put an end to the peculiar institution of Utah. Proving to be a dead letter in practice, this measure was succeeded by other acts of the same tenor until, in the Edmunds bill of 1882 and the Edmunds-Tucker law of 1887, a vital blow was struck at polygamy by a threat to confiscate property.

By that time Mormon communities had spread over the West from Iowa to California; the church, controlled by a small body of officials, had grown rich; individuals had amassed fortunes; the original communal economy had practically dissolved; and the Latter Day Saints, as the Mormons were now known, while still professing the creed of their fathers, had become as worldly-minded as the descendants of the Puritans. Monuments to their enterprise still stood in their Temple and Tabernacle, in their good roads, irrigation works, and industries. And scattered over the world from Hawaii to Scandinavia were congregations of Mormons who looked to Salt Lake City as the Rome of the new dispensation, the eternal home of the "Church of Jesus Christ of Latter Day Saints." But the pentecostal fervor of the early days and the serene assurance of Brigham Young's faith were hardly more visible in Utah than were the enthusiasm and somber resolution of Bradford and Carver in contemporary Plymouth.

CHAPTER XIV

The Sweep of Economic Forces

THE expansion of the United States to the Pacific—the acquisition of a vast territory adapted to plant ing in the South and to farming in the North—seemed to assure the indefinite predominance of the agr cultural interest, the main support of Jeffersonian demo racy as rededicated by Andrew Jackson. Indeed, for thre decades after the overthrow of John Quincy Adams, i 1828, the events of American politics appeared to confir the faith of those who upheld the banner of Jefferson an Jackson in a war on Hamilton's system of economy.

During these years, the Democratic party won all th presidential elections save two and the exceptions were hi torical accidents rather than direct defeats on questions o policy. On those two occasions the Whigs, who carried th day, nominated military heroes, made no declaration c principles, framed no platform, and swept the polls in th smoke and confusion of a general uproar. Had they de nitely confronted the country with a clear-cut program i cluding the bank, the protective tariff, ship subsidies, an the assumption of debts repudiated by states, it is doubtful whether they could have stampeded the voters into electing either of their martial statesmen.

While the Whigs were trying to capture the citadel of political power, under the cover of noise and evasion, the Democratic leaders worked toward a more and more specific definition of doctrines, making their appeal to the planting and farming classes more and more precise. In their platform of 1840 they wrote their dogmas in language so plain that the most simple-minded pioneer or mechanic could understand it. They declared their inflexible opposition to the tariff, a public debt, the bank, internal improvements, and all interference with the domestic institutions of the states—the labor supply of the planters. At every presidential election until the fateful campaign of 1860, Democrats reiterated this economic creed as their unchanging profession of faith.

In no official statements did they make any attempt to conceal the essential character of the conflict. On the contrary, their victorious candidates on the hustings and in state papers frankly and specifically named the place and the weapons. In any one of a sheaf of documents, the canonical articles could be found. For example, in a message to Congress in December, 1848, a message solemnly recording the views of his party, President Polk enumerated the regular devices of the Federalists and the Whigs against which the Democratic organization was arrayed—the bank, protective tariffs, the debt, internal improvements, and the recent project for the distribution of public lands among the states—scornfully referring to the "popular names and plausible arguments" employed by their champions in defense and justification. Then, in official form, he branded them all as schemes principally and deliberately contrived to transfer money "from the pockets of the people to the favored classes" and revealing a tendency "to build up an aristocracy of wealth, to control the masses of society, and monopolize the political power of the country."

The Whigs' victory in the presidential election of that year really meant no triumph for the party of Hamilton and Webster. Their candidate, General Taylor, a Louisiana planter and hero of the Mexican war, had no positive ideas on politics whatever; and in their appeal to the voters they deliberately avoided making any statement of principles at all. Hence, by electing Taylor they won no popular indorsement of their economic program. And this was their last victory—at all events, under the name which they had long utilized in conjuring the voters.

When the Whigs resorted to the same tactics again in 1852 under the leadership of Winfield S. Scott, also a general in the Mexican War, they were utterly discomfited; for the Democrats, besides distinctly avowing their agricultural program, gave the opposition a dose of its own medicine by also selecting as a standard bearer a man of Mars, General Franklin Pierce of New Hampshire. In the campaign that followed the Whigs were simply routed, the Democrats sweeping every state in the Union except Massachusetts, Vermont, Kentucky, and Tennessee. If the counting of heads meant anything, the party of Alexander Hamilton, Henry Clay, and Daniel Webster was dead and buried under an avalanche of public contempt.

At all events, with a grand air of assurance, Pierce announced that the general principle of tariff for revenue only could now be regarded as "the settled policy of the country." With equal confidence, the new President relieved the planting members of his party on the point of their labor system, waving aside with a disdainful flourish the agitators who tried to foment trouble "in the supposed interests of the relatively few Africans in the United States." The stars in the heavens were fixed. The American political system was rigid. At least so things appeared to the President of the United States in 1853, only ten years before the emancipation of the slaves.

Such assurance would doubtless have been justified if the American social order had been as unchanging as the structure of feudalism in the Middle Ages, but it happened to be at that moment the most dynamic society in the world. While it is true England was then gathering the fruits of triumphant industry and continental states were convalescing from the violent upheaval of 1848, in none of those countries was agriculture as well as manufacturing undergoing a swift and radical transformation.

In the United States nothing was static—not even the sacred and immutable Constitution. Inventors were altering the face of the earth and the sea; builders of factories and railroads were striding forward in seven league boots followed by their swelling army of industrial workers; steamships were beginning to drive sailing vessels from the deep; and packages of securities in strong boxes were growing bulkier day by day. Even the agricultural scene was changing, for the frontier was pushing westward as the economy of capitalism moved into the Ohio Valley, that stronghold of Jacksonian Democracy. From the Far West, California was pouring her golden stream into the national treasury, adding to the working capital of the nation. Moreover, the planting system, which in older days seemed to have a stability akin to that of the feudal order, was being turned upside down by the development of the cotton gin—undergoing a revolution scarcely less fundamental than that which had overtaken the handicrafts on the introduction of steam and machinery. Inevitably the intellectual life of the country was being stirred by fresh currents of inquiry and criticism, ranging from the Mormonism of Joseph Smith, through the transcendentalism of Ralph Waldo Emerson to the socialism of Horace Greeley. New England's dominant ideas were now as far from the mystic assumptions of Cotton Mather as the steam-driven spinning mill from the one-spindle wheel of Priscilla.

The history of technology, so vast and so vital, increasing in significance every year, belongs obviously to specialists in physics and chemistry. It cannot yet be written because the materials have not been assembled. The history of business likewise remains obscure because those who follow in the footsteps of Gibbon and Carlyle are prone to give more attention to the titled ruler of a little principality or the petty politician of Buncombe county than to the great captain of industry who takes the whole world for his realm. And as for the labor leaders of the middle period, marshaling their militant hosts, it is only necessary to note that the first comprehensive account of the American trade union movement came from the press in the second decade of the twentieth century. To this very hour, the marvelous development of American agriculture awaits the maker of its mighty sagas. Finally, psychology concentrating on the mind and its behavior has not yet explored the processes by which sentiment is woven in and out through the fabric of economy.

For these and other reasons the politician has continued to occupy the center of the historical stage, in spite of the fact that he is the shadow rather than the substance of things. Moreover, his proportions have been curiously distorted in the mirror of recorded legend by the contingencies of fate. The storm of the Civil War, the revolution wrought by the abolition of slavery, and the passions aroused by the conflict made it impossible for those who wrote immediately after the red years had passed to observe the "fabulous forties" and the "fitful fifties" in a clear perspective through the murky gloom. When at last the cloud lifts, when the fundamental course of American civilization is seen in a long, unbroken development, when the sharp curves of years are smoothed by the reckoning of centuries, then if all signs do not fail the middle period of American history will appear as the most changeful, most creative, most spirited epoch between the founding of the colonies and the end of the nineteenth century. The Civil War itself, called in these pages the "Second American Revolution," was merely the culmination of the deep-running transformation that shifted the center of gravity in American society between the inauguration of Jackson and the election of Lincoln.

On the material side, the leaders of this transformation were the inventors and the business men who, then as always, were bent on immediate ends and took little thought about the distant fruition of their labors. To the vast array of machines which revolutionized all industry, the United States furnished more than its quota during the Victorian age. Heavy borrowings, of course, were made from England—the steam engine of Watt, the locomotive of Stephenson, and the spinning machinery of Arkwright and Crompton—but in every case American inventors added to the contrivances they appropriated. Fulton put the steam engine into a ship and opened a new era of navigation; Howe created the sewing machine; McCormick and Hussey by giving the reaper to the farmer made obsolete at one blow the sickle and scythe that had come down from days beyond Tut-ankhamen; Morse, with his telegraph, spanned the continent, bringing around one table the business transactions of a whole nation; Whitney's cotton gin smashed an old economy created in the childhood of the race—challenging the spinners at their wheels in New England and the cotton planters with their armies of slaves far away under the burning sun of Mississippi and Louisiana.

For every inventor there stood a captain of industry ready to snatch the machine from the workshop, collect the capital to put it in motion, organize the labor forces necessary to production, and seek out the markets for the stream of goods that flowed from its whirling wheels. In every respect, the nature of American society in the North favored the enterprise of business men. No intrenched clergy or nobility overshadowed them in national life or branded their labors, as through all the long past, with the stamp of contempt.

Available for every kind of manufactures were unparalleled natural resources—timber, coal, iron, lead, and cop-

per—to be had in many cases from a friendly governmen
almost for the asking, if indeed that courtesy was mad
necessary by the easy ethics of the hour and place. Supple
menting the sons and daughters of American farmers wa
an ever-growing supply of stalwart European laborers from
which to draw recruits for mills, mines, and industrial un
dertakings of all grades and types.

Nor was capital wanting. As the flood of American
grain, cotton, and gold rolled into the Old World, Ameri
can credit was raised abroad. English and Continental in
vestors, though often pinched by the chicanery of Ameri
can communities, were eager to lend money at a higher
rate of interest than they could get at home. Finally, the
American manufacturer had an immense domestic marke
at his command; even when the Democrats managed to cu
the tariff down to the lowest point, the barrier of the sea
and the knowledge of the terrain gave him a distinc
advantage over his English competitors.

In these circumstances American business men rose exu
berantly to their opportunities, showing themselves in tal
ents and initiative not one whit behind their British
brethren. Beyond cavil, the Abbots, Lawrences, Astors
Browns, Forbeses, Vanderbilts, and Brookses of American
enterprise conceived and executed economic undertaking
of such magnitude and gathered in profits so princely as to
earn a just place among the heroes celebrated by that Plu
tarch of English capitalism, Samuel Smiles. They were al
flesh and blood men, keenly alive to every advantage, active
in promoting their political interests, and as determined in
their modes as the planters were in theirs.

By the middle of the century they were ready in num
bers, in wealth, and in political acumen to meet in the arena
of law or war the stanchest spokesmen of the planting
aristocracy. For every southern master commanding an
army of bondmen in the field, there was now a northern
captain of steam and steel surrounded by legions of work
ing people. If many a planter could boast of a thousand

slaves, many a captain of industry could pride himself on his thousand free laborers. On down the scale ran parallel the structures of the two economies, ending at the petty boss with two or three apprentices and the master with two or three slaves. When the Civil War came, the planting group of the South, high and low, could show an enrollment of 350,000 slave owners, large and small; in 1866 the treasury records of the federal government reported 460,000 persons, mainly in the North, paying income taxes. Both groups were ably led, well informed about the processes of government, and equally alive to the protection of their interests as they conceived them. One great difference was discernible, however: the planters frequently sent members of their own order to Congress to represent them, whereas the captains of industry relied mainly on lawyers to speak for them in the legislative chambers.

By an inexorable process beyond the will of any man or group, the sovereignty of King Cotton and the authority of his politicians were rudely shaken, the rapidity of the operation being recorded in ledgers and carefully set forth by the census. In the decade preceding Lincoln's election, the output of domestic manufactures, including mines and fisheries, almost doubled in value while the output of southern staples showed an increase of less than twenty-five per cent—a fact more portentous than all the oratory in Congress. In 1859 the domestic manufactures just enumerated yielded a return of $1,900,000,000 while the naval stores, rice, sugar, cotton, and tobacco of the South offered only a total of $204,000,000—a fact more ominous than Garrison's abolition. When Lincoln was inaugurated, the capital invested in industries, railways, commerce, and city property exceeded in dollars and cents the value of all the farms and plantations between the Atlantic and the Pacific —a fact announcing at last the triumph of industry over agriculture. The iron, boots, shoes, and leather goods that poured annually from the northern mills alone surpassed in selling price all the cotton grown in southern fields.

And the drift could not be reversed: the acreage of land available for farms and plantations was fixed by nature while the amount of capital that could be accumulated, the variety of machines that could be invented, and the number of people who could be sustained by manufacturing had no limits discernible to the human mind. By the middle of the century, the balance of power in the United States had already been shifted and every year saw the center of gravity advanced still further in the new direction. King Cotton had lost his scepter and nothing but a severe jar was necessary to overturn his throne. The supreme question to be debated, if contemporaries had only known it, was whether the political revolution foreshadowed by the economic flux was to proceed peacefully or by violence

§

No less significant in releasing dynamic forces and changing the direction of social currents was the rapid development of new means of communication, especially to the northwest. In whole sectors of the frontier transportation facilities now destroyed the economic basis of Jacksonian Democracy with its political and cultural reflexes. The revolution in this sphere began in 1807 with the successful trip of Fulton's little *Clermont* up the Hudson. Within four years there were steamboats on the Mississippi, inaugurating the age of thrilling adventure made epic by Mark Twain. The races, explosions, comedies, and tragedies of the mighty waterway, while they furnish color for the drama, were not the essence of the story, however. More fundamental was the prosaic fact that cargoes could now be carried up stream and to the eastern markets as well as to New Orleans.

A second stage in the evolution of transportation came with the construction of grand trunk canals. Two of these, the Erie opened in 1825 and the Pennsylvania system completed nine years later, linked the West with the eastern seaboard—with New York City and Philadelphia. Then followed swiftly the commencement of the third and still more revolutionary era; the banks of the new waterways were hardly carpeted with grass when they were sprinkled with the soot of locomotives. It was in 1828 that the ground was broken for the Baltimore and Ohio Railway, with great ceremony.

Within a decade or two, the chief cities of the coast were united by short lines; and railway promoters, with a keen eye upon the future, were reaching out along the trunk canals to the Mississippi Valley. By 1860 the Baltimore and Ohio, the Pennsylvania, and the New York Central systems had tapped the stronghold of Jacksonian Democracy. St. Louis, Cincinnati, Indianapolis, Chicago, and Cleveland by that date were brought within a distance from the Atlantic that could be measured in hours instead of in days. The stream of migration westward became a torrent; in return the stream of wheat, corn, and bacon from the farms became an avalanche.

The economic results flowing from this network of transportation were startling in range and intensity. With the swift expansion of the national market, textile mills in New England roared louder, blast furnaces in Pennsylvania flamed higher. As their crops multiplied and their land values increased, farmers of the old Northwest gathered in the increment, invested in government bonds and railway stocks, moved to neighboring county seats, started local banks, and passed out of the physical and moral atmosphere of the backwoods to other cultural circumstances. All over the Middle West, crossroads hamlets grew into trading towns, villages spread out into cities, cities became railway and industrial centers.

By 1860, the wide-scattered ganglia of the new economic system were well established: Cincinnati, Detroit, Cleveland, Sandusky, Columbus, Indianapolis, Madison, Terre Haute, St. Louis, Chicago, and Milwaukee were the scenes of lively business enterprise. Cincinnati was the pork-packing, clothing, and wine metropolis of the Ohio Valley. "I heard," wrote a visitor of that far-off time, "the crack of the cattle driver's whip and the hum of the factory: The West and the East meeting." Of the two thousand woolen mills recorded in the census of the year in which Lincoln was first elected President, one-fourth were in the western states. At the Republican national convention in Chicago, which nominated him, growers and carders of wool from Ohio and Indiana joined the spinners of New England and iron masters of Pennsylvania in cheering for the protective tariff plank. By 1860 the output of the grist mills, fed largely from the fields of the North and West, was almost equal in value to the whole annual crop of King Cotton.

In the presence of such indubitable and dynamic facts, the theories of Jacksonian Democracy lost some of their appeal—at least to the higher beneficiaries of the new order. As quick transportation carried farm produce to eastern markets and brought ready cash in return, as railways, increasing population, and good roads lifted land values, brick and frame houses began to supplant log cabins; with deep political significance did prosperity tend to stifle the passion for "easy money" and allay the ancient hatred for banks. At last beyond the mountains the chants of successful farmers were heard above the laments of poor whites, the equality of the primeval forest and stumpy field passing away forever, taking with it the psychological fringe.

Railroad lawyers now mingled in state legislatures with men in homespun from the farms, the great Lincoln himself serving as an efficient representative of the Illinois Central directors at Springfield. Well-groomed preachers damped the fires of Peter Cartwright's hell; while ladies formerly garbed in linsey-woolseys put on alpacas and silks, read Godey's Lady's Book on the fashions, and improved their grammar. From log academies the "Hoosier Schoolmaster" retired into the darker places of the backwoods, as teachers of the classics arrived on the banks of the Wabash and dancing masters came to introduce the manners of the ballroom—for a consideration.

In the sweep of things the old Northwest Territory was assimilated more and more to the economy and culture of the Northeast, the two sections drawing closer together every day in bands of steel and gold. By the railroads the trade and the interests of the upper Mississippi Valley were turned away from New Orleans to New York, Philadelphia, and the Atlantic seaboard generally. At the middle of the century an eminent southern economist complained, with full warrant, that "the great cities of the North have severally penetrated the interior with artificial lines until they have taken from the open and untaxed current of the Mississippi the commerce produced on its borders. . . . The Illinois canal has not only swept the whole produce along the line of the Illinois River to the East, but it is drawing the products of the Upper Mississippi through the same channel, thus depriving not only New Orleans but St. Louis of a rich portion of their trade."

To the mechanics of easy transportation, eastern capitalists added credit devices, advancing good bank notes of conservative eastern institutions to western operators on the security offered by commodities to be shipped to seaboard markets. "These moneyed facilities," lamented the same southern writer, "enable the packer, miller, and speculator to hold on to their produce until the opening of navigation in the spring, and they are no longer obliged, as formerly, to hurry off their shipments during the winter, by way of New Orleans, in order to realize funds by drafts on their shipments. The banking facilities of the East are doing as much to draw trade from us as the canals and railways which eastern capital is constructing." Thus planters who needed cheap corn and bacon for their slaves as well as political support from the Northwest found invincible competitors in eastern capitalists who, besides offering expansive credits and easy shipping facilities to the farmers, helped to make over the frontier in the image of great industry. It was all plain as day to southern statesmen, but no effort of will and imagination could overcome the flow of fortune. The economic basis was being laid for a new partisan adjustment—and in 1860 spinning fates wrought the patterns.

§

With the multiplication of manufacturing establishments and railways came another natural consequence: the rapid growth of a working class separated from the soil and congested in the cities. With every census the industrial army loomed larger on the horizon. In 1860, it was written down by the census taker that one-third of the entire population of the country was sustained by "manufacturing industry" and that the white population dependent upon daily wages for a livelihood, upon what Jefferson called the "caprices and casualties of trade," far exceeded the number of slaves laboring on the estates of King Cotton. And the rate of increase foretold in measured strokes the ultimate shift of the social base with riches from the country to the city.

Meanwhile the ranks of the working class were being transformed by new racial infusions—the supply of labor from the farms, men, women, and children of native stock, steadily augmented by a swelling stream of immigrants. As the Nordic planter of the South, in his passionate quest for wealth, was willing to submerge his own kind in a flood of Negroes from the wilds of Africa, so the Nordic mill owner of New England, with his mind on dividends, took little thought about the nationality or color of those who stood patiently at his spindles and looms or huddled into the tenements of his cities. A time was to come when the greatest industry in the land of John Alden and Cotton Mather was to be directed by a Portuguese Jew with an Anglo-Saxon name; when Governor Winthrop's Puritan capital was to be ruled by an Irish Catholic mayor. Under

he stimulus of feverish profit-making, the gates of the land
vere flung open to the peoples of the earth and it seemed
iighly moral to write over the portals the fine humane
ihrase: "Asylum for the Oppressed of Every Land."

America's inducements were made all the more alluring
o immigrants by the conditions of labor in the Old World
it the middle of the century. In those decades, the artisans
of England seemed to be sinking into hopeless poverty; on
iny reckoning the terrible picture of their state drawn by
he sharp pen of Friedrich Engels in 1844 was accurate.
The truth of this awful indictment was borne out by the
:hartist movement, which threatened the English ruling
:lasses with a revolution of violence, and by the eagerness
of skilled mechanics to escape from their native land to the
United States.

In worse distress, no doubt, were the peasants of Ire-
and, groaning beneath the burden of absentee landowners.
Celtic in race and Catholic in religion, they had for centuries
·hafed under the dominion of London. Forced to pay rents
o English lords, contribute tithes to the English Church in
Ireland, and obey laws made by the English Parliament in
vhich they had a minority of members, the Irish thought
heir wrongs too heavy for human endurance. Then as a
:limax came the potato famine, adding torment to despair.
Hundreds perished of starvation; travelers along the high-
vays reported that unburied dead lay where they fell, with
heir mouths stained green by weeds and thistles eaten for
iourishment in their last extremity.

Literally driven from home by starvation, the peasants
of Ireland swarmed to America. Within two decades, more
han one-half the laboring population of that unhappy coun-
ry was carried across the Atlantic and incorporated into the
iocial and political order of the United States. When the
:ederal government took its first census of the foreign born
n 1850, it found nearly a million Irish among them—in
:atios, forty-two per cent of the total; and, within ten years,
nore than half a million new immigrants from Ireland were

added to this brigade of industrial recruits. Coming with out capital, often with nothing better than rags on their backs, they flocked to the factories of the urban centers or joined the gangs of workmen busy on the canals, railways and other structures that marked the rise of American capi talism. If, in virtue of their economic status or their agri cultural inheritance, they generally joined the party that waged war on Hamilton's system, they contributed none the less to the fortunes of those who were soon to lay Jeffer son's planters low in the dust and multiply the demand for industrial labor.

During the same period, conditions similar to those pre vailing in Ireland sent a flood of German immigrants to seek their fortunes in the New World. The blight that blasted the potato crops of Ireland likewise visited the Rhine Val ley and sections of southern Germany, leaving in its wake misery equally galling if less widely extended. To this economic affliction was added political discontent. Though German peasants and laborers were not ruled by an alien race, they had in general no more voice in their government than did the Irish; and with a kindred zeal they united under bourgeois leaders in a national democratic move ment.

Taking advantage of the furor unchained by the French revolution of 1848, German radicals made heroic efforts to cast off the despotic rule of kings and princes by agitations and uprisings. At first success attended their revolts, only to be followed by a fierce reaction in which severe penalties were inflicted upon the defeated champions of liberty. To these victims of poverty and politics, Amer ica was indeed an asylum. In 1847 over fifty thousand Germans entered the United States; during the decade fol lowing 1850 they came at the rate of ninety thousand a year; and when the United States was to be tried by fire near the middle of the century over a million Germans were among the foreign born, some living in the towns as me chanics and merchants, others as farmers in the interior—

ven far and wide on the frontiers of Wisconsin and
Minnesota.

Another important element in the changing economic and
social order of the middle period was the women who
flocked from the native homesteads and from the immigrant
ships to the mills, offices, schoolrooms, and stores. Women
had laid the foundations of the textile business in colonial
America; at their wheels and looms they had nourished it
throughout the handicraft age. When at length the steam
engine drew the industry away from firesides to factories,
they naturally followed it, their labor remaining the
basis of that industry. Of the six thousand persons employed in the cotton mills of Lowell in 1836, nearly five
thousand were, according to a French visitor, "young
women from seventeen to twenty-four years of age, the
daughters of farmers from the different New England
states."

Indeed, in all except the heavier metal industries, women
were an essential factor; by the middle of the century more
than a hundred trades were employing them and they were
also to be found behind the counters in great mercantile
establishments. And as they streamed from their homes
the rigid domestic system inherited from the colonial age
began to crumble. The theory, the law, and the politics of
the facts soon reflected the economics. It was no accident
that "the women's rights movement" rose among the maids
and matrons of the industrial North with its relative
independence for those who labored, rather than in sheltered mansions on southern plantations where ladies still
bowed to the economic and social institutions of their grand-
mothers.

§

Like every other class in history called forth by economic
processes, the new industrial workers of America, as their
numbers mounted, began to draw together in associations
and evolve ideas of defense and aggression. Even before

the beginning of the transformation in society brough
about by steam and machinery, artisans in many stap
crafts had formed local societies and started can
paigns for higher wages, shorter hours, and milder legisl:
tion. In all the important towns of the young republi
such unions had appeared. While Washington was sti
President, the shoemakers of Philadelphia established
trade society and in 1799 they struck against their emplo·
ers, thus serving on the nineteenth century notice of even·
to come.

Startled by the growing power of their workmen, master
resorted to the courts, attempting through indictments an·
prosecution to dissolve the aligning forces that loome
before them. But they could not stay by judicial decrees th
movement of consolidation. By the time Jackson and hi
conquering hosts swept into the White House, artisans c
the standard crafts in every large industrial town wer
organized in unions and in each leading business cente
existed a federation of these "locals" for coöperative actio·
In 1836 there were fifty-three unions in Philadelphi:
fifty-two in New York, twenty-three in Baltimore, and si:
teen in Boston; among women workers as among men th
beginnings of association had appeared, especially in th
textile industry.

When once the labor groups of various localities ha
become well organized, a national federation seemed th
logical next step. Indeed, the course of American econom
required it, if efforts to control wages and other labor cor
ditions were to be successful; for the rapid rise of manu
facturing cities in the Middle West and the constant migra
tion of labor from town to town made coöperation ove
the whole area vital to effective action anywhere. Mean
while the development of the steamboat and railway, reduc
ing the cost of traveling, rendered centralization on a larg
scale apparently feasible. Believing that the time was ripe
labor leaders attempted in 1834 to bring about a solidarit
among workers of every craft and grade at a general con

vention of delegates of local unions held in New York "to unite and harmonize the efforts of all the productive classes of the country." Though auspiciously begun, the tentative federation formed at this conference just managed to stumble along for three years, meeting disaster in the panic of 1837. The foundations for a national structure were not yet properly laid.

Quick to catch the import of this failure, leaders in the most powerful trades set about the more business-like enterprise of consolidating for national action the local unions already formed in each of the great industries. So while Clay and Webster and Calhoun were arguing political questions in the Senate, obscure workers were traveling up and down the country in the interest of their crafts, welding the various local societies into separate national federations. Before the titanic social war broke in upon the peace of the land in 1861, printers, machinists, iron molders, stone cutters, hat finishers, and other special groups were well organized in the industrial cities and more or less effectively federated on the national stage. If it had not been for the multitudes of foreign immigrants, the constant drift of mechanics to the cheap lands of the frontier, and the possession of the ballot by practically all native and naturalized workingmen, the American labor movement of the mid-century would probably have matured in a national form as early as that of England. Even so, American trade unionists during the forties were more powerful in their influence on the course of domestic politics and legislation than were the disfranchised and uneducated laborers of the English mill towns.

Moreover, there was hardly a phase of the European labor agitation that was not duplicated in this country during the period. There were strikes and demonstrations, far-reaching, prolonged and repeated, never more volcanic in character than in the decade that preceded the Civil War. With the ebbing and flowing of strikes, surged a torrent of revolutionary theories that fired the imagination of working people and colored the thoughts of journalists and philoso-phers no less potent than Horace Greeley, Charles A. Dana, George William Curtis, Ralph Waldo Emerson, Margaret Fuller, and James Russell Lowell.

Especially did utopian socialism make a deep impression on the mind of the age. Profoundly moved by the poverty of industrial centers, intellectuals with tender sympathies freely declared that the solution of the problem of misery in the United States as in Europe lay in either communism or in phalansteries combining agriculture and industry. The way being prepared by native criticism, the teachings of French dreamers, particularly St. Simon and Fourier, were accepted with enthusiasm. No less hearty was the welcome given to the gospel of the British socialist, Robert Owen. Indeed, in more than one respect Owen belonged to the United States too; if he made a great social experiment at New Lanark in Scotland, he also established a communal colony at New Harmony in Indiana; if he appealed to the governing classes of Europe, he likewise addressed the House of Rep-resentatives in the United States with the same fervor; his New Moral World was read in Pittsburgh and Indianapolis as well as in London and Manchester.

Throughout the middle period, certainly after 1825, rad-ical beliefs kept the industrial section of America in constant turmoil. Numerous labor journals, some dedicated to politi-cal agitation, some to the promotion of labor solidarity and unionism, were issued under the direction of able edi-tors and exerted a strong influence in working-class districts. Long before the close of Jackson's first administration in 1833, there was in operation a labor press that compelled governing persons and artisans alike to give heed to new voices. Moreover, after repeated calls for independent political action, signs of revolt against party machines had become unmistakable in the cities of New England and of the middle states, with the nomination of labor candidates for local offices in many centers and their election in some instances. "The balance of power has at length got into the hands of the working people where it properly belongs," declared a reformist paper of Philadelphia in 1829. Premature as was this rejoicing, it took a good deal of skillful maneuvering on the part of regular politicians to quell the uprising; and in the operation the bulk of social legislation piled up in state capitals. Imprisonment for debt was abolished, the beginnings of free popular education were made, and laws safeguarding the life and health of workers in the factories were enacted.

Keen observers of the time, especially from the planting section, watching this turbulent current in the North, were moved to exclaim that the structure of industrial society was in imminent danger of dissolution, menaced by the rising tide of radicalism. "Do socialism and agrarianism and Fanny Wrightism find foothold at the North and threaten the destruction of private property and endanger private rights?" inquired an Alabama Congressman in 1858. The answer was inherent in the question: "At the South every man is secure from mobocratic misrule." Though no doubt there was a high pitch of excitement in such notes, a growing discontent in industrial districts did in fact offer burning issues to statesmen, economists, and manufacturers; if they had not exercised discretion and if the Civil War had not intervened, the labor movement might have taxed their powers of negotiation long before Samuel Gompers and Eugene V. Debs entered the arena.

But they had at their command the experience of the past. More than once in the history of humanity, popular distempers of revolutionary vehemence had been allayed, temporarily at least, by the confiscation and distribution of property. This had occurred in the plebeian uprisings of Rome, the peasants' revolts of western Europe, and the French Revolution of the eighteenth century. It was to occur again—in America, under another guise. The property that was now to be seized and tossed to the disinherited was not that of patricians, earls, marquises, or bishops. It belonged in law to the whole people of the United States and was held in trust for them by the federal government. It was the public domain of the West.

The disposition of that land in the form of a general largesse was, of course, not an idea created for the occasion. Jefferson had proposed to use the public domain for the purpose of building up a nation of free farmers, in his opinion the only enduring basis of a republic; and, before Jefferson died, Benton of Missouri had started to advocate a policy of free distribution. Politicians and speculators in the vanguard had been keeping their eyes on it for more than a generation. But a widespread propaganda in favor of relieving the poverty and discontent of the industrial East by giving away land in the West was a new emphasis in American affairs, producing a profound effect on the public mind. It touched all the radical labor leaders and brought even communists, such as Weitling, under the spell of an agrarian gospel. It appealed to the German immigrants who came in such throngs in the fifties. It crept up into the middle class of native Americans. Horace Greeley, who thought he had found a solution of the industrial problem in a kind of socialism, added the Homestead article to his profession of faith.

In this economic situation, so peculiar to American life, lay at least a partial explanation of the developments that took place in the labor movement of the middle period. Energies which in the normal course of affairs would have been devoted to building up trade unions and framing schemes of social revolution were diverted to agitation in favor of a free farm for every workingman whether he wanted it or not. A Homestead Act, ran the argument, would emancipate him from the iron law of misery; it would enable him either to go West and take up an estate or, as the price of staying home, to demand higher wages from his industrial employer. Thus, in the literature of the great social debate land reform assumed a radical color. Indeed, it was so tainted with communistic associations that President Buchanan, in vetoing the Homestead bill of 1860,

ould say with no little justice that the attempted raid on
he public domain had the savor of the subversive doctrines
hen fermenting in Europe.

In spite of Buchanan's protest the agrarian creed had
pread so far and penetrated so deeply that nothing could
top its progress. It was supported by the indisputable fact
of industrial misery, sustained by a promise of liberty.
Making a strong appeal to the urban masses, it sank like
a wedge into the ranks of mechanics and laborers who had
gathered under the standard of Jacksonian Democracy.
And when the Republicans in their platform of 1860 offered
free land to the workingmen of the world, in exchange for
a protective tariff, the way was already prepared for a
tumultuous response. When in the midst of the Civil War
he Republicans fulfilled their pledge by beginning to fling
he land to the clamoring multitude, the economic revolu-
ion was begun. If labor could continue its process of organization to win higher wages, there was little for the
socialists of the period to do except haul down the red flag.

§

On no point did southern orators dwell with more assur-
nce than on the stability and solidity of the social order in
he South, when compared with the turbulence and perils of
he North. The enslavement of the whole body of laborers,
s one of them remarked at the time, went "a long way to
neutralize the ruinous effects of universal suffrage and to
imit the absolute quality of popular sovereignty," while it
urnished to some extent a counterpoise to "liberty of con-
cience, free inquiry, and endless discussion." Every-
hing seemed to promise peace in the South. "The perfect
ubordination of the laborers, spread thinly over wide sur-
aces," continued the same philosopher; "the isolation of
amilies, forming diminutive centers of small communities
ound together by the closest ties of mutual affection, de-
endence, and interest; the peaceful occupations of hus-

bandry; the plenty which everywhere abounds; the almos
utter absence of want; the intimate communion with nature
all things, in short, tend to tranquillize society and exclud
the sentiments and riotous scenes so common in denser com
munities and in large manufacturing districts crowded witl
free white laborers who are at the same time noisy poli
ticians, debaters, and voters."

For the moment appearances seemed to support th
argument of the confident orator. Slavery stood fou
square to all the winds of agitation. The heavy sanctio
of the centuries was still upon it. When the curtain ros
on the historic stage bondmen were even then toiling unde
the lash, tilling the fields, guarding flocks, and rearing monu
ments to their rulers. Strange as it may seem, slavery ha
marked an upward stage in social evolution: prisoners o
war who had formerly been put mercilessly to the swor
were spared and sent to labor in servitude. Through th
long epochs of antiquity, slavery formed the foundation o
kingdoms, empires, and republics—the civilizations o
Babylon, Persia, Egypt, Greece, and Rome.

If with the collapse of the Roman empire and the ris
of Christianity slavery almost disappeared in the wester
world, the peasants who labored in the fields of Europ
during the Middle Ages were serfs bound to the soil, no
freemen in any modern sense. Though the Church frowne
upon the enslavement of Christians by "heathen" races
though medieval economy was unfavorable to chattel
bondage in any form, neither the Bible nor the Papacy lai
slavery strictly under the ban. If Christians on principle
cherished a deep-seated antipathy to the institution as such
most of them quickly overcame that repugnance when an
opportunity to profit from it was presented. At all events
it is not recorded that any of the great powers—either
Catholic or Protestant—whose conquerors and colonizers
followed in the wake of Columbus forbade their subjects
to enslave the natives in the lands they discovered or pro
hibited the practice of snatching Negroes from Africa for

servitude. Undoubtedly English theologians were for a time vexed by the question as to whether bondmen should be taught the Christian doctrine of salvation, but that problem in casuistry in no way involved the validity of slavery itself.

It was therefore under ancient and religious ordinances that the institution became lawful in all the thirteen English colonies in America. Under similar sanctions the carrying trade, traffic in Negroes, flourished. Puritan shipowners, who seized and transported Africans to the planting districts, seemed to suffer no more pangs of conscience than southern masters who bought them. Women like men shared in the trade and lived by the system.

Though chattel servitude was lawful in the northern states when the republic was established, there were then only about forty thousand slaves in that section as compared with seven hundred thousand in the South. And most of the northern bond folk were domestic servants rather than laborers in field and shop. Climate, soil, and economic practices, as already indicated, hindered the extension of slavery in the North, while the influx of free white laborers, more skilled and more industrious, also helped to restrict the area of its utility. Moreover, the growth of commerce and industry steadily diminished its relative importance in the North.

Hence, by the time the importation of Negroes was forbidden by federal law in 1808, chattel slavery was on the wane everywhere above the Delaware River—and the moral objection to the institution was deepening. The Massachusetts constitution of 1780 abolished it by implication and Pennsylvania in the same year made provision for gradual emancipation. In 1787, the Congress prohibited slavery in the Northwest Territory by the memorable ordinance for government and liberty. In 1799, New York declared that all children of slaves born after July 4 of that year should be free, though held as apprentices for a term; and about a quarter of a century later it removed the last dwindling vestiges of human bondage. By one method or another all the commonwealths north of Delaware gradually outlawed slavery.

If none of the southern states emulated these examples, it did not follow that opinion in the South was at first altogether unanimous on either the moral or the economic aspects of the subject. On the contrary, there were in the early days of the republic many southern statesmen who saw in slavery a wasteful system of labor and the one source of difference between the two sections that boded ill for the future. In Delaware and Maryland, the growth of trade and the increase in the number of free white farmers thrust slavery somewhat into the background. In North Carolina, where so much of the soil consisted of broken upland, slavery was confined by nature within relatively narrow bounds. In Virginia, likewise, the whole western region, unsuited to plantations, was possessed by white farmers who were in constant political conflict with their slave-owning neighbors on the coastal plain. Even the seaboard region of Virginia was being impoverished by slave labor and the number of slaves was multiplying too rapidly for the output of agricultural produce.

In these circumstances shrewd observers questioned the economic advantages of a system which in effect hindered the inflow of free artisans and adventurous capital, exhausted the primeval fertility of the soil, and created a master class steeped in pride and complacency. More than one Virginia thinker believed that the state would be better off in every way without slavery. Jefferson, as we have said, was opposed to it and at the time of the American Revolution was prepared to abolish it, believing that it was contrary to the genius of American liberty. "I tremble for my country," he said, "when I reflect that God is just; that his justice cannot sleep forever."

With his national outlook, Washington hoped that emancipation could be brought about in good time. "Not only do I pray for it on the score of human dignity," he once remarked, "but I can clearly foresee that nothing but the rooting out of slavery can perpetuate the existence of our union by consolidating it in a common bond of principle." Only in South Carolina and Georgia, where the high mortality of slaves in the rice swamps and the hotter climate made tropical labor seem more desirable, were the spokesmen of the planters fairly consistent champions of the institution from the beginning to the end. Even so, the planting interests in general were so pliant on the issue that the Missouri Compromise dedicating the lion's share of the Louisiana territory to freedom could be carried through the Congress of the United States in 1820.

§

During the next forty years, however, there occurred in the slave system itself a revolution almost as shattering as that wrought in handicraft industry in the North by steam and steel, drawing it into the very same economic transformation. While the spinning jenny and the loom altered the economy of New England, they introduced new elements into the planting system of the South, especially after Eli Whitney patented the cotton gin in 1794. Unaided by machinery a slave could extract the seeds from about one pound of raw cotton in a whole day; but with Whitney's first crude instrument a slave could clean fifty pounds and, when the invention was improved and harnessed to steam, a thousand pounds a day.

Henceforward, owing to the continual improvement of textile machinery, the use of power, and the perfection of the cotton gin, the earth's multitudes were to have cloth for a few cents a yard and the demand for raw cotton was to stretch to the breaking point the energies of southern planters. Until the end of the eighteenth century, rice, indigo, and tobacco had been the chief staples raised by the labor of slaves. The cultivation of rice was restricted by nature to certain areas and the demand for tobacco, though growing, was not equal to the demand for cloth to cover nakedness.

Under the pressure of the expanding textile market, the call for cotton rose from year to year, and before half a century had elapsed the economic order of the South was overturned. When the transformation began, planters of the old régime had settled down into a position very much like that of the English landed gentry—fairly content with established estates and the scheme of refinement transmitted by their ancestors. From generation to generation, their broad acres had been cultivated by slaves that had come down in the family. If masters frequently added new sections of land with the natural increase of their labor supply, they were seldom fired into feverish activities by the passion for making huge accumulations of riches. But under assaults by ruthless, aggressive, profit-making managers of slaves bent on an ever-increasing output of cotton to feed to hungry mills of England and the North, customary practices were compelled to yield—to give place to a force that was akin in spirit to the dynamic and acquisitive capitalism of the industrial world.

The results of this powerful surge were exigent and disruptive. A relentless drive was begun to secure more land for exploitation, additional areas in the old states and still more territory in the southwest, the Caribbean, and Central America. In this fierce quest for acreage, planters of North Carolina, South Carolina, Georgia, and Alabama advanced into the piedmont, adding small farms to their domains, enlarging the area of slavery, and thrusting their white neighbors into the mountains or out into the Northwest. Never satisfied, they pressed onward, across the Mississippi, through Louisiana and into Texas. After helping to bring an imperial realm into the Union, they turned their eyes southward for still new worlds to conquer, threatening in the flaming Ostend manifesto of 1854— issued by three American ministers abroad—to wrest Cuba from Spain. With equal urgency they placed a premium on large-scale production and multiplied their demand for Negro labor.

Stirred by the volcanic energies of capitalism, slavery of the traditional type underwent a drastic change. Even in the older sections where cotton culture did not flourish and where the law of diminishing returns had threatened the ultimate extinction of chattel servitude, the institution was now given a new lease on life. Since surplus men, women, and children could be sold to the planters of the cotton belt, the breeding of slaves for an expanding market became a highly lucrative business, stimulating the acquisitive instincts of masters in the border states.

So everywhere in the South the drive for profits now imperiled those practices of humanity which in the best of conditions had bound owners and slaves by cords of interest and sympathy—ties akin to those which had united the master workman and his employees in the days of the handicrafts. Just as the northern manufacturer often treated his laborers as mere commodities for exploitation and threw them into the streets in times of business depression, so the cotton planter of the new régime frequently looked upon his slaves as animals to be worked in gangs and driven to the limits of endurance under the pressure of immediate gain. An overseer who could not "make" the maximum amount of cotton in a year was in mortal dangeı of losing his position at the head of the human machine.

Forced ever onward by the cumulative passion for gain, cotton culture within the brief span of fifty years conquered the whole South, thrusting itself upward in the end as the dominant interest fated to rule all minor concerns with an iron hand. When George Washington was inaugurated President only two million pounds of cotton were produced annually in the United States; by 1860 the output had risen a thousandfold, to more than two billion pounds. When Jefferson Davis took his place at the head of the Southern Confederacy, nearly two-thirds of all the slaves in America were engaged in cultivating that crop alone. To this revolution in the internal economy of the South was added the centripetal influence of foreign connections. Furnishing the staple upon which a vast system of English industry depended for its very life, cotton growers were inexorably drawn into the sweep of English polity, with something approaching free trade as the logical and unavoidable corollary. Thus the cotton drive focused the attention of the slave states mainly upon a single interest and held it there with remorseless tension. According to outward signs, King Cotton seemed invincible at the middle of the century. Emerson, the idealist, confessed in 1854 that he did not know whether freedom or slavery would be abolished.

At that very hour, however, a crisis in cotton was in sight. The area of rich virgin soil to be exploited by slave labor had a fixed boundary in western Texas and when the last fertile belt was brought under the plow an amazing era of advance drew to an end. Though imagists dreamed of annexing Cuba and making excursions into Central America, their mirages dissipated in failure. By 1860 the limits of the American cotton kingdom were definitely fixed.

In the meantime the law of diminishing returns was beginning to tell in the older provinces of the realm. It had been by wearing out the land and moving on to new mines of fertility that the greatest fortunes were made in the grand years of prosperity. Hence a day of reckoning was inescapable: the necessity for applying expensive fertilizers and introducing more efficient methods of cultivation could no longer be avoided. Moreover, the margin of profit being thus put in peril, every kind of tribute collected on manufactured commodities bought by the cotton planters became doubly galling. Like Prometheus, the South was stretched upon the fateful rock, said Jefferson Davis, and only by an almost superhuman effort could the fetters now be broken. How was the impending crisis to be averted?

Several promising avenues of evasion seemed to open before those who scanned the horizon. If the federal government could be held in fee or a balance of power maintained at Washington, then the duties on goods bought by the planters could be kept at a minimum and all the advantages of independence be secured under the Constitution. Another solution offered was the introduction of manufacturing into the South. Under the tutelage of Webster, Whig leaders often counseled this procedure. Cotton mills at hand, they argued, would provide local markets, free them from the shackles of the New York exchange, and emancipate them from the servitude to distant spinners. Under the stimulus of this idea, societies were formed to encourage the development of industries; indeed some noteworthy experiments were made from time to time.

In the main these efforts bore little fruit. Planters did not take kindly to manufacturing; their rural habits of life ran against it—possibly they had the tribesman's instinctive dislike for unaccustomed ways. Skilled labor, as much as business enterprise, was wanting; white immigrants from Europe did not go in large numbers to a section where all manual toil, whether in the home, field, or shop, lay under a stigma; and slaves, though sometimes used in industries, afforded poor material for technical branches of manufacturing in which they had received no training. Further, there was a lack of capital for such undertakings. American financiers, finding abundant opportunities for profitable investments in the North and West, showed little disposition to push into unpromising regions dominated by slave owners.

Still another scheme for giving strength to the cotton kingdom was a proposal for a closer economic union with the Northwest. Observing the drift of trade away from New Orleans to the Atlantic ports, architects of southern fortunes sketched elaborate plans for linking the upper Mississippi Valley with the planting region. This was an engrossing theme and it was enthusiastically discussed at a railroad convention held in Knoxville, Tennessee, on July 4, 1836, under the presidency of Hayne, the famous orator who worked in economics besides constitutional law. One of the fine dreams of the hour was a line from Cincinnati to Charleston, making the South Carolina metropolis a rival of Philadelphia and New York; but it burst under the stern duress of realization.

Another project was a railway from the Lakes to the Gulf and, under the management of that astute Yankee, Stephen A. Douglas, this was finally accomplished. Though popularly known as the competitor of Lincoln in the momentous debates of 1858, and as the author of "squatter sovereignty," Douglas had a surer claim to distinction for his work on the Illinois Central Railroad linking two strongholds of Democracy—Illinois and Mississippi.

On his arrival in the Senate in 1847, he started a movement to wring from Congress a huge grant of federal land in aid of railway construction in his state and in spite of many obstacles he made his way to the goal. Chicago capitalists opposed his first plan for making Galena the northern terminus; he won them over by choosing their city instead. Southern statesmen offered grave constitutional objections to federal aid for internal improvements; by extending his line all the way from the Ohio to the Gulf he overcame their scruples. After much wriggling and writhing, enough votes were won, and in 1850 Congress dedicated an immense area of the public domain to the project for a "Lakes to Gulf" railway. The step was important but too late. Before the line could be completed, Baltimore, Philadelphia, and New York had rail connections with the Mississippi Valley and were weaving all parts of the North into one system of economy.

Notwithstanding every effort to give a new direction to the sweep of economic forces, the dominant interest of the South, the cotton planters, showed an increasing tendency to swing away from the center of American life. Their best market was England, then the textile center of the world, where they could both sell their produce and buy cheap manufactures of every kind. Confined by climate and soil to special regions, their main basis of operation was of necessity in the Far South, in the districts most remote from the citadels of northern industry and finance. By 1850, two-thirds of the cotton crop in the United States was produced west of Georgia.

In its onward march the cotton interest had borne its seat of power into the Mississippi Valley and worked a revolution in the Jacksonian frontiers of Alabama, Mississippi, and Louisiana. When South Carolina made her call for nullification in 1832, all those states had given her a sharp negative answer. In three decades, however, the face of things had changed. When South Carolina renewed her appeal in 1860, it was these very states of the Southwest that raised the flag of revolution while Virginia, North Carolina, Tennessee, and Kentucky still held back. Not until the Confederate government had been inaugurated and the first blow had been struck did the upper South cut loose from the national moorings. And to the end, four of the fifteen slave states—Kentucky, Maryland, Delaware, and Missouri—and the western half of Virginia remained in the Union. They belonged rather to the system of the North than to the specialized cotton system of the Far South.

Under the drive of economic forces, it was the cotton interest that led the slave states into the appalling crisis. European conflicts, such as the Crimean War of 1854-56. might raise hopes for an abnormal demand for cotton, but an industry founded on uneducated labor, an industry that was engaged in exhausting and selling the pristine fertility of the soil was fated for a crash. In truth a decline in its economic strength was under way while its faith in political action was mounting: capacity to endure the tax of a protective tariff was diminishing while the determination of the manufacturing interests to have their subventions was rising to the point of an explosion. Thus the cotton industry faced three choices: an internal reconstruction, independence, or a foreign war. Following the historic precedents set by interests in a similar plight, its spokesmen chose what seemed to them the easiest course and found, as often happens, not safety thereby, but ruin.

§

Like all the regions of the United States to the east and south, the western frontier underwent a striking transformation between 1830 and the Civil War. At the former date, the line of settlement, if we exclude a few communities around the mouth of the Mississippi and in the Missouri Valley, ran roughly along the western border of Alabama and Tennessee, crossed the Mississippi River into Missouri, and then turned back in a northeasterly direction through Illinois, Indiana, and Ohio to Lake Erie. Within three decades, it had moved hundreds of miles to the west and north; it had been broken by western trails and by the steady march of pioneers up the slopes of the treeless plains. Michigan had been admitted to the Union in 1837, Iowa in 1846, Wisconsin in 1848, and Minnesota in 1858.

In the meantime the new Middle West had been supplemented by a second frontier on the coast where California and Oregon stood as sentinels on the Pacific. They too had no special economic interests or continental ties to bind them to the cotton kingdom. Many Oregon farmers doubtless remembered that it was southern politicians who had been loudest in shouting "fifty-four forty or fight" and quickest in compromising the boundary dispute with England. In any event there was no slavery in Oregon. Neither was there any chattel bondage in California, a mineral state opposed, as Webster said, by the law of nature to the planting system. American traders had established commercial interests there and miners had made them secure beyond all cavil. "Gold is king," firmly announced a Californian member of Congress when he heard the praise of cotton sung once too often on the floor. If there was a touch of excessive pride in his boast, gold and grain, without doubt, were to be reckoned in every new political combination.

The frontier that had nourished Jacksonian Democracy had now moved far to the West and it had also altered its character, whereas the borders of the cotton kingdom had become fixed by a law that no political party could demolish, no act of Congress could repeal.

§

The revolution wrought by steam and machinery was by no means limited in its effect to factory districts, corn fields, cotton plantations, and mining camps. It widened the borders of economic empire by the extension of American commerce into the Far Pacific. Though obscured to the vulgar eye by the dust of domestic conflict, the construction of that commercial dominion went forward rapidly from the foundation of the republic. The very year after Cornwallis surrendered to Washington at Yorktown, the *Empress of China,* fitted out partly at the expense of Robert Morris, merchant prince and "financier of the American Revolution," sailed from New York to Canton, carrying the American flag into the midst of the Dutch and British pennants that fluttered in the breezes of Chinese waters. Before the Fathers completed the framing of the Constitution, at least nine voyages had been made to the Far East by enterprising Yankees.

In the year of Washington's inauguration, ten ships from Salem plowed the waters of the Indian Ocean. Before he delivered his "Farewell Address," warning his countrymen against foreign entanglements, American captains were at home in the ports of China, Java, Sumatra, Siam, India, the Philippines, and the Ile de France. In 1797, the date of his retirement to Mt. Vernon, a crew of thirty boys, the oldest not over twenty-eight, took the *Betsy,* a boat of less than a hundred tons, on a voyage around the world by way of the Horn, Canton, and Good Hope, netting on an outlay of about eight thousand dollars the neat profit of a hundred and twenty thousand.

Meanwhile Congress under a Constitution formed, as Webster remarked, mainly for the advancement of commerce, granted to merchants trading with the Far East protective rates and special privileges of royal generosity—advantages which assured magnificent returns except in the most adverse of circumstances. As Senator from Pennsylvania and a promoter of business with China, Robert Morris could speak with authority among his brethren in the Congress of the United States.

The trade thus begun at the very inception of the republic, while it waxed and waned with the fortunes of war, politics, and business in the western world, showed a general tendency to advance. In the decade ending in 1840, American business with China alone amounted to nearly seventy-five millions, a sum greater than the total debt of the American Revolution which timid souls in Hamilton's day thought the country could never pay. By that time American manufacturers, especially the cotton spinners, had come to view China's teeming multitudes as the marginal customers who were to keep their wheels whirling and their coffers full. In 1857 over a hundred and fifty American ships cleared from Indian ports carrying goods worth upwards of ten millions.

When the guns of Sumter echoed over the plains and through the valleys of the United States, shrewd American business men had already gathered into their ships more than half the trade to and from the port of Shanghai and had made themselves masters of the lion's share of the commerce up and down the turgid current of the Yangtze. The challenge of planters to captains of industry slowed down this enterprise in the Far East—but only for a day. Within a generation after the guns had ceased to fire on brothers at home, the Stars and Strips were flying over the American outpost of traffic in the Far East—the Philippines. In this titanic process, disputes over slavery and even the Civil War itself were incidents that delayed but did not halt the giant of steam in his seven-league boots.

CHAPTER XV

The Politics of the Economic Drift

THE distinctions which characterized the three great sections of the United States evolved in the sweep of economic forces were not fanciful; they were woven out of the tough facts of daily existence. The leaders in all these regions were of the same race, spoke the same language, worshipped the same God, and had a common background of law, ethics, and culture. Their differences in sentiments, patterns of thought, and linguistic devices—their social psychology—sprang mainly from divergences in necessary adjustments to environment: labor systems, climate, soil, and natural resources producing conspicuous variations in modes of acquisition and living.

Never before in the history of human societies had there been just such a disposition of affairs. Conflicts between agriculture and capitalism were, of course, as old as the empires of antiquity. The agrarian movements that shook Rome to her foundations, the first French Revolution which assured the triumph of the bourgeoisie and the peasantry, and the long partisan struggles in England were all the outward signs of internal divisions similar to those found in every civilized community. Nevertheless no European country had ever had a highly developed group of capitalists, a large body of independent farmers, and a powerful landed aristocracy each to a marked degree segregated into a fairly definite geographical area. No European country had ever had gigantic industries battling for the possession of the domestic trade and at the same time a highly specialized branch of agriculture, like cotton raising, almost solely dependent for its profits upon a wide and attractive market in foreign countries.

The social conflicts of the Old World arose from horizontal rather than from vertical divisions; that is, from the antagonism of classes dwelling together rather than from the friction of economic groups localized in separate districts. It is true that strife based largely upon economic differences had from time to time disturbed the various federations which had made their bow on the European stage, especially Germany, but in none of them did the contest bear exactly the signs that characterized the American schism. Moreover, no modern European country ever possessed an immense domain of virgin land available for distribution among the populace by political methods and viewed as a means of commanding party majorities requisite for other ends.

Hence it came about that what may be called the rhetoric of the American political process in the middle period differed widely from that employed in similar struggles in other countries of the world—a fact usually overlooked by Europeans who attempt to devise formulas for American social phenomena.

§

In each of the great geographical sections with its dominant economic interest was evolved a reasoned scheme of political action. Broadly speaking, the capitalists of the Northeast demanded from Congress a liberal immigration

policy to assure an abundance of cheap labor, ship subsidies
for the promotion of commerce, internal improvements in
the form of roads, canals, and harbor facilities, a sound
monetary system to guarantee that loans and interest would
be duly met in values at least equal to the nominal figure
in the bond, high tariffs for industries, and the preservation
of the protected market area by the retention of the southern states in the Union. This was a heroic program which
its sponsors could only realize by securing the possession of
the executive and legislative branches of the federal government.

To this scheme of positive action a supplement of negation was essential for capitalism, namely, a firm grip on the
federal Supreme Court, for that body alone could enforce
by appropriate interpretation those clauses of the Constitution which forbade states to issue paper money and impair
the obligation of contract—in short, interfere with the normal course of business enterprise. It was well known that
debtors of the rural regions, since the days of Daniel Shays,
had shown a strong penchant for easy money and loose
banking because an inflated currency enabled them to meet
their obligations with more facility and less labor. It was
equally well known that several states had repudiated their
just debts, imposed onerous burdens on business undertakings, and laid taxes objectionable to common carriers.

For these and similar reasons, the capitalist group required as a condition of highly successful operations the
enactment of a clear-cut program of federal legislation by
Congress and a friendly construction of the Constitution
by the federal courts. Of course it could be argued and
with cogency that such a program was designed ultimately
to benefit all interests and all sections of the country but
it is a significant political fact that the leaders of the planting and farming areas did not generally take this view of the
matter.

By their common agricultural interests, planters and
farmers were drawn together politically and thrown into

opposition to capitalists at many points. They were producers of raw materials and food stuffs and they were purchasers of manufactured goods. As far as they were conscious of economic processes, they naturally wished to sell in the dearest market and buy in the cheapest, namely, in Europe, and especially in England, where capitalist industry was far advanced in skill and technique while labor was ground to the very margin of existence. In brief, they wanted to sell their raw materials and foodstuffs to English manufacturers for high prices and buy English goods, made by cheap English labor, at low prices. Broadly speaking this meant that planters and farmers favored low tariffs—tariffs for revenue only—though not often free trade with the whole world, for that involved direct taxes on themselves for the sustenance of the federal government.

Yet another powerful bond of interest united these two agricultural groups, especially on the frontier belt: both were in need of capital and both were heavy borrowers in the eastern financial market. Farmers often mortgaged their lands and planters their estates and slaves for funds with which to embark on their respective ventures, or to expand them when once they were launched. Hence, being debtors instead of creditors, they were frequently the friends of easy money, of an elastic currency with varying degrees of soundness.

And to promote their monetary designs, they had an appropriate political scheme, supported by a full-blown constitutional theory. They had not yet formulated any project of national banking, dominated by "dirt farmers," that would yield the desired fruit under their control. In the national field their program was to destroy, rather than to construct—to abolish the United States Bank, prevent its revival, and put the issue of the currency in local hands, under the authority of state legislatures in which they were at home and easily supreme. The less scrupulous among the debtors openly favored inflation by local banks as a means of discharging their obligations in money of reduced value and advocated lenient bankruptcy laws for those who suffered a total shipwreck in finances.

Therefore, in the field of federal politics, the planting and farming groups asked for few favors; on the national stage they were in the main a party of laissez faire. And their constitutional doctrines naturally took on the color of their economic projects. Since they deemed it to their interest to have no protective tariffs and federal banks, it seemed reasonable to them to believe that Congress had no power under the Constitution to promote industries by special legislation and create banking institutions. They were, however, not beyond the necessity of consulting the auguries. They required at the hands of the judiciary a wide interpretation of the Constitution in one particular, at least; that is, a view of the revered document which would permit states to charter and manage banks, issue paper money, and make various modifications in the obligation of contract.

It must be conceded, no doubt, that every planter who stood like Horatius at the bridge for a strict interpretation of the Constitution and every Tennessee farmer who sprang upon a damask chair in the White House to cheer for Jacksonian Democracy had not formulated the whole scheme of things with meticulous precision but beyond question the great leaders of both groups thoroughly comprehended the economic processes of the age. There was ample proof of their understanding in the fact that the general drift of federal legislation and judicial interpretation after 1835 was directed to the interest of planters and farmers until suddenly reversed by the constitutional and social revolution popularly known in the North as the Civil War and in the South as the War between the States.

§

It is not here contended that all capitalists with mechanical exactness were drawn to one combination and all planters and farmers to another. Such a contention would be without historic warrant—contrary to the evidence in the case. In each of the three economic groups were represented varying degrees and kinds of property and prosperity. Planters were not all engaged in producing the same staples; neither did they enjoy the same rate of return on their capital or suffer the same pressure of adversity in times of financial depression. Some of them raised tobacco, some rice, others cane, and still others cotton—the last advancing to leadership in numbers and wealth. If cotton men were keen for a low tariff, cane growers and sugar makers were as eager for a high duty on their commodity as any woolen manufacturer in New England or iron founder in Pennsylvania for a tariff on his peculiar product.

Moreover, among planters of the same class there was inequality of status. Those who worked on the western margin, mining and selling virgin soil, often made huge profits while others to the east, who tilled land which had lost its original fertility, labored heavily under the law of diminishing returns. Account books of Calhoun's own estate reveal a moving story of a losing venture. It is not to be overlooked that the "hot-bed" of secession was South Carolina, where planters had been working worn-out land for a quarter of a century.

Nor did northern capitalists, any more than planters, present a perfectly united front on all matters. Manufacturers and their bankers were, on the whole, rather solidly behind demands for high protection against foreign competition. On the other hand capitalists engaged in the shipping business, while anxious for subsidies and other special favors, were by no means fervent in supporting revenue measures that cut down the volume of the carrying trade. Their intimate associates, importing merchants, although capitalists in a large way, were as enthusiastic as any southern planter for a low tariff admitting the easy flow of commodities into the United States. Furthermore it must be remembered that a large share of the importing merchant's business, especially in New York and Philadelphia, embraced the exchange of southern produce for European manufactures, linking merchandise with planting by substantial, if imponderable, bonds. Even finance was somewhat divided in its affections. In the strong boxes of northern investors mortgages on southern plantations rested by the side of industrial and railway securities; often a rich money lender was a perfectly good Democrat.

Among western farmers there were also divergences. Many of them grew hemp and wool and so welcomed protection by the government; some were prosperous either through industry, luck, or unearned increment in land values; others staggered under a burden of debt, tilling marginal land. Inevitably, therefore, the tension and patterns of their agrarian sentiments varied from community to community and with the seasons of prosperity and adversity.

Each of the three geographical sections, like each of the three classes of individuals, on minute examination, disclosed dissimilarities. The map of slavery giving the distribution of bondmen among the counties of the southern states was a document of prime importance in the economics of politics. Throughout large areas of western Virginia and North Carolina, northern Georgia, eastern Kentucky and Tennessee, northern Arkansas, and Missouri, excepting the river valleys, slaves formed less than twenty-five per cent of the population. The land of those regions belonged to free farmers who owned no slaves, or few, and who tilled the soil themselves; they, rather than the planters, furnished the original substance of Jacksonian Democracy, in their sections.

Nor were the manufacturing states of the Northeast a single economic unit, solely concerned with industrial enterprise. They possessed large agricultural interests likely to manifest varying degrees of agrarian temper. In addition, they had in their cities a growing working class which threatened from decade to decade to play an independent rôle in politics. Though generally thrown by social differences into opposition to the capitalists, especially in local affairs, the workingmen of the middle period were not all free traders; a large proportion believed that their bread was better buttered by protection than by a tariff for revenue only. Particularly was this true in New England and Pennsylvania with their great productive industries—as contrasted with New York City, the mercantile metropolis.

And the farming states of the West, as previously noted, were not without peculiar aspirations of their own. With astonishing swiftness they passed through the pioneer stage and began to supplement their rural economy by trading and manufacturing. Other times, other manners. A little woolen mill on the bank of an Indiana brook felt the beneficent shade of a high tariff quite as much as a huge building at Lowell, Massachusetts, filled with roaring machinery. Besides benefiting from such economic diversification, agriculture in the Mississippi Valley had its own psychological fringe. Certainly a wide gulf separated the independent white farmer who toiled like a slave in his narrow fields under the burning sun from the great planter who lived like an aristocrat on his broad acres.

While the farmer was as eager as the planter to buy his plows in the cheaper markets of England, he often found it difficult to think of himself in the same class as Louisiana cane growers who spent their summers at northern watering places and attended grand opera in New Orleans in the winter. He was by no means always sure that his interests lay in a pan-agricultural combination for political action. Very often the prospect of rising land values and better markets offered by railways linking the Northwest to Pennsylvania, New York, and Massachusetts had attractions for him that were hard to offset by pictures of the prosperity afforded by free trade with Liverpool and Manchester. It is not surprising therefore that the political architects of the middle period encountered grave difficulties in attempting to erect enduring political associations out of economic interests that were both sectional and diverse—difficulties which were increased by the periodic cycles of prosperity and panic.

§

Nevertheless, each of the three economic classes struggling for dominance in its own section and in the country at large had able spokesmen who attempted to formulate its program of political action, its scheme of ethical justification, and its line of attack on the opposing forces. In fact, all the resources of history, law, philosophy, logic, theology, and natural science, as they stood revealed at the time, were employed with amazing effect in a mighty triangular struggle that ran through politics, religion, journalism, education, and literature. Every orator who took part in it seemed sincerely convinced that his cause was righteousness itself and was apparently unable to understand why his own arguments failed to persuade others through the sheer force of compelling reasonableness.

If any satirical spectators ever perceived the incongruities of the rationalizing operation, they failed to turn the weapons of Juvenal and Swift upon the diligent apostles of rectitude. Those statesmen who raised themselves with heroic effort a little above the din of the partisan conflict and tried to emancipate themselves from the narrow confines of class psychology could not by the noblest exercise of imagination divine any solution for the contradictions except in some compromise or a balance of interests based upon the delusive assumption that stability and quiescence were possible in a swiftly changing society. Webster and Clay, oppressed by an awful foreboding of a crash to come, could only pray for a postponement of the deluge—ask God to grant that their dying eyes at least might behold no broken and dissevered Union.

§

Of the capitalistic interests in general—manufacturing, transportation, and banking—the one spokesman who towered above all others was, by common consent, Daniel Webster of Massachusetts. He was a true son of New England business enterprise, fully appreciated by those whom he served. When it was discovered that his salary as United States Senator was not sufficient to keep him in that style of living which he had chosen for himself, a number of wealthy men raised a capital fund and placed the income at his service. "Some of those who contributed," remarks Webster's admiring biographer, S. G. Fisher, "were interested in the industries sustained by the protective tariff; though by no means all."

Webster was a philosopher as well as a spokesman of economic forces. That he knew his Aristotle, Harrington, and Montesquieu, his Plymouth Rock oration abundantly demonstrated. He believed that the form and frame of governments were determined by the nature and distribution of property, that American institutions were founded on property, that property ought to have a direct representation in the government, and that the disastrous revolutions of the past had been revolutions against accumulations of wealth. Likewise a student of the Constitution, Webster correctly understood the economic features of that instrument. On this point, he gave the substance of his creed in a speech delivered at Andover in 1843: "We may look at the debates in all the state conventions and the expositions of all the greatest men in the country, particularly in Massachusetts and Virginia, . . . and we shall find it everywhere held up as the main reason for the adoption of the Constitution that it would give the general government the power to regulate commerce and trade."

That Webster firmly grasped the economic character of the political conflict in which he was a figure of gigantic proportions is also evident from numerous speeches. In none of these did he more effectively summarize the points of his doctrine than in an address to his party brethren of

THE POLITICS OF THE ECONOMIC DRIFT 673

Boston setting forth the objects of what was called "the Whig Revolution of 1840." With trip hammer strokes he drove them home: permanent peace with England, a stable revenue adequate to the needs of the federal government, the protection of domestic industry, the destruction of the compromise tariff of 1833 so inimical to the manufacturing interests, and finally a restoration of the currency and public credit by a sound banking and financial system.

Knowing very well that many a mechanic and farmer who had flocked to Jackson's conquering hosts regarded the tariff as a special privilege rendered by Congress to mill owners, Webster was careful on various occasions to meet the argument at the threshold. "I am looking," he once said, "not for such a law as will benefit capitalists—they can take care of themselves—but for a law that shall induce capitalists to invest their capital in such a manner as to occupy and employ American labor." Then he turned to the agrarian opponents of protection. "If all men in a country were merely agricultural producers, free trade would be very well," he remarked; but he quickly countered by saying that the interests of the United States were widely diversified, leading to a conclusion that seemed inevitable in his mind. "There are many false prophets going to and fro in the land who declare that the tariff benefits only the manufacturer and that it injures the farmer. This is all sheer misrepresentation. Every farmer must see that it is his interest to find a near purchaser for his produce, to find a ready purchaser, and a purchaser at a good price." Such in brief was Webster's view of the essential economic factors involved in the politics of the middle period.

On the outstanding moral issue of the hour, the abolition of slavery, Webster with unerring accuracy summarized the opinion entertained by the wealth and talents of Massachusetts. "I regret," he said, "that slavery exists in the southern states; but it is clear and certain that Congress has no power over it. It may be, however, that in the dispensations of Providence, some remedy of this evil may occur, or may be hoped for hereafter. But in the meantime I hold to the Constitution of the United States."

§

On the side of the planting interests, the issues of state-craft arising from the economic conflict were logically summarized and expounded by John C. Calhoun of South Carolina, a spokesman no less gifted than Webster. In a remarkable speech delivered in 1839 he traced the history of American politics from the foundation of the republic to his own time—covering in a summary interpretation the events we have already surveyed—and then sketched his map of the new battlefield. He opened by reviewing the old Jeffersonian case against the Federalists. Hamilton's policy, he said, had been to enlist "the more powerful classes of society, through their interests," to the support of his system.

The great Federalist statesman, Calhoun then continued, had chartered the Bank with a capital "to be composed principally of stock held by public creditors; thus binding more strongly to the government that already powerful class, by giving them, through its agency, increased profit, and a decided control over the currency, exchanges, and the business transactions of the country." This was not all; Hamilton had also proposed to pervert the taxing function "from a revenue to a penal power through which the entire capital and industry of the Union might be controlled."

Against this combination of economic forces, Jefferson strove with all his might but such gains as he made were transitory. After the War of 1812, Hamilton's system renewed its youth; the protective tariff, the United States Bank, internal improvements, and the other devices of the moneyed interests were approved again and John Quincy Adams, son of an old Federalist, was given a four-year term in the White House.

Then came the Jacksonian revulsion and the new revolution—the stages of which Calhoun proceeded to enumerate. The first stroke was the expulsion of Adams and his group from power; the second was the discharge of the funded debt; the third was the compromise tariff act of 1833, which professed to close "forever in this government a most prolific source of power, patronage, and corruption;" the fourth was the overthrow of the United States Bank; and the fifth was "the suspension of the connection between the government and the banks."

Calhoun now listed the remaining steps leading to his perfect order: the work of separating the government from banks must be completed; internal improvements must be stopped; the cost of the federal government enhanced by pensions and patronage must be reduced; and the tariff at the expiration of the compromise act in 1833 must be revised in such a manner as to put "an end to the protective system, with all the evils that follow and ever must follow in its train."

Of his real purpose Calhoun made no concealment: "My aim is fixed. It is no less than to turn back the government to where it commenced its operation in 1789; to obliterate all the intermediate measures originating in the peculiar principles and policy of the school to which I am opposed." As for slavery, the foundation of the planting system, that was in the circumstances "a good, a perfect good." There was thus no doubt about the character of Calhoun's economic-political argument. It was precisely stated and diametrically opposed to that of Webster.

In dealing with constitutional questions, the master logician of South Carolina also showed himself the peer of the Massachusetts statesman, though he drew exactly contrary conclusions from identical patterns of language. Notwithstanding the fact that he had himself supported the tariff of 1816, Calhoun came to believe and wrote powerful briefs to prove that the Constitution did not authorize the economic measures which Webster advocated and that his own latest program of low tariffs alone had the sanction of the Fathers. To their great covenant Calhoun's devotion was no less profound than that of Webster. His conviction that it proclaimed his gospel was no less firmly rooted. For him it simply had one meaning; for Webster another.

§

No towering giant like Webster or Calhoun rose from field and forest to formulate the political and constitutional creed of the independent farmers, East, West, and South; and yet the tillers of the soil had their spokesmen no less than the capitalists and planters. Orators of the second and third magnitude swarmed to their cause, filling pages of the Congressional Globe with arguments prolix and vehement. Two of these—both national figures for a day —presented their thesis with singular force and consistency. The first was Andrew Johnson of Tennessee, such a power in his realm that the Republicans, with an eye upon the farmer vote and additional strength for Lincoln, nominated him for the vice-presidency in 1864. The second was C. L. Vallandigham of Ohio, whom Lincoln later made temporarily famous by expelling him for intransigent opposition to the War. And the popularity which both enjoyed in the rural regions was no doubt largely due to the vigor with which they waged their political campaign against the capitalist class.

In the spirit of Jefferson, sometimes in the very words of the Virginian, Johnson again and again recited in Congress the creed of the farmer and rural mechanic. "The rural population, the mechanical and agricultural portions of this community are the very salt of it," exclaimed the tailor from Tennessee. "Mr. Jefferson never said a truer thing than when he declared that large cities are eye sores in the body-politic: in Democracies they are consuming cancers. . . . Build up your villages, build up your rural districts, and you will have men who rely upon their own industry, who rely upon their own ingenuity, who rely upon their own economy and application to business for support. . . . Our true policy is to build up the middle class; to sustain the villages, to populate the rural districts, and let the power of this Government remain with the middle class! I want no miserable city rabble on the one hand. I want no pampered, bloated, corrupted aristocracy on the other." To this representative of farmers and village mechanics sustained by agriculture, the policies of Webster and Calhoun were equally odious.

The other advocate of the small farmer, Vallandigham, sang the bucolic song to a similar refrain. According to his view, the conflict of the period was at bottom a contest between plutocracy on the one hand and labor in the shop and field on the other; but in the exigencies of politics he was willing to make use of an alliance with the planting aristocracy to realize his objects.

In a powerful speech delivered in 1861 he drew in bold strokes his history of the long political contest then merging into a revolution. "The great dividing line," he said, "was always between capital and labor—between the few who had money and wanted to use the government to increase and 'protect' it, as the phrase goes, and the many who had little but wanted to keep it and who only asked the government to let them alone." The issues arising from this conflict, he went on, had taken various forms: "a permanent public debt, a national bank, the public deposits, a protective tariff, internal improvements, and other questions of a similar character, all of them looking to the special interests of the moneyed classes." Around these issues the capitalists had rallied parties under various names, but each time they had encountered a formidable combination of sectional interests.

The planting South, he reasoned, "was the natural ally of the Democracy of the North and especially of the West." Why? "Partly because the people of the South are chiefly an agricultural and producing, non-commercial and non-manufacturing people, and partly because there is no conflict, or little conflict among them between capital and labor, inasmuch as to a considerable extent capital owns a large class of laborers not of the white race." Out of this national union of planters and farmers had sprung the powerful party of the Democracy and in each great open trial of strength between 1800 and 1860 the popular combination had emerged triumphant.

Then in utter despair, exclaimed Vallandigham, the champions of "the moneyed interest" resorted "to some other and new element for an organization which might be made strong enough to conquer and destroy the Democracy and thus obtain control of the federal government." Searching hungrily for a new combination of power, they eventually discovered "the nucleus of such an organization ready formed to their hands—an organization odious indeed in name but founded on two of the most powerful passions of the human heart: sectionalism, which is only a narrow and localized patriotism, and anti-slavery, or love of freedom, which commonly is powerful in proportion as it is very near coming home to one's self or very far off."

§

In this clash of sectional interests, the outstanding issue of the middle period was the tariff. From it sprang nullification in South Carolina and South Carolina finally led the way into secession. In general it was the representatives of the manufacturing group who fostered the demand for protection and showed the greatest facility in gathering recruits for that cause in national elections. On the whole, opposition to protection and support for free trade, or at all events low rates of duty, came from the agricultural and importing interests.

Yet the matter, as already indicated, was by no means simple. Every revenue law imposing taxes on goods coming into the United States was a complex of many items arranged under several separate schedules—a complex which in practice reflected the demands of many groups and factions, sometimes even conciliating opposing interests by compensatory favors of real or dubious utility. In these circumstances, American political society presented revolving kaleidoscopic patterns whenever the revenue question was up for controversy. Woolen manufacturers and sheep raisers might be united by a tariff that protected both cloth and raw wool but sent flying asunder by hardware schedules. Hemp and flax growers burned brown under blazing suns might be made to feel a common cause with steel and iron magnates bleeched white in shaded offices. Nevertheless two powerful agricultural groups, cotton and tobacco growers, supplemented by corn raisers, provided a fairly consistent leadership for a relentless war against the general principle of protection for manufactures.

Five times between 1830 and 1860 the tariff was revised, showing on the whole a downward tendency. A sliding-scale cut was made in 1833, as we have seen, under a threat of revolution on the part of South Carolina's planters, and, when, nearly ten years later, the Whigs with aid from the opposition forced the duties upward again, the champions of low tariffs swept the polls in the election of 1844. Then the tide definitely turned, the Democratic party under southern leadership driving the country steadily in the direction of free trade until the grand climax of 1860. By the tariff act of 1846, Congress struck a smashing blow at the protective system, the members of the South and West being in the vanguard of the majority that did the terrible execution; of the ninety-three votes against the measure in the House, New England and the Middle States furnished sixty-three.

As this law soon brought a surplus into the Treasury, triumphant Democracy delivered another savage thrust in 1857 making the rates still lower—in actual operation below the figure set in the famous compromise of 1833. Though the vote on this bill in the House seemed to reveal a confused state of public opinion in the large, it betrayed unmistakable tendencies. Members from the South and Southwest cast sixty votes for the measure and but two against it. More salient still was the fact that the West and Northwest furnished thirty-three votes against tariff reduction and only fourteen for it. The South was now almost solid; the West was evidently swinging away from its old moorings and was in a mood for a new political combination—one so adroitly effected at Chicago in 1860.

In the course of the long conflict over the tariff, statesmen from the South worked out a positive theory as to its practical effect on the distribution of wealth. The creed was perfectly formulated in a logical fashion by Senator McDuffie of South Carolina as early as 1830, all elaborations by those who followed in his footsteps being merely fine glosses on his protocol. In the Senator's own words, the argument ran as follows: "Owing to the federative character of our Government, the great geographical extent of our territory, and the diversity of the pursuits of our citizens in different parts of the Union, it has so happened that two great interests have sprung up, standing directly opposed to each other." The first of these interests embraces the manufacturers who cannot thrive in the face of European competition without protection and subsidies from the government; the second is composed of the producers of agricultural staples in the South—staples that can find a market only in foreign countries and can be advantageously sold "only in exchange for the foreign manufactures which come into competition with those of the Northern and Middle States. . . . These interests then stand diametrically and irreconcilably opposed to each other. The interest, the pecuniary interest, of the Northern manufacturer is directly promoted by every increase of the taxes imposed on Southern commerce; and it is unnecessary to add that the interest of the Southern planter is promoted by every diminution of the taxes imposed on the productions of his industry."

Thus the southern statesman reduced this phase of the political struggle of the middle period to its final terms: a conflict over the distribution of wealth. The planter desired a public policy that put money into his pocket, or, to use his customary language, enabled him to keep it there; the manufacturer of the North clamored for a policy that transferred it into his own. In McDuffie's mind it was the old and simple plan of getting and keeping; no political litany could obscure the issue for the initiates. Within two decades, practically all the statesmen of the planting interest were unreservedly committed to the Senator's faith.

No mere academic theory was this concept of the political battle. Statisticians of the South even tried to visualize it in terms of dollars and cents by figuring out the exact amount of "tribute" paid by the planting class to the capitalists of the North. In that calculation they estimated that forty million dollars in round numbers had been poured into the coffers of northern shipowners by 1850 in the form of freight rates. Finding that southern exports amounted to about one hundred millions annually, they came to the conclusion that this enormous sum was in fact lent without interest to northern merchants for use in the manipulation of foreign and domestic exchanges. The toll levied on the South by machine industry, they thought, was especially burdensome. "Were she to work up her 2,500,000 bales of cotton," exclaimed a southern economist, "and receive the profit of $40 each, she would realize 70 to 100 millions annually." To cap the climax, the calculators estimated that the southern people spent fifteen millions in the North traveling for health and pleasure.

If the figures sometimes missed the mark, the thesis was at least plain: through all the economic processes of trade, manufacture, exchange, merchandizing, and luxury, the South was taxed and exploited—in stark reality, brought down to the status of a tribute bearer to northern capitalism. "The South," lamented one orator, "stands in the attitude of feeding upon her own bosom a vast population of merchants, shipowners, capitalists, and others who, without the claims of her progeny, drink up the life blood of her trade. It cannot be here asserted that a deduction should be allowed for that portion of the southern crop which is shipped directly from the southern ports to foreign countries. The tonnage register will show that nine-tenths of the shipping employed belong to northern capitalists. . . . Where then goes the value of our labor but to those who, taking advantage of our folly, ship for us, buy for us, sell to us, and after turning our own capital to their profitable account return laden with our money, to enjoy their easily earned opulence at home?"

From this point of view the task before the planting states was, therefore, emancipation from the dominion of northern capitalism. "We confidently affirm," declared McDuffie, "that the people of the southern and southwestern states are invoked by considerations of the most enlightened patriotism, as well as of an enlightened self-interest, to apply a speedy and effective remedy. The means of achieving our commercial independence are abundant."

§

A second phase of this titanic conflict over the distribution of wealth involved the problem of controlling the currency and banking. Was it to be centralized under national auspices or dispersed among the states? As a rule, Hamilton's system of consolidation, while it was in effect, had been favored by northern business men because it afforded elastic credit facilities and guaranteed a sound currency for trade throughout the entire United States. Generally speaking, the opposition to that system had come from the agricultural sections. The party which destroyed the second federal bank so ruthlessly that the Whigs could never restore it was Jackson's farmer-labor combination, the new Democracy of the middle period.

And yet it would be a mistake to assume that the Democrats refused all political relations with banks. On the contrary, they adopted the policy of depositing federal funds in local banks, chartered under state authority, with a view to securing effective assistance akin to that furnished first to the Federalists and then to the Whigs by the United States Bank—a practice which helped to release the tension of "tight money" in the West and South and afforded funds for land speculation as well. It was not without some justification that the shrewd Davy Crockett, commenting on the fruits of the system, remarked: "It requires an eye as insinuating as a dissecting knife to see what safety there is in placing one million of the public funds in some little country shaving shop with no more than one hundred thousand dollars capital. This bank, we will suppose without being too particular, is in the neighborhood of the public lands where speculators who have everything to gain and nothing to lose swarm like crows about carrion. They buy the United States' lands upon a large scale, get discounts from the aforesaid shaving shop which are made upon a large scale, also upon United States funds; they pay the whole purchase money with these discounts and get a clear title to the land, so that when the shaving shop comes to make a Flemish account of her transactions, 'the Government' (*i.e.*, President Jackson) will discover that he has not only lost the original deposit, but a large part of the public lands to boot."

In fact, so notorious did the evils become that the Democrats in control of the federal government were forced to abandon the distribution of the revenues among banking concerns and safeguard their funds by establishing an independent treasury system. Thus the national government was cut loose from banks altogether. Neither the eloquence of Webster nor the persuasion of Clay could induce farmers and planters to agree to the creation of a third United States Bank; the obvious beneficiaries of such an institution were not as numerous and widespread as those who partook of the advantages of a protective tariff.

The destruction of the second United States Bank, of course, left unsolved the problem of the currency—that powerful engine which could be used for transferring wealth from one group to another as well as for supplying the means of commerce. Since the Constitution mentioned only gold and silver coin, there were in the early days of the republic a few statesmen who clung fiercely to hard money in the belief that the right to issue paper would be employed to favor the politicians, if exercised by the government, and to enrich the capitalists, if vested in private corporations.

But those who adhered to this view were soon overborne; the volume of metal was too small, the necessities of commerce too great. Accordingly, the first United States Bank founded in 1791 was authorized to emit bills and before it came to an end twenty years later, numerous local banks, chartered by the respective states, had also been empowered to scatter notes broadcast. In 1815 there were already in existence more than two hundred state banks; and after the abolition of the second United States Bank in 1836 they increased with extraordinary rapidity. Each year saw additions to the number until on the eve of the Civil War there were sixteen hundred institutions, with a circulation of $202,000,000 in bills based upon $87,700,000 in specie.

While many of these local banks were managed conservatively, others, especially in the South and West, were in the hands of inexperienced, often unscrupulous, operators; and every time there was a financial crisis some of them went to the wall, causing serious losses to the holders of their paper. For example, one of these "financial institutions," fittingly named "wildcat banks," wound up its affairs in chancery with bills to the face value of $580,000 in circulation and $86.46 in specie on hand for redemption. In vain did official inspectors of state banks seek to prevent such frauds: the devices of the "financiers" were too cunning for the best of watchmen. A specially clever manager, for instance, spread a layer of gold and silver on a foundation of nails and glass in his strong box, giving the appearance of "great resources." A whole group of banks conspired to defeat the law by sending specie from one to another in advance of the inspector. "Gold and silver," complained a perplexed commissioner, "flew about the country with the celerity of magic; its sound was heard in the depths of the forest, yet like the wind, one knew not whence it came or whither it was going."

With increasing velocity a flood of paper poured out upon the nation, some of it sound, some of it quickly depreciating, and nearly all of it fluctuating violently with the oscillations of business. As time passed, affairs grew worse rather than better. The development of railways spread all over the country the notes of local banks—frequently bills, known in the vernacular as "shin plasters," calling for sums as low as five cents. The growth of interstate commerce aggravated the disease until bewildered merchants and capitalists were driven to desperation trying to keep their accounts straight in paper that went up and down from day to day.

To make a long story short, on the eve of the final crash in 1860, the American currency system, under the drive of an agrarian democracy, had reached a state relatively more alarming, if possible, to business enterprise than it had attained under the Articles of Confederation in the previous century. Only a Daniel Shays was needed to reproduce the earlier terror.

So grave were the evils of loose banking that they could hardly be overlooked by anyone. Indeed they were early assailed by the radical agrarians themselves with scarcely less vehemence than by business men. As a matter of fact the banks chartered under state authority were corporations of capitalists and objects of suspicion to Jacksonian Democrats of the left wing; even farmers did not like to be cheated by bills founded on little or no specie. Accordingly the cry went up in favor of "notes inflated but sound" issued by and on the credit of state governments—in spite of the fact that the Constitution of the United States declared in words strong and exact: "No state . . . shall emit bills of credit; or make anything but gold and silver coin a tender in payment of debts."

Ignoring this clear prohibition Missouri farmers and planters, pinched for money, decided, as soon as they got into the Union, that they would make cash with the printing press. On their demand the local legislature provided in 1821 that the state treasury should issue two hundred thousand dollars worth of certificates in denominations of not less than fifty cents or more than ten dollars, the said bills to be distributed among the counties on the basis of population and lent to the needy on farm mortgages and personal property. The printing was done and the "certificates" were sent on their mission of relief.

Then the authors of the program had to reckon with John Marshall, Chief Justice of the United States Supreme Court, before whose august tribunal the issue finally came. In the course of time a Missouri debtor, with an ironic shrug, refused to pay the state government when it attempted to collect from him a loan originally made in its own notes, alleging in his defense that the issue of the bills was invalid from the beginning because forbidden by the federal Constitution. This case being taken to Washington, the Supreme Court, with Marshall rendering the opinion, sustained the debtor. Scarcely concealing his impatience, the stern old Justice turned a deaf ear to the eloquent argument of Senator Benton, who pleaded the cause of his state; in language that admitted of no ambiguity, Marshall informed the fiat-money party that no state could emit bills of credit designed to circulate as money on the faith of the state itself. So the Missouri paper money law was declared null and void. The chapter was apparently closed.

In fact, however, it was not really closed, for the neighboring state of Kentucky, shrewder in its generation than Missouri, had discovered a more subtle scheme for issuing paper money. Its legislature in 1820 established a bank in the name of the state, chose the directors and president of the institution, and authorized the corporation to issue notes, receive deposits, and make loans on real and personal property. In due course the validity of this act was questioned before the Supreme Court, where, at a preliminary trial, with two members of the tribunal absent, three of the five judges, Marshall in the lead, concurred in holding the Kentucky law void because in effect the state was issuing bills of credit under it. But since three justices did not constitute a majority of the full Court a rehearing was ordered.

When the case came up again, three years afterward, namely, in 1837, the composition of the bench had been changed; Marshall had passed from the scene and Jackson's stanch friend, Roger B. Taney, had taken his seat. Now dominated by western and southern men, the Court chose Justice McLean, a Jackson appointee from Ohio, to write the opinion in the Kentucky cause. After examining the statute enacted by his neighbors across the river from Cincinnati, the learned Justice came to the conclusion that, in spite of Marshall's declaration, the law did not conflict with the clause of the Constitution forbidding states to issue bills of credit. In other words, a state could charter a bank, hold all its stock, choose its officers, and empower it to issue notes and lend them to citizens, without imparting to the institution any of the "attributes of sovereignty."

With an eloquence marked by pathos, Justice Story dissented from this solemn judgment, speaking for himself and his dear colleague, the late Chief Justice Marshall. In a note of despair, Chancellor Kent of New York, on reading the report of the case, declared that he had lost his "confidence and hopes in the constitutional guardianship and protection of the Supreme Court." The Constitution remained just as written by the Fathers but new men were consulting the auspices. Well might the spiritual heirs of Shays rejoice in western cornfields. To private banks issuing notes could now be added state banks engaged in the same business.

Victorious in the currency field, the party of the easy way

began to draft bankruptcy laws and other legislation touching private rights in tender spots. Here, too, fine juridical points were involved; for it was necessary to take into account that clause of the federal Constitution which forbade states to impair the obligation of contracts. As interpreted by Chief Justice Marshall in the celebrated Dartmouth College case of 1819, and other opinions less famous in the history of constitutional law, those brief words, broadly speaking, commanded local legislatures never to repeal charters, land grants, and other privileges once issued to private persons and corporations, even if corruption had entered into the original transaction. In the same spirit, an act of the New York legislature authorizing bankrupts to discharge their obligations by turning their assets over to creditors in due form was declared invalid as to contracts, notes, and debts made previous to the enactment of the law.

In the course of time, however, changes in the personnel of the Court put Marshall in the minority and, much to his chagrin, his colleagues in the great tribunal sustained a bankruptcy law which applied to debts contracted *after* its passage. This was a decision of high consequence. Webster, who was of counsel in the case, put the situation in a nutshell. "Suppose," he said in his plea, "a state should declare, by law, that all contracts entered into thereafter should be subject to such laws as the legislature, at any time, or from time to time, might see fit to pass. This law, according to the argument, would enter into the contract, become a part of it, and authorize the interference of the legislative power with it for any and all purposes, wholly uncontrolled by the Constitution." Nevertheless, with Marshall vigorously dissenting, the Court declared in effect that whenever a state specifically reserved to itself the right to repeal or alter charters and contracts made in the future, such reservation gave it a free hand, in spite of the clause forbidding it to impair such obligation.

Quickly grasping the import of this decision, restive states cast off another federal shackle. Wisconsin, for example, in drafting her constitution of 1848 inserted in the article dealing with corporations the pertinent words: "All general laws or special acts, enacted under the provisions of this section, may be altered or repealed by the legislature at any time after their passage."

Thus, in solemn decisions, Jacksonian judges from agrarian states broke down the historic safeguards thrown around property rights by the letter of the Constitution and the jurisprudence of John Marshall. For practical purposes they declared the states to be sovereign. So in 1860 the country stood in fundamental respects just where it did in 1787 under the Articles of Confederation. Nothing but another radical change in the membership of the Supreme Bench or a constitutional revolution, such as that effected in 1789, could repair the havoc wrought in business enterprise by agrarian actions. This second revolution was to come—during the storm of war when the Fourteenth Amendment was forced on the nation by the military power of a Republican administration.

§

On the states' rights view of the Constitution, the reduction of the tariff, the overthrow of the United States Bank, and a general easing of the currency, Jacksonian Democracy presented a fairly united front at the turn of the half century, its future seeming to be assured beyond all question. However, among the irrepressible issues thrust upon the country during the middle period by physical fact was the land question, a partisan ghost that could not be laid by political verbalism. The immense public domain was a grim reality, and everybody was interested in its fate.

As we have seen, farmers and mechanics were determined to have it for themselves without paying anything for it; manufacturers were afraid of losing their workmen if this division was made; and in due time planters came to see in free states of free farmers a menace to their own supremacy unless the peril could be offset by acquisitions of new slave territory. All politicians were deeply enmeshed in the issue. Senators, Representatives, Judges, and Cabinet officers were quite commonly engaged in land speculations, watching like hawks every bill that promised to affect their acquired rights. Eastern capitalists had a stake in the affair; they bought large sheaves of the land warrants issued by the government to soldiers, secured choice sections of the public domain, and withdrew their property from the market in the hope of gain through appreciation. Squatters who had gone to the frontier and settled upon land without permit or title cried out continuously for measures of relief and confirmation. Highway, canal, railroad, and land companies, intriguing and lobbying for land grants, managed to get possession of magnificent principalities, frequently with the aid of members of Congress who personally profited from their projects. In the midst of this lively scramble over the distribution of the national domain towered one lonely figure of heroic stature, Dorothea Dix, laboring in vain for years to wring from the federal government an appropriation of land in aid of the insane poor whose treatment in that period was a disgrace to the United States.

As time passed, the agitation over free homes for the landless drowned all other clamor, swelling to proportions that seemed terrifying to the steersmen at the helm, as every turbulent element in the seething democracy of the age became enlisted in it. Summed up in the alluring slogan, "Vote yourself a farm," the creed appealed with equal force to radical workmen of the eastern cities and to radical farmers of the Mississippi Valley. Labor champions found in the Homestead project a solution for the problem of industrial misery; one of the outstanding agitators of the time, George Henry Evans, a leader in the National Reform Association, organized meetings, held conventions, and rallied the proletariat to the cause. Editors took it up as a popular movement. German immigrants, fleeing from poverty and oppression, added their pleas to the demands of native Americans. Abolitionists joined the chorus, for they saw in the advance of independent farmers a check on the spread of the slave empire. Philosophers who pondered on human rights shared in the hue and cry. "If any man has a right to life," asserted an apostle of this school, "he has, by inevitable consequence, the right to the elements of life, to the earth, the air, and the water."

Those who opposed the scheme were denounced as the enemies of mankind. "Both old parties" were condemned —charged with being "in favor of selling the fertile soil to mercenary wretches who might as well traffic in the life's blood of the poor." Thus the dangerous doctrines of liberty, equality, and the pursuit of happiness, so menacing to the planting order, were invoked in the struggle over the dispersion of the national domain.

Shortly after the log-cabin and hard-cider campaign of 1840 the homestead agitation, in full force, burst in upon the floor of Congress and from that time forward the drumbeat of the land reformers continued the uproar until an alignment was finally effected. In the process party ranks were broken to correspond more closely with the diversified interests of the country, as the Whigs and the Democrats both split, forecasting the great disruption just over the horizon. In the House of Representatives, that branch of the federal government "nearest to the people," many Democratic members, especially from the districts inhabited largely by independent farmers, voted for free homesteads when the question first came before them; in fact, a majority of the southern delegation favored the project at first. In the Senate, however, where planters were more powerful, opposition was resolute; it was the vote of southern statesmen that defeated the homestead bill of 1852. "The South opposes the movement," wrote a Whig editor of New York, "and to our mind correctly denounces it as a fraud and as a scheme that could proceed from no other source than demagogism itself."

Seven years later when the measure in a modified form was again pressed in Congress, the sectional pattern was almost perfect, only three southern members in the House placing themselves on the side of free distribution, while the whole northern contingent, except for a handful of Democrats and one Whig, voted solidly for the bill. Once more southern spokesmen in the Senate were obdurate; unable to secure the annexation of Cuba to balance free land in the West, they voted almost unanimously against the measure sent up by the House.

The result of this deadlock was a compromise which fixed a small price for homesteads and provided that, at the expiration of thirty years, any land remaining unsold should be ceded to the states. This measure, largely engineered by Andrew Johnson, the agrarian Democrat from Tennessee, was finally carried through Congress in 1860 by large majorities, to the delight of agitators; but it was killed in the White House by President Buchanan. Ignoring the pleas of the left wing, the President vetoed the Homestead bill, declaring in defense of his action that it would deprive the nation of a valuable heritage, "go far to demoralize the people," and perhaps "introduce among us those pernicious social theories which have proved so disastrous in other countries."

Thus a Democratic executive, who had on other occasions indicated his sympathy for the planting faction of his party, defeated an economic project resolutely backed by Democratic farmers and workingmen of the North and West. Already a third Republican party, bearing the name of Jefferson's old agricultural interest, had accepted the challenge and was rousing the masses with the new slogan, "Vote yourself a farm," while rallying the manufacturers with a kindred cry, "Vote yourself a protective tariff." The hour for the transfer of the public domain to private persons without compensation and the creation of protective safeguards for American industry was at hand.

§

In this clash of forces the two prevailing labor systems of the country—free and slave—inevitably became involved. From the beginning, as already noted, the planting statesmen looked upon the working classes of the industrial cities, in their struggle for power in the government, as a menace to the social order, no matter how much they rejoiced to receive the votes of mechanics. The Jeffersonian fear of the "mobs of the great cities," widely spread among the leaders of the South, had every appearance of being genuine. In the growing strength of an educated white proletariat they saw, or thought they saw, a rising peril to property, liberty, and the Constitution. Again and again, with tireless emphasis, they asserted that belief upon the floor of Congress. They did more than that; they insisted that the system of Negro slavery was not only safer to ruling classes but, considered in terms of humanity, superior to that of wage labor. In any event such was their official creed even though they gladly made use of the northern proletariat to defeat the party of Hamilton and Webster. In the taunt of John Randolph: "Northern gentlemen think to govern us by our *black* slaves; but let me tell them, we intend to govern them by their *white* slaves."

Of the many philosophers who expounded this doctrine, none displayed more dialectics than Senator Hammond of South Carolina. "In all social systems," he said, "there must be a class to do the mean duties, to perform the drudgery of life. . . . Such a class you must have or you would not have that other class which leads to progress, refinement and civilization. . . . We call them slaves. We are old-fashioned at the South yet; it is a word discarded now by ears polite; I will not characterise that class at the North by that term; but you have it; it is there; it is everywhere; it is eternal. . . . The difference between us is that our slaves are hired for life and well compensated; there is no starvation, no begging, no want of employment among our people, and not too much employment either. Yours are hired by the day, not cared for, and scantily compensated, which may be proved in the most deplorable manner, at any hour in any street of your large towns. . . . Our slaves do not vote. We give them no political power. Yours do vote and being the majority, they are the depositaries of all your political power. If they knew the tremendous secret that the ballot box is stronger than any army with bayonets, and could combine, where would you be? Your society would be reconstructed, your government reconstructed, your property divided. . . . You have been making war upon us to our very hearthstones. How would you like for us to send lecturers or agitators North to teach these people this, to aid and assist them in combining, and to lead them?"

On the other side of the line an equally vigorous indictment was formulated against slavery—the economic foundation of the planting class. Like Jefferson's antipathy for the urban "mobocracy," opposition to human bondage was as old as the republic. Many of the founding Fathers from the South as well as the North regretted the existence of slavery in the United States and hoped that the day of its disappearance would come somehow in the course of events.

After that generation had passed, Harriet Martineau, the English critic who traveled widely through the southern states in 1835, recorded that, in all her conversations with planters, she found only one who defended the system without reservations. About the same time the Virginia legislature seriously debated the issue of emancipation, many of the members indulging in the severest criticism of chattel servitude. "Slavery in the abstract," exclaimed Senator Benton of Missouri, a slave state, "has but few advocates or defenders in the slave-holding states." It was the seemingly insuperable difficulties inherent in the problem of free-ing slaves, rather than ethical and religious teachings, that afforded the best defense which the early spokesmen of slavery could advance.

And deeds spoke louder than words, From the founda-tion of the republic there had been an unmistakable display of good faith on the part of those who disliked slavery. Its exclusion from the Northwest Territory in 1787, the abolition of the slave trade in 1808, and the formation of colonization societies to encourage emancipation by the re-turn of slaves to Africa were all signs that the system of human bondage fretted the conscience of statesmen and pri--vate individuals. It is true that the territory south of the Ohio was opened to slavery, that some of the opposition to the slave trade came from the breeders of Negroes who wanted to shut off foreign competition, and that many advocates of colonization really desired to get rid of free Negroes whose presence among slaves was not conducive to order.

Yet running through all these movements was a sincere desire to curtail the area of slavery. Even a better evi-dence of this sentiment was to be found in the Missouri Compromise, by which many southern leaders, bending be-fore strong pressure from the North, agreed to surrender the bulk of the Louisiana territory to freedom. Indeed, it was not until the full effects of the revolution wrought by textile machinery were felt in the planting states, not until the northern attack on southern economic policies was launched all along the line, that opposition to slavery prac-tically disappeared among the statesmen of the cotton belt.

Naturally it was in the North where the value of slavery was slight that hostility to the institution—often mingled with hostility to the political economy of the planters—took the firmer root and flourished with the greater vitality. As early as 1775, before the battle of Lexington and Concord was fought, there was founded in Pennsylvania, under the presidency of Benjamin Franklin, a Society for Promoting the Abolition of Slavery, followed by the formation of similar organizations in other northern states and in Maryland. In 1794 these societies held a national convention, the first of a series assembled at more or less regular intervals for about a quarter of a century. Their discussions, however, were rather platonic and, after slavery was abolished in the northern states, their proceedings evoked no serious interest on the part of the public. It was not until the middle period when the economic struggle between the sections grew tense that the agitation against slavery became relentless and virulent.

It was in 1831, just a year before South Carolina threatened to leave the Union on account of the tariff of abominations, that William Lloyd Garrison issued from his press in Boston the first copy of a belligerent anti-slavery paper, The Liberator. Two forerunners had broken the path but they had been mild in comparison. The Emancipator, founded in 1820 at Jonesborough, Tennessee, by Elihu Embree, a Quaker of radical tendencies, had expired without making more than a ripple in public complacency. Neither did a second venture, called The Genius of Universal Emancipation, started in the summer of 1821 by another Quaker, Benjamin Lundy, ring a militant alarm bell. But Garrison, a man of different temper, had iron in his soul. He had been in prison in Baltimore for writing an article for Lundy's paper alleging that a certain New England merchant had allowed one of his ships to be used in carrying slaves down the coast, and while within the gloomy walls of his jail had meditated on powers and principalities. There he reached a high resolve, and on his release, hurried swiftly back to Massachusetts where, with a shrill cry of impatience, he issued The Liberator from a dingy back room in Boston.

Now an editor on his own account, Garrison broke away from the mild program of Lundy, taking his stand squarely in favor of "immediate and unconditional emancipation" and openly confessing repentance for having once accepted

"the popular but pernicious doctrine of gradual emancipation." His creed simple, his language as imperious as the
declamations of the ancient prophets, he contended that
slavery was "a crime—a damning crime" and hence that
all slaveholders were criminals and their supporters par-
takers of their guilt. No person or institution was great
enough to escape his passionate criticisms. Webster, Clay,
Calhoun, all statesmen and politicians, high and low, who
defended slavery, espoused compromises, or sought to avoid
the issue came in for a full measure of his scathing abuse.
To him the Constitution was no sacred parchment; it was
a slave-owners' document—a "covenant with death and an
agreement with hell." Day and night Garrison cried aloud
that "slavery must go!"

And yet he had no definite scheme for realizing his aim,
no method of politics or organization. He did not attempt
to marshal voters at the polls; neither did he preach revolution. Indeed he had little interest in politics and on principle he was bitterly opposed to violence, believing rather
in the doctrine of non-resistance. Just one consuming idea
possessed him: slavery is a crime. Just one message
poured from his soul: slavery must be abolished. On all
mankind he served notice that he would plow his furrow to
the end: "I am in earnest—I will not equivocate—I will
not excuse—I will not retreat a single inch—and I will be
heard."

Soon a band of adherents, men and women, as severe and
uncompromising as he, rallied around the Garrison banner.
Wendell Phillips, of a fine old New England family, laid
aside all plans for a reputable career to devote his consummate arts as an orator and agitator to the cause of emancipation. The Quaker poet, Whittier, turned his craft to
framing indictments that meted out rhythmic damnation to
slavery and politicians allied with it. In poem and in prose,
satire and argument, James Russell Lowell held up to scorn
the defenders of "our peculiar institution." Emerson
added the weighty words of the philosopher to the cutting

observations of the good hater. In 1852, Harriet Beecher Stowe dramatized the abolitionist creed in a novel, Uncle Tom's Cabin, which stirred the emotions of multitudes that had never read a political speech or heard a serious debate on any theme.

In arousing public sentiment every known instrument was utilized by the agitators. Local anti-slavery societies were formed and then federated into a national organization. Quakers, inspired by the teachings of Elias Hicks, inveighed against cotton broking and dealing in the products of slave labor, opening shops where "free goods" could be bought. Petitions denouncing human bondage were circulated by the thousands, signed, and showered upon Congress for the purpose of forcing debates there. Papers and tracts were widely distributed, even through the post offices of the South. References to slavery agitation were slipped into textbooks and popular works—much to the distress of editors and school trustees below the Potomac. Pressure was brought to bear upon northern legislatures to wring from them measures favorable to the cause, especially "personal liberty laws," granting to fugitive slaves the right of trial by jury, forbidding the use of local jails by slave catchers, and imposing heavy penalties on persons who tried to carry free Negroes into servitude.

Not satisfied with appealing to opinion and to law, many anti-slavery leaders, turning from words to deeds, laid out routes, known as underground railways, along which they spirited slaves from the South to safety in the North or in Canada. Advancing a step further, they occasionally organized mobs to rescue fugitives who were being carried back to bondage by their masters. In short, every conceivable agency was employed to arouse an undying hatred for slavery and the owners of slaves. If some of the agitators tried to keep the campaign on a high level of ethics and argument, others descended to the depths of abuse and scurrility.

The sources of this remarkable movement are difficult to

discover. Westermarck, in two huge volumes devoted to the history of moral ideas, gives no clue to the inspiration of such a crusade. Unquestionably, most of the men and women prominent in the anti-slavery agitation were deeply religious and made constant use of the teachings of Jesus in their appeals for support; Embree and Lundy were Quakers; Garrison was a Baptist in faith, if not in church membership. And yet on the other side were millions of Christians who saw in human bondage nothing inconsistent with their creed, who used the same Scriptures with equal zest in defence of the institution. Again, the abolitionists were also fond of appealing to Jefferson and the Declaration of Independence as their authority, but they could claim no monopoly in that sphere; for the last bulwark of slavery was found in the Democratic party, which professed to represent in politics the humanity of Jefferson.

Nor was sacrificial benevolence a controlling force in the abolition crusade. Indeed, the defenders of slavery taunted the agitators with calling for concessions at the expense of other people, and with a show of reason. Certainly the abolition movement was confined almost entirely to the North where there were no slaves to emancipate; the handful of southerners, such as the Grimké sisters, who freed their bondmen and dedicated themselves to Garrison's cause, merely offering exceptions that proved the rule. The only scathing indictment of slavery that came from the South after the agitation had reached serious proportions —The Impending Crisis by Hinton Rowan Helper—was penned by a man whom slave owners branded with the odious term of "poor white." And yet, conceding that the abolition cry appealed mainly to those who had nothing to lose by the revolution, it remained a fact that devotion to the creed sprang largely from sentiments of a moral nature.

How deeply this agitation went and how many people were really stirred by it can hardly be determined. According to all available figures the smoke was larger than the fire. One historian of the movement estimated that at the height of the struggle there were in the whole country about two thousand anti-slavery societies with approximately two hundred thousand members. Another reckoning placed the number of petitioners who signed the anti-slavery documents, presented by John Quincy Adams to the House of Representatives, at three hundred thousand. But when some of the abolitionists, greatly overrating their strength, entered the political field in 1844 with their Liberty party, they could muster only sixty-five thousand recruits from among the two and a half million voters who cast their ballots in that election. That was America's answer to a direct call for abolition and, now fully apprised of their voting strength, the advocates of the doctrine never again ventured to present a candidate to the suffrages of their countrymen.

In other words, immediate and unconditional emancipation as the rallying cry for a political party was from the beginning to the end a total failure. If, therefore, the realization of the abolition program had depended on the capture of a majority of the voters, if other factors than moral education had not intervened, the agitators might have waged a forlorn battle indefinitely. In any event, twenty years after Garrison launched The Liberator, the Democratic party on a positive pro-slavery platform carried every state in the Union except four; and that was in 1852, many months after the appearance of Uncle Tom's Cabin, which filled the country with the turbulence of debate. "It deepens the horror of slavery," wrote Ticknor of that novel, "but it does not change a single vote." The balloting seemed to warrant his assertion.

Nevertheless it appears that the influence of the abolition agitation far outran the measurements that were taken at the polls. Within six years after Garrison hoisted his flag in Boston, John Quincy Adams wrote in his diary—not for immediate political purposes—these revealing words: "The public mind in my own district and state is convulsed between the slavery and abolition questions, and

I walk on the edge of a precipice in every step that I take." In the same year, 1837, Webster openly declared that the anti-slavery feeling was not to be "trifled with or despised." In the Senate, his southern colleague, Calhoun, professed to be deeply frightened by it, making in reply, two years later, his famous speech in defense of slavery which called for an unconditional suppression of the abolition agitation as the price of continued Union.

If some were inclined to discount such alarms as mere political effervescence, the fact remained that in several northern states where the parties were fairly equal a few voters held the balance of power and on various occasions exercised their prerogative with deadly effect. In the elec-tion of 1844, for instance, the anti-slavery candidate, by taking a few thousand votes away from Clay, the Whig leader, gave the presidency to James K. Polk of Tennessee, spokesman of the Democracy. Continually haunted by fear of such schisms, politicians bent on the possession of office and power had to be careful lest a tiny minority of agitators throw their entire national machine out of gear.

So, after all, the abolitionists did not have to muster a conquering host to frighten the managers of party affairs and to advance their own designs. By little threats, they forced many a Whig candidate out into the open and in turn helped to consolidate all wavering forces in the South behind a single banner—safety to slavery. At the same time they compelled many a northern Democrat to speak softly on the excellence of "the peculiar institution" when he would fain have rallied whole-heartedly to his southern brethren. In a word, the fortunes of politics often hung upon the maneuvers of a "contemptible minority."

And yet it must not be supposed that even the opponents of slavery were solidly united in their creed or in their strategy. The reverse was true: they were divided among themselves into innumerable factions. On the right wing were sentimentalists who regretted the existence of the institution but thought that little could be done to mitigate its evils or remove it. On the left were Garrison's invincibles who condemned bondage as a crime and were prepared to abandon the Constitution and declare the Union dissolved to get rid of it.

Between these extremes were all shades of opinion. A large number of people were merely opposed to the extension of slavery into the new territories—a policy that seemed both humane and practicable since Congress had proclaimed freedom in the Northwest in 1787 and the northern part of the Louisiana Purchase in 1820 and a further application of accepted doctrine could be readily made. A smaller number, hostile to slavery everywhere on principle, yet hoping that planters could be persuaded to listen to the voice of sweet reason and accept compensation in return for emancipation, suggested that the revenues from the sale of public lands be devoted to this purpose.

Perhaps the major portion of all those who in their hearts disliked slavery were bewildered by the complex character of every solution offered. Lincoln himself, even though in his later years he fought consistently for freedom in the territories, could see no way to emancipation until a crisis forced a decision upon him. Nor is this a matter for wonder. The four million slaves represented a property interest amounting to billions of dollars, ramifying in every direction through the whole planting system and through numerous industrial and commercial activities that rested upon servile labor—involving the North almost as much as the South in its economic net.

Moreover, for the politician who respected established law there were insuperable obstacles in the path of abolition; for under the Constitution the national government had no authority whatever over slavery in the states where it already existed. And if emancipation came, what could be done with the four million slaves themselves? What civil, economic, political rights were to be given them on the morrow of liberty? Practical men simply could not visualize the fiscal and administrative measures necessary to effect such an enormous social revolution. Perhaps most practical men gave little or no thought to the finalities of the issue. If they felt in their bones that a crisis was ahead, they were in any case powerless to prevent the storm; and in the days to come the little plots and plans which they had evolved were tossed aside as the toys of children. In the economy of Providence, as the orators were fond of saying, abolition agitators were to be justified by history, not by the work of their own hands or by any of the political instruments they had forged.

§

On the planters the immediate effect of the anti-slavery clangor was a consolidation of forces and a searching of minds and hearts for an effective answer. Clearly the hour for apologetics had arrived and human intelligence was equal to the occasion. In the long history of defense mechanisms, there is no chapter more fascinating than that which recounts the rise and growth of the extraordinary system of ethics which, at the very height of the slave power, formed the moral bulwark of its established order.

The system did not, of course, spring full blown from the brain of any single thinker. It was the work of many minds, separate departments being added from year to year under the stress of attack from without and the pressure of fusion within. At length it was finished—an exhaustive compendium of historical, legal, constitutional, economic, religious, ethical, and philosophical arguments in support of slavery, a vast and intricate body of logic suffused with the glow of righteous sincerity and adorned with gems of classical eloquence—a ready and inspiring guide capable of sustaining those troubled by doubts and fortifying combatants on the firing line of politics. Representatives in Congress, newspaper editors in their sanctums, clergymen in their pulpits, professors in the institutions of learning, and political leaders ranging from national figures down to village politicians now had at their tongues' tips a reply to every attack, a foil for every thrust. By the irony of fate the great argument reached its perfection at the very moment when the economic class for which it provided moral assurance had passed the peak of its power and, unknown to its defenders, was tottering on the brink of doom.

On the economic side, the case for slavery was formulated by Calhoun in a powerful speech delivered in the Senate of the United States in 1839 with the precision and solemnity that marked all his great utterances. Advancing to the fray, lance in hand, Calhoun flung out the assertion that slavery, in the existing state of society, was not an evil but "a good—a positive good," a startling proposition which he sustained by two contentions.

First, the slaves had been brought from Africa "in a low, degraded, savage condition" and in the course of a few generations had been raised "to a comparatively civilized condition" under "the fostering care of our institutions." To this he added a second theorem even more fatalistic. In every civilized society, the bearers of culture must live upon the labor of others; this has always been true; it is still true; modes of exploitation merely differ. Under the "subtle and artful fiscal contrivances of modern times," the person who works for wages is exploited more severely than the chattel laborer, and then, in time of sickness, unemployment, and old age, he is committed to the tender mercies of the streets or of the almshouse. On the other hand, less is exacted from the slave and a solicitous attention is paid him in sickness and the infirmities of years. "Compare his condition," exclaimed Calhoun, "with the tenants of the poorhouses in the more civilized portions of Europe—look at the sick, and the old and infirm slave on the one hand, in the midst of his family and friends, under the kind superintending care of his master and mistress and compare it with the forlorn and wretched condition of the pauper in the poorhouse."

No less imposing was the political case for slavery.

Having demonstrated to their satisfaction the excellence of their economic system and the superiority of slave over wage labor, defenders of the institution argued that the relation established between master and servant in their section formed "the most solid and durable foundation upon which to rear free and stable political institutions," to use Calhoun's phrasing. This thesis was unfolded in a neat chain of reasoning: the slaves are of another race; they are kept in ignorance and take no part in government; they do not expect to improve their lot and are affected by no social ferment; they are widely scattered on lonely plantations and cannot be welded into unions for revolt. Thus the repose of the existing order is assured and the Constitution of the United States is afforded a stable economic bulwark; the "monstrous doctrine of equality" now making dangerous progress and threatening the security of private property throughout the civilized world meets in the South invulnerable barriers.

To the inescapable logic of economic and political science was added the authority of religion. While discussing "the moral aspect of this institution" in 1858 a southern member of Congress declared that slavery had the blessing of God and the Bible as well as of the Constitution and profane history. "We learn from the Holy Scriptures," exclaimed the orator, "that Abraham and many wise and good men of that day not only held slaves but exercised acts of ownership over them; and that God Himself, after he had rescued the children of Israel from the house of bondage, sanctioned and recognized slavery both in principle and in practice. In defining the rules for their government and their moral observance, it was prescribed that 'Thou shalt not covet thy neighbor's man-servant nor his maid-servant nor anything that is thy neighbor's.' Thus, sir, not only sanctioning slavery but providing for its protection for all time to come."

In the same vein a Virginia member of the House of Representatives, after a detailed presentation of the theological argument, summed up the whole case of morals and religion in a moving peroration: "I believe that the institution of slavery is a noble one; that it is necessary for the good, the well-being of the Negro race. Looking into history, I go further and say, in the presence of this assembly and under all the imposing circumstances surrounding me that I believe it is God's institution. Yes, sir, if there is anything in the action of the great Author of us all; if there is anything in the conduct of His chosen people; if there is anything in the conduct of Christ Himself who came upon this earth and yielded His life as a sacrifice that all through His death might live; if there is anything in the conduct of His apostles who inculcated obedience on the part of slaves towards their masters as a Christian duty, then we must believe that the institution is from God." This was both comprehensive and emphatic.

Although the "new psychology" had not yet risen above the intellectual horizon to contribute its decoration to the teachings of economics, politics, history, and religion, a Swedenborgian clergyman set forth "The Spiritual Philosophy" of bondage in the terminology of his sect. "By African slavery the sensual-corporeal principle of the African," he said, "is brought into obedience and subjection to the natural or scientific plane of the white man's life. The white man wills and thinks for him, determines his outgoings and his incomings, his food, his clothing, his sleep, his work, etc. . . . What is the result? His sensual-corporeal is adjusted as a servant to the regenerate natural of the white man and receives influx through it. His hereditary torpor is dissipated; the sphere of order, justice, and active use into which he is inserted is repugnant to his attendant evil spirits and they measurably leave him. . . . He is passing through the process which Almighty God has provided and which will eventuate in his true liberty and his final salvation. 'Bonds make free, so they be righteous bonds.'"

§

Those who resisted the agitation of the abolitionists did not confine themselves to arguments. Like their opponents, they seized upon all the weapons of law and custom, going occasionally beyond social peace—to violence and intimidation. When petitions for the abolition of slavery and the slave trade in the District of Columbia began to shower upon the House of Representatives like autumn leaves, in 1836, a member from Georgia proposed to reject them all, thus simply denying the ancient right of petition accorded by the express language of the American Constitution. After an impassioned debate a resolution known as the "gag rule" was carried, condemning slavery agitation and providing that petitions referring to the subject be tabled at once without consideration. Though this restraint on civil liberty was later removed from the records of the House on the insistent demand of John Quincy Adams, it betrayed a firm determination on the part of southerners to brook no interference with their peculiar institution, at any peril to constitutional forms.

In their own section where, of course, they had a free hand, the champions of slavery took even stronger measures in their efforts to stamp out propaganda. Defying the law, southern postmasters made a common practice of destroying abolition literature sent through the mails. Frightened by the specter of servile revolts, a number of states forbade the printing and distribution of attacks on slavery, Louisiana, for one, providing that persons guilty of this offense should be either imprisoned for life or put to death. With an eye to protecting the young, guardians of the established order also scrutinized school texts and other publications that came from the North and from foreign countries. In Appleton's dusty collection of facts, known as A Complete Guide of the World, one self-appointed inspector of public safety found "hidden lessons of the most fiendish and murderous character that enraged fanaticism could conceive or indite." To warn the unsophisticated, lists of dangerous books were compiled and published.

In the North, where abolitionists naturally carried on most of their work, the ordinary engines of resistance to criticism were supplemented by mob action. Garrison was beaten and dragged through the streets of Boston in 1835 by a maddened crowd, "including many gentlemen of property and influence," and escaped death only because the police seized him and put him into jail. One of his disciples, the Reverend Samuel May, was set upon at least six times in Massachusetts and Vermont. In Philadelphia, an attack on the abolitionists assumed the proportions of a riot. At Alton, Illinois, Lovejoy, a preacher and publisher, after suffering the loss of three presses at the hands of a mob, was shot to death while attempting to protect the fourth.

Such rioting, instead of meeting universal condemnation, was generally greeted by respectable people as acts of heroism directed against obnoxious pests who deserved death for disturbing the public and for abusing the grand statesmen of the time. Senator Benton of Missouri rejoiced that mobs had "silenced the gabbling tongues of female dupes and dispersed the assemblages whether fanatical, visionary, or incendiary." Before a great crowd in Faneuil Hall, the attorney-general of Massachusetts compared the Illinois mob that shot Lovejoy with the patriot Fathers who made up the Boston Tea Party and branded the victim as a "presumptuous and imprudent" man who had "died as the fool dieth." In fact all over the North the tactics of the abolitionists called forth denunciation and deeds of vengeance—an efficient counter-reformation. It is highly questionable whether they gained any important numerical strength after the uproar of the first decade that followed the establishment of The Liberator. Indeed, with a show of justification, the more confident statesmen referred to their activities as "a rub-a-dub" agitation.

§

But the slavery question, as we have seen, did not stand alone. Leaders among the planters not only wanted to conserve their labor supply. They also wanted free trade, or at least tariff for revenue only. They opposed a national bank and a national currency system built upon such an institution, they assailed ship subsidies, and they were generally against internal improvements designed to add to the ties binding the farming West with the commercial East. Declaring that the western territories "bought by common blood and treasure" should be open to slave owners and their bondmen as well as to farmers, they objected to the free distribution of the public domain among the landless— the peopling of new states with inhabitants not attached to the planting interest. Relying upon the mandate of the Constitution, they demanded a return of all fugitive slaves that fled to the North.

So while southern statesmen might speak with constitutional warrant of slavery as "a local institution solely within the sovereign power of the state," they were in fact themselves aggressively operating in the theater of national politics, and in their forward drive they accumulated a host of enemies who cared little or nothing about slavery itself. Many an orator who might have forgiven the South for maintaining a servile labor system could not forgive it for its low tariff doctrines and its opposition to centralized finance.

By forces more potent than abolition agitation, slavery was therefore swept along with vital economic issues into the national vortex at Washington. The institution itself, though under the control of the states, had many points of contact, under the Constitution, with the processes of the federal government. The importation of Negroes was subject to the control of Congress; it had been abolished in 1808 but the enforcement of the law was vested in the President of the United States, who could be either strict or lenient in his methods. Congress had power to make all needful rules and regulations for the government of the territories, the District of Columbia, the forts, and other lands belonging to the United States; in enacting laws for these regions it was compelled to decide whether slavery should exist in them. The admission of new states was entrusted to Congress; whenever a territory knocked at the door of the Union, the question of prohibiting or permitting slavery had to be squarely faced by the politicians of all schools.

Under the Constitution, slaves escaping from their masters and fleeing into other states were to be returned; Congress had the power to provide for enforcement of this rule. The postoffice was a federal institution; Congress, having the right to say what mail matter should be carried, was forced to consider projects for excluding abolition literature from the mails. Finally, the First Amendment to the Constitution, guaranteeing to citizens the right to petition, a right inherent in all free governments, gave the abolitionists express warranty for laying before Congress anti-slavery appeals of every character.

Hence, the restriction of slavery to the sphere of state politics was in fact as impossible as its isolation for consideration on intrinsic merits. Slavery was but one element, and if the number of abolitionists is any evidence, a minor element, in the sweep of political and economic forces that occupied the attention of statesmen throughout the middle period and finally brought on the irrepressible conflict.

§

By means of argument and bargain, for threescore years and more, representatives of the North and the South were able to make peaceable adjustments among the antagonistic groups in the American Union. The Constitution itself, as all the world knew, represented an exchange of concessions and guarantees. Under its beneficent shelter, the owners of slave property received ample protection in return for favors to northern merchants, financiers, and manufacturers. The continuance of slavery in the states was implicitly allowed; certainly Congress was given no power to meddle with the institution. Fugitive slaves were to be returned to their masters and three-fifths of the bondmen were to be counted as inhabitants in apportioning representatives in Congress among the several states.

It was not without some authority, therefore, that abolitionists spoke of the Constitution as "a slave-holder's document" and southerners boasted of the recognition which it accorded to their interests. As a matter of fact, it was a treaty of peace between the commercial and planting states. And the generation that made it showed the same spirit of accommodation in deciding the fate of the western territories: the Northwest being dedicated to freedom and the region below the Ohio opened to slavery.

A quarter of a century later, after slavery had been abolished in the original states north of Delaware, a similar facility for adjustment led the way to a peaceful settlement of another fierce dispute. In 1818 the territory of Missouri sought membership as a state in the Union—with slavery as a matter of course since the institution had been tolerated in that region from the early days of the French settlement. On the very threshold, the applicant was greeted in the House of Representatives by a proposal that no new slaves should be permitted to enter Missouri after the act of admission and that all slaves subsequently born there should be ultimately set free.

A deadlock ensued. The South, having half the Senators, could prevent the passage of this plan for the restriction of slavery and the North, commanding a majority in the House, could keep Missouri out of the Union. Only after a long and stormy debate, which filled the aged Jefferson with anxiety for the safety of his country, was the Gordian knot cut: Maine, separated from the parent state of Massachusetts, was admitted as a free state and Missouri with her slaves. In connection with this settlement it was agreed that the rest of the vast Louisiana territory north of the parallel of 36° 30′, like the old Northwest, should be for-ever free, while the southern portion, relatively small in extent, should be by implication open to slavery.

With this adjustment the extremists of neither party were satisfied. Brusque old John Randolph called it "a dirty bargain," sneered at its northern supporters as "dough faces," and mustered a large contingent to vote against it in the last ditch. Unbending critics of slavery, on their part —some of them especially concerned with maintaining the relative power of the Northeast in the Union—looked upon the settlement as an abject surrender to the South. But the leaders pledged to the middle course prevented a crisis. Without a dissenting voice, the members of Monroe's Cabi-net, which included Calhoun of South Carolina, Wirt of Maryland, and Crawford of Georgia, agreed to the ex-clusion of slavery from the northern portion of the Louisi-ana territory, displaying a conciliatory temper that augured well for the balance of power.

The next collision between the commercial and the plant-ing states, the nullification battle of 1833, did not involve slavery at all but merely the protective tariff so insistently demanded by manufacturing interests, wool growers, and hemp raisers. As we have said, it came nearer disrupting the nation than the battle over the Missouri question a decade before. In fact South Carolina prepared to leave the Union and the federal government made ready to use force against her to prevent secession, creating an emergency which was only resolved by the strenuous efforts of moderate men.

For nearly two decades the conflict of economic sections evoked no disturbing crisis. Then suddenly it again reached an acute stage with the shifting of the political scenery by the annexation of Texas, the war with Mexico, and the acquisition of additional territory stretching to the Pacific coast. The signal for this new test of strength was given on August 6, 1846, a few months after the armed contest with Mexico began, when David Wilmot, a Democratic farmer of Pennsylvania, introduced in the House of Representatives a resolution declaring that slavery should be entirely excluded from any territory which might be seized in the struggle—a resolution that was to become famous in American history as the Wilmot Proviso. "In the presence of the living God," cried Robert Toombs of Georgia, "if by your legislation you seek to drive us from the territories of California and New Mexico . . . I am for disunion."

The Proviso was voted down but, on the very mention of slavery in connection with the new possessions, a tempest swept the country. Abolitionists insisted that the Mexican War was nothing but a slave owners' scheme to get more land for cotton and bondage. Statesmen of the planting interest replied that it was an insult to deny them the fruits of a joint struggle in which the South had given its full portion of blood and treasure to punish the common enemy and sustain the national honor.

Like many others, this fresh battle of wits might have remained academic had it not been for the fact that, at the close of the Mexican War, arrangements of some kind simply had to be made for the government of the territories newly acquired. Accordingly when Congress met in December, 1849, a great controversy over this issue opened and continued to rage throughout the winter, transfixing the nation. In every way the debate was a memorable forensic contest worthy of a place in the annals of oratory beside the noblest intellectual tourneys of ancient and modern times. It was significant on account of the men who participated, the eloquence and cogency of their arguments, and the results that flowed from their deliberations.

Three masters, gray and bowed with some forty years of labor in the forum, dominated the scene: Calhoun from the Far South, Webster from the Far North, and Clay from the borderland. The first of them was destined to die before the grand argument came to an end. The last, bent with the weight of more than seventy years, had every reason to believe that his ambitions were at rest and that the veil of the dark portal was soon to part for him. Webster, to all appearances stronger in body and perhaps yet able to grasp the presidency, on which his heart was set, even so was soon to follow his colleagues to the grave. Around the masters were ranged the men of the younger generation who were to hear the tramp of marching armies and to lead contending forces through the four years of war that followed the failure of reason and eloquence.

For the planting interest, Calhoun issued the challenge and laid down the terms on which his section would remain in the Union. He opened by explaining the reasons for southern anxiety in the crisis. One of these was of course the long continued agitation of the slavery question in the North. But "the great and primary cause" of southern fears—lying behind the slavery issue and "intimately" connected with it—was the indubitable fact that the North through its amazing growth had now acquired "the exclusive power of controlling the government," whereas the South was without "adequate means of protecting itself against its encroachment and oppression." In other words, the delicate balance of former days was gone; the commercial and farming states could, if they would, henceforward dominate and oppress the planting states.

With his wonted logical exactness Calhoun then presented his ultimatum: the South was to have an equal right of way in all territories; the North was faithfully to fulfill the provisions for the return of fugitive slaves; the agitation of the slavery question was to cease; and finally there was to be an amendment to the Constitution restoring the equilibrium between the sections and giving the planting states security against the weight of northern majorities— an echo of the central idea of the Hartford Convention just reversed. His statement was clear and explicit—and historically impossible.

For the younger generation peering into the future, for the wing of the extreme left, spoke William H. Seward of

New York. He too was clear and explicit: slavery agitation would not cease. "Has any government ever succeeded in changing the moral convictions of its subjects?" he inquired. The fugitive slave law could not be enforced; the overwhelming weight of public sentiment in the North was against it. The territories would not be surrendered to slavery but consecrated to justice, welfare, and liberty. "There is a higher law than the Constitution," vowed the orator, "which regulates our authority over the domain and devotes it to the same noble purposes"—a battle tocsin which gave cold chills to lawyers who believed that life was encompassed by the walls of jurisprudence.

Having defied Calhoun on every point, Seward boldly declared to his astounded auditors that "emancipation is inevitable and is near; that it may be hastened or hindered; and that whether it shall be peaceful or violent depends upon the question whether it be hastened or hindered; that all measures which fortify slavery or extend it tend to the consummation of violence; all that check its extension and abate its strength tend to its peaceful extirpation."

Into this wide breach Clay flung himself with a compromise, the last of his distinguished career. By powerful speeches and skillful negotiations he labored to rally moderate men to a program of harmony that offered concessions to both extremes. A note of moving pathos ran through every plea that he made for freedom and slavery protected by the Constitution, for compromise as the only alternative to war and calamity. When he spoke of laying aside in a few days all earthly ambitions and honors for the habiliments of the tomb, of caring for nothing save his united country, even hardened cynics in the audience of anxious men and women dropped a tear. Once more, as in 1820 and 1833, Clay was to prevail.

But he won this time only through the aid of Webster. Day after day the Senator from Massachusetts sat in grim silence while the tumult raged around him, watching quietly with his sharp eye the winds that tossed contestants to and

716 THE RISE OF AMERICAN CIVILIZATION

fro. Then on March 7, 1850, casting off all doubts like a strong man preparing for a race, he rose and delivered the extraordinary oration that was fated for all time to bear the date of its utterance. Abolitionists had hoped that he would demand the express exclusion of slavery from all the new territories. Instead—to the dismay of the anti-slavery faction—Webster gave the weight of his great name and his eloquence to a plea for compromise on that point and, enlarging his tender to the planters, agreed to a drastic law for the return of fugitive slaves.

"He is a man who lives by his memory; a man of the past, not a man of faith and hope," was the comment of Emerson when the news reached his ears. "His finely developed understanding only works truly and with all its force when it stands for animal good; that is, for property." Lowell, Whittier, and Longfellow joined in the condemnation. Less generous critics charged Webster with having sold out to the southern Whigs in an effort to gain the presidency. His friends, practical men of affairs, replied that it was not ambition but an overmastering love of the Union that led him to risk all in an effort to preserve it.

At the close of a parliamentary battle that lasted for the better part of a year, the grand results were finally written into a series of laws, all of which were signed in September, 1850, by President Millard Fillmore, who had taken office on the death of General Taylor. To the great joy of the Texas bondholders who had labored long and hard in the interest of their depreciated securities, the boundaries of Texas were adjusted and a large payment was made to that state by way of compensation. On condition that in due course they should be taken into the Union, with or without slavery as their constitutions at the time might decree, the territories of Utah and New Mexico were formally organized—thus rejecting the Wilmot Proviso without guaranteeing the extension of slavery. Offsetting in some measure the concessions to the South, California was admitted as a free state.

The disposition of the new territories was supplemented by two measures touching the subject of slavery. The slave trade—not slavery itself—was abolished in the District of Columbia, an offering to liberty which was immediately counterbalanced by a new fugitive slave law extreme both in letter and in spirit. For the purpose of taking the business from the hands of state and local authorities likely to be swayed by a passion for freedom, the act provided for an array of federal officers to coöperate in the seizure and return of slaves. It laid heavy penalties on all who placed obstacles in the way of enforcing the law. It permitted a master or his agent by a mere affidavit to claim an alleged fugitive and to take the accused for a summary hearing before a federal commissioner—a hearing in which the Negro was denied the right of trial by jury and the privilege of giving evidence in his own behalf. If a federal marshal allowed a slave to slip through his hands, he was liable to a civil suit for damages. For a decision in favor of a claimant, a commissioner received a higher fee than for a judgment releasing a defendant. In this fashion the great statesmen of 1850 planned to put to rest the sectional conflict that threatened once more to destroy the balance of power in the Union.

§

The clash of interests and sections over questions of domestic policy was also carried into the sphere of foreign commercial relations, especially in the Orient. If Democratic low-tariff measures caused great shocks in the Northeast, they did not uproot the domestic enterprise of industrial captains or destroy their trade in China, India, and the East Indies. On the contrary, by cutting down the demand for American commodities at home, low tariffs drove northern manufacturers to search with still greater avidity for new outlets abroad—especially in the Far East where prospects were brighter than in the overcrowded markets of Europe.

Moreover, planting statesmen, as eager to make money as cotton spinners, took note of the fact that one of the great southern staples, tobacco, might find—as it ultimately did—an immense sale among the teeming millions of China. "There is reason to suppose," wrote a Democratic Secretary of the Navy to the Senate in 1853, "that our tobacco will be generally received there as a substitute for this poisonous drug [opium]. This article now so abundantly produced by our tobacco-growing states will then become the pioneer of our trade and open the way for our manufactures of cotton, wool, and particularly of cutlery and other manufactures of iron. . . . The production of tobacco would be increased in a measure corresponding to the increased demand of the two hundred millions of Chinese consumers and thus our national wealth would be greatly augmented." Even the stanchest Democrat had no objection if Yankee mill owners sold cloth in China. They merely protested against paying duties on goods they imported and they were only too happy when cargoes of tobacco could accompany boxes and bales of gray shirtings across the Pacific.

Nevertheless the major portion of the Far Eastern trade brought profits to northern ship owners and manufacturers rather than to growers of cotton and tobacco and it was natural that the Whig spokesmen of business, not the agrarian Democrats, should be eager to lend the protection of the State Department and the Navy to the advancement of foreign commerce. By no accident, therefore, did that loyal advocate of industrial prosperity, Daniel Webster, promote, while serving as Secretary of State under Whig Presidents, the three most startling achievements on behalf of American interests in the Pacific Ocean previous to the defeat of Spain by Dewey at the battle of Manila Bay in 1898—namely, the first commercial treaty with China, the specific reservation of Hawaii, and the opening of Japan's barred door.

Perhaps it was no accident either that the first American

naval officer to formulate and apply on the high seas imperial designs for taking naval bases and opening commercial ports by demonstrations of physical force—Commodore Perry who was selected to bring Japan into business relations with the United States—was a sailor from Providence, Rhode Island, long one of the chief centers of the China trade. It was certainly due to no mere whirl of fortune's wheel that the Secretary of State who pulled down the American flag in Formosa on the eve of the Civil War was a Democratic predecessor of the "peerless orator" from Nebraska, William Jennings Bryan, who later declared in favor of independence for the Philippines.

Appropriately enough, the first effective appeal for political and naval guarantees for Oriental trade was laid before the House of Representatives in 1840 by Abbott Lawrence, a cotton-mill owner of Massachusetts, bosom friend and financial backer of Webster. It came from American merchants in Canton asking for armed protection and a commission to secure a treaty of commerce with China. Knowing full well the importance of the China trade, so highly profitable to the metropolis of his state, the Democratic President then in power, Martin Van Buren of New York, ordered the East India squadron under Commodore Kearny, to sail for Chinese waters. Within a few months, the Whigs rode triumphantly into Washington behind their leader, General Harrison, but with their drums muffled.

Hands still more willing and expert, therefore, grasped the wheel. Daniel Webster became Secretary of State and, taking up the threads of Oriental policy, wrote for the President a special message on the China business which was promptly sent to Congress for approval. In this economic document, after calling attention to the fact that the China trade was now worth about nine millions a year, Webster proposed an appropriation for a special mission to visit the Son of Heaven in quest of commercial rights.

Interested and attracted by the idea, Congress voted the money—in spite of outcries on the part of the old Jacksonian Democrat, Senator Benton. Caleb Cushing, descendant of a Newburyport shipmaster—a man who knew about the substance of the China trade—was selected to head the delegation, with Webster's son, Fletcher, as secretary. The mission went, saw, and conquered, easily, as it happened, because Great Britain had recently beaten the Chinese in the Opium War and the Mighty One at Peking was in a chastened mood. With a flourish, Cushing signed, on July 3, 1844, a convention with the Imperial minister which secured for Americans commercial privileges in the open ports of China and the right to be tried in their own consular courts when charged with violating Chinese law. "By that treaty," wrote Cushing exultantly, "the laws of the Union follow its citizens and its banner protects them, even within the domain of the Chinese Empire." Thus was inaugurated a formal commercial and political connection between the government of the United States and the government of China.

A few years later, after the Whigs had again ridden into power, this time behind General Taylor, and Webster had once more become Secretary of State, the practices of a firm Oriental policy were resumed. On returning to authority, Webster found that a French naval officer, serving under the weird adventurer, Louis Napoleon, had just made a hostile demonstration against the Hawaiian Islands and was evidently in a mood to seize them. Now the Secretary could easily recall that when he was serving in the State Department under Tyler he had received a delegation of Hawaiians, then visiting America under missionary auspices, and informed them that the government of the United States would permit no European power to seize their country, colonize it, or overturn the native government. Remembering that pledge in 1851, Webster instructed the American minister at Paris to warn the French against undertaking imperial projects in that part of the Pacific.

Some Democrats, it seems, would have been willing to take possession of the islands then and there if details could have been agreed upon. At all events, Webster's Democratic successor, W. L. Marcy of mercantile New York, did draw up a treaty of annexation but he could not get it ratified by the Senate. It proposed large annuities to the deposed princes and that violated Jeffersonian simplicity. What was more significant, it provided for the ultimate admission of Hawaii into the Union as a free state. The time was not yet ripe.

Far more important than Webster's reservation of Hawaii for American usage was his prompt and efficient action in initiating the mission that opened Japan to American commerce. For over two hundred years the government of that island empire had kept its ports closed to foreign trade—save for one harbor where the Dutch were allowed to carry on a small amount of business—evincing an imperious desire to be let alone by aliens. That was the state of affairs when Americans began to search eagerly for markets all over the Pacific, resolute Americans who were not slow to protest against exclusiveness of any kind. From time to time United States naval officers cruising in the neighborhood were directed to sound the government of Japan on the subject of commercial relations as well as on the matter of protection for shipwrecked American sailors. But all such appeals failed to move the Shogun who ruled in the name of the Emperor over the Land of the Rising Sun.

Not dismayed by repeated rebuffs, merchants of the Atlantic cities, especially of New York, continued to press for action against the restrictive policy that prevailed in Yedo; and Webster now gave more heed to their demands. By way of a preliminary stroke, he issued a commission to an American naval officer in Chinese waters, instructing him to sail for Japan and do what he could to open the door. Among other things, Webster asked for the right to buy coal of the Japanese, informing them that this precious substance was "a gift of Providence deposited by the Creator of all things in the depths of the Japanese islands for the benefit of the whole human family"—a lofty sentiment that had peculiar reverberations in subsequent years. The appeal was eloquent but the first commissioner was not able to carry out his orders.

Undiscouraged, Webster then sent to Japan a second agent, Commodore Matthew C. Perry, with an imposing, if small, naval force. Having resolved in his own mind to seize neighboring islands by main strength, if necessary to execute his decrees, Perry was in the proper mood to frighten Yedo into concessions. To show his mettle, he ignored the traditional rights of the Japanese, violated their territorial waters, disregarded their laws, and spurned their protests.

But these actions might have been without avail had circumstances not helped the Commodore. Whatever their desires, the Japanese knew that the British had just broken down the barriers of China by arms and that both British and Russian battleships were at hand waiting to work their will on Japan. Moreover, the American sea captain at the front door, besides displaying tenacity, generously offered the Japanese facilities for trade, told them that the Chinese were coming to America, worshiping their own gods freely and growing rich, and gave them a cordial invitation to come and do likewise. So on March 31, 1854, after Webster had gone to his long home, the treaty that "gently coerced" Japan into friendship, to use the language of Seward, was duly signed and four years later, Townsend Harris crowned the work with a commercial treaty.

By this time, under the leadership of forth-putting men like Perry, professionals in the Navy Department had conceived a philosophy of action in the Pacific that was to accomplish results in the years to come. Though the Democrats were careful to oust civilians from office whenever they got possession of the federal government, though they were willing to send as consuls to the East planters who knew nothing of trade or the Orient, they never had the temerity to place vessels of the Navy in command of men who had never seen the sea. Favored by circumstances, therefore, a consistent naval tradition was easily framed and adopted by men in permanent tenure—and cherished even when triumphant agrarians were in the saddle at Washington.

That tradition, as set forth with great care by Commodore Perry, was startling in its simplicity. "We cannot expect," he said, "to be free from the ambitious longings of increased power, which are the natural concomitants of national success." This seemed axiomatic. "When we look at the possessions in the East of our great maritime rival, England, and the constant and rapid increase of their fortified ports, we should be admonished of the necessity of prompt measures on our part. . . . Fortunately the Japanese and many other islands of the Pacific are still left untouched by this unconscionable government; and some of them lie in a route of great commerce which is destined to become of great importance to the United States. No time should be lost adopting active measures to secure a sufficient number of ports of refuge."

Acting on such ethical assumptions, the Commodore seized the Bonin Islands, raised the American flag here and there, and set precedents. Then, as fate would have it, the Whigs were soon turned out of power and a Democratic Secretary of State, taking the Constitution seriously, told Perry that the President could not take possession of distant territory without the consent of Congress. Ere long, the flag was lowered in the Bonin Islands and Japan reasserted her sovereignty.

The same Democratic indifference to commercial considerations that wrecked for a time such imperial enterprises was also responsible for the loss of Formosa. Although very few citizens of the United States were aware of the fact, that "beautiful island" was actually brought within American grasp by the activities of a zealous commissioner in China, Dr. Peter Parker. Always searching for attractive opportunities, this enterprising official, a medical missionary translated to a government post, found that an American company, while engaged in exploiting the trade of Formosa, had raised the Stars and Stripes at Takow; and having an eye to good real estate Parker made haste to advise annexation.

With diplomatic instinct Parker immediately wrote to the State Department expressing the hope that "the government of the United States may not shrink from the action which the interests of humanity, civilization, navigation, and commerce impose upon it in relation to Tai-wan." In the meantime an American naval officer on the spot offered to keep the colors flying until word could be received from Washington. That was in 1857. When Parker's letter arrived, if Senator William H. Seward is to be admitted as a witness, the government was dominated by southern planters, cold to the pleas of the commercial interests. At all events the Democratic Secretary of State informed the impetuous Parker that the military and naval forces of the country could only be used "by authority of Congress." The proposal to annex Formosa was not even laid before that august body. So the flag came down in Formosa—to rise forty years later in the Philippines not very far away.

CHAPTER XVI

Democracy: Romantic and Realistic

THE grand political ideas stamped with popular approval by the American Revolution and by the triumph of Jeffersonian Democracy thrust themselves ever deeper into the thoughts and emotions of the people as the nineteenth century advanced, and shot out their ever-widening circles of implication as new problems of life, labor, and government were flung upward for consideration. Had there been no significant changes in the economic structure of the nation, had there been no novel social forces let loose in the national arena, had there been no additional impacts from revolutionary Europe, the great concepts of human rights and human equality, professed if not always followed by the Fathers, would have altered the intellectual climate for philosophy, letters, and the arts.

But on top of the expanding and reverberating notes of the Jeffersonian anthem, came the sharp vibrations of the revolution made by technology and applied science, doing more to shatter the old patterns of speculation and unfold vistas of endless progress for democracy than all the up-

725

heavals and renaissances of the centuries that had gone before. Though the age of machinery opened in the latter part of the eighteenth century, though Washington lived to see whirling spindles driven by water power, the machine process really did not get into high momentum until the era of Jackson and Lincoln.

Once the industrial revolution was fairly started, its effects upon culture—upon intellectual interests, æsthetic appreciation, and the institutions for the distribution of knowledge—were swift and cumulative. Under its stresses and strains the whole social structure was recast. To the old fortunes made from shipping and trade were added greater and more numerous fortunes wrung from textiles, steel, hardware, pottery, and railways. There were now large family estates to be taxed for popular education, to afford leisure for sons and daughters, and to offer patronage for letters, science, and the arts. As the shadow follows the sun, so in the wake of the expanding middle class came the ever-swelling industrial proletariat with its tendencies to radical opinion concerning society and government. Equally inevitable was the rise of a large body of women workers for factories, mills, and shops, with swift repercussions on the law and practice of domestic relations.

In the process occurred a rapid concentration of population—a condition so intimately related to stimulating and supporting cultural enterprises. During this middle period, roughly speaking between 1815 and 1860, overgrown villages suddenly became important cities; New York, which had a population of about thirty thousand when Washington was inaugurated, reached half a million before the election of Lincoln. At the latter date, Cincinnati and Chicago combined had more inhabitants than all the cities in the United States when independence was declared. With advancing capitalism came periodical industrial panics which shook the social order from top to bottom, intensified the poverty of the cities, and aroused deep public interest in all phases of social economy. By no means last in cultural significance, the avalanche of goods which flowed from the machines awakened new wants, created among the masses new desires, and stirred all society with aggravated acquisitive tastes.

Besides releasing terrific economic energies, the technology and science of the machine process thrust all kinds of material devices into inherited customs and modes. Expanding railway lines within the United States and the growing commerce of steam vessels in seven seas set in motion social currents ruinous to local rigidity in thought or practice. The telegraph and power-printing machinery transformed the newspaper business, gave to the country a penny press, made possible the instantaneous dissemination of news from Boston to San Francisco, and permitted the masses to break in upon the intellectual monopoly of the upper classes with relative ease. New magazines and publishing houses, called into being by social changes and technical apparatus, enlarged the market for literary wares and by enabling authors to live by the pen diverted more talent to the field of letters. The scientific spirit that accompanied the technical overturn spread into every department of life and opinion, applying its inexorable analysis to the mysteries as well as the materials of society.

In addition to these capital results of the industrial revolution, which were common to that economic upheaval in all other countries, there were a number of accessory features peculiar to America, in the middle period. For one thing, an increasing proportion of the men and women who worked in the new factories were drawn from alien nationalities; the flood of immigration broke all previous records, complicating the mixture of races and tongues. Parallel in time with this invasion were the gold rush to California and the steady opening of cheap lands in the West which, while disintegrating the older rural communities of the East, carried the center of population rapidly toward the setting sun. Men who were poor one day were millionaires the next; women who did the family washing on Monday moved into palaces on Wednesday and rode to church on Sunday in carriages. With the inrush of immigrants the Catholic Church, that ancient bugbear of Puritans and Presbyterians, multiplied the number of its communicants, forcing merchants and politicians to adopt circumspection in advertising their wares, and arousing once more the historic antipathy of Protestants.

Given all these turbulent factors, coupled with a surging Jacksonian Democracy of farmers and mechanics uncontrolled by a unified monarchy, clerical hierarchy, or aristocracy, the middle period was inevitably an age of mass movements—an age of lectures, public schools, circuses, museums, penny newspapers, varied propaganda, political caucuses, woman suffrage conventions, temperance reform, proletarian unrest, labor organization, Mormonism, Millerism, mesmerism, phrenology—an age of shoemakers, carpenters, and sons of poor parsons writing poems and essays, of women erecting colleges, asserting rights and taking part in every phase of the American opera, grand or comic—the martial notes of the agitator mingling with the vibrant tones of the moralist, preacher, and educator—pioneers in opinion marching forward, sometimes inspired, often ignorant and usually crotchety, to the conquest of the future in America. "Madmen, and women, men with beards, Dunkers, Muggletonians, Come-outers, Groaners, Agrarians, Seventh-Day Baptists, Quakers, Abolitionists, Unitarians, and Philosophers"—in these lines Emerson summarily described the seething democracy of his time.

The very exuberance of the age—an exuberance which amused and irritated foreign visitors, such as Dickens, and induced a modern writer, Meade Minnigerode, to fling at the decade the disparaging title, The Fabulous Forties—was no mere expression of democratic perversity. Rather did it flow from the dynamic efforts of the struggling multitudes, granted some leisure and an economic surplus, to entertain and decorate themselves after the fashion of classes supposed to be their "betters." Finding a limitless reproductive power in the machine, captains of industry borrowed, duplicated, and sold to the masses the things already available, the plumage of "superior" persons: oil paintings, pottery, spindle leg chairs, gilt frames, mirrors, and rugs copied after the designs of Versailles and London. Even the blazing chandelier of flashing crystal so conspicuous in the homes of the democracy was imported from drawing rooms soon to be celebrated for all time as Mid-Victorian. No doubt there was something bizarre about the wide distribution of goods, real or imitative, once restricted to limited classes, but whether bitter or sweet it was the natural fruit of the machine.

§

Among the many varieties of opinion that streamed from Europe into the deeply agitated America of the middle period were three which helped to deflect thought into novel channels. The first was a new philosophy or pattern of ideas evolved by doctrinaires to combat the scientific theories of the eighteenth century—that chain of theories, hard, mathematical, and mechanical, which stretched from Descartes to Laplace. To all such speculations concerning the nature of things, the political relations of the European powers, during the disturbances which preceded and accompanied the French Revolution and the Napoleonic wars, gave a decided bent. For nearly a quarter of a century, England and France were locked in a deadly war over commerce and empire, and French ideas were, therefore, made tabu in the polite circles of English society—notwithstanding the artistic forms given them by the poems of Wordsworth, Shelley, and Byron.

In this controversy, the ruling classes of Prussia and many minor German states were arrayed on the side of England; by reason of the war and their aristocratic pretensions, they too came to hate France and French radical views. Furthermore, during the armed contest with their redoubtable foe in Paris, the Germans, long divided among hundreds of principalities, were drawn together in an aggressive nationalism. Once Frederick the Great, despising the literature and language of his native land, had made Voltaire a bosom companion; after the outbreak of the French war and especially after the ruinous defeat at the hands of Napoleon, all Germany was thrown into an uproar over projects for creating a purely German culture—philosophy, science, and the arts. In this period of "Sturm und Drang" came a great flowering of the German intellect; Kant, Goethe, Schelling, Fichte, and Hegel wrought mighty tomes with their pens, sending reverberations around the world.

The outstanding figure in this Teutonic renaissance, a man destined to have directly or indirectly a powerful influence on American thinking, was the Prussian philosopher, of remote Scotch origins, Immanuel Kant. The son of a pious mother, Kant imbibed in his early youth the doctrines of a mildly evangelical Puritanism. Thrown by his early teachings athwart the mechanical creed promoted by scientific thinkers from Descartes and Locke to Hume and Voltaire, he turned with sympathy to the romantic enthusiasms of Rousseau, that arch-agitator and agricultural prophet, who regarded science as an enemy, not a friend of mankind.

Fortified by strong emotions, Kant worked out the Critique of Pure Reason, first published in 1781, a gigantic pile of thought, heavily laden with ponderous words, which kindled anew the philosophy of sentiments, and furnished somber authority for counteracting the destructive effects of analytical reasoning upon established concepts and institutions. The upshot of Kant's system for the man in the street was the declaration that the great ideas of God, soul, freedom, right, duty, and immortality cannot be tested at all by our contacts with the world of material things but "transcend" the experiences of our senses; they are intuitively inexorable and are discovered to be absolutely true by introspection, or the internal examination of our mental structure. Of course, apostles could light almost any kind of candle at Kant's altar, but in an age of revolt against France and French reason, it was the conservatives rather than the radicals, sentimentalists rather than scientists, who drew energies from the great philosopher of Koenigsberg.

And it was to Germany, at the opening of the nineteenth century, that American students, set free by new accumulations of industrial wealth, turned for light and guidance. They could not go very well to the English universities of Oxford and Cambridge where the monopoly of the Anglican Church was still unbroken. For sons of Northern Federalists, France was also anathema: French radicalism was associated with the devil and with defeat at the hands of Thomas Jefferson. Moreover, in France the reaction against the revolution, under the leadership of men like De Maistre, turned to Catholic doctrines for comfort—doctrines equally proscribed by descendants of Puritan divines.

On the other hand the North German states were Protestant, evangelical, and practically free of French taint. So it was to Germany that an increasing number of American students, especially from New England, flocked during the middle period. There they got transcendental philosophy, a thorough training in classical literature, and a fine hatred for the French "mechanical" school. Those who did not go to Germany got the same medicine indirectly from Thomas Carlyle, great feudal romanticist, and Samuel Taylor Coleridge, poet and dreamer, who made the English-speaking world acquainted with German writers and German philosophy.

The second nucleus of opinions imported from Europe in these decades was a new version of the concept of progress which had been so potent in the days of the early republic. It is one of the curious but neglected facts of history—illustrating again the irrefragable unity of all western thought—that a French army officer, who proudly wrote himself down as "a descendant of Charlemagne and a soldier under Washington," gave to the nineteenth century the doctrine of socialism as the goal of progress. That officer was Count de Saint-Simon, who fought in the American war of independence—interested, as he said, not in the war, but in its object—and in the New World got a glimpse of an order of things in which the humblest should be freed from the galling chains of poverty and disease.

Accepting at face value the theories of Condorcet and the dreams of the early American republicans, Saint-Simon announced in 1815 the coming "perfection of the social order." To summarize in the language of Bury the process by which this creed was reached: "As the goal of development is social happiness, and as the working classes form the majority, the first step towards the goal will be the amelioration of the lot of the working classes. This will be the principal problem of government in reorganizing society and Saint-Simon's solution of the problem was socialism." Of course elements of this idea were not new and thinkers such as Robert Owen and Charles Fourier reached similar conclusions by other routes, but Saint-Simon furnished the first dynamic drive for the economic dogma.

The third central pattern of theories derived from Europe in the age of Jackson and Lincoln was the thesis of evolution applied not only to society but to all living forms. Though popularly associated in its beginnings with the publication of Charles Darwin's Origin of Species in 1859, the idea was, as students of the history of science well know, long in the stage of formulation. The Greeks and Romans had vaguely hinted at the changing course of all things; and their concept of nature and man, submerged for centuries under Christian theology, finally began to work powerfully on the thought of western Europe, after the classical revival. Then, with the rise of modern science, the notion of development could hardly be escaped, as the various branches—such as botany, geology, zoölogy, and anatomy, and later biology and anthropology—flourished in the eighteenth century and foliated richly in the early decades of the nineteenth.

On the eve of the French Revolution, Buffon, the great naturalist, with an eye on clerical censorship, cautiously suggested the mutability of species. Across the Rhine, the poet, Goethe, boldly declared that all the more perfect organisms had sprung from a common stock. Meanwhile Lamarck, the distinguished professor of natural history at the Paris Botanical Gardens, caught faint sparkles of the electric word before he passed from the scene, blind and poverty-stricken, in 1829. In England, Lyell, carrying on the work of James Hutton, completed in 1833 his epochmaking treatise on geology, showing the evolutionary story written in the layers of the earth and striking a trenchant blow at traditional cosmogony. In short, Darwin and his co-discoverer, Alfred Russel Wallace, crowned labors that had been transforming all phases of natural science for many decades.

When at length at the close of the middle period, the Darwinian hypothesis was launched in finished form, its ruinous implications for the Miltonic hypothesis were quickly grasped. Disregarding accepted Biblical chronology, it asserted the antiquity of man and the earth. Rejecting the belief that each species of living beings was the result of an original divine act, it proclaimed the mutability of species. It alleged that there were no sharp lines between them; that they were gradually shaded into one another when classified according to characteristics; that they were all branches of a common tree of life; and that they had slowly evolved from simple to complex forms.

Moreover, this evolution was to be explained not by divine interposition but by natural causes—the struggle for existence, adaptation to environment, and the survival of the fittest. In every respect therefore the new theory ran counter to the Christian concept of creation, making grave difficulties for those who tried to reconcile it with the doctrines of the fall of man, original sin, Virgin birth, salvation by faith, and resurrection.

§

In the currents of religious life in America during this period was revealed in myriad forms the influence of new factors and forces—especially the machine, science, the expanding frontier, democracy, immigration, and imported thought-patterns. The power of devouring science and secularism was made manifest in the continued growth of Unitarianism among the Congregational churches and in the steady retreat of ancient tribal visions of the deity before the devices of rationalism.

At the opening of the epoch, in 1817, died Timothy Dwight, "the last of the Puritans" of the Edwardian lineage; in the hands of the new generation religion assumed a more "liberal" garb, namely, one in closer conformity to the revelations of naturalistic researches. Early in life, Emerson left the pulpit because he could not endure the ceremony of communion even in an attenuated symbolic form. His congregation, generous in its theology, sought to "induce him to remain, he administering the Lord's supper in his sense, the people receiving it in theirs" but the preacher of Concord would not bring himself to accept that charitable accommodation. An age was coming to an end. If Andover Seminary long continued to be the home of orthodoxy, such men as Horace Bushnell, Mark Hopkins, and Henry Ward Beecher carried into pulpits far and wide messages of Christianity that must have made Jonathan Edwards writhe in his grave. And the era had hardly closed when Beecher accepted a mild version of Darwin's evolution as the key to the creative process.

Conforming to the restless spirit of Jacksonian Democracy was a remarkable growth in the Methodist and Baptist churches, especially in the West and Southwest. Undoubtedly J. Franklin Jameson is right in relating the extension of political equality with the prosperity of the religious bodies that reject the Calvinist doctrine of election for the favored few. How could Jacksonian Democrats who exalted the masses of farmers and mechanics believe in a system of theology which condemned most of them to hell in advance without a hearing and reserved heaven for a select aristocracy favored of God? Of course the Presbyterians also flourished during the middle period, as the Scotch-Irish population increased, but the followers of John Calvin did not maintain the relative strength which they commanded in the colonial age. The unbreakable logic of Edwards still stood but it no longer had the same appeal in many sections of the country.

Intimately affiliated with effervescing democracy—particularly on the frontier—were the new sects and ebullient revival meetings that so distinguished the time. Of course the rise of visionaries and fiery apostles was not a strange phenomenon; Simeon Stylites, in sheer religious ecstasy, spent thirty years of his life on a pillar to demonstrate his devotion; St. Francis, St. Dominic, Luther, and Wesley, each in his day, made clarion calls for religious rededication. But when once the dominion of the hierarchy and clergy was badly shattered, as in America, and everyone, high and low, was permitted to express his religious sentiments and emotions, to declare and to exhort, a bewildering variety of dreams and professions was as natural as the unquenchable enthusiasms of a prosperous population.

It was inevitable therefore that the appearance of sects and schisms should be a matter of annual occurrence. Two-seed-in-the-spirit Predestinarian Baptists set themselves up against Free-will Baptists. Presbyterians broke into four or five divisions. Methodists, while managing to keep fairly close together on points of salvation, split over the slavery question into a Northern and a Southern wing. Still more radical on issues of faith, Alexander Campbell, calling for "a return to primitive Christianity," marshaled a host of followers. Prophesying in great enchantment the second coming of Christ and the end of the world, William Miller enrolled converts and in 1843 solemnly awaited the heralded occasion; though the failure of the prognostication damped the ardor of Miller's rank and file, the belief in the second advent exerted a continuous influence on religious thinking in America and even penetrated through its devoted evangels into the heart of Korea. In this fermenting era Mormonism also rose and prospered like the green bay tree.

As if to magnify the turmoil among established Protestant sects, whole communities were shaken by boisterous religious revivals. Frontier individualism brought forth fruits in theology and theories of salvation no less than in politics and fostered clerical notions as far removed from the administrative proprieties of Laud, Mazarin, and Bossuet as were its theories of self-government.

Only in one quarter was there a marked increase in the number of those who acknowledged obedience to high prerogative in matters ecclesiastical, namely, among the Catholics, most of whom were to be found in the industrial cities. But the multiplying communicants of that Church represented no wholesale return of American Protestants and skeptics to the ancient creed viewed with such horror in the colonial régime. It was due rather to the swarming invasion of well-disciplined peasants from Ireland and Europe, followed by Catholic clergy prepared to do their best to hold the faith against the swirling, sapping currents of American individualism. Unquestionably the task of keeping the ranks unbroken was difficult and a large portion of the former communicants was lost in the transfer of their political allegiance. Yet, on the whole, the Catholic body grew steadily in strength with the rise of immigration, affording elements of culture quite foreign to the heritage handed down by George Washington, Jefferson, Franklin, and Timothy Dwight.

§

With respect to intellectual interests of a secular cast, it was fitting that the age of machinery should give predominance to science, theoretical and applied, at least, in the Northeast where industrialism made its conquests. It is one of the significant phases of history that the development of political democracy during three revolutionary centuries was accompanied by the rise and growth of science and invention. Students have been baffled in their efforts to establish causal relations, to explain why the world had to wait thousands of years for the steam engine and the formula of atomic weights, why Rousseau was working on his Social Contract at the very time that Watt was bringing the steam engine to an operating basis.

Yet the fact remains that political democracy and natural science rose and flourished together. Whether in their inception there were deep connections, researches have not yet disclosed but beyond question their influence upon each other has been reciprocal. Democracy arrested the attention of idle curiosity and demanded that the man of microscope and test tube come into the street to invent, relieve, and serve. Science, on the other hand, helped to determine the course of democratic development. It was itself democratic in that it spurned nothing low or commonplace in its researches— the mold on decayed vegetables, the composition of the dirt in the field, the nature of curds in sour milk. Nothing was sacred to its relentless inquiry. Before it there was neither prerogative nor privilege.

More than that, science pointed the way to progressive democracy in its warfare against starvation, poverty, disease, and ignorance, indicating how classes and nations long engaged in strife among themselves might unite to wring from nature the secret of security and the good life. It was science, not paper declarations relating to the idea of progress, that at last made patent the practical methods by which democracy could raise the standard of living for the great masses of the people. Finally science gave to man revolutionary concepts of the world and of his place in the great scheme of nature, feeding the streams of thought which wore down ancient institutions of church and state.

Although there might have been no causal relation between science and democracy, it was a striking coincidence that, in the age of renewed revolution in Europe and the Jacksonian upheaval in America, epoch-making generalizations were made by scientists of the Old World and epoch-making machines for lightening toil and multiplying production of goods were invented in the United States. If Faraday could announce the law of electro-chemical equivalents in 1834, Morse could announce the completion of the first successful telegraph line in 1844. If Charles Darwin could span all creation, Cyrus Field could at least span the Atlantic Ocean.

§

While there were no kings and lords in Jacksonian democracy to patronize science, it was fostered by one means or another. To illustrate, Harvard subsidized Louis Agassiz, Yale financed Benjamin Silliman, and the federal naval observatory gave Matthew Maury some leisure for his researches. By way of supplement, the sale of textbooks for the multiplying colleges and secondary schools brought additional revenues to scholars and experimenters. Outside the academic world, the employment of scientists by the state and federal governments in the making of surveys and the management of museums also stimulated talent by giving it an opportunity and economic support. Finally, the revolution wrought in the art of printing by the power press and the growth of a huge literate population eager for more knowledge offered both a competency and an independence to writers who could popularize their specialties. Democracy thus had rewards of its own to offer—sometimes capricious, no doubt, but hardly more whimsical than that of noble lords, if Doctor Johnson's experience is a test, and with subtle influences on creative thought not yet clearly understood.

The advance of science in the middle period, as always, was marked by observation, the accumulation of data, generalization, and application. In this work of the age, American specialists rendered constructive services and their number was legion. Among the throng, five or six men stood out in bold relief: for example, Silliman at Yale collecting minerals, assembling a chemical laboratory, and promoting national interest in the leading branches of natural science; Audubon wandering with his wife in the wilds for long years to study and paint plants and birds, building an international reputation as an ornithologist; Agassiz at Harvard laying the foundation for teaching and research in zoölogy; Maury of Virginia exploring the mysteries of the sea's physical geography; Joseph Henry, tireless experimenter in physics and meteorology and creator of the first magnetic telegraph. Through the work of competent specialists, American botanists, with Asa Gray in the forefront, had taken over the study and classification of North American flora by 1850.

To the labors of individuals and colleges was added that of associations, local, state, and national, and the various surveys carried out under government auspices. In keeping with the trend, the older projects for general scientific academies were supplemented by specialization. Between 1815 and the Civil War, the geologists, geographers, ethnologists, and statisticians were separately organized on a national scale. And then these societies were crowned by the American Association for the Advancement of Science called into being at Boston in 1847 to "promote intercourse between American scientists, to give a strong and more systematic impulse to research, and to procure for the labors of scientific men increased facilities and wider usefulness." Shortly after its organization the Association began to issue annual publications.

Accordingly, before the middle of the nineteenth century natural science had become by various means a potent force in the intellectual life of America. Its great departments—geology, botany, zoölogy, ethnology, chemistry, physics, and the other disciplines—had been staked out here as in Europe. The collections of material objects and recorded data had attained impressive proportions; even the slow-moving federal government falling into line by establishing in 1846 the Smithsonian Institution and National Museum on the basis of a bequest from an Englishman, James Smithson. There were leaders of power, patience, and industry at work enlarging knowledge in every sphere. There were scientific societies and scientific journals available for the interchange of ideas and discoveries. There were constant voyages of exploration, survey, and inquiry in every direction unearthing more data and testing older hypotheses.

To consolidate gains and lay lines for the onward march, textbooks appeared in the several fields: such as Cleaveland's work on mineralogy and geology in 1816; Gray's survey of botany in the northern United States in 1847; and Silliman's elements of chemistry in 1830. Texts were supplemented by articles on the minutiæ of science and by special volumes on local phenomena.

The quality, variety, and amount of American work were so important that European scientists were compelled to take it into consideration. Many of them visited this country to see the huge terrain on which their colleagues were operating. The English geologist, Lyell, was well acquainted with students in the United States and made a long journey through the continent observing American society, studying natural objects, and conversing with the thinkers. Darwin kept a sharp eye open for new materials from this side the water. He was familiar with American publications and in communication with American workers in his particular field; for instance, his correspondence with Asa Gray at Harvard, opened in 1855 and maintained for more than twenty years, was close, frequent, and intimate. It involved a continuous exchange of ideas and information and it showed on the part of the great English pioneer a wholesome respect for the best expert opinion across the Atlantic. Only one who has spent weeks poring over the old textbooks, government reports, biographies, and records of museums can begin to appreciate the comprehensive, varied, and fruitful labors of scientists in that age, so often belittled by its successors.

Yet it must be acknowledged that the epoch which gave Faraday, Volta, Berzelius, Lyell, Wallace, and Darwin to the world produced in America no supreme generalizer in the realm of pure science. Altogether pertinently that keen French observer, de Tocqueville, profoundest of the Europeans who have surveyed the American scene, remarked of the Jacksonian era: "These very Americans who have not discovered one of the general laws of mechanics have introduced into navigation an engine that changes the aspect of the world. . . . If the democratic principle does not on the one hand induce men to cultivate science for its own sake, on the other, it does enormously increase the number of those who do cultivate it. . . . Permanent inequality of conditions leads men to confine themselves to the arrogant and sterile researches of abstract truths, whilst the social condition and institutions of democracy prepare them to seek the immediate and useful practical results of the sciences. The tendency is natural and inevitable."

In the main this stricture, if it be such, was justified by the facts; and there was doubtless something deeply penetrating in the philosopher's exposition of the course of American science. Absence of generalization may be due to ignorance or to a failure of supreme imaginative qualities—or to a recognition of the baffling complexity of things. Generalizations themselves are nearly always subject to later modifications and rejections; few of them escape the impress of continuous research. American society in this particular era was more fluid than that of any country in the Old World. In any case, American men of science were not ignorant; if they did not find what Emerson called the "electric word," they certainly helped to prepare the way for new explanations of man and nature and they were equipped by training and knowledge to grasp the import of all advances in European thought and speculation.

A long time before Darwin announced the consummation of his labors, the intellectual operations that were to culminate in his interpretation of life were shared by American scientists. When Benjamin Silliman, after receiving a call to a scientific post at Yale, sought to prepare himself for his teaching mission, he went over to study at Edinburgh where Hutton's cosmic theories, among the most advanced of his time, were being carefully expounded. Grasping the value of research, Silliman, on his return, founded the American Journal of Science and took an active part in promoting the new American Geological Society as a means of stimulating patronage and performance. When Lyell published his startling treatise on the creative process, as revealed by a study of the earth, American scientists were ready to appreciate it; when a few years later he came to this country to lecture, he found a wide and receptive public awaiting him.

The ferment was already at work. Indeed several years previous to that, the able Philadelphia botanist, Rafinesque, had advanced in a tentative fashion the thesis that "all species might have once been varieties and that many varieties are gradually becoming species by assuming constant and peculiar characters." At the same time Samuel Haldeman, the talented naturalist and philologist of Pennsylvania, was evolving the same startling hypothesis.

That Darwin himself was in constant touch with the progress of science in America is revealed in his correspondence with Asa Gray. As we have said, the two naturalists exchanged papers and memoranda, asked each other questions, and advanced theories about various subjects to each other. The year after their first exchange, namely, in 1856, Darwin gave Gray a glimpse of his secret and two years later sent him a long outline of the forthcoming treatise that was to shake the world. Toward the Darwinian thesis, when it came to him in sheets as they were printed, Gray was cautious, critical, and hesitant, pointing out errors which Darwin generously and apologetically acknowledged. Indeed, the English scholar placed Gray among the four contemporaries whose judgment he most valued. Eventually convinced that the theory of evolution was sound, Gray became an ardent champion carrying the fight for Darwinism all along the line.

And it must be conceded that the American public was as receptive to the revolutionary doctrine as that of any European country. If the Swiss scholar, Agassiz, rejected it as "mischievous," the head of Trinity College in Cambridge, England, refused to have a copy of Darwin's book in the library. Though many a clergyman in the American hinterland tore his hair and rent his garments, Henry Ward Beecher, the most popular preacher of his time, after much reflection, declared evolution to be the key to the natural world.

Darwin himself stated that "the two most striking reviews" of the Origin of Species appeared in the United States: in the North American Review and the New York Times. That was in April, 1860. The voice of American science was soon to be subdued to the roar of guns. "Great God! how I should like to see the greatest curse on earth—slavery—abolished," wrote Darwin to Gray a few weeks after Lincoln's call for arms. When his wish was consummated, he and Gray continued their correspondence until the long shadows fell upon them both.

§

If, through lack of talent, through timidity, or for want of a favorable environment, America made no great contributions to the hypotheses of pure science in the middle period, her advances in the application of physics and chemistry to the satisfaction of human needs were important enough to warrant a long chapter in any balanced history of western civilization. In the swift accumulations of the Patent Office in Washington a marvelous story was told. Perhaps it was no accident that the plot of land reserved in the original plan of the capital for a "national church square" was dedicated to the use of inventors in 1836 and that behind the façade of a Greek temple was opened in 1841 the largest exhibition room in the United States for the display of the devices which sprang from American inventive genius.

It was on American soil in this period that the idea of using chemicals for the prevention of pain in surgical operations was efficiently developed for the first time. No doubt the possibility of accomplishing this triumph had been sensed by the ancients; primitive races had used leaves as balms, such as the coca from which cocain is derived. Moreover, Faraday and Davy had advocated the trial of drugs as anæsthetics. But it was five American experimenters, Long, Jackson, Wells, Morton, and Warren, who carried vague speculation about anæsthetics into realization —and that in the age of P. T. Barnum and General Tom Thumb, so much better known.

The distribution of honors among these men is hazardous business; the French Academy after full investigation awarded the palm to Dr. Charles Thomas Jackson, born in the old Plymouth colony in 1805; but that decision has not been confirmed by the verdict of history. In any event, on the development of anæsthetics by American doctors was built not only a new surgery but also the science of dentistry, in which national skill has been so preëminently displayed. Within a few years practitioners in the United States had done more for the relief of human pain and suffering than all the soothsayers and shamans of ten thousand preceding generations. For the resignation of the mystics, they substituted the insubordination of the "hard" scientific mind dedicated to "the worship of progress."

It was during this so-called "vulgar" age that electricity, which had long occupied the attention of scientists on both sides of the ocean, was turned by American inventors to the transmission of messages. A score of individuals worked at this problem but Samuel Morse effected the happy combination of the scientific temper and practical understanding which bore the magnetic telegraph out into the world of affairs and placed it at the service of mankind. In the same age, Matthew Maury, exploring the mysteries of hydrography, became the "pathfinder of the seas," in luminous studies pointing out to captains the safest routes for their vessels and explaining the nature of the ocean bed to scientists dreaming of transatlantic cables. It was on his faith in the work of Morse and Maury that Cyrus W. Field of Massachusetts rested his confidence in the possibility of submarine telegraphy, organized a company, raised the capital, demonstrated the feasibility of the project in 1858, and opened the system to commerce and international relations in 1866.

Although leading in some phases, Americans were borrowing in others with increasing zeal. In fact, during the middle period all the great mechanical devices of the Old World were imported and adapted to American conditions —textile machinery, locomotives, and steam engines. So free, indeed, was the circulation of ideas, so close were the relations of explorers, experimenters, and inventors that it is perilous to attempt to cut the grand republic of science too definitely into independent national sovereignties.

§

Under the timid and uncertain patronage of the federal government a start was made toward making science a servant for tillers of the soil who in most countries and ages had been left to struggle along by rule of thumb close to the margin of subsistence. While President of the United States George Washington, a gentleman-farmer, had urged Congress to establish a department for the advancement of agriculture but provincial politicians, thinking that it would destroy local virtues, opposed it. Not until 1839 was a beginning made by an appropriation to the Patent Office, used in part for the purchase and distribution of new seeds and plants. The following year agents of the census began to collect the statistics of American agriculture which some day will be quickened by a writer of poetic gifts into the history of the land in the United States.

While politicians were debating the Wilmot Proviso, bleeding Kansas, and the fugitive slave law, men of science were urging, in the highways and byways, the conservation of natural resources and systematic aid from the government for the scientific use of our natural endowment. And this agitation bore fruit in the very midst of the Civil War in the establishment of the bureau of agriculture—a department without the rank—and provision for the creation of agricultural colleges in every state of a Union then hanging in a fateful balance.

In town, as well as country, applied science had work to do; there it had to face new problems created by the growth of huge industrial populations—problems in sanitation, transportation, public safety, and convenience. It is to this epoch that the historian traces impressive movements designed to make the city a safe, healthful, and comfortable dwelling-place. Of course, great waterworks, sewers, parks, and public baths were not novel in the nineteenth century. The chief cities of the Roman Empire, from the capital to the towns of the provinces, carried municipal improvements to an amazing degree of proficiency, but the mass of the people, slaves and artisans, derived small benefit from these mighty engineering achievements, except perhaps from the public fountains where they got their water supply.

The middle ages which followed the decline of Rome exhibited retrogression in every sphere of municipal science; for feudal wars forced the construction of walls around towns and the congestion of population within their confines. Narrow streets swimming in mud, open sewers, disease, and pestilence, no less than beautiful churches, mercantile palaces, and guildhalls, were the outstanding characteristics of the mediæval city. It was not until the seventeenth century that the larger municipalities, such as London and Paris, began to construct waterworks on a comprehensive scale; and at the opening of the nineteenth century most cities were still essentially mediæval in appearance and in practice.

Thus in municipal administration, unlike letters and pure science, America could not turn to the Old World for noble models. In fact, apart from pavements and public buildings, London and Paris were not far in advance of New York in Andrew Jackson's day; the revolution in steam and steel which made possible modern improvements came in America only a few years after it began its wonder-working transformation in England.

In most respects, therefore, American cities moved along lines almost parallel with those of European municipalities. It was in 1822 that Philadelphia opened the Fairmount pumping station which supplied the city with water. It was in 1842 that New York completed the Croton water system, one of the great plants of the modern age. Boston installed public sewerage in 1823; twenty-six years later New York created a sewer department and began to attack her sanitary problem in earnest. The bath tub made its way slowly into the homes of the best families. Sidewalks, extensively introduced in Paris in 1782, appeared in Philadelphia within four years and were afterward rapidly adopted by other cities. Pavements of cobblestones which had been popular in colonial days were gradually extended in some cities and in other places were supplemented by stone and wooden blocks. In 1849, New York made Broadway smoother by paving it with large granite squares. While revolutions and royal donations in Europe were throwing open to the masses magnificent gardens and parks, American democracy was faintly struggling to break the dreary monotony of streets with open spaces maintained at public expense. Boston continued to cherish the Common inherited from older days; Philadelphia made a striking departure in 1812 by buying a small private park; in 1858 New York started the construction of Central Park, a reservation of nearly a thousand acres.

The middle period also saw the beginnings of many important municipal agencies. It was in this era that the first regular public health service was organized, much to the disgust of citizens who, in spite of the plagues and fevers that periodically devastated their towns, looked upon their health as a strictly private affair. In 1853, New York, following an example set by London twenty-five years before, ordered policemen to don an official uniform—a blue coat with brass buttons, gray trousers, and a regulation cap. After a loud wail about "freemen wearing livery," the town constables succumbed and appeared in the new style. In the same decade, Boston and Baltimore, weary of constant fights among private fire companies, established municipal brigades. Before that decade closed, street cars were running in New York, competing with the hundreds of omnibuses that rattled up and down the main thoroughfares; the long battle over franchises and rates, attended by politics and corruption, had begun. William Marcy Tweed was mewing his mighty youth in the days of Andrew Jackson. If the modern reader gathers from reports of the time that American cities were dirty and unkempt places hardly fit for human habitation—and the impression is largely correct—he will do well to balance accounts by a study of European and Oriental cities, ancient, mediæval and modern.

§

In the field of social speculation, the idea of progress, so potent in the early republican era, foliated richly in the new setting afforded by natural science and technology, anticipating in every phase the progressive democracy of the twentieth century. The concept of the state as a humane institution for the promotion of public welfare, as distinguished from a mere military or police agency, was examined from all angles and vigorously expounded in the age of "Old Hickory" and "Honest Abe." "We believe that the government, like every other intelligent agency," said Horace Greeley, "is bound to do good to the extent of its ability—that it ought actively to promote and increase the general well-being—that it should encourage and foster Industry, Science, Invention, Social, and Physical Progress. . . . Such is our idea of the sphere of Government."

Emerson, in his fragmentary but deep-thrusting way, warned his contemporaries that the recent discoveries of science, in illuminating affairs of state, bade them think of the social order not as fixed but continually in the course of change. He was not sure of the social destiny of mankind but he was firm in his belief that the doctrine of evolution, which he vaguely discussed long before Darwin enunciated his thesis, would utterly "upset" traditional views of politics, trade, and customs.

It was within the framework of a large social philosophy that the most acute analyses of the prevailing issues were effected—banking and currency, free trade and protection, the land question, and the problems of labor. Writers on political economy had not yet committed the fatal error of separating economics from politics as if the production and distribution of wealth could be divorced from the civil law under which the process operates. The great theme, as Adam Smith conceived it, was kept intact; elements, outlines, and manuals of political economy pouring from the presses betrayed a deepening interest in the subject.

Moreover, as in other spheres, appeared some signs of emancipation from foreign dominance, particularly from England. Speaking for a country that had become the workshop of the world and for the moment faced no serious competition in any quarter, English theorists had found in free trade a policy that exactly fitted the occasion. English mill owners wanted cheap bread for their operatives; hence no tariff on food. Since they were not likely to be undersold in any market, they could incur the risk of competition in manufactured products at home. Seizing upon that peculiar condition, which, by the way, was never reproduced, English political economists proclaimed freedom of trade as a scientific doctrine—proclaimed it with such assurance and with such a display of logic that many American professors accepted it as if it were a decree of nature, in spite of the different economic conditions prevailing in their own country.

So it happened that the intellectual operations of the learned, especially in the colleges, did not always coincide exactly with the interests and opinions of practical men engaged in manufacturing. But the requirements of American industry were finally met by Henry C. Carey of Philadelphia, who published in 1837-40 three volumes on political economy in which he sharply criticized the leading preconceptions of the freetraders, sketched a nationalist basis for protection, and laid the logical foundations for a tariff system. To the doctrine of the economic man operated automatically by self-interest—fallacious at bottom and dangerous in application—Carey opposed the doctrine of national interest. Henceforward infant industries were to stand in no need of champions in the schools.

Meanwhile the rising labor movement found spokesmen who produced an immense literature sparkling with anticipations in every sphere. As early as 1826, L. Byllesby made pertinent inquiries into the origins of unequal wealth and the nature of its effect on human happiness. Three years later Thomas Skidmore declared the new rights of man—this time, to property. In a similar vein, Frances Wright preached radical labor doctrines from the platform, especially with respect to the position of women, her addresses issued as a "Course of Popular Lectures" winning a great vogue among working people. A decade later Albert Brisbane proclaimed the coöperative gospel of Fourier, who in spite of his fantastic schemes, "helped to familiarize the world with the idea of indefinite progress." Through translations from the French and in a book of his own entitled The Social Destiny of Man, Brisbane created a large school of reformers. Clinging still to their religion while recognizing new imperatives, the Christian Socialists found a genial spokesman in Adin Ballou. Anarchists won a hearing for their creed in trenchant works by Josiah Warren and Stephen Pearl Andrews. On the left also, The Communist Manifesto, of German origin, was given an English dress within a short time after its publication; and the German refugees fleeing to this country from the reaction that followed 1848 colored for a time the American stream of radicalism with this continental hue.

On the whole the note of coöperative idealism was strong and clear during the period, particularly in the eastern states where the population was becoming congested; where the fruits of machine industry, bitter and sweet, were falling upon the earth. Not until the national domain was flung by the Republican party to the hungry proletariat as a free gift, more significant than bread and circuses, did the socialistic idea sink into the background of the labor movement and the strictly realistic business of raising wages and reducing hours monopolize the thought of labor organizers.

This whole evolution was revealed in the case of Horace Greeley who, in the forties, vowed himself a socialist, opened the columns of his Tribune to Karl Marx and the communists, debated Socialism with H. J. Raymond, founder of the Times, threw himself into the Homestead movement, became absorbed in the slavery struggle, and ended in the embrace of respectability. The fact that men of Greeley's mental power and political standing were drawn to the socialistic philosophy is proof that the agitations of the middle period had reached far beyond the obscure circles of working people and were deemed worthy of serious consideration by some who sat in lofty places. Unquestionably the civil cataclysm of 1861 and the free land opened to labor by the Homestead Act of the following year checked for decades the strong radical drift.

§

By delving into the records of the past, historians now helped economists to detach, at least in some degree, the facts of social evolution in America from the glowing periods of revolutionary orators. George Bancroft, in 1834, began to issue a ten-volume History of the United States ranging from the founding of the colonies to the establishment of the Constitution. Though his New England origin and his Democratic politics gave many curious twists to the threads of his narrative, though an avowed intimacy with the purposes of Providence often lifted him far above the dusty way, his long and arduous researches gave his work a value which time has not destroyed.

In a less exalted strain, Richard Hildreth, one of Bancroft's contemporaries, a Federalist from New England, told the American story from the age of discovery to the Missouri Compromise. Declaring that of "centennial sermons and Fourth-of-July orations" there were "more than enough," he vowed that he wanted to portray the founders of the nation as they actually were, "unbedaubed with patriotic rouge, wrapped up in no fine-spun cloaks of excuses and apologies, without stilts, buskins, tinsel, or bedizenment." His inquiries were not as deep as those of Bancroft but his style was more restrained and more scientific.

A disillusioned Federalist, rather than an ardent Democrat, and claiming no special familiarity with the plans of the Almighty, Hildreth gave a colder and calmer view of the sacred past. When his first instalment appeared in 1849, a doleful sound went up from patriot quarters but scholars rejoiced in being able at last to discover something tangible through the mists. The editor of the Edinburgh Review, for example, even though he would have found it hard to discover anything but chauvinistic history at home, expressed his pleasure in seeing "the muse of American history descended from her stump and recounting her narrative in a key adapted to our own ears."

Not content, however, as a modern wit remarked, with this demonstration of "how civilization came into America by way of New England," writers in the middle and southern states began to take a look at the past for themselves. The novelist, Irving, long after composing a humorous history of the New York Knickerbockers which delighted everybody except some of the old Dutch families, wrote a substantial biography of George Washington in keeping with ponderous tradition. As if to offset the one-sided view of the country that came from the northern schools, George Tucker of Virginia gave a fine old southern gentleman's impression of the nation's historic past in a solid, if not brilliant, work which deserved deeper consideration than it ever received.

No less important for the development of accurate historical scholarship in America were the collections of original materials which industrious persons now began to assemble—collections from which searchers could form independent judgments. Foremost in this field was a Harvard professor, Jared Sparks, who labored long and hard at the work of compiling and editing. Besides making noteworthy contributions to American biography, he brought out the life and writings of Washington in twelve volumes and the works of Franklin in ten—correcting and polishing the letters of his two heroes instead of printing them exactly as they stood with all their errors in spelling, grammar, and diction. Still, in this editorial mutilation, Sparks inadvertently rendered a service to scholarship, for the opposition aroused by his easy liberties with the texts made his successors more wary and precise.

In the same business of collecting and editing, Sparks had an indefatigable contemporary, Peter Force, who projected a huge library of American archives and got several volumes through the press before the federal government, under whose auspices he was working, cut off its financial support. He managed to make important beginnings and to forward the spirit of scientific research. Thus the period, near its close at least, exhibited a growing interest in history and a bent toward that laborious hunting and assembling which were then making German scholarship the admiration of all students in this special field. In time so-called "scientific history" was to invade the realm so often monopolized by romance and mere convention.

By the side of the luminaries burned many lesser and local lights. In every section of the country, from Maine to Georgia and from the Atlantic coast to the Mississippi Valley, amateur historians and collectors were gathering papers, writing down folklore, and describing contemporary life. Timothy Dwight, journeying far and wide in New England and New York, left behind at his death four great volumes of his observations and impressions. Timothy Flint rendered a similar service for the Mississippi country. In one fashion or another an amazing pile of materials on local life and incidents was amassed. Illinois alone, to use a single example, was discussed under more than four hundred titles in works issued between 1818 and 1865. In college and private libraries and in state archives recorded data were preserved by a thousand hands. The age of oral tradition and gossip was merging into the age of sifted and tested facts. Herculean labor yet lay ahead but by 1860 much ground had been cleared and long strides taken in the work of placing the study of social evolution in the United States on a scientific basis.

§

The searches of the economists, historians, and scientists which threw such a flood of light on the nature of social origins and development inevitably reached the subject of the family. If the men had preferred to neglect it, circumstances did not permit them to exercise that prerogative; for in the forties feminism came to the front as one of the disturbing factors that could not be ignored. The accumulation of moderate fortunes which enabled the belles of New York to shine under the chandeliers also gave education and leisure to thousands of women who never saw the ballroom of a brownstone mansion.

Indeed, the significant feature of femininity in the middle period was not the inherited passion for salons done in red and green—that was as old as Trimalchio—but the invasion of women into fields of industry, science, education, letters, and civic affairs. Now thoroughly familiar with creeds such as Charles B. Brown timidly advanced in the eighteenth century, women, in open revolt against the masculine supremacy crystallized in the common law, energetically engaged in formulating political programs which contemplated sex equality. If liberty was the grand catchword for all, if opportunities for advancement were to be opened to all, high and low, then where did women stand? That question had been asked softly in the eighteenth century. In the mid-nineteenth it was asked in tones that could be heard by every editor, preacher, politician, and voter. The lone cry had become a chorus.

This was, as we have seen, the fruition of an agitation which began in the seventeenth century. Inevitably the discussion of the rights of man in America, France, and England raised the question of the rights of woman but, in the political reaction that followed the French Revolution, the hopes of women sank in the general disillusionment. Europe seemed sick, in spite of the continued debate on democracy; and radicals began to look for bold experiments to the United States, where the very newness of things gave promise of an earlier break in the bondage of law and custom. For this reason several keen and able women came from the Old World to study, lecture, or agitate in the democracy of America; from Poland Ernestine Rose, from Scotland Frances Wright, from England Harriet Martineau.

It was not mere unrest, curiosity, or agitation that commanded a hearing for women. They were already making themselves count in the affairs of the world. The age which produced in other countries George Sand, Charlotte Brontë, George Eliot, and Elizabeth Barrett Browning in literature, Rosa Bonheur in art, Caroline Herschell in science, Elizabeth Fry in humanitarian reform, and Florence Nightingale in nursing service on the battlefield also received offerings from America: Harriet Beecher Stowe and Margaret Fuller in letters, Harriet Hosmer in art, Maria Mitchell in science, Dorothea Dix in the care of defectives and delinquents, and Clara Barton in the hospital. Complacent political and military historians, following the traditions of their craft, had left women out of their chronicles of the American Revolution; Mrs. Ellet in a domestic history of that cataclysm partly restored the balance of justice.

With equal determination, Margaret Fuller reminded gentlemen of the pen that the women of the nineteenth century had a will and an understanding of their own. Pained by the slovenly style and the inaccuracies of the school books, Mary Lyon set to work to make a better series in history and geography. The recipient of the first medical diploma granted to women in America in 1849 Dr. Elizabeth Blackwell opened in New York an infirmary for women and children, soon adding to it a medical college for women. As if reëchoing the call of Anne Hutchinson, Antoinette Brown Blackwell, of the famous Morse family, a graduate of Oberlin in letters and theology, entered the pulpit as a fully ordained Congregational minister in 1853. While William Lloyd Garrison with little to lose was leading his crusade for emancipation, the Grimké sisters of South Carolina freed their slaves, braved the wrath of their class, and likewise gave their lives to liberty.

Besides making a real headway amid the turbulence of Jacksonian democracy, a large group of thoughtful women were deeply stirred by all the germinal ideas in theology, science, and social economy thrown up in that age. In an account of a brief conversation with Lucretia Mott in 1840, for example, Elizabeth Cady Stanton reveals what was going on behind the scenes. "She told me of the doctrines and divisions among the 'Friends'; of the inward light; of Mary Wollstonecraft, her social theories, and her demands of equality for women. I had been reading Combe's 'Constitution of Man' and 'Moral Philosophy,' Channing's works, and Mary Wollstonecraft, though all tabooed by orthodox teachers; but I had never heard a woman talk what, as a Scotch Presbyterian, I had scarcely dared to think."

Mrs. Mott herself was skeptical enough to have pleased Voltaire. "It is often a question," she wrote, "and still is unsettled with me, whether the various religious organizations, with all their errors, are more productive of good than evil. But until we can offer something better in their stead to a people largely governed by religious sentiment and a natural love for association, it requires great care how we shake their faith in existing institutions." In the age of zoölogy, Catherine Beecher dared to announce that "the time is coming when women will be taught to understand the construction of the human frame."

At every corner critical thought and economic change were eating away the foundations of the traditional family system inherited through the republican period from the colonial age. The abolition of primogeniture and the extension of civil marriage were bearing fruit; the factory system and the rise of public schools were offering women wider opportunities; easier divorce laws were giving them a new sense of independence. Furthermore, the opening of the West and the call of the growing cities made girls more defiant of parental authority and more determined to exercise their own pleasure both in the choice of work and of husbands. So marked were these features of American civilization that Harriet Martineau was amazed by the contrast with the subjection of women in England.

In the forties the scattering forces of feminism began to gather for a mass movement. True, a decade before, de Tocqueville, chiefly concerned with keeping French women in their ancient status, declared that he never observed in America an attempt on the part of women to subvert masculine power. "It appeared to me, on the contrary," he solemnly avowed, "that they attach a sort of pride to the voluntary surrender of their own will, and make it their boast to bend themselves to the yoke—not to shake it off." If the philosopher had come to the country in 1848, he might have noticed something else. In that year was held a Woman's Rights Convention at Seneca Falls in the state of New York and this was followed by other conventions, East and West, from Worcester, Massachusetts, to Dublin, Indiana.

In the strain of the eighteenth century document drawn by men, the Seneca Falls assembly issued a Women's Declaration of Independence setting forth again the grand principles of liberty and equality. Faithful to precedent too, it presented a list of grievances, after the manner of the bill of indictment launched against George III: the men had monopolized the lucrative professions and employments, they had closed the colleges of higher learning to woman, they had taxed her to support a government in which she had no voice, they had deprived her of property earned by her own labor, they had called her civilly dead at marriage, they had assigned her a lowly place in the church, and all in all they had put her in the status of serfdom. The implications were evident: political, economic, and intellectual equality. The note was defiant. Grave gentlemen, such as Richard Henry Dana, were shocked and indignant. Sapient editors laughed loud and long, flinging at the ladies their scornful headlines: "The Reign of Petticoats" and "Insurrection among Women."

In a little while the pioneer women in the movement, Lucretia Mott, Martha C. Wright, Elizabeth Cady Stanton, Lucy Stone—granddaughter of a captain in Shays' army of rebellion and Oberlin graduate—and Susan B. Anthony, were joined in their advocacy of woman's rights by a few men of distinction: Wendell Phillips, Garrison, Channing, Whittier, and Emerson. Far away on the western frontier Abraham Lincoln must have heard echoes of the strife in the early days of his career, for he declared that he favored sharing government with women. Without doubt the agitation for equal suffrage was gaining rapidly and would have gone far in the sixties if the anti-slavery movement and the Civil War had not induced women temporarily to put aside their cause for one that seemed even more impelling.

And yet in spite of that great diversion of feminine energy and enthusiasm, some victories were won by the forerunners before the second half of the century opened. In the domain of civil liberty, champions of the new cause demanded for married women, among other things, the right to hold and acquire property and to enjoy exemption from liability for their husbands' debts. In the masculine camp this claim raised a storm. The real reason was obvious but the good reason advanced was to the effect that the women, in managing property, would be thrust into the hard scenes of the busy world and suffer a diminution of their charms.

Nevertheless, a few outposts were carried with surprising ease. In 1839 Mississippi emancipated women from tutelage in the matter of property; in 1848 New York, Indiana, and Pennsylvania took a similar step; two years later California and Wisconsin swung into line. Once started, the march could not be stopped.

The growing respect for the rights of the individual, and the passion for leveling privileges which inspired the feminist movement also led to inquiries concerning the status of children. Under inherited usages they were in some respects the property of the father while he lived; and of the mother if she survived him. In part this subordination of children arose from the helplessness of infants and in part from the command of the parents over the earnings of their offspring. That parents were as eager as manufacturers to exploit youth appears written large in the documents of early investigators. Hamilton had boasted that the factory system would lead to the employment of children of "tender years" and fathers and mothers, either through necessity or selfishness, had responded to the call of the early mill owners, the sacredness of the home affording the plea of immunity from state interference.

This form of dominion, however, could not escape the surging forces of Jacksonian Democracy. From all sides parental sovereignty was assailed—by the trade unions which felt the competition of children and desired a restriction of apprentices, by the champions of popular education, by those who were caught in the tide of the new humanism, and by politicians who saw in illiterate citizens now enfranchised a menace to the institution of private property. It was no mere co-incidence, therefore, that the legislative inquiry into child labor undertaken in Massachusetts in 1825, perhaps the first in America, coupled a study of school attendance with an investigation into industry.

Within a little more than a decade there began to pour from state legislatures laws restricting the hours of labor for children, requiring a minimum allowance of time for elementary education, and otherwise restraining the power of parents to dispose freely of the services of their offspring. Before the mid-century was passed, the rights of children, conceived in the interests of humanity and of the community, were looming large in statute books and judicial decisions.

Yet the difficulties of enforcing the new laws were immense, for parents did not lightly surrender the ancient prerogative nor did the children, emancipated from the mill, turn joyfully to the schoolroom, in every case. Moreover, as the public mind was not prepared for drastic action, the legislatures usually left loopholes through which camels could pass. For example, New Hampshire in its law of

1847 provided that no child under fifteen should work more than ten hours a day—except with the written consent of parent or guardian. Halting steps were these but they were the beginnings of a transformation in the status of children. "The levelling system of the present age," lamented a Presbyterian magazine in the forties, "is nowhere more unfavorable than in the family. . . . The parents' authority ought to be early, absolute, and entire." It was a cry from the past.

§

The revolution in technology, the reconstruction of the social order under the impact of machine industry, the advance of science into the domain of cosmogony, the economic independence brought to the nation by increased wealth, the ferment of political equality, the changing status of women, the clash of parties over domestic issues, and the new contacts with foreign countries reset the intellectual stage for speculation about life and for all forms of imaginative literature. And the product bore the impress of its environment. After all, nearly everything that is written or painted bears some relation to the natural world, to the things that are done in it, and to opinions about its constitution.

Except for the monk marooned in a mountain fastness with nothing save the books of ancient lore, all artists of brush or word or chisel are caught more or less in the drift of society. That is inescapable even though some who enjoy private fortunes or special patronage may try to hold themselves aloof from contemporary currents and subdue their creative energies to the ancient patterns.

There is, of course, always a lag to literary and artistic culture for so much of it is traditional and cumulative. While the business man tears down his beloved factory when he finds that his profits can be enlarged by erecting a new one, no such transparent motive operates in the realm of the literary and plastic arts. Workers in those fields find at hand a great pile of conventional materials, often so beautiful that it seems a sacrilege to try to copy them—models by old masters. In any case it is usually more satisfying to bow to them than to break with them and apply naïve simplicity to current use and contemporary environment, infinitely easier than to attempt to pry open the barred gates of the future. All education inclines the mind to tradition; respectability generally urges one to accept it; genuine devotion to the creative achievement of the past often subdues the mind to worship; even a merely technical knowledge of dead languages and old art sets the possessor off from the common herd, giving him some of the distinction which all mankind covets so much.

Nevertheless, as William James cautions us, the worlds of fact and spirit evolve together; the changing circumstances that mark the economic and social development of nations into epochs also give periods to the evolution of arts and letters. Divisions are never sharp but they are undeniable. The America of cotton mills, blast furnaces, and a continental empire was not the America of stagecoaches, handlooms, and seaboard villages.

And the northeastern section now possessed just those conditions of life and economy that were favorable to the flowering of literary and artistic enterprises, being drawn into the center of the great vortex of industry, science, and secularism that was devouring the culture of feudalism and the soil and sweeping the social order inexorably forward into the future. First of all, in that section, the substance of urbanity had been provided by a marked growth in the density of population. The society of New England, besides being especially compact, had several centers of intellectual friction: Boston with its environs, Hartford, New Haven, Providence, and Newport; the inhabitants, relatively homogeneous, ingrowing, given to debate, and trained in self-expression, furnished a larger proportion of people who were city bred, had received a college education, and felt competent to instruct the multitude.

Not only was the rate of social exchange highest in the Northeast, but natural science was there made the servant of machine industry. If Virginia gentlemen or Philadelphia philosophers, like elegant amateurs, had dallied with physics and chemistry as "curious and interesting branches of polite knowledge," smudged and aproned men of affairs in industrial regions now turned those entertaining subjects to the uses of manufacturing, exalting them in the eyes of business practitioners willing to help with largesse and endowments the advancement of inquiries that brought returns to the counting house. In short, all the ruthless forces of the acquisitive instinct were, in the Northeast, put behind the scientific spirit—that protean and dynamic genius of the modern age, so devastating to the cultural legacy of agriculture. Those who believed with the theologians that it could be exorcised by appeals to the thought-patterns of Cotton Mather or with Georgia planters that it was all a perversion of good taste by willful men simply failed to reckon with fate and doom.

Besides cities, industries, and science, the Northeast had in virtue of its economic operations a strong passion for independence. A rising rival of England in the markets of the world, it felt its strength in riches and, while it desired protective tariffs against British competitors, it also cherished the sentiments of nationalism in letters and art. If American cottons and broadcloths were good enough for citizens to wear, why not American books and pictures attractive enough for them to buy?

Intimately related to these concrete economic factors were other conditions conducive to cerebration. The rise of cities, the appearance of the working class, the agitations growing out of strikes, industrial panics, and spreading urban poverty simply thrust into the faces of the most careless bystanders facts and sounds of a new order. With a rudeness that could not be ignored, a vast and complex array of phenomena and ideas broke in upon the calm of agricultural days, directing the sons and daughters of Federalists to the consideration of matters their ancestors had never dreamed of. At the same time, science driven forward by irresistible forces was disrupting the old and simple plan of salvation that had seemed convincing enough along the shores of Galilee, in the village churches of feudal Europe, and in the rural communities founded by yeomen and gentlemen in colonial America. With doubts about Biblical cosmogony came doubts about the whole epic, filling the air with criticism and speculation.

Stirred by the fierce debates, some thinkers turned one way and some another. Henry Thoreau sought solace in the offerings of sweet nature. George Ripley passed through unitarianism to free thought while his wife went back to the Pope, Saints, and the Church. New versions, guesses, and criticisms showered like sparks from the hot iron of the smith, kindling flames of excitement, large and small, in every direction.

With the ferment rose the demand for literary wares, with the demand the publishing houses, and with the publishing houses new wares feeding new anxieties and interests. In the middle period printing became an important business. The steam engine that drove a cotton mill could also drive a press. Capital that might be invested in a forge or weaving shed might be diverted to a newspaper, magazine, or book-publishing house. Every year saw the establishment of new publishing concerns, some destined to great careers; or of new magazines, fortunate enough to become household staples.

In this manner the market for literary goods was stimulated, and the cubic contents of printed stuff turned from the American presses rose from decade to decade. In 1820 not quite one-third of the publications issued in the United States came from American writers; before the middle period had reached its close more than four-fifths were of domestic origin. Thus the profession of letters was put on a firm economic basis; at all events the writers of good prose—women as well as men, for business enterprise kept its eyes on ledgers rather than ancient parchments—now had rewards that lifted them well above the seekers of patrons in Johnson's day and the hunters for dinners in Grub Street.

If, as Bryant remarked, poets still found it hard to combine the making of verse with fullness of stomach, writers of novels, stories, essays, reviews, and histories could count on respectable incomes. Harriet Beecher Stowe's Uncle Tom's Cabin ran into the millions of copies; Cooper and Hawthorne made more money with their pens than most preachers, bookkeepers, and pedagogues; Prescott drew perhaps a hundred thousand dollars from the royalties on his works.

Surrounded by a society becoming steadily more urban in composition, stimulated by new ideas, and furnished a market, young people of literary aptitudes in the Northeast could with relative ease embark upon that career. And circumstances favored the germination of just those aptitudes. The line of clerical, professional, and mercantile families had lengthened by two generations since the Declaration of Independence and more families with leisure had been created by the steady amassing of fortunes from manufacturing, merchandizing, and shipping. In this fashion an increasing number of boys and girls who in colonial times would have been submerged in the mere economy of living were now afforded opportunities for education and travel and experimentation.

Thus the personnel for the trade of letters—for letters is a trade—was enlarged. Thousands could be prepared for it, could face its economic risks, and could find a sale for their output. Only a few writers, of course, broke through the everlasting commonplace into fame; but without the market, without the intellectual friction of urbanism, and without criticism, how far could the genius of the middle period have advanced beyond the provincialism of colonial times?

§

Nothing more closely fitted the exactions of the age than the high note of nationalism that reverberated through the literature of the period. Clearly sounded in the days of the young republic, it had been amplified by the second war with England, reinforced by growing economic power under the shelter of tariff discriminations, and deepened by the pretensions of Jacksonian Democracy, especially as the countries of the Old World were subjected again and again to the storms of political revolution. All the American writers of the age were conscious of its reality and its appeal—even those who sought to employ the cultural implements of Europe in their intellectual operations.

Echoing the sentiments of Royall Tyler, James Dunlap, and Noah Webster, uttered when the struggle for independence was still keenly mirrored in their minds, Emerson issued a new manifesto in a Phi Beta Kappa Address delivered at Cambridge in 1837. "Our day of dependence, our long apprenticeship to the learning of other lands, draws to a close," declaimed the orator. "The millions that around us are rushing into life cannot always be fed on the sere remains of foreign harvests. Events, actions arise, that must be sung, that will sing themselves. . . . There are creative manners, there are creative actions and creative words . . . that is, indicative of no custom or authority, but springing spontaneous from the mind's own sense of good and fair."

In his view of things, it was subserviency and imitation that made Americans contemptuous of their own powers and hence sterile in the creative arts. With many perpendicular strokes, Emerson brought his hammer down on the American sycophant of his day: "It is for want of self-culture," he said in an essay on Self-Reliance, "that the superstition of Traveling, whose idols are Italy, England, Egypt, retains its fascination for all educated Americans. They who made England, Italy, or Greece venerable in the imagination did so by sticking fast where they were, like an axis of the earth. In manly hours we feel that duty is our place. The soul is no traveler; the wise man stays at home, and when his necessities, his duties, on any occasion call him from his house, or into foreign fields, he is at home still, and shall make men sensible by the expression of his countenance that he goes the missionary of wisdom and virtue, and visits cities and men like a sovereign and not like an interloper or a valet.

"I have no churlish objection to the circumnavigation of the globe, for the purposes of art, of study, and benevolence, so that the man is first domesticated, or does not go abroad with the hope of finding somewhat greater than he knows. He who travels to be amused, or to get somewhat which he does not carry, travels away from himself, and grows old even in youth among old things. In Thebes, in Palmyra, his will and mind have become old and dilapidated as they. He carries ruins to ruins.

"But the rage of traveling is a symptom of a deeper unsoundness affecting the whole intellectual action. . . . We imitate. . . . Our houses are built with foreign taste; our shelves are garnished with foreign ornaments; our opinions, our tastes, our faculties, lean on and follow the Past and the Distant. The soul created the arts wherever they have flourished. It was in his own mind that the artist sought his model. It was an application of his own thought to the thing to be done and the conditions to be observed. . . . Beauty, convenience, grandeur of thought, and quaint expression are as near to us as to any, and if the American artist will study with love and hope the precise thing to be done by him, considering the climate, the soil, the length of the day, the wants of the people, the habit and form of the government, he will create a house in which all these will find themselves fitted, and taste and sentiment will be satisfied also. Insist on yourself; never imitate. Your own gift you can present every moment with the cumulative force of a whole life's cultivation; but of the adopted talent of another you have only an extemporaneous half possession."

In the realm of imaginative letters, the independence which Emerson thus declared could, of course, take many forms, the simplest being to proclaim the new liberty by choosing American themes. That indeed was the procedure adopted by the most distinguished writers of fiction in the middle period, James Fenimore Cooper, William Gilmore Simms, Washington Irving, Nathaniel Hawthorne, Beverley Tucker, John Pendleton Kennedy, and Harriet Beecher Stowe.

If one of them be taken to illustrate the thesis, it may well be Cooper, whose first novel, published in 1820, was the direct outcome of a boast that he could write a better story than an English tale which he happened to be reading. Ashamed of this book turned out mechanically in the spirit of boyish bravado, Cooper then undertook to compose, as he said, "a work which should be purely American, and of which love of country should be the theme."

Happy circumstances prepared Cooper to be a pathbreaker. Brought up in his youth in the country, on the edge of the open wild, unlearned in the formal literary arts, tutored by a schoolmaster with a dislike for the Puritans, and early thrown against the raw materials of life as a sailor, Cooper was not inclined by nature or training to compete with a Scott or a Balzac in European patterns of thought, or to dabble in the theological ideas of New England. Driven to creative work by his own spirit, he was forced to choose his subjects from the life of his own people on land and sea rather than the shadow-haunted realms of Puritan repressions or the mediæval legends of feudal romance. If he was conventional in his treatment of women, he did but honor the letter and spirit of the common law, a jurisprudence accompanying manners that were beginning to dissolve, unknown to him, before his very eyes.

Without depreciating his experiments in European subject matter, it must be said that his most successful work was American to the core. In that medium he was at home and there he avowed a thesis: the story of liberty, clash of Patriot and Tory, ardent youth against surfeited age, the adventurous spirit in the primitive forest setting. With a broad and often stiff brush, Cooper painted the varied scene: Indians, pioneers, spies, pirates, slave traders, soldiers, sailors, planters, farmers, hunters, trappers, merchants, women, mountain and plain, lake and ocean. Admitting that he gave the Indian colors far too rosy, all must concede that he portrayed with a firm hand the American types of his age, revealing their ideas and passions, in lines bombastic at times but true to life.

And it was just this treatment of the scene he knew that gave Cooper his standing with contemporary critics abroad as well as at home, caused Thackeray to look upon him as the peer of Scott, induced Hugo to rank his work above that of Scott, and long afterward led Conrad to bow to him as to a master. Cooper was the first to thrust the Indian vividly into the foreground of fiction and that act alone was sufficient, given reasonable competence, to make him significant to the dreamers of the Old World still steeped in the romanticism of Rousseau's natural man.

Herein lay the secret of Balzac's exclamation that Scott was the historian of humanity, Cooper of nature. Indeed, so deep was this impression with Balzac that, one of his critical biographers remarks, "his usurers, his lawyers, his bankers, and his notaries owe too much to the sojourn of his imagination in the cabin of Leatherstocking or in the wigwam of Chingachgook and there are in the Comédie Humaine too many Mohicans in spencers and Hurons in frock coats." At all events, Cooper proclaimed the republic to the Old World for the first time in a form that made a wide popular appeal, making Europeans, young and old, who never heard of Emerson's essays or de Tocqueville's travel book aware of a dynamic country beyond the Atlantic Ocean. Moreover, in letters and essays, Cooper defended the government and people of the United States against European critics of aristocratic leanings—even though the conduct of the radical elements in Andrew Jackson's farmer-labor party was so hateful for him to contemplate that he opposed all such factions at home.

§

With regard to domestic affairs, as distinguished from the opposition of American civilization to that of other lands, the speculative and imaginative literature of the middle period, in so far as it dealt with the realities of American life, reflected all the issues of political economy and natural science thrown up in the seething democracy of the age. Far away on the right, the conservative agricultural thought of the period—forming one antithesis to the Hamilton-Webster-Clay system—was mirrored in the novels of Simms and Cooper.

The former, born in South Carolina and in his later years a slave owner and planter, represented in fiction the economics that Calhoun represented in politics. An opponent of tariffs and internal improvements, he became with the passing years an ardent advocate of secession as the price of economic freedom. With the same facile adjustment to concrete circumstance, Simms adopted the current defense of chattel slavery. "We beg once for all to say," he wrote defiantly in language echoing Calhoun's doctrines, "to our northern readers, writers, and publishers, that in the South we hold slavery to be an especially and wisely devised institution of heaven; devised for the benefit, the improvement, and safety, morally, socially, and physically, of a barbarous and inferior race." Believing slavery sound in morals, a champion of planting against industrialism, Simms gave his southern readers food seasoned to their palates. His novel, Guy Rivers, to use an illustration, presented to South Carolinians a planting gentleman for a "worn out English lord" and a Georgia outlaw for a "robber baron of the middle ages." In their ensemble, his writings drew a clear picture of southern aristocratic society, with its strong penchant for fighting men, fair women, fine sentiments, and moonlit romance. Even the very exuberance of his rhetoric merely flowered from the same stem as southern oratory. In the identical rhythmic category with Simms may be placed his friend and co-worker, Beverley Tucker, Virginia gentleman, jurist, and scholar, author of The Partisan Leader, a novel of peculiar power, defending the southern cause, and foretelling secession a decade before the event.

With equal fidelity the spiritual aspirations of the dying agricultural aristocracy of the Hudson River Valley gleam through the pages of Cooper. Springing from the landed patricians of New York, he inherited with his family estate his father's contempt for "the rabble." By economic origins, therefore, he was thrown into temperamental opposition to the financial and industrial classes for whom Daniel Webster's grand orations were delivered; and his early prepossessions were fortified by long sojourns in Europe where surviving feudalism was still strong enough to check the pretensions of the machine man.

To the end of his days, Cooper disliked the money-making bourgeois. With the true instinct of a landed gentleman, he regarded trade as "vulgar," and despised "the wine-discussing, trade-talking, dollar-dollar set" of New York City—which accounted for a great deal of the cursing he received at the hands of certain metropolitan editors. Through the pages of his Monikins the passions of the fight glow like smoldering fire. Of necessity, accordingly, Cooper rejected the Hamilton-Webster party and joined the Democrats, even daring in flashing articles to defend Andrew Jackson against the Senate—a thing as shocking to the "Best People" of New York as the defense of William Jennings Bryan in the great age of Marcus A. Hanna.

And yet for all that, much as Cooper hated the money changers, he had a contempt no less bitter for the rank and file of Jackson's farmer-labor party. Though agricultural in his sentiment, he was not agrarian—no debt-burdened plowman. In a tale of the anti-rent riots waged by tenants at the expense of the great landlords of the Hudson Valley, he gave vent to his feelings against the levelers—the Gracchi, the Shayses, Bryans, and LaFollettes of his time. "The column of society," he warned his readers in a preface, "must have its capital as well as its base. It is only perfect while each part is entire and discharges its proper duty. In New York, the great landholders long have, and do still, in a social sense, occupy the place of the capital. . . . We would caution those who now raise the cry of feudality and aristocracy to have a care of what they are about." Cooper's Ways of the Hour was frankly written "to draw the attention of the reader to some of the social evils that beset us," especially those springing from the course of democracy. "In trials between railroad companies and those who dwell along their lines," he lamented, "prejudice is usually so strong against the former that justice for them is nearly hopeless."

§

For the industrial right there were few novelists who ventured to draw near the all-devouring, all-becoming vortex, and justify its ways to mankind. In fact it was a bit too ruthless for mellowed men of letters; but its beneficiaries were not without sympathy in literary circles. If Oliver Wendell Holmes protested to James Russell Lowell that he was not "a thorough-going conservatist," he was none the less disinclined to be disturbed by the clamors of Jackson's democracy for what it pleased to call "justice." His general conspectus of the social order was neatly summed up in the following oracular statement made at the Breakfast Table: "The spiritual standards of different classes I would reckon thus: (1) the comfortably rich; (2) the decently comfortable; (3) the very rich, who are apt to be irreligious; (4) the very poor, who are apt to be immoral."

When taken to task for neglecting the agitations of his day looking to the improvement of the lot of the poor, Holmes replied: "I believe I have never treated them

unkindly in any way.   I am sure that I feel a deep interest
in all well-directed efforts for improving their condition,
and am ready to lend my cordial support to such practical
measures as furnishing them better dwellings and similar
movements."   In the main, however, he was personally
opposed to all the radical currents of his age, currents
which on the one side created the Jacksonian uproar among
the masses and on the other the socialistic furor among the
intellectuals—Lowell, Curtis, Emerson, and Ripley, for
example.   Against the abolitionist appeal Holmes was
equally dead set, holding until the eve of the Civil War that
"we must reach the welfare of the blacks through the
dominant race."

   Not in the same class as an artist in polite letters, but
far more outspoken in his championship of the Hamilton-
Webster system was John Pendleton Kennedy, the Baltimore novelist, friend of Thackeray and Poe.   From start
to finish a thoroughgoing Whig, Kennedy attacked "the
dangerous principles" of Jackson's administration, supported protection and the bank, cheered for Henry Clay,
and entered Congress as a devoted member of his party.
It is true that his best known pieces of fiction, Swallow Barn
and Horse-Shoe Robinson, are by no means stereotypes of
his political opinions; but his Quodlibet: Containing some
Annals thereof, by Solomon Secondthought Schoolmaster
is a broad satire on Jacksonian politics, written in a diffuse,
bombastic style appropriate to the theme—and to the campaign of 1840, the year of its publication.   In no way
a foe of those sound old planting Whigs of Virginia, whose
sympathies were with Webster rather than Jackson, Kennedy was primarily a friend of the new commercial and
industrial order, loyal perhaps to the mercantile traditions
in which he was reared.

   In that general direction also leaned Washington Irving,
son of a New York merchant, although he, like Oliver
Wendell Holmes, rather shrank from the fierce battles of
the forum.   Early in life he declared himself "an admirer

of General Hamilton and a partisan with him in politics," and in his latter years he avowed an equally deep admiration for Daniel Webster, from whom he received an appointment as minister to Great Britain. Though, during the high tide of Jacksonian Democracy, Irving softened in his antipathy for "popular politics," he declined Democratic nominations to public office in New York and a place in Van Buren's Cabinet.

At no time did Irving betray any sympathy for the farmer-labor wing of the Jacksonian army. On the contrary, he confessed in 1838 to "a strong dislike for some of those loco-foco luminaries who have of late been urging strong and sweeping measures subversive of the interests of great classes in the community. . . . I always distrust the soundness of political councils that are accompanied by acrimonious and disparaging attacks upon any great class of our fellow citizens. Such are those urged to the disadvantage of the great trading and financial classes of our country." In other words, with relation to Cooper's "trade-discussing, dollar-dollar set," Irving was on the opposite side of the arena.

§

Off to the left of Cooper, Holmes, and Irving—a sympathetic, though not passionately whole-hearted advocate of Jacksonian Democracy and its tendencies—was Nathaniel Hawthorne, the starveling author of Salem, poorer in purse in his early days than perhaps half the voters who cast their ballots for "Old Hickory." In a truly democratic spirit, Hawthorne accepted the people, instead of patronizing them after the fashion of the Brook Farm reformers. Moreover, he voted the Democratic ticket, called himself a Democrat, and was lifted out of semi-starvation by an appointment to a federal job in the customs service under Jackson's beneficent spoils system.

And this was perfectly natural. Hawthorne had no more faith in aristocracies of land or riches than had Jackson; like the General he belonged to neither. "The truth is," he said in The House of Seven Gables, "that once in every half-century, at longest, a family should be merged in the great, obscure mass of humanity, and forget all about its ancestors. Human blood, in order to keep its freshness, should run in hidden streams as the water of an aqueduct is conveyed in subterranean pipes."

Far from accepting at face value high-toned doctrines about the rich and well-born, Hawthorne had about as much reverence for the infallibility of superior persons as any humble professor of the Jacksonian creed. Once when dilating upon the fate of old Matthew Maule, executed for the crime of witchcraft, he remarked with a kind of cold precision: "He was one of the martyrs to that terrible delusion, which should teach us, among its other morals, that the influential classes, and those who take upon themselves to be leaders of the people, are fully liable to all the passionate error that has ever characterized the maddest mob. Clergymen, judges, statesmen—the wisest, calmest, holiest persons of their day—stood in the inner circle round about the gallows, loudest to applaud the work of blood, latest to confess themselves miserably deceived."

Certainly none of the persons, classes, institutions, or practices that agitated the Democrats and their reforming wings entirely escaped Hawthorne's pages—"this crowd of pale-cheeked, slender girls who disturb the ear with the multiplicity of their short dry coughs . . . seamstresses who have plied the daily and nightly needle in the service of master tailors and close-fisted contractors until now it is almost time for each to hem the borders of her own shroud. . . . The prison, the insane asylum, the squalid chamber of the almshouse, the manufactory where the demon machinery annihilates the human soul, and the cottonfield where God's image becomes a beast of burden."

And in a realistic spirit Hawthorne discarded the high theorizing of the transcendentalists. What did a Democrat and an office holder need with that frail support? In a brief but grinning paragraph, he disposed of the mystical Kant: "At the end of the Valley, as John Bunyan mentions, is a cavern, where, in his days, dwelt two cruel giants, Pope and Pagan, who had strewn the ground about their residence with the bones of slaughtered pilgrims. These vile old troglodytes are no longer there; but in their deserted cave another terrible giant has thrust himself, and makes it his business to seize upon honest travelers, and fat them for his table with plentiful meals of smoke, mist, moonshine, raw potatoes and sawdust. He is a German by birth, and is called Giant Transcendentalist; but as to his form, his features, his substance, and his nature generally, it is the chief peculiarity of this huge miscreant, that neither he for himself, nor anybody for him, has ever been able to describe them."

Still beyond Hawthorne, far beyond him, on the left, the ebullient and unreserved Whitman celebrated a whole-souled and jubilant faith in democracy, accepting and loving the masses as he found them, good, bad, and indifferent—Jackson's farmers and mechanics, rough of jacket and boisterous of word. Son of a farmer and apprenticed to a carpenter, was he not attuned to catch the rebellious spirit of the times? At all events, in Whitman the fermenting democracy of the age was incarnate; singing of America, he sang of himself, a spokesman of a pushing and defiant working class.

"Not a dilettante democrat," he said—"a man who is a double part with the common people and with immediate life—who adores streets—loves docks—loves to talk with free men—loves to be called by his given name and does not care that any one calls him Mister. Knows how to laugh with laughter—loves the rustic manner of workers—does not pose as a proper man, neither for knowledge or education—eats common food, loves the strong smelling coffee of the coffee sellers in the market, at dawn—loves to eat oysters bought from the fisherman's boat, loves to be one of a party of sailors and workers—would quit no matter what time a party of elegant people to find the people who love noise, vagrants, to receive their caresses and their welcome, listen to their rows, their oaths, their ribaldry, their loquacity, their laughing, their replies—and knows perfectly how to preserve his personality among them and those of his kind."

Born on American soil, Whitman dedicated his genius to it. "These states," he exclaimed, "conceal an enormous beauty, which native bards not rhymers manipulating syllables and emotions imported from Europe should justify by their songs, tallying themselves to the immensity of the continent, to the fecundity of its people, to the appetite of a proud race, fluent and free."

The swiftness with which Whitman's contemporaries responded to his melody and his strong notes confirmed him in his course. If Whittier thrust the first volume of Whitman poetry into the fire as something shockingly unclean, others of more patience and larger discernment saw gold shining through the dross. The ethereal Emerson sent a copy of Leaves of Grass to a friend with the words: "Americans who are abroad can now return: unto us a man is born."

To Whitman himself the Concord sage sent fine words of praise: "I find it the most extraordinary piece of wit and wisdom that America has yet contributed. I am very happy in reading it as great power makes me happy. It meets the demand I am always making of what seems the sterile and stingy Nature, as if too much handiwork or too much lymph in the temperament were making our western wits fat and mean. I give you joy of your free and brave thought. I have great joy in it. I find incomparable things said incomparably well, as they must be." Thoreau, though a sworn foe of the cities and mobs which Whitman praised, also paid tribute, declaring that the new author was the greatest democrat the world had seen, suggested something superhuman, and was the grand type. Bryant, then engrossed in his editorial labors and work as a good citizen, often went over to Brooklyn to walk and talk with the unconquerable American.

Before many years, Rossetti, Swinburne, and Tennyson saw a new planet swimming within their ken, and in the fullness of time, as the democratic surge shook thrones and classes, there were idolators and imitators the world over—in far off Japan, where ardent young students read Whitman's lines in the original tongue or in the soft cadences of Arishima's translation.

Appreciating on one hand the democratic spirit voiced by Whitman and yet affiliated by birth and training with the culture of the Hamilton-Webster economy, James Russell Lowell was to the end of his days torn by conflicting emotions, by his love of æsthetics and letters, and by his anxiety over the swift advance of industrialism in New England and slavery in the South. Early in his life he became entangled almost against his will in all the currents of agitation and opinion that surged through the society of the period. Taking the New England dialect as an instrument for his Biglow Papers, he attacked the Mexican War in vitriolic lines that scalded and seared the fustian patriots, the president of the peace society who rushed to the support of war, the demagogue who made votes out of it, and the "two-faced politicians" who throve by it—blasted them with a wrath that would have landed him in jail had he performed the ceremony in the era of "the new freedom."

About the same time Lowell wrote a letter to Oliver Wendell Holmes in which he put himself on record against war as a general proposition, against slavery, in favor of temperance, in favor of ameliorating the lot of the poor and reform in the large—foreshadowing a day when he was to describe socialism as a kind of applied Christianity. No matter how strong the artistic, classical, and traditional pull in his nature, Lowell never could resist the call of contemporary voices or forbear taking nervous glances into the future. If he was zealous in searching the past, he was equally eager in scanning the horizon. "My poems have thus far had a regular and natural sequence," he wrote in 1850. "First Love and the mere happiness of existence beginning to be conscious of itself, then Freedom—both being sides which Beauty presented to me—and now I am going to try more after Beauty herself. Next, if I live, I shall present Life as I have seen it." In homelier lines he expressed his inner conflict:

> There is Lowell, who's striving Parnassus to climb
> With a whole bale of isms tied together with rhyme.
> The top of the hill he will ne'er come nigh reaching
> Till he learns the distinction 'twixt singing and preaching.

Beyond the extreme confines of the left wing, beyond the reach of every "practical" concern labored David Henry Thoreau—ever to be remembered as the author of Walden —who like Whitman was true to the farmer-mechanic order from which he sprang. Deft with his own hands in garden and workshop, simple in taste as any rustic, desiring few things and able to secure them easily, Thoreau was as far removed from the over-elaborate manners of the rich bourgeois as from those of the slave-owning planter. He was of New England but no part of the great audience that cheered Daniel Webster. To him the huge Gothic retaining walls of an industrial and financial society were immense weights on the human spirit—a spirit born to be free in field, forest, and stream.

So he rejected both church and state, their demands, taxes, orders, fulminations, ceremonies, and pretensions, laughing at politics as dull futility—except where positively harmful—and orthodox religious professions as something entirely outside the range of intelligent human beings. "Know ye, all men by these presents," he once solemnly announced, "that I Henry Thoreau do not wish to be regarded as a member of any incorporated society which I have not joined." The state of Massachusetts commanded him to pay taxes for the support of the church; he refused and was imprisoned for his contumacy. A poll tax he likewise declined to pay and for that disobedience he also spent a night in jail.

Fiercely, with all the temper of one brought up as a child of nature, Thoreau resented the intrusions of a machine civilization, its routine, its brick walls and streets, its everlasting output of commodities, still more commodities, burying mankind alive in things and laws. "No truer American existed than Thoreau," once exclaimed Emerson; and he might have added "of primitive field and forest days, suffused with pagan culture."

§

Among the dissenters, himself apart from them all, taking the whole range of contemporary things within his catholic sweep, Ralph Waldo Emerson was easily first in penetration and high expression. Like Goethe he was no philosopher, in that he made no system after the fashion of Kant or Hegel; but, as Carlyle would say, by his flashing rush light he illuminated all corners of this dark vale. Six years before Marx and Engels startled Europe with their famous announcement that history is the story of class struggles, Emerson, in a lecture on The Conservative, delivered in Boston in 1841, declared: "The two parties which divide the state, the party of Conservatism and that of Innovation, are very old, and have disputed the possession of the world ever since it was made. This quarrel is the subject of civil history. The conservative party established the reverend hierarchies and monarchies of the most ancient world. The battle of patrician and plebeian, of parent state and colony, of old usage and accommodation to new facts, of the rich and the poor, reappears in all countries and times. The war not only rages in battlefields, in national councils, and ecclesiastical synods, but agitates every man's bosom with opposing advantages every hour."

No one in his time understood better the intimate relation of property to politics. "We might as wisely reprove the east wind, or the frost," he calmly remarked in his essay on Politics, "as a political party, whose members for the most part could give no account of their position but stand for the defence of those interests in which they find themselves. . . . Ordinarily, our parties are parties of circumstance and not of principle; as, the planting interest in conflict with the commercial; the party of capitalists and that of operatives."

When it came to their merits, he thought that the conservative party, "composed of the most moderate, able, and cultivated part of the population, is timid and merely defensive of property," and that Daniel Webster, the high priest of conservatism, was an exponent of property interests and fleshly living. In the circumstances, Emerson thought that "the philosopher, the poet, or the religious man will, of course, wish to cast his vote with the democrat for free trade, for wide suffrage, for the abolition of legal cruelties in the penal code, and for facilitating in every manner the access of the young and the poor to the sources of power and wealth." But he was under no idealistic delusions. On the contrary he looked upon the popular party with suspicion, as destructive and selfish in its aims, without ulterior and divine ends, lacking in those qualities that give hope and virtue to democracy.

Standing on this broad philosophic platform, Emerson slashed out in every direction—in poem, essay, and lecture —as the issues of the passing pageant filed before him. At an hour when Massachusetts respectability was as silent as the grave, he struck resounding blows at slavery as an institution. In the midst of the agitation over the public schools, he exclaimed that the furor about education among the rich, who had so long neglected the poor, sprang from a desire to subdue the rising generation to the dominion of law and order. "The cause of education is urged in this country with utmost earnestness—on what ground? Why, on this, that the people have the power and if they are not instructed to sympathize with the intelligent, reading, trading, and governing class, inspired with a taste for the same competitions and prizes, they will upset the fair pageant of Judicature and perhaps lay a hand on the sacred muniments of wealth itself and new distribute the land." Nothing silenced him, no institutional fear.

Then to the horror of the orthodox, he went on: "Religion is taught in the same spirit. . . . If you do not value the Sabbath or other religious institutions, give yourself no concern about maintaining them. They have already acquired a market value as conservators of property; and if priest and church members should fail, the Chambers of Commerce and the presidents of the banks, the very upholders and landlords of the country would muster with fury to their support."

Committed to this realistic view of the political and social scene, Emerson not unnaturally departed from current conventions in matters theological. Trained for the ministry, he left it after a few brief years for a life of literary freedom—for his world pulpit at Concord, where he spoke his mind as things came to him, to the great distress of most persons glued to reputability. Arriving at God through reason and nature—with the assistance of his heritage and Immanuel Kant—Emerson discarded, gently but firmly, most of the orthodox Christian tradition, so firmly in fact that, for an address delivered at the Divinity College in 1838, he was officially excluded from speaking at Harvard for nearly thirty years. Having put aside prescriptive articles of faith, running one, two, three, and so forth, Emerson remained all the rest of his days, as he said, "a chartered libertine," free to speculate on God and man as the foliation of his mind decreed.

Emancipated from all theological fetters, Emerson was prepared to grasp the implications of the new science, especially the notion of evolution, and its bearings upon life and letters. As early as 1833 he visited the Jardin des Plantes in Paris where Buffon and Lamarck had labored so patiently with such fruitful results; and not long afterwards he began to study both the developmental doctrines of the ancients and the bold hypotheses of the pioneers who were making smooth the way for Darwin. Several years before the Origin of Species appeared, Emerson discovered that the concept of evolution, in the general sense of change or progress as distinguished from Darwin's specific theory of causation, was destined to have a subversive effect on all theories of life, conduct, and religion.

In this connection, his penetrating discernment, as well as his varied knowledge, was amazing; his prescience was equally astonishing. In many passages of his works, the influence of the flying sparks of science was traced—with particular succinctness in his lecture on Poetry and Imagination delivered in 1854. "This magnificent hotel and conveniency we call Nature is not final," he said. "First innuendoes, then broad hints, then smart taps are given, suggesting that nothing stands still in nature but death; that the creation is on wheels in transit. . . . Thin or solid everything is in flight. . . . I believe this conviction makes the charm of chemistry—that we have the same avoirdupois matter in an alembic, without a vestige of the old form; and in animal transformation not less, as in grub and fly, in egg and bird, in embryo and man; everything undressing and stealing away from its old into new form, and nothing fast but those invisible cords which we call laws on which all is strung. Then we see that things wear different names and faces, but belong to one family; that the secret cords or laws show their well-known virtue through every variety, be it animal or plant or planet, and the interest is gradually transferred from the forms to the lurking method. . . . All multiplicity rushes to be resolved into unity. Anatomy, osteology, exhibit arrested or progressive ascent in each kind; the lower pointing to the higher forms, the higher to the highest, from the fluid in an elastic sack, from radiate, mollusk, articulate, vertebrate up to man; as if the whole animal world were only a Hunterian museum to exhibit the genesis of mankind." These words were uttered in

America five years before the Origin of Species rolled from the press!

Moreover, Emerson saw the coming revolution to be wrought in social thinking by the new scientific doctrine even before Herbert Spencer worked it out in close detail. "The hint of unity and development," he remarked in the lecture just referred to, "upsets our politics, trade, customs, marriages, nay, the common sense side of religion and literature which are founded on low nature—on the clearest and most economical mode of administering the material world considered as final." Many years afterward, in repeating this lecture, Emerson had merely to add a reference to the theories of Darwin announced since its original delivery. He had, of course, given an optimistic and lofty tone to the new gospel, affiliating it with, rather than substituting it for, the high philosophy of transcendentalism; but that did not identify him with the clergy of the traditional schools.

As he frankly said himself, the new view of nature ran to the roots of old religious dogma: "The narrow sectarian cannot read astronomy with impunity. The creeds of his church shrivel like dried leaves at the door of his church." The word had gone forth; a few had heard it; it could not be recalled.

Around Emerson, at various distances, gathered groups of reformers and speculators, dubbed by some one "The Transcendental Club," who made experiments in communal living at Brook Farm and in journalism with The Dial, wrote essays, lectured, and preached—among them several of the first thinkers of New England, such, for example, as Bronson Alcott, O. A. Bronson, W. H. Channing, Margaret Fuller, Elizabeth Peabody, and Theodore Parker. If, as some wit said, they were like-minded in that no two of them thought alike, they managed to make quite a stir among the intellectual classes of the period.

For the feminists Margaret Fuller spoke in new lines, carrying the political theories of Mary Wollstonecraft into the stage of social and economic exposition, and demonstrating by her wide knowledge of continental literature and her critical powers—as editor of The Dial for a time and then as special writer for Horace Greeley's Tribune—that women could be fair competitors of the leading men in matters of taste and opinion. For the experimenters who vainly imagined that the evils of industrial society were to be uprooted by the establishment of communities on utopian socialist lines, Bronson Alcott gave demonstrations, thereby helping to dispel unintentionally the communistic dreams of his generation. Although Alcott's colony Fruitlands, like the more pretentious scheme, Brook Farm, failed, as practical persons had predicted, it made reverberations in educational theory that outlasted the century. If, as scornful editors said, the promoters of The Dial were "zanies, considerably madder than the Mormons," the magazine, in fact, compared favorably in style and substance with the more bulky and lumbering reviews of England and the heavy magazines of the United States, containing articles more pertinent to life, as the future showed, than many a successful contemporary.

Had it not been for the slavery agitation ending in the crash of the Civil War, there is no doubt that the humanizing and urbanizing thought of the left-wing professors of letters would have given an entirely different direction to the intellectual life of the United States during the closing decades of the nineteenth century. But as things turned out no small part of the literary energies of the middle period were diverted to the slavery question. It haunted Lowell even when he explored the classics; it embittered Thoreau's already sharp antipathy to the state; it stirred Emerson to his angriest moods; it inspired Harriet Beecher Stowe to write Uncle Tom's Cabin, a book that was in the nature of things narrow in its range and transitory in its appeal, but a sensation in its day.

To John G. Whittier, slavery was an overpowering issue that appeared at every facet of his mind. Discovered by

that arch agitator, William Lloyd Garrison, and early enlisted in the abolition cause, Whittier could find little heart
in making verse for its own sake. While yet a boy, he
declared that he would rather be a Wilberforce than a
Byron; and drawn with all the intensity of his nature into
the contest over slavery, he could only think of the bondmen
entitled, as he said, to a full share in the fatherhood of God
and the brotherhood of man. Like Lowell, he admitted his
prime concern in that issue of the living present:

> And one there was, a dreamer born,
> Who with a mission to fulfill,
> Had left the muses' haunts to turn
> The crank of an opinion mill,
> Making his rustic reed of song
> A weapon in the war with wrong.

If with the passing of slavery reams of Whittier's verses
became mere historic documents, if the remainder were dismissed by severe critics as nursery rhymes and rustic jingles,
it remained true that the son of a farmer-mechanic etched
the life of the great body of home-owning yeomanry, industrious and God-fearing, with a surer hand than Whitman.
If the "Good Gray Poet" was a true singer of street car
conductors and engineers, their manners and morals,
Whittier, in spite of his preoccupation with slavery, was the
true singer of plowmen, haymakers, and farm housewives.
Those who have passed a long northern winter in a lonely
homestead shut in by the chill embargo of the snow know
with what varisemblance the poet caught the scene and its
moods.

§

Though it is a fact that the great creators of speculative
and imaginative literature moved in some relation to the
conflicts that engaged the attention of politicians and journalists and can be understood only in that relation, it does
not follow, of course, that the literature of the time is to be
classified under the head of social economy. Far from it.

While subtle emotions arising from their economic status colored in a myriad ways the work of men like Cooper, Simms, Irving, and Lowell, it did not follow that their prime concern every instant was the relevance of their work to the issues of the hour. That would be to assume a logical intensity of conviction never found in matters literary. On the contrary, in spite of the machine, science, slavery, and the clash of planter, manufacturer, operative, and farmer, all the old interest in problems of human destiny, roughly grouped as religious, in dramatic tales of hair-raising adventure, in the classical past, in sublimated gossip (the chief intellectual amusement of the human race), and in the diversities of American life on land and sea were fed by the imaginative writers of the middle period. Considered from that point of view, it can be said that no phase of American culture escaped their scrutiny. The times may be reconstructed through their eyes.

In New England, where the dissolving effect of science, secular thought, and the machine process upon inherited customs was the most acute, it was only natural that religious ideas and above all Puritan obsessions should be subjected to merciless analysis. That was the psychological operation that absorbed the highest talents of Hawthorne. Disillusioned by his experience with communal living at Brook Farm, caught in the swirl of surrounding skepticism, he became a student of manners and morals.

With merciless steel Hawthorne, the Democrat, dissected the conduct of the great and good, the high and respectable; with unerring accuracy he portrayed the pillars of society as executioners in unjust causes. In the same mood of the physician, he explored the deep recesses of the Puritan conscience, its fear of sin, its hard practical sense, its association of Providence with expediency and success. He also inquired into the new liberalism which, after rejecting established creeds, embarked without compass or rudder on the transcendental ship; and he considered the relation of the dissolving philosophy to Puritan culture. For sin, it offered self-reliance; for hell or heaven, it offered compensation; for authority, it offered freedom of thought—a procedure very disturbing to those who had a naïve scheme of salvation—but Hawthorne pursued his way to a logical conclusion without any support from Emerson's buoyant optimism. Indeed he may be called the realistic novelist of the crumbling order for which the Concord sage furnished the philosophy.

Another phase of Puritan dissolution was mirrored in the elusive lines of Emily Dickinson, secluded Amherst poet, who, after a sacrificial love affair, retired within her house and garden to brood upon the substance and mystery of life. With a certain relevance, she has been likened to a Hindu adept pondering in solitude over infinity, but the analogy is not altogether precise because an uncanny wit shines through her wonderment. "To multiply the harbors does not reduce the sea . . . No message is the utmost message, for what we tell is done . . . In a life that stopped guessing, you and I should not feel at home . . . A lonesome fluency abroad, like suspended music . . . To be singular under plural circumstances is a becoming heroism." In such vein did she too criticize the smooth and easy creed. And she did it with transparent sincerity, without pose and without care, for Emily Dickinson allowed none of her work to be published during her life, sought no applause, attended no banquets in her honor.

No less accurately were the physical setting for the American adventure and the manners of the several sections drawn by the writers of imaginative literature. New England, material and spiritual, is spread out before us in the pages of Hawthorne, New York in the stories of Cooper, the planting South in the novels of Tucker, Simms, and Kennedy, the southwestern frontier in the sketches of Joseph Glover Baldwin, David Crockett, and Augustus Baldwin Longstreet, and the Middle West in the turgid romances of James Hall and the clever etchings of Caroline Kirkland. Even the far Southwest over against the borders of Mexico was celebrated in the clear notes of Albert Pike's prose and poetry.

If we want to see a fine old plutocrat, we can find him in English guise in Cooper's Monikins. The slave-owning planter of the grand style passes through his manorial halls in Kennedy's Swallow Barn or a Sojourn in the Old Dominion. The lively horsetraders, planters, farmers, slaves, and poor whites of the Far South throng Longstreet's Georgia Scenes; while the shrewd pushing planters and lawyers of Alabama and Mississippi, too clever by far for old-fashioned Virginia gentlemen, live again in Baldwin's Flush Times. In the rough-hewn pages of David Crockett's Autobiography the political scenes of the frontier are preserved for all time.

Nor was the sea neglected. The middle period was the era of romantic maritime enterprise when clipper ships carried American trade into distant waters, enriching whole towns with the wealth of Cathay. And the hardy sailors who raised their anchors, unfurled their canvas, careened in the breeze, rounded every cape, and visited every port deserved—and found—their epic makers. In 1841, Richard Henry Dana, after two vivid years before the mast, brought the sea, the deck, the yardarm, the smell of salt and tar, and the drama of wide water-spaces to the door of every landlubber in a story that charmed the readers of his day and will live as long as the tongue in which it is written.

Out of wider and deeper experiences, out of a more playful and mystic nature, Herman Melville evolved still more powerful tales of life on the rolling deep. Renouncing the easy ways of clerks and merchants, he deliberately chose the hardships and oppressions of the forecastle, exchanging the dull routine of the quill and ledger for the excitements of shipwrecks, riots, mutinies, and cannibals. Moby Dick, wrought in the golden age of the sailing vessel, published in 1851, was a thrilling narrative, suffused by whimsy, doubts, and mystery that seemed to symbolize an eternal enmity between man and nature and yet suspend the reader between fact and fancy. So rich in color and philosophy was this romance that Melville could never again rise to the same height. Beyond all question he is one of the noteworthy figures of universal literature—though it was left for this generation to write his biography and pay full tribute to his genius.

§

While innumerable forces tended to direct American literary interest to domestic problems and themes, there were others which worked for continual subordination of the American mind to classical and contemporary European modes. Among them none was more potent than the use of the English tongue for it gave the American people immediate access to the established literature of Britain and helped to perpetuate in letters the provincial status that had been repudiated in politics by the war for independence. English writers still set models and styles; English criticism was keenly felt and usually disparaging; English praise was hungrily sought; and all this meant efforts to conform to sentiments alien to New World life, whether the conservatism of Sir Walter Scott and Sydney Smith or the radicalism of Byron and Shelley.

Moreover, the absence of a copyright law strengthened the yoke of foreign authority. Under the system then in vogue, American publishers could "pirate" at pleasure the works of English and European authors, that is, issue their books in the United States without asking their consent or paying them any royalties. As a consequence, foreign novels, plays, poems, histories, and criticism were reproduced in numerous cheap editions, flooding the market with a literature that was alien both in matter and in spirit in many significant respects. Harpers, for instance, began to publish in 1842 a library of select novels and, when the number reached more than six hundred, only eight or ten even then were the work of American authors.

American magazines, following the same practice, filched from their foreign contemporaries reviews, articles, and criticisms without paying a penny for their copy. What was the use of remunerating an American writer for commenting on a book when a review by the best critic of the Old World could be had for the taking? Of course in some instances sensitive publishers asked for publishing rights and paid for the privilege but competition was too strong to permit the exercise of such nice virtues on a large scale. It was not until 1891, when an international copyright law was wrung from Congress by American authors and honorable publishers, that gentlemen eager to protect American pig iron against English rivals consented to put letters on an equal plane and sweep piracy from literature as it had been swept from the high seas.

Inspired by European examples, faced every day by European competition in styles, and convinced that the fundamental lines in prose and verse had been laid for all time by the past, a number of American writers turned from the economic and religious conflict that surged around them to themes and rhythms of other lands. Some of them tried their best to fit their strong sinews into the stiff armor of European culture, daring to invite the Old World to examine their adaptability to its metal. Longfellow was of this school. A collegian, trained in the classics, an eager admirer of Dante, the president of the Dante Club at Harvard, he preferred the elegance which Whitman spurned. Whitman loved the divergent American language with its twists and turns, its prickly colloquialisms. Longfellow was a professor of established languages, a maker of textbooks, a lecturer on literature, fond of the middle ages, a good academician, essentially derivative rather than creative, true to conventional models even when writing Hiawatha, the Indian saga.

Underneath his load of learning, he was still a Puritan who shared the sentiments of the conservative, if not orthodox, clergy. While Whitman chose to roam with the commonalty, Longfellow remained a serene teacher in a quiet grove. Perhaps in that rôle he spoke to a wider audience of his countryfolk engaged in farming and manufacturing than did the roistering poet. At any rate he demonstrated that an American could polish his lines, like any good Victorian, and kindle some fire, even though he could not "strike the stars with his sublime head."

If not as deeply absorbed in European culture as Longfellow, the creator of the first great poem written on the soil of the United States, William Cullen Bryant, was in most of his verses equally remote as a poet, not as a citizen, from the uproar of the forum and marketplace. Starting in his New England youth an aggressive Federalist, he later became, as editor of the New York Evening Post, a mild free-trade Democrat—to the high pleasure of the importers, and then during the contest over slavery went over to the Republican ranks.

But the passions of the political debate did not surge through his rhythmic lines. Though often classed as a Puritan by casual critics, there was nothing Puritanic in his cosmic view of life as a solemn processional symbolizing the unity of man and nature, ending in their complete fusion. No doubt there were in Bryant many Puritan strains: correctness and serenity of private life, conscientious devotion to the task of editing, deep interest in public affairs, eagerness to praise nobleness of example in writers and statesmen, firm faith in the worth of American citizenship, purity of spirit, and respect for virtue. When all these qualities were enumerated and all his lines surveyed there was nowhere to be found Cotton Mather's rejoicing in the Providence of God or Roger Williams' acquaintance with the gentleness of Jesus. If the note of Thanatopsis is not that of lofty pessimism then it would be difficult to find it anywhere in universal literature.

That too was compatible with the stern discharge of duty —plowing the furrow, as it was started in youth, with dignity and contentment, to the end. Nor was it incompatible with a many-sided mode of living. Bryant could unbend in fairy tales and little lyrics of nature; he could rejoice in long walks and talks with the exuberant Whitman; he could serve as the councilor of statesmen. Still he was no intrepid knight thundering at turreted gates with an iron mallet. Neither was he a languid æsthete at home amid the perfumes of a salon sustained by fixed investments. Bryant was a substantial poet and a solid citizen.

At the opposite pole of temperament, though a warm admirer of Bryant, was the most exotic poet of the middle period, Edgar Allan Poe, in many ways unique. He did not love his own time and habitat like Whitman, flee from it like Longfellow, seek refuge in nature like Thoreau, or rest serene in optimism like Emerson. With all the power of his provocative intellect he sought a key to creative art and at a time when hero worship was the vogue in American literary circles, he so savagely attacked current modes that he won for himself the title of "the tomahawk man." As a critic he laid down dicta on the essence of wit, poetry, and humor; when he wrote romance or verse he bowed to his own rules.

Having defined poetry as "the rhythmical creation of beauty," Poe subjected himself with ascetic zeal to the laws of his own imagination, striving by mathematical calculation and composition in tones to find the music of prose. The result was not ideas but haunting, sonorous cadences that were saved from banality by a deep note of mystery. If, as Lowell said, two-fifths of Poe was "fudge," the remainder was powerful enough to make the age in which he lived noted in the annals of "beautiful" letters.

Among the romanticists who turned from American life for their materials must be reckoned four or five of the most distinguished historians of the period. After giving his countrymen a substantial though not brilliant life of George Washington, as if to pay a personal debt, Washington Irving chose Spain for his second home, charming the people of both nations with his story of Columbus and the

Conquest of Granada. Through years of travel, the mountains and valleys, the waysides and inns, the streets of crowded cities, and the quiet cloisters of monasteries in Spain became as familiar to him as the scenes of his native land; he loved "the rich ore of old, neglected volumes" in Spanish libraries even more than he did the newer manuscripts of his own young nation.

Likewise enamored of Spanish romance, William Hickling Prescott chose the conquest of Mexico and Peru as the subject of his luminous expositions, writing with such power that the authoritative scholars of Europe—Hallam, Guizot, Milman, and Thierry—accepted him as a peer in their realm. Given an alien bent early in life at the Northampton school of the German-trained Bancroft, James Lothrop Motley, a bit soured on Jacksonian Democracy, also exercised his talents on European material, adding a vivid, if thoroughly respectable, volume to the mountainous literature on the Dutch republic.

While confining his explorations mainly to this continent, Francis Parkman chose the conflict between England and France in North America for his deep and wide researches. Released from narrow local ties by the riches of his father, accumulated in the grocery business in Boston, George Ticknor, a ripe scholar and prodigious worker, wrote a history of Spanish literature so erudite and so charming that Macaulay recommended it to Queen Victoria. Thus in the very age when Hegel, writing his profound philosophy of history, saw in America a land of the future, some of the finest historical minds in the United States could find their most engaging themes only in the storied past of other countries.

§

The same interests, customs, conflicts which caught the attention of authors, editors, and publishers, the same competition with foreign appeals which ran through imaginative literature in general had their counterparts in the theater, the romantic drama running parallel with the romantic novel. From intellectual circles, the Puritan tabu had now definitely passed, lingering only among the evangelical sects wrestling with his satanic majesty on the frontier. So pure to the pure had all things become in the very section where once all things theatrical had been evil that even the ballet was enjoyed by Transcendentalists.

In the extension of the dramatic field, mechanical factors operated as effectively as in publishing. While money and leisure built upon money, as usual, provided local patronage for the drama, the development of railways and steam navigation transformed the continent—indeed, the whole Atlantic basin—into a theater for the production of plays. Greater wealth, spread widely over the country, and railways made it possible for the most eminent players to move swiftly from city to city, and encouraged capitalists to put money into the amusement business, as into industrial stocks and bonds—with such feverish haste in fact that overproduction ensued, Philadelphia, for instance, having five theaters fall into bankruptcy in a single season of 1828-29.

Before the period had come to a close, all the cities from coast to coast were bidding for playwrights and players. Scarcely had the miners of '49 erected their shacks in California when they declared that they must have a stage and no sooner did they get rough boards nailed together in a wooden hut than an Australian company arrived to present Othello to the serious and a French vaudeville troupe to raise boisterous laughter among the wielders of the pick. With the help of the railway, Edwin Forrest, Joseph Jefferson, James H. Hackett, and all the leading native actors "toured" the country, at least east of the Mississippi, with plays constructed in America included in their repertoire.

Had the railway developed without a correlative growth in steam navigation, it is conceivable that the course of the dramatic art in the United States would have been more nationalist. Certainly the upheavals of the age, obtruding themes, enthusiasm, and talent called into being native work of genuine power, while American actors capable of interpreting it gave their lives generously to the task of production. But oceanic navigation brought a rush of foreign performers with foreign plays to sue for favor behind the footlights, among them such celebrities as Edmund and Charles Kean, Charles Mathews, Junius Brutus Booth, William Charles MacCready, and Charles and Fanny Kemble, all with English plays in English interpretations. New York being the chief port of entry, the capitalists of the metropolis were quick to sense the size of gate receipts that would flow from making the outlying cities tributary to its successes. In this opportunity, the "star" system was created as a dramatic phase to business enterprise, throwing the profit-making instinct on the side of heavy importations and keeping the stamp of the province on American work.

Pitted against foreign actors and foreign plays, American actors and playwrights had stubborn problems to face, especially popular love of the exotic, continued emphasis on the traditional, and respect for the authoritative. However deep the actor's desire to give voice to American issues and psychology, he well knew from experience that his plays must be all the more convincing and artistic when handling the democratic theme. No one understood this better than Edwin Forrest, whose loyalty to American life led him, by personal appeal and by experiments in production, to stimulate the writers of Boston and Philadelphia—less submerged than New York by the European flood—to strain every nerve in creative work. So likewise James H. Hackett, famous for his impersonation of American types, though he loved Shakespeare's rollicking figures, never wearied in encouraging local playwrights. Even the poet Longfellow devoted his graduating oration at Bowdoin to an appeal for a greater appreciation of native drama and tried his own ability in that field, but with a foreign conception, The Spanish Student.

Under the stimulus of national idealism, in spite of formidable competition from every foreign quarter, at least seven hundred plays by American authors were produced before the close of the middle period in 1860. In all phases the output represented an immense growth in dramatic interest and power compared with the era of the early republic. Unhappily, however, owing to the absence of copyright protection, comparatively little of this work was ever published, especially in the South, leaving posterity to guess at its character and artistic competence. But from the printed plays and from news reports it has been shown that between 1825 and 1860 more than one hundred and fifty plays were constructed on the events and personages of the American Revolution alone; that all the economic and political struggles of the age invaded the actor's art—the battle over the Bank, the triumph of Jackson, campaigns of Whigs and Democrats, disputes over Maine and Oregon boundaries, the gold rush, the Mexican War, and the Mormon migration to Utah; that among domestic plays Rip Van Winkle took the lead; and that Yankees, planters, farmers, Negroes, countrymen, sailors, and townspeople were repeatedly, and often cleverly, portrayed.

It was significant that plays built around the theme of the masses casting off the classes were among the most popular dramas written and produced in America during the time. With Europe repeatedly stirred by political upheavals and America roused first by the Jacksonian battle and then by the struggle between planting and capitalism, Richard Montgomery Bird, a Philadelphia playwright, found the intellectual climate favorable to tragedy of a popular cast. Responding to this appeal, he wrote The Gladiator to celebrate the uprising of the slaves of Rome against their masters; Pelopidas picturing the revolt of the Thebans against Spartan tyranny and Oralloossa representing the Indian rebellion against Spanish conquerors. A Whig and stanch opponent of slavery, Bird made abolitionist opinion leap from the tongue of Spartacus once more, in the oratorical form still the vogue in that day:

Death to the Roman fiends, that make their mirth
Out of the groans of bleeding misery!
Ho, slaves arise! it is your hour to kill.
Kill and spare not—for wrath and liberty!
Freedom for bondmen—freedom and revenge!

More than a thousand times, Edwin Forrest played The Gladiator to cheering audiences in the North; and long after Bird and Forrest were dead and the slaves of the South had been emancipated, it still appeared on the boards of New York.

Conceived in the same spirit and appealing to the democratic sentiments of the time, Robert T. Conrad's historical play, Jack Cade, celebrating the courage of that Daniel Shays of Tudor England in a portrayal of an uprising by serfs and yeomen—as interpreted by Edwin Forrest—had a run that must have pleased Andrew Johnson and his followers. In short, the humors, gossip, customs, and deeper passions of the middle period all found their way into the theater, now accidentally, now subtly, now with gusto, making it seem as if a thousand years had passed since Jonathan Edwards preached damnation to the giddy.

§

Akin to the drama, especially on its operatic side, but more sublimated, more remote from the hard rationalizing processes of industry and science, the art of musical composition and production in America was subjected to even greater competition from abroad. French, Italian, and English opera companies boarded the swifter and safer steamers for experiments in the American marketplace, and singers and instrumentalists from Germany in particular surged in to exploit the concert and teaching field. After all, the roots of the world's musical masterpieces then as always lay deep in religious and martial sentiments older than reason or trade, and America of the middle period was essentially, almost crassly, economic.

In any event, the American people were dominated by no single church comparable to the state establishments of Europe which gave unity to religious emotions and patronage to the correlative elaboration of devotional music. Appealing primarily to farmers and mechanics, distrusting large military and naval establishments, Jacksonian Democracy, though it adored wars and military heroes, did not nourish the continuous martial ardors that often stimulate the production of music. In the rush and roar of economic development, moreover, little place was left for the quiet life of song and reflection conducive to lyrical compositions and nowhere in the country could be found a rich folklore upon which to build—save perhaps the elusive and exotic Indian mythology.

In the metropolitan centers offering the concentration of population necessary for æsthetic appreciation and the wealth for patronage, there was an extraordinary chaos in historical backgrounds for musical development. Boston, for example, long accustomed to the choral singing of hymns, now moving out and on under the influence of religious liberalism through oratorios into the sphere of secular music, displayed a coldness for the feudalism of European opera. In New York, where the Protestant Episcopal sect was strong and where Trinity Church had begun to give oratorios in the early days of the republic, it was easier to awaken an interest in anything Europe had to present, especially the opera with its social corollaries. Representing still a third type, the Quakers of Philadelphia had neither vocal nor instrumental music in their religious worship nor in the homes of the strict; nevertheless, with less of the Puritan passion in their make-up, they found it a simple matter to accept secular music when the Musical Fund Society, organized in 1820, opened the symphonic era in their city. It was New Orleans, Spanish and French in origin, possessing riches for patronage, mainly Catholic in religion, sustained under American possession by the economy of semi-feudal landlords, that first welcomed whole-heartedly French and Italian opera; for it was as far removed from Boston and Philadelphia in musical taste as it was in geography.

No city, however, had the conditions favorable to the flowering of native talent in the temper and cast of the Old World, even had such lain dormant. It was easier to make money from cod and cotton and pay foreign musicians than to foster native composition—if indeed by any method the creative musical faculty could have been awakened at that time. So leadership in such affairs passed naturally and completely into the hands of Europeans, of Germans especially. "The father of American orchestral music," for instance, was a Hanoverian, Gottlieb Graupner, who, after drifting through one of King George's regiments to London and thence to Charleston, South Carolina, eventually settled in Boston the year of Washington's death. There, with the assistance of such local and alien players as were available, he organized the first orchestra credited to America.

Another German, Carl Zerrahn, who came to the United States during the great exodus from his fatherland in 1848, became the leader of the Handel and Haydn Society in Boston and for more than forty years organized and conducted orchestral and choral festivals in various parts of the country, receiving in recognition an outpouring of money and appreciation that was lavish in proportions. German refugees also founded the Germania Orchestra, which gave concerts in the leading cities and helped to raise the level of orchestral music wherever budding experiments were made. To Theodore Thomas of Hanover belongs perhaps the highest honor of the middle period for enterprise and success in driving the New World along the musical paths of the Old; arriving in 1845, he inaugurated New York's first chamber concerts and devoted the remaining years of his long career to the development of the art in America. If none of these foreign musicians was a supreme master, yet the people of the United States owe heavy debts to them all.

Great as was this obligation to foreigners, it would be a mistake to overlook native participation and coöperation. Certainly, on the side of promotion, Lowell Mason of Massachusetts deserves a place in the chronicle. While a clerk in a Georgia banking house, he made a compilation of sacred music which won him immediate recognition; in 1827 he became the conductor of the young Handel and Haydn Society in Boston and, after holding that post for twenty-three years, transferred his interest with his residence to New York. As a compiler of church music, an organizer of choral societies, a partner in an organ factory, and an originator of conventions for the training of music instructors in the public schools, Mason impressed himself indelibly on the democracy of his time.

It would be an equal mistake, no doubt, to neglect the efforts that were made to resist the foreign invasion and the "systematized effort for the extinction of American music"—by the production of native composition. With this ideal in mind, William H. Fry of Philadelphia and George F. Bristow of Brooklyn attempted operatic flights. Fry's Leonora, performed in New York in 1858, was received with great applause—an applause that died away with ominous haste, however. Bristow's Rip Van Winkle was performed by one of the best of the foreign opera companies only to meet the same fate. Nor did his oratorios and symphonies prove to be more than transitory incidents in American cultural history. If these native artists built nothing enduring, if even they had to rely on European models, they at least labored sincerely and with slight commercial advantage to express and evoke creative genius in their own country. Whatever their natural talents they had to depend solely upon popular patronage, as few, if any, of the great composers on the world's roll had been forced to do, and the verdict of the people was against them.

As seemed congruous in a democratic society bent on raising the general level of culture, it was the institutions for interesting and educating the populace that made the striking music achievements of the day. Indeed the annals of the time were crowded with entries recording the formation of societies, academies, schools, conservatories, and publishing concerns devoted to this special art. Beginning with the Handel and Haydn Society, which was organized in Boston in 1815, successive decades saw the multiplication of all sorts of associations for the promotion of music, among the most notable being the Philadelphia Musical Fund Society established in 1820, the Boston Academy of Music in 1833, the New York Academy of Music in 1852, the Milwaukee Musikverein in 1851, and the New York Liederkranz in 1847. Popular enthusiasm was winning support also in institutions of learning where music courses were added to the curriculum, Boston setting a brave example in 1838 by introducing such instruction in the public schools. Old Federalists who thought that the end of the world had come when John Quincy Adams was rejected of Jacksonian Democracy could hardly say with justice that the artistic sense of the nation had been extinguished with the advent of the masses to political power.

Even the commercial enterprise that made new fortunes every year conspired in various ways to deepen the musical interest of the millions. This was the age which witnessed the rise of the regular manufacture of American pianos in something approaching mass production under the leadership of Jonas Chickering.

A cabinet-maker's apprentice who tempted fortune by going to Boston in 1818, Chickering joined the Handel and Haydn Society, penetrated into the fascinations of musical composition and instrument-making, and then embarked in business for himself. By numerous inventions, he soon made the American piano known over the world for its durability; while his business acumen put it on the market at a relatively low figure. Thus in making it possible for thousands to have pianos where but a few had enjoyed them before, Chickering contributed largely to the distribution of musical education and taste; and out of the riches he acquired from the trade in the instrument itself, he gave generous sums for the promotion of talent among the poor. One of the by-products of his industry was national concentration on piano-playing and piano-composition—the history of all music being interwoven with the instruments in favor at various times and for specific reasons.

§

The sweep of economic and social forces which carried America away from the cultural order of the colonial epoch, touching even the esoteric realm of music, influenced still more profoundly those arts which portrayed man and nature —painting, sculpture, and drawing. In this sphere as in music there was, of course, the cultural lag due to the load of tradition and classical training but the march of events was steady. Gentlemen of the old school who had fought a losing battle with Jefferson and another with Jackson had relied as firmly as any of Louis XIV's courtiers on the classics and on divinity for their verbal and moral support. Just as they had opposed the westward advance of the economic American empire under the drive of Jacksonian farmers they had looked to Europe rather than to native powers for guidance in matters of the spirit. To them the right of the rich and well-born to rule in the arts was as divine as the same right seemed to James I or Louis XIV in matters political.

It was therefore as natural for the wielders of the brush to carry on the ceremonial spirit of Trumbull in painting as for certain manipulators of the pen to concentrate on the classics. Indeed efforts to acclimatize traditional art became more numerous as students were enabled by new wealth and easier travel to study the old masters in Italy, as more models and copies of antique art were imported with the weakening of Puritan tabus, as rich patrons provided the means, and as schools in connection with the academies began to train Americans on the classical basis.

Of the artists of the middle period who painted in the grand style, John Vanderlyn, blacksmith-apprentice of Kingston, New York, won perhaps the most distinction, receiving for his picture of Marius among the Ruins of Carthage a medal from Napoleon the Great and for his Ariadne applause from the students who copied in Rome. In the same vogue sculpture, which now made its way with the aid of native aspirants, offered national statesmen in togas or with Greek draperies flung over frock coats and cylindrical pants. If Tories could not make Washington a king, they could at least make him over in the image of a Roman senator or emperor. For artists who chose themes out of a remote past unrelated to their own lives and times, it seemed perfectly congruous to use Greek columns draped with textiles as a background for heroic figures of American politics.

But the philosophy and practice of the grand style in art as in life had its antithesis. Faced by a monopoly of divinity in the persons of their opponents everywhere, advocates of democracy turned from God to nature for guidance and inspiration. Jean Jacques Rousseau, who went on before the democratic masses like a cloud by day and a pillar of fire by night, had preached the gospel of emancipation through a return to nature. In a like vein Thomas Jefferson, when he flung out the Declaration of Independence and blew the blast that echoed down through the middle period, appealed first to "the laws of nature" and then to the laws of "nature's God." It was the more devout and conservative brethren in the Continental Congress of 1776 who compelled him to insert at the end, "with a firm reliance on the protection of Divine Providence." What the democratic politician invoked for support—an all-surrounding and all-sustaining nature—poets of the new age celebrated and the men of science investigated with relentless and revolutionary persistence.

With the appeal for a "natural" government, the essence of democracy, as distinguished from an artificial and ceremonial government, there ran also through the arts a simple call for a return to nature. In Europe where revolutionary upheavals of the thirties and forties were keeping the intellectuals in excitement with the new ideas, American students of art came into contact with the rebellious spirit. And those who for one reason or other could not go abroad saw the modes of Peale and Trumbull disintegrating at home under the fire of Jacksonian democracy, under the influence of naturalism. With a flair for the temper of the new age an American art critic exclaimed in 1853: "The future spirit of our art must be inherently vast like our western plains, majestic like our forests, generous like our rivers."

In response to just such moods the most distinctive work was done by landscape artists, such as Frederick E. Church, John F. Kensett, S. R. Gifford, Thomas Cole, and Homer D. Martin—a group of whom were known as the Hudson River School on account of their intense preoccupation with the scenes of that great valley. Technically deficient as their work was, and photographic in minutiæ, still it could be said for them that they were nearer to reality—that is, to subjects within the range of their comprehension—than the expatriates who worked in mythology and the grandiose.

The shift of interest from imitative art was stimulated by the new technical processes which revolutionized printing and, besides making the reproductions of old masters in cheap form available, widened the market and opportunities for American artists who cared to work with the living things about them. This was the age of budding magazines, popular histories, travel books, gift books, and illustrated sets; it saw also the spread of the political cartoon.

And all this made for democracy in art, setting engravers and artists to work to supply the demand of a nation becoming literate and curious about its own scenery, its own people, urban and rural, Indians, city dwellers, rustics, fiddlers, Negroes, dancers, and politicians. Besides the serious and somber work done for The National Portrait Gallery of Distinguished Americans, issued in 1834-39, for the grand family Bible brought out by Harpers in 1843, "embellished with a thousand historical engravings," and for the Atlantic Souvenir, the Baltimore Book, the Lady's Album, and a hundred more ephemeral volumes, there was a perfect flood of political and social caricatures. In fact from the drawings of the artists who interpreted the passing show the politics and social life of the era could be reconstructed, if its printed words were destroyed: Whigs, Republicans, and Democrats, all the great figures from Andrew Jackson up or down, woman's rights, prohibition, slavery, abolition, labor, socialism, Catholicism, Mormonism, and Millerism.

In other directions than in the themes and affections of painters, sculptors, and engravers, the scientific and industrial drive of the middle period counted heavily. If domestic manufacturers were to get the full benefit of the protective tariff and make headway against foreign importations in clothing, furniture, and material commodities of every kind, they evidently needed the coöperation of artistic talent. With a closer reference to practical things, with a frank avowal of competing with the Academy of Fine Arts for public favor, the National Academy of Design was founded in New York in 1825. Under the leadership and inspiration of Samuel F. B. Morse, the painter-inventor, open criticism was made of the rival institution, charging its patrons and defenders with subservience to power, title, and rank. Tangent also to business requirements were the Philadelphia School of Design for Women opened in 1853 and the Cooper Institute of New York "devoted forever to the union of art and science in their application to useful purposes of life." Already it had become apparent that the handicrafts supported by apprenticeship had broken down before the steel fingers and the factory mind of the machine age and that some substitute comparable to the old affection for the product would have to be devised, unless.

forsooth, all art was to perish in the dry decay of everlasting copying.

§

The technical revolution which called into being the great urban centers, created a huge working class, accelerated the westward movement, spanned the region east of the Mississippi River with railways, and afforded a substantial basis for nationalistic democracy—a technical revolution which in short invaded every sphere—naturally destroyed the journalism of the handpress appropriate for local market towns and pointed the way to the monster journalism of the modern age. A demonstrated success by 1844 and used with great effect in the Mexican War, the telegraph completely changed the whole process of reporting events and made possible the newspaper as distinguished from the former political and literary organ. "You are going to turn the newspaper office upside down with your invention," said Horace Greeley to Morse when he witnessed a private demonstration of the magnetic telegraph. Within a few years, wires linked the editorial sanctum with Washington as well as with every other section of the country; political journalism was thus decentralized.

At the same time the steady development of the power press made possible large scale production. The London Times was printed by steam in 1814, an event more momentous than the downfall of Napoleon the next year, and the Hoe cylinder rotary press was installed in the office of the Philadelphia Ledger in 1846, announcing the triumph of the penny press. Without exaggeration it may be said that a new era was opened in America by the establishment of the New York Sun in 1833 as a one-cent daily paper. Two years later James Gordon Bennett launched the Herald, proclaiming at the outset his contempt for party principles and politics—"a sort of steel trap to catch the public"—and declaring that he would stick to the business of gathering and reporting the news of everyday life—interspersed as it happened with scandal and blackmail. It was not long before every city, East, West and South, had its cheap daily paper that reached far down into the lower strata of literacy.

In another generation the increasing requirements of capital to finance the new machinery of reporting and printing were to drive from the field the independent editors of the old school. But it was still possible at the middle of the century for a few men, such as Samuel Bowles of the Springfield Republican, Thomas Ritchie of the Richmond Enquirer, and Henry J. Raymond of the New York Times, to maintain the personal journalism of the early days—to make their principles and their courage count in spite of the approaching doom of anonymity which was destined to engulf journalism in time. It was yet possible for Horace Greeley to own the paper which he edited and, as he said, to "keep an ear open to the plaints of the wronged and suffering, though they can never repay advocacy, though those who mainly support newspapers will be annoyed and often exposed by it; a heart as sensitive to oppression and degradation in the next street as if they were practiced in Brazil or Japan; a pen as ready to expose and reprove the crimes whereby wealth is amassed and luxury enjoyed in our own country as if they had only been committed by Turks or Pagans in Asia some centuries ago."

In the technical advance of the printing and illustrating arts, appeared a whole flock of weeklies and monthlies, literally by the hundreds, to flourish as a rule for a few months and then pass into oblivion. Of the vast array Godey's Lady's Book, founded in 1830 and continued until long after the Civil War, reaped perhaps the richest harvest in cash, by making a successful combination of delicate fiction suited to chaste minds with tasteful articles on embroidery and dinner-table management. Having money with which to pay for manuscripts, it commanded while it lasted some of the best talent of the period to mingle with the banalities.

Of the monthlies devoted to letters, only two—Harper's Magazine established in 1850, and the Atlantic Monthly floated seven years afterward—managed to survive, together with the older North American Review, the buffets of fortune into the twentieth century. Scores of temperance, religious, anti-slavery, labor, reform, scientific, and special interest magazines borrowed and begged their way through varying periods, long or short, throwing high upon the neglected shelves of libraries the materials from which in due time illuminating chapters on the social and intellectual history of the United States will be written. Journalism and the lyceum were making "adult education" a factor in national life.

§

The social and economic conditions which so distinguished the middle period from the early republican era inevitably impressed themselves on educational institutions and practices—conspiring to give new powers and new direction to popular learning in America, enabling this country to lead all the world in removing the stamp of class-rigidity, sect, and charity from the training of the masses. England at that time still kept her universities and preparatory schools far removed from the commonalty, as centers for gentlemen who either intended to manage paternal estates or enter the Church, the army, the navy, or civil service, giving the poor almost nothing except bare rudiments offered in sectarian charity schools grudgingly aided by government doles. France, under Napoleon I, had subjected education to the dominion of the state, extending the elementary schools in the operation, and the successive governments continued the system with modifications; but the barriers that lay in the way of the ambitious poor had never been destroyed. Prussia had also established a program of class education. "The state," said the king after his ruin was recorded in the treaty of Tilsit, "must replace by intellectual forces the physical forces which it has lost"; but the educational scheme was worked out on the class basis; that is, the masses were to remain in the condition "prescribed by Providence" while the privileged were to enjoy the advantages of higher education. Such was the example set to American democracy by the older cultures of Europe at this time. At best they offered few adventures in intelligence—rather, scholastic devices for assuring the privileges and pleasures of the upper classes.

Now all the circumstances of the social order in America, especially in the North, worked against the maintenance of the rigid lines of feudalism in the sphere of education. In the industrial part of the United States there was no fixed landed aristocracy; nowhere was there a clerical or military establishment with its vested interests. With the working class and the farmers enfranchised and enjoying a certain economic surplus, it was impossible either to hold them in ignorance or to keep them contented with the charitable and "ragged schools" which had come down from colonial days.

For a nation of farmers and mechanics, bent on self-government and possessed of the ballot, there was only one kind of an educational program in keeping with self-respect, namely, a free and open public school system supported by taxation and non-sectarian in its control. Did not the grand Jeffersonian tradition, with its respect for human nature, require that careers should be open to talent? Did not the republican Fathers look to education as a source of republican strength?

In fact, a wide array of forces combined to translate the theory of popular education into practical achievement. With the rise of political democracy an effective drive was given to the demand of the idealists for public schools—organized labor, so restive in the age of the Jacksonian uprising, taking a lead in demanding from the legislators the establishment of free and equal common schools. While the spirit of natural science was transforming the mind of the intellectual classes and working for a secularization of social processes, the multiplication of religious sects and their unending rivalry speeded up the operation.

Moreover, the increasing flood of Irish and Continental immigrants, likely to fall under Catholic direction if educated at all in charity schools, frightened Protestants of every proclivity, making them willing to accept secularism rather than papal authority. Finally, as Emerson viewed it, the alarming radicalism of Jacksonian Democracy made property owners—who had once resisted the taking of money out of their pockets to educate the children of the poor—more amenable to appeals for funds to support institutions for popular discipline. Thus from many angles the problem of educating the masses was attacked when the republic became a democracy.

Of course the nature of the American federal system made impossible anything like the military uniformity of the Prussian system which was so often studied as a model. Hence the educational movement varied in form and force from state to state, becoming strongest naturally in the regions where political democracy was most advanced, namely, in the agricultural West and the industrial East.

Indeed it made the most rapid strides in the frontier states where there were fewer vested sectarian interests to hamper the action of government. Unquestionably, it seems, the honor of leadership belongs to Michigan, where, in 1817, the legislature sketched in detail on paper a full program of education from primary school to university, laid the foundations for common schools in 1827, and in 1837, after admission to the Union, created a university with four departments—Literature, Science and the Arts, Law, and Medicine. This was pioneer work in many respects for all the world. Other states had established fragments of such a system but none had constructed it from pediment to capital. Nothing remained for Michigan to do except to elaborate the details and enlarge the structure; in 1848 it added an institution for the instruction of the deaf, dumb, and blind; in 1855 it organized an agricultural and industrial college; fifteen years later the doors of its university were opened to women, thereby completing the democracy of the scheme.

It was not easy for the older states with traditions and vested interests to follow this radical example, because the sects were more firmly entrenched in their midst and numerous schools representing both religious convictions and economic endowments were already in full operation. The private academies, which had marked a forward step in former days, now with property rights at stake themselves, naturally resented the inroads of democracy. Where counties and towns had been empowered by state laws to raise money through taxation for local education, the prosperous districts had excellent schools but the backward regions had either wretched institutions or none at all; and those who were well provided under such a régime saw little excuse for changes and less reason for aiding the unfortunate. Notwithstanding Emerson's claim, many merchants and farmers were reluctant to endure taxes for the benefit of artisans and laborers; while the very notion that girls should share in continuous educational privileges was repugnant to respectable thinking.

Against these powerful forces the educational reformers of the East had difficulty in making headway. In breasting the current, they were forced to use even the argument of threat. They pointed out to property owners the peril that lay in an ignorant democracy just enfranchised, proving by investigations into illiteracy how great the danger already was. They demonstrated that the peril was rising as the stream of immigrants from Europe continued to swell; instruction in citizenship would prepare the alien for the right use of the ballot soon to be thrust into his hands.

Education was also offered as a panacea for every other ill—for pauperism and for the revolutionary distempers imported from Old World monarchies, for the growing radicalism among the ranks of American labor, for the spread of socialistic and anarchistic ideas, and for the opposition of the ignorant to the new scientific requirements of public health.   Arguments such as these were strengthened by events.   The strife among the religious sects, the struggle of each denomination to subdue all the pupils in its schools to its theological bias, and the resistance of parents all combined to augment the demand for general public schools supported by taxes and freed from clerical control. America had not become irreligious but no one sect was strong enough to dominate the whole terrain.   And secular instruction was the only thing on which all the sects could agree.   To these drives were added the upward thrust of Jacksonian Democracy, determined to destroy privilege in education as in politics and to provide ladders by which ambitious individuals could climb into the professions.

In the thirties and forties the educational movement became a potent political force.   Appropriations of money were multiplied, the salaries of teachers were increased to attract a better class, state supervision was introduced, the school year was lengthened, school buildings and textbooks were improved, societies for the promotion of education were founded, and educational journals were launched. By the middle of the century New York, Massachusetts, and Pennsylvania had built elementary systems on stable foundations but they still left higher learning to private enterprise supported in the main by fees and endowments.

In New Jersey and Delaware the reformers could not wring from the legislatures anything beyond permissive statutes allowing districts to act.   In the South no statewide system of public education was actually set working before the great cataclysm of 1860.   In the larger southern cities—Baltimore, Charleston, Savannah, New Orleans, and other centers—there were schools supported by taxation and in most of the southern states important beginnings were made in the creation of school funds, the enactment of permissive laws, and the subsidizing of elementary institutions for the poor.   Nearly every one of them like-

wise provided a state, county, and district organization—
thus framing the skeleton structure for the future. The
most advanced in democratic sympathies, North Carolina,
had made significant experiments and even when the Union
army was at her very gates in 1863 undertook to carry out
a project for grade schools and to provide systematic training for teachers. Dominated, however, by the planting
aristocracy and removed from the main currents of science
and industrialism, the South in general was content with its
few private institutions for the upper classes and with classical instruction as the basis of collegiate learning.

Meanwhile, as was to be expected in a farmer-mechanic
democracy, advocates of agricultural and technical education appeared on the ground. As usual, experiments were
first made with private funds. The Rensselaer Polytechnic, founded in 1824 by Stephen Van Rensselaer, flowered
by the middle of the century into a regular engineering
college with a four-year course. Under the patronage of
the state board of agriculture, a few energetic citizens of
Pennsylvania organized in 1855 the Farmers' High School,
which in due course became the Pennsylvania State College.
Two years after this institution opened its doors, Michigan,
as we have noted, established her Agricultural College.
About the same time the beginnings of scientific schools
were made at Harvard and Yale.

Thus the way was prepared for the great Morrill Act
of 1862, which dedicated an empire of public land to the
promotion of mechanical and agricultural education. The
spirit was already quickened when the financial support
came. Therefore, we may say that the foundations of
education in technology—the handmaid of democracy in
the conquest of the material universe—were securely laid
in the fabulous forties and the fermenting fifties. In the
same age schools of law and medicine were created by
private enterprise in many parts of the country and the
crude system of apprenticeship supplemented by opportunities for higher discipline in the classroom and laboratory.

In keeping with the humanism of the time, moreover, was the growth of interest in the special training of defectives and delinquents, as state institutions for the insane were established and efforts to segregate and heal the curable were developed into a system. Studies of the deaf, dumb, and blind were carried on in a scientific spirit and the preparation of that class of defectives for useful work in society was made a matter of public concern. Reform schools with provisions for industrial education, such as the New York House of Refuge, established in 1848, sprang up as the movement for salvaging juvenile offenders spread far and wide. A long stride was this from the treatment of "sinful" children under the blue laws of colonial New England! In the East these experiments were usually sectarian and only partly sustained by state subsidies; in the West they were as a rule carried out under official auspices with regular grants from the public treasury.

So it may truly be said that every essential feature of modern public education was either worked out or fairly anticipated in the United States by the middle of the nineteenth century. Unquestionably the borrowings from the Old World were immense, especially from the Prussian system, but in every case European ideas were put through the alembic of this democracy. Less rigid and stratified than the European, American society gave way quicker to the inexorable march of science and technology. With technology triumphant it was apparent in practice that a humble mechanic like Howe, or Richard Hoe, or McCormick, or Hussey might become more significant than a score of princes—nothing to boast about, just a revolutionary and indubitable fact. The pride of caste secreted by a feudal order was simply inappropriate to an industrial régime founded on applied science. Moreover, in such a society much of the higher learning which had been evolved in esoteric circles seemed akin to magic and occultism, from which no small part of it undoubtedly sprang. If the result of this natural course was the condition described in the oft-repeated observation that "America is the best half-educated country in the world," still it could be asked without invidious discrimination: "According to whose criteria and viewed from what immovable center?" With such bickerings, however, the historian has no more real concern than the biologist or physicist.

True to the processes of democracy, the educational revolution of the middle period was wrought by thousands of workers, nameless, from necessity, in the small compass of a general treatise. And yet it would be neglecting the powerful element of leadership to pass over in utter silence a few outstanding figures, for in the annals of this sphere there are names not less worthy of place than those in science, letters, and politics.

High in the list must be placed Horace Mann, a graduate of Brown University, abandoning jurisprudence for "the larger sphere of mind and morals," making the dead letter of the Massachusetts school law live in classroom and community intelligence, attacking child labor in factories as a bar to education, studying the educational value of physiology and hygiene, supporting the introduction of music and the expulsion of the rod, patiently seeking ways to help the defectives and delinquents, aiding women in the contest for equal privileges in the schools, visiting Europe in the search for germinal ideas, and finally going out to Antioch College in the Middle West to devote his last years to the cause of education in a virgin field.

A peer of Mann in every respect was Henry Barnard, trained at Yale and in Germany, making, in 1835, an American contribution to the literature of juvenile delinquency, establishing the first state teachers' association in the United States in 1845, organizing libraries with such vigor that in every town in Rhode Island except three there was soon a collection of five hundred volumes or more, writing a treatise on school literature, helping to found the American Association for the Advancement of Education, serving as its first president in 1855, publishing the first

American account of the Froebel kindergarten, founding the American Journal of Education, editing it more than a quarter of a century, translating the writings of Comenius, Rousseau, and Pestalozzi for the use of teachers, directing the young University of Wisconsin, toiling in the federal bureau of education—itself largely the outcome of his labors —and closing his career at the ripe old age of eighty-nine full of honors and appreciation, with his many monuments standing secure against time around him. Nor must we overlook Bronson Alcott, dreamer and humanist, who feared the growing power of the state and chose rather to set examples of private enterprise that nurtured wisdom in gentleness amid wholesome physical surroundings.

In this great warfare against illiteracy and ignorance were enlisted scores of able women, usually self-educated and burdened with heavy domestic responsibilities, who either fought all along the line for education or carried special redoubts for their sex alone. Emma Willard, the sixteenth of seventeen children, helped to refashion the whole program of education for women. Her activities were wide like those of her male contemporaries: she wrote texts on universal history, astronomy, and geography, translated Mme. de Saussure's Progressive Education to serve in her campaign, traveled in three years more than eight thousand miles on packet boats, canal barges, and stages to plead the cause before the multitudes, took her place among the pioneers in founding educational associations, went with Henry Barnard to an educational conference in London to demonstrate the new right of women to take part in public assemblies, and founded the Troy Seminary, forerunner of Vassar by half a century.

Emma Willard's sister, Mrs. Almira Phelps, if less varied in her labors, was no less indefatigable in chosen fields of education, waging the battle of science against the classics, for women. Catherine Beecher, the eldest of Lyman Beecher's thirteen children, while charged with the care of the flock, discovered the necessity for training in domestic science and with abounding energy promoted interest in the subject by writing and lecturing upon it. To assure continuity for her ideals and to advance the higher professional education of her sex, she founded, in 1852, the Woman's Education Association.

Another dynamic daughter of New England, Mary Lyon, starting out as a district school teacher at seventy-five cents a week with board, rose by combining teaching and study to a position of commanding influence in the educational world. Early in life she vowed that she would have a seminary for women and in spite of all the jeers at her "rib factory" and her "Protestant nunnery," she fulfilled her pledge by laying broad and deep the foundations for Mount Holyoke College.

After managing a publishing business in Boston and issuing The Dial for a season, Elizabeth Peabody, one of Emerson's transcendentalist group, acquired, through Mrs. Carl Schurz, an interest in the Froebel kindergarten, and became the dominant figure in the Froebel movement in the United States at the inception stage. She established an institution of her own, studied the experiment at first hand in Germany, and then organized in the United States a training school for kindergarten teachers in 1868. While Miss Peabody was widening education at the base, Dorothea Dix was humanizing philanthropy by arousing the country to the importance of separating the incurable insane from those that offered a promise of improvement and restoration to society.

§

In no department of education was the conflict of classes and ideals that surged through the politics of the middle period more subtly represented than in the realm of the higher learning, involving as a matter of course all questions of financial support, administrative control, and curriculum —inseparable elements of the collegiate system. In the nature of things, there were only four ways of supporting an

institution for advanced instruction, namely, tuition fees—
an impossible method as long as there was any eleemosynary
competition—endowments from persons of wealth, subscriptions in small sums from large religious bodies, and grants
from the public treasury.

Since the rich and well-born, particularly in the North,
were generally of the Hamilton-Webster party there was
not much likelihood of transferring to Jacksonian democracy the control of the higher learning as long as it was
monopolized by private institutions. If, therefore, the
popular party was to secure an easy access to that upper
realm—and such a ladder of access was demanded by its
highly vitalized individualism—then there were only two
choices before it: the conquest of existing institutions
by legislative action and the establishment of new state
colleges supported by land grants and public revenues, bringing the rich to book through the tax collector's office.

In the end, as things turned out, there was no choice at
all, for an attempt to conquer the older colleges by political
control was defeated by Chief Justice Marshall in the celebrated Dartmouth College case, decided in 1819—a spectacular event more important in American educational
history than the founding of any single institution of higher
learning. By securing the boards of trustees of endowed
educational institutions against political interference, the
Dartmouth decision in effect decreed that a large part of
the terrain of the higher learning should be forever occupied
and controlled by private corporations composed of citizens
empowered to select their own successors, collect and dis-
burse money, choose presidents and professors, and more
or less directly determine the letter and spirit of the
curriculum.

In the story of that famous lawsuit are revealed entertaining phases of the economics and politics of the period.
Dartmouth College was founded in the reign of King
George III by a royal charter and was managed by a
small self-perpetuating board of trustees, fashioned on the

model of the trading corporation. In the natural course of things the board passed into the control of stanch Federalists who adhered to the ways of their party. But with the uprush of Jeffersonian Democracy discontent appeared in the state of New Hampshire and also in the college. Under the pressure of the new forces, a Democratic legislature and governor attempted a conquest of the college by changing it into a university, enlarging the board of trustees, adding a number of political appointees, and in effect transforming it into a state institution.

Not to be outdone by this Jeffersonian maneuver, the Federalist faction began to fight the state legislature through the courts of law, carrying the case finally to the Supreme Court at Washington, where that loyal Federalist, John Marshall, still held the wheel, with failing grip, it is true, but yet powerfully. Very astutely, the old board of trustees engaged as its counsel Daniel Webster, that formidable opponent of everything Jeffersonian, to wage its judicial battle. When the case was tried at the state court in Exeter, Webster made the first of his sentimental speeches, introducing into a purely legal argument, as Rufus Choate said, a "pathos" that hardly seemed "in good taste."

Before the Supreme Court in Washington, Webster resorted to the same tactics, suffusing and crowning his legal argument with shrewd appeals to Federalist emotions and word-patterns, none of which was lost on Marshall, who hated Jefferson and all his works with an almost immeasurable intensity. Marshall was easily convinced, but at first, it appears, a majority of the Court, now coming steadily under current influence through judicious appointments, was against Webster and the old board of trustees. Discreet, as well as valorous, Marshall postponed the decision until his colleagues could be brought around to his views. When at length the decision was reached, it was announced that the charter granted by King George to the college was a contract; that the obligation of the contract was transferred to the state at the time of the Revolution; and that under the federal Constitution the state legislature could not "impair" its binding force. In short, there was to be no political interference with educational companies.

The way was thus definitely cleared for the development of control over the higher learning in America. Private corporations—usually religious in origins, for skeptics seldom endowed colleges—were free to go on with their historic mission secure from popular storms. Under the protection of the Dartmouth doctrine, established colleges, such as Harvard, Yale, and Princeton, continued, gathering in slowly, very slowly, gifts of money to augment their meager endowments. And under the same ægis, the religious sects, Methodists, Baptists, Presbyterians, and all the others, founded new colleges in the East and South—and all over the West as the frontier advanced toward the setting sun—small colleges usually, poorly endowed, mainly sustained by tuition fees and subscriptions of the faithful, theological in spirit, and generally managed by clergymen of the denomination, the most active and interested parties to the undertakings.

Running parallel with this development, nevertheless, was the growth of state colleges and universities in the South and West; a slow growth owing to the competition of private and sectarian colleges and the unwillingness of farmers to tax themselves heavily for the support of higher learning. If any one of these institutions is to be singled out for comment it must be the University of Virginia, inspired by Thomas Jefferson and opened in 1825, the year before his death. Created by the state legislature and governed by a board of visitors appointed by the governor and council, freed, in theory though not in fact, from sectarian control, and reflecting the spirit of its founder, this university broke from the classical traditions of the original semi-theological institutions, provided a broad curriculum, and permitted students to elect their course from among eight programs: ancient languages, modern languages, mathematics, natural philosophy, moral philosophy, chemistry, medicine, and law. To assure instruction of the highest grade, Jefferson selected the best professors he could find at home or abroad to fill the first chairs, setting a noble example to his successors, especially to the small sectarian colleges where denominational orthodoxy, rather than high competence, was the prime consideration.

Yet, notable as Jefferson's experiment was, it received small tribute from the organizers of public institutions in other states, even in the West in the days of triumphant Jacksonian Democracy, partly, perhaps, on account of clerical influences, the prevalence of New England traditions among the upper classes, and in the later period at least the influx of Prussian concepts of university organization, such, for example, as were adopted in the case of Michigan University, opened in 1841. After all it was not surprising that the democracy of the age found expression slowly in the higher learning—as in the upper ranges of judicial control.

With respect to curricula, the advocates of science and humanistic subjects were able to make only a few inroads upon the classical monopoly handed down from time immemorial. Clerical control in the old and new private colleges assured close adherence to Greek, Latin, logic, and moral philosophy; and the new state institutions, even Jefferson's defiant University of Virginia, could not escape the denominational drive on boards of trustees. Still, sheltered as they were from the wind and the rain, the colleges could not evade entirely the impact of worldly interests less subtly utilitarian than theology, law, and medicine.

Steadily, if gradually, science, called by a critic "the religion of modern industry," made headway in collegiate curricula, culminating near the close of the period in the establishment of the Lawrence Scientific School at Harvard, endowed by Webster's great friend and patron, Abbot Lawrence, and the Sheffield Scientific School at Yale, with the financial assistance of Joseph Sheffield, a rich merchant, one of the charter members of the New York and New Haven

Railway Company. In keeping with the growing recognition accorded to science was a rising appreciation of political economy and modern languages. Between 1820 and 1835, Harvard, Yale, Columbia, Dartmouth, Princeton, and Williams added the study of mercantile and business affairs to the respectable themes inherited from the landed clergy of medieval times, forecasting a time when "economics" was to become a favorite topic of instruction and learning.

With the drift of American students to Germany—a drift indicated by figures showing four of them in German universities in 1835 and seventy-seven in 1860—and their return to assume places of leadership in American university life, the secular and critical trend already evident in academic disciplines was accelerated, marking there as everywhere in culture the all-devouring operation of practical and earthly concerns.

§

However heavy were the borrowings of America from Europe, her political institutions, social customs, and intellectual development arrested the thought of those philosophers of the Old World who were trying to cast horoscopes of the future. The machine process was marching with seven league boots upon the already straggling ranks of peasants, feudal lords, and clergy. And all who stood upon the watchtower—those who faced to-morrow in confidence and those who filled the hours with lamentations—had to take note even of that Jacksonian democracy which the British Foreign Quarterly called "horn-handed and pig-headed, hard, persevering, unscrupulous, carnivorous . . . with an incredible genius for lying."

Like locusts a host of travelers descended upon the land and those given to literary expression wrote volumes on every phase of American life. And when their reflections and strictures were all thoroughly sifted, it was made apparent that both critics and friends of American institutions were addressing themselves to groups and classes in their native lands rather than to the experimenters on this side of the water. Every chapter of de Tocqueville's democracy in America mirrored his own political moods and bore a relation to the political currents in which he floated in France. The same was true of Harriet Martineau's volume on American society written in the midst of Jackson's triumphant career as President. Bringing to her travels in the United States a liberal and humanitarian mind, she saw clearest those phases of American life most directly tangent to the matters she was interested in at home. "Not by aggression," wrote Oliver Wendell Holmes, "but by the naked fact of existence we are an eternal danger and an unsleeping threat to every government that founds itself on anything but the will of the governed." As Maitland long afterward exclaimed in another connection: "Such is the unity of all history."

VOLUME II
THE
INDUSTRIAL
ERA

THE RISE OF
AMERICAN CIVILIZATION

CHAPTER XVII

The Approach of the Irrepressible Conflict

HAD the economic systems of the North and the South remained static or changed slowly without effecting immense dislocations in the social struc-ture, the balance of power might have been maintained in, definitely by repeating the compensatory tactics of 1787, 1820, 1833, and 1850; keeping in this manner the inherent antagonisms within the bounds of diplomacy. But nothing was stable in the economy of the United States or in the moral sentiments associated with its diversities.

Within each section of the country, the necessities of the productive system were generating portentous results. The

3

periphery of the industrial vortex of the Northeast was daily enlarging, agriculture in the Northwest was being steadily supplemented by manufacturing, and the area of virgin soil open to exploitation by planters was diminishing with rhythmic regularity—shifting with mechanical precision the weights which statesmen had to adjust in their efforts to maintain the equilibrium of peace. Within each of the three sections also occurred an increasing intensity of social concentration as railways, the telegraph, and the press made travel and communication cheap and almost instantaneous, facilitating the centripetal process that was drawing people of similar economic status and parallel opinions into coöperative activities. Finally the intellectual energies released by accumulating wealth and growing leisure—stimulated by the expansion of the reading public and the literary market—developed with deepened accuracy the word-patterns of the current social persuasions, contributing with galvanic effect to the consolidation of identical groupings.

§

As the years passed, the planting leaders of Jefferson's agricultural party insisted with mounting fervor that the opposition, first of the Whigs and then of the Republicans, was at bottom an association of interests formed for the purpose of plundering productive management and labor on the land. And with steadfast insistence they declared that in the insatiable greed of their political foes lay the source of the dissensions which were tearing the country asunder. "There is not a pursuit in which man is engaged (agriculture excepted)," exclaimed Reuben Davis of Mississippi in 1860, "which is not demanding legislative aid to enable it to enlarge its profits and all at the expense of the primary pursuit of man—agriculture. . . . Those interests, having a common purpose of plunder, have united and combined to use the government as the instrument of their operation and have thus virtually converted it into a consolidated empire. Now this combined host of interests stands arrayed against the agricultural states; and this is the reason of the conflict which like an earthquake is shaking our political fabric to its foundation." The furor over slavery is a mere subterfuge to cover other purposes. "Relentless avarice stands firm with its iron heel upon the Constitution." This creature, "incorporated avarice," has chained "the agricultural states to the northern rock" and lives like a vulture upon their prosperity. It is the effort of Prometheus to burst his manacles that provokes the assault on slavery. "These states struggle like a giant," continued Davis, "and alarm these incorporated interests, lest they may break the chain that binds them to usurpation; and therefore they are making this fierce onslaught upon the slave property of the southern states."

The fact that free-soil advocates waged war only on slavery in the territories was to Jefferson Davis conclusive proof of an underlying conspiracy against agriculture. He professed more respect for the abolitionist than for the free-soiler. The former, he said, is dominated by an honest conviction that slavery is wrong everywhere and that all men ought to be free; the latter does not assail slavery in the states—he merely wishes to abolish it in the territories that are in due course to be admitted to the Union.

With challenging directness, Davis turned upon his opponents in the Senate and charged them with using slavery as a blind to delude the unwary: "What do you propose, gentlemen of the Free-Soil party? Do you propose to better the condition of the slave? Not at all. What then do you propose? You say you are opposed to the expansion of slavery. . . . Is the slave to be benefited by it? Not at all. It is not humanity that influences you in the position which you now occupy before the country. . . . It is that you may have an opportunity of cheating us that you want to limit slave territory within circumscribed bounds. It is that you may have a majority in the Congress of the United States and convert the Government into an engine of northern aggrandizement. It is that your section may grow in power and prosperity upon treasures unjustly taken from the South, like the vampire bloated and gorged with the blood which it has secretly sucked from its victim . . . You desire to weaken the political power of the southern states; and why? Because you want, by an unjust system of legislation, to promote the industry of the New England states, at the expense of the people of the South and their industry."

Such in the mind of Jefferson Davis, fated to be president of the Confederacy, was the real purpose of the party which sought to prohibit slavery in the territories; that party did not declare slavery to be a moral disease calling for the severe remedy of the surgeon; it merely sought to keep bondage out of the new states as they came into the Union —with one fundamental aim in view, namely, to gain political ascendancy in the government of the United States and fasten upon the country an economic policy that meant the exploitation of the South for the benefit of northern capitalism.

§

But the planters were after all fighting against the census returns, as the phrase of the day ran current. The amazing growth of northern industries, the rapid extension of railways, the swift expansion of foreign trade to the ends of the earth, the attachment of the farming regions of the West to the centers of manufacture and finance through transportation and credit, the destruction of state consciousness by migration, the alien invasion, the erection of new commonwealths in the Valley of Democracy, the nationalistic drive of interstate commerce, the increase of population in the North, and the southward pressure of the capitalistic glacier all conspired to assure the ultimate triumph of what the orators were fond of calling "the free labor system." This was a dynamic thrust far too powerful for planters operating in a limited territory with incompetent labor on soil of diminishing fertility. Those who swept forward with it, exulting in the approaching triumph of machine industry, warned the planters of their ultimate subjection.

To statesmen of the invincible forces recorded in the census returns, the planting opposition was a huge, compact, and self-conscious economic association bent upon political objects—the possession of the government of the United States, the protection of its interests against adverse legislation, dominion over the territories, and enforcement of the national fugitive slave law throughout the length and breadth of the land. No phrase was more often on the lips of northern statesmen than "the slave power." The pages of the Congressional Globe bristled with references to "the slave system" and its influence over the government of the country. But it was left for William H. Seward of New York to describe it with a fullness of familiar knowledge that made his characterization a classic.

Seward knew from experience that a political party was no mere platonic society engaged in discussing abstractions. "A party," he said, "is in one sense a joint stock association, in which those who contribute most direct the action and management of the concern. The slaveholders contributing in an overwhelming proportion to the capital strength of the Democratic party, they necessarily dictate and prescribe its policy. The inevitable caucus system enables them to do this with a show of fairness and justice." This class of slaveholders, consisting of only three hundred and forty-seven thousand persons, Seward went on to say, was spread from the banks of the Delaware to the banks of the Rio Grande; it possessed nearly all the real estate in that section, owned more than three million other "persons" who were denied all civil and political rights, and inhibited "freedom of speech, freedom of press, freedom of the ballot box, freedom of education, freedom of literature, and freedom of popular assemblies. . . . The slaveholding class has become the governing power in each of the slaveholding states and it practically chooses thirty of the sixty-two members of the Senate, ninety of the two hundred and thirty-three members of the House of Representatives, and one hundred and five of the two hundred and ninety-five electors of the President and Vice-President of the United States."

Becoming still more concrete, Seward accused the President of being "a confessed apologist of the slave-property class." Examining the composition of the Senate, he found the slave-owning group in possession of all the important committees. Peering into the House of Representatives he discovered no impregnable bulwark of freedom there. Nor did respect for judicial ermine compel him to spare the Supreme Court. With irony he exclaimed: "How fitting does the proclamation of its opening close with the invocation: 'God save the United States and this honorable court. . . . The court consists of a chief justice and eight associate justices. Of these five were called from slave states and four from free states. The opinions and bias of each of them were carefully considered by the President and Senate when he was appointed. Not one of them was found wanting in soundness of politics, according to the slaveholder's exposition of the Constitution, and those who were called from the free states were even more distinguished in that respect than their brethren from the slaveholding states."

Seward then analyzed the civil service of the national government and could descry not a single person among the thousands employed in the post office, the treasury, and other great departments who was "false to the slaveholding interest." Under the spoils system, the dominion of the slavocracy extended into all branches of the federal administration. "The customs-houses and the public lands pour forth two golden streams—one into the elections to procure votes for the slaveholding class; and the other into the treasury to be enjoyed by those whom it shall see fit to reward with places in the public service." Even in the

North, religion, learning, and the press were under the spell of this masterful class, frightened lest they incur its wrath.

Having described the gigantic operating structure of the slavocracy, Seward drew with equal power a picture of the opposing system founded on "free labor." He surveyed the course of economy in the North—the growth of industry, the spread of railways, the swelling tide of European immigration, and the westward roll of free farmers—rounding out the country, knitting it together, bringing "these antagonistic systems" continually into closer contact. Then he uttered those fateful words which startled conservative citizens from Maine to California—words of prophecy which proved to be brutally true—"the irrepressible conflict."

This inexorable clash, he said, was not "accidental, unnecessary, the work of interested or fanatical agitators and therefore ephemeral." No. "It is an irrepressible conflict between opposing and enduring forces." The hopes of those who sought peace by appealing to slave owners to reform themselves were as chaff in a storm. "How long and with what success have you waited already for that reformation? Did any property class ever so reform itself? Did the patricians in old Rome, the noblesse or clergy in France? The landholders in Ireland? The landed aristocracy in England? Does the slaveholding class even seek to beguile you with such a hope? Has it not become rapacious, arrogant, defiant?" All attempts at compromise were "vain and ephemeral." There was accordingly but one supreme task before the people of the United States—the task of confounding and overthrowing "by one decisive blow the betrayers of the Constitution and freedom forever." In uttering this indictment, this prophecy soon to be fulfilled with such appalling accuracy, Seward stepped beyond the bounds of cautious politics and read himself out of the little group of men who were eligible for the Republican nomination in 1860. Frantic efforts to soften his words by explanations and additions could not appease his critics.

§

Given an irrepressible conflict which could be symbolized in such unmistakable patterns by competent interpreters of opposing factions, a transfer of the issues from the forum to the field, from the conciliation of diplomacy to the decision of arms was bound to come. Each side obdurately bent upon its designs and convinced of its rectitude, by the fulfillment of its wishes precipitated events and effected distributions of power that culminated finally in the tragedy foretold by Seward. Those Democrats who operated on historic knowledge rather than on prophetic insight, recalling how many times the party of Hamilton had been crushed at elections, remembering how the Whigs had never been able to carry the country on a cleancut Webster-Clay program, and counting upon the continued support of a huge array of farmers and mechanics marshaled behind the planters, imagined apparently that politics—viewed as the science of ballot enumeration—could resolve the problems of power raised by the maintenance of the Union.

And in this opinion they were confirmed by the outcome of the presidential campaign in 1852, when the Whigs, with General Winfield Scott, a hero of the Mexican war, at their head, were thoroughly routed by the Democratic candidate, General Franklin Pierce of New Hampshire. Indeed the verdict of the people was almost savage, for Pierce carried every state but four, receiving 254 out of 296 electoral votes. The Free-Soil party that branded slavery as a crime and called for its prohibition in the territories scarcely made a ripple, polling only 156,000 out of more than three million votes, a figure below the record set in the previous campaign.

With the Whigs beaten and the Free-Soilers evidently a dwindling handful of negligible critics, exultant Democrats took possession of the Executive offices and Congress, inspired by a firm belief that their tenure was secure. Having won an overwhelming victory on a definite tariff for revenue and pro-slavery program, they acted as if the party of Hamilton was for all practical purposes as powerless as the little band of abolitionist agitators. At the succeeding election in 1856 they again swept the country—this time with James Buchanan of Pennsylvania as their candidate. Though his triumph was not as magisterial as that of Pierce it was great enough to warrant a conviction that the supremacy of the Democratic party could not be broken at the polls.

During these eight years of tenure, a series of events occurred under Democratic auspices, which clinched the grasp of the planting interest upon the country and produced a correlative consolidation of the opposition. One line of development indicated an indefinite extension of the slave area; another the positive withdrawal of all government support from industrial and commercial enterprise. The first evidence of the new course came in the year immediately following the inauguration of Pierce. In 1854, Congress defiantly repealed the Missouri Compromise and threw open to slavery the vast section of the Louisiana Purchase which had been closed to it by the covenant adopted more than three decades before. On the instant came a rush of slavery champions from Missouri into Kansas determined to bring it into the southern sphere of influence. Not content with the conquest of the forbidden West, filibustering parties under pro-slavery leaders attempted to seize Cuba and Nicaragua and three American ministers abroad flung out to the world a flaming proclamation, known as the "Ostend Manifesto," which declared that the United States would be justified in wresting Cuba from Spain by force—acts of imperial aggression which even the Democratic administration in Washington felt constrained to repudiate.

Crowning the repeal of the Missouri Compromise came

two decisions of the Supreme Court giving sanction to the expansion of slavery in America and assuring high protection for that peculiar institution even in the North. In the Dred Scott case decided in March, 1857, Chief Justice Taney declared in effect that the Missouri Compromise had been void from the beginning and that Congress had no power under the Constitution to prohibit slavery in the territories of the United States anywhere at any time. This legal triumph for the planting interest was followed in 1859 by another decision in which the Supreme Court upheld the fugitive slave law and all the drastic procedure provided for its enforcement. To the frightened abolitionists it seemed that only one more step was needed to make freedom unconstitutional throughout the country.

These extraordinary measures on behalf of slavery were accompanied by others that touched far more vitally economic interests in the North. In 1859, the last of the subsidies for trans-Atlantic steamship companies was ordered discontinued by Congress. In 1857, the tariff was again reduced, betraying an unmistakable drift of the nation toward free trade. In support of this action, the representatives of the South and Southwest were almost unanimous and they gathered into their fold a large number of New England congressmen on condition that no material reductions should be made in duties on cotton goods. On the other hand, the Middle States and the West offered a large majority against tariff reduction so that the division was symptomatic.

Immediately after the new revenue law went into effect an industrial panic burst upon the country, spreading distress among business men and free laborers. While that tempest was running high, the paper money anarchy let loose by the Democrats reached the acme of virulence as the notes of wildcat banks flooded the West and South and financial institutions crashed in every direction, fifty-one failing in Indiana alone within a period of five years. Since all hope of reviving Hamilton's system of finance had been buried, those who believed that a sound currency was essential to national prosperity were driven to the verge of desperation. On top of these economic calamities came Buchanan's veto of the Homestead bill which the impatient agrarians had succeeded in getting through Congress in a compromise form—an act of presidential independence which angered the farmers and mechanics who regarded the national domain as their own inheritance.

§

Two incidents in this series of startling events deserve special consideration on account of their prominence in the forensics that decorated the struggle; namely, the repeal of the Missouri Compromise and the Dred Scott decision. In connection with the organization of two new western territories, Kansas and Nebraska, in 1854, Congress provided that, when they were admitted to the Union, they could come in, with or without slavery, as their respective constitutions might provide. Since these territories lay north of the Missouri Compromise line, the provision in effect set aside the solemn understanding which had bound the two sections of the country for so many years. To clear up all doubts, Congress expressly declared that the Missouri covenant of 1820 was null and void as contrary to the principle of non-intervention with the institution of slavery in the territories.

The authorship of this program is generally ascribed to Stephen A. Douglas, a Democratic Senator from Illinois, and his action in the premises imputed to his overweening desire to become President of the United States. Though Douglas took upon himself both the onus and the honor of the repeal, Senator Atchison of Missouri, a spokesman of local slave owners eager to break over into the rich region to the west, claimed to have inspired the stroke. The nature of American politics lends plausibility to this latter view.

However, the point is not important. The significant

feature of the maneuver was the vote on the repeal in Congress. In the Senate fourteen southern Democrats, nine southern Whigs, and fourteen northern Democrats voted in favor of the bill; while four northern Democrats, six northern Whigs, two Free-Soilers, one southern Democrat, and one southern Whig voted against it. In short, two southern votes were recorded against the measure in the Upper Chamber. Of the hundred votes cast against it in the House of Representatives, only nine came from the slave states while forty-two Democrats from the North broke from their party and joined the dissenters. Considered in any light, the division was ominous: the repeal represented the demand of an almost solid South supported by a wing of the northern Democrats—effecting a triumph for the planters that fell only a little bit below Calhoun's extreme demand. True, the Kansas-Nebraska act did not absolutely force slavery upon the states to be admitted from the region in question but it made slavery lawful in the territories and permitted the residents to decide the ultimate question for themselves.

Just one more legal step was essential to win for the planting interest the whole territorial domain of the nation, and secure its weight in the balance of power apparently for all time. That step was a decision by the Supreme Court declaring that Congress had no authority under the Constitution to abolish or prohibit slavery in any of the territories. If the Constitution could be so interpreted, then either a reversal of the decision or an amendment would be necessary before Congress could undo the effect of the decree. Since the judges held for life and the approval of the Senate was necessary to new appointments, the possibility of getting a fresh reading of the auspices was remote. On the other hand, approval by three-fourths of the states being required for the adoption of an amendment, a reversal by that means was inconceivable. If the coveted interpretation could be obtained, the planting states would be safe forever. At least so it seemed to those wise in their generation. But one point was overlooked in the calculations, namely, the likelihood of revolution.

Either by accident or intent the great issue was presented to the Supreme Court in 1856 by the celebrated Dred Scott case. Scott was a slave who had been taken by his master into the upper Louisiana territory in the days when, theoretically at least, the Missouri Compromise was still in force and slavery was forbidden in that region. After a term of residence there, the bondman had been returned to the state of Missouri where he sued for his liberty on the ground of having been in free territory. Was he then a free man or a slave? The whole affair could have been put under that simple rubric.

The Supreme Court could have answered the question in a few words without mentioning the Missouri Compromise or the power of Congress to abolish slavery in the territories owned by the United States. With perfect ease, the judges could have disposed of the case by saying: "Whatever was the status of Scott in the upper Louisiana region while he was there, he was restored to bondage on his return to slave soil and is now a slave." Indeed when the matter was first argued, a majority of the Court agreed among themselves that the issue should be decided without discussing the thorny question that was agitating the country. But after reaching this agreement, the majority for various reasons changed their minds and in the end Chief Justice Taney rendered an opinion not vital to the disposition of the case in which he declared that the act of Congress, known as the Missouri Compromise, was null and void; that Congress could not constitutionally abolish slavery in the territories. Thus he gave a stunning blow to the young Republican party whose cardinal doctrine was that Congress should establish freedom in all the territories; and evidently he had ignored all anti-slavery agitators of every sort and condition.

Thinking that the issue had now been settled by a decree of final authority, statesmen from the South called upon their countrymen to show proper respect for the highest tribunal in the land, a counsel of loyalty natural enough in the circumstances. And yet in a reaction equally natural, the Republicans rejected the advice. Under their influence northern legislatures denounced the opinion of Chief Justice Taney as extra-judicial in character, as sheer usurpation, and without binding effect upon the people. In Congress and outside, Democrats were taunted with having once opposed the constitutionality of the United States Bank after Chief Justice Marshall had set his high seal of legal approval upon it. Into their teeth Republican leaders flung quotations from Jefferson's attacks upon the Supreme Court made long before on similar occasions when that tribunal had pretended to act as the final arbiter in constitutional conflicts.

Convinced that the decision was a political trick, Abraham Lincoln said that, while Republicans would accept the decree of the Court remanding Scott to servitude, they would frankly reject its opinion respecting the power of Congress over slavery itself. Elaborating this idea, he declared that the President and Congress ought to disregard Taney's opinion as a rule of law, that slavery ought to be abolished in the territories in spite of the doctrines announced by the Court, and that the opinion ought to be reversed by a peaceful method—meaning of course a reconstruction of the Court through an efficient use of the appointing power. It had been done by Jacksonian Democracy. It could be done again.

The more Lincoln thought about the Dred Scott case, the hotter became his resentment. Finally he broke out in a militant note: "Familiarize yourselves with the chains of bondage and you prepare your own limbs to wear them. Accustomed to trample on the rights of others, you have lost the genius of your own independence and become the fit subjects of the first cunning tyrant who rises among you. And let me tell you, that all these things are prepared for you by the teachings of history, if the elections shall promise that the next Dred Scott decision and all future decisions will be quietly acquiesced in by the people."

Going beyond this view, some of his party colleagues openly denounced the action of the Court as a political conspiracy arranged by the President, certain members of Congress, and the pro-slavery judges of the Court for the purpose of fastening chattel bondage upon the territories forever. This extreme contention they rested on mere incidents. It so happened that Buchanan, in his inaugural address on March 4, 1857, a few days before the opinion of the Court in the Dred Scott case was made public, referred to the forthcoming decision and expressed his intention, in common with all other good citizens, to submit cheerfully to the ruling of the Court, "whatever this may be." To Senator Seward, Republican leader from New York, the President's declaration was sheer mockery. In a terrific indictment delivered in the Senate, he asserted that Buchanan "approached or was approached by the Supreme Court of the United States," arranged with that tribunal to hang the millstone of slavery on the neck of the people of Kansas, and knew very well when he blandly promised to abide by the will of the Court just what its decision would be.

Naturally this charge made a tremendous sensation, bringing down on the Senator's head the severest criticism from conservatives. On all sides he was accused of making assertions for which he had not the slightest proof. Indeed his attack was seemingly so rash and so unjustified that for more than half a century even northern historians agreed in condemning it. Professor John W. Burgess, for example, after looking over the evidence available in 1899, when he wrote on the middle period, declared that "both Mr. Buchanan and Mr. Taney were men of the highest personal and official character and possessed the most delicate sense of the requirements and proprieties of the great stations which they occupied. It is almost certain that the charge was an unfounded suspicion." James Ford Rhodes, in the first edition of his history, later modified, was still more emphatic: collusion between Buchanan and the impeccable Taney was simply impossible.

There the matter rested until the publication of President Buchanan's papers in 1910 revealed a portion of the truth. Among those records was a note from Justice Catron of the Supreme Court, dated February 19, 1857, thirteen days before the inaugural address in question—a note in which the Justice informs Buchanan that the constitutionality of the Missouri Compromise line will be decided by the Court shortly in the Dred Scott case and asks the President-elect to write to Justice Grier stating how necessary it is to "settle the agitation by an affirmative decision of the Supreme Court, the one way or the other." Acting on the suggestion Buchanan wrote to Justice Grier; just what we do not know for it seems the letter has been lost. Apparently he urged the Justice to fall in line; at all events a reply from Grier, dated February 23, 1857—nine days before the inauguration—acknowledges the receipt of a communication from Buchanan, gives a brief history of the Dred Scott case, discusses the forthcoming decision of the Court, states that the Missouri Compromise line will be declared invalid, and adds that the opinion will be rendered by March 6th. The Justice then concludes: "Though contrary to our usual practice, we have thought it due to you to state in candor and confidence the real state of the matter." So Senator Seward had a stronger foundation for his indictment than he himself imagined.

For a brief moment after the publication of the Buchanan papers, it looked as if the Dred Scott decision had really been framed by the President of the United States and certain Justices of the Supreme Court, but later revelations gave the matter still another aspect. Within a few years certain records belonging to Justice McLean of the Supreme Court were placed in the Library of Congress, opening to students a new chapter in the story of this crucial case.

In the light of unquestionable evidence, it appears that, when the majority of the judges decided at first to avoid the vexatious issue of the Missouri Compromise, Justice McLean announced to them his intention to file a dissenting opinion in the nature of a stump speech maintaining the power of Congress to abolish slavery in the territories— sound doctrine according to the politics of the Republican party. Now Justice McLean, like so many others in his day, was consumed by the ambition to be President of the United States and was in fact a strenuous seeker for that high office during more than a decade. Beyond question, he attempted to wring the nomination from the Republicans in 1856 and he sent active agents to present his appeal in Chicago four years later. And the dissenting opinion which he finally filed in the Dred Scott case upheld the power of Congress to exclude slavery from the territories, thus in effect setting forth the very political principles which he authorized his workers to employ in the quest for the Republican prize.

Beyond doubt accordingly the stiff insistence of Justice McLean upon the promulgation of his views at all costs was a leading factor in forcing the pro-slavery judges to come out against the validity of the Missouri Compromise. They were also aided in arriving at this conclusion by the knowledge that Wayne, a southern Justice, would announce pro-slavery doctrines in a dissenting opinion if they did not squarely face the issue. So the ambitions and passions of both political parties were in reality responsible for the judicial opinion that rocked the country from one end to the other. At any rate the Dred Scott decision was not a deliberate conspiracy on the part of the slavocracy.

§

The amazing acts of mastery—legislative, executive, judicial—committed by the federal government in the decade between 1850 and 1860 changed the whole political climate of America. They betrayed a growing consolidation in the planting group, its increased dominance in the Democratic party, and an evident determination to realize its economic interests and protect its labor system at all hazards. In a kind of doom, they seemed to mark the final supremacy of the political army which had swept into office with Andrew Jackson. During the thirty-two years between that event and the inauguration of Lincoln, the Democrats controlled the Presidency and the Senate for twenty-four years, the Supreme Court for twenty-six years, and the House of Representatives for twenty-two years. By the end of the period, the old farmer-labor party organized by Jackson had passed under the dominion of the planting interest and the farming wing of the North was confronted with the alternative of surrender or secession.

In this shift of power the Whigs of the South, discovering the tendencies of the popular balloting, moved steadily over into the Democratic camp. Though unavoidable, the transfer was painful; the planting Whigs, being rich and influential, had little affection for the white farmers who rallied around the Jacksonian banner. According to the estimate of a southern newspaper in 1850, the Whigs owned at least three-fourths of all the slaves in the country and it was a matter of common knowledge that leaders among them disliked wildcat banking as much as they hated high duties on the manufactured goods they bought. Indeed to a southern gentleman of the old school the radical agrarianism of Andrew Johnson was probably more odious than the tariff schedules devised by Daniel Webster. It was said that one of them, when asked whether a gentleman could be a Democrat, snapped back the tart reply: "Well, he is not apt to be; but if he is, he is in damned bad company."

But the rich planters were relatively few in numbers and virtue was subject to the law of necessity; the populace had the votes, northern manufacturers were demanding protection, abolitionists were agitating, and in the end all but the most conservative remnant of the southern Whigs had to go over to the party that professed the dangerous doctrines of

Jackson. The achievements of the years that lay between 1850 and 1860 seemed to justify the sacrifice.

Though the drift toward the irrepressible conflict was steady and strong, as events revealed, the politics of the decade had the outward semblances of dissolution. The abolitionists and free-soilers, while a mere minority as we have seen, were able to worry the politicians of both parties in the North. Largely deserted by their southern cohorts, the Whigs, whose organization had always been tenuous at best, could discover no way of mustering a majority of votes on the bare economic policies of Hamilton and Webster. Their two victories—in 1840 and 1848—had been dubious and their only hope for a triumph at the polls lay in a combination with other factors.

To this confusion in party affairs, the intellectual and religious ferment of the age added troublesome factional disputes. A temperance element, strong enough to carry prohibition in a few states, was giving the politicians anxiety in national campaigns. A still more formidable cabal, the Know Nothing, or American Party, sprang up in the current opposition to foreigners, the papacy, infidelity, and socialism. Combining the functions of a party and a fraternal order, it nominated candidates for office and adopted secret rites, dark mysteries, grips, and passwords which gave it an atmosphere of uncertain vitality. Members were admitted by solemn ceremony into full fellowship with "The Supreme Order of the Star-spangled Banner," whose "daily horror and nightly specter was the pope." When asked about their principles, they replied mysteriously: "I know nothing." Appealing to deep-seated emotions, this movement showed strength in many localities and was only dissolved by the smashing energy of more momentous issues.

§

The signal for a general realignment of factions and parties was given by the passage of the Kansas-Nebraska bill of 1854 repealing the Missouri Compromise. In fact, while that measure was pending in Congress a coalescing movement was to be observed: northern Whigs persuaded that their old party was moribund, Democrats weary of planting dominance, and free-soilers eager to exclude slavery from the territories began to draw together to resist the advance of the planting power. In February of that year, a number of Whigs and Democrats assembled at Ripon, Wisconsin, and resolved that a new party must be formed if the bill passed.

When the expected event occurred, the Ripon insurgents created a fusion committee and chose the name "Republican" as the title of their young political association. In July, a Michigan convention composed of kindred elements demanded the repeal of the Kansas-Nebraska act, the repeal of the fugitive slave law, and the abolition of slavery in the District of Columbia. This convention also agreed to postpone all differences "with regard to political economy or administrative policy" and stay in the field as a "Republican" party until the struggle against slavery extension was finished. All over the country similar meetings were mustered and the local cells of the new national party rose into being. Meanwhile the old Whigs who wanted peace and prosperity were floating about looking for any drifting wreckage that might hold them above the waves.

As the election of 1856 approached, the Republicans made ready to enter the national field. After a preliminary conference at Pittsburgh, they held a national convention at Philadelphia and nominated for the presidency, John C. Frémont, the Western explorer, a son-in-law of Benton, the faithful Jacksonian Democrat. In their platform they made the exclusion of slavery from the territories—and of necessity its economic and political implications—the paramount issue. So restricted, the platform offered no prizes to regular Whigs, no tariff, banking, or currency reforms; rather did it appeal to the farmers of the Jeffersonian school —men who were not slave owners and did not expect to enter that class, men who were determined to keep slavery out of the territories and to make the federal domain an estate for free farmers.

Lest there be some misunderstanding, they made it clear throughout their campaign that they were not trying to revive the Federalist or the Whig party. They were conscious of the fact that the name "Republican" of which they boasted was the device chosen by Jefferson for his embattled farmers and used by his followers until they fell under the sway of Jackson. "There is not a plank in our platform," exclaimed one of the Republican orators from Wisconsin before the great accommodation of 1860, "which does not conform to the principles of Jefferson; the man who, of all others, has ever been regarded as the true representative of the Republican party of this country. He was its representative in the Congress of 1776. He was its leader and representative in 1800; he was its true representative in 1812; he is the true representative of the Republican party to-day. We stand, Sir, upon his doctrines and we fight for his principles. We stand upon no sectional platform; we present no sectional issues . . . and we are coming to take possession of this government, to administer it for the whole country, North and South; and suffer monopolists neither of the North or the South to control its administration and so shape its action as to subserve the interests of the aristocratic few." On this platform those who opposed the plutocracy of the East and the planting aristocracy of the South could easily unite.

Replying to the Republican challenge the Democratic organization granted to its pro-slavery wing almost every demand. In its platform of 1856 it reiterated as a matter of course its fixed agricultural creed: no protective tariffs, no national banks, no industrial subsidies, and no Hamiltonian devices. It then commended the bargain of 1850, endorsed slavery as an institution, approved the repeal of the Missouri Compromise, and proposed that the new states to be admitted to the Union should come in with or without slavery as their constitutions might provide. In exchange the northern wing received honorific compensation in the nomination of James Buchanan of Pennsylvania. The South thus got the platform; the North, the candidate.

Defied by the Democrats in front and menaced by the Republicans on the left, the old Whigs, who hated the bother of slavery agitation and merely wanted to get government support for business enterprise, were sorely perplexed. They saw their southern brethren drawn away by the Democratic gift of the Kansas-Nebraska bill and yet they could not find in the Republican platform a promise of protection for industry or a pledge of currency reform. On the face of things, a combination with either of these political associations was impossible and so the Whigs decided to tempt the fates again and alone. At a convention held in Baltimore, they condemned "geographical parties," expressed a reverence for the Constitution and the Union, and nominated Millard Fillmore, a man "eminent for his calm and pacific temperament." As Fillmore had already been blessed by the American, or Know Nothing, party, there was some prospect of effecting a formidable bloc under his leadership.

When the votes were counted in the autumn of 1856, it was clear that a great majority of the people were opposed to anti-slavery agitation in every form. Not only was Buchanan elected by a safe margin on a strong slavery program; he and Fillmore together polled nearly three million votes against less than half that figure cast for Frémont. In other words, Garrison had been at work for a quarter of a century when, by a decision of more than two to one, even the mildest plank in the anti-slavery platform was overwhelmingly repudiated by the country at large. Still Frémont's poll revealed an immense gain in the number of free-soilers as compared with their trivial strength at previous contests, demonstrating in a striking manner that the fight for the possession of the territories, with all it implied in terms of political and economic power at Washington, could not be avoided. Especially did it show the Whigs that they would have to work out a new combination of forces if they expected to get business enterprise on an even keel again.

Fortunately for them, the way to the solution of their problem was pointed out by the election returns: Fillmore had received 874,000 votes, a number which, added to Frémont's total, would have elected a candidate. Given these figures, the question of how to unite free-soil farmers and timid apostles of prosperity became therefore the supreme issue before the political leaders who took their bearings after the storm of 1856 in the hope of finding some method of ousting the Democrats at the next tourney. Neither group could win without the other; the union of either with the planting aristocracy was impossible. Obviously an accommodation—a readjustment of the balance of power—and the right kind of candidate offered to Whigs and free-soil Republicans the only assurance of ultimate victory.

§

"The Government has fallen into the hands of the Slave Power completely," wrote Wendell Phillips in 1854. "So far as national politics are concerned, we are beaten—there's no hope. We shall have Cuba in a year or two, Mexico in five, and I should not wonder if efforts were made to revive the slave trade, though perhaps unsuccessfully, as the northern slave states, which live by the export of slaves, would help us in opposing that. Events hurry forward with amazing rapidity; we live fast here. The future seems to unfold a vast slave empire united with Brazil and darkening the whole West. I hope I may be a false prophet, but the sky was never so dark."

Three years later, when the inauguration of Buchanan had turned discouragement into despair, the only strategic stroke that Phillips and his colleagues could invent was to hold an abolition convention in Massachusetts and adopt a solemn slogan calling for the disruption of the Union with the slave states. And the events of the swiftly flowing months that followed, as we have already indicated, merely seemed to confirm the belief of Phillips in the supremacy of the Democratic party led by the indomitable planting interest; events such as the downward revision of the tariff, the withdrawal of the ship subsidies, and the Dred Scott decision opening the territories to slavery.

All the while the conflict was growing more furious. Advocates of protection, taking advantage of the panic which followed the tariff revision, organized a stirring campaign to wean workingmen from their allegiance to a free-trade Democracy. Advocates of a sound currency protested against the depreciated notes and the wildcat banks that spread ruin through all sections of the land. The abolitionists maintained their fusillade, Garrison and Phillips, despite their pessimism, resting neither day nor night. Going beyond the bounds of mere agitation, the slavery faction of Missouri in its grim determination to conquer Kansas for bondage and northern abolitionists in their equally firm resolve to seize it for freedom convulsed the country by bloody deeds and then by bloody reprisals. In a powerful oration, "The Crime against Kansas," done in classical style but bristling with abuse of the slavery party, Charles Sumner threw Congress into a tumult in 1856 and provided a text for the free-soilers laboring to wrest the government from the planting interest. Before the public excitement caused by this speech had died away, the attention of the nation was arrested by a series of debates between Lincoln and Douglas held in Illinois in 1858—debates which set forth in clear and logical form the program for excluding slavery from the territories and the squatter-sovereignty scheme for letting the inhabitants decide the issue for themselves.

Then came the appalling climax in 1859 when John Brown, after a stormy career in Kansas, tried to kindle a servile insurrection in the South. In the spring of that year,

Brown attended an anti-slavery convention from which he went away muttering: "These men are all talk; what we need is action—action!" Collecting a few daring comrades he made a raid into Harper's Ferry for the purpose of starting a slave rebellion. Though his efforts failed, though he was quickly executed as a "traitor to Virginia," the act of violence rocked the continent from sea to sea.

In vain did the Republicans try to treat it as the mere work of a fanatic and denounce it as "among the gravest of crimes." In vain did Lincoln attempt to minimize it as an absurd adventure that resulted in nothing noteworthy except the death of Brown. It resounded through the land with the clangor of an alarm bell, aggravating the jangling nerves of a people already excited by fears of a race war and continued disturbances over the seizure of slaves under the fugitive slave act—disorders which sometimes assumed the form of menacing riots.

The turmoil in the country naturally found sharp echoes in the halls of Congress. Buchanan's policy of aiding the slavery party in its efforts to get possession of Kansas and the taunting action of the free-soilers in their determination to save it for liberty, gave abundant occasions for debates that grew more and more acrimonious. Indeed the factions in Congress were now almost at swords' points, passion in argument and gesture becoming the commonplace of the day.

When Senator Sumner made a vehement verbal attack on Senator Butler of South Carolina in 1856, Preston Brooks, a Representative from the same state and a relative of the latter, replied in terms of physical force, catching Sumner unawares and beating his victim senseless with a heavy cane. Though the act was not strictly chivalrous—for Sumner, wedged in between his chair and his desk, could not defend himself—admiring South Carolinians gave Brooks a grand banquet and presented him with a new cane bearing the words: "Use knockdown arguments." On both sides of the Senate chamber all the arts of diplomacy were discarded, and the meanest weapons of personal abuse brought into play. Douglas called Sumner a perjurer who spat forth malignity upon his colleagues. The prim, proud Senator from Massachusetts, conscious of possessing a mellow culture, replied by likening Douglas to a "noisome, squat and nameless animal" that filled the Senate with an offensive odor.

Things were even worse in the lower house. Again and again debate was on the verge of physical combat, for which members equipped themselves with knives and revolvers. A Representative from Pennsylvania and another from North Carolina had to be put under bonds to keep the peace. A general mêlée occurred in the spring of 1860 when Lovejoy, whose brother had been shot by a pro-slavery mob in Illinois, made an unbridled attack on slave owners and Democrats, advanced to their side of the house shaking his fists in a terrible rage, and threw the whole chamber into such a confusion that all the resources of experienced leaders were needed to prevent bloodshed then and there. Without exaggeration did Jefferson Davis exclaim that members of Congress were more like the agents of belligerent states than men assembled in the interest of common welfare—an utterance that was startlingly accurate—born of prophetic certainty. After a few fleeting days, the irrepressible conflict that had so long been raging was actually to pass from the forum to the battlefield, to that court where the only argument was the sword and where the one answer that admitted of no appeal was death.

§

Every shocking incident on the one side only consolidated the forces on the other. By 1860 leaders of the planting interest had worked out in great detail their economic and political scheme—their ultimatum to the serried opposition —and embodied it in many official documents. The economic elements were those made familiar to the country through twenty years of agitation: no high protective tariffs, no ship subsidies, no national banking and currency system; in short, none of the measures which business enterprise deemed essential to its progress. The remaining problem before the planting interest, namely, how to clinch its grip and prevent a return to the Hamilton-Webster policy as the industrial North rapidly advanced in wealth and population, was faced with the same penchant for definition.

Plans for accomplishing that purpose were mapped out by able spokesmen from the South in a set of Senate resolutions adopted on May 24-25, 1860: slavery is lawful in all the territories under the Constitution; neither Congress nor a local legislature can abolish it there; the federal government is in duty bound to protect slave owners as well as the holders of other forms of property in the territories; it is a violation of the Constitution for any state or any combination of citizens to intermeddle with the domestic institutions of any other state "on any pretext whatever, political, moral, or religious, with a view to their disturbance or subversion"; open or covert attacks on slavery are contrary to the solemn pledges given by the states on entering the Union to protect and defend one another; the inhabitants of a territory on their admission to the Union may decide whether or not they will sanction slavery thereafter; the strict enforcement of the fugitive slave law is required by good faith and the principles of the Constitution.

In brief, the federal government was to do nothing for business enterprise while the planting interest was to be assured the possession of enough political power to guarantee it against the reënactment of the Hamilton-Webster program. Incidentally the labor system of the planting interest was not to be criticized and all runaway property was to be returned. Anything short of this was, in the view of the planting statesmen, "subversive of the Constitution."

The meaning of the ultimatum was not to be mistaken. It was a demand upon the majority of the people to sur-

render unconditionally for all time to the minority stockholders under the Constitution. It offered nothing to
capitalism but capitulation; to the old Whigs of the South
nothing but submission. Finally—and this was its revolutionary phase—it called upon the farmers and mechanics
who had formed the bulk of Jacksonian Democracy in the
North to acknowledge the absolute sovereignty of the planting interest. Besides driving a wedge into the nation, the
conditions laid down by the planters also split the Democratic party itself into two factions.

Soon after the Democratic convention assembled at
Charleston in April, 1860, this fundamental division became
manifest. The northern wing, while entirely willing
to indorse the general economic program of the planters,
absolutely refused to guarantee them sovereignty in the
party and throughout the country. Rejecting the proposal
of the southern members to make slavery obligatory in the
territories, it would merely offer to "abide by the decisions
of the Supreme Court on all questions of constitutional
law." Since the Dred Scott case had opened all the territories to slavery, that tender seemed generous enough but
the intransigent representatives of the planting interest
would not accept it as adequate. Unable to overcome the
majority commanded in the convention by the northern
group, they withdrew from the assembly, spurning the pleas
of their colleagues not to break up the union of hearts on
"a mere theory" and countering all arguments with a declaration of finality: "Go your way and we will go ours."

After balloting for a time on candidates without reaching a decision under the two-thirds rule, the remaining
members of the Charleston conference adjourned to meet
again at Baltimore. When they reassembled, they nominated Stephen A. Douglas of Illinois, the apostle of
"squatter sovereignty," who was ready to open the territories to slavery but not to guarantee the planting interest
unconditional supremacy in the Democratic party and the
Union. Determined to pursue their separate course to the

bitter end, the Charleston seceders adopted the platform rejected by the Douglas faction and chose as their candidate, John C. Breckinridge of Kentucky, an unyielding champion of planting aristocracy and its labor system. The union of farmers and slave owners was thus severed: the Republicans had carried off one large fragment of the northern farmers in 1856; Douglas was now carrying off another.

§

During the confusion in the Democratic ranks, the Republicans, in high glee over the quarrels of the opposition, held their convention in Chicago—a sectional gathering except for representatives from five slave states. Among its delegates the spirit of opposition to slavery extension, which had inspired the party assembly four years before, was still evident but enthusiasm on that ticklish subject was neutralized by the prudence of the practical politicians who, sniffing victory in the air, had rushed to the new tent. Whigs, whose affections were centered on Hamilton's program rather than on Garrison's scheme of salvation, were to be seen on the floor. Advocates of a high protective tariff and friends of free homesteads for mechanics and farmers now mingled with the ardent opponents of slavery in the territories. With their minds fixed on the substance of things sought for, the partisans of caution were almost able to prevent the convention from indorsing the Declaration of Independence. Still they were in favor of restricting the area of slavery; they had no love for the institution and its spread helped to fasten the grip of the planting interest on the government at Washington. So the Republican convention went on record in favor of liberty for the territories, free homesteads for farmers, a protective tariff, and a Pacific railway. As the platform was read, the cheering became especially loud and prolonged when the homestead and tariff planks were reached. Such at least is the testimony of the stenographic report.

Since this declaration of principles was well fitted to work a union of forces, it was essential that the candidate should not divide them. The protective plank would doubtless line up the good old Whigs of the East but tender consideration had to be shown to the Ohio Valley, original home of Jacksonian Democracy, where national banks, tariffs, and other "abominations" still frightened the wary. Without Ohio, Indiana, and Illinois, the Republican managers could not hope to win and they knew that the lower counties of these states were filled with settlers from the slave belt who had no love for the "money power," abolition, or anything that savored of them. In such circumstances Seward, idol of the Whig wing, was no man to offer that section; he was too radical on the slavery issue and too closely associated with "high finance" in addition. "If you do not nominate Seward, where will you get your money?" was the blunt question put by Seward's loyal supporters at Chicago. The question was pertinent but not fatal.

Given this confluence of problems, a man close to the soil of the West was better suited to the requirements of the hour than a New York lawyer with somewhat fastidious tastes, obviously backed by fat purses. The available candidate was Abraham Lincoln of Illinois. Born in Kentucky, he was of southern origin. A son of poor frontier parents, self-educated, a pioneer who in his youth had labored in field and forest, he appealed to the voters of the backwoods. Still by an uncanny genius for practical affairs, he had forged his way to the front as a shrewd lawyer and politician. In his debates with Douglas he had shown himself able to cope with one of the foremost leaders in the Democratic party. On the tariff, bank, currency, and homestead issues he was sound. A local railway attorney, he was trusted among business men.

On the slavery question Lincoln's attitude was firm but conservative. He disliked slavery and frankly said so; yet he was not an abolitionist and he saw no way in which the institution could be uprooted. On the contrary, he favored enforcing the fugitive slave law and he was not prepared to urge even the abolition of slavery in the District of Columbia. His declaration that a house divided against itself could not stand had been counterbalanced by an assertion that the country would become all free or all slave—a creed which any southern planter could have indorsed. Seward's radical doctrine that there was a "higher law" than the Constitution, dedicating the territories to freedom, received from the Illinois lawyer disapproval, not commendation.

Nevertheless Lincoln was definite and positive in his opinion that slavery should not be permitted in the territories. That was necessary to satisfy the minimum demands of the anti-slavery faction and incidentally it pleased those Whigs of the North who at last realized that no Hamiltonian program could be pushed through Congress if the planting interest secured a supremacy, or indeed held an equal share of power, in the Union. Evidently Lincoln was the man of the hour: his heritage was correct, his principles were sound, his sincerity was unquestioned, and his ability as a speaker commanded the minds and hearts of his auditors. He sent word to his friends at Chicago that, although he did not indorse Seward's higher-law doctrine, he agreed with him on the irrepressible conflict. The next day Lincoln was nominated amid huzzas from ten thousand lusty throats.

A large fraction of Whigs and some fragments of the Know Nothing, or American, party, foreseeing calamity in the existing array of interests, tried to save the day by an appeal to lofty sentiments without any definitions. Assuming the name of Constitutional Unionists and boasting that they represented the "intelligence and respectability of the South" as well as the lovers of the national idea everywhere, they held a convention at Baltimore and nominated John Bell of Tennessee and Edward Everett of Massachusetts for President and Vice-President. In the platform they invited their countrymen to forget all divisions and "support the Constitution of the country, the union of the states, and the enforcement of the laws." It was an overture of old men—men who had known and loved Webster and Clay and who shrank with horror from agitations that threatened to end in bloodshed and revolution—a plea for the maintenance of the status quo against the whims of a swiftly changing world.

§

A spirited campaign followed the nomination of these four candidates for the presidency on four different platforms. Huge campaign funds were raised and spent. Besides pursuing the usual strategy of education, the Republicans resorted to parades and the other spectacular features that had distinguished the log-cabin crusade of General Harrison's year. Emulating the discretion of the Hero of Tippecanoe, Lincoln maintained a judicious silence at Springfield while his champions waged his battles for him, naturally tempering their orations to the requirements of diverse interests. They were fully conscious, as a Republican paper in Philadelphia put it, that "Frémont had tried running on the slavery issue and lost." So while they laid stress on it in many sections, they widened their appeal.

In the West, a particular emphasis was placed on free homesteads and the Pacific railway. With a keen eye for competent strategy, Carl Schurz carried the campaign into Missouri where he protested with eloquence against the action of the slave power in denying "the laboring man the right to acquire property in the soil by his labor" and made a special plea for the German vote on the ground that the free land was to be opened to aliens who declared their intention of becoming American citizens. Discovering that the homestead question was "the greatest issue in the West," Horace Greeley used it to win votes in the East. Agrarians and labor reformers renewed the slogan: "Vote yourself a farm."

In Pennsylvania and New Jersey, protection for iron and

steel was the great subject of discussion. Curtin, the Republican candidate for governor in the former state, said not a word about abolishing slavery in his ratification speech but spoke with feeling on "the vast heavings of the heart of Pennsylvania whose sons are pining for protection to their labor and their dearest interests." Warming to his theme, he exclaimed: "This is a contest involving protection and the rights of labor. . . . If you desire to become vast and great, protect the manufactures of Philadelphia. . . . All hail, liberty! All hail, freedom! freedom to the white man! All hail freedom general as the air we breathe!" In a fashion after Curtin's own heart, the editor of the Philadelphia American and Gazette, surveying the canvass at the finish, repudiated the idea that "any sectional aspect of the slavery question" was up for decision and declared that the great issues were protection for industry, "economy in the conduct of the government, homesteads for settlers on the public domain, retrenchment and accountability in the public expenditures, appropriation for rivers and harbors, a Pacific railroad, the admission of Kansas, and a radical reform in the government."

With a kindred appreciation of practical matters, Seward bore the standard through the North and West. Fully conversant with the Webster policy of commercial expansion in the Pacific and knowing well the political appeal of Manifest Destiny, he proclaimed the future of the American empire—assuring his auditors that in due time American outposts would be pushed along the northwest coast to the Arctic Ocean, that Canada would be gathered into our glorious Union, that the Latin-American republics reorganized under our benign influence would become parts of this magnificent confederation, that the ancient Aztec metropolis, Mexico City, would eventually become the capital of the United States, and that America and Russia, breaking their old friendship, would come to grips in the Far East—"in regions where civilization first began." All this was involved in the election of Lincoln and the triumph of the Republican party. Webster and Cushing and Perry had not wrought in vain.

The three candidates opposed to Lincoln scored points wherever they could. Douglas took the stump with his usual vigor and declaimed to throngs in nearly every state. Orators of the Breckinridge camp, believing that their extreme views were sound everywhere, invaded the North. Bell's champions spoke with dignity and warmth about the dangers inherent in all unwise departures from the past, about the perils of the sectional quarrel. When at length the ballots were cast and counted, it was found that the foes of slavery agitation had carried the country by an overwhelming majority. Their combined vote was a million ahead of Lincoln's total; the two Democratic factions alone, to say nothing of Bell's six hundred thousand followers, outnumbered the Republican army. But in the division and uproar of the campaign Lincoln, even so, had won the Presidency; he was the choice of a minority—a sectional minority at that—but under the terms of the Constitution, he was entitled to the scepter at Washington.

§

From what has just been said it must be apparent that the forces which produced the irrepressible conflict were very complex in nature and yet the momentous struggle has been so often reduced by historians to simple terms that a reëxamination of the traditional thesis has become one of the tasks of the modern age. On the part of northern writers it was long the fashion to declare that slavery was the cause of the conflict between the states. Such for example was the position taken by James Ford Rhodes and made the starting point of his monumental work.

Assuming for the moment that this assertion is correct in a general sense, it will be easily observed even on a superficial investigation that "slavery" was no simple, isolated phenomenon. In itself it was intricate and it had filaments through the whole body economic. It was a labor system, the basis of planting, and the foundation of the southern aristocracy. That aristocracy, in turn, owing to the nature of its economic operations, resorted to public policies that were opposed to capitalism, sought to dominate the federal government, and, with the help of free farmers also engaged in agriculture, did at last dominate it. In the course of that political conquest, all the plans of commerce and industry for federal protection and subvention were overborne. It took more than a finite eye to discern where slavery as an ethical question left off and economics—the struggle over the distribution of wealth—began.

On the other hand, the early historians of the southern school, chagrined by defeat and compelled to face the adverse judgment of brutal fact, made the "rights of states" —something nobler than economics or the enslavement of Negroes—the issue for which the Confederacy fought and bled. That too like slavery seems simple until subjected to a little scrutiny. What is a state? At bottom it is a majority or perhaps a mere plurality of persons engaged in the quest of something supposed to be beneficial, or at all events not injurious, to the pursuers. And what are rights? Abstract, intangible moral values having neither substance nor form? The party debates over the economic issues of the middle period answer with an emphatic negative. If the southern planters had been content to grant tariffs, bounties, subsidies, and preferences to northern commerce and industry, it is not probable that they would have been molested in their most imperious proclamations of sovereignty.

But their theories and their acts involved interests more ponderable than political rhetoric. They threatened the country with secession first in defying the tariff of abominations and when they did secede thirty years later it was in response to the victory of a tariff and homestead party that proposed nothing more dangerous to slavery itself than the mere exclusion of the institution from the territories. It

took more than a finite eye to discern where their opposition
to the economic system of Hamilton left off and their affection for the rights of states began. The modern reader
tossed about in a contrariety of opinions can only take his
bearings by examining a few indubitable realities.

§

With reference to the popular northern view of the conflict, there stands the stubborn fact that at no time during
the long gathering of the storm did Garrison's abolition
creed rise to the dignity of a first rate political issue in the
North. Nobody but agitators, beneath the contempt of the
towering statesmen of the age, ever dared to advocate it.
No great political organization even gave it the most casual
indorsement.

When the abolitionists launched the Liberty party in the
campaign of 1844 to work for emancipation, as we have
noted, the voters answered their plea for "the restoration
of equality of political rights among men" in a manner
that demonstrated the invincible opposition of the American
people. Out of more than two and a half million ballots
cast in the election, only sixty-five thousand were recorded
in favor of the Liberty candidate. That was America's
answer to the call for abolition; and the advocates of that
policy never again ventured to appeal to the electorate by
presenting candidates on such a radical platform.

No other party organized between that time and the clash
of arms attempted to do more than demand the exclusion
of slavery from the territories and not until the Democrats
by repealing the Missouri Compromise threatened to extend
slavery throughout the West did any party poll more than
a handful of votes on that issue. It is true that Van Buren
on a free-soil platform received nearly three hundred
thousand votes in 1848 but that was evidently due to personal influence, because his successor on a similar ticket four
years afterward dropped into an insignificant place.

Even the Republican party, in the campaign of 1856,

coming hard on the act of defiance which swept away the Missouri compact, won little more than one-third the active voters to the cause of restricting the slavery area. When transformed after four more years into a homestead and high tariff party pledged merely to liberty in the territories, the Republicans polled a million votes fewer than the number cast for the opposing factions and rode into power on account of the divided ranks of the enemy. Such was the nation's reply to the anti-slavery agitation from the beginning of the disturbance until the cannon shot at Sumter opened a revolution.

Moreover not a single responsible statesman of the middle period committed himself to the doctrine of immediate and unconditional abolition to be achieved by independent political action. John Quincy Adams, ousted from the presidency by Jacksonian Democracy but returned to Washington as the Representative of a Massachusetts district in Congress, did declare that it was the duty of every free American to work directly for the abolition of slavery and with uncanny vision foresaw that the knot might be cut with the sword. But Adams was regarded by astute party managers as a foolish and embittered old man and his prophecy as a dangerous delusion.

Practical politicians who felt the iron hand of the planters at Washington—politicians who saw how deeply intertwined with the whole economic order the institution of slavery really was—could discover nothing tangible in immediate and unconditional abolition that appealed to reason or came within the range of common sense. Lincoln was emphatic in assuring the slaveholders that no Republican had ever been detected in any attempt to disturb them. "We must not interfere with the institution of slavery in the states where it exists," he urged, "because the Constitution forbids it and the general welfare does not require us to do so."

Since, therefore, the abolition of slavery never appeared in the platform of any great political party, since the only appeal ever made to the electorate on that issue was scornfully repulsed, since the spokesman of the Republicans emphatically declared that his party never intended to interfere with slavery in the states in any shape or form, it seems reasonable to assume that the institution of slavery was not the fundamental issue during the epoch preceding the bombardment of Fort Sumter.

§

Nor can it be truthfully said, as southern writers were fond of having it, that a tender and consistent regard for the rights of states and for a strict construction of the Constitution was the prime element in the dispute that long divided the country. As a matter of record, from the foundation of the republic, all factions were for high nationalism or low provincialism upon occasion according to their desires at the moment, according to turns in the balance of power. New England nullified federal law when her commerce was affected by the War of 1812 and came out stanchly for liberty and union, one and inseparable, now and forever, in 1833 when South Carolina attempted to nullify a tariff act. Not long afterward, the legislature of Massachusetts, dreading the overweening strength of the Southwest, protested warmly against the annexation of Texas and resolved that "such an act of admission would have no binding force whatever on the people of Massachusetts."

Equally willing to bend theory to practical considerations, the party of the slavocracy argued that the Constitution was to be strictly and narrowly construed whenever tariff and bank measures were up for debate; but no such piddling concept of the grand document was to be held when a bill providing for the prompt and efficient return of fugitive slaves was on the carpet. Less than twenty years after South Carolina prepared to resist by arms federal officers engaged in collecting customs duties, the champions of slavery and states' rights greeted with applause a fugitive slave law which flouted the precious limitations prescribed in the first ten Amendments to the Constitution—a law which provided for the use of all the powers of the national government to assist masters in getting possession of their elusive property—which denied to the alleged slave, who might perchance be a freeman in spite of his color, the right to have a jury trial or even to testify in his own behalf. In other words, it was "constitutional" to employ the engines of the federal authority in catching slaves wherever they might be found in any northern community and to ignore utterly the elementary safeguards of liberty plainly and specifically imposed on Congress by language that admitted of no double interpretation.

On this very issue of personal liberty, historic positions on states' rights were again reversed. Following the example of South Carolina on the tariff, Wisconsin resisted the fugitive slave law as an invasion of her reserved rights —as a violation of the Constitution. Alarmed by this action, Chief Justice Taney answered the disobedient state in a ringing judicial decision announcing a high nationalism that would have delighted the heart of John Marshall, informing the recalcitrant Wisconsin that the Constitution and laws enacted under it were supreme; that the fugitive slave law was fully authorized by the Constitution; and that the Supreme Court was the final arbiter in all controversies over the respective powers of the states and the United States. "If such an arbiter had not been provided in our complicated system of government, internal tranquillity could not have been preserved and if such controversies were left to the arbitrament of physical force, our Government, State and National, would cease to be a government of laws, and revolution by force of arms would take the place of courts of justice and judicial decisions." No nullification here; no right of a state to judge for itself respecting infractions of the Constitution by the federal government; federal law is binding everywhere and the Supreme Court, a branch of the national government, is the final judge.

And in what language did Wisconsin reply? The legislature of the state, in a solemn resolution, declared that the decision of the Supreme Court of the United States in the case in question was in direct conflict with the Constitution. It vowed that the essential principles of the Kentucky doctrine of nullification were sound. Then it closed with the rebel fling: "that the several states . . . being sovereign and independent, have the unquestionable right to judge of its [the Constitution's] infraction and that a positive defiance by those sovereignties of all unauthorized acts done or attempted to be done under color of that instrument is the rightful remedy."

That was in 1859. Within two years, men who had voted for that resolution and cheered its adoption were marching off in martial array to vindicate on southern battlefields the supremacy of the Union and the sovereignty of the nation. By that fateful hour the southern politicians who had applauded Taney's declaration that the Supreme Court was the final arbiter in controversies between the states and the national government had come to the solemn conclusion that the states themselves were the arbiters. Such words and events being facts, there can be but one judgment in the court of history; namely, that major premises respecting the nature of the Constitution and deductions made logically from them with masterly eloquence were minor factors in the grand dispute as compared with the interests, desires, and passions that lay deep in the hearts and minds of the contestants.

§

Indeed, honorable men who held diametrically opposite views found warrant for each in the Constitution. All parties and all individuals, save the extreme abolitionists, protested in an unbroken chant their devotion to the national covenant and to the principles and memory of the inspired men who framed it. As the Bible was sometimes taken as a guide for theologians traveling in opposite directions, so the Constitution was the beacon that lighted the way of statesmen who differed utterly on the issues of the middle period. Again and again Calhoun declared that his one supreme object was to sustain the Constitution in its pristine purity of principle: "to turn back the government," as he said, "to where it commenced its operation in 1789 . . . to take a fresh start, a new departure, on the States Rights Republican tack, as was intended by the framers of the Constitution."

This was the eternal refrain of Calhoun's school. The bank, subsidies to shipping, protection for industries, the encouragement of business enterprise by public assistance were all departures from the Constitution and the intentions of its framers, all contrary to the fundamental compact of the land. This refrain reverberated through Democratic speeches in Congress, the platform of the party, and the official utterances of its statesmen. "The liberal principles embodied by Jefferson in the Declaration of Independence and sanctioned by the Constitution . . . have ever been cardinal principles in the Democratic faith"— such was the characteristic declaration of the elect in every platform after 1840. The Constitution warrants the peaceful secession of states by legal process—such was the answer of Jefferson Davis to those who charged him with raising the flag of revolution. Everything done by the Democratic party while in power was constitutional and finally, as a crowning act of grace, the Constitution gave approval to its own destruction and the dissolution of the Union.

It followed from this line of reasoning as night the day that the measures advanced by the Whigs and later by the Republicans were unconstitutional. In fact, Calhoun devoted the burden of a great speech in 1839 to showing how everything done by Hamilton and his school was a violation of the Constitution. Party manifestoes reiterated the pronouncements of party statesmen on this point. In their platform of 1840, the Democrats highly resolved that "the Constitution does not confer upon the general government the power . . . to carry on a general system of internal improvement . . . the Constitution does not confer authority upon the federal government, directly or indirectly, to assume the debts of the several states . . . Congress has no power to charter a United States Bank . . . Congress has no power, under the Constitution, to interfere with or control the domestic institutions of the several states." This declaration was repeated every four years substantially in the same form. After the Supreme Court announced in the Dred Scott case that Congress could not prohibit slavery in the territories, the Democratic party added that the doctrine "should be respected by all good citizens and enforced with promptness and fidelity by every branch of the general government."

In the best of all possible worlds everything substantial desired by the Democrats was authorized by the Constitution while everything substantial opposed by them was beyond the boundaries set by the venerable instrument. Hamilton, who helped to draft the Constitution, therefore, did not understand or interpret it correctly; whereas Jefferson, who was in Paris during its formation was the infallible oracle on the intentions of its framers.

On the other hand, the Whigs and then the Republicans were equally prone to find protection under the ægis of the Constitution. Webster in his later years devoted long and eloquent speeches to showing that the Constitution contemplated a perpetual union and that nullification and secession were utterly proscribed by the principles of that instrument. He did not go as far as Calhoun. He did not declare free trade unconstitutional but he did find in the records of history evidence that "the main reason for the adoption of the Constitution" was to give "the general government the power to regulate commerce and trade." A protective tariff was therefore constitutional. Furthermore "it was no more the right than the duty" of Congress "by just discrimination to protect the labor of the American people." The provision of a uniform system of currency was also among "the chief objects" of the Fathers in framing the Constitution. A national bank was not imperatively commanded by the letter of the document but its spirit required Congress to stabilize and make sound the paper currency of the land. In fact Webster thought the Democrats themselves somewhat unconstitutional. "If by democracy," he said, "they mean a conscientious and stern adherence to the Constitution and the government, then I think they have very little claim to it."

In the endless and tangled debates on slavery, the orators of the age also paid the same sincere homage to the Constitution that they had paid when dealing with other economic matters. Southern statesmen on their side never wearied in pointing out the pro-slavery character of the covenant. That instrument, they said, recognized the slave trade by providing that the traffic should not be prohibited for twenty years and by leaving the issue open after that period had elapsed. It made slavery the basis of taxation and representation, "thus preferring and fostering it above all other property, by making it alone, of all property, an element of political power in the union, as well as a source of revenue to the federal government." The Constitution laid a binding obligation upon all states to return fugitive slaves to their masters upon claims made in due course. It guaranteed the states against domestic violence, not overlooking the possibilities of a servile revolt. "Power to abolish, circumscribe, or restrain slavery is withheld but power is granted and the duty is imposed on the federal government to protect and preserve it." The English language could hardly be more explicit.

All this was no accident; it was the outcome of design. "The framers of the Constitution were slave owners or the representatives of slave owners"; the Constitution was the result of a compromise between the North and the South in which slavery was specifically and zealously guarded and secured. Such were the canons of authenticity on the southern side.

This view of the Constitution contained so much sound historical truth that the opposition was forced to strain the imagination in its search for an answer. In an attempt to find lawful warrant for their creed in 1844, the abolitionists made a platform that became one of the prime curiosities in the annals of logic. They announced that the principles of the Declaration of Independence were embraced in the Constitution, that those principles proclaimed freedom, and that the provision of the Constitution relative to the return of fugitive slaves was itself null and void because forsooth common law holds any contract contrary to natural right and morality invalid.

Although the Republicans did not go that far in their defensive romancing, they also asserted, in their platform of 1860, that the principles of the Declaration of Independence were embodied in the Constitution and they claimed that neither Congress nor a state legislature could give legal existence to slavery in any territory of the United States. But there was one slip in this reasoning: the Supreme Court of the United States, with reference to the Dred Scott case, had read in the same oracle that Congress could not deprive any slave owner of his property in the territories and that the abolition of slavery there by Congress was null and void.

Nevertheless, the Republicans neatly evaded this condemnation of their doctrine, by calling it "a dangerous political heresy, at variance with the explicit provisions of that instrument itself, with contemporaneous exposition, and with legislative and judicial precedent." In short, the Republicans entered a dissenting opinion themselves; while it was hardly authentic constitutional law it made an effective appeal to voters—especially those fond of legal proprieties.

Even in their violent disagreement as to the nature of the Union, the contestants with equal fervor invoked the authority of the Constitution to show that secession was lawful or that the perpetuation of the Union was commanded as the case might be. With respect to this problem each party to the conflict had a theory which was finely and logically drawn from pertinent data and given the appearance of soundness by a process of skillful elision and emphasis.

Those who to-day look upon that dispute without rancor must admit that the secessionists had somewhat the better of the rhetorical side of the battle. Their scheme of historicity was simple. The thirteen colonies declared their independence as separate sovereignties; they were recognized by Great Britain in the treaty of peace as thirteen individual states; when they formed the Articles of Confederation they were careful to declare that "each state retains its sovereignty, freedom, and independence and every power, jurisdiction, and right, which is not by this Confederation expressly delegated to the United States in Congress assembled." These were undeniable facts. Then came the formation of the Constitution. The states elected delegates to the federal convention; the delegates revised the Articles of Confederation; the revision, known as the Constitution, was submitted for approval to the states and finally ratified by state conventions.

Q. E. D., ran the secessionist argument, the sovereign states that entered the compact can by lawful process withdraw from the Union just as sovereign nations may by their own act dissolve a treaty with other foreign powers.

There was, of course, some difficulty in discovering attributes of sovereignty in the new states carved out of the national domain by the surveyors' compass and chain and admitted to the Union under specific constitutional limitations—states that now outnumbered the original thirteen. But the slight hiatus in the argument, which arose from this incongruity, was bridged by the declaration that the subject territories when taken in under the roof were clothed with the sovereignty and independence of the original commonwealths.

The historical brief of those who maintained, on the other hand, that secession was illegal rested in part on an interpretation of the preamble of the Constitution, an interpretation advanced by Webster during his famous debate with Hayne. "It cannot be shown," he said, "that the Constitution is a compact between state governments. The Constitution itself, in its very front, refutes that idea; it declares that it is ordained and established by the people of the United States. . . . It even does not say that it is established by the people of the several states; but pronounces that it is established by the people of the United States in the aggregate." That is, the Constitution was not made by the states; it was made by a high collective sovereign towering above them—the people of the United States.

This fair argument, which seemed convincing on its face, was later demolished by reference to the journals of the Convention that drafted the Constitution. When the preamble was originally drawn, it ran: "We, the people of the states of New Hampshire, Massachusetts, &c., . . . do ordain and establish the following Constitution." But on second thought the framers realized that according to their own decree the new government was to be set up as soon as nine states had ratified the proposed instrument. It was obviously undesirable to enumerate the states of the Union in advance, for some of them might withhold their approval. Therefore the first draft was abandoned and the words "We the people of the United States" substituted. The facts of record accordingly exploded the whole thesis built on this sandy foundation.

This fallacy Lincoln was careful to avoid in his first inaugural address. Seeking a more secure historical basis for his faith, he pointed out that the Union was in fact older than the Constitution, older than the Declaration of Independence. It was formed, he said, by the Articles of Association framed in 1774 by the Continental Congress speaking in the name of revolutionary America. It was matured and continued in the Declaration of Independence which proclaimed "these United Colonies" to be free and independent states. It was sealed by the Articles of Confederation which pledged the thirteen commonwealths to a perpetual Union under that form of government; it was crowned by the Constitution designed to make the Union "more perfect."

Far more effective on the nationalist side was the argument derived through logical processes from the nature of the Constitution itself, by Webster, Lincoln, and the philosophers of their school. It ran in the following vein. The Constitution does not, by express provision or by implication, provide any method by which a state may withdraw from the Union; no such dissolution of the federation was contemplated by the men who drafted and ratified the covenant. The government established by it operates directly on the people, not on states; it is the government of the people, not of states. Moreover the Constitution proclaims to all the world that it and the laws and treaties made in pursuance of its terms, are the supreme law of the land and that the judges of the states are bound thereby, "anything in the constitution and laws of any state to the contrary notwithstanding." Finally, the Supreme Court of the United States is the ultimate arbiter in all controversies arising between the national government and the states. Chief Justice Marshall had proclaimed the doctrine in beating down the resistance of Virginia, Maryland, and Ohio to federal authority; Chief Justice Taney had proclaimed it in paralyzing the opposition of Wisconsin to the fugitive slave law. Such being the grand pledges and principles of the Constitution it followed, to use Lincoln's version, that no state could lawfully withdraw from the Union; secession was insurrectionary or revolutionary according to circumstances.

What now is the verdict of history on these verbal contests? Did the delegates at the Philadelphia convention of 1787 regard themselves as ambassadors of sovereign states entering into a mere treaty of alliance? Did they set down anywhere a pontifical judgment to the effect that any state might on its own motion withdraw from the Union after approving the Constitution? The answer to these questions is in the negative. Had they thought out a logical system of political theory such as Calhoun afterward announced with such precision? If so, they left no record of it to posterity.

What then was the Constitution? It was a plan of government designed to effect certain purposes, specific and general, framed by a small group of citizens, "informed by a conscious solidarity of interests," who, according to all available evidence, intended that government to be supreme over the states and enduring. They were not dominated by any logical scheme such as Calhoun evolved in defending his cause; they were engrossed in making, not breaking, a Union; they made no provision for, and if the testimony of their recorded debates be accepted as conclusive, did not contemplate the withdrawal of the states from the federation by any legal procedure. Surely it was not without significance that James Madison, the father of the Constitution, who lived to see secession threatened in South Carolina, denounced in unmistakable terms the smooth and well-articulated word-pattern of Calhoun, condemning secession as utterly without support in the understandings of the men who made, ratified, and launched the Constitution.

But it may be said that the men of Philadelphia merely drafted the Constitution and that what counts in the premises is the opinions of the voters in the states, who through their delegates ratified the instrument. Did, then, the men who chose the delegates for the state ratifying conventions or the delegates themselves have clearly in mind a concept that made the great document in effect a mere treaty of alliance which could be legally denounced at will by any member? The records in the case give no affirmative answer. What most of them thought is a matter of pure conjecture. Were any of the states sovereign in fact at any time; that is, did any of them assume before the world the attributes and functions of a sovereign nation? Certainly not. Did the whole people in their collective capacity make the Constitution? To ask the question is to answer it; they did not.

When the modern student examines all the verbal disputes over the nature of the Union—the arguments employed by the parties which operated and opposed the federal government between the adoption of the Constitution and the opening of the Civil War—he can hardly do otherwise than conclude that the linguistic devices used first on one side and then on the other were not derived from inherently necessary concepts concerning the intimate essence of the federal system. The roots of the controversy lay elsewhere—in social groupings founded on differences in climate, soil, industries, and labor systems, in divergent social forces, rather than varying degrees of righteousness and wisdom, or what romantic historians call "the magnetism of great personalities."

CHAPTER XVIII

The Second American Revolution

IN the spring of 1861 the full force of the irrepressible conflict burst upon the hesitant and bewildered nation and for four long years the clash of arms filled the land with its brazen clangor. For four long years the anguish, the calamities, and the shocks of the struggle absorbed the energies of the multitudes, blared in the headlines of the newspapers, and loomed impressively in the minds of the men and women who lived and suffered in that age.

Naturally, therefore, all who wrote of the conflict used the terms of war. In its records, the government of the United States officially referred to the contest as the War of the Rebellion, thus by implication setting the stigma of treason on those who served under the Stars and Bars. Repudiating this brand and taking for his shield the righteousness of legitimacy, one of the leading southern statesmen, Alexander H. Stephens, in his great history of the conflict, called it the War between the States. This, too, no less than the title chosen by the federal government, is open to objections; apart from the large assumptions involved, it is not strictly accurate for, in the border states, the armed struggle was a guerrilla war and in Virginia the domestic strife ended in the separation of several counties, under the ægis of a new state constitution, as West Virginia. More recently a distinguished historian, Edward Channing, entitled a volume dealing with the period The War for Southern Independence—a characterization which, though fairly precise, suffers a little perhaps from abstraction.

As a matter of fact all these symbols are misleading in that they overemphasize the element of military force in the grand dénouement. War there was unquestionably, immense, wide-sweeping, indubitable, as Carlyle would say. For years the agony of it hung like a pall over the land. And yet with strange swiftness the cloud was lifted and blown away. Merciful grass spread its green mantle over the cruel scars and the gleaming red splotches sank into the hospitable earth.

It was then that the economist and lawyer, looking more calmly on the scene, discovered that the armed conflict had been only one phase of the cataclysm, a transitory phase; that at bottom the so-called Civil War, or the War between the States, in the light of Roman analogy, was a social war, ending in the unquestioned establishment of a new power in the government, making vast changes in the arrangement of classes, in the accumulation and distribution of wealth, in the course of industrial development, and in the Constitution inherited from the Fathers. Merely by the accidents of climate, soil, and geography was it a sectional struggle. If the planting interest had been scattered evenly throughout the industrial region, had there been a horizontal rather than a perpendicular cleavage, the irrepressible conflict would have been resolved by other methods and accompanied by other logical defense mechanisms.

In any event neither accident nor rhetoric should be allowed to obscure the intrinsic character of that struggle. If the operations by which the middle classes of England broke the power of the king and the aristocracy are to be known collectively as the Puritan Revolution, if the series of acts by which the bourgeois and peasants of France overthrew the king, nobility, and clergy is to be called the French Revolution, then accuracy compels us to characterize by the same term the social cataclysm in which the capitalists, laborers, and farmers of the North and West drove from power in the national government the planting aristocracy of the South. Viewed under the light of universal history, the fighting was a fleeting incident; the social revolution was the essential, portentous outcome.

To be sure the battles and campaigns of the epoch are significant to the military strategist; the tragedy and heroism of the contest furnish inspiration to patriots and romance to the makers of epics. But the core of the vortex lay elsewhere. It was in the flowing substance of things limned by statistical reports on finance, commerce, capital, industry, railways, and agriculture, by provisions of constitutional law, and by the pages of statute books—prosaic muniments which show that the so-called civil war was in reality a Second American Revolution and in a strict sense, the First.

The physical combat that punctuated the conflict merely hastened the inevitable. As was remarked at the time, the South was fighting against the census returns—census returns that told of accumulating industrial capital, multiplying captains of industry, expanding railway systems, widening acres tilled by free farmers. Once the planting and the commercial states, as the Fathers with faithful accuracy described them, had been evenly balanced; by 1860 the balance was gone.

§

When the armed contest was precipitated, the eleven states in the southern Confederacy were confronted by twenty-three states in the federal Union. Nine million people, more than one-third of whom were slaves, faced

twenty-two million people nearly all white. Before the
strife was over there had been 2,898,000 enlistments in the
federal armies and approximately 1,300,000 enlistments in
the confederate armies; on the basis of men and terms of
service, the ratio of the contending forces was about three
to two. Practically all the iron, steel, textile, and munition
industries of the country were in federal control. By far
the major portion of the foreign commerce had long centered in the ports above the Potomac; even most of the
foreign goods destined for the South had poured through
the warehouses of northern cities. More than two-thirds
of the banking capital of the country was in northern hands.
The North also had an almost complete monopoly of the
science and skilled labor required to furnish the sinews of
warfare. In fact the real revolution—the silent shift of
social and material power—had occurred before the southern states declared their independence and precipitated
the revolution of violence. As Seward had warned the
planters, they could accept the inescapable either in peace
or in battle.

How then could the planting aristocracy hope to form a
combination of interests strong enough to resist such superiority in men, money, and metal? Only by seeing things
through the eyes of the confederate leaders of 1860 can
the question be answered. They faced an unknown future
and made their calculations on what appeared to be cer-
tainties at hand. They had long been taught and they
were convinced that Cotton was King and that their control over staples essential to northern industries would enable them to bring on a ruinous crisis in the manufacturing
states in case force was applied against them. "I firmly
believe," exclaimed Senator Hammond of South Carolina
in the year of secession, "that the slave-holding South is
now the controlling power of the world; that no other
power would face us in hostility. Cotton, rice, tobacco, and
naval stores command the world; and we have the sense to
know it and are sufficiently Teutonic to carry it out success-

fully. The North without us would be a motherless calf, bleating about, and die of mange and starvation."

The same mastery of raw materials, they thought, would induce England and France to recognize their independence, grant them aid, keep the seas free, and permit them to exchange their output for the materials of war. To such substantial interests, they added sentimental considerations. They knew that the aristocracy of England and Napoleon III, Emperor of the French, looked with pleasure upon the prospective break-up of the American republic—the failure of that disturbing experiment in democracy. So they planned to paralyze northern industries by cutting off their supplies and to gather abundant assistance from a sympathetic England and France.

Those southern statesmen who sought to save the planting aristocracy from its doom by withdrawing from the Union had also other grounds for optimism. They expected to push the Confederacy up to the Ohio River and with the aid of Missouri to lay hold of the Mississippi Valley, the granary of the nation, overestimating the power which they could wield in that region through their control over the outlet at New Orleans and undervaluing the efficiency of the railways which bound the Middle West with the seaboard.

At the same time they attached, and apparently with good reason, a very great importance to the internal conflict which promised to weaken the North. Facts betraying that division were patent to all: Lincoln had received just a little more than one-third of the popular vote; he confronted a formidable opposition on his own ground; and his mandate at best was vague. No issue of secession and civil war had been submitted to the country in the election of 1860. In condemning slavery in the territories, the Republicans did not say that they would fight, if necessary, to gain their ends, or to keep the South in the Union. Indeed, the new party embraced a large number of people interested primarily in the protective tariffs, free homesteads, and related matters, practical people who thought the less said about slavery the better.

Nor were the Republicans when safely installed at Washington in a position to exert force on a large scale; the national government which passed into their control had an empty treasury, a mounting debt, a sorry navy, and a pitiable army. Whether the southern members of Buchanan's Cabinet had deliberately weakened its military strength for ulterior purposes was a matter of debate. Whatever the cause the fact remained that the Union government was not prepared for any great demonstration of armed might whereas the Confederacy had taken care to seize practically all the available munitions within its domain.

Finally, in striking their balance sheet, the mettlesome planters of the South placed on record their low opinion of the northerners generally, declaring that "the greasy mechanics" would not fight, thus discounting the numerical superiority of the North. With confident assurance they cited historical parallels showing how on numerous occasions small but valiant armies had vanquished hosts. "Our fathers, a mere handful," said John Tyler of Virginia, "overcame the enormous power of Great Britain." Even those who believed with Jefferson Davis that the war, if it came, would be long and awful, did not foresee the terrible struggle which was to mark its course.

§

So it was with fairly buoyant hopes that the southern leaders sought to retain their economic and political power by cutting loose from the dominion of northern capitalists —by taking the southern states out of the Union. Jubilant spirits in South Carolina had announced during the campaign that they would withdraw from the federation if the balloting gave victory to "the Black Republican nominee and his fanatical, diabolical Republican party." The news of Lincoln's election was, therefore, merely a long-awaited signal for action. The planters had threatened to leave the Union thirty years before on account of the high tariff— at a time when slavery had not become the subject of serious agitation; by resistance then they had forced a reduction of the hated duties and won nearly three decades of economic security. Now they were about to be ruled by a party openly committed to high protection, slightly tainted with abolitionism, and avowedly in favor of excluding slavery from the territories.

In this crisis the most dogmatic group among the planters acted with decision. A few days after Lincoln's election, namely, on November 10, the state legislature of South Carolina, without a dissenting voice, called a popular convention to choose the course appropriate to the emergency. In December the convention met in a thrill of excitement. The galleries and lobbies of the assembly hall were crowded with ladies in gala attire, soldiers in bright new uniforms, judges, editors, and officers, all in high spirits and sanguine as to the outcome. The delegates were nearly all old men or men beyond the middle years, too old to fight but too proud to let the Lincoln menace pass without an answer. Divine blessings were invoked, the issue was submitted to debate, and then by a unanimous vote South Carolina declared her independence. As soon as the momentous verdict was rendered, a shout of triumph ran through the streets of Charleston and the night was made joyous with merrymaking, enlivened by song and wine, dancing and fireworks. Those wiseacres who thought they saw dark shadows in the background slunk away or held their tongues. The jubilee was perfect.

As in the time of the nullification struggle, South Carolina now called upon her neighbors to follow her example; and before Lincoln was inaugurated six of them—Florida, Georgia, Alabama, Mississippi, Louisiana, and Texas—had proclaimed their union with the northern states at an end. Though in Alabama and Georgia a respectable minority was opposed to secession, in the other four states only a few malcontents could be mustered to resist the flushed and confident majority. Having declared their independence, the seceded states, acting on a summons from Mississippi, sent delegates in February, 1861, to Montgomery, Alabama, where a plan of union was adopted and preparations were made for the establishment of a new general government.

This was the posture of affairs when Lincoln took the oath of office on March 4, 1861. Virginia, North Carolina, Tennessee, and Arkansas trembled in the balance. Conventions had been called in these states but they had all refused to take the fatal step, preferring to await the course pursued by the incoming President. In Virginia, North Carolina, and Tennessee there was a large majority against secession on the issues presented before Lincoln's inauguration. Though they all upheld slavery, their economy was more diversified than that of the cotton belt; they had wide upland sections occupied by small farmers who had no special love for the planting aristocracy at the head of southern affairs.

Even after Fort Sumter fell, when the call for blood was running through the land, there was still a formidable opposition to secession in each of these states. In North Carolina, the federal faction resorted to the tactics of indifference and obstruction; in Virginia, it managed to tear away several disaffected counties, organize them into the new state of West Virginia, and enter the Union as a separate commonwealth; in Tennessee, it furnished thousands of soldiers for the northern army and kept whole counties in constant turmoil. Hence it happened that Lincoln on the day of his coming to power found secession menacing but by no means triumphant. The chemicals for a crisis were prepared but some stroke was necessary to explode them.

§

From the early days of November, 1860, to March 4, 1861, while planters prepared for the worst, the government at Washington drifted, helpless in the conflicting currents. According to the terms of the Constitution, Lincoln could not be inaugurated until the day lawfully appointed, and so for four critical months the Democratic party, which had been split wide by the campaign and defeated at the polls, continued to hold the reins of power. Its titular leader, President James Buchanan, had no popular mandate to deal with the question of secession. Nor had he any overmastering will of his own in the premises. Obviously bewildered by the stirring events taking place about him, he exclaimed in one breath that the southern states had no right to withdraw from the Union and in the next that he had no power to compel them to retain their allegiance. His Cabinet crumbled away, his host of advisers wrangled among themselves, and inaction seemed to him the better part of valor—at least it could be defended on the ground that nothing should be done to embarrass the incoming President.

On every side were heard the buzzing voices of politicians attempting to forecast the future, effect compromises, soothe angry passions. The Congress which assembled in December had no mandate from the election of the preceding month; the House had been chosen two years earlier and the Senate piecemeal over a period of six years. Congressmen were as perplexed as the President. To the public generally it seemed as if the solid earth were dissolving.

Southern residents of the capital were rapidly closing their houses and leaving for "their own country," most of them with confidence in coming events. Henry Watterson of Kentucky, who was on the ground, tells of a southern belle who drove away waving the Palmetto flag defiantly as her carriage rolled toward the blue hills of Virginia. She was a type of her class.

"She truly believed secession a constitutional right, slavery a divine institution. To her the mudsills of the North, as she dubbed them, were an inferior people. Cotton was king and she preferred a monarchy to a republic. If there should be any war at all, which was unlikely, it would be short-lived. Washington would become quickly the seat of the Confederate government. . . . All Europe would welcome the New Aristocracy of the South into the firmament of nations."

During the winter preceding Lincoln's inauguration the whole Washington scene was dismal beyond description. In an imperial system when Cæsar rides in state to the capitol, with unclouded brow and firm-set jaw, he spreads around him, no matter how great the perturbation of his inner spirit, an atmosphere of authority, stability, decision, and prescience. In the swirling democracy of Washington there was no Cæsar, though Sumner and Seward at least felt competent to steer the ship of state away from the rocks. Instead of Augustan assurance, confusion, difference of opinion, and uncertainty as to the outcome prevailed among the victorious Republicans. When it rained or snowed the unpaved streets of the uncouth city swam in mud; when they were dry the wintry winds swept clouds of dust up and down the thoroughfares—a physical condition that typified the mental atmosphere. The air was thick with gossip and opinion.

Amid the babel of tongues, presumably speaking for the North, only three clear notes were discernible: far to the left declaimed the professors of a simple doctrine—let the seceding states depart in peace; far to the right shouted the professors of immediate and unconditional coercion, with Sumner and Chase in the lead; in the middle were the conciliators and opportunists led by Seward, the former fire-eating promoter of the irrepressible conflict. In the Autobiography of Charles Francis Adams these anxious saviors of their country are represented as rushing to and fro in eager haste to be doing something. Charles Sumner, who did not take the Adams view of the dilemma, was "a crazy man, orating, gesticulating, rolling out deep periods in theatrical whispered tones—repeating himself and doing everything but reason." William H. Seward was always running in and out of the Senate, "the small, thin, sallow man, with the pale, wrinkled, strongly marked face—plain and imperturbable—the thick, guttural voice and the everlasting cigar," the Wellington of the picture, at Waterloo, praying in vain for night or Bluecher. In the White House, poor distraught Buchanan, he of "the wry neck and dubious eye," was wringing his hands, proclaiming the Union indissoluble, and himself unable to prevent it from dissolving. Meanwhile the unknown and unfathomable Lincoln "was perambulating the country, kissing little girls, and growing whiskers."

In that milling tumult, not one statesman foresaw the immediate future or read correctly the handwriting on the wall. Those oldest in experience and most learned in the arts and sciences of the schools turned out to be no wiser than the rough men of the frontier who stumbled and blundered along in the dim light of their conscience and understanding. All were caught up and whirled in a blast too powerful for their wills, too swift for their mental operations.

§

Even the safe inauguration of Lincoln and the straightforward words of his first address made no immediate change in the situation. The new President took a positive stand on the nature of the Union: it was perpetual and no state could lawfully withdraw from it. He was equally firm in declaring that he would enforce the Constitution and the statutes against states that sought to violate or defy the law but his tone was conciliatory and he closed with a simple and moving appeal to sentiments of union, peace, and friendship.

Still these were merely spoken words which left the affairs of state exactly as they stood, great events continuing to wait on action, on the movement of federal authorities, on some overt physical stroke, on some outward manifestation of will and decision. Though on both sides hotheads clamored for bloodshed, all hesitated to make the fateful thrust that was to draw it. Day after day passed with the ship of state rolling erratically in the trough. April came and the warm spring sun seemed to beckon the nation to the pursuits of peace; dark clouds on the horizon looked dim and far away. In the White House, plagued by the horde of office-seekers hungry for jobs and by advisers swollen with infallibility, Lincoln wrestled with the multiplicity of minor questions permitting of decision.

Beyond all dispute Lincoln's problems in those tense days were stupendous. He spoke for a minority. He was no dictator standing for a triumphant majority and commissioned to carry out its appointed task. On the contrary he was aware, as southern planters were aware, that the North was torn by factions and he had no way of discovering how the bulk of his own party wanted him to act in the crisis. He knew that the anti-slavery sentiment in the country, though strong, was limited in its appeal; that, except in the hearts of the abolitionists, it was timid; that the Quakers who professed it were in general against emancipation by war.

Moreover abolitionists were divided on secession. Henry Ward Beecher, when informed that the southern states were withdrawing from the Union, burst forth: "I do not care if they do." Horace Greeley wrote in the Tribune: "If the cotton states shall decide that they can do better out of the Union than in it, we insist on letting them go in peace. The right to secede may be a revolutionary one but it exists nevertheless." It required events to drive that editor into the ranks of the coercionists.

Few, indeed, were the prophetic opponents of slavery who welcomed the test of battle and believed that the great solution of force foretold by John Quincy Adams was at hand. To no one except the fanatic was the issue simple. A wide belt of slave states had not seceded: a single utterance or act by Lincoln savoring of a war on slavery would have sent them all into the arms of the Confederacy. Nor could Lincoln count with certainty on undivided economic support above the Potomac. Ardently as they desired the preservation of the great customs union, northern business interests did not want war, save in the last bitter extremity. With respect to this problem Greeley estimated that southern debtors owed at least $200,000,000 to creditors in New York City alone, drawing from his figures the conclusion that a resort to arms meant general ruin in commercial circles. Unless human experience was as naught, the watchword of the solemn hour was Caution.

For good reasons, therefore, all practical men, including Jefferson Davis on the one side and Abraham Lincoln on the other, feverishly sought some middle ground of compromise. Speaking for eastern finance, Thurlow Weed, an Albany journalist and politician, who had done valiant work in carrying New York for the Republicans, proposed that the Missouri Compromise line be extended by common consent to the Pacific. Though this offer called for a partial surrender, Davis, warning his followers that a war would be terrible, expressed a willingness to accept the adjustment. But Lincoln stood rigid as a rock against it, pointing to his own pledges and to those of his party—promises to drive slavery from the territories. Eastern business men might bargain over the matter but the western farmers had decided that national lands must be dedicated to freedom and the President could not ignore their resolve. In Congress, Senator Crittenden of Kentucky proposed a compromise similar to that offered by Weed but Lincoln's followers could not be induced to support it.

On this point the fate of the nation seemed to turn. Lincoln was prepared to give any reasonable guarantee to the slave owners against interference with their peculiar institution as it stood. As evidence of his sincerity, he wrote to Alexander H. Stephens of Georgia, assuring the planters that the Republican administration would not "directly or indirectly interfere with their slaves or with them about their slaves"; that "the South would be in no more danger in this respect than it was in the days of Washington".

Not only that; Lincoln and his Republican brethren, offering proof of their readiness to seal the covenant forever, supported and carried through Congress an amendment to the Constitution declaring that for all the future the federal government should be denied the power to abolish or interfere with slavery in any state. On March 4, 1861, the resolution was sent forth to the states for their ratification, with Lincoln's approval, and three states had actually ratified it when the outbreak of physical combat stopped the operation. By the irony of fate, not the deliberate choice of men, the Thirteenth Amendment to the Constitution when it finally came was to abolish slavery in the United States, not to fasten it upon the continent to the end of time.

Why was the fatal blow that substituted armed might for negotiation ever struck? According to all outward and visible signs the opposing sections might have stood indefinitely in the posture of expectancy. Why did any one seek to break the spell? In whose brain, in the final analysis, was made the decision which directed the hand to light the powder train and blow up the wall of doubt that divided peace from war? No unanimous verdict on that point has yet been rendered by a court of last resort; one more question of war guilt remains unsolved.

It has been said that Lincoln, by deciding to send relief to Fort Sumter in the harbor of Charleston, splashed blood on his own head. The answer to such a thesis is that the relief sent to the beleaguered fort consisted mainly of provisions for a starving garrison and offered no direct menace to the Confederacy. It has been alleged that the inner leaders of the Confederacy, feeling the ground slipping from under them, thought bloodshed necessary to consolidate their forces and bring the hesitant states into their fold. The answer commonly made to this argument is that President Davis, in his final instructions to General Beauregard, commanding the Confederates at Charleston, spoke merely in general terms about the reduction of Sumter and advised action only if certain conditions of evacuation were rejected.

As a matter of fact, Major Anderson, in charge of Union forces, offered a compromise which should have been sent to Davis for review but Beauregard's aides, spurred on by an ardent secessionist from Virginia, made the decision on their own account in favor of audacity and at 4:30 on the morning of April 12, started the conflagration by firing on Fort Sumter. This bombardment and the surrender of the fort had just the effect foreseen by the extremists: the South, by striking the first blow and hauling down the Stars and Stripes, kindled the quivering opinion of the North into a devouring flame. Lincoln's call for volunteers and answer of force by force pushed Virginia, North Carolina, Tennessee, and Arkansas into the Confederacy. The die was cast.

§

The event at Fort Sumter, by quickening the revolutionary zeal of the South, gave heart to the Confederates who for two months had been engaged in constructing a new union at Montgomery. Early in February, 1861, after adopting a tentative plan of government, they put it into effect by electing Jefferson Davis of Mississippi provisional president. In due course Davis appeared to deliver his inaugural address.

Cheer on cheer rose from the throngs gathered from far and wide to view the spectacle. "The man and the hour have met"; clear as the snap of a rifle rang the words of the orator who presented the hero of the occasion and the crowd replied with the voice of thunder.

This man of destiny was indeed an arresting figure. He was lithe and sinewy, just above the middle height. A square chin, thin lips, a firm nose, deep-set eyes, and a high, noble brow revealed a thoughtful spirit and a strong will. "He is certainly a very different looking man from Mr. Lincoln," wrote the correspondent of the London Times; "he is like a gentleman." And yet in birth the social gulf between the two presidents was not as deep as sometimes imagined; for Davis was the son of a Kentucky farmer, and he, too, had no mansion for his birthplace. His father, however, unlike the luckless Thomas Lincoln, moved South instead of North and acquired a modest fortune as a planter in Mississippi. Well endowed with earthly goods, Jefferson Davis enjoyed the advantages of a college education in Kentucky, finished by a military training at West Point. Having chosen the profession of arms and politics, he served with distinction in the Mexican War, and after the close of that struggle, spent much of his time in Washington, either in the Senate or in the Cabinet. He was a United States Senator when the fateful "hour" drew near.

Throughout his career Davis had been loyal in defending the planting interest but he was not as caustic and unbending as many on his side. With Calhoun he believed that "African slavery, as it exists in the United States, is a moral, a social, and a political blessing." He favored the repeal of the Missouri Compromise and the extension of slavery throughout the territories. Penetrating the verbalism of the contest, he plainly grasped the economics of the political conflict. The South, he said repeatedly, was an agricultural section whose interest demanded the freest possible trade with other nations. The protective tariff was to him merely a tribute laid on the planters for the benefit of northern capitalists and accordingly he opposed it to the bitter end. And yet he was no extremist; he was ready to accept the project for extending the Missouri Compromise line to the Pacific, which Lincoln so resolutely rejected. Davis foresaw that the war would be long and desperate if it came and he took up the sword with anything but a light heart.

A short time after the inauguration of Davis as provisional president the congress at Montgomery drafted a permanent constitution for the Confederate States of America. In November, 1861, the elections were held and on the 22d of the following February Davis, already worn and haggard, took his place at the foot of the Washington Monument in Richmond, the capital chosen for the Confederacy, to deliver his inaugural. By this time Fort Donelson had fallen and gloom had begun to settle down on the southern cause. Rain poured from heaven on the assembled throng as an evil omen but Davis was not daunted in the "darkest hour of our struggle." Disaster would only call forth renewed effort. "To thee, O God!" he exclaimed at the end of the ceremony, "trustingly, I commit myself and prayerfully invoke Thy blessing on my country and its cause."

The confederate constitution which thus went formally into effect was in most respects like the instrument drafted by the Fathers at Philadelphia in 1787 for the whole Union. It provided for a president, a senate, and a house of representatives and it empowered the congress to give department heads seats upon the floor of either house and to confer upon them the right to take part in debates. Echoing the long economic contest between North and South, it withheld from the congress, however, certain significant powers: it forbade appropriations for internal improvements, the granting of bounties to private enterprise, and the levy of import duties for the purpose of fostering any branch of industry. For the silence of the federal Constitution with regard to the nature of the Union it substituted the express declaration that each state acted "in its sovereign and independent character." The cornerstone of the new system rested, as the vice-president, Alexander Stephens, said, "upon the great truth that the negro is not equal to the white man, that slavery—subordination to the superior race—is his natural and normal condition. This our new government is the first in the history of the world based upon this great physical, philosophical, and moral truth."

As to the ethical character of their enterprise, the confederate leaders were somewhat confused. In his first inaugural address, Davis rested the case on the natural right of the people to alter or abolish their governments and on the legal nature of the constitutional compact; he objected to calling secession "revolution." His colleague, Stephens, however, boldly spoke of the dissolution of the Union as "this revolution." Senator Iverson, of Georgia, also took the ground that the secession of a state was "an act of revolution" and that the question of attempted coercion by the national government was one of policy and expediency. Using almost the same language Robert E. Lee declared in 1861 that "Secession is nothing but revolution." Robert Toombs, of Georgia, said with engaging frankness to the North that he did not care about the language of the occasion: "You may call it secession, or you may call it revolution; but there is the big fact standing before you ready to oppose you—that fact is, freemen with arms in their hands."

But as time advanced and as doom loomed larger and larger on the horizon, especially after the battle of Gettysburg in 1863, southern leaders in high places began to lay increasing emphasis on their constitutional and legal right to withdraw from the federal Union. Triumphant revolution carries its own moral justification; a revolution suppressed wears another aspect. So the official tradition in due course came to be that secession was an act solemnly sanctified by the federal Constitution—not revolution, not rebellion, not insurrection, but due process of law.

§

When the southern leaders turned from legal theory to the task of raising money, materials, and men for the titanic struggle, they faced problems of a different order. The North had a national currency system, such as it was; the South had to create one. Though its finances were at a low ebb, the North had a treasury and a scheme of taxation; the South had to build its fiscal structure from the base up. At first, the Confederacy placed its main reliance for current income on customs duties levied for revenue rather than for protection—a frail reed soon broken by the blockade of southern ports which Lincoln proclaimed in April, 1861. Resort was then had to a direct property tax apportioned among the seceding states; but this also proved disappointing to its sponsors.

There was but one prime resource left—paper; so bond issue after bond issue flowed from the central and local treasuries in a steady torrent. Southern patriots bought confederate securities by the ream. Large blocks were sold in London, Paris, and Amsterdam; many an English lord sought to combine profit with sympathy for the planting aristocracy, only to lament in later years the proofs of his nescience. To bonds were added bills of credit; all in all the confederate treasury issued more than a billion dollars in paper. States, banks, city governments, and business men contributed floods to the main stream. Even grocers, barbers, butchers, bakers, and candlestick makers floated bills of small denominations. But all this paper brought little cash. During its entire existence the Confederacy gathered in less than thirty millions in hard money, a large part of which was sent abroad to pay for goods.

It could, therefore, make no pretense at keeping its currency on a specie basis. The old yet ever new story was repeated. Attempts were made to prevent depreciation but they were all in vain. Though the paper rose and fell with the fortunes of war, it exhibited on the whole a marked downward tendency. Before two years of the struggle had passed, one gold dollar was worth twenty-two in confederate paper and an ordinary dinner in a good Richmond restaurant cost from fifty to a hundred dollars in currency. And yet the printing presses had difficulty in keeping up with the call for paper—more paper—until at length the vast house of rags and pulp came down in complete collapse. That the smash finally came was not surprising; the amazing thing was that the southern people were able to carry on the unequal contest with such enthusiasm and effect in spite of their chaotic currency.

Though enjoying a far more strategic position, the federal government was itself driven to its wits' ends in financing the war. The enormous and unexpected cost of the undertaking was bewildering to officials accustomed to handling only petty sums. During the four years of the conflict, the army and navy departments alone disbursed over three billion dollars—more than twenty times the outlay of the preceding four years of peace. In meeting these charges, Congress resorted to loans at high rates rather than to heavy and drastic taxes. In the first year of the war, it borrowed $8.52 for every dollar of revenue it raised by taxation and at the end the ratio was still as high as three to one.

Most of the federal bond issues were floated on a liberal commission basis through the banking house of Jay Cooke. With astonishing energy, "the financier of the Civil War" organized bond "drives" from Boston to San Francisco, which supplied Lincoln's administration with funds in fair weather and foul. In this operation of course Cooke did not escape criticism: charges were made repeatedly by the press that he reaped exorbitant profits from his transactions; and it is true that he grew immensely rich during the war. Nevertheless an investigation showed that his earnings from bond sales were on the whole as moderate as the people had a right to expect from bankers in circumstances that were highly speculative. At all events, Cooke's gains were relatively small as compared with the magnitude of his undertakings. In September, after the close of the war, the national debt stood at $2,846,000,000 as against $74,-985,000 on the day that Lincoln took over the administration of affairs.

By that time the revenues from taxation had risen to the highest point in the history of the country. After dodging the question for many months, Congress eventually came face to face with reality. It increased the rates on imports, more than incidentally pleasing the protected interests; it imposed direct taxes on the states according to their respective populations; and it laid duties on luxuries, occupations, incomes, the earnings of corporations, and almost every other available object. The fiscal year ending in June,

1862, showed a revenue from taxes of only fifty millions; the year 1865 reported nearly three hundred millions—one-tenth from the income tax.

In addition to laying taxes and issuing bonds, the federal government, driven to desperation for funds, began in 1862 to issue bills, popularly known as "Greenbacks," unsupported by specie. At the end of two years over four hundred million dollars' worth of such paper had poured from northern printing presses into the market to pay the Union soldiers and meet current expenses, except interest on the debt which was paid in specie. When this paper began to decline, as it naturally did, those who sold supplies to the government, in keeping with historic practices, raised their prices to cover the differences—but the soldiers whose wages were fixed could not recoup their losses so easily. In the dark days of 1864, it took nearly three dollars in Greenbacks to buy one dollar in gold.

§

The same experience of initial buoyancy and later depression was reported by the departments of government that raised the armed forces for the struggle. At the outset both sides were able to rely on the enthusiasm of the masses to fill the ranks of fighting men. Lincoln called for seventy-five thousand volunteers when the news from Sumter reached his ears; by the first of the following July more than three hundred thousand soldiers were at his command. Similar loyalty was shown in the South. "The anxiety among our citizens," said Howell Cobb of Georgia, "is not as to who shall go to the war but who shall stay at home." When Davis faced a special session of his congress on April 29, he could boast that forty-five thousand men were under arms for the Confederacy and that volunteers were rushing in faster than they could be equipped and trained.

Then the tide turned. After the appalling magnitude of the struggle became evident and the passions of the early weeks cooled in the grim test of actual fighting, neither government was able to rely upon volunteers to fill the gaps and enlarge the forces necessary to meet the rising call of necessity. In 1862 the confederate government resorted to the draft; the next year the federal government was driven to the same expedient. In 1864 the Confederacy prepared to enlist all white males between seventeen and fifty, thus, as the phrase went, robbing the cradle and the grave; in its dire need at the last it decided to enroll slaves. On each side the great principle of universal liability was at first violated by invidious exceptions which were made doubly odious by the provision that persons drafted might by hiring substitutes escape service altogether—a privilege so crass and so plainly favoring the rich as against the poor, that it sowed seeds of bitterness everywhere.

In both sections of the country hostile demonstrations greeted the conscription acts. The beginning of the drawings for the federal service on July 13, 1863, was the signal for a serious riot in New York City which to timid civilians seemed like a revolution. The draft headquarters were destroyed; the office of the Tribune was gutted; Negroes were seized, hanged, and shot; the residence of the mayor was attacked; the homes of several Unionists were burned to the ground; and pitched battles were fought in the streets between the rioters and the police. For three days the revolt raged. Not until a large contingent of troops arrived on the spot was the insurrection quelled. By that time at least a thousand people had been killed or wounded and a million dollars worth of property destroyed. In other parts of the North there were evasions and desertions; the number who bought substitutes was also beyond all expectations.

The South, too, had its heartburnings. The governor of Georgia declared to President Davis that no law passed by the Congress of the United States had ever struck such a fell blow at liberty as the conscription act of the confederate government. In the mountain districts of North Carolina,

Tennessee, Georgia, Alabama, and South Carolina there was open resistance to the draft; public meetings were held to denounce it; throngs of eligible men fled to escape it; and in some places lawless men gathered in bands to overawe the officers engaged in executing it. Everywhere resentment was aroused by the provisions which allowed the rich to avoid service by money payment and in effect exempted owners of the larger plantations. Finally under pressure, the confederate congress, against the hot protests of those who had hired substitutes, abolished the practice and made liability universal, subject to the usual exemptions and special considerations for the owners of more than fifteen slaves. At the end both governments were displaying relentless vigilance in combing the populace for recruits to fill the gaps and swell the ranks of their armies; but the Confederacy proved unequal to the task. During the closing months of the war, conscription "utterly failed" in the South and the authorities at Richmond had to report a hundred thousand deserters.

§

Another task which confronted the belligerent governments, in some ways more baffling than that of raising money or organizing armed forces, was the mobilization of public opinion and civilian forces in support of the war. In a large measure, of course, that operation was at first automatic; the clash of arms, the shock, the challenge rallied masses of people on both sides to the battle standards. While youths rushed to the colors, older men of affairs, laying aside their private concerns, dedicated themselves to the official and unofficial assistance of their respective governments, often allowing their emotion to outrun their discretion.

Responsible statesmen and politicians, it seems, were on the whole more temperate than the vociferous among their constituents. "The truth is," recorded Jefferson Davis, "the southern people were in advance of their representatives throughout"—an opinion underlined by the newspapers. The Charleston Mercury, for example, could not conceal its impatience at all attempts to effect a compromise at the opening of 1861. "Southern Senators upon the floor of Congress," wrote the editor, "demean themselves by pitiable lamentations and lachrymose appeals to haughty, contemptuous, and openly threatening enemies—Republicans—Yankees." The English journalist, Russell, writing from New Orleans to the London Times in May, 1861, declared: "There is no doubt of the unanimity of the people. If words mean anything, they are animated by only one sentiment and they will resist the North as long as they can command a man or a dollar."

If on the other side there was no such singleness of purpose, there was a resolution no less grim. The shot at Sumter produced a mass response; as Garrison remarked, sent a "mighty current of feeling . . . sweeping southward with the strength and impetuosity of a thousand Niagaras." Other witnesses confirmed that view. "That first gun at Sumter," said Lowell, "brought all the free states to their feet as one man."

The rolling tide of war swept women with men into its current. Until the end of the eighteenth century war had been almost exclusively a man's business—a trade followed by kings to acquire territory and renown—a trade carried on with the aid of feudal retainers and bands of professional soldiers—a trade in which peasants and merchants had little part—a trade in which women were even less involved except as victims or as camp followers. But the democratic movement of the eighteenth century which culminated in the French Revolution lifted merchants and peasants to the enjoyment of rights and privileges, gave them the ballot, thrust muskets into their hands, and made them patriots. It was the French who, under Napoleon, instituted the practice of general conscription and taught the art to Europe. As democracy advanced on universality, the principle of general liability to military service became widely fixed; inevitably, therefore, as women won economic independence, gained legal rights, and demanded equality in politics and every other sphere, they too were drawn into, or entered of their own accord, the trade of war. A logical outcome of Jacksonian Democracy was a new relation of women to the business of fighting, in all its branches and agitations.

So the Civil War in the United States marked the next era in the history of American feminism. Previously men had done the nursing at the front as well as the fighting and cooking. Now northern women, under the leadership of Clara Barton, in spite of bitter official opposition, insisted on bearing all the hardships and enduring all the perils of nursing and cooking in the field hospitals just behind the battle front, carrying into warfare woman's passion for order, comfort, and cleanliness. Southern women also took up these burdens: "the exception," said Mrs. Jefferson Davis, referring to her Richmond friends, "was a woman who did not nurse at a hospital."

The introduction of the feminine arts at the battle front in turn induced an enormous demand for hospital supplies, conveniences, and delicacies—a demand which was in its turn met largely by the efforts of women themselves. In the organization and management of the United States Sanitary Commission they were especially active; the sanitary fairs which received such high praise from Lincoln were almost entirely their work. Nor were the women of the Confederacy backward in this respect; in the letters and memoirs of southern writers are recorded strenuous labors of women in preparing and forwarding supplies for hospitals and camps. Writing of her neighbors at Richmond, Mrs. Davis said: "They clothed and cared for their own households, sewed for the soldiers, made our battle flags, and sent their dearest and only breadwinners to give their lives for them. They fed the hungry, cared for the orphans, deprived themselves of every wonted luxury to give

it to the soldiers, and were amid their privations so cheerful as to animate even the men with hope."

Apart from rendering wider services in direct connection
with the fighting, women extended the range of their economic and political activities as a result of war necessities,
especially in the North. They entered the new industrial
enterprises which made supplies for the armies by the factory process. They poured into the recently established
schools to take the places of men summoned to the front.
On hundreds of farms where there were no slaves to till
the soil, women picked up the lines and plow handles as the
men dropped them, assuming the burden of the heavy work
in the fields. On that scene Anna Howard Shaw raised the
curtain in her vivid reminiscences of war days in Wisconsin.

Throughout the North where women had waged a long
and bitter struggle for platform privileges, they now became accepted speakers at public meetings held to raise
money, sell bonds, and keep alive the martial spirit. The
young "spellbinder," Anna Dickinson, became so indispensable during the war to the Lincoln party that at its close
Republican politicians made a special appeal to her to postpone still longer her woman suffrage activities to help maintain them in power. In fact, in 1872, so grateful were they
for such support that they recognized the rising power of
women to the extent of a plank in their platform reading:
"The Republican party is mindful of its obligations to the
loyal women of America for their noble devotion to the
cause of freedom. Their admission to wider spheres of
usefulness is viewed with satisfaction; and the honest demand of any class of citizens for additional rights should
be treated with respectful consideration." North and
South, women of every rank felt the old order falling down
about them as the tide of battle flowed on to its inexorable end.

§

Notwithstanding the yearning for war service that was evident among great masses of people, men and women alike, both governments found it difficult to maintain the morale of the public, especially after a few months of bloodshed had cooled the ardor of zealots. In controlling opinion and rallying scattered forces, each had its peculiar difficulties. According to outward signs, the resolve of the South to carry the struggle through to the end was more completely fused in the white heat of unity; at all events the confederate administration was harried by no such formidable opposition as that presented to Lincoln by the Democratic party and its press.

Still it would be a mistake to speak of a "solid South" at that time. In large sections of the upland and mountain region were powerful unionist movements. During the course of the war peace societies, some of them clearly disloyal to the confederate cause, were discovered in North Carolina, Alabama, Georgia, Virginia, and Mississippi. A few newspapers openly refused to give wholehearted aid to the Richmond administration. The editor of the Raleigh Standard, for instance, consistently adhered to policies that bordered on rebellion and even ventured to run for governor of the state in 1864 on a platform that was called "a peace-at-any-price proposal." When his printing plant was wrecked by irate soldiers, his civilian patrons replied by smashing the office of a rival secessionist organ. Furthermore the anarchic force of states' rights, invoked by the confederates against the government at Washington, raged against the government of their own making. In the final stages of the awful struggle, the governors of North Carolina and Georgia were on the verge of revolt against the Davis régime. Indeed in February, 1864, the southern president was moved to send a special message to his congress directing attention to "secret leagues and associations" and to the "disloyalty and hostility to our cause" shown in various quarters.

With a view to counteracting disruptive tendencies, the

confederate government resorted to special measures. Early in 1862 the writ of habeas corpus was suspended by a general act; later the suspension was renewed in more sweeping terms; and many citizens were imprisoned under military authority. But on the whole Davis had to walk warily in employing repressive tactics. On every side he heard vigorous protests, made in the name of civil liberty, against martial rule, against centralized and autocratic government even though southern in personnel and temper. When near the end an effort was made to ignore them and erect a dictatorship under General Lee, the design was quickly frustrated. The states' rights bias of the confederate constitution ran against all strong measures, thus contributing to the ultimate ruin of the southern cause.

The federal government was better equipped than its southern rival to exert heavy pressure on the public; and from the beginning of the war to the conclusion, it made constant and drastic use of its military power in dealing with speech and press. At the very start of the conflict, Lincoln as Commander-in-chief authorized the suspension of the writ of habeas corpus along the lines of march between Philadelphia and Washington. Later the martial area was extended, likewise by proclamation.

In the spring of 1863, Congress, bent on laying all doubts as to the President's power, provided that he might suspend the writ anywhere in the United States and after a few months of hesitation Lincoln destroyed this ancient weapon for the defense of civilian rights throughout the length and breadth of the land. Thus autocratic prerogatives could be exercised, under the President, by military officers authorized to arrest without warrants, imprison, and mete out penalties at the drumhead. While the military arm was made in effect omnipotent, the civil arm of the government was strengthened in 1861 by an act which imposed heavy penalties on all persons who interfered by threats, intimidation or force with the prosecution of the war.

Of the powers just enumerated, the federal government

made extensive use against persons accused or suspected of southern sympathies. Editors of hostile journals were put in prison, their papers suspended, their newsboys arrested. Peace meetings were broken up and the organizers sent to jail. Members of the Maryland legislature, the mayor of Baltimore, and local editors accused of holding obstructive views were arrested on military order; though they were charged with no overt act of any kind, they were held in jail and denied the privilege of a hearing before a civil magistrate. All over the country, the net was thrown out to catch offenders—in the theater of war, in the border states where there was constant danger of new uprisings, and far away in the North to the boundaries of Canada, where the ordinary criminal courts were competent to handle the most fiery advocate of secession. With devotion to the national cause went zest for persecution, that persistent passion of mankind, and thus a kind of iron discipline was spread to the remote recesses of the continent.

Such measures and activities on the part of the federal administration naturally aroused deep hostility among the victims—among Democrats on whom most of the stigma fell and among Republicans who disliked harsh policies of coercion. Meetings of protest were held in the great cities; deputations of dissenters besieged the White House; and members of Congress sought to put on record a resolution of objection to the suspension of the writ of habeas corpus. In an effort to uphold civil liberties, Roger B. Taney, Chief Justice of the Supreme Court of the United States, before whom the case of a man arrested on military order was brought for a hearing, declared, in an opinion bristling with citations, that the President had no power to suspend the writ of habeas corpus. Lincoln put the opinion of the learned Justice in a pigeon hole. A Democratic leader in Ohio, C. L. Vallandigham, kept up a defiant criticism of the federal government, insisting that oppression would produce a reign of terror, and declaring the war "a costly and bloodly failure"—until he was finally banished to the

South on military order. Wendell Phillips assailed Lincoln as "a more unlimited despot than the world knows this side of China."

At heart a friend of liberty and a foe of wanton oppression, Lincoln sought to adjust the rigors of the military régime to evident necessities. In the very midst of the war he granted amnesty to all "political prisoners" who would promise to give no aid or comfort to the enemy. He endured without murmuring personal abuse at the hands of hostile editors and politicians who, while they were declaiming against restraints on their liberty, were carrying it to the extreme of license. Yet in general Lincoln held strictly to the view that strong measures should be used in dealing with those who "talked against the war." On one occasion, after listening to arguments from a committee of objectors, he asked in his quiet way: "Must I shoot a simple-minded soldier boy who deserts, while I must not touch a hair of the wily agitator who induces him to desert?" When accused of violating the Constitution, he replied that he had taken an oath to uphold it and that any action necessary to carry out his oath was lawful. This was "liberal construction" with a vengeance but it pleased Lincoln's supporters; so the rigor of the law was invoked against "political offenders," with varying emphasis, to the end.

§

Among the many threads that were woven into the web of fate, diplomacy figured beside finance, armies, and opinion. The facts of 1861 burst the shibboleth of isolation. If England and France had recognized the independence of the Confederacy, forced the North to relax the blockade, and opened the way for money and supplies to pour into the South, the history of the Second American Revolution would have been far different. Fully alive to the perils of this situation, Lincoln gave constant attention to the task of conciliating English opinion and counteracting movements looking toward foreign intervention. More than once he softened the language of diplomatic notes; continuously did he sustain Charles Francis Adams, federal minister in London, in the diplomacy of patience and firmness.

Happily for the Union cause, the North had many loyal friends among the people of England—sympathizers who believed that the issue of slavery *vs.* democracy was really hanging in the balance. Despite sneers from the upper classes, liberal leaders, such as John Bright, worked night and day to convince their countrymen that aiding the slaveowners' Confederacy was striking at liberty throughout the world. And the textile workers of the mill districts applauded that sentiment. Even in the gloomiest hours when the cotton famine had brought them to the verge of starvation, they petitioned their government to aid the North by allowing the blockade to continue unmolested.

Especially after Lincoln's "Proclamation of Emancipation" did popular opinion in England run clear and strong in favor of the North. "Bondage and the lash can claim no sympathy from us," exclaimed Spurgeon the famous preacher, to his vast congregation; "God bless and strengthen the North; give victory to their arms!" By immense public meetings held in the industrial centers of England, the anti-slavery passion was kept at white heat. At one assembly Bright declared that, while statesmen were hostile or coldly neutral, while many rich men were aiding the Confederacy, while the press betrayed the Union cause, the English masses believed in the triumph of freedom and prayed for the success of northern armies. Diplomatic strategy, wheat, and fate crowned Lincoln's efforts in England with success.

President Davis likewise grasped the significance of the foreign problem and spared no effort to propitiate the powers of the Old World. Early in the struggle he sent special commissioners abroad and until its close he did everything he could to win foreign aid. At first the omens were favorable. With the ruling classes of Europe, the southern cause was undoubtedly popular, since they felt instinctively that the triumph of the North would imperil their dominion at home. In England a majority of both houses of Parliament was in open sympathy with the Confederacy; leading statesmen, especially among the landed aristocracy, hoped that the war would end in the downfall of "the contemptible democracy" beyond the sea.

Across the Channel, Napoleon III was anxious to throw himself officially on the southern side. In 1861, he proposed to Russia a coalition against the North. Defeated in this, he suggested to England joint intervention. Receiving a non-committal answer from her wary Cabinet, he ventured in 1863 to offer his services directly to Lincoln as mediator. Again he met a rebuff; Lincoln declined the offer politely while Congress suggested in a sharp resolution that he attend to his own affairs.

From time to time throughout the war, however, it looked as if England and France were about to recognize the Confederacy. On one occasion Gladstone, whose family fortune contained profits from the slave trade, speaking as a responsible officer in the British government, virtually acknowledged southern independence. In a speech at Newcastle in 1862, he announced: "Jefferson Davis and other leaders of the South . . . have made a nation. . . . We may anticipate with certainty the success of the southern states so far as their separation from the North is concerned."

In dealing with practical concerns, the British ministry also showed a certain benevolence toward the South. With indifference, if not approval, it permitted war vessels to be built for the Confederacy in English shipyards and allowed them to sail forth to prey upon Union commerce. It looked calmly on while one of these ships, the Alabama, constructed in Liverpool by an English firm and paid for by bonds sold to English investors, destroyed more than fifty merchantmen before she was brought to book by the

Kearsarge in 1864. Again and again did the American minister in London protest that such actions were unlawful —merely to meet indifference. It was only by a threat of retaliation in the form of war on England that Lincoln was able at last to arouse the British authorities to stop the sailing of ships built for the confederate service.

Nevertheless it must be admitted in all fairness that the British government had good reasons for entertaining some ill-will toward the North. Viewed in a detached way, the pleas of English democrats in behalf of the Union on the score of liberty were without justification, for the Lincoln government, far from vowing a war on slavery in the early days of the conflict, offered to guarantee the institution forever if the secessionists would only come back into the Union. It was not without excuse that English critics cried: "The Yankees are after all only fighting for the tariff and hurt vanity." And the English government, it must be remembered, years before had adopted the "grand principles of free trade" which the Confederacy professed to the world. Nor must immediate economic considerations be overlooked. The English cotton business was hard hit by the blockade, especially after the stocks on hand were consumed—hard hit in spite of the compensations offered by the federal purchases of war supplies and the great inpouring of American wheat.

To make irritating matters worse, the spokesmen of the Union were not always as tactful in their foreign relations as they might have been. In his capacity as Secretary of State, Seward was often curt with England, even though Lincoln more than once toned down the acerbity of his diplomatic notes. Inflexible in its support of the government, the administration press was frequently needlessly severe, especially the New York Herald which kept declaring that the English aristocracy was conspiring against American liberties and every now and then hinted that war with England would be a desirable thing. "Let England and Spain look well to their conduct," the editor of that paper once roared, "or we may bring them to a reckoning." Unquestionably American explosions of that kind had unfortunate reverberations abroad. With a great show of authority, Herbert Spencer could argue that English sentiment was less friendly to the North after months of such bickering than at the beginning of the civil conflict.

This state of affairs was partly the result of a single untoward incident. In the autumn of 1861, two confederate agents, Mason and Slidell, appointed by Davis to represent the Richmond government at London and Paris respectively, sailed for their posts on the British steamer, the Trent. Getting wind of this adventure, Captain Wilkes, in command of a Union vessel, overhauled the English ship and took off the two confederate commissioners, giving the world a fine example of search and seizure and thereby raising anew burning questions in the law of the sea. On her part, England had often resorted to analogous, though not identical, practices before the War of 1812 and the United States had hotly objected on the ground that such deeds violated American rights. Now the tables were turned.

Without any ado, England demanded the release of the two men and a proper apology for their seizure. Incensed by this peremptory call, belligerent politicians at Washington wanted to fight; but both Seward and Lincoln kept their heads. Calmly reviewing the merits of the case, they decided to surrender Mason and Slidell and disown the action of Captain Wilkes. So the cloud passed and the following autumn, after the emancipation of slaves was announced, the sentiment of the English public, as distinguished from the ruling classes, began to veer more strongly than ever toward the northern side.

§

Supplementing their formal diplomatic negotiations, Lincoln and Davis both paid court to the art of propaganda. The extent to which the federal government engaged in frank and covert efforts to influence foreign opinion is not easy to discover because all the official papers are not available. But there is reason to believe that it neglected no opportunities. The State Department had at its disposal a secret service fund which it had used on at least one occasion to sway opinion at home and had it neglected opportunities abroad during the war it would have been strangely remiss. At all events when the confederate commissioner visited the Pope in the interest of the Richmond government, he found His Holiness duly informed that "Lincoln and company" were waging a war against slavery.

As to the propaganda of the Confederacy in foreign fields, more is actually known because its archives, seized after the war, were thrown open by the national government, revealing to the public the official efforts of President Davis to win support by the circulation of prepared ideas. Hoping to win a recognition of independence, if not direct assistance, the Confederacy placed money at the disposal of its agents to be devoted to "the enlightenment of public opinion in Europe through the press." It freed the directors of this secret service from the necessity of furnishing vouchers for their expenditures, if circumstances did not permit an accounting. For the propaganda in England "the chief editor of one of the leading journals" was engaged and every occasion was seized to strengthen the intimacy of the confederate agents with "established organs of public opinion." In France chambers of commerce were induced to petition Napoleon III for intervention with a view to restoring commercial relations with the South. Beyond the Rhine the support and encouragement of Prussian army officers and upper classes were enlisted, a fact reported to Richmond with no little satisfaction.

Paying respect to the utility of religious emotions, a carefully selected Catholic priest was dispatched to the Continent—to work especially in Paris, Madrid, Vienna, and Rome. As a stimulus to action, the confederate secretary of state, Judah P. Benjamin, an astute Jewish lawyer, informed this clerical diplomat that a recent raid had been made on Richmond for the purpose of committing it to flames, exposing its women to nameless horrors, and putting to death the chief magistrate and principal officers of the government; and by way of elaboration, Benjamin added that the fury of the federals "spares neither age nor sex, nor do they even shrink from the most shameful desecration of the edifices in which the people meet for the worship of God." News of such things the priest was told to distribute among foreign religious bodies where it would serve the southern cause.

Keeping in mind similar ends, the confederate secretary announced to his commissioners abroad that "the time is not far distant when the massacre of Catholics at the North will exhibit the full spirit of the Puritan on a scale of which mankind has yet had no example." As if to confirm the prophecy, he added that New England soldiers were even then desecrating Catholic churches and suggested the dissemination of statements to that effect in Catholic countries.

For the purpose of checking Irish emigration, a special agent, a Catholic priest, was instructed by Secretary Benjamin to visit Ireland and enlighten her people on the American situation: to tell them that the United States government was enticing laborers to migrate ostensibly for work on the railroads and then forcing them into the army; and to suggest that it was shocking for the Irish to leave their own land "for the purpose of imbruing their hands in the blood of a people that has ever received the Irish emigrant with kindness and hospitality."

To engage the sympathy of the Vatican, the Confederacy sent to it an envoy of peculiar accomplishments. Bearing an official letter from President Davis, this commissioner was duly received and reported a touching interview at the reading of his state paper to the Pope: "When the passage was reached wherein the President states in such sublime and affecting language, 'we have offered up at the footstool of our Father who art in Heaven prayers inspired by the same feelings which animate your Holiness,' his deep sunken orbs, visibly moistened, were upturned toward that throne upon which ever sits the Prince of Peace. . . . At length His Holiness asked whether President Davis were a Catholic. I answered in the negative."

Not inclined to be captious on that point, the Pope inquired whether it would not be judicious for the confederate government to consent to the gradual emancipation of the slaves. Thereupon the envoy explained the mysteries of constitutional law which gave the government at Richmond no control whatever over the domestic institutions of the states, suggesting in conclusion that if slavery were an evil, "there was a power which in its own good time would doubtless remove that evil, in a more gentle manner than that of causing the earth to be deluged with blood for its sudden overthrow." This position, having met the approval of His Holiness, the commissioner then went on to say that "Lincoln and Company" were decoying Irishmen to America "to be murdered in cold blood" and that northern "pulpit buffoons whose number is legion" were teaching shocking doctrines of cruelty to the people. By all these things too His Holiness was visibly moved.

§

The long conflict which ended in the downfall of the Confederacy thus had many phases. It was waged on land and sea by arms, in the capitals of Europe by diplomacy, and in the sphere of morals by propaganda, publicity, and coercion. Descriptions of the war itself must be entrusted to those who have charted the science of military tactics or mastered the art of depicting tragedy and romance. Since every one of its great battles has been the subject of fierce debate among experts, the layman does well to leave the technical issues to them. In the large, however, the problem for the South was mainly that of defense, although one heroic effort was made to push the war into the enemy's domain by a thrust into Pennsylvania—a thrust parried at Gettysburg in July, 1863. On the other hand, the problem of the North, to state it simply, was one of invasion and conquest. Lincoln's task was that of beating southern armies on their own soil or wearing them down to exhaustion.

Geography, as often happens, gave a distinct turn to the military process. The Appalachian mountains, stretching through the Confederacy into Alabama, divided the theater into two immense sections, in each of which, east and west, were prizes sought by northern armies. If Richmond, the confederate capital, could be taken by a bold stroke, the moral effect would be electric of course. If a wedge could be driven down the Mississippi Valley to the Gulf, the Confederacy would be severed and the southwest cut off from the center of power. Moreover victories in the west were necessary to hold the wavering states of Kentucky and Missouri in line with the Union. All this was patent to Lincoln and his advisers and on such theories they started operations in both areas.

To the armies of the western arena, victory came first. In February, 1862, General Grant captured Fort Donelson on the Cumberland River, offering to his defeated foeman the ultimatum: "No terms except unconditional and immediate surrender." At Shiloh, Murfreesboro, Vicksburg, Chickamauga, Chattanooga, and other points desperate fighting occurred, with varying results, but with an unmistakable drift. Within little more than a year after the fall of Donelson, the Mississippi Valley was open to the Gulf. "The Father of Waters again goes unvexed to the sea!" exclaimed Lincoln when he heard of the surrender of Vicksburg on July 4, 1863. The initiative in the West had passed to the Union commanders who continued to hammer the wedge, making wider and wider the rift between the two sections of the Confederacy. In the autumn of the next year, Sherman was at Atlanta and soon on his devastating march to the sea. To the complaint against his ruthless severity, he had an emphatic answer: "War is hell!" On Christmas day, Savannah was in his hands; the ocean was open before him.

Contrasted with the successes in the West, Union operations in the East during the first two years of the war presented an almost unbroken series of misfortunes. Hurried into action against better counsels by the popular cry, "On to Richmond," the federal army rushed into the enemy's country in July, 1861, to meet a terrible disaster at Bull Run. For four years periodical advances were made on Richmond without important military results. General after general—McClellan, Pope, Burnside, Hooker, and Meade—was tried and found wanting; none could administer the fatal blow. Their highest achievements amounted to little more than successful defense. McClellan checked General Lee at Antietam in September, 1862; and Meade paralyzed his northward thrust at Gettysburg in July of the following year; but nothing decisive was accomplished. At last in February, 1864, Lincoln turned to General Grant whom he placed in command of the armies of the Union. After surveying the ground, the new military master, supported by unlimited supplies, commenced a pitiless drive on Lee's army in Virginia. Though every inch of ground was stubbornly contested, the relentless pressure told in the end. Richmond fell, the Confederacy collapsed, Lee surrendered at Appomattox on April 9, 1865. The war was over.

To this outcome the contest on the sea, though less dramatic than that on the land, bore a vital relation. There, too, the task was cut out by remorseless fact: the South, an agricultural region, was largely dependent upon Europe for manufactured goods and in turn had to pay its bills in cotton and other raw materials. Once more, therefore, the sea power loomed large on the horizon of those who weighed national destinies. Quick to perceive it, Lincoln, on April 19, 1861, proclaimed a blockade against southern ports and, to make his order more effective, proceeded to increase the naval forces depleted by neglect. As time moved on, the iron grip of the northern patrol upon the sea-borne trade of the Confederacy grew tense. Only once within the four years was the blockade in serious peril— in the spring of 1862 when the confederate ironclad, the Merrimac, steamed out into Hampton Roads, crushed two federal vessels as if they were paper, and spread consternation far and wide in the Union ranks. At that very moment, however, a northern ironclad, the Monitor, was ready for the test and met it, ending the depredations of the Merrimac. A new epoch in sea fighting was opened; the success of the blockade was assured; the fate of the Confederacy was sealed.

Day and night, through winter and summer, the war vessels of the Union patrolled the coast, performing a relentless routine that was only now and then enlivened by an exciting chase when a blockade runner hove in sight. Though many adventurers, European and southern, equipped swift ships and risked lives and fortunes trying to break the cordon, the unresting vigilance of the federal navy steadily raised the hazards of the game. In 1860, the value of the cotton exported amounted to about two hundred million dollars; two years later it had fallen to four millions. Correlatively the foreign trade of the Confederacy in commodities of every kind was also cut to trifling proportions. Near the end of its career, the Richmond government could not get enough high-grade paper for its bonds and notes or enough iron to keep up the tracks and rolling stock of its railways. Southern business men no doubt showed great energy and capacity in building plants and furnishing supplies but they could not repair the industrial neglect of two centuries during the four years of the war.

§

The armed combat which called forth so much heroism and sacrifice was accompanied by all those darker mani-

festations of the human spirit that always mark great wars:
corruption in high places, cold and cynical profiteering, extravagance, and heartless frivolity. Before six months had
passed, the air of Washington was murky with charges of
fraud. "We are going to destruction as fast as imbecility,
corruption, and the wheels of time can carry us," said a discouraged Senator. A congressional investigation revealed
startling facts: contractors had made fat profits; they had
charged outrageous prices; they had deliberately cheated
the government by the delivery of inferior goods. The trail
led in the direction of the War Department; thereupon Lincoln removed the Secretary, a machine politician from Pennsylvania, and with a touch of poetic justice sent him as
minister to the court of the Tsar. An eminent authority
estimated that from one-fifth to one-fourth of the money
paid out of the federal treasury was tainted with the tricks
of swindlers.

Troubles of the same nature plagued the South. Richmond newspapers were full of complaints about robberies
by "official rogues." A Georgia editor lamented that
"quartermasters and commissaries grew rich by speculation
and robbery." In fact allegations of this type became
so numerous that the confederate congress enacted a special
law against knavery in the bureaus charged with buying war
materials. But apparently the disease could not be stamped
out; for one competent southern writer attributed the downfall of the Confederacy to the curse of corruption. Men of
more moderate temper on both sides ascribed the evils that
worried their respective governments more to inefficient administration than to the inordinate rapacity of merchants
and capitalists.

Luxurious living and profiteering on the part of civilians
as well as official transgressions characterized the struggle.
The new rich could not restrain their emotions. "We are
clothed in purple and fine linen," exclaimed the Chicago
Tribune, "wear the richest laces and jewels and fare sump-
tuously every day." When Secretary Chase visited New

York on urgent treasury business in the spring of 1864, he found men of affairs more interested in the stock market than in the awful news of bloodshed at the battle front. Running through the letters and papers of the time was the continuous dirge that contractors and profiteers were hoping for a long war and still better "pickings." "No one can fail to perceive," declared Robert C. Winthrop in 1864, "the danger that a real or even a professed patriotism may be made the cover for a multitude of sins and gallantry on the field of battle be regarded as a substitute for all the duties of the decalogue."

Notwithstanding the poverty of the Richmond government, chances to make huge profits and live on the fat of the land were also abundant in the South. Blockade-running presented prizes especially tempting: one ship alone yielded to her owners seven hundred per cent profit before she was captured. Some of the railways paid dividends ranging from thirty to sixty per cent and politicians waxed rich from army contracts. "The passion for speculation," cried President Davis in 1863, "has seduced citizens of all classes from a determined prosecution of the war to a sordid effort to amass money." Though the curtailment of foreign commerce made it difficult to import European finery, editors daily lamented that, while confederate soldiers were dying for the lack of medicines, the shops of the cities made more extensive displays of foreign fabrics than ever before. "On with the dance!" bitterly commented a southern writer when he read in the columns of the same newspaper that flour was more than a hundred dollars a barrel and that five grand balls were announced.

Over against stories of profiteering and luxurious displays were equally insistent tales of poverty and suffering among the working classes. It is easy to pile up illustrations from the daily press. To be sure, the wages of skilled artisans, especially in the North, rose rapidly and gross figures were often cited to silence the mutter of misery; but a scientific study of the facts long afterward showed conclusively that earnings did not keep pace with commodities and that the loud protests of factory operatives had a basis in reality. As a matter of course also the prices of agricultural produce shot upward but they did not tally in any way with the cost of the manufactured goods which the farmers had to buy. On the whole therefore the balance tipped sharply in favor of the entrepreneur. Prices were not checked by government intervention; loose buying in huge quantities for war purposes tended to push them still higher; while rich winnings escaped heavy taxation to pay current bills. In the general ruin at the end, southern profiteers lost most of their ill-gotten gains but northern capitalism certainly grew fat on Cæsar's meat.

§

All the passions of the war inevitably got into politics, giving intensity to emotions naturally bitter enough. The confederate administration, although it was not shaken from center to circumference by a presidential election in the midst of the conflict was continually disturbed by dissenters. On every hand, doubters and critics assailed the policies of the Richmond government, making the days of President Davis heavy with jarring discords and heedless abuse. Indeed recent historians, such as Frank L. Owsley and A. B. Moore, are inclined to attribute the final collapse of the Confederacy not so much to a failure of material goods as to a lack of support from state authorities, to evasions of the draft, and to discouragement among the masses; above and beyond everything, to the growing conviction among the southern farmers of the uplands that the confederate government was a slave owners' agency of power given to class favoritism, that the conflict was "a rich man's war and a poor man's fight," all the more poignantly evident when the draft laws exempted first the owners of at least twenty and then fifteen Negroes from military service on the ground of supervisory requirements.

No less trying perplexities vexed Lincoln to the day of

his death. Constantly was he reminded that he was the leader of a minority. Democrats of all schools and Whigs of the old line who wanted to preserve the Constitution and maintain "business as usual" could not forget their partisan interests even when they cordially supported the Union. And many of them were aggressively hostile to the administration. Stephen A. Douglas did indeed pledge his allegiance to Lincoln at the opening of the war but death soon laid that masterful leader low, leaving no Democrat of equal power to succeed him as a unifying force.

Never for an instant was Lincoln allowed to forget politics, either by his followers or by his opponents. At the outset, he was simply besieged by office-seekers. "I seem like one sitting in a palace, assigning apartments to importunate applicants while the structure is on fire and likely soon to perish in ashes," he said in his direct way a short time after his inauguration; and until the last shadows fell, job hunters asking for places in the administration and in the army tormented his waking hours. Nearly every action, civil or military, had to be taken with reference to politics. Frémont was given a high position in the army, not for his talents, but to satisfy the radical Republicans who had once voted for him. Battles were fought and blood was shed with relation to election returns. And so the story ran. No matter what he did, Lincoln came under the censure of editors who had no respect for the bounds of propriety. On one occasion, a New York paper went so far as to inquire: "Mr. Lincoln, has he or has he not an interest in the profits of public contracts?" and then without giving any evidence, answered its own query in the affirmative. Members of his Cabinet esteemed him lightly and thought themselves far wiser than he; one of them, Chase, Secretary of the Treasury, thought it not unworthy of his honor to carry on a lively backstairs campaign to wrest the presidency from Lincoln in 1864.

Attacked on all sides, Lincoln held true to his central idea of saving the Union and when the end of his first term arrived the Republicans decided that they would not "swap horses while crossing a stream." Taking the name Union Party as their title, they renominated Lincoln for President and selected as his associate a southern man, a Unionist from Tennessee, Andrew Johnson. Having to meet this call for an endorsement of the administration, northern Democrats, in their platform, denounced the war as a failure, advocated an immediate peace, and favored a restoration of the federal system—with slavery as before. Choosing as their candidate, General McClellan, who was in their eyes "a military hero," they tried to carry the country by means of drum and trumpet, expedients that had so often brought victory in the past. The appeal and the array of strength were ominous, especially as McClellan took the sting out of his platform by saying that he could not look his soldiers in the face and pronounce the war a failure.

But the answer of the people at the polls was decisive. The Republicans, besides reëlecting Lincoln, returned enough Senators and Representatives to force Congress to adopt the Thirteenth Amendment abolishing slavery forever within the jurisdiction of the United States. The war was to go on, therefore, until peace could be won by the sword. Thus the voters vindicated the great mystic in the White House, disclosing as if by some subtle instinct the fateful mission of their generation.

At this distant day it is difficult to discern the man Lincoln through the clouds of myth that surround him or to imagine what his status in history would have been had the war ended in defeat or had he lived through the reconstruction scandals and the malodorous frauds of the gilded age. If we look at him through the letters and diaries of the men associated with his administration in the early days of the war, we certainly see a person far removed from the picture of the neat bourgeois which Ida Tarbell has drawn. Taking as authoritative the testimony of men like Sumner, Chase, Seward, and Charles Francis Adams, Lincoln displayed a lack of sensibilities, an uncouthness of manner, and a coarse jocularity that were shocking to persons of taste two or three generations removed from the soil. He told tales none too elegant for chaste ears. "An ignorant Western boor," sniffed a hostile New York editor. His pictures reveal him as a tall, lanky, homely, awkward countryman.

And yet the severest of his critics was arrested by something impelling about the personality of Lincoln—something transcending the roughness of the frontier. In his face during repose, in his glance, in his messages and decisions, lay proof that he "knew the sadness of things," as the Japanese would say. It was his nature to temper official words and deeds with moderation. He was in very fact President of the United States in a tragic hour, measuring up in full length to his Augustan authority and responsibility. When the more cultured Seward proposed to act with churlish rudeness in foreign relations, Lincoln softened his caustic notes by words of wisdom. While men like Adams who could boast of education and refinement were cocksure that they could avoid war and save the Union, Lincoln was the soul of modesty. If politicians besieged him with their personal bickerings, he tried to draw them to high ground by fixing their attention on the main challenge of the moment. He never heedlessly turned a deaf ear to the plea of mercy. When he addressed the country through a message to Congress, wrote a letter to a mother who had given her sons to the supreme sacrifice, or made a speech dedicating a battlefield, he emphasized great issues, offered wise counsel, revealed the "deathless music" of his spirit. In all things, however, he was practical, watching the strategy of the war with the eyes of a hawk and giving advice at every crucial point.

Notwithstanding the elusive phases of his character, Lincoln was an astute politician rather than an idealist or a doctrinaire. He was made the "Emancipator" by circumstances and expediency rather than by his own initiative.

When it became necessary to traffic in petty jobs to get votes with which to carry the Thirteenth Amendment abolishing slavery, he made use of the tools of the trade. He never invited the purist's doom by flying in the face of organized society but he had the good sense to grasp the inexorable by the forelock. With a resignation that seemed to betray a belief in the philosophy of history cherished by Bishop Bossuet, he wrote in the spring of 1864: "I claim not to have controlled events but confess plainly that events have controlled me. Now at the end of three years' struggle, the nation's condition is not what either party or any man devised or expected. God alone can claim it. Whither it is tending seems plain." It was fate that gave Lincoln the martyr's crown and the good fortune of being justified by events. He steered the ship of state with the gale, not against it, and it was one of the ironies of historic destiny that he was assassinated, on April 14, 1865, as the spokesman of the triumphant cause for which Wendell Phillips and William Lloyd Garrison had defied mobs and courted the fate of Lovejoy.

§

When at the close of the great tragedy, the statisticians came upon the scene to make their calculations, the world was astounded to read the record of the awful cost in blood and treasure. Comprehensive and accurate figures were not available and the most cautious estimates varied but there were gross totals that staggered the mind. On the northern side, the death roll contained the names of three hundred and sixty thousand men and the list of wounded who recovered two hundred and seventy-five thousand more. On the southern side, about two hundred and fifty thousand men had given their lives to the lost cause and an unknown number had been wounded. According to a conservative reckoning, therefore, six hundred thousand soldiers had paid the last full measure of devotion.

In treasure the cost was not as easily appraised. The mere war expenses of the belligerents amounted to about five billion dollars in round numbers. The outlay for three years of reconstruction was placed at three billions more. In a strict sense the property destroyed in the struggle, the pensions paid to the surviving soldiers, the economic losses due to the immense diversion of energies were all a part of the price paid for the preservation of the Union. A grand assessment of values was therefore impossible but one thing was certain: the monetary cost of the conflict far exceeded the value of the slaves. *Felix qui potuit rerum cognoscere causas.*

§

Neither the losses nor the costs of the war, not even the heroic deeds on the field of battle—so lovingly described in a thousand memoirs and histories—were after all the final phases of the great process that flowed through the years of the conflict and transformed American society. From one standpoint they were means to ends, ends that usually outran the purposes and visions of the masses who played their several rôles in that long drama. Viewed in the large, the supreme outcome of the civil strife was the destruction of the planting aristocracy which, with the aid of northern farmers and mechanics, had practically ruled the United States for a generation. A corollary to that result was the undisputed triumph of a new combination of power: northern capitalists and free farmers who emerged from the conflict richer and more numerous than ever. It was these irreducible facts, as already noted, that made the Civil War a social revolution.

And that revolution was thoroughgoing. Beyond a doubt the ruin of the planting class through the sweep of the war was more complete than the destruction of the clergy and the nobility in the first French cataclysm because the very economic foundations of the planting system, including slavery itself, were shattered in the course of events.

In wide regions of the South, estates had been devastated by fire and pillage, buildings had decayed, tools and live-stock had wasted away. The bonds and notes of the Con-federacy had fallen worthless in the hands of their holders and there was little fluid capital available for the restoration of agriculture to its former high position. To pile calamity on calamity, the old debts due northern merchants and capitalists, long overdue indeed, could now be collected by distraint through the medium of the federal courts sus-tained by northern bayonets. To complete its ruin, the planting aristocracy was subjected to the military dominion of the triumphant orders ruling through Washington while its own leaders, with some exceptions, were excluded by law from places of trust and influence in their respective states as well as in the national government. Finally the new combination was supported by the emancipated bond-men into whose hands the ballot was thrust by the white victors.

A crucial stroke in this revolution—though by no means as significant as sometimes suggested—was the confiscation or, to use a more euphonious term, the abolition of the planter's property in labor. Whatever may be the ethical view of the transaction, its result was the complete destruc-tion of about four billion dollars' worth of "goods" in the possession of slave owners without compensation—the most stupendous act of sequestration in the history of Anglo-Saxon jurisprudence. Even that was not drastic enough for some radicals. Extremists wanted to make the execu-tion still more crushing by transferring to the slaves the estates they tilled but this was too much for the temper of those who directed the course of federal affairs in Washington.

Indeed emancipation itself was not effected hastily at one fell blow directed by abstract policy; it was only brought to pass when the conquest of the South on other terms seemed impossible. At the commencement of their adminis-tration in 1861, as we have seen, the Republicans were willing to guarantee slavery in the southern states if they would return to the Union and peacefully accept the clear verdict of the census returns. The war had been raging a year before Congress attacked even the outworks of slavery. Not until April, 1862, did it begin to move by resolving to offer financial aid to any state that would start gradual emancipation. A few days later it abolished slavery in the District of Columbia.

Within two months the tide rose higher. Summoning all its courage on June 19, Congress fulfilled the Republican pledge by sweeping slavery from the territories forever. Lincoln had said that if the opportunity was given him he would strike at slavery in the territories in spite of the Dred Scott decision. Chief Justice Taney still lived; his solemn opinion stood unaltered in the law books; the letter of the Constitution was unmodified; it was time, circumstance, and sentiment that had changed.

By these acts all the normal powers of Congress over slavery under the Constitution, even as construed by radical Republicans, were exhausted. Negro bondage stood unscathed in the states where it was lawful. But the Second American Revolution was still making headway. The government of the United States was at war; the President was Commander-in-chief of its armed forces; and there were precedents for aggression. In the days when American troops were marching on Mexico, enlarging the slave empire, President Polk had declared in effect that, in exercising his war power in enemy country, he was limited only by the law of nations and could blockade ports, capture property on the high seas, levy tribute, and do all things necessary and proper to vindicate the rights and honor of the country. Long before Polk's announcement, John Quincy Adams had foreseen that a revolutionary blow at the vested interests of the slavocracy could be struck in a time of crisis by the use of extraordinary military authority.

The crisis had arrived. Abolitionists urged Lincoln to seize the opportunity and attacked him bitterly for every sign of hesitation. Through many weary months, unperturbed by their criticism, he bent his energies to his major task of saving the Union, knowing that the country was not generally abolitionist in sentiment, that hasty action might drive into the arms of the Confederacy the border slave states still loyal to the federal government. He was likewise aware that thousands of soldiers in the army and some of the high commanders, such as McClellan, were utterly opposed to a war on slavery; that as long as the issue on the battlefield was uncertain, emancipation would be an empty, futile, ridiculous measure, even if he desired to proclaim it himself. Though the whirling currents for a long time seemed to have no forward direction, the brooding man in the White House kept his own counsel and his balance.

At last, in the summer of 1862, Lincoln reached the great decision. He then drafted the Proclamation of Emancipation, read it to his Cabinet, and laid it aside until some military achievement might beckon him on the shadowy way. In September, McClellan rolled Lee's forces back at the awful battle of Antietam. It was a doubtful victory, if a victory at all, but Lincoln felt that the omen was favorable. Consequently on the twenty-third of that month, he sent forth his immortal document announcing that, unless the confederate states returned to the Union by the first of the following January, all the slaves in every place under arms against the federal government would be given their liberty.

On the appointed day, duly informed that the aforesaid states had ignored his appeal, Lincoln fulfilled his decree to the letter; the drastic act of emancipation—in language that seems cold and formal when compared with the language of Jefferson's Declaration of Independence—was spread on the pages of time's ledger. Within a few days President Davis made answer in a scornful message to the confederate congress: "Our own detestation of those who have attempted the most execrable act recorded in the history of guilty man is tempered by profound contempt for the impotent rage which it discloses."

Whether Lincoln's Proclamation was an act of futile wrath or not, the issue raised by it was certainly clouded. Slavery as a system was not in fact then and there abolished; only bondmen dwelling in those states and parts of states in arms against federal authority were declared free; in all other places the peculiar institution, according to the outward signs of law, stood unimpaired. Moreover the freedom of the emancipated rested upon a mere ukase of the President issued with doubtful constitutional warrant. What would happen when peace came and civil authority supplanted the military régime no statesman could divine.

Oppressed by apprehension about the future, Lincoln urged upon Congress the adoption of a resolution proposing an amendment to the Constitution to prohibit slavery forever throughout the length and breadth of the land. At the conclusion of a long and bitter fight, this project was carried and sent to the states for ratification in January, 1865.

Clearly a great advance had been made but the goal was still far off. It was obvious that extraordinary methods —methods hardly contemplated by the founding Fathers —would be required to win the approval of three-fourths of the commonwealths then theoretically composing the Union. Appreciating full well the necessities of the case, the sponsors of the proposal bent to their task. By trading federal patronage for Democratic votes in Congress, Lincoln secured the admission of Nevada, adding one more sure vote in the North for the Amendment. A few months later Lee surrendered, the Confederacy collapsed, and the work of the Emancipator, now laid low by an assassin, was brought to fruition. Under the pressure of federal military authorities enough southern states were forced to ratify the Thirteenth Amendment to give it the requisite semblance of propriety, and on December 18, 1865, the momentous resolve was proclaimed in effect.

At last the unconditional emancipation demanded by Garrison three decades before, to the horror of his countrymen, had come, sealed by blood and authorized by law; and with it a grand moral victory for its champions. By the same act, the destruction of the slavocracy that had dominated the country for a generation was assured: the Republicans had accomplished amid the crash of arms what neither the Federalists nor the Whigs had been able to achieve in time of peace.

The prostration of the planting aristocracy was made more thorough by the Fourteenth Amendment ratified three years later. Besides attempting to confer certain civil rights on all Negroes and to assure political rights to Negro men, that amendment struck at the political and economic powers of the leaders in the Confederacy who were the spokesmen of the planting interest. It declared that no person who had once taken an oath as a federal or a state officer to support the Constitution and then had participated in the "rebellion" or given aid and comfort to it should hold any state or federal position, civil or military, until Congress by a two-thirds vote removed the disability. In other words, until an extraordinary majority could be mustered in the national legislature, the statesmen of the planting interest were to have no share in the governing process. Freedmen were to enjoy political privilege. White leaders of the South were to be deprived of it.

In addition to suffering the loss of their slaves without compensation, men of property in the South were further penalized. All the war debts and obligations incurred by the Confederacy and the states under its jurisdiction were abrogated by the Fourteenth Amendment and payment of the same by the United States or by any state was absolutely forbidden—a pronunciamento that caused intense grief in London and Paris as well as below the Mason and Dixon line. This cancellation of the whole confederate debt was attended by a provision that the validity of the public debt of the United States and also pensions and bounties for services in suppressing insurrection or rebellion should never be questioned. Consequently the securities of the Confederacy fell dead in the hands of the owners while the obligations issued by the Washington administration were given a constitutional status. In this manner bonds and other paper to the value of millions were destroyed by the stroke of a pen and their repudiation placed beyond all hope of revival. The financial circles of Europe, accustomed in new settlements to funding the debts of both parties to every revolutionary struggle in Latin-America, were excited over what appeared to be an act of bad faith but their complaints fell upon Republican hearts that were like stone.

§

While the planting class was being trampled in the dust —stripped of its wealth and political power—the capitalist class was marching onward in seven league boots. Under the feverish stimulus of war the timid army marshaled by Webster in support of the Constitution and Whig policies had been turned into a confident host, augmented in numbers by the thousands and tens of thousands who during the conflict made profits out of war contracts and out of the rising prices of manufactured goods. At last the economic structure of machine industry towered high above agriculture—a grim monument to the fallen captain, King Cotton. Moreover, the bonds and notes of the federal government, issued in its extremity, furnished the substance for still larger business enterprise. And the beneficent government, which had carefully avoided laying drastic imposts upon profits during the war, soon afterward crowned its generosity to capitalists by abolishing the moderate tax on incomes and shifting the entire fiscal burden to goods consumed by the masses.

To measurable accumulations were added legal gains of high economic value. All that two generations of Federalists and Whigs had tried to get was won within four short years, and more besides. The tariff, which the planters had beaten down in 1857, was restored and raised to the highest point yet attained. A national banking system was established to take the place of the institution abolished in 1811 by Jeffersonian Democracy and the second institution destroyed by Jacksonian Democracy in 1836. At the same time the policy of lavish grants from the federal treasury to aid internal improvements so necessary to commerce was revived in the form of imperial gifts to railway corporations; it was in the year of emancipation that the construction of the Pacific railway, opening the overland route to the trade of the Orient, was authorized by the Congress of the United States. With similar decisiveness, the federal land question which had long vexed eastern manufacturers was duly met; the Homestead Act of 1862, innumerable grants to railways, and allotments to the states in aid of agricultural colleges provided for the disposal of the public domain. As a counter stroke, the danger of higher wages, threatened by the movement of labor to the land, was partially averted by the Immigration Act of 1864— an extraordinary law which gave federal authorization to the importation of working people under terms of contract analogous to the indentured servitude of colonial times.

While all these positive advantages were being won by capitalists in the halls of Congress, steps were taken to restrain the state legislatures which had long been the seats of agrarian unrest. By the Fourteenth Amendment, proclaiming that no state should deprive any person of life, liberty or property without due process of law, the Supreme Court at Washington was granted constitutional power to strike down any act of any state or local government menacing to "sound" business policies. Finally the crowning result of the sacrifice, the salvation of the Union, with which so many lofty sentiments were justly associated, assured to industry an immense national market surrounded by a tariff wall bidding defiance to the competition of Europe.

§

Since this view of the so-called "Civil War" or "War between the States" will appear novel to many, it seems desirable to reinforce it by some illustrative details. First of all a word may be said on the methods employed by the federal government in financing the war—methods which served to increase the amount of fluid capital in private hands. As we have noted, the profitable principle was adopted that the generation which directed the war should not bear the main burden of paying for it. At the very start, the Secretary of the Treasury took the position that there should be no extraordinary taxes except to meet the interest on the new loans and redeem a small part of the debt annually; so the first year of the war saw loans amounting to nearly half a billion dollars and no material increase in taxation. Later this easy-going philosophy was modified; taxes were increased in all directions; and an income tax running as high as ten per cent on incomes above five thousand dollars was imposed; but at the close of the conflict it was found that in the operation the government had floated loans to the amount of $2,621,000,000 and collected from various sources taxes totaling only the sum of $667,000,000.

Although the bonds issued from time to time varied greatly in their stipulations, according to the prospects of ultimate success which seemed to lie before the Union cause, their provisions were seldom ungenerous to the money lenders. Often the rate of interest ran to seven per cent, occasionally slightly higher. In some cases certain depreciated Greenbacks were received in exchange for bonds payable, interest and principal, in gold, thus giving the holder two or three times the rate of annual return nominally written in the contract. As always, necessity was the mother of policy: the exigencies of the federal government were great; the risks incurred by money-lenders were serious though time proved their faith well justified; and in its distress the federal treasury had to deal gently with its creditors. If the Union had been dissolved their losses would have been overwhelming; as things turned out, their earnings were immense.

Industry as well as finance had its reward in the Second American Revolution. The armed conflict, the withdrawal of southern members of Congress, and the demand for revenue enabled the advocates of a high protective tariff to push through measure after measure and to fasten their system upon the nation so tightly that it was not even shaken for nearly half a century. Until the eve of the war the doctrine of free trade, or rather of tariff for revenue only, had been steadily gaining under southern leadership; suddenly this process was completely reversed. When secession came, the cotton planters, long the bulwark of low duties or no duties, passed from the picture; an enormous economic power exercised against protection was shattered.

Relieved of heavy pressure from this quarter, the protectionists, now firmly in the saddle, were able to frame tariff bills primarily designed to afford advantages to industries. Even after the federal government had been at war for many months and the treasury was on the brink of bankruptcy, customs schedules were still drawn up mainly with reference to protection rather than revenue. At no time was the issue lost to sight as Congress ground out act after act with mechanical regularity. In the operation the general average of tariff rates was raised from about nineteen per cent as fixed by the measure of 1857 to forty-seven per cent in the law of 1864. Furthermore when it was found that other internal taxes bore heavily upon manufactures, "proper reparation" was made in the form of higher and countervailing tariff duties. The demands of the war gave excellent justification for the inevitable. There were protests from some agricultural districts—echoes of former days—but there were no longer any powerful southern planters to direct the low-tariff hosts and turn the engines of the federal government against the spokesmen of machine industries.

That other great requirement of business enterprise—the

national banking system—was also scrutinized by the politicians during the storm of the war. As a matter of prosaic fact, in those dark and trying days, the statesmen of sound money found a chance to return to the policies which had been so ruthlessly discarded by Jacksonian Democracy. When the Republicans came to power in 1861, local banks, either managed or chartered by states, possessed the field, having in circulation seven thousand kinds of paper notes, to say nothing of more than five thousand varieties of counterfeit and fraudulent issues.

Viewed in any light, the confusion was unendurable to Secretary Chase, long a foe of all agrarian devices, especially of easy money; and soon after his installation in the Treasury Department he took up the problem of ending the financial chaos. In the first year of his service, he recommended to Congress the establishment of a new national banking system; and, when he was defeated on the merits of his case, he made full use of the opportunity presented by the necessity of selling war bonds, wringing from Congress at last the national banking act of 1863. By express terms, this law authorized the formation of local banking associations under federal authority and empowered them to emit notes on the basis of United States bonds up to ninety per cent of the par value. In other words, a local bank could buy federal securities, receive interest from the government on its holdings, and then issue on the strength of those securities paper bills to be lent to borrowers at the current discount.

Having driven this wedge into the system of local currency and having attracted the support of powerful banks by favorable terms, the party of sound money completed its program in 1865 by carrying through Congress an act which imposed a tax of ten per cent on all state bank notes, absolutely wiping them out by a single stroke. In this fashion sweeping designs, which neither Clay nor Webster had been able to accomplish by oratory in days of peace, Republican leaders effected by arrangement during the pressing time of war. When southern statesmen returned to the Union after the curtain was rung down on the battlefield, they found the national banking system intrenched in the financial structure of the nation.

§

But capital, no matter how enormous or carefully buttressed by tariffs and sound finance, was helpless without an adequate labor supply—a plain economic truth well known to the industrial members of the Republican party. Their forerunners, the Federalists, had understood that; Hamilton, in his Report on Manufactures in 1791, had spoken about the necessity of drawing upon Europe in addition to native sources for labor to operate the machinery set in motion by tariffs. His Whig successors often emphasized the point.

Continuing the refrain, the Republicans, known temporarily as the Union party, declared in their platform of 1864 that "foreign immigration, which in the past has added so much to the wealth, the development of resources, and the increase of power to this nation—the asylum of the oppressed of all nations—should be fostered and encouraged by a liberal and just policy." Responding to the new demand that very year Congress incorporated the policy in law by creating a bureau of immigration and, as pointed out, authorizing a modified form of indentured labor which permitted the importation of workers bound for a term of service. Though the latter feature of the law was soon repealed, the corresponding practice was long continued, eastern capitalists bringing in laborers from Europe under contract and western railway builders drawing upon the inexhaustible supplies of the Orient.

To the cry of survivors from the Know-Nothing faction that the old Anglo-Saxon stock was being diluted and submerged, the champions of free immigration answered that America was the asylum of the oppressed. So it was—

and incidentally the coming of the oppressed augmented the earnings of stockholders and land speculators tremendously. Thus light and shadow continued to play down the ages.

§

While winning its essential economic demands in the federal sphere, the party of industrial progress and sound money devoted fine calculation to another great desideratum —the restoration and extension of federal judicial supremacy over the local legislatures which had been so troublesome since the age of Daniel Shays. Restoration was heartily desired because the original limitations imposed by the Constitution on the power of the state to issue money and impair contracts had been practically destroyed by adroit federal judges imbued with the spirit of Jacksonian Democracy. An extension of federal control was perhaps more heartily desired because, for nationalists of the Federalist and Whig tradition, those limitations had been pitifully inadequate even when applied strictly by Chief Justice Marshall—inadequate to meet the requirements of individuals and corporations that wanted to carry on their business in their own way, immune from legislative interference.

In all this there was nothing esoteric. Among conservative adepts in federal jurisprudence the need for more efficient judicial protection had been keenly felt for some time; and when the problem of defining the rights of Negroes came before Congress in the form of a constitutional amendment, experts in such mysteries took advantage of the occasion to enlarge the sphere of national control over the states, by including among the safeguards devised for Negroes a broad provision for the rights of all "persons," natural and artificial, individual and corporate.

Their project was embodied in the second part of the Fourteenth Amendment in the form of a short sentence intended by the man who penned it to make a revolution in the federal Constitution. The sentence reads: "No state shall make or enforce any law which shall abridge the privileges or immunities of citizens of the United States; nor shall any state deprive any person of life, liberty, or property without due process of law, nor deny to any person within its jurisdiction the equal protection of the laws."

Just how this provision got into the draft of the Fourteenth Amendment was not generally known at the time of its adoption but in after years the method was fully revealed by participants in the process. By the end of the century an authentic record, open to all, made the operation as plain as day. According to the evidence now available, there were two factions in the congressional committee which framed the Amendment—one bent on establishing the rights of Negroes; the other determined to take in the whole range of national economy. Among the latter was a shrewd member of the House of Representatives, John A. Bingham, a prominent Republican and a successful railroad lawyer from Ohio familiar with the possibilities of jurisprudence; it was he who wrote the mysterious sentence containing the "due process" clause in the form in which it now stands; it was he who finally forced it upon the committee by persistent efforts.

In a speech delivered in Congress a few years later, Bingham explained his purpose in writing it. He had read, he said, in the case of Barron *versus* the Mayor and Council of Baltimore, how the city had taken private property for public use, as alleged without compensation, and how Chief Justice Marshall had been compelled to hold that there was no redress in the Supreme Court of the United States—no redress simply because the first ten Amendments to the Constitution were limitations on Congress, not on the states. Deeming this hiatus a grave legal defect in the work of the Fathers, Bingham designed "word for word and syllable for syllable" the cabalistic clause of the Fourteenth Amendment in order, he asserted, that "the poorest man in his hovel . . . may be as secure in his person and prop-

erty as the prince in his palace or the king upon his throne."
Hence the provision was to apply not merely to former
slaves struggling for civil rights but to all persons, rich and
poor, individuals and corporations, under the national flag.

Long afterward Roscoe Conkling, the eminent corporation lawyer of New York, a colleague of Bingham on the
congressional committee, confirmed this view. While arguing
a tax case for a railway company before the Supreme Court
in 1882, he declared that the protection of freedmen was
by no means the sole purpose of the Fourteenth Amendment. "At the time the Fourteenth Amendment was ratified," he said, "individuals and joint stock companies were
appealing for congressional and administrative protection
against invidious and discriminating state and local taxes.
. . . That complaints of oppression in respect of property
and other rights made by citizens of northern states who
took up residence in the South were rife in and out of Congress, none of us can forget. . . . Those who devised the
Fourteenth Amendment wrought in grave sincerity. . . .
They planted in the Constitution a monumental truth to
stand four square to whatever wind might blow. That truth
is but the golden rule, so entrenched as to curb the many who
would do to the few as they would not have the few do to
them."

In this spirit, Republican lawmakers restored to the
Constitution the protection for property which Jacksonian
judges had whittled away and made it more sweeping in its
scope by forbidding states, in blanket terms, to deprive any
person of life, liberty, or property without due process of
law. By a few words skillfully chosen every act of every
state and local government which touched adversely the
rights of persons and property was made subject to review
and liable to annulment by the Supreme Court at Washington, appointed by the President and Senate for life and far
removed from local feelings and prejudices.

Although the country at large did not grasp the full
meaning of the Fourteenth Amendment while its adoption

was pending, some far-sighted editors and politicians realized at the time that it implied a fundamental revolution in the Constitution, at least as interpreted by Chief Justice Taney. Ohio and New Jersey Democrats, reckoning that it would make the Supreme Court at Washington the final arbiter in all controversies over the powers of local governments, waged war on it, carrying the fight into the state legislatures and forcing the repeal of resolutions approving the Amendment even after they had been duly sealed. As a matter of course all the southern states were still more fiercely opposed to the Amendment but they were compelled to ratify it under federal military authority as the price of restoration to the Union. Thus the triumphant Republican minority, in possession of the federal government and the military power, under the sanction of constitutional forms, subdued the states for all time to the unlimited jurisdiction of the federal Supreme Court.

§

While business enterprise received its share of the advantages accruing from the Second American Revolution, other elements in the combination of power effected in 1860 —namely the free farmers of the West and the radical reformers of the East—also had their rewards. On the outbreak of the war, their old opponents on the land question were no longer in a position to dictate. The planters of the South were out of the political lists and northern mill owners, who had feared that free farms would lure away wage-workers, were shown the possibilities of a counterpoise in the promotion of alien immigration. If some were unconvinced by such reasoning, they could at least see that the agrarian element in the Republican party was too strong to be thwarted by the business wing. So eventually in 1862 the hard contest over the public domain came to an end with the passage of the Homestead Act which provided for the free distribution of land in lots of one hundred and sixty acres each to men and women of strong arms and willing hearts, prepared to till the soil. In this action, the appealing slogan, "Vote yourself a farm," was realized and before the ink of Lincoln's signature was dry the rush to the free land commenced.

To northern farmers who had no thought of going to the frontier, the war likewise brought marked advantages. Especially did the Mississippi Valley, former home of agrarian discontent and Jacksonian Democracy, reap immense gains in inflated prices paid for farm produce, in spite of the mounting cost of manufactured goods. At one time wheat rose to more than two dollars and a half a bushel and other commodities followed its flight. From overflowing coffers debt-burdened tillers of the soil who had once raged against the money-power now discharged their obligations in Greenback "legal tenders" received for the fruits of their labor. The more fortunate farmers collected large returns from rising land values, accumulated capital, and became stockholders in local railway and banking enterprises. For many years a prosperous farming class, tasting the sweets of profit, could look upon the new course of politics and pronounce it good. There was discontent, no doubt, and a reaction against industrialism was bound to come but the political union of 1860, though strained, was never successfully broken.

§

The main economic results of the Second American Revolution thus far noted would have been attained had there been no armed conflict for the census returns with rhythmic beats were recording the tale of the fates. But one great outcome of the war itself was the sudden creation of a large and anomalous class in the American social order—a mass of emancipated slaves long destined to wander in a hazy realm between bondage and freedom. Emancipation cut two ways: it ruined the planting class and it threw into the turbulent forces of democracy a strange and distracting element.

Nothing just like this had ever happened in history, at least on such a scale. On the Continent of Europe, the liberation of serfs generally left them freeholders or tenants on the land which they tilled. In the South, on the other hand, where slaves were chattels bound to their masters and not to the land, their emancipation sent them flying off into social space as "a laboring, landless, and homeless class," to use Lincoln's phrase. Moreover most of the upheavals in other times and countries had been due to the growing power of the subjected orders. No such thing occurred in the case of the slaves. They had not essentially improved their status through their years of bondage; at any rate they had made no striking development in intelligence; nor had they succeeded in acquiring property to any extent. If many of them yearned for freedom, few took any steps to gratify their desire. In fact the overwhelming majority were loyal to the masters who were fighting against their freedom—proof of their contentment, their affection for their owners, their inertia, or their helplessness—or all four combined. So when the abolition of slavery was assured by the adoption of the Thirteenth Amendment the freedmen were in no way prepared to become an effective factor in the new order of society to which they were admitted. For practical purposes they were powerless in the hands of the governing group that directed the revolution and reconstruction from Washington, a group naturally concerned, among other things, with maintaining its supremacy.

It was accordingly an almost insuperable task which the Republican administration encountered in trying to give civil rights to a class that had no economic power or social organization. Seeing the logic of the situation, the radical wing of the party proposed to face it by transferring to the freedmen a part of the soil they had tilled; but, when asked for a bill of particulars, the advocates of this heroic remedy surrendered. The slaves had not been accustomed to any village coöperation akin to that practiced by the servile peasants of old Europe. They did not have historic rights in cottages and plots of land. They knew little or nothing about the managerial side of agrarian economy. If land was given to them outright, there was little reason to believe that they could find the capital with which to develop it or could show the proprietary skill or knowledge necessary to hold it against speculators and sharpers in general. Obviously any effort to establish the ex-slaves on an economic foundation involved immense difficulties even if the idea of confiscating the land as well as the masters' personal property had been acceptable to the majority in Congress.

In these circumstances, the Washington government, apart from attempts to give temporary economic relief through a freedmen's bureau, confined its work on behalf of the Negroes mainly to conferring civil and social rights upon them in paper proclamations. Indeed some action of this nature was rendered imperative by events. Soon after slavery was legally abolished the former masters, working through state legislatures, r stored a kind of servitude by means of apprentice, vagrancy, and poor laws. This strategical movement the radical Republicans in Congress answered by passing the Civil Rights Bill of 1866 designed to assure American citizenship and the legal rights of citizens to all freedmen—a mere statute which a succeeding Congress could undo.

Anticipating such a reaction as the tide of northern war passion receded and knowing that they were in a minority in the country as a whole, the Republicans undertook to place the civil rights of freedmen beyond the reach of an ordinary majority forevermore—in a constitutional provision. If the opportunity was lost it might never come again; so the joint committee on reconstruction drafted the necessary instrument which now appears upon the books as the Fourteenth Amendment, a complicated device already considered in another connection. But when the proposal was sent to the states in 1866 for approval, it was definitely rejected. Three former slave states which had not seceded

—Delaware, Maryland, and Kentucky—registered their disapproval and the Amendment was also repudiated by nine slave states which had seceded.

Realizing that it was impossible to win ratification by the ordinary procedure of voluntary authorization as contemplated by the Constitution, the sponsors of the proposal in Congress then resorted to peculiar measures. After terrific arguments in Republican ranks, intransigent members of the party forced through Congress the drastic Reconstruction Act of 1867, an elaborate statute which put ten of the former confederate states under military rule, provided for the organization of local governments under federal supervision, and declared that the said states should not be entitled to representation in Congress—in effect denied them readmission to the Union—until they ratified the pending Fourteenth Amendment. Unquestionably this heroic project for military occupation placed a severe strain upon the consciences of some Republicans; but, driven by an emergency that seemed to call for a broad interpretation of their rights and duties under the Constitution, they gave their consent to the bill.

Face to face with the iron regimen of martial rule, the southern states capitulated. The Fourteenth Amendment was ratified and proclaimed a part of the law of the nation on July 28, 1868.

Aside from the sections which repudiated the confederate debt, disfranchised certain participants in the confederate war, and established broad rights of persons and property, the Fourteenth Amendment made three general offerings to Negroes. It assured them citizenship by declaring that all persons born or naturalized in the United States were citizens. It promised them certain civil rights by asserting that no state should ever deprive any person of life, liberty, or property without due process of law or deny to any person equal protection of the law. It attempted to confer the vote on Negro men by the negative provision that, if any state refused the ballot in specified elections to any adult male citizens, its representation in Congress should be proportionately reduced.

All these stipulations seemed to be pointed but in practice they proved to be little more than platonic theories. Connecticut, New Jersey, Pennsylvania, Ohio, and other northern states still excluded Negroes from the suffrage, the voters of Connecticut having rejected a proposition to enfranchise them as late as the summer of 1865. And the South, in no mood to grant what these commonwealths withheld, simply declined to confer the ballot on the freedmen. Defeated in the attempt to enfranchise all Negro men by indirection, Congress passed and the states ratified, while the South was still under military rule, the Fifteenth Amendment to the federal Constitution, declaring that the right of citizens to vote should not be denied on account of race, color, or previous condition of servitude. That provision, formally ratified, in 1870, was apparently invulnerable but it failed to reckon with the political and juristic ingenuity of the Anglo-Saxon race.

§

The process of reconstruction in the South helped to accelerate the revolution hastened by the war. A man of moderate temper, Lincoln would have restored each of the seceded states to the Union as soon as a body of citizens qualified under the old laws and equal to one-tenth the number of the voting population in 1860 stood ready to take the oath of allegiance to the United States and to establish a formal government again—a program for rapid rehabilitation cut short by the deed of an assassin. Lincoln's successor, Andrew Johnson, a southern Democrat, proposed to follow with some modifications the same general course with respect to reconstruction but he was blocked by a hostile group of Republicans headed by Thaddeus Stevens of Pennsylvania and Charles Sumner of Massachusetts. Though Johnson managed by a narrow margin to escape conviction when he was impeached before the Senate by the House of

Representatives in 1868, he was from first to last helpless in the presence of his foes. In fact Congress, not the President, now held the whip hand. It alone had the power to admit states to the Union and each house had the right to pass judgment upon the qualifications of every person claiming to be elected to membership, whether his seat was contested or not.

Thoroughly intrenched the determined majority in Congress proceeded to pass a series of complicated reconstruction acts, in addition to the three amendments to the Constitution already described. It laid out the prostrate southern states into military districts, each in command of an army officer, conferred the right to vote on Negro men, disfranchised most of the leading Confederates, and empowered the military authorities to proceed to the organization of state governments with the aid of Negro voters and such white men as were left in possession of the ballot. It forced the southern states to ratify three amendments to the constitution as the price of admission to the union and not until 1870 did the last one find shelter again under the national roof.

But when all the states of the Confederacy were back in the Union the Republicans continued to maintain their strong grip on the helm. Seven years more elapsed before the last military commanders were withdrawn from southern capitals. And after every vestige of the armed occupation had been removed, various civilian agencies of northern dominion remained in operation. In 1870, 1872, and 1873 Congress enacted three drastic measures, sometimes known as "force bills," providing for the use of federal officers in the supervision of elections throughout the Union, measures necessary, the framers argued, to sustain the Negro in the exercise of his new political rights and to prevent fraudulent voting in the crowded cities of the North. Admitting that their force laws were stringent in terms, the Republicans long defended them against Democratic assaults, yielding with deep reluctance to a pressure which abrogated one section after another and culminated in the repeal of the last fragment in 1894.

The same radical majority in Congress that sought to uphold the legal rights of the Negro, with equal insistence tried to keep the surviving members of the planting aristocracy, battered and beaten, in complete subjection. Seven years passed before Congress could be induced to grant, in 1872, a general amnesty, and at that late hour it sternly resolved upon exceptions which remained in effect until 1898 when the Spanish-American War finally brought about a union of hearts and spread the mantle of oblivion over the past. Thus in addition to working a profound social and economic transformation, the leaders of the government at Washington sought to guard themselves as long as possible against the expected reaction. Seldom, if ever, before had there occurred in the affairs of a nation a revolution so drastic, so effective, and so well protected against the inexorable recoil.

CHAPTER XIX

Rounding Out the Continent

ONE of the richest prizes at stake in the physical combat of the early sixties was, as we have seen, the huge territorial spoil lying beyond the outpost states of the Mississippi Valley—a prize which fell to farmers and capitalists victorious in the struggle. In superficial area this magnificent domain was almost equal to all the states in the Union combined. The half-way point along the fortieth parallel between the Atlantic and the Pacific lay in the heart of the Kansas-Nebraska district where the first blood of the civil conflict was shed, where the tocsin was rung for the gathering of the armed hosts.

Though rivaling in extent the older East, this dominion differed from that section in nearly every other respect. More than half of it was arid plain and broken land. It is true that in the region adjoining Minnesota, Iowa, and Missouri and in broad belts near the Pacific shore there was fertile soil fit for the plow of any pioneer. But on the western border of the Mississippi Valley the land began to rise steadily across semi-arid reaches to the foothills of the

122

Rockies. Beyond those towering piles of stone lay more than a thousand miles of plateau and basin serried by mountains, slashed by valleys, blistered into deserts by a burning sun. At the western edge of this huge stretch rose the Sierra Nevada buttressed by coastal ranges and the Cascades that sloped rapidly down to the Pacific, spreading out occasionally into swards and mesas made arable by seasonal rains.

If in the dry and hilly regions, the offerings of this territory to the farmer were rather niggardly, the same could not be said of the booty presented to miners, cattle barons, and lumber kings. Hidden under the mountains and the wild wastes were gold and silver surpassing in bulk the wildest dreams of the Spanish conquerors of the sixteenth century; even transcending the fancies of medieval alchemists who sought a magic way to transform baser into finer metals. Here were copper deposits wide and deep and rich. Here were pasture lands for flocks and herds vaster than any assembled on the deserts and steppes of the Old World. Here was a supply of timber to fill the gap caused by the disappearing forests in the settled sections of the country. Here were ranges of climate cold enough to make the Scandinavian feel at home and warm enough to attract Orientals whose original habitat lay under the mild skies of the South Seas. And the western shores looked out upon the Pacific to fabled Cathay, to realms of mystery and unknown potentiality. Still the star of Manifest Destiny hung high in the heavens. Ambitious leaders in Lincoln's party, such as William H. Seward, saw it beckoning Americans across land and wave to battle for empire on the plains of Asia.

Huge and significant as was this territorial prize little had been done to exploit its resources and not much was known about it in detail by the busy masses of the East when Lincoln was inaugurated. The explorers, Lewis and Clark, Pike and Frémont, had, indeed, tramped over wide reaches of it and written bulky reports for them that cared to read. Gold had already made California famous and paved its way into the Union in 1850. Persistent advertising had drawn to the fertile valleys of Oregon enough settlers by 1859 to warrant the admission of that territory to statehood. Under the leadership of Brigham Young, Mormons were turning a Utah desert into a garden spot and giving to their strange colony a notoriety that echoed far into Europe. Across plain, desert, and mountain, trails had been worn deep by the tread of oxen and the grind of wheels that marked the westward migration of settlers. A stage-coach line connecting St. Joseph on the Missouri with the Pacific offered passengers a trip to the coast in twenty-five days; while a pony express carried letters into San Francisco in ten days. Travel books and tales of life in the Wild West had appeared in the bookstalls and lively journalists, with Horace Greeley in the lead, had gone over the Rockies to see the western heritage with their own eyes. But on the whole the wide expanse of plain, mountain, and desert between Iowa, the last state on the Mississippi, and California on the Pacific coast was, at the opening of 1861, an undeveloped land awaiting the prospector, surveyor, pioneer farmer, and capitalist. In all the territories combined were not more than half a million people. Over this imperial domain, Indians and buffalo roamed at will, unvexed by the pressure of the white man's enterprise.

§

Such was the stage upon which the last scenes in the drama of the movement to the Pacific were to be enacted. Here the frontier, long a striking characteristic of America, was kept open for a generation and then closed for all time. Here the old processes of colonization were repeated but with distinct features that gave a different twist to the story, making it more varied and colorful. With the farmer who again assumed his familiar task came cowboys, miners, cattle kings, Mexicans, Chinese, Japanese, Indian outlaws, highwaymen, female adventurers, and "bad men" playing new

rôles in American history. The Far West soon had mining
camps and boom towns as well as prim villages on the New
England model—bustling cities putting on the airs of financial centers—princely estates tilled by labor imported,
not from Africa, but from Mexico and the Orient, some of
them great baronies held by foreign owners—and special
industries based on migratory labor, restless and tempestuous. In the Far West, Nordic stocks received their first
experience with aridity and large scale irrigation. There
vast areas devoted to agriculture were plagued by periodical
drouths that brought crop failures, followed by agrarian
revolts against the eastern plutocracy, revolts that culminated in populist uprisings in national politics. It was
the Far West that yielded to the American pioneer for the
first time a rich treasure of precious metals; it was in the
Rockies and beyond that the dream of Sir Walter Raleigh's
men and John Smith's companions of the seventeenth century was finally realized.

Even the political conditions of colonization were in some
respects unique. Unlike the settlers of the Mississippi Valley, the pioneers of the Far West for a whole generation
could deal with a lenient body of politicians in Washington
who had definitely abandoned the idea of securing revenue
from the public domain and were committed to a wholesale
free distribution of the land. Under federal patronage,
arable soil was now given outright to farmers and capitalists; timber, stone, and mineral grants were sold on nominal
terms; the Indian menace was removed by troops paid and
commanded from Washington; and means of rapid communication with the two oceans were provided. And after
all the territories were erected into commonwealths and admitted to the Union, the nature and disposition of the soil
created peculiar relations with the federal government, for
at the expiration of nearly half a century at least one-half
the land in eleven states—Washington, Oregon, California,
Arizona, Idaho, Nevada, Montana, Utah, Wyoming, Colorado, and New Mexico—was still held in national owner-

ship; and problems of conservation, reclamation, and administration were being pressed upon Congress and the executive departments of the government. Finally, the immigrants who crowded into the region, with the exception of the Mormons, were not primarily seeking a haven for religious and political liberty or interested in building another New Canaan in the wilderness. Rather were they directly and frankly interested in improving their economic lot—in making money. Some of them found great riches; others comfort; many of them, like the wanderer in Hamlin Garland's tale of the middle border, nothing but a mirage at the end of the long trail.

Innumerable factors, therefore, conspired to give the Far West a singular place in the annals of American culture. In the beauty and majesty of the natural setting and in its types of settlement, it presented amazing contrasts with the relative uniformity of town and country in the Northeast, the serried monotony of the Middle West, and the planting levels of the South. The very magnitude of the theater and the gargantuan shapes of the rocks and hills gave a grandiose flare to the thought and gestures of the people and high pretensions to their oratory. Torrential rushes to the mineral fields, to the rich arable lands, and to the luxuriant timber resources produced varied social groupings unlike those left in the wake of the advance into the Mississippi Valley. In the process novel modes of conduct were evolved; throughout immense areas, where the population was thin and the yoke of law sat lightly on every shoulder, the primitive instincts of an adventurous people, tinged with anarchy, found free play, providing shooting affrays, robberies, murders, as daily diversions. In the frenzy of speculation let loose by miners and prospectors and in the swift acquisition of fortunes effected by the hurried partition of the federal domain, the construction of railways, and the opening of new mineral deposits, breaking all precedents, the whole continent was agitated from axis to periphery.

In many ways a new tone was given to American nationality by this last westward movement. A dash, verve, and flourish, supposed to be appropriate to the life of the "Wild West," became the symbols of all America in the eyes of those who hankered after the bizarre. Stories of stage-coach and conestoga wagon robberies, bad men and coarse women, Indian massacres, and sudden riches poured from the pens of facile writers and were sold by the millions. A whole generation of boys was brought up on the deeds of Wild Bill, Buffalo Bill, and other heroes of the Nick Carter and Diamond Dick library. A quarter of a century later the moving picture carried on this entertainment, providing for a sober and industrious multitude the vivid reproduction of life on a surging, drinking, fighting frontier. Thus in fiction and in film, business enterprise advertised to the world a passing phase of sectional development as the typical product of American culture. In fact, laying out homesteads on the plains, driving cattle from Texas to Montana, wielding the pick and shovel in mines and on railway embankments, and cooking in tents, huts, and shanties were the modes by which the Far West was subdued; but, offering tamer themes for the romancers, they received little attention save at the hands of a few realists.

§

Control over the territorial prize of the West had hardly passed definitely to the Republican leaders in 1861 when the government at Washington undertook the task of developing its holdings. Every year of the decade which opened with Lincoln's first election witnessed some important action designed to draw the region into closer relations with the Union and promote its interests. In 1861, telegraphic communications were established with the Pacific Coast, Kansas was admitted as a state, and the Colorado, Nevada, and Dakota territories were organized. The following year, 1862, Congress, no longer hampered by fearsome slave owners, passed the Homestead Act offering free farms to all adult citizens and to aliens who had filed their declaratory papers, thus in effect inviting the laborers of the Old World and the farmers and mechanics of the East, women no less cordially than men, to come and share the bounties of nature, and setting in motion a swift partition of riches which, before twenty years had elapsed, transferred over fifty million acres from the national domain to private ownership.

Forty-one days after Lincoln signed this sensational act came the settlement of another long contested issue, the railroad to the Pacific. Since the very opening of the railway age, statesmen of all sections had grasped the import of a transcontinental system and had discussed with no little acrimony the subject of the proper route. One grand scheme, a Charleston-Vicksburg-San Diego line, promised facilities for the expansion of the planting area. Another project, linking St. Louis with Sacramento by way of Salt Lake City, was especially attractive to miners and the shippers of manufactured goods.

But no agreement on the route could be reached until the Republicans ousted the southern contingent from the federal government. Then, true to their sectional loyalty and interests and under the constraint of necessity, they chose a northern route—beginning at Omaha in Nebraska and running across Wyoming, Utah, and Nevada to California—and by two acts of Congress, the first passed in 1862 and the second in 1864, they conferred lavish grants upon private corporations enlisted for the enterprise. To the Union Pacific Railroad Company, authorized to build the line from Omaha almost to the California border, Congress gave a right of way across the public domain, all the timber, stone, and earth needed for the undertaking, twenty sections of land with every mile of road constructed, and a credit ranging from sixteen to forty-eight thousand dollars a mile, secured by a second mortgage on the completed system. To local corporations organized in California for the construction of the western end, Congress offered similar generous subsidies, thereby assuring the completion of the project all the way to the Coast.

This magnificent program, advancing so eminently the commercial interests of the Pacific Ocean, cherished by Webster, and bringing appreciably nearer the goal of Asiatic empire eloquently portrayed by Seward in the campaign of 1860, conciliated all elements of the Republican party. It pleased the northern manufacturers, now exfoliating into new life under the influence of high tariffs, for it offered to them in place of the long and perilous voyage around the Horn a more direct route to the trade of the Far West and the Orient. On the completion of the transcontinental railway, as one of their distinguished merchants proclaimed, "the drills and sheetings of Connecticut, Rhode Island, and Massachusetts and other manufactures of the United States may be transported to China in thirty days; and the teas and rich silks of China, in exchange, come back to New Orleans, to Charleston, to Washington, to Baltimore, to Philadelphia, New York and Boston in thirty days more."

The northern course chosen for the Union Pacific was equally satisfactory to farmers because it was to open the fertile prairies of Kansas and Nebraska to settlement and provide an outlet for their grain, pork, and cattle. Miners of the West were likewise gratified by the prospect which promised them an easy channel to eastern markets for their mineral output and cheaper foodstuffs and other supplies in return. To the capitalists who furnished the directive impulse the outlook was especially pleasing because they were called upon to contribute so little money relatively and yet were assured handsome profits from the construction of the roadbed and tracks and from the land endowments accompanying the long mileage. Secretly awarded compensation for their interest, in the form of stocks and bonds, many of the leading politicians who voted for the railway bills also took comfort from the proceedings.

In 1863, the year following the passage of the first Union Pacific bill, Congress created a territorial government for Idaho. The next year it gave Montana a territorial status and admitted Nevada to the Union to furnish more votes for the Lincoln policies. Only one more obstacle had to be removed to clear the way for acquisition on a mammoth scale; it was necessary to determine the final position of the Indians in American economy. At that time it seems there were about three hundred thousand Indians in the West. A large district known as the Indian Territory was occupied by peaceful tribes which had been pushed beyond the Mississippi in Andrew Jackson's day; to the north were the Sioux; to the west, the Cheyennes and the Arapahoes; to the south, the Apaches, Comanches, and other minor groups. By the federal government all these tribes were regarded as "nations" and many of them held large tracts of land under solemn treaties duly negotiated and ratified. Living on subsidies from Congress, on the produce of a crude agriculture, and on the wild game of plain and mountain, enjoying nearly half a continent as their preserve, they were on the whole content with their lot; at all events they seldom molested the white pilgrims who crossed their hunting-grounds on the way to the Coast. Such in general was the state of affairs when the Lincoln administration launched its great drive to possess, organize, and develop the West at the opening of the Civil War—the last phase in the long struggle between the white man and the red.

Homesteaders and the prospectors now looked upon the remaining Indian lands, pronounced them good, and from time to time served notice on Washington that "the savage must go." Usually the federal government complied with the lightest demand of the white man for the opening of new regions to settlement. If it delayed a few months now and then, pioneers were likely to seize any coveted district even though the title was solemnly guaranteed to the Indians by treaty. As a matter of fact, therefore, the prime question before the government was one of means: the subjugation of the Indian by the slow process of industry or by the quicker arts of war.

To the political managers in Washington, the conven·tional resort to physical force seemed the easier way and it was chosen. In the second year of the war for the maintenance of the Union, accordingly, a military campaign was started against the Indians, which lasted for a quarter of a century and ended in the removal of that long-standing issue for all time. It was marked by more than a thousand armed clashes, many desperate and deadly, a few disastrous to federal troops, all pointing pitilessly to the expulsion of the red man from lands coveted by farmers, prospectors, and railway builders. "There are no good Indians but dead Indians," exclaimed General Philip Sheridan, who, after Appomattox, was commissioned to "pacify" a wide section of the frontier. In that spirit no small part of the undertaking was realized. "Many, if not most, of our Indian wars have had their origin in broken promises and acts of injustice on our part," laconically remarked President Hayes in a message to Congress in 1877.

§

Since the federal government, even while engaged in a struggle for self-preservation, could find leisure to work out a legislative program for western development and could wage war on the Indians as well as on southern armies, it is not surprising that the energies and resources of private citizens could be enlisted to promote every form of economic enterprise in the Far West. Indeed the civil conflict at once stimulated rather than retarded the exploitation of the empire beyond the Mississippi. The "terrible sixties" of suffering in the East and South were the "roaring sixties" of prosperity in the West. While the war drew its thousands to the battlefields, it also sent thousands on the long trails to the Pacific. In many parts of the country, especially in the border states of Missouri and Kentucky, were discontented people who regarded the war as a folly or had no stomach for fighting or were noncombatants harassed by guerrilla bands. To them the distant frontier offered a haven from the turmoil of the war.

So the westward current, instead of diminishing, increased with the progress of the civil conflict. According to estimates, in the single year of 1864, at least one hundred and fifty thousand emigrants fled from the Missouri River country into the Far West, mostly to the mines. In the same year, it is recorded, seventy-five thousand people passed through Omaha on the westward march, taking twenty-two thousand tons of freight, thirty thousand horses and mules, and seventy-five thousand head of cattle.

Under the stimulus of war, the agricultural regions of the West, enlarged by the army of immigrants and enriched by inflated war prices, entered upon an era of booming prosperity. With amazing speed the cultivated area of the Mississippi Valley spread out toward the arid uplands of the plains, pouring millions of bushels of wheat into eastern markets to feed the Union army and to supply the pressing needs of English buyers. Far out beyond the Rockies, the Columbia River Valley teemed with new life. Walla Walla in Washington territory, already a lively trading center, fairly hummed with activity as caravans were being outfitted there for ranches and mining camps near and far, as families seeking homesteads, miners, prospectors, cattlemen, missionaries, and adventurers of every brand passed through it in a steady stream in search of fortune. All the way from Walla Walla to the Pacific Coast could be seen the frames of farmhouses rising on unbroken ground, wagons heaped with wheat and oats destined for the mining camps of California, and cattle wending their way to coastal markets.

To the south the agricultural settlements of the Mormons flourished with increasing vigor on the traffic with the prospectors and miners who poured in an endless procession through Salt Lake City to and from the gold fields. Well supplied with cash from this trade, agents of the Mormon Church carried on their operations unabated during the darkest days of the war, removing other members of their original congregation from the Missouri region and enlisting recruits in the East and in Europe by giving them the financial aid necessary to reach a haven of peace in Zion.

Even the lure of California gold failed to check the growth of the Mormon settlement. When the young men, naturally dazzled by it, proposed to leave Zion for the mines, Brigham Young urged them to stay in Utah where diversified industry and agriculture offered comfort and security. "In a few years," he argued, "you will be able to buy out everyone who goes to California—tenfold over"— a prophecy strangely accurate, as events proved. Within a short time enormous coal fields were discovered in Utah; silver, copper, lead, and even gold mines were unearthed. Accordingly the Saints, by hard labor, wise economy, and good luck waxed rich and powerful in the tempestuous days between Sumter and Appomattox.

Scarcely less important in an economic sense than the opening of new agricultural lands during the stern days of the war—with its devastating effect on large areas of the South—was the development of western mining. On the very eve of Lincoln's election, the gold fields of California that had poured their stream of wealth into the national treasury for ten years were enlarged by new discoveries. Far and wide in the vast region of mountain and basin embraced between the Rockies and the Coast, as the years flowed on, rich mines one after another were uncovered, stirring even the war-worn nation with sensational reports of fortune piled on fortune. Between 1861 and 1865, the annual output of gold rose from forty-three to fifty-three millions.

To this hoard was now added a treasure of silver, drawn from great beds unearthed in Nevada, Colorado and Montana in the late fifties and early sixties by the prospectors, miners, and promoters who swarmed out in all directions, exploring, washing, digging in a feverish search for wealth.

Every year was marked by increased earnings; in 1860 they wrung nearly a million dollars worth of silver from the soil; five years later their annual findings totaled more than eleven millions. When Lee and Grant made the great peace, there was hardly a spot in the mineral belt that had not been visited, mapped, and described by aggressive fortune-hunters.

As soon as a fresh deposit was revealed by a miner's pick, a rush to it commenced; if the vein was thick enough, a town of wooden shanties sprang up on the site almost overnight. Before the decade of the Civil War had closed, every mountain territory was boasting of swelling populations and metropolitan enterprise. Nevada pointed with pride to her capital, Carson City; Montana to Missoula, Helena, and Alder Gulch, rechristened Virginia City; Idaho to Boise City; and Colorado to Denver. Nothing like the speed of this occupation had ever before occurred on the soil of the New World save perhaps in the mining camps of California in the days of the gold rush. "Only eighteen months ago," wrote a miner in 1863 describing the Alder Gulch district, "this was a howling wilderness. . . . Truly truth is more wonderful than fiction and excels in marvelousness even the Arabian Nights, but truth and the marvelous go hand in hand when Young America finds a good gold gulch."

And in their early days these mining communities were the strangest aggregations of human beings ever brought together on this continent of diversities. It was fortunate for posterity that no less a genius than Mark Twain caught the spirit and drew a picture of the mining frontier. In the autumn of 1861, shortly after his arrival in Carson City, he characterized that wooden village of two thousand souls— and the surrounding regions—in a breath-taking letter to his mother. "This country," he wrote, "is fabulously rich in gold, silver, copper, lead, coal, iron, quicksilver, marble, granite, chalk, plaster of Paris (Gypsum), thieves, murderers, desperadoes, ladies, children, lawyers, Christians, Indians, Chinamen, Spaniards, gamblers, sharpers. coyotes

(pronounced ci-yo-ties), poets, preachers, and jackass rabbits. I overheard a gentleman say the other day that it was
'the d——dest country under the sun'—and that comprehensive conception I fully subscribe to." Later he portrayed
the scene, with its actors undisguised, in his incomparable
Roughing It.

Among the adventurers who opened up and exploited the
natural resources of the Far West were some whose ambitions did not stop at the water's edge. Far to the north
beckoned Alaska and American explorers soon answered its
call. Fishermen, following the lure of their craft, nosed
about its shores and, becoming aware of the opportunities
for profits, urged the authorities at Washington, D. C., to
secure fishing rights from the Russian government, the
owner of the distant peninsula. In 1859, Joseph Lane
Mac Donald, one of the watchers for new things, began to
communicate directly with officials at the national capital
on this subject and in the course of time the legislature of
Washington Territory re-enforced his plea for action by
addressing a memorial to the President on the matter of
opening Alaska to American enterprise. Thus Seward's imperial designs were supported by local pressure for a right
of way and fortified by the energies of a propagandist who
longed to see a transcontinental railway linked by steamboat connections with that far-off region. No doubt the
Washington memorial proved to be a useful document when
the negotiations for purchase were opened with Russia.

Out of effort and fortune came the purchase of Alaska
just two years after Grant made terms with Lee. "We
could have bought a much superior elephant in Siam or
Bombay for one hundredth part of the money," groaned a
resentful editor. "We have in our grasp the control of
the Pacific Ocean and may make that great theatre of action for the future whatever we may choose it shall be,"
remarked a member of Congress. The victorious party in
the Civil War thus bore the western front out on the Pacific
to a point not far from the sentinel islands of the Japanese

Empire so recently visited by American gunboats under the command of Commodore Perry.

§

With the program of the federal government fully outlined and the economic development of the Far West already in rapid swing, the release of national energies at the close of the war gave a terrific impulse to frontier ventures. The first heavy task was of course the construction of the railways which Congress had duly authorized and in 1866 the drive on the Union Pacific line began in deadly earnest. At the eastern end, great gangs of Irish immigrants and veterans fresh from the battlefields of the South began to grade, cut, and bridge their way across plains, mountains, plateaus, and rivers. At each stage of the progress a movable town was erected, pleasantly dubbed by the workmen, "Hell on Wheels," where an army of cooks, sutlers, harpies, and gamblers assembled to serve, entertain, and fleece the brawny sons of toil. With incredible haste the eastern company carried its track forward across Nebraska and Wyoming into Utah. Simultaneously an army of Chinese coolies marshaled under the direction of California capitalists pressed eastward over towering mountains and yawning gorges across California and Nevada, overcoming physical barriers that seemed insurmountable and finally reaching the upper region of Utah.

On May 10, 1869, the two advancing hosts met at Promontory Point, near Ogden, where their tracks were united with an imposing ceremony. Peace had its victories, no less renowned than war. The last spikes were connected by telegraph wires with leading cities in all sections of the country so that the final strokes of the hammer could convey to the uttermost parts some of the thrilling pride that animated the conquerors of plain, desert, peak, torrent, and ravine. The work that Lincoln had sanctioned was now finished. The age of the pony express, overland coach, and wagon train had closed. Steam and steel were to master a continent.

Before the work on this central line had been fairly started, projects for three additional railways to the Pacific Coast were afloat. In 1864, Congress chartered the Northern Pacific, under the direction of Jay Cooke, financier of the war, who sold huge issues of securities in America and in Europe to provide the capital for uniting Lake Superior with Puget Sound. Two years afterward Congress authorized lines to the Far South which, later fused under the name of the Southern Pacific, in due course linked New Orleans with San Francisco. About the same time it chartered the Atchison, Topeka and Santa Fé, projecting a route that finally cut through the center of Kansas, crossed a corner of Colorado, ran through New Mexico and Arizona, and found an outlet at the Pacific.

Endowed by Congress with magnificent gifts of land but given no such assistance in credits as the Union Pacific and the Central Pacific had received, these later companies found the task of financing their schemes exceedingly difficult. Moreover, construction was delayed by the panic of 1873 which temporarily paralyzed capitalist undertakings of every kind. Collapse succeeded collapse; one group of promoters followed another into chancery; and yet defeat was never confesssd. By 1884, there were four railway lines connecting the Mississippi Valley and the Pacific Ocean, opening up the intervening region to settlement and exploitation.

§

Before long, however, railway promoters learned that they had built on flimsy foundations. In the very year which witnessed the completion of the three new lines to the Coast, another financial panic sent scores of companies into bankruptcy courts producing a search for more freight and passenger business. With relative ease, the inquiry showed that the western concerns which held imperial domains of

public lands could turn their claims into profitable properties if they had labor to develop their resources—presenting to railway managers the task of securing a closer
settlement of the regions penetrated by their lines. The
need, once firmly grasped, was answered in a truly American
fashion—by an army of aggressive promoters who inaugurated a "boom." Land speculators and railway operators
—the Baltimores and Penns of the new day—commenced
to colonize on a colossal scale. Widespreading towns were
platted on treeless plains that had not a house in sight as
yet. Advertising campaigns were organized. Eastern
states and the Old World were scoured for settlers to take
up federal lands under the Homestead Act or to buy tracts
from railway companies or from forehanded real estate
agents. Sometimes schemes for the occupation of whole
counties were announced in advance and the brave of all
nations invited to help realize the paper project with its proposed railway, its towns to be built on virgin prairie, and
its farms to be staked out and brought under cultivation.

Among the hundreds of leaders in the westward movement that rounded out the continental domain there was
none more forceful or spectacular than James J. Hill of
Minnesota, who in later years became head of the Great
Northern and allied railway lines. Reared on the frontier,
Hill knew its people and its potentialities; and turning to
railroading as a business, he early grasped the key to successful operation. Unlike the land gambler in search of
instant profits at any expense to his victims, Hill took a
long view of things, basing his vision on definite realities:
every state should be closely studded with homesteads; all
the arable land should be tilled by competent farmers; every
facility should be afforded them to help improve their crops
and their livestock; and markets should be developed in
Europe and the Orient to provide freight for the long haul.

With these ends in mind, Hill set to work to conquer the
Northwest. He sent agents into the older states to tell the
farmers and their wives of the wonderful opportunities on

the advancing frontier. Warning them against allowing their children to become "farm hands" or factory workers, he urged, as a preventive, migration into the West where rich lands could be obtained so easily. Not content with words, Hill organized excursions and carried train loads of prospective settlers to see for themselves the kind of soil that awaited their plows. "You farmers talk of free trade and protection and what this or that political party will do for you. Why don't you vote a homestead for yourself? That is the only thing Uncle Sam will ever give you." In that vein his publicity men appealed to the people of the East and of the Middle Border.

Tens of thousands answered Hill's appeal. Whole communities of farmers and merchants, hoping for "better luck" in the new country, indicated their desire to migrate to it. Religious congregations sometimes offered to move en masse as in the days of the Puritan exodus from Europe. Whenever a large company of prospective settlers assembled at one place, Hill's agents provided trains of passenger and freight cars to carry the emigrant families with their livestock and household goods to their destination.

After the settlers arrived, Hill did not leave them to shift for themselves. On the contrary, he took a continuous and profound interest in the welfare of every community along his railway lines—in its tillage, ditching, highways, credit facilities, and improved methods of production. Going still further in his imperious dream, he sent representatives to China and Japan to discover what American products those countries might consume and what they had to give in exchange. In line with this interest he established direct steamship communication between his Coast terminals and the Orient, encouraging Japanese railway engineers to buy supplies in America and ship them by his lines.

Through a long and active life, Hill carried on this process of promotion, passing from the primitive stage of frontier society through the pioneer epoch into the age of high finance. All the way from the Dakotas through Montana and Idaho to the Coast, his enterprises bore fruit in prosperous farms, thriving towns, and great industries. Before he died in 1916, Hill had the satisfaction of seeing the wheatfields of the northwest bound by economic ties to the mill towns of the Old World and the cities of the Far East. What he did with a grand sweep, others accomplished on a smaller scale, giving to the last strong tide of westward migration in the United States a peculiar direction, character, and force.

§

Railways and promoters, however, merely accelerated a westward movement that was inevitable and indeed was in progress even while the Union Pacific track layers were grading and driving spikes. At the close of the Civil War, when thousands of able-bodied young men anxious to win economic independence were released from the armies, the federal government encouraged them to go West by allowing them to count their term of military service as a part of the five years' occupancy required for the permanent possession of a free homestead under the act of 1862. From this source the migration into Kansas and Nebraska, which had continued during the war, was especially augmented—now that the strife between slaveholders and free farmers was laid to rest. Within twenty years the population of Kansas leaped from one hundred thousand to a million, an increment greater than that of New England between the landing of the Pilgrims and the eve of the American Revolution. In the two decades between 1860 and 1880, Nebraska's twenty-eight thousand increased to nearly half a million; in 1867 the territory was admitted as a state to the Union.

Before General Grant, the victor at Appomattox, died in 1885, the central frontier had reached its last belt of arable land and had merged into the treeless and arid regions of the plains that sloped upward toward the Rockies. By that time the stream of migration had been turned northward beyond Minnesota into the Dakotas where the rich soil of the Red River Valley lay fallow for the plow. Within a few years more, even the frontier of the northwest had been pushed beyond the fertile regions into the barren lands and forbidding hills that announced the mountain ranges.

In settling the upper reaches of the Mississippi and the Missouri, pioneers from the older states had the help of new racial stocks from Scandinavia, as well as of the Germans who continued to come though after a while in diminishing numbers, and of their Russo-German kindred. The Swedes had first appeared in the New World in a colony of their own on the Delaware founded long before the days of William Penn and all through the succeeding generations immigrants from Denmark, Sweden, and Norway had filtered into the country—in these later years into Wisconsin and Minnesota mainly; but it was not until after the Civil War that their small number became a multitude.

By that time the pressure of population upon the limited agricultural resources of Scandinavian countries had reached an acute stage. A man in Denmark who had enough land to support two or three cows and a horse was considered independent and prosperous while tenant farmers and day laborers of Norway or Sweden who netted fifty or a hundred dollars a year were deemed among the fortunate of the earth. Even the grassy walls of the fjords were close cropped by hungry herds, the daring goat was hoisted or lowered to little niches of grass that could not be reached in any other way. Evidently conditions were ripe for another Viking movement, not to conquer the towns of England or the fair lands of Normandy, but to occupy by peaceful penetration wide-stretching prairies of virgin soil beyond the Mississippi River.

News of opportunity in America had already reached Scandinavia through the letters of forerunners in Wisconsin and Minnesota when the signal for a general exodus was given by the restoration of peace in 1865—a signal which started a migration so enormous that it frightened the

Scandinavian governments. Within one generation, Norway lost a larger percentage of her population to America than any other Old World country save Ireland alone. One-third of Denmark's Icelandic subjects crossed the Atlantic in search of fortune. Before half a century had passed, the Scandinavians in the United States were equal in number to one-fourth the combined population of Denmark, Norway, and Sweden.

By use and wont these new stocks were well fitted to occupy the upper Mississippi country and build prosperous communities there. They were skilled in agriculture and forestry; they were hard-working, Puritan in temper, devoted to education, and frugal in habits. Accustomed to the cold climate of northern Europe, they did not quail in the stinging blasts of the American northland. Before the railways offered them easy transportation, they advanced on western Minnesota and the Dakotas, pressing upward into the Red River Valley where the trappers of the Hudson's Bay Company were making their last stand. By 1870, there were more than two thousand farmers in the valley, announcing the doom of the fur monopoly in that region. With astonishing energy the Scandinavians then spread out in all directions, seizing every opportunity to develop the resources at hand. They fished in the Red River, contrasting it no doubt a bit ruefully with the salt waters of the North Sea where their ancestors had plied that trade for a thousand years; they worked on the flat boats carrying hay and grain to market; they hauled their produce to shipping points in wagons, picturesque like the carts of Peking; they established tiny trading towns here and there in the forests and on the plains; as lumberjacks they cut and hewed timber for houses and barns.

Though their life in the New World was hard, their labor brought material rewards which, in comparison with their meager earnings at home, seemed riches indeed; while some amassed millions from crops grown on their broad acres. In an appealing vignette Henry Goddard

Leach has etched the life history of a family of Norwegians that garnered a fortune from the golden grain of the Red River Valley. The father was a bronzed pioneer of the frontier; the mother came to America "a Valkyrie in a red bodice and a black shawl with the bright mountain bloom of Norway on her cheeks"—a vigorous couple blessed with many stalwart sons and daughters who bent to heavy work with strong arms and willing hearts. Year after year the family treasury swelled with fresh returns from crops, the old couple retaining the simplicity of earlier days in the midst of plenty, while their grandsons studied at Yale and Harvard and took on urban airs. At the age of seventy-five the woman, then a widow, erect as a Viking still, "great-limbed and competent," though she could count her millions drawn from wheat, proudly wore, even at parties given in her honor, a black shawl such as she had when she came in the steerage more than a half century before.

Within twenty-five years after the passage of the Homestead Act all the best land between the Mississippi and the mountains, available under that statute, had been staked out and transferred to private ownership, except the rich Indian Territory occupied by red men. Already the longing eyes of a soil-hungry people were turned upon the acres still lying fallow or only half-tilled under Indian ownership. Already a clamor had been heard in Washington for the removal of this barrier to the march of Manifest Destiny. Since, without legal authority, land jumpers had begun to invade the red man's domains staking out homesteads in defiance of the law, the inevitable could not be turned or stayed.

Yielding finally to political pressure, the federal government bought from the Indians a large region known as Oklahoma and in 1889 threw it open to an army of white invaders encamped on the border awaiting the sign to rush in. At the appointed moment a stampede of settlers swept into the coveted region. Within twenty-four hours colonies had risen at Guthrie and Oklahoma City; within ten days frame buildings appeared; within one year there were churches, schools, banks, newspapers, and with them saloons, "bad men," and reckless women. Having occupied that much of the Indian Territory, the settlers then demanded the rest and bit by bit it was subjected to similar invasions until nothing was left to the former Indian owners save a small strip in the southwest. In 1890, the territory of Oklahoma was organized and the drive for statehood had begun.

§

When the combing outriders of the homestead frontier reached the semi-arid borders of western Kansas and Nebraska, a new conflict arose—this time with cattlemen who claimed as their special preserve a vast unfenced domain stretching from Texas to Canada. For many years, without interference from any one, rangers had been breeding cattle in Texas and driving them north with the advancing spring, fattening them for market on the way as they grazed across the plains to ever fresher grass and herbs. Within the twelve months of 1884, for example, nearly a million head of livestock, it is reckoned, were moved to the north by four thousand cowboys. In area the cattle dominion claimed by these nomads embraced 1,300,000 square miles or more than one-third the total expanse of the United States and on its wide acreage huge fortunes were continually made from grazing. There cattle kings and queens flourished, accumulating wealth which enabled them to rival the pretensions of the sovereigns enriched by cotton, gold, silver, and wheat. There immense quantities of beef were produced at a nominal cost, supplying an abundance for the meat-eating American nation and for untold millions of Europe. In short, like railroading and cotton-spinning, cattle-raising had become a staple industry, a formidable vested interest. Now it was menaced by a powerful combination of men who possessed hard fists, weapons, keen eyes, and political power in Washington, to wit, farmers and sheep raisers.

Both parties to this masterful combination were bent on fencing the plains and making them private property. To the homesteader, of course, fences were necessary as a protection for crops against animals, wild and tame. Similarly the prosperity of the sheep raiser depended on enclosures; Texas steers might defend themselves with hoof and horn against dogs, wolves, and other beasts but sheep needed careful safeguards; moreover cattle in great herds tramped down the vegetation of the plains, ruined water holes, and made great tracts useless for the producers of wool and mutton. Without much difficulty, therefore, farmers and sheep raisers reached a common conclusion, namely, that the free play of the cattle rangers must be reduced to barbed-wire limitations. Hard battles and desperate skirmishes followed their decision but in the end the cattlemen lost the war: their dominion was broken up into enclosures and their grand drive from Texas northward had to be abandoned. Eventually no wild grazing land was left except in the forests and reserves of the federal government.

Even in that last stronghold the cattlemen lost their traditional liberties at the opening of the twentieth century. Under President Roosevelt the national forestry service deliberately favored the settler as against the large stock raiser and, in the summer of 1906 for the first time, cattle and sheep owners were both forced to pay for their privileges on the American public domain. No doubt the new rule was painful to men accustomed to freedom; and in attempt to regain their old rights, they kept up a running battle with the officers in charge of the federal reserves. Though they never raised the white flag, in the dissolution of their empire that picturesque figure of American romance—the cowboy with his broad hat, his pistols, his lasso, his shining spurs—definitely lost his vocation. Grazing had also become a form of capitalist enterprise.

In place of the adventurer who had rounded up cattle, half for the fun of the game, had come a matter-of-fact laborer, a wage worker, who, in his wildest moments, seldom commanded the imagination required for shooting up a town or the sentiment necessary for yodelling melodies to frightened flocks and herds. On "dude" ranches and at show places in the national parks, it must be admitted, a few gaily caparisoned horsemen tried to maintain frontier appearances but only in fiction did the historic cowboy continue to ride and shoot as in the "good old days." Moving picture stars might make money portraying him to gaping multitudes of many lands—alike in Nara, the ancient capital of Japan; in Oxford, home of the classics; and in Venice beside the storied pile of St. Marks and the Bridge of Sighs. Students of folklore and professors of anthropology might gather up and treasure his yodels, his musings under the starry sky, and his ballads thrown off in lonely hours; but the real cowboy was seen no more in all the land. One more primitive phase of society had passed.

In the same relentless economic process that destroyed the free cattle range, the wild Indian at last disappeared. The warfare of subjugation, begun by the federal government in 1862, was continued for nearly thirty years, accompanied by cruelty, treachery, and injustice on both sides, the white man proving himself on the whole little if any above the red man in morals or humanity. To such a conflict, whatever its merits, there could be only one conclusion. Of course the Indians occasionally won battles that deceived them with hopes; for example in the summer of 1876 the Sioux, angered at the invasion of their Black Hills by prospectors, put on the war paint and destroyed General Custer's command on the Little Big Horn. But such transient victories only nerved the federal authorities for more effective fighting. When in 1886 the Apaches of the Southwest gave up the cause as hopeless, the long armed contest between the European and the Indian for the possession of the American continent came to an end. Even the recorder with no illusions about "the noble savage" had to draw a black border around that page in American history —that story of one elemental force, the eternal clash of races, illustrating Anaximander's thesis.

While remorselessly closing in on the Indians, the federal government made attempts to work out a system of control that would assure some protection to those who survived the heroic remedy prescribed by General Sheridan. In 1869, upon reading the report from a special committee of inquiry, Congress created the Board of Indian Commissioners charged with caring for the nation's wards, and two years later the practice of dealing with the tribes through the formalities of treaties was abandoned. Pressed by the friends of the red men for more liberal treatment, Congress in 1887 passed the Dawes Act which offered citizenship to Indians and permitted them to take up land in individual holdings, allowing them to merge their race in the body politic. Though many availed themselves of this invitation, the great majority preferred to settle down on government reservations where they were supported in part at least by federal doles; for at any rate life according to that plan, such as it was, offered security and no responsibility.

Three hundred years after the arrival of the white man and the founding of Jamestown, there were probably as many Indians in the area now embraced within the United States as there were when Captain John Smith landed on the shores of Virginia; and the latest census reported an increase within the decade. It is not exactly correct, therefore, to speak of the "extermination" of the red man. Indeed it is doubtful whether the arms and whisky of his white competitor were more destructive than his own diseases, such as smallpox, his tribal wars, his clannish jealousies. Neither Rousseau nor Cooper, in their most restrained moments, came near the realities of the matter —this without any apologies for cruelties inflicted by the rifleman of the frontier, the mistakes of the government, or the rapacities of liquor dealers and land grabbers. Some things seem to be deeply rooted in the very constitution of the universe.

§

When the rangers and the Indians were overcome and deprived of their free dominion, the western pioneer still had contests enough to fill his days with trouble—against his fellow-men and against nature. Angry and incessant were his wrangles with the railway companies which, in several of the western states and territories, held one-third or more of the land under titles acquired from the federal government. In some cases, squatters, anticipating such grants, had settled upon soil afterwards claimed by railway promoters; in other cases, concessions to railways were vague in terms and contingent upon the final location of their lines, thus jeopardizing the farms of homesteaders who had entered their holdings in due form. Disputes arising from such collisions were thick as autumn leaves, crowding the federal land office with claims and counter-claims and the courts with litigation. Whoever lost in a suit before administrative or judicial officials turned to Congress for relief, asking indemnities or compensating favors.

From these appeals sprang repeated debates in the Senate and House, studded with eloquent pleas for the settlers in their struggle against railways. "These citizens are humble," exclaimed James Wilson, of Iowa, stating their case with reference to one issue, "but their rights . . . should be as sacred in the contemplation of the Government as though they were the owners of principalities of lands and millions of invested capital. A government can be as truly great in guarding the comparatively insignificant rights of its humblest citizens as in contests of empire." Another congressman, defending the claims of some constituents against ouster proceedings, hinted that justice was hardly to be expected in the other branches of the government. "When laws are passed for their protection it is meet that those who sit upon the softly-cushioned seats of advantage should heed these laws—in a contest of abstractions (corporations) and such men. . . . The history of these cases would seem to illustrate the unhappiness of those who do business with a department of chance (Interior) and afterward are so unfortunate as to encounter the over-ruling Providence of that department which alone is a law unto itself (Judicial)."

In this prolonged controversy, both political parties tendered their good offices to voters in quest of relief. "These settlers," lamented a Nebraska statesman, "read the platform of the great Republican party which promised them the earth if they would vote the straight ticket and then they read the platform of the great Democratic party which promised them not only the earth, as the other platform did, but everything over it and under it, and they said: 'We are safe; our friends, the politicians, will take care of us.'" When the politicians did attempt to fulfill their pledges, they usually compensated railways that lost to the settlers, by giving them grants in other places, thus saving them from material damage. Indeed it frequently happened that all parties to hotly contested transactions were gratified with the outcome of their disputes.

On two other counts the western pioneer had quarrels with the common carriers. The first of these related to the lands held for appreciation in price by the railways under grants of apparent validity. Although the companies always sold large areas of their imperial domains at reasonable rates with a view to developing the country along their tracks, they generally retained a substantial portion for speculative purposes—waiting on an unearned increment that would flow from the intensive development of adjoining regions. Naturally the settlers, who bore the brunt of the labor involved in pushing land values upward, looked with some envy upon the corporate beneficiaries, especially after all the choice land available under the Homestead Act was gone. If by any chance therefore a flaw could be found in the title of an offending company, an agitation was started to annul by judicial or legislative process its unlawful claims. In this way millions of acres were wrested from the railways for entry by farmers and grazers.

If there was no possibility of victory in that direction, the feeling against the railways as landowners could easily be merged in the resentment aroused against them on account of their high rates and their practices as carriers. Accepting the Manchester creed for gospel truth, the railroad corporations, as one of their competent lawyers explained, like other capitalists, "charged all the traffic would bear." Bent upon the profitable business of the long haul, they often refused to build extensions, side tracks, and collateral lines demanded by local patriots, thereby opening springs of ill-will which burdened the politics of western states and territories with interminable controversies and forced the statesmen who managed affairs at Washington to keep a watchful eye on "the demands of the western farmers."

Scarcely less irritating to the possessors of small freeholds were the huge estates of landlords, both American and alien, often secured by fraud and usually held for speculative increments or developed by tenant and wage labor—the alien owners naturally receiving the heavier condemnation because they had no patriotic interest in the prosperity of the West, were actuated by motives purely mercenary, and held areas regal in size. From colonial times Old World capitalists had been accustomed to making handsome fortunes in American land speculation but after the Civil War their avidity was even more marked than in the days of King Charles II. Now besought by American railway promoters to buy blocks of stocks and bonds, they looked into the nature of congressional grants and acquired a lively interest in the general free-for-all distribution of land and resources in the Far West.

"The glittering accounts of our prolific soil and the immense area of our pasture lands," explained a congressman from Pennsylvania, "soon caught the eye of European capitalists. And our railroad companies with a thrifty purpose of their own stimulated the interest already aroused by free excursions in well-stocked palace cars, by which noblemen and other men of wealth saw the bounteousness of our prairies through the sparkle of champagne and the delicate smoke of pure Havana; and the enormous returns which foreign investors received from their American cattle ranches still further inflamed the cupidity of their countrymen and many others sought these rich fields of gain." By 1884, approximately twenty million acres had passed into alien hands. Lord Dunmore had one hundred thousand acres; Lord Dunraven had sixty thousand; the Duke of Sutherland, who owned so much of Scotland, had nearly half a million acres of American soil; an English syndicate headed by the Marquis of Tweedale had more than a million and a half; two English syndicates over seven millions in Texas alone; and a German concern more than a million acres.

In the aggregate the large estates in the hands of American and alien investors constituted at the opening of the twentieth century a huge dominion. Almost one-half the farm land in the Mountain and Pacific states was then laid out in lots of a thousand acres or more, occupied by tenants or laborers; making the absentee landlordism that had plagued Ireland for centuries a familiar thing in an area of the United States many times the size of the Emerald Isle. Throughout wide reaches of territory, something like the plantation system of the Old South was being reproduced in different circumstances, frequently with Japanese and Mexicans as laborers instead of slaves imported from Africa—a method of exploitation which, in its social consequences, approached chattel servitude rather than the freedom of the system obtaining in the Middle West. If after a while the bars had not been put up against Oriental labor, there is no doubt that one of the striking features of civilization in the lower South would have been duplicated in large sections of the Southwest and the Far West;

a minority of whites would have been ruling a majority of laborers drawn from other races not readily assimilable—Chinese, Hindu, Japanese, and Mexican. Unquestionably the exclusion of Orientals slowed down this process but it went forward inexorably, if at a slower pace, as the flood of Mexican Indians rolled over the border and streamed out in every direction.

The forces of nature, no less than the systems of land tenure and tillage, gave a peculiar direction to agricultural development in the Far West. Neither the farmers from the older East nor the immigrants from Europe had ever faced exactly such conditions. In the northern reaches of the Mississippi and Missouri valleys frequent hurricanes spread wreckage in their wake, and blizzards isolated lonely farms for weeks at a time. Often mountains of snow almost buried houses, barns, and cattle pens; in the autumn of 1881, for example, an avalanche of snow, which came down early on the cornfields of North Dakota before the crop could be gathered, held it for months in an icy embrace. In summertime came pests, locusts and grasshoppers, that devastated thousands of acres as if by fire, bringing poverty and misery to prosperous communities.

If insects did not devour or snows cover, droughts were apt to wither and blast the grain in the field. This alternative the pioneers in western Kansas and Nebraska soon learned to their sorrow. When they first entered the lands of the distant plains, a series of unusual rainfalls had given false notions of the weather, but in 1887 the course changed and for several years there was not enough rain to sustain the crops. "Week after week," wrote an eyewitness of one awful summer, "the hot, burning sun glared down from a cloudless steel-blue sky. The dread hot winds blew in from the south. Day after day they continued. All fodder, small grain, and corn were cut short." Economic ruin followed; debts were unpaid; mortgages were foreclosed; men, women, and children were driven homeless out into the world. A wave of agrarian unrest swelled up into the great populist movement that alarmed political leaders from Penobscot to the Golden Gate.

Beyond the drought-harassed regions of the plains lay arid lands that would yield no crops at all except under irrigation, presenting an entirely new problem to the American farmer. In ancient times, the Indians of Arizona and New Mexico had attacked it by constructing dams and ditches, displaying in their work an engineering skill of high order. Long afterwards, the Mormons in Utah, at first baffled by aridity, took the offensive and mastered it, their irrigation works serving as inspiration to the pioneers about them. When eventually the watered lands of the Mississippi Valley were practically all entered by homesteaders, the oncoming hosts of settlers had to face in all seriousness the task of reclaiming the desert. And they set to work on it with a will. Some ranchers with an instinct for water like that of the miner for metal "located" supplies, sank wells into dry, parched soil and brought forth water that "soused the thirsty desert and turned its good-for-nothing sand into good-for-anything loam." Private capitalists entered the lists, buying up large areas, erecting irrigation plants, and selling their watered lands in small lots at good prices. Joint stock concerns organized by farmers and financed by local resources made successful demonstrations in cooperative irrigation.

Near the turn of the century when the magnitude of the problem was realized, western Senators and Representatives in Washington drew the attention of the nation to the war for the conquest of the desert. In 1895, Congress authorized the transfer of arid lands to the states on the understanding that irrigation projects were to be constructed. Seven years later a program of reclamation under federal authority was sanctioned and the construction of immense works begun. In 1911 coöperation between the national government and the states was inaugurated. Thus by individual and corporate enterprise, by federal and state assistance, millions of acres were redeemed and transformed into fertile farms for producing hay, corn, fruits, and vegetables. Whole communities were founded on the science and art of irrigation—communities that were as different from the great estates and ranches of the West as from the farming regions of the East.

§

Before the restless drive on the agricultural, mineral, and timber resources of the great West had gone very far, local patriots in the several territories started pressure for statehood on grounds not difficult to trace. As long as a region was governed from Washington through officers appointed by the President, pioneers on the spot were prevented from disposing of lands, mineral rights, forests, and water power sites at pleasure and compelled to bargain and truck with politicians at the national capital. In their battles against aridity, alien landlords, cattle rangers, and railways, they had to petition for federal aid through agents who had no votes in Congress; and often for the want of adequate powers they saw victory snatched from their hands by puissant cattle, railway, and lumber kings possessing the ear of the national administration. Such obstacles, they said, put a damper on their prosperity and hindered the development of their resources. In any case the condition was intolerable to them, especially to passionate individuals brought up on the gospel of self-determination. Embittered by experience they resolved to be their own masters.

But resolution was simpler than achievement for there were colossal barriers in the way of mastery. As a rule, eastern investing interests with high risks in the West, fearing the radical politics of the frontier, preferred to operate under the ægis of federal authority rather than to entrust themselves to the mercies of local patriots striving for independence. Railroads, badly stung by the granger legislation of the seventies, had enough trouble on their hands without taking on more state legislatures—and they were the greatest single force in western politics. Furthermore, the Democrats, suspecting that the northwest, inhabited by men owing their very farms to Republican generosity under the Homestead Act, would support the ticket of that party in all national elections, could see no reason for making a party sacrifice. So the enlargement of the Union halted. Except for Nebraska admitted in 1867 and Colorado nine years later, no new state was organized until the end of the century approached.

Fretted by delays, the people of southern Dakota called a convention in 1885, drafted a constitution, and pressed their claims with vigor. "Every printing press that is whirling to-night," declared a champion of Dakota, "has advertised to the world that you have 600,000 people, over 4,000 miles of railway, over 100,000 farms and happy homes and lowing cattle and mines of precious metal— more and better than all the other territories put together and far in advance of many states. What more does Congress want to know than all this?" The figures were a little high but the argument was sound. Yet Congress hesitated. "We have seen people fighting to get out of the Union," lamented a disappointed spokesman of statehood, "amid the protests of the national government; it is a novel sight to see 500,000 people struggling to get into the Union without being heeded." With equal force the territory of Washington on the Pacific coast could plead for the privileges of statehood; with less justification intervening mountain territories could demand their place at the national council table.

It was only after prolonged debate and much political intrigue that the federal government could be induced to move, and when action came it was in the form of "omnibus bills." In two years, 1889-90, Congress admitted six states —the two Dakotas, Washington, Montana, Idaho, and Wyoming—the last with the innovation of woman suffrage. After the lapse of six more years the Mormons bowed to the necessity of prohibiting polygamy, a requirement imposed by national legislation, and were taken into the Union in spite of strong protests from conscientious objectors who held that longer probation was imperative to "wipe out the stain." In 1907, Oklahoma, entitled to statehood on the score of population and economic prosperity, managed to wring that prize from a reluctant Republican Congress; and five years later the last of the continental territories, New Mexico and Arizona, came under the national roof. Thus in the administration of President Taft was finally brought to a close the long process of creating self-governing commonwealths, begun in the days of President Washington.

Before its admission each new western state was required, in accordance with time-honored custom, to present a constitution drafted by a convention representing the local voters. In the main, of course, these new fundamental laws followed the models of older states, offering in only a few cases marked departures from accredited usage. Wyoming went beyond the standards of the time by insisting upon the continuance of woman suffrage established in territorial days; since the feminine voters were likely to be Republicans the innovation was accepted by a Republican Congress with a wink and a nod—to conciliate the region. Oklahoma and Arizona, entering the Union at the time of a Progressive wave, brought the initiative and referendum with them and the latter state, the greater experimenter of the two, added the recall for all public officers, including even judges— after getting safely past the gates.

The assemblies that framed these constitutions naturally mirrored the varied interests of their constituents, with gentlemen of the bar usually at the head of the steering committee. In the North Dakota convention of 1889, for instance, were twenty-nine farmers, twenty-five lawyers, nine merchants, five bankers, three real estate dealers, two publishers, one doctor, and a railroad man. The Washington convention, embracing besides native Americans a remarkable number of Scotch, English, Irish, Canadians, and Germans, divided according to occupations into twenty-one lawyers, five bankers, six doctors, fifteen farmers, four stockmen, two hop growers, six lumbermen, three teachers, one preacher, one mining engineer, and a few editors, surveyors, and real estate men. In every case the transactions of the constitutional assembly were carefully scrutinized by able counselors for the railway companies having extensive property rights involved in the deliberations. Whole sections of the South Dakota constitution, for example, were framed by a distinguished professor of law in the service of Henry Villard whose large railway holdings and knowledge of the Far West gave him a peculiar interest in the political affairs of that region. Nor was this solicitude without warrant. The haste with which local legislatures began to regulate and tax showed the perspicacity of such general oversight on the part of those whose property was subject to special burdens.

Admission to the Union, in a few cases, heralded a struggle over the location of the state capital. In South Dakota where competing railway lines held large blocks of land, the battle assumed a sensational form. The Chicago and Northwestern, which had extended its lines as far as Pierre, presented to the voters the superlative merits of that particular town as a prospective metropolis. It organized excursions and carried farmers, their wives, children, and "hired hands" to its favorite village. On one such occasion, the little place of two thousand inhabitants had to entertain five thousand guests brought by the railroad company "to view the sights." For months the state indulged in a general picnic while "threshers stood unfed among the grain shocks, plows rusted in their furrows, and the potatoes crowded undug in the hills. Merchants locked their doors and schools closed to permit the people to visit the rival cities." At the close of a lively agitation, Pierre won the honor. The victory was great but the seat of government never showed any signs of rivaling Chicago or New York —at the end of half a century its population was under three thousand. The number who could thrive on politics alone was apparently limited.

§

Besides producing colorful local incidents, the development of the Far West exercised a profound influence on the politics and economy of the entire nation. It bore the frontier, which had been a characteristic feature of American life since colonial times, steadily away from the Mississippi toward the Pacific and finally extinguished it completely. With the movement of that belt line of pioneer farmers engaged in breaking virgin soil, usually poor in earthly goods and in debt for capital advanced to finance the operation, went the political belt line of agrarian unrest, a ferment that was periodically whipped into an explosion by crop failures and business panics. At no time between the Civil War and the end of the century was any administration in Washington able to move hand or foot without considering members of Congress from the Far West, whose constituents, toiling under the open sky, felt that they were bearing American plutocracy on their backs.

To make politics more ticklish, those laborious voters had a representation in the Senate all out of proportion to their numerical strength. Unlike the older middle states, such as Ohio and Illinois, the new commonwealths did not grow rapidly after their admission to the Union; by 1900 nine western states—Montana, Wyoming, Colorado, Utah, Idaho, Washington, Nevada, Oregon, and California—had fewer than four million inhabitants but nevertheless sent eighteen Senators to the national capital to offset the weight of an identical number from nine industrial states on the Atlantic Coast speaking for twenty-one million people. Nevada with its forty-three thousand had the same voting power in the Senate as New York with its seven million. Had it not been for the fact that in the worst of the rotten boroughs copper, silver, lumber, railway, and cattle kings could usually buy their way into the upper chamber the western states would have proved still more irritating to the directors of national politics in the age of Marcus A. Hanna.

Hardly less disturbing to the managers of the federal government were the agitations on the western coast that grew out of the conflict between domestic and Oriental labor. The Chinese were the first to bear the impact of the collision with the Nordic. In the days of the gold rush they had come in throngs with immigrants from all parts of the world to seek their fortune in California. Later, railway and mining corporations imported them in large numbers as cheap and patient laborers who did not organize and never struck. To meet this demand the Pacific Mail Steamship Company established in 1866 a regular traffic between Hong Kong and the Golden Gate, deriving a large part of its revenue from the steerage business. Setting an official seal on such operations by a treaty signed in 1868, the Republican administration in Washington, in keeping with the liberal policy recently written into the contract labor statute, authorized the wholesale immigration of Chinese, specifically recognizing their right to come and go at will—to enjoy all the privileges and immunities of citizens of the most favored nation. At the end of the decade consequently there were approximately sixty thousand subjects of the Peking emperor in the region west of the Rockies, nearly half of whom were engaged in industries.

Just as the Chinese were about to settle down to the enjoyment of the welcome extended to them by the government, they became the objects of a bitter attack launched by California workmen aided by discontented farmers, under the leadership of Dennis Kearney, an Irish drayman and orator of undoubted parts. Day and night this intrepid master of invective carried on an agitation of whirlwind intensity, closing every speech after the fashion of Cato with the thunderous command: "The Chinese must go!" Kearney's progress, swift enough without artificial stimulus, was helped by the business panic started in 1873 which sent multitudes of American workers into the streets to beg for work or bread and also by the local contest then raging between the railway and ranch kings on the one hand and farmers and laborers on the other—a conflict that resulted in the formation of a new and radical constitution in 1879. Not until the federal Congress in 1882 gave heed to the agitation by enacting the Chinese Exclusion law did the storm blow over and the hatred that had flamed out against the Chinese die down. Even then it was not expedient for any candidate for public office or employer of union labor to show too much open sympathy for immigrants from the Celestial Kingdom.

Out of similar social forces sprang a few years later a kindred hostility for the Japanese. Like their Oriental neighbors, the Chinese, they too had been cordially invited by the United States government to settle in America—by Commodore Perry when he forced the gates of Japan with the mailed fist in 1854 and by a special treaty flinging wide open to them the ports of this country. Though at first indifferent to the invitation, the Japanese, near the end of the century, began to take advantage of the proffered hospitality, attracted by the congenial climate of the Coast and by the varied industries adapted to their versatile talents. In 1900, there were about twenty-five thousand Japanese in the continental United States; during the next decade their number multiplied three-fold, owing in a large measure to their extremely high birth rate.

As the representatives of the only non-Caucasian nation on the globe that had been able to hold off the imperial powers of western civilization and defend their own soil against foreign invaders, these later immigrants from the Orient raised again all the issues generated by the Chinese and several in addition. They were more eager to acquire property, more zealous in educating their children, and quicker to resent demands for servility. In such circumstances, Californians reasoned that the Japanese if not checked would, within a relatively short span of time, occupy a large part of the Pacific slope and, being backed by a powerful government of their own at home, would present grave problems in American local administration, domestic economy, and international relations. Dennis Kearney was dead but there were more leaders, some of them Irish also, ready to take his place and blazon on their escutcheons: "The Japanese must go!"

In 1906, the racial conflict flared up over an order of the school board of San Francisco proposing to segregate Asiatics. Although there were not many Japanese among the thousands of white children enrolled in the local schools, the government of Japan, sensing the discrimination inherent in the regulation, lodged protests at Washington claiming rights under treaties. With an eye to the balance of power in the Orient, President Roosevelt, while sympathizing with the desire of the Californians to restrict Oriental immigration, promptly objected to the school decree and by patient, but firm, negotiation reached a compromise. As a part of this settlement, Washington and Tokyo concluded a secret understanding, known as the Gentlemen's Agreement, in which Japan undertook to stop the emigration of her laborers to America in exchange for a promise on the part of the United States to make no open discrimination against her people. That was in 1907.

If this adjustment relieved diplomatic tension, it did not check the agitation against the Japanese, for a few years later California passed a law forbidding aliens ineligible for citizenship to hold land anywhere in the state. In vain did Roosevelt's successor in the White House, President Wilson, stand out against this law in the name of international harmony. Besides rejecting advice from Washington, leaders in the exclusion movement continued to advance relentlessly, enacting legislation which made it impossible for Japanese adults to acquire land in trust for their children born on American soil and entitled under the Constitution to all the rights and privileges of American citizens. Flushed with local victories, champions of exclusion now demanded the abolition of the Gentlemen's Agreement and the sealing of American ports to Japanese immigrants.

To this proposal the Tokyo government objected, citing the bilateral provisions of the compact but offering to make concessions—even to accept a quota arrangement that would admit to the United States not more than one hundred and fifty Japanese annually. Giving no heed to such overtures, Congress in 1924, against the protests of President Coolidge and the Secretary of State, Charles E. Hughes, met the call of the Pacific Coast by passing an Exclusion law which placed the Japanese in the same category as the Chinese. "Now," it was said, "the Yellow Peril is laid to rest." And yet the protectors of the white race saw no incongruity between the total exclusion of Orientals and the free admission of more than one hundred thousand Mexican Indians every year, raising a question as to whether after all it was a desire to protect the Nordic stock that primarily produced the drive against the Japanese. In any event the planters of the Southwest and the ranchers on the Coast wanted laborers who were not likely to acquire land, push into business, or organize under the ægis of revolutionary socialism.

With respect to other phases of the labor question, the Far West also presented features not to be found in the eastern sections of the country. In the Coast cities, of course, trade unionism of the conventional type flourished, often assuming dictatorial powers, but on the great cattle, sheep, and fruit ranches and in the mining and lumber camps, laborers worked under conditions so different from those of urban employees and indeed under conditions so different from those prevailing among freehold farmers that a new type of organization arose among them. In ranching, mining, and lumbering industries, employment was more seasonal and fluctuating, utilizing armies of workers at high tension in certain periods and turning them off to shift for themselves in the intervening times. Wages were often low and standards of living unspeakable; while constant migration from camp to camp, from ranch to ranch, made the normal home life prevailing in other agricultural and industrial communities practically impossible.

Among these migratory workers efforts at union organization and the improvement of hours and wages and conditions of labor by collective effort naturally presented problems of peculiar difficulty. Miners, lumberjacks, and roving harvesters, brawny in frame and accustomed to a life of hardship, were more ruthless in temper and independent of routine habits than the ordinary craftsman of the cities, less interested in the formation of permanent locals, the holding of business meetings, and the creation of enduring ties in harmony with the regular trade union principles.

For these and other reasons, there arose from the peculiar labor conditions of the Far West a type of unionism formed on the radical pattern of the old Knights of Labor rather than on the craft basis of the American Federation of Labor. The new organization was all-embracing in membership, loose in government, supported by stanch individualists usually of ripe American stock and frankly built on revolutionary aims, taking the catholic name of Industrial Workers of the World, a title soon shortened by the public to the I. W. W. In the opening decades of the twentieth century, therefore, the most radical leaders of American labor were to be found in the camps, fields, mines, forests, and cities of the Far West rather than in the cotton centers and steel mills of the East, even though for a brief moment they seemed to be making headway with their form of unionism in the East. At that time, the most lawless conflicts of capital and labor occurred in Idaho, Montana, and Colorado rather than in Massachusetts, New York, and Pennsylvania—a frontier phase of American civilization, perhaps a passing phase.

The development of the Far West after the Civil War did more than raise new problems in politics and labor organization. It helped to effect an economic transformation in the regions beyond the Mississippi. The gold, silver, grain, and meat that moved eastward and on across the ocean to Europe, in addition to paying off gigantic debts to creditors, brought fresh capital with which to push the exploitation of American resources. With payments made from the riches of the West—especially from its agricultural produce and bullion—the dependence of the United States upon foreign capital, which had been such a striking feature of American economy since Alexander Hamilton's day, was steadily diminished.

In the same process the agriculture of the older East was brought under a severe pressure that drove whole sections of the poorest land out of cultivation, the abandoned farms of New England bearing mute witness to the competing power of western fields. It is true that after the first shock was over, tobacco raising, truck gardening, and dairying made up some of the loss while summer visitors and tourists and "gentleman farmers" who bought up the old homesteads helped to restore life to desolated regions; but the former economic security of well-balanced farming could not be recalled. The same movement that produced such depressing effects on eastern agriculture also contributed to the gradual shift of industrial power into the Mississippi Valley, by inducing manufacturing corporations to discontinue their local expansion in the East and build their new plants beyond the Alleghenies in order to escape the long haul and get nearer to their customers.

§

As the star of empire moved with the riding sun, enthusiasts on the western coast began to speak in grand style of the Pacific as the center of the coming civilization. With growing emphasis they repeated the saying that, whereas the civilization of antiquity had flourished on the shores of the Mediterranean and the culture of the modern age on the Atlantic, the future belonged to the Pacific where the oldest and the newest were meeting in trade and eco-

nomic rivalry. Though there was exaggeration in that outburst of anticipation, the development of American interests
on the Pacific Coast and in the distant islands of that ocean
undoubtedly gave a powerful impetus to all the imperial
enterprises of the United States in that sphere. As long
prophesied by political soothsayers, the extension of American sovereignty over islands in the Pacific—the Philippines
and Hawaii—soon followed the rounding out of the continent, and in a few years more controversies over the Boxer
rebellion in China and contests with Russian and Japanese
capitalists in Manchuria indicated that Seward's early
prophecy might soon be fulfilled. When at length the
Washington Conference of 1921 assembled, it was hailed in
some quarters as a sign that the supremacy of the Pacific
was at hand.

But as a matter of fact that view of the situation was
eminently one-sided. Seven of the nine nations that participated in the Washington Conference were primarily Atlantic, not Pacific, powers and the significance of the diplomatic gathering was due essentially to imperial rivalries in
which the trade of the Far East was but one factor. In
the very year that the Conference was held, "the declining
nations of the West" purchased in American markets goods
worth five times the commodities bought by all the teeming
millions of the Orient combined; even the workmen of war-
sick Germany showed on the average a buying capacity ten
times as great as the laborious coolies of China. With
reference either to economy or culture, therefore, the
peoples of the Orient could not by any conceivable operation
supplant the Europeans in influencing the onward course of
civilization in America. Far from transferring the center
of gravity to the Pacific, the rounding out of the American
continent really emphasized the closely-knit unity of the
world.

CHAPTER XX

The Triumph of Business Enterprise

THE Second American Revolution, while destroying the economic foundation of the slave-owning aristocracy, assured the triumph of business enterprise. As if to add irony to defeat, the very war which the planters precipitated in an effort to avoid their doom augmented the fortunes of the capitalist class from whose jurisdiction they had tried to escape. Through financing the federal government and furnishing supplies to its armies, northern leaders in banking and industry reaped profits far greater than they had ever yet gathered during four years of peace. When the long military struggle came to an end they had accumulated huge masses of capital and were ready to march resolutely forward to the conquest of the continent—to the exploitation of the most marvelous natural endowment ever bestowed by fortune on any nation.

History was repeating old patterns in a new and more majestic setting. In the development of every great civilization in the past, there had come to the top groups of rich and enterprising business men devoted to commerce, industry, and finance. The sources of their fortunes varied and their modes of acquisition differed from age to age, but they formed a dynamic element in every ancient society that passed beyond the primitive stage of culture and everywhere they advanced with deadly precision on the classes which derived their sustenance from agriculture. In the documents which record the rise of civilization in Egypt, Babylonia, and Persia and in the trading centers of Tyre, Sidon, and Carthage, the immense operations of business men can be traced, though priests, singers, poets, philosophers, and courtiers were the chief masters of the written word.

Even in Athens, acclaimed the cultural center of antiquity, the directors of trade and industry played a powerful rôle that can be discerned through the thick layers of clerical and classical tradition. With full and sufficient warrant, a competent modern historian, W. L. Westermann, commenting on Alma Tadema s famous painting, A Reading from Homer, remarks that the conception would be equally applicable to the ancient Hellenes "if the roll from which the rhapsodist is reading were a business document; if the subject of rapt attention were the possibility of a profit of twenty-five per cent a year instead of the deep-sounding harmonies of Homeric hexameter."

Nor were the noble Romans from Remus to Cicero merely engaged in demonstrating their excellence in law or their proficiency in arms. Long before the era of the republic had drawn to a close, the forum at the capital had become the center for the greatest network of commerce and finance that the genius of man had yet woven out of economic enterprise. When the ears of antiquarians are correctly attuned, they can hear the clank of the money-changer's metal above the measured periods of Marcus Aper, Cicero, and Julius Secundus. At the opening of the Christian era, the Appian Way was lined by banking houses which carried on transactions with Athens, Alexandria, and every important city of the republic—then slowly changing into an empire while still paying homage to its ancient constitution. Wide spaces of the Forum and halls of official buildings were crowded with *publicani* and *negotiatores* chaffering, haggling, and closing deals.

The former, the publicans, hated of the populace, did business with the state and made their fortunes in political undertakings. They lent money to the government in times of necessity, collected taxes in the provinces on a contract basis, and constructed the highways, aqueducts, and public buildings which expressed the economic and martial power of an imperial race. As the Roman state had no administrative agencies for executing such projects directly, it let them at auction to companies of promoters headed by the Morgans, Vanderbilts, and Goulds of that period—masterful capitalists whose augmenting riches and luxurious lives shocked stern old patricians drawing meager revenues from estates tilled by slaves. The other leading group of Roman business men, the negotiators, were mainly engaged in brokerage and banking: they accepted deposits, managed checking accounts, sold drafts and bills of exchange on distant cities, dealt in securities, lent money to farmers, merchants, and manufacturers, and carried accounts for the politicians.

In fact the relations between the statesmen and capitalists of Rome seem to have been more than intimate. Proud members of the old aristocracy, who depended upon their estates for their income, finding it increasingly difficult to keep pace with the rising publicans and negotiators, supplemented their landed revenues by investments in business themselves. They took stock in the contracting companies upon which they bestowed favors as senators and speculated in financial ventures which were contingent upon the fortunes of war waged under their direction.

By the life of Cicero the run of affairs was abundantly illustrated. Though not of blue blood, he was intimately affiliated with the patricians as their orator. Like Edmund Burke, who centuries later served well the English Whigs, Cicero loved lavish living and was always borrowing from the money lenders. Having the reputation of an honest man according to the standards of the Forum, his influence in the councils of state was enormous, his standing in the market place was good, and his shares in economic concerns both diversified and lucrative. Indeed during the latter days of the Empire, the publicans, money lenders, politicians, and military men had become so closely united that no one could tell where private enterprise ended and the business of the state commenced. By that time the doom of all was at hand.

As medieval civilization rose on the ruins of the Roman system, business men appeared once more at the center of things. The Italian fortunes that fertilized sources of letters and art in Venice, Florence, and Genoa and sustained the Renaissance, which in turn introduced the modern age, were made mainly by trade, barter, and industry. Many a noble plutocrat was created out of the toll taken from the goods of the Orient which flowed through the peninsula on their way to the markets of Lisbon, Paris, Rouen, and London. The Bardis from the banks of the Arno, who financed more than one royal war, were valiant successors of the Roman negotiators on the banks of the Tiber and equally valiant forerunners of the Rothschilds on the shores of the Thames. As Manifest Destiny made its way westward, merchants and manufacturers of the Hanse towns, of France, and of England grew rich from the profits of trade. Sagacious cobblers, astute weavers, and clever tailors, who began in a small way at stalls in the public square, often ended as wealthy and mellow gentlemen in grand establishments surrounded by choice bits of art collected from the treasuries of the known world.

When again a new epoch was opened by mechanical inventions, when Arkwright, Crompton, Watt, and Stephenson turned the medieval civilization upside down, the business man rose to heights undreamed by his predecessors. In medieval cities, as in Rome, he was always conscious of the fact that the barons of the crags looked down upon the barons of the bags; if perchance an impoverished nobleman married one of his children into a mercantile family, stifling his instinctive repugnance to the alliance by the thought of the economic advantage carried with it, the practise was never regarded as altogether proper in feudal societies.

But in the nature of things the hereditary exclusiveness of the clan could not last forever: the domain of the landed aristocracy was limited—the acreage of a country is fixed —whereas the empire of capital was apparently infinite and birth was no key to authority within its portals. So from small beginnings, merchants, weavers, dyers, fullers, and tailors, incipient capitalists of the Elizabethan age, could develop into the mill-owning and banking magnates of the Victorian age. They bought, earned, intrigued, and forced their way into the aristocracy until that ancient landed class was subjected to the sovereignty of trade.

§

Compared with their historic forerunners, the triumphant business men of America had a freer field and a richer material endowment. Their planting opponents were laid lower in the dust by one revolutionary stroke than the nobility of France or the landed gentry of England by the upheavals which had broken their ranks. In the United States, no royal families, no great landed aristocracy, no heavily endowed clergy owned the forests, plains, and mountains where lay the natural resources so necessary to the development of business. More than one-half of the whole area of the country, to be exact, 1,048,111,608 acres, belonged to the government in 1860—a benevolent government in the hands of friends, ready to sell its holdings for a song, to give them away, or to let them pass by mere occupation. The rest belonged in large part to farmers and could be easily bought, leased, or rented for mineral exploitation. So no ancient titles, parchments, and seals prevented an enterprising individual from getting at the materials for his operations; vast mining royalties did not flow into the coffers of an opposing class to enrich it and give more substance to its power in the state. In short, much of the land for industrial exploitation could be had for the asking or at the price of a little political manipulation; the rest could be obtained in a fairly easy market.

Equally available were willing hands to develop the natural endowment. On the shores of the Old World stood a limitless supply of laborers, reared to manhood and womanhood at the expense of their mother countries, awaiting an opportunity to take part in the American advance; and competing steamship companies were now prepared to bring them across at a mere fraction of the passenger rate imposed by shipmasters in the days of Alexander Hamilton.

The American stage furnished by nature to business men for the fulfillment of their customary rôle was magnificent beyond comparison. Counting Alaska, it embraced 3,600,-000 square miles—an area nearly equal to that of all Europe. Within the geographical limits of the domain beyond the Mississippi, the entire Roman Empire, so marvelously described in the first chapter of Gibbon's imperishable work, could be comfortably tucked. The principality of American coal alone included more than 335,000 square miles; under the coal and often beyond its boundaries lay priceless stores of oil. The principality of iron offered treasures of astounding riches in the Pennsylvania, Lake Superior, and Appalachian regions. The principality of copper and precious metals, though not fully explored in 1865, was dimly outlined and its significance was comprehended by those who stood in the vanguard of business enterprise. The principality of timber, covering more than a third of the whole American estate, contained nearly every variety of wood needed for industrial and domestic purposes.

On the border of these principalities and in and out through their confines were waterways opening practical channels of commerce, the Mississippi and its tributaries alone draining one-third of the continental area. The reaches of the navigable rivers and the shore lines of the Great Lakes exceeded in mileage the ice-free seashores of all Europe; and a coast nearly equal in length, washed by the Atlantic, the Mexican Gulf, and the Pacific offered harbors and bays for ships of every class. And widely distributed over the arable portion of this spacious realm were millions of hard-working farmers exploiting fertile soil and wistfully watching every chance to exchange their produce for the commodities that streamed from mine and forge and loom. Special laws kept foreign ships from the coastwise trade while all around the vast American dominion rose a wall of high protection which sheltered capitalists from the keen and cutting competition of their European brethren.

§

With capital at hand, with natural resources to be had for the asking or the taking, with stalwart labor ready for the fray, with a vast domestic market assured, with politicians impatient to coöperate and share the fruits, and unhampered by a powerful aristocracy, lay or clerical, attached to other manners and other ideals, American business men leaped forward as strong runners to the race when the news of Lee's surrender boomed throughout the land. Just how many notables of various degrees took part in directing the exploitation of the continent is nowhere recorded in the census, but above the multitude who worked in the sphere of business towered a few figures as imposing in their day as the barons of Magna Carta, rulers of England in the days of King John.

There are, of course, good grounds for differences of opinion as to the names to be enrolled first in the peerage of the new industrial age; yet none will exclude from it Jay Gould, William H. Vanderbilt, Collis P. Huntington, James J. Hill, and Edward H. Harriman of the railway principality; John D. Rockefeller of the oil estate; Andrew

Carnegie of the steel demesne; Jay Cooke and J. Pierpont Morgan of the financial seigniory; William A. Clark of the mining appanage; or Philip D. Armour of the province of beef and pork. To draw the American scene as it unfolded between 1865 and the end of the century without these dominant figures looming in the foreground is to make a shadow picture; to put in the presidents and the leading senators— to say nothing of transitory politicians of minor rank—and leave out such prime actors in the drama is to show scant respect for the substance of life. Why, moreover, should any one be interested in the beginnings of the house of a Howard or a Burleigh and indifferent to the rise of the house of a Morgan or a Rockefeller?

From a review of the American business peerage, it appears that the eleven men just named had so many things in common that they can be treated collectively. All were of north European stock, mainly English and Scotch-Irish; Gould alone, according to Henry Adams, showing a "trace of Jewish origin." The old planting aristocracy of the South furnished no major barons of business. Of the group here brought under examination only two, Morgan and Vanderbilt, built their fortunes on the solid basis of family inheritances while only one had what may be called by courtesy a higher education: Morgan spent two years in the University of Göttingen. Carnegie began life as a stationary engineer; Jay Cooke as a clerk in a general store in Sandusky; Jay Gould as a surveyor and tanner; Huntington, Armour, and Clark as husky lads on their fathers' farms; Hill as a clerk for a St. Paul steamboat company; Harriman as an office boy in a New York broker's establishment; and Rockefeller as a bookkeeper in Cleveland.

All but Carnegie, who was tinged with skepticism, were apparently church members in good and regular standing. Jay Cooke, his biographer tells us, was "a liberal patron of the Evangelical Christian Church and of those who preached its doctrine." He was a strict and conscientious observer of the Sabbath, displaying during the Civil War a great deal of anxiety about "the laxity of Lincoln and Grant on the Sunday question." In addition to setting apart one-tenth of the profits from his business for charitable uses, Cooke gave bells, steeples, organs, Sunday-school books, rectories, and silver communion services to churches, while bestowing generous subsidies on deserving ministers—at least until he was overwhelmed by bankruptcy. He taught a Sunday-school class at great personal sacrifice and, although he disliked ritualistic controversies, was loyal to the Episcopalian Church unto his death. His faith he summed up in the words: "We must all get down at the feet of Jesus and be taught by no one but Himself." Rockefeller was a no less active and devoted member of his church, the Baptist denomination. Armour gave liberally to a non-sectarian Sunday school. Hill, though a Protestant, settled more than half a million dollars upon a Catholic seminary, thinking that the papal organization was best fitted for the task of bringing immigrant workingmen under civic discipline in America. "What will be their social view, their political action, their moral status, if that single controlling force should be removed?" he once asked in cautious tones. Morgan seems to have been reticent on religious as well as other matters but his semi-official "Life" shows him contributing generously to the Episcopalian Church of which he was a consistent member.

Those leaders in the new capitalist baronage who were eligible for military service seem to have been alike also in their relation to martial glories. If none of them was a theoretical pacifist or lacking in affection for the national cause, none, for one reason or another, was found in the ranks of the Union army in the fateful months when Lincoln and Grant were saving the republic. Three—Cooke, Huntington and Vanderbilt—all born in 1821, were mature men when the first call for volunteers was issued and perhaps felt handicapped for military service by age. Harriman, then but thirteen years old, was too young for the warrior's life. Hill was ineligible on account of his defective vision. Carnegie, Armour, Clark, Gould, Rockefeller, and Morgan, though born in the thirties, found services in other spheres more to their taste than carrying the sword or musket. Armour was merchandising in Chicago when Grant started his drive through the shambles of the Wilderness and he made his great "killing" by selling pork "short" on the strength of his faith in the indomitable hero of Donelson and Vicksburg.

Above all else, the new economic barons were organizers of men and materials—masters of the administrative art—who saw with penetrating eyes the wastes and crudities of the competitive system in industry and transportation. Possessed of a luminous imagination they could think imperially of world-spanning operations that lifted them above the petty moralities of the village-smith or of the corner-grocer. In coöperation with tireless workers in science and invention, they wrought marvels in large-scale production, bringing material comfort to millions of people who never could have wrung them barehanded from the hills and forests. "Two pounds of ironstone mined upon Lake Superior," to use a single illustration, "and transported nine hundred miles to Pittsburgh; one pound and one-half of coal, mined and manufactured into coke, and transported to Pittsburgh; one half-pound of lime, mined and transported to Pittsburgh; a small amount of manganese ore mined in Virginia and brought to Pittsburgh—and these four pounds of materials manufactured into one pound of steel, for which the consumer pays one cent." With natural pride did Andrew Carnegie, the recorder of this achievement, put it among the wonders of the world. Compared with the complicated Pittsburgh operation, the deeds of the pyramid builders—who merely commanded under the lash armies of slaves to drag by brute force huge blocks of stone into one enormous pile—sink into banalities, inviting respect neither for the intelligence displayed nor for the object in view.

§

In four great provinces bound together by ever-constricting ties of federation—manufacturing, extractive industries, transportation, and finance—the leaders of business enterprise, sustained and assisted by a host of liegemen, marched from victory to victory in the decades that followed the triumph of Grant at Appomattox. Statistics but dimly shadow their progress. In 1860, just a little more than a billion dollars was invested in manufacturing and only 1,500,000 industrial wage earners were employed in the United States. In less than fifty years the capital had risen to more than twelve billions and the number of wage earners to 5,500,000. During the same period, the value of manufactured products had leaped to fourteen billion dollars a year, fifteen times the total at the beginning of the epoch. The output of American iron and steel—that measure of modern power—was, in 1870, far below the tonnage of England or France; within twenty years the United States had outstripped them and was pouring from its forges more than one-third of the world's total annual supply. The iron crown, as Andrew Carnegie said, had been placed on the brow of Pennsylvania.

With a stride that astounded statisticians, the conquering hosts of business enterprise swept over the continent; twenty-five years after the death of Lincoln, America had become, in the quantity and value of her products, the first manufacturing nation of the world. What England had once accomplished in a hundred years, the United States had achieved in half the time.

In this development industry had moved swiftly through three stages. The little old-fashioned mill on the river's bank turned by a lumbering water wheel, marking the first step in machine manufacture, had given way to the immense plant driven by engines or turbines of gigantic power. Then in turn the isolated establishment under the ownership of a single master or a few masters had surrendered to the corporation. At the end of the century three-fourths of the manufactured products came from factories owned by associations of stockholders; in each great industry was a network of federated plants under corporate direction; by 1890 combination was the supreme concept of the industrial magnate. Oil products, iron, steel, copper, lead, sugar, coal, and other staples were then in the hands of huge organizations that constituted, if not monopolies, efficient masters of their respective fields. During the following decade, the work of affiliation went forward with feverish haste, culminating in the billion dollar United States Steel Corporation of 1901.

§

Since generalizations about the barons of capitalist enterprise give but a pale and colorless picture of their cyclopean operations, one concrete and detailed analysis seems worth a volume of miscellanies. And the best example of all is offered by the oil business, for in its development is illustrated in clear and vivid outline the whole gigantic process—industrial, political, and legal—which followed the overthrow of the planters and revolutionized the heritage bequeathed by Washington, Jefferson, and Jackson. In the unfolding of this single industry, we see modern science, invention, business acumen, economic imagination, and capacity for world enterprise at work creating material goods and organizing human services to supply not only every nook and cranny of this country but the uttermost parts of the earth with useful commodities of a high standard.

In the record of this industry lies the story of aggressive men, akin in spirit to military captains of the past, working their way up from the ranks, exploiting natural resources without restraint, waging economic war on one another, entering into combinations, making immense fortunes, and then, like successful feudal chieftains or medieval merchants, branching out as patrons of learning, divinity, and charity. Here is a chronicle of highly irregular and sometimes lawless methods, ruthless competition, menacing intrigues, and pitiless destruction of rivals. Private companies organize armed guards and wage pitched battles over the possession of rights of way for pipe lines. Men ordinarily honest are seen slinking about in the cover of night to destroy property and intimidate persons who refuse to obey their orders. Agreements are made with railway companies to obtain secret rebates on shipments of oil and, what is more astounding, rebates on the shipments of rival concerns. Newspapers are purchased; editors are hired to carry on propaganda and to traduce respectable citizens whose sole offense is the desire to handle an independent business. The most astute counsel, occupying conspicuous positions in public service and social esteem, are employed to sustain the rights of defendants in litigation.

In the same chronicle, the relations of economics and politics are unfolded. The sources of attacks on trusts are exposed. Combinations and their enemies are seen operating in legislatures and courts, drawing lawmakers, governors, and judges into one structural pattern. Bribery, intrigue, and threats are matched by blackmail until the closest observer often fails to discover where honor begins and corruption ends. Public policies, lawmaking, and judicial reasoning become unintelligible except in relation to the interests of oil producers, shippers, and refiners.

Meanwhile, as this running warfare goes on from year to year, the production, refining, shipment, and selling of oil concentrate in the hands of one gigantic combination. Legislatures assail it; courts declare it dissolved; but its economic power is steadily augmented. And all through this drama, from the start, dishonesty, chicane, lying, vulgarity, and a fierce passion for lucre are united with an intelligence capable of constructing immense agencies for economic service to the public and a philanthropic spirit that pours out money for charitable, religious, educational, and artistic plans and purposes.

Like all other great American industries, the oil business had its small beginnings, its day of romance, its period of consolidation and regular routine. Long before 1850, "rock oil," as it was known, had been found in various parts of Pennsylvania, Kentucky, Ohio, and the region now embraced in West Virginia. Sometimes it appeared on the surface of streams and creeks; sometimes it broke into wells driven to tap supplies of brine for the manufacture of salt. At first oil was sold as a medicine, those who put it on the market having the temerity to say that, taken in liberal doses, it was good for "cholera morbus, liver complaint, bronchitis, and consumption." By chance or experiment, one of the vendors, Samuel Kier, who had a bottling plant near Pittsburgh, found his medicine also useful as a lubricant and luminant and, after having a sample studied by a chemist in 1849, commenced to refine crude oil by the process of distillation.

Attracted by an advertisement of Kier's medicine, G. H. Bissell, Dartmouth College graduate, wandering teacher, and journalist, had some of it analyzed independently by Professor Silliman of Yale. Receiving favorable reports on its value for lighting and lubrication, Bissell turned to the art of promotion, interested some capitalists in a speculative venture, and in 1854 organized a company to begin productive operations. With these preliminaries out of the way, the corporation leased land in northwestern Pennsylvania and sent its representative, Edwin Drake, a former clerk, express agent, and railway conductor, to sink a well on the property. Amid the amused pity of the local wisemen, Drake commenced his labors near Titusville and day after day worked on his "folly," as they named it, until at last late in August, 1859, while John Brown was gathering the forces for another "folly" at Harper's Ferry, Drake struck oil on his own.

Those who had watched with laughter now began to applaud and then to lease land themselves in the surrounding region while the whole East was set aflame by a frenzy almost equal to the gold fever that had swept through the country ten years before. Farmers, who had been wringing nothing but a scanty living from the soil with their gnarled and knotted hands, suddenly found themselves millionaires, with town houses, bank accounts, bonds and stocks—and culture. A country doctor, who gave up pills for oil, drew a fortune of $1,500,000 from a single well. Prospectors, investors, workingmen, speculators, gamblers, and women of easy virtue rushed into the enchanted kingdom. Towns sprang up like magic. The hills were dotted with derricks. Fields, roads, and grass were splashed with oil. Backwoods trails were crowded with swearing teamsters hauling barrels of the precious fluid to the railways and to flatboats on Oil Creek, which carried it to Pittsburgh by way of the Allegheny. In short a novel and powerful economic force was released in the world of business enterprise.

Owing to the play of many factors, the oil industry was highly dynamic. In the first place, the supply of raw material fluctuated widely, for it cost but a few thousand dollars to drill a well and the operation might yield a million dollars worth of oil—or nothing. If a gusher was tapped, it might deliver thousands of barrels every day for weeks and then suddenly dwindle to a trickle or even dry up completely. Thus as the old fields were exhausted, additional sources were hunted with hysterical energy. The same uncertainty permeated the business of refining—a simple process involving no immense and expensive machinery and permitting individuals with little capital to push their way into the trade. Hence competition in refining was keen and variable, keeping the whole industry in a constant flush of speculation. Oil was twenty dollars a barrel in 1859 and fifty-two cents in 1861; it was over eight dollars a barrel in 1863 and under three dollars two years later. And in spite of these oscillations, the industry was rapidly expanding. The domestic demand continually mounted and by 1871 the oil men were sending one hundred and fifty million gallons abroad: to Europe, Egypt, Syria, India, the East Indies, China, and South America. To meet the increasing orders for deliveries, the number of refineries multiplied at Pittsburgh, Cleveland, Philadelphia, and New

York, cities favorably located for selling and shipping but remote from the fields, thereby creating a huge carrying business which augmented the cupidity of the competing railways to the point of open violence.

Early in the stages of this remarkable development, the genius of the new industry entered the arena—John D. Rockefeller, son of a farmer, born in Richford, New York, in 1839. While yet a boy, he was taken by his father to a farming community in upper Ohio where he received the bare rudiments of formal education. At the age of sixteen, after tramping the streets of Cleveland many weary hours in search of work, young Rockefeller found a position as clerk and bookkeeper at an initial salary of $12.50 a month, a princely income which enabled him with his thrifty habits to pay his board and save money. Having accumulated some capital, he embarked in 1858 in the produce commission business and, all during the Civil War, remained at his desk adding to his tiny fortune as the price of commodities soared with the demands of the government.

Cautiously branching out in 1862 Rockefeller invested some of his savings in oil, in a Cleveland refinery, and three years later when the battle-scarred veterans who had fought under Grant and Lee were making their way back to their homes or their ruined fields, he organized an oil concern of his own. These efforts crowned with success, he then helped to establish in 1870 the Standard Oil Company, an Ohio corporation, with which were associated two other men famous in the kingdom of oil, H. M. Flagler and S. V. Harkness.

By this time Rockefeller was well started on his dominating career—a thrifty, silent, tireless worker at the oil industry. With unrelaxing scrutiny, he watched every department of the business to ferret out waste and inefficiency, to improve its processes, to effect economies, and to enlarge its sphere. He made no display of wealth for a long time and took little part in the political and social affairs of Cleveland. Apparently he had but one consuming passion

—organizing the oil industry and reaping his reward. To accomplish his purpose he could be as suave and compromising, as hard and relentless, as informed or as forgetful, as occasion necessitated.

When Rockefeller entered upon his career with the Standard Oil Company, the industry was in one of its periodical depressions: the prices of kerosene were falling, refineries were multiplying, and ruin was staring the weaker operators in the face. With a view to eliminating just such accidents of fortune, a group of men at this juncture set about stabilizing the whole business by bringing it under the "South Improvement Company," a mysterious corporation founded on the authority of a charter bought from a defunct concern in Pennsylvania. To this maneuver Rockefeller's own relations were shadowy. He has been accused of swearing at one time that he was a member of the Company and denying it on another occasion; but this accusation rests upon a legal technicality susceptible of a double interpretation.

At all events, the corporation managed to unite a number of Cleveland, Pittsburgh, Philadelphia, and New York refineries in a federation and then arranged a secret plan with the Erie, Pennsylvania, and New York Central Railway managers for rebates on its oil shipments—a scheme requiring all the carriers to return to the Company $1.06 out of the $2.56 charged per barrel for hauling crude oil to New York, $1.06 on every barrel sent by its competitors, and similar drawbacks on shipments to other points than New York. No doubt the conception was Napoleonic and if it could have been realized, rebates alone would have brought in $6,000,000 a year; but unfortunately for the officers on the bridge, the ship could not get under weigh. As soon as the increased freight rates were announced, producers of the oil district, in a towering rage, organized and declared war on the South Improvement Company. A congressional committee characterized it as a "gigantic and daring conspiracy" and the Pennsylvania legislature, aroused by popular indignation, was forced to annul its curious charter.

After this grand plan for organizing the oil industry was defeated, Rockefeller went about his purpose in a more circuitous way, using the Standard Oil Company, of which he was the driving genius, as the instrument for his proceedings. Within a few months after the South Improvement Company lost its charter, he made a compact with the New York Central for secret rebates—a structure of freight rates which he readily extended to other lines. From time to time, these agreements were interrupted but insistence on such favors continued to be a part of the systematic policy of the Standard Oil Company, as of many other concerns. Occasionally there were no rebates; frequently they were high and yielded immense profits.

Having established among the railways its right to special privileges, the Company then began to buy out competitors under propitious conditions. By the close of 1872 it had acquired nearly all the refineries in Cleveland, twenty out of twenty-six. In 1874, it secured control of the Warden Refinery in Philadelphia, the Lockhart concern in Pittsburgh, and the Pratt interests in New York. The next year a Central Association of Refiners was formed with Rockefeller at the head. In 1876, the Harkness plant in Philadelphia passed under the Standard Oil yoke, followed in 1877 by the last adversary in Pittsburgh. Meanwhile the argus-eyed Company had got control of its rivals in the oil-producing districts and in the city of Baltimore. In other words, before it was ten years old, the Standard group had possession of the refining field. Independents there were still, struggling along against adversity, but the Standard's holdings and its railway connections made it the master of the industry.

At this point the business of transporting oil became the next link in Rockefeller's administrative chain. The barreling and shipping of crude and refined products had been from the beginning of course an important factor in the industry and in its early phases a number of concerns specializing in that operation had appeared—some independent and others affiliated with railways. Generally speaking, all had gone merrily enough until 1876 when the Empire Transportation Company, closely associated with the Pennsylvania Railroad, found its customers dropping off as they were absorbed one after the other into the Standard Oil federation and sought to recoup its losses by investing in independent refineries with a view to controlling their shipments.

When this new combination rose above the horizon, Rockefeller protested vigorously against the union of shipping and refining. In a cavalier manner, he told the directorate of the Pennsylvania Railroad that it would get no more Standard Oil freight until it broke with its Empire confederate and he then enlisted the Erie and the New York Central railroads in this attack, thereby making the storming party too strong for the adversary. Already half paralyzed by a formidable strike among its employees, the Pennsylvania capitulated in August, 1877, forcing its ally, the Empire Transportation Company, to sell out to the Standard Oil Company. The objection which ran against a combination of shipping and refining evidently did not apply to refining and shipping.

This specter had hardly been laid when another broke in upon Rockefeller's peace, namely, the independent pipe line to the Atlantic Coast. In 1878, the Tidewater Company began to pump oil over the Alleghenies to Williamsport, announcing to producers that oil could now be carried to the seaboard for about sixteen cents a barrel as against $1.25 or $1.40 by rail. In reply, the Standard Oil group secured a right of way from the Bradford oil field to Bayonne, New Jersey, organized the National Transit Company, and acquired by purchase a large block of stock in the competing Tidewater concern. With two weapons in hand, it finally got complete control over its rival in 1883 and then having a new outlet to the sea eliminating dependence upon the railways, it spoke to their managers in more magisterial tones. If they did not come to terms, oil could be carried without them.

Having secured for all practical purposes control over the transporting and refining business, the Standard Oil concern now pushed forward with great energy the work of perfecting its selling system. For this purpose the country was laid out into districts and subdistricts; companies and individuals were selected to undertake the distribution of oil; cities, towns, villages, and hamlets were covered by an immense network of agencies. In technique and management, the system became a model for all captains of business enterprise. The ideal, generally realized in practice, was to deliver goods of a standard quality promptly to merchants and consumers as ordered, while making desperate and unremitting efforts to kill off competitors and maintain prices at a level yielding enormous profits. Whenever necessary, rates were cut until competitors were ruined; then raised to recoup the losses. With the same remorseless precision, devices of doubtful legality and questionable morality, including espionage and intimidation, were used to compel merchants to sell only Standard oil.

While control over selling was being pushed to the very door of the consumer, a similar dominion was carried back into the extraction of crude oil. In 1887, the Standard group entered the drilling and pumping field on a large scale and after that date steadily extended its authority over oil lands and leases, until within ten years it was practically master of the oil business from the well to the lamp. And within this economic kingdom, its services to the public were immense and efficient, its administrative organization marvelous in structure and performance, its earnings as high as the managers cared to make them. No competition worthy of the name remained to reduce prices, and the consumers, incapable of organization themselves, lay at the mercy of the Standard Oil satrapy.

In the expansion of its business, the Standard Oil system

grew to unwieldy proportions, taking the form of a loose federation grouped around the original company as the owner of the controlling interest in all affiliated plants. An awkward arrangement, requiring the direction of widely scattered subsidiaries from a single center, it naturally produced a dispersion of forces and a great deal of friction, especially since the major portion of the stock was held by about fifty individuals. Obviously a closer organization was prescribed by the canons of efficiency, if nothing more, and this centralization was finally effected. In the transaction, separate Standard Oil corporations were formed in the strategic states and then fused into one grand combination by placing all the shares of the various concerns in the hands of nine trustees who in turn issued trust certificates to the respective holders and took over the management of the entire enterprise. Such was the nature of the Standard Oil Trust formally created in January, 1882, bringing the direction of an enormous economic empire under the authority of nine men, among whom Rockefeller was the first consul.

§

It is impossible, and it would be unjust, to attempt to characterize by a phrase the business methods of the Standard Oil group. For many of the evil deeds laid at its door, it disclaimed responsibility, declaring that its agents had showed excessive zeal or had violated their instructions. As to many acts only inferences could be drawn. When, for an example, armed thugs assailed the workmen of an independent pipe line company, the assumption usually was made that the assailants did not act without motive or direction; but it was one thing to assume, another thing to prove, and a nice problem in ethics anyway to render a just judgment in a baronial epoch when physical force was a normal part of high business procedure. Only one case of this nature ever came to trial in the courts, the famous Buffalo case of 1886, and it ended in a divided verdict: two men connected with a local Standard Oil subsidiary were found guilty and three representatives of the Trust, indicted in connection with the crime, were cleared of all complicity. The evidence in the case revealed a sordid story from which neither side emerged with any credit; and the historian of the distant future will probably call it a case of the kettle and the pot.

Whatever the merits of the leading actors in this particular affair, many counts in the indictment of the Standard Oil group as a community and as individuals were well established. It did receive rebates from time to time on its own and on its competitors' shipments of oil; it did crush out by methods none too delicate its rivals and adversaries; its agents did resort to espionage and intimidation in destroying opposing concerns; its high spokesmen either lied deliberately or suffered from deficient memories on various stands; it had prominent politicians on its pay roll as counselors; and it contributed heavily to party campaign funds. On the other hand it was constantly assailed and blackmailed by men whose motives were no better and whose principles were no higher than its own.

By reason of the general animus in her remarkable account of the Standard Oil Company, Ida Tarbell is partly responsible for the distorted view of its history mirrored in the popular mind. Her record is a drama with heroes and villains, rather than a cold and disinterested summary by an impartial student. In her first chapter she draws a picture of upstanding and adventurous American citizens developing the resources of the oil district, building homes for themselves and their families, erecting altars for the worship of God, establishing schools and hospitals, and founding happy and prosperous communities. Then the villain comes upon the scene stealthily and under the cover of darkness to bring ruin and desolation. "Life ran swift and ruddy and joyous in these men. . . . They would meet their own deeds. They would bring the oil refinery to the region where it belonged. They would make their towns the most beautiful in the world. There was nothing too good for them, nothing they did not hope and dare. But suddenly, at the very heyday of this confidence, a big hand reached out from nobody knew where, to steal their conquest and throttle their future. The suddenness and blackness of the assault on their business stirred to the bottom their manhood and sense of fair play, and the whole region rose in a revolt."

But in depicting the contest between the upright, God-fearing oil heroes and the wicked oil villain, Miss Tarbell incidentally portrays the former as reckless in their methods, wasteful in their operations, and contemptuous of moderate profits which other men in business would have been glad to earn. She shows that they were willing at almost any time to make terms with the Standard Oil group as against the public and failed not because their system of morals was different but because they were unable to hold their bargains on account of treacherous defections in their own ranks. Again and again they sought to keep up the prices of crude oil by curtailing extraction, and, for the purpose of intimidating independents who insisted on drilling and pumping in times of over-production and low prices, they resorted to tactics certainly as reprehensible as those employed by the villain in the play. "Men who appeared at church on Sunday in silk hats, carrying gold-headed canes—there were such in the Oil Region in 1872—now stole out at night to remote localities to hunt down rumors of drilling wells. If they found them true, their dignity did not prevent their cutting the tools loose or carrying off a band wheel."

In the end the failure of the producers to cope with the Rockefeller interests was due to no lack of will but to their own incapacity—their inability to restrain their profit-taking instincts and to maintain a producers' combination equal in strength to that of the refiners. One of their own number, after battling for years in their behalf, spoke of them as "a cowardly, disorganized mob." Some of their leaders, no doubt, assumed heroic proportions but the question may well be asked: "Would the public, the politicians, and the consumers have been more fortunate in the hands of a grand consolidated producers' union composed of Miss Tarbell's heroes than under the imperial sway of the Standard Oil Trust?"

In this stirring contest between major and minor barons over dominion in the kingdom of oil were revealed the processes of American politics as well as the nature of the economic drama. From its very inception, the Standard Oil group encountered investigations and hostile legislation, injunctions and judicial orders, lawsuits and prosecutions. As soon as the South Improvement Company embarked upon oil in 1872, it faced an attack in the legislature of Pennsylvania, directed by independent producers, and lost its anomalous charter—without suffering any material damage. About the same time a congressional committee pried into the case, denounced the Company as a conspiracy—and gracefully withdrew.

Foiled in these attempts to break down the Rockefeller alliance, the oil producers again appealed to Congress in 1876 for an inquiry into the growth of combinations in the refining field. The appeal was heard and an investigation was made under the direction of H. B. Payne, chairman of the committee on commerce, father of O. H. Payne, treasurer of the Standard Oil Company—an investigation which failed to develop any substantial evidence showing irregularity in the methods of the Company. Three years later, the Hepburn commission in New York, acting under the authority of the state legislature, managed to wring from the leaders of the oil industry important testimony as to the extent of their control and the character of their operations—also without any ponderable effect. In 1888, the senate of New York ordered another inquiry into trusts and during the same year the committee on manufactures in the House of Representatives at Washington conducted a searching inquest along similar lines. Ten years later, an industrial commission established by Congress once more surveyed the ground with thoroughness, filling bulky volumes with their findings.

At first the representatives of the Standard Oil interests either flouted official investigators or treated them with scant regard. Then as time passed, they adopted more conciliatory tactics. They no longer refused to testify before tribunals of inquisition but appeared when summoned and spoke softly under the promptings of cunning and distinguished counsel. For example, when Rockefeller himself was grilled by the New York senate commission on trusts in 1888 he showed no extreme irritation at the interference with his private affairs but amiably remembered or forgot under the guidance of competent lawyers. If the arts of diplomacy failed, his personal adviser, the Honorable Joseph H. Choate, could usually find a refuge for him in the dædalian technicalities of jurisprudence.

Altogether, the numerous legislative inquiries, while producing bales of information on the practical methods of the Oil Trust, had little or no influence on the progress of its business. They harassed its officers but did not impede its development. It would be surprising if the representatives of the industry did not secretly regard these researches as the necessary devices of gentlemen engaged in "playing democratic politics."

Perhaps somewhat more alarming to them was the petition filed in the Supreme Court of Ohio in 1890 by the attorney-general of the state, David K. Watson, asking for a dissolution of the Standard Oil Company on the ground that it had violated its charter in entering the Standard Oil Trust—a suit famous in the annals of American politics, especially because McKinley's manager, Marcus A. Hanna, appeared in the background as a moderating spokesman of the oil interests. The battle, at least to spectators, assumed regal proportions. Powerful attorneys were employed by the Standard Oil Company; Mr. Choate, who had so ably managed the trust investigation two years before, again bringing his genial wits to bear on the strategy of the litigation. And yet for a moment the state seemed victorious—to the inexperienced eye of the layman. The Ohio court ordered a dissolution of the Trust. But the charter of the Company remained intact and the decree of the tribunal could not be enforced. Supplementary proceedings, instituted to bring about the overthrow of the Trust, dragged through eight weary years—until public interest waned and the case was finally dropped by a capable politician, John M. Sheets, who came to the attorney-generalship at Columbus in 1900.

Though finally successful in the Ohio action, the leaders in oil felt the need of a more elastic organization. Accordingly in 1899, they reconstructed the Standard Oil Company of New Jersey, incorporated seventeen years before, by securing an amended charter broad and sweeping in its scope, comparable to the rights of the defunct South Improvement Company—a legal bull which permitted them to engage in almost any kind of business that pleased their fancy.

Thus equipped in law, the Company flourished and waxed fat under the congenial skies of New Jersey, until 1911 when another wave of anti-trust feeling culminated in a decree from the Supreme Court of the United States ordering its dissolution into constituent elements. Still the New Jersey corporation did not perish; it declared a sixty per cent dividend in 1913 and a 400 per cent stock dividend in 1922. By that time much water had run under the bridge.

§

With the high velocity that marked the advance of manufacturing and the extractive industries, the system of transportation passed through many phases during this period. Naturally the first railroad builders had concentrated their efforts on short lines between important cities, such as Baltimore and Washington, Philadelphia and Reading, Boston and Springfield, New York and New Haven; for the prospects of profitable business on such roads were good, the terrain offered no great obstacles, the capital could be obtained with relative ease. By 1860, nearly all the important cities of the East were connected by one or more tracks and the railway leaders were taking up the next obvious task: that of uniting short lines and forming continental projects. Indeed by that time the chief seaboard cities were already linked with Chicago and St. Louis by various systems and the call for the advance to the Pacific was heard in the land.

This movement the Civil War expedited rather than checked. During the gloomiest days of the conflict, as we have seen, Congress gave a strong impetus to it by authorizing railway companies to bridge the gap between the Atlantic and the Pacific. That undertaking, pushed with lightning speed, heralded still more magnificent adventures. Congress now granted public lands to railway corporations in imperial domains; states, cities, and counties bonded themselves for staggering debts to get rail connections; farmers and merchants along projected lines invested their savings in securities; and European capitalists were induced to take heavy risks. Sustained by lavish financial backing, construction and consolidation swept on at a magic pace up and down the continent.

Fifteen years after the completion of the first road to California, the Southern Pacific had linked New Orleans with the Coast; the Atchison, Topeka and Santa Fé had united the waters of the Mississippi with the Western Ocean; and the Northern Pacific had cut a path from the Great Lakes to Puget Sound. By 1890, America had 163,-562 miles of railways, more than all Europe had and indeed nearly half the mileage of the world. At that date, the nominal capital represented by the business had reached a total of almost ten billion dollars or about one-sixth of the estimated national wealth—easily twice the value of all the slaves on whose labor the planting aristocracy of the South had once built its political power. Moreover the process of consolidation had gone so far that seventy-five companies, out of about sixteen hundred, dominated more than two-thirds of all the mileage in the country.

Notwithstanding the high degree of concentration thus attained, there was evidently room for still greater confederacies, promising returns still more colossal to their architects. Besides the lure of larger profits, the casualties of competition were driving railway promoters to seek closer affiliations; rate cutting, rebating, and promoters' wars, coupled with periodical panics, had brought financial difficulties even to the strongest lines. Only one American railroad listed on the London Exchange in 1889 was paying dividends on its common stock; within less than fifteen years more than four hundred companies, representing two and a half billions in capital, had perished in bankruptcy.

It was such calamities, no less than colossal ambitions, that moved the empire builders, like Morgan, Harriman and Hill, to attack the problem of unification, thereby opening a new era in transportation. Certainly it was just such economic anarchy that brought the first of these three giants to the conclusion in 1885 that he must "do something about the railroads" and led him in the short space of seventeen years to gather under his control thirteen systems having a mileage of fifty-five thousand and a capital of three billion. With the same volcanic energy and feudal ruthlessness Harriman united thousands of miles under his sovereignty and was in a fair way to encircle the globe when death overcame him. He made his most daring stroke in combining the Union Pacific and the Southern Pacific—more than fifteen thousand miles—and he had his eyes on Siberia when the long shadows closed upon him.

The work of the railway men, like that of the oil magnates, involved political complications; but the former, compelled to deal with organized farmers and manufacturers, were subjected to a control far more stringent than that imposed upon the oil interests. In fact they were harassed almost beyond endurance, so they thought, by the hue and cry of shippers and travelers and threatened on all sides by prosecutions under the Sherman Anti-Trust law enacted in 1890.

Even Morgan and Hill, powerful as they were, could not escape political entanglements. After effecting a vast consolidation of the Northern Pacific, the Great Northern, and the Chicago, Burlington and Quincy under the Northern Securities Company chartered in New Jersey, they found themselves face to face with the redoubtable Theodore Roosevelt in the White House, a man who genuinely loved a good fight. "If we have done anything wrong," said Morgan to the President, "send your man (meaning Attorney-General Knox) to my man (naming one of his lawyers) and they can fix it up." But Morgan was not now dealing with Grover Cleveland. Roosevelt replied: "That can't be done"; and pressed the suit until the Supreme Court in 1904 by a decision of five to four declared the merger illegal. "It really seems hard," complained Hill on hearing the outcome, "when we look back upon what we have done . . . that we should be compelled to fight for our lives against political adventurers who have never done anything but pose and draw a salary."

Faced always by the danger of dissolution at the hands of the government, subjected to the rule of "reason" in fixing rates, and compelled to deal with national trade unions in arranging wage schedules, promoters and organizers in the railway sphere at length found the range of their activities materially limited. Moreover the collapse of many a grand structure, such as the New York, New Haven and Hartford system, bringing sickening losses to "innocent investors," intensified the rising hostility of the public in every direction and drew the net of official control still tighter. With the pleasures and profits of the game abated and its hazards raised, railway construction and consolidation were brought almost to a standstill.

Yet the evils of disjointed and conflicting lines inadequate to the requirements of national transportation remained painfully manifest—so impressive to the doubting Thomases among manufacturers and farmers that Congress in the Railway Act of 1920 actually sought to encourage more and greater railway federations under government supervision. By that time the capital of the lines, real and fictitious, was set down at more than twenty billion dollars.

§

With the consolidation of industries and railways and the necessary financial maneuvers went a fundamental shift of economic authority from promoters to financiers. In the old days of petty industry, the master of each plant extended his operations by means of his savings and profits, supplemented occasionally by loans from local bankers. The latter stood, so to speak, on the edge of the industrial realm; the isolated bank, employing neighborhood savings and deposits, served the isolated plant. In those more primitive times, opportunities for investment were limited mainly to government bonds and the stocks of minor canal, turnpike, industrial, shipping, and railway concerns; accumulations of capital were small and the area of speculation, except in public lands, was narrowly bounded. It was perfectly natural, therefore, that local sovereignty in industry should be associated with states' rights in banking politics; that attempts of Federalists and Whigs to force the barriers of tomorrow by creating a permanent national banking system should be effectively blocked by the Democratic party.

Broadly speaking, such was the state of affairs when the Civil War broke rudely in upon the old order, setting in train forces that changed the face of things within a few years. The very financing of the conflict itself taught countless thousands, through public drives and the ownership of "baby bonds," the mysteries of interest and saving while the profits of war manufacturers furnished vast reservoirs of active capital seeking general investment, thus amalgamating local publics into a national public. Far from stopping at the close of the military struggle this process was quickened by the sale of securities for the building of continental railways supported by national credit, which in turn paved the way for the sale of securities issued by distant industrial corporations.

As such transactions multiplied and opportunities to amass new capital by the manipulation of paper increased, the New York Stock Exchange raised its economic forum to the position of an all-American tribunal. Thus localism in finance broke down and the banks of the strategic cities, meeting the new demand, began to operate on a national scale, somewhat as the Bank of the United States was operating when destroyed by Jackson's farmer-labor party. It was to their hoardings, to their stock and bond departments, that promoters of railways and industrial corporations now had to turn for assistance; and in the course of time bankers learned that they could in reality become masters of the economic scene—were in some measure forced to assume that rôle. If industrial magnates could visit them, they could pay visits in return. In the exchange of courtesies, it was soon discovered that the weapon of the hour was finance and that the possession of the weapon had passed to the bankers.

With financial control, managerial sovereignty was transferred from the operators of industries and railways to the directors of capital accumulations—a fact illustrated in a striking fashion when Morgan brought about the union of fifteen great railway organizations and created a steamship trust, a harvester trust, the United States Steel Corporation, and numerous other combinations less pretentious in scope. By the end of the century the government of American railways and staple industries, with exceptions of course, had been lost by the men who had grown up in the roundhouses and the mills through all the technical processes. On the whole, the high command in the empire of business was now in the hands of great banking corporations, and captains of industry were as a rule no longer evolved by natural selection; they were chosen by the dominant bankers who served as financial guardians.

And these dominant bankers were so united by treaties of alliance and by conversations, to use the language of diplomacy, that the boundaries of their respective dominions were difficult to delimit. In 1911, Morgan's semi-official biographer, after enumerating the giant banks under his sovereignty, placed his total banking power at more than a billion dollars and the assets of the railway and industrial corporations under his paramount influence at ten billions. About the same time, the authority on trusts, John Moody, recorded that two mammoth financial complexes—the Morgan and Rockefeller interests—had gathered under their suzerainty a network of enterprises which constituted "the heart of the business and commercial life of the nation."

Of course there was always warfare on the borders of this new Roman empire; novel industries were continually springing up with the progress of invention; and minor princelings and earls, as long as they restrained their pretensions, enjoyed a high degree of local autonomy. But new enterprises of any moment found it hard, if not almost impossible, to obtain a foothold without paying tribute to the grand seigneurs; certainly no large issue of stocks and bonds could be floated in defiance of their orders.

By the end of the nineteenth century the hegemony of American financiers was supreme at home and they were ready for foreign conquests. It was in 1899 that Morgan and Company floated the first significant foreign loan ever issued in America, the bonds of the Mexican republic. This was followed in two years by a fifty million loan to the government of Great Britain to help pay the expenses of conquering the Boer republics. Soon after this came another opportunity, the Russo-Japanese War; while the Tsar's agents were begging and borrowing in Paris and London, fiscal agents of Tokyo, in dire straits for money, were copiously supplied by New York banking houses until the danger point was reached. So American capital contributed to the extension of English supremacy in Africa and Japanese supremacy over Manchuria. A little later with the aid of President Roosevelt, China was forced to grant American bankers a share in a fifty million dollar loan negotiated with Germany, France, and England; the House of Morgan floated it. In the meantime American capital directed by New York bankers poured down into the Caribbean, making smooth the path of American dominion there.

Roads from four continents now ran to the new Appian Way—Wall Street—and the pro-consuls of distant provinces paid homage to a new sovereign. The land of Washington, Franklin, Jefferson, and John Adams had become a land of millionaires and the supreme direction of its economy had passed from the owners of farms and isolated plants and banks to a few men and institutions near the center of its life.

§

The methods by which this immense concentration of wealth and power was effected have never been subjected to scientific analysis. With all the endowments for research into everything from plant rust to hookworms, no considerable sum, perhaps for obvious reasons, was ever devoted to a thoroughgoing and dispassionate inquiry into the fundamental economic processes that created modern America —inquiries so essential to the formulation of a sound public policy. Though no balance sheet can be struck at this time, therefore, note may be taken of many factors lying on the surface of the development. For one thing, all the manufacturing operations were carried on behind the walls of a high tariff which protected the profits of American enterprise against the competition of European capitalists. While cheap products were barred, the cheap labor of the Old World poured through the wide open gates to man the mills, forges, and looms, and native labor, unorganized or but half-organized, was long forced to accept wages determined by highly competitive conditions.

In the next place, the extractive and lumber industries owed a large part of their prosperity to the benevolent paternalism of a government that sold its natural resources for a song, gave them away, or permitted them to be stolen without a wink or a nod. Indeed until the second administration of Cleveland, the public land office of the United States was little more than a center for the distribution of plunder; according to President Roosevelt's land commission, hardly a single great western estate had a title untainted by fraud.

Any one who was squeamish about bald prehension could obtain generous gifts with a show of legality. Within a quarter of a century ending in 1872, the government granted to railway concerns more than one hundred and fifty million acres of public land—an area equal to Maine, New Hampshire, Vermont, Massachusetts, Rhode Island, Connecticut, and New York, with a large slice of Pennsylvania thrown in. During the same period, states, cities, and counties bonded themselves heavily to underwrite such enterprises. To the Union Pacific alone Congress granted a free right of way through public lands, great blocks of land on both sides of the line, and an enormous loan secured by a second mortgage. A chart of the railway land grants in the West looms up like the map of the Roman Empire in the age of Augustus.

To the fortunes made in industries protected by a paternal government and those accumulated by the acquisition of natural resources were added others reaped by manipulations in paper. The watering of stocks, namely, the issue of securities in excess of physical values, early became a favorite device among the lords of business enterprise. On the testimony of Charles Francis Adams, an expert in railway affairs, the promoters of the New York Central injected fifty thousand dollars of "absolute water" into the value of every mile between New York and Buffalo. In the five years between 1868 and 1872, the share capital of the Erie jumped from $17,000,000 to $78,000,000 and most of the increase was pure fiction. The company that built the Central Pacific made a profit of about sixty millions. The Louisville and Nashville added twenty millions of fiction to its stock in 1880, an example followed by the Boston and Albany two years later. About 1902 the Rock Island Company acquired the Chicago, Rock Island and Pacific "capitalized at $75,000,000 and substituted therefor its own stock to the amount of $117,000,000 together with $75,000,000 of collateral trust bonds, secured by the stock of the property acquired." Near the same time sixty million dollars of Alton securities were issued during the short course of seven years "without one dollar of consideration." According to the United States bureau of corporations the stock commission gathered in by the Morgan syndicate for underwriting the Steel Corporation was $62,500,000 in cash value and the tangible worth of the property of the giant concern in 1901 represented $682,000,000 as against $1,400,000,000 outstanding securities.

In several cases the increased earning power of the watered concerns, due partly to higher efficiency, quickly absorbed the shock. But in many conspicuous instances—for example, the New York, New Haven and Hartford, the International Mercantile Marine, the Southern Railway, and the United States Steel Corporation—crashes sooner or later carried thousands of "innocent" investors down to ruin. Completeness in figures is, of course, impossible but beyond all question an enormous proportion of the capital amassed between 1860 and the end of the century represented profits arising from protective tariffs, from natural resources fraudulently or surreptitiously acquired, and from water injected into industrial and railway corporations. It is a commentary on the intellectual life of the time that no scientific inquiry into complex facts so tangent to public policy was ever begun.

Whatever may be said on fine points of legality it is certain that the methods used by the giants of industrial enterprises were artistic in every detail. Undoubtedly in versatility and ingenuity these new lords far outshone the princes of the middle ages who monotonously resorted to the sword, marriage, or poison in the building up of family estates. Related to more complex situations, the modern modes were more varied. If the barons of capitalism did not themselves put on armor and vanquish the possessors of desirable goods in mortal combat at the risk of their lives, they did sometimes hire strong-arm men to help them seize the property of a coveted company; and occasionally they planned real battles among workingmen in an effort to appropriate a railway or pipe line. Usually, however, they employed less stereotyped means to attain their ends; namely, stock manipulation, injunctions, intimidation, rate cutting, rebates, secret agreements, and similar pacific measures.

By a single case of authentic record the martial diversions of the process may be illustrated. In the late sixties Jay Gould and Jim Fisk of the Erie started a war on a neighboring barony—to get possession of the Albany and Susquehanna Railway. Through a clever stratagem they drove the coveted line into bankruptcy and Fisk took a gang of Bowery toughs to a stockholders' meeting in Albany to close the deal. When Fisk reached the head of the stairs leading to the board room, the doughty president of the endangered railway knocked him down to the ground floor, and his army of retainers, frightened by this unexpected display of physical energy on the part of a high railway officer, fled from the scene in disorder. Dazed by the sudden onslaught, Fisk himself was seized by one of the company's men masquerading in the garb of a policeman and taken to a police station.

Defeated in this turn at open diplomacy, Gould and Fisk thereupon declared war, issuing a challenge which was accepted by the lords of the Albany and Susquehanna. Fisk opened the fray. Putting a brigade of fighting men in charge of an Erie train, he sent them full steam on to the rival line for the purpose of confiscating its rolling stock. On the other side, the Susquehanna company, after waving in the face of the enemy a judicial order obtained by J. P. Morgan, turned to counter-violence, dispatching a train load of men at top speed down the track to meet the invaders. When the two engines collided with a terrific impact, bands of workmen leaped from the cars, marched on each other in close array, and waged a pitched battle in the darkness of the night.

At this point the majesty of the commonwealth being defied, the governor of the state intervened. Then under martial law, the disputed line was wrested from the grasp of Fisk and Gould and leased to the Delaware and Hudson, sending the stock of the company, which had been selling as low as eighteen, all the way to one hundred and handsomely rewarding those who had labored for the grand seigneurs of the Susquehanna.

Less entertaining but more imperial in its range was a contemporary operation in transcontinental railway politics, known as the Credit Mobilier scandal. After Congress authorized the Union Pacific line, a construction company, called the Credit Mobilier, was formed, mainly among Union Pacific stockholders, and given the task of building the railway at a profit estimated at from ten to twenty millions. Although the shares of the railway company, according to acts of Congress, were to be sold for cash at par, they were in fact handed over to the construction ring at about one-third their face value in exchange, not for money, but for road-making at handsome prices.

Beyond all doubt, this was high finance with a vengeance and rumors of the fancy "killing" made in the transaction were not long in reaching Congress. At length when some prying statesman stirred restlessly, Oakes Ames, a member of the House of Representatives and a leader in the railway enterprise, fearing unfriendly legislation, began a "back fire" in a tactical war of defense. As a part of his program, he had Credit Mobilier stock transferred to him as trustee, saying to his colleagues in the business that, since he was on the ground in Washington, he could put the shares "where they will do most good to us."

His expectations were quickly realized, many members of Congress welcoming the chance to take part in so great an undertaking, especially as a generous reward followed a display of their interest. All went well until the Credit Mobilier in 1868 "cut a melon" in the form of dividends composed of the stocks and bonds of the Union Pacific, an allotment amounting in cash to nearly $3500 for every thousand dollars invested. The story of this juicy transfer, too good to keep, leaked out filling the air with charges and suspicions and finally in 1872 forcing a congressional inquiry. Besides several other diverting truths, the investigation disclosed the fact that many men of the highest political standing had taken the profitable stock without realizing that they were "guilty of any impropriety or even indelicacy." Still Ames was censured; a Senator from New Hampshire was found guilty of corruption and perjury by a committee of his colleagues; all without making any change in the distribution of the Union Pacific returns.

Indeed any radical alteration in financial policy would have checked railway construction. Risks in those days were large; losses were gigantic; and, taking the bitter with the sweet, the earnings of the railways in 1870, according to Charles Francis Adams, did not run much above a fair return on the actual money put into them. Yet the same authority felt compelled, on a candid review, to say that "every expedient which the mind of man can devise has been brought into play to secure to the capitalist the largest possible profit with the least possible risk." That was natural, if not magnanimous, and revealed the inward spirit of business enterprise.

§

The devious operations that went with industrial progress in its normal days were varied by periodical panics which shook the structure of national economy from top to bottom. Such an industrial depression opened in 1873 and lasted for five years. In 1884, came a crash on Wall Street that wrecked bankers and brokers, carried General Grant's financial house into bankruptcy, and shattered the business of the whole country. Another prolonged and widespread industrial upheaval followed nine years later. The captains of industry, victims of cyclical disasters, evidently could not keep their headquarters in order.

Neither could they adequately feed their armies. Strike after strike, many of them long and bloody, pitched battles between Pinkerton detectives and discontented workmen, clashes between soldiers and employees, and widespread destruction of property periodically disturbed their sovereignty, raising in the minds of anxious observers like John Hay, within a decade of Appomattox, the question whether the republic that had survived the civil conflict was to be destroyed by social wars. Every panic was shadowed by strikes, and Pittsburgh, Haymarket, Homestead, Leadville, and Cœur d'Alene were made significant names in the annals of industrial progress, as important there as many a battle in the records of armed might. In some of these contests loomed labor leaders of high character and great talent for strategy; in others strike directors as reckless and vulgar as Jim Fisk with his diamond shirt studs, his retinue of women, and his bands of thugs; and in a few cases violent men who, when restraints were unleashed, stopped at nothing. The land of rocks and rills, of woods and templed hills, was being shaken by industrial earthquakes—just as Calhoun had prophesied.

§

When the twentieth century dawned, the statisticians of the census bureau and the sociologists, in constructing the mathematics of human life, unfolded a story that made the political rhetoric handed down from the days of the Fathers seem strangely formal and antiquated. They recorded a growth in population unprecedented in western history, passing from thirty-one millions in 1860 to seventy-six millions in 1900, a population exceeding that of England in 1860, France in 1870, Germany in 1880, and standing at last without a peer in Europe save great Russia alone. Hopeful prophets could look forward, as Andrew Carnegie exclaimed, to the day "when five hundred millions, every one an American, and all boasting a common citizenship, will dominate the world—for the world's good."

Statisticians also showed how the United States which, at Webster's death, did not have national wealth equivalent to one-third that of the United Kingdom had in fifty years piled so high its money bags that it could boast of property estimated at thirteen billions more than Britain's fifty-two billions. "The sixty-five million Americans of today," shouted the happy ironmaster of Homestead in 1893, "could buy up the one hundred and forty millions of Russians, Austrians, and Spaniards; or, after purchasing wealthy France, would have pocket money to acquire Denmark, Norway, Switzerland, and Greece"—yes, even Greece, the discus-thrower and all!

The same statisticians revealed a national market extending from coast to coast, surrounded by a wall of protective tariffs, offering to American industrial captains an internal commerce exceeding the combined foreign trade of Great Britain, France, Germany, Russia, Holland, Belgium, and Austria-Hungary. They then described the new industrial structure itself. In the place of innumerable isolated plants owned by natural persons engaged in competitive production to meet local needs, was exhibited a network of corporations controlling enormous establishments from which issued three-fourths of the annual output of manufactures—indicating that the anarchy of competition was held in check by combinations, conversations, and understandings competent for most eventualities.

Only on one important point were statisticians in doubt. For reasons, not mysterious even to laymen, they could not discover in what shares this immense economic estate was distributed among the seventy-five million triumphant democrats. They could tell how many slave owners there had been in the South at every decade from the founding of the republic to the Proclamation of Emancipation; they could calculate the number of pigs raised for the stockyards; but they did not know how many persons owned the major part of the physical layout of the United States after a century of unparalleled progress. Certainly at one end of the scale were millionaires whose riches would have made the eyes of Crœsus start from their sockets. At the other end of the scale was poverty widespreading and degrading enough to arouse fear among those who scanned the horizon of the long future. Between these extremes was a middle order of prosperous farmers, professional workers, and small merchants larger in proportion and enjoying a higher degree of material comfort than in any other country on the globe.

In the swift transformation of the whole economic order, the very texture of American society had been recast. A rural scene had become urban. On the day of Lincoln's first election, not more than one-sixth of the people lived in towns of eight thousand and upwards; by the end of the century one-third of the people were in centers of that class. Reckoning as rural only those who lived on farms, then less than two-fifths of the people were on the land in 1900. In a word, when McKinley was inaugurated the second time, the day so dreaded by Jefferson had arrived: the people were "piled high up on one another in cities." The area now embraced in Greater New York, which contained a population of less than seven hundred thousand in 1850, had more than three millions at the end of the fifty years that followed. Chicago, a frontier town with a hundred thousand inhabitants in 1860, boasted more than a million when the administration of Roosevelt began. Towns that had not appeared on the map at all in 1860 or were set down as mere villages—such as Milwaukee, St. Paul, Minneapolis, Omaha, Denver, Portland, Seattle, Houston, and Birmingham—had grown to proportions that would have made Senator Benton exhaust his vocabulary if he had lived to see them.

And in these urban areas, statisticians went on mercilessly to record, was an increasing mass of landless, toolless, homeless people dependent upon the caprices of trade, as Jefferson put it, with nothing but their labor power to sell and hence never far from the gates of poverty. In Manhattan, the heart of Greater New York, more than ninety per cent of the inhabitants lived in rented homes and tenements in 1900; in Boston, Fall River, Jersey City, and Memphis four-fifths of the people were renters; Detroit, standing at the head of cities for its proportion of home owners, could only show a little more than one-fifth of the population possessing houses free from mortgage.

Nor was the home itself always that closed, sheltered, and sacred circle pictured in Godey's Lady's Book. In 1870 fifteen per cent of the women were engaged in gainful pursuits, a proportion which moved up steadily to sixteen per cent in 1880, to nineteen in 1890, and to twenty when the curtain of the century was rung down. At that hour one-third of all the females over ten years of age in Philadelphia were employed away from the domestic hearth; at Fall River more than one-third of them were dedicated to the machine. Evidently swift currents of change were bearing the nation on through the pillars of an unknown future.

§

While the industrial structure had sunk its roots deeper into the social order of the Northeast, it had shifted its center of gravity. The old valley of Jacksonian Democracy had become the home of modern capitalism. Of the ten states standing highest on the census returns for the value of their annual output of manufactured products in 1910, only four, New York, Pennsylvania, Massachusetts, and New Jersey, lay on the Atlantic seaboard, while six, Illinois, Ohio, Michigan, Wisconsin, Indiana, and Missouri, were in the region long ruled by agrarians. By that time many a captain of industry beyond the Alleghenies could boast of a private fortune larger than the total stock of the United States Bank, which had been overthrown in 1836 as a terrible "money power." In the region beyond the Mississippi the railway mileage had increased from 1,840 in 1860 to 114,465 in 1910, making the wilderness to which Daniel Boone had fled from advancing civilization in Kentucky to vanish as if in a dream. Like a colossus, machine industry stood astride the continent.

Having swept triumphantly to the Pacific, the industrial system invaded the planting South. If some of the old Bourbons stood wringing their hands around "this once fair temple of liberty rent from the bottom, desecrated by the orgies of a half-mad crew of fanatics and fools, knaves, Negroes and Jacobins," other Southerners, such as Benjamin Hill of Georgia, advanced on the future, demanding that the people forget the dead past, which was largely imaginary at best, and seek their salvation in science, industry, and popular education. After wordy battles and years of hesitation, the advice began to sink in and, once opened, the way was found surprisingly smooth. In many respects the South was in a position more favorable to industrial development than New England. Southern states had at hand unlimited power in the form of waterfalls, an abundant supply of labor unrestricted by state legislation and uncontrolled by trade unions, raw material such as coal, cotton, tobacco, oil, and iron, and a climate as hospitable to man as that of Italy. All that was needed was business enterprise and in time that was supplied.

Under the direction of descendants of old planting families, aided by young men who had made their way up from the bottom and by northern capitalists, many sections of the South were swiftly transformed into manufacturing districts. Whereas in 1860 cotton spinning was a negligible matter in the southern states, they had in 1880 one-fourth of all the mills in the country; at the end of the next decade their quota had risen to one-half. When the new century turned its first quarter, the cotton states reported that they were doing each year nearly five-eighths of all the spinning in the country. Likewise in the iron, lumber, mining, and tobacco industries and in the construction of railways, the South went forward with a speed that overwhelmed those who still stood around the once fair temple of liberty, thinking of plantations and slaves, Calhoun and Jefferson Davis. So rapid was the stride that all New England became worried by the competition from the land of Washington, Davis, Pinckney, Toombs, and Stephens. Southern statesmen, gray and bent, who had looked upon Grant's victory at Appomattox as marking the conquest of the cotton kingdom by northern capitalism had at last their revanche, but with the sweet the bitter—science, labor agitation, trade unions, radical politics, free thought, and feminism, those corroding forces so menacing to all that was left of the aristocratic order and its clinging culture.

§

When near the end of the nineteenth century, watchmen from their turrets scanned the landscape, they saw various visions. Carnegie, announcing his book, Triumphant Democracy, in 1893, joyfully declared that it was written "at high noon, when the blazing sun right over head casts no shadows. . . . There is not one shred of privilege to be met with anywhere in all the laws. One man's right is every man's right. The flag is the guarantor and symbol of equality. There is no party in the state that suggests or which would not oppose any fundamental change in the general laws. These are held to be perfect and differences between parties are limited to questions of their proper or improper administration."

From other angles the view seemed less roseate. The year before Carnegie proclaimed perfection, a million voters set their approval on a Populist platform which declared that America was ruled by a plutocracy, that impoverished labor was laid low under the tyranny of a hireling army, that homes were covered with mortgages, that the press was the tool of wealth, that corruption dominated the ballot box, "that the fruits of the toil of millions are boldly stolen to build up colossal fortunes for a few unprecedented in the history of mankind; and the possessors of these in turn despise the republic and endanger liberty." It seemed that a trial at politics was impending between the party of high noon and a host of doubters. And so it was.

CHAPTER XXI

The Rise of the National Labor Movement

INHERING in the onward flow of stubborn facts which shook to pieces the planting aristocracy and assured the triumph of business enterprise were the inevitable factors foreseen by southern statesmen—a growing army of wage workers haunted by poverty, an increasing solidarity among skilled craftsmen, and periodical uprisings of labor in industry and politics. While vainly attempting to stem the course of machine production and natural science, Calhoun had warned his countrymen against their fated fruits. "It is useless to disguise the fact," he announced from his place in the Senate while Lincoln was yet a young man. "There is and always has been in an advanced stage of wealth and civilization a conflict between capital and labor. . . . We have, in fact, but just entered upon that condition of society where the strength and durability of our political institutions are to be tested."

Within little more than a decade after Lincoln's death, to be precise in 1877—the very year in which the last northern bayonet was withdrawn from the capital of Calhoun's state

211

—the social order of the victors was threatened by a violent railway strike stretching from Pennsylvania to Texas. More years rolled on and the Congress of the United States, under the command of labor leaders sitting in the gallery with stop watches in their hands, dictated to the owners of railways the hours of work for their trainmen. And a successor of Thomas Jefferson signed the bill.

The clash of arms started at Fort Sumter compelled the labor leaders, who were directing the trade union movement at the close of the middle period, to make the first in a series of momentous decisions, for the sectional strife had passed from debate to action. As American citizens, they had to choose their cause. Until that hour their sympathies had been on the whole with southern planters rather than with northern capitalists. Certainly the bulk of the mechanics had been enrolled under the Democratic standard.

Beyond all question the officials of the American labor movement, such as it was in 1860, were opposed to Garrison's uncompromising theories of emancipation. Apart from the immediate problems of their respective crafts, those officials were more interested in free land than in the slavery question, moving on to the latter in some cases largely because free land and slavery in the territories had become reciprocally involved. At any rate, during the hectic days that immediately followed Lincoln's election, the leading trade unionist of the time, W. H. Sylvis, head of the iron molders, and many of his strongest colleagues worked for an adjustment that would protect chattel bondage in its existing domain and avoid war by taking the issue out of Congress. When that effort failed, however, and the military struggle actually came, organized labor in the North gave its support to the federal government in a manner fairly ungrudging.

For the workingmen who remained in civilian pursuits, the war raised perplexing economic problems—especially competition and mounting prices of goods. Business enterprise, quickened into life by the demand for military supplies, called to loom and forge and throttle thousands of new laborers—men and women—from the farms of America and from the fields and shops of the Old World, unorganized, unacquainted with trade union principles, and frequently accustomed to low economic standards. Financing its armies mainly by bond issues and inflated currency, without taking effective action to control prices in any sphere, the federal government allowed the cost of living to shoot skyward like a rocket. It cannot be denied that wages moved in the direction of prices but they lagged far behind and at no time during the armed conflict did they fairly correspond with the level of commodities or place labor in the happy realm of those who gathered great fortunes from the necessities of the perilous hour. If the war assured employment. it also raised the cost of everything the workers had to buy and sharpened their struggle for existence.

To meet a crisis of this kind labor was ill-prepared. In 1861, only a few of the standard crafts were organized into unions, amalgamated on a national scale, able to lay down terms in the market place. More than that, there was among the unions so organized no common association to operate throughout the country, no federation of all organized labor to give solidarity to opinion and power to demands. It was not until rising prices began to pinch severely and the closing of the war began to send wages down, that working people, driven by hardships, commenced to draw together in large bodies. Between 1861 and 1865 the number of local unions multiplied nearly fourfold; at the end of the decade, the number of strategic crafts nationally organized had risen to at least thirty, claiming a total strength of more than two hundred thousand enrolled members.

§

From that time forward the history of the labor movement ran parallel in many respects to the history of business enterprise. With increasing tenacity the work of organizing was pushed through the decades that followed, on the whole with an enlarging measure of substantial results. When the full story of self-government in America is written, reviewing the commonplace no less than the spectacular, pages on the cellular growth of local craft unions will be placed beside the records of town meetings; while chapters on the formation of national labor structures will complement the sections on the origin and development of the federal Constitution. Although the prosaic effort of trade union agents and secretaries did not arouse the interest or the fear evoked by the brusque language and hostile acts of the agitators, it was more significant in fact because it brought about an immense and compact organization of industrial workers capable of supporting their demands by something more potent than words.

Compared with the task of the rich capitalist organizer, that of the labor leader was infinitely severe. The former, in effecting combinations in industry and transportation, dealt with relatively few people and had the assistance of the ablest attorneys, technicians, and editors that the whole country could provide. On all counts the status of the trade union director was decidedly inferior. Often he himself was harassed by the kind of sacrificial poverty that is etched with steel in the early pages of Samuel Gompers' Autobiography; never did he have at the outset a full treasury or the aid of powerful figures from the ranks of law and journalism. If the capitalist suffered a serious curtailment of his income in a panic, the labor leader in his time of crisis usually faced starvation, the deadly blacklist, or prison bars.

Moreover the organizer in the labor world, in marshaling his forces, had to weld together not simply a few stockholders and directors but thousands of people of every race, tongue, and opinion. He could not appeal merely to the investor's instinct of acquisition for, among the masses with whom he dealt, the most active workers were often obsessed by theories about a social order far removed from the immediate test of dollars and cents. Through the records of the American labor movement during the seventies stalk German refugees, English chartists, Italians of Garibaldi's red-shirt army, Irish Fenians, French communards, Russian nihilists, Bismarck's exiles, and Marxian socialists bent on nothing less than a world revolution, philosophers of every school mingling with those hard-headed craftsmen who were indifferent to utopias and principally concerned with matters of fact—shorter hours and better wages.

Three social groups in the industrial field made the problem presented to labor organizers especially perplexing: women, aliens, and Negroes. Upon the labor of women and children the Hamilton-Webster program for industrial America had largely rested from the beginning. But, tossed from one industry to another with the changing course of business enterprise, women had never been accepted in social fact and economic theory as an integral and permanent part of the machine system either by the capitalist or by the labor leader. The necessity that drove them to the mills had been generally ignored by the philosopher of ethics and matrimony, their industrial occupation regarded as transient, and their proper sphere held to be romantic—husbands, babies, and kitchens. In general, it seemed to be taken for granted that, if women insisted on remaining in industry, long hours and low wages were the unavoidable concomitants of their perversity. Whenever they chafed against their conditions of labor and asked for a more generous consideration, they were likely to be told that a husband or his substitute was the proper provider and that, anyhow, adequate economic independence for them was an impossible ideal. They managed, it is true, to organize unions occasionally, especially in the textile trades, but seldom were their efforts at improving their lot strong enough to command authority in the wages market. And the women themselves, heirs of an older tradition and pitched about in the dissolving forces that destroyed their hand looms and their village life, could hardly discern on their part any fixed relation to the industrial process.

The confusion brought about by the wholesale movement of women into industry was confounded by the swelling stream of alien immigrants—men and women from almost every country of the globe—that poured into the United States after the Civil War. In two respects the foreigners made the task of the labor statesman working for national organization particularly arduous. They represented many races, divided into factions by long standing grudges and historic wrongs, by diversity of languages, religions, and customs, making it often necessary to form separate locals in each craft for each nationality and to publish the journal of a trade in as many languages as there were races in the industry. If perchance several nationalities were united in a single union, its business had to be transacted and controversies adjusted in a perfect babel of tongues.

In case such obstacles were surmounted, one equally perplexing remained to plague the labor organizer, namely, the practice of importing laborers in armies bound by contract to specified employers, coupled with the reduction of the ocean fare by competing steamship companies which kept the tide of immigration at its flood. When a union successfully organized a craft and struck, either against a wage cut or in favor of an increase, it was comparatively easy for the employer to cable to Europe for a new supply of workers and have them on the spot within a fortnight, if indeed a shipload of competent workers, brought by the latest steamer, did not stand at the moment on the docks in New York waiting for jobs. That a trade union movement was able to get under way at all is a marvel.

A third distracting factor for the labor organizer was the Negroes, northern and southern, all freed at tne end of the war from ties of slavery and thrown into competition at several points with white wage earners. Though few of the freed men had ever come into contact with machinery before 1865, many had acquired by hook or by crook some skill in various handicrafts and it was evident that, with the multiplication of educational opportunities and the removal of apprenticeship obstacles, an increasing number would advance into the mechanical trades. Moreover, owing to the constant dislocation of craft lines by technical changes, Negroes were often able to penetrate into the industrial field through the ranks of casual or semi-skilled laborers. Hence they were an ever present element that could not be ignored in any attempt to control the labor market.

And yet, when trade union organizers came to face this novel feature in the economic situation, they were embarrassed by puzzling problems. On every side they saw white craftsmen, impelled by racial antipathies or a desire to limit the labor supply in their own protection, insisting on the exclusion of Negroes from employment as well as from their local unions, even calling strikes to force the dismissal of colored workers. If, however, Negro laborers, thus subjected to discrimination by the rank and file, were neglected by union organizers, they naturally acquired a still stronger hostility toward the unions and seized with even more eagerness all opportunities to serve as strike breakers and so get a foothold in industry. In the most favorable circumstances, therefore, Negro laborers, especially the unskilled, could not be readily organized and brought into close harmony with the general labor movement.

§

It was in the face of such obstacles that American labor leaders undertook to accomplish among industrial workers a solidarity of interest and purpose comparable to that achieved by captains of business enterprise among investors, large and small, through trusts and combinations. Like the creative capitalist, the constructive trade unionist moved from the particular to the general. As the former operated first in specialized fields concerning which he had immediate knowledge, so the latter began by organizing employees in the particular trade with which he was himself conversant. From this it resulted that the basic cell of each labor structure was the local union of the workers in a single craft, such as a town or district society of cigarmakers, iron molders, carpenters, or printers. Following the formation of basic cells in a given industry usually came a federation of such cells in a national association.

Among all the great crafts, events in detail took much the same course. Forceful leaders appeared; locals were formed, sometimes shattered and then reassembled; federations were built up, often dissolved and then re-formed; battles were fought over hours and wages; journals were published; and common standards were evolved.

Paralleling the craft movement, sometimes cutting athwart it, were efforts to form a single grand society of industrial workers—either by federating existing federations or by drawing into one big union all wage earners without respect to trade, race, sex, color, or peculiar interest of any kind. Although the fusion of so many diverse elements under one emblem would evidently tax the ability of union organizers, the idea of a national movement on some line appealed to their imagination and met their need for cooperation on a large scale in controlling wages. Inspired by this dream of universal labor solidarity, W. H. Sylvis, head of the ironmolders, started on a quest for the successful formula some time before the close of the Civil War. Knowing that the chief industrial centers already had city assemblies composed of representatives from the local unions of the various crafts, Sylvis proposed that these municipal federations be welded into a superfederation under a national constitution. Among his labor colleagues the project aroused high hopes and steps were taken to realize it. It was extensively discussed at many conferences and in 1866 the new organization, known as the National Labor Union, composed of various types of labor associations in addition to trades assemblies, was formally launched.

For six years this National Union weathered a stormy sea while many captains struggled for place on the bridge. A few stalwarts wanted to steer for the well-known port of short hours and high wages for skilled craftsmen but they could not hold their ship to that specific course. At one time the association veered in the direction of the farmers who were founding granges; at another time it lent aid to the woman movement represented by suffragists and leaders among the textile and laundry workers; in 1869 it gave its blessing to a small but determined band of Negroes who were trying to form unions of their own. Even casual observers could see that the National Labor Union, animated by generous social ideals, was finding it hard to decide upon a definite route.

Its difficulties were increased by the refusal of its strongest members to accept the capitalist order as the end of all creation. Sylvis himself, though a strict unionist with a practical mind, was ever casting about for some scheme with which to emancipate labor from the dominion of employers. At one time he thought he had found it in the coöperative society of skilled craftsmen possessing their own plant and operating it under their own management, a solution received with enthusiasm by many of the union men. Scores of such producers' organizations were formed —by ironmolders, bakers, tailors, and printers—only to fail for want of capital, technical direction, and ability to compete with giant industrial concerns already in the field. Besides making these efforts to escape from capitalist control, the directors of the National Labor Union tried to use the government in the realization of their purposes; in addition to many general propositions, they advocated, concretely, the exclusion of Chinese coolies from the country, a universal eight-hour day, and the establishment of a national bureau of labor.

While the leaders in this national organization were fixing their attention on complicated enterprises, the very foundations of their structure were crumbling away. The city federations on which the National Union partly rested became more interested in local affairs and municipal politics than in vague projects for general improvement. Skilled craftsmen, indifferent to utopias or stung by the failure of coöperation, drifted back to concentration on their own peculiar problems. Turning from platform oratory, practical organizers devoted their energies to directing battles over wages and to holding the rank and file of single trades in line. Gradually the National Labor Union dwindled away until only the reformers and idealists were left. In 1872 it ceased to function even as a body for the formulation and approval of resolutions.

§

Just as the National Labor Union was perishing in an unfriendly world, a new type of labor organization, taking the name of the Noble Order of the Knights of Labor, was making ready to enter the national field—an association that had originated in a secret society formed among the garment workers of Philadelphia in 1869. Declaring that open societies of labor had for decades failed to cope with the power of capital, leaders of the Knights decided to create a union which could operate behind the screen of secrecy, binding its members with oath and ritual. "We but imitate," they said, "the example of capital, for in all the multifarious branches of trade, capital has its combinations and, whether intended or not, it crushes the manly hopes of labor and tramples poor humanity into the dust." Fired by their success in Philadelphia, the Knights branched out, organizing local societies in neighboring cities and in 1875 transferring their efforts to the national arena by the formation of "one big union" on principles akin to those expressed by Sylvis. Casting off secrecy at this juncture they frankly announced their purposes.

In the promotion of their Order, catholicity of the broadest kind was displayed by the Knights. They summoned all laborers, skilled and unskilled, white and Negro, male and female, to band together in a mighty association without distinction of trade, race, sex, or nationality. For reasons of expediency they were compelled to admit trade unions and socialist groups as such to their fellowship; but in managing their own lodges and locals they tried to live up to their universal faith. Their consuming idea was to fuse all labor into a single consolidated mass.

The operating methods of the Knights, like their organization, were modeled in the main on the examples set by the National Labor Union; that is, they resorted to economic pressure in the industrial sphere and to political action in the realm of government. In their economic rôle, they carried on aggressive campaigns for higher wages, declared strikes right and left when their demands were refused and, in the returning prosperity of the late seventies and early eighties, won many notable successes over their capitalist employers. For instance, by belligerent tactics, including sabotage, they were able to bring the powerful Gould railway combination to its knees in 1885 and demonstrate to an amazed country the potency of organized labor. Intoxicated by such triumphs, their leaders came to believe that there were no limits to achievement. Not until they suffered many severe defeats in a falling market did they lose their faith in the invincibility of organization, boycotts, and strikes.

In the sphere of politics, the Knights also had large plans, both immediate and remote. They favored Chinese exclusion, the establishment of state and federal labor bureaus, an eight-hour day on public works, legislation prohibiting the importation of working people bound under contract to specific employers, and other measures conceived in the interest of labor. Supporting these projects by a lively political agitation, they had the satisfaction of seeing many of their demands enacted into law by pliant legislatures.

Then, encouraged by minor accomplishments, leaders among the Knights formulated plans for the reorganization of industrial society as a whole. They advocated the public ownership of railways, water works, gas plants, and other utilities, the establishment of productive coöperative societies in order to fuse labor and the ownership of capital; they flirted with socialists, greenbackers, populists, and even revolutionaries who talked eloquently about the overthrow of the wages system. By such radical tendencies and by their appeals to unskilled workers, the Knights raised up a host of enemies—capitalists who resented this menace to their mode of production and distribution and skilled workmen who did not want their ranks diluted by casual laborers.

§

Among the leaders of various craft unions, opposition to the Knights of Labor made continuous headway, mainly on the theory that the association was doomed by inherent weakness; and, after carefully observing for many years the drift of labor events, two members of the cigarmakers' organization, Adolph Strasser and Samuel Gompers, decided that the time was ripe to attempt the formation of a new national federation. Both Strasser and Gompers were experienced operators in the labor movement, thoroughly familiar with the American terrain and also with the methods by which their British colleagues had recently built up compelling associations. Though not without social theories of their own, though conceding that there was something fine in the appeal for labor solidarity, they urged that working people could not live by discussing utopias alone and they pleaded for a combination of sentiment and substantial considerations in labor statesmanship. Furthermore they had given demonstrations of their policy in their own craft union by choosing a practical and intelligible goal of higher wages and shorter hours, assigning complete authority over locals to the officers of their national organization, increasing the dues of members, and establishing a benefit fund; in a word, by creating an efficient central government and a prosperous treasury—a system that would hold the rank and file together by tiding its members over strikes and industrial depressions.

With solid results accomplished in a limited field, Strasser and Gompers believed that their policies would afford a realistic basis for a wide and effective labor organization on the national stage. Joined by other labor leaders with similar views and aspirations, they decided to make the great experiment in 1881. In response to a formal call, a conference was held in Pittsburgh which, after due deliberation, undertook to establish the Federation of Trades and Labor Unions of the United States and Canada. In spite of the enthusiasm generated at the moment by the adventure, the Federation, inaugurated with high hopes, languished for want of funds and, some of its promoters thought, on account of the lack of interest among the members in the political demands embodied in its program.

Instead of discouraging its promoters, however, the decline in the strength of their organization moved them to renewed endeavors. In 1886, accordingly, they called another grand convention and succeeded in bringing together a large body of forceful delegates from all parts of the country, including representatives of strong unions not drawn into the first experiment. Now at last, a solid corps of statesmen was ready for business—the men of authority in the great national unions, such as the iron and steel workers, boilermakers, tailors, coal miners, and printers. They spoke for powerful units of industry, each composed of workers in a given craft organized first into locals and then into a national association, forming what proved to be the substantial basis for a vast partnership of labor.

The prime problem before this labor assembly of 1886 was to work out a plan of government which would give sufficient strength to a central agency and yet grant requisite autonomy to each trade. With the experience of years to guide them, the leaders in the conference finally agreed upon a fundamental law for industrial workers. Taking as their basic unit the national craft union, they formed a super-government for common purposes, a federation in which each affiliated national union of the standard type was given due representation while local or sporadic unions were recognized only in case they were not yet welded into some larger association. Such was the general structure of the American Federation of Labor created in 1886.

In the distribution of powers the new constitution makers, like all statesmen, were compelled to be tender of vested interests. So they left to the individual national union of each craft the right to issue charters to its locals, arrange wage schedules, conduct negotiations with employers, and carry on strikes. To the central association of all crafts were assigned only limited functions, such as helping in the organization of more labor unions, local and national, lending aid and comfort to each division in the conduct of its labor disputes, and watching over the legislative interests of all. Educated by events the delegates did not bind the Federation itself to come to the assistance of any craft by ordering a general strike but left it free to determine the degree and kind of assistance to be rendered to any union engaged in an industrial dispute, according to time, circumstance, and discretion. Thus the framers of the charter of the American Federation of Labor made tangible gains in the direction of unity, avoided too much detail in the constitution of their government, and left many things to the future. One of the leaders in the convention, Samuel Gompers, was chosen first president of the new association and, except for a single year, held that post until his death in 1924.

§

Throughout his career as President of the American Federation of Labor, Gompers adhered with tenacity to certain principles laid down in the beginning. Whatever he may have thought about the future of capitalist society—in his early life he had socialist leanings—he made from the housetops no call for revolution. Practically, he accepted the capitalist order and concentrated his efforts on high wages, short hours, and favorable conditions of labor within its metes and bounds. In short, he sought to make labor a contented and prosperous partner of business in the American system of acquisition and enjoyment.

With a view to advancing this design, Gompers coöperated cordially with the American Civic Federation, an association of business men and professional people, formed in 1900 to promote friendly relations between capitalists and trade unionists and aid in settling specific disputes as they might arise. With the same goal in mind, Gompers steadfastly opposed the endorsement of any revolutionary theories by the American Federation of Labor; whenever the socialists sought to commit it to their program at an annual convention, they were defeated in each passage at arms on an appeal from the indomitable president. "It will divide us over mere theory and display our weakness at the polls" was the burden of an argument so realistic that no passionate fervor for reform could overcome it.

While rejecting socialism and independent political-party action Gompers did not, however, ignore the rôle of the state. On the contrary the American Federation of Labor, like every other strong economic group, had a program of legislation which it proposed to realize by the ordinary means of citizenship. It pressed its measures upon the attention of the country, urged them upon legislative bodies, supported individual candidates who favored them, and assailed candidates who opposed them; but it never sought to form a class party designed to capture the government. Pragmatic in its views, it adopted the policy of rewarding friends and punishing enemies, on the theory that a few thousand voters, easily mobilized and shifted from one candidate to another, were more powerful in politics than a million or two separatists formed into a minority party of their own.

§

Based upon a closely-knit alliance of craft unions and disavowing all forms of economic radicalism, the American Federation of Labor naturally came into collision with the Knights of Labor. At first the leaders of the two associations thought of coöperation but in practice they found that there was an incurable antagonism between them. The Federation spoke primarily for the skilled trades. The Knights, numbering over six hundred thousand, had within their ranks an army of unskilled workers—the very casual laborers who were always sapping away the foundations of the partial monopoly enjoyed by regular craftsmen, breaking through the rigid apprenticeship system and other restrictions set up by the unions for the protection of their members. "Help us organize the unskilled that we may present a united front to capitalists," said the Knights. "Very good," replied the craftsmen, "but let us proceed along trade lines." For a time conciliatory experiments were made in an effort to blend oil and water but before long the two factions of the labor movement were openly at war.

Losing the support of the better-paid workers who went over to the Federation, the Knights suffered from steadily diminishing financial resources. Their coöperative enterprises failed and with increasing frequency their strikes, waged for the most part by a floating body of workers, came to naught. Forced into competition with the Federation and suffering from structural weakness, the Knights saw their membership fade away until at the end of the century their organization passed into the dusty records of history beside the National Labor Union. Their grand master, Terence V. Powderly, whose very name had once caused investors to shudder, now found a haven in the federal bureau of labor which he had helped to call into being and spent his declining years in the service of the national government, assisting the labor movement from that side in a conservative fashion. Other leaders who had been towers of strength for the Knights in their youth became, in many cases, agents for the Federation of Labor, a number of women going over with the men.

Though it gained a victory over the rival organization, the Federation by no means had smooth sailing on its own sea. It failed to secure the affiliation of the powerful railway unions and even found difficulty in winning recruits among the skilled workers to whom it especially appealed. In the year of its formation—1886—its membership was reckoned at about one hundred and fifty thousand and when the century closed, its enrollment had little more than doubled. Then things began to move perceptibly. The next sixteen years raised the membership to two millions and brought prestige with power, making the federated forces of the American labor movement at last a formidable factor in industry and politics.

§

Keeping pace with the prosaic process of forming local and national trade unions, though often unconnected with it, ran a series of industrial struggles which menaced the structure of the capitalist system and seemed about to fulfill at times the prophecy of the planters that another irrepressible conflict would plague the victors. In 1873, while the hero of Appomattox was still President of the United States, a devastating panic arrived, scattering unemployment, poverty, and bitterness of soul in its wake. Late in the following year the anthracite regions of Pennsylvania were terrorized by crimes of violence which threatened the social order of the state. During the boom which accompanied the Civil War those districts had been flooded by unskilled laborers, many of whom were homeless and reckless characters; and mining had been carried on in feverish haste under conditions that made the lot of slaves on Jefferson Davis's plantation seem pleasant by comparison. Though efforts to organize regular unions with a view to raising standards had failed, secret societies, known as the

Molly Maguires, sprang up in the leading anthracite centers, followed by numerous outrages in which mine owners, foremen, and bosses were cruelly beaten, in some cases murdered in cold blood.

For months this terror reigned, defeating all attempts to ferret out the guilty, until by prolonged intrigue a detective wormed his way into the inner ring, and in 1875 sprang a deadly trap, revealing the operations of the conspirators, and sending several to the gallows and others to prison. When duly unfolded at the trial of the criminals, the story proved to be a curious mixture of industrial strife and private revenge, forming an important episode in the relations of capital and labor, a phase of a raw and unrelieved war over the distribution of wealth, comparable in its lawlessness, though more cruel, to the physical contests that took place between capitalists sparring for supremacy in the early days of oil and railway consolidation.

In the midst of the excitement over the Molly Maguires came a far more ominous struggle—a railway strike that involved more than one hundred thousand workers, paralyzed nearly all the lines between the Atlantic coast and the Mississippi, and reached out into allied industries. This explosion, like the upheaval in the anthracite districts, had been long in gathering and before it was over made manifest all the elements common to modern industrial conflicts. It opened in a determined resistance to falling prices. After the collapse of the war inflation in the devastating panic of 1873, railway companies began to reduce wages by successive orders, ending in the summer of 1877 with a horizontal cut of ten per cent, apparently effected by concert. In connection with the wage reductions, many managers, plainly declaring their intention to smash trade unions, adopted the practice of discharging without ceremony all the men who dared to serve on grievance committees. On the other side, the Brotherhood of Locomotive Engineers, founded in 1863, made rapid progress in organizing highly skilled engine drivers and in lining up brakemen, conductors, and trackmen until by 1875 it could boast of fifty thousand members, a reserve fund of a million dollars, and many a decree dictated to railway presidents in minor disputes.

To the fuel for a conflagration already collected, a match was applied on July 17, 1877, when some employees of the Baltimore and Ohio, having appealed in vain to the company for relief from a cut in their wages, stopped work and called upon their comrades to prevent the movement of trains. Apparently without prearrangement and without any active direction from the officials of the Brotherhood, the strike spread rapidly all over the East.

Cessation of work was followed by the mobilization of the state militia at strategic centers, and the appearance of the state militia was frequently in turn a herald of open warfare. In Baltimore nine strikers and bystanders were killed soon after the soldiers came upon the scene. In Pittsburgh a regular pitched battle was fought; when the militiamen marched into the midst of the assembled strikers, they encountered a resistance which developed into a guerrilla war ending in several deaths and the destruction of the railway station, roundhouses, and hundreds of freight cars, causing losses running into the millions. The striking workmen of Columbus made a tour of the city, using intimidation to close industrial plants on every side. At Buffalo and Reading, skirmishes with the militia resulted in many casualties. In Chicago, where the police tried to break up a meeting of strikers in the streets, an all-day battle took place in which nineteen persons were killed and a large number wounded. When a huge crowd of labor sympathizers jeered and challenged the police in St. Louis, the latter retaliated by arresting all the trade union delegates mobilized at the central labor hall to discuss the situation. Even far away on the Pacific Coast were heard echoes of the strife as workers and vigilant committees came into combat.

For two weeks this nation-wide struggle between strikers and soldiers continued, until finally the militia, supplemented at many points by federal troops, succeeded in getting the upper hand. The governor of Pennsylvania, for example, by sending a detachment of armed men over the railway between Philadelphia and Pittsburgh and by threatening "a sharp use of the bayonet and musket," set trains in motion to the West. By similar methods in course of time the strike was broken everywhere, forcing most of the workers to resume their places at reduced wages or on the former terms.

This deadly grapple between capital and labor, the most serious and most extensive in the history of the country, exhibited in its progress the gravest aspects of economic warfare. On the one side, the railway managers declared that they would not allow labor to lay down the law to them, asserting that wage reductions were made necessary by the state of business. On their side, labor men replied that they would not submit to dictation by the managers, that their wages were below the point of decent existence, that the railway companies, besides watering their stocks, had been guilty of perpetrating frauds on the public, and that railway directors rode about the country in luxurious private cars proclaiming their inability to pay living wages to hungry working men.

According to a judicious reporter who surveyed the field during this conflict, all the elements usually arrayed against capitalists were found in action: railway strikers, miners, and other industrial workers in various parts of the country whose wages were "oppressively low," trade unionists in general who naturally sympathized with their brethren at war, communists who hoped "for no immediate benefit from the strike unless it should lead to a general social revolution and disruption of property tenures," idle laborers of the tramp class accepting temporary jobs as strike-breakers, and the criminal fringe rejoicing in any disorder offering an opportunity for revenge and robbery. Every engine of agitation was also employed. While the strike was in progress, "knots of men gathered in all the large towns and industrial sections to listen to harangues upon the oppressions of capital, the social revolution, and the labor republic." At a monster mass meeting held under socialist auspices in Tompkins Square, New York City, on the evening of July 25, eight or ten thousand people cheered impassioned speeches by labor orators; and this was followed the next night by a similar gathering in Cooper Union under trade union management.

In the course of the warfare the public was deluged by propaganda. Whenever a fray ended in bloodshed, the press published charges and countercharges of the kind that have since become familiar items in the records of industrial conflicts. According to the employers, the strikers were guilty of starting each riot. According to the strikers, the blame rested on the militia and the proof lay in the fact that nearly all the deaths were among the ranks of workmen. Popular sympathy for labor was enlisted by pictures of starving women and children. Appeals were made on behalf of the suffering, collections for them were taken at public meetings, and farmers sent food from their fields by the wagon load.

When the awful battle was over, philosophers rushed forward with reflections on the lessons of the day. Conservative capitalists, though somewhat frightened, rejoiced in "the end of trade unionism." Strikers went sullenly back to their tasks. Socialists exulted in the fact that the skirmish had revealed so much revolutionary spirit. As the decade closed, the flames died down, the ashes grew cold, and returning prosperity brought a welcome truce. Other battles came in time but none so widespread in their menace to the American social order.

Later labor disputes were usually confined to a single industry or were localized in one or more districts. And yet, more restricted in area as they were, they were numerous and bitter, ringing out like rifle shots with deadly regularity—to the amazement of those respectable citizens who believed that all the problems of democracy had been solved with the emancipation of the slaves—and occasionally transfixing the nation by ominous bloodshed. For instance in the spring of 1886, the entire country was startled by the news of an anarchist outbreak in Haymarket Square in Chicago. This incident, like most industrial storms, had a long series of events leading up to it. For several weeks regular trade unionists in Chicago had been conducting a verbal agitation for an eight-hour day and a small group of radical anarchists, fishing in troubled waters, had been urging a resort to the argument of the "deed." In the course of this movement a dispute occurred at the McCormick harvester works, ending in a lockout of the men, a local disturbance, a collision with the police, and the death of several laborers.

If society at large was inclined to take little note of this eventuality, friends of the obscure dead, quite naturally, refused to let it pass unheeded. While the air was still charged with electricity, a protest meeting, called by labor leaders, was held in Haymarket Square, and speeches made livid by high temper were delivered to a responsive throng. For some time the oratory ran on without producing any untoward results—in fact with such conformity to the ceremonials common to similar gatherings that the mayor of the city, who had attended the meeting in the public interest, left the scene with the assurance that the crowd, already breaking up in a peaceable fashion, had no evil intent. But near the close of the speaking, a group of policemen, for no apparent reason, marched on the remnants of the assembly that remained on the ground as if to disperse them by force. In a flash a bomb was exploded with terrific force, killing one policeman and wounding several others, making the square a place of death and desolation.

In the excitement which followed, the leading newspapers, now in a high temper themselves, called for summary vengeance and eight anarchists, some of whom had advocated violence on various occasions, were rounded up and put on trial for murder in an atmosphere more like that of a battlefield than a court room. Contrary to normal procedure, men were admitted to service on the jury who confessed that they had read about the case and had made up their minds against the prisoners arraigned before them. As the proceedings dragged on, the lust for blood became more intense. Press and pulpit throughout the length and breadth of the land called for short shrift, even though the evidence as unfolded from day to day failed to show that a single one of the prisoners had anything whatever to do with the throwing of the bomb or knew anything about the person who did throw it. In the end no trace of the man actually responsible for the deed could be discovered, but the jury found all the defendants guilty.

In a laconic summary, the presiding judge, Joseph E. Gary, disclosed the spirit of the trial when he said: "The conviction has not gone on the ground that they did actually have any personal participation in the particular act which caused the death of Degan; but the conviction proceeds upon the ground that they had generally by speech and print advised large classes to commit murder and had left the commission, the time, place, and when to the individual will, whim or caprice or whatever it may be of each individual man who listened to their advice." Admitting that the evidence did not convict the accused of taking any part in the crime, the judge declared that in consequence of their "advice, in pursuance of that advice, and influenced by that advice somebody, not known, did throw the bomb that caused Degan's death."

Though the data brought out at the trial did not show and could not show that the unknown offender who threw the bomb was in fact influenced by the speeches or writings of the accused, the judge insisted on his view to the end and on that theory of justice seven of the men were sentenced to death and one to the penitentiary. Of the seven, four were hanged, one committed suicide, two escaped the gallows by the intervention of the governor who changed their sentence to life imprisonment. In vain did one of the condemned men beg the governor to spare the others and execute him to "satisfy the fury of a semi-barbaric mob." In vain did men like William Dean Howells, Lyman J. Gage, Robert G. Ingersoll, and Samuel Gompers protest against executing men on the assumption that their spoken or written words might have induced some unknown person to commit murder.

When the passions of the hour had subsided and national interests were again diverted to business, politics, and sports, the voice of the American dissenters was finally heard for a moment above the din of democracy. Six years after the execution of the four men, Governor John P. Altgeld, on reviewing the case, pardoned the three men who were still in the penitentiary, thus reopening the wound and unleashing the old public fury. Notwithstanding the fact that scholars, editors, bank presidents, and heads of railways had signed a petition for executive clemency, Altgeld was savagely scored by the conservative press and portrayed by cartoonists as an anarchist himself with a dagger between his teeth and a bomb in each hand.

To the end of his days Altgeld's act of clemency plagued him, partly perhaps for the reason that he had used highly critical language in discussing the judicial proceedings in the case. From the pulpit Dr. Lyman Abbott, the great religious leader, lashed him as "the crowned hero and worshiped deity of the anarchists of the Northwest." Theodore Roosevelt, the idol of the reform wing of the Republican party, flayed him as a man who "condones and encourages the most infamous of murders." More years went by. The grave closed upon the central figures in the tragedy. Then sober students of history, poring over the moldy records at a safe distance, came to a general agreement that "the trial of these men showed that a panic had seized not only Chicago but the whole nation"—to use the moderate language of Professor L. B. Shippee. Then lovers of the Greek tragedy with its inexorable law drew the veil of charity over the American drama.

No doubt some of the bitterness shown toward Altgeld

was due to the fact that the country was at that moment passing through another industrial crisis. The year before the Governor opened the prison door to the surviving anarchists, there had been a bloody battle between the employees in Carnegie's plants at Homestead, Pennsylvania, and a band of Pinkerton detectives hired by the company to protect its strike-breakers and its property. After several desperate clashes between the guards and the strikers, the management carried the day and smashed the amalgamated association of iron and steel workers which had directed the strike. The corporation also profited from a revulsion of popular feeling when a young anarchist, Alexander Berkman, filled with rage over the death of workingmen, made an attempt to kill Henry Clay Frick, the company's captain-general, who, in the absence of Carnegie, managed the contest with the workmen. Though the effort at assassination failed, it shocked the country of course and led uninformed persons to lay the blame on organized labor, thereby identifying trade unionism with anarchy.

Within two years the tragic events at Homestead were followed by a still more significant labor quarrel also marked by disorder, namely, the Pullman strike at Chicago. In that case, President Cleveland used federal troops, in spite of a strong protest from Governor Altgeld; and the local federal court sent Eugene V. Debs, head of the American railway union, to jail for disobeying a sweeping injunction which practically forbade any kind of activity on the part of the unions involved in the contest. If the Homestead skirmish introduced the nation to the use of private armies by captains of industry, the Pullman conflict made it familiar with two powerful engines of the federal government—the judicial ukase, known as the writ of injunction, and the use of regular soldiers in industrial disputes.

These engines, it is true, were not novel. They had been brought into service during the great strike of 1877, but the attacks on them by organized labor had awakened no great popular response. By 1894, however, sentiment had changed and there were now hundreds of labor champions, supported by competent lawyers, ready to denounce what they were pleased to call "the prostitution of the government to the service of capitalists." And the platform of the Democratic party in the next presidential election echoed their denunciation.

§

In no small measure the industrial disputes associated with the advance of capitalism were due to the flat refusal of employers to recognize labor organization as an inescapable outcome of the economic process and to accept collective bargaining as a peaceful mode of reaching agreements on hours and wages. During the contest of 1877, the uncompromising resolve of the leading railway managers to brook no interference with their business helped to precipitate the strike and then to embitter the warfare that ensued. The same factor weighed heavily in the Homestead affair of 1892 and still more heavily in the convulsive struggle at Chicago two years afterward. Although the capitalists of nearly every great industry had by that time protected themselves by combinations against falling prices and the stress of competition—against the law of supply and demand—neither they nor their spokesmen were willing, as a rule, to concede to labor the same right or necessity.

In their opposition to collective bargaining, they were supported by many learned economists who, after more or less research, discovered that trade unions violated the natural right of men to buy and sell labor and "other commodities" to the best possible advantage. Speaking for this school, William G. Sumner, for example, while teaching a whole generation of young business men at Yale, continually employed heavy-shotted batteries of argument against labor organizations, laying down the law with Mosaic finality. "If any man is dissatisfied with his position," exclaimed the Professor from his chair, "let him strive to better it in one way or another by such chances as he can find or make, and let him inculcate in his children good habits and sound notions. . . . But every experiment only makes it more clear that for men to band together to carry on an industrial war, instead of being a remedy for disappointment in the ratio of satisfaction to effort, is only a way of courting new calamity."

From no mere prejudice against organized labor sprang this dictum; at least not in the opinion of the Professor. On the contrary, it flowed inexorably, he thought, from the iron laws of political economy as disclosed to the adept: "Wages of employees and the price of products have nothing to do with each other; wages have nothing to do with the profits of the employer; they have nothing to do with the cost of living or the prosperity of business. They are really governed by the supply and demand of labor, as every strike shows, and by nothing else." Applying this doctrine to the telegraph strike of 1883, Sumner announced oracularly: "The only question was whether the current wages for telegraphing were sufficient to bring out an adequate supply of telegraphers." Still he was not without hope of amelioration. "The way to improve the relation of employer and employee," Sumner suggested at a later date, "is not to get sentiment into it, but to get sentiment out of it"—a statement put forward not as sentiment but as obstinate fact discerned by the author.

To all political economists, however, these infallible dogmas were not as plainly revealed. At Johns Hopkins University, for instance, Richard T. Ely, fresh from long and laborious studies in the Old World, was teaching historical rather than pontifical economics; and in his book on the American labor movement issued in 1886, he seemed to recognize in the formation of trade unions a drift of things quite as decisive as the facts covered by Sumner's prelatical dicta. And one of his associates, John R. Commons, much to the dismay of several college presidents, was distributing the news abroad that the organization of labor was as natural as flowing water—a means of raising the standard of life for the masses and a procedure worthy of approval in polite society.

The way being thus broken, other recruits from the middle classes joined the pioneer professors in asserting that employers should recognize unions and accept the practice of collective bargaining. "I believe in strikes. I believe also in the conservative value of the organization from which strikes come," declared the eminent Episcopal Bishop, Henry Codman Potter, in 1902. Sentiment was suffusing iron law, in spite of all the warnings.

By that time the National Civic Federation, composed of capitalists, labor leaders, and professional people, and dedicated to the fostering of harmony between organized capital and organized labor had begun to function. Marcus A. Hanna, master in industry, finance, and politics, had joined it and was pointing out what seemed to be the handwriting on the wall. Once outlawed and hunted to its lair, trade unionism was now mounting high on its dusty way toward reputability. The president of the American Federation of Labor had the support of many professors and was dining with magnates in New York. There were Mirabeaus of industrial democracy at the court of capitalism.

§

Long before this demonstration, statesmen had become acutely conscious of a new factor in the noble art of politics. According to reports, that gruff old warrior, General Grant, on hearing of the disorders arising from the strike of 1877, wished once more for the presidential scepter that he might use the effective tactics of the Wilderness on leaders of labor, but that was only a lingering touch of the old régime. Other presidents may have enjoyed the emotion; none expressed it as freely. Indeed Grant's successors—whatever their actions—spoke softly on the subject of capital and labor.

During his first term, President Cleveland wrote a message to Congress recognizing the place of trade union organizations in modern life and urging voluntary arbitration as a solution of the problems of industrial strife. Congress also took note of changing currents, enacting in 1888 a law which created a federal commission charged with the duty of tendering its services to employers and workers whenever they entered upon an industrial dispute in the field of interstate commerce. Four years later a congressional committee made a searching inquiry into the conditions of labor at Homestead and into the circumstances of that violent outbreak of labor—an inquiry that was not all whitewash. When the Pullman strike soon afterward shook the country, President Cleveland, though uncompromising in the use of federal troops, sent a special commission to Chicago to bring out the facts in the case. Upon full investigation it rendered a verdict which, in effect, condemned the Pullman company and suggested that employers should recognize trade unions in the interest of capital as well as of labor. Theory was altering in the realm of statecraft.

Under the American constitutional system, the federal Congress possessed a large authority over interstate and foreign commerce—the right to deal with labor controversies arising in that sphere; and the state legislatures, according to the same legal arrangement, enjoyed important prerogatives over manufacturing and mining in general. Thus the politicians in both spheres, national and state, had to face problems presented by trade unions.

While nominally operating within the realm of private economy, as they bargained with employers over hours and wages, such unions in fact came in contact with all branches of government at numerous points. Being huge societies with potential power to restrain trade, their very right to existence depended upon the sanctions of law. On this point questions had been raised at the end of the eighteenth century and for several decades they were debated with acrimony. Although some courts declared labor associations as such to be illegal conspiracies, the issue was decided mainly in favor of the unions long before the Civil War. By 1865, as a general principle, therefore, labor had the right under state laws to form societies for mutual benefit.

But what could such organizations do in advancing their aims? The answer to that question depended upon the jurisprudence of each state, in theory at least, and in the best of circumstances it was by no means clear. Evidently trade unions were not authorized to violate state law in any particular while bargaining and conducting strikes; and after Congress passed the federal anti-trust act in 1890 they were forbidden to operate as combinations in restraint of foreign and interstate commerce. What labor unions could actually do to realize their purposes also depended, even to a greater extent, upon the way in which mayors of cities, sheriffs of counties, governors of states, and the President of the United States made use of the police and military arms entrusted to them. In short, the right to strike, picket, persuade, hold meetings, parade, and coerce at any specified time and place depended more upon the authorities in control of physical force than upon any fine theories embodied in the law books.

Into the contest between capital and labor the judiciary as well as other departments of government was continually drawn. The courts of law tried persons arrested in times of industrial disputes, decided in final analysis what particular deeds were permissible, and, subject to vague words in statutes, defined the area of prohibited actions.

Nor was this the limit of their jurisdiction. Under American practice, the courts, state and federal, could employ the bill of injunction in labor controversies; for an ancient prerogative authorized judges, by such a bill or writ, to order corporations or persons to do specific things or to refrain from doing specific things likely to cause irreparable damage. The same prerogative conferred upon judges the right to punish by fine and imprisonment, without jury trial, any one who disobeyed a decree of this nature duly signed and sealed. By long-standing custom, the courts had freely used the injunction in the transaction of their regular business and in the course of time attorneys for employers engaged in contests with labor discovered its utility with respect to strike-breaking. It was brought into play during the railway battle of 1877 and again with special severity in the Pullman dispute seventeen years later.

Naturally, therefore, if trade unions and their tactics were matters of intimate concern to legislators, executive officials, and judges, the law and its administrators were in turn the objects of grave consideration for the unions. Accordingly, with increasing diligence, organized labor scrutinized candidates for public office and worked its way into the processes of politics—always preferring to incline government agents in its direction by threats or promises rather than to declare war on intrenched party machines. At the strategic points of the political conflict, especially in the industrial states, and in all the great contests at the polls, from the close of the Civil War to the end of the century, labor sought to enlarge its sphere of liberty for coercive action in struggles with employers, while capitalists pursued their interests with vigilance and on the whole with more noteworthy results.

§

Fundamental as it was, freedom of action was by no means the sole demand which craft unions made of the government. From the founding of the National Labor Union onward, labor leaders and conventions put forth with steady persistence their programs of positive legislation. They favored, for instance, the creation of special offices or departments to serve labor interests in various ways and to accord to the trade union a certain dignity in the scheme of social economy. As early as 1869 they induced the Massachusetts legislature to establish a bureau of labor statistics; within a decade nine additional states followed this example;

and between 1880 and 1900 twenty-six more states made a labor agency of some sort a part of their administrative machinery. In the meantime Congress took cognizance of this general tendency by creating in 1884 a federal bureau of labor—an action which immediately started a movement to elevate this bureau to the position of a Cabinet Department, a goal reached in 1913. Although the powers of these labor agencies differed from place to place, the collection, analysis, and dissemination of information relative to labor conditions was for them all an essential function—a function that carried the weight of authority in promoting a wider knowledge of trade union principles.

In the field of general legislation the gains of labor were even more important, involving as they did such matters as the payment of wages in goods or store orders, the use of prisoners in the manufacture of commodities for the open market, the importation of aliens to work under contract, the encouragement of heavy immigration, and the exemption of employers from responsibility for injuries incurred in industry save in special cases. On these and other customs legally authorized, labor kept up a running fire, making advances year by year and altering in many ways both the spirit and the letter of statutes and judicial rulings.

To cite one illustration: under the common law, an employer was not liable for damages in an accident case if the injury to the worker came from unpreventable causes or from the negligence of the employee or one of his fellow-workmen. Against this ancient theory of the master and servant relation, labor leaders early lodged complaints, insisting that physical injuries to the human factors in industry were as inevitable as damages to plants by fire and should be covered by insurance in the same way—demanding that the employers, consequently, should be held liable in every case which did not result from the willful act of the victim. After a long agitation, the spell of the common law was broken and at the turn of the century the doctrine of social responsibility was gaining ground all over the country.

Meanwhile labor was also making headway in a campaign for factory codes requiring proper ventilation and sanitary appliances, the provision of safety devices, and similar measures for the regulation of employers' plants in the interest of employees. In the operation, there were many contests and many verbal battles over the "rights of property" and "liberty of contract" but, with the aid of a few stanch friends among the professional classes, organized labor eventually rewrote whole chapters of inherited law and covered new areas of human action with its special legislation.

§

In another field of social relations, intimately related to American nationality, organized labor also sought government aid, namely, in the control over the immigration of competing laborers. For nearly a century after the founding of the republic the gates of the country were wide open to aliens. Whenever Congress, under whose jurisdiction the subject came, made laws pertaining to immigrants, it sought to encourage rather than restrict the foreign invasion —an invasion that promised to transform this country as radically as the Teuton inroads had altered the social structure of Rome.

Into the formation of this liberal policy, practical interests and idealism had both entered. Land speculators who wanted to raise the value of their western holdings invited aliens to come and settle there, sometimes luring individuals with the glowing language of the promoter, sometimes importing settlers in companies. Owners of mills and mines were no less avid in their search for stout arms and strong hands to "tend" their forges and machines. Hamilton, in his first report on manufactures, called attention to the supplies of labor in the Old World waiting to be tapped by American business enterprise, and capitalists who followed his teachings never lost sight of that fact. Co-operating with these interested parties were the proprietors of the swift steamers which had made the Atlantic a mill pond by the middle of the nineteenth century—most of them foreigners themselves—for they naturally approved the free movement of passengers so essential to large profits. And orators, applauded by these mighty friends, were fond of portraying America as the asylum for the oppressed of the world suffering from wars, revolts, pogroms, and persecutions of every kind. Seldom had economic gain and lofty idealism coincided with such mechanical precision.

True, the torrential sweep of the invasion stimulated by these forces awakened an intense opposition. In the early fifties arose a lively anti-foreign movement, directed by the American or Know-nothing party, composed mainly of Protestants who looked with alarm on the throngs of Irish and German Catholics that crowded through the gates at Castle Garden. Especially were the conservatives pained to find German socialists, fresh from the revolutionary upheavals of 1848, holding meetings to condemn American capitalism, calling upon working people to overthrow the order established by Washington and Jefferson, and demanding a voice in the government "proportionate to their numbers." With particular warmth did southern Whigs demur when these "foreign atheists" condemned in radical tones their peculiar institution. But this phase passed. The demand for laborers in the rising industries and for settlers on the vacant lands became so urgent that the voice of hostility was almost stifled.

In the grand alliance of farmers and industrialists effected at Chicago in 1860, there was no opposition to immigration. On the contrary, the Republican platform of that year specifically favored throwing wide the doors of "the asylum for the oppressed." And in 1864 a Republican administration enacted the contract labor law, to which reference has already been made, authorizing the importation of laborers under terms akin to the bonded servitude of colonial days. It is true that the law was soon repealed but the practice continued without express legal warrant and companies were organized to supply employers with European labor in any quantity, anywhere, at any time.

With the gates of the nation flung ajar, eager capitalists bidding for cheap labor, free farms awaiting strong muscles, and greedy steamship companies drumming up steerage passengers, the surge of immigrants broke all precedents in the new age of business enterprise. From all parts of the world —from the Orient as well as from every section of Europe—laborers poured into the United States in quest of employment, a movement of peoples that was watched with growing anxiety by trade union men.

Engaged in the task of raising the American level of living by controlling the labor market, union leaders saw that their efforts were like bailing the ocean as long as employers could import at will armies of Europeans and Orientals, accustomed to low standards, whenever a demand was made for higher wages or a strike was called to resist a cut. If they had accepted the situation without a murmur, labor organizers would have been false to their chosen mission and they were not lacking in alertness on that score.

Indeed the era of triumphant industrial enterprise had scarcely dawned when they sounded a warning note. In 1872, the shoe workers of Massachusetts, the land of John Alden and Cotton Mather, cried out that the Chinese, subjects of the Son of Heaven and worshipers of strange gods, were taking bread out of their mouths. In coöperation with labor leaders and farmers on the Pacific Coast they were able, as we have seen, to drive Congress a decade later into the enactment of the Chinese exclusion law.

Flushed with this victory, labor leaders turned their guns on the practice of importing laborers under legal contract and called upon Congress to prohibit it. The battle that followed was intense, for by this time the doctrine of "the asylum for the oppressed of every land" had become intrenched in popular psychology. Defenders of the contract system, reviving the mode of slave owners who had in the old days advocated the slave trade as a means of raising Negroes from African barbarism to American Christianity, now urged assistance to European immigrants as a method of bringing the poor of the Old World to the land of liberty and opportunity. The appeal had a fine moral ring and it was backed by fierce economic passions. But organized labor had another ethic which in the end prevailed. In 1885, Congress forbade in a tentative way the importation of laborers under contract and a few years later made the bar complete and secure.

Having carried two strategic points—the exclusion of the Chinese and the prohibition of the contract system—trade union representatives began to consider other expedients for curtailing the labor supply. All through the years the deluge of immigrant competitors had continued to rise as the steerage rates of fiercely competing steamship companies fell. Checked temporarily by the Civil War and again by the panic of 1873, the current soon swelled to a torrent; by 1880 the annual invasion was almost half a million; within a quarter of a century it passed the million mark.

As the number increased, the proportions of the nationalities changed. The first great influx in the forties had been largely Irish; this was quickly followed by the German and Scandinavian waves; in fact previous to 1880 about three-fifths of the immigrants were from these sources. Then by the time the Irish and the Germans had well established themselves in industry, agriculture, and politics, the dikes burst in other quarters. From southern and eastern Europe now came strong laborers to mine coal, work at the flaming forges, or ply the needle in the garment trades—Italians, Greeks, Croats, Czechs, Slovaks, Poles, Hungarians, Rumanians, Russians, and Jews. At the opening of the twentieth century the immigration of the Irish and the Teutons had dropped far behind; while the Iberic, Slavic, and Jewish races furnished three-fourths of the people who poured into the asylum.

Like the southern planters who, in their quest for riches

from the labor of hands other than their own, had flooded their land with Negroes from the wilds of Africa, the captains of industry, in their feverish search for profits, welcomed invaders from the ends of the earth. Not since the patricians and capitalists of Rome scoured the known world for slaves—Celts, Iberians, Angles, Gauls, Saxons, Greeks, Jews, Egyptians, and Assyrians—to serve them and then disappeared themselves under a deluge of strange colors had the world witnessed such a deliberate overturn of a social order by masters of ceremonies. Nothing save the peculiar circumstances of the case prevented general consternation. Until about 1890 a free farm in the West awaited every able-bodied laborer who wanted it and dared to advance to the frontier. When the free land was gone, the expanding railways, mills, and mines furnished employment for a large part of the earth's multitudes. But finally when the point of saturation seemed to be at hand, political captains who had long tossed on the main with utter indifference to the objections of trade union leaders began to take weather observations.

Though some descendants of colonial families had grown restive as they were elbowed aside by Irish mayors and policemen, it was the labor leaders, headed by an Anglo-American Jew, Samuel Gompers, who first lifted their voices effectively against the alien invasion, pointing out in unmistakable terms those features of capitalist evolution in the United States that looked particularly evil to them. In other manufacturing countries, such as England, France, and Germany, industrial workers were largely of the same stock as their employers; masters and workmen were united by ties of blood, language, and tradition. In America, on the other hand, the armies of labor became, to a surprising extent, alien in origin, divided in patriotic allegiance, given to constant argumentation, difficult to organize on account of racial and lingual barriers, and excluded from the higher social and political life of the country by their ignorance of its language and codes. While arraying themselves on the side of loyalty in the matter of nationality, trade union leaders also urged that the tender regard for high wages made manifest, at least in orations, by advocates of protective tariffs required restraints on the free importation of competing workers just as on goods. So by one appeal or another, powerful sentiments and interests were enlisted in a crusade to restrict immigration. Before the twentieth century was very old the agitation bore fruit in federal statutes broad and strong.

§

Zealous attention to legislative issues of immediate concern to working people did not prevent leaders in that sphere from making wider excursions. The National Labor Union, the Knights of Labor, and the American Federation of Labor, each in its turn, endorsed from time to time measures falling in the general domain of politics, rather than the specific field of labor legislation. Of such were the popular election of United States Senators, woman suffrage, equal pay for equal work, municipal ownership of public utilities, generous support of public schools, and the establishment of a national department of education. In all the currents and drifts that bore America in the direction of social democracy, organized labor was one of the dynamic factors, even though it rejected officially the socialist demand for independent political action.

There was nothing paradoxical in this. The philosophy of schematic socialism—with its version of the "downtrodden proletariat"—did not grip American workingmen. Trade unionists in the United States could vote and hold office; in the cities they were actually courted by the politicians rather than feared or despised as in parts of Europe; and many of them passed lightly from the payrolls of their unions to comfortable berths in municipal, state, or federal service. More than this, American society was more fluid than that of the Old World and workers could rise more readily from the bench to the swivel chair, from poverty to ease. Indeed one of the most prominent labor leaders, without becoming a captain of industry, amassed a fortune of a quarter of a million dollars at the turn of the century. There were class lines but not caste lines in the social order of the gilded age.

Impervious to the socialist creed though the ranks of organized labor seemed to be, exponents of that doctrine kept up their agitation without despair, the course of their thought in the United States running all the time rather close to that of the Old World—through utopianism to political action. Before the Civil War there was, as we have said, a wave of idealism which inspired the formation of numerous communistic colonies. Though all, except a few subject to severe religious discipline, soon passed into the limbo of defeated hopes—Owenite, Icarian, and Fourierist alike—the sentiments that animated their founders had more vitality than their experiments in application. In any event, the ferment reflected in the utopian undertakings of the middle period touched and tinged many intellectual currents, from New England transcendentalism to western agrarianism. It sparkled in the writings of Emerson, Curtis, and Lowell. It crept into the editorials, articles, and reminiscences of Horace Greeley and Charles A. Dana.

Among the writers on economic questions who contributed articles to Greeley's Tribune was a European correspondent destined to become the philosopher of the most formidable working class movement in the history of the world. This once obscure journalist was Karl Marx—a dogged thinker who combined the laborious researches of the savant with the aspirations of the humanist and the bitterness of the social outcast. While Abraham Lincoln was busy with Illinois politics, Marx in collaboration with his friend, Frederick Engels, issued the challenge of the Communist Manifesto to the ruling classes of the world: "Workingmen of all lands, unite! You have nothing to lose but your chains!"

With the advent of this new force the European labor movement and its radical fringe began to throw aside utopian idealism—the concept of a beautiful society created by kindly efforts to fit the dreams of philanthropists—and to veer in the direction of the Marxian prophecy. Socialism thus acquired a business-like gospel of blood and iron: the story of mankind is the history of class struggles; the modern conflict is between the bourgeoisie and the proletariat; in the end the death knell of capitalism will be rung and a triumphant working class will rule the earth. Such was the essence of the Communist Manifesto made public late in 1847.

Within a short time the Manifesto crossed the Atlantic. As far west as Illinois and Missouri, sermons were preached on the new articles of faith by German immigrants expelled from their Fatherland in the deadly reaction that followed the revolution of 1848. Defying the "republic of the bourgeois," a socialist paper, *Die Republik der Arbeiter,* was founded in 1850 by William Weitling; and in the same year a socialist gymnastic society was organized in New York. While Garrison was proclaiming abolition and Everett praising peace with prosperity, little knots of radicals in the industrial cities were tirelessly debating over foaming pots of beer the impending revolution, thus arousing a great fear in the minds of native Americans and furnishing the chief bugbear for the crusade which the American or Know-nothing party carried on against aliens, atheism, and anarchy.

Though never very numerous, the socialists might have raised a considerable tempest in the United States by 1860 if their energy had not been diverted by the agitation over free land, if fiery apostles of revolution had not turned from advocating the expropriation of capitalists to shouting for the expropriation of the federal government, if a bigger cataclysm than they had ever proclaimed—the Second American Revolution—had not come down upon agitators of all kinds with a terrible crash, rolling the tide of war over all the little debating and gymnastic societies in the country.

During this storm in the United States, the first world union of the proletariat, the International Working Men's Association, was organized in Europe with Karl Marx as one of its active promoters. That was in 1864, the year before the surrender of Lee at Appomattox. Within a few months socialist branches of this Association appeared in American industrial centers, at first among Germans and then among French and Bohemian workers, supported by some native Americans who claimed to be the successors of the old land and labor reformers. In 1873, the German section issued the first number of its weekly, the *Arbeiter-Zeitung,* calling for solidarity among the working people of the United States and using the misery of the current industrial panic to illustrate the Marxian argument.

Now furnished with an organ of news and opinion and given a living theme of discourse, leaders of the socialist societies decided that the time had come to start a national movement. At a general convention held in 1874, the Social Democratic party was formally organized and the radicals, thus strengthened by union, commenced to "bore within" the Knights of Labor to whose fellowship their association was soon admitted. But the way of the agitator was thorny. The hard Marxian gospel of the class struggle grated on the ears of Americans then preparing for the nation-wide conflict between the capitalists and trade unionists which broke out in the terrible railway strike of that decade. Socialist meetings were raided by the police or by indignant civilians and the Social Democratic party, scarcely more than a shadow, sank into oblivion.

On its ruins was established in Newark, in 1877, the Socialist Labor party which managed to survive the vicissitudes of many decades—a party for various reasons largely German in spirit, like its predecessor. Sponsored at first mainly by immigrant workmen from Germany, it adopted the program of the Marxian movement then growing to huge proportions in the Fatherland, and was later recruited by exiles driven from the Empire by Bismarck's draconian law of 1878. Supplied with a coherent body of doctrines and with forceful leadership, the Socialist Labor party made a considerable furor in the late seventies and early eighties.

Indeed the lively agitation of its orators, the echoes of the recent Paris commune, and the violence of the great American railway strike—all vibrated so widely that they even reached the arguments of lawyers delivered in the calm, judicial atmosphere of the Supreme Court at Washington. Many a statesman now spoke with trepidation of the dangerous revolt raised against the republic but recently purified by fire; and a cry of horror added to the panic when John Most, an anarchist of the deed, marched into the arena in 1882 with his gospel of social war which seemed to bear bitter fruit in the Haymarket riot in Chicago and the recurring strikes after that tragic episode.

As a matter of fact, however, the numerical strength of the radicals in the United States was greatly overestimated by their foes. When the Socialist Labor party ventured in 1892 to nominate a candidate for the presidency on the mildest kind of platform, it could command only about twenty thousand votes. Like the contemporary British trades union conferences, the conventions of the Federation of Labor remained utterly impervious to socialist appeals, while American unionism continued to steer its way on an even keel toward its chosen haven of high wages and short hours within a capitalist society.

Yet socialist doctrines, seeping generally unseen through the crevices in the solid structure of acquisition and enjoyment, soon reached the most unexpected places. Radical farmers of native American stock, for example, were all through this period engaged in a class enterprise of their own which was certainly tinged with socialist theories. Many a grand bourgeois rubbed his eyes in 1884 when he read in James Russell Lowell's valedictory on democracy that socialism means "the practical application of Christianity to life and has in it the secret of an orderly and benign reconstruction." And four years later the entire nation was stirred by Edward Bellamy's lively romance, Looking Backward—the first utopia of applied science—which naturalized socialism and baptized it anew in the name of business efficiency. At the end of the nineteenth century, therefore, fresh winds of opinion were blowing hither and yon. The organization of labor, like that of capital, was proceeding in regular form. The creeping tide of discussion and agitation was depositing new labor laws on the statute books. Though legislatures continued to meet under the guise of old formulas as did the Roman senate in the days of the divine Augustus, strange things were being done in the sacred name of tradition.

CHAPTER XXII

The Triple Revolution in Agriculture

TRIUMPHANT business enterprise, with its rush and roar of train and mill, its ostentatious display of overtopping riches, and its convulsive struggles with organized labor, gave the dominant tone to the intellectual and moral notes of the nineteenth century's closing decades, leading those who cast horoscopes in the national watchtower to neglect the quiet places of the countryside. Nothing could have been more natural. The great fortunes of the new bourgeois were heaped up in the urban centers where their retainers and vassals gathered to serve them. Of necessity, the culture that wealth attracted and fostered took on the flavor of the metropolis rather than the country house. In the cities were the industries and their hordes of employees, the newspapers, writers, publishers, libraries, parliaments, forums of discussion, and makers of opinion.

What is more, there was not, and never had been, in the United States a landed aristocracy exactly comparable to the social orders of that type in other civilizations. In the Roman empire, it was the patricians of rural origins who ruled in the senate and gave direction to public policy even under powerful Cæsars. Men of no less consequence than Cicero, orator and rich man's client, spoke with cunning deference when they addressed a superior person from a country estate and the most gorgeous plutocrat of the Appian Way bowed more low in the presence of a scion of noble stock. It was the Junker of old Prussia who formed the pillar of the Hohenzollern state and still, after the shock of a World War, seemed to offer to the Reventlows and Spenglers of Germany the only bulwark—except possibly in desperate straits, Bolshevism—against the all-conquering power of international capitalism. At Versailles in the old régime, landed nobility and landed clergy, besides furnishing talents for war and peace, made the court of His Most Christian Majesty the envy of all princes by their lavish display and finished etiquette. In England, gentry of the same economic resources for centuries wrote the law of the land, supplied officers for state and church, served in Parliaments, and shed luster on royal houses at court. And, if one of her most penetrating wits is to be believed, to this hour there is not a plutocrat of soap or coal who would not rather be seen walking down Pall Mall with a duke on each arm than with a brace of the richest cotton spinners the broad empire of Britain could furnish. Far away in the Orient, landed samurai, proud and haughty as any courtier of Louis XVI, sustained the authority of the Shogun at Tokyo and later that of the restored imperial family, shaped the moral code, and directed the affairs of state and society.

But in America, as we have said, there never had been any such class dominant throughout the country. Practically all the soil of New England and the Middle States was divided into relatively small farms, owned by the freeholders who tilled them, the handful of great proprietors in the Hudson River Valley forming an exception of diminishing importance. Though embracing many families of seasoned stock and long monopolizing the politics of the section, the landed gentry of the South never had a capital of concentration comparable to Rome, Berlin, Paris, London, or Tokyo and after the Second American Revolution the whole class lay prostrate before victorious capitalism

§

And yet, through the furious years of the commercial development that followed the Civil War, American agriculture, so little noticed in the writings of philosophers and economists, underwent a transformation hardly less dynamic than the revolution that overtook manufacturing and transportation; and remained at the end of the century a productive estate of the highest importance for the whole of American civilization. While the cities were growing like magic, the countryside was also growing in strength. The total population of the United States in 1850 was less than thirty millions; the first census of the twentieth century reported more than fifty millions living on farms or in villages sustained by agriculture.

America had not yet, like England, devoured her farms—drawn three-fourths of her people into industrial cities. Neither had her felicity become primarily contingent upon the casualties and caprices of foreign and imperial trade or in any respect dependent on the sale of gray shirtings to savages in Africa or Brummagem trinkets to them that sit in darkness. Until near the end of the century, the domestic market maintained by agriculture, with farming people as great purchasers, absorbed practically all the products of American mills and mines.

In short, the expansion of agriculture almost paralleled the expansion of industry. During the era that lay between Lincoln's first election and the outbreak of the World War, the mere increase in the number of farms was more than twice the total number of homesteads and plantations brought under cultivation between the landing of the Pilgrims and the victory of the Illinois rail-splitter at the polls.

In round numbers, there were two million farms in the United States in 1860; fifty years afterward there were more than six million.

Comparatively speaking, the new farming homesteads added to the national heritage in the age of business enterprise were alone greater in number than all the industrial workers enrolled upon the books of the American Federation of Labor at the moment of its supremest strength. Expressed in terms of area, the additional farms brought under cultivation embraced over three hundred million acres of improved land or a dominion larger than the productive area of France and Germany combined. During that span of years the output of wheat rose from 173,000,000 bushels to nearly 700,000,000 bushels—one-sixth the total crop of the world.

Frequently overlooked by those who imagined that prosperity and power were the fruits of urban genius alone, agriculture in reality furnished the nutriment for flourishing industry and profoundly altered the relations of the United States with the countries of the Old World. Produce from the farms supplied huge quantities of freight for the railways, thus becoming one of the main supports for that important branch of American capitalism. It fed the armies of factory workers and by a rising purchasing power steadily enlarged the demand for the commodities they manufactured. It yielded materials for domestic packing and canning industries and tonnage for fleets of merchant vessels in the seven seas. A heavy element in the discharge of American debts to European capitalists, it thus aided in the rapid promotion of economic independence for the United States.

By way of illustration, during the Civil War the increase in the wheat export to England furnished an offset to the stoppage of southern cotton, helping to turn the balance in the mind of English statesmen against any open action in favor of the Confederacy. In economic terms, the choice lay between cotton and bread and bread won. The total export of wheat in 1860 was 17,000,000 bushels; it rose three years later to 58,000,000; at the end of the century it had gone well over the 200,000,000 mark. While advance agents for the cotton spinners of England and ironmongers of Germany, in the piping days that followed the Franco-German War, marched with measured tread into the backward and waste places of Asia, Africa, and South America and invaded islands of distant seas, the farmers of the United States poured their swelling avalanches of wheat, corn, and pork into the markets of Europe to supply food for the laborers of Manchester, Birmingham, and Essen. With true insight, a distinguished Austrian economist declared that the flow of American agricultural produce to the Old World in the latter part of the nineteenth century made a revolution in its economy comparable to that produced by the flow of gold and silver in the age that succeeded the discoveries of Columbus.

§

These bald facts, hard and impressive, though striking enough to command the attention of those who reckoned national destiny in terms of the balance sheet, did not tell the whole story. While heaping its produce higher and higher, American agriculture underwent a triple revolution no less Sibylline in its social implications than the conquest of manufacture by science and the machine. First of all, this era of triumphant progress in agriculture witnessed the dissolution of the slave-owning aristocracy—a landed estate —with a correlative influence on Negroes, white farmers, southern economy, and national politics. Next, it saw the long process of colonization and settlement opened at Jamestown in 1607 brought to a close by the exhaustion of the arable land on the far frontier with its sharp repercussion on labor, farm values, tenantry, and migration. Finally, this era marked the absorption of agriculture into the industrial vortex, endlessly sustained by capitalism, science, and machinery.

By this triple revolution, basic problems of population, food supply, and social policy were raised for the consideration of economists and statesmen. At the end of the epoch the protests of the agrarian or the discontented laborer could no longer be silenced by the command to go West and exploit the fertility of fresh soil. Within less than a hundred years after Jefferson's death, his "republic of free and independent farmers" had come to the end of its rope and it was far from clear by whose hands the soil of America would be tilled at the close of another century. The experience of Rome, France, Germany, Denmark, England, Italy. and China began to have an import for those who searched the future.

§

In order of time, the agricultural revolution in the South occupied first place and it displayed the most spectacular features. To that transformation there were three parties: slave owners, slaves, and freeholders. In the old régime, the first of these groups enjoyed undoubted primacy; certainly the white master's estate with its servile workers was the center of the agricultural scene, at least according to the books and the orators. Beyond all question, political leadership in the South was taken by the planters who, besides devoting great energies to the development of their holdings, insisted on directing affairs of state. Socially, the widespreading acres of the plantation with the classical mansion and imported decorations served as the symbol of southern prowess and prestige. According to outward signs the slave-owning planter was riding from victory to victory when the Civil War sent his system crashing to earth.

Working for three hundred and sixty thousand slave owners of varying fortunes were about four million slaves. These bondmen were not only chattels; they were Negroes whose original ancestors had been imported from the forests of Africa. Whether handicapped or not by innate disabilities for life in America, as frequently argued, they certainly had never been subjected to any such cultural discipline as the European peasant or artisan and they seldom had been inspired through opportunity, property, and competition to raise themselves in the economic scale by industry and thrift. Whether bond or free, they were poorly equipped for developing prosperity on the land.

Outnumbering the slave owners and their chattels were the free farmers of the South whose families constituted at least two-thirds of the total white population. Of this group, the majority, industrious and self-respecting, lived in the broad belt of upland that stretched all round the coastal plain; and though deficient in formal education, these sturdy tillers of the soil showed capacity for raising their standard of living. Hanging on the lower ranges of the yeomen, but usually widely separated from them in cultural equipment, were the "poor whites," despised alike by master and slave. Scattered over barren pinelands and in mountain notches they waged a spiritless battle for existence against poverty and the hookworm. Economically futile, the poor whites were politically as negligible as the indentured servants of colonial times, from whom a large part had descended.

Between the freehold farmers and the planters there had been from the beginning a deep gulf. The latter, content with their power, were more concerned with the interests of their own class and their slaves than with the advancement of their white neighbors of the upland. Able to educate their children without the aid of public schools, they gave little thought to the intellectual needs of the white community beyond their pale. Indeed the genius of the planting system was hostile to the spirit of science, competition, and popular education so supreme in northern economy, urban and rural—a fact well known to leaders among free white farmers of the South long before the crisis of 1861.

Whatever the grounds, it was certain that the more

radical thinkers among the yeomen had come to look upon slavery as a curse to their class and upon the planters as the natural enemies of "the white democracy." Inspired by this conviction, thousands of southern farmers, especially in the mountain regions, clung to the Union during the civil conflict, and served valiantly in the federal armies waging war on their sectional brethren. Though the majority, in the exigencies of the hour, supported the Confederacy and improved their political status by their services to the common cause, they did not succeed altogether in breaking down the barriers that separated them from the planting aristocracy.

§

When the curtain was rung down at Appomattox, however, all the parties to the southern triangle were forced to adapt themselves to novel conditions of life and labor. The planters, burdened by debt, restricted in their enterprises by lack of capital, and stripped, for the most part, of their complaisant labor supply, such as it was, had to devise other methods of cultivation than those they had practiced—or forsake agriculture completely for business, industry or the professions. Some who chose the first of these alternatives tried to hold their domains intact by employing their former slaves as wage earners to till the soil, but this was a strange relation both for masters and servants and only the most skillful managers could make it very productive. Other planters sought to keep their estates together by resorting to the practice of renting; dividing their land into convenient plots, they now leased it to white farmers or freedmen, receiving in return either cash or a share of the produce.

Since money was scarce, the "cropping" system was generally the method chosen. In that case the planter furnished the land and often a part of the capital while the tenant supplied the labor and occasionally some of the equipment; at the end of the year the fruits of the combination were divided according to the terms of the contract. In this fashion a tenant or cropper economy with its social implications supplanted tillage by slaves throughout immense areas formerly occupied by unified plantations under superior direction. Moreover, since the Negro or poor white seldom had any money in hand, he was usually under the necessity of receiving an advance of capital from his landlord and was thus tied to his patron by a chain of debts that never could be broken, unscrupulous landowners often taking advantage of both poverty and ignorance of bookkeeping and law.

Tested by results, none of the methods adopted by the planters was remarkably efficient. In truth the War had brought to a head a long-impending crisis in southern economy as well as the conflict between the sections of the country—an economy based on the exploitation of virgin soil by slave labor, that was already staggering under heavy burdens when the Second American Revolution struck it a mortal blow. The Virginia seaboard had been exhausted; the fields on the coastal plains of North Carolina, South Carolina, and Georgia, though still fairly prosperous, were feeling many sharp pinches; and the black lands stretching from Alabama to Texas were wearing down under Negro labor with its incessant cropping unsupported by proper rotation and fertilization. On the whole, southern agriculture was in a backward state when the crash came. In 1860 the average value of farmland and improvements per acre in the South was less than half the figure in the stony New England section—with all that meant in terms of money for homes, stock, schools, roads, public institutions, and standards of living. And even that value was due in no small part to the vigilance of the plantation owners in directing their laborers.

Although the abolitionists attributed the languor of southern agriculture to slavery alone, the fruits of emancipation, at least as carried into effect, did not sustain their contention. At the end of forty years of liberty, the acre-value of farms in the South was relatively lower than on the eve of the civil conflict—only about one-third the amount then attained by New England with all its abandoned farms.

Unwilling to cope with the hazards of agriculture in the new conditions, a large number of planters surrendered in despair and went into business or industry. Selling their estates on the auction block, often at ruinous prices, to capitalists who felt competent to make the wage or renting system work or disposing of their property in small plots to the white farmers on their borders, these planters turned high abilities once devoted to agriculture to the service of business enterprise their ancestors had so despised. Indeed one of the foremost historians of the South, P. A. Bruce, is authority for the statement that "the higher planting class . . . so far as it has survived at all, has been concentrated in the cities. . . . The transplantation has been practically universal. The talent, the energy, the ambition, that formerly sought expression in the management of great estates and the control of hosts of slaves, now seek a field of action in trade, manufacturing enterprises, or in the general enterprises of development." Moreover, a large number of the planters, particularly the younger generation, abandoning their estates, moved from the South to northern cities, particularly the Democratic stronghold of New York, where they helped to give direction and tone to business and society.

A dead past was ready for burial. While tender memories of the old régime, often highly colored by imagination, were fondly retained and long continued to engross intellectual powers worthy of creative work in their own time, the lordly planter, real or mimic, like the hardy pioneer and the dauntless prospector, now belonged only to history and romance.

§

Although, as already noted, the overthrow of the planting aristocracy was in some respects analogous to the subversion of the landed classes in England and France, the process was by no means identical, especially as far as the servile bondmen were concerned. The serfs of the Old World were as a rule as white as their masters; if they were branded with social inferiority, they were separated by no indelible color line from the ruling orders. Nor was their social heritage comparable to that of the Negro slaves. Usually their liberation, at least in western Europe, came about gradually as by industry and thrift they worked their way steadily, if slowly, upward into freedom; and the crowning act of emancipation simply granted the inevitable. Moreover, the serfs had always been accustomed to the ownership of personal property and to the management of fields and gardens; their children sometimes escaped from bondage, rose in the church or through marriage, and served at the courts of kings. When at last their fetters were broken, they generally received land in outright ownership, if burdened by taxes—a stake in the country of their birth.

In all vital respects the status of the southern freedmen was different from that of emancipated serfs. They were of another race from their masters; the seal of color was upon them; go where they might they could not escape the ancient sign of servitude. Except for a few thousand who had passed by devious routes into the farming, professional, business, and even slave-owning classes, Negroes were not used to holding property, working for wages, or managing anything directly. Emancipation came to them as a result of no potent striving on their part but as the by-product of a war which broke the power of their masters. When their fetters were struck off, they were given no lands, no claims against their former landlords. On the day of their freedom they stood empty-handed, without property, without tools, without homes, hardly the possessors of the clothes on their backs.

It was, therefore, impossible for the Negroes to strike out boldly in the white man's world, especially as their hope for free land, which vague rumors had awakened in them, was dashed by the federal government. It is true that thousands fled to southern cities or made their way to the distant North but the vast majority remained in their cabins on the plantations, continuing to till the fields by old methods and for wages that afforded them, for a long time at least, little more than their former standard of living.

As the decades passed, a large number became the renters of small plots on a cash or share basis, while the more enterprising and the more fortunate succeeded in passing into the realm of ownership. Ten years after emancipation, the bureau of agriculture at Washington found that about five per cent of the freedmen of the cotton belt had become freeholders. At the end of the century, one-fourth of the colored laborers on the land owned the soil they tilled, but frequently under heavy mortgage. Those who looked backward or compared the Negro with the least prosperous whites saw promise in the toilsome upward climb from bondage; those who simply looked around were apt to be discouraged.

No doubt the general course of economic affairs was unfavorable to the Negro as a farmer. The changing technique of agriculture in an age of machinery and science baffled the men and women of the colored race as well as their untutored white neighbors. Familiar with only two or three staple crops, limited in their skill to the primitive tillage of plow and hoe, they clung with pathetic devotion to tradition. They had raised three-fourths of all the cotton grown in the days of slavery, they knew how to plant, cultivate, and harvest it, they found it a commodity for which they could always get some cash at the end of the season, and they kept loyally in the way of their ancestors.

But they had not advanced very far in their freedom when they encountered formidable obstacles to continued and easy progress, namely, exhaustion of the soil, necessity for scientific fertilization, the ravages of the boll weevil, and the competition of Texas cotton culture under the stimulus of other labor, particularly Mexican. Though Booker T. Washington and his valiant assistants made heroic efforts to meet the novel problems by education and annual conferences, the direction of the current was against them. By the end of the century only one-half of the cotton crop was produced by Negro labor. Nor were the freedmen more fortunate in the higher mechanical pursuits. In slavery they had enjoyed relatively little opportunity to test their powers as artisans; and after emancipation lack of training, deficiency in aptitude, or the jealousy of white workers—or all three—prevented them from going far in the skilled trades. Given these realities, the inevitable drift of Negroes from the land and domestic employment was toward the lower ranges of industry; only four per cent of the Negroes were in the higher mechanical ranks thirty-five years after Lincoln's death.

Unable to make rapid strides in the economic field, Negroes found themselves losing the political and civic privileges which the emancipators had tried to thrust upon the race in the days of reconstruction. After 1880 colored men were virtually disfranchised by law and social pressure in large sections of the South, especially the lower seaboard. The grand words of liberty and equality still stood in the Fourteenth and Fifteenth Amendments, but they were defied in practice. In short, after the passion of the Civil War cooled and northern bayonets were withdrawn from southern capitals, the Negro was again subjected to white government as he had been before the war. Since he was seldom rich in worldly goods, he also suffered the disabilities of the poor in the courts, high and low, receiving as a rule dubious justice from judges and jurors everywhere and often terrible punishment under lynch law for alleged offenses against the white community. Thus the Negro lost most of the power for social improvement that may inhere in the processes of politics.

If the mass of the colored population in the South took small notice of such matters, restive individuals made use of the discriminations to stir a resentment that reacted unfavorably on southern agricultural economy, especially as avenues of escape were now opening northward. The enormous growth of northern industry, the increasing demand for unskilled labor, the relatively high wages offered by business enterprise, and above all the curtailment of European and Asiatic immigration multiplied the opportunities available to that portion of the negro race energetic enough to cast aside the hoe and incur the risk of migration to the cities beyond the Ohio and the Potomac.

The velocity of this movement from the land was augmented after the World War when negro soldiers, drafted into the "army of democracy," returned from camp and trench where, inspired by the lofty ideals of President Wilson, their Commander-in-chief, they had acquired sentiments that made them unwilling to wear with complacency the former badges of servitude. Moved by new theories and encouraged by active propaganda, multitudes of Negroes now chose the hard struggle of northern cities rather than the more leisurely and perhaps more healthful life on southern fields and in southern homes where reminders of fixed discriminations met them at every hand.

In fact this northward movement was so strong during the opening decades of the twentieth century that it presaged yet more radical changes in the economic and social basis of southern agriculture. Some prophets were rash enough to say that in the end the results would be beneficial to the South, on the assumption that the old-fashioned planter and the inefficient Negro on the seaboard would both be pushed aside by an invasion of white settlers from the piedmont and the North—by new stocks capable of applying thrift, capital, and energy to land which under slavery had never risen to the levels of northern production and was but little, if any, more fruitful under the labor system that superseded it. Whatever the future had in store, it was a fact that, after almost fifty years of freedom, southern agriculture stood low in the national scale, the average value per acre of lands and improvements being only $8.96 in that section against more than four times the amount in the central states.

§

The families of the white freeholders—the third party to the triangle—won more immediate benefits from emancipation, as Hinton Rowan Helper had prophesied, than the freedmen themselves. They cast off in some measure the stigma of contempt from which they had suffered in a society where all labor was regarded as servile. If the gulf that separated them from Helper's "haughty cavaliers of shackles and handcuffs" was not entirely bridged by the overthrow of the cavaliers, it was at all events no longer as obvious.

Instead of the neglect or contumely of former days, the white farmers now encountered a little respect and occasionally some flattery. Their valor had been useful to the slave owners in the war and their continued support was necessary to prevent domination by the Negroes. So faced by this direct menace, planters and small farmers rallied under the Democratic flag, buried their grudges and, making a common cause at the ballot box, created in a few years a "solid South" bent on holding the Negro to something approaching his historic status in matters social and political.

In addition to gaining prestige in the Second Revolution, white freeholders reaped economic advantages from the new order. While slavery lasted they were subject to the constant pressure of planters driving steadily onward into the piedmont in a quest for additional lands to be tilled by gangs of bondmen. With little capital at their command and unable to resist the force of rising land values in their neighborhood, the yeomen had been compelled to move higher into the hills or to betake themselves into the western country beyond the Ohio or the Mississippi.

But when the planters were wrecked by the war, the farmers began to return to the lowlands and acquire small holdings as the great plantations were broken up for sale. During the decade that followed the election of Lincoln, the size of the average farm in the ten cotton states fell from about four hundred acres to two hundred and thirty; while the number of freeholds embracing a hundred acres or less rose from three hundred and thirty thousand to five hundred and seventeen thousand. In the next thirty years the number of farms south of the Potomac and Ohio River line doubled in every state except Arkansas and Louisiana. Thus the abolition of slavery altered the status of the white farmer in a fashion that offers an interesting analogy to the change in the position of the French peasantry after the mighty cataclysm of 1789.

§

Whatever the interpretation of the southern tendencies, there was no question about the reality of the second phase in the triple agricultural revolution, namely, the final closing of the frontier, the disappearance of cheap or free land. By 1900, the outstanding characteristic of American development, colonization and settlement, was brought to a dead stop and American society finally reduced to the economic laws of older societies, a dénouement startling in its swiftness. In 1827, the Secretary of the Treasury had reported that "it would take five hundred years to settle the public domain"; after that declaration the state of Texas and the fruits of the Mexican War were added to the possessions of which he spoke.

And yet within the brief space of seventy years the impossible had happened. In 1860, the free soilers voted themselves farms, to use the current phrase, and while their opponents in the South were engrossed in the war for southern independence, they legalized their expectations. In 1862, Congress passed the Homestead law, already so fully described, and the Morrill Act assigning to each state a share of the public lands, proportioned to its representation in Congress, for the support of agricultural and mechanical education. Two years later—the year of Sherman's memorable march to the sea—came another important measure which threw upon the market an empire of coal land at a minimum figure of twenty-five dollars an acre, a nominal price which was later further reduced in the interest of purchasers. This was quickly followed by a more sweeping provision which abolished the practice of leasing, more honored in the breach than in the observance, and opened to general exploration and occupation vast areas of mineral lands in the public domain. Meanwhile huge blocks of the national estate were turned over to railway companies in aid of their enterprises. So by one legal phrase or another and by administrative procedure, the federal government prepared the way for the rapid seizure and exploitation of all the remaining lands on the western frontier.

The rush for which preparation was thus made exceeded every estimate. Within thirty years after the enactment of the Homestead law all the choice arable land on the continental domain had been staked out and occupied. By 1890, according to the historians of the West, the frontier had disappeared; the federal government had no more rich farming land to give away. Even wide semi-arid plains where the buffalo and the cowboy once roamed at will were being swiftly enclosed by wire fences; dry farming was being introduced on lands once scorned by the pioneer; and a clamor for appropriations to irrigate the deserts was already raised in Washington. A grand drama had come to an end; the doors of a great economic theater were closing. The United States was at last beginning to encroach upon marginal land and to pass into a stage which Europe and the Orient had reached centuries before.

The shock of this stupendous climax was felt throughout America and indeed throughout the world. No longer was the native farmer to enjoy the advantage of mining virgin soil and underselling his competitors in the Old World working fields that had been tilled for ages. No longer could the wage earners of the eastern cities or the laborious peasants of other hemispheres look for freedom and a secure living on the ample domain of the United States. No longer were members of Congress to rise on the floor and advocate the settlement of the West by Orientals. The world's chief outlet for economic unrest was now shut and no political legerdemain could open it again. The frontier which had nourished the pioneering spirit and given such a peculiar flavor to the social order for three centuries had vanished forever; there were to be no more Boones, Houstons, and Frémonts; the long wagon trains of homeseekers had gone down over the western horizon for the last time.

And with the passing of romance slowly dawned an age of realism. The army of untrained and wasteful farmers who had prospered by raising huge crops on virgin soil, in spite of their methods, could never again take refuge from themselves by leaving the exhausted lands of their first settlements for new sections in the West. At last they had to face the science of farming and marketing; and the politicians who now spoke for them in Congress stood in the presence of economic problems that could no longer be exorcised by the cabalistic phrases of Andrew Jackson, Abraham Lincoln, or William Jennings Bryan. Whether they could acquire new habits and discover new modes of agriculture was hidden somewhere in the depths of the twentieth century.

§

The third phase of the revolution in agriculture was the subjection of the farmer to the processes of capitalist economy—a movement accelerated by the destruction of the slave plantation and the exhaustion of free land on the frontier. A striking characteristic of the old farming unit had been its capacity for self-sufficiency—an ideal that was never fully realized, of course, but none the less gave a decided bent to rural life. Bread came from the corn and wheat fields; milk, butter, cheese, and meat from the pasture; clothing from the backs of the growing flock; wood from the forest; sugar from the maple grove; and leather from the neighboring tanyard. Horses and oxen raised on the farm furnished the motor power and a few simple and inexpensive tools made up the mechanical equipment. Of the annual produce a certain amount was sold to bring in cash for current expenses including taxes and some was exchanged at the village store for necessities not made at home. The essence of that system, like the economy of the middle ages, was production for use rather than for exchange or profit and the psychology of that mode of life inhered in all its transactions.

Into this order so often idealized by the sentimentalist, the American inventor and manufacturer thrust their instruments with ruthless might. Their reaper had started a revolution on the land before the Civil War and the range of its coming empire had been indicated by the establishment of the McCormick works in Chicago. But that crude affair, which merely cut the grain and left it unbound in piles, was superseded in the seventies and eighties by the automatic self-binder and later, in the Far West, by a machine that cut, threshed, and bagged wheat ready for market all in a single operation. In 1870, the chilled steel plow, light and durable, was made available at a low cost to farmers long accustomed to the heavy, back-breaking implement of ancient memories. Swift in succession came mechanical corn planters and wheat drills that drove from the fields the men who dropped or sowed grain by hand to the song of the lark. Corn huskers, shellers, riding plows, hay loaders, potato diggers, tractors, gas engines, and other prime devices of the inventor made a change in the cultivation of the soil scarcely less profound than that wrought by the spinning jenny, the loom, and the blast furnace in the methods of manufacture. The man or woman with a hoe, bowed by the weight of centuries, now mounted a tractor and drove the furrow with the mechanical ease of the motorist. If, unlike the industrial operative, the farmer worked alone in the open country, still the automobile, telephone, and radio now gave him quick communication with the market, bank, and grange. Agriculture of the hoe and spade was reduced to a subordinate position in national economy.

Supplemented by other factors, the introduction of machinery made capital almost as important to the farmer as to the manufacturer. Formerly agricultural implements were simple and cheap, often home-made; for a thousand years the heavy hoe had served the Italian peasant; the ax, hoe, plow, and scythe had met most of the needs of the American farmer for two centuries. Then suddenly the bewildering variety of novel and expensive machinery was pressed upon him. He was urged to lay aside his scythe and cradle, which cost but a few dollars and lasted a lifetime, to buy in its place a self-binder which cost twenty times as much, was in need of constant repair, and wore out in three or four years of hard usage even if not left out in the rain and snow to rust and rot, as it often was. And as a matter of fact the farmer had no choice. The price of his grain in the market being fixed by the cost of production on the most fertile and best-equipped farms, he was compelled to buy machinery or to work for somebody who could, just as the handicraftsman had been at the start of the industrial revolution. Consequently the value of farm implements and machines per acre of land almost doubled between 1890 and 1910.

To the financial problems raised by the inventors were added economic difficulties springing from the rise in land values, especially after the closing of the frontier. So in the strategy of its advance, farming, like manufacturing, called for more and more capital, an ever larger investment to keep pace with competition—more debts and a closer reliance on banks and bankers. Swiftly and silently it became capitalistic in nature and spirit without at the same time acquiring the social technology which capitalism had evolved to marshal its forces, command governments, break into foreign markets, scale debts by facile bankruptcy, and engage the services of experts in production, promotion, and sales.

A second capitalist tendency in agriculture was the drift toward specialization in crops—a drift aided by the introduction of machinery, the stimulus of business enterprise, and the pressure of competition. In this run of things, King Cotton was not only restored to his throne, but was given a still greater monopoly in southern rural economy than he had enjoyed in earlier days. According to the returns of 1866, the cotton crop was reckoned at less than a million bales; five decades later it had risen to more than ten million bales; and cotton culture had encroached on the fields devoted to other southern staples. At the opening of the twentieth century the per capita output of wheat in the southern states was far below the figure for 1860, the percentage of the total national crop falling even lower in the scale. In the reign of Andrew Jackson, six of the ten leading maize states were in the South; at the end of the century only three southern states were found among the ten that poured into the national market seventy-five per cent of the corn crop.

While cotton thus outstripped its competitors in the South, wheat and corn were conquering the Northwest. At the middle of the nineteenth century the center of wheat production was near Columbus, Ohio; before the Victorian age closed it had crossed the Mississippi and passed through Des Moines, Iowa, to a point seven hundred miles beyond Columbus. During this period the center of the corn area moved from southern Ohio five hundred miles in a westward direction. In the process of concentration the live-stock industry, once widely scattered on the farms and plantations of the seaboard and middle west, fixed a seat of empire in the Missouri Valley. Sustained by immense energies and huge accumulations of capital, the cotton, corn, wheat, fruit dairy, and live-stock industries now loomed like giants on the field of national enterprise. Now American farmers, dependent upon one or two specialties and forced to buy large quantities of supplies at stores, found their personal fortunes, like those of manufacturers and capitalists, linked with the caprices and casualties of domestic and foreign trade, though not yet primarily dependent on them. There was admonition in that for all who pondered on national destiny.

Especially distressing to those in terror about "the passing of a great race" was the rapid growth in tenant farming, a striking increase in land values, and the multiplication of farm mortgages. The old Jeffersonian ideal, never in fact realized, had been the division of the continent into single farm units worked by the owner and his family—people of North European stock—owing no tribute to any man. For a long time it seemed that this goal was within the range of possibility but the flow of facts finally turned against it.

The overthrow of slavery, unattended by any heroic effort to settle the Negroes on the soil, let loose a flood of landless people destined to wage labor or tenancy. By way of supplement, the closing of the frontier, the rise in land values, the advent of capitalist competition, and other pitiless forces drove northern agriculture in the direction of ancient servitudes. In 1880, the year of the first census of tenancy, twenty-five per cent of all the farms in the United States were tilled by renters; at the opening of the twentieth century the proportion had risen to thirty-five per cent and the curve was clearly upward. Throughout wide reaches of the country, from New England to California, the sons and daughters of the pioneer generation had moved to towns, throwing their ancestral homes upon the market for sale or rent; in Iowa, for instance, more than two-fifths of the farms were tilled by renters. No longer beckoned westward by free land, the ambitious farm laborer, bent on winning a homestead for himself, had now no choice except to plod on through tenancy and debts to his goal; and if ill-health or crop failures fell to his lot, he remained all his days in the tenant class.

Great as they were inherently, the exigencies of the process were intensified by an invasion of laborers from other lands where different standards of life obtained—standards sometimes lower than those of the Americanized Negro. Poles and Italians from the Old World spread over New England and the Middle States; Indians from Mexico seeped out over the Southwest; Orientals, multiplying in spite of the bar on new immigration, redeemed waste places on the Pacific Coast. Those given to monitory gestures pointed to a day when the soil of America would be tilled by alien and colored races under semi-feudal tenures; with what degree of prevision no one could tell.

Even though about two-thirds of the farmers owned the land they tilled at the opening of the twentieth century, a large proportion of these more fortunate individuals labored under heavy debts which imposed servitudes on them no less real, if more euphonious, than the burdens laid upon the cottars and bordars of the middle ages. In 1910, the burden of farm mortgages stood at seventeen hundred million dollars; within another decade it leaped to more than four billions, a sum almost equal to the value of all the farm property in America seventy years before. It is true that, in no small measure, heavy indebtedness as well as tenancy represented an advance among farm laborers engaged in buying land and an increase in capital that spelled enlarged production. To some extent it was the outcome of the American mania for speculation; but viewed in the light of statecraft it meant that the early dream of a nation chiefly sustained by free, independent, home-owning farmers of North European stock had been exploded in one-fourth the time it took Rome to evolve from the economy of Cincinnatus to that of Augustus.

Nor was there any sign on the horizon of a turn in the sweep of agricultural enterprise. On the contrary an almost steady rise in land values under the new influences made more difficult the position of laborer, tenant, mortgagor, and owner. In the decade of the seventies in spite of the panic, they rose about forty per cent; in the decade of the World War they almost doubled. Naturally there were ups and downs; there were enormous depreciations in the South and East; but in the main each generation of laborers, tenants, and land-hungry immigrants in their toilsome battle upstream to ownership had to breast, especially between 1890 and 1920, a rising tide of capitalization. Every generation of farmers, whether owners or not, in competing with foreign agriculture, as well as in the struggle for a livelihood, had to carry an ever-mounting burden of capital charges. If the extraordinary demand for foodstuffs during the World War gave some relief to those who carried the load, the aid was temporary.

An epoch had come to an end and the iron gates were locked. Industrial capitalists were organized to make their own prices; industrial workers were organized to fix wages; whereas farmers, with the exception of a few powerful groups, were still incorrigible individualists at the mercy of the market. Throughout wide areas, the independent, self-sufficient farm unit of Lincoln's era had become a specialized concern producing for profit, forced to employ large capital in the form of machinery and fertilizers, compelled to compete with European agriculture on more equal terms, and obliged to carry the weight of an increment in land values which had mounted with the years. With energetic members of the younger generation escaping to the cities to share in capitalist enterprise, with new racial stocks occupying ancestral homesteads, with a remorseless competition determining the prices of produce, with industrial capitalists and industrial workers compactly united to dictate terms on manufactured commodities, the economy and culture of historic American farming were crumbling into ruins. Against that fact the rhetoric of Jeffersonian banquets echoed with strange hollowness; while orations on free trade and the currency seemed almost as irrelevant as the admonitions of Buddha.

§

A revolution in rural economy so vast and so deep-thrusting could not fail to cut great gashes in the texture of American sentiments and politics, changing the psychology of the countryside. In the days of frontier independence and self-sufficiency, a spirit of stubbornness and of more or less contented ignorance characterized farming communities. Often satisfied with the rough necessities of food, clothing, and shelter, they were likely to be indifferent to the amenities of science, art, and urbanity. Heirs of historic mythology, signs, omens, and rules of thumb, they remained, in the backward regions at least, the last bulwarks of magic and credulity. But assailed by machinery, science, capitalism, and education they could not hold to their ancient customs. When the lamp of science, kindled in the laboratory of the city, was carried to farm and plain and mountain cove, the tyranny of habit had to retreat before experiment and demonstration; guesses of wiseacres had to give way to reports of the weather bureau. With their own eyes farmers now saw, what Buckle long before observed in industrial affairs, that exorcism could not meet their daily needs—repair reapers, make balky engines run, or unite broken electric connections. Forced to become realistic by the demands of their craft, they commenced to discard folklore for the substance of science and technology.

By such routes, the farmers were drawn closer into all the currents of modern life; assimilated more and more to the mechanical process that was reshaping the whole world. As the capitalist and stockbroker took large risks in the hope of large gains, so the farmer now speculated in single crops and in land values with similar expectations. As the families of the cities raised their standards of living and increased their wants, the families in the country came under the same spell. Consequently the feverish search for material possessions and a richer economic life thus engulfed the nation, reducing traditional differences between rural and urban types, and tending to create a standardized cultural unity from coast to coast. Italians on the stony hills of Connecticut, Negroes in southern cotton fields, Mexican Indians under the burning sun of Texas, and Orientals on the Pacific coast all showed signs of sloughing off age-old habits as they were swept forward into the irresistible stream. In fact no small part of the economic distress that overtook American agriculture from time to time was due to this rising desire for more worldly goods—a desire that would not brook the hard and barren fare of the European or Oriental peasant, baffled by severe economic limitations and held in place by church and state. When once the flame was kindled, no one could tell how far it would spread or how long it could be nourished by new fuel.

In the economic changes on the land were implicit new attitudes toward the state and society. It is true that farmers had figured largely in politics from the earliest time in America, but mainly as a negative and dissolving force. They finished the war on the British commercial empire which the American merchants had unwittingly started in 1765. They supplied the discontented members for Daniel Shays' rebellious army and afforded most of the opposition to the adoption of the Constitution. To them Jefferson appealed in express terms and their answer was the upheaval of 1800. To them Jackson appealed, after the notables had recovered some of the lost ground in an age of good feeling, and for a long time they formed whole battalions of Jacksonian Democracy, accepting the leadership of the planters in the war on capitalism. In the main it was farmers who started the independent movement that shattered the Democratic party and called into being the Republican opposition of 1856. If they had little love for the manufacturer who sought to place a tariff on their plows and cloth, they had less for the aristocratic planter who tried to block the way to free land in the territories. Confronted, however, by the necessity for an alliance, the western farmers who established the Republican party on free-soil principles in 1856 found it possible four years later to effect a combination with the cotton spinners of Massachusetts and the iron founders of Pennsylvania, receiving, in the Homestead Act and other measures opening wide the treasury of western land, their share of the common rewards of victory.

But the Chicago union stayed no tide in the affairs of agriculture. The westward movement of the corn and wheat belt shifted the center of agrarian discontent from the first home of Jacksonian Democracy into new areas where at each recurring panic it flamed up again. The spreading monopoly of cotton in the South, the concentration of both planter and farmer on that one crop, linked the fortunes of those ancient foemen, adding another seal to the bond that made the Solid South—a seal that could only be broken in days of distress and agrarian upheavals. The creation of a huge tenant and debtor class, a class augmented at every cycle of depression, furnished the substance for the Greenback explosion of the seventies, the Populist revolt of the nineties, the Non-Partisan uprising of the new century, and the Farm Bloc of "normalcy." Although to the casual eye, the currents of unrest seemed to be revolving in a vicious circle, they were not in truth; for among the farm leaders there was a growing recognition of the fact that the ancient weapons of currency inflation and tariff reduction would not break the grip of industrial capitalists and industrial workers on the prices of commodities bought by the farmer or bring permanent prosperity to his class.

Casting about for other methods of improving their economic status, agrarian leaders decided at last to learn lessons from dynamic capitalism itself—to attempt a control of prices through the union of producers on the land and to make a positive use of the engine of the state in the promotion of their interests. Under their direction the National

Grange, founded in 1867, flourished, languished, and flourished again; at the end of half a century it could boast of a "powerful organization of farmers, active in thirty-three states, with its own press, its own body of organizers, its own lecturers, its own literature, poems, music, and traditions."

As in the labor movement there were special and general tendencies. While the industrial workers of the trades were drawing together in craft unions, wheat, cotton, and fruit growers also strove to stabilize production and control prices through the agency of organization. Though many of these efforts proved futile, others achieved permanent results. For example, a local association of orange growers appeared in California in 1888; it soon was followed by a district organization; in 1905 a federation was brought to pass; and in the course of a few years the California Fruit Growers' Association became as effective in its peculiar sphere as the Brotherhood of Locomotive Engineers in its domain.

By that time the country was literally covered by a network of farmers' societies, some of them founded on the stable basis of a special-product interest, indicating that the hour of federation had arrived. In fact, two efforts were now made to bring about a grand consolidation: by the establishment of the Farmers' National Headquarters, somewhat radical in tendencies, and the National Board of Farm Organization, more conservative in tone. Both favored an amalgamation of the agricultural forces throughout the country; both approved a plan for erecting a Temple of Agriculture in Washington to stand beside the headquarters of the American Federation of Labor. So at the opening of the new century a closely-knit farm lobby appeared in the halls of the people's Congress to jostle the elbows of labor agents and experts speaking for industrial capital.

Besides drawing together in unions and displaying an increasing consciousness of solidarity, farmers revealed a changing attitude toward the state—a resolve to use the government for group designs. As is so often the case in history, the idea had long preceded the deed. George Washington, that practical farmer and persistent experimenter, urged, in his annual message to Congress in 1796, a federal appropriation to stimulate enterprise and experiment in agriculture, to draw to the national center the results of individual skill and observation, and to spread the collected information far and wide throughout the nation. But the seed sowed by Washington fell on barren ground. Hamilton's party, engrossed with subsidies, bounties, and tariffs in aid of commerce and manufacturing, gave no serious thought to the wise suggestion of the planter-President. Its competitor, the agricultural party, which swept Jefferson into power in 1800, felt satisfied with the existing knowledge and understanding or at all events preferred to leave the cause to state action and private patronage.

Accordingly for half a century after the adoption of the Constitution, the curious philosophy of Manchester held sway whenever the federal government considered agriculture: each farmer, relying upon his instincts and following his nose amid the commonplaces of life, knew what was best for himself and needed no aid from common effort and no illumination from universal experience. During this period, Congress gave no direct assistance to the agricultural arts and the states did little more than bestow an occasional blessing or a petty appropriation upon local agricultural societies.

It was almost by inadvertence that the first slight departure was made in an action recalling the initiative of that restless genius, Benjamin Franklin, who, while in England, had kept his eye open for better seeds, plants, trees, and domestic animals than the common stock afforded and had started the practice of sending good things across the sea. Inspired by this example, American consuls, after the establishment of the federal government, casually continued the custom; while the patent office in the Department of State on its own motion distributed the agricultural products sent in by its agents abroad. At last in 1839 Congress, largely in response to insistence on the part of the commissioner of patents, appropriated one thousand dollars for "the collection of agricultural statistics and for other agricultural purposes." From time to time small additions were made for chemical analyses, the assemblage of data, the purchase of seeds, and special investigations.

Nothing of note was done, however, until the swelling tide of farmers enrolled under the new Republican pennant swept into Washington in the train of Abraham Lincoln. While the manufacturers were then getting their share of the Chicago bargain in tariffs and other specific aids, representatives of the farmers, going beyond the terms of the Homestead Act which merely threw open to the plow more bare land, carried through Congress that very same year a measure creating the bureau of agriculture—and also the Morrill law dedicating an immense area of the public domain to education in the agricultural and mechanical arts.

The constitutional barrier now being forced, the course of federal farm legislation widened, slowly at first because many, who favored protective tariffs for industries, shrank from "class measures" in favor of agriculture. In 1884, the bureau of animal industry was organized and given a regulatory power over important branches of rural economy. Three years later Congress, by the Hatch Act, provided for the establishment of experiment stations in each of the once sovereign states. Two years more passed and the bureau of agriculture became a Department raised to Cabinet rank.

The agrarian drive was now on in earnest. It furnished a great deal of the momentum behind the passage of the federal interstate commerce law of 1887 aimed at the control of common carriers. Its power was reflected in the rural free delivery act of McKinley's administration, the irrigation act of 1902, the farm credits legislation of the Wilson-Harding régimes, the coöperative marketing act of silent normalcy—all of which bore the impress of the agricultural solidarity. In the states as well as in the federal sphere, swelling pages of the statute books and mounting appropriations for boards and departments of agriculture recorded the insurgency of agrarian leaders. Before the twentieth century was well out on its course, farmers, while rejecting the doctrines of socialism, were, like all other powerful groups, in practice making use of the government to promote collective advantages and to force other interests into acceptable lines of action. Though the fickle tides of populism flowed and ebbed, the volume of farm legislation and the activities of administrative agencies showed no signs of retreat. Agriculture had passed out of the age of mere uproarious protest into the age of collective effort and constructive measures. That too was something to be observed by those who searched for omens.

CHAPTER XXIII

The Politics of Acquisition and Enjoyment

GEARED by constitutions and laws to the processes of the sun as in the age of the slave power, the American political machine ran on through the three decades of triumphant business enterprise, but driven by new motive forces and grinding out different legislative, executive, and judicial products. Whenever the earth had rotated on its axis the appointed number of times, members of state legislatures, city councils, and the House of Representatives were duly chosen by popular balloting, governors were elected, and a new President of the United States was inaugurated. At the close of each biennium, a portion of the federal Senators put off their togas to make way for successors designated by legislative caucuses. Whenever a judge of the Supreme Court at Washington died or resigned, another incumbent was nominated by the President and confirmed by the Senate.

During those three decades, therefore, a veritable army of politicians strode in upon the floors of state houses, council chambers, and the national capitol, enjoyed a brief moment of power, and then dropped silently, most of them, into the deep valley of obscurity from which they had emerged. Seven men in due course sat in the presidential chair—Johnson, Grant, Hayes, Garfield, Arthur, Cleveland, and Harrison—and although a few Senators managed to retain their honors and emoluments for several terms, the personnel of that august body also altered swiftly with the running currents of time. Only the judges of the federal Supreme Court who held a life tenure offered a semblance of permanency; Field of California was in office from 1863 to 1897; Bradley of New Jersey from 1870 to 1892; Harlan of Kentucky from 1877 to 1911; but even they were not immortal and within a decade after Appomattox a new majority had been installed in the tribunal of John Marshall and Roger B. Taney.

In the transfer of the federal ship of state from one titular master to another, little consistency was shown in the selection of mates or crew. Indeed the nautical analogy is hardly appropriate at all; for instead of looking like a ship of state, built on the English model at least, with a captain premier and his cabinet mates theoretically commissioned to sail by a plotted chart, the American political vessel had the appearance of a loose-seamed and leaky scow, on which there were many captains and many mates contesting for cabins, rooms, and corners; and divided among themselves even as to the position of the fixed stars. During a large part of the time between 1865 and 1897, Republican Presidents faced Democratic majorities in the lower house of Congress. In Cleveland's first administration, a Republican Senate contended with a Democratic executive and a Democratic House for possession of the tiller. For only two years out of the thirty-two did the Democrats command both the political departments of the federal government; and never in all that time did they possess the citadel of the judiciary. For place and power in state and local governments, politicians also waged battles at regular intervals, in a guerrilla warfare even more confused. On a casual view, the whole political world seemed without form and void, swept by gusts as wayward as seasonal winds.

With its fitful changes and its divided leadership the political machine presented a strange contrast to the business machine which worked endlessly, without periodic revolutions, controlled by a directorate that was unbroken in time and fairly united in purpose. In the economic world there was no electoral calendar. John Pierpont Morgan was born only a few weeks after Andrew Jackson left the capital for the blessed Hermitage in Tennessee; he entered economic life in 1857 when James Buchanan was in the White House; he was doing business as usual when Woodrow Wilson rode down Pennsylvania Avenue to his inauguration. John D. Rockefeller, born in the days of Martin Van Buren, was in active managerial life for more than half a century; in the span of his manhood years, he saw Buchanan, Lincoln, Johnson, Grant, Hayes, Garfield, Arthur, Cleveland, McKinley, Roosevelt, Taft, Wilson, and Harding come and go. If few of Rockefeller's industrial generation ran such an extraordinary gamut, still all the giants of his time outlasted at least half a dozen Presidents and many of them left heirs-apparent to maintain through the coming years the unity of their houses. Thus, while political power was being shifted from party to party and dissipated among an ever-changing army of captains and subordinates, most of them nameless in history, the sovereignty of the business empire was kept continuously in the hands of a relatively few dominant figures whose grip was firm, whose experience was cumulative, and whose goal was clear.

§

In the variable game of politics, two great parties according to American usage carried on the contest with the customary weapons. The Republicans, however, found themselves in a particularly fortunate position after 1865— a position far stronger than their predecessors, the Federalists and Whigs, had ever occupied at any stage in their careers. On the right wing of the Republican party were, to be sure, the same elements that had supported Hamilton and Webster, namely manufacturers, financiers, and capitalists in general, but in this new era the captains of business enterprise were no mere handful of men struggling to maintain strategic citadels in an agricultural country directed principally by planters and farmers. In numbers and riches they were more powerful than ever. According to the measurement of dollars, the value of the mills, mines, railways, and urban property of the United States by 1865 had well overtopped the agricultural resources and continued to rise swiftly in the scale with the passing years as the petty manufacturers and bankers of the Whig régime gave place to a generation of giants in steel, copper, oil, and sugar. Moreover the scanty brigade of bondholders, such as the Federalists and Whigs had mobilized in their days, had grown into a militant army. In 1865, $2,700,000,000 in federal securities—thirty-five times the amount which Hamilton had funded and used as a buttress for the Federalist organization—was outstanding in the hands of public creditors, every one of whom looked to the Republicans, rather than to the Democrats, for the faithful discharge of interest and principal.

Other recruits, equally practical in their interests, added to the strength of the Republican right wing. The railway corporations which had received enormous grants from the public domain, not yet through with their business in Washington, had to adjust innumerable controversies with government officials over the fulfillment of contracts and over the titles of land seized or claimed by farmers or squatters; and fresh companies with fine projects on paper offered to build additional lines if adequate favors could be wrested from the Congress of the United States. With a ferocity that seemed to increase as the federal possessions diminished, individuals and corporations clamored for princely patents to timber and mineral resources, to exploit or hold according to the requirements of the traffic and the prospect of profits.

Last but not least, everybody who had any industrial property liable to be regulated or otherwise attacked by an agrarian legislature or a proletarian city council was, in the nature of things, drawn to the cohorts of the Republican right wing; for, according to American political practice, relief to persons, natural or corporate, thus adversely affected was provided by the Supreme Court at Washington —a tribunal not composed of Delphic oracles but of statesmen and politicians appointed by the President and Senate. It did not call for much knowledge of American history to discover that satisfactory judicial protection was more likely to come from the spiritual heirs of Hamilton, Marshall, and Webster than from those who wore the Gracchian mantle of Jefferson, Jackson, and Taney. Verily, it was a formidable combination of economic powers that gathered on the right under the ægis of the Republican party in the decades that followed the surrender of the planters in 1865.

On the left wing of the Republican phalanx was an immense body of farmers, more numerous, more prosperous, and more closely consolidated than the agricultural regiments which the Federalists and Whigs had assembled in days gone by. Indeed there was justification for the claim that the Republican party itself was agrarian in origin and that the capitalistic troops had merely joined it in 1860 in time to turn the tide of battle. At any rate, the union effected in Chicago in that year was cemented by the discharge of the agricultural terms written in the bond and strengthened by other factors, economic and racial.

It could be said with justice that millions of people owed their very homesteads to the bounty of the Republican party. It was also a matter of common observation that the frontier, which had furnished the crude substance for Jacksonian Democracy, was advancing westward and that the farmers of Ohio, Indiana, Illinois, Wisconsin, and Michigan were gathering in neat fortunes from the unearned increment of rising values in land. In the best of times, a considerable portion of the farmers, perhaps as many as one-third, were able to save money, invest it in securities, and attach themselves through local banking enterprises to the higher ranges of the American system of acquisition and enjoyment. So agrarian calamities could come and go without breaking off from the Republican enrollment a formidable body of farmers whose sires had proudly worn the regalia of Andrew Jackson. From another direction the Chicago vincture was also heavily reinforced—by the German and Scandinavian recipients of Republican homestead bounties, recent immigrants who had never owed allegiance to the Democracy but had started on their careers with the Republican organization, unhampered by any former connections. Whenever they grew discontented with their party, they did not, as a matter of course, turn back with affection to the slogans and symbols of their first love.

The partnership of farmers and manufacturers, so formed and cemented, was strengthened by clever management on the part of Republican directors. At each recurring presidential election they remembered that the happy settlement at Chicago could only be maintained on a reciprocal basis. When dividing patronage and legislation, therefore, spokesmen of both contingents made concessions. In the general apportionment, the capitalistic wing usually thought it wise to give the presidency to the Mississippi Valley, once the fastness of Jacksonian Democracy where agrarian grievances might become virulent under neglect. Managers of that group had been shrewd enough in 1860 to put aside Seward of New York, an avowed imperialist, a high protectionist, and an uncompromising foeman of the planting aristocracy, in favor of Lincoln, the rail-splitter of Illinois; and they seldom forgot the lesson they learned on that occasion. So it was no mere accident that the Middle West furnished all the successful Republican candidates for the presidency between the close of the Second Revolution and the end of the century. Grant, Hayes, Garfield, Harrison, and McKinley were all born in Ohio; the only Republican candidate defeated during the period between 1860 and 1892 was Blaine of Maine.

In addition to the broad support afforded the Republican party by its host of embattled farmers were other popular elements arrayed on its side at the ballot box. A million northern veterans of the Civil War, nearly all organized into the Grand Army of the Republic, remembered that their Commander-in-chief, the immortal Lincoln, had been a Republican, and none of them, not even Democrats in the fellowship, could ignore the service of the Republican party in obtaining pensions for Union soldiers—pensions in generous totals amounting to more than half a billion dollars between 1879 and 1889 and over a billion in the succeeding decade. Neither could they fail to observe that Cleveland vetoed more pension bills in one year than all the Republican presidents from Grant to McKinley, incidents tending to confirm the veterans in their historic faith.

Equally reliable in their political orthodoxy were the million freedmen. Their shackles had been struck off by the Great Emancipator, a Republican, and to Republicans they owed the ballots in their hands. With an affection altogether natural, they remembered their debt on election day in the South as long as the whites would permit it, while their Negro brethren in the North, already free and enfranchised, voted their appreciation with ceremonial regularity.

By no means negligible in this enumeration of popular forces, must also be reckoned the host of federal officeholders who formed an industrious and vigilant rank and file for the Republican general staff. During the period from 1861 to 1897, the Republicans held the presidency for twenty-eight years, distributing the spoils of government almost without let or hindrance, even after the Civil Service Act of 1883 threatened to make inroads upon the patronage that fell to the victors.

To practical considerations were added ethical and sentimental factors. The Republican party had originated in an age of profound moral enthusiasm. If it did not win the allegiance of unconditional abolitionists, it did command the affection of many idealists, such for instance as James Russell Lowell and George William Curtis, who had denounced slavery day and night when it was neither safe nor popular to oppose that pillared institution. In the afterglow of victory the spirit of the crusaders descended upon party managers. "When in the economy of Providence, this land was to be purged of slavery," orators were fond of saying, "the Republican party came to power." In vain did the Democrats reply that the Republican party in 1861 had spurned abolition as poison, that it had offered to fasten slavery on the republic forever by a constitutional amendment, that it had accepted emancipation only as a desperate war measure, and that it had wrought the great moral achievement at the expense of the slave owners whose property had been confiscated. In vain did the abolitionists recall older days when some of the new knights in shining armor had thrown bad eggs at anti-slavery agitators. On any count the ethical issue was debatable and historical memories were short; so the Republicans were able to capitalize at par their services as emancipators.

Less controversial, indeed indisputable, was the declaration that under Republican auspices the Union had been saved and the Stars and Stripes kept floating in the heavens over a nation, one and inseparable, now and forever, fulfilling Webster's beautiful vision. Thousands of northern Democrats, it is true, had fought in the Union armies, and had served the national government faithfully in the darkest hours of its distress but there was something more than political fiction in the assertion of the stump-speaker that every soldier who fought under the confederate flag was a Democrat.

At all events in minds of a certain type the Republicans managed, bv adroit appeals to war passions, to make party loyalty equivalent to national patriotism and voting the opposition ticket identical with sedition. Though Democrats scornfully called that practice "waving the bloody shirt," it gave Republican spellbinders a sway over popular psychology which no Federalist or Whig had ever commanded. Year after year it appeared in campaigns, encouraging a wit, as late as 1884, to express the hope that they might "wring one more President" from the folds of that battle-stained garment. And long after martial sentiments began to wane, conflicts over reconstruction in the South, the use of federal troops in the elections, and the protection of Negroes in their civil and political rights aggravated the wounds of the war, making the "salvation of the Union" a long proceeding as well as a patriotic deed.

Another moral asset of undoubted potency in the Republican cause was the Lincoln tradition. The Emancipator had been a Republican; his tragic ending at the hands of a sympathizer with the South had hushed the savage voice of criticism; and around the solid substance of his deathless fame had clustered some of the sweetest memories and noblest traditions of American democracy. Lowell had shot a winged shaft with his words: "New birth of our new soil, the first American."

Besides such ethical resources, the Republicans had martial glories at their command—war heroes to offer to the populace as candidates for the presidency, not minor figures, such as William Henry Harrison who had killed a handful of Indians or Zachary Taylor who had overwhelmed bands of ragged Mexicans, but knights-errant of the first magnitude with General Ulysses S. Grant at the head. Again and again did the Republican directors in search of available nominees resort to the temple of Janus. And with telling effect, for every one of their successful contestants for the office of chief executive between the close of the Second American Revolution and the end of the century was a soldier of rank from the Grand Army of the Republic. Grant had saved the Union as the commanding general; twice was he elected to the presidency and almost a third time. His successor, Rutherford B. Hayes, had been wounded on the battlefield and had been promoted to the status of major-general. James A. Garfield who followed Hayes had served with honor under the colors and had risen from the position of lieutenant-colonel to that of major-general. Then came a break in the martial roll; in 1884 the Republicans deserted the military list by nominating James G. Blaine who had been a mere member of Congress during the Civil War, only to meet defeat. Warned, perhaps, by this untoward incident, they presented General Harrison at the next election and finally for the last campaign of the century, they nominated Major McKinley.

Sustained by such forces, economic, ethical, and sentimental, the Republican party moved forward with confidence through the political calendar between 1864 and 1896. Neither the leaders of business enterprise on the right wing nor the farmers on the left embarrassed it by making impossible demands upon the directorate. In fact the re quirements of the industrial captains were mainly on the negative side anyway. During the Civil War they had accomplished most of the positive designs for which Federalists and Whigs had struggled for generations, wringing from the distracted country, while the opposition was broken by the armed contest, high protective tariffs, a sound national banking system, generous land grants to railway corporations, and a constitutional amendment which permitted the Supreme Court to strike down state and local legislation dangerous to acquired rights—no matter how recent. Under the Homestead Act, supplemented by later Timber and Stone Acts, they could easily acquire any additional portions of the federal domain necessary to the profitable development of their enterprise. Beyond these things, they needed only one more great piece of positive legislation to complete the circle of their felicity, namely, a law establishing the currency system on a firm, metallic basis. Having already won from the government substantially all their historic demands, the prime consideration of leaders in business enterprise was to secure a liberal administration of existing statutes and the maintenance of *laissez faire* in the midst of law and order. Given the prevailing pattern of economic relations, it followed that the political program favored by the industrial baronage was simple in structure. Naturally it desired to see all branches of the federal government in the hands of its friends but it could make headway with a President and a Senate favorable to its requirements, even if it lost the House of Representatives.

The executive department was invested with a positive power of immense economic utility; if so disposed, it could operate the land office munificently, distribute the natural resources of the nation in generous fashion, and manage foreign policy with reference to the demands of trade. It could also wield a negative authority; the President had the legal right to veto acts of Congress; he nominated Supreme Court justices who, in the grand manner of jurists, could set aside legislative measures. With respect both to action and negation the Senate of the United States likewise had its uses; as the upper house of Congress, its consent was necessary to the passage or defeat of any new legislation and to the confirmation of the President's nominees for important public offices, including the federal judiciary. Fortunately for business enterprise, the machine for electing the President was cumbersome and costly to move; Senators were chosen indirectly by state legislatures; and federal judges were selected by the President and the Senate for life.

§

Against this huge and formidable Republican combination, the Democrats, split by a furious dispute and separated into two factions for four years by a wall of fire, undertook to do battle in a struggle for the possession of political authority. Though they had constituted an overwhelming majority of the nation when Lincoln brushed them out of office, they labored under severe handicaps in 1865. They were composed in rank and file of farmers and mechanics, who had never produced at the plow and bench leaders capable of coping with the industrial baronage.

In the old days the planters had supplied most of the high officers for the war on protection, ship subsidies, centralized currency, and national banks, but in 1865 there was no longer a united aristocracy of slave owners, rich, educated, and domineering, able to measure strength with corporation lawyers in the political forum. The surviving directors of the planting class had lost most of the economic substance that had once given lusty energy to their leadership and argument. Their property in slaves was gone, all gone, and they could not hope, like the clergy and nobility of revolutionary France, to recover a shred of it in the calmer days of reaction. Their property in confederate bonds was also gone—abolished by the Fourteenth Amendment to the Constitution of the United States. And other bitter dregs were in their cup. A large proportion of them were disqualified for voting and holding office until Congress saw fit to remove their disabilities; and that body was slow to forget the poignant sufferings of the four terrible years, loath to grant sweeping measures of amnesty. Besides losing their property and political rights, southern leaders, for many years, were mere residents of conquered provinces governed by soldiers under the authority of Republican Presidents in Washington, with the aid of Negroes. Though every confederate state had been nominally restored to membership in the Union by 1870, it was not until seven years later that federal troops were removed from the last southern capital; and it was not until 1898 that the last supporter of the Confederacy was fully restored to citizenship, spreading the mantle of kindly oblivion over the harrowing past.

As the business of party management required at least some money, leisure, and education, it was evident that the

Democratic masses would have to look to new quarters for direction; and they found it mainly among the merchants, lawyers, financiers, and office-holders of the eastern cities. From time immemorial importing merchants, ably assisted by editors of metropolitan newspapers sustained by advertising, had furnished nutriment for low tariff politics. There was no mystery about that: the more goods imported, the larger the profits.

Closely affiliated with the merchants were the bankers who brought over from Europe immense quantities of capital, principally for railway construction. Inasmuch as their imports, in the long run, came in the form of manufactured commodities rather than gold, they too looked with favor upon low tariffs, or at all events opposed a high protection which interfered with their business—with the free inflow of capital and outflow of agricultural produce to discharge the principal and interest. Even the railway financiers did not always see eye to eye with the manufacturers; they had little relish for tariffs on steel rails and rolling stock and it made little difference in their balance sheets whether the goods they hauled were imports or domestic commodities.

Thus it happened that, except on sound money and correct banking, capitalism was divided against itself. If the heaviest battalions were clearly on the Republican side, the Democratic masses could nevertheless count on securing a small directorate from the body of wealth and talent as long as they were willing to support sound money. It was, however, a timid right wing thus assembled, a contingent that could be easily driven out of the party or into retirement by an ominous action on the left.

In the matter of issues as well as leadership the Democrats suffered from embarrassments after 1865. The destruction of the planting aristocracy and the invasion of the Mississippi Valley by machine industry subdued some of the old zeal for immediate and unconditional free trade, to say nothing of tariff for revenue only. Moreover the southern sugar planter, the hemp grower in the border states, or the wool raiser in Ohio, even though he might call himself a Democrat in principle, was as doughty in defending his particular infant industry as any cotton spinner from Massachusetts. So while many congressional districts sent ardent foes of protection in general to Washington, the directorate of the Democratic party had to be careful about defining the national battle lines too precisely, about a wholesale assault on the tariff. To attack the new banking system of 1863 after the fashion of the Jacksonian Democrats was also out of the question; for the financial wing of the party was easily frightened by menacing gestures of that sort. To strike at the industrial baronage with the implements of social democracy was likewise impossible because a program of that kind called for a revolution in the campaign curriculum, which merchants and financiers could not approve.

Committed by affiliations with agriculture to a creed of *laissez faire* adopted in the age of stage coaches and tallow-dips, having utterly rejected all doctrines of paternalism, the Democratic party, as things stood in 1865, could not readily endorse the kind of state interference required to scale the accumulations of the bourgeois by taxation or to hold down their earnings by regulation. In short, by its time-honored doctrines, it was pledged to administrative nihilism.

Casting about for presidential candidates capable of arousing popular enthusiasm, the Democrats ran into snags in every direction. They could not expect either the southern contingent or the lukewarm brethren of the North to endorse a military hero chosen from the Grand Army of the Republic. But they tried that expedient twice, once with General McClellan in 1864 and again with General Winfield S. Hancock in 1880, and in vain. Neither could they hope that their colleagues engaged in the mercantile and importing business would rally with enthusiasm around an agrarian hailing from the Valley of Jacksonian Democracy, however much he might praise free trade; when they resorted to that stratagem in 1896, enlisting under William Jennings Bryan of Nebraska, they were simply routed.

Their best hope, so they reasoned, was to hover around the mercantile metropolis of the country when searching for available standard bearers. It was in the state of New York accordingly that they found Horatio Seymour, a gentleman of the old school, selected in 1868; Horace Greeley, the Republican editor whom they accepted in a forlorn delusion in 1872; Samuel J. Tilden, the able corporation lawyer presented in 1876; and Grover Cleveland, a "safe and sane" politician put forward in 1884, 1888, and 1892. Of the entire list, only Cleveland was able to lead them to victory—on one occasion a dubious victory at that—during all the years between Appomattox and Manila Bay.

In only one quarter and as a result of a gradual process did the Democrats capture a stronghold from which they could not be shaken in any crisis. That was the Solid South. In Hamilton's time a large regiment of prosperous lawyers and planters from that region, fearing like poison the radical agrarianism of Jefferson, had voted the Federalist ticket. Long afterward the social successors of the same class had gone with Webster rather than with Jackson, preferring the risks of high tariffs to the perils of a leveling democracy. Even in the fateful election of 1860, the South had been seriously divided. In only six of the fifteen slave states did the extreme pro-slavery candidate receive a majority of the votes cast; and throughout that section the moderate candidate, Bell, appealing to old Whig sympathies made a good showing: 42,000 in Georgia, for example, against 51,000 for Breckinridge. In a word, there was a marked cleavage between the seaboard planter and the upland farmer.

But in the clash of arms and reconstruction, it was largely overcome, except in the border states where a strong Union faction survived even that heroic welding operation. Faced by a military government directed by Republicans in Washington and supported by Negroes at hand, the white men of the South forgot ancient divisions in the presence of forces more formidable. Having determined to recover their dominion, their first task was, as a matter of course, to wrest the ballot from the newly enfranchised freedmen —the ballot conferred upon them by the Fourteenth and Fifteenth Amendments, supplemented by various federal force bills for the supervision of elections.

This they accomplished, in the early stages, by forming secret societies, such as the Ku Klux Klan and the White Camelia which, by warnings, nocturnal visits, impressive parades in white hoods, and other methods, sometimes including murderous violence, managed to frighten great masses of the colored voters away from the polls, in spite of federal protection there. Very generally the freedman into whose hands the ballot had been thrust by the Republican victors did not care to risk his head in exercising his political rights, so that the mere show of force materially reduced the number of ballots cast against the Democrats.

Finding such tactics highly effective and the resistance of the northern Republicans weakening as the passions of the late war cooled, the southern whites moved from intimidation to legal procedure by writing into their state constitutions various provisions which lawfully deprived Negroes of the ballot, without disturbing the political prerogatives of the Caucasian race. Since the Fifteenth Amendment forbade them to deprive any person of the right to vote on account of race, color, or previous condition of servitude, they hit upon devices of indirection. The most easily administered was an ingenious provision requiring the voter to read a section of the state constitution or a statute or "understand and explain it when read" by election officers. Negroes who experienced no difficulty in meeting this requirement might be caught upon an alternative, such as a taxpaying or property qualification on voting. And to let illiterate and poverty-stricken whites through the net, the inventors constructed the so-called "grandfather clause"—a plan which admitted to the suffrage any man who did not have the property or educational qualifications, provided he had voted on or before 1867 or was the son or grandson of such person.

Although the federal Supreme Court finally annulled the grandfather clauses, the various restraining measures were strikingly effective, especially in the Far South. In 1896, for illustration, Louisiana had 127,000 colored voters enrolled; and under the reformed constitution adopted two years later the number fell to 5300. To make a long story brief, after 1890 there were at least nine southern states in which no Republican candidate for President could hope to win a single electoral vote. The South was solid. There were indeed from time to time desperate battles between the prosperous white planters and manufacturers and the populistic white farmers over state politics and seats in Congress, but only in crucial contests did either faction call upon Negro support or permit differences of opinion to cut down the Democratic vote for presidential candidates in local areas. Still, as time passed and manufacturing increased, Republicans lifted their heads in southern states, particularly in the industrial belt—indicating an economic thrust too strong for many old loyalties.

§

The task of aligning party masses for hand-to-hand encounters in the political arena was further complicated by administrative factors thrown up in profusion during the era of business enterprise. All functions of government were now becoming more complex, the number of public officers was mounting, campaign funds from corporations were growing, railways, telegraph lines, and newspapers were multiplying—in combination making the work of marshaling voters, providing appropriate publicity, and managing party machinery more tortuous. In other words, the duties and emoluments of politics were increasing and the talent employed in party manipulation foliating in richer diversity. Entrusted with more devious exercises and sustained by larger treasuries, the directorate within each party, therefore, became more redoubtable, assuming after a fashion the nature of an economic estate or class, and enjoying the fruits of returns as sweet to politicians as the revenues of farms, railways, and mills to their respective recipients.

With his party institutionalized, the solemn obligation of the professional politician, high and low, whatever his campaign label, was to hold office if he had it and to get it if he was out of power, for without office he could collect no tolls, fees, or imposts. If to accomplish this purpose it was necessary to tack and trim, the requirement could be met by steering carefully between the sinuosities of indifference and indignation. As a result, directors of national, state, municipal, county, township, and village political engines often served those who paid them best and devoted little attention to the rhetoric of the orators as long as it was within the bounds of reason. If, perchance, the political managers of the two parties found their mutual trade in peril they could ordinarily make common cause against the menace—enter into conversations and understandings with a view to conserving their earnings.

Accordingly, in normal times, it made little or no difference to the Napoleons of business enterprise what party directorate commanded the field as long as the requirements of their political economy were met in a satisfactory manner. This fact, though generally known, was illustrated in a manner peculiarly picturesque during a federal investigation of 1893 when it was shown how the Sugar Trust gave money to both parties without prejudice. "The Sugar Trust is a Democrat in a Democratic state and a Republican in a Republican state?" queried the senatorial inquisitor. "As far as local matters are concerned, I think that is about it," replied the genial Mr. Havemeyer for the Sugar interests. "The American Sugar Refining Company has no politics of any kind. . . . Only the politics of business," continued the robust man of affairs.

Corroborating this testimony not long afterwards, an expert witness, an outspoken member of "the idle rich," Frederick Townsend Martin, remarked with charming frankness: "The class I represent, care nothing for politics. . . . Among my people I seldom hear purely political discussions. When we are discussing pro and con the relative merits of candidates or the relative importance of political policies, the discussion almost invariably comes down to a question of business efficiency. We care absolutely nothing about statehood bills, pension agitation, waterway appropriations, 'pork barrels,' state rights, or any other political question, save inasmuch as it threatens or fortifies existing conditions. Touch the question of the tariff, touch the issue of the income tax, touch the problem of railroad regulation, or touch the most vital of all business matters, the question of general federal regulation of industrial corporations and the people amongst whom I live my life become immediately rabid partisans. . . . It matters not one iota what political party is in power or what President holds the reins of office. We are not politicians or public thinkers; we are the rich; we own America; we got it, God knows how, but we intend to keep it if we can by throwing all the tremendous weight of our support, our influence, our money, our political connections, our purchased senators, our hungry congressmen, our public-speaking demagogues into the scale against any legislature, any political platform, any presidential campaign that threatens the integrity of our estate. . . . The class I represent cares nothing for politics. In a single season a plutocratic leader hurled his influence and his money into the scale to elect a Republican governor on the Pacific coast and a Democratic governor on the Atlantic coast."

Another factor which helped party directorates to avoid sharp and dangerous battles likely to unhorse them and deprive them of the emoluments of power was the fluidity of classes. Always a striking characteristic of American society, it was even more marked after 1865, especially as the growth of corporate enterprise worked for a wide and invisible distribution of ownership through stocks and bonds. In former days, when a southern planter rose solemnly in a political assembly, buttoned his frock coat over his bosom, and delivered his defense of slavery and free trade in Ciceronian periods, there was no doubt in the minds of his auditors about the nature of the play.

But in the new industrial age, statecraft became less obvious in its methods. When a gentleman garbed in fustian rent the skies with pleas for "the downtrodden people," there was no assurance that the raiment was not chosen for effect or that the orator did not have a strong box in a neighboring bank. Especially did lawyers crowding into politics help to blur the social dichotomy. Enjoying a certain leisure for party affairs, accustomed to rendering opinions on call, and supple in arguing causes, they were usually preferred as candidates, especially by captains of industry who were as a rule too busy or too disinclined by taste for the peculiar life of the forum. Indeed in the grand era of acquisition and enjoyment, it was the lawyer, with his special system of ethics, who appeared in leading rôles before the footlights on the political stage.

Thereupon, the substance of politics became too elusive for the eye of the inexperienced; what was going on behind the scenes was seldom fully known to the audience. For instance, until a scandal exploded the inner works, it was not disclosed that several powerful members of Congress who spoke earnestly on the urgent necessity for progress in the Far West during the sixties had handsome gifts of Union Pacific or Credit Mobilier securities safely laid away. To use a later illustration, until the agents of William Randolph Hearst purloined the papers in the case, the great American electorate was unaware that the Honorable Joseph B. Foraker of Ohio, who represented the generality of that state in the Senate and who wrote the Anti-Trust plank for the Republican platform in 1900, had received generous retainers from the Standard Oil interests. Neither did that electorate know that the Senator had received, while in office, a large sum from the same source for the purpose of aiding in the purchase of a Republican newspaper.

§

If the professional members of political machines frequently softened the animosities of political warfare by acting as "honest brokers" between contending economic forces, they also occasionally added to its acerbity by scandalous and corrupt practices which furnished targets for the enemy. Whenever any political party enjoyed a long tenure of power in federal, state, or municipal offices, ringleaders were sure to accumulate large profits and hereditaments without regard for public decorum or at least without sufficient command over discretion. "What are we here for?" was the popular slogan of those who made politics itself a form of business enterprise. At Washington where the Republicans ruled the administration for more than two decades without interruption, the major delinquencies were assignable to members of their society; while in states and cities where the Democrats were in power, most of the letters of marque and reprisal were ascribed to them.

Year after year, in spite of the best efforts of those who sincerely desired clean ceremonials, scandals in high places broke out with distressing regularity at the national capital. After Jay Gould and Jim Fisk attempted to corner the gold market and brought about the financial crash of Black Friday in 1869, an investigating committee reported that President Grant's brother-in-law, a notorious speculator, had maintained a curious subterranean connection between the government and the conspirators. No one questioned for a moment the personal honesty of the President in the matter but he had undoubtedly been exploited in the operation. At all events, a few days before the grand "killing," the General and his wife had been taken by principals in the transaction to see Offenbach's La Périchole at the Fifth Avenue Theater, thus impressing intended victims by their access to the presence of the mighty. Three years later came the un-savory exposure of the Credit Mobilier which involved many Republican congressmen of good standing; though the curtain was drawn with decent celerity, an inquiry revealed the Vice-President of the United States as a man who had sworn falsely to conceal improprieties.

Before another year elapsed, the most brilliant party leader of his era, James G. Blaine, was openly accused by the Springfield Republican of using his powers in Congress to favor high tariffs and railway corporations in return for monetary considerations. After ignoring the charge for a time, Blaine finally took notice of it, securing at the hands of a congressional committee an official examination conducted according to accepted use and wont. This inquiry failed to disclose corrupt actions on the part of the accused; but Blaine, besides exhibiting during the furor a bearing that was not conspicuous for candor and nicety, told, as the record showed, six separate falsehoods. More than that, he seized a collection of papers, known as the Mulligan letters, which, it was alleged, contained incriminating statements from his pen and, after reading in Congress what purported to be certain extracts from these documents, declined to show the actual dossier to the investigating committee. Though his Republican friends refused to believe that there had been anything improper in his conduct, the flavor of the affair was not exactly suited to an enlightened public taste.

The Blaine incident had not yet closed when the Secretary of the Treasury unearthed frauds in the collection of internal revenues from certain distilleries, revealing in the operation a "Whisky Ring" composed in part of high politicians thriving on profits derived from that form of economic endeavor. Additional inquiries made with the aid of the Attorney-General led quickly to the door of President Grant's private secretary, arousing the General once more to military wrath. When his secretary was brought to trial, the President voluntarily intervened to give testimony, swearing that he had never seen anything in the conduct of his friend which indicated any connection with the Whisky Ring and declaring that he had "great confidence" in the integrity and efficiency of his assistant. In the end, although a few of the participants in the fraud were duly convicted and duly pardoned, Grant's secretary, sustained by high authority, was adjudged innocent and restored to his position in the bosom of the official family. But the respite was short, for into that privacy the scorn of the public penetrated, forcing the President's trusted servant to resign at last. Even in such an extremity, Grant's faith remained unshaken; nor did it fail later when the hunted man was indicted for an alleged connection with plans for breaking open a safe and getting possession of incriminating documents.

On top of the Whisky Ring scandal came startling charges respecting the Secretary of War, General William W. Belknap, accusing him and his wife of collecting for their private purse large sums of money from federal officeholders. Stirred to action by insistent rumors, a congressional committee took damning testimony on the subject in 1876 and promptly reported to the House of Representatives a resolution calling for the impeachment of the Secretary for "high crimes and misdemeanors while in office," buttressed by evidence so conclusive that the House approved it without a dissenting vote. Reading the handwriting on the wall, Belknap tried to escape his fate by resigning, to the "great regret" of President Grant; but the trial took place before the Senate in due form with distressing revelations marking every step of the inquest. At the close, thirty-seven Senators voted "guilty" and twenty-five "not guilty," some of the latter taking the ground that it was impossible to impeach a man after he had left office. In any case, the requisite two-thirds vote had not been obtained, so nothing came of the grand flourish.

Just as the interest in this affair began to wane, public excitement was renewed by a revelation of frauds in the carriage of mails over certain lines—roads marked by asterisks in the official records and popularly known as "star routes." It was shown by competent evidence that the men operating such lines were often paid more money than their contracts stipulated and that the secretary of the Republican national committee, which managed Garfield's campaign in 1880, had been the beneficiary of benevolence, if nothing more. Indictments followed. Some minor figures in the scandal, duly convicted, won a reversal of the verdicts against them on technicalities in the higher courts and all the prime actors in the drama were declared innocent. Distracted by the assassination of President Garfield, whose name had been unhappily dragged into the affair, the country heaved a sigh of relief on seeing the veil quietly drawn.

When the best aspect was put on all the untoward events which accompanied the triumphant march of business enterprise across the continent, a certain degree of resentment was felt by the more ingenuous masters of statecraft. In a great speech, delivered during the trial of Secretary Belknap, the Honorable George F. Hoar, a Senator from Massachusetts, soon to be a distinguished national leader, reviewed in a pathetic strain the grievous cases that had recently come to his notice. He had seen five judges of a high federal court driven from office by threats of impeachment for corruption or maladministration. He had seen four judges of New York impeached for corruption and the chief city disgraced throughout the world by the machinations of the Tweed ring. He had listened with astonishment to a demand from the chairman on military affairs that four congressmen be expelled for selling cadetships at West Point. Then he moved on to the worst. "When the greatest railroad of the world, binding together the continent and uniting the two great seas which wash our shores, was finished, I have seen our national triumph and exaltation turned to bitterness and shame by the unanimous reports of three committees of Congress—two of the House and one here—that every step of that mighty enterprise had been taken in fraud. I have heard in the highest places the shameless doctrine avowed by men grown old in public office that the true way by which power should be gained in the Republic is to bribe the people with offices created for their service. . . . I have heard that suspicion haunts the footsteps of the trusted companions of the President."

§

Inferior in pretensions to the misdemeanors committed in the national sphere by the machine politicians of the Republican affiliation, but no less commensurate with the facilities offered, were the deeds of state and municipal directors, frequently of Democratic proclivities. If the Republicans at Washington furnished flaming scandals as targets for their opponents, the Democrats in New York City proved themselves worthy rivals on a smaller stage. From the age of Jefferson forward, they had enjoyed an almost uninterrupted control of that growing metropolis while their directors were becoming firmly knit together in a sovereign association, known as Tammany Hall—a private society for good fellowship and charitable works, founded in the age of the American Revolution. Entering politics actively during the campaign of 1800, Tammany waxed fat from decade to decade, welcoming the poor immigrants who landed at the port, carrying municipal elections, and gathering in the spoils of federal and local offices. As technology revolutionized the city, as gas, transportation, and other utility corporations sought franchises and privileges, as the municipality undertook new functions in the interests of public health and safety, opportunities to make money out of the business of politics multiplied until even Clive with his Oriental imagination would have been dazed at their magnitude.

About the end of the middle period appeared a leader in Tammany Hall who was not hampered in his ambitions by any such moderation as stayed the hand of the English administrator in India. This man was William Marcy Tweed. Born in 1823 in the city of New York, educated at a public school, introduced to ward politics as a fireman in a volunteer company, Tweed knew the local terrain as well as any general who ever won a battle. Carefully choosing the site for his operations, he had himself elected to the county board of supervisors which had large powers, distinct from those of the city government, in levying local taxes and spending money for buildings and improvements. On this board he served for thirteen years, four times as president, making it the point of vantage from which to effect an organization of kindred spirits in Tammany Hall for the purpose of controlling more places of power and pelf. By 1869, the Tweed group had possession of the mayor, the common council, the district attorney, the municipal judges, the legislature at Albany, and even the governor of the Empire State.

With reckless indifference to all amenities, Tweed and his band scooped in the rewards of their labors, multiplying the debt of the city tenfold in a decade and putting no small part of the proceeds into their own pockets. The construction of a county court house, which was supposed to cost a quarter of a million dollars, in fact involved an outlay of eight millions in which the city was charged $470 apiece for chairs and $400,000 apiece for safes in which to store valuable papers. In collateral transactions, huge sums were fraudulently paid out of the city treasury under the specious title of "general purposes," enriching politicians, contractors, and real estate speculators at the expense of the taxpayers.

According to all signs, there seemed to be no limit to the ambitions of Tweed's cohorts and indeed they might have gone on indefinitely if they had not fallen out among themselves over the division of the loot, creating dissensions which led to exposures in 1871. On the motion of a committee of indignant citizens formed to prosecute the malefactors, Tweed was arrested on a charge of having stolen

$6,000,000, convicted, and sent to prison. Escaping by connivance, he fled to Spain in 1875, only to be discovered, rearrested, brought back to New York, and kept in jail until his death soon afterward. Other members of the circle being also caught in the toils of the law, Tweed's inner Tammany ring, a closed corporation for exploiting the backward places of politics, was temporarily broken, to reassemble some years later under the more subtle and careful direction of Richard Croker.

Sensing opportunities highly attractive, if less munificent, politicians of other cities—Philadelphia, Chicago, Cincinnati, St. Louis, and nearly every municipality of importance—emulated the Tweed performance and evolved similar machines under Republican or Democratic auspices according to circumstances, with results alike in kind if not in degree. If, therefore, a Democratic orator pointed the finger of political scorn at Credit Mobilier or Star Route frauds, he was sure to receive in return a volley on the score of his own party's municipal scandals.

§

With the advent of the political machine as a special form of business enterprise, farmers and mechanics, who had formed the bulwark of Jacksonian Democracy, found all the more intractable the task of forming an effective combination against the dominant Republicans. Indeed under the American system of government, it was hard for humble men of no wealth and little leisure to operate directly in any political theater larger than a town or county; the involutions of the organism were too labyrinthian.

Leaving aside the perplexities of state and local administrations, federal politics alone was divided into two great spheres—an upper and a lower. In the former took place the election of the President which required a huge, expensive, and unwieldy party machine. There also occurred the choice of United States Senators which involved neat management in the caucuses of state legislatures; and there likewise fell the selection of federal judges, which called for quiet ingenuity on the part of the appointing President, the confirming Senate, and their counselors. In this upper range, wealth, leisure, talent, finesse, discretion, negotiation, and a good press were the prime desiderata of statecraft.

In the lower sphere of federal politics occurred the operation of choosing members for the House of Representatives—a transaction conducted in relatively small districts, as a rule remote from the economic and political metropolis and attended by more or less activity on the part of the rank and file. Though in such elections there was usually pressure from above, the candidates for the House, being always brought personally into contact with the voters themselves, were forced to heed more closely the opinions and passions of the multitude.

It is only with reference to the upper and lower ranges of the federal government that the course and results of political warfare during the interval between the Second Revolution and the first inauguration of McKinley can be understood. In connection with the former were the presidential campaigns and elections which came along every four years, as required by the American political calendar, even though no vital issues called for popular judgment. Involving large scale exploits, they fell mainly into the hands of professional politicians who devoted their lives to their respective organizations and on both sides were consumed by the same desire to hold or to obtain offices.

Consequently caution was their supreme watchword. It is vain to search the Republican and Democratic national platforms between 1868 and 1896 for any clear-cut antithesis on any issues, economic or ethical. Democratic directors, as we have seen, could not in the nature of things agree to declare a holy war on the national debt, the national banking scheme, the protective idea, or the centralized currency system; while Republican directors, always under the necessity of placating their agrarian wing, could not be too intransigent on either side of the monetary question. In fact, about the only substantial materials for political debate in the presidential campaigns of this period, apart from the waning war issues, were furnished by the scandals in the federal administration.

Naturally these outrages were odious to a large number of industrial barons who desired to see the process of economic development go forward with all the respect for legal proprieties that was possible under prevailing conditions. They were equally odious to a considerable estate of "intellectuals," comprising such high characters as James Russell Lowell, George William Curtis, and Edwin L. Godkin, all men of education and refinement. So unbearable indeed did the scandals become that some of the insurgents, calling themselves Liberal Republicans, broke from the party organization in 1872 and united with the Democrats on Horace Greeley as a candidate. In their desperate effort to prevent the reëlection of General Grant, they only met a humiliating disaster at the polls, which drove most of the dissidents, chastened by the experience, back to the Republican fold. Not more than a handful continued their independency—to be assailed for their "base hypocrisy and insincerity" by young Theodore Roosevelt at the beginning of his political apprenticeship.

After the ruin of the Liberal Republican movement, the rôle of organized opposition was left mainly to the Democrats. Unable, for reasons already given, to fuse all their factions on the old issues of free trade, localized banking, easy money, and their legal corollary, state sovereignty, the directors of that party devoted themselves in the presidential campaigns chiefly to the business of consolidating the elements that were discontented with the Republican régime. In 1876, they made a shrewd stroke of state by nominating Samuel J. Tilden, an able, conservative, and rich corporation lawyer of New York, sixty-two years old and beyond the age of dangerous political emotion, who, as governor of the state and as a private citizen, had fought valiantly against corruption in his own party and promised to purify politics in Washington, if elected. With Tilden at their head, they almost captured the presidency in a contest with a "dark-horse" Republican of Ohio, Rutherford B. Hayes. Indeed, the Democrats asserted that they had in truth carried the country, pointing to the records which gave Tilden a plurality of the popular vote and claiming for him a majority of the electoral college. But, citing documents equally impressive, the Republicans asserted that Hayes was lawfully elected, precipitating on that account a dispute over the returns which raged for months while the fate of the candidates hung uncertain in the balance.

On any view of the case, the merits of the controversy were confused owing to the peculiar condition of several southern states, still disorganized from the effects of the Civil War. By both sides frauds were probably committed —or at least irregularities so glaring that long afterwards a student of the affair who combined wit with research came to the dispassionate conclusion that the Democrats stole the election in the first place and then the Republicans stole it back. Whatever the virtues of the contestants, the country was in an ugly temper for several weeks and civil strife again seemed imminent, when suddenly the managers in Congress agreed to submit the issues to a commission of fifteen. This special body, embracing eight Republican members who voted solidly on all crucial questions, surveyed the disputed election and awarded the palm to Hayes.

Having had enough strife for the time being, the Democrats acquiesced in a verdict which they detested, hoping that, on appeal, the voters would condemn it at the polls in succeeding elections. In due time they were permitted to rejoice over what seemed to be a rebuke to the Republicans, when in 1878 the people returned a Democratic House of Representatives and the state legislatures a Democratic Senate. But the emotions which produced this result were short lived; for two years later the same people, riding on a high tide of economic prosperity, elected to the presidency the Republican candidate, James A. Garfield, with a plurality that could not be questioned in any tribunal, indicating that if any wrong had been done in 1876 it was hardly grave enough to demand reparation in the form of a political revolution.

At that juncture, however, fate turned the iron leaves in her book. Garfield was assassinated by a disappointed office-seeker and his place was taken by the Vice-President, Chester A. Arthur, a machine politician of New York who did not understand the Valley of Democracy and who could not keep in lockstep the federal office holders in the South, the "bread and butter brigade," as they were called at the time. When the campaign of 1884 approached, the Republican directorate was in a dilemma. Arthur was impossible, Grant lay upon his deathbed; and Blaine's public record, after every defense had been made and every apology uttered, was distressing for the reformers to contemplate. Nevertheless on the plea that Blaine had "earned the nomination," the coveted prize was given to him.

Now for the first time in their history, the Republicans in the quest for a leader had turned away from the Mississippi basin and selected as their candidate a man closely associated with that ancient demon—the money power. Besides that departure from tradition, they chose a statesman whose mercantile affiliations in politics had aroused the distrust of those reputable citizens whom Roosevelt styled the "most virtuous and desirable men of the great seaboard cities." The signs of the Republican zodiac were far from propitious.

At that very moment the Democrats were at last favored by fortune, in finding for their standard bearer a man of peculiar availability, Grover Cleveland. Though not born in a log cabin, Cleveland had made his way upward from poverty and could drink beer from the bar in a fashion approved by any mechanic in his party. Though his "moral character" had been impugned by Roosevelt, he had a general reputation for sterling honesty. He knew the ways of politics and had displayed his talents in that line as sheriff and mayor of Buffalo and as governor of his state, one of the strategic commonwealths of the Union.

Beyond all question Cleveland was conservative—and from New York, where dwelt most of the mercantile and financial Democrats. His respect for acquired rights had been demonstrated by his refusal to sign a bill fixing a five cent fare on the elevated railway in New York City; and men of substance, especially those with no investments in protected industries, believed that Cleveland would prove trustworthy in most emergencies and conduct public business with due regard for proprieties. At any rate he was not associated with a demand for radical changes in the common run of usage; rather was he wholly innocent of convictions on that score. To complete the list of his political virtues, he had never held a post in the federal government and so had no irreconcilable enemies in the national sphere.

The whole burden of the argument for Cleveland could therefore be summed up in the ancient and persistently popular slogan, "Turn the rascals out," an appeal which Republicans answered in a manner fitted to the gage. From the beginning to the end the campaign was primitive in its tactics. Without respect for parlor etiquette, Republicans attacked the personal character of Cleveland, who was not devoid of frailties of course, who in fact confessed them; while in behalf of the Democracy a famous cartoonist drew a horrible picture of Blaine which in the eyes of decent citizens must have damned the author rather than the victim. And when the dust, smoke, and stench died down, it was found that Cleveland was elected President by a slight plurality, owing his success to a victory won in New York by methods which the Republicans called fraudulent— methods none too dainty even when viewed in the light of vulgar custom. At best the popular verdict was dubious, for the state legislatures kept an opposition majority in the United States Senate during Cleveland's entire administration.

Much to the chagrin of Republicans, the country survived

the shock of having a Democrat in the White House again after the lapse of twenty-four years, and the mills of the gods continued to grind as of yore. If the new President had cherished any plans for unique and constructive legislation, the Republican Senate would have checked him, making the security of the status quo doubly sure; but as a matter of fact Cleveland's attitude toward the state was that of classical negation with respect to business and his conduct of public affairs bore the stamp of his philosophy. Vetoes were the most significant feature of his presidency; he killed more than two hundred pension bills, thus destroying the hopes of many thousand Republican applicants; he struck down a great river and harbor bill, therewith snatching from contractors and commercial communities benefits which they had been taught to expect by long-established practice.

From the Republican standpoint, Cleveland's administrative acts were also mainly negative; for, within two years of his inauguration, he had removed four-fifths of the fourth-class postmasters, all the internal revenue collectors, and ten-elevenths of the collectors of customs—a veritable army of Republican politicians who, to use the language of the trade, had long "battened at the public crib"—and had appointed in their places deserving Democrats, to the great sorrow of the civil service reformers who had supported him at the polls. Broadening the range of his activities, the President wrested from corporations and private persons more than eighty million acres of public lands illegally obtained from the generous land office of the federal government during the benevolent régime of his predecessors. It did not entirely destroy the merit of such actions to point out, as his enemies were fond of doing, that they represented virtues exercised chiefly at the expense of Republican mesne lords.

In any case Cleveland soon accumulated a host of foes among those who lived by politics and near the end of his term he aroused consternation, real or feigned, in the hearts of industrial captains, by assailing the moral principles of the protective tariff itself. That was the last straw; apparently the violation of a long-standing truce. In spite of more or less tinkering with the tariff schedules, the rates on the average had not been cut below the high levels established in the crisis of the Civil War. On their part, Republicans had been content to let well enough alone; while the Democratic national directorate, in its thirst for political power in Washington, had avoided making a direct attack on the whole system, after the manner of the forefathers in the day of Calhoun. So things stood in 1887 when Cleveland, taking a fresh view of the matter, announced in his annual message that the protective tariff, besides being vicious and inequitable, taxed every consumer in the land "for the benefit of the manufacturers."

If New York importers of capital and merchandise now rejoiced, the great industrial barons shouted for help like drowning men and the Republican managers made the most of the occasion. Putting aside Blaine, who was thoroughly weary of politics, they nominated Benjamin Harrison of the Middle West, a shrewd Indiana lawyer and a reticent politician who had committed no known indiscretions. To expedite his candidacy, they selected an efficient collector of campaign funds, who with charming simplicity asked manufacturers to contribute to the party war-chest on the basis of the benefits to accrue from Republican insurance against a tariff reduction. As expectations were large, the free-will offerings were generous. Cleveland was defeated.

Imagining that the old mandate had now been definitely renewed, Republicans set to work under the leadership of William McKinley in the House of Representatives to raise many notches the tariff which Cleveland had so recently condemned as exorbitant. Expecting for this achievement a chorus of approval, they were much astounded to find their work rejected of the populace. While the ink was still wet on the McKinley bill, they lost the congressional campaign in the autumn of 1890, and, two years later, they saw Harrison overwhelmed at the polls by his old antagonist, the author of the terrifying message of 1887, Grover Cleveland. They were even more amazed to learn that over a million citizens in the same election had repudiated both established parties—had voted the populist ticket and demanded something more drastic in the line of political action than the observance of obvious decencies in the process of acquisition and enjoyment, indicating that the end of a period had come.

If, at the close of thirty years of campaigning in the upper range of American politics, any Herodotus had inquired into the grand measures of national policy consistently advocated by the victorious candidates previous to their nominations, he would have met disappointing results. Grant had been a grim and silent soldier who knew little about politics before he took office in 1869; his opinions on the subject, such as they were, rather inclined him to the Democratic side; at least he voted the Democratic ticket in 1856 and would have done it again in 1860 if he could have acquired a residence in Illinois in time to cast a ballot against Lincoln. Hayes and Garfield were "dark horses," that is, they were nominated, not for their outspoken championship of noteworthy measures, but because the prominent figures in the party so split the convention vote that only politicians of the second order could be chosen. Cleveland had been sheriff of Buffalo county, mayor of Buffalo, and governor of New York but he had given little thought to national questions and with genuine feeling distrusted his capacity to fill the office of President. Harrison's chief asset was his descent from William Henry Harrison, the hero of Tippecanoe. Not one of these men was elevated to the presidency because he had formulated and defended in the theater of national politics a large or definite program of measures and policies. Indeed it was the very leaders associated with positive ideas and practices in the House and Senate who were deemed by party managers unavailable for a national campaign.

§

Surface indications afforded by party platforms, official orations, and statistics of presidential elections did not, however, accurately reveal the political state of the Union in detail. The people were not as contented with the operations of party captains as superficial appearances seemed to imply; nor was the triumph of the Republicans entirely unmixed with bitterness. It is true that they carried every presidential campaign in this period except two and, saving two brief interruptions, commanded a majority in the Senate continuously; but they were by no means fortunate in the popular congressional tourneys. In that sphere—the lower range of federal politics—they lost more elections than they won.

Between the restoration of the last southern state in 1870 and Bryan's first battle twenty-six years later, the Democrats triumphed in eight of the twelve contests for the possession of the House of Representatives. And through all those years the Republican directorate was made still more nervous by the agitations of recalcitrant members on the left wing of the party, especially by the spokesmen of the agrarian West where the original union of capitalism and agriculture effected in Chicago in 1860 was attacked, first by the Greenbackers and then by the Populists. In short, in the lower ranges of politics, nearest the electorate, the old currents of agrarian and labor unrest continued to run as before the Civil War, now sluggishly, now swiftly, with the ebb and flow of business prosperity.

Although that armed conflict and the prosperity associated with it in the North for a time obscured former economic antagonisms and silenced insurgency in many quarters, what seemed to be a political peace was after all only a partial truce. The philosophy and sentiments of Jackson's farmer-labor party never vanished completely and when, in the garnering of the war's aftermath, the high prices of agricultural produce collapsed—while the interest and principal of farm mortgages remained as before—and industrial workers were compelled to face severe wage reductions, historic schisms reappeared so plainly that all could see them. Everywhere among distressed farmers and suffering laborers in the cities, advocates of change and apostles of revolt once more raised their voices against the prevailing order of the rich, if not the well-born. In the councils of both established parties, in independent agitations, and especially in elections to the House of Representatives, where the popular influence more easily became effective, the spiritual descendants of humble Jacksonian leaders made their voices and their creeds count in the tussles of political life.

If most of the restless politicians who came to the front in this new age could find comfortable quarters and occasionally official berths in the left wing of an accredited party, there were always extreme innovators content with nothing less than a complete declaration of independence; and from 1872 forward at each successive presidential election one or two minor parties appeared: Labor Reformers in 1872; Greenbackers in 1876 and in the two following campaigns; United Laborites in 1888; and Socialists and Populists in 1892. In every case leaders of these factions made their appeal to farmers and laborers unhappy about their share in the annual output of wealth. Even the Prohibitionists, who in launching their national party in 1872 emphasized the abolition of the liquor traffic, made professions of faith on other matters and split temporarily over the currency question in 1896. But none of the minor parties ever succeeded in establishing a permanent organization among farmer-labor constituents. The Greenbackers whose vote in the congressional elections of 1878 rose to the million mark and the Populists who fourteen years later cast more than a million ballots for their presidential candidate were equally powerless to effect a revolution in the American two-party system.

Against all efforts of new factions to get a firm foothold on the political stage many forces operated. As such insurgents usually rose in periods of economic depression, so they were generally overwhelmed by returning tides of prosperity. Subsisting on temporary distress and having no spoils of political preferment on which to maintain a skeleton army of officers in lean years, their capacity to resist adversity was pitifully inadequate to the demands of party warfare. Often their most princely leaders fell under the lure of comfortable jobs in the departments at Washington; Terence V. Powderly, for example, head of the Knights of Labor and once the terror of respectables gathered over their tea cups, was at last brought into the fold and lived to a ripe old age on a government salary. Others, less prominent, were frequently accommodated in state and municipal offices.

This process of attrition was also hastened by concessions from one or both of the canonical parties. True to the traditions of Jackson, the Democrats always made special efforts, particularly in congressional elections, to win votes in farmer-labor circles, while stalwart Republicans were sometimes stained green or red according to the favorite color of the current independency. Blaine, for instance, was accused by righteous eastern papers of wanting to inflate the currency for the benefit of farmers and McKinley was an ardent bi-metallist in his early days. Nor were the oblations from regular shamans always perfunctory. From time to time significant pieces of legislation were granted at state capitals and grand overtures were made at Washington, for reasons patent and unavoidable. As a matter of fact, in a country so closely divided between Republicans and Democrats all political leaders had to walk warily; a few thousand, nay a few hundred, votes shifted here and there meant the gain or loss of the presidency with all the honors, profits, and emoluments thereunto attached. So the astute managers of independent fragments were occasionally able to wrest substantial discounts from the harassed and anxious directors of the main spectacles and, still more prophetically, to set the issues for the coming decades.

Whatever their fortunes as organizations or political traders, the third parties as a rule included in their professions of faith certain large assumptions and a number of concrete items. Orthodox rebellion always required from them of course a condemnation of both old parties. "We denounce," exclaimed the United Labor party in 1888, "the Democratic and Republican parties as hopelessly and shamelessly corrupt and by reason of their affiliation with monopolies equally unworthy of the suffrages of those who do not live upon public plunder." The Greenbackers broke a lance on the august Senate of the United States, declaring it to be composed "largely of aristocratic millionaires who according to their own party papers generally purchased their elections in order to protect the great monopolies which they represent."

While condemning the major parties and their practices, the sectaries advanced from time to time specific articles of salvation. Collectively their programs embraced standard elements: the earliest possible extinction of the national debt —that ancient bugbear of Jeffersonian Democracy; the abolition of the national banking system—after the fashion of Jacksonian Democracy; the substitution of notes issued by the government—awakening echoes as old as 1765; the unlimited coinage of silver as well as gold to enlarge the volume of currency—a new statement of the ancient plan for easy money; the reduction of the tariff particularly on articles bought by farmers—a return to the state of things on the eve of Lincoln's fateful election; the regulation of railway and other public utility rates by government action— a departure from Democratic *laissez faire* for obvious reasons; the recovery of public lands from railway and other corporations that had been negligent in observing the law— to be turned over free of charge to farmers and laborers; inheritance and income taxes tapping the wealth of those who had come to the top in the struggle for existence—lightening the taxes on goods consumed by the masses; the popular election of United States Senators with a view to changing the economic composition of that body; woman suffrage as an act of tardy justice in keeping with the national creed; the defense of labor against the use of the injunction and military force in time of industrial disputes; and certain pieces of social legislation, such as the prohibition of the contract labor system and the exclusion of Chinese coolies. To such professions of faith must be added of course the larger generalities of the Socialist Labor party which made its appearance on the national stage in 1892 with a declaration that "man cannot exercise his right of life, liberty and the pursuit of happiness without the ownership of the land and tools with which to work."

§

If these proposals, which seemed so revolutionary when first advanced in "thunders on the left," found little or no favor in the upper sphere of American politics during this period, if they were not approved by Presidents, Senators, or Federal Judges, they were none the less popular in the lower range, in congressional elections and legislative debates. In fact, the record of orations delivered in the House of Representatives shows a continuous division over economic issues along the lines of the cleavage which existed in Jackson's day, often without respect for the symbols of established parties.

In that "people's forum," under various guises, the old struggle of farmers and laborers to get a larger share of the golden stream which flowed from industry was waged with all the rancor that had marked the controversies in the middle period and the Hamiltonian age. It is true that the battles usually ended in smoke; the contest over the Mills tariff bill in 1888, for example, evoked a flood of speeches which if printed in full would occupy at least twenty massive volumes and yet modified not a line in the statutes; but it was the debate, not the lawbook, that revealed the prevailing tempers of the multitude.

If the English parliamentary system had been in vogue in the United States, the Democratic masses that dominated the House of Representatives for sixteen out of the twenty-four years between 1872 and 1896 would have ruled the upper works—the Senate, the President, and the Judiciary—as well as the chamber of loquacity and effected more than one radical change in the Jacksonian direction. Under the American system of checks and balances, however, they could do little more than elect spokesmen to give vent to their feelings on the tariff, trusts, railways, currency, and other economic issues involved in the distribution of the annual national income.

§

In these circumstances nothing disruptive could be done in the way of tariff reform. With the power of the federal government often divided between the two parties and with both organizations suffering from vexation on the wings, it was difficult to move the rates up or down. There were, to be sure, reductions in duties in 1872—quickly offset by increases—and there was another revision in 1883 when the Republicans, finding the treasury loaded with a surplus, decided to forestall action too sweeping on the part of the opposition. But Calhoun's historic doctrines had not a ghost of a show among the directors of the upper range of federal politics.

When the Democrats won the presidency and the House of Representatives in the election of 1884 and after long debates put a tariff-reduction bill through the lower chamber, their measure was promptly killed by the Republican majority in the Senate. Then emboldened by a swing of the political pendulum, the advocates of protection under the leadership of William McKinley tried an upward push. This new champion, as his biographer states, had become "the guardian angel, in the halls of Congress, of the industries of the country. . . . His father and grandfather were both manufacturers of iron, an industry which depended heavily upon the protective tariff," and his district was full of industries that "had been started under the fostering care of protective duties." Carefully engineered by the "guardian angel," the bill of 1890 bearing McKinley's name carried the rates to a point far above the Civil War tariffs.

Against what they were pleased to call the Republican levy on their toil, importing merchants, angry planters, and discontented farmers now made a great outcry and in the elections of 1892 the Democrats captured both the executive and legislative departments. On the assumption that they had at last a clear mandate from the country, their left wing leaders in the House of Representatives drove through a bill that frightened manufacturers more than any tariff measure since the crisis of 1857—a project putting sugar, lumber, coal, iron, and wool on the free list while subjecting the duties on cotton, woolens, and linen to severe cuts. Going still further, they imposed a tax on the incomes of the rich for the avowed purpose of easing the burdens of the masses. Amplifying the sentiments of their proposed statute, the Democrats, in supporting the measure, made speeches that sounded like echoes from the tomb of Calhoun.

Exultant over their victory, they laid the fruits of their labor before the Senate, transferring the business to the higher sphere of American politics. When the performance was concluded in that chamber, the result was a measure—the Wilson bill of 1894—that resembled the design of McKinley rather than the patterns of McDuffie and Walker. Completely disappointed with this outcome, President Cleveland, who had now advanced to the point of declaring that "a tariff for any other purpose than public revenue is public robbery," refused to sign the bill, allowing it to become a law without his approval. Soon afterward a congressional inquiry into the pressure of interests on specific schedules spread an unsavory odor over the whole affair, convincing the left-wing Democrats that a revolution would have to be accomplished in the upper realm by establishing the popular election of United States Senators. This revision of the work handed down by the Fathers was to be achieved in time.

If little could be done with the tariff by champions of reduction, still less could be accomplished in the enterprise of forcing down what the Populists called "the annual tribute levied by the trusts upon the people of the country." Although the directorates of both parties, in formulating national platforms, were either silent or inscrutable on the issues afforded by the new economic leviathans, the left-wing factions, true to form, were both vociferous and assertive. They filled acres of print with denunciations of corporate wealth and they offered a prescription which they deemed a remedy for the disease—the dissolution of all great industrial associations into competing parts, cutting prices for consumers.

In fact they were able to frighten the right wing into concessions with reference to this proposal and to force through Congress, in 1890, the Sherman Anti-Trust Act which, in impenetrable language, forbade all combinations in restraint of foreign and interstate trade. As a plain-spoken Senator from Connecticut remarked, no one knew what the bill would do to the trusts, but a majority agreed that something must be flung out to appease the restive masses.

In the general attack on corporate wealth which ran true to Jacksonian formulas, the managers and owners of railways came in for more than their share. They had made swollen fortunes in building, operating, and manipulating systems of transportation; they had granted rebates and privileges to favored persons and corporations; and they had fixed freight and passenger rates with an eye to large returns. By obvious methods of learning and reasoning, western farmers reached the opinion that the railway companies had received doles too generous from the government, had fallen into the hands of promoters bent on quick profits rather than efficiency, and were in fact heartless enterprises engaged in garnering "all the traffic would bear."

By the same logical route they arrived at the conviction that the shippers of grain were the chief tributaries to the strong boxes of the "railway magnates," especially in the West where "the long haul" was the significant feature of transportation.

From idea to action the road was not long. During the general upheaval of the seventies, farmers, already extensively organized in benevolent lodges known as Granges, managed to capture the legislatures of several states, notably Illinois, Wisconsin, and Iowa, in campaigns waged largely on railway issues. Once in possession of the local strongholds they enacted laws fixing rates for carrying freight and passengers and charges for warehousing grain, thus making known their determination to use political weapons in the contest over the distribution of wealth.

Immediately a shrill chorus of rage arose from the ranks of railway security holders. Speaking for their interest, the editor of the New York Nation, doubtless regarding rate regulation as an unforeseen tendency of democracy, declared such legislation to be in principle "confiscation, or, if another phrase be more agreeable, the change of railroads from pieces of private property, owned and managed for the benefit of those who have invested their money in them, into eleemosynary or charitable corporations, managed for the benefit of a particular class of applicants for outdoor relief —the farmers. If . . . we are going back to a condition of society in which the only sort of property which we can call our own is that which we can make our own by physical possession, it is certainly important to everyone to know it, and the only body which can really tell us is the Supreme Court at Washington."

For a time, that is, until competent adjustments could be made in the personnel of the judiciary, that eminent tribunal failed to make the expected answer. In fact in the first cases presented for hearing, it upheld the local rate legislation against the most vehement pleas of skilled railway lawyers. It refused, however, to sanction state laws hampering the course of interstate commerce, thereby forcing the farmers to carry their agitation to Washington.

At the national capital, as indeed in their own communities, the agrarians received aid and comfort from manufacturers and business men of the middling order who had suffered from rebates, secret rates, and other discriminations at the hands of the railway companies. In a grand rush this powerful economic combination carried through Congress the Interstate Commerce Act of 1887—a measure couched in uncertain terms which were soon hopelessly buried in the glosses of the Supreme Court and rendered practically innocuous to those who had invested their money in railways.

§

In this endless contest over the annual output that flowed from mill, mine, and farm, the battle over the currency loomed far larger than did the struggle over tariffs, trusts, or railways. This was entirely natural. From the uprising of Daniel Shays, indeed from colonial times to the latest hour, debt-burdened farmers with their eyes fixed on the volume of currency had sought to control it to their own advantage. If it was enlarged in generous proportions through the agency of a government in their hands, they could expect rising prices and the easy discharge of their obligations in interest and principal. About this reasoning there was no mystery.

On the other hand, capitalists who held mortgages and bonds drawing a fixed rate of interest were equally concerned over the amount and character of the money in circulation If the volume was restricted and the basis sound, they could count on receiving their interest and principal in dollars of the same purchasing power as those they had originally lent to their debtors. If, however, the volume was contracted or at all events not made adequate to the swelling currents of business, so the theory ran, prices would fall and the bondholder would reap the advantage of a return in dollars of a greater buying power than those originally lent. There was no mystery about this exploit in logic either.

So the one party held that the government itself should issue all money and make the volume generous, if not immense; only on mathematical measurements did the gentlemen of this school have differences of opinion. With kindred inferences the other party looked favorably upon a steady currency, or at least one not too expansive, and declared that the emission of paper notes should be confined principally to national banks for the benefit of those who invested their money in that form of business enterprise. Whatever the intrinsic merits of the respective arguments, it was made manifest that in the struggle over the distribution of wealth a considerable stream could be deflected one way or another through the use of the government's power over the issue of money.

Until the eve of the Second Revolution, as we have seen, the party of easy money, with varying fortunes, had waged a contest that was on the whole highly gratifying to its leaders. The national banking system had been destroyed a second time and state banks were issuing currency with a more than generous regard for the requirements of the occasion. Then in a moment victory was snatched from the agrarians and all aspects of public finance transformed. During the Civil War, as noted above, the Republicans in Congress wiped out state banks of issue by one stroke and established on their ruins a national banking system. At the same time, however, the exigencies of war, as often happens in such cataclysms, made it imperative for the national government itself—still compelled to be tender to agrarian interests—to float immense quantities of paper money, not founded on gold, known as "Greenbacks." Thus, in spite of protests from advocates of sound money, the currency was inflated, prices were enhanced, and the northern farmers could rejoice.

When the internecine struggle was over, however, grave questions arose as to the future of this paper money. Was it to be kept on its fiat basis, maintained in its existing volume or enlarged on the original principles? Was it to be ultimately cancelled or placed on a metallic basis? Naturally the agrarian section gave one answer; the investing section another, the latter with increasing influence in party councils. After a long and bitter struggle, Congress enacted in 1875 a law providing that, at the end of four years, the legal tender notes then outstanding should be redeemed in specie when presented to the treasury in sums of not less than fifty dollars. "Now we know," remarked a political wag, "that our redeemer liveth." The captains of business enterprises and the financiers heaved a sigh of relief. "By five o'clock," noted the Secretary of the Treasury on the day when resumption began, "the news was all over the land and the New York bankers were sipping their tea in absolute safety."

This news about the bankers happy at tea was by no means pleasing to the debt-burdened farmers who saw in resumption an act that forced them to yield a larger share of produce in paying each coupon due on their mortgages. With no little heat, therefore, they refused to accept the verdict as final and cast about for another method of attaining their ends. Fortunately for them there was upon the carpet at that very moment a second phase of the same issue, namely, the free coinage of silver into dollars.

In this matter also, legal as well as economic points were involved, for the Constitution gave Congress power to coin money and evidently contemplated the use of gold and silver. On this theory Congress had operated for many years without ever being able to get into the gold and silver coins the exact proportion of precious metal necessary to keep them circulating equally. If the gold in a gold dollar exceeded in market value the silver in a silver dollar, the former was hoarded and the latter alone used in business. If the balance tipped the other way, silver went into hiding and gold held the field. Frustrated by this problem in higher accountancy after more than one attempt to reach a precise poise, Congress stopped the coinage of the standard silver dollar altogether in 1873, just as new mines were being discovered in the West and the volume of the world's silver was rising to an unprecedented level. For one reason or another the price of the precious white metal was now borne steadily downward until by 1890 silver was worth in gold only about half the price it commanded twenty years before.

This course of events led the advocates of easy money, defeated on the resumption issue, to begin a desperate fight to restore the silver dollar by compelling the federal government to adopt the free and unlimited coinage of silver at its old ratio to gold, sixteen to one, the proportion in force when the so-called "crime of '73" was committed. In making their demand, they denied that there had been an actual decline in the value of silver and alleged that in reality gold had risen because it had been given a monopoly in the mints of all the leading governments of the world.

Applying the argument, they contended that the contraction of the currency—the elimination of silver and the adoption of specie payments for Greenbacks—had in effect lowered the price received for all products of labor and in that way had increased the real income of all who held mortgages, bonds, and other investments yielding a fixed return. With persistent reiteration they pointed out that the holder of such securities had been able to buy less than half a bushel of wheat in 1865 with each dollar of interest received and then, in the course of years, without any labor on his part, had seen his coupon dollar rise to the purchasing power of more than a bushel. In the meantime intense business depressions had added to the misery of the farmers during those troubled decades and when the crisis of 1893 arrived, their desperation, especially in the heavily mortgaged sections of the West and South, reached the breaking point.

A matter of such acute economic strife inevitably became a prime issue in the political arena, raising up advocates of free silver in the councils of both parties, especially in the left wings. Naturally most of them came from the West and South—from agrarian districts far removed from the seats of the mighty; but even in the East some of the political observers thought they saw a certain justice in the plaintive argument of the farmer. Blaine, with the presidential aspirant's feeling for the temper of the West, once declared that the single gold standard would be ruinous for all forms of property except investments yielding a fixed return, and McKinley, who was later to march to battle for gold, clad in righteousness, was a bi-metallist until he was shown the rescript of those who directed his party. In fact, there was no lack of moderate men who believed that the gold standard was too narrow, tending to enrich the rich while bringing adversity to debtors of every class.

By 1878 those who held this view had become so numerous that the silver faction mustered a majority in the House of Representatives and, notwithstanding obstacles put in its way by a Republican Senate, carried a bill providing for a huge monthly purchase of silver to be coined into standard dollars and given a legal tender quality, even though lower than gold in value. Amplifying this measure, the same faction later enacted additional legislation requiring the Secretary of the Treasury to purchase a certain amount of silver monthly for coinage and issue for it notes redeemable in either metal at his discretion. But in spite of these half-hearted efforts to placate the agrarian faction, silver with some fluctuations continued its downward course, or to use the language of the bi-metallists, "gold went soaring to the sky," making the circulation of the two metals on a parity increasingly difficult.

Opposed to inflation in any form, President Cleveland hastened the oncoming crisis by insisting, during his second administration, on the redemption of silver notes, as well as all other paper, in gold, though not legally required to do so, making it impossible to keep an adequate gold reserve in the federal treasury. Then powerless to stem the current which he had himself helped to set in motion, Cleveland adopted the policy of selling interest-bearing bonds for the purpose of bringing gold to the reserve; only to see the precious metal brought in by bond sales immediately withdrawn by bankers in exchange for notes, creating a vicious circle. In the language of the silver orators, the President of the United States was as clay in the hands of New York bankers directed by J. P. Morgan; in the language of reputable economics both the politician and the financier bowed to natural laws.

This spectacle aroused deep interest in Congress. The populist faction demanded that, at least, the bond sales should be thrown open to the general public instead of being negotiated behind closed doors with the gentlemen of high finance—a petition which was granted, after considerable uproar, and with decided advantage to the government. Encouraged by this concession, the radicals then went on to urge that the existing law providing for the redemption of notes in either gold or silver be enforced and that the two metals be freely coined at the old ratio of sixteen to one, notwithstanding the disparity in their market price. To this extreme proposal, the conservatives replied by calling for the total repeal of the silver purchase acts and by condemning free silver as a form of confiscation made at the expense of bondholders and creditors in general. Beset on both sides by determined sectaries and forced to make a choice, Cleveland threw in his lot with the party of "sound money." And supported by right-wing Republicans, he induced Congress to erase from the statute books the troublesome provisions for the purchase of silver, bringing to a sudden end the business of selling bonds to get gold.

For this action, Cleveland was immediately denounced by partisans of the left wing as a traitor to the Democracy, a supine servant of high finance, the storm of criticism raging with increasing force when it became perfectly clear that the repeal of the silver clauses would bring no permanent relief to the panic-stricken country. In fact with the passing months, the intensity of the business depression deepened

and the falling prices of farm produce or, as the radicals contended, the rising value of gold coupons heaped still greater
treasure in the chests of creditors.   All over the South and
West where the sound of the sheriff's hammer was heard
thumping off the sale of farms and stock to meet mortgages
foreclosed, farmers' families, driven from their homesteads,
piled maledictions on the heads of those who sat comfortably veiled at the feast.   The flame of popular wrath licked
the very doors of Congress.

§

Meanwhile in the dreary wastes of the industrial cities
another cyclical paralysis was sending regiments of men and
women into the streets unemployed and embittered, adding
the discontent of the working classes to the unrest of debtor
farmers.   Falling wages exasperated labor and this in turn
involved Cleveland's administration.   The Pullman strike,
we have seen, culminated in the dispatch of federal troops to
Chicago by the President, armed intervention in the contest,
and the imprisonment of the trade union leader, Eugene V.
Debs, for disobeying a blanket injunction issued by a district
judge.   In vain did Debs invoke the Constitution and the
right of trial by jury.   The Supreme Court at Washington
answered his appeal by declaring that in injunction cases a
federal judge could issue orders, command the arrest of
offenders, try without jury, and sentence to prison at
pleasure; drawing down upon that puissant tribunal the
wrath of organized labor.

During the very same year, the protection of the same
Constitution was invoked by gentlemen in high places who
objected to paying the new federal income tax laid upon
them by Democrats and Populists in 1894.   On their behalf,
the Hon. Joseph H. Choate, who had recently steered John
D. Rockefeller through the sinuosities of legislative inquiries, was employed to defend the rights of those who
received large portions in the annual distribution of national
wealth.   In an eloquent plea the advocate warned the judges

that it was "now or never"; that the "communist march" must be stopped; that property demanded immediate and unconditional security in its rights. After some vacillation a majority of the Court came to agree with the eminent counsel and, looking into the sacred letter, found indisputable justification for blocking the communist march. "The present assault upon capital," said Justice Field in his opinion, "is but the beginning," such a fearful beginning that, in his judgment, it promised the arrival of a terrible day on which boards of walking delegates would be fixing taxes for the rich. The very thought was shocking to the judicial conscience and five of the judges united on rulings that substantially destroyed the income tax law.

A pæan of approval greeted their solemn determination —at least in certain quarters. "The wave of the socialist revolution had gone far," exclaimed the editor of the New York Sun, "but it breaks at the foot of the ultimate bulwark set up for the protection of our liberties. Five to four the Court stands like a rock." If the figure of speech was somewhat awry, the news was good. Equally jubilant, the editor of the Tribune saw, in "the influence behind this attempt to bring about a communistic revolution in modes of taxation," an un-American and unpatriotic effort to destroy domestic industries in the interest of foreigners—foreshadowing the day when the responsibility for such untoward incidents could be ascribed to the Russian Bolsheviks. "Thanks to the Court," the editor gravely continued, "our government is not to be dragged into a communistic warfare against the rights of property and the rewards of industry." In this light the incident gleamed from one angle.

But there was dissent. Four judges out of nine, looking just as carefully into the Constitution, failed to discover there the general justification so clearly visible to the majority of their brethren. One of the doubters, Justice Harlan, was venturous enough to remark that the decision was without warrant and calculated to give to "aggregated wealth" a position of favoritism as objectionable as the dominion of the lawless. And the populistic press, supported by some metropolitan journals, including the New York World, flayed the majority of the Court in language that seemed horrible to those who had so recently received the benefits of its thoughtful protection—to say nothing of the old Republicans who but dimly remembered what they had said forty years before when the same Court had rendered the Dred Scott decision so pleasing to the slavocracy. In the West, Governor John P. Altgeld, in keeping with his principles, declared in so many words that the income tax judgment was on all fours with the Dred Scott opinion and that the Supreme Court and the other branches of the federal government were dominated by capitalists in 1895 just as they had been by slave owners before the revolution of 1861.

§

That a great campaign of education or a foreign war, or both, were required to allay the distemper of the time was now apparent to persons of conservative inclination. The Populists had polled more than a million votes four years before and were making impressive gains among the masses of the Democratic party, disclosing an unflagging discontent with the empire of business enterprise which promised embarrassments for those at the center of things. Forewarned by flashes on the horizon, the directors of the Republican party made ready for the domestic fray by choosing the gold issue as the central theme and the protection of industries and the Constitution as the other grand object of desire.

At this juncture Marcus A. Hanna, a retired business man, weary of the routine of the counting house and enamored of Warwick's rôle, entered the lists in full panoply. By a liberal expenditure of money, judicious publicity, and an early management of Negro politicians from the South, he made William McKinley the man of the hour. On the otherwise stainless shield of his hero there was only one fleck: McKinley had voted in Congress for the free coinage of silver and was widely known as a bi-metallist. But by prudent negotiation that conviction was overcome, and McKinley was nominated as the Republican candidate for the presidency on a platform favoring the gold standard and opposing the free coinage of silver except by international agreement. With the gravity that was his wont McKinley now appealed to the country to support him as the foe of the whole populist program—"that sudden, dangerous, and revolutionary assault upon law and order."

When the Democratic convention met in Chicago the nerves of the politicians in attendance were taut with excitement. For months the agrarian radicals of the West and South had been seeking delegates of their own kind and their labors had been crowned with success. Even the opening prayer of the vast assembly vibrated with "sympathy for our toiling multitudes, oppressed with burdens too heavy for them to bear." Every roll call, every vote revealed a triumphant majority for the left wing.

In vain did the faithful old guard on the right seek to stem the tide. David B. Hill of New York, whom the cartoonists loved to picture with a feather in his hat, labelled "I am a Democrat," marched into the arena, looking more like Robert G. Ingersoll's plumed knight than Blaine ever did, and with fitting eloquence stormed against free silver, income taxes, and criticism of the Supreme Court. Senator Vilas of Wisconsin stretched the tension almost to the breaking-point when he hinted at a possible repetition of the atrocities which had stained the French Revolution and with dark solemnity warned the convention that "in the vastness of this country there may be some Marat unknown, some Danton or Robespierre." But the gentlemen of the right addressed ears that were deaf, appealed to hearts that were as flint.

The climax came when William Jennings Bryan, "that Tiberius Gracchus of the West," as he was called, flung the gage full and fair in the face of the enemy, naming defiantly those for whom he spoke—the wage laborer, the country lawyer, the cross-roads merchant, the farmer, and the miner—Andrew Jackson's farmer-labor cohorts—and summoning them with the zeal of Peter the Hermit to the silver standard, that waved above his head, in a fateful battle against the plutocracy. "It is for these that we speak," he said. "We do not come as aggressors. Ours is not a war of conquest. We are fighting in defense of our homes, our families and our posterity. We have petitioned and our petitions have been scorned. We have entreated and our entreaties have been disregarded. We have begged and they have mocked when our calamity came. We beg no longer; we entreat no more; we petition no more. We defy them. . . . We shall answer their demands for a gold standard by saying to them: You shall not press down upon the brow of labor this crown of thorns. You shall not crucify mankind upon a cross of gold."

Almost by acclamation Bryan was declared the nominee of the Democratic party. Cleveland was repudiated with contemptuous scorn; free silver was endorsed; injunctions in labor disputes were assailed; jury trial in such cases was demanded; and the Supreme Court was criticized for its income tax decision in language as shocking to the new guardians of the sacred covenant as that employed by Republicans in the Dred Scott affair had once been to leaders of the Democracy.

With the opposing forces sharply aligned, the great battle of 1896 was on. In due time, not far away, the country was to see a progressive income tax laid, bank notes issued on the basis of something even less material than silver, an inflation worse than that threatened by a fifty-cent dollar, a reform in the use of injunctions approved in high places, and innovations still more significant than the belligerent Democrats under Bryan's banner had yet imagined; but in the summer of 1896 all that lay beyond the sealed portals of the unknown. Now the roll of martial drums called the country to take part in the most clearly defined struggle of economic groups since the first campaign of Lincoln.

Conscious of the real gravity of his task, Hanna, the director of Republican headquarters, as his biographer remarked, "hit the high places" in America's Via Appia, levied staggering assessments on those who feasted at the national banquet, and organized such a campaign of education, information, and effective influence as the American populace had never witnessed in all its history. Inflamed by a spirit almost as revolutionary in its intensity, Democrats on their side collected funds from the owners of silver mines and small contributions from the rank and file, and waged open and deadly war on the "plutocracy."

The rhetoric of the campaign was that of the battlefield, the pirate ship, and the cave of forty thieves. Democratic orators fumed against "English toadies and the pampered minions of corporate rapacity—the divinity of pelf." Republicans answered in kind. The editor of the New York Tribune found the inspiration of the Bryan faction in "the basest passions of the least worthy members of the community. . . . Its nominal head was worthy of the cause. Nominal because the wretched rattle-pated boy, posing in vapid vanity and mouthing resounding rottenness, was not the real leader of that league of hell. He was only a puppet in the blood-imbued hands of Altgeld, the anarchist, and Debs, the revolutionist, and other desperadoes of that stripe. But he was a willing puppet, Bryan was—willing and eager. None of his masters was more apt than he at lies and forgeries and blasphemies and all the nameless iniquities of that campaign against the Ten Commandments."

Since this was the language of cultivated and educated gentlemen, the argument of the street must be left to the imagination. Of course the magnificent passions of the occasion were sometimes refined, tempered, and clothed in economics and statistics; but on the whole the battle was waged without mercy to the bitter end. When the votes were counted, it was found that a solid East and Middle West had overwhelmed Bryan, giving McKinley a plurality of more than half a million. The campaign of education had succeeded beyond all calculations—and there was soon to be a foreign war to clinch the results.

§

The age of negation was drawing to a close. There had been seven presidential campaigns since Grant's election in 1868 and fourteen congressional campaigns. Yet when the outcome and aftermath were reckoned in terms of achievement written in the statute books, the results seemed meager in comparison with the efforts. All in all, between 1865 and 1897, there were put upon the federal law books not more than two or three acts which need long detain the citizen concerned only with those manifestations of political power that produce essential readjustments in human relations.

There were, it must be conceded, many laws pertaining to reconstruction in the South but most of these were either temporary in character or were quickly riddled by decisions of the Supreme Court and by illegal actions of white men resolved to be masters of the scene once more. In the realm of positive legislation the civil service act of 1883 imposed restraints upon the President's power over patronage so limited in scope that with the multiplication of federal functions the actual number of desirable plums for deserving partisans did not materially diminish. The interstate commerce act of 1887, hailed as a triumph of society over one branch of business enterprise, was cautiously administered by the executive department and adroitly interpreted by the Supreme Court; at the end of twenty years the act was hardly more than a scarecrow. On the open confession of those who passed it, the Sherman anti-trust law, signed in 1890, was nebulous in meaning and for ten years practically nothing worthy of note was done under its prohibitions. The income tax law of 1894, imposing tribute on accumulated wealth, as already noted, was quickly struck down by the Supreme Court, standing "like a rock, five to four." If, as an apparent offset, farmers snatched a few favors in the silver purchase acts, they soon lost them all by defiant repeal. Labor received some crumbs from the table in the measures excluding Chinese coolies and prohibiting the entrance of European workmen under contract but through the wide gates of the eastern ports swift-steaming ships poured a swelling stream of unindentured labor from every part of the Old World—a stream more than sufficient to meet every need of business enterprise.

In every respect, therefore, the essential achievements of the Second American Revolution remained secure after the lapse of thirty years. On no front had there been a dangerous reaction; the tariff, the banking system, the currency sustained by the specie resumption act of 1875, and the accepted methods for disposing of the public domain stood unshaken by all the storms. Nowhere in the realm of practical politics did the philosophy and practice briefly characterized as Darwinism encounter any formidable doubters. And soon the gold standard law of 1900 was to lay the specter of Bryanism.

In this flow of things, even refractory state legislatures and city councils in the far corners of the provinces—likely to be the seats of agrarian and labor troubles—were subdued to the doctrines of use and wont prevailing in higher places, through the progressive development of the Fourteenth Amendment in the hands of the Supreme Court. When the power of local authorities to regulate the rates of railways and grain warehouses had been impugned before that high tribunal in 1876, in the famous Granger cases, a majority of the judges, whose memories yet ran back to the days of the stagecoach, upheld the sovereignty of the state, in an opinion containing the ominous line: "For protection against abuses by legislatures, the people must resort to the polls, not the courts."

Profoundly perturbed, but determined not to be thwarted

by any such ratiocination, utility corporations kept up the fight, allowing scarcely a year to pass without raising a new issue involving the right of state and municipal governments to regulate their rates and services. In learned briefs and prolix arguments, counsel for these harassed concerns warned the Supreme Court with emphatic repetition against the oncoming hosts of communism and anarchy—sending through American jurisprudence echoes of the Paris Commune of 1871—and demanded that the Court stem the tide by assuming the function of passing upon the reasonableness of all menacing legislation.

Time flowed irresistibly on. Judges died. New appointments were discreetly made by the President and Senate. The law grew. At length the great goal was reached in 1889 when a railway company called upon the federal Supreme Court to annul an act of the Minnesota legislature authorizing a state commission to fix freight and passenger rates—and received from the judges an answer in words that admitted no doubt: the question of the reasonableness of rates is ultimately a judicial question requiring for its determination due process of law and due respect for the rights of property guaranteed by the Fourteenth Amendment.

Thereafter the validity and effect of the acts of all state and local governments, even village councils, touching the earning powers of business enterprise, might be determined finally, not at the polls, but in the council chamber of the august Supreme Court composed of judges appointed by the President and Senate and serving for life. Unlike the statesmen of the forum, these remote authorities spoke not as men but as justices, not their will but a higher will, not the language of the street and shop but the austere tongue of juristic technology. The age of miracles had not come to an end. Indeed all things seemed possible now that jurisprudence was brought into line with the political economy of giant industry.

CHAPTER XXIV
More Worlds to Conquer

THE renewal of the Hamilton-Webster system in the field of domestic affairs after 1861—protective tariffs, sound currency, centralized banking, and federal benevolence for business enterprise—brought with it a resumption of the old solicitude for the promotion of foreign commerce. If planters had lost their lust for new soil with the forfeiture of their slaves, manufacturers and merchants still had an appetite for new markets beyond the seas and officers of the Navy were as eager as ever to sail to fame and power in the wake of Commodore Perry. Even during the engrossing struggle of the Civil War itself, as we have said, the Republican administration did not overlook its obligations abroad to its constituents at home. The Pacific railway which opened a quick route through California to the "Gold of Ophir" and the coercive policy of Seward which raised American naval prestige in the Far East foretold greater events to come. And as industry advanced with lightning rapidity after Appomattox, as the domestic market was saturated and capital heaped up for investment, the pressure for the expansion of the American commercial empire rose with corresponding speed. Irresistible forces were mobilizing; the parallax of economic realities was becoming clear to adepts at the center of things.

Fortunately for them, the President, as manager of foreign relations and head of the Navy Department, had a fairly free hand in caring for business interests abroad—especially in distant and backward countries. Only in case he had to call upon the Senate to ratify a treaty or the House for a vote of money in aid of his efforts did he arouse any popular hostility to interfere with the onward sweep. From the election of Lincoln to the triumph of McKinley, the process had moved forward.

§

On the very day that Seward took office in 1861 he faced a crisis in the affairs of Mexico—a crisis created by the effort of Napoleon III to reap advantage from a civil conflict which had been raging in that unhappy country for more than ten years. Although superficially the new contest, like all previous revolutions in Mexico, seemed to be a war between kites and crows, it really bore a striking resemblance in several respects to the social upheavals which had racked Europe for centuries.

It was in essence an economic struggle between great land owners who possessed the soil and servile peons who tilled it—an antagonism of classes sharpened by distinctions of race, the masters of the country being mainly of Spanish origin and endowed with the fierce spirit of the old war lord, whereas the serfs were Indians in blood and subdued to bondage by force of arms. As in Europe during the middle ages, the clergy in Mexico were large owners of estates, drew princely revenues from the labor of the peons in their fields, and like their brethren of medieval times, added to their incomes by fees of many kinds and earnings from the administration of ecclesiastical courts in which important cases were tried. Affiliated with the lay and clerical landlords was a substantial body of military men pledged to uphold the ancient heritage; and between the upper strata and the lower orders stood a middle class of merchants and professional men—a class too large to be completely ignored but too small to make a successful revolution akin to the conquest of power effected by the bourgeois of France in the eighteenth century.

As in Europe, the conflict in Mexico lay, in the main, between the serfs and the middle class on the one hand and landlords, lay and clerical, supported by the soldiers, on the other. In general too it ran true to historic forms. The peons and the intelligentsia in assailing the privileges of the landed proprietors resorted to the economic and legal devices of liberalism. According to their program, the Church was to be stripped of its estates, the feudal domains dissolved into small holdings, serfdom abolished, church courts suppressed, and the power of the monastic orders broken. For autocratic rule the liberals proposed to substitute trial by jury, religious toleration, freedom of the press, popular education, and democratic government. On the other side the lay and clerical landlords, in defending their economic rights, proclaimed themselves the protectors of religion, morality, the home, and legitimacy. In its constitutional aspects the struggle took the guise of a contest over federalism and centralization. The feudal party— landowners, clergy, and military men—championed the idea of a powerful government at Mexico City; the liberal element, finding itself dominant in some of the states, laid stress on the doctrine of local autonomy. Both parties were pacific or revolutionary according to the safety or jeopardy of their respective interests.

Just previous to the opening of the Civil War in the United States the struggle of these forces for supremacy in Mexico was especially keen. It broke out in open violence with the overthrow of the liberal government which had been set up under American auspices at the close of the war over Texas and California. And it ran through alternating revolution and reaction until brought to a temporary close with the triumph of the popular faction under the leadership of Benito Juarez, a Zapotec Indian of remarkable talent and courage. Ecclesiastical courts were suppressed, the Church ordered to sell its estates in small lots to tenants, and the liberal constitution of 1857 put into effect. Now in their turn the conservatives took up arms against law and order, making Mexico the scene of a ghastly racial, economic, and religious war, until the party of Juarez, driven to desperation, overcame the reactionaries by a Herculean rally.

With its finances thrown into disorder by this struggle, the Mexican government felt compelled in 1861 to defer for two years the interest on its external debt, much to the irritation of European investors. England, France, and Spain were especially aggrieved; for their citizens, besides holding defaulted bonds, alleged that the Mexican government owed them enormous sums on account of property destroyed, relatives killed or injured, and private debts suspended. As usual, these demands were inflated, but Mexico was not strong enough to scale them down; so Juarez was compelled to approve British bills to the amount of $69,900,000 and Spanish claims computed at $9,400,000— exactions flagrant enough to make Captain Kidd weep with envy.

Still more unsavory were the French pretensions; if there had been any humor in international finance, many of their pleas would have been laughed out of court, especially a case hatched up by a Swiss adventurer, named J. B. Jecker. This stormy petrel of speculation, in 1859, negotiated a loan with Mexico to the amount of $15,000,000; bonds bearing the face value of $16,800,000 were issued and $1,470,000 was paid into the Mexican treasury. Thereupon Jecker went into bankruptcy, became a French citizen by connivance, and called upon the government of France to help collect the face of the loan. Sensitive to the tones of the Bourse, Napoleon III supported Jecker's demands and finally broke off diplomatic relations with Mexico when Juarez refused to acknowledge any indebtedness in excess of the sum actually received on the bonds.

No doubt all the powers engaged in pressing claims on Mexico had legitimate grievances but other motives also influenced the conduct of the governments at Madrid and Paris. The Spanish monarch, besides being interested in a return of the clergy to their former high estate, cherished a vague hope that a reunion with Mexico might be some day effected. Far more ambitious and definite were the designs of Napoleon III. Having just got his crown through a coup d'état, he felt obliged to amuse his subjects by a vigorous foreign policy and remembering the adage of his illustrious uncle to the effect that France loved glory, he sought the bauble for her first in one place and then in another until he met his fate at Sedan. In the course of his checkered career, Napoleon conceived the idea of establishing a great power in Mexico under his patronage to offset the strength of the United States and add to the prestige of his family.

Without making all his motives clear at first, Napoleon associated himself in 1861 with England and Spain in an armed demonstration against Mexico, ostensibly to collect debts. When his partners in this undertaking discovered that they could get nothing out of it and withdrew entirely from the business, he cast off all disguise. The very stars seemed to be marshalled on his side. He was relieved of embarrassing friends; the United States appeared to be on the verge of dissolution; and the mastery of the New World might easily fall to his hands. It was a glorious dream.

After pressing upon the Juarez government demands which were wholly indefensible, including the notorious Jecker claim, Napoleon ordered his troops to start the march on the Mexican capital. Though the task proved surprisingly difficult and costly, his commanders cut their way to Mexico City in the spring of 1863, summoned a council of conservatives, and issued a proclamation calling for the establishment of a Catholic empire in Mexico. An "assembly of notables," hastily collected, then formally invited Maximilian, a brother of Francis Joseph, emperor of Austria, to assume the crown; and the sovereign-elect, aided by Napoleon and accompanied by his young wife, Carlotta, landed in Mexico hoping for a magnificent ovation.

Scarcely had he reached his new capital when the glorious dream exploded. Instead of a united nation waiting to cheer his imperial eagles and rally about his throne, he found a divided and sullen country, torn by factional quarrels, monarchists more interested in recovering property lost in the recent revolutions than in building his house upon a rock and republicans already under arms in the field. Trying the wiles of conciliation in vain, Maximilian finally surrendered control to the conservative party and ordered rebels caught with weapons shot on sight—a fatal policy that made still more precarious his dubious title. Nothing but French arms sustained his shadow authority while events inexorably paved the way for his tragic end.

From the very beginning of this episode the government of the United States had watched the trend in Mexican affairs with anxiety. At first it could do little more than deplore and regret the course of Napoleon for it was itself engaged in a life and death struggle, but, as the fate of the Union unrolled, it spoke with increasing assurance. After the battle of Gettysburg, it addressed a curt note to the French emperor and, receiving in reply an invitation to recognize his puppet at Chapultepec, it squared away for action. In 1864, Congress by solemn resolution declared that "it does not accord with the policy of the United States to acknowledge any monarchical government erected on the ruins of any republican government in America under the auspices of any European power."

The next year, after Grant's triumph over Lee, the federal government, having concentrated troops on the Mexican border, politely but pointedly called on Napoleon to withdraw his soldiers from the western hemisphere. In making this request, the State Department did not rest its case on the moral mandates of the Monroe Doctrine; it simply informed the emperor of the French that any attempt of a foreign power to erect a monarchy in Mexico was a menace to the people of the United States and it stood ready to say so with guns if necessary. Thus halted in his imperial game, the emperor of the French had to beat a retreat with as much grace as possible. As soon as the last French regiment withdrew from Mexican soil in 1867, the republicans in the capital seized the reins of power, captured Maximilian, tried him by court martial, and executed him. Carlotta, who had shared in his adventure and had outshone him in the arts of negotiation, lived on in Europe for more than half a century, insane from grief over the scenes of the Mexican tragedy.

§

While removing the foreign menace from Mexico, Secretary Seward was revolving in his mind a project for acquiring Alaska from Russia. He had long believed that this territory was necessary to the extension of the American empire in the Pacific and he was afraid that it would, if neglected by the United States, fall into the possession of England. Happily for Seward's purposes, the owner of the coveted domain, the Tsar, occupied at the moment with a Slavic drive to the south which might bring him again into collision with the Mistress of the Seas, was also thinking of the possible loss of Alaska, and on due consideration he authorized his minister in Washington to negotiate the sale. On an evening in March, 1867, when Seward was playing whist in his home, the Russian official called to announce this news and to suggest the completion of the transaction on the following day. "Why wait till tomorrow, Mr. Stoeckl? Let us make the treaty to-night," said the American Secretary with alacrity; and sometime before dawn the document was completed and signed.

This preliminary out of the way, the next thing was to win the approval of the Senate and induce the House of Representatives to appropriate $7,200,000 to pay the bill of purchase. Without difficulty the upper chamber was managed but certain members of the lower house saw only foolish extravagance in the purchase of "a vast area of rocks and ice" at a time when the country was groaning under an immense war debt and still had millions of acres of undeveloped land in the West. Only by skillful negotiation sweetened by bribery was the money wrung from the national legislature and the treaty of transfer duly executed, adding to the American estate an area twice the size of Texas. Thus Seward, who had in 1860 forecast the march of events, beheld within seven years the realization of his plan for carrying the flag to the Arctic and pushing American dominion along the outlying islands up to the very gates of the Orient.

With equal zest Seward labored to fulfill his dream of expansion in tropical waters. Through the good offices of the Navy Department he negotiated a treaty for the acquisition of Samana Bay in Santo Domingo, another for the purchase of the Virgin Islands from Denmark, and a third assuring American control over the Isthmus of Panama; but the Senate, to his chagrin, refused to approve his agreements and the House of Representatives expressed its unwillingness to appropriate money for such undertakings. So Seward passed out of the State Department with his structure of empire commenced but unfinished. The southern planters, now that slavery was gone, had lost their fervor for expansion in Latin-America, and it required more time to educate the left wing of the Republican party to the imperialist view.

Unabashed by this setback, President Grant, coming to office in 1869, decided to see what he could do in imperial matters. Indifferent to Seward's defeat, the Navy Department had again asked for a base at Samana and local circumstances seemed to be more favorable to the consummation of the project. At this moment the little republic of Santo Domingo was suffering from one of the periodical revolutions that had long vexed it; and taking advantage of the occasion, President Grant sent down a personal agent to sound the ground. Just what happened is not clear but when the curtain was raised this unofficial assistant emerged with a treaty providing for the annexation of Santo Domingo to the United States. It had been negotiated, it was explained, with a gentleman who bore for the time being the title of President of the Republic of Santo Domingo. Duly signed and sealed, the document was sent to the Senate with Grant's cordial approval.

To the amazement of its sponsors, the air of Washington was soon made heavy with charges and counter-charges. In the heat of the argument, it was alleged that the Dominican president who had signed the treaty was only a puppet held in office by American naval power and that at the bottom of the transaction lay nothing but naked aggression at the expense of a weak and helpless country. Though able replies were made on the other side insisting on the formal correctness of the procedure, the scheme for annexation was rejected by the Senate, amid much uproar.

Still convinced that his policy was sound, Grant continued until the end of his second administration to urge on his party expansion in the Caribbean. In his last regular message to Congress in 1876, he lamented the interference of the Senate with his designs on Santo Domingo and said that, had his first stroke of policy been approved, "the soil would soon have fallen into the hands of the United States capitalists." That was frank, to say the least, but the country at large was unresponsive and the United States capitalists for the moment had many other places for the profitable investment of their surplus.

§

Not in the least discouraged by the defeat of his Caribbean policy, President Grant turned his imperial glance upon the fair lands of Samoa, a tiny archipelago in the southern Pacific on the route from Honolulu to Australia. Those distant principalities, inhabited by untutored tribes, had been made known to America long before by merchants, missionaries, and whalers from New England; and in 1872, the year of Grant's second election, as if by accident, Admiral Meade of the United States Navy, while cruising in the South Seas, discovered a strategic center for sea power in the island of Tutuila. Without difficulty the enterprising officer secured from a native prince a treaty granting the United States a naval base at Pago Pago.

When the Senate at Washington, failing to appreciate the delicate diplomatic action, ignored the document, President Grant, pressed by "certain highly respectable persons," sent out a confidential agent, Col. A. B. Steinberger, a Quixotic gentleman with a past, to investigate the Samoan problem on the spot. With Gilbertian humor the redoubtable Colonel fomented a revolution upon his arrival, made himself prime minister, and placed the islands under American protection. When, once more, the Senate turned a cold shoulder on a tiny bit of humanity laid at its doorstep, a second uprising followed in Samoa, the American flag was boldly hoisted above the official thatch in the native "capital," and a high chief, Mamea, moved by some mysterious impulse, made a tedious and expensive journey to the banks of the Potomac. By princely artifices, accompanied by local aid, he at last obtained in 1878 a treaty which, among other things, ceded a part of his country to the Great White Father.

Before many moons had passed, troubles appeared in the offing. The Germans in Samoa, already enjoying the lion's share of the local trade and industry, redoubled their efforts to extend the blessing of Teutonic culture to the entire collection of islands, while their competitors, the English, ever mindful of business opportunities, likewise started a feverish expansion of their economic operations. In the meantime, the natives commenced to quarrel over the pretensions of rival princes who had been aroused, abetted, and supplied with ammunition by their foreign friends.

For ten years mighty disputes and petty wars were waged over the "royal claims" of half-naked aborigines, over consular jurisdiction, and over such issues as the theft of some pigs belonging to an American half-caste known in the records by the name of Scanlon. During these lordly disputes, the Germans favored "King Tamasese" and the English, supported by the Americans, bolstered up "King Mataafa." There were protests and counter-protests; flags were hauled up and pulled down; national honors were insulted and apologies were demanded. Eventually things came to such a pass that the three great powers involved—the United States, England, and Germany—decided to bring their armed might to bear upon the tempest in the Samoan teapot. Their battleships were riding sullenly in the chief harbor of the islands and the air was tense with bad temper when an awful hurricane burst upon them like the wrath of God, destroying every vessel save one lone English steamer that managed to escape to the wide sea. After this calamity, the three governments concerned agreed to a truce and in 1889 arranged for a tripartite protectorate over the Samoan group.

If the high contracting parties hoped to establish peace in Samoa by this agreement, they were quickly disillusioned. The native king whom they made secure in his hut, far from being content with his estate, was highly incensed by the budget plan which allotted him an income of ninety-five dollars a month while assigning six times as much to a Swede employed under Christian auspices to administer justice in the kingdom. Local chieftains, excluded from the throne by the settlement, were still more unhappy. Though the revenue of the crown was small, they coveted the treasury as well as the title and they tried again and again, with the aid of alien adventurers, to wrest the tinsel throne from its lawful owner by armed revolts. In the fighting that accompanied their efforts, cruel deeds were committed by the white soldiers employed to suppress them, adding anguish to Samoan misery. Without avail did Robert Louis Stevenson, then gradually dying at Vailima, protest against atrocities, perhaps with a certain tenderness to British concerns, and plead for peace.

As a matter of fact the invaders to whom Stevenson appealed were themselves torn by jealousies as bitter as those of the island natives—except when engaged in putting down uprisings against common authority. Their merchants struggling for the petty markets, their capitalists buying up native lands, their missionaries saving souls for the hereafter, their consuls sparring for fine diplomatic points, and their naval officers punctiliously watching with eagle eyes for imperial advantages filled the foreign colony in Samoa with gossip, intrigue, and rancor. So from one incident to another, events dragged on until the Spanish-American War when the seizure of the Philippines lifted the veil and revealed America as a world power to the esoteric circles of the domestic hinterland. Now ready for positive action, the Senate of the United States, ratified in 1900 a treaty disposing of Samoa. Tutuila and a few islets came under the Stars and Stripes; Germany got the remainder; and England was satisfied with concessions elsewhere —until the German heritage fell to her in 1919 as a fruit of the war for democracy. Thus by a procedure which seemed aleatory to some and inexorable to others, American suzerainty was established far away under warm southern skies. Probably not one citizen in ten thousand was aware of the fact but those who assumed the duty of taking thought for to-morrow knew full well the nature of the new obligations.

§

In this sweep of Manifest Destiny across the Pacific, it was inevitable that the Hawaiian Islands should be brought into the fold. American relations with those islands had opened in Washington's administration. When the Columbia, the first ship that carried the starry flag around the globe, rode into Boston harbor in 1790, it brought a Sandwich Islander to astound the Puritans. How their mouths gaped as Captain Gray turned out in state to call on Governor Hancock, escorting up the street the strange guest garbed in his helmet and cloak of flaming red! Into the ken of the Yankee trader swam a new opportunity to sell goods.

Soon afterward bold seamen, already accustomed to rounding the Horn, trafficking in furs along the west coast of America and trading skins in Canton for tea, silks, Chinaware, and nankins, put the newly discovered islands on their commercial routes—first as a stopping place on long voyages and then as a source of sandalwood so desired by the Chinese. From the closing decade of the eighteenth century onward, their trade with Hawaii prospered. In 1822, sixty New England whalers, while scouring the seas from Behring Straits to Tierra del Fuego, called at Honolulu; two decades later four hundred whalers cast anchor there in a single year.

In connection with the coming and going of many ships sprang up a brisk local traffic followed by an invasion of foreign immigrants. New England merchants opened stores; capitalists organized bands of workmen to cut sandalwood; and often a sailor, weary of the lash and salt pork on shipboard, deserted his command, fled into the interior, and settled down with a native wife to a softer life under genial skies. Among the motley throngs came also the fishers of men, the first vanguard of Congregational missionaries landing in 1820 to prepare the way for a conquering church militant. Hence, in the course of time an American colony grew up in Honolulu; warehouses, saloons, shops, residences, and steeples in the New England style rising beside the thatched huts of the villagers. With the Americans came Europeans of many nationalities, Chinese in their everlasting search for a new breathing space, and later the indomitable Japanese already too congested in their narrow home. It was soon made patent that a struggle for possession of the islands was to engage the diplomacy of three continents.

The physical setting for this play was both weird and charming. Although the islands revealed their volcanic origin in the jagged mountains thrown against the skies and seemed like barren rocks from a distance, the appearance was deceptive. The larger members of the group, especially Oahu, the seat of Honolulu, were dotted with rolling fields and narrow niches of fertile soil. A semi-tropical sun and a misty rainfall brought forth a luxuriant growth of fruits and vegetables with little labor, while adjacent seas yielded fish in abundance.

Into this picture, the Hawaiians whom the white men found in possession of the little paradise fitted with strange exactness. Primitive in their culture, they wore scanty clothing adapted to the climate, and lived in a tribal state under a warrior-chieftain called by a stretch of courtesy the king. They were simple in heart and unvexed by literacy; if they lacked the virtues of civilization, they were fortunate in escaping most of its vices. And yet the idyllic picture drawn by sentimentalists was not altogether without blemishes. The masses were in fact bent to earth under a remorseless servitude; women were degraded almost to the level of the beasts in the fields; and the whole population was occasionally thrown into distress by intertribal wars.

Whatever their merits in the way of civilization, the Hawaiians could not possibly hold their own in a contest with pushing Yankees, thrifty Chinese, and tireless Japanese. Though they were converted to Christianity and taught to read and write, economic competition, whisky, and disease cut them down like grain before a sickle. And in the process the whites got control of nearly all the land in the kingdom, overcoming the cupidity and resistance of the dusky proprietors by the lure of money and pressures of various kinds. By 1890, most of the crown domain had been alienated by native statesmen and their "advisers";

more than half the real estate was owned by foreigners; and about two-thirds of the personal property was in alien hands—the Americans leading the British and the Germans in the extent of their holdings. At the end of five more years, the Hawaiians owned less than one-third of the land and only six per cent of the capital invested in commerce and industry. It was then boastfully claimed, perhaps with some exaggeration, that two-thirds of the sugar business belonged to Americans, many of whom were sons of missionaries, who had chosen the way of Dives rather than the thorny path of Paul.

Thus after a hundred years of promotion the land and the resources of Hawaii had passed under the direction of foreigners. In spite of the royal government maintained in the "palace" at Honolulu approximately five thousand whites, mainly Americans, were the real masters of eighty thousand natives, Chinese, and Japanese. In short, the fate of the Hawaiian Islands was already sealed. They were to become an imperial province inhabited by Orientals and directed by white capitalists, operating under a contract labor system more efficient than the old plantation methods of Virginia and South Carolina. It was equally manifest that the American flag would soon follow American economic supremacy.

Indeed as the interests of its citizens had multiplied in the islands, the government of the United States, in its upper range, had given increasing attention to the business of drawing them within its sphere of influence. More than once the State Department served notice on foreign powers to beware of treading on its preserves. In 1851 Admiral Du Pont, an out-sentinel of the American Navy, reported home that "the Hawaiian Islands would prove the most important acquisition we could make in the whole Pacific Ocean—an acquisition intimately connected with our commercial and naval supremacy in those seas." In 1875 a treaty with the ruler of Hawaii included a pledge on his part not to alienate any territory except to the United States;

and twelve years later a supplementary treaty gave Americans exclusive use of Pearl Harbor.   Henceforward the
State Department and the Navy kept their eyes even more
firmly fixed on the star of destiny.   During Cleveland's
first administration, Bayard, the Secretary of State, outlined
the policy of his office in this vein: "to wait quietly and patiently and let the islands fill up with American planters and
American industries until they should be wholly identified in
business interests and political sympathies with the United
States.   It was simply a matter of waiting until the apple
should fall."

The maturing stage was hastened by the enactment of the
McKinley tariff bill in 1890.   That measure, while removing
the duty on raw sugar imported into the United States, compensated domestic farmers and manufacturers by giving
them a handsome bounty on the output of their fields and
mills, producing on competitors in Hawaii an effect that was
immediate and ruinous.   Already the growth of the beet
sugar industry in the United States had caused a depression
in the islands and the McKinley law deepened it into a genuine distress, a calamity which pinched with special severity
American owners of Hawaiian plantations and mills, oc-
casioning a loss estimated by the minister of the United
States at approximately twelve million dollars a year.   "Unless some positive action of relief be granted," he said, "the
depreciation of sugar property here will go on.   Wise, bold
action by the United States will rescue property holders
from great losses."

There were, of course, other grounds for "wise, bold
action."   It was said that the native monarchy was corrupt,
that better roads and sanitary arrangements were needed,
and that Pearl Harbor should be fortified by the United
States—an undertaking that would contribute to national
defense and assist in a pecuniary way American contractors
and merchants in Honolulu.   Still it was mainly sugar that
precipitated the crisis.   "What do you think were the causes
of the revolution?" asked the American commissioner after-

wards sent into the islands to conduct an inquiry. "Simply two cents a pound on sugar—to get some treaty or some arrangement with America," laconically answered a sugar planter from Lanai.

On top of the economic calamity induced by the McKinley bill came difficulties in local politics. The very next year after the passage of that measure, the Hawaiian Queen, Liliuokalani, gave the tree a shake which helped to bring down the ripened fruit. Having acquired in her youth a hatred for missionaries and foreign invaders, she started a policy of exclusion when she came to the throne in 1891. In keeping with her theories, she overthrew the constitution of 1887 which gave generous rights to aliens—rights wrung from her predecessor by substantial pressure—and then sought by various means to restore "the good old days," adding a ceremonial insult to the economic injury done by William McKinley.

Replying brusquely to the reactionary policies of the Queen, the foreigners in Honolulu, mostly Americans, fomented a revolution and upset her tottering throne. In the course of this revolt, American marines were landed from a warship conveniently at hand, a provisional government was erected, and the flag of Washington and Lincoln was hoisted by the United States minister, J. S. Stevens. These things safely accomplished, a commission composed of four Americans and one Englishman—to give it an international character—was immediately sent to the White House to seek annexation. On arrival there, the envoys were cordially received by President Harrison and within a few days a treaty adding Hawaii to the American empire was laid before the Senate.

There it rested when Harrison left office on March 4, 1893, surrendering control over foreign affairs to President Cleveland, head of the party founded by farmers and mechanics in the time of Andrew Jackson. Hearing that all the proprieties of international courtesy had not been observed by the American minister in Honolulu, the President dispatched the Hon. James H. Blount to the scene to investigate and report. After making a searching inquiry, Blount came to the conclusion that the American minister in Hawaii and certain associates of his nationality were the real authors of the upheaval which ousted the Queen.

In a final memorandum the Commissioner stated that the revolutionists had disclosed to Stevens in advance all their plans and had received in return assurance of protection. "They needed the troops on shore to overawe the Queen's supporters and government," ran the document. "This he agreed to and did furnish. . . . The leaders of the revolutionary movement would not have undertaken it but for Mr. Stevens' promise to protect them against any danger from the government. . . . Had the troops not been landed no measures for the organization of the new government would have been undertaken." Emphasizing the alien character of the coup d'état, Blount went on to say that, had the foreigners in the islands been excluded from voting, the plan for annexation would have been defeated "by more than five to one." If, as Stevens asserted, "politics" was involved in the Commissioner's inquiry, there was no uncertainty as to the real character of the revolution.

On receiving the findings of the Commission, Cleveland was much embarrassed. He was a bit awkward in dealing with ironies which European chancelleries could lightly turn into pleasantries; but he plunged into the current, instructing the new American minister at the capital of Hawaii to negotiate in a friendly spirit with the deposed Queen. When, in accordance with his orders, the envoy called at the royal establishment, he found Her Majesty obdurate, fully determined to get her throne back, to cut off the heads of the "traitors" who had overthrown her rule by violence, and to confiscate their property.

A painful pause ensued. The Cleveland administration, desiring to be just to the intransigent sovereign and yet unable in the nature of things to surrender American citizens and property to her tender mercies, resorted to a policy of delay until the Queen, finally persuaded that everything would be lost by insistence on what she was pleased to call her "rights," came to terms, promising amnesty and full pardon to the participants in the recent rebellion. By that time it was too late.

On July 4, 1894, an appropriate day, the party of revolution in Honolulu, having resolved not to lose by diplomacy what it had won by action, declared the independence of the Hawaiian republic and as a sovereign state sought recognition by the powers. Faced with this stern fact, Cleveland put aside the original idea of saving the primitive monarchy and, after a month elapsed, cordially greeted the new nation, to the utter consternation of the moralists who had thus far applauded his course. After all, its government had been in existence more than a year; it had kept order—with the assistance of American forces; and reasoning from events, Cleveland thought it entitled to recognition "without regard to any of the incidents which accompanied or preceded it," thus summarily dismissing the ethical questions that had formerly vexed him. Secretary Bayard's fruit had fallen and it was to be picked up in due season: the Hawaiian Islands were to be annexed to the United States when the Spanish War made Manifest Destiny a little more manifest to the American nation.

§

If circumstances produced a vigorous foreign policy in Mexico, the Caribbean, Samoa, and Hawaii during the years that followed the overthrow of the planting aristocracy, the affairs of Europe on the whole, by way of contrast, called for suavity and moderation. American citizens had little or no money invested in European enterprises and for nearly half a century there were no disturbances in the Old World which seriously jeopardized American commercial interests in any quarter. It is true that more than forty wars were fought in this period by various European powers, but most of them were brushes on the frontiers of expanding empires in Africa and Asia—British, French, German, and Italian.

Even the graver Franco-Prussian War of 1870 failed to ruffle the academic calm of the State Department; for during its course neither party assailed American commerce by ruinous blockades or reprisals and at no time did the balance of power seem to be disturbed by the shock of battle. In any event the people of the United States, remembering the recent attempt of Napoleon III to establish an empire in Mexico and sympathizing, in the main, with Germany, saw no ground for intervening in the struggle or traversing the verdict. Generally speaking, American newspapers rejoiced in the downfall of Napoleon and looked upon the annexation of Alsace-Lorraine by Germany as an act of justice, taking in this matter the same view as the London Times.

In its necessary dealings with European powers during this period the government of the United States, therefore, had little reason to make radical departures. On various revolutionary occasions it simply recalled the sentiments of former days: long ago the American public had cheered the Greek revolt against Turkey; and Louis Kossuth, fleeing from the wrath of Vienna, had been cordially received by applauding multitudes, by Daniel Webster as the Secretary of State, by the President, and by the houses of Congress. The traditions still lived and it was easy to refer to them. When, for example, Napoleon III was overthrown in 1870, President Grant recognized the third French republic within forty-eight hours. Again when the Spanish monarchy was upset by revolt three years later, our minister at Madrid, on instructions from the State Department, paid his respects to the new republic the day after its proclamation, only to be chagrined by its early death.

All this was true to form. Catholic influence in Washington had as yet reached no substantial proportions and

in none of the revolutions was the principle of private property impugned; at any rate in these acceptable convulsions
no American investors lost any large sums of money.
Moreover as a matter of fact the several gestures to revolutionary movements in Europe were platonic in character.
When, for instance, Paris, London, and Vienna asked Secretary Seward to join in a formal protest to the Russian
Tsar against his cruel treatment of the Poles after their uprising in 1863, the Secretary declined to intervene, remarking in passing that, while American institutions, founded on
the rights of man, were the hope of revolutionists everywhere, our influence should be moral rather than physical.
The number of Russian Jews in the United States was still
small.

Other interests, however, other manners. When in 1880
the great powers of Europe held a conference about the
division of the Morocco estate, the government at Washington gladly accepted an invitation to join in the deliberations and the Senate ratified the settlement devised by the
diplomats. An American representative four years later
shared in the discussions of the Berlin Congress which
dealt with the economic affairs of the Congo Free State and
the trading rights of other countries within the territory of
that anomalous corporation. Though fair beginnings in international coöperation under the auspices of a Republican
President moving in the higher ranges of observation, these
adventures, especially participation in the Berlin conference,
were harshly attacked by spokesmen of the left wings in the
House of Representatives; and President Cleveland, wearing somewhat gingerly the mantle laid aside by Jackson,
flatly advised the Senate in 1885 not to ratify the Berlin
agreements. When a second assembly was summoned on
the same subject at the German capital, he declined to do
more than permit American agents to appear as observers
and the Senate merely ratified the conventions respecting
slavery and tariffs. It was thus made evident that the impacts of domestic partisanship were to be felt in the realm of

foreign affairs even if politics was supposed to stop at the water's edge.

Though Cleveland shrank somewhat from formal association with European governments, he seemed to welcome an opportunity to give Great Britain some curt instructions on the Monroe Doctrine. Relations with that country were running smoothly when he assumed office the second time in 1893—unmarred for twenty years by any untoward incident. The hostile feelings aroused by the negligence of the British government in allowing the construction of confederate cruisers in British ports during our Civil War had been allayed. It is true that England at first disclaimed responsibility in the matter but, eventually induced by the unremitting insistence of Washington to approve a project for arbitrating the issues, she accepted the decision of the high court agreed upon—the Geneva Tribunal of 1872; and paid with a gracious bow the lavish award to American claimants in spite of her legitimate objections to some aspects of the decree. In this manner the controversy came to a peaceful ending and the conversations of the two governments returned to the formal amenities of diplomacy.

Not until the summer of 1895 was the placid current broken by another clash of any moment and this new brawl, for such it was, arose over a collateral issue: an appeal from Venezuela for assistance in a dispute with London about the western boundary of British Guiana. Asserting in its memorandum that England was in fact trying to extend her dominions in the New World, the government at Caracas maintained that it was entitled to claim protection under the shield of the Monroe Doctrine. Regardless of the merits of the argument, the plea fell on sympathetic ears in Washington, inducing the Secretary of State, Richard T. Olney, in July, 1895, to make upon London a demand that the quarrel be submitted to arbitration—a demand couched in the language of a decree rather than an invitation and accompanied by remarks of a magisterial quality which, if they had come from the English foreign office, would have raised a furor in America. "The United States is practically sovereign on this continent," Olney informed England, "and its fiat is law upon the subjects to which it confines its interposition. Why? It is not because of the pure friendship or good will felt for it. It is not simply by reason of its high character as a civilized state, nor because wisdom and equity are the invariable characteristics of the dealings of the United States. It is because in addition to all other grounds, its infinite resources combined with its isolated position render it master of the situation and practically invulnerable against any or all other powers."

The pretensions of this manifesto, clothed in diction not unfamiliar in London, brought from the English government a direct reply denying the applicability of the Monroe Doctrine to the matter in question and declining to arbitrate the issue. Then, applauded by belligerent sections of the populace, not excluding large Irish contingents in New York and Boston, President Cleveland entered the lists. In a message inviting Congress to create a commission for the purpose of ascertaining the truth in the boundary controversy, the President announced in vivid language that it would be the duty of the United States "to resist by every means in its power, as willful aggression upon its rights and interests," the appropriation by Great Britain of any lands which, "after investigation, we have determined of right belong to Venezuela." Lest there be some doubt as to the strength of this resolve, the President served general notice that war was better than "a supine submission to wrong and injustice and the consequent loss of national self-respect and honor."

To the surprise of every one who watched the course of events, the British foreign office, evidently impressed by Cleveland's determination and knowing that the aid of the United States might be needed in a coming conflict with Germany, did not meet the President's message with a counterblast. On the contrary when the American commission began work, the English government, knowing that its case would brook daylight, courteously replied to all requests for information on the boundary question and in the end agreed to arbitrate the whole controversy.

As things now turned out, this concession required no great sacrifice for, when the matter was finally reviewed by an impartial tribunal, it was found that the British claims in South America were, on the whole, well-grounded. So the affair closed happily for all parties. England got her land. Cleveland had the pleasure of vindicating his version of the Monroe Doctrine and pulling the Lion's whiskers a bit in the bargain. Moreover, he made it obvious to the world that, while he could not set the seal of his approval on transactions of dubious correctness in Hawaii, he was no pacifist; he was prepared to have American soldiers make the supreme sacrifice to prevent "wrong and injustice" in this hemisphere.

§

An opportunity to apply the high principles announced by President Cleveland in this case was also offered in a still graver controversy not as far from our shores as Venezuela. At the very moment when the quarrel with Great Britain was becoming acute, another one of the periodical revolutions that had long plagued Spain broke out in Cuba —the usual uprising of peons on the land and working people in the towns against the Spanish upper classes sustained by church and state. The immediate and efficient cause of the revolt was an economic crisis.

For several years the chief industry of the island had been the cane sugar business and it had been suffering from the increasing competition of beet sugar manufacturers in Europe and the United States, the output of European beet sugar alone rising from two hundred thousand tons in 1850 to nearly four million tons in 1894. And instead of offering relief to her Cuban planters in their deepening distress,

Spain forced them to endure discriminatory tariffs on their imported manufactures, tariffs that maintained at a high figure the prices of their purchases while their buying power in terms of sugar was being diminished—all for the plain purpose of keeping business in the hands of Spanish merchants. In its extreme application, this colonial policy resulted in the carriage of goods from the United States to Spain, the payment of handsome profits to local traders, and shipment back across the ocean to Cuba. Only prosperous planters exploiting virgin soil for a strong market could bear such a heavy burden and Cuban planters were far from prosperous when the last decade of the nineteenth century arrived.

The breaking point in this strain came with the passage of the Wilson tariff bill at Washington in 1894. Ardent reformers in the House of Representatives, as we have seen, without reckoning on the bloc of high protectionists in the Senate, had planned to put sugar on the free list but, under the leadership of Senator Gorman of Maryland, cane-sugar Democrats, beet-sugar Republicans, and tariff warriors of the McKinley discipline united in forcing through a bill that placed duties on low grade sugars and "compensating rates" on refined sugars. In its effect on the Cuban sugar business, the Wilson law was ruinous; taken in connection with Spain's tariff policy, it spread swift disaster among Cuban planters and their laborers, a process explained by the American minister to Spain in two sentences: "There can be no doubt that the economic crisis which followed that event (*i.e.,* the passage of the Wilson bill) precipitated the present revolution. When exposed without mitigation to two systems of hostile tariffs, at a time when the price of cane sugar had been reduced by competition to a very low point, the Cuban producers threw up their hands in despair and the bands of laborers thus deprived of work were the first to swell the ranks of the insurgents." The next year, 1895, all Cuba was aflame with revolution and the usual atrocities were committed on both sides, the intensity of the contest making them more numerous and more horrible than ever. Almost immediately a Cuban junta of agitation was established in the United States to carry on propaganda and to purchase on shaky credit, at high prices, American munitions for the insurgents.

Substantial interests were now rudely disturbed. American trade with Cuba was practically destroyed by the paralysis of economic life in the island and American investments in Cuban plantations and mills were being wiped out by war and pillage, thereby furnishing abundant fuel for the moral fire kindled by the sensational press in the United States and the revolutionary committee on public information. It was true that there were crimes equally hideous to be discovered in many other parts of the world at the time but none were so widespread; none were so near to American shores; none could command such generous resources for the manufacture of opinion. In accordance with the nature of the case, the Cuban revolt had not advanced very far when a shout for American intervention on behalf of an oppressed people began to run up and down the land.

To this outcry President Cleveland paid no heed, assuming for the government an attitude of correct neutrality and denying to the insurgents the status of belligerents. Enlarging upon this pacific policy, he sought to bring the revolution to an end by officially tendering the services of the United States in mediation—an offer which Spain declined with a polite hint that her gratitude would be forthcoming if the Americans would cease aiding the rebels with money and munitions in violation of international law. Winning few supporters at home by his program of peace and rebuffed by Spain in his effort at conciliation, Cleveland, now repudiated by his party on the silver question, relapsed into the position of a passive observer of Cuban affairs, remaining in that attitude until the close of his term.

§

On its return to power in 1897 under the leadership of McKinley, the party of business enterprise gave a new tone to American foreign policy. In their national platform of the year before, the Republicans had declared in favor of using influences and good offices to give peace and independence to Cuba and had taken note of the fact that Spain was unable "to protect the property or lives of resident American citizens," referring to economic interests which included more than fifty millions in invested capital, sixteen million dollars worth of damages done, it was alleged, to American citizens, and a trade reaching approximately a hundred millions annually.

Between the summer of 1896, when this Republican manifesto was issued and the inauguration of the McKinley administration, affairs in Cuba went from bad to worse. Correctly gauging the pressure of property in certain American circles and bent on ruining Spanish landlords, the insurgent general, Gomez, made a fine point of destroying sugar plantations. In retaliation the Spanish general, collected men, women, and children from the areas of disturbance and concentrated them into wretched camps where they died like flies. Horrors succeeded horrors. And when transmuted into American news, they made the blood of gentle folk boil, thereby affording opportunities of which William Randolph Hearst, not hitherto regarded in polite society as a special apostle of righteousness, made the most in editorials and in headlines of lurid carmine; while his rival journalist, Joseph Pulitzer, fishing for more profits, also fumed and stormed over the plight of the poor Cubans. Here was a combination of economic interest, appealing humanity, "good journalism," and popular tumult which drove the United States steadily toward war.

By two spectacular events, one of them a tragic verity, the torrent was hurried on. In February, 1898, the Hearst papers published under great headlines a letter written by the Spanish minister at Washington in which contempt was expressed for President McKinley—a letter stolen from the mails. Thereupon a tempest raged for several days over the "insult to national honor," forcing an apology from Spain and the recall of the offending diplomat. Hard upon this episode came the destruction of the battleship Maine, in the harbor of Havana, bearing to death two officers and two hundred and fifty-eight members of the crew in a terrific explosion. Though the cause of the disaster was unknown, it was ascribed by the American public to the malice of local Spanish officials. In spite of the fact that the government of Spain was more than solicitous in its attempts to do the proper thing in the circumstances, no note of apology or condolence, no appeal for arbitration could rise above the shrill popular cry, "Remember the Maine," which ran from shore to shore in America, from the Great Lakes to the Gulf of Mexico.

Meanwhile McKinley was pursuing a course that bore all the outward signs of studied restraint. He protested with dignity against the atrocities of Spain in Cuba and received promises of reform, assurances that the cabinet at Madrid, eager to avoid a war that could have but one end, was prepared to make every concession permitted by Spanish public opinion. Yielding to his importunities, it assured McKinley, early in April, 1898, that it was ready to suspend hostilities, call a Cuban parliament, and grant a generous local autonomy, thus complying substantially with every demand that the President had made. Reinforcing this pledge, the American minister in Spain, General Woodford, cabled McKinley about the same time that, if Congress would agree to a settlement, the Madrid government was willing to grant any autonomy which the insurgents would accept, even complete independence for Cuba or a cession of the island to the United States.

In short, the President knew that Spain had offered to surrender as unconditionally as popular sentiment would warrant, but he was beset by the war party calling for extreme measures. "Every congressman," exclaimed a Representative from Maine, "has two or three newspapers in his district—most of them printed in red ink . . . and shouting for blood." Many of McKinley's advisers were equally bent on a resort to arms. "McKinley had no more backbone than a chocolate éclair," was the taunt Roosevelt flung at him. Overwhelmed by such pressure, the President surrendered such pacific intentions as he had entertained and, without making public the latest concessions from Madrid, sent a militant message to Congress, on April 11, 1898, declaring that his efforts were brought to a standstill and the issue was in the hands of Congress.

War was now inescapable. With lightning speed a resolution authorizing the President to use the armed forces of the nation against Spain went through the House of Representatives, the advocates of peace and mediation being swept aside in a whirlwind of passion. In the Senate, however, the war resolution encountered a brief check at the hands of a few Populists who suspected that it was a signal for conquest under the guise of service; but they were unable to do more than force the adoption of a supplement disowning all such subterfuges—a proposition to which the Republican sponsors, having proclaimed the conflict a war for liberty, could hardly demur.

In its final wording the resolution announced the independence of Cuba, called upon Spain to withdraw from the Island, authorized the President to use armed forces to carry the resolve into effect, and disclaimed any "disposition or intention" on the part of the United States "to exercise sovereignty, jurisdiction or control over the said Island except for the pacification thereof." Porto Rico, lying peacefully near by and the Philippines lying far away under Pacific skies, apparently did not come within the ken of the Populists. On April 19, 1898, the United States was at war, triumphantly and gloriously, with the most decrepit and powerless imperial nation in all Europe.

The conclusion was foregone. The Navy, owing in no small measure to the alertness of its administrative officers and its technicians, was ready for the trial by battle.

Within two weeks Commodore Dewey had shattered the enemy's fleet in Manila Bay and rung the doom of Spanish dominion in the Pacific. On July 3, the Spanish ships that had crossed the Atlantic in safety under Admiral Cervera were destroyed, while attempting to escape from Santiago, by American vessels in charge of Admiral Schley. On July 17, Santiago, invested by American troops under General Shafter and shelled by American ships in the offing, gave up the forlorn struggle. A week later General Miles landed in Porto Rico, adding that pearl to the American empire. In August General Merritt and Admiral Dewey carried Manila by storm

The war with Spain was at an end; its consequences were at hand. Defeated and helpless, Madrid now begged for peace through the good offices of the French ambassador in Washington, M. Cambon. Upon official inquiry at the White House, the mediator reported that the victorious power was "resolved to procure all the profit possible from the advantages it had obtained," but in the circumstances he advised Spain to accept her fate. With the preliminaries out of the way, Spain agreed in a protocol signed on August 12, 1898, that Cuba should be independent, that Porto Rico and an island in the Ladrones should be ceded to the United States, and that the Philippine Islands should be held under American authority pending the final settlement. After all, the resolution of Congress declaring war had not applied the self-denying ordinance to any territory except Cuba. So that the provisional enlargement of the American empire was not out of harmony with that historic manifesto.

§

To suppose that the State and Navy Departments of the United States were at that point unconscious of the economic and strategic utility of the Philippines, especially in view of American operations in the Pacific for a century past, is to imagine that they were lacking in the sophistication commonly displayed by the Anglo-Saxon peoples on such occasions. Yet it would be a mistake to say that all Republican leaders were solidly united on annexation, that the country was fully informed about the matter, or that the development of an imperial mind through the press and political speeches had reached an acute stage. As a matter of fact, in his message of December, 1897, President Mc-Kinley had declared that "forcible annexation . . . cannot be thought of, by our code . . . would be criminal aggression." It is true he later remarked that "when the war is over we must keep what we want," but the orientation of the masses called for discrimination and caution. Even late in the autumn of 1898 when the American commissioners sailed away to Paris to meet the Spanish diplomats at the peace table, they received from McKinley no positive instruction as to the fate of the Philippines and were compelled to wait several weeks for final orders in that relation.

On this account it is sometimes said that the directors of American affairs in the upper range of politics had no intention in the beginning of using the war for the liberation of Cuba as a pretext for the enlargement of the American empire. That the yeomanry of the domestic hinterland had any such purpose in mind in the spring of 1898 is hardly to be supposed; nor is there any reason for believing that all who sat at the President's inner council table had at the time any such definite imperial design. And yet the managers of the federal administration did not merely wander without effort in "the wide, gray, lampless depths of human destiny." It would have been possible to drive Spain out of the western hemisphere without waging war on her in the Philippines, but for efficient reasons the strategists in Washington, long before the outbreak of the conflict, decided upon another course. They knew very well that for more than half a century American naval officers and merchants, familiar with the Far East, had coveted Oriental bases to serve as points of support for martial adventures and commercial enterprise. If they had ever referred to the earlier chapters of American history, they must have learned that the flag had once been hoisted over Formosa, not far away from Manila, and that Commodore Perry had, in a moment of enthusiasm, seized the Bonin Islands off to the northeast.

That a number of active politicians had early perceived the wider implications of a war with Spain is evident from the letters and speeches of the time. On September 21, 1897, several months before the sinking of the Maine, Theodore Roosevelt, Assistant Secretary of the Navy, wrote to Senator Lodge that, in case of a collision with Spain, "our Asiatic squadron should blockade, and if possible take Manila." In May of the next year, Lodge informed Roosevelt that substantial land and naval forces were to be sent to the Philippines and that there was no need for hurry about Cuba. "Porto Rico is not forgotten," he added, "and we mean to have it. Unless I am utterly and profoundly mistaken, the Administration is now fully committed to the large policy that we both desire." In July, the Senator confirmed this impression when he discovered that McKinley evidently wanted to hold the Philippines but was "a little timid about it." He also cited the seizure of Guam as proof that the administration "expects to hold on to the Philippines." A month later he found McKinley apparently hesitating but still he expressed the hope that "they will at least keep Manila which is the great prize and the thing which will give us the Eastern trade." Just what was going on in the bottom of McKinley's mind is not entirely plain but soon afterward he announced his conviction that America should retain all that had been won by the sword.

The intellectual and moral methods by which he resolved his perplexity the President later explained to some of his Methodist brethren in a brief address. "I walked the floor of the White House night after night," he said, "and I am not ashamed to tell you, gentlemen, that I went down on my knees and prayed Almighty God for light and guidance more than one night. And one night late it came to me this way—I don't know how it was, but it came. . . . There was nothing left for us to do but to take them all, and to educate the Filipinos, and uplift and civilize and Christianize them, and by God's grace do the very best we could by them as our fellow-men for whom Christ also died. And then I went to bed, and went to sleep and slept soundly." Of course he was fully alive, as he said on another occasion, to "the commercial opportunity to which American statesmanship cannot be indifferent. It is just to use every legitimate means for the enlargement of American trade."

So, in the end, as Secretary Hay cabled the peace commissioners, the President could "see but one plain path of duty—the acceptance of the archipelago," compelling Spain to surrender the islands in return for a gratuity of twenty million dollars. Anticipating the exalted strain that later characterized President Wilson's appeal to the nation, McKinley declared in 1898 that the war had brought new duties and responsibilities "which we must meet and discharge as becomes a great nation on whose growth and career from the beginning the Ruler of Nations has plainly written the high command and pledge of civilization."

§

While certain German journalists read the phraseology of annexation with an amused shrug, Englishmen appreciated the quality of sincerity which made it ring true to the Anglo-Saxon mind. Among the royal family our ambassador at the Court of St. James's found "nothing but hearty kindness and—so far as is consistent with propriety—sympathy." Joseph Chamberlain, that arch apostle of British imperialism who was soon to play a high rôle in the war with the Boer republics in South Africa, unable to contain his joy when he heard of America's challenge to Spain, declared in a public address that an armed conflict, terrible as it was, would be cheap "if, in a great and noble cause, the Stars and Stripes and the Union Jack should wave together over an Anglo-Saxon alliance." And he said privately to Ambassador Hay that he did not "care a hang what they say about it on the Continent," meaning, significantly enough, the French and the Germans. "If we give up the Philippines it will be a considerable disappointment to our English friends," the American Ambassador wrote home after the fighting was over.

While Henry Adams, recalling the days of the Civil War when his father, as American minister, had been a hundred times humiliated in London, coldly remarked on reading Hay's exuberant notes that "the sudden appearance of Germany as the grizzly terror" had "frightened England into America's arms," the Republican administration was more than grateful for the sympathy and kindly solicitude of the English. Irrespective of the explanation for the new affection, the United States enjoyed the benefit of England's benevolent neutrality during the war and her cordial patronage during the conclusion of the peace.

German imperialists, on the other hand, in their natural ambition to acquire spoils of the kind that had made the British empire fat, pursued a policy which strengthened the Anglo-American entente, and in after years came back to plague them. As soon as McKinley began his diplomatic sparring with the Madrid government in 1897, the Kaiser became excited over the dangers to "the monarchical principle" likely to flow from a war between Spain and republican America. Grieved to observe what he described as "the overseas covetousness" of the United States, especially as it promised to interfere with his own, he tried to work up a European combination to save Spain from an armed attack. Austrian sympathies were readily enlisted. The Pope was approached and, after canvassing the ground, the Holy Father instructed Archbishop Ireland, who enjoyed the confidence of McKinley, to visit Washington and "work diligently with the President" in the interest of peace—and the salvation of the decrepit Catholic monarchy. England, for obvious reasons, was cold to the Kaiser's project. It cannot be denied that the English ambassador in Washington did finally join in the collective appeal of the diplomats to McKinley in behalf of peace but his government showed no spirit of coercion.

When at length all the Kaiser's efforts failed and war was declared, the Teutonic press on the whole continued to favor Spain, thereby driving the United States still closer to the British system. In fact German newspaper comments, widely circulated in this country by the guardians of the Anglo-American entente, stirred up so much ill-will toward Berlin that the American ambassador on the spot, Andrew D. White, had to make special efforts to allay the irritation while the war was in progress.

Immediately after Admiral Dewey's smashing victory at Manila, the German foreign office was again aroused to feverish activity and expectation, especially as the government of the United States had apparently disclaimed all intention of making forcible annexations. Over a report from the German consul in Manila to the effect that the Filipino revolutionists had rejected the idea of an independent republic and would probably offer the throne to a German prince, the Kaiser became positively inflamed. Appreciating his inability to defy England, he proposed that London be sounded, suggesting to Lord Salisbury through official channels that "the fat spoils" be shared in some measure between the two empires.

Bluntly informed by the British government in reply that the United States would resent any interference with the settlement of the Spanish estate and at almost the same moment warned by his consul in Manila that an Anglo-American understanding had been reached in the Philippines, the Kaiser still remained hopeful. As late as July the German ambassador in Washington was instructed that "His Majesty, the Emperor, regards it a principal object of German policy to leave unused no opportunity which may arise from the Spanish-American war to obtain maritime fulcra in East Asia." And by way of reinforcement the American ambassador in Berlin was also presented with a statement showing the amount of spoils that would be satisfactory to the Kaiser. Awaiting eventualities, German warships were held in Philippine waters.

Thoroughly familiar with German intentions and already approaching the shadows of the impending World War, the English foreign office countered the German thrusts at every turn. On July 28, 1898, Ambassador Hay cabled from London that England preferred to have the United States keep the Philippines, thus indicating that the Kaiser was balked in all projects for dividing the plunder. When the armistice terms were announced in August, the hopes of the Berlin government were seen to be crushed and during the ensuing peace conference at Paris its spokesmen were genially circumspect. Asked by Spain for aid in overcoming the "ever-growing covetousness" of the Americans, the German ambassador politely declined to intervene—no doubt with a sardonic smile, for "covetousness" was a strange word to use confidentially in diplomatic circles. Nevertheless in the hurly-burly Germany did manage to effect a secret arrangement with Madrid for the purchase of Yap and two other small islands in the Far Pacific, a pitiful reward for earnest labors which must have amused the directors of the British Empire. Concerning such minor things they cared little. The stage was being cleared for a larger imperial spectacle than the world had yet seen and at the prodigious dénouement the United States government was to remember ancient favors well.

§

When the program of annexation was completed and the treaty of peace with Spain was laid before the Senate of the United States for ratification, a bitter opposition arose, particularly among the Populists and Democrats, aided and

sustained by a few Republicans of the old school, led by
Senator Hoar of Massachusetts. The country was also
divided into quarrelsome factions. Andrew Carnegie, the
great peace advocate who had so recently issued a new
edition of his Triumphant Democracy, was indescribably
hurt by the swing to imperialism; according to John Hay,
he really seemed to be "off his head." Many other idealists, who accepted literally and at face value the Declaration of Independence, insisted that just governments derived
their powers from the consent of the governed, that ruling
conquered provinces was contrary to the genius and spirit of
American liberty, that the Constitution did not authorize
the processes of the proconsul. On the other side answers
were made by logicians more supple in their imagination.
Able Senators of the new direction, such as Beveridge of
Indiana and Platt of Connecticut, saw Manifest Destiny
once more written vividly on the western sky and spoke
with moving eloquence about our high and sublime mission
in carrying the torch of civilization and Christianity around
the world.

After weary days of fretful argument, the champions
of empire were still unable to muster the necessary two-
thirds vote in the Senate and President McKinley was
visibly worried: perhaps after all the vision which he had
seen on his knees in the White House at midnight was to
be blotted out by politicians. But at this crucial juncture
when all seemed lost, William Jennings Bryan, the New
York Tribune's "wretched, rattled-pated boy" appeared in
the arena and for some strange reason, by dint of much
persuasion, induced several Democratic Senators to change
their minds and carry the treaty with its program of annexation, by the narrow margin of one vote, thus saving William
McKinley from a defeat akin to that which befell Woodrow
Wilson two decades later. To facilitate the operation, a
little sop was thrown to liberals in the form of a resolution to the effect that the policy to be adopted in the Philippines was an open question. It was still open--at least

until the Republicans, once freed from the Democrats and Populists tearing at their flanks, found a voice in which to answer it.

§

The year that saw the establishment of American dominion in the Caribbean and the Far Pacific also witnessed the conclusion of the little drama in the Hawaiian Islands, a finale played by McKinley according to instructions from the Republicans who elected him. In their platform of 1896 they had called for a "firm, vigorous, and dignified" foreign policy, one which would guard "all our interests in the Western hemisphere," amplifying their creed by a plain declaration that the Hawaiian Islands "should be controlled by the United States." Informed by this specific article of faith and fortified by a mandate in the election that admitted of no dispute, McKinley, shortly after his inauguration, laid a treaty of annexation before the Senate only to have it defeated by Democratic maneuvering under the two-thirds rule. A year elapsed. Then Dewey fired at Manila another shot "heard round the world" and the impatient Republicans, tired of what they deemed factious opposition, resorted to the expedient of annexing the Hawaiian "republic" by a joint-resolution which required merely a majority in both houses—the same procedure used by the Democrats to annex Texas in 1845.

In every respect the debate on the Hawaiian resolution ran true to form. At the outset the Republican view was tersely expressed by the chairman of the House committee on foreign affairs: "The importance of the question lies first of all in the necessity of possessing these islands for the defense of our western shore, the protection and promotion of our commercial interests, and the welfare and security of our country generally." Equally characteristic was the Democratic reply: the revolution had been effected by chicane; annexation was being fostered by American speculators who had purchased $5,000,000 worth of Hawaiian bonds at thirty cents on the dollar; the passage of the resolution meant the assumption of all or a large part of this inflated paper by the government of the United States. The plea of naval defense was flouted as nothing but the professional rhetoric of the professional imperialist. "We are told," said the Democratic spokesman, "that we need these islands as a strategic base in military operations. All the admirals, rear-admirals, commodores, generals, colonels, majors, and captains say so. How does it happen then that we have gotten along splendidly for one hundred and nine years without these volcanic rocks? If we did not need them when we were only three millions strong, why are we likely to perish for the want of them now that we are seventy-five million souls?"

In their counter-blast by way of replication Republican orators declared the Hawaiian Islands necessary to the defense of the Philippines which in turn were necessary to the defense of American interests in the Far East. After all, besides the strength of their arguments, the Republicans had a majority in each house, so the Hawaiian Islands were formally annexed by a joint-resolution adopted on July 7, 1898. Then under the stimulus of business enterprise, the American residents entered upon an era of marvellous prosperity; the native population kept on declining; the multiplying Japanese and Chinese continued to till the soil either as laborers on plantations or as the masters of small holdings; and the city of Honolulu, with its paved streets, its electric lights, and other urbanities of civilization, became one of the garden spots of the Pacific.

CHAPTER XXV

The Gilded Age

IF the era of triumphant business enterprise witnessed a continuance of the old strife between financial and industrial interests on the one side and agricultural and labor interests on the other, which had characterized the middle period giving substance and color to its culture, the struggle now presented novel features, both quantitative and qualitative. It was on a scale more vast, stretching across a continent; its participants were augmented in numbers and strengthened by additional resources; its course was unimpeded by the pressures of a slave-owning aristocracy; its technical instruments for productive and intellectual operations were infinitely more varied and flexible; and the rhetorical discourses associated with the contest were embroidered by new logical, scientific, and factual designs.

Above all, the masters of great urban wealth now dominated the social plain. Statisticians could only roughly estimate the strength of the spreading plutocracy and the size of its share gathered from the golden flood, but, according to one guess, there were only three millionaires in the United States in 1861 and at least thirty-eight hundred at the lapse of thirty-six years. If the calculations of the economist, Charles Spahr, be accepted, one-tenth of the American people owned nine-tenths of the wealth by the end of the century. Though precaution suggested doubts about all such reckonings, two facts remained indisputable: the richest class in America was composed of those who owned factories, mines, railways, and urban property, not the possessors of plantations and farms; and the swiftness of their accumulations outrivaled all previous achievements in the history of lucre.

In another respect the Second American Revolution, thus described in the parabola of riches, differed from its prototypes in other lands and ages. True to historic rules, of course, the recruits for the plutocracy came up from the ranks of small farmers, artisans, petty traders, and day laborers, but they did not rise slowly in the midst of a society dominated by patricians and they did not retain their former masters as ornaments after destroying all superior authority. From the beginning, the capitalists and the planters had been separated by wide geographical boundaries, and when the war was over there was hardly enough left of the planting aristocracy, if it ever deserved that name in a strictly cultural sense, to give a decided tone to its own section. So the new bourgeois, who spurted up into wealth and power with the ruin of the slave owners, were not curbed by surviving members of an older order who could serve as models in matters of restraint, taste, scorn, and drawing-room procedure. Except for a few select segments on the Atlantic seaboard, the new age of American culture was without form and void; the young plutocracy had yet to acquire canons of propriety and æsthetics. Unchecked by classical traditions, unhampered by the contempt of strong upper classes, and not yet disciplined into culture by generations of leisure, it attacked its problems of living unusually free from customary repressions—emancipated from the inferiority complexes of European peasants and merchants.

Yet, after all, these departures from European traditions were somewhat superficial and temporary. Fundamentally, the American bourgeois were fairly true to classical types and even to contemporary models abroad. Rome had her *novi homines,* France her *nouveaux riches,* Spain her *ricos hombres,* and England her *nabobs.* In one deep-rooted instinct, the plutocrats of all lands were alike, resembling for that matter potentates in church and state of every age and every civilization: they loved color, glitter, pomp, and display. Why be rich if one could not throw off the mantle of obscurity? Why have the substance of power without the shadowing glory? What are the pleasures of display without admiring and applauding masses to impress? These were emotions as old as the days of Pericles and the members of the American plutocracy, of the same clay as their predecessors, presented the same psychological reaction to munificent circumstances.

Since they could cut their coupons and cash their dividend checks anywhere, they gravitated to the places where gorgeous objects could be had for money and shown to gaping multitudes, the bravest of the socially venturesome migrating to the most powerful center of accumulation, New York City. "Into the mighty cities of the East," wrote one of their number, "there moved an ever-growing army of those who had gathered from the mines of California, from the forges of Pittsburgh, from the forests of Michigan, from the metalled mountains of Montana, wealth beyond the dreams of Midas." On their arrival in a metropolis, they advertised their advent in the most obvious manner by erecting palaces, buying art, and giving social exhibitions. Along the streets, avenues, and boulevards where the birds of a feather flocked together, rose châteaux of French design, mansions of the Italian renaissance, English castles of authoritative mien—a riot of periods and tastes—with occasionally a noble monument to the derivative genius of some American architect trained in Europe and given freedom to create. As in old Yedo of the Tokugawa era, merchants and artisans assembled to serve the daimios and samurai under the frowning castle of the Shogun, so on all sides of the new American plutocracy swarmed maîtres d'hotel, shopkeepers, artists, writers, lecturers, art dealers, musicians, tutors, beggars, and lackeys—a motley array of the high and the low bent on sharing the crumbs that fell from Dives' table.

Housed in a grand style, like the great of old, the American captains of business enterprise poured out their riches in the purchase of goods. As the new men of Rome in Cicero's day, more acquisitive than creative, despoiled Egypt and Greece of their treasures, so the plutocracy of the United States ransacked the palaces, churches, abbeys, castles, and ateliers of Europe for statuary, paintings, pottery, rugs, and every other form of art. Even the Orient was forced to yield up graven goddesses of mercy and complacent Buddhas to decorate the buildings of men absorbed in making soap, steel rails, whisky, and cotton bagging and to please the women who spent the profits of business enterprise. The armor of mediæval knights soon stood in the halls of captains of industry whose boldest strokes were courageous guesses on the stock market or the employment of Pinkerton detectives against striking workingmen; while Mandarin coats from Peking sprawled on the pianos of magnates who knew not Ming or Manchu and perhaps could not tell whether their hired musicians were grinding out Wagner or Chopin. Grand ladies, who remembered with a blush the days when they laundered the family clothes, shone idly resplendent in jewels garnered by a search of two hemispheres. European tutors were imported to teach the "new people" and their offspring "parlor and table etiquette," music and "appreciation," as Greek preceptors had served Roman families in the time of Cicero. European artists were brought over to design and decorate for them as the artists of Athens were summoned to beautify the homes of Trimalchio's contemporaries. Private libraries of the "sets," rare editions, and rich bindings

were quickly assembled in job lots to give tone to establishments—a diversion that afforded gratifying appearances of
culture with none of its laborious penalties.   Almost buried
in a deluge of alien goods, the vestiges of colonial taste,
which though derivative had become acclimatized, survived
only in rural districts, North and South, out of the range
of the grand plutocracy.

Having discovered that they could buy palaces and import them to America, sticks, stones, carvings, and tiles,
the *novi homines* assumed, by no means without respectable
sanction, that they could buy their way into "the best
families" of two hemispheres.   On the eve of the Civil War
there had been many "seasoned clans" on the eastern seaboard, some of them dating their origins back a hundred
years or more, and boasting of ancestors who had served
as preachers, judges, warriors, and statesmen in colonial
times, in the heroic epoch of the Revolution, and in the
momentous age of the new republic.   Able to hold their
own socially, if not politically, these select families had
absorbed with facility the seepage of rising fortunes that
gradually oozed into their ranks—until the flood of the new
plutocracy descended upon them.   In that crisis all who
were not fortunate enough to multiply their estates had
to be content with genteel poverty or surrender to the owners of riches reeking of the market.

The possessors of gold now thundering at the social gates
would not be denied entrance; they demanded admission to
charmed circles, just as the English invaders of New
Netherland in the seventeenth century had demanded recognition from the old Dutch burghers and patroons.   Some of
the newcomers, frankly offering money bags as credentials,
were able to work magic by skirting along the edges of prudence.   If in groups especially choice, social arbiters demanded references—character witnesses, so to speak—
leaders of the storming party engaged genealogists to trace
their lineage as far back as William the Conqueror, if need
be, in that way furnishing many good dinners to the starve-

lings of Grub Street who worked in the London heraldry records.

Thus by one process or another amalgamation was effected and new varnish softened by the must of age. As the landed gentlemen of England had on various occasions saved their houses from decay by discreet jointures with mercantile families, so many of the established people of Boston, New York, Philadelphia, and Baltimore escaped the humiliation of poverty by judicious selections from the onrushing plutocracy. This matrimonial transaction was not as vexing as society editors imagined, for the smell of cod, soap, hides, tallow, and spices was on most of the sea-coast fortunes and association with the new railway princes and smelter kings was not very fantastic after all. The one source of serious anxiety was the fact that there were not enough old families to go around; the struggle had to end in the triumph of lucre. "We are all descended from Adam," laughed Mark Twain, reëchoing the shot of Petroleum V. Nasby—"We are all descended from grandfathers."

New times, new manners. In the leisurely days before the telephone and the express train, merchants, even though devoid of classical training, often took pride in knowing something of books and matters of the spirit. The father of Henry Cabot Lodge, for example, according to the memoir of the son, attended to the duties of citizenship, read history, and loved Shakespeare, Gray, Pope, Southey, Cervantes, and Scott, presenting, in the light of a misty past, a strange contrast to "the modern and recent plutocrat" who "knows nothing of the history or traditions of his state and country and cares less." When farmers and village artisans, who had suddenly acquired bulging purses, invaded the social arena, they could not help bringing with them the atmosphere of the market place and calling attention again to the earthly sources of culture. At the dinner-table and in the drawing-room they could not ignore what they knew at the desk, so, as Frederick Townsend

Martin recorded, tales of the conquests made by hard cash constituted the staple conversation of ladies and gentlemen in the gilded age.

Even the casual chatter of the idle moment was colored with the verbiage of trade. When Martin once remarked to a railway magnate during soft days on the Florida coast, "How lovely the earth is! I wonder if Heaven will be more beautiful than this scene," he received in reply: "Well, Fred, I guess I'll have no use for Heaven unless there are railways to be constructed there." Far away in New England, Lodge confirmed Martin's lament. "I was taught in my youth," he wrote gravely, "and vigorously taught, that it was not good manners to discuss physical ailments in general society and that it was the height of vulgarity to refer to money or to what anything cost, whether in your own case or in that of other people. I now hear surgical operations, physical functions, disease and its remedies, freely and fully discussed at dinner and on all other occasions by the ingenuous youth of both sexes. Money is no longer under taboo. One's own money and that of one's neighbors is largely talked about, and the cost of everything or anything recurs as often in polite conversation as in a tariff debate."

Yet there was development among the possessors of riches as everywhere; and soon some of the older families, assisted by the more supple or more discreet among the later arrivals, determined to attain distinction through organized exclusiveness. Since there was no legalized aristocracy into which Dives could be compelled to win his way by purchase, politics, cajolery, or philanthropy, it was necessary to resort to a kind of dictatorship. It was by this process that a portion of the plutocracy of New York was brought for a time under the sway of a social sovereign, Mrs. William Astor, capable of setting a fashionable standard for the city and thus for the nation. The founder of the house had come over as a penniless immigrant at the close of the eighteenth century but had quickly laid the basis of a family fortune by operations in furs, hides, and real estate, making it possible for his children to work wonders in the cultural line.

At last when the queenly heiress by wifely right assumed the reins in New York society, she had all the material substance required for her rôle. She wore regal jewelry and wore it regally; she erected a court and selected its courtiers —limited to four hundred because that was the number which her ballroom would comfortably hold; she had heralds to announce her activities, a public dazzled by her splendor, and newspapers, as eager as any court gazette, to make known her magnificence to those that sat in outer gloom. Moreover, she was ably assisted by a southern gentleman, Ward McAllister, the last Beau Brummel of his school. Thus conditioned, her experiment was successful beyond all hopes for many years—indeed until the invasion of "steel barons, coal lords, dukes of wheat and beef," described by Mrs. John King Van Rensselaer, broke the floodgates at the close of the century. But by that time the dictatorship had won recognition abroad; it had paved the way for the leaders to ascend into English society; and it had won titles for many of the high participants.

In its social aspirations, the American plutocracy inevitably turned to Europe. For a brief day after Appomattox it looked as if Paris under Napoleon III and Eugénie was to prescribe the modes of elegance and splendor for the western world, as in the age of Louis XIV, but the downfall of the Second Empire in 1870 put an end to that régime. Precedence then passed to the court of London. "Venus Victrix," wrote Martin in his society chronicle, "dowered with loveliness and dollars, set forth to conquer England." Though the timid had prophesied an early frost, the victory was simpler than the most ambitious had expected; for they had not read in advance the history of the British peerage from James I to Victoria.

With extraordinary swiftness a wedge was driven into the English line in 1874 by the marriage of Miss Jennie

Jerome, daughter of a Wall Street broker, and Lord Randolph Churchill. There had of course been earlier conquests; Miss Bingham, daughter of a rich Philadelphia merchant in Washington's time had married Alexander Baring, later Lord Ashburton, but that leap into the nobility had been by accident rather than carefully nourished design. It was the marriage of Miss Jerome that broke the ice, for her exploit was quickly followed by other international matches. The daughter of a railway king married a descendant of the hero of Blenheim; a granddaughter of a daring speculator in stocks and gold wedded a French count; the Leiter millions of Chicago were merged with the estate of Lord Curzon, that "very superior person." Finally the conquering power of the almighty dollar was completely demonstrated when William Waldorf Astor shook the dust of the United States from his feet, invaded the British Isles, acquired an English peerage by the usual method, and landed in the House of Lords among a host of English cotton spinners, soap magnates, tobacconists, journalists, and successful brokers.

Building town houses, buying art objects, and twisting into European society by no means exhausted the energies of the plutocracy now merging with the "old families" of fifty or a hundred years' standing. Its members, sated with ordinary things, sought amusement in Lucullan feasts and often in bizarre pranks borrowed from the underworld. For what an over-fond memory called an age of "plain living and high thinking" they substituted an age of "high living and plain thinking." As one of their number recorded, "in spite of ourselves we drifted into a period in which idleness became the fashion. . . . It was the poison of idle wealth. . . . It came at first like a little spot upon the body of man. Quickly it spread from limb to limb and part to part, until, in the fullness of time, it was a leprosy, following the body of society almost from head to foot."

Animated by fantastic passions, this idle set supplied

amazing sensations to the public in the ample days of Cleveland and Harrison. At a dinner eaten on horseback, the favorite steed was fed flowers and champagne; to a small black and tan dog wearing a diamond collar worth $15,000 a lavish banquet was tendered; at one function, the cigarettes were wrapped in hundred dollar bills; at another, fine black pearls were given to the diners in their oysters; at a third, an elaborate feast was served to boon companions in a mine from which came the fortune of the host. Then weary of such limited diversions, the plutocracy contrived more freakish occasions—with monkeys seated between the guests, human gold fish swimming about in pools, or chorus girls hopping out of pies.

In lavish expenditures as well as in exotic performances, pleasures were hungrily sought by the fretful rich delivered from the bondage of labor and responsibility. Diamonds were set in teeth; a private carriage and personal valet were provided for a pet monkey; dogs were tied with ribbons to the back seats of Victorias and driven out in the park for airings; a necklace costing $600,000 was purchased for a daughter of Crœsus; $65,000 was spent for a dressing table, $75,000 for a pair of opera glasses. An entire theatrical company was taken from New York to Chicago to entertain the friends of a magnate and a complete orchestra engaged to serenade a new-born child. In a burst of sentimental benevolence a family of destitute Negroes in the South was suddenly dowered with riches, garbed in luxury, and placed in a gorgeous house.

Unable to temper his culture with refined patience, a copper king turned connoisseur overnight and bought a complete museum of art. As if to put a climax to lavish expenditure, the Bradley Martins in 1897 gave a ball in New York that dazed the entire western world. "The interior of the Waldorf Astoria Hotel," according to a member of the family, "was transformed into a replica of Versailles and rare tapestries, beautiful flowers, and countless lights made an effective background for the wonderful gowns and their wearers. I do not think that there has ever been a greater display of jewels before or since; in many cases the diamond buttons worn by the men represented thousands of dollars and the value of the historic gems worn by the ladies baffles description. My sister-in-law personated Mary Stuart and her gold embroidered gown was trimmed with pearls and precious stones. Bradley, as Louis XV, wore a court suit of brocade. . . . The suit of gold inlaid armor worn by Mr. Belmont was valued at ten thousand dollars."

When described with journalistic gusto in the daily press, this grand ball of the plutocrats astounded the country, then in the grip of a prolonged business depression with its attendant unemployment, misery, and starvation, and called down upon the heads of the host and hostess a shower of invectives from the populist newspapers, which even the plea that the ball was given to help the poor by stimulating trade could not avert—a shower that increased until the sponsors of the ball sought refuge abroad.

§

Housed in the back streets and alleys behind the symbols of riches and power lived the urban masses who washed the linen, dug the trenches, served the wheels, and watched the forges for Midas and Dives. Whether the styles of Queen Anne or Louis Quatorze ruled along the boulevards made little difference to Mary, Tom, Dick, and Harry at the rear. With scarcely any direction other than that given by avid real estate speculators and greedy landlords, the tenements of the poor stretched and sprawled forward and outward in haphazard fashion, devoid of beauty, comfort, or health—made worse by the incoming hordes of Europe who pressed of necessity into the cheapest districts already cursed by squalor, dirt, and disease. Where literary effort fails to describe, the reports of the tenement house commission in New York may complete the picture.

History seemed to be repeating itself. Ancient Rome had its proletarian quarters; London, Paris, and Berlin their slums. Nero's House of Gold rose near the waste of dark tenements in which his subjects of the artisan and slave classes lived. The courtiers who hovered around Louis XVI wrested their incomes from the gnarled hands of burdened peasants; Queen Victoria drew revenues from rack-renting in London misery; Diaz decorated Mexico City with money wrung from wretched peons. As Calhoun remarked, somebody had to pay for culture.

In a general way, of course, there was nothing new about the juxtaposition of mammon and poverty in American cities but there were features in the situation that distinguished it from the urban life of other civilizations. Especially striking was the fact that the masses in the great cities of the United States were not slaves or the submerged offspring of slaves; neither were they the descendants of twenty generations of urban starvelings. They were free men, a large portion of whom had wandered into the cities from the farms bearing with them the notions fitted to rural economy; others had come straight from the fields of Europe. Even the oldest of American cities were new by comparison with those of England or the Continent. They had no traditions of royal patronage, noblesse oblige, or princely æsthetics. The feudal nexus had been dissolved; the cash nexus substituted.

Now the cash nexus pure and simple was the outstanding characteristic of social relations during the gilded age in America. On the plantation of the old South, the laborers were housed near the residence of the owner; their living quarters, whether comfortable or wretched, were known to the members of the planter's family; sickness was looked after and old age supported, at least in a way, authentic records telling us of many generous masters and mistresses who carried heavy burdens of human management. In contrast, the industrial labor which served the plutocracy housed itself, clothed, fed, and took care of itself as best it could on the wages received. Its living quarters stood apart from the seats occupied by the captains of industry, even if sometimes only a stone's throw from the boulevards, and families of the new lucre might live their entire lives without catching a glimpse of the districts in which their servants, immediate or remote, dwelled, reared their children, and passed from the scene. Commenting on this sharp separation of classes, Henry Cabot Lodge declares in his memoirs that not until the great fire of 1872 in Boston destroyed acres of tenements rendering their occupants utterly homeless, did he have any knowledge at all about how the other half of the world lived. And yet, though there was poverty in American cities, stark and galling enough to blast human nature, there was no proletariat in the Roman sense of the word.

Among the American working classes, all save the most wretched had aspirations; there was a baton in every toolkit. The public schools which flung wide for all the portals to the mysterious world of science, letters, and art opened the way for the talented to rise into the professions—at least that of politics. No tokens of garb, tongue, accent, or grammar marked them off as hopelessly from the upper ranges of society as the English cockney was separated from superior persons of Rotten Row. Brawny boys were constantly climbing upward to riches and circumstance; Patrick O'Riley of the saloon gang, who became Patrique Oreillé in Mark Twain's caricature of the passing show, was no mere creature of the imagination. There was misery enough no doubt; there were occasional outbreaks of political unrest which seemed to indicate a class upheaval, such for instance as occurred during Henry George's New York campaign in 1886; there were strikes longer and bloodier than ever before; there were a few hole-in-the-corner anarchists who compared the assassination of Garfield with the murder of the Tsar, Alexander II; but there was no multitudinous, grim, sodden, submerged industrial mass beaten to the status of permanent servitude. Certainly the majority of the craftsmen were not political pariahs; they could vote; and they had to be treated with wordy respect by statesmen and politicians.

In fact, the party machines that governed Boston, New York, Philadelphia, Chicago, and many lesser cities responded, at least in minor matters, to the will and desire of the working classes, rather than to the whims of the plutocracy—one of the strange ironies of the situation. Though the reformers fumed and raved, the hated political bosses were in truth, as that cool observer, James Bryce, quietly remarked, buffers between the rich and the poor, buffers who taxed the one to keep the other in good humor. The political levies and sometimes the flagrant corruption to which party managers resorted were chiefly for the purpose of acquiring the funds necessary to "take care of the boys," that is, to amuse them with balls, outings, and picnics, to supply them with clothing and funds in hard times, and to lend them money on occasion. Naturally there were brokers' charges on the collections but these were small as compared with the cost of riots and revolutions.

Expanding its functions, the political machine, hated of the righteous, also performed another service of mediation; it provided an avenue by which the humblest could get his grievances before the municipal government. It did more. It opened careers to ability. Many a ditcher, blacksmith, or trade union official, marked off from his fellows by shrewdness and will, was lifted by his party organization into a municipal berth, furnished what seemed to be a princely salary, and garbed in the frock coat and top hat of political respectability. Of course in all the operations of this character keeping open the channels between the classes, the saloon—the workmen's club—lent its assistance to the politicians; while the associated trades of the liquor industry, gambling and prostitution, were frequently made to yield their tribute to the cost of the general spectacle. No doubt the scene was far from pleasing to æsthetes and there were occasional outbursts of moral indignation against the party bosses but caution in that respect was exercised even by the highest and best. National elections could not be carried without the help of ward managers and their superior officers; many fine old families and at least one of the most fashionable churches in New York City drew large rents from slum tenements not fit for swine.

Besides the political outlets through which the surplus energies of the urban working classes found an easy vent, were other opportunities for relieving the tension induced by poverty and mechanical routine. The Catholic Church, with its gorgeous ceremonials and its sublime consolations for suffering and wretchedness, followed the poor everywhere, building edifices in the grayest and gloomiest wastes of the great cities. If its hierarchy gave sharp orders and insisted on adequate tribute, it none the less offered to the humblest and meanest a cordial welcome and a psychic pleasure that were not found in the cold orthodoxy of middle-class Protestantism. For that service the Salvation Army with drum and tambourine could tender but a feeble substitute.

More numerous and more continuous in operation, however, were the commercial "palaces of entertainment." For those who found little release in religious worship, and for some who did, were provided gaudy and lively amusements organized and managed on mercantile principles. Vaudeville shows, prize fights, circuses, dime museums, and cheap theaters, like the spectacles of ancient Rome, kept countless millions happy in penury, not at public expense, as in Cæsar's day, but at the expense of those who enjoyed them and to the advantage of those who owned them. Indeed, tickling the urban masses—creating popular tastes and standards of culture—now became one of the large and highly lucrative branches of capitalistic enterprise.

Into this business all the feverish passions of money-making were thrown, in efforts to arouse one sensation after another to sustain box-office receipts. The Paris "can-can" was imported in 1872, becoming quickly a high favorite and bringing heavy revenues into the pockets of promoters. Whole armies of scribblers were kept busy plotting hair-raising melodramas based on love, suicide, rum, and murder. "Cheap and nasty" were the watchwords of the new festivity and nothing could break their spell. The few aspiring actors who tried to "refine" the "thriller" met the same revolt which had long before defeated soulful Roman playwrights and had outraged contemporary improvers of the London music hall. Sothern, in his autobiography, relates that some reformers who tempted fate in New York were compelled to play behind meshed nets to protect themselves against eggs, vegetables, and other evidences of resentment hurled at them by the audience.

Into this grand game of amusing the multitude, P. T. Barnum, whose career had begun in 1835, entered with joy in spite of his advancing years and repeated threats of retirement. After experimenting in New York with museums containing "curiosities" of every sort from "roaring baboons" to "interesting relics from the Holy Land," Barnum joined his talents with two other entertainers and in 1871 launched the "Greatest Show on Earth" which was hauled on trains from city to city to divert the crowds, rural and urban. Nothing of the kind had ever been seen in western civilization and its success was stupendous.

Taking his cue from this venture, "Buffalo Bill," Colonel Cody, who had been fascinating audiences of eastern "tenderfeet" with desperate Indian melodramas, startled the country in 1883 with his "Wild West Show" portraying life on the plains—Indian fights, buffalo hunts, desperate brawls, and stagecoach robberies. For years it was a national rage. Then it was transferred to London where royalty and costermongers went equally wild with delight over its boisterous and exotic scenes, demonstrating that, after all, the tastes of the American democracy, in some respects at least, were not so far removed from those of the Victorian era in England, either in the higher or the lower ranges. Nor was that astonishing, for aged journalists could easily recall that, nearly half a century before, the great Queen had been pleased to entertain P. T. Barnum and Tom Thumb. A little entertainment seemed to make the whole world kin.

§

Between the urban masses with their circuses and prize fights and the plutocracy with its "palatial" mansions and its social aspirations stretched a wide and active middle class engaged in professional, mercantile, and clerical pursuits. It was within this group that the early Puritan characteristics of thrift, sobriety, and self-denial appeared to survive and unfold in the most natural fashion. It was into this class that sons and daughters of old colonial stock made their way by the thousands from farms and mills as their places were taken by the aliens who surged into the country to do the "rough work."

Whether the members of this order were the possessors of superior Nordic talent, as some said, or advanced by climbing upon the backs of untutored immigrants, as others argued, their cultural operations beyond question set the central pattern for the future in America. They were predominant in the schools, colleges, and professions. They supplied the higher politicians and makers of opinion— statesmen, journalists, and literary craftsmen who figured conspicuously in the run of intellectual interests. Members of this class also formed the backbone of Protestant Christianity. They set the taste in art and letters throughout a large area of the American landscape.

Often they appeared to be, in the imagination of their spokesmen, the entire American public. "I would rather address a Methodist audience than any other audience in America," Roosevelt once privately remarked. "You know for one thing that every one there is an American. . . . Next to the Methodists I prefer to address Episcopalians. They are all American likewise, usually representing the higher or else the lower social class. The Methodists represent the great middle class and in consequence are the most representative church in America. I think the Methodists and the Episcopalians increase more rapidly than any other churches in this country. They appeal to the genius of our institutions more than any other denominations. . . . The Catholic church is in no way suited to this country and can never have any great permanent growth except through immigration for its thought is Latin and entirely at variance with the dominant thought of our country and institutions."

In the main this great middle class met the requirements of Aristotle's golden mean. Though members of its upper ranges, fired by the ostentatious display of the plutocracy, crowded the hotels at Saratoga Springs and Long Branch, bought the cheaper seats at the Horse Show, attended the opera, and made "the grand tour" of Europe, the large majority was composed of people who possessed only moderate incomes or were in fact struggling along on the margin of subsistence to maintain appearances—hard-working husbands and pinching wives fighting desperately to keep their heads above water, support their sons in college, and marry their daughters into a better status. While the plutocrats built their palaces, this class filled the land with Italian, Tudor, French, Gothic, and castellated villas and cottages, large and small, which still rear their bizarre fronts beside the modest structures of earlier times. If the occupants of this social order could not buy Rembrandts with gleanings from lucky strikes in "the Street," they could often afford Winged Victories in replica for their mantels. If they could not rival copper kings in the purchase of whole art galleries, they could at least buy pianos, wax flowers, steel engravings, four-dollar opera tickets, statuary, Browning's poems, dyspepsia, and lawn tennis—to use the list of a contemporary.

Those who missed a college education or were unable to spend their summers in Europe found some satisfaction for their spiritual cravings in the "polite magazines," lec-

ture courses, and various schemes for popular adult education of the better sort. "The Concord School of Philosophy and the religious and ideal assemblies at Chautauqua
have developed into what we are accustomed to call 'institutions,'" gravely explained the New York Times in 1880.
"A few years ago they had not been heard of or had attracted the attention of only a small and interested circle.
They have now passed from experiment to success. They
seem this year to have reached the full maturity of vigor
and to have taken on a national character. Philosophers
from beyond the Mississippi are lecturing at Concord and
men and women from all over the country give and receive
instruction in the groves at Chautauqua. . . . If we were a
sluggish-minded people or imbued with a pedantic spirit,
we would show nothing like this. . . . To a great extent
knowledge sought at these academies is for its own sake.
Our young and new nation has at length reached a point
where a portion of its people can leave practical questions
to pursue purely intellectual questions having no relation
to dollars and cents. That is a mark of growth!"

It was after lecturing to comfortable and excellent people at Chautauqua that William James heaved an immense sigh of relief as he escaped into the freight yards
at Buffalo where the noise, grime, and jar of reality broke
the monotony of moderation, purity, and median lines of
thought. Nevertheless it was this respectable middle class
that in the main sustained the churches, filled the colleges
with sons and daughters, supported the "clean" press, kept
alive foreign and domestic missions, supplied the sinews for
the anti-saloon movement, backed the Women's Christian
Temperance Union, and, according to Matthew Arnold,
carried the burden of American civilization in the gilded
age.

§

Except in some of the mountain regions of the South, the
aspirations of the middle class were on the whole joyously

emulated by the agricultural masses and by the merchants of tiny villages who throve upon local trade. Though constituting, even at the end of the nineteenth century, a majority of the population, farmers and small-town folk, with respect to the tendencies of their cultural life, were drawn into the urban vortex. Handicraft arts which once gave distinction to European peasants and small-town artisans had never flourished to the same extent in the United States and with the advance of machinery those that had been introduced in earlier times practically disappeared.

So while the farming population supplied the middle class with a large number of leaders in politics, business, education, and religion, it threw up no dominant group of its own, evolved no culture peculiar to the soil comparable to that created by the European peasantry—consisting of music, dancing, folklore, costume, and mythology—and it received scant aid or comfort from the upward climbers who deserted it for the cities. If on occasion it furnished savage critics of the plutocracy and made noisy disturbances in the political sphere, it took its general ideas, tastes, and tones largely from the press, pulpit, and publishing modes directed and supported by the middle class. Composed largely of landowners, actual or potential, it had few ties of sympathy with the propertyless urban proletariat—except such as came from a mutual dislike for the "malefactors of great wealth." Limited in income to a meager margin of surplus, it found the qualities of thrift and temperance virtues as well as necessities.

The planting division of the agricultural population that had previously sent many haughty rulers to the national forum, although able to create a Solid South, could not retain its social prestige after the destruction of its economic and political supremacy. It had never been an aristocracy formed exactly on the European model for, deprived of the rights conferred by entails and primogeniture, it had been constantly diluted by invaders from the yeomanry. While it had furnished many statesmen, orators, and military officers in the days of its glory, it had produced relatively few writers, painters, sculptors, inventors, or scientists. Its culture was largely that of leisure, bought with the surplus of slave labor—conspicuous and lavish expenditure on articles of refinement made elsewhere. It had never possessed a social capital such as the landed gentry of England enjoyed in London or the daimios of Japan in Yedo. It must be conceded that in the days of slavery New Orleans and Charleston in particular had just pretensions as centers of taste but, after the Second Revolution spread disaster among the ranks of the planters, those cities turned more and more to trade.

A few southern orators continued to protest against the sacrilegious conduct of the deserters who, "ignoring the elevating influence of heroic impulses, manly endeavor, and virtuous sentiment, would fain convert this region into a money-worshiping domain; and careless of the landmarks of the fathers, impatient of the restraints of a calm, enlightened, conservative civilization, viewing with indifferent eye the tokens of Confederate valor, and slighting the graves of Confederate dead, would counsel no oblation save at the shrine of Mammon." But such reproofs buttered no parsnips. Survivors among the planting aristocracy and their children now moved into the towns as leaders of business enterprise or strove to place their estates on a money-making basis. When Senator Benjamin Harvey Hill made his memorable address before the University of Georgia at Athens in 1871, he raised his eloquent voice without apology in behalf of applied science, urging the people to develop the practical "facilities by which to retain the possessions they occupy." He advised them not "to pine away or fret to exhaustion for imaginary treasures hopelessly lost" but rather to "reach out their hands and gather richer treasures piled up all around them." The land of Calhoun was being assimilated finally to the realm of Yankee ingenuity.

§

Within the ranks of the several classes so deeply affected by the progress of business enterprise, women found the direction of their cultural concerns also changed by the drive of economic forces. Among the plutocrats, it was they more than the men who set the pace in the new vogue of "conspicuous waste." Among the working classes, the women who labored for wages got a certain amount of money they could now call their own and by their expenditures helped to give a trend to taste, at least in mass production. In the middle orders, especially the more prosperous ranges, thousands of women, escaping completely from the grind of factory, office, and kitchen, secured leisure and means for reading, traveling, and social undertakings. Supplementing these economic resources was the system of inheritances which, by giving wives and daughters control over large estates, set many of them free to follow their whims, to patronize artists, musicians, lecturers, and writers as few had done heretofore—except in the case of queens and other ladies of high degree—to indulge in amateur excursions on their own account. Under various pressures therefore the gravity of women's interests steadily moved from the center of the family outward toward the periphery of that circle where it merged into the larger humanities.

On the left of the feminist movement, the leaders, Elizabeth Cady Stanton and Susan B. Anthony, who had launched their revolutionary cause before the Civil War, took up once more the strategy of the battle for equal suffrage after the slavery question was settled. Far on the right, less concerned with matters of historic status, a host of women in a great zeal for self-culture in arts and letters formed a club movement which unwittingly prepared the way for political action on a national scale. The Sorosis of New York, founded at the home of Jane C. Croly in 1868, called forth a thousand imitations, covering the land with Monday Clubs, Rainyday Clubs, Browning Societies, and Shakespeare Coteries, expanding the market for magazines, prints, books.

and musical instruments in swiftly widening rings. Then local societies were united in state federations, women imitating the politicians, the Knights of Pythias, and the Elks in making excursions away from home to great assemblies of their kind, which like men's conventions furnished more or less news for the press. Finally, in 1889, a national union was effected by the formation of the General Federation of Women's Clubs, which drew within its fold a multitude of organizations with varied aims.

Once federated on the national scale, club women began to take a broader outlook. Though timid in discussing questions long reserved for the masculine mind, though inclined to stick tenaciously to their cultural program, they could not successfully resist the beat of opinions that thrummed on every side of them. Little by little, self-centered groups, bent on improving their personal standards of refinement, found social and political questions seeping into their papers and debates. While they kept on patronizing polite letters and the fine arts in a genial fashion, their intellectual interests drifted out into the broader and deeper streams of national life and opinion.

By the opening of the new century, American women had broken down the walls of the traditional sphere. "When I read in the paper and heard in the Club that a dozen women of great wealth were standing along Broadway handing bills and encouragement to the girl shirtwaist strikers of last winter, I was not a bit surprised," wrote a diarist member of the plutocracy as the century turned. "It is just what you might have expected. Nowadays I can hardly go to a reception or a ball without being buttonholed by somebody and led into a corner to be told all about some wonderful new reform. It is perfectly amazing, this plague of reform, in its variety, in its volume, and in the intensity of earnestness with which it is being pushed." Seed sown in the distant middle period had, in the more favorable conditions, sprung up many fold.

8

Mingling with the social ferment created by these changing domestic forces were surging currents of opinion borne into America from Europe by cables and by books—above all by home-coming travelers and scholars increasing in numbers as steamships multiplied and passenger rates declined. Among the imported scientific theories of the age were two clusters of ideas which immediately turned the course of thought in the United States. The first, closely related to the old warfare between science and religion, had Darwinism as its center.

Although the Origin of Species was published in 1859 it was not until the Civil War had blown over that the full effect of the doctrine was felt in America and it was not until 1871, during Grant's administration, that the Descent of Man sprang detonations which shook from top to bottom the traditional concept of human origins. After that explosion, the fire spread. In the age of Garfield and Cleveland, Bellamy and Henry James, the evolutionary strife was carried deliberately into the theological camp by Thomas Henry Huxley, furnishing for Robert G. Ingersoll in the United States the kind of ammunition that Voltaire had given Paine a hundred years before.

Associated with Darwinism, but far more disconcerting for the defenders of "permanent institutions," was the synthetic philosophy of Herbert Spencer which applied the evolutionary concept to ethics, politics, economics and ceremonials in general—thus fulfilling the prophecy made by Emerson in the middle period. If uncertainty hovered over the Darwinian account of organic evolution, there was no doubt about the general doctrine of social development: the career of mankind, as now revealed by the sociologist, opened in a remote past far beyond the limits of Eden's chronology and was marked by many steps leading away from primitive savagery to modern civilization. While the mutability of species was still awaiting indubitable proof, the mutability of customs, beliefs, and institutions was demonstrated with a wealth of evidence that could not be controverted. If Spencer's personal antagonism to social-ism, his invincible preference for "anarchy plus the police constable" was assuring to the leaders in the American acquisitive process, his broad theory of social evolution was ruinous to any perfection of wisdom, even though embodied in the Fourteenth Amendment to the federal Constitution, and it offered the starting point for dynamic speculation in every department of thought and action.

Certainly nowhere in the world was Spencer's work more cordially received than in the United States. Admirers in America gave him several thousand dollars in 1866 to help in the prosecution of his studies; the sale of his books was larger here than in England; and the Popular Science Monthly, founded by E. L. Youmans, afforded the English philosopher an audience that was astounding in its range and enthusiasm. Suffused with the optimism dominant in New World life, Spencer's theories were employed to fortify at every point the idea of progress that had been so potent in earlier years.

Of a different character and yet strongly supporting the concept of progress were European achievements in natural science during this epoch. No previous age had given to mankind so many discoveries of utility in its war on disease and pain or made so many revelations as to the constitution of matter and force. From 1860 to the end of the century, the years were crowded with intellectual triumphs of the first order. Pasteur by his work in bacteriology and by his invention of serum inoculations proclaimed an effective war on devastating plagues. In the same field, Lister revolutionized surgery by the application of antiseptics, striking down at one blow the black horror of blood poisoning. Complementing these victories, though of wider implications, were the labors of Crookes and Roentgen which produced the X-ray apparatus so useful in surgery, medicine, and dentistry. Quickly following the discovery of the X-rays by Roentgen came the epoch-making stroke of Professor and Madame Curie in extracting radium from Austrian pitchblende, which opened a new era in physics. By the close of the century, Marconi had begun the emancipation of telegraphy from cables and wires. These exploits, coupled with the feats of countless other workers in many fields, brought about nothing short of a revolution in the scientific outlook of the Old World.

To a Europe now fired with a glowing curiosity about everything past and present, flocked a host of American students in search of wisdom. Owing to peculiar circumstances, most of them went to Germany to school. The ancient universities of England, still under the dominance of clerical and classical traditions, had no equipment for advanced research and as yet extended scant welcome to American students. France, long in confusion after the downfall of the second Empire, presented no special attractions either. On the other hand, the universities of Germany greeted American graduate students hospitably and conferred the degree of doctor of philosophy upon those who complied with the requirements for that honor. The response from the United States was in keeping with the generosity of the German welcome. In all the German institutions of higher learning, American college graduates were soon pursuing advanced studies in science, economics, history, theology, and classical literature and acquiring habits of independent research that transcended the restraints of current conventions. On their return home, these young doctors taught the progressive philosophy of Hegel, the socialistic economics of Wagner and Schmoller, and the historical methods of Mommsen and Gneist. At last, American colleges and intellectual interests, as far as they were affected by collegiate discipline, felt the shock of critical inquiry and the impact of ideas wholly foreign to the heritage handed down by the theological educators of the middle period.

§

In the religious life of America during the gilded age

there were also novel developments, apart from the influence of new social opinions upon theology and ethics,
namely, the remarkable growth of the Roman Catholic
Church and the rise of the Christian Science movement
under the inspiration of Mary Baker Eddy.   The first of
these departures in historic American tendency—continuing
the beginnings of the middle period—was due of course to
the steady influx of immigrants from Catholic regions of
Europe rather than to any marked revulsion of religious
sentiment among original Protestant stocks.   But whatever
the prime cause, it gave a new cast to culture and shifted
the balance of ecclesiastical power within American society.
By 1890, the Catholics possessed a majority, or at least a
plurality, of the Christian communicants in thirteen states;
twenty years later the number of such commonwealths had
increased to eighteen, mainly the industrial sections with
large factory and mining populations.

This spectacular growth of Catholicism, though it amazed
some defenders of the inherited order, was really welcome
to many Americans of colonial descent who were now recoiling before the advance of radical ideas and scientific
thinking.   Priests of the Catholic denomination were found
in practice to have, as a rule, a moderating influence on
strikers and labor agitators; and often a Protestant capitalist, such for example as James J. Hill, looked to the
Catholic hierarchy for support in the maintenance of law
and order.

Moreover the large right wing of the Protestant clergy,
engaged in sustaining the accepted dogmas of their respective denominations, were happy to reckon the Catholic clergy
among their allies in throwing up bulwarks for the faith.
If the more intellectual among the latter exercised great
discretion in dealing with scientific discoveries and opinions,
it remained a fact that the Catholic Church was no more
willing to surrender the Bible and Virgin Birth than the
most invincible Baptist or Presbyterian of the southern
highlands.   Besides, the Catholics had before them the

410 THE RISE OF AMERICAN CIVILIZATION

plain instructions of the Syllabus of Errors issued by Pius IX in 1864, stigmatizing as false the doctrine that "the Roman Pontiff can and ought to reconcile himself to, and agree with, progress, liberalism, and civilization as lately introduced." In the presence of a common foe, the ancient enemies found themselves comfortably enlisted in the same campaign.

Additional recruits for the struggle against what appeared to be materialistic tendencies in natural science were drawn from the adherents of the new sect founded, in 1866, by Mary Baker Eddy of New England, home of Transcendentalism and mystical visions of varied types. The creed was not entirely original but it was emphatic in its dissent from the dogmas of the naturalists. "There is no life, truth, intelligence, nor substance in matter," wrote Mrs. Eddy. "All is infinite Mind and its infinite manifestation. . . . Matter is mortal error. . . . Man is not material; he is spiritual." For the serums of Pasteur and the antiseptics of Lister, believers in Christian Science offered the healing balm of religious conviction; in accord with their Catholic contemporaries they proclaimed their faith in the existence of miraculous powers capable of giving sight to the blind, strength to the cripple, health to the sick, and courage to the faint in heart.

Making a wide appeal to the middle classes, they were soon able to build up rich and flourishing congregations all the way from Boston, the seat of the Mother Church, to San Francisco at the Golden Gate, to say nothing of congregations in Europe, Africa, South America, the Orient, and islands of the seas. Though the practice of the sect forbade "numbering the people," estimates made by students at the end of the century placed its membership above that of many important denominations claiming ancient origins. Moreover the teachings of the Christian Scientists affected the thinking of other Protestants, including doctors of medicine, who, without denying the efficacy of material cures for human diseases, recognized the power of the mind over the body. And the creed also got into the new psychology—the latest religion of skeptics.

§

Notwithstanding the growth of Catholicism as the number of immigrant workers increased and the rise of Christian Science, especially among the comfortable middle classes, the general process of secularization wrought by business enterprise, technology, and natural science, so vigorously advanced in the middle period, now hurried forward with a quickened pace. As in the earlier age, leadership went to the inventors: Charles Brush, Peter Cooper Hewitt, Charles P. Steinmetz, and Thomas Edison in electricity; George Pullman in sleeping car construction; George Westinghouse, creator of the air-brake; George B. Selden, Charles E. Duryea, R. E. Olds, and Elwood Haynes, designers of automobiles in the seventies and eighties; James Oliver, inventor of the chilled plow; Samuel P. Langley, Glenn H. Curtiss, and the Wright brothers in aeronautics; Ottmar Mergenthaler, William Bullock, the Hoes, Tolbert Lanston, and Henry A. Wise Wood in the arts of typesetting and printing; Christopher Latham Sholes, a pioneer in the development of typewriting machines; Alexander Graham Bell in the sphere of telephonic communication; Hannibal Goodwin and George Eastman in photography; and Edward Muybridge and C. Francis Jenkins in motion picture production.

Nearly every year between the close of the civil conflict and the end of the century witnessed some signal achievement in the realm of applied science. In 1865, Bullock built in Philadelphia the first continuous web-printing press. In 1866, cable communications with England were opened under the indomitable captaincy of Cyrus W. Field. In 1867, John F. Appleby exhibited the working model of his self-binding reaper. In 1868, the Sholes typewriter was put to commercial use. In 1869, Westinghouse took out the initial patent for his railway air-brake. In 1870, H. H.

Marvil invented a machine for making fruit and berry baskets. In 1872, Edison announced his duplex telegraph which made it possible to send two messages over the same wire at the same time. In 1875, G. F. Swift built the first refrigerator car. In 1876, Alexander Bell sent his historic telephone message by wire. In 1877, Edison heard "Mary had a little lamb" on his phonograph. In 1879, Selden applied for a patent for a gasoline carriage. In 1880, Edison built an electric railway at Menlo Park. In 1886, Mergenthaler's linotype machine rang out the coming doom of typesetting by hand in the great newspaper offices. In 1887, a vestibule train was put on the tracks by Pullman. In 1888, A. N. Hadley patented his corn cutter and shocker. In 1891, Strowger formed a company for the manufacture of automatic telephone exchanges. In 1892, Bell opened telephonic communication between New York and Chicago. In 1893, Henry Ford tested his first automobile on the road. In 1894, Jenkins gave a motion picture show with his new machine at Richmond, Indiana. In 1895, Elwood Haynes drove a motor car through the streets of Chicago. In 1896, Langley's airplane flew three thousand feet. In 1897, Lanston's monotype machine was patented. In 1900, Henry A. Wise Wood began making stereotype plates by an automatic process. In 1901, the Wright Brothers completed their first glider.

All along the frontier where machine industry came into contact with the natural world, constant experimenting was creating a new social climate for men of bench and forge. The era of the cloistered inventor was drawing to a close. In every branch of science a host of searchers was at work; news of strange undertakings flew about on the wings of the winds; two or three persons often applied simultaneously for the same patent. Frequently American achievements were so closely paralleled in Europe that it was hard to apportion honors among the competitors of two hemispheres.

As the collective character of advancing technology became more marked, coöperative plans were deliberately adopted with a view to promoting systematic inquiry and discovery—"the invention of invention," contrived by the Germans, becoming the outstanding feature of American enterprise. In 1876, Edison, for instance, established with his own earnings a huge laboratory at Menlo Park in New Jersey where he assembled a body of experts and began to create machines on a wholesale principle. By the opening of the twentieth century, the General Electric Company had ceased to rely on sporadic outcroppings of genius and had organized the work of invention on severely methodical principles under the leadership of competent masters. Technology was passing into a social phase of apparently limitless possibilities.

In pure science, a field separated by indistinct boundaries from that of applied science, American work in general, as during the middle period, took the form of painstaking and important researches in every field—biology, chemistry, physics, botany, geology, and astronomy—now supported however on a more extensive scale by large endowments. No epoch-making discoveries comparable to the work of the Curies, Pasteurs, and Roentgens of Europe were made, a fact of peculiar significance, but nevertheless descriptive and analytical studies were pursued with zeal and intelligence. Geological surveys, botanical expeditions, the collection of specimens, the foundation of great institutions, such as the Natural History Museum of New York established in 1869 and the Columbian, later the Field, Museum of Chicago in 1893, the construction of laboratories, and the publication of articles in technical journals all marked a steady progress in the exploration of the natural world.

In this onward movement there was developed a body of technically competent scientists equal in talent to the same class of workers in Europe. In the domain of ethnology, Lewis H. Morgan, a Rochester lawyer, did work of permanent value, his accounts of Indian tribes and his extraordinary book on Ancient Society producing a deep impression on the social thought of the Old World and the New. Besides making him a recognized master at home, the original researches and publications of James D. Dana, the Yale geologist, won for him the Copley prize from the Royal Society of London, the Wollaston medal from the London Geological Society, and honorary degrees from Munich and Edinburgh. In 1895, the Institute of France paid tribute to American genius by electing Simon Newcomb, the astronomer, to membership after he had already received the Copley prize, degrees from leading universities, and the Huygens medal from Leyden for the best work done in his science for a period of twenty years. The achievements of Samuel P. Langley in solar physics and Henry Draper in photo-chemistry revealed high powers of penetration and imagination, placing them both among the outstanding figures of their era in America and Europe. As head of the Smithsonian Institute, Joseph Henry, generally conceded to be "the foremost American physicist" of his time, pursued his restless inquiries in many directions, and continued to make original contributions to electrical science, meteorology, and acoustics until his death in 1878 at the ripe old age of eighty-one.

In the same class of creative spirits, perhaps a little higher in the galaxy, was Josiah Willard Gibbs, who, after studies in Paris, Berlin, and Heidelberg, began in 1871 his thirty-two years of service as professor of mathematical physics at Yale University. By accomplishments of a superior order, he won for himself a position of commanding importance in the international republic of science. Competent experts hailed him as the founder of "a new department of chemistry"; his illuminating papers were translated into French and German; he was greeted by the celebrated Ostwald as the "founder of chemical energetics"; and in 1901 the Royal Society of London awarded him the Copley prize as "the first to apply the second law of thermodynamics to the exhaustive discussion of the relations between chemical, electrical, and thermal energy and capacity for external work." A critic no less severe than Henry Adams put Gibbs on the "same plane with the three or four greatest minds of his century."

That phalanx of scientists who sought some kind of key to the riddle of the universe as a matter of course had their task cut out for them in the gilded age by the revolutionary work of Charles Darwin and Herbert Spencer. By no equivocation could America escape the mental challenge of these English thinkers; every student of philosophy and the natural world had to declare allegiance or dissent, at least with respect to general principles. As we have already seen, Asa Gray, a leading botanist of the preceding period, early expressed his approval of the evolutionary thesis and began to champion it in the public forum.

Before Gray retired from Harvard in 1873, John Fiske, a more popular writer and speaker, without special training in natural science, took up the cudgels for Darwin and Spencer and with the aid of his friend, E. L. Youmans, led the fight all along the line on the tenacious Miltonic hypothesis of creation. This militant campaign Fiske started at Harvard in a series of lectures delivered in 1869-71, later incorporated in his Outlines of Cosmic Philosophy, a work which quickly ran through many editions. Terrific was the burst of fury which greeted Fiske's first assault; newspapers and clergymen made vehement protests; and the Lowell Institute would not allow the "agnostic" to deliver his message to its select body of thinkers. Unshaken by the opposition and cordially supported by Charles W. Eliot, the new president of Harvard, Fiske went on with his crusade, steadily gaining adherents, especially after he began to emphasize the possible reconciliation of the Spencerian theory with the ancient concept of a personal God. By the end of the century, evolution in a variety of linguistic patterns stretching from the defiant skepticism of Huxley to the genial Christian theories of Drummond had become thoroughly naturalized in the United States with widespread influences in every branch of mental activity.

The secularizing process stimulated by Fiske and his colleagues was advanced by scientific writers who made direct frontal attacks on theological traditions. In the course of this paper war, John William Draper, the eminent chemist, choosing the instrument of historical exposition, published in 1862 a survey of the intellectual development of Europe which treated the clergy and their allies after the cavalier fashion of Buckle; and twelve years later Draper brought up new artillery—a version of the conflict between science and religion. The schism which Draper created was afterward widened by Andrew D. White, who crowned his labors in 1896 with a great work on the warfare between science and theology in Christendom. After that day there were few thinkers in higher university groves, who accepted without fatal reservations the simple epic made immortal by Milton. Indeed science was now so enthroned in America that it became a kind of dogmatic religion itself whose votaries often behaved in the manner of theologians, pretending to possess the one true key to the riddle of the universe.

§

Upon religious concepts and Christian ethics, especially in Protestant circles, the influence of scientific thinking was immediate and emphatic. Although the ponderous theologian, Charles Hodge, in presenting his view of Darwinism in 1874, declared that "a more absolutely incredible theory was never propounded for acceptance among men," President McCosh of Princeton, whose orthodoxy was flawless, boldly undertook to reconcile a kind of evolutionary doctrine with the Christian idea of God. The theory, said McCosh, "makes God continue the work of creation, and if God's creation be a good work, why should he not continue it?" Thus given a high recommendation, the evolutionary view of the universe soon permeated Protestant theology everywhere except in the intellectual hinterlands of the country.

Also disconcerting to the theologians of the old school was the contemporaneous development of higher Biblical criticism—an examination of the authorship, textual composition, and plain meaning of the Bible in the cool light of historical science. "In every department of Biblical study we come upon errors," exclaimed Charles Augustus Briggs, one of the most cautious of the new scholars; for his temerity he was convicted of heresy and suspended in 1893 from the Presbyterian ministry. Nevertheless he found a home in the Protestant Episcopal Church and a generous hearing throughout the country. Within a few years his doubts about the inerrancy of the Bible had become commonplaces in all the theological schools that paid any attention to the voice of reason.

In spite of the fact that the clergy who disagreed with the conclusions of the higher critics declared them more damaging than Ingersoll's popular lectures on the mistakes of Moses and ancient conceptions of Hell, the process of scientific invasion and historical research could not be stayed by any verbal fiat. In every quarter insistent issues simply had to be met. Preachers of all schools, disturbed by the steady secularization of intellectual interests, were compelled to face the dilemma of losing doubters by sticking fast to old creeds or losing their creeds in trying to keep up with the sweep of science, philosophy, commercial amusements, and acquisitive obsessions. The reconciliation of religion with the new science called for supreme abilities.

While the Catholic Church was able to escape in some measure the dissolving effects of this intellectual movement by falling back upon traditions older than any version of the Bible, all the Protestant denominations that did any reading or thinking were forced to make new reckonings. Of their religious convictions the very center and support was the Bible, especially the King James version, and as advancing science questioned its astronomy, biology, ethnology, physics, and historical canons, there was no choice except surrender or answer. Consequently those who refused to throw overboard their heritage cast about for buoys of various shapes and materials.

In meeting the mixed array of disturbing doubts now set afloat, the heroic Briggs freely declared that "the religion of Jesus Christ is not only the religion of the Bible, but the religion of personal communion with the living God." Among the Protestant masses at large, those who paid any heed to such perplexities probably found their state of transition very well described in the amazing scheme of liberation devised by Professor William N. Clarke of Colgate. "I have described the change, " he wrote, in his Sixty Years with the Bible, published in 1909, "by saying that I passed on from using it in the light of its statements to using it in the light of its principles. At first I said: 'The Scriptures limit me to this'; later I said: 'The Scriptures open my way to this.' As for the Bible, I am not bound to work all its statements into my system; nay, I am not bound to work them all in; for some of them are not congenial to the spirit of Jesus and some express truths in forms which cannot be of permanent validity."

Equally troublesome to the theologians was the new philosophy imported from Germany, principally by college professors. Owing to their extraordinary growth in the gilded age, American universities afforded economic support for a numerous class of intellectual workers not connected with the churches on the one hand, as in colonial times, or with the substance of industry on the other—a class of workers to whom the anomalous title of "educators" was given. In these circumstances philosophy, natural and theological, once the monopoly of the clergy, passed gradually into the hands of secular newcomers.

Among the pioneers of this group, William T. Harris stood preëminent. During a long life devoted to educational work, he sang the praises of the profoundest German thinkers, above all of the kingly Hegel, who though religious in outlook were primarily secular in interest. In 1867, Harris founded in St. Louis the Journal of Speculative

Philosophy, which for a quarter of a century promoted contemplative studies and encouraged young American scholars, such as Josiah Royce, Charles S. Peirce, William James, and John Dewey, to employ their talents in examining cosmic problems from the earthly side. While plunging into the secular current, Harris had no desire to affront the theologians. He constantly assured them that genuine philosophy supported rather than undermined the grand doctrines of Christianity; but in practice the results were not exactly as prophesied.

It is true that Royce, by the performance of marvelous intellectual feats, managed to stay within the hazy bounds of authentic religion, but Peirce, James, and Dewey swung gradually over toward the mathematical and scientific wing. And in the end philosophy, which in America had hitherto served as the handmaid of theology, deserted her employer, showing in the eighties and nineties an independence that bordered on insolence, at least as things were mirrored in the minds of the former initiates. It was then too late however for theologians to recover the chairs of philosophy established in the leading universities and filled by laymen in correspondence with the intellectual trend.

§

While theology was being forced to reform its verbal modes under the stimulus of science and secular philosophy, Christian ethics had to reckon with the thundering facts of the new economic order and with all the varieties of social thinking thrown up so profusely in the conflict of capital and labor. In reality, by reason of its Oriental emphasis on things of the spirit, an emphasis natural enough among a people lacking in material goods and living on the margin of subsistence, Christianity ran counter to the acquisitive drift in American life. If the ethics of the historic faith continued to satisfy pulpit and pew in many rural regions, doubts and quandaries certainly appeared in the great centers of industry, wealth, and poverty, particularly as the blows at Pittsburgh, Homestead, and Pullman came ringing through study walls.

While T. DeWitt Talmadge went serenely on preaching salvation in another world as the chief aim of man, a number of lesser lights in the clerical profession began to hunt through the words of Jesus for pertinent truths applicable to capitalists and workingmen engaged in a desperate struggle over the possession of worldly goods. Turning also to the illuminating experience of England, they read the writings of Kingsley, Ruskin, Maurice, Carlyle, and Ludlow. After much searching of hearts, a small group, calling themselves Christian Socialists, came together in Boston, under the inspiration of W. P. D. Bliss, in 1889, and put forth an American declaration of faith, asserting that "the control of business is rapidly concentrating in the hands of a dangerous plutocracy" and that "the teachings of Jesus Christ lead directly to some specific form or forms of socialism." Small as their circle was, the range of their influence, as events later proved, was wider than it was thought to be at the moment.

Many a clergyman who did not accept with a whole heart the radical creed of the Boston party was caught in the drift of current social thinking and borne along part of the way. At the Rochester Theological Seminary, Walter Rauschenbusch, recasting his scheme of reasoning in the light of Christian Socialism, frankly placed social service above pious profession. "This high task of making human life and human society the realization of the Father's loving will for his children; this is the real substance of the spiritual life, of which the services and devotions of the church are but outward forms." At the Chicago Theological Seminary, the industrial implications of Christianity were given frank recognition in the establishment of a chair in Social Economics which was filled by Graham Taylor, fresh from the Hartford Seminary, where he had been emphasizing, in the terms of religion, the collective obligations of the new epoch. In Ohio, Washington Gladden, though opposed to Socialism, flayed the plutocracy in scorching words and pleaded for a mild form of municipal ownership and state control that looked like anarchy to the philosophers of the full dinner pail. Beyond the Mississippi, George D. Herron, from his chair of Applied Christianity at Grinnell College, preached a gospel of "social redemption" which turned scores of Methodist clergymen from the traditional themes of card-playing and dancing to the conflicts of the market place. With growing insistence it was asked in nearly every quarter whether Christianity had any message for thinkers who were trying to construct a fairer order or at any rate to reduce the frictions of the lucrous game.

This new Christian interpretation of human obligations, combined with the study of ethics, bore practical fruit in the college settlement movement—that social adventure of the eighties. The original attempt to bridge the gulf between rich and poor, by establishing residential centers in slum areas, was made at Toynbee Hall in London under the influence of Samuel A. Barnett, a clergyman of social leanings in the Church of England; and from that English experiment, Stanton Coit, who founded the Neighborhood Guild in New York in 1886, drew direct inspiration. It was with emphasis on religious sentiments that Professor Vida Scudder, of Wellesley College, appealed for student volunteers to break down the barriers between the classes, called for "a new Franciscanism" to overcome the brutality of the acquisitive process, and gave unstinted service to the settlement movement. In opening the Hull House amid the dreary industrial wastes of Chicago in 1889, Jane Addams likewise ascribed no small part of her initiative in the enterprise to "the impulse to share the lives of the poor, the desire to make social service, irrespective of propaganda, express the spirit of Christ—an impulse as old as Christianity itself."

Whatever the dominant force behind this effort to cross the social divide, it exerted, beyond all question, a direct and immediate influence on American thinking about industrial questions and on the course of social practice. It is safe to say that few economists grew to maturity in the gilded age without some association with a college settlement where first-hand contacts with labor could be made. In fact the contribution of the institution to the education of the middle classes was perhaps greater than its services to the poor; for one of its prime functions was to interpret to the boulevards and avenues the life and aspirations of the factory quarters. Moreover through the practical experiments of such agencies fresh approaches were revealed to workers tackling the problems of urban misery. For instance the value of organized district nursing was concretely demonstrated by the Henry Street Settlement of New York under the direction of Lillian D. Wald.

With no exaggeration did Robert Woods, the experienced Boston leader, declare in his survey of thirty years that the college settlement had brought representatives of the working class into conferences affecting the whole community; that it had provided the first laboratory for the study of the immigrant question; that it had revealed to the prosperous the life and problems of the poor; that it had promoted realistic studies, social surveys, kindergartens, free libraries, recreation, the enforcement of industrial and sanitary codes; that it had waged war on the sharpers who played upon the weakness of the masses; and had effected a union of forces against the more flagrant abuses of American industrialism.

Indeed, any search for the origins of social practice in the United States meets at some point the work of settlements. One example will illustrate the wide range of their activities. It was the residents of Hull House who led the first effective fight against child labor exploitation and sweat shops in Illinois. It was one of this group, Florence Kelley, who, on the basis of first-hand experience, suggested to the state bureau of labor an investigation into these long accepted evils. The inquiry was made. A legislative committee appointed to examine into the state of affairs in Chicago

held meetings at the Hull House. Members of that institution were selected by organized labor to coöperate in the
formulation and enactment of protective legislation. Under
this pressure was passed "the first factory law of Illinois,
regulating the sanitary conditions of sweatshops and fixing
fourteen as the age at which a child might be employed."
Immediately afterward, Mrs. Kelley was appointed the first
factory inspector, given a staff of deputies, and put at the
task of enforcing the law, with the aid of another Hull
House resident, a young lawyer, who helped in prosecuting
violators of the factory act reported by the inspectors.
This was the beginning of a long career of service on the
part of Mrs. Kelley in promoting better standards of industrial practice and in educating consumers with respect to
responsibilities to the producers of their goods. It was
no accident that Jane Addams, head of Hull House, stood
with Theodore Roosevelt at Armageddon in 1912 when
the plutocracy was challenged in the name of "decent government and fair play."

§

Changing industrial processes, ostentatious riches, novel
adventures of the scientific spirit, and new interpretations of
Christian duty ran deeply into political opinion, economic
doctrine, ethics, and esthetics. As the plutocracy shot upward into power and fame above the low levels of the social
plain, it naturally became the target of criticism on every
side. Farmers and industrial workers who enjoyed neither
the hope nor the possibility of great fortune, old families
of talent and lineage who were content either through
choice or necessity with modest estates, the shattered aristocracy of the South that clung to the rhetoric and philosophy of the manor house, the middle classes which had a taste
of wealth with irritation rather than emancipation—all took
a less rosy view of the economic universe than millionaires
fresh from business victories surrounded by their admiring
retainers.

Centuries before, in the momentous decades of ancient Rome when new men swollen with the proceeds of commerce and speculation astounded the Eternal City by their luxurious display, plebeians and patricians of seasoned stock united in expressing anger at self-centered, vulgar parvenus and anxiety for the safety of the state. Cato the Elder, offspring of a farmer, Cicero of dubious origin—probably artisan—and Juvenal, descendant of a freedman, concurred with the flower of the landed aristocracy in the belief that lovers of great riches and effeminate luxury were a menace to morals and patriotism. In similar fashion, during the uprush of the plutocracy that followed the Second American Revolution, those who for one reason or another garnered no huge stakes from the lucrous game were moved by doubts and misgivings as to the future of the republic. Labor leaders, like Powderly and Gompers, and agrarian champions, like Peffer, Simpson, and Bryan, joined thinkers from other realms, for example, Emerson, Lowell, Henry Adams, Lodge, and Roosevelt, in expressing the conviction that there was something alarming in the drift of American affairs.

In no contemporary documents can the direction of such opinions be traced with more precision than in the writings of Henry Adams, who, after serving as secretary to the legation in London, carefully studied and observed the course of American economy until his death in 1918. In his early years, Adams said, he struggled in a half-hearted way against "State Street, banks, capitalism altogether, as he knew it in Old England or New England," but in the end he gave up the battle, confessing defeat. "A capitalistic system," he wrote in 1893, "had been adopted and if it were to be run at all, it must be run by capital and by capitalistic methods; for nothing could surpass the nonsensity of trying to run so complex and so concentrated a machine by southern and western farmers in grotesque alliance with city day laborers, as had been tried in 1800 and 1828, and had failed even under simple conditions." A few years later Adams warned his countrymen that in the end they would have to choose between the pessimism of European politicians, religious reaction, and the communism of a labor dictatorship.

Henry Adams' bosom friend, Henry Cabot Lodge, the successor of Webster in the Senate, though regarded in radical quarters as a spokesman of the plutocracy, entertained fears scarcely less poignant. He declared that he could not be "oblivious to the darkest sign of all, the way in which money and the acquisition of money by taking it from some one else through the process of law seems in the last analysis rampant in every portion of the community, and at the bottom if not at the top of almost every proposed reform, every political issue, and every personal ambition." In 1913, he openly confessed his uneasiness at "the gigantic modern plutocracy and its lawless ways" and even more uneasiness at the restless desire of the populace to escape hard labor and to despoil Dives of his pecuniary rewards. All society, all art, all letters, all manners, the distressed statesman saw afloat in an age obsessed by money and amusement.

Less guarded than the Senator from Massachusetts in his verdict upon the gilded age was another offspring of old stock, Theodore Roosevelt. As early as 1897, before he loomed large upon the political horizon, Roosevelt, writing to Lodge about a municipal campaign, exclaimed: "The really ugly feature of the Republican canvass is that it *does* represent what the populists say, that is, corrupt wealth. . . . Both Platt and Tracy represent the powerful, unscrupulous politicians who charge heavily for doing the work—sometimes good, sometimes bad—of the bankers, railroad men, insurance men, and the like." Later experience confirmed him in this analysis of politics. In explaining to Sir Edward Grey the campaign of 1912, he declared with evident feeling: "We had against us . . . ninety-nine per cent at the very least of the corporate wealth of the country and therefore the great majority of the newspapers. . . . We were fought by the Socialists as bitterly as by the representatives of the two old parties and this for the very reason that we stand equally against government by a plutocracy and government by a mob. There is something to be said for government by a great aristocracy which has furnished leaders to the nation in peace and war for generations; even a democrat like myself must admit this. But there is absolutely nothing to be said for government by a plutocracy, for government by men very powerful in certain lines and gifted with the 'money touch,' but with ideals which in their essence are merely those of so many glorified pawnbrokers."

§

In spite of all this concern about the course of events in America during the gilded age there appeared no social philosopher competent to survey the society from top to bottom, plot the trajectory of plutocratic ascendancy, or interpret the sweep of things in the large. Of course, the socialists were active in obscure corners offering the gospel of Karl Marx in pamphlets and brochures, but they produced no critique of the capitalist procession in America worthy of more than a passing glance. Disgruntled populists, deprived of planting leadership and finding no clergymen or college professors to write for farmers as they had once written for slave owners, did nothing but pepper Mæcenas with bird shot.

Perhaps the first approach to a critical diagnosis that made a rift in American complacency was Henry George's Progress and Poverty, published in 1879, a trenchant volume drawing the deadly parallel of riches and misery, sun and shadow; proposing to apply to the complexities of the capitalist order a physiocratic doctrine of the eighteenth century in the form of a single tax designed to absorb unearned increment in land values and strike at the root of gross inequalities of wealth. By his livid description of the carking desolation spread under the high noon of American prosperity and the assurance he displayed in prescribing a remedy, George sounded a new note in American criticism. Within a decade, he became famous at home and across the seas; radicals and trade unionists in New York tried to elect him mayor; owners of factories patronized him—he offered no disturbance to their economic operations. In England and Ireland he was hailed as a conquering hero, and, owing to the acuteness of their land problem, made a profound impression on current economic opinion. Through countless channels, George's ideas filtered out into varied types of American thought, helping to make the country at least dimly aware of the social question; but the single-tax creed bore little fruit in legislation and gave no serious qualms to the managers of politics.

In a different vein, but with effects on complacent opinion almost as subversive, was James Bryce's American Commonwealth issued in 1888. For the first time since the days of de Tocqueville, a philosophic foreigner, in this case an Englishman, had surveyed the whole American tableau, if, as someone remarked, "over the rim of a champagne glass," and described it with elaborate precision. Hitherto, most of the books on American government had dealt with the subject in the terms of pious constitutional fiction; but Bryce laid bare the anatomy and morphology of politics—rings, bosses, frauds, machines, intrigue, and chicane. It was devastating, especially that part of it written by a young professor at Columbia University, Frank J. Goodnow. Though Bryce did not speak in the language of a medical man or offer specifics for the ills he exposed, his book made a sensation among those who, to use Ruskin's phrase, had sat with joyful faces at the banquet table—blindfolded.

Before their serenity was completely restored, they were given a more violent shock in 1894 by a volume from the pen of a fellow-countryman, Henry Demarest Lloyd, bearing the pointed title, Wealth against Commonwealth. For a long time Lloyd had been studying closely the methods used by the giants of capitalism in disposing of petty competitors. In 1881, to the distress of respectable readers, he published in the Atlantic Monthly a merciless attack on the Standard Oil group. After devoting more laborious days to amassing data, Lloyd then opened a general campaign, using the records of judicial trials and legislative inquiries to convict capitalists of the crimes usually ascribed to those inclined, like Napoleon, to neglect minor conventions in the pursuit of major aims. Some of his evidence was sedulously controverted; yet there was enough truth in his sweeping indictment to spread among the mighty much trepidation over the safety of their institutions. Doubtless the effect of Lloyd's arraignment would have been more terrifying if he had not offered social democracy as the answer to the questions raised by his analysis—a particular solution no more palatable to the American middle class than the doings of John D. Rockfeller's South Improvement Company.

Upon the members of the plutocracy at large, the criticisms of Henry George and of Henry D. Lloyd made no very lasting impression; though, as time moved on, a few of them began to manifest doubts more or less philosophic. If none followed the Christian injunction to sell his goods and give to the poor or emulated the example of the Grimké sisters who, freeing their slaves, took up abolition, one at least, Frederick Townsend Martin, gave his whole class a terrible lashing in a book, called The Passing of the Idle Rich, published in 1911. "It is strange to me," he said, "and it always has been strange to other men who have studied those things, that a plutocracy can be so long maintained; for a plutocracy, of its very nature, is the weakest possible form of government. It lives either by force or fraud. It lived in Rome before the days of Marius by force alone; and the lower orders of Rome were slaves. It lived in Paris before the Terror by a combination of force and fraud. . . . It lives in America by fraud alone; and what may we say of the people of this nation that permit it to live? . . . Today we are studying the sources of our wealth, finding out for ourselves the real price paid by humanity to give us the privilege of the social life which we and our fathers have enjoyed." Thus the American leisure class was invited to turn in upon itself, inspect its economic position, and consider its place in the general social structure. Naïve acquisition and enjoyment were coming under the scrutiny of sophistication.

§

A counter-reformation, as always, followed the assaults of the critics. The capitalist system, in which the plutocracy flourished, like every other social organism, had to evolve a scheme of defense and, as things turned out, the task of justifying to man his own handiwork fell mainly to the economists in the universities that sprang up like mushrooms as the gilded age advanced. At Yale, William G. Sumner vindicated in lecture and treatise the economics of Manchester so acceptable to captains of industry eager to be left alone—at least in domestic affairs if not in the matter of tariffs. At Columbia, John Bates Clark, in his Philosophy of Wealth and later in his Distribution of Wealth, showed with a lavish display of learning and logic that on the whole the capitalist system worked for justice, rough-hewn, but still justice; to put his system in more severe terminology, each factor of industry, particularly capital and labor, is rewarded in the main according to its contribution and thus business enterprise partakes of even-handed equity. Under the terms of a gift from a wealthy manufacturer, the Wharton School established in 1881 at the University of Pennsylvania was expected to expound the protective tariff as a highly praiseworthy economic device. All that was needed to make the circle complete was another Calhoun to celebrate the theme: "Capitalism a Perfect Good!"

That task, however, proved impossible; for academic economics was not at bottom altogether unified by any such simple faith. When viewed closely from the standpoint of business enterprise, it showed cracks and flaws in its retaining walls. If Professor Sumner rained resounding blows on the heads of trade unionists, who, as he thought, were trying to make water run up hill, he also struck out at the beneficiaries of protective tariffs and commercial imperialism, taking his canons from the Cobden-Bright school without reference to the peculiar problems of the American order. Even more disturbing to "sound economy" was E. B. Andrews, who, at Brown University, in the old home of Federalism, upheld the heresy of free silver until for reasons of weight he was compelled to transfer his scene of activity to the Middle West. In the same institution, Lester F. Ward declared that the social process was highly dynamic, jarring perceptibly the solid structure of orthodox economics built on concepts essentially static in nature. Though far more radical in the import of his teachings, Ward managed, by refraining from meddling too much in practical affairs, to keep his chair to the end.

In other halls of learning the crucible was bubbling. At Johns Hopkins and later at Wisconsin, Richard T. Ely, who had studied among the Germans their strange mixture of feudalism, cameralism, and capitalism, known as social economy, expounded a critical and constructive creed that looked to the elect like the threat of socialism. Indeed, his teaching made such a furor that a legislative investigation was held and peace was not restored until it could be shown that his frightful doctrines were merely a mild brand of "reform." About the same time John R. Commons, after amazing academic experiences, began to introduce the learned world to organized labor as an inevitable accompaniment of capitalism. In 1899, at the turn of the century, Thorstein Veblen printed the Theory of the Leisure Class, a merciless analysis of bourgeois reputability, the first of a long series of ironic books from his bewildering pen.

Evidently social criticism had crept into scholarship. Indeed, university teachers were openly proclaiming that science had nothing to do with bolstering up or assailing any social order; its business, they said, was the search for truth—that corroding acid more disruptive to prevailing modes than any force except the discovery of new ways to easy profits. In other words, the creed of unrestrained acquisition was growing soft. When the American Economic Association was founded in 1883, under the presidency of General Francis A. Walker, it boldly engraved on its shield the devices of science rather than the dogmas of any static concepts. And before long younger members of the society began to play havoc with general economic theory by making innumerable concrete studies of taxation, railways, trusts, labor unions, wages, profits, panics, and other details in the progress of business enterprise, with little or no reference to any exigencies of capitalist defense.

While masculine economists occupied themselves with capital, interest, land, profits, labor, and wages, a feminist leader of no academic pretensions, Charlotte Perkins Gilman, half as advocate and half as prophet, demanded and received a national hearing on the relation of women to the new order of things. After a season of lecturing, she published in 1898 two works, one in prose, called Women and Economics, and another in verse, entitled In This Our World. With much ingenuity and a great deal of humor, she propounded the thesis that woman was enslaved by tradition and could only regain her primitive vigor and creative power by securing complete economic independence from "the nearest male relative by birth or marriage." So stirring was her analysis of historic reverence for "the holy stove" and so clarion was her call for freedom in mind and labor that a new school of feminist thinkers was raised up in America and Europe which sent reverberations as far afield as awakening Japan. Moreover, the system of co-operative living, with its enlarged leisure for women, which seemed when proposed by Mrs. Gilman a utopia more chimerical than Bellamy's romance, proved to be in the hands of real estate promoters the soundest economy for urban development. Though shocking to defenders of inherited matrimonial institutions, the idea of economic independence for women, if extremely difficult to define in practice, was continuously illustrated by the multiplication of women wage workers in industry, by new adjustments in marital relations, and by a constant increase in the number of divorces granted at the instance of discontented wives. Concepts which had been broached as revolutionary in the early days of the republic or even in the middle period became commonplaces at the close of the gilded age.

§

The general process of bringing ideas into closer relation with changing circumstances was also aided by the rise of a school of "scientific historians," who, like the economists, were largely sustained by the colleges and universities. Before the nineteenth century closed a revolution had been started in the spirit of historical research and composition; the old romantic craft, ornamented by Bancroft and Prescott, had passed away; and an army of doctors of philosophy, trained in Germany or in the new American institutions of higher learning, had taken the seats of the mighty. Announcing as their slogan the dictum of Ranke that it was the business of the scholar to see the past as it actually was, they invaded every important field in a critical mood, challenging respectable dogmas with a rudeness that alarmed the amateur guardians of national traditions. In 1884, the American Historical Association was founded, followed eleven years later by the publication of the American Historical Review. Before long the collection and interpretation of materials passed largely into the hands of professional workers who, unlike Bancroft, made no claims to special knowledge concerning the ways of God and in theory at least were committed to the search for mundane truth. In due course this change in the affairs of Clio was to bear strange fruit.

For the time being, however, historical writing in "the grand style" remained largely in the hands of men who dropped into the business more from accident than design. Indeed most of the ambitious work of the period was done by students who had little or no connection with the schools, at all events as professors. A great history of Lincoln in ten volumes was written by his former secretaries, Nicolay and Hay. A practising lawyer, Henry Harrisse, of French origin but a graduate of the University of South Carolina, achieved monumental results by researches in the period of discovery and exploration. From his office in the Harvard library, Justin Winsor issued huge volumes of narrative and critical history which still stand as staples in the studies of scholars. Another son of Harvard, Francis Parkman, continued with increasing success his series on the struggle of England and France for the possession of North America. And his neighbor, John Fiske, turning from cosmic philosophy, retold the early period of American history with no little literary skill—discarding the canons of his master, Herbert Spencer, in favor of interesting episodes and actions. With a decided penchant for realism, two grandsons of John Quincy Adams, Charles Francis and Henry, finding political careers closed to them, devoted their high talents to works presenting significant phases of national culture.

If no one followed in the footsteps of Irving and Motley, European themes were not wholly neglected. In Philadelphia a prosperous business man, Henry C. Lea, more than made up for the general indifference of his contemporaries. Retiring from commercial affairs with a competency in 1880, he indulged himself in his affection for mediæval studies, and published, eight years later, a great history of the Inquisition, which was followed by other works in the same field. With a more practical purpose in mind, Captain Alfred Mahan, at the Naval War College, employed history to stimulate interest in enlarging the Navy at the very moment when American capitalism was looking for more worlds to conquer. In rapid succession he turned out volume after volume on the influence of the sea power in destiny, visibly impressing the governing classes of England and encouraging the German Kaiser to redouble his efforts in naval construction. Although the secrets of social evolution in the United States received little attention from such masters of the grand style, the materials for that more or less esoteric inquiry were being heaped up in the modest brochures and articles which flowed from the pens of professional students.

§

For imaginative literature, as for history and other factual subjects, the conditions favorable to creative work, already rich in the middle period, were intensified by the economic development of the gilded age, multiplying the demands of the market, schools for training, and facilities for the nurture of hereditary power. Now the makers of novels, stories, poems, and essays had a larger and more varied audience—with the shift of industrial and population centers into the West, the absorption of the South into the machine process, the expansion of urban civilization, the multiplication of literates through the public schools, the opening of colleges to women, and the general extension of the middle-class area of comfort and leisure. In magnitude the demand of this continental audience could be measured according to financial terms: the annual output of book and job presses was approaching a hundred million dollars at the end of the century, a sum greater than the national debt of Washington's day, which croaking pessimists thought the people of America could never pay.

In response to this enormous demand for literary wares was called forth a corresponding body of workers possessing fair technical competence, among whom occasionally appeared a personality hailed as a genius—how and why no one can exactly tell. No doubt, as Edwin L. Clarke proves in his study of American letters, heredity has been an important factor in the production of talent: during the nineteenth and early twentieth centuries sixty-eight families conspicuous for literary power furnished nearly one-sixth of the one thousand leading American authors. But this is not the whole story. In those select families, nurture—the climate of books and learning, the occupations and conversations of parents and adult friends—was an element to be placed in the scales with heredity. Any way, among the distinguished literary families, only a few heirs-apparent were writers of the first magnitude. More pertinent to intellectual evolution in the large are Clarke's conclusions respecting the whole group of authors under survey. He shows that "in proportion to numbers, families in comfortable circumstances had produced more literary children than had families living in poverty"; that birth into the more fortunate social classes had given ability exceptional opportunities to secure advantageous training; that the richest and most dissident religious denominations had brought forth the largest numbers of authors; that the stimulus of the cities had fostered creative work; and that, as the education of women advanced, they had become more prominent in the world of letters.

If the economic development of the gilded age increased the demand for imaginative literature and enlarged the supply of competent writers, the social conflict of the period furnished stirring themes for their versatile pens. By the authors of the first rank who rose above purely local portraiture—authors of the quality of Mark Twain, Whitman, Lowell, Hay, and Howells—the great questions of national destiny which perplexed statesmen and economists were proclaimed, hinted at, etched or shown through a glass darkly according to mood and circumstance. In Letters as well as in orations, editorials, and treatises were reflected the deeds of industrial captains, the doings of the plutocracy, the clashes of capital and labor, the schemes of reformers, and the protests of the agrarians. Nearly every line written by Walt Whitman after 1865 mirrored some aspect of the immense and varied economic processes of America, the hopes and doubts that ran with them.

> Race of veterans! Race of victors!
> Race of the soil, ready for conflict! Race of the conquering march!

Whitman cried triumphantly in the hour of the great peace. But in his Passage to India written five years later the exultant note was somewhat subdued to an inquiry about the inner meaning of the rush and roar.

> A worship new, I sing;
> You captains, voyagers, explorers, yours!
> You engineers! you architects, machinists yours!
> You, not for trade or transportation only,
> But in God's name, and for thy sake, O soul.

One year more and acrid doubts had begun to corrode the poet's confidence: "I say that our New World democracy, however great a success in uplifting the masses out of their sloughs, in materialistic development, products, and in a certain highly deceptive superficial popular intellectuality, is, so far, an almost complete failure in its social aspects, and in really grand religious, moral, literary, and esthetic results. In vain do we march with unprecedented strides to empire so colossal, outvying the antique, beyond Alexander's, beyond the proudest sway of Rome. In vain have we annexed Texas, California, Alaska, and reached north for Canada and south for Cuba. It is as if we were somehow being endow'd with a vast and thoroughly appointed body and then left with little or no soul."

Whitman's humorist contemporary, Mark Twain, fresh from Missouri, Benton's old agrarian stronghold, was equally outspoken in condemning the achievements of American Mammon—at least until prosperity and his wife took the edge from his wrath temporarily. When in 1871 he and Charles Dudley Warner surveyed the ground for a novel of their time, they decided that the title, The Gilded Age, covered their view of the scene; and, under that head, which we have used from their coinage, they portrayed the social structure from top to bottom. In the guise of fiction they displayed the new plutocrats, ignorant in mind and vulgar of tongue, assuming the airs of the grand style; a raw, rough, uncouth nation obsessed by the acquisitive passion; a scrawny country of villages striving to rival New York and Chicago with the aid of congressional plunder; corrupt politicians, municipal, state, and national, given to high sounding verbalism and low pillage; the roaring mobs of great cities fed on murder and scandal by a sensational press—an unlovely mess without beauty and prospect of taste. In a similar vein James Russell Lowell, when called upon in 1876 to write a centennial ode, blew a blast against rings, bosses, and plunderers which aroused a storm oɩ objections among the super-patriots. Taken to task for his bitterness, Lowell asked: "Is ours a 'government of the people, by the people, for the people' or a Kakistocracy, rather for the benefit of knaves at the cost of fools?"

In spite of Lowell's strictures on American society, the industrial magnates of Chicago invited him to deliver his mind before them in a public address, and on his arrival they tendered him a magnificent reception; one so gorgeous in fact that it inspired Eugene Field, then a young journalist in the western metropolis, to comment on Literature and Riches and shoot a few barbed shafts at the local exponents of culture. With much gusto he quoted Varro's lines about patronage in a gilded age long buried:

> Mæcenas is a model host,
> Who o'er his viands nice,
> Is wont to name each dish and boast
> Its quality and price.

Then in a burst of merriment he declared that "the mantle of the most luxurious, the most fastidious, and the most refined of the grand old Roman times" had fallen, so to speak, "upon the shoulders of the representatives of Chicago wealth and culture. . . . It is understood that the private dinners given to Mr. Lowell during his stay here have called for an expenditure of not less than forty thousand dollars. Yet there are carping critics who say that Chicago is not a great literary center!"

In a flare of whimsy Field called himself the Chicago Dante, "bard of pork and lard," and with the capricious comments that filled his column in the Chicago Daily News, one of the pioneers of these modern literary channels, he continually mingled quips on lucre and respectability, which carried a flow of humor that was both gentle and careless, for the pageant evoked in him no Puritan wrath. He was no bigot; if every day's calendar of events drew his attention to irritating things, it awakened in him no rancorous bitterness. When a great circus came to Chicago, for example, he linked the episode with the appearance in London of a new edition of Sappho: "As the cage containing the lions rolled by, the shouts of the enthusiastic spectators swelled above the guttural roar of the infuriated monarchs of the desert. Men waved their hats and ladies fluttered their handkerchiefs. Altogether, the scene was so exciting as to be equalled only by the rapturous ovation which was tendered Mlle. Hortense de Vere, queen of the air, when that sylphlike lady came out into the arena of Forepaugh's great circus tent last evening and poised herself upon one tiny toe on the back of an untamed and foaming barb that dashed round and round the sawdust ring. Talk about your Sapphos and your poetry! Would Chicago hesitate a moment in choosing between Sappho and Mlle.Hortense de Vere, queen of the air? . . . If it makes us proud to go into our bookstore to see the thousands upon thousands of tomes waiting on customers, if our bosoms swell with delight to see the quiet and palatial homes of our cultured society overflowing with the most expensive wall papers and the costliest articles of virtue; if we take an ineffable enjoyment in the thousand indications of a growing refinement in our midst—vaster must be the pride, the rapture we feel when we behold our intellect and our culture paying the tribute of adoration to the circus."

In a similar light, other phases of the American spectacle in the gilded age passed under Field's genial review—splashes of color taken from it appearing in his "Culture's Garland; being Memoranda of the Gradual Rise of Literature, Art, Music, and Society in Chicago and other Western Ganglia" collected in the year 1887. Nothing escaped his wit, not even the practices of village statesmen. When, for instance, a crowd of Illinois politicians set out on a junket to New Orleans at public expense, he wrote a "fake" telegram from "Blue Cut, Tenn.," stating that "the second section of the train bearing the Illinois legislature to New Orleans was stopped near this station by bandits last night. After relieving the bandits of their watches and jewelry, the excursionists proceeded on their journey with increased enthusiasm."

Harping upon same string, two other funmakers of the gilded age—as yet unchecked by the deadly standardization of the machine and unoppressed by the monetary morals of the counting house—took special note of the follies in current political economy. Under the lackadaisical bantering and uproarious explosions of Artemus Ward often lay piercing observations on the paradoxes of the American republic. During the tense days of the Civil War, Lincoln had found relief from his agony in the absurd humor caught by Ward from the life of the trains, canal-boats, and small towns of the Middle West and in the shrewd comments of the satirist on the acquisitive instinct in politics. When, in a joke, Ward described the swarms of office-seekers who descended upon Lincoln at Springfield, when he attributed the disastrous defeat at Bull Run to a rumor of three vacancies in the customs house at New York, he reached deeper down into the substance of popular conventions than any of the long-faced pretenders would ever admit. If Stanton could not see the flash of the rapier, his once-snubbed chief was fully able to appreciate it.

In a far wider range of daring and with a surer grasp of details, Peter Finley Dunne, speaking in the language of

"Mr. Dooley," depicted the American process as he saw it at the end of the century. With sparkling laughter he exposed the theories, conceits, lies, and corrupt practices of his time, displaying such rich humor that he received storms of applause from the generality as well as the scoffers. His phrase "the Supreme Court follows the election returns" —a doctrine that might have cost a professor his chair— was greeted with vociferous cheers and passed immediately into current coin among people who would brook not the slightest disrespect for that great tribunal, who certainly would not admit that human passions ever interfered with the consultation of the divine auspices. Fully as popular was his casual remark that a law which looked like a stonewall to a layman was a triumphal arch to the eye of a corporation lawyer. His three words on Roosevelt, "alone in Cuba," were worth a volume on that warrior's official claims to distinction in the Spanish War. With a touch of the same severe irony, Mr. Dooley discoursed on imperialism in the Philippines, "irradyatin' civilization," selling men's shirtings to the "natives iv neighborin' Chiny"— "with a holy purpose in our hearts, th' flag over our heads, an' th' inspired wurrud iv A. Jeremiah Beveridge in our ears." If Dooley's version made no votes for the anti-imperialists, it at least relaxed the tension of the "moral overstrain."

With kindred stress, the transformation of the social order which arrested the thought of poets and humorists struck into the pages of the novelists, furnishing themes and drives for countless tales—and money and leisure for rising above the eternal commonplaces of the humdrum. As in the days of the early republic and in the middle period, writers of fiction, who did not flee to other countries or devote their talents to the portrayal of local scenes and characters, arrayed themselves from right to left on the issues of the social conflict that ran through the gilded age like a livid scar; though none ventured a whole-hearted defense of the plutocracy. Perhaps the best vindication of raw capitalism was the Breadwinners, a novel on the great railway strike of 1877, written by John Hay, who was in time to become a high Republican politician, a trusted associate of Marcus A. Hanna, the accomplished diplomat of William McKinley's imperialism.

For the poignant middle class of seasoned families, equally distressed by the doings of the plutocrats and the vulgarisms of democracy, spoke Henry James. The grandson of a millionaire, a whole generation removed from the odors of the shop, and granted by good fortune a luxurious leisure, James steered his way into a more rarefied atmosphere, normally as the sparks fly heavenward. In a loftier altitude he found many superior people "cultivated" in taste, languid in habits, and desirous of elegant manners if they had not fallen heir to them in a natural way. Of such upper class persons and for them, James wrote most of his novels, using the crude, rising, bourgeoisie of America to emphasize the prettiness of the English landed aristocracy which had subdued even its latest cotton-spinning recruits to some accord with manorial taste. Possessing an assured income from fixed investments, he took time in his writing to evolve a meticulous and fine-spun style, one so vague and so intricate that it moved even his brother, William, the pragmatic philosopher, to explode in a letter to the novelist: "Say it out, for God's sake." Accustomed by his position to the society of people not wholly engrossed in business, James found a home in England, where at last, during the World War, he renounced his American citizenship and became a subject of King George.

Somewhat in the same fashion that more versatile genius and more powerful improvisor, Francis Marion Crawford, after drawing a picture of Boston politics in 1884, fled from the "thin and vulgar life of America" to the mellow civilization of Italy, where he devoted his talents to exploiting European scenes and personalities. Though such withdrawals were alarming to patriotic Americans and soothing to the nations thus classed as more exquisite, the practice was by no means new among literary people.   Byron, Keats, Shelley, and the Brownings seemed to prefer Mediterranean to English culture; Heine enjoyed his days in Paris more than in Hamburg or Düsseldorf; Turgeniev died in the capital of France though he might have returned to Russia.

To the left of the center were the most penetrating makers of fiction.   There Mark Twain belonged, by birth and by nature, retaining in his mental make-up to the end of his days some of the twists of Missouri's agrarian democracy; though apart from occasional thrusts at "privilege," particularly in the Yankee at the Court of King Arthur, he attempted no general analysis of American society after the merciless scrutiny of The Gilded Age.   Turning aside to safer themes, he left to his less gifted and milder-mannered friend, W. D. Howells, the task of discovering fiction in the roaring vortex.   Like Twain, Howells was from an old agrarian region; born in Ohio, he knew the frontier; in his youth he had cut trees, plowed corn, and dug potatoes. It was by sheer force of mind that he made his way into the higher economic stratum where, as a boy from the soil, he encountered the frost of culture two or three generations old, giving him a shock that vibrated through his tale of The Rise of Silas Lapham.

Early drawn into the struggle of labor against the plutocracy, Howells not only wrote of that conflict and its antithesis, the Socialism of Altruria, but he descended into the forum to champion the right as he was given to see it— even to protest against the execution of the Chicago anarchists as "a grotesque perversion of law," knowing full well, as he said, that his action was distasteful to "the immeasurable majority of the American people."   If his wrath never burned to high heaven and his stories of the times, realistic as they were, marked no epoch in American letters, there was no doubt about the locus of his soul in the curve of the American economic alignment.

Still to the left of Howells, at least in the baldness of their fictional structures, were two writers of the period far more dogmatic in their style. Accepting the machine system at face value Edward Bellamy wrote a frank novel of Socialism, Looking Backward—the first American utopia of the industrial age, glorifying science and invention as the savior of mankind from the curse of nameless and unhonored drudgery. With an extraordinary swiftness it caught the imagination of the whole country, led to the formation of a short-lived Nationalist Party, and gave to the hard Marxism of the German Socialists a deep tinge of American sentiment. If Bellamy's furor soon died away in the storm of the generality, his influence on social thinking was never lost. Of a different order but radial to the same center, was The Bomb written several years later by Frank Harris. In none of Zola's terrible descriptions of Parisian degradation, was the devastating brutality of modern poverty, a root of industrial revolt, more accurately presented than in this picture of Chicago slums, a tale of social unrest in the submerged wilderness of that ruthless city.

Intense as was the pulling power of the machine vortex, drawing sections and provinces into one simple crucible, the great majority of the popular novels turned out in the gilded age derived their substance from geographical peculiarities and ancient triangles. After writing one national novel, The Gilded Age, Mark Twain portrayed life on the Mississippi and in the West, a life that was peculiar to the New World in many ways, and made a few excursions into European scenes, ending in bitter doubts about all so-called eternal values. In the Hoosier School-master, Edward Eggleston etched with deadly accuracy a poor white community in the Indiana of pioneer days; and afterward tossed off occasional pictures of the frontier that was passing. From the Old South came the voices of Joel Chandler Harris, who made the southern Negro to laugh and weep in his pages, and of George Washington Cable, who, with rare sympathy, caught the spirit of his particular section, notably New Orleans. In the far North, Sarah

Orne Jewett saved pictures of fading New England, while Margaretta Deland reflected in John Ward, Preacher, the sinking flickers of religious passions that still divided families. From the Pacific Coast to New York and London, Bret Harte carried the roar of the mining camps; and in the pages of Helen Hunt Jackson's Ramona the dying years of Mexican California were clearly painted.

So rich indeed was the harvest of this period that a present-day critic, Carl Van Doren, reviewing the whole gamut of American fiction, is persuaded that the decade between 1880 and 1890 produced more good novels than any similar span in American history. Why so many of them perished quickly, like the grass that is cut down and withereth, must be left to those who preside over the battle of the books. Perhaps, however, mass production in letters as in pig iron, the pressure of publishers for new stocks to sell, and the dynamic drive in American economic evolution account for most of the oblivion that overtook them.

Whatever may be the arbitrament of time in this matter, it can be safely said that the best selling books of the gilded age were of a different order. In that uproarious era, the American masses cherished what a clever writer has called "dime-novel theories of the world." They were not interested in esoteric, impersonal, futurist or vortical speculations. They were obsessed by the concrete, personal, primitive, material zest for life—for a life that was to last but a brief moment until the free land was occupied and the waste places were conquered by man with his machines, his codes, his arts, and his standardized reputations. In every respect the epoch was distinguished by what John Hay called "the restless haste and hunger which is the source of much that is good and most that is evil in American life."

So in those epic days, while the women and girls of the middle class throve on Godey's Lady's Book and Bok's Ladies' Home Journal, the men and boys consumed tons of "thrillers" that represented almost without exaggeration the adventures in tragedy, lust, hot passion, mystery, and riches which were indigenous to the soil of the New World. For every copy of Howells' Traveller from Altruria or Henry James' Portrait of a Lady that was sold in the marts of trade, doubtless a thousand copies of Buffalo Bill's desperate deeds, Diamond Dick's frantic exploits, and Beadle's blood-curdling jeopardies were consumed by the men who, with the consent of their wives, governed the country in the gilded age and by the boys who were to possess the future.

That other branch of imaginative literature, the drama, ran true to the laws which governed fiction. There were heavy borrowings, as always, from Europe, while the themes evolved in America often corresponded with ceremonial usage. Yet it is significant that two of the most conspicuous dramatists, Bronson Howard, styled the "dean of American drama," and James A. Herne, creator of American types, were both deeply affected by the economic processes that were swirling around them. Capital and labor, the amusements and diversions of the plutocracy, and the disasters of frenzied speculation formed underlying patterns for Howard no matter how thickly he overlaid them with French persiflage and conventional entertainment. That affection for nearness to the soil which marked the spirit of Howells was also in the drive of Herne's work. A student of Darwin and Spencer and deeply impressed by the economic tragedy portrayed in Henry George's story of progress and poverty, Herne tried to reach down into fundamentals. Still, for every one of these efforts motivated by an intense reaction to the substance of American life, came a thousand plays adapted from European writers and designed for those who took especial pride in being cosmopolitan or who preferred technique to strife; a thousand more or less refined melodramas for the middle classes; and a thousand blood-curdlers, like Nellie the Beautiful Cloak Model, for the proletariat, "at popular prices."

Perhaps this was to be expected, for one of the striking facts of the gilded age was the conquest of the theater by business enterprise and the organization of dramatic production on a trust basis. The cost of management, the expansion of the market with the rise of new cities all the way to the Pacific coast, and the enlarged opportunities for profit conspired to place theaters like newspapers in the hands of men economically competent. In these circumstances, the old-fashioned stock company, organized by one or more actors or actresses, free to produce plays that suited their fancy and directly dependent on the earnings of the box-office, steadily gave way before the theatrical manager who supplied the capital, searched out the national market, selected his own plays with reference to potential earnings, and chose his own stars. Like the industrial capitalists who frequently climbed from the boiler room or the clerk's desk to the direction of industry, these theatrical magnates often rose from the position of boy ushers taken from the streets, through libretto writing, to the high adventure of production and management. By 1900, the theatrical trust had the drama as firmly in its grip as the oil trust had the petroleum business.

In both cases there were some independents and many protestants, but their operations were confined to side eddies in the main current, and to criticisms of the victors. It was alleged, for example, that the new type of manager stifled both acting and playwriting; to which the defendants replied that they were hungry for signs of genius and found them not. Considered on its intrinsic merits, the discussion which raged was much like the old controversy over the advantages of French academies and English literary anarchy. In any event, the theater, as it always has been, was subdued to the forces that were uppermost in the world of business— and philosophers were unable to break the whirling circles of cause and effect.

§

For the fine arts as for imaginative literature, the economic and social setting of the gilded age provided specific conditions of development. The mounting riches of the plutocracy, the growing wealth of the middle classes, and the construction of public buildings and monuments expanded the market for painting and sculpture.

While the market was being extended, ways and means for artistic aspirants to secure technical training were multiplied. The passage to Europe was made easy and inexpensive; more Americans than ever before could study under the best teachers of the Old World and see the originals of great work from the historic past. Meanwhile, the facilities for stimulus and training at home were enriched and drawn more closely to those of Europe. At the celebration of the centennial of independence in Philadelphia in 1876, a great display of European, Oriental, and American paintings, sculpture, porcelains, and textiles gave the general public its first chance to get a glimpse of the world's masterpieces.

From wider interests of this nature sprang, during that decade, museums of the fine arts, such as the institutions in Boston and New York, under the inspiration of professional and business leaders, with the support of popular subscriptions and municipal grants. Within a few years, it was a mean city indeed that could not boast of a public art collection, or at least an occasional exhibition. In connection with the museums and independently as well, centers of instruction in the fine arts rose on every hand in bewildering confusion; the new high schools, spread all over the country from Maine to California, were adorned with reproductions of classic art which students were set to copying with such skill as they could command. And so out of the unknown masses emerged a host of men and women to use the brush, pencil, and chisel in response to an enlarging market that was offering inducements for a professional career. These were the substantial and realistic forces which helped to shape the progress of the fine arts in the era that followed the Second American Revolution.

The weight of power was, therefore, on the side of imitation rather than creative feeling. Both the plutocracy that patronized and endowed the arts and the democracy that took its cue from striving respectability shrank from daring innovations. To them the common life of fields, factories, workshops, and commercial cities seemed to furnish no inspiring themes for grand strokes. So the owners of great riches, clinging to representations of the displays and ceremonials of popes, kings, and queens, instructed their clients to adhere as closely as possible to the authentic canons of the old masters, whatever their imagery, technique, or inspiration. In the same mood, committees of state legislatures and city councils, when choosing schemes for the adornment of public buildings, selected murals of stainless knights, fair ladies, and idealized nudes, ordering acres of such decorations from European and American ateliers.

As yet there was no seasoned security of the kind that immemorial inheritance brings. Neither was there any eager searching of the future to call into being a revolt against the scholasticism of art comparable to that raised in the realm of reason against the scholasticism of religion and learning. Instead, a powerful pressure was brought to bear on American artists to restrain their natural emotions and remain content with their pale imitations of classical form, forgetting that Michelangelo's Moses, could it have been copied with a skill equal to that displayed in the original, would have been almost as incongruous in a land of roaring industry as a placid Buddha cunningly fashioned after the Daibutsu of Kamakura. The pall of unreality hung heavily over stimulus, training, and product. Sargent's Dogma of Redemption, painted for the Boston Public Library, seemed strange in the old home of Unitarianism in an age when Harvard was governed by Charles W. Eliot, a serene skeptic, trained in chemistry rather than dialectics. A very climax of formalism was reached by John W. Alexander when, in a great mural, he personified Pittsburgh as a man in medieval armor receiving a crown from a modern high school girl stripped to the waist.

But within these limitations, work of undoubted competence was produced by some American artists. There was a polished finesse and steel-like accuracy in the portraits of the lords, ladies, and rich bourgeois that sprang into phantom life under the brush of John Singer Sargent. In fact those who took their rulings from London had every reason to rejoice in American achievement. Sargent received commissions from England's oldest and richest. Abbey was chosen to paint the official picture of King Edward's coronation; Whistler's Carlyle was cherished in London as well as Boston, Kansas City, Walla Walla, and Rushville; and American canvases hung in the gallery of the Louvre.

If the formalism of standardized painters, museums, schools, and academies, European and American, seemed absolutely rigid at a casual glance, appearances were in some measure deceptive. Everywhere in the period were artists who knew that, try as they would, they could not by imitation reach in the same modes the heights of the originals handed down by the masters. The very comparison of ancient, medieval, modern, and primitive art, Western and Oriental, made possible by the museums, had a dissolving effect in time upon the pure classicism inherited from Mediterranean antiquity. Even the iron discipline of the schoolmen itself produced an antithesis in the minds of refractory students who, as Voltaire cast off the regimen of his Jesuit teachers, were galled by the yoke of tradition. Moreover, artists were human beings subject to the impact of ideas from contemporary science, industry, and politics. They read books and newspapers. They could not by any route escape altogether the shock of democratic doctrines which shook thrones and established orders in Europe during the nineteenth century and brought on the débâcle that closed the drama of the World War. If America seemed relatively calm after 1865, the Europe in which so many American painters received their early training was seething with popular ferments, later intensified by the communist uprising in Paris in 1871.

In this intellectual effervescence new concepts of art flashed out in all parts of the Old World, sending vibrations even through the gates of Japan so recently opened to Occidental influences. Common things of common life now thrust themselves deeper into the realm of the arts. In France, Millet put aside the admonitions of his master to paint in immortal form the simple peasants he had known in his youth when he himself toiled in the fields; it was no accident in æsthetics that the first sum of money which set him on the path to freedom came, in the revolutionary year of 1848, from the Socialist, Ledru-Rollin, who was soon to flee from France to the life of an exile.

Similar revolts occurred in other quarters. "Ideal nudes" gave way gradually before genre painting and sculpture. "Realism" and "sincerity," so potent in fiction, became watchwords for wide circles of artists, as for scientists and students of mankind. "It is the effect of sincerity," wrote Manet, the leader of French dissidence in 1867, "to give to a painter's works a character that makes them resemble a protest whereas the painter has only thought of rendering his impression." This was an insurgent note in art. Whether intended as a protest or not, "impressionism" represented the rise of a new school of painters, with right and left wings, who ignored many rules of the disciplinarians, even though its chief masters were all children of the galleries, and flung upon their canvases anything that interested them. The spirit of this revolt against the schoolmen was surging up in Europe when, in the gilded age, American youth rushed there in such numbers to study.

To the ateliers of the French impressionists many of these aspiring young Americans drifted, though not always to remain enchained. William Morris Hunt, George Inness, and John La Farge, for example, were profoundly stirred by the new school, and brought back to the United States the devotion of reformers. In 1878, the American Academy, which had continued to uphold the older and more rigid standards of excellence since its foundation, was challenged by a new organization known as the Society of American Artists, headed by La Farge. Though the rebellious association did not succeed in keeping all its members firmly attached to its canons of faith, it did produce a movement of realism in æsthetics akin to the scientific movement in philosophy which drove scholars away from cloisters and historic models to the world of nature and experimentation.

While democratic currents were thus modifying the themes and emphasis of painting, in spite of the classical schools, science was also affecting the arts. Physicists had long been breaking substances into their component parts; so a few artists taking a cue from this operation began to use the spectrum in their quest for a better understanding of light. They worked in the laboratory, they studied the writings of Helmholtz, Chevreul, and Rood. They went far in their examination of the relations of line to line, plane to plane, angle to curve, and the kinship of the hues and colors in nature.

Among the Americans who took this scientific tack, La Farge accomplished the most striking results. In the opinion of Henry Adams, La Farge had the most complex American mind of his day; at least he was both sophisticated and primitive; both mediæval and modern; both American and European—able "to burn incense at enough shrines" to give him a claim to universality. To this mental equipment, he added the spirit of the artisan, for he worked in his own glass factory to create by experimental methods windows that would rival the stained glass of old. Though custom laid a heavy hand upon him, there was in his work a faint adumbration of the freer impressionism to come.

If, however, a search is made in the welter of color and form and imagery that flowed from the brushes of the artists trained abroad for a distinct note of American dynamics, it will hardly be found, so strong was the grip of formal tradition conserved in the museums and taught by the men of the schools. Through the thick layer of that imported culture, the passions and ideas which characterized

American life in the gilded age could seldom break. Rather did they find expression in the work of men less subjected to the discipline of the masters—in the paintings of Winslow Homer, Alexander Wyant, Albert Ryder, and Ralph Blakelock, none of whom spent long formative years under the iron rule of authority. Certainly Winslow Homer was close to the substance of the United States. Born of American parents in New England, he came to art through apprenticeship to a lithographer and sketching for Harper's Weekly, achieving recognition by the sheer strength of his genius. Knowing nothing of the luxurious salons supported by the plutocracy, he became absorbed in the primal struggle of man with nature; he painted sailors, fisherfolk, workmen, and farmers in their setting of land or sea—mankind and nature all of one element wrapped in the mystery of life. Of the same vagrant type was Wyant, the son of an Ohio farmer-carpenter; though sadly deficient in technique, he revealed in his American landscapes the instinct of the creator. More romantic and subjective but equally independent in expressing his own vision was the third of this group, Ryder, whose best work displayed, as a critic observed, the "obscure, elusive quality that is to painting what Browning is to poetry." Away on the wings still more to himself was Blakelock, a weird and formless spirit, untutored, simple friend of nature and companion of Indians, whose subtle play with color and feeling for the esoteric kept him ever aloof from the successful clients of the plutocracy.

In the kindred art of sculpture were betrayed the same obedience to classical traditions and signs of a movement nearer to the heart of American culture. The acquisition of riches, the growth and rivalry of cities, and the quest for respectability expanded the market until there was an almost unlimited demand for busts of the rich, for soldiers' and sailors' monuments, for grand decorations at successive national expositions, and for ornamental attachments to public buildings. The result was a profusion of products by both men and women, nearly every section of the country making contributions. Saint-Gaudens though born in Ireland was reared in New York; Daniel Chester French was a native of New Hampshire; Bissell was a Connecticut boy; Barnard, a son of Pennsylvania, spent his impressionable years in Muscatine, Iowa; Gutzon Borglum was born in Idaho; Niehaus was a son of Cincinnati. Geographical divisions as well as history furnished the themes of sculpture: the Far West gave Indians and hunters; the Civil War, generals and privates.

Here and there flashed out evidences of an emancipation from mere imitation, especially as allegorical extravaganzas sank slowly, but steadily, in public favor, as statesmen lost their Roman togas and put on frock coats and trousers. Near the end of the century, a still freer drift appeared in the recognition accorded to the power of common life—the strength of labor, the art of the machine, the protean might of industry. With full authority could Lorado Taft say in 1903, that "where once was indecision and a timid leaning on the past, there exists today a valuable nucleus of artistic consciousness. The American sculptor no longer puts himself deliberately out of touch with his time, but endeavors to be a part of the life about him. He realizes that, in order to exert an influence, his art must speak no alien tongue, but must follow the vernacular of his day and race."

§

Fortunately for the future there was a growing recognition that the fine arts and industry, put asunder by the machine, must be somehow reunited. Even the old Puritan antagonism to gauds, which had long lingered among men of substance grown rich through the exploitation of the New World, began to relax before the necessity of improving designs with a view to holding the market for textiles and other commodities. In time it became evident that commercial art was shut up in no water-tight compartments, that it must depend for its growth upon nourishing the higher forms of imagination. But the captains of industry, faced by domestic and foreign competition, at first found little help from the somewhat exclusive masters of the fine arts and little encouragement from the directors of museums filled with classical treasures.

Driven to other expedients in their efforts to relate industry to beauty and imagination, they turned to the established educational system near at hand; in 1870, Massachusetts, the home of the textile industry, made drawing compulsory in the public schools. This innovation was followed three years later by the foundation of a Normal Art School to train teachers of art—a movement which the Centennial Exposition of 1876 helped to make national. Organized immediately afterward, the Philadelphia School of Industrial Art set an ambitious example that was observed from all the segments of the educational field. By the end of the century every state had one or more normal schools offering instruction, of a kind at least, in the fine and industrial arts. Accordingly as the handicrafts, such as they were in this country, declined, "technically competent" training began to take the place of apprenticeship discipline to supply industries with new patterns, figures, and colors, much to the horror of those esthetes who had forgotten, if they had ever learned it, that in great creative periods there had always been a vital relation between the crafts and the arts.

§

If meager results were accomplished in the fine and industrial arts as a whole, certainly one branch, often disowned by its relatives, showed distinction of the first order. That was the graphic arts. The magazines founded by commercial publishers, the newspapers run on business principles, the processes of engraving created by the technologist, and the market daily enlarging with the spread of literacy called for genius to illustrate stories, editorials, headlines, and political rhetoric. In this field the American temper flowered with prolific skill, perhaps because it could here be more natural, nearer to the realities of life as it throbbed from day to day in the conquest of a continental domain. Certainly it was the graphic talent which drew closest to the events, ambitions, passions, hopes, and interests that made up the passing show of the gilded age. It was from the pictures of the illustrators liberated from the formalism of anatomy, grammar, and patterns of logic, that life and action stared with the starkest verity, reflecting the spirit of American civilization more powerfully perhaps than the written word.

For example, the age of the Civil War, the Credit Mobilier scandals, and the Tweed Ring was immortalized in the defiant cartoons of Thomas Nast whose Tammany Tiger survived the devastations of time. The New York World's concept of the battle between the democracy of mechanics and farmers and the plutocracy of the Goulds and the Vanderbilts was made vivid in the horrible black and white lines of "Belshazzar's Feast" hurled at Blaine in the campaign of 1884. Homer C. Davenport's cartoons of Hanna, covered with dollar marks, expressed the passions of Bryan's "crown-of-thorns" speech with more deadly accuracy than the words of the orator and clung to the popular imagination when the echoes of his eloquence were as silent as the tomb. On the other side the portraiture of Bryan and Altgeld in the fustian and grinning terrorism of anarchy struck deeper into the memories of their foes than all the pointed and rabid rhetoric of editors and reporters.

The same market that gave support to the cartoonist gave sustenance to the general illustrator, in spite of the steady encroachment of photographic reproduction upon the field of engraving. Winslow Homer got his start toward fame when he was commissioned to make sketches of Lincoln's inauguration for Harper's Weekly. The wide social orders that read the Ladies' Home Journal saw their ideal of femininity projected in the American girls drawn by Charles Dana Gibson. Humanitarians of the middle class who founded social settlements dropped tears on M. A. Woolf's sketches of lowly life in a great city and the children of the "mobility." It was for the publishers of books and magazines that Howard Pyle, Frederic Remington, Howard Chandler Christy, Joseph Pennell, and Mary Cassatt drew, painted, limned, and etched all phases of national life and interest, some of their work revealing a vibrant power.

While Whistler was finding inspiration in Venice and London, Pennell beheld through the eye of imagination not only European life but the course of American business enterprise; with a sure hand he portrayed the elements of modern industry—mechanics, steel, labor, energy, mass production, and power. Had they not said in olden times that to labor was to pray and did not Calvin Coolidge say that the business of America was business? It really required no uncanny vision for Pennell to serve as the prophet of the future rather than an imitator of a past that was, at all events, dead. Nor was it a mere accident that novel representations of womanhood and child life wrought upon the mind by the social changes of the gilded age now took their place beside the conceptions of the schoolmen who copied canvases of the middle ages.

§

On the course of musical development, the economic and imitative factors so powerful in the realm of the fine arts during the gilded age exerted still stronger pressures. Riches gave patronage and endowments; prosperous middle classes the wide market. It was a banker of State Street, Henry L. Higginson, who assumed, in 1881, the task of supporting the Boston Symphony Orchestra and who, by relieving it of anxiety over box-office receipts, enabled it to devote its talents to pure art, unvexed by the distractions of American competition. From the plutocracy of New York City came the money to build, in 1883, the Metropolitan Opera House, planned with reference to the social aspirations of the rich who held the parterre boxes. It was the rich iron-master of Pittsburgh, Andrew Carnegie, who gave to that city a great music hall, equipped it with a fine organ, and added a generous fund to provide free concerts for the people. In other places also millions were poured out of the earnings of industry for concerts, operas, schools, and conservatories, just as thousands had been poured from the coffers of the princely and clerical landlords of Europe for musical production. And to the endowments and gifts of the rich was now added the patronage of the multitude—a patronage which came mainly from the women of the middle class given leisure by the surplusage of prosperity and drawn in their quest for diversion, reputability, or inspiration, to the charms that inhere in music.

Indeed, women played a dominant rôle in American musical history during the gilded age. Millions of daughters thrummed and strummed in parlors while pinched mothers washed dishes and hard-pressed fathers toiled at trade, happy to purchase at any price the signs of good breeding and "accomplishment" or to carry the training forward to flower on the concert stage or in operatic performance. Women constituted the major portion of the audiences at concerts and the opera, furnished most of the students who in turn sustained the teachers, bought the printed music and the literature on the subject, subscribed to the trade journals, themselves became teachers of music, and talked the art in season and out. And some of the women won high honors as musicians as well as patrons. For instance, Mrs. H. A. Beach received an open and generous recognition at home and enjoyed the distinction of having her work rendered by important artists in London, Berlin, and Paris. "I do not think," said Walter Damrosch out of his wide experience, "that there has ever been a country whose musical development has been fostered so exclusively by women as America."

To the sway of riches and women was added the pressure of business enterprise—market, organization, and mass production—so potent in that age. Already well started in the middle period, the manufacture and sale of musical instruments by the millions became an important branch of industry; pianos and organs were made by the trainload and sold on the installment plan, like sewing machines, by smooth and loquacious salesmen, until an instrument stood in nearly every home that had risen above the margin of subsistence. Improvements and inventions put novelties in the field besides. Whatever was profitable to business was praiseworthy in culture. With a passion for organization akin to the aggressiveness of instrument manufacturers—and certainly not without an eye to salaries and fees, promoters spread all over the United States the forms and methods of musical education recently established in Europe. Indeed, in some respects Europe was outdone in this relation; at every stage from the kindergarten to the university, instruction in music received an official recognition in the American academic system, and was given a more extensive and elaborate equipment than in the Old World.

With characteristic energy, efforts were made time and again to produce the most gigantic music festivals, establish the biggest orchestras, and assemble the largest number of devotees. As if to announce the booming era of prosperity and the full dinner pail, a chorus of ten thousand voices and an orchestra of one thousand pieces celebrated at Boston in 1869 the close of the Civil War by a festival of peace given under the direction of Patrick S. Gilmore, an Irishman from Dublin. Apparently discontented with this paltry effort, Boston did honor to peace a second time in 1872, with a chorus of twenty thousand and an orchestra of two thousand members. Determined to surpass his first effort, Gilmore now had artillery reinforcing the strains of voice and instrument; firemen pounding fifty anvils to give a realistic ring to the Anvil Chorus of Il Trovatore; German, French and English military bands mingling their notes with the roar of native talent; and forty thousand people listening and clapping their hands. On this occasion

Johann Strauss and Franz Abt were shown how a great nation could render their music when it set about the task. With the same genius for organization which produced such mammoth festivals, the energy of the country found expression in countless music conventions, societies, guilds, teachers' associations, schools, lectures, concerts, recitals, quartettes, quintettes, orchestras, and choral associations from shore to shore. Americans demonstrated their willingness to attend musical conferences with as much enthusiasm as party assemblies and meetings of fraternal orders.

In this musical furor, as in the promotion of the fine arts, Americans leaned heavily on European guidance, at least during the early stages. With the timidity of a new people suddenly released by economic prosperity from drudgery but conscious of a deficiency in technical training, musical aspirants naturally turned to the reputable masters, making a rush to the conservatories of the Old World that paralleled the rush to the galleries and studios of the European centers of art. Moreover, the immense American market for teachers, conductors, and directors, protected by no such tariff as sheltered the manufacturers of steel and cotton goods, drew Europe's leading artists of voice and instrument to the American field of exploitation. This alien invasion was augmented by the German migration of the early seventies bringing with it, as a by-product, a veritable flood of music lovers to join clubs and assume leadership in organization.

After all, teaching, directing, and selling had been old trades in music as in the other arts. From time immemorial artists had shifted with the market from one country to another, from one patron to the next, as necessity or mood directed; so the European musicians who flocked to America to pursue their trade were merely following accredited practices. Even stars of magnitude were lured by the earnest solicitation of Americans who offered substantial remuneration. For example, Dr. Leopold Damrosch, having made a brilliant success at Breslau, was brought to

America by the Arion Society of New York in 1871 to serve as its conductor; and Wilhelm Gericke was enticed from Vienna by Higginson in 1884 to conduct the Boston Symphony.

Confronted by European influences wherever they turned, the American composers who won highest distinction in the era—among whom were John K. Paine, George Chadwick, Edward MacDowell, Horatio Parker, and Arthur Foote—were almost completely subdued to the music of the Old World. They produced works which won the applause of both hemispheres, overcoming the stigma of the province; but they could hardly be called American in anything but birth.

Against the alien musical dictatorship there were from time to time nationalist waves of protest, but with little or no avail. America had nothing distinctive to say in music. There was no rich heritage of indigenous folk song to serve as the base of elaborate and sophisticated superstructures; attempts to utilize Indian and Negro strains yielded slight results, for those exotic notes were also foreign to the white composers who sought to handle them. Equally unsuccessful were efforts to strike chords common to all American life. They evoked no divine response such as came to the music masters of Europe working with the unities of racial states—Slav and Latin, Celt and Teuton; royal families—Hapsburg and Romanoff, Bourbon and Hohenzollern; and ecclesiastical hierarchies—Roman, Russian and English. That MacDowell could command the respect of the best critical opinion abroad proved that somewhere in the vast continent slumbered the fire of genius but at no hour in the gilded age did a flame illuminate the heavens.

§

On the form and spirit of journalism the triumph of business enterprise and technology laid a heavier hand than on the arts. Established newspapers, such as the New York

Evening Post, which had been founded to represent and promote commercial interests, continued to meet oncoming issues with appropriate phraseology, and Charles A. Dana lived until 1897 to protest in the editorial column of his Sun against offenses of "impersonal journalism"; but the days of somber dignity and caustic wit were passing fast. Inventors had so revolutionized printing, engraving, and typesetting that it was no longer possible for an impecunious printer, such as Horace Greeley, to found and develop a metropolitan daily as an organ of opinion. Large capital was now necessary to provide the great mechanical outfit, purchase the requisite literary and artistic talent, and provide the worldwide news service demanded by the age. At the same time the enormous growth in commercial advertising and the reduction in the price of newspapers inevitably made editors more and more dependent on those who manufactured and sold goods. Daily journalism, therefore, became a branch of machine industry. Without advertising no great paper could thrive; without circulation advertising was not forthcoming; without a wide appeal no extensive circulation could be obtained.

Given these conditions, acquisitive sagacity was not long in realizing that it paid to champion, amuse, and entertain the urban masses, and in due time a new type of newspaper undertaking that function burst into the streets. The designer of this departure was Joseph Pulitzer of Magyar-German-Jewish descent, a restless, driving, erratic editor who forged to the front in St. Louis during the seventies as owner of the Post-Dispatch. In 1883, Pulitzer went to New York, bought the World from Jay Gould, and opened what his foes called the era of "yellow journalism."

Though some critics imagined that the enterprise was nothing more than a sensational pandering to the tastes and passions of the mob, that rough judgment betrayed neither insight nor discrimination. The World in Pulitzer's hands had a social program that pleased the lower middle classes and workmen who enjoyed no large taxable incomes, a program that was strangely clear-cut for a land fond of re-sounding platitudes. For instance, it declared an open war on the plutocracy, on Martin's "idle rich." On the third day of his reign, Pulitzer wrote irately: "There is the aristocracy of Central Park. The low Victoria, adapted to exhibit boots, stockings, and skirts as freely as hats and shoulder wraps. . . . There is the sordid aristocracy of the ambitious matchmakers, who are ready to sell their daughters for barren titles to worthless foreign paupers. . . . The new World believes that such an aristocracy ought to have no place in the republic—that the word ought to be expunged from an American vocabulary." By way of starting the extinction, Pulitzer proposed that the government should tax luxuries, inheritances, large incomes, monopolies, and privileged corporations, reduce the tariff to a revenue basis, reform the civil service, and punish political corruption. "This is a popular platform of ten lines," he added. "We recommend it to the politicians in place of long-winded resolutions."

Having announced a spirited campaign against the possessors of swollen fortunes, the World proclaimed itself "the organ of a true aristocracy—the aristocracy of labor— the man who by honest, earnest toil supports his family in respectability," thus drawing the lines of its class appeal so plainly that none could mistake its animus. But, of course, Pulitzer's paper could not be sustained by intense reformers alone. To secure and hold the necessary circulation, it made use of innumerable devices to catch the fancy of the populace—cartoons, comic cuts, elaborate news service, expert reporting, and costly special articles; and it exploited to the utmost limit the tragedy and comedy of contemporary life, in all its component elements of sex, society, crime, perversion, love, romance, and emotion generally. Nobody and nothing were spared in the quest for a thrilling subject to furnish the pretext for towering head lines. Thus a new journalism was born of the changing social conditions and the changing technology of the printing industry. The *populi* were to be entertained while the *ordo equester* was being bated and taxed. Cicero, as well as Catiline, would have understood the transaction.

Before Pulitzer had gone far on his uncanny way, a formidable competitor arose in the person of William Randolph Hearst, son of a California railway and mining millionaire, who, like Cæsar before him, had found his ambitions cramped by the limitations of his class. After toying for a time with the San Francisco Examiner, Hearst went to New York in 1896, bought the Journal, employed Arthur Brisbane, past master of the galvanic arts, and outdid Pulitzer in all the tricks of the sensational game. The same appeal to the masses he intensified and made more vivid and violent; the same apparatus of large type, red strips, flaming headlines, crude drawings, and cartoons he employed with more cleverness and profusion. Reaching out for "the man in the street and the woman in the kitchen," he gave them what he thought they wanted. While flaying the plutocracy to the measure of their anger, he gratified their natural curiosity about "superior persons" by recording the doings of the idle rich with meticulous detail.

Within a short time these new methods cut a wide swath in American journalism. Fastidious citizens who prided themselves on their moderation attributed this result to national depravity, but that was a hasty view of the matter. No small part of the success achieved by the yellow press was due to its fierce denunciation of flagrant abuses passed over in silence by timid editors who fancied themselves more respectable. The severest critic could hardly deny that the sensational editors of the eighties and nineties, by resorting to merciless attacks and repeated exposures, contributed powerfully to the improvement of the methods pursued by American capitalists and politicians. They also aroused the interest of unknown millions never before reached by the daily newspaper, thereby making a contribution to the democratic process. They likewise nourished patriotism; Hearst probably did more than any single private citizen to bring on the Spanish-American War; and Pulitzer supported the same cause with loyal fervor, convinced, as he said, that it would boost his circulation. At any rate, whatever its merits or demerits, the yellow press rose and flourished in the gilded age preparing the way for the cheap illustrated daily which sank its tentacles still deeper into the strata of the faintly literate.

In the sweep of this enterprise, Pulitzer was finally outclassed; before the nineteenth century closed, he became milder in manner, departing so far from his early theories that he was prepared to support for the presidency Admiral Dewey, a brave warrior but a naïve politician, wholly innocent of social or economic opinion. Perhaps the wiser editor remembered from what quarter Cæsar drew his loudest cheers; perhaps his constituency was growing more prosperous and respectable.

For the middle classes, with their left wing touching the proletariat and their right the plutocracy, was also created an appropriate journalism—a periodical type which in the ordinary course of events called for no such capital outlay as a metropolitan newspaper. There was in fact a large, if somewhat bewildered, army of editors who refused to surrender to the methods of the strong characters in the economic conflict—to figures of Homeric proportions like Jay Gould, Jim Fisk, and J. P. Morgan. These editors of milder emotions, the intelligentsia of the gilded age, sought to apply historic ethics to the changed situation. The Independent, for example, a religious weekly founded in 1848, when committed to the direction of Henry Ward Beecher in 1861, announced that it would "assume the liberty of meddling with every question which agitated the civil or Christian community." Combining the powerful editorials of George William Curtis with the staring cartoons of Thomas Nast, Harper's Weekly assailed scandals of the Credit Mobilier age. Bent on still more purist designs, E. L. Godkin founded The Nation in 1865, as a critical weekly, and for thirty years poured broadsides into the corruption and vulgarity of the plutocracy. But when his editorials were carefully analyzed, it was evident that he was mainly pleading for better manners—the manners of a well-ordered bourgeois society not subject to the swift and rude changes in technology so characteristic of the times. In any event, as soon as the western agrarians made their populist assault upon the perquisites of railway bondholders in the seventies, Godkin showed that he could be as firm and harsh as the Wall Street Journal in sustaining the authenticity of the acquisitive process.

To meet the demands of the great democracy of the median orders now rising into literacy through the ministrations of the public schools, new popular magazines entered the field. For the women came the Ladies' Home Journal; started in 1883 under the shrewd management of Mrs. Cyrus Curtis, it opened the modern phase of its career six years later when Edward Bok took the helm. Casting aside the severe formalism of Godey's earlier offerings, this journal now united "polite" literature of a kind with a skillful treatment of the humblest domestic arts, thereby answering all the imperious requirements of the woman in the kitchen who aspired to ultimate liberation in the parlor. "The great heart of the people" was reached; their response was a circulation running above a million.

Deeply as this downward thrust penetrated, it left a great majority of the literates of the United States still untouched. In the country districts and small villages especially were multitudes of men as well as women whose ambitions soared above the local weeklies with their community gossip—men and women a bit interested in "the big doings of the big world." Clearly here was an alluring opportunity for business enterprise and it was grasped by S. S. McClure who, as a peddler of pots and pans in the Middle West, had come early in life to grips with the strong common people dwelling in the Valley of Democracy. From first-hand experience McClure learned that the staid Atlantic Monthly, with its longing for a more exotic culture than the one available, could not transfix the imagination of the farmers and storekeepers who bought his wares. They and their wives and children wanted gleams in their gray lives.

Sensing the nature of this higher longing the clever itinerant merchant laid McClure's Magazine before the multitude in 1893, giving the people safe fiction, sprightly stories about great folks, and lively pictures of the passing pageant in general. Within three years his journal had a circulation greater than the combined list of three of the noblest older monthlies. Vivid lives of Napoleon and Lincoln, told serially by Ida M. Tarbell, brought enthusiastic purchasers from the byways and hedges. Portraits of actresses (as yet somewhat garbed), generals, politicians, athletic heroes, prize fighters, and statesmen (American and foreign) lifted dull domiciles into the realm of "interesting people and things."

When once the trick was turned, other magazines, taking their cue from McClure, changed their nature; while many new ventures of a similar type were made in quick succession, assuming such democratic names as the Cosmopolitan or Everybody's—until the newsstands and mails fairly groaned with garlands of pictures and romances. In this vein the editors of the new direction ran prosperously until the passions of the Bryan revolt against the plutocracy, calling for critical nutriment, set them furiously at work on the business of "muck-raking" the rich and the politicians, a performance that made a tremendous uproar and yielded golden returns for a season. Silenced eventually in this diversion by weariness, consolidations, the resentment of their victims, and radical fright, the traffickers in popular interests began to offer the masses "literary goods" which reflected the social and economic proprieties of American life, praising Dives and pointing the easy way to riches and fame.

Even the peculiar brand of humor hitherto characteristic of America came under the sway of business enterprise.

The success of popular laugh-producers, such as Artemus Ward, Bill Nye, and Petroleum V. Nasby, proved that "there was money in it." If jokes could be sold from the platform, they could be sold in print; so Puck was founded in 1877, Judge in 1881, and Life in 1883. In such commercial undertakings, matters unpleasant to powerful economic elements in the great democracy were usually avoided, the caustic wit which European weeklies applied to the thin cuticle of current reputability being one phase of Continental culture not widely imitated in the United States. Rather was it the Mormons, undertakers, mothers-in-law, Jews, and woman-suffragists that enlisted the energies of the professional humorists who wrote weekly stints for the "funny papers." After all, customers who had dimes and quarters for the magazines wanted the soothing jocularity of satisfaction, not the acid drops of skepticism, and consequently the broad jest and hearty roar of the frontier which had often pierced to the fundamentals of the social process sank down to the drollery of contentment, preparing the way for the light Ford witticisms of the machine age to follow.

§

Organized learning, also, in spite of its classical heritage and its theoretical insulation from practical affairs, was reconstructed from top to bottom in the great age of riches, business, and science. The growth of national wealth now made funds available for the multiplication and improvement of the public schools. Seventy million dollars were dedicated to this purpose in 1871; at the end of the century the annual amount had risen to more than two hundred millions. Transformed into human equivalents this increased outlay meant a steady reduction of illiteracy, notwithstanding the handicap imposed by the growing Negro and immigrant population; in 1880 the percentage of illiterates stood at seventeen; twenty years later at less than eleven; and in 1910 at below eight. In this development, the rural education described in Eggleston's Hoosier School-master disappeared even from the remote mountain districts of the hinterland.

With the improvement of the common schools went an expansion of public education to meet the new demand of the artisans, farmers, and the lower middle classes for a bridge over the gulf separating them from the college. Concretely, this expansion took the form of multiplying high schools, institutions supported by taxation and designed to serve parents who, while relieved from the necessity of putting their young children to work, could not afford to send them to private academies. When Lincoln was inaugurated there were only about one hundred public high schools in the country; by 1880 there were eight hundred; at the opening of the new century the figure had passed six thousand. Though there was some grumbling among labor leaders about the shares of revenue allotted to the respective divisions of the educational system, patrons of high schools were strong enough in politics to force a steady development in this upper range.

The influences which promoted the high school were also effective in establishing new state universities, especially in the West, and in enlarging the plants already in the field. At the end of the period all but nine or ten of the states offered, in addition to free elementary instruction for the masses, a regular program of free education extending through the high school and college. Thus the monopoly of the higher learning, once enjoyed mainly by the prosperous, was punctured at the expense of taxpayers; its academic facilities were made generously available to that portion of the people who either had a margin of economic surplus or possessed special talents and energy. So thousands of youths, who in the older days or in contemporary societies elsewhere would have remained at the plow or the loom, squirmed their way into the middle class as lawyers, doctors, writers, teachers, and professional workers of every kind. Especially did girls take advantage of the new opportunities, flocking in increasing numbers to high schools and colleges—in this fashion augmenting the independence of women and enlarging their empire over national culture.

Supplementing the great outpouring of public funds for education were huge gifts made to colleges and universities by those who had won high stakes in the contest for riches. Such gifts, of course, were not unknown in earlier times; the famous merchant, Stephen Girard, on his death in 1831, had left two million dollars for a boys' college in Philadelphia; but his example was not widely followed at the time. Indeed there were in the middle period few millionaires with handsome surpluses to throw at the feet of learning; but with the triumphs of the gilded age vast supplies became available for that purpose.

The epoch had hardly begun when Johns Hopkins, a Baltimore merchant, set a precedent in American opulence by dedicating his fortune to the foundation of a new university which was formally opened in 1876. In the next decade, the American Baptist Education Society, finding its college at Chicago dying on its hands, appealed to the grand seigneur of the Standard Oil principality, John D. Rockefeller, for help, receiving in acknowledgment the first of his lavish gifts which later grew into a total of more than twenty millions. In the meantime the older colleges, taking advantage of the suggestion thus offered, began to collect large tribute from the favored disciples of Plutus besides smaller sums from those less fortunate in the acquisitive process—with results astounding in their range. At the end of the century the private colleges and universities of the United States had endowments yielding revenues approximately equal to those derived from public funds by the state institutions of higher learning.

One grand outcome of this development in higher learning was the practical emancipation of colleges and universities from clerical dominion, excepting of course the realm ruled by the Catholic hierarchy. The new state universities and women's colleges prepared primarily for secular avocations, not for the church, and it was only natural that laymen rather than preachers should direct their affairs. As the flood of gold rolled into the chests of the various colleges of religious origins, the power of the clergy in management correspondingly declined. Depending no longer, save in some freshwater districts, upon collections taken up by local parsons in connection with levies for domestic and foreign missions, college administrators paid less and less attention to the thunders of the pulpit. Appealing now to the leaders of business enterprise for endowments, they drafted men of money into the service of collegiate direction until at the end of the century the roster of American trustees of higher learning read like a corporation directory.

In the transaction havoc was played in the neat little scheme of classical discipline transmitted by the theologians. Having immense sums at their command, many of the older colleges, such as Harvard, Columbia, Yale, and Princeton, branched out into universities in the German style, sometimes overwhelming their once glorified academies with graduate and professional schools. Scarcely anywhere could the new intellectual interests banging at the gates be denied.

Paralleling in time the revolution in administration were drastic changes in the requirements of the clients; for in ever-increasing proportions students who frequented the halls of higher learning demanded "subjects" which prepared for business and secular professions. In any case, from the thoughts, interests, and aspirations of youth reared to trade, the flowing periods of Greek and Latin poets and orators were far removed. Finally the dissolving processes were accelerated by the growth of natural science as a theme of collegiate instruction—a growth inseparable from machine industry resting immediately upon the practical findings of physics and chemistry. Thus by a multitude of forces quite beyond the will of any group of persons, large or small, or the conscious desires of a nation profoundly religious in its professions, the theological and classical atmosphere of learning was dissipated in Protestant quarters. Religion, of course, remained but not as the lodestar of higher studies. The revolution could be easily grasped by comparing a baccalaureate sermon of Timothy Dwight with one by Arthur T. Hadley.

If a date must be fixed for the beginning of this secular upheaval, it may very well be 1869, four years after the death of Abraham Lincoln, when Charles W. Eliot, a young chemist, was made president of Harvard College. Exercising the firm will associated in popular opinion with business enterprise, he swept out of the institution most of the old-fashioned teachers whose minds and methods belonged to the eighteenth century. He then called in young men fresh from European experience, shattered the classical prescriptions for graduation, and inaugurated an elective system from which the students could select almost at pleasure their own program of studies.

The idea was magnificent—in complete harmony with the catholic spirit of the modern science, constantly widening its borders to include new dominions. At the same time, the scheme was incidentally well fitted to the spiritual requirements of rich men's sons who now flocked to the seats of higher instruction. Under the old compulsory plan, as Lodge once remarked, "a certain amount of knowledge, no more useless than any other, and a still larger amount of discipline in learning were forced on all alike. Under the new system it was possible to escape without learning anything at all by a judicious selection of unrelated subjects taken up only because they were easy or because the burden imposed by those who taught them was light." When Professor Henry Adams asked one of his pupils in the new régime what could be done with the education imparted, he was surprised, he said, to receive the answer: "The degree of Harvard College is worth money to me in Chicago."

So the destruction of the narrow but formidable classical plan produced extraordinary results. On the one hand, it enriched the curriculum with the new sciences, natural and humanistic, and was accompanied by a multiplication of the opportunities offered to those competent to make use of them. On the other hand, it eased the preparatory strain on the plutocracy. The old system, whatever its faults, was both democratic and disciplinary, if desiccated and narrow; only boys, rich or poor, who could work set problems and read set lines were admitted and graduated. Under the new system there was more flexibility; those who enjoyed the leisure born of wealth could more easily enter and more easily remain to the end. Thus two causes were served.

Less than a decade after the initiation of Eliot's experiment at Harvard came the opening of the Johns Hopkins University at Baltimore. Everything about the procedure breathed the secular spirit of the business age. The endowment was bestowed by a man of affairs; laymen, not clergymen, ruled the board of trustees; and scientific research in its higher ranges was announced as the dominant feature of the institution. An avowed champion of agnosticism, Thomas Henry Huxley, plumed knight of the Darwinian battle then raging throughout the world, delivered the inaugural address. The devout were shocked when they heard that the new seat of learning was opened without clerical benediction. "It was bad enough to invite Huxley," lamented one parson. "It were better to have asked God to be present. It would have been absurd to ask them both." But in spite of the lamentations of the clergy, the new institution, by its insistence upon graduate work and advanced research, set the model for higher learning in the United States for nearly a quarter of a century—in fact until many colleges had transformed themselves into competing universities.

This secular tendency, strong as it was, did not completely meet the requirements of business enterprise. Graduates of "literary" colleges were usually superficial in their equipment; lacking the precision, the knowledge of material things and forces, the mathematical ability, and the laborious habits essential for efficient results in machine industry. They were accused, though not always justly, of being "too cultural" in their aims if not in their achievements. In any case the exactions of the machine process demanded a type of education which only technical schools could supply. A few lines from the chronicle of the era illustrate the rise of a new power in the world of learning: the Columbia School of Mines was opened in 1864, the Massachusetts Institute of Technology and the Worcester Polytechnic in 1865, Lehigh University in 1866, Stevens Institute in 1871, the Case School of Applied Science in 1880, Rose Polytechnic in 1883, and the Brooklyn Polytechnic Institute in 1889. To this development of private endowments, the operations of the Morrill Act, which inaugurated in 1862 the policy of granting federal lands in aid of industrial and mechanical education, gave additional velocity. By the close of the era technical discipline was becoming a fundamental part of the American system of education and a sharp distinction was being made between the training of those who were to direct the material modes of industry and those who were to manage its finances, sell its bonds, and distribute its goods.

While this was the general situation, it would be a mistake to imagine that the whole bent of education in the gilded age was toward luxury on the one side and technology on the other. If the widened elective curriculum allowed the sons and daughters of the rich to flit lightly through the academic course, if it merely prolonged infancy for multitudes with little brain capacity, it likewise offered to those who cared for learning opportunities of incomparable richness to acquire it, in a hundred fields closed to all former generations of college students. Wholly new departments of instruction were organized and opened freely to those who loved knowledge for its own sake. Physics, chemistry, and biology received a prominence that had once been accorded only to Greek and Latin. Art, music, and letters were recognized by the creation of separate chairs and then special departments to handle their many phases.

Social studies crept into colleges and universities, usually through the back door, through history, moral philosophy, or law, it is true, but once in, they stayed and received more generous treatment. In 1880, eight years after Professor Sumner began to thunder on sociology at Yale, the Columbia faculty of political science was organized with divisions of history, economics, and public law. Not to be outdone by allied and associated kingdoms, philosophy proceeded to shake itself loose from its theological bondage and to divide into departmental sectors. The Philosophical Review founded in 1892 followed up the work begun twenty-five years earlier by the Journal of Speculative Philosophy in voicing critical opinions concerning traditional doctrines and in 1890 the graduate school of philosophy was opened at Columbia.

In the course of academic events, pure science, freed somewhat from purposes immediately practical, received an increasing support. By 1899 it was possible to organize an American Physical Society for the promotion of that speculative type of inquiry which promised nothing but intellectual rewards—this, as its first president said, "in the midst of a world which gives its highest praise, not to the investigator in the pure ethereal physics which our Society is formed to cultivate, but to one who uses it for satisfying the physical rather than the intellectual needs of mankind." It was this spirit which Andrew D. White, president of Cornell, voiced when he declared the allegiance of his institution to "this zeal for truth as truth, this faith in the good forever allied to the truth."

The satisfaction of that zeal, in every field, called for special training. For some time that discipline was largely supplied by American graduates of foreign universities. Indeed the direction of higher learning in the United States during the gilded age was to an amazing extent in the hands of teachers who had acquired their knowledge and technique in Germany. It was not until the last decade of the epoch that domestic graduate schools were able to supply an annual grist of scholars large enough to meet the demands of colleges for teachers and deans. But whether trained at home or abroad the doctor of philosophy finally managed to take the place of the doctor of divinity so effectively that a habit of respect for scientific method, minute research, and objective thinking became well established in academic groves, by the turn of the century.

If, as sometimes alleged with good reason, the change frequently substituted for a generous interest in the important, a passion for the insignificant, at all events many of the rhetorical approaches beloved of clergymen, literary historians, and professors of belles lettres were badly damaged in the operation. On the whole, society gained even though the study of literature and the arts suffered more than one grave injury at the hands of mechanicians wearing the garb of cap, gown, and hood. Certainly a large number of the crude acquisitive assumptions which ran current among masses and classes in the gilded age received in the universities a calm analysis which was destined in time to work havoc with the commonplaces of reputability. By 1900, the cloud was as big as a college president's hand.

In such an era, while the spirit and method of collegiate instruction were in process of revolution and while women were pushing intrepidly from the kitchen and nursery into every corner of economic and cultural life, it was impossible for men to retain their age-long grip upon higher learning. In fact educators, who scanned the horizon in the fermenting days of Andrew Jackson, had then begun to discover that the masculine dominion over colleges could not be preserved forever. And it was fitting that the first important experiments in co-education should be made in the Valley of Democracy. Oberlin invited women to share its facilities on the day of its opening in 1833 and Antioch, under the benign sway of Horace Mann, followed that example twenty years later. The state universities of Utah and Iowa, established in the middle period, proclaimed equality in the beginning. During the gilded age the wedge was driven deeper and deeper into the old monopoly. State universities in the North, one after another, abandoned the policy of exclusion: for illustration, Michigan in 1870 and Wisconsin definitely in 1874. Private institutions soon began to pursue the same course: Cornell was opened to women in 1872; the Massachusetts Institute of Technology in 1883; and Chicago University in 1892. A few of the older colleges that could not break so suddenly with custom made a compromise by establishing annexes for women: Barnard College was thus founded in 1889 at Columbia and Radcliffe in 1894 at Harvard.

Meanwhile colleges designed exclusively for women were springing up in the East where their demands met no such generous response as in the state universities of the West. It had long been the dream of leaders among the women, such for example as Mary Lyon, founder of Mount Holyoke, to have colleges of their own amply endowed and equal in standards to the best of the institutions for men. The new day so longed for dawned in 1865 when Vassar College, financed by a rich brewer of Poughkeepsie, was opened with much ceremony, setting a contagious object lesson. Within five years Wellesley and Smith in Massachusetts had been chartered. In 1885, Bryn Mawr in Pennsylvania received its first class of young women. Besides making entrance examinations obligatory and severe, Bryn Mawr offered in a few branches graduate work comparable in quality to that at Johns Hopkins or Harvard.

In the realm of professional education, the feminist advance was not as rapid. It is true that the Massachusetts Institute of Technology and Cornell University both offered engineering instruction to women but the law and medical schools of the first rank refused to capitulate. In 1865, women could secure medical instruction at only a few places in the country and at the end of the century their position in that respect was hardly improved. Though law was also somewhat obdurate, at the close of the epoch several high-grade institutions offered them legal training. As a matter of fact, among the thousands of girls who crowded the colleges, relatively few desired to study engineering, medicine, or law; it was teaching, letters, and the arts, that attracted the majority, thus promoting the transfer of supremacy in questions of culture and taste to feminine hands.

§

Inevitably the fervor for popular education, fanned into a glow by enthusiasm for democracy, touched also the advanced guard of the Negro race. Northern whites who in the old days had opposed slavery felt under some obligations to aid in the process of lifting the freedmen from their slough of illiteracy. The requirements of industry and agriculture, in transformation under the sway of machinery and science, called at least for the spread of the rudiments of learning among those who were to work in shop and field. But if the reasons for change were cogent, the task of educating the Negro was infinitely difficult.

In the first place there was a patrimony of inveterate opinion to overcome, to say nothing of the force of inertia. Before the Civil War, teaching slaves to read and write was a crime in some parts of the South; and in the North the repugnance to Negro education was almost as intense as the hatred for abolition. When, for instance, it was proposed to found a college for colored youth at New Haven, Connecticut, the citizens and the municipal authorities of the town made an angry outcry, declaring officially that the project should be resisted by all lawful means. When in 1833 Prudence Crandall admitted a few colored girls to her boarding-school at Canterbury in the same state, she was attacked by a mob and then imprisoned under a special law making it a crime to admit Negroes to any institution of learning. In other places in the North, the opposition was almost as fierce; but in spite of it all the number of primary schools open to the colored race was steadily increasing when emancipation put a new face on the whole problem.

It was too much to expect the southern states, impoverished by war and traditionally negligent of education for the masses, white or black, to assume at once the immense burden of educating the freedmen. In the circumstances the responsibility rested quite as much on the North as on the South and to some extent northern philanthropists attempted to discharge that obligation. A considerable part of the fund given by George Peabody in 1867 to the cause of southern education was granted to Negro schools and fifteen years afterward John F. Slater of Connecticut dedicated a million dollars to "the uplifting of the lately emancipated people of the South." Northern capitalists also came to the help of Booker T. Washington who opened in 1881 with local aid an institution at Tuskegee for training Negro students in the arts of self-help.

Such gifts, splendid as some of them were, did not of course touch more than the fringe of the problem. The main burden of educating the Negro fell upon the southern taxpayers who assumed it with perhaps as much alacrity as could be expected in the circumstances. By the close of the century, they could show large results, at all events in a relative sense. According to the best estimates, forty years after emancipation, at least one-half of the Negroes in the United States were reported as able to read and write. Moreover the number of schools for higher learning, such as Howard University and the Hampton Institute, had multiplied and the leaders of the colored race could secure in their own institutions, to say nothing of other colleges now open to them, an efficient training in the arts and sciences.

During this intellectual advance the old-fashioned Negro preacher gradually lost his prestige. Historically he was "a descendant of the medicine man of the African clan" and when Christianity was added to his spiritual equipment, he was possessed by a strange medley of beliefs. In the plantation days he had been, as Du Bois says, "the healer of the sick, the interpreter of the unknown, the comforter of the sorrowing, the supernatural avenger of wrong." After emancipation, the colored preachers, as masters of a technique that gave them power over their race, grasped the reins of authority among the helpless communities of freedmen, proclaiming a gospel of equality according to the Scriptures and adding to their ecclesiastical functions the art of political manipulation as soon as the suffrage was thrust upon them. Though some of these preachers were educated, the great majority were at the time, little, if any, above their parishioners in knowledge and understanding.

But as the general level of Negro culture rose above the primitive conditions of slave days, the sovereignty of the pulpit declined. With the spread of secular education, the multiplication of institutions for technical training, and the increasing prominence of science in the curricula of the schools, telling inroads were made on the kingdom of "singing and shouting parsons." "Dey ain't no Holy Ghos in it at all," cried one of them on examining the contents of the new program. And in a sense he was right. The change flowed logically from the conquest of learning by practical interests and the direction of the Negro's mind to the white man's major concern—the acquisition and enjoyment of goods. However rigid might be the social discrimination, therefore, it was no longer possible to erect water-tight intellectual barriers between the two races. For weal or woe the Negro race, in its varying shades and types, was a part of the American economic system—a fact which no linguistic flourishes could obscure. The forces of the age beating pitilessly upon the whites were also driving colored men and women before the storm.

CHAPTER XXVI

Imperial America

WITH the growing economic surplus which sustained the colorful and exuberant culture of the gilded age ran an increasing pressure for foreign markets and investment opportunities. And since America was now fairly out upon the imperial course, all the interests and ambitions usually associated with that form of human activity, centering in the captain's quarters in the upper sphere of politics, conspired in a cumulative fashion to hold the ship of state steadily in the chosen way. McKinley, Roosevelt, Taft, Wilson, Harding, and Coolidge occupied the presidency in due succession, according to the chronology and accidents of politics, without making any sensational changes in the sailing charts throughout the years of their service.

The Republicans inherited a sanction of tradition from Webster, Seward, and Grant; so McKinley, Roosevelt, and Taft, finding no difficulty in adhering strictly to the policies outlined in the doctrine of Manifest Destiny, applied the creed from time to time as new occasions carried new duties. Although the Democrats, goaded by Bryan's agrarian faction, were committed by their platform principles to a return upon the course, Wilson in fact made no revolution in the practices bequeathed him by his Republican predecessors, at least, in this hemisphere. If he granted the Philippines a larger autonomy and looked coldly upon capitalist expansion in China, he bore down with special vigor in the Caribbean, adding the Danish Islands by purchase and valuable protectorates by an energetic use of the navy. If Harding and Coolidge sought to give formal legality to operations in Central America and the Caribbean generally, they were resolute in restoring imperial authority over the Philippines and in warning Japan against open excursions in China and Siberia where economic, opportunities imposed moral mandates upon the American government.

§

In laying out his sailing directions with respect to details after the peace was formally concluded with Spain in 1899, McKinley had to study dangerous reefs and foggy headlands, for obstacles lay on every side. The social order in Cuba was disturbed; the Philippines were in open revolt against American authority; legal uncertainties clouded the status of the conquered provinces. And to make prudence still more cautious, the opinion of the American nation on the policy of annexation was not yet clearly developed and registered. In short, the government at Washington was in a position akin to that of the Roman Republic in 242 B. C. at the end of the Punic War.

Viewed from any angle the first of the problems before the administration, the Cuban question, presented thorny phases, especially to politicians disposed to be fastidious. Boldly before them in resplendent diction, stood the solemn resolution of Congress passed by the advocates of the attack on Spain, under Populist pressure, vowing before all the world that the United States had no intention of exercising any sovereignty or jurisdiction over Cuba except to restore peace. And yet if the government of the island was transferred without restraint to the insurgent peons and proletariat, that gloated triumphantly over the old Spanish ruling classes, would landed property and capital be safe? The question was by no means academic. Everybody knew that the revolutionary junta in Havana was in a bad temper, decidedly inclined to deal in no mincing way with the local Spaniards who, besides remaining loyal to Madrid in the recent social war, had all along sneered at the pretensions of the populace. If things came to a dangerous pass on the withdrawal of the United States troops, the interests of American business men in the island as well as the estates of the old rulers would be in serious jeopardy. The situation was delicate, involving both honor and necessity.

Out of this perplexity, an ingenious Senator, O. H. Platt of Connecticut, discovered a way, by evolving a set of principles which restricted the relations of the Cuban government with foreign countries, limited its debt-creating power, forced it to concede certain coaling stations for the American navy, and proclaimed the right of the United States to interfere in insular affairs, whenever necessary, to protect life and property. To the purists in Congress this looked like a violation of the solemn pledge made a short time before, but in spite of their objections the new doctrines were incorporated in an annex to the army and navy appropriation bill of 1901—hence the name Platt Amendment—and the Cubans were compelled, after they had made an impotent gesture, to embody the self-denying ordinance in their new constitution. Thus the substance of American control was assured while the trappings of sovereignty were handed over to the independent republic.

Within five years, that is, in 1906, President Roosevelt found it expedient to intervene, under the Platt decretal, establish a military régime, and restore local formalities, at considerable expense to the Cubans. Although he ordered a withdrawal as soon as matters were running smoothly, Cuba was given to understand that she received freedom, sovereignty, and independence, as written in the terms of the bond, subject to a moral mandate.

§

The Philippine problem was still more complicated. Discontented elements among the natives had been on the verge of an armed revolt in 1898 when the war between Spain and the United States broke in upon their plans. At the opening of this crisis the leader of the insurgents, Aguinaldo, receiving an invitation to join the American forces in overturning Spanish dominion, threw himself promptly and heartily into the fray, taking it for granted, without warrant, so the Americans claimed, that his native islands would receive their independence at the close of the war. But whatever the basis of his hopes, he was doomed to disappointment; for in the end a new alien power was substituted for the former authority of Spain.

When the news of this change in masters reached Manila, a certain tension appeared in Filipino quarters. In circumstances that are clouded by obscurity a war broke out in February, 1899, between the American troops and the forces of Aguinaldo. According to official reports, it seems that four native soldiers, on approaching an American outpost, failed, possibly through a misunderstanding, to obey the command of the sentinels to halt. The result was more shots heard round the world. Since the officers of the native high command were absent at the moment and the number of the advancing men was small, it is hardly probable that the Filipinos then had in view a general assault upon the American lines. Indeed the eagerness with which Aguinaldo afterward begged for a truce lent color to the opinion that no aggressive movement was then intended.

As soon as the first native blood was shed, American military authorities on the spot absolutely refused to parley and widened the incident into a general conflict. After some serious fighting in which American forces were easily victorious, the struggle settled down to a guerilla war which lasted for nearly three years. In the course of this confused contest, atrocities were committed by the native soldiers and apparently repaid with compound interest; in fact in such a struggle it proved exceedingly difficult to observe the etiquette of civilized combat. So by heroic efforts and a generous use of what the Americans called "the water cure," the insurrection against the dominion of the United States was put down, at the expense of many lives and about one hundred and seventy-five million dollars.

News of this imperial process, filtering home in spite of a rigorous military censorship, evoked some discontent among old-fashioned Americans. Senator Hoar of Massachusetts, assuming that the Declaration of Independence was a part of the Republican creed, openly declared in the upper chamber that there was not a supporter of the war within the sound of his voice who, if he were a Filipino, would not fight for liberty just as the Filipinos were fighting and would not despise them for doing otherwise. In a towering rage, Mark Twain dipped his pen in vitriol and wrote a savage article on civilizing and Christianizing insurgents by the use of the rifle and the water cure. Senator Tillman of South Carolina laughed loud and long. "Republican leaders," he exclaimed, "do no longer dare to call into question the justice or the necessity of limiting negro suffrage in the South. . . . Your slogans of the past—brotherhood of man and fatherhood of God—have gone glimmering down through the ages!"

To such criticisms replies equally direct were made. With righteous indignation, McKinley and his advisers denied that there was in the Filipino war any analogy whatever with the American struggle for liberty in 1776. To them the very mention of Aguinaldo and Washington in the same breath was nothing short of sacrilege; while praising the insurgent army of 1899 for resisting American dominion was worse than quixotic; it was akin to treason, to lending aid and comfort to the enemy.

Turning then to concrete issues, they pointed out the difficulty inherent in giving self-government to seven million people scattered on hundreds of islands and ranging in culture from primitive hill-folk to polished urban dwellers. They scouted as fanciful Hoar's program for immediate peace, the recognition of independence, friendly assistance in establishing self-government, and an invitation to the powers of the world to join in assuring continued freedom to the insular republic.   In short, the McKinley administration could see no solution of the problem except that of conquest, to be followed by the slow and orderly development of education and local autonomy under American tutelage.

§

Given this difference of opinion over the imperial adventure the Philippine question became a leading issue in the campaign of 1900. On their part Republicans faced it squarely. By acclamation they renominated McKinley, author and defender of the forward course. Ignoring dissenters in their ranks, they vowed that there was no other choice than pacification by war; that responsibility for the peoples freed from Spain fell upon the United States as an outcome of victory; that "it became the high duty of the government to maintain its authority, to put down armed insurrection, and to confer the blessings of liberty and civilization upon all the rescued people." With a view to enlivening their campaign the Republican managers sent their candidate for Vice-President, Theodore Roosevelt, popular "hero of the Rough Riders," through the country in a tempest of oratory and ovation, flaying as "mollycoddles" the softlings who opposed Manifest Destiny. On the other side, the Democrats, still under the spell of Bryan, nominated the Commoner again and made imperialism an issue comparable in gravity to trusts and free silver.

In the contest that ensued, the methods and passions of 1896 were revived. Once more Hanna took charge of

486 THE RISE OF AMERICAN CIVILIZATION

the Republican campaign chest and, as Hay said, by crying "Wolf, Wolf" all summer, wrung adequate revenues from the leaders of business enterprise. Through fear or financial necessity, Bryan was now called the enemy of empire as well as property. Even Hay, a man with good claims to sophistication, denounced the Democratic candidate as "a frank anarchist," darkly hinting that "nobody knows what Jack Cade may do." Nor was invective of this type spared by Democrats. Scorning the moral pretensions of their opponents, they declared that "a greedy commercialism" had dictated Philippine policies and that the effort of the American army to restore law and order was "a war of criminal aggression."

On the merits of this debate, the popular verdict was conclusive, for the election returns gave McKinley a majority over his rival far in excess of that won four years before, commanding him to hold his place on the captain's bridge. Rejoicing in this vindication, he had just given the order for full steam ahead when a tragic fate overtook him. While attending the Buffalo exposition in September, 1901, McKinley was shot in cold blood by an anarchist, and died at the home of a friend a few days afterward. In an instant even the harsh voice of partisan criticism was hushed; the whole nation united in paying tribute to the virtues of the dead President as he was laid to rest amid the strains of his favorite hymn: "Nearer, My God, to Thee." The principal author of the new course was dead but his policies, according to the announcement of his successor, Theodore Roosevelt, were to be continued "absolutely unbroken"—a pledge soon redeemed by an energetic prosecution of the war on the Filipino insurgents to a victorious finish.

§

After American supremacy was assured by arms, came the task of establishing political institutions for the provinces. With respect to that subject, too, President Roosevelt received from his predecessor full guidance. Shortly after possession had been wrested from Spain, a commission of distinguished citizens was sent out to study economic and social life in the Philippines and to report findings pertinent to the adoption of a final policy. On the basis of that inquiry a second commission headed by William Howard Taft was placed in temporary charge of civil affairs, pending the ultimate extinction of the military régime. Early in 1900, in an organic law for the government of Porto Rico, Congress had demonstrated that American imperial ideas were to be tempered somewhat by democracy—certainly by a larger measure of self-government than any of Spain's colonial provinces had ever enjoyed in their centuries of development or the peoples conquered by the imperialist powers of contemporary Europe had ordinarily received. Provision was made for a governor and six cabinet heads appointed by the President and Senate; and for a local legislature of two houses, one chosen by popular vote and the other composed of the department chiefs and five other persons selected at Washington.

With such directions already in hand, President Roosevelt had no difficulty in formulating projects for the administration of the Philippines. In his first message to Congress, he laid stress on the problem and in 1902 an organic law for those islands was duly enacted. Five years later, after peace was fully established, after a census was taken and preparations formally made, elections for the popular branch of the legislative body were held and the new system was duly installed. The Philippine government then consisted of the governor and a civil commission, which also acted as the upper chamber of the legislature, chosen by the President and Senate, and a lower house elected by popular vote.

In thus determining the fate of the new possessions, Congress, operating under a Constitution which contained no express provisions respecting imperial provinces, had to face some legal questions never encountered before in exactly the same form. One of these, the most perplexing, was summed up in the popular query: "Does the Constitution follow the flag?" Among adepts in public law nothing but an affirmative answer seemed possible for, according to time-honored judicial precedents, Congress was clearly restrained in the government of territories by the provisions of the Constitution—in any case by the clauses establishing freedom of the press, trial by jury, and other formulas of Anglo-Saxon jurisprudence. But it was obvious to every one that such refined notions of American policy, though well known to high-class Spaniards, could not be lightly applied to primitive people in tropical islands. Doubtless the Sultan of Sulu had never heard of Magna Carta.

An awkward pause therefore occurred among the lawyers until the Supreme Court, in a series of decisions known as tht "Insular Cases," cut the knot, or rather discovered that the obstacles were really not in the Constitution after all. The way was smooth at last. Though in the most important case four of the nine judges dissented and the five who formed the majority differed in their reasoning, this incident, if tormenting to precisionists, made no lasting impression on the populace. Its conclusions, the genial Mr. Dooley no doubt fully expressed in the passing remark that "the Supreme Court followed the election returns." At all events Congress was authorized to go forward on the hypothesis that in governing the dependencies it could do anything that did not violate a "fundamental" part of the Constitution, that is, prove too brusque for the judicial conscience. When a Philippine editor went to some lengths in questioning the beneficent intentions of the American administration, he was quickly shown by the Supreme Court that under the First Amendment to the federal Constitution no specious pleas for license could be made.

The years that followed the creation of the new system witnessed no serious revulsion in policy. Regarding its mandate as secure, the Republican administration continued the progressive application of its educational and economic policies in the colonial possessions. The Democrats, in each succeeding presidential campaign, repeated in varying form the criticisms of 1900. On the constructive side their general idea was to give Porto Rico the legal status which had been accorded to the older continental territories since the enactment of the Northwest Ordinance and to grant independence to the Philippines "as soon as stable government can be established." When at length under the administration of President Wilson, the Democrats finally got a chance to test their theories, Congress, by an act passed in 1917, provided that the upper house of the Porto Rican legislature should be made elective and the natives were given a larger share of the local offices. In 1916 Congress solemnly resolved that the Philippines should become independent, when the time was ripe, and made a promising gesture by granting the islands an elective senate. As in Porto Rico, lucrative and important posts hitherto reserved to Americans were bestowed upon natives and the management of finances was allowed to slide into their hands.

Instead of bringing harmony in the Philippines, these concessions merely fired anew, as was natural, the ardor of the independence party and moved the local legislature at Manila to repeat its resolve in favor of an immediate separation from the United States. They also worried American interests in the islands, both financial and industrial, inspiring them to make vigorous demands in Washington for a stern Philippine policy. For a few years it seemed as if a crisis might come any time but in due course President Wilson passed out of office and it was discovered that his acts of grace were not beyond recall. In any case, they did not prevent General Leonard Wood, sent out by President Harding to serve as governor, from bringing the ship to an even keel again in 1921.

For American consumption it was then reported that only a few politicians and agitators desired independence, that the withdrawal of American power would leave millions of helpless wards to the tender mercies of local satraps. To the Filipinos, it was gradually revealed that the Wilson rainbow was a mirage and that the American people, or at least the plurality of those that took the trouble to cast their votes, desired no reversal of the imperialist policies adopted at the opening of the century. As the years passed preponderance in the commerce and industry of the islands shifted steadily from native to American hands and the possibilities of rubber culture became poignantly evident, making Manifest Destiny doubly appealing.

In the illuminating language of a telegraphic dispatch sent from Baguio, the summer capital of the American administration, in September, 1926, to reinforce the coming report of Carmi Thompson, a member of the Harding-Daugherty group of Ohio statesmen sent by President Coolidge to collect information, "If we withdraw from these fertile tropical islands, strategically located at the Orient's gateway, we would have to relinquish our position as an Asiatic power. Without the Philippines as a commercial and military base, it is said, we could not enforce the open door policy of equal trade opportunities for all nations in China, could not issue [sic] the limitless economic opportunities sure to accompany the awakening of the East, and could not wage war effectively to protect our interests. The argument advanced to support this contention is that the Philippines strategically are the only place available to the United States as a base. The Philippines are a part of a group of islands from Japan on the north to Borneo on the south, which form a screen across the Pacific to the coast of Asia, constituting the door to the future possibilities of the Far East. As long as America holds this strategic position, it is argued, she will remain a powerful factor in the Orient's economic and international life."

§

The seizure of the Philippines, by providing a splendid base for economic operations in the Far East, brought nearer to fulfillment an old dream of American imperial states-men. In Lincoln's day Seward had declared that the United States ought to command the empire of the seas and that the vast Pacific basin was to become the chief theater of world events in the coming years. With inflexible tenacity, in his relations with the Orient, he pursued as Secretary of State the policy of the "open door," although he did not invent that clever phrase to catch, if not inform, the public imagination.

As we have shown, he coöperated with other western powers in forcing Orientals to throw wide their gates to commerce. With Seward's approval, American naval officers joined in bombarding the Japanese town of Shimonoseki in 1864 in retaliation for hostility displayed by local lords. With his sanction, the American representative in Tokyo united with the agent of Great Britain in compelling Japan to accept a commercial convention which, as Payson J. Treat well says, kept her "in bondage to British commercial interests for nearly half a century." In accord with these measures, Seward also proposed to France common action in punishing Koreans for murdering French missionaries and American traders who had insisted on going where they were not welcome. If the State Department and the Navy could have found adequate support in Congress, the American flag would have been hoisted in Eastern waters long before the Philippines were wrested from Spain in 1898.

But it took some time for the country at large to see the spheres of usefulness early discovered by the men in high posts of observation. Indeed the tariff policy introduced by Seward's party colleagues helped to relax temporarily the early economic interest in Pacific imperialism. Well protected by high duties on competing goods, American manufacturers commanded for many years after 1861 an immense and growing market at home and, until that was saturated, felt no overpowering need for more foreign trading facilities.

Meanwhile other imperial powers were aggressively busy in the Orient—waging war on China and parceling her ancient dominions among themselves. In southeastern Asia, France tore away an immense estate. Intrenched at Hong Kong in command of the Canton trade and aided by their banking operations at the treaty ports, the English gathered in a lion's share of the Empire's commercial business. At the close of a victorious war on China in 1895, Japan annexed Formosa and would have taken more if Russia, Germany, and France had not intervened. Two years later, Germany, offering as a pretext the murder of a missionary, seized Kiao-chau and brought the whole province of Shantung under the sway of her administrators. The very next year, Russia wrung Port Arthur from China on a lease and secured the right to build a railway through Manchuria to Harbin, connecting with the Trans-Siberian line. Not to be left out of the feast in the North, Great Britain then laid hold of Wei-hai-wei, a strategic port lying between the new bases seized by the Germans and Russians.

While these things were being done, European capitalists were lending money to the tottering Chinese Empire, acquiring exclusive rights to build railways in different parts of the country, and annexing most of the mineral resources within reach of tidewater. In this fashion China was divided into "spheres of influence" and when finally American merchants and capitalists, having saturated their home market, as they thought, turned to distant places for new opportunities, they found themselves hampered at every turn by grants and monopolies in rival hands.

At this very juncture there occurred in China an uprising against aliens, known as the Boxer Rebellion. For a long time the conservative leaders in Peking had looked with dismay on the course of events—their religion assailed by Christian missionaries, their government attacked by revolutionary advocates of democracy, their lands divided among foreign powers like "meat flung to tigers." From the capital, dismay spread to the illiterate masses, causing secret societies of patriots, known as Boxers, or "fists of righteous harmony," to spring up in all quarters. And when enough materials for an explosion had accumulated, an omen of a coming storm was flashed on the sky near the close of 1899 by the murder of an English missionary in Shantung.

In the summer of the next year the crash came. The German minister, on his way to the imperial palace to protest against the conduct of the Chinese, was killed in the streets of Peking and violence broke out on every hand. Terror-stricken, the foreigners in the capital fled to the British legation, threw up defenses against besieging insurgents, and sent forth a call for help that rang throughout all Christendom, uniting the great powers in a relief expedition to Peking. After many lively squabbles over precedence and spoils, the associated forces finally occupied the capital, freed the imprisoned aliens, and pillaged shops and palaces. Brought thus to its knees, the imperial government of China was forced to pay a huge indemnity for the murder of foreigners and the destruction of their property, compelled to make abject apologies, and required to erect in Peking a monument in memory of the German minister.

In the invasion of China and the settlement that followed, the United States government took an active part. Indeed the Boxer Rebellion afforded it an excellent opportunity to bring to the notice of the world its own special policies and claims. Having established a strategic base in the Philippines, the McKinley administration had already given thought to the promotion of American interests in China— or at least in that part of the country not yet seized by foreign powers and their enterprising capitalists. By a little economic analysis it easily discovered that, unless the United States was to join in the dismemberment and demand a share of the territorial spoils, American business men could only hope to get their part of Chinese trade by checking the greed of others. In short, the obvious remedy was an "open door," that is, the maintenance of Chinese national unity and the establishment of equal trading privileges for all foreigners—saving, of course, the acquired rights already won by aliens. With the advantages of such a program clearly in mind, John Hay, as Secretary of State, had addressed a note to the great powers in 1899—before the Boxer outbreak—asking them to adhere to the doctrine of restraint and equality.

Taking advantage of the opportunity offered by the Boxer negotiations, Hay again invited the other governments concerned "to seek a solution which may bring about permanent safety and peace to China, preserve Chinese territorial and administrative entity, protect all rights guaranteed to friendly powers by treaty and international law, and safeguard for the world the principle of equal and impartial trade with all parts of the Chinese empire." Since the only alternative seemed to be a scramble among the victors that might end in a world war, the American formula was accepted in theory. "The moment we acted," said Hay, "the rest of the world paused and finally came over to our ground; and the German government, which is generally brutal but seldom silly, recovered its senses and climbed down off its perch." Besides this friendly gesture, the United States, finding its share of the indemnity wrung from Peking far in excess of the damages incurred, returned the remainder to China in the form of a fund dedicated by secret negotiations to the education of Chinese students in American schools.

In this manner the American government demonstrated to the powers that, while it had profited from British aggression and treaty-port rights, it would not approve any more seizures of Chinese territory or any more monopolies within the boundary of that ancient Empire. Though devised with realistic and practical ends in mind, the policy of the open door also had a lofty moral flavor, pleasing to Chinese, missionaries, anti-imperialists, and pacifists alike. At the same time it gave American economic interests in the Far East about all the guarantees that the state of popular sentiment at home warranted. "We do not think," laconically remarked Secretary Hay, "that the public opinion of the United States would justify this government in taking part in the great game of spoliation now going on." That was the heart of the matter. President McKinley was personally willing to take a hand in the carving up of China, if it was to come about, but feared that the hinterland of America was not yet fully indoctrinated with any such view of Manifest Destiny.

§

With the high sanction of the open-door policy, Secretary Hay and his successors under Roosevelt and Taft bent their energies to the work of securing for American citizens equal trading privileges in all parts of China and equal opportunities for investment in the development of railways and natural resources. In particular they gave continuous attention to the economic penetration of Korea, Manchuria, and Mongolia, thereby coming into collision with Russian enterprise. "I have been thinking a great deal about Manchuria," wrote Senator Lodge of Massachusetts to Roosevelt on May 21, 1903. "Our trade there is assuming very large proportions, and it seems to me we ought to take very strong grounds. . . . I have had letters from Lawrence where some of the mills make cotton goods which go to Manchuria, urging the strongest possible action and then demanding that a fleet be sent. . . . It is the same way with the cotton mills of the South and much the same with the flour interests of the Northwest, who send a great deal of flour to China."

If, however, American capitalists who owned cotton mills and flour mills thought the problem of possessing the trade of northern China was simple and could be solved by dispatching a fleet of battleships, they were mistaken. Politicians knew better; for, taking a longer and broader view of the matter, they discovered that the business of exploiting Chinese resources involved a vast network of international rivalry and called for finesse in diplomacy as well as saber-rattling. Even the most obtuse among them saw at the opening of the twentieth century that Russia, backed by French capitalists, was for the moment a menace to all the other powers eager to extend their economic operations in North China. With the terrific pressure of a glacier the Muscovite was bearing down toward the ice-free waters of the Asiatic coast.

In the presence of this gigantic force, it was the part of discretion for the administration at Washington to make common cause with other governments in the quest for a counterpoise against the Tsar in the Far East. To President Roosevelt the elements of the situation were perfectly visible. As he well knew, England, threatened by Russia on the Anglo-Indian frontier and in China, had entered into an alliance with Japan in 1902, and had made friendly overtures to the United States during and since its war on Spain. Meanwhile Japan had already begun an economic invasion of the mainland by way of Korea.

Given this state of affairs, sympathetic coöperation with these two countries seemed to Roosevelt the only possible choice, and when in 1904 the economic contest between Russia and Japan on the banks of the Yalu ended in a resort to arms, he immediately served notice on France and Germany that, in case they entered the affair in support of the Tsar, he would "promptly side with Japan and proceed to whatever length was necessary on her behalf," fully confident all the while that the English government "would act in the same way." This, of course, meant war for the United States if either France or Germany refused to heed the warning. In substance it also meant that the government at Washington was not willing to allow the rich resources of northern China to fall under Russian monopoly sustained by French capitalists.

Happily for Roosevelt, the fortunes of the Russo-Japanese conflict favored his program. It was his supreme wish to prevent either party in the contest from winning an absolute dominion over all northern China; while the French, English, and American bankers who floated the loans of the warring countries were equally anxious to see their respective principals escape from their war with ability to pay what they owed. When, at length, the contestants in the struggle approached bankruptcy without reaching a decision, financiers served a stop notice on their debtors and closed their purses. Caught in this economic trap, Japan then turned to Roosevelt for help and received it. After discreetly sounding the ground in Europe, the President acted as mediator, with a fine flourish bringing the representatives of Russia and Japan together at Portsmouth, New Hampshire, in the summer of 1905. There the compromise which the President desired with reference to American interests was reached: Japan got Russia's rights in Port Arthur, Dairen, and the South Manchurian Railway, but she won no indemnity to repair her impoverished treasury. So the two belligerents faced each other weakened and divided and northern China was still without an absolute master.

Continuing this policy of balancing the powers in the Far East, Roosevelt opened secret negotiations, in the summer of the Portsmouth conference, with Japan and England for the purpose of upholding order in the Orient. Though personally in favor of a regular alliance, he said that the Senate would never approve it and that he "might as well strive for the moon." So he had to be content with sending an emissary to Tokyo and making a simple agreement with the premier of Japan recorded in a highly confidential memorandum.

In this secret convention, Japan on her part undertook to respect American dominion in the Philippines; while the President of the United States agreed on his part to accept the establishment of Japanese dominion over Korea by force of arms, thus setting the imperialist ventures of one country over against kindred enterprises of the other.

At the same time, Roosevelt's emissary in Tokyo assured the Japanese premier. that the people of the United States were "so fully in accord with the people of Japan and Great Britain in the maintenance of peace in the Far East that, whatever occasion arose, appropriate action of the government of the United States, in conjunction with Japan and Great Britain, for such a purpose, could be counted upon by them quite as confidently as if the United States were under treaty obligations." "In fact it is a Japanese-Anglo-American alliance," blurted out a well-known Tokyo publicist on hearing by an underground route of this secret agreement. Such it was, at least while Roosevelt was in the White House, although the people of the United States knew nothing about it until Tyler Dennett, finding the document among the President's personal papers, made it public in 1924.

While Japan was willing to subscribe to peace in 1905 when she was on the verge of bankruptcy, she had no intention of allowing American business enterprise to snap up the rich prizes recently wrested from Russia at a cost of so much blood and treasure. As an evidence of its resolve, the Japanese government refused to permit the American railway Napoleon, Edward H. Harriman, to make the Manchurian railway a part of his "round the world system" and it also politely declined to allow Jacob Schiff, its New York financial backer in the war with Russia, to revive that project a year later.

Indeed, on seeing formidable American interests at work in their special preserves in northern China, both Japan and Russia quickly forgot their recent hatreds, composed their quarrels, united to protect their winnings—and to gain more. Together they held the key to the situation. Japan controlled lower Manchuria through her mastery of the strategic railway and Russia was strong in upper Manchuria and Mongolia where the Chinese Eastern Railway, under her sovereignty, offered connections with Vladivostok and the Trans-Siberian line. Policing their long stretches of track with trained soldiers and fixing the freight rates for the entire region with reference to their requirements, the two powers virtually occupied northern China and were in a position to exploit for their own benefit the vast undeveloped country at their very doors.

In an effort to break the grip of Japan and Russia on Chinese territory, American capitalists proposed, and the Department of State attempted to secure, the "neutralization" of the important railways described above—an action designed to open the whole district to American enterprise. During this operation steps were also taken in 1910 to float a large Chinese loan through banking houses in the United States on the understanding that the money was to be used in developing, among other things, railways and commerce in Manchuria. At this juncture, the Russian foreign office learned, through French sources in Washington, that Secretary Knox, in supporting the loan, proposed to have an American supervisor put in charge of the disbursement, therewith in effect setting up American political influence in Peking and Manchuria.

Frightened by the news, St. Petersburg and Tokyo, now convinced that the open-door policy was in reality a subterfuge to cover an American invasion of their Chinese property, started negotiations looking to advantages in their mutual concerns; and in a series of secret conversations and treaties, made public only after the Bolsheviki threw open the Tsarist archives in 1918-19, united in protecting each other's interests. Frankly flouting the open-door creed, they divided Manchuria into spheres and promised to assist each other in case of an armed conflict with any other power aiming at political supremacy in China—solemn agreements referring without question to the United States since England was bound to Japan by a treaty of alliance and was apparently fully aware of the Russo-Japanese understanding.

Chinese affairs were undoubtedly taking a serious direction when there came a slight release of the tension under President Wilson. Determined, he said, to free the federal government from the dominion of financial and industrial interests, he turned a cold shoulder on proposals to continue in the Orient the forward policy pursued by Roosevelt and Taft. In fact, he expressed his hearty sympathy with the popular party in China which had overthrown the empire in 1912, announced its resolve to shake off alien interventions, and tried to establish democratic institutions in the oldest civilization in the world. To show that his sympathy was more than nominal, Wilson seized an opportunity then before him to give a practical demonstration. At the very moment, American bankers were coöperating with foreign financiers in arranging a Chinese bond issue, known as the "consortium," or five-power loan, a venture to be made secure by a firm grip upon specified revenues, administered under semi-official direction. Confronted by a request to approve this project, Wilson refused to endorse it on the theory that it was an effort of "high finance" to control the destiny of the Chinese people.

While expressing his interest in an "independent" China, Wilson also made a friendly overture to Japan. In 1917, he authorized his Secretary of State, Robert Lansing, to make an agreement with Viscount Ishii, the Japanese ambassador, recognizing that "Japan has special interests in China." Though the language of this understanding was as elusive as moonshine, it was taken to mean that Japan was to have a freer hand in promoting her concerns on the mainland. At any rate, it was received with delight in Tokyo and with consternation in Peking. To the American minister in China, Paul S. Reinsch, it was a shocking surprise. He had long been complaining to the State Department about the neglect of American interests in that country and the Lansing-Ishii understanding proved to be the last straw for him. In a short time he resigned with ill-concealed disgust at the cautious and timid policy of the Wilson administration in the Orient. The truth was that the President confined his active participation in imperialism to one sphere, the Caribbean, where the opportunities were less dangerous and the effective use of the Navy, in promoting law and order, was far easier.

§

The annexation of Porto Rico and absorption of Cuba under Republican auspices had been merely a prelude to the transformation of the Gulf of Mexico and the Caribbean into an inland sea of the United States. In the nature of things, to use the language of diplomacy, the region was a part of the American empire; for a lion's share of the commerce with nearly all the islands scattered between the Bahamas and Trinidad had been readily gathered into American hands. Even British and French traders could not resist the pull of the powerful market in the United States; while the combined efforts of Britain and Canada could not make water run up hill. On the mainland also, in Mexico, Central America, Colombia and Venezuela, American business enterprise marched from one victory to another.

Political as well as economic processes favored the development of American hegemony. In those places where European powers did not keep order, there were periodic uprisings against the titular governments, revolts often purely factious, sometimes the efforts of honest men to oust corrupt and tyrannical adventurers, occasionally the outcome of a failure to appreciate the merits of foreign investors. Regardless of their source, they were always disturbing to business interests, particularly to the holders of local bonds. As a rule the outstanding obligations of Latin-American republics were large for the pertinent revenues. In fact they were generally inflated to a high pressure; for at each uprising the debts of the defeated party were added to those of the victors, thereby preventing any such magnificent repudiation as had occurred when the government of Abraham Lincoln triumphed over that of Jefferson Davis in the Second American Revolution. It required, accordingly, no sweeping derangement of the social order in a Latin-

American country to fetch down a high structure of finance.

In every crisis the government of the United States was involved, and given new occasions for assimilation. Besides being pledged under the Monroe Doctrine to prevent European powers from occupying more territory in the western hemisphere, even in the honest performance of collecting debts, it was continually besieged by American bankers and business men to help them save endangered revenues. At no time did it feel inclined to say that it would neither allow European governments to succor their nationals among the bondholders nor make any movement itself on their behalf. If the duties imposed by the necessity for action were slight, the mere presence of American battleships in the offing might enable bankers to take possession of customs houses and effect amicable settlements of debts by negotiations. If, however, local leaders refused to listen to the voice of warning and forced the landing of American marines, a limited warfare sometimes had to be waged on the basis of presidential orders to the Navy Department. And yet in no case did the parties of interest feel constrained to invoke the constitutional provision vesting the power to declare war in the Congress of the United States. As things turned out, American economic and political sovereignty was steadily advanced in the Caribbean without breaking the legal peace of the western hemisphere or disturbing the party of pacific intentions in the domestic hinterland.

A brief illustrative chronology hints at the process. In 1903, Germany was compelled by a threat of force from President Roosevelt to withdraw from Venezuela and submit certain financial claims to arbitration. In 1905, Roosevelt, by executive action, took over the customs houses of Santo Domingo and stationed war vessels in Dominican waters to give point to the argument. Under the Platt amendment, he interfered in Cuba in 1906, giving the natives a convincing proof that American warnings against disorder were to be respected. By a formal treaty ratified by the

Senate of the United States, the pecuniary protectorate over Santo Domingo was made regular in 1907. The next year Secretary Knox broke off relations with the President of Nicaragua; a little later an American warship served notice on local contestants for power that there was to be no fighting in Bluefields—"thus protecting the preponderating American and other foreign interests," as the State Department in Washington put it. In 1911, on the suggestion of New York bankers, a treaty was negotiated with Honduras, extending American authority over that republic; though ratified by the United States Senate, it was rejected by the native authorities.

During the same year an American warship was sent to Nicaragua, a loan arranged, and a treaty drawn, reciting "the benevolent intentions" of the United States and putting the customs into the hands of a presidential appointee. When, in spite of three urgent messages from President Taft, the Senate declined to ratify the agreement, marines were landed in Nicaragua and business was restored to a normal course. In 1914-16, a treaty with Nicaragua was at last adopted ceding a canal strip and naval bases to the United States in return for three million dollars in cash to be expended largely for American goods in coöperation with American authorities. In 1915, the marines carried the flag into Haiti and established American suzerainty there after killing more than two thousand natives who, for one reason or another, got in the way of the operation. In 1916, Admiral Knapp—"to maintain domestic tranquillity"—took possession of Santo Domingo and declared that "republic" subject to the military government of the United States. In 1917, the Virgin Islands were purchased from Denmark. In 1920, the American navy was employed in helping to stabilize Guatemala. In 1921, after some American marines had smashed the office of the *Tribuna* in Managua, for printing critical articles, the minister of the United States requested the local Nicaraguan government to set apart adequate space outside the capital for drill grounds, a dance hall, and a moving picture theater to be used by American forces and also to designate special liquor saloons for their convenience. In 1923, the national assembly of Panama approved a large loan for highway construction to be secured by investments correctly placed in New York City. In 1924, the American marines once more came to the aid of public order in Honduras. In 1927, the marines were again in Nicaragua. Such was in brief a partial chronicle of what Secretary Knox called "dollar diplomacy."

The series of events here recited were accompanied by no expressions of ill-will on the part of the American government. On the contrary, Roosevelt, Taft, Wilson, Harding, and Coolidge all agreed that, in this connection, there was nothing either sinister or ungenerous in the purposes of the United States. Wilson was especially emphatic on this point. Speaking cordially of the Latin-American countries, he said: "We must prove ourselves their friends and champions upon terms of equality and honor. . . . We must show ourselves friends by comprehending their interests whether it squares with our interests or not."

Harding was also solicitous in the matter of fraternal relations. Thinking that, perhaps, there had been some needless severity in the treatment of the countries to the south, he declared that he would never permit any officer under his authority to "draw a constitution for helpless neighbors in the West Indies and jam it down their throats at the point of bayonets borne by United States marines." Undoubtedly Coolidge agreed with the Republican platform of 1924 which asserted that "new sanctions and new proofs of permanent accord have marked our relations with all Latin America." It could not be said, therefore, that the steps which indicated the march of Manifest Destiny were taken with reference to any deliberate or frank design of empire.

In fact, each of the numerous incidents in the extension of American authority over the Caribbean was marked by colors and episodes peculiar to the occasion. For that reason, the bare chronicle of the forward movement as a whole fails to give a correct impression of the higher law in its specific application. To gain an insight into that phase it is necessary to examine somewhat minutely an entire chapter of contingencies, and for the purpose of illustration the case of Haiti offers a sufficient revelation. That little island republic became the scene of revolutions and assassinations as soon as it cast off the yoke of France in 1803 and at all times thereafter showed an evident need for law, order, good roads, sanitation, education, and industrial progress. But the southern planters who ruled the United States in the middle period of national expansion, although they were ready to raise the flag over good land fit for cotton culture, shrank from relations too cordial with a spot where slaves had made a successful revolution and were trying to govern themselves. Moreover, their successors at Washington, the masters of business, were also largely indifferent to the requirements of Haiti as long as domestic enterprise—even farm mortgages—yielded ten or fifteen per cent or happy negotiations with the federal land office brought larger returns on smaller risks. But at the end of the century, when the southern slavocracy had moldered in its grave and the pecuniary equipment of the United States had been well rounded out, there arose a marked solicitude about the welfare of Haiti.

In 1902, one of the periodical rebellions that had plagued that small republic sent it swimming within the range of American kinetics. Turning for aid to the United States, the Haitian government floated a loan in New York at twelve per cent and invested large sums in ammunition at two or three times the usual price. Unabashed by these commitments, American munition makers showed an equal interest in the revolutionary forces fighting for "liberty" and sold them instruments of destruction, also on profitable terms. Observing the scrimmage from afar, European capitalists tendered their good offices with the same devotion to both parties, everyone of them knowing, as the American minister on the spot remarked with casual directness, that the civilized powers concerned would make the Haitians pay all bills no matter which side won in the civil war. Now, among the countries involved in this crisis, none was more anxious than the German Empire. German merchants controlled about nine-tenths of Haiti's foreign trade and showed a concern in local affairs that was artistically proportioned to the flow of goods. In the press of things, they were able to place a loan of half a million at thirty-five per cent interest and later they managed to float a smaller issue of three hundred thousand dollars which yielded a net sum of about half that amount to the Haitian treasury.

Naturally vexed by this precocity on the part of the Germans and fearing utter discomfiture at the hands of their rivals, American business men began to display great consternation, the State Department sharing their fear. Although an American company had got important railway and land concessions and although the National City Bank of New York had gathered in much of the Haitian debt on terms presumably not adverse, it was thought that the American share of the local proceeds was entirely too small. Moreover, there were irritations connected with an affront to national honor; open discrimination was shown by Haitians against some American citizens of Syrian origin who had been very active in bringing local trade into American hands. And this annoyance was augmented by an untoward incident, arising from an attempt of the Haitian president to seize the gold reserve in the local national bank, a design foiled by the intervention of American marines, and the transfer of the treasure on an American war vessel to New York, where it was safely deposited at a low rate of interest, leaving the government of Haiti to clamor loudly for a return of the funds.

Since it was now evident that the friendly concern of the State Department in Washington must take a more practical form, President Wilson sent commissioners to Haiti charged with the task of persuading Vilbrun Guillaume Sam, president of the republic, to accept the benevolent protection of the United States. At the same time American bankers served notice on him that no more loans were to be expected without adequate guarantees, placing him in a real dilemma. Procuring aid from Berlin was out of the question, for Germany, in the toils of war, was blockaded by an invincible sea power. Neither was assistance from France forthcoming; that country, far from indicating a desire to help President Sam out of his pinch, dispatched a naval force to his republic to protect French lives and property.

Given this signal for action, the government of the United States, in the summer of 1915, ordered Admiral Caperton, in command of the good ship, Washington, to Haitian waters, just in time to learn that President Sam, enraged by the turn of events, had ordered the murder of more than a hundred prisoners and had been himself assassinated in retaliation. Visibly disturbed by such cruel deeds, the Admiral directed his marines to seize the local political theater and some blood was shed in the operation, but not enough to cause a declaration of war by Congress. Competent directors now being in charge, martial law was instituted under American auspices and the Haitian national assembly was permitted to elect as president, General Dartiguenave, a candidate acceptable to Admiral Caperton and apparently disposed to coöperate with American representatives on the ground.

At all events, as soon as he was installed, the General signed a treaty with his new friends. In the preamble, the document stated that it was the desire of the "High contracting parties . . . to confirm and strengthen the amity existing between them by the most cordial coöperation in measures for their common advantage." According to the terms of the bond the United States was to use its good offices in developing the agricultural, mineral, and commercial resources of the little republic, to name engineers whose advice was to be binding in the management of the said resources, to take over and administer the customs of the republic, and to select the financial adviser charged with directing the fiscal affairs of the local government.

Thus, in a single stroke, the United States undertook to promote private enterprise and safeguard the public finances upon which large bond issues afloat in the United States rested for security. With the restraint that characterized Clive's course in India, the American administration refrained from annexing Haiti; indeed this would have been inconsistent with Wilson's lofty declaration of two years before to the effect that this country would "never again seek one additional foot of territory by conquest." In this spirit the Senate ratified the Haitian treaty of amity in the spring of 1916.

It is due to historical accuracy, however, to say that this assistance from the United States was not unanimously approved by the citizens of Haiti. Indeed, no little dexterity and some show of force were required to secure a ratification of the treaty of amity by the local congress. Moreover, in the lapse of five years the American troops on the spot felt impelled to kill more than two thousand natives. Though most of the victims were called "bandits" by the military and naval agents of the United States, some of them were probably actuated by resentment at the "alien invasion." In fact a number of foreigners joined the natives in deprecating the new course in Haiti. An American missionary who had spent years in the tiny republic took it upon himself to protest indignantly against the conduct of the American authorities and would not be silenced even after he had been thrown into a dungeon. An American real estate speculator in Haiti also lodged charges against the marines and the gendarmerie; shortly afterward he was murdered. Although no political significance was attached to these incidents, they certainly revealed a measure of discontent with the order of things established under the auspices of the United States.

If all the Haitians shot and murdered deserved their fate, it was none the less evident that many who survived the process of pacification were not entirely pleased with the new régime. In any case, when attempts were made to develop the agricultural resources of the interior in conformity to the provisions of the amity treaty, it was found necessary to use force in holding natives at the task of roadbuilding. Moreover, local orators and editors, according to American reports, conducted such an "agitation against the United States officials who are aiding and supporting the constitutional government of Haiti" that vigilance dictated the suppression of newspapers and public meetings and the institution of trial by court martial.

In connection with the land question, local discontent was particularly marked. By the old constitution of Haiti land ownership was restricted to natives, thus handicapping by a legal barrier American business leaders, impatient to get at the work of developing the agricultural resources, as stipulated in the treaty of amity. With a view to removing this obstacle to "the advance," a new constitution, omitting the objectionable clause, was framed by skilled draftsmen in Washington and submitted to the Haitian assembly for approval. At this point the wrath of disgruntled natives, who resented the alien invasion as bitterly as Californians resented the intrusion of the Japanese, broke all bounds, giving the assembly such a fright that it did not dare to agree to the constitution proffered by Washington. Defeated in its desire to proceed with respect for the forms of law, the American administrators now dissolved the legislature, instructed the marines to drive out recalcitrant members by force, and decreed that the revised constitution, authorizing alien corporations to hold land in Haiti, should be submitted to a popular referendum under American military supervision.

At the election, held with due regard to formalities, sixty-three thousand votes, according to the returns, were cast in favor of the proposal and two or three hundred against it—a ludicrous outcome that induced some wag to suggest that American marines had put in the negative ballots merely to avoid the specious appearance of enthusiastic unanimity. Indeed the transaction was so indecorous that Americans at home, hearing of it, added their demur to the remonstrances of the natives. In a short time, Senator Harding, campaigning for the presidency, joined them in declaring that if elected he would never jam constitutions down the throats of his West Indian neighbors at the point of bayonets borne by marines.

Soon after Harding entered the White House, a number of prominent citizens presented to his Secretary of State, Charles E. Hughes, a petition against the activities in Haiti to which the chief executive had adverted while a candidate. In response to the appeal, the Secretary, with that judicial calm which always characterized him, declined to be hurried into a complete reversal of policy by stories of atrocities and by indictments of American banking interests; that, he thought, would be sacrificing to sentiment an opportunity "to promote the tranquillity and well-being" of Haiti. Support for that view now came from other directions.

A senatorial committee, headed by the Honorable Medill McCormick, witty son-in-law of Marcus A. Hanna, after a long inquiry reported that, in spite of the unfortunate things done under the Wilson administration, the emergencies of the occasion required the United States to continue its work of instituting a local government "as nearly representative as might be" and coöperating with the Haitian authorities for "the development of the Haitian people." Grave moral responsibilities had been incurred and national honor, as well as many minor things, bade the United States carry out the terms of the treaty of 1916, namely, "to confirm and strengthen the amity" existing between the two republics—one small and harassed by poverty, the other great and magnanimous.

§

The growing interests of the United States in the Caribbean made inevitable the fulfillment of an age-old dream— a canal across the Isthmus of Panama to shorten by thousands of miles the ocean passage from the Atlantic to the Pacific. By military and commercial men the hour of realization was announced. In a dramatic manner the naval advantages of the waterway had been emphasized during the Spanish war when the battleship Oregon made her tedious voyage around the Horn while the nation waited anxiously through many weeks for news of her safe arrival. Manufacturers and merchants complaining of high railway rates across the continent, steamship companies engaged in coastwise trade, and Gulf cities hoping for a livelier traffic through the Isthmus let their desires be known in the lobbies at Washington.

Obviously the time had come to beat down the barriers that nature had lifted between the two oceans—barriers that had stood in the way of European peoples since the days of Magellan. But neither Colombia nor Nicaragua, the two nations that owned potential routes, could command the wealth or the engineering skill required for the Herculean undertaking. French capitalists, under De Lesseps, the hero of Suez, had attempted it only to meet disaster. Evidently the task belonged to the United States, whose increasing needs demanded the canal and whose preponderant position in the Caribbean would not permit any other great power to assume the work of constructing it.

Many difficulties, however, stood in the way of beginning the project. First of all was the Clayton-Bulwer treaty drawn up with Great Britain in 1850 at a time when the latter possessed a larger stake in Central America than did the United States. In that agreement the two powers had made a pledge that they would seek no exclusive control over the canal route and bound themselves to coöperate in encouraging any private capitalists who might undertake to build the waterway "for the benefit of mankind." About the terms of the contract, there was no doubt; it contemplated a joint enterprise. If, therefore, the United States was to do the work alone, especially through government agencies, courtesy, if nothing more, required a new arrangement with Great Britain. After much diplomatic skirmishing, this international adjustment was effected by the Hay-Pauncefote treaty of 1901, abrogating the old agreement and thus removing one stumbling block from the path.

Other problems, even more troublesome, yet remained for solution. Should the Nicaragua or Panama route be chosen? Apparently a scientific question, it involved other considerations. To speak concretely, the old French company still held a concession from Colombia authorizing it to build a waterway through Panama; it was bankrupt; a large part of its stock had passed at a nominal figure into the hands of American speculators; and its rights were to expire in 1904 unless some action was taken under them. As the months passed without any decision on the question of the route, the anxiety of the American promoters who held the French securities drove their lobby in Washington to redouble its efforts to force the hand of Congress.

In a little while the momentous verdict was rendered. Notwithstanding the fact that two federal commissions, advised by experts, had recommended the Nicaragua route, Congress in 1902 approved the purchase of the French company's Panama claims at a figure not above $40,000,000. At the same time it provided that a canal strip should be bought from the republic of Colombia, adding that, in case this could not be done, the Nicaragua route was to be chosen. In conformity to these instructions, President Roosevelt immediately negotiated a treaty with Bogota granting the coveted zone to the United States in return for a promise of $10,000,000 down and an annual rental.

At that point proceedings were brought to a sudden halt. The Colombian senate demanded a large increase in the cash payment and, failing to get it, unanimously rejected the treaty, thus blocking President Roosevelt, who was impatient to get at the enterprise, frightening the speculators in the old French company whose year of doom was near at hand, and irritating the people of Panama eager to taste of the prosperity that the canal would naturally bring. It was patent that if a long delay was to be avoided, the forms of legality would have to be breached.

And in this emergency two stormy petrels of revolution, Dr. Manual Guerrero, a Panama conspirator, and Philippe Bunau-Varilla, a French adventurer, deeply involved in the intrigues of the French canal company, realizing that the hour had struck, hurried to the United States to raise money for an upheaval in Panama and to gain assurances of protection from the federal government in case such a revolt could be engineered. Bunau-Varilla saw Roosevelt in the White House and visited Secretary Hay in the State Department. Though he got no official guarantees he at once sent word to the strategists in Panama that American war vessels would stand by them in an uprising against Colombia. After the ships arrived, the revolution broke out, American troops were landed, one Chinaman was accidentally killed, and the independence of Panama was proclaimed on November 3, 1903. Within three days President Roosevelt recognized the new republic as a member of the family of nations. Within a few weeks a treaty was negotiated between the interested parties, in which the independence of Panama was guaranteed and the United States granted the right to construct a canal across the Isthmus in a return for a cash payment and a deferred annual rental.

"If I had followed traditional, conservative methods," said Roosevelt, "I would have submitted a dignified state paper of probably two hundred pages to Congress and the debate on it would have been going on yet; but I took the Canal Zone and let Congress debate; while the debate goes on the Canal does also." In these few words, the transaction was neatly described by the chief actor in the drama.

Having thus cut the legal knot by one swift blow, the administration at Washington pressed rapidly forward toward its goal. The forty million dollars allotted by Congress was paid in full to the French canal concern, rewarding in a heaping measure those far-seeing American capitalists who had invested heavily in the defunct French company and had argued their cause so effectively in the lobbies of Congress. At last, after a tedious, ardent, and expensive campaign, they could breathe freely once more. Extraordinary in every respect, the incident did not pass, of course, without arousing the customary uproar in the newspapers, but the storm raged for only one brief moment; then, borne on the wings of forgetfulness, the affair dropped into the archives with the Star Route episode and the Yazoo land fraud.

One lobby at least was now out of the halls of Congress and other questions could be considered somewhat on their merits. How was the work of building the canal to be supervised? Following a long wrangle between Congress and the President, a curious compromise was reached; Congress insisted on commission management but Roosevelt finally made George W. Goethals master of ceremonies and reduced the other members of the canal board to the status of advisers. "A board is a long, narrow and wooden thing," Goethals is reported to have said. How was the menace of deadly tropical diseases to be overcome? They had mowed down the employees of the French concern like grain before a sickle and it was perilous to touch even the border of their kingdom. So the aid of science was invoked and Dr. William C. Gorgas won a brilliant victory in the name of preventive medicine. What kind of canal was to be built? The debate on that point also covered reams of the Congressional Record but it was decided eventually to overcome the grades by a system of locks instead of cutting a sea-level channel. How was the work to be done: by private contractors or by public enterprise? It was at length agreed that the government should employ the labor, buy the materials, and do the work directly.

In the spring of 1904 the "dirt began to fly," as Roosevelt

put it in his pithy language.   Nine years later, after over-coming formidable obstacles—labor, engineering, and sanitary—the directors of the enterprise united the waters of the Pacific and the Atlantic.   Science, capital, technology, skill, and toil had wrought a miracle greater than Balboa could have conjured up in his imagination when four hundred years before he first saw the South Seas from the isthmian heights.   In 1914 the new waterway was open to the commerce of the world.

Before the work was done the question of the tolls to be charged for the use of the canal was brought up for decision.   Though apparently simple, it involved delicate relations with England and many vested economic interests besides.   In specific phrases, the Hay-Pauncefote treaty, which released the United States from the stipulations of the old coöperative agreement, provided that the canal should be open to the vessels of all nations on equal terms. While on its face explicit, the nature of the pledge, under the drive of acquisitive talent and political passion, became a subject of debate in Congress and throughout the country.

It was said on the one side that the promise was unmistakable and the obligation was binding in law and conscience—exactly the same rates should be charged to all vessels, American and foreign.   On the other hand it was urged that American ships engaged in coastwise trade did not come within the scope of the equality clause, that the original treaty had been wrung from the United States merely because Great Britain had planted her flag in Central America in defiance of the Monroe Doctrine, and finally that the Hay-Pauncefote understanding was not a contract at all but a unilateral declaration on the part of the United States which could be modified at pleasure.   On these lines the debate ran for many months, the railroad and the steamship lobbies vigilant in directing the fight.   Duly impressed by the arguments in favor of discrimination, Congress passed and President Taft signed in 1912 a bill exempting

American coastwise ships from the charges imposed on foreign bottoms.

To this action England objected at once and with increasing emphasis voiced her protest as the time for the opening of the canal drew near. Confronted by a categorical demand from London and compelled by the revolution in Mexico to reckon with English interests there, President Wilson, on whose shoulders the business now fell, was placed in an embarrassing position, especially since the platform of his party contained a clear pledge against the repeal of the tolls law and the usual elements were vociferous against "bowing the knee to England." Nevertheless, in the spring of 1914, the President went before Congress and asked for a reversal of the action taken under his predecessor, basing this request on the ground that the statute transgressed the treaty with England, was indefensible economically, a violation of explicit promise. Then having in mind the Mexican problem, he added in cryptic language: "I ask this of you in support of the foreign policy of the administration. I shall not know how to deal with other matters of even greater delicacy and nearer consequence if you do not grant it to me in ungrudging measure."

Amazed by this appeal, some Democratic congressmen declared that they would not "truckle" to Great Britain, in any circumstances, while others took refuge in rejoicing over the chance to abolish what they called Taft's "tribute to the American shipping trust." When the hot debate over the proposal died down and the whip of executive leadership was applied, Congress yielded, repealing the tolls law of 1912 and substituting a schedule of equal charges for all vessels of all countries.

The only serious problem now left for solution was the renewal of cordial relations with the republic of Colombia from whose side Panama had been so suddenly and so unceremoniously torn by revolution in Roosevelt's administration—a task of reconciliation gladly undertaken by President Wilson. After some skirmishing, his Secretary of

State, William Jennings Bryan, reached an understanding with Bogota in a solemn treaty expressing regret that the Panama incident had marred the friendship of the two countries and binding the United States to pay twenty-five millions to the government of Colombia as a balm for its wounded feelings. When published, this document was greeted with a chorus of wailing and derision among Roosevelt's friends. It was a shameful confession of error and wrong-doing, they said; an affront to American honor; a symbol of folly and weakness; "sheer blackmail," as the Colonel put it himself. Under the influence of such arguments the Senate refused to approve the treaty, and the incident appeared to be closed.

Shortly after things came to this pass, the news leaked into the lobbies of Congress that there were rich oil fields in Colombia, that American capitalists were losing a fine harvest of profits on account of the ill-will cherished in Bogota. Something had to be done, therefore, to rectify the wrong to business enterprise. So indignant friends of Roosevelt swallowed their wrath while a bargain was struck. The express apology was dropped, saving American points of propriety; the pecuniary balm was retained, conciliating Castilian pride; and in 1922, during Harding's administration, the treaty was finally ratified. Senators who had earlier opposed it rose on the floor and freely confessed that for economic reasons they would do a thing which a short time before had been called "a stain on the national honor." And they did it, thus assuring American hegemony in Colombia.

§

In the very midst of the advance on the Caribbean a revolution occurred in Mexico, raising in many parts of the United States a call for a similar forward policy beyond the Rio Grande. That there was a real basis for such a demand could not be denied. For nearly fifty years American capitalists had been steadily increasing their investments in

Mexico, reaching, at the opening of the twentieth century, a total of more than half a billion dollars. During that long period local conditions had been especially favorable to their enterprise. In the intrigues which followed the expulsion of the French and the execution of Maximilian, one of the Mexican military leaders, Porfirio Diaz, managed to raise himself to the presidency and established social order. Except for an interregnum of four years, he occupied the executive palace from 1876 to 1911, enjoying for practical purposes dictatorial powers. From the first to the last Diaz gave American capitalists a cordial welcome, encouraging them to build factories, bestowing upon them generous mineral rights, and helping them to acquire immense sections of arable land.

His generosity, it seems, outran his discretion. At least it was alleged that, in disposing of natural resources, Diaz violated the Mexican constitution of 1857, under which he nominally ruled, and that many of his grants to promoters were tainted by fraud. While such assertions were hard to prove, the history of the public domain in the United States and the respect shown by American prospectors for the law in the premises lent color to the charge that Diaz had been negligent if not worse. Moreover, the ethical notions of such men as E. L. Doheny and the Hon. Albert B. Fall, who operated in both countries, indicated that it must have been difficult for even the most scrupulous officials in Mexico to avoid hazards of various kinds in dealing with capitalists from beyond the Rio Grande. In any case it was largely owing to American enterprise that Diaz was able to collect enough taxes to meet his obligations, pay his soldiers, and keep himself in the saddle.

To the foreigners operating under his beneficence, Diaz was "the strong man" who knew how to rule Mexico in the only possible way, namely by physical violence, but in truth underneath the outward calm were smoldering embers liable on the slightest disturbance to spurt up in jets of fire. Viewed from any angle, the land question which had vexed the country for more than a hundred years offered materials for an explosion. If anything, conditions were worse because greedy landlords, aided by pliant judges, had steadily enlarged their estates at the expense of the small holders— to speak plainly, by stealing village property. To the grudges of the Indian peons were now added the grievances of organized labor. The development of railways, mines, factories, and oil wells called into being a large body of industrial workers, recruited mainly from Indian sources and under the Marxian formula open to revolutionary suggestions. In the same economic process the number of "intellectuals" was also increased, especially among the people of mixed Spanish and Indian stock, and liberal support was found for a movement against the iron dictatorship of the "president."

All the while Diaz sat serenely on his volcano, doing nothing to postpone impending calamity. He adopted no effective measures for lifting the peon out of the age-old state of degradation or for raising the standard of life among the industrial masses. A large part of the revenues from foreign enterprise he spent upon grand buildings, boulevards, and plazas in Mexico City: attempting among other things to outdo Paris and New York by erecting a marble opera house, the finest in the western hemisphere. Such was the social "order" which Diaz and his American advisers thought "solid": at the top a small luxurious plutocracy headed by a hard, unimaginative autocrat; at the bottom a semi-servile mass, agrarian and industrial, sunk in the depths of poverty and poorly prepared for any concerted action save passionate revolt.

Unfortunately for those foreigners who built their castles in Mexico, Diaz was not immortal and as the shadows of his years lengthened, that fact was poignantly realized. Even before he was ready to relax his grip, Mexican politicians began to talk of dividing his estate and at length in 1911, after he had passed beyond the span of four score years, his dictatorship was broken by a revolution that set in motion a swift train of startling events. To the place of Diaz dethroned by this uprising was elevated a mild liberal, Francisco Madero, with many followers of dubious ambitions. Two years later Madero was murdered in cold blood and a military adventurer, General Huerta, came to the helm with a flourish that led business enterprise to hail him as the "strong man," so heartily desired again.

Taking a practical view of the issue, European governments, especially those whose nationals had money invested in Mexico, quickly recognized his authority and made ready for a return to prosperity; but President Wilson dashed their hopes by withholding his support and by lending aid to Mexican liberals in arms against the new régime. In 1914, Huerta was in turn driven out of power and an opposition, headed by Carranza and Villa, rose to the top, only to divide over spoils and policies. In the fighting that ensued Carranza slowly gained the ascendancy and seemed in a fair way to get the battered ship of state into seaworthy condition when he was murdered in 1920. At this stage, another combination, under Obregon and Calles, got the symbols and substance of authority over a people worn out by a decade of revolution, disorder, and economic distress.

The tangled story of these troubled years yields to no simple hypothesis. There was a substantial basis for rebellion in agrarian and industrial discontent, but it was often exploited by bandits and other adventurers. There was a natural enthusiasm for fair play in the opposition to foreign capitalists, but jealousy was often mixed with patriotism in the movement to cast off their supremacy. Cynics said that the fighting was merely a contest between the Spanish and the Mestizos over the right to rob the Indian but that easy version of the revolution ignored idealistic elements among the upper classes. For, although Diaz had done practically nothing to prepare the people for self-government, there was in Mexico a democratic ferment which could not be utterly despised. If any evidence was needed it could be discovered in the constitution of 1917—an amazing document betraying a sincere desire to promote popular education, to safeguard the public domain from private rapacity, to create freeholds by the dispersion of great estates, to limit the power of the Church in politics, and to raise the standard of living for industrial workers. Indeed the instrument exhibited a humane radicalism too bold for the government at Washington.

During the course of events that followed the overthrow of Diaz, the government of the United States, in common with interested capitalists, faced many thorny diplomatic questions. When the first revolt broke out, President Taft promptly warned those concerned that American lives and property must be respected but he made no effort to uphold his warning by a display of martial prowess. When Wilson took up the reins, he informed the Latin-American states, in a startling speech delivered at Mobile, that they were now about to witness one of the miracles of the modern world—emancipation from the dominance of foreign capitalists. So explicit and so frank was this announcement that it puzzled foreign offices everywhere, causing Sir Edward Grey, the English master of the diplomatic art, to wonder whether Wilson was not actually planning something unusually subtle in the interest of American promoters.

In truth it was President Wilson who was confused. He could not allow matters in Mexico to follow their own course; neither could he bring himself to intervene effectively at any time—a policy called "watchful waiting," meaning in practice many things besides quiescent observation. As a matter of fact President Wilson more than once took an active part in Mexican quarrels. By refusing to recognize General Huerta he made certain the downfall of that adventurer. On a point of national honor he landed marines at Vera Cruz in 1914 and waged a petty war without asking Congress to declare it; after several American marines and many more Mexicans had been killed without effecting a decision, he accepted in the premises the mediation of Argentina, Brazil and Chile, the "A.B.C." powers. On some occasions Wilson placed an embargo on arms for export to Mexican belligerents; at other times he lifted it. About the merits of the contestants in Mexico his opinions varied. For many months after the expulsion of de la Huerta, he refused to recognize Carranza; finally he accorded that favor only to inflame Villa, to whom he had once lent some countenance. Then, after Villa in impotent rage had invaded New Mexico on a murderous expedition in 1916, Wilson dispatched American troops to capture the offender, dead or alive, on Mexican soil, a task in which they were engaged until February, 1917, without success and at a cost of more than $130,000,000. After the opening of that year, the President was too deeply occupied with world affairs to devote serious attention to oil, revolution, banditry, and politics in Mexico.

Left practically to her own devices Mexico then drifted from one desultory fight to another until the murder of President Carranza in 1920 again aroused at Washington a lively interest in events across the southern border. Compelled now to act upon the question of recognizing the dead man's successor, Wilson's Secretary of State, Bainbridge Colby, took a firm stand in support of the customary political sacraments declaring that, as the price of lawful friendship, Mexico must show respect for American lives and property, pay damages for American losses in the revolution, and abrogate decrees that were confiscatory in nature. In vain did Mexicans point out that the United States had not paid for the property of foreigners destroyed in the Civil War which raged on its own soil from 1861 to 1865. In vain did they urge that many "objectionable" decrees were aimed at restoring property illegally obtained by foreign concessionaires. Whether or not such arguments were pertinent or ingenuous, they had no effect on Washington. Still it was one thing to inform the Mexican government that it must pay and repair; another thing to collect and enforce.

Somewhat astounded at interminable delays and fruitless

negotiation, observers who had watched American progress in the Caribbean during this period naturally wondered why the Wilson administration did not swiftly apply in Mexico the principles of law and order which it enforced so summarily in Haiti and Santo Domingo. Doubtless, the question could not be lightly answered but some things seemed relevant. The Caribbean countries were tiny republics. Within their boundaries operations could be executed by the Navy under presidential orders alone—without requiring the approval of Congress. Once on the spot American authorities could establish martial law, censor dispatches, and manage affairs with military decorum, awakening no outcry in the United States to embarrass the administration.

In the case of Mexico matters were not so simple. Besides having about fifteen million inhabitants, Mexico was so large in area and so close at hand that a few marines could not seize it quietly, set up a pliant government, and restore the normalcy of Diaz. On the contrary an effective occupation of Mexico meant a war of such proportions that the President could hardly wage it without an express declaration by Congress, at least without giving the legislative branch of the government some information on the subject. Moreover a movement of troops on so extensive a scale would have attracted public notice in the United States, arousing, perhaps, obstructive hostility in many directions. Certainly it would have evoked angry assertions to the effect that the invasion of Mexico, even though nominally undertaken in behalf of general welfare, was in truth designed to benefit the oil and banking fraternities. Indeed, against just that eventuality the American Federation of Labor, for example, was defiantly on guard, maintaining continuous relations with the labor movement below the Rio Grande and taking a positive stand against intervention.

Nevertheless materials for a crusade in favor of forcible mediation also lay at hand. American lives had been destroyed, the flag desecrated, and historic claims of the Catholic Church, especially to property rights, flatly rejected by

Mexican revolutionists. By the summer of 1919 claims against Mexico for half a billion dollars in damages had been filed with the State Department mainly by oil groups, to say nothing of the demands of financiers distressed by the sight of unpaid coupons piling up and Mexican bonds sinking lower and lower. Responding to these forces as the helm to the compass, Republicans in the Senate, having acquired a majority in the election of 1918, created a sub-committee of the committee on foreign relations, with Senator Albert B. Fall as chairman, for the specific purpose of making an investigation into the Mexican situation. In obedience to instructions, the sub-committee held hearings, formulated American demands on Mexico, and advised a military occupation of the country if compliance was not forthcoming.

Immediately after this ominous action came the election of Senator Harding to the presidency and the elevation of Senator Fall to a seat in his Cabinet. Pleased with the new outlook American investors in Mexican oil, powerfully organized, now prepared to realize some of their long-delayed expectations; while bankers and owners of Mexican bonds, also well-knit together in eastern strongholds of finance, presented rights and claims both huge and valid. It was accordingly assumed in various quarters that there was to be a restoration of American property in Mexico by force of arms if necessary; certainly the materials for propaganda were abundant and inflammable. But the Republican administration refused to answer Fall's demand for money or war. If it displayed firmness, it also showed patience; instead of rattling the saber, it sent a mission to Mexico City and accorded recognition to the hard-pressed Obregon-Calles government in exchange for promises respecting American claims. Contrary to the predictions of cynics, the resolution and the martial power displayed in the Caribbean were not employed in this instance; and Seward's dream of incorporating the Mexican republic in the United States once more failed to materialize.

With respect to Latin-American affairs, the procedure of the United States government naturally involved many references to the Monroe Doctrine—all sorts of issues in the name of that early manifesto. Did the Doctrine strictly forbid all attempts of European powers to add new territories in this hemisphere? As interpreted by President Polk long before the Civil War it did not even call for a strong protest against the extension of British dominion in Central America. As interpreted by President Cleveland half a century later the same creed commanded the country to go to war on England if necessary to prevent her from occupying territory to which she had at least some historic claim.

Did the Monroe Doctrine compel the government of the United States to intervene when European powers sent battleships to Latin-American countries to collect debts for their merchants and investors? The records give two answers. When in 1859 Great Britain proposed a naval demonstration at Vera Cruz to collect debts, the Secretary of State said on that occasion that the United States assumed "no right to sit in judgment upon the causes of complaint which Great Britain may prefer against Mexico nor upon the measures which may be adopted to obtain satisfaction." Again in 1897 a similar position was taken when the German imperial government sent war vessels to Haiti, demanded an indemnity of thirty thousand dollars for a subject imprisoned as the result of a curious part in a wrangle involving approximately twenty-five cents, and called for an apology satisfactory to German national honor. In this affair also the State Department at Washington declined to interfere or to assume the duty of protecting its American neighbors from "the responsibilities which attend the exercise of independent sovereignty."

But that was an echo of a dying age. By the dawn of the new century, the investments, claims, and hopes of American capitalists in the Caribbean region had mounted so high that no quarrel could now arise between a European power and Latin-American governments without drawing the attention of Washington forcibly to the existence of positive interests—besides vague responsibilities under the Monroe Doctrine. As the needle the magnet, so public policy followed the course of economic events, and it so happened that the German Emperor felt the first shock of the reverse drive.

When in 1902 Germany, Italy, and England united in a naval demonstration against Venezuela with a view to collecting bills presented by their citizens, President Roosevelt sprang upon the stage with alacrity, proposing arbitration as a means of settlement. According to a story in Thayer's "Life of John Hay," published in 1915, and re-inforced by a letter from Roosevelt in 1916, Germany was the leader in this undertaking, refused at first to arbitrate, and did not yield until Roosevelt threatened to use naval force. This account, made public during the World War, was effective propaganda and was generally accepted as authentic. Later researches, however, especially H. C. Hill's book on Roosevelt and the Caribbean, have practically destroyed the Roosevelt-Thayer thesis. In fact, Great Britain was the leader in the enterprise; Germany had decided to accept arbitration before the receipt of the American suggestion. Roosevelt's own papers do not show that he threatened the Kaiser in particular. Neither do the German documents. But in any case the Monroe Doctrine was a brake on Anglo-German ambitions.

Successful in this episode, Roosevelt gave the screw another turn in applying the Monroe Doctrine to a similar crisis in Santo Domingo. When certain European powers threatened armed intervention there on behalf of their citizens, the United States, besides objecting to the procedure in accordance with the Venezuelan precedent, traveled beyond the confines of that incident. It did not even suggest arbitration; it seized the bankrupt republic, adjusted its assets, and ordered a settlement of its bills—not without appropriate consideration for American investors, some of

IMPERIAL AMERICA

whom had acquired Dominican bonds on favorable terms.
Before long, as we have seen, American hegemony was
spread far and wide in Latin-America.

Although the government of the United States made it
plain, in the course of the forward movement, that it did
not rely for moral sanctions on the Monroe Doctrine alone,
a great deal was said about that historic creed during those
adventurous years. Roosevelt warned all the parties involved that wrongdoing, disorder, the lessening of the ties
of civilized society, and the failure to pay debts would force
the United States to exercise its international police power.
That was specific. Taft, angered by the assertions of critics
to the effect that the Monroe Doctrine was only a shield to
cover the seizure of lands and privileges by the United
States, replied that such base insinuations would not prevent
this country from discharging its duty as occasions arose.
That was the age of "dollar diplomacy."

It was followed by the age of "the new freedom." Soon
after his inauguration Wilson, as we have said, announced
in a speech at Mobile a humanistic twist to the Doctrine.
Turning the tables on his predecessors, he bluntly declared
that capitalists, not content with getting into Latin-American republics, were trying to dominate their domestic affairs; and he informed the world that those states were
about to be emancipated and treated as friends and equals
on terms of honor. That manifesto too was perfectly explicit as far as the language went, but the natives of Haiti,
Santo Domingo, Mexico, and Nicaragua found difficulties
in grasping its practical implications—difficulties not entirely dissipated when Charles E. Hughes, as Secretary of
State, in a carefully prepared address explained that the
Monroe Doctrine did not infringe upon the sovereignty of
the Latin-American states or exhaust the rights and responsibilities of the United States in the Caribbean.

To various professions on the part of the Washington
government, more or less official, a host of Latin-American
statesmen, politicians, editors, and publicists replied that

the Monroe Doctrine was only a Yankee scheme for staking out claims and preëmpting territory until the United States was ready to seize it. From the standpoint of this school, the grand old Doctrine which was so excellent when employed to protect them against European debt-collectors was nothing but a cloak for American imperialism when used to preserve order and advance American business interests. As a matter of fact it could not be truly said that the government of the United States was operating deliberately upon a policy of imperialistic domination; for the simple reason that the Anglo-Saxon mind never did work that way. The British empire was not charted in advance by a Treitschke or a Bernhardi; it slowly broadened out from episode to incident. In a similar fashion the American empire sprang from what seemed, in the view of the Washington government, to be unavoidable concrete circumstances and specific moral duties.

Moreover, all through the official declarations of American policy ran a strong note of good-will to the neighboring countries at the south. If the mailed fist was brought down on the table in Haiti and other places with a bang, the hand of friendship was often extended too. Deeply appreciating economic opportunities to come, James G. Blaine, for example, while Secretary of State, made a special point of cultivating cordial relations with Latin-America, declaring his belief that peace in this hemisphere under the leadership of the United States was the best guarantee of commercial prosperity. Going beyond platonic professions, Blaine, with justifiable pride, called to order in 1889 a Pan-American conference, the first of the kind ever assembled on this continent, to symbolize coöperation as the new watchword. The precedent thus set was followed from time to time by similar meetings, in 1901, 1906, 1910, and 1923, supplemented by scientific, financial, labor, feminist, and educational conventions, making Pan-Americanism a mystic word.

In principal and detail, the results of these conferences

were difficult to appraise. One tangible outcome no doubt was the formation of a permanent coöperative bureau which was given the name of the Pan-American Union and housed in a beautiful building in Washington. The imponderables were less easy to assay. One competent historian, after examining the work of the several conferences, came to the conclusion that the principal fruits were "spiritual" rather than economic and substantial. In the eyes of another historian the Pan-American Union promised to substitute coöperation for imperial dominion and offered an antidote to the Pan-Hispanism which sought to redress the uneven balance of the New World by calling upon the Latin nations of the Old World for help.

With reference to practical matters, however, the government at Washington did not receive much assistance from efforts to form cultural bonds among Latin peoples or from the resolutions offered at Pan-American conferences. After all was done and said, its sources of inspiration lay in other quarters. Its ability to rely upon English support, its material strength, and its naval power permitted it to assume and discharge its obligations without aid from the Latin-American nations themselves. Indeed it could not rely upon those countries to coöperate effectively on any program, economic or political—a fact the State Department learned to its sorrow in 1921 when it gave its blessing to the short lived Central American Union and again in 1924 when it made another attempt to bind those tiny states into a federation.

§

The effect of the imperial advance in the Pacific and in the Caribbean on American concepts of national grandeur are not readily traced in the tangled record of those crowded years. In the beginning was the deed, as the poet wrote of life in general, and long afterward came the idea. So while the American flag was raised first over one place and then over another, the several acts constituted no part of a logical pattern formed beforehand. On the contrary there was much confusion in the pertinent rhetorical discourses of the age. Constant dissent indicated that the country was not unanimous in approving the conquest of alien races and territories as a regular function of the federal government. The fact that a Democratic Congress declared in favor of ultimate independence for the Philippines, though withholding it for the time being, was doubtless of some significance —how much is not yet revealed by fate. The fact that Senator Harding, while campaigning for the presidency, assailed the Wilson administration for using American bayonets to shove constitutions down the throats of West Indian neighbors, conveyed the impression that he regretted such untoward incidents or at least, as his critics alleged, thought his protest in the premises likely to attract votes. In either case Harding's declaration manifested some national tenderness on the point of imperial conduct.

On the other side of the ledger, however, were many entries which implied that the populace was glad to have new colonial possessions, protectorates, spheres of influence, and moral mandates added to the American heritage. The defeat of Bryan on the issue of imperialism in 1900, the cheers that greeted Roosevelt's vigorous use of the "big stick," the rise of American prestige in the Caribbean under Wilson, and the return to stern measures in the Philippines under Harding and Coolidge bore witness to a general contentment with the course of Manifest Destiny.

Nevertheless, no philosophy of empire was worked out to systematic perfection and fused with the Constitution into the current system of ethics. Either on account of logic or Christian training, American thinkers shrank from an overt application of the Darwinian law to the struggle of nations for trade and territory. They were of course not unaware of the ancient creed, for they had heard about the theory and practice of Rome. In their school books they had read Pro Lege Manilia, the panegyric by Cicero, which summed up in a single sentence the old doctrine of might: "Do not hesitate for a moment in prosecuting with all your energies a war to preserve the glory of the Roman name, the safety of our allies, our rich revenue, and the fortunes of innumerable private citizens." They had before them also the voluminous writings of European imperialists who scorned the more tender sentiments of liberals and frankly advocated war and expansion for glory and emoluments. "Was für Plunder!" roared General Blücher when he first viewed London from the dome of St. Paul's.

If such bald tenets made any appeal to American statesmen or editors, few traces of the fact were to be found in their professions of faith. Critics, it is true, accused the directors in high places of believing at the bottom of their hearts in such dogmas but indignant denials were always forthcoming. As a matter of record, Anglo-Saxons seldom looked upon imperial conquests so simply and so harshly as Roman and German philosophers; according to their cosmic view, there were always ethical elements to be taken into account. When Drake and Hawkins overhauled a Spanish galleon, relieved it of its treasure, and sent ship and crew to the bottom of the sea, they felt that they enjoyed, besides the rewards of their labor, the approval of the Virgin Queen and the sanction of the Protestant faith. When Clive had access to the treasure of an Indian state, he refrained from taking all of it and was delighted as well as surprised at his own self-restraint. When Edmund Burke made his celebrated speech indicting Warren Hastings at the bar of the House of Lords, in vain, he assumed that British imperial dominion was founded "not upon the niceties of a narrow jurisprudence but upon the enlarged and solid principles of state morality." A hundred years later, the poet Kipling voiced the same spirit in his lines celebrating the imperial call as a solemn command to take up the White Man's burden, to seek another's profit and work another's gain, a flame communicated to the American branch of the race. German imperialists made a fatal error, therefore, when they questioned the sincerity of the poet's sentiments

—when they failed to see that a high sense of moral responsibility could accompany security for invested capital and the conquest of smaller social groups troubled by disorders and revolutions.

§

That practical considerations and humane sentiments could flourish in the same political and economic climate was abundantly demonstrated by the fact that the movement for universal peace found its strongest support among the two branches of the English-speaking empire, nowhere more enthusiastically than in America. The age that witnessed the transformation of the American republic from an association of equal and self-governing states into a consolidated system ruling distant provinces and subject races also saw the rapid rise and phenomenal growth of a propaganda to outlaw war and establish permanent concord among the nations of the earth.

During this period, local, state, national, and international peace associations sprang up with bewildering rapidity in all parts of the United States, especially in the commercial East. In 1906, the New York Peace Society was founded and the startling announcement made that Andrew Carnegie had given ten million dollars to advance the cause of international good-will which lay so close to his heart. The following year a national peace conference was held in New York, the beginning of annual sessions, and the National Association of Cosmopolitan Clubs was instituted under the leadership of Louis P. Lochner, who was later to sail in Henry Ford's peace ship, carrying the olive branch to war-worn Europe. Emulating the example of Carnegie, Edwin Ginn, a rich publisher of Boston, dedicated a part of his fortune in 1911 to the creation of the World Peace Foundation. In 1912, the American Peace Society, organized in New York nearly a hundred years before, the first of its kind in the world, fixed its headquarters in Washington and embarked upon a new career. Echoes of the agitation reached the educational world where the American School Peace League was formed to push propaganda in the schools under William Lloyd Garrison's international banner: "My country is the world, my countrymen all mankind." Clergymen of every denomination took up the cry, creating the Church Peace League to work in the religious field.

Associated with these societies as members, leaders, and orators were some of the first citizens of America, including Lyman Abbott, Jane Addams, James M. Beck, Nicholas Murray Butler, Andrew Carnegie, Carrie Chapman Catt, Charles W. Eliot, Hamilton Holt, David Starr Jordan, A. Lawrence Lowell, Joseph H. Choate, Thomas Edison, James J. Hill, and William Howard Taft. On the far left wing were extremists who called for the absolute and unconditional abolition of war as a sin and a crime.

Given this membership and this support, the activities of the peace advocates were naturally varied and far-reaching. Conferences were assembled, sermons preached, researches made, propaganda carried on, literature circulated, professors exchanged among the nations, banquets held, and orations delivered. Nothing seemed more respectable than the condemnation of war as barbaric and the advocacy of peace as an enduring ideal. In the common assault on militarism men and women of widely divergent views could unite.

Perfect harmony, of course, was not attained, at first, even in the peace movement. Pro-British elements had doubts about the merits of the German-American concord; German-Americans saw portents in the Anglo-American entente; and the Irish took their historic attitude toward the latter affiliation.

In fact, in the run of the debates by these parties, the idea got about that the German Empire was no friend of international peace, and special efforts were therefore made to reassure the public on that score. Examining the charge from one angle Richard Bartholdt declared his "honest opinion that William II is for permanent peace." After a similar inquiry Edwin D. Mead expressed the conviction that "German thought is now swinging toward a new idealism of the Kant type." By way of supplement, a distinguished German clergyman, sent over to attend an important conference in 1911, informed his American auditors that he had talked with the Kaiser before setting out and that his Majesty "took a good deal of interest in the movement for international peace." On various occasions, Nicholas Murray Butler, who was personally acquainted with William II, added his guarantees; and under his inspiration, in 1913, the twenty-fifth anniversary of the Kaiser's coronation, the New York Peace Society struck a beautiful medal which it sent with an appropriate address to the master at Potsdam. As if to confirm this manifestation of faith, Andrew Carnegie, also on friendly terms with the All-highest War Lord, announced to doubting Thomases that his imperial friend was "a peace lord" and that "whatever impressions exist to the contrary are based on ignorance of the Emperor's true nature." So eventually great and good citizens all over the land came to believe that humanity was finally nearing the goal of universal peace—in spite of the Spanish-American war of 1898, the Filipino War of 1899, the Boer War of 1899, the Russo-Japanese War of 1904, the Turco-Italian War of 1911, the Balkan War of 1912, and minor disturbances on the borders of expanding empires.

In truth there were a number of ostensible signs which seemed to indicate that governments were inclined to shrink somewhat from the dangerous arbitrament of arms and to favor amicable methods of settling their disputes. By enthusiasts, at least, two conferences held at the Hague, in 1899 and 1907, on the call of the Russian Tsar, were hailed as portents of the new order; although behind the scenes the diplomats of England, France, and Germany were laughing up their sleeves. At the first of these assemblies, three agreements of mild promise were reached. One of the covenants provided that at any time during an international dispute, or even during war, a neutral power might, without offense, tender its good offices to contestants with a view to effecting a peaceful solution or bringing hostilities to an end. In another compact, it was stipulated that any party to a controversy might, without prejudice, call for an impartial commission of inquiry to make an investigation into the facts of the case. These two declarations were crowned with an arrangement for an international court at The Hague to which disputants might, by agreement, submit issues that could not be adjusted by diplomatic methods.

Suggestions for disarmament, however, came to nothing and the proposal for banning poison gas was rejected by the American delegates. Indeed the fatal animus of the powers was clearly manifest at the second conference when practically the only points on which concord could be reached were new rules for "civilized warfare," legal rules which were soon to be treated by them all as mere scraps of paper, incapable of restraining armed forces facing each other.

If Christendom did not agree on a program of peace, the government of the United States did in good faith testify on occasion to its general belief in pacific principles. It is true that President McKinley refused to arbitrate the Maine incident, rejected offers of mediation in the contro- versy with Spain, and declined to bring pressure on Eng- land with a view to drawing the Boer war to an end; but he declared publicly that "peace is preferable to war in almost every contingency." In 1903 a long-standing dispute with Canada over the Alaskan boundary was settled by a joint tribunal in London—in favor of the American claim. On the receipt of pertinent information, President Roosevelt in 1905 tendered his good offices to Russia and Japan, both near to exhaustion, and helped them bring their war to a conclusion at Portsmouth. Three years later, England and the United States agreed to submit to arbitration all ques- tions not involving "vital interests" or "national honor," and in 1910 the two countries closed an old quarrel over fishing rights by submitting it to judicial determination at The Hague.

Concrete projects for peace were now in the air. As if to illustrate the change of heart, Secretary Knox signed treaties with France and Great Britain in 1911 undertaking to submit all disputes to international arbitration, but his plans were defeated in the Senate by a powerful and determined opposition. The Irish and German elements bitterly attacked the proposal for obvious reasons and the representatives of several states which had repudiated their bonds opposed it because they feared that European creditors would attempt to collect through a court of inquiry. Undaunted by the fate of the Knox treaties, Secretary Bryan took up the issue when he entered the Cabinet under the Wilson administration. Displaying his characteristic zeal, he effected agreements with about half the independent powers of the earth, providing that all disputes of whatever nature should be submitted to an international commission for inquiry and that in no case should war be declared before the tribunal had made a formal report. With surprising alacrity the Senate approved these conventions, sending a note of triumph through the peace movement in America.

At this very moment the outbreak of the World War rudely dissolved the spell cast by the treaties and placed the advocate of peace in an awkward position. Overnight, these ardent apostles, once applauded as the wise friends of humanity, became the objects of menacing hostility, denounced as traitors by the Anglophiles and treated as suspects by the man in the street. Increasingly tragic became their dilemma as the cry for war intensified, reaching a climax when President Wilson called upon Congress to take up arms against Germany. By that act the die was cast, compelling all, save scoffers, to make a choice. On the left, extremists, especially those who entertained doubts about the finality of capitalist economy, still clung to peace and many of them were sent to prison as transgressors under the espionage and sedition acts. On the right, prudent plead-ers of the cause cleared themselves of taint by ample displays of militancy, while the leading peace societies, as a matter of course, rallied to the support of the government, taking consolation, perhaps, in the thought that the war was waged "to end war." In this spirit, the Carnegie Peace Endowment announced that it could serve the ideal of its founder best by lending all its strength to the prosecution of the armed conflict to a triumphant conclusion. Occupying the middle ground, groups of liberals, such as the Union against Militarism, which had unsuccessfully opposed intervention in the European war, turned to the advocacy of "a democratic peace" and assisted in the organization of the Civil Liberties Union, a society for the maintenance of individual rights against governmental action.

When the end came, the path of the peace advocate was still strewn with thorns, particularly after the country rejected the League of Nations and took its stand in favor of an armed isolation. A strenuous apostle of peace thereupon became *ipso facto* something of a traitor in the eyes of professional patriots, the War Department, the Navy Department, and the various leagues for the support of the military establishment. Even an agency as powerful as the Carnegie Peace Endowment, gathering up the fragments after the wreck, felt impelled to move with caution. It devoted a huge sum to preparing a monumental history of certain aspects of the World War, sent generous gifts to help repair the ruin wrought by the German armies in France and Belgium, made an expression of good-will for Great Britain by contributing fifty thousand dollars to the restoration of Westminster Abbey, that great Pantheon of the Anglo-Saxon dead. Thus, after the age of empire had worn on a few decades, it became necessary to examine pacific doctrines and test categorical ethics with reference to new duties and new potentialities.

CHAPTER XXVII

Towards Social Democracy

MATHEMATICAL politicians who kept their minds on the course of empire, on tons of coal, miles of railway, and bales of cotton, at the opening of the twentieth century, had good reason for supposing that the gilded age of the full dinner pail and the unrestrained exploitation of the American estate would never pass. But unknown to them other factors than commodity output were at work in the United States. Farmers, feeling the pinch of the agricultural revolution, were becoming restive under the new application of the Hamilton-Webster creed. The growing army of industrial workers was attaining a closer solidarity. In the sphere of social reasoning, science was challenging the intellectual patterns handed down from the epoch of the stagecoach.

In a word, cumulative forces, complex and interacting, were beating upon the accepted order of things. Almost too young to be called accepted that order itself was born of an industrial transformation which touched every phase of life and labor; was indeed still in constant change under the drive of invention, technology, and capitalist ambition. And this relentless drift in national life was strengthened by the activities of two political personalities, the most dynamic raised to high authority since the age of Andrew Jackson—Theodore Roosevelt and Woodrow Wilson—statesmen who were, in the course of events, by accident rather than the intent of party managers, placed on a throne of power that Cæsar might have coveted.

§

The logical starting point for a survey of these unforeseen tendencies in American democracy is a summary view of the system of acquisition and enjoyment at high noon. As already indicated, the general cast of thought and scheme of political practice in the United States corresponded for a long time to the requirements of the substantial owners of industrial property who ruled the country with the aid of the more fortunate farmers. The philosophy which they affected was Doric in its simplicity: the state and society were nothing; the individual was everything. A political party was a private association of gentlemen and others who had leisure for public affairs; its functional purpose was to get possession of the government in the name of patriotism and public welfare as a matter of course and to distribute the spoils of office among the commanders, the army, and its camp followers. How the party managed its caucuses, conventions, and committees was none of the general public's business; if leaders sometimes bought voters and marched them to the polls, they were only engaged in doing unto others what they expected others to do to them. Propriety merely warned them against atrocities.

Thus organized and directed in those good old days of liberty, the political party was in effect a standing army; if encamped in possession of the government, its officers and men lived on the fat of the land; if driven from the field in defeat, it closed its ranks, reduced the rations, and prepared with the passion of desperation to recover the lost paradise. When in control of a government, state, local, or national, a party could make laws and carry on administration in caucuses and cabals behind closed doors without much risk of an intrusion by the citizens—until the next election when stale issues were likely to be overwhelmed in the flood of time and events. If signs of a popular revolt did appear on the horizon, officers of opposing forces could unite with marked facility in the face of a common danger and control the polling. If necessary, elections could be held in saloons, accompanied by drunken orgies and physical violence or resort could be had to ballot box stuffing —a practice so common as to excite humor rather than indignation.

As was appropriate to the age, the grand political world was a man's world. When a few bizarre women ventured to ask for the ballot as a gift from a benevolent patriarchate, they were answered by a writer in Godey's Lady's Book in this fashion: "How many are there possessing the modesty, the delicacy, the withdrawing spirit, the gentleness of the sex, who would not rather delegate to their husbands, their fathers, their brothers, those arduous and disagreeable duties? How many, who in addition to the duties of love, of friendship, of education, of charity, all of which society imposes, would willingly assume the burden of politics? I believe, I hope, there are very few." The belief and the hope seemed well founded.

In managing his property, the individual in the gilded age was about as immune from interference on the part of the state as was the caucus. Government intervention was an evil, a violation of the inexorable laws of nature, save when practiced to preserve order, grant subsidies to railway promoters, or afford protection and bounties to manufacturers. With these subtle exceptions, the solemn duty of the state was to keep its hands off private affairs. The immense national capital in arable land, forests, water power, and minerals was to be given away or sold for a pittance without any limitations or reservations as to use or potential monopoly. Getting a generous portion of the national spoils for nothing, the farmers saw no reason why railway corporations, lumber companies, and mining concerns should be seriously handicapped in taking their particular allotments. Though the law for seizure and exploitation was liberal in all conscience, in actual practice those who entered and occupied the public domain were none too fine in their observance of the letter and spirit—so careless in fact as to move President Roosevelt to exclaim, after reading the report of his Public Lands Commission, that the taint of fraud was everywhere in the process of alienation. While the national domain was thus being carved up and parceled out, railway companies were ruling their respective dominions with a high hand; they made mergers and combinations without restraint, granted rebates to favorite shippers, discriminated against towns and ports for a consideration, issued unlimited quantities of stocks and bonds to the gullible public in the New World and in the Old, went into bankruptcy with cheerful insouciance, and made rates based on the current principle of "what the traffic will bear."

Besides nourishing by benevolence the enterprises of capitalists, the national government was tender in imposing burdens of taxation on great possessions. In fact, it derived practically all its revenues from indirect duties on imported goods, whisky, tobacco, beer, and wine—judiciously distributed among the consuming masses. Even state and local governments, although operating on the theory that all property should be taxed alike, found it difficult to discover and list illusive stocks and bonds hidden in boxes so strong that they could not be penetrated by the eye of the shrewdest tax assessor; state commission after state commission declared that the general property tax was a farce and that the evasion of taxes on intangible securities was almost universal. In a word, nowhere did heavy income and inheritance taxes vex the lives of those closely engaged in the great game of acquisition.

Nor were they harassed by responsibilities for workers

killed or injured in their industries. A victim who lost an arm in a factory, the family of a man crushed to death in a rolling mill or suffocated in a mine had to assume the risks of the occupation; damages could be secured only when the employer was in some special sense guilty of negligence and even then as a rule only after a long, tortuous, and expensive lawsuit. Under an ancient quirk of legality, therefore, the sacred rights of property owners could not be invaded with the object of compelling them to carry the burden of their own social wreckage. According to the same canons of excellence, industrial workers, unlike the slaves of the Old South, were no charge on business when unemployed; that risk they assumed also under the beneficent laws of political economy.

The jurisprudence of the acquisitive instinct, as well as justice in general, was administered by the judicial branch of the government with circumspection. When at length it was fully demonstrated that the state legislatures were bent on establishing by law the rates of railways and other utility corporations, the courts felt compelled by the irrefragable logic of the federal Constitution, to determine in cases properly presented whether such rates were reasonable or not, that is, yielded a fair return to the owners, as guaranteed by the due process clause of the Fourteenth Amendment. When the New York legislature in a reforming mood fixed the hours of labor in bake shops at ten per day or sixty per week, the Supreme Court at Washington found the act a clear violation of "the liberty of the individual protected by the Fourteenth Amendment." When another session of the same legislature sought to make it easier for a workman to recover damages for an injury sustained in industry, the high court of the commonwealth struck down the law in the name of constitutional freedom.

Such in general was the great complex of use and wont in politics and economics during the early stages of triumphant business enterprise. In this limited space, naturally, the strokes and lines are bolder and sharper than they would be on a larger canvas admitting of shades, distinctions, and exceptions; but the essential outline of the picture, limned by the testimony of private letters and public papers, is sound and authentic. If the year of its finest perfection must be fixed, then 1880 may be chosen, exactly half way between the election of Lincoln, which sounded the doom of the planting dominion, and the end of the wonderful century. The magnificent system of acquisition and enjoyment then stood full blown without a serious fault to mar the beauty of its symmetry. Those who acquired and enjoyed pronounced it good and appeared to assume that it would last forever in its splendid form. Yet at that very moment it had already become the object of lively assaults from many directions; before the lapse of a generation it was so battered and undermined at the base that the men of the age which had constructed it imagined, perhaps with undue fright, that the solid earth was crumbling beneath their feet.

§

In tracing the changes wrought by this conflict—changes that would have been called revolutionary if they had been effected all at once by some such convention as the French National Assembly of 1789—the processes of American democracy are to be observed working through our intricate federal system of government. Each separate battle in the general campaign was carried on by some active group of private citizens driving upon some particular angle, redoubt, turret, or gateway of the mighty structure thrown up by the drift of three hundred years. In a thousand obscure corners, as well as in great open assemblies, the forays and agitations were organized: in city councils, state legislatures, women's clubs, trade unions, grange conferences, reform associations, party caucuses and conventions, the Congress of the United States, the chambers and public rooms of judicial courts, executive mansions, and editorial sanctums.

Trading, bartering, and huckstering as well as fighting accompanied the operations. No statesman conceived the minor adjustments in terms of a larger whole or foresaw the trend of destiny; no political party could claim special credit for results or escape responsibility for the outcome. Certainly no political messiah pointed the way or inspired the participants in the fray from a height seen by all. If any responsible person had mirrored to the American mind of 1880 the American system of 1927, he would have been laughed out of court. Such havoc does fate play with the little schemes of men!

Hegel's theory of history was being illustrated once more: the system of acquisition and enjoyment was calling into being its own antithesis—forces that challenged its authority and conditions that required a reconsideration of its laws and ethics. In the fullness of time, factors which had long worked in obscurity thrust themselves upward in bursts of power which could not be ignored by the most hardened man of affairs. Physical realities, always vivid enough to those who worked in shop, factory, and mine, swam at last into the ken of those whose business it was to understand the intricacies of modern society and to proclaim the right and wrong of things. Ideas born in the evolving clash of mind and matter altered the range of America's "intellectual climate," made obsolete phrases that had once contained substance and driving energy, and in due time shook themselves down into divergent patterns of thought. "Is there nothing eternal in the world?" cried a distinguished educator of the age. "Nothing except change," replied one of his colleagues.

Among the many forces that swept political activities into novel channels, none was more potent than the increasing organization of industrial workers. After the skirmishes of the gilded age, the American Federation of Labor began to make amazing strides in membership and financial power. In 1900 it could claim only 548,000 wage workers; fourteen years later the number had passed the two million mark. Outside its affiliation, but in fraternal sympathy with its aims, were the Railway Brotherhoods and in an independent position several minor associations whose combined strength added half a million more to the total enrolled under trade union emblems. In the second decade of the twentieth century, the Federation, which had started its career in a dingy back room in New York City, dedicated an imposing seven story office building in Washington, in the presence and with the benediction of the President of the United States. On the cornerstone were carved these words: "This edifice erected for service in the cause of Labor, Justice, Freedom, and Humanity." Within a hundred years from the payment of Hamilton's last federal bond, a single great labor society, the Brotherhood of Locomotive Engineers, was in control of enterprises and banks with resources greater in extent than the total national debt which the redoubtable secretary of the treasury had funded in 1790. All these things were ponderables coming within the scope of William James' "stubborn and irreducible facts."

Equally obdurate were the changing verities in the life of American women, recorded in returns of the industrial census. By 1870, the proportion of women engaged in gainful pursuits had reached about fifteen per cent of the total; when the end of the century came, it had passed twenty per cent. At the latter date, nearly one-third of all the females over ten years of age then living in William Penn's Quaker city of Philadelphia were working for wages; while in many new industrial towns, such as Fall River, Massachusetts, more than one-third of the females were in the mills, stores, and offices. Moreover no fewer than half a million married women were wage earners in 1890 and the proportion was steadily increasing; by 1910 it was nearly one-fourth the total number of women gainfully employed throughout the country.

Evidently the system of manufacturing inaugurated by Hamilton was permanent and in 1892 the American Federation of Labor finally took official notice of the fact. In that year its president, Samuel Gompers, commissioned

Mary E. Kenney to head a crusade for the mobilization of industrial women. Of course, women had formed many transitory societies in the early days of the factory system; they had been admitted to some of the regular trade unions, local, national, and international, including the Knights of Labor, that had risen during the nineteenth century; and they had taken part in numerous battles over hours and wages. But up to this point their continuous rôle in industry had not been appreciated by most of the leaders highest in the American Federation of Labor.

The designation of an official organizer among women, marking a new phase in the American labor movement, was followed soon by the formation of the Federal Labor Union at Chicago, a similar society at Boston, and finally, during the annual convention of the American Federation of Labor in 1903, by the National Women's Trade Union League charged with the function of bringing women into the main stream of associated effort. Pledged to the organization of all workers, the League demanded equal pay for equal work, an eight hour day, the maintenance of the American standard of living, and full equality for women in the rights of citizenship. Slowly but steadily the militant crusade among women began to count in numbers and in the spread of ideas. Seven years after the formation of the League less than six per cent of the women employed in manufacturing industries were enrolled in unions as against eleven per cent of the men; at the end of the next decade the proportions were eighteen and twenty-three respectively.

Striking as were these figures, they did not tell the whole story; for the activities in the industrial field thus reported by accountants agitated a wide fringe of the middle class, carrying the strife and problems of the labor movement into circles of leisure, and aiding in the dissolution of the comfortable social thesis acquired from the gilded age. Thus energetic and persistent wage-earning women, educated women pressing into the competitive world, and rich women now enjoying the possession of property in their own right even though married, refashioned many modes of thought handed down from the era of Millard Fillmore and James Buchanan. The kaleidoscope was swiftly turning and amazing were its new revelations.

This drift in human relations and the stream of ideas that flashed up as it swept forward, changing the social order and its intellectual imagery, naturally provoked doubts with respect to current political practices. The costly conflicts of capital and labor, the diligence of Marxians, the milder but insistent discussions of Christian Socialists, the percolations of Bellamy's utopian nationalism, and the haunting queries of academic economists unsettled the opinions of thousands who had once found peace and security in the party of Thomas Jefferson or that of Abraham Lincoln. At length in 1900 the time seemed ripe for another crystallization and a new political organization, the Social Democratic Party, was formed. It nominated for the presidency Eugene V. Debs, still smarting under the judicial lashing received during the Pullman strike, and polled ninety-six thousand votes for a general revolution.

Encouraged by the result, meager as it was, Debs and his supporters decided to put their party on a permanent basis. Adopting the name Socialist in 1901, they concentrated on the formation of local branches in the industrial regions, undertaking in the operation an active popular propaganda. In the next election, over four hundred thousand ballots were cast for Socialism; even in 1908 when Bryan drew off the lukewarm regiments, a slight gain was made; and four years later, in spite of Wilson's new freedom and Roosevelt's progressive offerings, the Socialist party more than doubled its vote. By that time it could boast that its candidates had captured several hundred offices in various sections of the country, including a seat in Congress, and were actually making inroads upon established political ceremonies.

Although there was no little difference of opinion among the Socialists, as indeed among Republicans and Democrats, concerning the exact character of their principles and tactics, their professions conformed with fair precision to certain general concepts, more closely adapted to the actual trend of business and science than the utopianism of the middle period had been. Modern industry, they all held, necessarily creates a division of society into contending elements—the capitalist class which controls the machinery of production and the working class composed of landless, homeless, toolless people dependent upon the sale of labor for their livelihood. There is, continued the thesis, an inherent antagonism between these two classes, for each seeks to secure all it can from the annual output of wealth, an antagonism manifest in organizations of capital and labor, in industrial disputes, and in open social warfare; out of this contest the former gain security and luxury and the latter misery and poverty, while the frightful wastes of competition levy a toll on both parties to the struggle. In the realm of politics and education, the Socialists maintained, capitalism is dominant. "The capitalist class," ran their platform in 1912, "though few in number, absolutely controls the government—legislative, executive, and judicial. This class owns the machinery for gathering and disseminating news through its organized press. It subsidizes the seats of learning—the colleges and the schools—even religious and moral agencies." Then came the synthesis: the working class is becoming conscious of its position and its potential strength; it is being consolidated by coöperation, economic and political; and in the course of time it will conquer the government and seize the machinery of production and distribution.

To the middle classes this creed seemed menacing enough but to those who marched in the left wing of the Socialist movement it was tepid doctrine. Demanding something hotter, the intransigents formed in 1904 a still more revolutionary society known as the Industrial Workers of the World and announced that they would carry the struggle from the realm of theory to that of action. Inspired largely by William D. Haywood, a western miner who was destined to have a checkered career that carried him all the way to Moscow to coöperate with the Soviet Republic after the Russian revolution, the new group of radicals proposed, after the fashion of the Knights of Labor, to build one big union of all industrial workers. With that instrument they planned to conquer the capitalist system in a series of mass strikes, accompanied by sabotage. With a burst of enthusiasm, Jack London described "the day" in his proletarian novel, Revolution.

In harmony with the law of social trepidation, these preachers of defiance created more commotion than the numerical strength of their adherents warranted, driving statesmen and politicians, ever sensitive to seismic disturbances, to display their customary apprehensions. "The labor men are very ugly and no one can tell how far such discontent will spread," wrote President Roosevelt to Senator Lodge in 1906. "There has been during the last six or eight years a great growth of socialistic and radical spirit among workingmen and the leaders are obliged to play to this or lose their leadership. Then the idiotic folly of the high financiers and of their organs such as the Sun helps to aggravate the unrest."

Replying, the Senator reported back from Massachusetts a few months later that, according to information from a trade union leader, "there was nothing to fear from the labor unions . . . but there was great danger in his opinion from the socialistic movement led by men of some education who made incendiary appeals to all laboring men. I think he is right." Startled by their findings in this relation, both the President and the Senator expressed a profound conviction that, unless strong measures were taken to curb the plutocracy and the proletariat, property in general might suffer grievous injury at the hands of the socialists and that, even in the best of circumstances, the clash of the contending forces might come to a dangerous crisis in a great political campaign. So after all it appears that the era of the full dinner pail was not an age of static security either in economics or politics.

§

One of the first dents in accepted political use and wont was made by the civil-service reformers, inspired by middle-class notions, rather than labor, agrarian, or revolutionary ideas, to attack the spoils system, the general distribution of public offices to victorious party workers. Unwittingly, perhaps, they assailed a conservative institution—one that damped the ardor of agrarian and proletarian discontent by a judicious partition of loaves and fishes and at the same time prevented the erection of a permanent government bureaucracy coveting powers and policies not entirely pleasing to industrial captains. But without inquiring too narrowly into the distant implications of their work, they condemned the practices of the spoilsmen wholesale and advocated a program of reconstruction in administration, proposing that the major portion of the public offices should be open only to persons of demonstrated fitness selected by examinations, that partisan influences should be eliminated in such cases, and that tenure should be during good behavior, not at the behest of politicians.

The group of reformers who espoused this cause was never very large. When one of their lecturers widely advertised a discourse on the subject in Chicago in 1880, he was greeted by seven or eight more or less curious auditors. But their influence could not be measured solely by numbers. Some of their strategists were writers and speakers of singular force; such for instance as E. L. Godkin, whose vitriolic editorials in the Nation made the politicians wince every week; George William Curtis, editor of Harper's Weekly, a skilled penman and magnetic orator; and Carl Schurz, a veteran of the Civil War and energetic leader in public affairs. Moreover, they kept up their campaign in season and out, in spite of the laughter of men wise in the partisan game.

For a long time of course, though they won a hearing from a select audience of citizens, they were largely ignored by the strongest political directors. In fact their foes marveled at the temerity of their agitation and wondered just "what these fellows want." Speculating on their motives, Senator Roscoe Conkling of New York, past master of the art of manipulation as then practiced, answered: "Some of them are man-milliners, the dilettanti and carpet knights of politics, men whose efforts have been expended in denouncing and ridiculing and accusing honest men. . . . They are wolves in sheep's clothing. Their real object is office and plunder. When Dr. Johnson defined patriotism as the last refuge of a scoundrel, he was unconscious of the then undeveloped capabilities of the word 'reform' "—an explosion that passed for convincing argument among the political giants of the established order.

Nevertheless the agitation over the spoils system went on, making ripples here and there on the smooth surface of orthodox custom without alarming the politicians. Such was the situation in 1881 when President James A. Garfield was done to death by a disappointed and demented office-seeker. The shot then fired rang throughout the land, echoes of the cruel deed driving into the dim and addled brain of the most hardened henchman the notion that there was something disgraceful in reducing the Chief Executive of the United States to the level of a petty job broker. Even men who had laughed with Flanagan of Texas when, with reference to dividing the spoils, he cried out at a Republican convention, "What are we here for?" could not smile at that.

Overnight what had been "snivel" service reform became popular. Within a year a committee of the United States Senate brought in a report condemning the spoils system in stinging terms. It pictured the President giving audiences to beggars and flinging offices to "a hungry, clamorous, crowding, and jostling multitude." It portrayed the poor congressman confronted by the spoils system at his door in the morning and haunted by it in his chamber at night; the specter "goes before him, it follows after him, and it meets him on the way."

Driven by public opinion and the necessity for self-defense, Congress enacted in 1883 a civil service law that promised a large measure of reform. In express terms the act authorized the President to appoint a supervising commission of three, not more than two from the same political party, and empowered him to extend the merit system to specified classes of federal offices. It also stipulated that admission to those branches of the public service was to be granted only to persons who passed appropriate examinations and that their tenure was to last during good behavior. Although at first only a few thousand offices were brought within the scope of the law, the number was afterward gradually increased—sometimes in the interest of efficient government and occasionally in the interest of partisans bent on making secure jobs already obtained by political influence. Within forty years the proportion of federal employees under the merit system had risen to three-fifths of the total, namely, about three hundred thousand out of approximately half a million.

The example set by the federal government was slowly followed by the states; at the opening of the new century ten commonwealths had civil service commissions. In the municipal sphere, where administration had a peculiarly vital relation to public welfare, the advance on the spoilsmen was swifter and wider in its reach; in more than three hundred cities, with varying results, the merit system of recruiting public service had been adopted by 1927.

Thus by legislation and the growth of public functions a kind of independent *imperium in imperio* was set up, composed of permanent civil servants primarily engaged in technical work. Inspired by common purposes, they began to draw together in organizations and in trade unions; to develop professional standards and take a hand in politics themselves, introducing a new factor into the political system—a large bureaucracy offering advantages in expert service on the one side and perils to personal liberty and free experimentation on the other. As a collateral incident, party managers, now finding their supplies in the form of levies on office-holders reduced, were compelled to rely more and more on the long purses of rich men and business corporations.

§

Having made this successful raid on the commissariat of the partisan armies, the "men-milliners and carpet knights of reform" demanded a change in some of the most authentic and approved campaign methods. According to election customs handed down from the early days of the republic, every voter came under the scrutiny of party captains at the polling place. Even after the use of printed lists superseded open or viva voce voting everywhere, it was a common practice for political organizations and candidates to furnish their own ballots, each machine or group choosing a distinctive color for its papers—a system from which two major evils flowed. The cost of the necessary printing was so high that, as a general thing, only party treasuries could bear the burden; hence independent candidates and factions incurred financial handicaps at the start. The custom also made it possible for party captains who distributed election papers to watch the voter from the moment he received his ballot outside the polling place until he deposited it in the box, enabling the directors of each fray to make sure that "the goods had been delivered."

In this fashion bribery was encouraged because the briber could not lose in the transaction; intimidation was fostered because secrecy was impossible. To make doubly sure, a practice known as "straight arm voting" was invented and applied: venal voters were lined up near the election room, into their extended hands brightly colored ballots were placed, and then they were marched to the polls with their arms raised like semaphores.

Such, broadly speaking, was the second cherished institution of the inheritance attacked by the "little contemptibles" who proposed as a substitute that all ballots be furnished by public authorities at public expense and that arrangements be made for secret voting—a reform drawn from Australia. Though immediately branded by the custodians of tradition as a foreign contraption, un-American in principle, the Australian ballot was adopted with impunity by Massachusetts in 1888 and by every state in the Union except two, within twenty years. If, contrary to fond hopes, it wrought no sudden miracle in elections, it did wrest a great weapon of coercion from the hands of a hundred thousand petty captains who helped to form the nation's "will" at the ballot box.

Shifting its emphasis, discontent with the management of elections now ran deeper until it touched the very engines of party organization. According to long custom, the chief agency used by political leaders in selecting candidates and training their hosts for the capture of the government was the convention, local, state, and national, "fresh from the people," as Jackson was wont to say. Delegates to such conferences were chosen by party members at elections known as "primaries" or by subordinate assemblies made up of representatives so chosen in smaller units. In general not more than ten or fifteen per cent of the party voters attended the primaries or paid any attention to the selection of delegates; when therefore the army of party captains, office-holders, and office-seekers was counted out, the number of disinterested citizens active in political affairs was manifestly small. What was the use for untrained and unorganized individuals to oppose the swarm of professional manipulators and their friends?

So the convention, even when ornamented by dignitaries, was usually swayed by spoilsmen who received petty offices themselves, if no payments in cash, and yielded the choicer fruits to gentlemen of more distinction, greater wealth or larger imagination. Whenever a party congress assembled, as a rule a few old and experienced managers would meet in a little room in a local hotel, choose the candidates, and write the platform while the rank and file of party members loafed around awaiting orders. In the circumstances, the voice of delegates fresh from the people was a still small voice; for men of independent minds, known to have ideas nowhere authorized by the canons of party orthodoxy, could be quickly silenced as the captains of politics drove the "steam-roller" over them when the votes were taken.

After a while, however, a number of independents sorely bruised by this ruthless procedure began to rebel. Thereupon a demand arose for the abolition of the party convention. In its place was proposed the choice of all party candidates for public offices at formal elections within the party surrounded by legal safeguards—elections known as "direct" primaries in contradistinction to ordinary primaries at which only delegates were chosen. The idea was not an innovation in local politics for under party rules county officers, especially in the Middle West, had often been nominated by this method. But imposing leaders, whose ceremonials were now rudely invaded by reformers, made a loud outcry. With tearful eloquence, they spoke of "the great representative principle" embodied in the party assembly and of the ancient virtues given to the institution by conscript fathers, as if the nominating convention was hoary with age and respectability instead of being a contrivance hurriedly created in Jackson's time by radical Democrats for the purpose of ousting the opposition from comfortable posts in the American system. In any event, the reformers gave no heed to the lament. "Abolish the caucus and the convention; go back to the first principles of democracy; go back to the people!" exclaimed Robert M. La Follette in an address to the students of Chicago University on Washington's birthday in 1897.

Under La Follette's leadership, Wisconsin six years later

enacted the first state-wide direct primary law with provisions for searching scrutiny over the election process. From this experiment, the idea swept rapidly through the West and then gradually awakened reverberations in the staid old East. In New York Governor Hughes, thwarted in a fight with a bi-partisan combination of political leaders, sought an escape in 1907, urging the adoption of the direct primary; across the river, in New Jersey, Governor Wilson, four years afterward, pressed upon the legislature the same reform.

When the first decade of the twentieth century was safely turned, two-thirds of the states were nominating candidates for most of their offices by direct primaries; in a few more years all save a handful of recalcitrant commonwealths were operating on the new basis. It is true that in the inevitable reaction two or three states, including New York, later restored the convention as an instrument for making nominations for state offices, but the recoil was not severe; perhaps because the politicians, by taking their bearings with new instruments, found navigation under the reformers' rules not as difficult as they had anticipated. Still the highest beneficiaries in acquisition and enjoyment never ceased to condemn the direct primary, because it paved the way for more lay interference with the professional interests, bruited abroad news of subtractions and divisions once made quietly in caucus chambers, compelled their candidates to spend more money openly in campaigns, and forced into the upper works of politics some of the beliefs and passions hitherto confined largely to the lower ranges.

§

Reinforcing this attack on the citadels of party manipulation, the left-wing reformers, particularly those of a farmer-labor persuasion, finally decided to strike at the very structure of the government under which the American system of acquisition and enjoyment had so long flourished. To some extent, they were moved to take this course by authentic reports on the transaction of public business at state capitals.

For a hundred years the conduct of legislatures had been notorious; even P. T. Barnum, though long accustomed to taking money for curious services, had been shocked while a member of the Connecticut assembly at the lack of good taste shown by his colleagues in pecuniary matters. At frequent intervals investigations had revealed popular representatives selling franchises and charters to private corporations, blackmailing companies into paying "hush" money, defeating salutary measures demanded in the interest of public welfare, interfering corruptly with the affairs of cities, and squandering revenues from taxation in questionable undertakings. At each new state constitutional convention, additional limits on the powers of the legislature were devised, nearly every one indicating an increased distrust of the people's chosen agents. With distressing frequency, startling revelations of lobbies, rings, and caucuses, operating behind closed doors, and dictating laws and resolutions, broke into the columns of the newspapers; and finally in 1888, that detached English observer, James Bryce, drew a picture of the system in his American Commonwealth that even caught the eye of contented respectability.

In a short time a small band of sturdy democrats offered their remedy. They proposed to transfer the ultimate power from the state legislature to the voters, that is, to vest in the people the right to suggest laws by petition and enact them directly at the polls. As a necessary supplement, they also proposed to subdue the legislature by authorizing petitioners to lay its measures before the electorate for approval or rejection. All hail, they said, to the initiative and referendum! With great enthusiasm the Populists espoused the cause; Bryan set his seal upon it in 1896; and two years later theory bore fruit in South Dakota where a combination of labor leaders and radical farmers drove through a constitutional provision establishing the initiative and referendum. Encouraged by this adventure, a fusion of Democrats and Populists won a similar victory in Utah, though held up temporarily by the refusal of a Republican legislature to pass an enabling act putting their amendment into effect. In 1902 Oregon adopted the device; before the first decade of the new century closed, Oklahoma, Missouri, Maine, Arkansas, and Colorado had also turned to direct government for relief from legislative ills.

The progressive wave was now rolling in and larger figures, such as Roosevelt and Wilson, who had once opposed or ignored the initiative and referendum, gave their high approval to the innovation. On the other side, equally significant figures, long accustomed to defend with bold and trenchant rhetoric our immutable inheritance, saw Catiline lurking in the shadows of the polling place and caught visions of agrarians and proletarians dividing property, menacing liberty, and destroying the rights of those who had achieved success in the aleatory enterprise of acquisition and enjoyment. "It is radicalism run rampant!" cried a congressman from South Carolina. "The ultimate issue is socialism!" exclaimed President Taft.

But before the eventful year of 1912 had passed, sixteen states, principally in the West, laughing at the advice of the doubters, had assumed the risks of direct government. Then the radical current was checked; within the next decade only four more states joined the forerunners "in undermining the great and cherished principle of representative government"—Michigan, North Dakota, Mississippi, and Massachusetts. On the final reckoning, twenty states were committed to what Taft called "dangerous changes in our present constitutional form of representative government." A smaller number, eleven in all, had added to their armory of democracy yet another institution, known as the recall—a scheme which enabled the voters, by the use of the petition and special election, to oust public officers at any time during their term. Seven of these states even applied the system to judges; to employ the language of an agonized opponent, "they proposed to submit the solemn decrees of justice to the whim of demagogues." But the great fear was hardly justified by practice, for a decade of usage failed to produce either the grave evils that had been foretold by the prophets of calamity or the drastic changes dreamed of by the apostolic Populists who brought the new engines of democracy upon the American political scene.

§

In this general movement upon local institutions, the national form of government—particularly the upper works—was also assaulted. Since the state legislature was under suspicion as a law-making authority, why should it be entrusted with the privilege of choosing United States Senators to serve at Washington? Such was the pertinent inquiry made by those sponsors of direct government who now favored the election of Senators by popular vote. Indeed, a long time before South Dakota adopted the initiative and referendum, the senatorial issue had been raised, a natural outcome of the consideration given to the rôle of government in the process of acquiring and holding property.

In providing that Senators should be chosen by the state legislators, the framers of the federal Constitution had intended to establish a conservative body to represent the substantial economic interests of the country and to act as a check on "popular distempers" made manifest by the lower house. As things turned out, their plans succeeded beyond all expectations; certainly during the closing decades of the nineteenth century, the Senate was crowded with rich men, occasionally by railway and industrial barons but more frequently by their able advocates in matters of law. Some of them were political leaders of genuine talent but a majority possessed no conspicuous merits except the ownership of strong boxes well filled with securities. "I sometimes think," said Senator Lodge in 1902, "that the business man in politics is too often one who has no business there."

For the unruly sections of the populace, the reputation of the Senators was lowered by the methods through which they sometimes won their seats. Though the state legislatures nominally chose in solemn assembly, in reality the assignment was made at a party caucus held behind closed doors where pecuniary bargains were frequently consummated. Every now and then a magnate, accustomed to buying engineers, lawyers, managers, palaces, and works of art, brushed aside the decorum of constitutional propriety and bought a seat in the Senate with such disregard for the refinements of easy ethics that investigations, revelations, and alarms inevitably pursued him. Indeed from year to year the country was shocked by noisy scandals connected with the elevation of plutocrats to the august body once ornamented by Calhoun, Webster, and Clay, until eventually the weary public was led to suspect that even in unknown cases the senatorial toga had been secured by something other than high and meritorious statesmanship based on patriotic principles.

Among the Populists at least every scandal was greeted as another proof that the malady was universal, an argument in favor of requiring the election of Senators by popular vote. As a matter of fact that primitive agrarian, Andrew Johnson, foe of capitalism and slavocracy alike, nominated with Lincoln to catch votes in the South and West, had early emblazoned on his banner a demand for this reform, and, as President of the United States, had suggested to Congress, in 1868, a constitutional amendment to give effect to the idea. From time to time thereafter the subject was broached in the lower chamber and at last, in 1893, after a great influx of Populists, the House of Representatives actually passed the amendment, only to find the Senate unconvinced by the reasoning advanced in support of the scheme.

Again and again the House insisted, always to be blocked by the Senate under the influence of mighty orators, such as Senator Foraker of Ohio, later revealed as a stipendiary of the Standard Oil Company, and Senator Hoar of Massachusetts, a man after Cato's own heart, who leveled the heavy batteries of their eloquence against the proposal "to undermine the foundations" of the most excellent existing order. Lesser lights sparkled and twinkled but the sappers and miners continued unabated their agitation for the amendment, gaining steadily in state after state as the direct primary was rapidly applied to the nomination of candidates for the Senate. Indeed they made headway so fast that by 1912 three-fourths of the Senators had to run the gauntlet of that popular fire even though, under the federal Constitution, the state legislatures nominally retained the right to elect.

From a contemptible populist storm in a teapot, the agitation had now grown to such proportions that there were signs of unwonted stirring in the Republican camp and nearly all the distinguished Democrats, following in Bryan's lone trail, were exclaiming in speeches and interviews: "Let the people rule!" By 1908, the upward thrust had become so strong that Taft, bidding for votes as the Republican candidate for President, decided to endorse the popular election of Senators in spite of the ominous silence of his party platform on the subject. Two years later Woodrow Wilson, long opposed to that radical scheme, saw the light on his path to the White House. To employ political language, the bandwagon was rolling swiftly along in a great cloud of dust with statesmen of the most cautious temper scrambling for seats beside the veteran Populists who rode on the box.

In 1912, the necessary two-thirds vote in favor of the resolution was mustered in both houses of Congress and the next year the Seventeenth Amendment to the Constitution, establishing the popular election of Senators, was ratified by the requisite number of states. Slowly, for better or for worse, the composition of the Senate changed, as shouting from the housetops in senatorial elections was substituted for the negotiation of the caucus. One by one those who had wrung their hands from fear of change passed away and a new generation was taught in its books to revere as part of the sacred letter a provision which good and wise men a short time before had abhorred as treason to the principles transmitted by the Fathers. Such is the burden carried by that weary Titan, Time.

§

Amid the turbulence connected with this reconstruction in political machinery, woman suffrage was once more brought out of the parlor and the academy, reviving an agitation which, after giving great umbrage to the males of the fuming forties, had died down during the Civil War. For this renewal of an old campaign a rallying command was given in the late sixties when Congress was attempting to nationalize suffrage by enfranchising the freedmen of the South and champions of the colored man were declaring that no person's civil liberties were safe without the ballot. With a relevancy that could hardly be denied the feminists now asked why the doctrine did not apply to women, only to receive a curt answer from the politicians that sent them flying to the platform to make an appeal to the reasoning of the public at large.

For the purpose of giving a concrete point to their agitation they drafted a brief amendment to the federal Constitution, in express terms conferring the suffrage on women, and they secured its introduction in the House of Representatives in 1869. With that as the symbol of their high resolve, under the leadership of Elizabeth Cady Stanton and Susan B. Anthony, later supported by Anna Howard Shaw and Carrie Chapman Catt, they launched a campaign destined to last for half a century before attaining its goal.

The invincible minority of women who engineered this movement concentrated their forces on two redoubts of political power with varying emphasis. From time to time they were able to raise a debate on their federal amendment in Congress and occasionally they commanded for it a "respectful consideration," though seldom even that much honor. Discovering however that the drive on Washington brought scant results the suffragists devoted more labor to winning the ballot in individual states, each of which under the federal Constitution had the right to decide who should vote within its borders. Thus they hoped through state enfranchisement to get a leverage strong enough to move things at the national capital.

In that sphere also gains were exceedingly slow for the traditions of all the ages were against the measure. It is true Wyoming, while yet a territory, granted the suffrage to women in 1868 and as a state reapproved the innovation twenty years later but that single exception only seemed to prove the rule that politics was a man's world. For three decades the feminists beat their bare fists against granite, winning here and there the right to vote in some local elections, but awakening little more than amusement among those who sat on high political thrones.

Then the unexpected happened. Engulfed in the rising tide of populism which swept through the West in the early nineties, Colorado, Utah, and Idaho gave the ballot to women, leading the dauntless minority to announce the beginning of an immediate landslide. While their prophecy was somewhat premature, within but a few years their cause was lifted to the headlines by the militant suffragists of England striking hard blows, if not firing the customary shots heard round the world.

At last the avalanche really began to move. The progressive surge added Washington to the suffrage states in 1910 and before five years had gone, California, Oregon, Kansas, Arizona, Nevada, and Montana had completely enfranchised their women; while Illinois had given them a right to vote for President of the United States. Having now in their hands the fate of many presidential electors, Senators, and Representatives, the petitioners could no longer be scorned by the gentlemen who managed national affairs, for a minority of feminine votes, shifted from one side to the other, might elect or defeat a candidate.

Grasping that fact with clear understanding, a group of rebellious young advocates, who had not grown up in the state campaign atmosphere, led by Alice Paul and Lucy Burns, began to organize women voters in an effort to wring an endorsement of equal suffrage from the major political parties and carry the national amendment through Congress without further delay. Henceforward no politician with his ear to the ground in Washington or his eye on federal patronage for his home town could be unmindful of women already enfranchised, however indifferent he had been in the past.

So there was an unwonted bustle even among the seared and hardened painters of political scenery. In 1916 the Republican nominee for the presidency, Charles Evans Hughes, endorsed the federal suffrage amendment in spite of the fact that his party platform gave him no authority for that action. In a similar spirit ex-President Roosevelt, who a few years previously thought the matter too trivial for mention in one of his voluminous messages on things in general, now declared it a significant issue in the campaign. Not oblivious to practical considerations, President Wilson, while he had always entertained a deep-seated feeling against every form of feminism, on chivalric grounds, as a candidate to succeed himself conquered his instinctive repugnance and praised woman suffrage in principle. But he approved it in the form of state action over which he had no direct control, not the federal amendment laid at his door.

The victory of Wilson in the ensuing election seemed to mark a set-back for the national enfranchisement of women but appearances were illusory. Other states, including the great commonwealth of New York, were soon swung into line by popular vote in the peculiar confluence of political strategy induced by the World War. This gave greater encouragement to all the suffrage associations; more power to the conservative groups and more audacity to the militants campaigning in Washington. By picketing at the White House and by hunger strikes in jails, the latter dramatized the struggle for a nation devoted to sensations.

Words which formerly only amused the commonalty now became living facts—of which President Wilson himself took cognizance. In September, 1918, with a congressional election at hand, he went before a joint session of the Senate and the House in person to urge the passage of the national suffrage amendment, yellow with age, as a measure "vital to the winning of the war." By June of the following year, the requisite two-thirds vote was assembled and the resolution was sent to the states for ratification. After three-fourths of the commonwealths had approved it, the Nineteenth Amendment was proclaimed in the summer of 1920 a part of the law of the land. The fruit of a hundred years of agitation and social development had finally been garnered.

§

While they flowed from complex causes, the readjustments in the political machinery just described, particularly direct elections, were to some extent intended to forward the plans of agrarians and organized labor for diverting from the treasure chests of the fortunate a portion of the golden stream that poured there under the beneficence of a government which granted privileges and abstained from obstruction. It is true that, except in obscure and esoteric circles, there was little precise agreement as to the intimate essence of the political drama, if in fact it had any such metaphysical substratum. On the whole the reformers of the gilded age were eclectic in philosophy.

Perhaps a majority of the orators who inveighed against bribery in elections and sought to wrest from political managers the tools of their trade saw nothing in the struggle beyond civic purity or democratic and sex equality; observed no relation between the election of United States

Senators by state legislatures, with or without venality, and the safety of property or income. E. L. Godkin, for example, while condemning the spoils basis of conservative politics—for spoilsmen never entertained any invidious designs on settled economic institutions—was utterly amazed to learn that the western agrarians, who agreed with him when he lashed corruptors and corruption, were in fact primarily interested in cutting down railway rates by legislation, on principles which seemed to the sapient editor to involve sheer confiscation.

If, however, Roscoe Conkling's "carpet knights" and the feminists shrank from attacks on fundamental pecuniary practices, there was no doubt about the purposes of the Grangers and the Populists: the latter intended to dip their broad hands into the golden treasury of the railway kings or, to speak with due deference to constitutional forms, they planned to diminish the revenues of security holders by reducing rates through appropriate legislative action. During the tempestuous seventies they had managed to cut local railway charges in the Middle West; and, foiled by a decision of the Supreme Court in their attempts to lower rates on interstate consignments, they carried their agitation to Washington where, with the aid of other shippers, they secured the passage of the Interstate Commerce Act of 1887.

Instead of taking a stronghold, as they thought, they had really deluded themselves. Within a few months the federal courts began to pare down their great statute by adverse rulings and finally the whole structure was shattered by a judicial decree declaring that the federal interstate commerce commission, instituted by the Act, had no authority to fix rates for carrying passengers and freight. That was a clean victory for the holders of railway securities, a victory that moved the commission itself, with the insistent support of shippers, to take up the gage of battle.

Year after year the commission asked Congress for power to determine reasonable rates for common carriers engaged in interstate commerce. With evident concern it pointed out the steady increase in the economic strength of the railways through mergers and deplored their tendency to charge their customers all the traffic would bear, going so far as to assert in its 1905 report that over $100,000,000 a year was being collected from the people through increased tariffs that had no fair basis. But occupied with other matters and loath to disturb settled institutions, Senators and Representatives declined to act on the recommendations of the commission or the promptings of the shippers.

Observing their negligence in the matter, President Roosevelt finally intervened stating, in a message to Congress in 1904, that "the commission should be vested with the power, where a given rate has been challenged and after full hearing found to be unreasonable, to decide, subject to judicial review, what shall be a reasonable rate to take its place." Two years later, the House of Representatives, sensing indications of an agrarian upheaval, showed a willingness to accept the advice and the Senate, now aroused by potent forces pressing hard upon the gates, was compelled to heed the agitation.

At this very juncture, Robert M. La Follette, straight from victories over railways in Wisconsin, arrived upon the floor of the upper chamber to open his terrific barrage on the plutocracy before an audience of once languid Senators representing the old régime, thereby transforming their calm indifference into purple wrath. On one occasion the leaders of the right wing walked out just to show their contempt for his discourse, stinging La Follette to remark with prophetic gift that the seats of some members temporarily empty, would soon become permanently vacant. When the Wisconsin Senator proposed an amendment to a bill, forbidding a judge to hear and decide a case affecting a railway company in which he was personally interested as a security-holder, only three Republican Senators favored the proposal. Nevertheless, after much haggling over terms, Congress passed, in 1906, a railway bill known as the

Hepburn Act which extended the authority of the inter-state commerce commission over pipe lines, express companies, sleeping car companies, and railway terminals and gave it the power, not to fix rates, but to nullify rates found to be discriminatory or unreasonable on complaints of shippers adversely affected.

Far from satisfying agrarian demands, the Hepburn Act only stimulated the progressive surge which was soon to induce a political earthquake, causing tremors that registered even on the crudest instruments for recording seismographic phenomena. When the great railways announced a general increase in rates in 1910, Congress countered by passing the Mann-Elkins Act—a measure which empowered the interstate commerce commission to investigate proposed charges before permitting them to go into effect and authorizing it to determine maximum rates on its own initiative. In 1913, the commission was instructed to establish, once for all, the "physical valuation" of the railways, as a basis for rate control. Without going into greater illustrative details, it may be sufficient to say that by these and other laws the right of railway owners to manage their property fundamentally in their own interest was seriously limited.

With their rates fixed by state and federal commissions, acting always under the eagle eyes of shippers, and with their wage schedules prescribed by trade unions, railroad companies found it impossible to increase freight and passenger charges at will to meet the rising costs of operation or to cut wages at their pleasure for the purpose of enhancing profits by reducing expenses. So, through political action in one sphere and direct labor action in another, a large and important class of American property owners suffered a substantial diminution in their incomes for the benefit of wage-earners, travelers, and shippers. In other words, by a gradual and peaceful operation was effected a transfer of economic goods greater in value than the rights shifted from the French nobility to the peasantry by the national assembly on the night of the famous fourth of

August, 1789. Reputable American historians now recorded in their books that the theory of the public interest was being substituted for the older doctrine of *laissez faire*. Apparently it pleased everybody except holders of railway securities.

§

This abridgment of the incomes enjoyed by common carriers was only one phase of the general assault upon the chief beneficiaries of the prevailing system of acquisition and enjoyment. Vast as it was, the capital invested in the railroads, real and fictitious, represented the finances of only a minor portion of the complex mechanism employed in producing and distributing wealth in the United States. Indeed, the railways were simply strands of a larger network of corporate business enterprise—an enterprise impersonal in form and centralizing in tendency, that continued to occupy, with the passing years, an ever larger area of the economic field.

In the path of the rolling ball of accumulation, the Sherman Anti-Trust Act of 1890, penalizing combinations which restrained trade in the sphere of interstate and foreign commerce, proved no barrier at all. The Act was vague in language and not enforced in practice. During Harrison's administration there were three indictments under the law; during Cleveland's second term two indictments; under McKinley not one. Roosevelt, although he believed and said publicly that anti-trust legislation was about as effective as a papal bull against a comet, instituted twenty-five indictments; and Taft, his successor, placed forty-five to his credit. Considering the multitude of combinations and the fact that each act in restraint of trade was an indictable offense, the prosecutions in the days of highest tension were few in number.

What is more to the point the most severe judicial decisions, if they caused a furor in the news, made small impression on the captains of industry. The latter paused now and then to cry out against "Theodore the meddler" or to direct an editor to write a double-shotted leader on the inspiring topic of "Let us alone"; but ordinarily they had their minds fixed on things more substantial than the verbiage of the conflict.

As a matter of fact the years that followed the enactment of the Sherman law witnessed the formation of combinations on a daring scale that would have amazed the promoters of the seventies and eighties. In 1899, the Standard Oil Company took the place of the old trust; about the same time the Copper Trust and the Smelters' Trust were formed under the beneficent laws of New Jersey. The next year the National Sugar Refining Company came into existence with a capital greater than the total national debt in Washington's day; and at the opening of the new century that towering genius of finance, J. P. Morgan, completed the edifice of the United States Steel Corporation with more than a billion dollars in outstanding paper. As the chief element in these operations was the ability to float huge issues of stocks and bonds, primacy in such matters passed to large banking houses and heavy investors. So an immense collection of great and small interests was knit into a compact fabric under the management of two or three potent financial groups in New York.

This course in human events was naturally alarming to the middle classes, to philosophers of the cross-roads store and isolated factory, and to all the armchair speculators who saw a certain incongruity between political democracy and financial concentration. Inevitably also a mass of discontent accumulated among the people at large. Normal grievances were aggravated by untoward incidents which seemed to indicate a want of foresight and consideration on the part of the masters of the capitalist ceremony. For example, hundreds of petty manufacturers were frozen out by high-handed competitive methods and driven to raise plaintive voices about their vanished rights. Useless plants, offices, and mills were closed in many communities, causing resentment among local merchants. For one reason or another the general level of prices seemed to be rising and this produced anxiety among consumers. To make matters worse, leaders in the formation of great combinations often showed an arrogant severity in dealing with those who came across their path, a quarterdeck bluntness that savored of the methods applied by stalwart characters, like Drake and Hawkins, to Spanish sea-captains who objected to being robbed in the days of the Virgin Queen.

Even the investors who relied with child-like faith on the legerdemain of financial wizards had grounds for complaints. Either through inadvertence or calculation, some of the gigantic corporate structures revealed distressing flaws in their masonry. For instance, the New York, New Haven and Hartford Railway combination, effected under Morgan's tutelage, was so loaded with stocks and bonds that it collapsed with an awful crash, spreading ruin far and wide among widows, orphans, and other security holders in New England and giving an awful shock to those who had bought common shares at a high figure in the old days of prudence. In other cases thousands of small investors who tried to partake of the feast likewise found themselves reduced to scanty fare; those enthusiasts who bought common stock at the inception of the United States Steel Corporation were fated to see their paper fall to eight and not a few perished in the hour of disenchantment. In fact when everything seemed possible to the titans, huge quantities of water had been injected into the system of corporate finance, and, except where monopoly or good fortune attended the operation, the commonalty was called upon to pay the bill. All such things awakened emotions of hurt surprise among four influential classes of American citizens: petty investors who had tried without avail to turn an honest penny; bystanders who had merely been permitted to view the lucrous combat from afar; consumers, particularly farmers and planters, who could not raise their incomes by organization and suspected that they bore some share of the expense;

and philosophic politicians who entertained misgivings about the safety of the republic.

So, as the new century dawned, a demand for more legislation against the trusts arose on all sides. Having in mind western farmers, southern planters, people of the smaller towns, and workingmen of the cities, Democratic chieftains with a radical cast of thought inveighed against the trusts as a matter of course and conviction. Socialists hailed the new giants as proof that competition destroyed itself and prepared the economic structure for the inevitable Marxian transition. Feeling the solid earth tremble under their feet, Republican leaders spoke in favor of cutting away the "evils" of the trusts by regulation. Even the astute Hanna, on whom fell the burden of collecting campaign funds in "the high places of Wall Street," thinking that the Republicans should break their reticence in 1900, approved a cautious anti-trust plank drafted by Senator Foraker for the party platform of that year. Unwittingly, therefore, Theodore Roosevelt, raised to the presidency by a stroke of Atropos, was furnished a canonical text for many prolix messages and impetuous speeches on the trust question and given the color of justification for instituting several prosecutions against corporations accused of restraining trade. His successor, Taft, pressed forward along similar lines and in 1911 actually secured at the hands of the Supreme Court a dissolution of the Standard Oil and the American Tobacco companies into several individual but friendly concerns.

Still the Democrats were not appeased. Their spokesman, Woodrow Wilson, in proclaiming the New Freedom, promised to restore the old and happy days of competition when every person with a little capital could go into business and taste the wine of liberty—and profits—for himself. So on coming to power, the Democrats proceeded to enact the Clayton anti-trust law of 1914, an elaborate measure which in letter at least threatened to tear apart all combinations large enough to control prices in their respective areas. But the mild fright that it immediately caused in business circles was allayed in time by a decision of the Supreme Court, to the effect that so great a giant as the United States Steel Company was not proscribed by the terms of the law.

In truth, grave doubts existed in many places as to whether pains and penalties of any kind could restore the era of petty industry and unrestrained competition. Though appealing to the masses, the Democrats came to think more kindly of federal regulation; for they supplemented the Clayton Act by a bill which contemplated the control rather than the destruction of huge industrial combinations. Besides declaring unfair methods of competition illegal, the law in question created a federal trade commission and authorized it to coöperate with business men in establishing equitable practices.

As the new century advanced, intransigent hostility to great organizations of capital seemed to be on the wane. At any rate, the threat of horrible dissolution almost vanished as their securities flowed out into the hands of small investors, profit-sharing employees, savings banks, and endowed institutions. Socialistic proposals to transform the new leviathans into national property produced practically no response. Price-fixing devices, similar to those used with such effect against railways, apparently could not be brought into play against the trusts, perhaps partly for the reason that attempts of farmers to apply regulation to corporations or to break them asunder received no material support from industrial shippers as in the case of the joint war on common carriers. Neither could the trade unions get a grip on the basic industries comparable to their hold on systems of transportation, for the want, they alleged, of effective barriers against the flood of European immigrants ready to work at any price on any terms. After forty years of political campaigning therefore, the solid structure of manufacturing enterprise remained intact throughout the land.

§

Far more effective than the efforts of reformers to reduce the absorbent propensities of the great industrial combinations was their attempt to check the free and easy use of the national domain which, through custom, had come to be regarded among leaders in acquisition and enjoyment as a normal part of their property. From the foundation of the republic the vast empire of land held by the government of the United States—amounting in all from first to last to more than twenty times the area of Great Britain and Ireland—had been managed on the assumption that it must ultimately find its way into private hands.

For a time, as we have noted, Congress sold arable lands at a low figure for the purpose of raising revenue, with particular reference to extinguishing the public debt, and made experiments in leasing its mineral holdings on a rental basis; but under the pressure of the agrarian democracy and business enterprise, Congress adopted more facile methods for disposing of its estate. By granting free homesteads to farmers, huge areas to the states in aid of education and public improvements, and princely domains to railway companies, it quickly stripped the government of its agricultural property. Abandoning the policy of leasing in favor of sale at nominal prices, it transferred to private parties most of its timber, mineral, stone, and waste lands. Besides alienations made in the regular course with due respect for the proprieties of the law, others were effected by fraud and chicane so daring and so colossal as to exceed the imagination of the innocent and make the brazen looting of the Tweeds and Crokers sink to the level of petty frivolity.

While the democracy of the East was attending Barnum's circuses and museums and intellectuals were discussing strictures on American culture by foreign travelers, alert pioneers and the agents of far-sighted capitalists on the distant frontier were enclosing, slashing, burning, and despoiling, without let or hindrance, national property that had been bought with the blood or the money of the whole country. While orators were loudly praising American institutions, members of Congress and high administrative officials were continuously engaged in land speculation and it was a rare estate of generous proportions that was not tainted with irregularity in its acquisition. With feverish haste, this sequestration of the public domains went on unabated until, at the close of the nineteenth century, all the arable land had been given away and most of the timber and waste land had been transformed into private property. In such an urgency, the few scientists, who pointed out the perils bound to flow from a devastation of natural resources, could make little impression on hard-headed men of affairs acquiring and enjoying or on the vast mass of voters absorbed as ever in their fated routine.

Near the end of the saturnalia, however, Congress, almost by inadvertence, acting on the initiative of a small group of enlightened citizens, inserted in the General Revision Act of 1891 one of the most noteworthy measures of law ever passed in the history of the nation, a clause authorizing the President to set aside and withhold from sale public lands covered wholly or in part with timber and undergrowth. Thus the far-reaching principle of national ownership of forests was established by a few lines written into a general statute and pushed through Congress toward the close of a session when the faithful champions of fixed custom seem to have been asleep.

Perhaps the bill was deemed harmless as long as vast areas were still open to occupation or the matter was left to presidential discretion. In fact the law produced no radical change immediately for Harrison and McKinley were cautious in the exercise of the authority so conferred upon them and Cleveland instituted no revolution under the act. Not until President Roosevelt explored its terms were its latent powers fully realized, in sweeping decrees enlarging the forest reserves to the point where the national area withheld from sale embraced a hundred and fifty million acres, thus making conservation a national issue.

Then came of course the inevitable recoil. Individuals and companies that felt the pinch made vehement objections to the interruption of their progress. Western states, or at least the vocal and interested elements in them, declared their property and welfare in jeopardy. For good and sufficient reasons therefore Congress reversed the order of events in 1907 by declaring that no new reserves should be created without its express consent; and had it not been for Roosevelt's spirited fight, the remnants of the public domain already reserved by executive action might have been thrown to the hungry accumulators at the portals. As affairs worked out, the national forests were saved but, in the heat of the fray, it became impossible to agree upon consistent policies for the economical management of the common estate. If the doctrine of conservation had found lodgment in the American mind, the philosophy and practice of efficient use were still to be established.

After a brief revulsion against the Roosevelt policies, forward steps were taken with respect to the development of the minerals found on public lands. In the good old days, a farmer entering a homestead, a lumber company purchasing a principality, or a railway granted an empire secured title to everything below as well as above the ground. So national gifts intended to make homeowners or promote some public enterprise often made coal or oil barons instead. In such transactions there seemed to be at first nothing contrary to the public interest; such at any rate was the opinion of the beneficiaries while others for a long time gave little heed to the matter.

But in the contest over the distribution of national goods which grew sharper near the turn of the century, new views, favoring a return to the former practice of leasing, forged to the front. In response to a popular demand Congress, while legislating on the sale of public lands during Taft's administration, provided for the separation of the surface from the subsoil and reserved to the government the ownership of minerals. Expanding this idea, Congress in 1920 applied to millions of acres of coal, oil, and phosphate lands the principle of public ownership, leasing such holdings to private parties for development on a rental basis. In the same year a similar rule was adopted for the use of water power on national property, saving to cities and states the free utilization of sites devoted to public purposes.

By this halting procedure the remaining fragments of a domain once imperial in its area, fragments of no small magnitude however, were in theory at least brought under permanent social ownership. Time-honored practices approved by "the very best people" now stood condemned in the light of new policies while the federal government was called upon to devise a technique for controlling the exploitation of public property by private parties accustomed to operate under other disciplines according to individualistic dogmas. No doubt a people that elected to Congress an adventurer dismissed from a federal office for complicity in fraudulent transactions, that regarded the conviction of a United States Senator for the common crime of land-stealing as "the most brutal outrage ever perpetrated on mortal man," found it hard to summon the sacrificial courage required to administer an immense heritage for the common good; but perhaps, in reality, the task was not insuperable. In any case it was argued that, with the passing years, the scientific understanding and moral fiber necessary for the work would spring from the bosom of a democracy gradually rising to meet the need of all things. Otherwise those would administer who could.

§

The idea that the power of the state belonged to the majority of the people and that it could be avowedly employed to control, within uncertain limits, the distribution of wealth among the masses was inherent in all the projects for direct government and in the legislation pertaining to railways, trusts, and the national domain, which occupied the attention of statesmen in the new century. A similar doctrine was implicit in many proposals relative to currency, banking, and taxation advanced during the same period and, whenever carried into the sphere of practical policies, it found opposition or support according to social form. Certainly, those whose purses were well lined with the fruits of American economy saw in the exercise of power over the monetary system a utility of the highest order. To this party, the affair seemed simple enough: it was the duty of the government to maintain all its currency on a gold basis, entrust to private banks the mission of issuing paper money for discount at their own profit under certain safeguards, and then keep its hands off the running machine. Only one major problem perplexed those who sat safely within the scope of this simple thesis, namely, how to make the currency elastic, how to inflate it to meet the needs of business or contract it as the demand for money slackened.

Those without the gate at the dawn of the twentieth century had other views on the subject. To them the prevailing system, based on the national banking law of 1863 and the gold standard act of 1900, formed a part of the grand mechanism for augmenting the possessions of those to whom much had already been given. According to this hypothesis, the law authorizing private associations to buy federal bonds and issue paper currency on that security merely permitted them to subtract from the annual income of the country the interest collected on the notes placed in circulation; while the gold standard act, restraining the volume of money and holding down the prices of farm commodities, simply compelled debtors to pay their obligations in dollars of rising value. That was only a part of the indictment. The system, it was said, also permitted a concentration of financial power in New York, enabled the large banks to dictate to the small, and encouraged them all to restrict the credit of the petty merchant and manufacturer in the interest of the great corporations that were drawing the resources of the country within an ever-narrowing circle.

During the controversial years that succeeded 1896, Republicans in the main saw no reason for serious alterations in the currency system. They did enact in 1908 the Vreeland-Aldrich bill which sought to offset in a limited way some of the stringency induced by the gold standard and they appointed a congressional committee which made a monumental report on all aspects of money and banking. On the whole however the Republicans were satisfied. It was the Democrats who kept hammering at the money portals and presenting novel expedients for easing the strain in the interest of planters, farmers, and the people of the middling order in general.

Returning to power on an insurgent wave in 1913, the Democrats took advantage of the opportunity to try their theories by enacting, though not without concessions to redoubtable opponents, a new banking and currency law, establishing what is known as the federal reserve system. Combining Jacksonian hopes with more financial propriety, they put the emission of notes under the supervision of a federal board, divided the country into twelve banking districts, placed a federal reserve bank in each, and authorized the issue of currency on the basis of bonds and commercial paper representing credit and wealth in various forms while retaining the gold basis in theory. With this banking machine they made an attempt to distribute "the money power" throughout the nation, to block the centripetal energies of New York, and to make smoother the way of borrowers by weakening in fact the complete monopoly of gold. The radicals by no means got all they demanded nor even a major part of it but whereas their leader, Bryan, had once advocated what Republicans dubbed a "fifty-cent dollar," they all lived to see, at least for a period, something that approached a thirty-cent dollar, and the note-issuing banks making huge profits.

Having relaxed the currency strain, Jefferson's historic

party turned its attention to improving the lot of the rural debtor. On inquiry the Democrats found that tillers of the soil in the South and West were often paying ten or twelve per cent on borrowed money; and shocked at the discovery they sought to divert a share of the golden stream from the pockets of bondholders to the pockets of the farmers. With this end in view they drove the federal government into the money-lending business by the Farm Loan Act of 1916, placing the financial strength of the nation and the privilege of tax exemption at the service of those laborers on the land who were in need of funds; through a semi-public banking scheme the rate on loans was lowered and economic currents were shifted.

Under the new régime a farmer, who had once been paying one hundred dollars every twelve months in interest on a thousand dollar note, could borrow at six or even five per cent, thus keeping in his own coffers two-fifths or one-half the previous annual tribute to his creditor. Such items, multiplied by the thousands, ran into enormous totals. And this material result was attained by a stroke of state which philosophers of the old school regarded as an artificial interference with the wisdom of Providence made manifest in the distribution of wealth according to merit under natural law. Evidently the honored doctrine of "the less government the better" now had limitations—in the eyes of beneficiaries.

§

A government that could deflect golden streams hither and yon by currency, banking, and farm-loan legislation could also bear down on the rich in other ways and ease up on the poor through the exercise of the taxing power. It was no accident therefore that in the movement toward social democracy a deliberate and overt attempt was made to shift a part of the burden of sustaining the federal government from the consuming masses to the possessors of great fortunes. It is true that the Supreme Court had declared the income tax law of 1894 unconstitutional and that citizens who enjoyed large revenues from enterprises and investments imagined themselves securely wrapped in the strong mantle of protective legality. But Bryan and his legions were still active in the field, vociferously demonstrating to farmers and wage earners the justice of a levy on the incomes of the prosperous. In fact at the turn of the century discontent with established practices in taxation—that is, collecting federal revenues from the masses by indirection—was spreading like a virus through the left wings of both political parties, especially in the regions where great estates were few in number.

Already a fever was about to break out when President Roosevelt, in a message to Congress in 1907, frankly advocated taxes on incomes and inheritances with a view to leveling down some of the inequalities of fortune prevailing in the United States. Though to the occupants of high places in the lucrous game, this strange proposal from the White House seemed like a betrayal in their own establishment, it merely showed that a tide was rolling in and that Canute would have to move his chair to safer ground. Acutely sensitive to such tremors, the Democrats, in preparing for the campaign of the next year, cast off the timidity of the last election, renewed their challenge to the plutocracy by demanding an income tax amendment to the Constitution, and nominated Bryan to give point to their argument. The velocity of their propaganda was increasing when, without any warrant from his own party program, the Republican candidate, Taft, after consultation with Roosevelt, personally endorsed a levy on incomes as a fiscal device, "stealing Bryan's thunder." After the election returns were counted a decision on action had to be made.

When Congress assembled in the special session called in 1909, it was found that there were enough insurgent Democrats and fretful Republicans to force an income tax provision into the tariff act—this in spite of what seemed to be the clear mandate from the Supreme Court in 1895 declaring such a tax unconstitutional. Naturally a heated debate on the proposition followed. On their side, sponsors of the proposal were indecorous enough to point out that the decision invalidating the last income tax law had been made by a Court divided five to four, that some of the judges who made it had died, and that as the Stygian River flowed on in its course, the Constitution had really changed in spirit without being altered in letter. To this argument the friends of clean ceremonials made reply that the passage of an act in flagrant defiance of a decision by the Supreme Court would unloose the foundations of the social order. When the debate threatened a storm and the passage of an income tax measure actually became imminent, President Taft threw himself into the breach bearing a compromise, namely, that Congress should put aside the thorny bill and submit to the states an amendment to the Constitution authorizing the collection of taxes on incomes from whatever source derived. With alacrity, this proposal was accepted, since the danger of an income tax was postponed indefinitely while proper respect was paid to the prestige of the Supreme Court.

By a curious turn in political fortunes the Sixteenth Amendment was ratified by the states and became a part of the federal Constitution in 1913, just in time for the triumphant Democrats to make the beginning of a revolution in the national fiscal system by imposing a tax on incomes, with exemptions high enough to avoid offense to the major portion of the rank and file. By such means the way was now cleared for progressive levies that mounted during the war days of 1918 to two-thirds of the incomes enjoyed by the chosen few in the uppermost social ranges. So the "communist march," which Honorable Joseph H. Choate feared and denounced before the Supreme Court in 1895, had eventuated in a vivid realism. If Hanna had not died in 1904, it is hardly possible that he would have survived this shock, especially as Bryan was Secretary of State when the Amendment was put under the great seal.

§

To add to the discomfiture of the new burden-bearers, a large part of the national revenue derived from taxes on incomes and excess profits was devoted by devious methods to social purposes which anxious guardians of the American heritage deemed wholly beyond both the spirit and the letter of the Constitution. During the administration of Wilson, leader of the party originally dedicated to states' rights, old appropriations in aid of state agricultural and mechanical colleges were supplemented by astounding departures made in the name of "general welfare." Large sums were voted by Congress for the promotion of forestry in the states, educational work in agriculture, trades, industrial subjects, and home economics, the construction of highways, and the advancement of public health. If there is a national wrong, said a member of Congress, let us provide a remedy for it; if the Supreme Court declares the remedy unconstitutional, then let us devise a constitutional amendment to give effect to our policies.

Accepting the new creed at face value, social reformers pointed out that the number of workers annually injured in industry exceeded the total number of American soldiers wounded during the World War, indicating a problem and the need of action. Yielding to importunities, Congress passed the Industrial Rehabilitation Act of 1920 proffering federal aid to the states in restoring to civil employment the wounded "soldiers of the ploughshare and the hammer." In the same spirit, the reformers, with women predominating, cited figures showing an appalling death rate among mothers and infants due to ignorance with respect to the hygiene of child-birth and Congress answered with gifts of money to carry the light of science to them that sit in darkness here in America now.

In vain was the thaumaturgy of the Constitution invoked by those who viewed with dismay "this awful waste of the taxpayers' hard-earned money." Despite all protests advanced in the name of precious local autonomy, Congress continued to manifest a resolve to make the existence of poverty, disease, and ignorance in any part of the Union a national question—a determination to create American standards and stimulate the states to action by offering subsidies on specific conditions. And with a swiftness that surprised even the advocates of the new course, the states accepted the federal grants, made appropriations of their own in addition and complied with the requirements imposed in the general interest.

In a thousand other ways the driving spirit of the new century was revealed in attacks upon the aleatory system of acquisition and enjoyment. Among the cardinal notions arising from historic conflicts was one which the early economists had rationalized and made sacred under the term "freedom of contract." According to this concept, practice produced perfect good when employer and employee were at liberty to make any bargain they pleased as to hours, wages, and conditions of labor. No doubt a class less avid and less serious than that which presided over the industrial enterprises of America in 1900 would have been struck by certain quixotic lines in the picture of a single workman with a two days' bread supply in his domestic larder waiting at the gates of a giant factory to negotiate with the management on a basis of equality a contract for entering the employment of the plant.

But captains of industry were resolute in the heroic age and swore gravely by those sections of political economy which seemed reasonable to them. They could not understand the reformers at state capitals and in Washington who kept sapping and mining the foundations of their most excellent order. "Very wealthy people," said President Roosevelt in the midst of this conflict, "usually entirely without meaning it, are singularly callous to the needs, sufferings, and feelings of the great mass of the people. They show this in their attitude toward such a matter as the employers' liability bill. They are simply unable to understand what it means to a working man's family to have the bread winner killed or crippled. . . . Heaven knows how cordially I despise Jefferson, but he did have one virtue which his Federalist opponents lacked—he stood for the plain people whom Abraham Lincoln afterwards represented."

Going far beyond earlier laws restricting the hours of women and children in industry and prescribing certain sanitary standards in plants and shops, leaders in the swing toward social democracy now resorted to bolder projects. In the name of general welfare, they secured state legislation fixing the hours of men in employments that were especially dangerous or involved public health and safety in some peculiar fashion. When once the wedge was driven into freedom of contract, the scope of such legislation was widened until at length Oregon with utter impunity established a maximum of ten hours in all manufacturing plants.

With a similar reference to the public good, even the hallowed wage contract was touched by lawmakers: Massachusetts in 1912 adopted a measure designed to assure a minimum standard to women and children and within a few years one-fourth of the states had followed suit with still more drastic provisions. From the states, as in other cases, the movement for social legislation spread to Washington. In 1908, Congress limited the hours of railway employees engaged as trainmen and telegraph operators on interstate lines, taking away a part of the socialist taint by intimating that the main object of the act was to promote the safety of the traveling public. Eight years later, with the threat of a nation-wide strike impending, Congress, directed by the firm hand of President Wilson, proclaimed a universal eight-hour day for all trainmen on rail lines engaged in interstate commerce—the Adamson law.

In other important relations besides hours and wages, freedom of contract was materially abridged by statutes. A part of the liberty enjoyed by working people was the right to assume practically all the risks of injury and death that inhered in industry. Under the time-sanctioned common law doctrine, as we have already seen, employers were not liable for such damages except when they were themselves personally responsible, that is, they were not held legally accountable when an accident was due to "unpreventable causes or the carelessness of the employee himself or one of his fellow employees." Moreover damages in any case usually had to be won by a lawsuit that was likely to be long, tedious, expensive, and uncertain of conclusion. If a workman was seriously injured, he and his family often dropped down into poverty, into the ranks of the poor who are always with us; if he was killed, his family frequently drifted into the wreckage at the bottom of the best of all possible civilizations—so eloquently challenged in The Pittsburgh Survey, directed by Paul U. Kellogg.

Having enjoyed this kind of liberty for a century or more industrial workers, aided by reformers, began to insist that business should automatically bear the costs of all injuries not due to willful conduct of employees—a demand which seemed to the possessors of good things just another attempt to confiscate a portion of their property in the interest of those who had nothing. After a long public argument, the trend of opinion began to run clearly in favor of the proposed shift in economic burdens. On the insistence of Roosevelt, Congress in 1906 made common carriers engaged in interstate commerce liable for injuries sustained by working people in their service and when the Supreme Court intervened on technical grounds, the law was reënacted with the unconstitutional features removed.

Subjected to the same influences, the states had by that time taken up the matter. Some of them, sweeping away the old rules of the common law, made employers responsible for injuries arising from the necessary and inherent risks of their industries; while others provided insurance schemes designed to obviate lawsuits and make compensation for accidents simple and automatic. As the result of a hard battle, employers in the leading manufacturing states were compelled to insure their employees against dangers to life and limb as well as their buildings against fire and cyclone. On second thought, when the revolution had been accomplished, the requirement did not seem so unjust.

§

Among the incidents of this long and varied campaign to force *noblesse oblige* upon the third estate, concerning which only hints can be given here, were numerous and fierce collisions with the state and federal judiciary. Relying of necessity upon precedents, the courts looked to the past for guidance; whereas the reformers appealed to the future. No doubt the future was as real as the past, but judges as a general thing did not take cognizance of that theorem in metaphysics. Moreover the ablest lawyers, whose prime function was then as always to protect and enlarge the pecuniary advantages of their clients, as a rule held with Hon. Joseph H. Choate that "the preservation of the rights of private property was the very keystone of the arch upon which all civilized government rests." To seasoned members of the judiciary, this doctrine seemed axiomatic and, in following it, courts invalidated hundreds of legislative acts—laws regulating the hours of labor in bakeshops, providing compensation for people injured in industry, and making other invasions into the ancient practices agreeable to the beneficiaries.

Of course in nullifying social laws, judges confessed to no emotional bias. Instead they usually announced with somber mien that they were merely applying the Constitution, the higher law made by the people, to the statute made by the legislature. It was with tongues of logic, not of fire, that they spoke. Only now and then did a judge let his temper get the better of his rationalizing faculties and express a personal dislike for reformers and all their works. Only occasionally did any of the judicial oracles threaten to disclose the mysteries of the craft to the vulgar; few ventured to follow the example of Mr. Justice Holmes who, to the consternation of his colleagues no doubt, once allowed his genial wit to melt the frosty verbalism of the law by declaring in a dissenting opinion that "this case is decided upon an economic theory which a large part of the country does not entertain. . . . The Fourteenth Amendment does not enact Mr. Herbert Spencer's Social Statics."

But such admissions by connoisseurs in the course of time led the sophisticated to the conclusion that after all the courts were not expounding theorems in mathematics or dealing with mysteries akin to Einstein's doctrine of relativity, unintelligible to laymen possessing no technical apparatus for comprehension. So there arose among the intellectuals the belief that the judges were making the higher law out of their sentiments and intuitions; while the plainer people in the reforming army, especially labor leaders, became convinced, by less devious reasoning, that the courts were simply the bulwarks of those who had acquired and wished to live at peace.

From these and similar convictions sprang the movement to apply the recall to judges and then to judicial decisions. In fact a few western states actually raised before their tribunals the specter of the plebiscite; while others provided that their courts could nullify statutes only by extraordinary majorities—four votes to one or five to two as the case might be. Creeping upward to Congress, the same unrest appeared in the form of various proposals to restrain the power of the federal Supreme Court, such for example as measures requiring the approval of seven judges to invalidate an act or bills empowering Congress to overcome a judicial veto by a special majority in both houses. Less censorious commentators were content with the suggestion that erudite criticisms of judicial opinions would be sufficient to prevent grosser abuses of oracular authority.

§

At bottom the wide agitation that ran with the conflict over economic legislation and judicial interference represented a profound movement of social forces which finally breached the philosophy of "Let us alone." Yet that movement as a whole represented no articulate social theory; the varied measures thrown up by it fitted into no political mosaic.

If a Martian visitor had examined the statutes as they flowed year after year from the legislative bodies of the country, he could not have discovered from their volume and nature that the people were divided into two major parties which were in turn possessed of the power of governing, for the oscillations in the fortunes of parties in presidential elections bore little or no relation to the course of legislative action. Democrats did not repeal Republican measures assuring compensation to workers injured on railways; Republicans did not strike from the book Democratic measures fixing the hours of trainmen.

Indeed not often did the vote at Washington or a state capital on the measures of the new social democracy fall exactly into party lines. Rather did the division of Republican and Democratic forces into right and left wings, already described, account for more law-making than the partisan oratory true to dogma. Roosevelt succeeded McKinley; Taft followed Roosevelt; Wilson enjoyed eight years of power; Harding came into a brief tenure and dying in 1923 bequeathed his honors to Coolidge. With every one of these Presidents are associated legislative acts of one kind or another; and yet it would be difficult to find a single statute which any of them originally conceived in general or in detail and made a party issue before the country. Presidents came and went, governors and legislatures came and went but the movement of social forces that produced this legislation was continuous. It was confined to no party, directed by no single organization, inspired by no overpowering leadership. Such were the processes and products of American democracy when the mind was left free to inquire, to propose, and to champion.

If the story of any particular federal statute is traced

minutely, it ordinarily reveals strange involutions. An individual, often in the beginning obscure, occasionally unknown throughout the procedure, proposes a measure to somebody; discussion follows; perhaps a society is founded to promote the cause. In due time it either commands attention in Congress or becomes entangled in the debates of partisan politics. In some cases it never reaches the political stage but is enacted into law without coming under the party whip.

Take by way of illustration the momentous measure of 1891 which prepared the ground for the permanent public ownership of an immense forest reserve. The historic roots of that provision ramify into fibers that are lost to sight. As early as 1867 an unhonored land-office commissioner suggested such a reservation; six years later a committee of the Association for the Advancement of Science inclined a friendly ear to the idea; in due time the American Forestry Association, under the direction of a handful of enthusiasts, notably Dr. B. E. Fernow and E. A. Bowers, educated the Secretary of the Interior, John W. Noble, in their creed; a few Senators were persuaded and then some members of the lower house; finally Congress, wholly unaware of the implications inherent in the bill, enacted it into law. Cleveland with some hesitation and Roosevelt with characteristic audacity struck out under the authority conferred upon them. The grand result was accomplished before any considerable part of the country was conscious of the play. In the course of time the conservation of natural resources became a fixed concept in the national mind.

In other cases where larger or at least more spectacular interests were drawn into conflict, legislation took a regular political course, originating in obscure quarters, passing through the stage of tense discussion, and finding lodgment at last among accepted things. Indeed nearly all the major propositions that have been written in the federal statute books during the last quarter of a century, such as the regulation of railway rates, employers' liability, the graduated inheritance tax, the income tax, and popular election of Senators, were first urged upon the public by petty minorities—Greenbackers, Populists, Socialists, and other varieties of restive agitators. In each instance the leading parties at first denounced the suggested innovation, maintained a discreet silence concerning it, or recognized it with a meaningless phrase. But as the leaven of propaganda worked and the necessity for action pressed, political captains in high places espoused the once horrible reform and finally arranged to have it embodied in specific legislation.

By such routes outcast ideas were gradually gathered to the bosom of reputability. "We demand a graduated income tax," declared the Populists in 1892. "The act of Congress which we are impugning before you is communistic in its purposes and tendencies and is here defended upon principles as communistic, socialistic—what shall I call them—populistic as have ever been addressed to any political assembly in the world!" exclaimed the Hon. Joseph H. Choate, that great pillar of the Republican party, in assailing the income tax law of 1894 before the Supreme Court. "A graduated income tax of the proper type would be a desirable feature of federal taxation," suggested Roosevelt in his message of 1907. President Taft who succeeded him had no choice; in 1909, as we have seen, Congress laid before the states a constitutional amendment authorizing federal income taxes. In four short years, during the administration of Wilson, whose party had been afraid to make any avowal on the subject in 1904, Choate's "communistic" tax became a part of the federal fiscal system. Such was the strategy of the "new" democracy.

By a somewhat similar course of gradual seepage was spread abroad the opinion that the whole system of acquisition and enjoyment was really dominated by a few high beneficiaries who under varied forms and phrases ruled the country. "We have witnessed for more than a quarter of a century the struggles of the two great political parties for power and plunder," cried the Populists in 1892. "We protest against the domination of politics by predatory corporations," wrote Bryan not long afterward. "Behind the ostensible government sits enthroned an invisible government owing no allegiance and acknowledging no responsibility to the people. To destroy this invisible government, to dissolve the unholy alliance between corrupt business and corrupt politics, is the first task of the statesmanship of the day"—so ran the Progressive platform in 1912.

"Suppose you go to Washington and try to get at your government. You will always find that while you are politely listened to, the men really consulted are the men who have the biggest stake—the big bankers, the big manufacturers, the big masters of commerce, the heads of railroad corporations and of steamship corporations. . . . The government of the United States at present is a foster-child of the special interests"—such was the gospel according to the New Freedom preached by Woodrow Wilson, Democratic candidate for President that same year.

Twelve months later, an Ex-President, Professor Taft, looking out upon the world through the academic groves of Yale, declared that he was in no mood "to minimize the critical nature of the conditions which prevailed in politics and business and society after the Spanish War, and which seemed to have crystalized into a rigid control of all by great business combinations. . . . That the occasion for the general alarm was justified, no one who has studied the situation can deny."

Not long afterward the Honorable Elihu Root, who had once been sent by President Roosevelt to inform the voters of the Empire State that "the people rule," exclaimed in the constitutional convention of New York that in point of fact they had been ruled for nearly forty years by "an invisible government" of party bosses. Speaking of modern times, he said: "Mr. Platt ruled the state; for nigh upon twenty years he ruled it. It was not the governor; it was not the legislature; it was Mr. Platt. And the capital was

not here [at Albany]; it was at 49 Broadway; Mr. Platt
and his lieutenants. . . . The ruler of the state during the
greater part of the forty years of my acquaintance with the
state government has not been any man authorized by the
constitution or by law." With such strange doctrines falling from the lips of men eminently respectable, it is not
astonishing that persons of ruder culture and position began to wonder whether the theory of representative government by mathematical majorities actually functioned in the
manner prescribed by the canonical works for the education
of the faithful.

§

Broadly speaking this was the drift of practice and opinion that produced a schism in the Republican organization
in 1912 and an attempt to form a new party consciously
dedicated to social politics. Evidently the event had been
long in preparation. Though conservative Republicans appeared scatheless in their unchanging world with the banner
of prosperity floating proudly above their heads and the
symbol of the full dinner pail held firmly in their hands, the
very fates were working against them. After the Spanish
War, it is true, there was a revival of business enterprise
which outran the predictions even of the optimists; in fact
it seemed that the mouths of the "calamity howlers" were
effectively closed by big loaves and that populism was as
dead as Daniel Shays. But in the very hour of invulnerable
security, tragedy altered the face of things—in the assassination of President McKinley—transferring the scepter to
Theodore Roosevelt whom Senator Platt, "the easy boss"
of New York, had intended to bury alive in the office of
Vice-President. While the new chief executive tried to calm
the directors of his party by announcing at once that he
would hold the ship at the old moorings and retain his
predecessor's Cabinet, skeptics had their worries.

In almost every respect Roosevelt was a unique figure
in the Republican great headquarters. He had not risen

to high position from humble beginnings through the approved stages of party discipline. Springing from a prosperous middle-class family in New York City, Roosevelt was not a conventional self-made man; money had smoothed his path in boyhood, carried him through college, and guaranteed him a competence for life. No pleasing assurance that his success had been accomplished by his own unaided efforts toughened the fiber of his individualism. No hard battle up from the ranks through the system of use and wont, gathering in handsome retainers' fees from the possessors of great riches, gave him the psychology and mannerisms of the successful lawyer. Early discovering indeed that he had no taste for the ethics of the bar, Roosevelt spent many years of uncertainty, tossing about restlessly, dabbling in letters and politics without finding a solid footing anywhere.

In a kind of ambulatory course Roosevelt served as a member of the New York legislature, as police commissioner of the metropolis, as civil service commissioner under Harrison, as assistant secretary of the navy under McKinley, and as colonel in the Spanish War. In the intervals he studied and wrote history always with an eye to fine moral points, praising and condemning with elaborate flourishes. For recreation he rode to the hounds and played tennis. Unlike politicians of the log-cabin or clerical-manse school, he was of the great city, acquainted with its dark alleys, where misery and suffering lurked, as well as with the broad avenues where prosperity laughed and danced. In fact he was full of the insouciance and sentiment that distinguished the man of the world from the hero of Samuel Smiles who climbed the ladder from honest poverty by sheer tenacity. Born and reared in the comfortable middle class, his mind fitted into the philosophy of that order as the hand fits into the glove.

Thus endowed by nature and nurture, Roosevelt did not understand or sympathize with the radical rich man or the radical labor leader. The mighty business organizers with

Napoleonic imaginations who consolidated railways and integrated anarchic industries, amassing millions and more millions in the operation, were to him, as a class, enemies of society and personally objectionable. That beneficent fruits of their achievements, transcending all party politics and all bourgeois morality, might lie beyond the horizon never occurred to him. "I do not dislike but I certainly have no especial respect or admiration for and trust in the typical big moneyed man of my country," he wrote in 1906. "I do not regard them as furnishing sound opinion as regards either foreign or domestic policies." Again a year later: "I neither respect nor admire the huge moneyed men to whom money is the be-all and end-all of existence; to whom the acquisition of untold millions is the supreme goal of life and who are too often utterly indifferent as to how these millions are obtained. . . . I despise him if he does not treat other things as of more importance in his scheme of life than mere money getting; if he does not care for art, or literature, or science, or statecraft, or war craft, or philanthropy."

More than that, Roosevelt was convinced that such big-moneyed men were unfit to govern the country, that they had corrupted politics, and had been responsible in part for "the enormous increase in the Socialistic propangada." If, however, he condemned Edward H. Harriman, the railway magnate, as an "undesirable citizen," he was equally bitter in applying the epithet to Eugene V. Debs, the labor leader and Socialist candidate for President. Without reservation, he declared that men of the Debs school "have done as much to discredit the labor movement as the worst speculative financiers or the most unscrupulous employers of labor and debauchers of legislatures have done to discredit capitalists and fair-dealing business men."

Having grown up naturally in the doctrines of the middle class, Roosevelt adjusted his politics to the acquisitive modes of that order. The idea of basing politics on economics, of course, was not entirely original. Jefferson thought the republic would endure as long as there was an abundance of free land for farmers—until the people were piled up on one another in cities as in the Old World. Foreseeing a time when the mass of people would be without any kind of property worthy of note, Madison sought to break the force of majority rule by checks and balances in the government. Looking to similar ends, Webster frankly wanted to limit the government to property owners, trusting to a wide distribution of land to save the forms of democracy.

But Roosevelt was the first President of the United States who openly proposed to use the powers of political government for the purpose of affecting the distribution of wealth in the interest of the golden mean. In a letter to the reformer, Jacob Riis, in 1906, he avowed his intention, "so far as it can be done by legislation, to favor the growth of intelligence and the diffusion of wealth in such a manner as will measurably avoid the extreme of swollen fortunes and grinding poverty. This represents the idea toward which I am striving." The very suggestion that such purposes could be accomplished by the state was a heresy of the rankest kind to regular politicians, and Roosevelt himself, apart from proposing the taxation of "swollen inheritances and incomes," never made it very clear just how a political system in which, according to his creed, wealth was so powerful could be turned into an engine for the more equitable distribution of wealth.

Although Roosevelt had made no radical public utterances in his early political days, old and seasoned leaders in the Republican party—men who had made money and appreciated the art—suspected him and never took to him kindly. The potentate of New York, Senator Platt, frankly had no use for him; yet in searching for a man who could carry the state in 1898, he selected the young Colonel fresh from the Spanish War, knowing full well the appeal of a hero to the populace. Indifferent to the purisms of historical research and in no mood to give any heed to the cloud of dubiety resting on the fame won by Roosevelt at San Juan Hill, the voting public sent him with great acclaim to Albany. From that post, after two years of service, Governor Roosevelt was pushed into the office of Vice-President by Senator Platt with an evident sigh of relief.

This was the man set by fate at the head of the party led by Marcus A. Hanna, Joseph G. Cannon, Nelson B. Aldrich, Boies Penrose, Joseph B. Foraker, and John C. Spooner. Contrary to their expectations, however, the President moved forward with caution. The spirit of his first administration Roosevelt summed up in a single sentence: "We are neither for the rich man as such nor for the poor man as such; we are for the upright man, rich or poor." He expressed the belief that publicity would cure the evils of wicked trusts, that railway rates should be "just to and open to all," that natural resources should be conserved, that the navy should be strengthened, and that combinations which violated the anti-trust law should be prosecuted. In all this there was nothing very extreme. "I cannot say," he remarked afterward, "that I entered the Presidency with any deliberately planned and far-reaching scheme of social betterment." Still, by denouncing "malefactors of great wealth," "reckless agitators," "frauds on the public domain," "corruption in office," and "wrong-doing of every kind" and by vigorous executive declarations that broke into headlines nearly every day, Roosevelt alarmed those who hankered after "subtraction, division, and silence."

Mainly by manners that seemed dangerous to readers of financial papers, Roosevelt convinced the general staff of the Democratic party that it could carry the country in 1904 with a conservative and colorless candidate. So Bryan, the hot-tempered, was cast aside in favor of Alton B. Parker, a calm judge presiding over the highest court in New York; and a platform of avoidance, including an evasion of the income tax issue, was put forth to lure the voters.

On the other hand, if some of the Republican rajahs turned longing eyes backward to older and better days, they had no choice but to nominate Roosevelt to succeed himself. Hanna died before the contest started and there was no other politician strong enough to bend his bow. In the campaign the great corporations with unwonted profusion contributed to the funds of both the major parties, more liberally of course to the Republican chest, yet without failing to remember the needs of the opposing force.

Elected by a huge majority to reign in his own right now, President Roosevelt grew more severe in dealing with the directorate of his party and more precise in his recommendations. His first administration had been almost barren of important legislation; but the second produced some measures of outstanding significance. The powers of the interstate commerce commission were enlarged and it was given authority on application to pass upon the reasonableness of railway rates. Sponsored by Senator Beveridge, laws directed against adulterated and impure food, drugs, and meat were enacted in 1906 with a din that seemed to shake the pillars of heaven. The hours of certain railway employees were reduced and common carriers were compelled to compensate those injured in service.

In the meantime several important prosecutions were commenced against trusts; public land thieves were pursued with surprising energy; and a number of smaller fry guilty of evil deeds were driven from the temple with whips of scorpions. Moreover the volume of presidential messages, interviews, and speeches swelled to impressive proportions. In a nomenclature that frightened those accustomed to the economic patois of the early nineties, Roosevelt freely discussed social questions hitherto ignored in the White House. Income and inheritance taxes were commended, on the startling theory that wealth was not already distributed with justice and mercy; and gentlemen of the robe were shocked to hear a President confess that jurisprudence was not a mathematical science, that there were "some members of

the judicial body who have lagged behind in their understanding of these great and vital changes in the body politic, whose minds have never been opened to the new applications of the old principles made necessary by the new
conditions."

§

When the political season of 1908 came around, leaders of the Republican right wing indulged in the hope that
they might return in safety to the era of the full dinner
pail. Every suggestion that he should again be a candidate
Roosevelt had resolutely put aside and with him out of the
way many things seemed possible. In Ohio, Warren Gamaliel Harding, pledging the loyalty of the Republican
League "to that robust Republicanism expounded by its
great leaders of the past—John Sherman, Marcus A.
Hanna, and William McKinley"—pressed the candidacy of
Senator Foraker, distinguished counsel for the Standard Oil
Company.

But party masters of this school had not reckoned with
their host. Knowing, as he said, that he could not nominate "an extreme progressive or an extreme conservative,"
Roosevelt chose as his heir-apparent William Howard
Taft, his Secretary of War, who had been drafted from the
bench to a life of administrative service first in the Philippines and then in Washington. And by the effective use of
federal patronage, the President corraled enough delegates
to ensure the nomination of his friend. Even the stoutest
apostle of regularity knew that, without an endorsement
from the White House, no Republican could carry the fermenting West.

Taking note of these activities in the other camp, the
grand seigneurs of the Democratic party, having suffered
an awful disaster in 1904 by trying to rally under Cleveland's old flag, surrendered again to Bryan. At their national
convention in Denver, the Nebraska statesman wrote a
radical platform and nominated himself to a chorus of tu-

multuous applause that recalled the dazzling triumph of twelve years before. When the issue was joined in November, however, Bryan went down to defeat for a third time. "I can never forget," wrote Taft to his great patron soon after his inauguration as President, "that the power I now exercise was voluntarily transferred from you to me, and that I am under obligation to see that your judgment in selecting me as your successor shall be vindicated."

"The historical accident," as one trained observer remarked when Roosevelt left Washington in 1909, "is now out of the way." President Taft, a lawyer by preference, a judge by temper, conservative in affiliation and thought, and guided by a firm faith as he said, "in the fixedness of moral principles which we learned at our mother's knee," simply could not spring into the limelight booted and spurred, grinning from ear to ear. Matter-of-fact in outlook and procedure, he thought it was his duty to take stock rather than to drum up trade and keep the public excited every moment.

Nevertheless Taft really induced, or at all events presided over, more legislative activity than his predecessor. He tackled the thorny question of the tariff which Roosevelt had studiously avoided but he assumed no dictatorial rôle. When two gentlemen of the old school, Payne in the House and Aldrich in the Senate, made a revenue bill that reminded the country of 1897, the President stood genially by while his party was rent asunder, ten eminent Senators from the agrarian West voting against the measure. When an income tax bill was pressed in Congress, he went to the aid of the conservatives by urging a constitutional amendment instead. On the other hand, Taft gave his support to a measure establishing a postal savings system, once denounced as socialistic but later discovered to be a help to savings banks—in operation drawing from hiding places a vast sum and placing it at the disposal of private bankers at a low rate of interest. Another "socialistic" proposal, the parcels-post, Taft also endorsed; and after long resistance on the part of the express companies, it was carried through Congress at last.

In his executive capacity the President pressed a number of lawsuits against great corporations charged with restraining trade, having the satisfaction of winning from the Supreme Court judicial orders which dissolved the American Tobacco Company and the Standard Oil Company into several presumably competitive concerns. But this triumph, if such it was, the Court marred, unfortunately for Taft's political future, by expressing the opinion that only those combinations which "unduly" restrained trade were banned by the law—a dictum which roused the ire of Bryan and all advocates of a relentless war on the trusts.

With respect to the administration of the natural resources, Taft became embroiled in a quarrel between the orthodox school of conservationists and the upholders of ancient liberties. Driven into a corner against his will, he took the side of the latter, dismissing from his post the chief forester, Gifford Pinchot, a close friend of Roosevelt and the inspiration of the conservation movement. During the spectacular newspaper battle over personalities that resulted, the public took little or no notice of two fundamental laws signed by the President in the summer of 1910 —one separating the surface of the agricultural lands on the public domain from the mineral rights beneath and the other withdrawing water power sites from entry.

As a matter of fact, a political storm was now raging; left wing insurgency was lifting its head in the House of Representatives. Early in 1910 a combination of agrarian Republicans and jubilant Democrats concentrated their fire on the Speaker, Joseph Cannon, who for years had manipulated the legislative machine in the interests of the old régime and, after a dramatic contest, ousted him from his place at the head of the rules committee. In the autumn elections of that year, the Democrats carried everything before them, sending a large majority to take possession of the lower chamber. From sea to sea the air was now charged with the kind of "assaulting" and "assailing" which made big headlines and delighted the people at large.

True to political traditions, the Democrats did all they could to embarrass the President by passing, with the aid of refractory Republicans, various bills reducing the tariff on commodities of general consumption—bills which were promptly vetoed. Plagued by factions, the Senate mangled the arbitration treaties which Taft had negotiated so enthusiastically with England and France, forcing him to abandon his project for advancing the cause of international peace. To cap the climax, after he had driven through Congress a bill providing for reciprocity with Canada, in defiance of many insurgent and regular Republicans, the President was chagrined to have his plans ruined by the defeat of the program in the Canadian parliament. Thus on every side Taft raised up a host of critics without gaining any points of advantage.

§

By way of preparation for the opening of the coming presidential campaign, dissenters in the Republican party, adding the prefix "Progressive" to their historic title, began to draw together under the leadership of La Follette. They formed a league for the express purpose of defeating the renomination of Taft, invited Roosevelt to join them in the fray, and, undismayed by his refusal, commenced to urge the candidacy of the Wisconsin Senator.

While these insurgents were incurring the hazards of party rebellion, Roosevelt was watching the battle from afar, and occasionally sending up ammunition in his own way. At strategic points in the country, he made ringing speeches, advocating doctrines that shocked his former colleagues, such as Platt, Aldrich, Barnes, and Cannon, leading them to think that he had completely lost his head. With a high visibility unusual among politicians, he endorsed a strict regulation of the trusts, a graduated income tax, a thoroughgoing conservation program, an elaborate scheme of labor legislation, direct primaries, the initiative and referendum, the recall of executive officers, and the popular review of judicial decisions involving the constitutionality of social reforms. At length in February, 1912, when seven Republican governors declared that the requirements of good government demanded his candidacy, the indomitable Colonel replied that, if tendered the nomination, he would accept it.

"My hat is in the ring!" shouted Roosevelt with great gusto, making a slogan that appealed to sporting elements in the political game, and sounding the gong for a spirited struggle over the possession of the Republican convention. Pursuing customary methods, President Taft proceeded to capture delegations from the southern states, where the dominant Republicans were federal office-holders, and to use the engine of patronage at other points with skill and discretion. In the chief Republican states of the North, however, especially where the new primary system permitted the voters to express their opinions directly, the two distinguished aspirants were compelled to take the stump— attacking each other from the platform before cheering multitudes.

When the contest was over and the convention assembled, the returns showed that 252 seats were "disputed." With a certain show of judicial calm the national committee, which was controlled by regular Republicans, set about hearing the pleas of the rivals but the conclusion was foregone. After the usual display of legal arguments, the controversies were decided in such a way as to give Taft a safe majority in the convention, causing most of the Roosevelt delegates to withdraw, amid cries of "fraud." As soon as the smoke had cleared away Taft was renominated by the rump parliament in a sincere belief that the country was being saved from a tidal wave of dangerous radicalism.

Having broken from the regular organization, the Progressives, except those loyal to La Follette, went to work to form a new party. In August they assembled their hosts in Chicago—the strangest political convention that had been called to order by competent directors on this continent since the Republican insurrection of 1856. Typical politicians, seasoned office-holders, and hardened managers of local captains were conspicuous by their absence; reformers, idealists, and members of Roosevelt's "lunatic fringe" filled the seats and packed the committee rooms. Eighteen of the delegates were women and one of the keynote speeches was delivered by Jane Addams of Hull House, the famous social settlement in Chicago.

To complete the picture, Roosevelt was present himself, made a confession of faith, accepted the nomination tendered in thunderous applause, and joined enthusiasts of every school in writing the platform. As finally adopted, the composite profession of faith denounced the old parties as "tools of corrupt interests," approved the political devices of direct government, and endorsed with a precision not ordinarily found in partisan documents a vast array of specific proposals then already in process of realization or at least of exigent agitation. For the first time the major tendencies in American economic legislation that had been pursuing their course beneath the furor of partisan contests for a quarter of a century were brought to a focus in the expressed creed of a political organization.

Meanwhile the Democrats had made the most of their opportunities. On the forty-sixth ballot on the seventh day of their national convention in Baltimore they had nominated Woodrow Wilson, governor of New Jersey, as their candidate for the presidency—a man whose availability was in many respects superb. Wilson had sprung from the clerical middle class of the prosperous hamlet. Born in the village of Staunton, Virginia, he had been reared in Augusta, Georgia, and in Wilmington, North Carolina, under strict Presbyterian auspices. Apart from a brief residence in Baltimore while he attended Johns Hopkins University, his whole life was spent in small towns. Trained in the classics and mathematics at Princeton, he escaped the more dissolving influence of natural science and the socializing provocations of political economy. But brought up in the South, he was accustomed to using the rhetoric of Jeffersonian democracy as employed by the slave-owning aristocracy and he had himself some of the planter's hatred for the classes that flourished under the protective tariff.

Having found the practice of law in a Georgia country town neither lucrative nor pleasant, Wilson turned to the business of teaching jurisprudence and political science, moving from the woman's college at Bryn Mawr through Wesleyan University at Middletown, Connecticut, to the Princeton faculty. In the course of his academic career he wrote voluminously on law, history, and politics but none of his works betrayed any marked interest in the misery of the great industrial wastes or the contest between the plutocracy and the masses described by Roosevelt.

Judged by his career and his writings, Wilson was everywhere regarded as a conservative Democrat of the old school who detested alike the paternalism of the Republicans and the socialism of the new democracy. Speaking concretely, his philosophy was a concept that pleased southern planters without alarming merchants who imported goods and capital. Indeed it was in the rôle of a Cleveland individualist, stanch and safe, that George Harvey, editor of the North American Review and Harper's Weekly, both approved Morgan publications, presented Wilson to the public as a candidate for the presidency; and not without reason, for in his academic groves the professor had once confidentially expressed the hope that Bryan might in some way be "knocked into a cocked hat."

But for all that, Wilson had made no irreconcilable enemies among the followers of the Nebraska Gracchus by open warfare upon him. If he had passed his fiftieth birthday without endorsing any of the heresies that had been advanced by the Populists, on the other hand he had never been intimately associated, save for a short time as president of Princeton, with the masters of great business enterprises—Napoleons of finance and organization. And that slight exception had made a profound impression on Wilson's psychology. When for instance he had tried, in the interest of scholarship, to break down the system of exclusive clubs maintained by rich students at Princeton, he had been battered and beaten by the men of money who acted as the beneficiaries of the institution and dictators in the case.

While enjoying the popularity that flowed from this Princeton contest, Wilson was nominated for governor of New Jersey by old-line Democratic bosses who felt that local unrest at the moment called for a candidate known as a good man rather than a veteran of political wars. Once safely installed in office, to the dismay of his backers Wilson struck out on a new course. He pressed through the legislature a direct primary law, a workmen's compensation bill, and a plan for regulating public utilities, all symbols of the progressive dispensation. On a western tour, he visited Bryan to pay his respects to the skillful warrior who held the balance of power within his party. About the same time he declared himself in favor of the initiative and referendum and gave other signs of sympathy for insurgent advocates of direct government. If the conservatives felt they could trust a man who had steered a safe course in his youth and through his middle period, backers tinged with radicalism could now point to the cautious scholar made progressive by experience; and his managers could employ either chapter in his history according to the requirements of the occasion.

Immediately after his nomination for the presidency, Wilson embarked on a campaign that displayed a mastery of tactics. In speeches of great oratorical power, he stated that the national government had long been dominated by captains of industry and announced that the time had come for the "new freedom," that is, for a restoration of the lower middle class, hard pressed farmers, and working

people of the cities to their rightful authority in Washington. When asked for his bill of particulars, Wilson replied
that he was not discussing "measures or programs" but
expressing "the new spirit of our politics."

There was strength in this procedure: progressives were
assured by the blows struck at the "interests" and timid conservatives were not aroused by terrifying specifications of
the Bryan type. There was weakness in it also—as the
elections revealed—for, while Wilson's popular vote on that
plea was greater than Parker had received, it fell below the
standard reached by Bryan in every one of his sensational
campaigns and two million below the combined total of his
opponents. In fact he did not win a majority of the ballots
in any of the industrial states. Beyond question it was the
internecine strife in the Republican party, not the mere
appeal of his program, which enabled Wilson to win an
overwhelming number of the presidential electors and to
restore the party of Jefferson and Jackson to the direction
of the federal government. So after trying radical and
conservative candidates in vain and wandering for sixteen
lean years in the desert, the Democrats accidentally rode
into power as a minority group amid the whirlwind of national confusion.

As soon as he was inaugurated, President Wilson put an
iron hand upon his party in Congress and, before he laid
down his office, gave the country the implications of his
theories in the most remarkable program of national legislation enacted within the same length of time since the stirring epoch of the Civil War—legislation conceived principally in the interests of "small folk," planters, farmers, and
organized labor. For the first time in half a century, the
tariff was materially reduced, awakening ancient memories.
The currency and banking system was overhauled in a spirit
somewhat Jacksonian with a view to securing greater flexibility, a wider distribution of financial power, and a broader
basis than that given by gold alone. An anti-trust law, the
Clayton Act, containing prolix specifications, was hurled at

gigantic corporations and a federal trade commission was instituted to prevent unfair business practices. Labor received an installment in La Follette's Seamen's Act, in a measure purporting to exempt trade unions from the operation of the anti-trust laws, and in an eight-hour day for trainmen. To farmers the portion allotted included many tariff favors and the Farm Loan Act giving them the aid of the government in bearing down the rate of interest. "We found our country hampered by special privilege, a vicious tariff, obsolete banking laws and an inelastic currency. Our foreign affairs were dominated by commercial interests for their selfish ends. . . . Under our administration, under a leadership that has never faltered, these abuses have been corrected and our people freed therefrom." This was the triumphant note sounded in 1916 by the Democrats, reviewing the achievements of their redoubtable President.

CHAPTER XXVIII

America in the Balance of Power

WITH flaming headlines newspapers announced on a quiet summer day in 1914 that the Archduke Francis Ferdinand, heir to the Austro-Hungarian throne, and his wife had been murdered in Sarajevo by Serbian conspirators, giving a violent shock to the balance of power and raising in every European capital the specter of War. All through the month of July the world watched with bated breath while the diplomats of Germany and Austria-Hungary on one side and the diplomats of England, France, Russia, and Serbia on the other haggled over the incident, offering slight concessions to propriety but doing nothing substantial to prevent the recourse to arms.

At noon on July 28, Austria declared war on Serbia. Two days later, the Tsar of Russia ordered a general mobilization—an action which, according to understandings with the government of France, meant an armed challenge to the German Empire. On August 1, Germany replied by declaring war on Russia. Reasonably sure that England would not keep out of the fray even on condition that the neutrality of Belgium, the unity of France, and the integrity of the French colonies be fully respected, the German government announced to the King of the Belgians, on August 2, its preparations for the invasion of his realm on the route to Paris. That very afternoon, Great Britain, anxiously besought by the French government, promised the aid of the British navy in case German warships made hostile demonstrations in the Channel. August 3, Germany declared war on France. The following day after demanding unconditional respect for Belgian neutrality and receiving a negative answer, the English government broke off diplomatic relations and cleared for action. The storm now broke with pitiless fury—the Central Powers, Germany and Austria-Hungary, arrayed in deadly combat against the Entente Allies, Russia, France, England, and Serbia with Italy waiting on the course of events to decide her rôle in the struggle. Soon the hurricane was spread around the world.

For the State Department in Washington, the culmination of age-long rivalries in this terrible calamity was by no means a complete surprise; it was familiar with the questions big with national destiny that the war raised. Under the administrations of McKinley and Roosevelt, there had been a deep and lively interest on the part of the American government in the bitter contest of the great industrial nations for trade, territories, and concessions; with reasoned consistency the doctrine of the balance of power had been followed by the directors of foreign affairs. As we have seen, at the time of the Russo-Japanese War, Roosevelt notified Germany and France that, if they took the part of Russia, he would "promptly side with Japan and proceed to whatever length necessary on her behalf"; and when that struggle drew to a close, he deliberately sought to prevent a knockout blow, "so that each may have a moderative influence on the other." Three years previous to the outbreak of the World War, Roosevelt, in giving his private opinion on American foreign policy, stated that, if England failed to keep the scales level, "the United States would be obliged to step in at least temporarily, in order to reëstablish the balance of power in Europe, never mind against which country or group of countries our efforts may have to be directed. In fact we ourselves are becoming, owing to our strength and geographical situation, more and more the balance of power of the whole globe." If William Jennings Bryan, Secretary of State in 1914, did not thoroughly appreciate this point of view, certainly his distinguished chief, President Wilson did, for he said to Colonel E. M. House on August 30, 1914, in effect, "that if Germany won, it would change the course of our civilization and make the United States a military nation."

In keeping with this historic anxiety, the President had realized, several weeks before the tragedy at Sarajevo, that Europe was a powder house which might blow up any time with fateful consequences for the United States. With an idea of forestalling disaster, he had sent Colonel House to Europe for the purpose of forming some kind of general entente cordiale capable of preventing the war that loomed on the horizon. If the President's views at the time were vague, they were soon given precision by a letter from his emissary, dated May 29, 1914, warning him that "the situation is extraordinary. It is militarism run stark mad. Unless some one acting for you can bring about a different understanding, there is some day to be an awful cataclysm. No one in Europe can do it. There is too much hatred, too many jealousies. Whenever England consents, France and Russia will close in on Germany and Austria. England does not want Germany wholly crushed, for she would then have to reckon alone with her ancient enemy, Russia, but if Germany insists upon an ever increasing navy, then England will have no choice."

Besides being admonished about the imminence of war, Wilson was specifically informed by Colonel House on June 26, that, as all the world knew, the competition of the "money-lending and developing nations" was responsible for "much of the international friction." When the war did break, the Colonel gave the President his solemn judgment that "there is no good outcome to look forward to. If the Allies win, it means largely the domination of Russia on the Continent of Europe; and if Germany wins, it means the unspeakable tyranny of militarism for generations to come. . . . Germany's success will ultimately mean trouble for us." These opinions Wilson apparently shared. At all events in the early stages of the European struggle, while he deplored the invasion of Belgium and was indignant about the reported version of Bethmann-Hollweg's reference to the Belgian treaty as "a scrap of paper," he viewed the European War rather neutrally, regarding it as another of the hate-born conflicts that had plagued the Old World for two thousand years and of significance to America mainly in the possible destruction of the balance of power.

But the mass of the people of the United States had no such direct warning and no particular philosophy of foreign affairs as a background for understanding the outbreak of war. Though some Americans knew that the governments of the embattled nations had long been preparing for a trial at arms, the great majority seemed secure in the faith that business would go on as usual for time without end. As previously indicated, no cause was more prominently before the public or more widely endorsed by high respectability than international peace.

Even the political parties had thought the peace movement significant enough to receive a benediction. Only two years before, both the Republicans and the Progressives had approved the pacific settlement of international controversies. The latter, going up to Armageddon under the leadership of Colonel Roosevelt and Jane Addams, had deplored "the survival in our civilization of the barbaric system of warfare among nations" and favored the substitution of civil means for settling disputes.

In those piping days of innocence and peace, few there were who looked with fear and dread upon the German Empire as a huge war machine prepared for "the Day." On the contrary the closest ties of friendship existed between the upper classes of Germany and prominent American citizens. German-Americans who had wrung money from beer or pork or sugar found no trouble in breaking into the court at Berlin and many Americans of native stock, sated with the culture of the local bourgeoisie, got thrills in the presence of His Imperial and Royal Majesty at Potsdam. Dinners in select New York circles were enlivened by choice bits of gossip straight from the entourage of the "All Highest." Professors were exchanged with much ceremonial. Prussian decorations of the second and third class were bestowed with lavish, yet thoughtful, care upon a chosen regiment of American celebrities. Presentation to the Kaiser became as much an event as presentation to Edward VII or George V.

No less a personage than President Roosevelt, when preparing for a European trip, fished for an invitation to Germany, caught the coveted prize, and thoroughly enjoyed the hospitality extended to him by William II, especially the opportunity to review the German army from the back of a mettlesome charger, with the Kaiser on his left. With transparent glee, Roosevelt reproduced in his autobiography, issued in 1913, the famous cartoon of Punch portraying His Imperial Majesty and himself as apostles of the strenuous life. In an outburst of enthusiasm, a distinguished university president, deeply impressed by the gracious beneficence of William, declared that, if Germany were a republic, the people would unanimously elect the splendid Hohenzollern president. Of course a few radicals laughed at the Kaiser's speeches studded with references to God and himself and regarded William II as the greatest menace to democracy outside St. Petersburg; but the sober, respectable part of the American nation knew little about German politics and thought that little good as the great shadow fell athwart the eastern horizon.

§

With England also relations had been increasingly cordial. The open hand which the English ruling classes extended in welcoming the United States as a recruit to the conquering and imperial nations of the earth in 1898 had caused the country to forget many old wounds. Whether, as Henry Adams said, it was the fear of the German specter that produced the change of heart in London, it made little difference to the American public not given to the study of diplomatic history. The fact of England's friendly support during the Spanish-American War stood in plain view.

And the ties thus woven were strengthened by King Edward VII, chief architect of the Anglo-French understanding which brought England and France into the war together against Germany. While engaged in perfecting that continental adjustment, in February, 1905, the King approached President Roosevelt on his own motion saying: "You, Mr. President, and I have been called upon to superintend the destinies of the two great branches of the Anglo-Saxon race and this trust should in my opinion alone suffice to bring us together."

The personal friendship thus opened by correspondence was deepened by later communications. In 1905, the secret understanding which Roosevelt reached with Japan and England with respect to Anglo-Japanese-American coöperation in the Orient was fortified by Senator Lodge's visit to King Edward with instructions to inform the King "that we intend to have the United States and England work together [in Europe] just as we are now working together in the Far East." Indeed such communications had gone so far that in 1913 an American historian of undoubted competence, Roland G. Usher, declared that a secret agreement had been reached, binding the United States to come to the aid of England and France in case of a war against Pan-Germanism. While this allegation was officially denied, there was unquestionably substantial reality behind it. At any rate the way had evidently been so carefully smoothed that there was no possibility of a serious irritation between England and the United States in the summer of 1914.

§

Given this state of affairs at the opening of the great war it seemed perfectly natural for President Wilson—awaiting clearer intimations as to the outcome—to proclaim American neutrality in the language and form sanctioned by custom from the days of Washington down to his own time; and this solemn ceremony he supplemented on August 18 by a warning to his fellow-citizens to be impartial in thought as well as action. Reinforcing this official position Ex-President Roosevelt, then communicating to the country regularly through the columns of The Outlook, endorsed Wilson's policy of non-intervention, in an article published on September 23; for he was not taken by surprise even by the invasion of Belgium or hurried into premature judgment. Three years before, he had written to Senator Lodge that "the German war plans contemplate, as I happen to know personally, as possible courses of action, flank marches through Belgium and Switzerland"; and in his Outlook article he confessed that "very probably nothing that we could have done would have helped Belgium. We have not the smallest responsibility for what has befallen her." In general Roosevelt urged American neutrality, gave thanks that the United States had been "free from the working of the causes which have produced the bitter and vindictive hatred among the great military Powers of the Old World," and declared significantly that "nothing but urgent need would warrant breaking our neutrality and taking sides one way or the other." Reversing himself impatiently in a few weeks, however, Roosevelt repudiated his doctrine of evasion and his theory respecting Belgium, swinging violently over to the English view of the crisis.

If a former President, long intimate with the inner gyrations of diplomacy, could entertain directly opposite opinions within such a short time, it is no wonder that among the people at large there was much confusion in thought. In truth impartial judgments were hard to reach or maintain, for the country was deafened at once with the clamor of propaganda, which steadily increased in volume and intensity. Among Americans of German descent, moved by inherited sentiments of affection for their Fatherland, there was a frank sympathy with the Central Powers; while among Americans of Irish ancestry who recalled in bitterness the long struggle of their people against British dominion, there was an equally frank expression of hope that England's doom had come at last—sources of pro-German opinion which were openly and secretly stimulated by the governments of the Central Powers. On the other hand thousands of citizens of English and Canadian origin were no less zealous in whipping up fervor for the Entente Allies— actively supported by the English government in the business of drenching America with propaganda giving its official syllabus of the war. If Americans of the old stock who had no immediate connections with any of the belligerents, either by blood or by trade, resented the frantic cries of partisans for war, they were seldom heard above the roar of the factional controversy which raged over the merits of the European belligerents.

In their work of "educating the United States" the propagandists soon discovered that the American people were more easily moved by stories of atrocities than by the folios of Red, White and Yellow books packed with carefully selected diplomatic documents, issued by the belligerents in their own defense. On this score the Germans had laid themselves especially open to attack by their invasion of Belgium whose neutrality, including the British guarantee, was as Delphic mysteries to a nation that found high entertainment in the comic sections of Sunday newspapers. Taking advantage of this psychology, the British government made a master stroke by inducing James Bryce, so widely esteemed in America, to sign its report on German "frightfulness" in Belgium—a weighty state paper of dubious contents and worse propriety but none the less a horrible tale that sent shivers through the spines of those who read the newspaper headlines purporting to summarize it. Though the balance sheet of offenses against American intelligence committed by both belligerents in the days of President Wilson's neutrality cannot now be struck for want of totals, the slight revelations already made show how desperate were the designs pursued and how venomous was the poison fed to the public by interested partisans.

With a view to perfecting the technique of Entente propaganda a complete official thesis was evolved for the guidance of those who needed a creed to support their emotions. It ran in the following form. Germany and Austria, under autocratic war lords, had long been plotting and preparing for the day when they could overwhelm their neighbors and make themselves masters of the world. England, France, and Russia, on the other hand, all unsuspecting, had pursued ways of innocence, had sincerely desired peace, and made no adequate preparations for a great cataclysm. When England and France were trying to preserve equal rights for all in Morocco, Germany had rattled the sword and now, taking advantage of the controversy over the assassination of the Austrian archduke, the Central Powers had leaped like tigers upon their guileless victims.

To further their ends, the story for babes continued, the Germans had hacked their way through Belgium, a small and helpless country whose neutrality had been guaranteed by all the powers in their fond desire to safeguard the rights of little countries; and in cutting their way through this defenseless kingdom, the Germans had committed nameless and shocking deeds, crimes against humanity, offenses not justifiable in the name of war, horrors not usually incident to armed conflicts. To crown their infamy, so ran the Entente articles of faith, the Germans did what no other Christian people would do, namely, employed the submarine, a new instrument of warfare, against unarmed merchant vessels, sending cargo, crew, and passengers alike to the bottom of the sea. Embellished in many details, embroidered with rumors and ghastly stories, this Entente war creed was pressed upon the people of the United States with such reiteration and zeal that in wide and powerful circles it became as fixed as the law of the Medes and Persians. To question any part of it in those spheres was to set one's self down as a boor and a "Hun" and, after 1917, as a traitor to America besides.

§

If American property and lives and the balance of power had not become involved in the European conflagration, the battle of propaganda might have ended in words. But something more than words was at stake. As at the time of the Napoleonic conflict, the right of Americans to trade with belligerents and neutrals on land and sea, besides being limited by the laws of war, was frequently flouted by both parties to the struggle. Naturally, since oceanic commerce was the substance of the business, England, mistress of the seas, following the general practice of dominant governments in all times, had evolved the rules of international law which took into account her own requirements. Indeed the law of the sea, in spite of the repeated protests of land powers, was what England permitted and little more.

Among the principles of that law established by long usage were three of special pertinence for the quarrel now raging. First, it was generally agreed that a belligerent might blockade the ports of his enemy, but a blockade to be legal had to be effective, that is, maintained by a close patrol of the coast line by ships of war—a patrol which the menace of the submarine made impossible for all the warring powers. A second rule of law provided that contraband of war, that is, materials of utility in armed conflicts and the ships carrying such goods were liable to seizure on the sea— a doctrine applied with terrific force by the Entente Allies in destroying German trade. Exercising her undoubted powers as a belligerent, England steadily widened the list of goods marked contraband, until it included almost every conceivable commodity of importance, smashing in this way the entire direct sea trade of the Germans.

But that was not enough. Owing to her geographical position—her proximity to neutral powers, the Scandinavian countries, Holland, Switzerland, and Italy—Germany could purchase supplies from neighbors that could in turn buy from countries whose goods came safely by the sea lanes. So in the third place, the Entente Allies, using a precedent set by the United States during its Civil War, made the final destination of cargoes, rather than the port to which they were shipped, the test of ownership and purpose, in applying the contraband rule. In this widely stretched net the trade of the whole world was caught and, by whatever obscuring subtleties of the law defended, was subjected to such treatment as England, the principal sea power, thought conducive to her interest.

Finding that the submarine made it dangerous for captors to stand by and search ships at sea, in accordance with old practices, English commanders, under orders, adopted the custom of carrying merchantmen into port where they were sometimes held for months before their fate was officially determined. In this operation mails, packages, and boxes were searched and seized; the correspondence of American merchants with their factors abroad was ransacked; checks and money orders were impounded; and business secrets were explored. Moreover, though the high sea was nominally open to all powers, England, alleging that the Germans had sown deadly contact mines in the North Sea, proclaimed this entire area a military zone on November 2, 1914, and three days later ordered ships bound for Scandinavian countries to take the northern route, through her lanes of search and seizure. When the German government in January, 1915, nationalized food stocks, except shipments from the United States, English authorities declared grain and flour destined to Germany conditional contraband.

At this juncture Berlin, after asserting that the Wilson administration had failed to enforce American rights against England, declared the waters around the British Islands a theater of war, announced its intention to destroy enemy merchant ships wherever bound, and warned neutrals that, since English captains often flew false flags, the vessels of all countries were in peril. As a matter of fact the United States itself had protested emphatically and repeatedly against infractions of the rules of war by England—so strongly and so frequently indeed that Walter Hines Page, American Ambassador in London, who boasted that he was no neutral in thought or in fact, fairly apologized when he presented the notes from Washington to the English government.

Without undertaking to bargain between Great Britain and Germany in an effort to maintain the laws of war, however, President Wilson quickly and firmly warned Berlin that the government of the United States would hold the Imperial German authorities strictly accountable for the destruction of American lives and property. To this admonition Germany replied that, if England would pass food supplies through the blockade, the submarine campaign would be dropped. Adhering to his original position the President still refused to bargain.

Evidently every element in the situation was delicate. The submarine, invented by an American, was a new instrument of warfare and no rules for its use had been devised. Accepted law, evolved before its advent, held that whenever a warship overhauled a merchant vessel liable to seizure and destruction, provisions must be made for the safety of passengers and crew. Since the operation of that law ran in favor of England, she saw no reason for modifying it; all the more because in its ancient form, it had the merit of humanism which was in the circumstances gratifying to the English people. On the other hand Germany, being strangled by the blockade, sought to legislate for novel conditions and her new law threatened to bring to the civilian population of her enemies primarily and to neutrals incidentally the horrors of trench and battlefield. Undoubtedly moral sentiments in the United States ran heavily against the Germans in their contentions, even though many American naval experts, foreseeing the possible need for the submarine in future wars and anticipating the ultimate extension to non-combatants of destruction by bombs, fire, and gas, thought the German precedent an example not to be lightly rejected.

§

A test of fact soon made a decision unavoidable. Having failed in their effort to relax the British grip through American pressure, the Germans began operations against merchant vessels in accordance with their threats. As anticipated, American ships, passengers, and sailors became involved in these maneuvers from time to time, each new incident increasing the tension. The strain was already great when on the morning of May 1, 1915, there appeared in American newspapers an advertisement signed by the German Embassy at Washington, which warned American citizens against the dangers of the war zone and especially against the perils of sailing on British ships. On that very day the British steamer, Lusitania, listed as an auxiliary war craft, carrying ammunition and a large number of passengers, dropped down the Hudson River and steered for the open sea. Six days later without receiving any warning, the ship was struck by two torpedoes and in a few minutes sank by the bow, taking to a watery grave more than a thousand people including over one hundred Americans.

When the news reached this country, a shudder of horror ran through the nation followed by instant cries for vengeance. A few editors and publicists, it is true, argued that the victims of the disaster, duly admonished of the peril, had taken the risks voluntarily, that American lives had already been destroyed by British mines unlawfully sown in the North Sea, that the captain of the Lusitania had invited destruction by steaming slowly, and that the calamity, deplorable and awful as it was, constituted only one of the numerous ghastly phases of the war. But President Wilson took no such view of the matter. As soon as the facts were in his possession, he dispatched a note to Berlin, calling upon the German government to disavow the act, make reparations, and prevent the recurrence of such a deed. Then, solemnly, as if pronouncing a doom, he stated that his government would not "omit any word or any act necessary to the performance of its sacred duty of maintaining the rights of the United States and its citizens and of safeguarding their free exercise and enjoyment."

At that moment the die was cast. In reply Germany temporized and again sought to make a bargain by offering in effect to respect American rights if England would do the same. Against this trading policy, Wilson set his face like flint, driving the Secretary of State, Bryan, who indignantly resented this refusal to bargain, to resign from the Cabinet, protesting privately that he could not see the fairness of coercing the German government which was willing to arbitrate while dealing gently with the English government which stood resolute on its interests. Finally, after weeks of haggling, Germany agreed on September 1, 1915, not to sink liners without warning and without providing for the safety of non-combatants. "It is a triumph not only of diplomacy but of reason, of humanity, of justice, of truth!" exclaimed the New York Times on hearing the news. Yet it marked a truce, not peace.

§

Reverberations of the desperate conflict in Europe, the constant thrumming of propaganda, fears of investors who had bought Anglo-French bonds and of manufacturers who had sold enormous quantities of supplies to the Entente Powers, the continuous insistence of citizens who genuinely feared the menace of a German victory, and the strained tension of diplomatic relations—all combined to beat the domestic politics of the United States into a boisterous storm. Advocates of "preparedness" were given an impressive theme and hearing. The National Security League, organized in December, 1914, mainly with the support of eastern capitalists, joined the old Navy League in demanding a more adequate equipment for fighting; when the combination failed to denounce Democratic congressmen with sufficient force, the American Defense Society came to the rescue. Then the American Rights Committee rushed upon the stage with a demand for immediate war on the Central Powers. On the other side of the line, peace propaganda began to drift into the control of extremists who imagined that pacifism could be urged with safety when war was imminent, in their temerity redoubling the fury of the party bent on war.

Being in power, the Democrats naturally had to endure the assaults of all factions, their leader, President Wilson, bearing the brunt of the shock. Busy with negotiations among the nations looking to a fair peace, hoping in vain that a proposal to England suggesting an equitable settlement would bring the conflict to a close, the President long resisted all demands for additional military equipment—until 1916 when, for reasons not made public in specific form, he made concessions in that direction without going far on the way to adequate preparation for actual war. Probably more as a gesture than an act of defiance, Congress passed in that year four special measures strengthening the forces of the country. One enlarged the regular army and the national guard; another authorized the construction of ten dreadnoughts and six battle cruisers within three years; a third established a council of national defense; a fourth, the Shipping Board Act, provided for the creation of a mercantile marine at public expense.

By this time the country was in the throes of another presidential campaign. Putting aside their former grudges in a common opposition to Wilson, Republicans and Progressives united in calling Charles Evans Hughes from the Supreme Bench to be their candidate. "We desire peace, the peace of justice and right," ran the Republican platform, "and we believe in maintaining a straight and honest neutrality between the belligerents in the Great War in Europe. We must perform all our duties and insist upon all our rights as neutrals without fear or favor." With so much judicial skill was this lofty sentiment reiterated by Hughes in his campaign speeches that active supporters of the Entente powers and equally active Irish and German elements in the electorate found no difficulty in uniting under his banner. By some means, however, he gave the impression that his election meant war—war on Germany; at all events, he captured the imagination of the industrial and financial sections already deeply involved in the fate of the Entente.

Fearing that the election of Hughes meant the triumph of capitalistic imperialism, radicals and pacifists of all schools turned to Wilson as the best hope for continued peace. Nor did the Democrats reject these recruits or deny the pacifist implications of such support. Nominating Wilson by acclamation, they reviewed the party's legislative achievements with the customary pride and commended "the splendid diplomatic victories of our great President who has preserved the vital interests of our government and kept us out of war." On the issue of peace a special appeal was made to enfranchized women of the West. Frightened by the rush of militant suffragists to Hughes after the latter's declaration in favor of the national amendment, Wilson sent the "spellbinder," Dudley Field Malone, to the Pacific Coast with a commission to rally the women, to promise peace in exchange for votes, and to offset by other pledges the known hostility of the President to modern feminism—a strategy that proved exceedingly effective. Turning the scales by a few hundred votes, California assured the re-election of Wilson.

Generally speaking, the West and South, agrarian states that had been the bulwark of the Jacksonian party, returned Democratic majorities whereas the eastern centers of industrial and financial power went to Hughes in a landslide. Even the Socialist vote fell heavily as party members rushed to the pacific camp of the President, acting perhaps on the advice of the Socialist candidate, Allan Benson, who frankly declared that Wilson should be the second choice of all good comrades. Though the Democratic victory in the electoral college was narrow, the popular majority in favor of Wilson was decisive.

§

Taking the mandate as a verdict in support of conciliatory policies, President Wilson, soon after the election was over, addressed open notes to the belligerent powers proposing a negotiated settlement and asking them to state the terms upon which the war might be brought to an end—an action in keeping with the negotiations which he had long been carrying on with the belligerents through the agency of Colonel House. Early in 1916 he had approached the Entente powers with a peace project which savored of democratic theories and contemplated no imperialist gains of great magnitude for any party, even going so far as to indicate that he might take the United States into the war on their side if Germany proved recalcitrant. But, having experienced on that occasion a chilling rebuff from the masters of England and France who, without his knowledge, had already divided the spoils of war in advance by secret treaties with Russia, Italy, and Japan and did not then want any military aid from the United States, at least on pacifist principles, Wilson decided in December, 1916, to make his bid for a negotiated peace open to all the world. In reply to his manifesto the Central Powers, then enjoying the better of the fight, stated that they were ready for a conference while the Entente Allies laid down drastic conditions as the price of their acceptance, bringing to naught the effort at mediation.

Not discouraged by the results of his previous attempts, Wilson returned to the theme on January 22, 1917, declaring in a speech before the Senate that it was the duty of the United States to take part in restoring international harmony on the basis of certain principles. These he enumerated in a short form: "peace without victory," the right of nationalities to liberty and self-government, independence of Poland, freedom of the seas, reduction of armaments, and abolition of entangling alliances. If no new factors had entered the contest, the program suggested by Wilson might have provided the only solution of the peace problem for, while his terms were abhorrent to the war party in each belligerent country, the long conflict now promised a stalemate, causing the peoples of Europe to be sick at heart and augmenting social unrest in every quarter. But events decreed another fate, making a break in the long monody with startling suddenness on January 31, when the German Ambassador at Washington, Count von Bernstorff, announced the purpose of his government to renew the submarine campaign. Within three months after that the United States was involved with the Entente Allies in the war on the German Empire.

§

What was running through Wilson's mind in those harrowing times when he was engrossed in "waging neutrality" —how did he view the conflict that was shaking the world? Obviously the answer to this question is not to be found in biographies and eulogies written after Wilson carried the United States into the war. Neither can it be discovered from his own writings for his intimate papers revealing the trend of his thinking during the first years of the struggle in Europe have not yet been laid before the country. Nevertheless the mystery is not completely sealed; for in the correspondence of Walter Hines Page, American Ambassador in London, in the papers of Franklin K. Lane, Secretary of the Interior, written between 1914 and 1917, fortunately, if indiscreetly, made public, and in the letters of Colonel House, can be caught illuminating glimpses of the President's thought as it developed before the measures of the German imperial government, coupled with the pitiless beat of propaganda and the ceaseless din of war voices, bore him into the fray.

In these records it seems to be made plain that, until the United States entered the war, Wilson, in spite of fluctuations in his temper, looked rather coldly on the pretentions of both the embattled forces, being inclined to regard the conflict as a war of commercial powers over the spoils of empire. "The President," complained Page, "started out with the idea that it was a war brought on by many obscure causes—economic and the like. . . . Thus we have failed to render help to the side of Liberalism and Democracy which are at stake in the world."

When the Ambassador came back to America in 1916 to impress Wilson with the righteousness of the English case, he found his chief rather frigid as he presented that particular appeal. According to Page, Wilson, on this occasion, "described the war as a result of many causes, some of long origin. He spoke of England's having the earth and Germany's wanting it. Of course, he said, the German system is directly opposed to everything American. But I do not gather that he thought that this carried any very great moral responsibility." Such apparently was the position of President Wilson at the end of two years of the war although, as Page records in another place, "when the war began he and all the men he met were in hearty sympathy with the Entente Allies."

In the letters of Lane, the opinion expressed by Page is amply confirmed. As late as February 2, 1917, even after news had come that Germany would renew her submarine warfare, Wilson was asked at a Cabinet meeting which side he wished to see victorious in the European conflict. Without equivocation, he replied that "he didn't wish to see either side win—for both had been equally indifferent to the rights of neutrals—though Germany had been brutal in taking life and England only in taking property."

A little later Wilson added that "the country was not willing that we should take any risks of war." When Lane, holding the opposite view, reasserted that, if the people knew about the treatment of American consuls' wives in Germany, there would be no question as to public sentiment, the President resented this "as a suggestion that we should work up a propaganda of hatred against Germany." Seeing three other members of the Cabinet, McAdoo, Houston, and Redfield, join Lane in the contention that the people were entitled to know the "facts," "the President turned on them bitterly, especially on McAdoo, and reproached all of us with appealing to the spirit of the Code Duello."

After this passage at arms, Lane wrote with a touch of bitterness: "I don't know whether the President is an internationalist or a pacifist; he seems to be very mildly national—his patriotism is covered over with a film of philosophic humanitarianism that certainly doesn't make for 'punch' at such a time as this." When, at last, the die was cast Lane recorded on April 1 that the President was "for recognizing war and taking hold of the situation in such a fashion as will eventually lead to an Allies' victory over Germany. But he goes unwillingly. . . . We can stand Germany's insolence and murderous policy no longer."

During this period of American neutrality Wilson's public utterances were fairly in accord with the private opinions so recorded. Evidently he believed that the unconditional triumph of either party would be undesirable. In a speech delivered on May 27, 1916, he expressed the conviction that this country was not concerned "with the causes and objects of the war." In his peace communication to the contending powers, in December of the same year, he took "the liberty of calling attention to the fact that the objects which the statesmen of the belligerents on both sides have in mind in this war are virtually the same, as stated in general terms to their own people and to the world." No doubt he knew that such a declaration would make a painful impression in England and indeed it did. According to Page, Lord Northcliffe blurted out: "Everybody is mad as hell ... The King, expressing his surprise and dismay that Mr. Wilson should think that Englishmen were fighting for the same things in this war as the Germans, broke down;" while Lord Robert Cecil was "deeply hurt."

If such objections were communicated to Wilson, they had little effect on his views, for he continued to use similar language in public and in private. Even after he took the United States into the conflict, he adhered to his conviction that the primary interest of Great Britain in the war was commercial and imperialistic. With that in mind, he objected to a proposal to send Ex-President Taft to England in December, 1917, as a messenger of good will to cement the ties of the two powers then aligned side by side on the battlefields of France; saying bluntly that the United States should not be "in a position of seeming in any way to be involved with British policy." To clinch his argument, he cited as proof one of the secret treaties, made public by the Bolsheviki, by which the Entente Allies had divided the spoils of war in advance of victory. From no record at present available does it appear that Wilson ever surrendered his personal conviction that, as far as the causes and objects of the war were concerned, there was no ground for assuming that either party to the conflict had any special merit of righteousness to be accepted at face value.

What then eventually turned the scale in Wilson's mind and within two months changed him from a man who "didn't wish either side to win" into an ardent advocate of war "without stint" against Germany. No easy answer is forthcoming, if indeed the psychological process of human decision is fathomable at all; but many of the factors that profoundly influenced him were patent to every one. First among them certainly was Germany's announcement of a general submarine campaign practically without let or hindrance, followed shortly by the destruction of six American vessels, in a majority of cases without warning, three of them carrying American citizens to death. Unless the President was to repudiate his previous position on that issue and now accept submarine warfare with all its consequences as approved by the laws of combat, there was no other choice than an appeal to arms. In any event, this was the official thesis for, when Wilson called upon Congress for the fateful war resolution, he declared that the German imperial government had in fact driven the United States into the position of a belligerent, that the nation had no alternative except a reply by force—a judgment which he confirmed in defending the postponement of hostilities against Austria, saying "We enter this war only where we are clearly forced into it because there are no other means of defending our rights." Such even was the verdict of the German Ambassador in Washington for he attributed to the action of his own government the rupture of relations adding that, in his opinion, affairs were not only distinctly favorable to Germany at the moment but moving, under the President's policy, in the direction of a fair peace.

There were of course other forces that helped to form the President's crucial decision. It was clear by the spring of 1917 that without American aid the Entente Allies could hardly hope for anything more than a stalemate if indeed they could escape defeat at the hands of the German war machine which for nearly three years had held its lines against astounding odds. At best, American investors who had staked money on the Anglo-French side, munition makers who had accepted the paper of London and Paris in return for supplies, merchants and manufacturers who had huge Entente credits on their books were placed in a serious dilemma; they were in danger of immense losses unless the

United States government came to their rescue. No doubt the war dirge raised by these selfish factions was adequately financed, astutely managed, and effectively carried into strange out-of-the-way places as well as into the main highways.

Encouraged by this interested domestic support, the Canadian, British, and French propagandists increased their drive, going to such lengths indeed that President Wilson, angry at their insistence, was at last moved to exclaim that there were too many Englishmen pushing their cause in America and to ask the British Ambassador late in 1917 to send some of them home. In addition to the professional profiteers and propagandists engaged in fomenting the war fever was a large body of Americans of English stock who felt bound to England by ties of blood and affection and who urged upon Wilson a war in the name of kinship.

Finally a considerable number of people, who looked upon the intrinsic merits of the European quarrel with relative indifference, believed that the United States had a genuine reason to fear the triumph of the German military caste in the Old World. As a distinguished professor of European history phrased it in unacademic mode: "England is a retired old sea robber in possession of immense imperial spoils, more interested in keeping peace with America than the young German pirate at the beginning of his career; for the latter can only hope to win his place in the sun by a general dislocation in the present distribution of the world's booty." That was the philosophy of some practical Americans who begged the President to make war on the German imperial government.

§

While the evolution of Wilson's opinion respecting the war in Europe may be traced according to the above design from the letters and papers of his contemporaries, it cannot be denied that there is authentic evidence for another view of the case, namely, that the President, having come practically to the end of his rope as regards domestic policies—offerings to planters, farmers, and trade unionists, as he himself confessed to Colonel House on September 28, 1914—reached the conviction in 1915 or early in 1916 that he could play a masterful rôle on the international stage by taking the United States into the war on the side of the Entente Allies, irrespective of German submarine tactics. The support of this hypothesis is twofold.

First, there is convincing proof that sometime late in February, 1916, Wilson called into conference at the White House certain leaders of his party in Congress and intimated to them, to use the language of Hon. Thomas P. Gore, in a speech delivered in the Senate on March 2, 1916, that "if Germany insisted upon her position the United States would insist upon her position; that it would result probably in a breach of diplomatic relations; that a breach of diplomatic relations would be probably followed by a state of war; that a state of war might not be of itself and of necessity an evil, but that the United States by entering the war now might be able to bring it to a conclusion by midsummer and thus render a great service to civilization." In other words, in February, 1916, the President was contemplating war and sounded out his party in Congress to see whether his project was acceptable.

That he did at the time also sound the Entente Allies and suggest taking the United States into the war is conclusively demonstrated in the memoirs of Sir Edward Grey and Colonel House. Early in February, 1916, Wilson undertook, through the mediation of House, "on hearing from France and England that the moment was opportune," to propose a conference to end the war, and in case the Allies accepted and Berlin refused, "probably" to direct the United States into the struggle against Germany—all on the understanding that there was to be a fair settlement, including the restoration of Belgium, the transfer of Alsace-Lorraine to France, the assurance of a sea-outlet to Russia, and compensation to Germany by "concessions to her in other places outside Europe."

But England and France, having already agreed with their associates on a different division of the spoils and still confident that they could win without American aid and American interference at the peace table, declined to accede to the project for such a conference, thus taking upon themselves full responsibility for putting off American support in men, metal, and money until defeat threatened them. Again and again House and Wilson tried to get England to agree to action on the part of the President under the terms of this secret protocol, without avail until the renewal of the submarine warfare by Germany in 1917 and the peril of disaster at last made such coöperation imperative. In the light of these facts—which by the way illuminate all the ethical questions of the peace settlement and the debts—it cannot be denied that while "waging peace," President Wilson was revolving in his mind the question of his leadership and mission in world affairs, and kept revolving it until he finally broke with the German Empire.

§

On the opposing side the most cogent argument against the declaration of war was delivered by Senator La Follette of Wisconsin, one of the little group branded by Wilson as "willful" obstructionists. Considered in the large, the Senator's plea for peace fell into three general divisions. First in his bill of indictment was the contention that the administration had not pursued an impartial policy in dealing with Germany and England. The latter, he asserted, had begun the violation of American rights by unlawful orders, searches and seizures and by closing the open waters of the North Sea with deadly mines. Out of the illegal practices of England, German submarine tactics had sprung inevitably—even Germany's subsequent promises to abstain from sinking merchant ships without warning being based on the assumption that the United States would fetch England to book for her unlawful decrees and unlawful destruction of neutral trade.

Instead of bringing pressure upon the first wrongdoer, the President, continued the Senator, had departed from the traditions of America and from the path of justice by insisting that one of the belligerents should obey the rules of international justice while the other refused to be bound by them. It followed, therefore, that Germany was within her rights in resorting to retaliatory measures after failing to enforce upon England obedience to recognized law. But it was said that Germany had taken lives while England had merely stolen and destroyed property. The plea was specious, the Senator replied, because England, by sowing deadly contact mines in the open sea, had raised a menace as terrible as the submarine and had in fact destroyed American ships and American lives. Was the life of a sailor on a merchant vessel less precious than the life of a tourist or merchant or financier traveling in luxury on the Lusitania? So in spirit and in reality, La Follette declared, England as the original miscreant was even a greater offender than Germany against the law of nations and the rights of neutrals.

The second count in the Senator's argument pertained to the thesis that we were about to take up arms in a war to make the world safe for democracy against Prussian autocracy. What about England with its hereditary monarchy, its hereditary House of Lords, its hereditary landed system, its grinding poverty for wage workers, its dominion over Ireland, Egypt and India? asked the orator. Would we refuse to go to war if Russia were still ruled by a Tsar? What about the autocratic institutions of Japan, Italy, and the lesser European powers arrayed with us in this democratic crusade?

Passing, finally, from the ethics and embellishments of the case, La Follette declared that the people of the United States had never by their votes given the slightest countenance to the idea of plunging into the European conflict, that if the supporters of the war resolution dared to submit the issue to a referendum they would be defeated by a vote of ten to one. "The espionage bills, the conscription bills, and other forcible military measures which we understand are being ground out of the war machine in this country," urged the Senator, "are complete proof that those responsible for this war fear that it has no popular support and that armies sufficient to satisfy the demands of the entente allies cannot be recruited by voluntary enlistments." Such in brief was the case against the war filed in the court of opinion by the leading champion of peace in the Congress of the United States.

§

When hostilities were once declared gigantic economic and military tasks had to be undertaken. Nations were embattled, not simply armies of volunteers and mercenaries; before the war was over more than 3,700,000 American soldiers, including the marines, were under arms while not less than ten million adults were engaged in sustaining them on the firing line. "It is not an army that we must shape and train for war," said the President, "it is a nation."

And Congress gave Wilson power with a lavish hand, outlining statutes in broad terms and leaving him free to fill in the details at his own pleasure. In a series of the most remarkable laws ever enacted in Washington the whole economic system of the country was placed at his command. Under their provisions, the President was authorized to requisition supplies for the army without stint, to fix the prices of commodities so commanded, arrange a guarantee price for wheat, take possession of mines, factories, packing house, railways, steamships, and all means of communication and operate them through public agencies, and license the importation, manufacture, storage, and distribution of all necessities. For the actual exercise of these powers, many agencies were specifically established by Congress but the

President was authorized to consolidate, abolish, and establish bureaus, offices, and divisions in any fashion demanded by the exigencies of war. "We might as well abdicate and make the President a king," lamented a member of the Senate, but his wail changed no votes.

The dictatorial powers thus conferred on the President were extensively employed. Wheat was fixed at a figure far below the relative prices of the manufactured goods which the farmer had to buy. Railway, telegraph, telephone, and cable lines, express companies, and coastwise and high seas shipping were taken over by the government, and an Emergency Fleet Corporation was created to mobilize the ship-building forces of the country; the stocks of common carriers, long suffering under a drag, rebounding quickly in the hope of generous terms during occupancy. But cotton went free to catch the favors of a swelling market and the South was happy beyond measure, counting this boon from a Democratic President some atonement for fifty years of Republican high protection. To assume the new functions, innumerable agencies were organized; and hundreds of captains of industry flocked to Washington to serve their country at the rate of one dollar a year.

In mobilizing men and materials for war, a sincere effort was made to avoid the scandals which had marred previous armed conflicts: numerous contracts for supplies were made on the basis of cost plus a reasonable commission, an idea alluring but expensive. Although the type of fraud that had been perpetrated in earlier days when contracts were let on the lump-sum principle was thus avoided, other evils scarcely less distressing were called into being. Under the cost-plus system no one was interested in economy; if the producer of raw materials raised his prices, the war contractor could smile and pass on the extra charge with an increase in his commission. If a trade union struck for higher wages, the manufacture could grant the demand with a friendly shrug for the additional expense meant a larger commission garnered from the beneficent government. Only the wheat growers suffered severely in this procedure, their commodity being held down to a low level whereas the prices of nearly all other essentials went shooting to the sky. So the war led by a Democratic President strengthened his opposition by making several thousand millionaires in the course of two years and by pouring out billions in extra dividends frequently in the form of stock, thereby enabling holders in effect to escape taxes on income. Only the stanchest patriots could restrain their emotions as they contemplated the possibilities of the economic scene.

In only one respect, namely taxation, did the beneficiaries of war prosperity suffer grave disappointment. If former practices had been followed, the bills incurred by such lavish expenditures would have been met from the sale of bonds bearing a high rate of interest and discharged at last by indirect taxes on consumption. This had been in the main the fiscal procedure adopted by the directors of the federal government at the time of the Civil War and the Spanish-American struggle; but during the populist surge of the intervening years, political manners had changed. In radical quarters the demand was now pressed for "the conscription of money as well as men." Indeed it was frankly urged that the entire cost of the war should be charged up to possessors of large fortunes and that all the special gains and benefits accruing from war business should be taken from profiteers by taxation.

Although extreme counsels did not prevail, Congress laid heavy, progressive taxes on incomes and inheritances and burdensome levies upon the excess profits of corporations and partnerships. In spite of the fact that many marvelous schemes were devised by lawyers and accountants for absorbing the shock, including the ingenious device of issuing new stock in lieu of dividends, a weight of taxation that would have seemed revolutionary to the age of Lincoln fell upon the rich and the comfortable during the war for democracy. "This," exclaimed the leading authority on the subject, Professor Edwin R. A. Seligman, speaking of the upper range of the tax structure, "is the high water mark thus far reached in the history of taxation. Never before in the history of civilization has an attempt been made to take as much as two-thirds of a man's income by taxation."

The levy was not only serious; it was prophetic, foretelling a day not far distant when both the great political parties would endorse the demand of the American Legion for a universal draft act "to place at the disposal of the government, without profit to any one person, the men, money, and material resources of the nation." If the radicals did not have their way in 1917 they flung a dash of bitters into the cup of industrial and financial barons, by showing how in a crisis the sacred right of private property to collect all the revenues the traffic can bear might disappear in a wave of nationalization.

In the sacrificial ardor of 1917, however, all profits were not lost, for the major portion of the current expenses during the war years was met by the sale of interest-bearing securities—not by direct levies on accumulated and accumulating fortunes. Counting the Victory Loan of April, 1919, five great blocks of bonds were floated, making a total of $21,448,120,300, each of them on severe terms that would have astounded the bankers of the Civil War period. Only the first of these issues, the smallest in amount, conceded the sweeping exemption from taxation which had been customary in national loans; the others, while granting favors to small holders, carried liabilities for federal taxes under specific rules. Moreover the bonds were not sold through syndicates on a generous commission basis, but "over the counter" with specific compensation for financiers.

In the popular "drives" the whole nation was invited to share—and recalcitrants were compelled to join. To float the loans, every engine of social control was brought into play: banks, churches, industrial plants, theaters, moving picture shows, associations and societies of every type, as well as public-spirited individuals, sales agents, and organizers. All the vociferous advertising methods so characteristic of American business in general were mobilized to force each issue "over the top." Not a latent sentiment of loyalty, fear, love, or hate was left unstirred. Immense posters bearing the imprint of a bloody hand and carrying the legend, "The Hun, his Mark. Blot it out with Liberty Bonds," were flung upon the hoardings to move one type of investor. Streamers bearing the inscription, "Ask his Mother How Many Bonds You Should Buy," appealed to another class.

No person, native born, naturalized, or alien, escaped the universal dragnet. Workmen in factories, farmers in fields, clerks in stores, members of lodges, children in school, bank depositors, government employees, travelers on trains, pedestrians in the streets, were all invited, besieged, and belabored to "buy until it hurts." Whoever refused to answer the call was liable to be blacklisted by his neighbors or associates and enrolled in the Doom Book in the Department of Justice as a potential traitor to his country. The sovereignty of the war passion admitted no exceptions. Nationalism was in full flower.

§

These material activities were merely a phase of the general mobilization of the whole people in a conflict which, until April 6, 1917, had been stanchly opposed by a large part of them. About one week after the declaration of war, President Wilson organized a committee on public information for the purpose of "selling the war to America." At the head of this agency, he placed George Creel, a versatile journalist of socialist affiliations, well fitted accordingly to reach critics and malcontents. Under Creel's directions, masters of the printed word, adepts in advertising, university professors, facile magazine writers, and popular novelists were enrolled in regimented ranks assigned to "educating" the United States and in turn deluging the world with American propaganda.

To the necessities of this campaign, trained historians bent their supple discipline while the sciences and arts rendered their full tribute to the cause. With the higher mental order thus arranged, the entire school system of the country was easily brought into line with mechanical precision, subduing even the minds of tender children to the official thesis concerning the origins and merits of the contest. Bulletins, tracts, leaflets, and flyers in all languages by the billions were poured out in unending streams. Heavy, documented articles were devised by men of learning for the intellectuals; pungent sayings and slogans were invented to supply substance for the less sophisticated.

Never before in history had such a campaign of education been organized; never before had American citizens realized how thoroughly, how irresistibly a modern government could impose its ideas upon the whole nation and, under a barrage of publicity, stifle dissent with declarations, assertions, official versions, and reiteration. Organized to sell the war to a divided and confused nation, the committee on public information succeeded beyond all expectations.

With adversaries who were not convinced or cowed by its publicity campaign, the government dealt mercilessly under drastic statutes. In June, 1917, Congress passed the Espionage Act, laying heavy penalties on all persons who interfered in any way with the effective mobilization of the military and naval forces of the nation. Not content with the sweeping provisions of this law, the President asked and received from Congress a still more severe measure, the Sedition Act of May, 1918, a statute which in effect made any criticism of the Wilson administration illegal.

Though this measure surpassed in violence the Sedition Law of 1798, so hotly denounced by Thomas Jefferson, it was enacted without difficulty. It is true that twenty-four Republicans and two Democrats voted against it in the Senate; it is true also that a few independent Senators, such as William E. Borah and Hiram Johnson, condemned it as unconstitutional and unnecessary; but the pressure of the

administration could not be stayed. An attempt was likewise made to lay on the press the iron hand of an official
censorship but associated editors, unlike unorganized and
inert citizens, were able to defeat that design. Yet theirs
was a bootless victory as practice showed, for under the
general terms of the Espionage and Sedition acts, newspapers were continually silenced by orders and prosecutions.
Individual critics of the war and the Wilson program were
rounded up by the government, often without warrants of
arrest, hustled to jail, held incommunicado without bail,
tried in courts where the atmosphere was heavily charged
with passion, lectured by irate judges, and sent to prison for
long terms—in one case an adolescent girl for twenty
years.

Armed with the elastic provisions of the penal statutes,
the various branches of government, national and state,
that could find a color of justification, set in motion machines
of inquiry and arraignment. The Departments of War,
Navy, State, and the Post Office created "intelligence" agencies which directed professional and amateur detectives in
collecting and filing information of every kind concerning
citizens of every class, ranging from radical members of
the Industrial Workers of the World to simple-minded
professors who entertained philosophic doubts about the
plenary authenticity of the canon delivered to President
Wilson. Under the direction of A. S. Burleson of Austin,
Texas, the Postoffice Department found the defeat of the
censorship bill no bar to the suppression of newspapers that
failed to measure up to its standards of propriety and taste.
In the War Department an army of clerks and investigators
assembled mountains of "data" bearing on the opinions of
private persons; a swivel-chair chauvinist, thrown up from
obscurity for an hour and drawing a dollar a year for his
services, gave to the press under the color of dubious
official authority a long list of citizens branded as traitors
in his own patriotic eyes.

Naturally the great burden of work under the Espionage

and Sedition acts fell upon the Department of Justice, a small bureau of investigation, erected in Roosevelt's administration, being transformed into a nation-wide spy system, with millions of money and thousands of employees at its service. Judging by its official reports, the main business of the Department was not the apprehension of the people who gave aid and comfort to the Central Powers with which the country was at war but rather the supervision of American citizens suspected of radical opinions about the perfection and perpetuity of the capitalist system of economy at home. According to authentic evidence, every practice dear to the Russian police of the old régime was employed by federal agents: provocative "tools" were "planted" among organizations of humble working people, supposed to have dangerous tendencies, and were instructed to incite them to unlawful acts; meeting places of such associations were raided without proper warrant, property was destroyed, papers seized, innocent bystanders beaten, and persons guilty of no offense at all rushed off to jail, subjected to police torture, held without bail, and released without recourse.

To the official army of the grand inquest was added a still greater force of more than two hundred thousand private citizens enrolled by the Department of Justice in the work of watching neighbors. To these volunteers no test of intelligence or efficiency was applied; any person, man or woman, willing to play the rôle of informer was admitted to the fellowship. So in offices, factories, mines, mills, churches, homes, schools, restaurants, trains, ships, ferries, and stores, government watchers could be found listening to conversations, insinuating and suggesting, noting prattle and tattle, and reporting "findings" to Washington to be filed in huge dossiers of "information"—recalling the fateful days of 1692 in Salem.

Private associations and societies conformed to the prevailing mood of the bureaucracy. From institutions of higher learning, professors were expelled, frequently on evidence that would not convict a notorious cut-purse in normal times, Columbia University leading off in this kind of "purification." "It is very difficult to discharge professors once employed," wrote A. Barton Hepburn, the banker-philanthrophist on its board of trustees. "They make common cause and howl about academic freedom. We have had trouble along this line in Columbia where they taught sedition and disloyalty and that enabled us to get rid of eight or ten at the time." Clergymen were unfrocked and sent to prison for overemphasizing the Sermon on the Mount. Members of clubs were ostracized for failure to conform.

And yet when all these immense inquisitorial activities were sifted down to the very bottom, only two conclusions of significance remained. The first is that not a single first-class German spy or revolutionary workingman was caught and convicted of an overt act designed to give direct aid or comfort to the enemy. The second is that, as in England during the period of the French Revolution, the occasion of the war which called for patriotic duties was seized by emotional conservatives as an opportunity to blacken the character of persons whose opinions they feared and hated.

Undoubtedly the great body of citizens would have given the Wilson war administration unstinted support without the whip of coercion. Even in the ranks of labor, where hostility to the doctrines of the established order is usually most marked, opponents of the war gained few recruits. No doubt, the proletarian revolution in Russia in November, 1917, caused a flurry in radical circles and alarmed old ladies and gentlemen at their tea and cakes but it made no perceptible drag on the mobilization of national forces for the war. Hitherto pacifist in profession, the Socialists split asunder and grew more and more impotent as the days lengthened into the months; a small faction, adhering to the Marxian creed, denounced the conflict as a capitalist quarrel but an equally able group of leaders lent their pens and voices to the government in the prosecution of "the war for democracy to end war." At all events, organized labor stood firmly behind the President. Speaking in the name of the American Federation, Samuel Gompers declared that "this is labor's war," pleading for the undivided support of all the bodies under his jurisdiction.

In return, union labor was given a high position in national affairs. Besides being granted representation on important boards and commissions in charge of industrial relations, its standards for hours and wages were generally accepted and widely applied. While the Department of Labor, headed by a trade unionist, spared no efforts in stimulating the loyalty of workers in mills, mines, and factories, their demands for higher wages to meet the mounting costs of living were granted with an alacrity that amazed the veterans of stubborn battles, who could recall the scenes at Homestead and Pullman. As labor became more revolutionary in Europe, during the course of the war, the importance of conciliating it temporarily in America loomed especially large in the minds of government officials and industrial captains.

In this war of arms, industry, and politics, the women of the nation, like the men, were completely absorbed. As in Napoleon's time, as we have seen, the bayonet had been thrust into the hands of the common man together with the ballot, making war democratic and national, so in the age of industry and equal suffrage, the age of belligerent economic titans, all services short of fighting in the trenches fell to the lot of women and were radiantly accepted by them. In the Civil War they had served as nurses, organized hospital relief, furnished supplies for the wounded, flocked to the factories that made war materials, labored on the farms, and participated in charity drives.

In the World War, they did all these things and more. Now organized in clubs and associations of a thousand varieties, they were easily drawn individually and collectively into the main war currents. They established all-women hospital units; they acted as doctors, nurses, ambulance drivers, camouflage artists, propagandists, entertainers, hostesses at canteens and dance halls, spies at home and abroad, members of government defense and war committees of all kinds, and informers under the Sedition Act—in short in every capacity save that of the soldier at the battle front, foreshadowing, perhaps, the day when equal opportunity will have no limitations or exceptions even there.

§

While capital, materials, opinion, labor, and women were mobilizing for the gigantic struggle, the army and navy were being organized to carry the weight of the United States to the battle lines of Europe. At the outbreak of the war, the general public was in doubt about the best method for providing man power for the front. Although Old World experience pointed to universal service as the inexorable solution of the problem, American tradition ran against military compulsion as an aid to patriotism. Only as a last resort had conscription been accepted during the Civil War and the enforcement of the draft at that time had been the occasion for desperate rioting in New York City and bitter opposition in other quarters.

If, however, any one high in authority felt inclined to appeal to history in the spring of 1917, he was quickly overruled. President Wilson immediately crystalized vague and fluid ideas by declaring in favor of conscription; all the more readily because volunteering for the regular army did not proceed with expected rapidity and the grim business ahead as unfolded by daily bulletins admitted of no temporizing. "The whole nation," said the President, "must be a team in which each man shall play the part for which he is best fitted." Under his direction Congress, by an act of May 18, 1917, provided that the military and naval forces for the war should be recruited by lot from among the adult males of the land, excluding alien enemies, between the ages of twenty-one and thirty inclusive—limits which were extended the next year to eighteen and forty-five. This decree, calling the entire manhood of the country to the colors, was accepted by the people of every section and so smoothly administered that it surprised all prophets of adversity.

Effective coöperation with the Associated Powers, the great goal for which national energies were being mobilized, was facilitated by expert assistance. As soon as the proprieties admitted, Allied commissions appeared in Washington with the Rt. Hon. Arthur James Balfour and General Joffre as the most impressive leaders. The former with the quiet dignity of an English gentleman captivated those members of the public who had the privilege of meeting him personally; when he turned aside from diplomacy to confess his faith in a personal God, the efficacy of prayer, and the immortality of the soul, he linked himself with hooks of steel to the great heart of America. He was cheered to the echo when he declared at the Chamber of Commerce in New York City that "since August, 1914, the fight has been for the highest spiritual advantages of mankind and without a petty thought or ambition." His colleague, General Joffre, hero of the Marne, though reserved, paternal, circumspect, and given to silence on momentous matters, was also received with tumultuous acclaim by the masses for his martial glory.

In quiet conferences with President Wilson, these commissioners described the desperate plight of the Entente Allies and demonstrated the imperative need for immediate help with money, supplies, and men at the front. In response, loans running into the billions were granted with alacrity, and provisions made for united action in controlling world trade and pouring an unbroken stream of materials into the Allied countries, in spite of the submarine menace, then growing deadlier every hour.

"Send us American soldiers!" was the universal cry from the Associates of the United States. "Let the American flag be unfurled on the fields of France and let the tramp of American armies thrill anew the worn spirits of those who have borne the brunt of battle for three long years." So it was decided to dispatch at the earliest possible moment contingents from the regular army and the state militia mustered into national service.

Resolutely putting aside a plea that Colonel Roosevelt be placed at the head of an advance guard of soldiers, Wilson chose as commander of the American expeditionary forces, General John J. Pershing, who had seen service in the Philippines and had directed the recent punitive invasion into Mexico. In June, General Pershing went to France to prepare the way for the coming hosts, followed in a few days by the first units of the regular forces which marched through the streets of Paris as a pledge of America's determination. Until the draft army was ready, of course, the transport of forces was inevitably slow, but in the opening weeks of 1918 the tiny current became a torrent; by July a million American soldiers were on the scene of action. When at last in November the curtain was rung down on the world tragedy, the number had doubled, belieing the contemptuous prophecies of German critics and astounding the world by the miracle wrought through the transformation of America into a fighting machine.

Naturally the posture of military affairs decided the disposition of American forces along the front. The English held the western section near their base of supplies; the heart of France was concentrated on the defense of Paris; accordingly the most tranquil section toward the east was first assigned to the American associates. With incredible swiftness a huge American war mechanism was created on the basis of this arrangement, with its chief port of entry at Bordeaux and its headquarters at Chaumont, below Verdun. Slowly the regular soldiers, forerunners of the draft army, as soon as their elementary instruction in the arts of local warfare permitted, were filtered into the trenches. By October, 1917, a few of them were on the firing line;

in November they had their first severe clash with the enemy.

After a winter of such cautious preparations, General Pershing, now strengthened by increasing forces from America, was ready to work effectively with General Foch in breaking the shock of the mighty German offensive launched in March. Again in the summer when General Ludendorf's last desperate drive threw the French and Allied forces back upon the Marne, American soldiers at Château-Thierry, Belleau Wood, and other points along the flaming line played well their part in the awful fighting that turned the tide of battle. In September, with French assistance, they wiped out the German salient at Saint Mihiel and then joined in the fierce surge from the mountains to the Channel that burst wide the gates of victory.

On the ocean, American coöperation with the Allied powers, though less spectacular, proceeded with equal resolve. Already aware that the crash was imminent, President Wilson, in March, 1917, sent Admiral Sims, whose English descent on his mother's side made him peculiarly acceptable, across the sea to prepare the way for united action and on May 4 American destroyers steamed into Queenstown. Meanwhile the manufacture of submarine chasers and scout cruisers was hastened in American shipyards; recruiting and training of the naval forces were carried on with high speed; and new types of deadly contact-mines were turned out by the shipload. In protecting the American coast, in patrolling the war zones for submarines, in sowing mines through the North Sea, in bombing submarine bases, and in convoying troop ships, the American navy rose to the requirements of the combat. When at length the long conflict was over and the armistice was proclaimed on November 11, 1918, more than three hundred American war vessels and seventy-five thousand sailors were operating in European waters.

§

Besides economic might and military power, new social and intellectual forces were thrown into the balance. In days of old when kings made war with mercenary armies, no grand proclamation of aims and purposes was required; the royal will was made known and good subjects obeyed. That was the state of affairs when the French Revolution altered the face of politics, thrusting the ballot and the bayonet into the hands of peasants, hairdressers, and carters, and making it expedient, on summoning them to arms, to accompany the call by a declaration of principles answering to their moral aspirations. In this service the resourcefulness of the human mind never failed. Napoleon was pastmaster of the publicity art and his successors imitated him at a distance. When the statesmen of Europe blindly blundered into war in the summer of 1914, as Lloyd George, who sat at the council table of the great, bluntly described the tragedy in after years, belligerent managers on both sides engaged an army of philosophers and scribes to formulate convincing reasons for each turn in affairs, manufacturing in this fashion a literature that was immense and imaginative.

In addition to designing moral patterns for popular use, European statesmen in charge of the war had also to agree upon more substantial objectives. Of course there was little doubt about the character of the settlement that the German militarists would have imposed upon the world if victory had perched upon their banners; out of their historic past and out of their mouths they stood confessed—the treaty of Brest-Litovsk forced on Russia revealing in drastic terms in 1918 the range of their ambitions. It was not even necessary for the Central Powers to enter into secret understandings as to the division of the booty to be acquired; they formed a solid bloc under German dominion.

But the case of the Entente Allies was different in that no single power was dominant. Italy, for example, had been brought into the war only by heroic bargaining which resulted in a secret treaty stating exactly what her reward was to be; and all the Associates were afraid of defections induced by favorable offers from the enemy. To make sure of their unity, therefore, the diplomats of France, England, Russia, and Japan in 1915 set projects for distributing the spoils, on the fine old Roman principle of "Woe to the Vanquished!" If the Bolsheviki had not torn open the secret archives of Petrograd and flung the documents in the face of mankind in December, 1917, these plighted war aims of the Entente Allies would have remained unknown perhaps forever and their official hypothesis would have been questioned only by the cynical at home or abroad. But the Russian Revolution made the facts public property, enabling the generation that fought the war to get its sources and origins straight from authentic records. This was a novel chapter in the story of diplomacy.

To these European understandings America had been no party. President Wilson privately believed that both embattled hosts were fighting for the same thing, namely, to relieve historic grudges and gain material advantages. It was this conviction, as we have said, founded on no mean knowledge, that kept him aloof in the early years of the war while hysterical compatriots raged around the White House.

But, as he watched the smoke and flames of burning Europe month after month, the President came to certain general conclusions relative to the kind of settlement that ought to be made—long before he threw the American sword into the scales. These conclusions he expounded in a peace address before the Senate in January, 1917: recognition of the rights of small nations, independence of Poland, government by consent of the governed, freedom of the seas, outlets to water for landlocked countries, and a concert of powers to preserve the peace of the world. By the managers of Europe this address, in which lay the germs of the President's later program, was greeted with doubts and derision. The thundering editor of the London Daily

Mail laughed loud and long at this "abstract pontifical statement of a future international morality."

Yet water flowed swiftly under the bridge. In less than a year, while the decision on the battle fronts still hung in the balance, the Russian Revolution of November, 1917, shook the social order of Europe to its very foundations, making the whole earth vibrate with the tramp of the proletariat and tremble at the most daring call for a universal uprising against governments issued to mankind since the French Declaration of Rights in 1789. At once it became evident that Russia could be held in line and the war morale of Germany undermined only by liberal statements of a democratic policy flatly contradicting the imperialistic aims hidden in the secret treaties of the Allied Powers.

It was then that President Wilson, renewing his former professions, came to the rescue of his hard-pressed associates of little faith. In the tempestuous days of January, 1918, when the Bolsheviki were staggering before the harsh terms proposed by the imperial governments of Germany and Austria at Brest-Litovsk, Edgar Sisson, representative of the American committee on public information at Petrograd, cabled to George Creel, its director in Washington, a request that the President "restate the anti-imperialistic war aims and democratic peace requisites of America, thousand words or less, short, almost placard paragraphs, short sentences." If the President would do this, Sisson added, he could "get it fed into Germany in great quantities in German translation and utilize Russian version potently in army and everywhere." Five days later Wilson went before Congress and proclaimed his Fourteen Points in ringing periods that flew on the wings of lightning to the remote corners of the earth, even into Korea, Cambodia, Siam, India, the Philippines, and the Islands of the South Seas— wherever subject peoples were ruled by imperial powers.

Briefly digested these articles of political faith embraced the following items: open diplomacy, freedom of the seas, removal of hampering trade barriers among nations, reduccion of armaments, adjustment of colonial claims in the interests of the populations involved, fair treatment for Russia, restoration of Belgium, righting the wrong done to France in 1871, adjustment of Italian frontiers on principles of nationalism, more autonomy for the peoples of the Austro-Hungarian empire, restoration of Rumania and Serbia, an independent Poland, reorganization of the Turkish empire, and finally an association of nations to uphold a peaceful world order.

Such was the American creed formulated by the spokesman for the nation and received with a shout of approval from coast to coast, except in conservative and radical circles where such lofty sentiments were viewed with equal suspicion. Like drowning men grasping at straws, responsible statesmen among the Entente Allies gave their sanction to the Wilsonian formulas "in principle"—privately subject to discreet and appropriate reservations. With revolutionary doctrines thus phrased and approved, the people of the Central Powers, soldiers and civilians, were drenched in a propaganda for liberty and democracy, warning them that they were fighting for imperialist masters against governments that offered them a peace of justice and freedom. Assailed by Bolshevik propaganda from the East, filtering into the army by fraternization, and by no less effective propaganda from the West, the flame of German ardor was slowly dampened down.

§

Yet it would be a mistake to lay too much stress on the achievements of this indoctrination. It was the weight of materials rather than of words that defeated Germany and Austria. On August 14, 1918, Ludendorf, according to secret papers now unfolded, confessed to his imperial master that the great game was over, that German armies were beaten, and that the one remaining task was to wring from the victors the best possible terms.

At first the discomfited directors of the German government thought of sounding out the Entente powers through the good offices of some neutral country but, as days wore on and the raging hail of steel and fire and gas beat on their western front with increasing severity, they conceived the idea of appealing directly to Wilson in the language of his Fourteen Points. By way of preparation, they admitted a large number of the Socialists to their council, introduced the English parliamentary system of government, and called a mild liberal, Prince Max of Baden, to the imperial chancellorship. Now, they said, since the German people rule in place of an autocracy, let us have an armistice followed by a peace fashioned after the doctrines of liberty and democracy laid down by the President of the United States. In a startling call sent to Wilson through the mediation of Switzerland, on October 5, 1918, the new German government asked him to take steps to end the war because, forsooth, the principles proclaimed by him were in accord with the "general ideas cherished by the new German government and with it the overwhelming majority of our people." Prince Max afterwards admitted that he had no faith in Wilson's ability to fulfill his pledges but he thought that the opportunity for embarrassing the great pacificator was not to be missed.

Amid trying circumstances Wilson faced the test of his hypothesis. In formulating American moral principles into linguistic patterns, he was his own master but on the field of battle the army of the United States was only one among many. Moreover, when it came to laying down the exact conditions of an armistice, political theories had to descend to concrete realities: there had to be precision in terms of men, money, munitions, and movements of troops. In this sphere it was General Foch, responsible head of the Allied and associated armies, who was the natural master of ceremonies. Now this seasoned soldier, who did not take the Fourteen Points at face value, showed no signs of a hurried belief in German conversion to democracy and certainly wanted no revolution across the Rhine anyway. So for more than a month the discussion of provisional conditions for peace went on while the German armies in France crumbled before the relentless drive of the Allied and associated forces.

On all sides, in fact, the Central Powers were revealing a fatal weakness. At the end of September, Bulgaria had surrendered unconditionally. Late in October, Austria, after suffering ruinous reverses on the Italian front, begged for peace, and on November 3 laid down her arms. Two days later President Wilson transmitted draconian armistice terms, drawn by military men, to the authorities in Berlin where revolution had already raised its red specter.

In this crisis, the German Kaiser, still undefeated in his ambitions, proposed to use his soldiers on the wavering civilians in the rear, only to find that even his choicest men had no stomach for such an enterprise. Confronted by an implacable foe and deserted by his weary nation, he laid down the insignia of his imperial office and fled with the Crown Prince to personal safety in Holland. On the morning of November 11, at eleven o'clock, the armistice went into effect and the roll of guns that had thundered along the front for four agonizing years died away. A tumult of thanksgiving surged throughout the world, even the Germans finding crumbs of comfort in the fact that there was to be no triumphal march of victors into Berlin.

§

Wilson now had to meet the greatest crisis of his life— and without the support of a united country. At the congressional elections held a few days before the armistice the American voters, spurning his appeal for a Democratic House of Representatives to sustain his hand in negotiating peace on his avowed principles, had returned a majority of Republicans after a savage campaign in which many outstanding leaders had demanded the unconditional surrender of Germany, a Spartan peace for the vanquished, and the utter rejection of the proposed league of nations. "In no other free country in the world today would Mr. Wilson be in office," was the taunt flung at the President on the eve of his departure for the peace conference in France, a taunt taken up with glee by the imperialist press of London and Paris.

On his arrival in Europe to realize the dream of his Fourteen Points, President Wilson was, therefore, a broken instrument compelled by fate to engage in high diplomatic combat with the most astute politicians thrown to the top in the volcanic upheaval of the war, everyone sustained by powerful chauvinistic passions at home. To them it made little difference if the President was acclaimed by the radical masses everywhere as the Moses of the new day who was to lead them away from the bloody sands of the European desert to the promised land of peace or if, on his journey through England, France, and Italy with Mrs. Wilson at his side, he received a triumphal ovation that would have turned the head of a Cæsar or a Napoleon.

When Wilson reached Paris in the early days of December with a veritable army of American experts in history, geography, economics, and diplomacy, and four commissmissioners chosen by him to serve as his aides, he found his Entente associates—Lloyd George of England, Clemenceau of France, and Orlando of Italy—unready for immediate action, while the manager of the Japanese delegation was engrossed in reading French novels. Knowing that the singing masses would soon lose their fervor and shift to new attractions, these experienced statesmen played safely for delay. As a result of this strategy more than a month was allowed to elapse before the plenary peace council of the thirty-two victorious belligerents met formally, on January 18—to receive the information that all important business would be transacted by a supreme council composed of the representatives of the United States, Great Britain, France, Italy, and Japan.

When eventually the diplomats got down to determining boundaries and distributing goods, a contest of wits commenced—a contest held behind closed doors at Wilson's request, with the ready acquiescence of his colleagues. As time passed and the antagonisms around the council table grew sharper, the supreme council narrowed down still further. Assured in the matter of Shantung, Japan dropped out; and Orlando, angered by Wilson's flat refusal to yield to Italy's intransigent demands, withdrew amid the cheers of his countrymen. So in the end, "the big three"—Lloyd George, Clemenceau, and Wilson—in their private chambers shaped the significant clauses for the voluminous treaty of peace, including the section putting the responsibility for starting the war on the Central Powers. The German delegation, on June 28, 1919, having filed vigorous protests, entered the Hall of Mirrors in the palace of Versailles, the scene of the Hohenzollern triumph in 1871, to sign on the dotted line. In due course Austria, Hungary, Bulgaria, and Turkey were also brought to book.

The details of the grand settlement were spread over many pages but the principles of historic importance were few and simple. Like all such human arrangements, the outcome was in some respects a compromise. Certain elements of the Fourteen Points were realized: for example, nine independent states, most of them in eastern Europe, were called into being under the principle of self-determination and Alsace-Lorraine was restored to France. The boundaries of Italy, Greece, Rumania, Serbia, Belgium, and Denmark were enlarged on the theory of nationality, with many glaring violations of the creed. Germany was reduced in size and power and Austria-Hungary broken up. While conforming in some respects to the Wilsonian doctrines, these arrangements added to the security and strength of France without jeopardizing, at least immediately, any British interests.

In the distribution of imperial spoils slight concessions were made to Wilson's feelings. Germany's former colonies in all parts of the world were transferred to the victors, merely as mandates to be held under the League of Nations as "a sacred trust for civilization." The Saar Valley, purely German in population but possessed of rich coal fields, was assigned to France simply for temporary exploitation. Shantung, wrested from Germany by Japan, was won by the diplomats of Tokyo, against the loud protests of the Peking delegation, only under a promise of ultimate return to China, later carried out to the letter under interesting circumstances. But in the main and substantially, the arrangement of boundaries and the division of booty outlined in the famous Secret Treaties of 1915 were realized in the Versailles treaty—with a noteworthy exception. Russia, given no voice in the council chamber at Paris, did not receive the share originally allotted to her; on the contrary the territory of the old Russian Empire was cut and carved at will by the mapmakers of the supreme council. Subject to these limitations, the proceedings at Paris ran true to careful plans and immemorial usage.

Nothing was omitted that promised to break the power of Germany as a competitor in the markets of the world. Her navy was turned over to the victors. Her army was reduced to a negligible figure. She was deprived of her colonies, her merchant marine, her property in foreign lands, and her trading bases and banks in all parts of the world. Under the guise of reparations, including the cost of pensions for the veterans of the Allied armies and their families, the Germans were forced to pledge themselves to payments totaling in the end about thirty-three billion gold dollars, a staggering sum that made the punitive indemnities of earlier settlements seem pitiably small.

In short, the law of vengeance was to be applied. By way of preliminary, Lloyd George had said: "In substance the Allies have one common principle which I once set forth thus: 'Germany must pay up to the last farthing of her power,'" a prophecy that neatly foretold the results of the peace conference on the point. Finally, to complete the picture the Germans were compelled to acknowledge that on the Central Powers rested the full responsibility for bringing upon humanity the curse of the World War—a solemn declaration that must have brought an exquisite smile to the lips of Lloyd George and Clemenceau as they thought of the secret archives in London and Paris.

In this great bargain President Wilson got no indemnities and no territory for the United States, nothing comparable to McKinley's winnings in 1898. In fulfillment of his principles, he sought no national gains. Looking to the long future, he labored rather with unbending will and great stress of spirit to secure agreement on a plan for a League of Nations, counting all temporary provisions as minor matters to be adjusted in the coming Parliament of Man. Keeping always before him that more distant ideal—suggested to him by Sir Edward Grey through the instrumentality of Colonel House—the President contested every inch of the ground in Paris, once even going so far as to threaten a rupture of negotiations by ordering his steamer to make ready for departure. Undoubtedly his perplexity was deep. If he had defiantly refused to make any prime concessions to the diplomacy of historic subtraction and division, he would have pleased a little band of faithful liberals at home, but by the same token he would have brought down upon his head the wrath of an army of Republicans bent on the ruin of Germany and the recovery of power at Washington. So in the end, the President made his choice and completed the treaty, reckoning the settlement with the Central Powers, however open to criticism, as lighter in the balance than a pledge of perpetual peace. Weltgeschichte, as the Germans say, ist Weltgericht; and long after all now living are in their graves the far judgment of destiny may be rendered on this man.

§

The Covenant of the League of Nations incorporated in the structure of the treaty and brought home by the Presi-

dent provided for the creation of three permanent international agencies: a Secretariat, finally located at Geneva;
an Assembly consisting of one deputy from each nation, dominion, and self-governing colony; and a grand Council
composed of representatives from the United States, Great
Britain, France, Italy, and Japan and four other representatives selected from time to time by the assembly. Numerous and weighty were the duties imposed on the League and
the obligations accepted by its members. All the associated
powers bound themselves to respect one another's territorial
integrity and to coöperate in preserving it against external
aggression. They agreed to submit to arbitration or inquiry by the Council every dispute that could not be adjusted
by diplomacy; on no account were they to resort to arms
until three months after the decision of that tribunal and in
case the verdict was unanimous they were bound to abide
by it. If any member declined to observe its covenants,
drastic retaliation could be lawfully invoked; the refusal
was to be viewed as an act of war against the League, the
trade of the offending member could be cut off, and the
Council after deliberation could recommend to the associated governments the military measures to be adopted.
At last a World Parliament, so celebrated in prose and
poetry, seemed within a measurable distance of realization.

On submitting this program to the judgment of the American people, champions of the new order encountered a
hostility which dazed those who thought the war had been
waged to end war. During the longdrawn proceedings at
Paris the air had been filled with discordant notes and when
the treaty finally appeared, the forces of opposition, conservative and radical, coalesced in shouting a mighty negative. With grim determination Wilson's adversaries carried their battle into the Senate, now in Republican hands,
where under the Constitution a two-thirds vote was necessary to the ratification of the Versailles document.

Inevitably, therefore, the affections and hatreds of domestic partisanship were injected into the discussion of the

great international issue; and according to time-honored custom, opinions on the merits of the treaty were scattered along the political line from right to left. A small group of "irreconcilables," mainly Republicans, would have nothing but quick and unqualified rejection; a body of Democrats, closely marshaled under Wilson's rule of unquestioning obedience, demanded ratification without material change; while between these two uncompromising regiments were strung at varying intervals the advocates of ratification subject to amendments, reservations, or interpretations. Some of the moderates were prominent Republicans like Elihu Root, William Howard Taft, and George W. Wickersham, well-known advocates of peace; others were Democrats entertaining doubts.

With political forces so divided there was bound to be a long and bitter contest and it came with a startling impact. From every angle the Versailles settlement was assailed. German sympathizers attacked it for the severe terms imposed upon the vanquished. Irish sympathizers advanced upon it because it gave representation to the self-governing dominions of Great Britain while offering no sign of recognition to Ireland, then deep in her struggle for independence. On the other hand, if some thought the burdens laid upon Germany too heavy, or the claims of Ireland shamefully neglected, perhaps as many were discontented because the rights of America and American citizens had received too little attention in the gathering up of the fragments at Paris.

But the heaviest barrage of fire was concentrated on the Covenant of the League of Nations by those who clung to the American doctrine of isolation. The project, ran the argument of this party, would involve America in European entanglements, by binding the government to coöperate with other powers in maintaining the independence and integrity of all members associated in the League; it would erect a super-state that might invade the domestic interests of the United States, such for example, as the control of immigration; it would impose a moral obligation on our government to take part "in the disturbances, conflicts, settlements, and wars of Europe and Asia"; it would lay the same obligation on other countries to concern themselves in the affairs of the Western Hemisphere.

Nor did the personal tactics pursued by President Wilson from the beginning have a mollifying effect on political passions. Departing from all precedents, he had gone to the Paris conference himself, taking no member of the Senate, not even one of the Republican majority, with him to the peace table. He had practically ignored the four men who did accompany him, with the possible exception of Colonel House, and had assumed the whole burden of responsibility for the final settlement, in effect inviting his enemies to transfer to his handiwork the full brunt of their animosity against him and his domestic policies.

Moreover, during the negotiation of the treaty, the Senate itself had been neglected, receiving from Wilson no conciliatory messages. Worse than that; on the completion of the document, copies of it found their way into the hands of bankers and journalists before the Senators were given a glimpse of the text, an ominous incident; and as if to increase partisan tension, already high, Wilson addressed Senators in reference to the treaty with an air of finality not calculated to soothe the opposition. "The stage is set," he said; "the destiny disclosed. It has come about by no plan of our conceiving, but by the hand of God who led us into this war." Though willing to allow "interpretations" of particular clauses, the President would accept no essential changes in the great structure he had helped to erect. He now endeavored, it is true, to disarm his critics in the Senate by personal conferences but his efforts in that direction were too late and too evidently marred by appearances of awkwardness and restraint.

Fearing defeat in the end the harassed President, taking the stump in September, made a grand tour to the Pacific Coast appealing to the American people at large over the heads of the recalcitrant Senators in Washington. But the effort was too much for him. While engaged in this battle for his treaty, Wilson became desperately ill and was taken back to the capital broken in body if not in spirit. Save for occasional hours of feverish activity, he never recovered his power. During the remainder of his term the affairs of his administration drifted; his Cabinet fell to pieces with resignations and dismissals; and Congress, dominated by Republicans, devoted itself in accordance with canonical party custom to the politics of obstruction and recrimination preparatory to the coming election. Unable to agree on reservations and worn by the long debates, the Senate, on March 19, 1920, definitely rejected the treaty by announcing that the constitutional majority could not be obtained. The campaign being now at hand, Wilson insisted that the people should hold "a solemn referendum" upon the League of Nations. His desire was gratified.

CHAPTER XXIX

The Quest for Normalcy

FINANCIAL feudalism died in the United States when Woodrow Wilson took the oath of office as President. . . . Mr. Hanna and Mr. Morgan both believed that the country should be governed by property and that the power over both property and Government should be centralized. . . . Hannaism died a lingering death, but it died, root, branch, and twig. With the election of Woodrow Wilson to the presidency in 1912, the last spark of life had vanished. Outside the select circle of Privilege, there were no mourners. . . . The new Banking and Currency law has destroyed the conditions under which a Morgan was possible." Thus, in language that recalled the celebration of Jefferson's great revolution in 1800 and, long afterward, Jackson's triumph of 1832, the editor of the New York World tersely presented a popular view of the economic result achieved by Wilson's election.

Both the style and the form of the argument were beyond reproach; but a large part of the country did not approve either the diagnosis or the announcement of the cure.

"America's present need is not heroics but healing; not nostrums but normalcy; not revolution but restoration; . . . not surgery but serenity." In these brief phrases, delivered to an audience of responsive captains of industrial enterprise in Boston, in May, 1920, Senator Warren Gamaliel Harding, of Ohio, expressed another opinion of Wilson's services to American society. Though the word "normalcy" was not in the household dictionary, it was caught up with enthusiasm, especially by applauding business men, as the symbol of their poignant yearning for a return, how far no one could tell, upon the route along which they had been carried by Wilson. No political manometer registered the exact degree of pressure.

With reference to foreign affairs, any program of healing, restoration, and serenity implied a repudiation of Wilson's high internationalism including its tenderness for subject races, a reliance upon the safeguards offered by the balance of power, a revival of the Webster-Seward-Hay policy in the Pacific Ocean, the hard-headed promotion of foreign trade by the engines of state, the development of the Navy as the forerunner and defender of commerce, and firmness in the government of imperial provinces. Equally realistic, essentially economic, were the insinuations of normalcy in domestic politics.

There was, of course, some grumbling about the popular election of United States Senators, the direct primary, woman suffrage, the initiative and referendum, and the other instruments of the new democracy, but they were more easily manipulated than destroyed. After all none of them had made any serious dislocations in the system of use and wont—for example, by distributing their votes among the parties largely in accordance with their social groupings women placed no insuperable obstacles in the way of Harding's renaissance. There was also a great deal of smothered conversation about the juristic process of healing and serenity; the Supreme Court under the influence of liberal members picked by Roosevelt and Wilson had showed a

tendency to relax the rigidity of the Constitution as read
in the era of the full dinner pail and to tolerate legislation
thrown up in the sweep of social democracy. If Phœnix was
to get clear of the ashes a number of discreet judicial appointments would have to be made.

But all this was by way of preliminary and incident; the
real bill of exigent particulars presented by those who demanded a general retreat to the old régime referred primarily to economic legislation touching the distribution of
wealth. To them the revival of McKinley's learning sig-
nified a repeal of the taxes on incomes, inheritances, and excess profits, especially the higher schedules, and a shift of
the burden of federal support from wealth enjoyed by the
rich to goods consumed by the masses. It likewise involved
a fair recovery of the Hamilton-Webster-McKinley system
of tariffs, subsidies, and bounties for the owners of industries and merchant vessels. Apart from such paternal assistance, it meant, as the phrase ran current, "no government interference with business"—no official meddling with
mergers, combinations, and stock issues, no resort to harsh
price-fixing or regulatory schemes, and a release of the tense
pressure exerted upon railways. Finally, normalcy implied
the immediate opening of the remaining fragments of the
national domain to rapid development; if not by outright
gift or easy sale, then by a generous exercise of the leasing
powers recently conferred upon the executive department
by acts of Congress. Other specifications similar in character were included in extreme projects for normalcy; some
champions of recession proposing to go the full length to a
logical conclusion, defying time and flood.

§

The ladies and gentlemen who pined for a recovery of
the Hamilton-Webster-McKinley system had valid reasons
for desiring to turn their backs upon the policies of Woodrow Wilson. Early in his first administration, he had openly

warned the masters of business enterprise that their grip
on the federal government would be broken and, except during the urgent years of the war, including its aftermath, he
had been cold to their pleas and threats. Indeed he had, in
their eyes, violated the rules of the political game by denouncing the lobbyists in the corridors of Congress and by
stating baldly that capitalist interests were trying to drive
him into a war with Mexico. Few of the schedules in his
tariff bill of 1913 had pleased leaders in great industries.
None of his subsequent laws, except perhaps the Federal
Reserve Act, had exactly met their requirements.

Moreover, Wilson had gathered around him in his official
family several liberals approved only by farmers and industrial workers. He had permitted, if not encouraged, high
talk about a grand "reconstruction of the existing order"
on the return to peace—giving a kind of second-hand benediction to those philosophers of social inclinations who contended that the extraordinary productivity which resulted
from the intense coöperative effort of the war had proved
the soundness of their theories. During his administrations, and with presidential blessings, organized labor had
rapidly extended its membership and attained a power both
in private industry and in public affairs most disconcerting
to men brought up in the liberty of the gilded age. Under
the patronage of Wilson's indulgent government in the years
of the war, at a time when labor was scarce and profits
high, when labor costs could be shifted to a complacent
public or to generous taxpayers, demands for wage increases
had been granted with unusual urbanity and trade unions
had been distinctly favored in their efforts to get a strong
grip on the manufacturing processes. The phrase "industrial democracy" leaped into popular conversation. Under
the stimulus of federal action, it became the fashion to talk
about shop committees, personnel administration, and self-
government in industry, as if the echoes of the Russian Revolution and socialistic Germany were to be heard tolerantly
in America. All this was bitter medicine for business men

desirous of managing their own affairs in their own way, of shutting off dictation by labor and by government.

Examining the ground when the tumult and the shouting of war died away, they found reasons for indulging in expectations. After all, the opulence which Roosevelt disliked and Wilson snubbed had not been dissipated in the era of the new freedom. On the contrary, at the head of the list of rich men paying taxes on annual incomes of more than a million dollars in 1920 were the old leaders reporting augmented estates and a great many fortunes had been added to the original roll, the four years of the war for democracy alone making more millionaires in America than a whole decade of aleatory peace. In spite of everything Roosevelt and Wilson had said or done, the captains of business enterprise were still in the arena; they were conscious of no wrong-doing such as had been ascribed to them in the tempestuous days of 1912 and they were not convinced that the drift in politics since the close of McKinley's era had been either just or inherently necessary.

In fact they could find some support for the belief that the course of recent events had been wholly fortuitous. Neither Roosevelt nor Wilson had ever received a favorable verdict on his program of domestic economy. The former had been elevated to the presidency in the first place by an accident, the tragic death of McKinley; when the public elected him in his own right in 1904, the salient features of his philosophy had not yet been disclosed; and he had been emphatically repudiated eight years later when he offered his well-articulated Progressive program.

Nor was Wilson's case much better. He too had been rejected by the popular vote in the election of 1912 that made him President—the majority against him was more than two million; he had not won a majority in a single industrial state, in any state in fact outside the solid South; coldly stated, he owed his election simply to divisions among his opponents. The circumstances of his reëlection had also been abnormal: at that time the storm of a World War was beating against the doors of America and no decision on controversies over domestic issues could be obtained.

Moreover opponents of Wilson could assert with some show of authority that nothing but the World War had prevented the country from reaping a harvest of economic ruin under his policies. Certainly, business depression had begun early in his first administration; the construction of railways had been practically stopped by the rate-making and wage-regulating measures of the government; and industrial enterprise, harried by prosecutions and new anti-trust legislation, had slowed down its rate of progress.

Relying upon facts of this class, critics who resented the progressive upheaval under both Roosevelt and Wilson felt justified in saying that only the prosperity won by the sale of supplies to the Entente Allies at enormous profits enabled the people to escape gathering the "bitter fruits of fanaticism." So all in all, it could be urged with some display of reason that the majority of the people had never approved "the war on business" and that the attempt of planters, mechanics, debt-burdened farmers, and importing merchants to govern the country had been intrinsically a failure. These were the conditions that gave heart to the masters of machine economy who buoyantly made ready in 1920 to restore Warren Gamaliel Harding's normalcy and serenity.

§

To their designs the general state of the Wilson régime was distinctly favorable. Immediately after the armistice, the administration commenced to disintegrate. Patriotic dollar-a-year men, who had hurried to Washington to serve during the war, rushed home at its close with equal speed to attend to their private affairs. Departments and bureaus fell into disorder as secretaries and chiefs withdrew from the sinking ship to recoup losses incurred during their arduous public services or to enjoy returns amassed during their absence.

While the federal machine was falling apart, President Wilson was engrossed in the work of the peace conference and in the realization of his project for a League of Nations. Then to cap the climax, just at the hour when domestic leadership was more imperative than ever, the President, worn out by long and trying labors, became desperately ill and was never able to resume his former empire over the course of party affairs. It is true that when Robert Lansing, his Secretary of State, undertook to keep the vessel up against the wind by holding Cabinet meetings on his own authority, Wilson, hearing of these sessions behind his back, roused himself from his sick-bed and dismissed his active Secretary with a haughty gesture of contempt; but that was a temporary flare. Physical weakness had, in fact, stripped from him the grand manner of earlier days. Besides he had been repudiated at the congressional election held near the close of the war in 1918 and political custom made a third-term out of the question.

Even if circumstances had permitted Wilson to remain in his former vigor at the helm, it is not certain that more changes of a radical character would have been made in the American system of acquisition and enjoyment. It does not appear that he had in mind after 1918 any material additions to his program of economic legislation; at all events, if he had, he did not exhibit them to the public. Indeed he admitted to Colonel House that he had exhausted his armory by 1914. In any case, one incident indicated the direction of his thinking. In October, 1919, when his conference representing capital, labor, and the public, called to consider the state of industrial democracy, was thrown into confusion by hopeless diversity of opinion, Wilson accepted the outcome with seeming apathy.

In truth, by long training and sincere belief Wilson was an economist of the Manchester School. No deep-rooted conviction therefore urged him to maintain any part of the special control over transportation and industry which had been built up during the war. With logical consistency, he

declined to accede to the request of William G. McAdoo,
director of the railways, for a test of government operation
in time of peace and made no strong objection when Congress, in Republican hands, returned the lines by the Transportation Act of 1920 to their former owners on terms more
favorable than they had reason to expect. Though the
prices of commodities continued to rise above the highest
war levels, federal control in this sphere was likewise dissipated by judicial decisions, administrative action, and
congressional repeal. As a matter of fact, since most of
the emergency statutes providing for federal supervision
over private economy were general in character, leaving the
details, as well as the enforcement of the law, to presidential
discretion, it was easy for the executive department to relax
the rigor of such legislation before Congress found time to
remove it from the books. Thus the country was already
drifting rapidly into normalcy when Harding made his plea
in Boston for a return to the good old days.

In only one relation did the Wilson administration per-
sist in exercising unsparing control over private affairs once
justified by the demands of the war, namely, in the suppression of critical opinion. To the petition for a general amnesty and oblivion which circulated soon after the armistice,
the President turned a face of steel. With his approval,
the Postmaster General, Burleson, continued to exercise a
stringent supervision over the press and the mails. With
the same high benediction, the Attorney General, A. Mitchell Palmer, candidate for the Democratic nomination, kept
himself in the public eye by a hot "war on the Reds," arresting suspected persons wholesale, permitting the use of
provocative agents to stir up "seditious meetings," insisting on the deportation of aliens rounded up by detectives
from the Department of Justice, and tolerating if not authorizing constant resort to the third degree, that is, the
physical abuse of accused persons.

Indeed the inquisitorial activities of the Wilson administration after the close of the "war to make the world safe

for democracy" became so vehement that a committee of prominent lawyers filed a memorandum of remonstrance. In the name of constitutional rights, Charles E. Hughes, a man given to measured language, warmly protested in an address delivered in the summer of 1920 before the Harvard law alumni, speaking with deep concern about inflammatory appeals to prejudice made by district attorneys and about the browbeating of witnesses during trial by judges in every kind of court and in every part of the country. "We may well wonder, in view of the precedents now established," exclaimed the former Justice of the Supreme Court, "whether constitutional government as heretofore maintained in this republic could survive another great war even victoriously waged." It was only by the most strenuous efforts that persons of liberal tendencies were able to prevent Congress from passing, in days of peace, a new sedition bill more drastic than the measure enacted ostensibly for martial purposes; and in spite of their efforts many war statutes affecting civil liberties were retained in force long after the close of the European conflict.

By many hands, therefore, the stage was set for a strong reaction against everything that had a Wilsonian flavor. Business men could not forgive him for the tariff act, the Adamson law fixing an eight hour day for trainmen, his Mexican policy, his indifference to many appeals for favors, and the heavy taxes laid on private and corporate incomes—to mention some of a hundred items. German-Americans were resentful because he had helped to effect the downfall of the German Empire. Irish-Americans were furious about the aid rendered to Great Britain. Liberals fumed over "his surrender to British and French imperialism at Paris," his blunt refusal to approve a general amnesty for political offenders, and his continued prosecution of persons accused of harboring radical opinions. Republican statesmen who had endured and even ostentatiously approved Wilson's lofty sentiments about the objects of the war now felt free to deny the official hypothesis, assail it violently, and substitute for it the simple and less seraphic reason that we had taken up arms "to save our skins."

§

In fact on all sides the canonical creed of the war, the enthralling idealism with which Wilson had sustained his grand crusade, was now attacked with relentless analysis— much to the amazement of the Socialists in jail for the objections they had so recently put on record in the court of opinion against the official hypothesis. At the origin of the conflict, the European belligerents later associated with the United States in that high enterprise had not made professions directly contrary to their real sentiments incorporated in the Secret Treaties, and in the hour of distress they had accepted Wilson's ethical flourishes merely as a garnish to the substantial aid that accompanied them. Once safely over the hazards of war and in secure possession of the fruits of a draconian peace, they indulgently allowed critical writers to turn heavy batteries upon the most elaborate of their former defense mechanisms.

With an unconcern that astounded the generality, Sir Philip Gibbs now characterized the Belgian atrocity stories as pure war myths and portrayed the Allied leaders as cynical and contemptuous gamblers in the lives of boys. Freed from official censorship this brilliant journalist, whose livid etchings of the war had thrilled millions during the tragic years and had given the Allied leaders heroic proportions, angrily dubbed the patriot statesmen of the war for democracy "the Gang." In vitriolic language, he condemned the "hard materialist outlook" of Balfour, Law, Curzon, and Carson in his own country.

Then after exclaiming contemptuously "Is there any soul in England who believes in the wisdom of Winston Churchill?" Gibbs laughed at Clemenceau, "the indomitable Tiger of French victory," declaring that "he looked more like a walrus than a tiger, a poor old walrus in a traveling circus."

Having thrown Clemenceau from his pedestal, the indignant journalist paid his respects to that "peerless champion
of liberty and the right," Raymond Poincaré, M. le Prési-
dent de Bordeaux, "with plump waxen face, expressionless
and, I thought, merely stupid." Through with them as individuals, Gibbs rendered a collective judgment: "The old
politicians who had played the game of politics before the
war, gambling with the lives of men for territories, privileged markets, oil fields, native races, coaling stations, and
imperial prestige, grabbed the pool which the German gamblers had lost when their last bluff was called and quarrelled
over its distribution."

To the confessions of once-muzzled journalists were added more impressive documents. When Russian, German,
and Austrian archives were torn open by revolution, the secret negotiations, conversations, agreements, and treaties by
which the Entente Powers had planned to break Germany
and divide the spoils of war according to the ancient rules
were exposed to the public gaze. In all its naked horror the
sordid and grimy diplomacy which had precipitated the
bloody conflict was revealed; and by way of supplement
memoirs, papers, treatises, and articles on the background
of the war began to flow from the presses. Though cautious editors long ignored the researches of scholars, though
aged club men and embattled women continued to fight the
war along canonical lines, the task of keeping alive the old
reverie was far beyond their powers.

And after a while misgivings leaked into the very Senate
of the United States. In the chamber that three short years
before had carried the war resolution in a tempest of enthusiasm, the question was now calmly asked: "Why after
all did we enter the war?" To most Democrats this inquiry
was worse than indecent; it was profane. But Republicans
pressed it and Senator Harding answered. Referring to the
preamble of the measure declaring hostilities against Germany, he recited the acts of violence committed by the German government against the people of the United States.

Then he closed laconically: "There is the whole story. Nothing there especially proclaiming democracy and humanity." This he said in no captious mood; at bottom it expressed his mature conviction. A little later in his speech accepting the presidential nomination, Harding took pains to state formally that "we asked the sons of this republic to defend our national rights" rather than to "purge the Old World of the accumulated ills of rivalry and greed." So the politicians seemed to blow mists of doubt athwart the sunlight that streamed down on the poppies in Flanders fields, bringing anguish to those who felt with Wilson that the heart of humanity would break if the United States did not enter the League of Nations.

§

By the spring of 1920 the spell of the war to end war was shattered. "Any good Republican can be nominated for President and can defeat any Democrat," remarked Boies Penrose, grand seigneur of the Republican machine in Pennsylvania, encouraging many of his colleagues to offer themselves to their party for consideration. A hero of Belgian relief, Herbert Hoover, seemed to command the practical skill required by the age of "reconstruction," but he made little headway among political experts. Gathering about him Roosevelt's mantle and well sustained by funds from the heir to a famous soap establishment, General Leonard Wood opened a hopeful campaign of generous proportions in the way of publicity. In the Valley of Democracy, Governor Frank Lowden, of Illinois, who attracted national attention as an administrator and was deeply interested in agriculture, entered the lists with great prospect of victory. Far away on the Pacific coast, Hiram Johnson, of California, who had run for the vice-presidency with Roosevelt eight years before but had been sobered by recent contact with public affairs, forged to the front with his customary confidence.

In due form all these candidates and some minor lay figures in politics submitted their respective merits to the judgment of their party, without obtaining any decisive verdict at the primaries. Receiving thus no explicit mandate from the rank and file, the leaders of the Republican national convention at Chicago, after days of hard wrestling, broke the deadlock by selecting a "Dark Horse," Warren Gamaliel Harding, the apostle of normalcy and serenity.

From many points of view, Senator Harding, like General William Henry Harrison in 1840, was admirably qualified for the business of leading the Republican party out of the wilderness in which it had been wandering since the advent of Roosevelt. From his youth the Senator had been a faithful and unwavering member of the party organization, never attempting to exalt himself above its operations, to thrust his opinions upon its managers, or to ignore its decrees. Publicly avowing his loyalty to the McKinley-Hanna-Foraker school of political economy, in spite of the fact that Hanna had distrusted his methods, Harding said with an air of tenderness that he loved "the good old times when the Republican protective tariff policy filled the treasury and at the same time gave that protection to American industry which stimulated the development which had made our record a matchless one in the story of the world." He favored subsidies to private companies engaged in building up the merchant marine. He knew the ways of Ohio politics—ways so vividly illustrated in the careers of Hanna and Foraker—and party workers felt sure that they would receive appropriate recognition at his hands. In the crisis of 1912 he had remained faithful to the covenants of the organization, opposing the heresies of Roosevelt without pushing anything to the point of extremes. To complete his record of availability, Harding had served a term in the Senate, without making enemies by pressing any particular piece of legislation or delivering any speeches that excited severe criticism east of the Hudson River.

Above everything, Harding was specially qualified for

making an appeal to the Middle West and leading it back into the party fold. His home was in the Valley of Democracy that had once voted for Andrew Jackson and afterward furnished so many distinguished Republican Presidents. The brand of the prosperous corporation lawyer was not upon him; far from it; he was merely the editor of a country paper at Marion, Ohio. In the language of journalism, Harding was "an average American," a boon companion; as one of his neighbors remarked, "the best fellow in the world to play poker with all Saturday night." No one loved the common people more sincerely or understood them better or had less of Wilson's penchant for "the moral overstrain."

Proud of being just a plain citizen among the folks of an ordinary community, Harding avoided the pretensions of urbanity. In one of his most popular addresses, he sang the praise of the small town, recording how the village "bruiser" was tamed and became the head of the local bank; how a carpenter's son became a Chicago captain of industry at twenty-five thousand a year; how a grocer's offspring developed into one of the great lawyers of Ohio; and how "the brightest boy of the class," the teacher's pride, became the janitor of his village lodge and "the happiest one of the lot." Then came his peroration: "What is the greatest thing in life, my countrymen? Happiness. And there is more happiness in the American village than in any other place on the face of the earth." Such sentiments struck home; for more than half the people of the United States lived on farms or in villages of less than twenty-five hundred inhabitants.

With his sincere democratic simplicity, Harding combined a religious nature. He spoke from the bottom of his heart when he said soon after his election: "It will help if we have a revival of religion. . . . I don't think any government can be just if it does not have somehow a contact with Omnipotent God. . . . It might interest you to know that while I have always been a great reader of the Bible, I have never read it as closely as in the last weeks when my mind has been bent upon the work that I must shortly take up. I have obtained a good deal of inspiration from the Psalms of David and from many passages of the four Gospels, and there is still wisdom in the sayings of Old Solomon. . . . I don't mind saying that I gladly go to God Almighty for guidance and strength in the responsibilities that are coming to me." He confessed that he was disturbed because "in the conception of Versailles there was no recognition of God Almighty." And yet Harding was no Puritan; he enjoyed life, its amenities, and its pleasures. It was not without reason that the people in offices, shops, Pullman smokers, and moving picture palaces felt that the Ohio Senator was near to the great throbbings of American humanity.

In a quiet campaign conducted on his front porch in Marion, Harding continued to broadcast the issue of normalcy throughout the country; while the Democratic nominee, James M. Cox, with equal insistence urged on the stump the issues presented by the League of Nations, advocating an immediate ratification of the Peace Treaty without any reservations impairing its efficiency. The League question, of course, made some difficulties for the Republican candidate because he had to conciliate extremists, such as Senators Johnson, McCormick, and Brandegee, men absolutely opposed to ratification in any form or manner whatsoever, and to keep in the same step strong supporters of an international union, such as George W. Wickersham, Charles E. Hughes, A. Lawrence Lowell, and William H. Taft. But if the task had its perils, Harding adroitly surmounted them by condemning the League of Nations devised at Paris and proposing instead "a free association of nations." There he cautiously stopped, declining to make it clear just what kind of association he had in mind or how it was to be brought into existence.

In the confusion that arose, one wing of Harding's political army could appeal for votes on the ground that he was in favor of the League while another wing could assure its friends that under his direction the nation would maintain its splendid isolation. This looked like a contradiction but in the hurry of the campaign only a few dialecticians of the Wilson school seemed disturbed by the evident dichotomy in Harding's logic. Indeed, the precaution was after all unnecessary as the election returns proved; for the repudiation of the Democratic party was staggering even to the coldest observer. Cox did not carry a single northern state; even Tennessee went Republican. Besides a popular plurality of seven millions, Harding received 404 out of 531 electoral votes.

§

Although there were many agrarians and progressives among the Republican majority returned to both houses of Congress, Harding naturally felt authorized to direct the upper range of the federal system with what he once called "loyalty to that robust Republicanism expounded by its great leaders of the past—John Sherman, Marcus A. Hanna, and William McKinley; and as advocated to-day by their able and distinguished successor in leadership, Joseph B. Foraker." In choosing his Cabinet, he completely ignored even those Progressives who stood repentant in sackcloth and ashes at the gates. As if in contempt, he picked for three important posts men especially objectionable to practitioners of the Roosevelt school: for the Treasury, Andrew Mellon, one of the richest men in the Cameron-Penrose wing of the Republican organization in Pennsylvania; for the Interior, Albert Fall, sworn foe of all liberal opinion, vigorous manipulator in oil and advocate of war on Mexico; for the Department of Justice, Harry M. Daugherty, a prominent politician of Ohio who, to say the least, had long been associated with the conservative forces of his party in that commonwealth. Likewise, in making selections for the Supreme Court, Harding returned to the course from which Roosevelt and Wilson had departed upon occasion. His four appointees, Taft, Sutherland, Butler, and Sanford, were all apostles of the Hamilton-Webster-Mc-

Kinley school and on mounting the bench they tipped the scales of justice once more on the side of normalcy.

The nature of the recoil in the upper range of the federal system was soon made apparent in various particulars. For example, normalcy meant no special tenderness to radicals from the fringe of the labor movement who had been sent to prison during Wilson's era of the new freedom. It is true that President Harding extended executive clemency to Eugene V. Debs, former candidate for the presidency on the Socialist ticket, but he refused to grant a broad pardon to political prisoners. Having appointed his old friend and gay companion, Harry Daugherty, to the office of Attorney General, he gave his official sanction to a continued prosecution of radicals by the agencies of the federal government.

Assisted by William J. Burns, a prominent private detective, who, after serving the German government in the early days of the World War, had turned his versatile powers to "running down Reds," Daugherty devoted great energies to "stamping out Bolshevism." To facilitate their designs these two champions of the moral order employed all the methods and tactics which Charles E. Hughes had found so dangerous when used by the Wilson administration. In dealing with striking workmen, the Attorney General was equally vehement; when in 1922 railway shopmen, after demanding wage increases commensurate with the rising cost of living, laid down their tools and therewith disrupted the railway service, Daugherty sought and obtained from the federal district court in Chicago the most sweeping injunction ever issued in the history of labor disputes in America. By its terms practically all activities on the part of trade union officials were forbidden—even communications by telephone or telegrams encouraging persons to leave their employment. Drastic as this action appeared, it was sustained in the courts on appeal by the unions and greeted by manufacturers' associations as calculated to "end the labor menace."

On other occasions the wheel also responded to the compass. In the leasing of federal oil lands for exploitation, for instance, there was a return to the more sympathetic policy of earlier days. Recent acts of Congress dealing with the subject were not repealed; the public domain reserved since the act of 1891 was not parceled out; but hard bargains were avoided by the Hon. Albert B. Fall when he turned over certain large oil pools to the Doheny and Sinclair interests. On jurisprudence, the effect of the new drift was also observable. The Constitution stood as of yore but the judicial decisions rendered on labor issues and social legislation carried the minds of lawyers back to the times of McKinley. Indeed in one case under the new dispensation, Chief Justice Taft, who sometimes tempered the angularity of his logic with humanity and good humor, felt compelled to file a dissenting opinion.

§

With respect to foreign policies, Harding had reason for feeling that the verdict of the election permitted the repudiation of Wilson's internationalism and a return to the more aggressive ways of Webster, Seward, Hay, and Knox. And yet while the mandate at the polls was overwhelming, there was some uncertainty as to just what had been decided in the matter of the Versailles treaty. Responding vaguely to that ambiguity, Harding seemed inclined at first to look favorably on some indefinite form of coöperation with the powers of the world. "I have every faith that our nation will take its fitting place in an association of nations for world peace," he said one day after his election, "and I believe that we are going to be able to do it without the surrender of anything we hold dear as a heritage of the American people."

But gradually the idea faded out of Harding's mind, or at all events, any thought of acting upon it was abandoned. Once safely installed in the White House, he flatly refused to revive the Versailles treaty and eventually he came to the conclusion that the American people had settled this issue forever. To invite the other countries of the world already bound together in the League to join the United States in forming another "association of nations" on a new American model, as he had suggested during the campaign, was evidently out of the question, if not whimsical.

Having finally arrived at an adverse conclusion, the Harding administration placed the Versailles pact in the official wastebasket and Congress, hearing news of this action in the White House, by a joint resolution, signed by the President on July 2, 1921, declared the war with the late Central Empires at an end—expressly reserving to the United States and its citizens all the rights and privileges to which they were entitled under the armistice and the final settlement. Thereupon separate treaties of peace were negotiated with Germany, Austria, and Hungary and duly ratified by the Senate. Thus in an unexpected fashion "the war to end war" was formally brought to a close, as far as the United States was concerned, nearly three years after the fighting ceased on the battlefield.

Annoyed by the lag in events, a few critics felt impelled to suggest that there was something wrong with a constitutional system which kept the country in the iron grip of a political deadlock for two years; and they offered a remedy in the form of a constitutional amendment permitting the ratification of treaties by a bare majority of the Senate. To the vestal virgins guarding the sacred fire, this proposal savored of sacrilege but any fears on that score were unjustified. There was little likelihood that many of the Senators would vote for an amendment that promised to deprive them of any prerogatives. The general public was indifferent. The cloud blew over.

Having come to terms with the governments of the Central Powers, the Harding administration took up in a pragmatic fashion those international questions which appeared to be of practical concern to the United States and its citizens. It declined to participate officially in any of the numerous European conferences summoned for the purpose of settling the troubled estate of the Old World but it did remind the several constituent powers of the dangers arising from association with Bolshevik Russia and it did give attention to all matters of moment to substantial interests in America. It continued the policy, inaugurated under the Wilson administration, of protesting whenever foreign governments tried to deprive any American company of the right to drill oil wells in their territories and dependencies, especially if held "in sacred trust for humanity" under the League of Nations. It gave the former associated powers to understand that, while the United States did not propose to ratify the Versailles treaty, it would surrender none of its legitimate claims upon the former German colonies, notably the island of Yap, a strategic cable station in the Pacific, assigned as a mandate to Japan. Gently intimating to Tokyo its displeasure about Japanese occupation of Siberia, it assumed a certain "moral responsibility" for that part of Russia, while refusing to consider a mandate for Armenia.

To speak summarily, in negotiations over Dutch Sumatra, Mesopotamia, the Near East generally, Russia, the Mid-Pacific, Siberia, and China, the Harding administration took all necessary and appropriate steps to protect and advance the claims of American business enterprise to goods of a ponderable character. In the Caribbean and in Latin-America generally, as already noted, it followed the policies of the Wilson administration. To preserve the integrity of the American empire in the Philippines, it hoisted once more the pennant of William McKinley. "Let the internationalist dream and the Bolshevist destroy," intoned President Harding. "God pity him 'for whom no minstrel raptures swell.' In the spirit of the republic, we proclaim Americanism and acclaim America!"

§

Peace with Germany and Austria having been restored and the diplomacy of economic opportunism renewed, the next major question of foreign concern before the Harding administration was a readjustment in that strategic theater of American commercial and naval ambition, the Pacific Ocean. After eight years of neglect and uncertainty, threads of policy spun by Secretary Webster and Commodore Perry, by Secretary Seward and Admiral Dewey were taken up anew. In language harmonizing with their traditions, President Harding made the nature of the business perfectly clear to the country. "We have seen the eyes of the world," he said, "turned to the Pacific. With Europe prostrate and penitent, none feared the likelihood of early conflict there. But the Pacific had its menaces and they deeply concerned us. Our territorial interests are larger there. Its waters are not strange seas to us, its further shores are not unknown to our citizens. . . . We covet the possessions of no other power in the Far East and we know for ourselves that we crave no further or greater governmental or territorial responsibility there. Contemplating what is admittedly ours and mindful of a long-time and reciprocal friendship with China, we do wish the opportunity to continue the development of our trade peacefully and on equality with other nations." Stripped of all embellishments there was the crux of the matter: "The Pacific had its menaces and they deeply concerned us."

And there was no doubt about the sources of these menaces. Russia, long a chief engineer of high intrigue in China and the Far East, was temporarily paralyzed. Neither France with her Indo-Chinese possessions nor Holland with her East Indian dominions offered any serious challenge. Germany, flat on her back, was unable to make even a commercial stab at American prestige in the Orient. There remained England and Japan closely united by a treaty of alliance—a pact useful to England in checking the pretensions of Russia and Germany and keeping order in her Indian empire but the object of constant criticism in Australia and Canada where fear of Japanese power was a psychic factor of moment. Besides being caught between these two fires, the British foreign office dreaded the coming naval supremacy of the United States: it wanted the security of the Japanese alliance without its galling yoke. In the eyes of English experts, a triple adjustment seemed to be the only possible way out of the dilemma.

Though reluctant to dissolve the dual arrangement, Tokyo was not lacking in discernment. Under the ægis of the alliance and during British preoccupation in the World War, Japan had strengthened and extended the net of her economic hegemony in the Orient. In August, 1914, with a show of assistance from England, she seized the German province of Shantung in China. When President Wilson relaxed somewhat the aggressive economic policy pursued by McKinley, Roosevelt, and Taft in the Far East, the business men of Nippon made the most of the commercial opportunities afforded by the circumstance.

Indeed with England distracted by the war, Russia paralyzed, Germany eliminated, and the United States less watchful, Japan developed a local Monroe Doctrine and Caribbean policy of her own: declaring in effect a kind of protectorate over neighboring lands and waters. In 1915 she made her famous, or notorious, Twenty-one Demands on China which promised to give her the substance of sovereignty over that distracted country, and immediately sent her merchants, capitalists, and army officers swarming into the new preserves in search of trade and privileges.

Before the uproar over the Twenty-one Demands had died away, President Wilson permitted Secretary Lansing to exchange notes with Viscount Ishii, the Japanese Ambassador, acknowledging the obvious fact that the Island Empire had special interests in China. The very next year, namely, 1918, Japan made another strategic advance by joining the United States and the associated powers in occupying Eastern Siberia, "to protect supplies and steady efforts at self-government" as the phrase ran. And once firmly installed in that desirable section of the mainland, so alluring to concession hunters, the Tokyo militarists declined to withdraw their forces when the other countries recalled their troops. Then came the crowning bargain at Paris—where Wilson, eager to win the support of the Japanese delegation for his League of Nations, let Japan have Shantung on a promise of ultimate restoration to China and allowed her to take over the German island of Yap as a mandate, without objection.

Not unnaturally these events in the Orient caused intensified agitation in the United States, raising a great outcry against Japanese imperialism. Among American liberals such assumption of rights, titles, privileges, and property, unaccompanied by any mitigating ethical pretensions, was regarded as positively shocking. Distressed for other reasons, stanch advocates of the American forward policy in the Caribbean and the Philippines joined the humanists in denouncing the machinations of Tokyo; while American merchants and capitalists interested in the development of China composed a threnody on rights and prospects threatened by the closure of the open door. On the Pacific Coast, the immigration question was again stirred into flame; and among Christian missionaries in China and their supporters at home voices calling for a holy war on "Pagan Japan" were heard. In Congress baiting Tokyo became popular. Looking upon himself as a sort of heir-apparent to Webster's throne and being in fact a tuneful mouthpiece for cotton spinners hunting for Oriental markets, Senator Lodge hurled one philippic after another against Japan, striking at President Wilson and the Versailles treaty through the flowing robes of the Samurai.

Consequently when Harding began in 1921 to apply the Seward-McKinley policy once more, a real crisis in Far Eastern affairs was precipitated, bringing forward the grave question whether Japan could be forced to drop her new harvest fruits without disturbing the imperial holdings of America or England in the Orient; by peaceful methods, if possible; by war if certain energetic men in the Navy Department and Hearst's editorial rooms could have their way. And ethical reasons for coercion were not wanting. To break the grip of the Japanese on the mainland would be to uphold the grand principle of the open door: equal opportunity for the commercial interests of all countries. To come to the rescue of China would be to protect a weak and defenseless republic of four hundred million people against a haughty empire of sixty millions. There was something in the proposal that appealed to the heart of American humanity.

In this agitation against Japan, England was inevitably caught. Her people, groaning under a mountain of war taxation, were begging for relief and yet no deliverance could be granted while preparations were being made for a great fight in the Pacific, with the United States building battleships at a breakneck speed that promised to wrest the trident from the Mistress of the Seas within five years. In the book of fate it was clearly written that England could not stand idly by and allow any single power to become supreme in an ocean where her imperial interests were so exigent. But her choice was not to be made easily. Her nationals would benefit, of course, from any reduction of Japanese trade in China, even though they already had a major portion of the business in that dissolving republic and held most of the strategic centers for new operations. Moreover, the opposition of Canada and Australia to English coöperation with Japan in case of a war with the United States was so intense that it could not be ignored in London without grave peril to the Empire.

Meanwhile forces undeniably strong were pulling in the other direction. Pledged to friendship and aid by the Anglo-Japanese alliance, the English ministry shrank from offending the cabinet of Tokyo by any unfriendly action; such ties were not to be lightly snapped. The Japanese navy had helped to check the Indian revolution during the World War; the conquest of Shantung, effected by Anglo-Japanese coöperation, had been sealed by a secret treaty; England held Hong Kong and Wei Hai Wei on conditions similar in moral obligation to those on which Japan rested her claims to valuable concessions; and if any punitive expeditions were to be undertaken against China, assistance seemed more likely to be forthcoming from Tokyo than from Washington—from a military empire rather than from a government harassed by pacific sentiments, and often timid about making predatory raids in distant lands without high ethical attachments.

Altogether the situation was delicate for Downing Street; but prudence clearly suggested some kind of alliance or agreement that would reduce the burdens of the English taxpayers, prevent the navy of the United States from outstripping the strength of Britannia, shake Japan's grip on the trade and resources of China, assure the three powers the continued possession of the imperial dominions they had already gathered unto themselves, and in the process preserve all the suavity of friendly intercourse. England, Japan, and the United States had once come to a secret understanding, in Roosevelt's administration, and a renewal of the pledges might be more effective in open covenants openly arrived at.

In the circumstances, Japan, threatened by isolation and vexed by taxes that bowed her peasantry to the earth, had little to choose. To the most ardent Japanese imperialist, fighting both the United States and England seemed to be quixotic, if desirable; so responsible statesmen in Tokyo were prepared by necessity to accept a proposal for an exchange of opinions relative to the "menaces of the Pacific." "The divine winds" had long favored the Island Empire and they might not fail even in Washington. All signs, therefore, pointed to a new adjustment of forces.

§

An international conference was evidently in order and the idea admirably fitted the temper of the United States at the moment, for a certain amount of interest in peace as an ideal had survived the insinuations of the recent political campaign. Neither Wilson's passionate plea for the League of Nations, placing the stamp of high authority on the outlawry of war, nor his fierce indictment of militarism had been wholly forgotten in the clash of politics; and after the angry tumult of the presidential contest died away, many who had once cheered his lofty sentiments of humanity returned to their former emotions. Peace associations began to show their heads above the clouds of suspicion spread abroad by the War and Navy Departments and by private societies for the promotion of "adequate defense." For a time, at least, that portion of the American populace which loved combat for its glory, rank, profits, emoluments, promotions, and decorations had been sated; while business men, disquieted by heavy taxation on incomes and profits and by the rumblings of the Bolshevist revolution, were in no mood for more heroics.

Nor was this all a matter of speculation. With an alacrity that astonished all super-patriots, the country at large repudiated the efforts of General Pershing and other army officers, supported by active propaganda on the part of civic associations, to establish universal military service as a permanent phase of American culture. Even General Leonard Wood, one of the chief advocates of that Napoleonic remedy for weakness, on sounding the ground in his presidential campaign, found it expedient to disclaim with scurrying haste any intention of forcing any such program on the people. In fact, the army of the United States was quickly reduced to 125,000 men and the ultimate reliance for national defense was once more placed on a citizen soldiery. The time was ripe for some dramatic move in the direction of peace.

Senator Borah was the first responsible statesman to announce the play, at least in the open, by securing from the Senate the adoption of a resolution requesting the President to call an international conference on the reduction of armaments. In the summer of 1921, it was made known that Harding had asked Great Britain, France, Italy, and Japan to take part in such a convention, and that he had invited China, Belgium, Holland, and Portugal to share in the deliberations pertaining to the Far East and the Pacific. With expressions of pleasure, all the powers answered the appeal and sent their shrewdest diplomats to sit at the council table.

On November 12, President Harding, in a felicitous speech, opened this pageant in Washington. Immediately afterwards, Secretary Hughes, coming to the heart of the business with breath-taking directness, proposed that Japan, Great Britain, and the United States stop building capital ships, reduce their sea power, and proclaim a naval holiday—a clear and ringing call for specific action that transfixed the conference. According to the Japanese journalist, Kawakami, a falling pin could have been heard as the Secretary moved from point to point in his great argument. All over the country, peace enthusiasts saw the dawning of a new day, the beginning of general disarmament and the furling of flags in the Parliament of Man. Nor were they entirely squelched when Harding quickly warned them that there was nothing chimerical in his designs, that he had in view a reduction in the cost of preparedness, relief for the taxpayers, and the settlement of concrete matters which threatened to cause serious friction among certain great powers.

The substantial results of the Washington conference, including those embodied in treaties and those effected by amicable conversations, may be summed up under three heads. First of all was the substitution of the four-power compact for the Anglo-Japanese alliance; England, Japan, France, and the United States agreed to respect one another's insular possessions in the Pacific and to settle all disputes growing out of Pacific issues by conciliatory negotiations. Was this an alliance? If not, what was it? Some of the United States Senators insisted upon regarding it as a union guaranteeing to the four signatories the undisturbed tenure of their imperial holdings in the Pacific—peace among themselves and a solid front against other ambitious nations.

But President Harding opposed this view, saying to the Senate that "nothing in any of these treaties commits the United States to any kind of alliance, entanglement, or envolvement." If no commitments had been made, what then had been accomplished? Harding sought to resolve this difficulty by adding: "It has been said, if this is true, these are meaningless treaties and therefore valueless. Let us accept no such doctrine of despair as that."

The second result of the conference, ultimately effected with the aid of some quiet coercion on the part of the United States, was the withdrawal of Japan from Shantung, the surrender of that province to China, and finally, the evacuation of Siberia by the Japanese troops. In this relation also may be cited the treaties binding the high contracting parties to respect the principle of "the open door" in China, as defined anew in various particulars, and pledging them to confer in due time on an increase in Chinese customs duties and on the abrogation of extra-territorial rights enjoyed by foreigners in that republic. Apart from ousting Japan from Shantung and Siberia, the conference, by its several solemn agreements, made little actual change in the affairs of Asia. It is true that Secretary Hughes soon afterwards announced the end of the Lansing-Ishii understanding which recognized Japan's special interests on the mainland, but that return to normalcy was a transaction in paper rather than an economic fact.

Crowning the work of the Washington conference was the five-power treaty in which Italy, France, England, the United States, and Japan agreed to limit their capital battleships to a fixed ratio for ten years. The truly significant feature of this project was the establishment of equality between the two Anglo-Saxon nations and the allotment to Japan of a tonnage equal to three-fifths that assigned to each of the major partners. In this way, the construction of capital ships was effectively stopped.

Attempts were also made to limit the submarine and to relax the tension in other branches of naval competition; but without avail. Indeed many naval experts took the view that sea warfare in the future would be mainly under the water and in the air, and that dreadnoughts and super-dreadnoughts, as obsolete as wooden hulks, could be scrapped with perfect safety. At any rate, the Washington conference effected great savings in capital ships, tacitly approved the unrestrained construction of other war craft, and gave experts a breathing space in which to study the respective merits of the various engines for fighting on the sea.

The last formal session of the Washington conference was held on February 6, 1922. By that date the negotiations, or at least the discussions known to the public, had demonstrated that the diplomats assembled at the national capital were practical men bent on substantial results, not dreamers wrestling with the task of creating a new order. With this understanding, England and Japan quickly ratified the agreements and the Senate of the United States, after a mild reservation in the case of the four-power compact, set its seal of acceptance on the entire program of commitments. By these approaches the strain was unquestionably reduced in the Pacific. Every one of the high contracting parties could point to some material benefits gained at the council table; and yet none was pledged to any kind of pact that forbade taking up arms at any time in defense of national interests and national honor.

Encouraged by the success of the conference, the Harding administration began to show a more lively interest in other projects for the pacific settlement of international disputes. Though it continued to assume that the national verdict of 1920 had condemned the League of Nations for all time, it watched with peculiar interest the proceedings of the Permanent Court of International Justice, established under the auspices of the League and opened for business at The Hague, in February, 1922. In a little while faint movements in its direction were observed in Washington. Secretary Hughes made a declaration in favor of a world tribunal standing on an independent basis. That was a concession but as nearly all the nations of the earth were operating under the League court, there was a distinct air of hauteur in an American call for another institution of international justice.

Perceiving this paradox, perhaps, Harding himself then indicated a desire to participate in the existing World Court if it could be so constituted "as to appear and to be, in theory and practice, in form and substance, beyond the shadow of a doubt a world court and not a League court"— adding specific conditions designed to assure the equality of the United States with other powers and to guarantee American independence of action in all circumstances. In a word, the benefits of international coöperation were to be sought, without incurring any of the attendant entanglements. Yet even that quest raised domestic vexations. Though supported by many League advocates, both Republicans and Democrats, Harding encountered on the threshold of his undertaking the old relentless hostility of the isolationists. His message to the Senate in 1923 urging coöperation with the tribunal at The Hague was received with chilling formality.

§

In Congress where the multitudinous voices of the masses were more potent in driving and checking, the effects of the mandate delivered in the election of 1920 were not as striking as in the executive and judicial departments. By the popular election of Senators the upper chamber had been brought nearer to the level of the House of Representatives and under the constitutional rule two-thirds of the old members had survived the cataclysm that shook down the Wilsonian edifice. Though it is true that the Republicans

won a majority in both branches, agrarians in their ranks
and among their Democratic neighbors were so powerful that Harding had to pick his way with cautious realism.

Nor were things made any easier for him in the congressional election of 1922. On the contrary it reduced the
Republican majority in the Senate as well as the House, ousting in the procedure two reliable party Senators from the
Northwest in favor of a Farmer-Labor candidate and a
champion of the Non-Partisan League, a radical farmers'
organization that had taken up the scepter of Populism. As
a matter of fact, agriculture was passing through another
ruinous depression, the prices of produce had fallen to an
alarming degree, and the Republican union formed at Chicago in 1860 showed signs of cracking again.

Owing to these circumstances the doctors of the McKinley
school in Congress were in a genuine quandary during the
opening years of the quest for normalcy. Only by remarkable concessions to left-wing Republicans and Democrats,
organized in a vociferous Farm Bloc, concessions in the
shape of high duties on raw materials and agricultural produce, were they able to enact tariff bills restoring the system
of protection for manufacturers—an emergency law followed by the Fordney-McCumber Act of September 21,
1922. On several important issues, especially ship subsidies and taxation, the instructors in normalcy were utterly
routed.

For many years the question of bounties for private companies engaged in operating merchant ships had been warmly
agitated. Once such aid had been a part of the Hamilton-
Webster system, but the Democrats had brusquely withdrawn it on the eve of the Civil War, and the captains of
business enterprise in the Republican party had never been
able to bring the agricultural wing around to supporting a
restoration of the practice. That was the state of affairs
when the outbreak of the World War played havoc with
shipping, making it impossible to find enough bottoms to
carry to the Entente powers the munitions and food sold to

them at good stiff prices. At last the shoe pinched corn and cotton growers as well as the makers of steel and gunpowder. In these circumstances, the farmer-labor-planting representatives aligned on Wilson's side, though still unwilling to grant subsidies to private capitalists, agreed that they must all have ships. Accordingly in 1916, Congress passed the Shipping Board bill providing for the purchase, lease, and operation of merchant ships by the federal government.

To this pass things had been brought when the skies began to brighten for healing and normalcy. Responding to the cry of industrial barons, "Get the government out of business," President Harding now proposed that the government vessels be turned over to private companies on generous terms and that substantial appropriations be voted to help them operate on a comfortable margin. With surprising vehemence the project was rejected by Congress under the drive of the Farm Bloc.

Undeterred by defeats in this connection, the Harding administration made a demand for the reduction of direct taxes on the more fortunate diners at the table of acquisition and enjoyment. Beyond all question, the collectivist principle embodied in taxes on incomes, inheritances, and excess profits was contrary to the historic policy of the Republican party. That great association had financed the Civil War and the Spanish War largely on bond sales and had sustained the government in times of peace principally by indirect taxes imposed on goods consumed by the masses. Moreover it had shown no disposition to disturb by drastic levies any of the high profits made by masters of business during the wars managed under its auspices.

Nothing was, therefore, more natural than for the prophets of normalcy on coming to power to expect, if not a revolution in the Wilsonian program of taxation, at least a radical modification of its harshest terms. Finding approximately one-half the federal revenues derived from income and inheritance taxes, they insisted on immediate relief. By way of concrete suggestion, Secretary Mellon, praised in eastern circles as the greatest financier since Alexander Hamilton, urged slashing cuts, especially in the upper brackets—cuts lowering the surtax on the highest incomes from sixty-five to twenty-five per cent. But the insurgents in Congress refused to accept the proposal and in the revenue law of 1921 kept the supreme surtax levy at fifty per cent, causing much bitterness in the hearts of those who paid the bill.

Besides rejecting a downward revision of taxes on the rich, Congress declined to abandon the centralizing and socializing program built up in the drive toward social democracy. In fact, not a single one of the great statutes enacted under this head was completely repealed after the Republican victory in the congressional election of 1918. While continuing federal grants in aid of highway construction and education, Congress made new excursions in the field of social work. An Industrial Rehabilitation Act passed in 1920 set the stamp of national approval upon the idea of community responsibility for industrial accidents, by offering federal funds to states to assist in restoring to civil employment persons injured in industry or any legitimate occupation. An equally novel departure was made the next year when Congress appropriated money for the purpose of safeguarding the welfare of mothers and infants at the time of childbirth. Forced upon the consideration of Congress by women's civic societies, this project raised great outcries in the name of states' rights and sacred individualism; but without avail. Defeated in the national legislature, opponents appealed to the Supreme Court where they likewise received a rebuff.

With a kind of grim determination, the apostles of general improvement by collective action moved forward. Blocked twice by the Supreme Court in their efforts to restrict child labor by federal legislation—once by regulating interstate commerce and once by taxation—they promptly proposed an amendment to the Constitution permitting the specific enactment of national child labor laws. Again great lamentation was heard among the guardians of the covenant; but Congress in 1924 passed the resolution authorizing that form of federal intervention in labor conditions throughout the Union. While the amendment met a frigid reception in the states, that was no fault of Congress.

In its halls the collectivist principle continued to be invoked. The Wilson organization for furnishing federal aid to agriculture was not only kept intact; it was enlarged by new laws extending rural credits, encouraging farmers to form coöperative societies, and spreading federal control over stockyards and speculation in grain. Similarly, in dealing with two great national industries, railways and coal mining, Congress refused to rely solely upon the beneficent working of competition and private enterprise; no matter how savagely Attorney General Daugherty might be prosecuting advocates of socialistic creeds. When the railways were returned to their owners by the Esch-Cummins act of 1920, no attempt was made to break up great systems and stimulate competitive strife; on the contrary, the interstate commerce commission was authorized and instructed to plan for new consolidations among existing carriers. Going beyond this provision, Congress sought to make the strong roads carry the weak by ordering them to pay half of their earnings above a fixed percentage into a national fund for common railway financing. Though this project was denounced in tribunals of law as a scheme for seizing private property in the general interest, it was sustained by the Supreme Court, Chief Justice Taft rendering the opinion.

Even in a sphere rather remote from interstate commerce, responsible politicians resorted to the principle of collective action. Alarmed by a coal strike which began in the spring of 1922, Congress enlarged the powers of the interstate commerce commission, authorized it to control coal shipments during the emergency, empowered it to beat down "unjust prices," provided for the appointment of a federal coal director, and created an agency to investigate the industry. In the course of time, this agency reported that coal mining, formerly regarded by sound thinkers as a branch of private enterprise solely within the jurisdiction of the states, was not only "affected with public interest," but was also a proper subject for federal regulation and control by governmental agencies. Evidently, in the opinion of Congress, the country did not want a restoration of all the great customs and usages of the McKinley era. In matters of national legislation, Harding was still far from the goal of normalcy when death overcame him at San Francisco in August, 1923.

§

Harding's successor, Calvin Coolidge, of Massachusetts, Daniel Webster's state, had just the training, temper and opinions required to promote the administrative policies of restoration and healing. Coolidge had likewise come up through the great American school of village politics to high places by cautious steps always in line with the measured tread of his organization leaders. He had long served his party, rising from membership in the town council of Northampton through the offices of city solicitor and clerk of the court to the state legislature, passing on to the post of lieutenant-governor and finally reaching the governor's chair. Never in all his career had he shocked his neighbors by advocating strange things prematurely; neither had he been the last of the faithful to appear upon the scene in appropriate armor. Conciliation and prudence had been his watchwords; patience and simplicity his symbols of life.

Only one action among his varied local achievements had excited national interest. In 1919, while he was still governor, the policemen of Boston, who were affiliated with the American Federation of Labor, made a plea for a wage adjustment to meet the rising cost of living and, failing to secure it, went on strike, leaving the city for a few days without protection. After disorder and looting had occurred and the air had become tense with strife and passion, Governor Coolidge called out the state militia and wrote a ringing note to Samuel Gompers informing him that "there is no right to strike against the public safety, by anybody, anywhere, any time." The language was so decisive that President Wilson congratulated the Governor on his stand and a friendly press began to praise him as the silent man of iron, afraid of nothing.

In critical circles, however, the idea of Coolidge as a figure of heroic proportions was ridiculed and attempts were made to show that, far from doing his duty promptly and courageously, he had in truth evaded his responsibilities as long as possible, had refused to act until the mayor of Boston, aided by the police commissioner, had got the situation well in hand, and had moved at last only when he could come upon the stage in a burst of red fire, with full political safety. On these allegations there was a long and acrimonious debate; though it was not necessary for any one who wanted to know the facts to remain in darkness. In words that admitted of no double interpretation, Governor Coolidge himself told directly and simply just what happened; and he did this in a speech delivered at the Republican state convention in 1919 before the incident became obscured by partisan dispute. "Some urged me," he said, "to remove the [Police] Commissioner, some to request him to alter his course. To all these I had to reply that I had no authority over his actions and could not lawfully interfere with him. . . . To restore order, I at once and by pre-arrangement with him and the Commissioner offered to the Mayor to call out the State Guard. At his request I did so." There in the plain, unaffected language appropriate to the man was the record over which journalists and campaign managers worked up such a fierce debate.

Called by his favorable press a silent and restrained statesman, Coolidge was in truth a facile and versatile speaker and writer. His collected orations and addresses in two or three volumes, as well as numerous public letters and articles, bore witness to his genius for expressing opinions on a wide range of topics, resounding with a native shrewdness and an open sincerity that reminded his friends of Lincoln. In one series of speeches, historical and philosophical in character, tracing the evolution of political economy in America, Coolidge revealed a firm grasp on the nature of the partisan battles that had raged from the days of Washington down to his own time. With bold strokes he sketched the system of Hamilton and the policies of the organizations which had held the inheritance intact. "The party now in power in this country," he said in 1922, "through its present declaration of principles, through the traditions which it inherited from its predecessors, the Federalists and Whigs, through their achievements and its own, is representative of those policies which were adopted under the lead of Alexander Hamilton,"

Growing more specific in his bill of particulars, Coolidge frankly expressed the belief that manufacturing was the motive power of American civilization. "The driving force of American progress," he declared, "has been her industries. They have created the wealth that has wrought our national development. . . . Without them the great force of agriculture would now be where it was in the eighteenth century." In keeping with this view, he saw in William McKinley, that outspoken champion of industries, a successor to Alexander Hamilton, Washington's famous Secretary of the Treasury. The Ohio statesman, he said, had taken up "the work of Hamilton and Clay . . . reëstablished their principles, and under his leadership the government re-adopted their policies."

And yet Coolidge was not oblivious to the charges brought by Roosevelt and Wilson against the leaders of business enterprise; he agreed that there had been "growing up an attempt to exercise an improper control over the affairs of the government." Speaking in 1921, he said that "this condition culminated about twenty years ago." But the evil had been overcome. Roosevelt, he declared, "broke the menace of monopoly. He made the sovereignty of the people supreme. . . . He was . . . the defender of the republic. He found it menaced and he left it free." The conclusion was inevitable; there was nothing to do but to move forward along the lines marked out by Hamilton, Clay, and McKinley now that the ogre of "special privilege" had been destroyed by Roosevelt.

Though laying great stress upon economic forces in the evolution of American society, Coolidge by no means looked upon the acquisition and enjoyment of wealth as ends in themselves. His system of political economy was suffused with a moral glow. "If society lacks learning and virtue," he said, "it will perish. . . . The classic of all classics is the Bible. . . . Civilization depends not only upon the knowledge of the people but upon the use they make of it. . . . The nation with the greatest moral power will win." When dealing directly with politics and economics he spoke in the same vein: "What we need is thrift and industry . . . Let everybody keep at work . . . We have come to our present high estate through toil and suffering and sacrifice . . . Not by revolution but by evolution has man worked out his destiny . . . The man who builds a factory builds a temple, the man who works there worships there, and to each is due not scorn and blame, but reverence and praise . . . We are all members of one body . . . Industry cannot flourish if labor languish. Transportation cannot prosper if manufactures decline . . . Large profits mean large payrolls . . . Politics is not an end, but a means . . . It is the art of government . . . In Massachusetts we are citizens before we are partisans . . . We do not need more government, we need more culture . . . Abraham Lincoln was not a radical, but a conservative. He never sought to waste, but always to save . . . Democracy is not a tearing down; it is a building up . . . Man's nature drives him ever onward . . . McKinley was the 'advance agent of prosperity' that he might be the prophet of the intellectual and moral forces of mankind."

§

President Coolidge's practical program, based upon this combination of economic and ethical philosophy, was transparent in its simplicity. Taxes were to be reduced—not indeed on goods consumed by the masses but certainly on the incomes of those who sat highest at the American feast. This was to be done, he urged, with a view to leaving more money in the hands of the rich for investment, so that the opportunities of the poor to gain profitable employment might be multiplied. Correlatively, there was to be less interference with business through administrative orders and through the prosecution of trusts before the courts; for Roosevelt had destroyed the threat of monopoly. With genuflections in the same direction, the practice of taxing the industrial East and distributing the revenue all over the country in the form of subsidies for roads, health, education, and other social purposes was to be discountenanced as a violation of the sacred creed of states' rights so long honored by the Democrats.

Invoking the same economical spirit, Coolidge condemned the use of the government's financial strength and organized power to aid the farmers in offsetting, by price-control devices, the menacing lag between the selling values of agricultural produce and the cost of manufactures protected by the tariff. Harmonizing with this tenderness for the treasury and the taxpayer was the President's refusal to endorse the idea of a huge appropriation in the form of a bonus to the soldiers in the late war for democracy. Finally, the ship of state which Hamilton launched, which Clay, Webster, and McKinley had steered successfully on its course, was not to be disturbed by minor scandals below decks; the wicked were to be punished but eyes were to be fastened on the stars.

As long as the Senate and the House of Representatives, left over from the previous régime, held power, Coolidge found it hard to cut his way through the entanglements thrown up by the backwash of recent years. He opposed a bonus for the soldiers; Congress passed it over his vote. He demanded a heavy cut in the surtaxes; Congress in the revenue act of 1924 fixed the surtax on incomes of over $500,000 at forty per cent and even voted that the amount returned by all income taxpayers should be made public. To the legislation already enacted for the farmers were added new laws and new forms of financial assistance. An effort to get a man of "constructive economic imagination" into the department of justice was defeated by insurgency in the Republican ranks, for a large number of agrarian congressmen wearing the Republican label were now coöperating with the Democrats rather than with the Coolidge administration. In short, the healing and restoration promised by Harding in 1920, after long and arduous labors, had not been effected to the satisfaction of the Republican high command.

§

Convinced that larger areas of normalcy could be recovered by a frontal assault, the managers of the Republican organization renominated Coolidge by acclamation in 1924 and in keynote speeches and platform planks flouted and repudiated the Republican congressional program. Confronted by formidable opponents in partisan array with this standard of healing and serenity floating high overhead, the Democrats, amid great confusion, tried to prepare for the tourney. For many weary days, in convention assembled, they tossed about in a raging fever while William G. McAdoo, champion of the radicals, and Governor Alfred Smith, spokesman of the moderates, wrestled for mastery within the party.

When at length the deadlock was broken, the palm went

to a third contestant who aroused no great enthusiasm save on the right wing—John W. Davis, of West Virginia and New York. No doubt Davis was a gentleman of taste with a flair for good form; his deportment during his service under Wilson in the department of justice and as ambassador to Great Britain had been impeccable; but he lacked the warmth of Bryan, had none of the oratorical suppleness of Wilson, and was handicapped by his connections with the banking house of J. P. Morgan and Company. Moreover his platform, if it seemed good in the sight of importing merchants, was lacking in appeal to the American Federation of Labor and the agrarian battalions of the Great Commoner.

There was evidently room for an insurgent candidate and all signs pointed to Senator Robert M. La Follette as the logical man for the rôle. Author of luminous pages in the statute books of progressive democracy and leader of the fight in Congress against the hosts of normalcy, he could not consistently support either Coolidge or Davis. Having announced his nonconformity in an unmistakable manner, the Wisconsin Senator was nominated for the presidency at a hastily assembled convention composed largely of delegates representing farmer and labor elements, supported by progressive sympathizers among whom were many women. Even the Socialists endorsed him, leaving to a few intransigent Communists the business of working for an overturn of capitalism root and branch. Treated with scanter courtesy than usual by the directors of the two major parties, the American Federation of Labor also gave its official benediction to La Follette, leading unseasoned politicians to imagine that the great economic combination had been made at last.

A triangular battle was now fought to a finish. Coolidge stood fast by "normalcy and common sense"—the Constitution and the wisdom of the Fathers. Davis bore down heartily on the revelations of corruption and malfeasance in office laid at the door of the Republican directorate by congressional investigations. La Follette sought to unite agrarians and industrial workers in a frontal assault on trusts and monopolies, on the Supreme Court as the defender of current use and wont, and on the policy of imperial advance in the Caribbean and the Orient. Again the verdict at the polls was decisive: Coolidge was given a clean majority of more than two millions over the combined vote of his opponents and a Republican Congress more effectively attuned to normalcy was returned.

In the new intellectual climate the policy of the administration was consistent with the election returns. Income taxes were reduced and projects for cutting the rates of the upper brackets were now accepted by Congress. Though legal action was begun against one of the fresh crop of industrial mergers, the general policy of non-interference with business was pursued. Discarding the precedent set by Roosevelt in the coal strike of 1902, Coolidge allowed the anthracite operators and miners to wear themselves out in a long battle extending from September, 1925, into February of the following year. Thus, it was made manifest that economic enterprise was not to be harried or hampered by prosecutions. And the prosperity that spread throughout the industrial states lent color to the claim that at least temporarily the application of the Hamilton-Webster-Clay-McKinley-Coolidge principles brought a greater abundance of good things to the masses than either the régime of progressive democracy or the program of the new freedom. To them that had labored hard for a recovery of normalcy, this was a sufficient reward.

With reference to foreign affairs, the Coolidge administration moved forward cautiously after the election of 1924. The broad way was, of course, as clear as it had been in the days when the Republican party formally inaugurated the second stage in its advance policy with the Spanish War. Indeed, those economic forces that had driven the country out upon the seven seas were more powerful and more insistent than ever: investments and trade abroad had multiplied many fold and the swelling industrial equipment, especially stimulated by the World War, needed ever wider markets for its increasing stream of goods.

Tersely and neatly the new situation was summarized by the Secretary of the Navy, Curtis Wilbur, in a speech before the Connecticut Chamber of Commerce on May 7, 1925, about two months after the inauguration of Coolidge: "Americans have over twenty millions of tons of merchant shipping to carry the commerce of the world, worth three billion dollars. We have loans and property abroad, exclusive of government loans, of over ten billions of dollars. If we add to this the volume of exports and imports for a single year—about ten billion dollars—we have an amount almost equal to the entire property of the United States in 1868 and if we add to this the eight billion dollars due us from foreign governments, we have a total of $31,000,000,000, being about equal to the total wealth of the nation in 1878 . . . These vast interests must be considered when we talk of defending the flag . . . We fought not because Germany invaded or threatened to invade America but because she struck at our commerce on the North Sea and denied to our citizens on the high seas the protection of our flag . . . To defend America we must be prepared to defend its interests and our flag in every corner of the globe . . . An American child crying on the banks of the Yangtse a thousand miles from the coast can summon the ships of the American navy up that river to protect it from unjust assault."

Immense as were the diplomatic requirements of this economic strain, they were met by President Coolidge with pragmatic realism. First of all, the problem of the debts owed by European powers to the government of the United States had to be handled with regard for both domestic opinion and foreign relations. A majority of the American taxpayers evidently thought they were entitled to relief by a recovery of the total amount lent to friendly belligerents during the World War. But to American bankers the matter had other aspects; drastic efforts to collect the foreign debts would make it more difficult for them to float additional loans abroad, public and private, and would check the gathering of rich commissions from that form of enterprise. If the banking and investing interests could get a reduction in their heavy income taxes and could then shift to consumers the burden of paying off the federal bonds issued to provide the money originally lent to the Entente powers, they could count themselves doubly fortunate in having the debts canceled and the decks cleared for new foreign financing under their management.

Among American manufacturers enjoying the benefits of the protective tariff similar reasons prevailed for tenderness with respect to the obligations incurred in the common war for democracy. If the debts were paid, of necessity payment would have to be made in goods, starting a heavy influx of foreign commodities—exactly the thing they did not want. Besides, there were pleas for compassion on the score of comradeship in "the great humanitarian crusade," poignant longings for European affection, and touching appeals from the citizens of the debtor nations. Hence a widespread propaganda was begun in favor of canceling the debts. Crowning it all were obvious difficulties in collection and payment; though none of the debtor countries ventured to defend on simple confiscatory grounds a repudiation far greater than the Bolsheviki had made in Russia.

Between the general taxpayers on the one hand and parties to the case on the other, the federal government had to steer a ticklish course, tacking rather in the popular direction. The Harding administration negotiated a settlement with Great Britain on terms which seemed severe to the British though they fell short of the amount written in the bond. Swinging over to the view of the investing fraternity, the Coolidge administration granted more generous terms to France, Belgium, and Italy and showed no disposition to be harsh or too urgent. How much of the grand total would ever be collected or whether in fact collection was possible at all, was still uncertain a decade after the United States entered the World War.

Entangled with the debt question was the issue of European relations as a whole. While bitter critics of the League of Nations continued to oppose joining that fellowship for adjusting international disputes, it was becoming increasingly manifest that, as Secretary Wilbur indicated, the practical stake of American investors in European countries called for coöperation of some kind. If the federal government could not take part in European conferences, American bankers could participate in the councils of European financiers. As a matter of fact, they gave material strength to the movement which put into effect the Dawes plan for stabilizing the economic system of Germany, and for collecting at least a part of the reparations. Moreover, they floated in the United States, naturally on terms advantageous to themselves, a huge German loan issued to give support to the new order of things.

From economic coöperation it was but a step to political or at least juristic coöperation. So many who favored the former joined the Wilsonian idealists in promoting the latter. After all, the arbitration of international controversies had long been a prominent feature of American theory and, as the country was already a member of the international tribunal established by the Hague conference of 1899, it seemed no radical departure to join the World Court set up by the League of Nations. Following the example of his predecessor, President Coolidge, accordingly, gave the project his blessing; and in 1926 the Senate, with abundant reservations and conditions, assented—provided the other powers would accept the stipulations laid down by America as the price of her affiliation. Though a great deal of feeling was displayed in the controversy over this cautious action, the degree of commitment involved in it was not serious, especially as compared with the entanglements implicit in pledges already made in Hague conventions and arbitration treaties. Indeed, it was so slight that the leading nations associated with the League took steps which amounted to a rejection of the American terms.

Viewed in the large, the proposed entrance of the United States into the World Court seemed to be a part of general plans for assuring international concord. Like Cleveland, McKinley, Roosevelt, Taft, and Wilson, President Coolidge boldly proclaimed himself an advocate of peace. He openly repudiated those spokesmen of the navy and air defense interests who rattled the sword when appropriation bills were pending in Congress and on one occasion he went in person to tell the graduating class at Annapolis that in this country the civil branch of the government was supreme over the naval and military divisions. For the purpose of preserving friendly relations with Japan, Coolidge opposed the provision of the act of 1924 which expressly excluded Japanese immigrants from the United States—adding that, had it not been incorporated in the body of the bill, he would have applied his veto. "In peace," he said, "there lies the greatest opportunity for relief from burdensome taxation."

Yet when American property rights or claims were jeopardized within the borders of any minor country, President Coolidge let it be known that neither love of peace nor desire for normalcy would prevent the use of military engines in the protection of vested interests. On the occasion of renewed disturbances in Nicaragua in 1927, marines were again employed in that tiny republic, and when civil war in China interfered with American operations, large naval forces were dispatched to the scene to await eventualities. Taking advantage of the furor over Nicaragua and the continuation of the contest with Mexico over the application of her land laws to American owners and lessees, the President bluntly declared through the White House spokesman that the whole issue could be "boiled down to the simple question, 'Shall the property of American citizens in Mexico be confiscated without being paid for?'" And when the Senate unanimously voted in favor of arbitrating the Mexican controversy, saving American rights, the President did not commit himself to that platonic proposition but by innuendo implied that the United States was prepared to defend the claims of its citizens in certain countries, to define them on its own authority, and to enforce them by arms if necessary—this even though a claims commission for the adjustment of Mexican difficulties had been provided by negotiation and officials of the Mexican government asserted that only one-seventh of the oil companies representing about one-twentieth of the property involved, especially the so-called Doheny and Mellon interests, had declined to comply with the land laws in question. Perhaps Coolidge was screwed up to this firm resolve by alarmist reports from the State Department hinting that Bolsheviki were lurking around every corner.

§

Surveying the ground after ten years of labor for restoration and healing, the warriors of normalcy, in spite of their overwhelming victory in 1924 and the reduction in the taxes on the rich, could not feel sure that ultimately they were to be transported all the way back to the era of the full dinner pail. As a matter of disconcerting fact the economic world in which they moved and the intellectual climate on which they relied for ideas and phraseology were not the same as in the piping days of McKinley and Hanna. If organized labor was less intransigent—more intimately associated with capitalist methods and philosophy on account of high wages, labor banks, huge accumulations of funds, and wide investments in every form of business enterprise—the setting for capitalist operations had been radically altered by the economic events of the past fifty years and by the transformation of Europe in peace and war.

In the good old days, American money lenders had practically nothing invested abroad and American manufacturers made goods almost entirely for a home market that was rapidly expanding with the development of virgin soil in the West. While that condition prevailed, American bankers were on the whole sympathetically allied with the captains of industry whom they helped to finance; and the state of European civilization made relatively little difference to those who owned forges in Pennsylvania or spindles in North Carolina.

But in the new age when heroic efforts were being made for a recovery of serenity, the face of the wide world had been transformed. American manufacturers, always multiplying their facilities in the hope of larger profits, had pushed out into the markets of South America, Asia, and Africa—on which England, France, Italy, and Germany were trying to thrive—and even into the very shops of London, Paris, Berlin, Rome, and Tokyo. Moreover American bankers, glutted with profits and savings won from business enterprise, had lent billions abroad and were lending more millions every year—billions on which constant returns had to be made to the United States in interest and principal installments, inevitably bound to take the form of manufactured goods, raw materials, and agricultural produce, at least in the main, unless of course canceled in Europe's next cataclysmic upheaval. At this very juncture, the great nations of the Old World whose growing industries had once made enormous demands for American farm produce were suffering from the devastating effects of the World War, were heavily in debt to the United States, and were fated either to repudiate their bonds flatly or in some respectable manner or to send huge exports to America with which to discharge their obligations.

Considered realistically, therefore, the era of normalcy was an age of paradox. Could the United States continue to supply unlimited streams of farm produce and manufactures to the world except in the guise of credits? And if in the form of credits, would there not come a time when the burden of interest and installment payments must result either in imports ruinous to American business and agriculture or in repudiations ruinous to American investors? Furthermore in this seemingly inexorable flow of things was there not bound to arise sooner or later a terrific struggle between the American banking interests engaged in foreign financing on the one side and American businessmen engaged in manufacturing on the other? Indeed the financial columns of the newspapers reflected every day flashes from the conflict between the advance guards of these now opposing forces—never more signally than in October, 1926, when J. P. Morgan announced himself in favor of free trade for Europe. If the light seemed to shine brightly on the pathway of normalcy, shadows lurked there also.

On the left flank the new agricultural forces had to be taken into the reckoning. Led by the cotton planters and the corn-belt farmers, agrarians were now more versed in the ways of the world than Daniel Shays, Andrew Jackson, or Jerry Simpson had ever been. By recent legislation it was absolutely demonstrated that they had put aside the simple gospel of inflation in favor of something more substantial and it was further evident that they were in no complacent mood. Caught between organized capital and organized labor sustaining prices of manufactures on one side and the relative decline in the European market for their produce on the other, the farmers were in something of a panic. With land values blown up to the bursting point and the wages of farm labor at urban levels, they faced more than losses on current crops. They saw ahead the possibility that a large part of their property might be confiscated through an increasing disparity between income and outlay spread over a long period of years.

Respecting the political arts, agrarians had more elaborate views than in 1860 or 1896 and they now had the support of a few competent statesmen who looked upon the salvation of the native farming population as more important than multiplying urban industrial centers peopled by imported aliens or swelling the profits of manufacturers already rich. If the engines of state—diplomats, gunboats, marines, and armies—could be used at great cost to protect and promote banking and industry at the ends of the earth, why not a public service no less energetic on behalf of agriculture, they inquired. If manufacturers closely organized in combinations could charge high prices for their goods at home and dump their surplus abroad at heavy discounts, charging the differential, if any, to domestic consumers, why should the federal government not accomplish the same legerdemain for the farmers? With such queries in mind, agrarians cried out: "Protection for all or none." Or as a philosopher given to lightning summaries stated it, "If we can't all sit at the table, let's kick the legs out from under the table and all sit together on the ground." While there was nothing revolutionary in this slogan, it implied trouble for the apostles of serenity and it meant that their problems of statecraft were not as simple as those so easily solved by the political school of William McKinley and Marcus A. Hanna—whose banner Harding tried to hoist again over the White House.

CHAPTER XXX

The Mirage Dissolves

DURING the closing years of President Coolidge's administration, the economic scene as viewed from the portico of the White House was clear and pleasing to the observer. The clouds which critics thought they saw on the horizon did not seem to be visible at all from the President's angle of outlook. Only two problems, therefore, engaged his attention. The first was to put a few finishing touches to the fair pageant of prosperity and the other to prevent any disturbance of the exhibit by agrarian members of Congress on the left wing. As a result, his last years were singularly barren of significant legislation. His recommendations were sparing and his vetoes effective.

On the positive side, the Merchant Marine Act of 1928 brought the powerful aid of the government to the side of the shipping interests. Once the Democrats had denounced ship subsidies as a bare-faced fraud upon the public, but, as we have said, during the World War, when farmers and cotton planters needed bottoms for their exports, President Wilson had put the government into the shipping business. Now the issue, as President Coolidge saw it, was how to get the government out of private enterprise and secure enough money from the Federal Treasury to enable private concerns to operate at a profit. A direct subsidy was out of the question, owing to opposition in Congress. So an expedient was chosen. The new Act provided that the Postmaster General could award mail contracts to the lowest American bidders for the carriage of mails to all ports not covered by the coastwise shipping acts. The maximum rate to be granted could run as high as twelve dollars a mile, without respect to the mail tonnage aboard. In this manner there was granted to American shippers a favor which a commissioner of the Shipping Board called "the most lucrative mail subsidy in the world."

Under this Act and other measures, ships owned by the government were sold at low prices to private concerns, mail subsidies were granted, money was lent by the government at a low rate of interest for construction, and American naval officers were permitted to serve in the merchant marine, receiving half their pay from the Federal Treasury. As an additional relief for business Congress provided that until 1932 only fifty per cent of the crews on American vessels need be American citizens. Ultimately the entire shipping business was to be restored to private hands with a substantial aid from the government. During the transition period the government was to continue to operate "pioneer lines," which did not pay their expenses, transferring them to private concerns as soon as a profit showed up on the balance sheet. Under official stimulus American shipping was expanded just at a moment when the maritime powers of Europe were also subsidizing their merchant lines, in one guise or another. By this process were multiplied the empty vessels available for the world's carrying trade.

While urging and approving this form of federal beneficence for commerce and industry, President Coolidge was hostile to certain measures sponsored by agrarian leadership in Congress. The first of these was the McNary-Haugen bill for agricultural relief, passed early in 1927. This measure contemplated, in effect, dumping abroad surpluses of six chief products at a loss if necessary and making up the difference by an "equalization fee" charged against the producers of the respective crops—all under government auspices. In this way, it was argued by the sponsors of the bill, agricultural prices could be raised in the United States to a satisfactory figure. In addition, certain features were introduced with a view to the stabilization of agriculture. Expecting prosperity from the measure, the Western radicals handed this project—their Magna Carta of Farmers—to the White House for approval.

President Coolidge replied with a veto couched in terms even more severe than he was wont to use. He declared that the bill really imposed on the Government a price-fixing function—"an economic fallacy from which this country has every right to be spared." The equalization fee he denounced as "a tax for the special benefit of particular groups," without distinguishing it from tariff duties on particular manufactured commodities. The whole measure, he thought, was complicated, unworkable, and unsound in principle and concept. Moreover a part of it was characterized as unconstitutional by his Attorney General. But undisturbed by their defeat, the agrarians passed a similar bill the following year, only to receive a second veto more vigorous, if possible, than the first blast delivered during the previous season. No additional proof was required to demonstrate to the Farm Bloc that President Coolidge did not intend to set his signature to any such elaborate measure for drawing the government into the operation of raising the prices of prime farm produce. That much was definitely settled as the campaign of 1928 approached. The issue, still alive and hot, was handed to his successor.

A second proposition, framed under the direction of Senator Norris and supported by agrarian members of both houses, dealt with the government's power plant at Muscle Shoals. This huge establishment, built during the World War as a part of the munitions-producing program, had been lying almost idle for years while the debate over its disposal raged in Congress. At last in 1928 Senator Norris was able to carry through Congress his bill authorizing government operation of the plant for the production of power and nitrates. To this measure President Coolidge applied the "pocket veto." Breaking his silence later, he expressed objection to putting the government "into the retail business" and announced that he was willing to sign a bill authorizing the lease of Muscle Shoals to a private concern. Neither the pocket veto nor the subsequent criticism had a mollifying effect upon the opposition, and so that issue continued to vex the country.

More neutral in aspect, though marked by highly controversial features, were two other measures approved by President Coolidge, after negotiation and compromise. The first authorized an enormous federal expenditure to carry out a system of public works designed to control floods in the Mississippi Valley. The second provided for the erection of a great dam at Boulder Canyon or Black Canyon for power, water, and irrigation purposes. Besides invoking the wrath of some of the states involved in the transaction, the latter bill raised the old specter of government ownership and operation. A compromise was the outcome. Large authority was vested in the Secretary of the Interior to be exercised at his discretion. After a sharp contest in Congress, it was stipulated, however, that in disposing of the water and power available at the new dam the Secretary must give preference to public bodies—states and municipalities—over the private companies that applied. In due course the project was started and the Secretary, under constant fire from public-ownership advocates, made generous, though not full, concessions to their insistence. The principle of public ownership was firmly fixed, operating rights were leased, and public bodies were promised the major part of the output in water and power. Something had happened since the days when power sites were given away or sold for a song.

In the sphere of general international relations, President Coolidge continued the policy of compromise which had been inaugurated under Harding. At the close of the World

War, the United States was in a position to realize the principle of *Machtpolitik* which had been implicit from the beginning in Federalist-Whig-Republican tradition—full freedom to define national interest without foreign intervention and to enforce it by adequate naval power. But the Washington Conference had called a halt on naval rivalry with its prospect of ruinous ultimates. And this surrender of sovereignty the Coolidge administration confirmed by signing the Kellogg-Briand Peace Pact of 1928. By Article I of this pact, the high contracting parties "solemnly declare in the names of their respective peoples that they condemn recourse to war for the solution of international controversies and renounce it as an instrument of national policy in their relations with one another." In Article II they "agree that the settlement or solution of all disputes or conflicts of whatever nature or of whatever origin they may be, which may rise among them, shall never be sought except by pacific means." In other words, the reservation of "national honor" and "vital interests" as items to be defended in the last ditch by war, if necessary, was finally and positively discarded and henceforward the settlement of all disputes was to be sought by peaceful means. Such excursions as the war against Spain in 1898 were thus formally renounced.

The sweeping language of the Kellogg-Briand Pact, however, was restricted by subsequent definitions. Under its terms, as explained by the signers, nothing "restrains or compromises in any manner whatsoever the right of self-defense"; and as every country now claims that its wars are fought solely for that purpose, the loophole seems big enough for almost any eventuality. Furthermore, according to interpretations, resort to war by one party "would automatically release the other parties from their obligation to the treaty-breaking state." Agreements to employ arms under the Covenant of the League of Nations also stand unimpaired under the new pact. Defensive alliances concluded between France and certain powers in Eastern Europe are in effect likewise excluded from the scope of the pact. By way of supplement, the British Government declared that its renunciation of war does not apply to those regions of the world which have a special interest for British peace and safety. According to a tacit understanding, the Monroe Doctrine is not affected by the outlawry of war. Hence it is difficult, in speaking of the commitments under this international agreement, to say just what it means in any concrete case of controversy and conflict. Nevertheless the bold principle of renunciation stands clearly written in the Kellogg-Briand document. It marks a transition in the literature, if not the substance, of diplomacy.

As if kindled by a special enthusiasm for peace, President Coolidge put forward anew the issue of the World Court. For a time, however, the outlook for American entry seemed dark. After powerful members of the tribunal declined to accept the reservations laid down by the Senate of the United States in 1926, all prospects for an agreement seemed to be at an end. Yet the President did not surrender. Near the close of his administration, he sent Elihu Root to Europe for the purpose of working out a compromise which would permit American membership without commitments too shocking to the senatorial conscience. The enterprise was successful, in part at least, for Mr. Root was able to reach an agreement on formulas which seemed to meet all the reasonable demands of the isolationists. Duly signed by the contracting parties, the document was presented during the administration of President Hoover to the Senate for ratification, but it was coldly received and laid aside in the dark recesses of a committee room. Arduous labors by advocates of the Court could not stir the Senators to action.

Amid all these efforts to establish peace, nothing impractical was done. After the Geneva naval conference broke up in 1927 without arriving at any conclusions respecting the reduction of fighting craft not included in the Washington Conference treaties, President Coolidge recommended to Congress the construction of fifteen new cruisers, specifying no time limits for laying down the ships. Interpreted on the one side as a threat designed to force England and Japan into a reduction agreement and on the other as the sign of a naval revival, the bill was passed by safe majorities. Its advancement, however, was doubtless facilitated by the powerful lobby maintained by the ship-building interests and a liberal use of money in "entertaining" and "educating" members of the national legislature—as a Senate investigation revealed in 1930.

Moreover, it was made perfectly clear that the Kellogg-Briand Peace Pact did not alter the status and operations of the United States in the Caribbean. Worried by renewed disturbances in Nicaragua, President Coolidge dispatched a force of marines to that country and after some fighting restored again the semblance of peace. When criticized for this action and accused of departing from the spirit of the Peace Pact, he replied tartly: "We are not making war on Nicaragua any more than a policeman on the street is making war on the passersby. We are there to protect our citizens and their property from being destroyed by war and to lend every encouragement we can to the restoration of peace." In order to regularize activities, the President sent Henry L. Stimson to Nicaragua as a special representative and a plan was evolved, after conferences with leaders of various factions, providing for American supervision of the coming elections. The following year, the elections were held; a new president was then installed; and a small American force was placed in charge of pacification. It was said by the administration that in due course complete withdrawal would be possible, as in the case of Santo Domingo, after full guarantees of American rights had been obtained. This occurred in January, 1933. Similar efforts to arrange for the restoration of full sovereignty to Haiti, with appropriate guarantees, under the administration of President Hoover, encountered endless delays. Thus American hegemony in the Caribbean remained undisturbed.

In American relations with Europe, the last days of normalcy brought no significant changes. Negotiations for the settlement of the debts owed by the Allied powers to the government of the United States were carried to completion, save in the case of Soviet Russia, and payments were duly made until the close of 1932. Early in 1928, it was evident to all students of finance that the Dawes plan for adjusting German reparations was breaking down, but that was not regarded in Washington as an affair calling for action on the part of the United States. The great powers of the Old World recognized Russia and sought to develop commercial relations with the Soviet government, but the United States clung to the position early announced by Secretary Hughes: If Russia intends to pay what she owes, she can do so without calling a conference and that will be the proper time to consider recognition.

The chilly attitude which the Harding régime had taken toward the League of Nations was relaxed however; indeed, from time to time, official representatives of the American government participated in conferences held under the auspices of the League and treaties drawn under its authority were ratified by the Senate. But the doctrine of isolation remained sacred. From year to year more millions were poured into the foreign investment market; the Department of Commerce, under the direction of Herbert Hoover, kept an army of agents abroad drumming up trade; American business men were told to "get into the foreign game," to lend money to foreigners, to seek outlets for goods, and, if necessary, to enlarge their plants for the purpose of meeting swelling demands. The Navy League urged the expansion of the navy and merchant marine to provide protection for American lives and property at the ends of the earth. Yet in all these things there appeared to be no "entanglements" and "involvements," as the late President Harding had been fond of declaring.

Never had the world seemed brighter to those who enjoyed the brightness than at the hour when the curtain descended on the Coolidge administration. There were signs of distress and discontent, to be sure. Farmers and planters sank deeper and deeper into debt and calamity. Business triumphant had been, after all, decidedly "spotty" and microscopic searchers had discovered disconcerting movements among the indices of production and transportation. A few agitations—about the execution of Sacco and Vanzetti, the prolonged incarceration of the Centralia prisoners, and the "affair of Tom Mooney"—were kept alive by a handful of intellectuals and radical sympathizers. But, on the whole, important and respectable people busy with the stock market, selling goods, floating "investment" trusts, and making loans to foreigners paid little or no attention to such alarms and tremors. With some spectacular ups and downs, the stock market had displayed unwonted strength since the election of Mr. Coolidge in 1924. If symptoms of weakness and distress appeared around the national shrine, the President or his distinguished Secretary of the Treasury, Andrew W. Mellon, issued official statements to the effect that the fundamental economic basis of the country was "sound." On the day of President Harding's death, United States Steel stock stood at eighty-seven; on September 3, 1929, it stood at 261¾. Religion, education, publishing, and "the arts" were all vibrant with the upward surge; and as the austere man from Vermont with a strange reputation for silence rode away from the White House on March 4, 1929, the chorus of press praise drowned all minor strains of dissent. The perfect symbol of perfect business enterprise had passed from official life to the pleasures and emoluments of retirement.

§

It seemed written in the stars that President Coolidge could have been elected to succeed himself in 1928. There were, in fact, insistent demands that he should be "drafted." All these appeals, however, he put aside firmly, as if with uncanny prescience, and let it be known that he "did not choose to run" again. At this signal, various candidates for the Republican nomination flung out their banners. Head and shoulders above the throng stood Herbert Clark Hoover. He had been long in the public eye. As head of Belgian relief he had captured the imagination and sentiment of millions during the early years of the World War. After the entrance of the United States into that contest he had continued his conspicuous war services under American auspices. By 1920 he had become so distinguished that there were movements among the Democrats and Republicans alike to elevate him to the presidency. When that proved to be a forlorn hope, Mr. Hoover had cast in his fortunes with the Republican party and had been chosen as head of the Department of Commerce by President Harding. From this point of vantage he was able to form vital contacts with the business interests of the country, keep himself in the eye of the public engrossed in commercial activities, and build up a strong following. In addition, he carried on various philanthropic enterprises, gaining more honors, especially through the American Relief Association and the American Child Health Association. In the natural course of events there emerged a popular image of Mr. Hoover as a great engineer, an efficient executive, a rugged individualist, and a tender humanitarian. The combination was irresistible and he won the Republican nomination in a whirlwind of votes.

Confronted by Mr. Hoover as a guarantee of Coolidge prosperity for the coming years, the Democrats decided that an appeal to agrarianism in the style of William Jennings Bryan would be inappropriate. They chose for their candidate Alfred E. Smith, of New York, the old stronghold of the Cleveland wing. Unlike his opponent, Mr. Smith had seen political service from his early youth. He had been a member of the state legislature, sheriff of New York county, president of the board of aldermen, and governor of the commonwealth. Starting as a loyal member of Tammany Hall he had played the political game according to its rules, while revealing deep human sympathies as he rose from post to post. As the curve of his career bent upward, he drew to himself several judicious advisers who introduced him to the ideas and phrases of social reform and gave to his speeches and writings the flavor of modern liberalism. Thus a poor boy from the sidewalks of New York, closely associated with machine politics, was made to stand apart from his political origins as a peerless leader of the people. Indeed Tammany Hall was itself refurbished for the occasion and the tradition of "a new Tammany," purified by Governor Smith, was created by ardent publicists. The strength of the appeal was not to be denied. Furthermore Mr. Smith was "a wringing wet," as the current slang expressed his attitude toward the liquor question. Besides all this he had the support of personalities powerful in the financial world —Bernard M. Baruch and John J. Raskob, for example— who could supply funds for the campaign chest. To his availability there was only one serious drawback: Mr. Smith was a Catholic in a country overwhelmingly Protestant and, therefore, in the same relative position as a Protestant would have been in a country overwhelmingly Catholic.

During the campaign that ensued, there was no very sharp definition of political divisions. Mr. Hoover laid emphasis on the desirability of cleaning up a few dark corners left in the midst of glamorous prosperity. In his acceptance speech, he said: "One of the oldest and perhaps noblest of human aspirations has been the abolition of poverty. . . . We in America today are nearer to the final triumph over poverty than ever before in the history of any land. The poorhouse is vanishing from among us. We have not yet reached the goal, but, given a chance to go forward with the policies of the last eight years, we shall soon, with the help of God, be in sight of the day when poverty shall be banished from this nation. There is no guaranty against poverty equal to a job for every man. That is the primary purpose of the policies we advocate." Beyond that it was impossible for Mr. Smith to go. On the tariff, likewise, neither he nor his platform differed in any respect from the promises of the opposite side: all pledged protection for American industry and labor. While Mr. Smith attacked prohibition and Mr. Hoover defended it with faint praise, the performances of their respective parties in Congress offered no precision or certainty. Both candidates were for the traditional isolation, big navy, and firm foreign policy; neither devoted much attention to pressing international questions on the horizon, East, West, and South.

In the circumstances, the Democrats sought to raise a furor over the oil scandals and other corruption of the Harding régime. This malodorous subject was made the theme of the keynote address at the Democratic convention, and it was not allowed to drop out of sight during the campaign. In fact, from month to month, since the death of President Harding, news of dragging trials and investigations had kept the theme more or less in the headlines, despite intense preoccupation with money-making. The case of E. F. Doheny and Albert B. Fall, accused of bribery and misconduct in connection with oil leases, was in process of formulation. It was revealed that H. F. Sinclair, also involved in the oil transactions, had contributed liberally to the Republican campaign fund in 1920 and that a block of Liberty bonds, bought from the profits of oil, had figured strangely in Republican finances of that year under the management of Will Hays, chairman of the committee. Other noisome facts were unearthed about the same time. And all of them bulked large in Democratic political oratory; but apparently the voters took little interest in the retailing of past scandal. Perhaps they thought that emphasis on corruption did not come with good grace from the party of Tweed, Croker, and Murphy—which was soon to produce James J. Walker with his mysterious bank accounts and other Tammany leaders with "tin boxes" full of cash derived from unknown sources. At all events they elected Mr. Hoover by an overwhelming vote, giving him forty states out of the Union and throwing only eight to Mr. Smith—six in the ever solid South and two in New England: Massachusetts and Rhode Island.

§

Among the pledges made by the Republicans during the campaign was a promise to place agriculture upon an equality with industry; and shortly after his inauguration, President Hoover called Congress in a special session to redeem the obligation. He did not himself offer an economic project for raising the prices of farm produce to higher levels, but merely suggested the creation of a Farm Board charged with the duty of finding the remedy, if one could be discovered. The response of Congress was the Agricultural Marketing Act of 1929. By express declaration the purpose of the law was to minimize speculation, prevent wasteful methods in distribution, encourage the organization of producers into associations for self-government, and assist in "preventing and controlling surpluses in any agricultural commodity through orderly production and distribution," all with a view to eliminating undue fluctuations and depressions in prices. The Act created the Farm Board and placed in its hands a revolving fund amounting ultimately to five hundred million dollars. After its establishment the Board made loans to farmers' coöperative associations to aid in the enlargement of old societies, the formation of new organizations, and the provision of facilities for handling, storing, and marketing produce. Through stabilization corporations, the Board entered the market for the purpose of buying commodities and pegging prices.

After a few months of operation the Farm Board, even though under competent direction, encountered baffling difficulties. Despite the millions which it poured into the markets, prices of agricultural produce fell—and continued to fall—until in 1932 the price of wheat was forty-two cents a bushel, the lowest level reached in more than three hundred years. With high taxes to pay for the support of state and local government, with high prices to pay for all manufactured goods, even farmers with good land free of mortgage could scarcely make ends meet, while those possessing marginal land or land burdened by debt incurred in boom days simply dropped into the abyss. In every part of the country, particularly in the West and South, banks, land banks, and money-lenders foreclosed mortgages and garnered in millions of acres which they could neither sell nor manage to advantage. All that could be said, therefore, for the Farm Board was that, without its assistance, things might have been worse, but this declaration of faith could not be substantiated in differential equations. The Board was caught in a general down swing and was powerless to stop the avalanche.

Next upon the carpet was the revision of the tariff. Relatively little had been said about it in the campaign and that little referred, in the main, to giving agriculture an equality of protection with manufacturing. But the tariff interests, alert as usual, as Joseph B. Grundy, President of the Pennsylvania Manufacturers' Association, later testified, had contributed a huge sum to Mr. Hoover's campaign fund, and felt that the Republican victory sanctioned an upward revision. And the upward revision came, but amid a prolonged and angry debate over favors, especially in the Senate, and a barrage of propaganda and lobbying seldom, if ever, exceeded in the history of tariff legislation. In the course of the proceedings it came out, for example, that Senator Hiram Bingham, of Connecticut, had introduced into the Senate finance committee, of which he was a member, an agent of the Manufacturers' Association from his state to help in the writing of schedules. For months the discussion went on, but at last, in the summer of 1930, with the aid of Democratic votes, the Hawley-Smoot tariff bill was sent to the White House for approval. Then a new storm broke. Leading economists and publicists from every part of the country protested vigorously against the measure and Democrats who had not voted for it condemned it as "a Republican steal." Yet President Hoover signed it, explaining that any objectionable features could be removed by executive action, in coöperation with the Tariff Commission, under the flexible provisions of the law. So the tariff act went into effect —to encounter not a burst of McKinley prosperity but a disconcerting downward movement of all business enterprise.

While the tariff bill was still under discussion, President Hoover turned to the subject of reducing naval armaments by international agreement. Early in his administration he had allowed the American representative in the Geneva Preparatory Commission, Hugh S. Gibson, to make a declaration in favor of drastic curtailment in arms, which startled the cabinets of Europe. In England conditions were now more favorable, for a Labor premier, Ramsay MacDonald, was at the head of affairs. In the autumn of 1929, Mr. MacDonald paid a personal visit to President Hoover and shortly afterward his government issued a call for a naval conference to be held in London. In response to the invitation the delegates of the chief powers assembled early in 1930. This time naval experts were thrust into the background and civilian agents took the helm. As a result, England, Japan, and the United States reached an agreement applying the ratio principle of the Washington Conference to cruisers, airplane carriers, destroyers, and submarines, subject to the escape clause providing that any of the three powers might increase its armaments if its security were menaced by a fourth party.

Immediately a howl of rage went up from naval circles in England, Japan, and the United States. With striking unanimity it was declared by navy propagandists in each of the countries that security had been surrendered; something akin to treason committed. In the United States the Navy League made "a smashing attack" on the London treaty; a long list of admirals registered protests against it, to offset the advocacy of the Secretary of the Navy, Charles Francis Adams, and a few admirals enlisted under his banner; and isolationist Senators, supported by the heavy batteries of the Hearst papers, smote the document with all their wrath. But in the end the requisite two-thirds vote was mustered in the Senate and the London agreement became law. President Hoover had won the mortal enmity of powerful interests in the bureaucracy and the naval supply industries.

This was intensified when he refused to throw his weight on the side of naval officers and congressmen bent on "building up to the limits of the London treaty." The Navy League accused him of "abysmal ignorance" and of betraying the interests of his country—of subordinating its interests to those of Great Britain and Japan. In fact, he was the only President for many years who had openly defied the naval bureaucracy. Wilson had talked of naval supremacy; Coolidge had declared that citizens and dollars abroad were as much a part of "the national domain" as if they were in the United States and had insisted that the navy must be strong enough to defend them everywhere. The Navy League had demanded a navy large enough to carry on a major operation, presumably against any or all powers in combination, in the waters of Europe, Asia, and Africa. But President Hoover said laconically that the function of the army and navy was to protect the United States against invasion, and that was treason to the cause of *Machtpolitik* espoused by Admiral Mahan, Theodore Roosevelt, William Randolph Hearst, and other disciples of Kipling.

§

Before President Hoover had fairly embarked on his program, the clouds which had long been hovering on the horizon of Coolidge prosperity rolled up swiftly toward the meridian and burst with a frightful crash. Flashes and distant mutterings had given ominous but neglected signals early in the year 1929. The election of Mr. Hoover had been greeted by a spurt in the stock market, though the major indices of business had pointed toward a recession. Blind and

heedless, leaders of business and finance, seconded by politicians, encouraged the public to keep up the "money-making
orgy" and, through the summer, stocks soared, until early
in September they reached a region described by Frederick
Lewis Allen as "the blue and cloudless empyrean." American Telephone and Telegraph rose to 355, General Electric
to 396, Montgomery Ward to 466, and United States Steel
to 279, taking account of adjustments. Then came the drop,
followed by thunderous detonations running into October.
Billions in paper values and alleged fortunes were destroyed.
In the mighty torrent, actresses, doctors, professors, school-
teachers, office boys, truck-drivers, small-town merchants,
Tom, Dick, Harry, Will, Susan, Bridget, and Jane, drawn
into the gambling madness by the advice and example of their
"betters," were swept into ruin as calls came for bigger mar-
gins and their holdings were sold in the wild scramble on the
Stock Exchange.

Bewildered by the downward rush and unable to believe
that an end had come to a perfect day, the nation's business
and financial leaders, with a few honorable exceptions, sought
to stem the tide by declaring that nothing serious could happen to America. Charles E. Mitchell, of the National City
Bank, declared that "the industrial situation of the United
States is absolutely sound and our credit situation is in no
way critical." Thomas Lamont, of J. P. Morgan and Company, Richard Whitney, vice-president of the Stock Exchange, John D. Rockefeller, Sr., and gentlemen of their
light and understanding issued reassuring statements indicating that the great fear was unwarranted, that the flurry
would soon pass, and that it was a genuine lake of fresh
water, not a mirage, that lay before the thirsty country.
Andrew W. Mellon, from the Treasury Department, lent
the weight of his name and fortune to that hypothesis, and
President Hoover insisted that "the fundamental business of
the country, that is, production and distribution, is on a
sound and prosperous basis." From day to day such statements were issued from high quarters, with slowly diminish-

ing confidence, until the stark and black facts of ruin silenced all save the most romantic. As investors in "prime securities" gazed upon defaulted bonds, or read notices of dividends passed, as men and women by the millions were turned out of factories, shops, offices, schools, and kitchens, the cruel truth percolated down to the bottom: the mirage had been a mirage after all.

Being mortal and unable to divine the future, the directors of affairs continued to hope against hope. By way of precaution, which seemed unduly pessimistic to some, President Hoover called the leaders of industry, agriculture, and labor to a conference in the White House and asked them to do their best to keep economic enterprise on an even keel. Then he issued an appeal to the governors of all the states urging them to coöperate with the federal government in an expansion of public works, national, state, and local, in order to take up any slack in employment that might arise. With unwonted harmony Republicans and Democrats in Congress rushed through a bill cutting taxes on income, as an assurance to the possessors of wealth, thereby curtailing the revenues of the Federal Treasury on the eve of the greatest deficit ever encountered in a time of peace since the establishment of the Republic. All through 1930 stocks wavered and flurried, recovering in many cases from the low levels of the preceding October, but on occasion displaying a sickening weakness that pointed to worse troubles ahead. Relief committees were established and presidential commissions were set to work, but neither the President nor Congress presented any program of concerted action to the country. In this fashion things drifted and eddied until the summer of 1931.

In the spring of that year the tinsel house of cards built in Central Europe, largely on lavish loans and credits from the United States and England, with certain supplements from France, collapsed amid world-wide alarms. Early in the spring, it was announced that the Kredit Anstalt of Austria, founded by the Rothschilds in 1855, was in peril and the banks of the world were called upon frantically for help. This crisis was sufficient to push over the financial structure in Germany, if structure is the appropriate term. And finally it was made so clear that even bankers could comprehend that the economic consequences of the Versailles "settlement," as J. M. Keynes had foretold, were bound to be disastrous. The Young Plan, substituted for the Dawes Plan, in 1929, could only stay the judgment of doom for a few months.

Doubly warned of Germany's desperate plight, President Hoover began cautiously to discuss a program of action with the leading bankers, and then after a cry of despair from President von Hindenburg on June 20, he issued a proposal for a moratorium of one year on the payment of interest and principal on account of the intergovernmental debts. France balked for a moment at the suddenness of the announcement and in the end accepted the inevitable. There was no alternative. If the governments had not given up their claims, private bondholders and financiers with investments and short-term credits in hand would have confronted bankruptcy—not frozen assets in Germany, but petrified assets. Since President Hoover had taken the precaution to consult leaders of Congress in advance, that body yielded at its December session, proclaiming anew its resolve against debt cancellation and rejecting a suggestion that a committee of inquiry be appointed. The financial world breathed more easily.

For a moment the moratorium relaxed the world tension, and there were upward flurries on the stock market. But the renewal of foreign trade did not follow and soon declines and disillusionment set in again. By autumn, as the session of Congress approached, bank failures, falling prices, defaults, and increasing unemployment indicated a deepening crisis. The handwriting on the wall was too large and firm to be misread. What was to be done? In previous panics the capitalist system had been allowed to work its own cure through the ruthless process of bankruptcy and liquidation which reduced debt charges, capital overhead, and commodity prices to low levels, where reduced buying power could become operative and start up the cycle of production. Could the old course be repeated? Two things were against such an outcome. In the first place, the concentration of nearly half the business wealth in the hands of two hundred corporations with strong reserves and close control over prices meant a long delay in the customary liquidations and price reductions. In the second place, if, as in previous panics, ten or fifteen great railway systems should go into receivers' hands, the life insurance companies, savings banks, and other institutions holding huge blocks of railway bonds would crash, spreading greater havoc far and wide. In these circumstances President Hoover threw himself into the breach with a project for sustaining the gigantic capitalist structure by government credit and for preventing, if possible, the cruel liquidation required by the laws of capitalist production and distribution.

On the President's recommendation Congress created the Reconstruction Finance Corporation with a capital of two billion dollars and gave it general authority to make loans to banks, life insurance companies, building and loan associations, farm-mortgage associations, railroads, and live-stock associations. Within a few months more than five thousand loans were made by the Corporation and numerous bankruptcies postponed, if not escaped entirely. Meanwhile there was a growing demand in Congress for federal appropriations for the relief of distress in all parts of the country. It was said, as Will Rogers light-heartedly put the case, that the bankers had received their dole and that the time of the starving unemployed had come. Against projects for the latter, however, President Hoover took a firm stand. At first he had insisted that at least the major portion of the funds for the unemployed should come from private charity—to avoid anything that savored of the English dole. Then he dwelt upon the responsibility of each community for the care of its destitute. When these expedients proved inadequate, and Congress seemed on the verge of making a large blanket appropriation for relief, the President forced a compromise. The adjusted scheme provided for loans to states and municipalities for "productive public works" self-supporting in character, with a view to affording employment for the idle. Although criticized for not going far enough, President Hoover made radical departures from the precedents of previous depressions and involved the government of the United States deeply in the financial structure of private business enterprise, with what long outcome only time could tell.

While the administration wrestled with the problems of the crisis, various agencies under the authority of Congress carried on investigations which added to popular knowledge of the political arts. Instructed by a Senate resolution of 1928, the Federal Trade Commission inquired into the organization and methods of public utility corporations with special reference to propaganda, and made startling discoveries of high-powered publicity. It showed that these concerns, individually and collectively, had declared war on public ownership and every form of regulation deemed too strict. They had surreptitiously insinuated miles of printed matter into the editorial and news columns of newspapers, censored textbooks on economics and civics, showered the public schools with propaganda, introduced speakers into classrooms, hired professors by means of retainers, and given money to institutions for subsidizing "research." Inquiries into lobbies, campaign funds, and campaign methods also produced data which cast doubt upon the authenticity of many public acts. And when President Hoover vetoed the Norris bill for public operation of Muscle Shoals it was alleged by his critics that he was either victimized by propaganda or governed by too much sympathy for "the power trust."

In other respects relations between the President and Congress were strained. When he nominated Charles E. Hughes to the post of Chief Justice of the Supreme Court as the successor to William Howard Taft, he was startled to find, instead of a chorus of approval from the Senate, a stubborn and bitter opposition led by Western Senators. During the debates on confirmation the latter declared that Mr. Hughes had for years been representing the most powerful corporations in the country as attorney before the Supreme Court, that he was a spokesman of great interests, and that if placed on the bench he would support property to the neglect of human rights. In the end the nomination was ratified but the dispute left deep scars. When President Hoover presented to the Senate the name of Judge John J. Parker, of North Carolina, for a place on the Supreme Bench, another storm was precipitated; Mr. Parker was accused of being unfair to organized labor and to the Negro race; his selection was attributed to the President's desire to pay a political debt; and after an angry dispute the nomination was rejected. Thereupon Owen J. Roberts was appointed and approved. Perhaps chastened by this experience and, it was alleged, warned by Senator Borah, President Hoover, on the retirement of Justice Holmes, crowned with years and honor, chose for the vacancy Judge Benjamin Cardozo, of New York, a jurist worthy in learning and intelligence of succeeding so discerning a man and fitted by humanistic outlook to take his place beside Louis D. Brandeis and Harlan F. Stone, thus helping to maintain the historic balance of three or four to six or five.

As usual, domestic conflicts produced repercussions in colonial affairs. The imperial mirage painted by Theodore Roosevelt, Henry Cabot Lodge, and Alfred Thayer Mahan, strenuous professor of *Machtpolitik,* began to fade. The question of Philippine independence was raised anew and a limited bill passed in December, 1932. Once it had been advocated by a few Boston Puritans who believed in the Declaration of Independence; now it was demanded by militant economic groups—farmers who felt the competition of imports from the Philippines and organized labor protesting against the competition of the cheap labor supplied by Filipino

immigrants.   Capitalistic interests with investment and commercial opportunities at stake protested, but the tide was
running against them.   After the Wall Street débâcle, the
downhill movement of Porto Rico became more obvious; the
swelling population stimulated by sanitary measures beat
remorselessly against the material resources of the Island;
Porto Ricans, good American citizens, by the thousands
crowded into the already overpacked sections of New York
and other continental cities, adding more color to the social
complex and new tongues to the babel; and at last in 1932
the Governor of Porto Rico openly proclaimed birth control
the only remedy for the disease of degradation, much to the
horror of the Catholic clergy and other people who did not
like to have the phrase mentioned.   In Cuba, "our economic
colony," nothing but the despotism of Machado, supported
by American interests, official and private, prevented a revolution, and it was questionable how long that iron régime
could last, especially if the depression in sugar continued.

In the realm of foreign relations, President Hoover pursued a policy of cautious moderation, without any sabre-
rattling.   Before taking office he had made "a good-will
tour" to Latin America, and afterward he sought to promote
friendships favorable to commercial intercourse.   The "stabilization" process was continued in Nicaragua, with emphasis on actions favorable to the speedy withdrawal of the
American marines.   With Haiti an adjustment was sought
which would permit the retirement of American forces, while
providing guarantees for American property and investments.   Since the pressure of American oil interests on the
government of Mexico had relaxed and a conservative
régime, akin to the system of Porfirio Diaz, had been established in that troubled country, it was easy to carry forward
the mollifying measures inaugurated by Dwight W. Morrow,
whom President Coolidge had sent as ambassador to Mexico
City.   American losses were enormous but no one north of
the Rio Grande wanted to fight about them, especially after
the retirement of Albert B. Fall.   Nibbling and procrastina-

tion were the only alternatives before the administration. After all, revolutions in South America and the collapse of business had eased the strain of promoters and concession hunters, giving a breathing spell to the State Department.

Beyond the Pacific Ocean, however, signs of tension appeared late in 1931, threatening for a time that tenuous affiliation known as the concert of nations. Harassed by twenty years of disorder in China, injurious to trade, and angered by the American Exclusion Act of 1924, the government of Japan developed a Monroe practice if not a Monroe Doctrine for itself. Taking advantage of incidents in Manchuria, either bona fide or manufactured, Japan dispatched large military forces to that region, waged war on local Chinese armies and bands, extended control beyond her treaty zone, occupied Manchuria, and set up there a puppet republic headed by Henry Pu Yi, the former boy emperor of China. Meanwhile for the purpose of suppressing a Chinese boycott, about which the government at Nanking either would or could do nothing, Japan enlarged her contingents at Shanghai and by some mysterious maneuvers came into collision with Chinese forces. Unlike other recent affairs in which bombardments by British or American gunboats had soon silenced opposition, this incident widened into destructive warfare. Before it ended, the Chinese city of Chapei had been burned, hundreds of lives lost, and devastation spread through the outlying regions. While seasoned observers of world events came to the conclusion that these operations merely demonstrated that Japan had learned well the lessons which Western powers had been teaching her for three hundred years, the smaller countries in the League of Nations—with no large territorial or commercial interests at stake in the Far East—and idealists who took the letter of the Kellogg-Briand Peace Pact seriously were visibly disturbed.

It was said flatly that Japan had violated the Pact and had made war on China, but the government in Tokyo would admit no such charge. It took the view, expressed privately by the Japanese ambassador in Washington to a New York group of specialists in foreign affairs, that its operations on Chinese soil did not differ in kind or intent from the "stabilizing" operations of American marines in Nicaragua. Unable to accept this version, the Secretary of State, Henry L. Stimson, openly declared that his government, bound by the Peace Pact, could recognize no territorial changes made in violation of its terms and in repeated notes and public statements informed Japan that her conduct was highly reprehensible. He even went so far in a letter to Senator Borah as to hint that the changed circumstances might lead to a modification of the treaties which restricted American naval power in the Orient. He also coöperated with the League of Nations. When China appealed to the League against Japan, invoking the Covenant, and the Council of the League invited the United States to send a delegate to sit with it during its consideration of the Kellogg Pact, Secretary Stimson instructed the American consul at Geneva to take part in the deliberations. Meanwhile, in defiance of all protests, Japan pushed her expansion in Manchuria and resented interference by the League. But the strain was temporarily relieved by an agreement in the League to send an impartial commission of investigation to the Orient under League auspices and headed by Lord Lytton. When its report came out in 1932, the deep complexities of the Oriental scene were made clearer to the West. If negotiation seemed to offer no solution, neither did war, and the drift of opinion appeared to favor a settlement by the parties directly concerned, China and Japan, under the constraints of world pressure—as the only alternative to war.

Toward Europe President Hoover's administration maintained the traditional attitude of isolation, at least so far as formulas went, even after the party of President Wilson came to power in Congress following the elections of 1930. Russia was not recognized although business relations were unofficially approved. Debts and reparations were treated as separate branches of economy and the former were to be paid, whatever happened in the Old World. Yet account was taken of the movement of things. When the League of Nations began to deal with economic matters in which the United States had an interest, American delegates took part in League conferences and helped to draft treaties which the Senate ratified. When the Council of the League took the Kellogg-Briand Pact under its wing in the Manchurian case, a representative of the United States, as we have seen, participated in its deliberations. The draft convention prepared for the disarmament conference, opened in 1932, was drawn with the coöperation of American representatives and a project for a consultative pact was included in the final project. Moreover there was discernible a growth of opinion in favor of uniting debt reduction or cancellation with the general curtailment of expenditures for armaments. Thus, while the theory of no "involvements" was rigidly observed, the facts remained what they were.

§

As the summer of 1932 approached and advanced, the long and ruinous downward trend of business and stock prices seemed to reach bottom. At all events values turned upward and displayed a growing strength until September arrived. Even optimists admitted that the signs warranted no general rejoicing, but hope deferred found a faint encouragement. In a scene of great uncertainty both the major parties prepared for the coming campaign, while the Socialists and Communists made ready to capitalize the breakdown of the industrial system. Without any serious opposition President Hoover and Vice President Curtis were renominated by the Republicans. Among the Democrats a lively contest added to the somber gayety of the scene. Smarting under the defeat of the previous election, Alfred E. Smith assembled a small but loyal group of delegates in the hope of vindication. Supported by William Randolph Hearst and William Gibbs McAdoo, John N. Garner,

Speaker of the House of Representatives, appeared in the arena with a compact and useful contingent. The popular verdict, however, was clearly in favor of Franklin D. Roosevelt, Governor of New York, for he swept into the convention with a safe majority, if not enough to meet the requirements of the two-thirds rule. Before the balloting had gone far, Mr. McAdoo, head of the California delegation, swung his regiment into the Roosevelt camp and settled the contest. Roosevelt and Garner became the Democratic candidates. Once more the Socialists put forward Norman Thomas. The Communists offered W. Z. Foster. Under these leaders the war of words began.

With respect to concrete issues, the differences between the major parties were slight. Touching foreign affairs, important but sadly neglected, no significant divergences could be discovered. In the field of tariff legislation, the Republicans clung to their traditional position, while the Democrats picked their way with caution. Retreating somewhat from their protective policy of 1928, they declared in favor of a "competitive tariff for revenue," omitting the old word "only," promised reciprocity, which the Republicans had once advocated and then abandoned, and offered a revival of trade by "an economic conference." This profession of faith in the platform Mr. Roosevelt accepted, with the comment, reassuring to industry, that "it would protect American business and American labor." Only on the vexatious question of prohibition did a sharp antithesis emerge. The Democrats demanded a repeal of the Eighteenth Amendment, promising at the same time to safeguard the dry states against the unlawful importation of liquor—an impossible bracket which was soon lost to sight in the dust of the campaign. Bowing to the clear movement of public opinion, the Republicans offered to submit the question of repeal or modification to the states for review, on the understanding that there was to be no return to the outlawed saloon. Although the economic disaster from which the nation was suffering occupied the center of discussion, the two parties presented no precise and opposed programs of relief, restoration, constructive action. On election day Governor Roosevelt carried the country in a landslide comparable to that on which Mr. Hoover had ridden into office, and took with him majorities in both houses of Congress. Another battle had been fought—and won; perhaps another battle of Blenheim.

While the gloom deepened around the witches' cauldron of depression, many incantations were heard. The party of good cheer on the right insisted that this was just another periodical distemper, that it would soon be over, and that bigger and better prosperity would follow. Some who had once been highly intoxicated with enthusiasm, however, seemed to imagine that the end of the world had come and, with the same insight into the nature of things, sold at fifty cents a share stocks for which they had eagerly paid twenty-five dollars in 1929. Economists, as far as they agreed at all, offered a simple remedy: cancel debts and reparations, lower the tariff, and renew lending abroad; then the dawn will come. Communists, excited by the fulfillment of certain predictions, prophesied the collapse of capitalism, the dictatorship of the proletariat, and a repetition in America of the Russian experiment. Great bankers still counselled faith in the soundness of American institutions, and laid a large share of the blame for the trouble on the follies of the people in 1929, who had then followed banking prognostications and bought into rising prosperity. Cynics, impressed by the relativity of all things, dryly remarked that the human race was still on its old treadmill and would keep up its antics to the end of time. So the pot bubbled and boiled to the tune of many words.

In the realm of labor, employed and unemployed, a comparative calm prevailed. By the close of 1932 there had been no widespread strikes and intransigence, such as had characterized the panics of 1873 and 1893. The American Federation of Labor offered no radical program, unless its conversion to unemployment insurance could be placed in that category. Hunger marches on city halls and state capitols stirred momentary sensations and occasional disorders; enraged farmers in some western regions blocked highways leading to markets and dumped milk into gutters; but there was no drawing together of forces for concerted action, either political or direct. The vote for Norman Thomas in the most congested quarters of Philadelphia was almost negligible as compared with his returns in the sections occupied by the moderately well-to-do middle classes.

Only among the veterans of the World War did insurgency on a national scale occur. By the Adjusted Compensation Act of 1924, passed over President Coolidge's veto, they had secured a bonus in the form of insurance certificates; by a supplementary law of 1931, passed over President Hoover's veto, they had extended their capacity to borrow on the basis of their certificates; but still dissatisfied they now demanded payment in full. In support of this project groups of veterans from all parts of the country marched on Washington and encamped by the thousands in old buildings and on vacant lots. Failing to obtain their objective, they "dug in" for a siege and threatened to remain indefinitely. Confronted by this "bonus army," statecraft in Washington exhausted its imagination in employing armed forces, tanks, and gas to drive the campers out of the city and destroy their shacks and tents. After the famous "battle of Anacostia" all was quiet on the Potomac again, until the "hunger marchers" arrived, under Communist leadership, for a brief stay.

On the whole, the scene displayed but one novel aspect. In previous panics men of affairs in business and statecraft had taken the position that there was nothing that the government could do to level off the peaks and valleys of depression, but the calamity that opened in 1929 had not advanced far when other opinions were heard. Indeed, before it broke, a preparatory plan for a huge stabilization fund for public works in anticipation of a slump had been presented to the annual conference of governors and so warmly endorsed by the President that it became known as the Hoover

Plan. Later in the season of distress a flood of plans descended. Adelbert Ames, Stuart Chase, and George Soule presented schemes. Gerard Swope, of the General Electric Company, proposed a charter for the stabilization of the electrical industries and informed them that if industry could do nothing about the wrongs of unemployment the government would. A committee of the United States Chamber of Commerce laid out an elaborate program for trade associations, production control, and unemployment reserves. On one significant particular most of these proposals agreed: the prime cause of cyclical disasters is the inefficient distribution of wealth which diverts too much income to capital and plant extension and too little to the buying power of consumers. Whether all this was mere diversion in the gloom, to be swiftly forgotten during the next rush on the stock market, or presaged some modifications in historic capitalism was the theme of a lively discussion in press and forum.

While planning was under consideration a new American slogan, Technocracy, broke into headlines, editorial sanctums, dining rooms, and all up-to-date conversations. Under the direction of Howard Scott, engineering investigators discovered by prolonged researches that labor-saving machinery was saving labor, that technological unemployment was bound to increase, and that the United States, given its enormous resources, could produce an almost unlimited amount of goods. The country could be rich and yet it was poor and headed for disaster. What was the cause? The technocrats found it in the "price system," based on gold instead of productive energy, that is, in old-fashioned terms, in the wage system under which labor is unable to buy all the goods it produces. Capitalists, socialists, and fascists were wrong. The technocrats alone could turn the great trick. But just how? That was the enigma.

Judging by the movement of opinion, however, it seemed that the mild project of unemployment insurance might receive endorsement in the coming years. Many manufacturers advocated it; organized labor approved it; Communists concentrated their propaganda upon it; and a few professors of economics agreed that it was the only "practical" program in sight. Yet it was attacked on three sides. Experts in actuarial accounting found it difficult to make estimates for unemployment contingencies on a large scale and to discover methods for covering them adequately. Conservatives rejected it as imposing an intolerable burden on the rich and "pauperizing" the poor. On the left of the Communists, unemployment insurance was regarded in small circles as reflecting the intellectual and moral bankruptcy of capital and labor, as promising a degradation of labor to the point of despair and inefficiency, as repeating the bread and circuses of old Rome, which demoralized government and governed, and as deliberately avoiding the imperative of planning in favor of the easiest way to temporary social peace and the ultimate paralysis of society.

CHAPTER XXXI
The Machine Age

THE cumulative forces of machine industry, which began to dissolve the agricultural order of the Fathers in the days of Jacksonian Democracy, swept the nation into and through the holocaust of the Second Revolution, and assured the supremacy of business enterprise in the gilded age, widened in range and increased in momentum during the opening decades of the twentieth century. These forces made a steady growth in the volume and velocity of mass production the outstanding feature of American economy, with correlative influences on American slants of thought, modes of living, manners, and æsthetic expression. Year by year new mechanical inventions encroached on the area occupied by hand workers: ingenuity gave a pneumatic drill to the miner underground, electric appliances to the woman in the kitchen, a tractor to the farmer, and a radio to the child. At length the day arrived when in all the land save in out-of-the-way places, there could be found none but machine-made objects, duplicated by the ton, impersonal, standardized according to patterns adapted to fingers of steel, and circulated by publicity drives.

Measured in money value the manufactured products of the United States reported by the census bureau amounted in round numbers to one billion dollars in 1849, eleven billions in 1899, and sixty-one billions in 1923. The variety of the mass was even more astounding than its size, whether revealed by a comparison of the encyclopedic catalogue issued from a great mail order house in 1926 with an industrial inventory of 1880 or by a study of the multitude of things presented at the Sesquicentennial Exposition at Philadelphia in 1926 contrasted with those shown in 1876.

More fraught with social destiny than this mass production of things in dazzling variety were the radical departures effected in technology by electrical devices, the internal combustion engine, wireless transmission of power, the radio, and the airplane—changes more momentous even than those wrought by invention in the age of Watt and Fulton. In that earlier industrial revolution the steam engine, associated with a fixed kind of social apparatus, gloomy and depressing, had furnished the motive power for industry and transportation. Now the steam engine was big and heavy; it was as a rule attached to a definite spot or driven along metal rails. When used in manufacturing, it promoted concentration in the cities, thereby sharpening the line between town and country. It was expensive to install, moreover, and ordinarily every increase in the size of the plant added to the economy and profits of the business built around it. At best it was cumbersome and crude. While augmenting enormously the output of goods, the steam engine marred landscapes, defied æsthetics, filled the air with smoke and gases, and became the center of dull, dreary, dispiriting wastes of railroad yards, warehouses, and slums.

However, just at the moment when the belching smokestack seemed finally accepted as the symbol of western civilization, new motive forces and new instruments began to rearrange the American social pattern that had apparently crystallized around steam economy. Though their full import for the generations to come could hardly be foretold, certain of their tendencies were obvious. By distributing power in any quantity to shop, forge, house, or highway, electricity and the gas engine offered to emancipate mankind from utter dependence on the fixed plant and railway. They quickened travel and transportation, spread new arteries for the distribution of goods, and brought backward places within the grasp of urban modes and manners. Through the agency of the automobile the normal cruising radius of the average family, limited to four or five miles in the days of horse-drawn vehicles, was widened to forty or fifty miles. To farmers as well as villagers, the moving picture machine made manufactured amusement and urban mental patter swiftly available; while the radio carried the ideas and noises of the city to every nook and cranny of the country as if on the wings of the wind.

Almost immediately these new inventions began to break down the barriers recently erected between city and country by the steam engine, checking the rate of concentration in the great municipalities and strengthening the economy of the small town. By carrying into the family circle labor-saving machines, "canned" information, and sterotyped mental excitements, they invaded every relation of life, business, and society, spreading urban standards, values, and types of conduct over the whole nation. In comparison the effects of the steam engine on the civilization of the stagecoach and hand loom were grossly material and superficial. It could not be denied that the influence of the new motors and machines was as subtle as the electricity that turned the wheel, lighted the film, and carried the song.

In swiftness and variation their processes were such as to defy all efforts at logical representation. An illustration merely illuminates the edge of the vortex. When the first quarter of the twentieth century had closed, there were over twenty million automobiles in a nation of approximately twenty-five million families; there were more than fifteen million telephones and at least three million radio sets. It was then established that the average daily attendance at the moving picture houses was about twenty-five millions—equivalent to one person a day for every family in the land.

§

The effect of mass production on class arrangements was more measurable than the subtler social bearings of gas and electrical technology. For example, there was no doubt that the number of millionaires had been augmented with the volume of commodity output. On every side the families of the older plutocracy established by heroic efforts in railroading, mining, ranching, lumbering, and manufacturing during the gilded age were now surrounded by fresh nabobs who had made money out of automobiles and accessories, electrical appliances, moving pictures, and other standardized goods of the day. Between 1914 and 1919, the number of persons in the United States returning taxable incomes ranging from $30,000 to $40,000 a year increased from 6,000 to 15,400 and the number returning between $50,000 and $100,000 per annum rose from 5,000 to 13,000, in round figures. Reckoning as millionaires all persons reporting $30,000 a year or more in 1919—and this seems conservative in view of tax exemptions, stock dividends, and other technicalities—there were 42,554 millionaires in America at the close of the war for democracy. Those who thought that the age of great fortunes had passed when the simple exploitation of natural resources had about come to a close were dazed by the immense facility of business enterprise, perhaps capable of indefinite expansion.

In fact the accumulations of the machine age made those of the gilded age seem slow and pitiful by contrast, outrunning in rapidity and force all calculations and defeating all attempts to establish levels and barriers, while the pace of lavish spending and lavish giving set by the older plutocracy seemed like the movement of a snail. At the close of the World War millionaires were almost as common in Detroit, Toledo, Indianapolis, Cincinnati, Denver, and Seattle as they had been in Boston and New York in the age of McKinley. In the single year of 1925, the income of private persons from rent, interest, and dividends, reported for tax purposes, showed a jump from $5,900,000,000 to $8,200,000,000—the mere increase alone amounting to more than twenty-five times the national debt in Washington's day.

While a new plutocracy was continually boiling up from below, the older families of that order were growing into maturity. Children of the second and third generations were enjoying fortunes acquired by pioneering fathers untrained in the schools and innocent of the restraints imposed by the graces of the drawing-room. As a rule they could boast of a college education with its peculiar manners and codes, which occasionally softened the fine assurances inherited from acquisitive ancestors and sometimes corroded by philosophic doubts transmitted views of government, economy, and social values—if indeed it did not supplant ancient anarchy by constructive proposals. Under the satire directed against raw plutocracy by novelists and essayists of their own and other countries, these educated possessors of seasoned estates writhed and twisted, casting about for more respectable mantles of security and atonement. Pelted by criticism and stormed by appeals they came to imagine that wealth, after all, owed obligations to society or at least that it was more pleasing in the eyes of democracy, especially the middle classes so potent in matters of opinion, if it was tinctured by the spirit of *noblesse oblige*.

In short, by 1925, a whole generation of men and women who had inherited fortunes reeking with the odors of the market place had been to college and had gone abroad on the grand tour. Lincoln was the last of the true log-cabin presidents of the United States—though others made high pretensions to such honors. After Cleveland, there was no occupant of the presidency who could conjure the masses with the magic of an education won in the university of hard knocks. Harvard, Yale, and Princeton in succession sent sons to the White House and then Amherst sent Calvin Coolidge. Even the chief executive of the United States Steel Corporation, Judge Gary, could hang a college diploma on his office wall. The world of books and trade had touched.

As the stream of commodities flowing from the factories broke every barrier, the business of selling goods employed an ever larger army of commercial officers and privates, swelling the ranks of the middle classes with recruits of the mercantile color. Huge areas of American social power were now occupied by huckstering shock troops who, with a technique and a verbiage all their own, concentrated on ogling, stimulating, and inveigling the public into purchases. By raising the business of advertising to the intensity of a crusading religion, embattled vendors gained an almost sovereign sway over newspapers and journals, as they pushed goods, desirable and noxious alike, upon a docile herd that took its codes from big type and colored plates.

Under this economic drive the psychology of the sales-man—as distinguished from that of the warrior, organizing capitalist, and creative inventor—became the dominant spirit of an immense array of persons who, in the view of "thoughtful editors," constituted the "sound heart of the nation." In this intellectual climate, trades which the landed gentry had formerly scorned as vulgar were crowned with respectability: real estate agents became realtors, under-takers assumed the rôle of morticians, and clerks expanded into salesladies. When the second census of the twentieth century was compiled there were seen to be at least four million people engaged in trade, including retailers, sales agents, and collateral forces under this general head.

With these increases and changes in commodity produc-tion and selling, the older professions—law, medicine, preaching, and teaching—engaged ever-growing armies of recruits. At the taking of the last census there were in the United States 200,000 physicians and dentists, 122,000 lawyers and judges, 785,000 teachers, 127,000 clergymen, and more than 1,000,000 public servants in addition to those employed in the public schools.

To summarize in consolidated figures, allowing a wide margin for error, the number of Americans engaged in trade and in professions in 1920, including of course their families —the substantial bulk of the middle class—was about equal to the entire population of the northern states in 1860 when the election of Abraham Lincoln marked the transition from an agricultural to an industrial civilization. The number of persons returning taxable incomes ranging from $2,000 to $10,000 in 1919 was 3,189,080.

Moreover through investments in odd lots and baby bonds, through stock-owning and profit-sharing schemes, through savings banks and insurance companies, this large middle class had become part owners, usually absentee, of the enterprises managed by captains of finance. By this unforeseen development the Marxian prediction that the middle class would be ground to pieces between the plutoc-racy and the proletariat was so far unrealized in the United States. Unquestionably, President Coolidge expressed a widespread conviction when he stated that the prosperity of the middling and lower orders depended upon the good fortunes and light taxes of the rich.

Deep down into the laboring and farming groups ran the filaments of interest and enjoyment which connected the plutocracy and the middle class. It appears from the best of estimates that American workmen received a real increase of wages between the opening of the World War and the flood tide of normalcy and that the farmers, while they suffered terrible reverses after the collapse of inflated prices, did not exactly return to their former standard of life. By the millions, cheap automobiles, new and second-hand, tele-phones, radios, labor-saving implements and other com-modities, classed in more sparing societies as luxuries, found their way into the possession of those who labored with their hands at plow or forge. Whereas the proletariat of older cultures, Rome for instance, had to be amused with circuses and supplied with free bread, the industrial multitudes of the United States, like the middle class, paid for their own diversions and bought their own loaves. To their prosperity labor banks, labor investment enterprises, insurance schemes, and housing programs bore convincing testimony while the rise of whole trades, such as the garment workers, from low standards of living based on sweatshop labor, demonstrated an economic resilience that seemed to discredit the iron law of wages. No doubt there were dark sides to the picture—shadows blacker and more depressing than the comfortable trading and professional classes liked to admit; but the area of grueling poverty was relatively so limited that revolutionary calls to working people to shed their chains met with no wholesale response.

If there was any danger in the social order it seemed to lie in the possibilities of a breakdown from prolonged war or a Malthusian crisis that would snatch from a nation accustomed to luxury surplus goods and pleasures deeply embedded in national psychology as indispensable necessities. Indeed biologists warned the nation that, under prevailing standards of agriculture, the country could support only one hundred sixty-six million people whereas at the current rate of increase the population would be two hundred fourteen millions in 1964. But little heed was paid in the street to such predictions and, besides, some leading scientists argued that there was no limit in sight to the potentialities of agricultural and machine production. Whether the age of acquisition and enjoyment had reached its apogee or had centuries to run with increasing measure remained merely a matter for alluring speculation.

§

Apart from their effect on the structure and prosperity of classes, the extension of mass production and the achievements of the new technology brought complicated influences to bear on the American family, especially on women and children. The multiplication and subdivision of trades, professions, arts, and crafts, and the development of training schools of every kind enlarged the routes by which women could gain that coveted "economic independence" so celebrated by Charlotte Perkins Gilman in the last years of the gilded age. It is true that there was no marked growth in the relative number of women wage earners between 1899 and 1909; the proportion of females over sixteen employed in the standard industries of the country as compared with the males stood still; and in the next decade the proportion of women gainfully occupied, considered in relation to the female population of the country ten years of age and over, actually declined from 23.4 to 21.1 per cent.

But in absolute figures the number of women in trade and mechanical industries increased materially, certainly the number in trade between 1910 and 1920. Moreover the accumulations of the middle classes, schemes of insurance, and the laws of inheritance giving women larger, if not always equal, shares in parental estates, helped to lift thousands of them out of the necessity of working for a living. These factors, coupled with the introduction of labor-saving tools and the growth of coöperative living in apartment houses with their central heating, lighting, and cleaning systems—if not in every case with a common dining service —gave to American women an amount of economic power and leisure that was the envy of their sisters in every other land.

Immediately reflected in the activities of women, this expansion of the middle class hurried forward the club movement which had been such an innovation in the gilded age. By 1926, the General Federation of Women's Clubs boasted of a membership running almost to three millions, making it "the largest organization of women in the world." With the numerical growth and national enfranchisement went a widening of the intellectual horizon; literary yearnings, originally so predominant, sank into the background before the work of eight grand departments fostered by the Federation: American citizenship, the American home, applied education, fine arts, international relations, legislation, press, and publicity.

More directly political in its emphasis was the National League of Women Voters formed by leaders in the suffrage movement immediately after the ratification of the Nineteenth Amendment. A federation of state and local associations of women from both parties, it gave its attention to the study and promotion of specific legislative measures. Though it brought the general range of politics within its purview, it took special pains to interest its membership in laws pertaining to social welfare, the election and appointment of qualified women to office, and international relations. In order to draw all the feminine concerns to a focus, and to profit by the strength of unity while eliminating duplication, there was formed in 1920 a Women's Joint Congressional Committee representing more than twenty national societies and speaking for over four million members, dedicated to the advancement, in a non-partisan fashion, of a legislative program formulated at annual conferences.

Individually and collectively, as wage earners, members of clubs and professions, housewives, politicians, and heiresses, American women now assumed an unquestioned rôle in shaping the production of goods, material, humanistic, literary, and artistic. They were the chief spenders of money: while accurate figures could not be obtained, it was estimated that they bought personally at least seven-tenths of all the manufactured commodities sold each year in the country. Books, magazines, newspapers, and moving pictures were modeled to suit their purses and their fancies. Lines of automobiles and plans of houses were drawn to please their imagination. Objects of domestic adornment—rugs, wall papers, lamps, chairs, tables, curtains, and pictures—had to conform more and more to their standards of taste. Since they were the great consumers of fiction also, romance was chiefly pitched to their key. Music and drama tallied with their requirements, real or assumed. Possessors of leisure as well as money, women forged rapidly to the front as leaders and patrons in education, charity, social work, and civic affairs in general.

Already potent by that time, their influence in politics was immensely enlarged when the ballot was placed in their hands. Besides sharing offices and party jobs with women, the politicians now had to tread more warily as they threaded their various ways among their constituents. Having the means to buy and to command, education to guide them, and freedom to superintend, women became powerful arbiters in all matters of taste, morals, and thinking. In short, they called the tunes to which captains of industry, men of letters, educators, and artists now principally danced.

Without avail did alarmists of the old school cry out as Cato had done that those things which tended to effeminacy were signs of national decay. In vain did European critics from other societies where male tastes predominated offer dire forebodings—usually to audiences of the American women themselves—at large fees from beaded bags. It was difficult to discover how, in a machine age devoted chiefly to making, selling, and enjoying material goods, the martial virtues of feudalism and primitive society or the ethereal speculations of aristocratic leisure founded on other modes of economic exploitation could be exalted to pristine excellence. Indeed in the eyes of the true soldier, the merchant had always been the contemptible promoter of comfort and luxury; so officers of the American army and navy often repeated the historic protest against an effeminacy that tended to encourage pacifism.

Far from producing contentment with the conjugal yoke, the ease of life and opportunities for personal adventure steadily augmented dissatisfaction with all the offices of matrimony. The economic independence of women and the coöperative living, which hopeful feminists often had heralded as signs of a better day in marital relations, were in reality accompanied by an increasing weakness in the nuptial bond and all it implied. In 1900, the ratio of divorces to marriages was one to twelve; in 1916, one to nine; in 1924, one to seven. Equally impressive was the fact that the major portion of the applicants were women.

Even to the light-hearted this record was startling; while to those accustomed to measure morality in marital terms it was appalling. Though the purveyors of remedies ascribed the tendency to the facilities afforded by lenient divorce laws, the case was not so simply stated. It is true that a number of states, especially in the West, dissolved marriages on slight grounds, such as incompatibility of temper, but others were almost mediæval in their severity. South Carolina for instance forbade divorce absolutely and New York granted it only in circumstances that covered one or both parties with scandal and shame.

The disintegration of the colonial family régime marked by the increasing freedom of divorce was no doubt hastened by the expansion of woman's authority over her children. Under the old law of England which was generally binding in America, the father could assign a guardian to his children under age to take charge of them in the event of his death; only when no such guardian was appointed could the mother act in that capacity. Under the common law too, as transplanted, when parties were divorced the father retained possession of the children, even though he had been the offender whose conduct gave grounds for the separation. While in the early course of American development, divorce was being made easier and traditional patterns of law were being altered in many respects, the disabilities imposed on women in matters of guardianship were long retained in whole or in part.

But naturally with the rising tide of feminism, sprang up a lively demand for a new adjustment of rights over children as well as property, an adjustment generally covered in the terminology of propaganda by the phrase, "equal guardianship." By the constant sapping of state

legislation, man's inherited prestige in this matter underwent radical modification until in the high noontide of the
machine age it seemed that this phase of the old régime
was also doomed. Over law and precedent piled on law
and precedent, women advanced steadily toward the goal
of equal rights in their children.

Having won the ballot, enlarged economic opportunities,
freedom to bob their hair, wear men's clothes, smoke and
swear, and extensive powers in the domestic relation, women
looked for new fields of enterprise. At this point a group
of the more intransigent demanded "absolute and unconditional equal opportunity" in every sphere. To give effect
to their doctrines, they proposed an amendment to the
federal Constitution providing that there should be no discriminations against women on account of sex in any national or state legislation.

If the full import of this demand was difficult to grasp,
its implications in many details were readily defined. Certainly the more extreme of this feminist school called for a
repeal of all protective legislation not applicable also to
men, such as laws limiting the hours of women workers and
closing to the sex the heavier and more dangerous trades
such as mining and brickmaking. In other words they asserted in effect the physical equality of the sexes and insisted
upon freedom to compete with men on the same footing all
along the line. Thus by one of the curious ironies of history they were seeking the overthrow of factory legislation
just at the moment when young industrial nations like Japan,
long accustomed to equal rights in the hardest and most
degrading labor, were trying to create "enlightened" codes
to safeguard the health of women and home life. However
it is necessary to add that among the advocates of equal
opportunity were those who looked forward to a day when
industry would be regulated, if at all, on the basis of the
common interests of men and women, whatever those might
be.

The dissolution of patriarchal authority indicated by the

rising power of women was no less evident in the relations of parents and children. That ancient law which placed the father at the head of the family and the mother and children below him in the firmament represented with fair accuracy a stage of military and economic facts. In a sentence Edmund Clarence Stedman summarized it when he told how his grandfather rebuked a clergyman who prayed for the "united head" of the house, exclaiming: "Sir, there is but one head of the house, and I am the head; a united head would be a monster."

In those far-off times, the father read the Bible, said the prayers, and asked the blessing on his family while the regimen of work and play for the entire group was adjusted to his purse and convenience with such deference to the wishes of the mother as time, her will, and circumstances permitted—by no means always slight. "It was an accepted tenet," wrote Henry Cabot Lodge of his boyhood days, "that children not only ought to honor their father and mother, but that they owed them a great debt and were bound to respect it, to help them, to sympathize with them, and, if need be, to care for them."

No doubt such morals fitted very well into the system of economy prevailing in Lodge's youth but the machine age altered the scene for the management of the family by its male head. In the new order prodigal members of the plutocracy set standards of reckless expenditure and high living which spread like a virus among all ranks of society, making the spending of money a national mania and casting the stigma of contempt on previous virtues of thrift, toil, and moderation. The public schools which gave boys and girls of the middle and working classes an education, together with the business enterprise which offered them employment beyond the hearth, made them both increasingly independent of the chief breadwinner. Under the drive of profit-making or of well-subsidized philanthropy, the multiplication of boarding schools, summer camps, organizations for supervised amusements, dance halls, vaudeville houses, cabarets, moving picture theaters, and public eating places, to say nothing of the automobile, young people were weaned from the restricted living-rooms of their urban homes during the leisure hours left by the school or factory. They now played as well as worked and studied outside the home, for the most part. Finally the dress of youth in the machine age, modeled for life in public places, cheap and flaunting, or costly and dazzling, was another sign of contempt for parental restraint. So the home, especially in the larger towns, became little more than a place for sleeping and an occasional meal, the decline of domestic authority paralleling the velocity of mass production and publicity. "The present view seems to be," wrote Lodge in 1913, "that parents owe an unlimited debt to children because they brought them into the world and are bound to defer to them in all possible ways."

Consequently the father, in losing his prerogatives, lost few of his obligations; indeed they were multiplied rather than diminished, especially for the male of the upper classes. Ever more relentlessly the increase in the number of things that could be bought with money and the rising standard of life drove him to the task of acquiring wealth. And his wife, besides defying and divorcing him, could still secure alimony if he possessed an estate or any earning capacity. The "lord of creation" appeared to be on the verge of an eclipse.

§

The whole scheme of American life, as well as the structure of classes and the economy of the family, felt the impress of the changing machine process as mass production and the vivid selling operations which attended it scattered the same commodities and identical ideas over the entire country. Even distant lands were being transformed by an Americanization on the pattern which Matthew Arnold had so dreaded fifty years before, their more ancient arts and moralities also corroding under the invasion of

technology and standardized wares. Queens on thrones
were soon endorsing American facial creams, for a price,
and ex-premiers approving American cigarettes. With all
his energies every great manufacturer in the United States
strove to capture at least the national market. Makers of
phrases also wrought for a continent. The slogans and
catchwords of advertising sped from sea to sea on the
morning of their publication—photographs and designs
eventually flying as quickly as words on the wings of
electricity.

Within the week of their announcement the modes of
New York, Boston, and Chicago became the modes of
Winesburg, Gopher Prairie, and Centerville and swept on
without delay into remote mountain fastnesses. Thus the
technology of interchangeable parts was reflected in the
clothing, sports, amusements, literature, architecture, manners, and speech of the multitude. The curious stamp of
uniformity which had arrested the attention of James Bryce
at the dawn of the machine age sank deeper and deeper into
every phase of national life—material and spiritual. Even
those who bent their energies to varieties of social reform,
to the improvement of education, the management of drives
for benevolence, the distribution of knowledge, and the advancement of public health brought the nation within their
purview and utilized the advertising courage of the market-
place. And all these tendencies, springing naturally out of
the whirl of business, were encouraged by the conscious
struggle for efficiency in every domain, by the discovery and
application of the most economical apparatus for the accomplishment of given ends.

Under the remorseless hammering of the machine was
effected a standardization of American society that daily
increased in precision and completeness. Nothing escaped
its iron strokes. Those who apparently directed and those
who labored became one in the routine. "It is the age of
the machine triumphant," wrote a contemporary journalist.
"We are but ants in the machines; the wheels revolve and

we revolve with them. Can any man look at the subway rush and then speak of those jammed midges as 'lords of creation'? Alarm clocks, time tables, factory whistles, ordinances, rules, the lock step of industrialism—the lock step of paternalism!" Plastic youths who sought education found it graded and measured by "points." Adults who turned to the libraries for wisdom were offered "handy guides" to reading which laid out by foot rules the paths to culture or a knowledge of business enterprise. Like the professions the great departments of business and industry, aided by the schools, worked persistently at perfecting uniformity in methods and practices, codifying trade and professional ethics.

When work was laid aside for amusement, the masses listened passively to manufactured music, watched moving pictures portray with endless reiteration identical plots and farcical acts, sat on the bleachers at games, in vicarious playing, to cheer their favorite teams. When they gratified their thirst for the open country, they did so in standardized automobiles wheeling along standardized highways, past standardized signboards and standardized "soft-drink" huts, to conventional places of entertainment packed with masses of their kind, to the White Mountains, Florida, or the Yellowstone Park where business enterprise offered the comforts of metropolitan hotels or of camps serving tinned milk and biscuits. The towering climax seemed reached in 1925 when Bruce Barton, a rich advertising agent and proud member of the Republican party, presented Jesus Christ to his countrymen as The Man Nobody Knows—a joyous, ripping good fellow, the perfect image of a "go getter" from the Jazztown Rotary Club— an effusion which the historian, Hendrik Willem Van Loon, limned in a cartoon showing God as at last worthy of being naturalized into American citizenship.

To artists of a classical bent and to spectators of a soulful temper the pageant in its deadly uniformity was no doubt rather agonizing. But neither could explain how an age of machinery might by any magic retain the flexibility inherent in a system of handicrafts. Indeed that older flexibility had itself been exaggerated in the imaginations of the modern philosophers who knew it not at first hand. As a matter of chill reality all previous societies had been standardized at some level of poverty or wealth, none more rigidly, save for a fortunate few, than those of the ancient world or of modern China. The slaves who rowed the quinquiremes of Nineveh bowed their scarred backs in mechanical unison and the chant of Oriental coolies bearing horses' burdens had the monotony of the shuttle's steady clangor.

§

Paralleling the extension of manufacturing and selling which gave uniformity to life from one end of the continent to the other was a multiplication in the number of associations for profit, pleasure, diversion, and improvement. The tendency of Americans to unite with their fellows for varied purposes—a tendency noted a hundred years earlier by de Tocqueville—now became a general mania as the means of communication and the routine of economic activity grew to be national in scope. Thousands of new organizations were founded on trades, professions, and the many subdivisions of lucrative enterprise. For instance, in towns and cities business men united in boards of trade or chambers of commerce; local units were in turn knit together in state federations; and finally the whole complex was crowned by a central combination—the United States Chamber of Commerce—whose agencies were housed in an imposing structure in Washington where they could keep in touch with political affairs.

In addition to organizations primarily for mutual advantage, new types of fraternal societies were created, distinct from the established orders like the Masons, Odd Fellows, and Knights of Pythias. Business and professional men now flocked to Rotary Clubs, Kiwanis Clubs,

Lions' Clubs, and a score of other associations where they listened to speeches without number, gave dinners to dignitaries, raised money for worthy causes, and played pranks on their comrades. In strange mixture they combined what one of their leaders called "fun, fellowship, profit, and service," setting the hallmark of symmetry on the liverymen of trade. Drawn into the same vortex, business and professional women formed their leagues and strove for power and place on standardized levels. As if to aid the course of nature, rapidly multiplying business schools, with a scholastic passion for system, devised schemes of economic thought and disseminated knowledge about uniform standards that were good for trade or gave a better position to those that followed them.

In other spheres than the economic, enthusiasm for organization also produced a bewildering number of clubs, orders, and societies—political, social, benevolent, religious, and reform. The directory of charitable enterprises in New York City alone in 1925 embraced more than 345 pages of fine print. It was a rare American who was not a member of four or five societies. Every person who evolved a new idea or a variant on an existing doctrine strove at once to found a fellowship for propaganda and promotion. Any citizen who refused to affiliate with one or more associations became an object of curiosity, if not of suspicion. If he isolated himself, he could hardly hope to succeed in any trade, business, or profession, no matter how great his talents. Moreover the opportunity to attend conventions in distant cities, wear highly colored uniforms, and participate in festivities offered both to men and women diverting releases from the routine of employment and domesticity—freedom which they seized with avidity since they could pay for it. This longing for diversion and this herd distinct, quite as much as hatred for Catholics, Jews, and Negroes, was no doubt responsible for the revival of the Ku Klux Klan with its weird ritual and hooded regalia, its parades, and its outbursts of violence.

When social philosophers tried to unearth the roots of the ardor for association in the United States, they could not advance far beyond the explanation offered by de Tocqueville, namely, that in a democracy which professes equality, the individual without special titles, riches, distinctions, or gifts feels an oppressive sense of weakness alone in a vast mass of general averages; and thus bewildered he seeks strength and confidence in an affiliation with kindred spirits. Unquestionably the leveling modes of democracy, intensified by the technology of standardization in mass production and distribution, accounted for a large part of the federations and super-federations which knit the American nation into a crisscross of a thousand unities.

§

Another motive for collective enterprise, sometimes infused with economic designs, was certainly the passion for governing which Jefferson noted as a source of tyranny— that hot desire to force ideas and moral standards on one's fellowmen. It was under this head that the critics of prohibition usually classed the associated effort which abolished, nominally at least, the manufacture and sale of intoxicating liquor as a beverage. Their assignment, however, is not altogether exact. It is true that since the middle of the nineteenth century there had been a well-organized temperance movement in America, inspired by moral fervor, and that it was given a decided impetus by the Woman's Christian Temperance Union founded in 1874 with Frances Willard as a dominant leader. It is true also that the Prohibition Party, which nominated its first candidate for the presidency in 1872 and continued its agitation with unabated zeal, was largely supported by religious ardor. But while these movements flourished, the liquor business likewise flourished.

It was not until the Anti-Saloon League, founded at Oberlin, Ohio, commenced its nation-wide campaign in 1895 that war on the traffic took on a formidable aspect. Now the Anti-Saloon League which bent its energies to abolishing the saloon in villages, towns, counties, and states in a piecemeal fashion no doubt made an appeal to the moral elements of the population—particularly the Methodists —but it had also practical ends in view. It did not ask its members to take the total abstinence pledge; rather did it summon them to battle against the saloon, the workingman's club. In the South, the League was strongly supported by business men who saw in the abolition of the "dram shop" an increase in the sobriety and regularity of their colored personnel. In other parts of the country, especially in the West, employers of labor in quest of efficiency gave money and support to the new crusade, for drunken workmen were a danger as well as an economic loss to machine industry. Moreover, it must not be forgotten, the saloon and liquor dealers were frequently in politics— Democratic politics at that—and as a rule engaged in activities of no marked benefit to the business community. So under the influence of forces not merely moral in purpose, the work of extinguishing the saloon was expedited during the opening years of the twentieth century. Then came the World War, a life and death struggle, calling for the conservation of grain as a food supply, a vital element in sustaining the military machine and its civilian auxiliaries and resulting in the temporary suppression of the saloon.

These were factors often overlooked or minimized by critics who imagined that a tyrannical minority of Puritans suddenly compelled Congress in 1917 to submit to the states the Eighteenth Amendment to the Constitution prohibiting the manufacture and sale of liquor as a beverage and then browbeat local legislatures into ratifying it within two years. The operation was by no means a stampede. As a matter of fact as early as 1914 a prohibition amendment had received a majority in the House of Representatives then dominated by Democrats under southern leadership. Furthermore at the time the Eighteenth Amendment went into effect, namely, on January 16, 1920, two·

thirds of the states had already adopted prohibition by popular vote, about ninety per cent of the land area was at least theoretically dry, and nearly seventy per cent of the American people nominally lived under a dry regimen.

It is a fact that none of the populous industrial commonwealths had as yet adopted state-wide prohibition and that a large portion of their inhabitants, especially organized labor, were emphatically opposed to it. Nor can it be denied that astonishment reigned in many quarters when Congress passed the resolution of amendment in December, 1917. But in view of the history of the preceding twenty years and the economic factors operating in the war on the saloon, the adoption of prohibition could not be called with accuracy, as it was, "a trick played upon an indulgent nation by a belligerent minority of moral fanatics working in underground passages."

Probably many supporters of the Anti-Saloon League were amazed when they discovered that the total abolition of the saloon implied the extreme doctrine of unconditional prohibition. Even as things turned out, the middle and upper classes with money to spare could always get good liquor of any kind, in any quantity, for a price. Therefore, from one point of view it was possible to say that, while prohibition was a failure, the abolition of the old-fashioned saloon was fairly successful. At all events, ascribing prohibition to nationalized Puritanism betrayed a forgetfulness of leading features characterizing colonial life, for the old Puritan loved fine liquor, mild and strong, and none of the original Puritan states was dry when the Eighteenth Amendment went into effect. It was safe to venture a guess that the desire of business men for efficiency and safety in labor was as potent in bringing about the new régime as the wanton lust of moralists determined to impose their own standards upon the nation.

The same economic factor was also effective in the promotion of another type of routine requirement—the intense nationalism which followed the participation of the United

States in the World War. By the strife in Europe the American people were made acutely aware of the alien races in their midst and aroused to the perils of a dual allegiance in the case of wars affecting the interests of this country. In addition, the proletarian revolution in Europe which had repercussions among the working classes of America, though exaggerated in significance in all probability, gave timorous employers of labor even more concern than did the corner saloon which made for drunkenness and inefficiency. For these and other reasons there arose at the close of the World War a crusade for "Americanization"—a movement organized to force certain patterns of thought, linguistic performances, and professions of loyalty upon the population from Maine to California.

While the program of this movement was often noble in conception, if nebulous and vague in details, the net result was usually to exalt uniformity and discourage all inquiry disturbing to those who sat high at the table of enjoyment. In concrete effect it produced numerous state statutes intended to purge historical works of all doubts about the immaculate character of American government and policy, to impose on teachers newly-devised allegiance tests, and to compel the dissemination of purified doctrines of patriotism as understood by chauvinists in good standing.

Distrusting the efficiency of the government they praised, private associations of "minute men" and other self-appointed guardians of American morals undertook to supplement the efforts of public authorities in forcing conformity to type—adding the terrors of private vengeance to the rigors of official justice. Inspired and financed, an army of writers poured out a flood of literature praising the conservative Nordic elements in the national stock and inveighing against Latin, Hebraic, and Slavic contributions to American civilization. Pageants were directed and moving pictures produced to create a correct doctrinal thesis. Prizes were given to school orators who celebrated the perfection of the American Constitution. Even an "authentic" history of the nation was prepared under the ægis of patriotic societies to transmit to the youth of the land an authoritative canon, claiming the intimate favors of God from first to last. The utility of all these things became quickly apparent to the directors of Manifest Destiny.

Connected with this intensification of the nationalist spirit and the agitation of the American Federation of Labor against competition and communism was a series of federal laws restricting immigration. In 1903 anarchists were expressly excluded and four years later the bar was put up against persons suffering from physical and mental defects. In 1917 organized labor won a thirty-year battle in the passage of a bill over President Wilson's veto, excluding all aliens over sixteen years of age "physically capable of reading, who cannot read the English language or some other language or dialect, including Hebrew or Yiddish." Not content with this restriction, which in fact made no very great reduction in immigration, Congress adopted a new rule in 1921, limiting the number of aliens admitted from most countries to a certain percentage of their citizens already in the United States in 1910. Advancing beyond this very effective slash, Congress in 1924 abolished the Gentlemen's Agreement with Japan and cut the number of immigrants to be admitted to "two per cent of the number of foreign born individuals of any nationality resident in continental United States, as determined by the census of 1890, with a minimum quota of one hundred, subject to certain exceptions." It also provided "that the annual quota of any nationality for the year beginning July 1, 1927 [postponed to 1929], and for each year thereafter, shall be the number which bears the same ratio to 150,000 as the number of individuals of continental United States in 1920, having that national origin, bears to the number of inhabitants of continental United States in 1920," with a minimum quota of one hundred. The undoubted design of all these later acts, taken with the measures respecting Asiatic immigration already considered, was to reduce the immigration from Asia and from southern and eastern Europe for the purpose of preserving the racial balance and keeping out radical ideas. As one member of Congress put the matter: "Now asylum ends. The melting pot is to have a rest. The nation must be as completely unified as any nation in Europe or Asia."

§

If such standardized processes making for mechanical uniformity of mind and manners seemed to have a metallic ring, they were in fact associated with a general affability and tenderness of feeling, respecting other matters, not usually found in any feudal society. In accordance perhaps with the law of contrasts, which appears to govern human affairs, a nation thoroughly absorbed in the mass production of material goods at the same time displayed a spirit of charity, generosity, and benevolence astounding in its fruits. In two words the humanistic keynote of the new century was summed up, "uplift and service," words which though soon tarnished by vulgar usage none the less expressed a prevailing American mode almost as engrossing as national sports. From the topmost pinnacles of society, the plutocracy showered millions on universities, hospitals, churches, foundations, and other institutions not conducted for immediate gain. In the twenty-five years that followed the opening of the century, more than two billion dollars were given for benevolent purposes. No human interest seemed overlooked: knowledge, health, welfare, peace, and comfort were to be promoted by lavish monetary endowments. Lest time produce unforeseen developments and new needs be neglected, givers of great wealth established permanent foundations and community funds from which directors were to make appropriations to meet the requirements of coming generations.

By this enthusiasm for the general welfare all classes of American society were stirred to action. Associations of business men, though rigorously observing the rules of their callings, grew ashamed of any program that did not include some elements of "civic improvement." The women's clubs, which in the early nineties had been absorbed in Shakespeare and Browning, turned from mere self-development to public service and social uplift. Drives for hospitals and charitable institutions swept city, town, and countryside producing sums of money that ran into incredible totals. If leading citizens tarred and feathered and outlawed obstreperous members of the Industrial Workers of the World and Communists, they showed equal zeal in providing institutions for dependent orphans and the feeble-minded. If southern gentlemen sometimes administered bitter medicine to Negroes who tried to ride in Pullman cars, they also gave large sums to schools for the education of colored children in the manual arts.

Paradoxical as it seemed there was perhaps some justification in the exclamation of a visitor from a foreign country, which had received great largess from the United States in the form of charitable relief, to the effect that "the American people have the softest hearts and hardest heads of any race on earth," combining under one mental roof "pep, thrift, and service." Nor was it without warrant that an American critic, W. J. Ghent, coined the phrase "benevolent feudalism" to characterize exactly the peculiar union of ruthless business methods with lavish benefactions for humane purposes. In any case the phenomenon was not easily explained. It found no parallel in Roman society of the Cæsars or in English society of the Victorian capitalism. While all the original content of the Latin word *religio*—awe and propitiation of the gods—was not lost in the course of centuries, the human implications of those deepseated emotions in the America of Calvin Coolidge were quite different from the same manifestations in the Rome of Cicero.

Certainly it cannot be proved that those ancient factors in charity, the satisfaction of conscience or the fear of the gods, played any important part in the new benevolence.

Perhaps some old-fashioned pietists hoped that the poor would always be with us so that the rich could display their virtues, but in fact the keynote of American generosity in the period of mass production was no longer charity or *noblesse oblige*; in that realistic age it became prevention. No doubt there was a notable improvement in the institutions for the care of defectives and dependents; millions of dollars were given annually for hospitals and other eleemosynary institutions; these things revealed humanism at work.

Far more significant, however, was the opening of the attack on the roots of poverty and distress, the program of social legislation devised to reduce the need for asylums and poor houses, the construction of "daylight" factories giving air and sunshine to the workers, and the persistent effort in every direction to get at the causes of human suffering and provide effective therapeutics. It was a sign of the new times that schools of philanthropy changed their names to prove that social work rather than charity was their main concern, that the immense endowment of the Rockefeller Medical Board was dedicated not to the relief of suffering but to the eradication of diseases, that the Russell Sage Foundation, created from the fortune of a close-fisted banker, and the Commonwealth Fund, established by the Harkness family a few years later, were both devoted to the humanities, and in practical operation made generous contributions to the war on sickness and misery and to community planning in the large.

Under the stimulus of such preventive ideals, the social settlement, that novel humanistic experiment of the gilded age, found its mission and its outlook subjected to severe tests. On the one side, many of the evils against which it had originally inveighed were removed by collective action while several of its experimental functions were now assumed by public and private agencies. On the other side, its educational work among the middle classes and the plutocracy was largely taken over by college departments of economics and sociology. In these circumstances, one of the leaders in the movement felt impelled to say at a great international conference in 1926 that "settlement work has shifted from the question of community welfare to the broader field of social education."

The outward-reaching community sentiment which inspired benevolence and social legislation touched at last the fringes of the perplexing racial question, North and South. For a time at the turn of the century the increase in collisions and lynchings seemed to betray the smoldering passions of a coming race war; but the development of more constructive enterprises on the part of Negro leaders, the labors of the American Association for the Advancement of Colored People, the exodus of colored workers from the cotton belt to northern industries, and the scientific study of race relations gave another direction to thought and practice in this sphere. Moreover, in the long and painful way from 1865, the formation of the Interracial Commission in 1920 marked an unmistakable milestone. Providing for direct and friendly coöperation between the leaders of the white race and the black, this Commission undertook to substitute for historic prejudice and suspicion mutual help in searching for a path out of common difficulties. Carrying the same spirit into scientific inquiry more than sixty southern colleges undertook to give courses of instruction in the race question, thereby recognizing its importance and seeking a more impartial approach to its troublesome involutions.

§

As if to accentuate a paradox already great, in the general emphasis on the utilities of benefactions and the practical ends of humane endeavors, æsthetics for the multitude, pure science, and polite letters were patronized by hardheaded men of trade. Throughout the gilded age the possessors of great wealth ransacked the galleries, palaces, private collections, and auction rooms of the Old World, purchased objects of art at fabulous prices, and brought home their harvests for their private enjoyment. Now in the machine age, with increasing frequency, these great hoardings were presented to the public in the spirit of generosity. In 1897 J. P. Morgan made the first of his lavish gifts to the Metropolitan Museum, and in 1924, the splendid Morgan collection of books, manuscripts, paintings, tapestries, and the beautiful building in which they were housed were turned over by his son to a board of trustees for the benefit of the commonalty. About the same time, H. C. Frick, the steel magnate, gave to the public in New York City, subject to certain restrictions, the treasury of paintings he had assembled. In 1925, the collection of the copper king, W. A. Clarke, went to the Corcoran Gallery in Washington, and within twelve months the entire fortune of Frank Munsey passed to the Metropolitan Museum in New York. All over the country, in fact, the artistic riches of Midas were being given to "the folks," California vying with New York for honors. When the cynics laughed at money, steel, and copper barons despoiling Europe of her treasures, they were reminded by historians that textiles, metals, spices, and banking had supported most of the original owners under whose benign pleasure the precious objects had been created in the Old World. But what effect Rembrandt, Holbein, Fragonard, Turner, and Chavannes would ultimately have on a race of salesagents and on American taste in general remained in the lap of the gods.

Besides the facilities for conventional æsthetic study and appreciation afforded by benevolence in the machine age, the opportunities for people who wished to pursue intellectual careers, gross or subtle, were multiplied many fold by the creation of foundations, by an increase in the scientific activities of governments, federal, state, and municipal, by the establishment of new professorships in every field, by the development of special institutions for research, and by the endowment of fellowships. Biologists could boast that Woods Hole had been expanded to "the largest and best equipped marine laboratory in the world." The Rockefeller

Institute in New York supplied all the favorable conditions for medical research that wealth could buy or the art of man conceive.

Whereas amateurs, such as Lyell, Wallace, and Darwin, men of modest but sufficient competence, had pioneered English science in the nineteenth century, the direction of science in America was now assumed by a corps of professionals, trained according to the formulæ of the schools, and solemnly dedicated to teaching and inquiry. If occasionally some undiscovered genius was born to waste his powers on the desert air, it certainly could be said that, by and large, careers were open to talent in America. Indeed those who had occasion to fill professorships constantly lamented the dearth of first-rate candidates and those charged with administering fellowships frequently found themselves required by the terms of benevolences to endow mediocrity. If free tuition and wide gateways to colleges and universities, research laboratories and institutions, could have made a nation of intellectual supermen, the America of the new century should have led the world.

Keeping pace with the multiplying institutions which furnished support for brain workers were expanding markets for ideas which could be transmuted into commodities or technological improvements and for literary products, high and low. Day and night, leaders in business enterprise clamored for novelties to make and for unique devices to promote selling. New magazines, trade, fiction, cult, special organs and general, jostled for place on the stands. Printing and publishing became one of the major branches of capitalist undertaking, ranking not far behind lumber, iron, and steel in the value of the annual output. If, in this trade, fiction, short and long, brought the greatest rewards, still it could be said that the more serious products of the mind enjoyed a respectable buying public and showed signs of steady gain.

While a few aspiring authors insisted that they could not find appreciation for their genius and were thwarted by a lack of sympathy or opportunity, a still larger number gave thanks for a generous nation that bought books, magazines, and newspapers with the same prodigality as chewing gum and theater tickets. Taken all in all, if it is safe to generalize about a matter not capable of mathematical measurement, it would appear that America of the machine age offered material subsistance for a life of the mind more varied and more lucrative, both relatively and absolutely, than any nation that had flourished since the beginnings of civilization in the Nile Valley.

§

Before the machine age had advanced very far, intellectual modes carried from Europe to America by ever multiplying lines of contact brought disruptive shocks to the patterns of culture inherited from the era of the full dinner pail. At the dawn of the twentieth century the main streams of European interest seemed to be running true to definite forms. Darwinism, elaborated by testimony from biology, anthropology, and sociology, had apparently triumphed beyond all question. Political democracy, especially the parliamentary institutions evolved by England, promised to conquer all the capitals of the earth, including St. Petersburg and Tokyo. According to the election returns from England and the Continent, Socialism marched from victory to victory, presaging a transformation of the capitalistic system, the substitution of coöperation for war and competition. Those who did not get the gospel straight from Karl Marx received it in a diluted state from the writings of Tolstoy, Anatole France, and George Bernard Shaw. With perfect confidence anti-clericals, inspired by emotions born of an age-long conflict, continued their bombardment of the Catholic Church, effecting in 1905 a separation of state and religion in France which caused great trepidation in Rome. If the bourgeois who ruled western Europe did not approve radical creeds in any guise, they looked upon the future with apprehension, and proclaimed their benevolence by offering an improvement in the lot of the people as the goal of industry, business, and government. "Peace, Science, Democracy, and Progress"—such was the grand slogan blazoned on the banners of the liberals and accepted by the conservatives, perhaps a bit ruefully, as inescapable prescriptions of the modern epoch.

Under the surface of things, however, were flowing deeper currents of inquiry and speculation which were destined to put new aspects on the outlook of the world before the lapse of many years. By minute researches into the problems set by Darwin a generation of scientists completely shattered the simple mechanistic ideas, such as the struggle for existence and survival of the fittest, offered as the keys to the riddle of the universe; and under the leadership of Hugo de Vries reintroduced into man's concept of the creative process inexplicable cataclysmic doctrines—sudden and swerving transformations not to be explained by any simple chain of material causation. In short, in the light of the new biology, the neat creed of evolution received from the Victorians appeared about as inadequate to the requirements of science as the epic contained in the Book of Genesis.

To the disconcerting effects of biologic researches were added startling discoveries in the department of physics. Indeed it was this branch of learning rather than biology that now occupied the center of intellectual interest, resuming its old empire while presenting novel phases. From the age of Newton that noble science had been largely dominated by a mechanistic view of the universe; and its early doctrines had been formidably buttressed by the first law of dynamics, known as the conservation of energy and the indestructibility of matter, expounded in the nineteenth century, and by the Darwinian hypothesis advanced in the same period.

But long before the turning of the century, the solid mechanistic structure of physics received terrific jolts in the house of its friends. From the laboratory of Lord Kelvin came a manifesto denying the validity of the earlier law of dynamics and substituting for that doctrine an equally confident assertion "that all nature's energies were slowly converting themselves into heat and vanishing in space, until, at last, nothing would be left except a dead level of energy at its lowest possible level. . . . incapable of doing any work." Many years later, to be exact, in 1898, from the laboratory of the Curies was hurled a "metaphysical bomb" in the form of radio activity. A new era was at hand. Within twenty-five years, the philosopher, Alfred N. Whitehead, could say: "Science is taking on a new aspect which is neither purely physical, nor purely biological. It is becoming a study of organisms. Biology is the study of the larger organisms; whereas physics is the study of smaller organisms."

To make a complicated matter simpler than science really permits, earlier concepts of matter and force, which had once been set forth in the physics books as firmly as the laws of the Medes and Persians in the jurisprudence of the ancients, were thrown into the discard. The foundations of confident materialism were dissolved; in place of the old dogmas was offered a curious combination of physics and biology for which philosophers could find no better word than "organic mechanism." Even the certitudes of logic were shaken. When the distinguished French mathematician, Poincaré, asked whether Euclidean geometry was true, he answered himself by saying that the question had no sense: "Euclidean geometry is and still remains the most convenient." When Haeckel, with Teutonic thoroughness, dared the riddle of the universe, he broke down at the crucial point and confessed that the "proper essence of substance appeared to him more and more marvelous and enigmatic as he penetrated further into the knowledge of its attributes." No less revolutionary for the Victorian outlook were the explorations of the new psychology, particularly researches into the nature and functions of the subconscious life, the rôle of defense mechanisms in thinking, real and feigned, and the wider implications of sex for the expression of life in all its forms.

While the masters of microscope and test tube were penetrating deeper into the substance of all things, the World War took the direction of affairs out of the hands of debaters and placed them in charge of primitive force. As every student of war foresaw, the conflict produced convulsive results wholly outside its mere range of death and destruction. With frightful emphasis the fragile character of "law and order" was demonstrated by ruthless violations of "international comity" on every side, and by domestic upheavals against accredited governments. After preaching the coming "revolution" with religious fervor for a whole generation, Marxian Socialists of the chair were startled into frenzy by the sight of mass energy ripping up the old Tsarist régime and enthroning Bolshevism or a proletarian despotism as a working scheme of politics. On all scores this was distressing enough to orthodox believers in parliamentary institutions and democratic apparatus for counting heads, but they had scarcely got their attack on the Soviet dictatorship in working form when they were invited to stop and applaud dictatorships in Italy, Hungary, and Spain established in the interest of property, not against it —putting yet another aspect on political ethics.

Then, in the aftermath of the war, in the period of reaction and dismay that always follows such volcanic efforts of mankind, pessimists, unable to endure the necessary strain of the age, led by Oswald Spengler in Germany, announced the doom of western civilization. It was gravely asked whether science, the great god of the nineteenth century, was not to be the destroying Frankenstein of the twentieth century. To this challenge the optimists could only answer by promising a return to the old course of "peace and progress."

And they too had some justification; for when the vapors sank down around Russian Bolshevism and Italian Fascism, it was seen that the goal set by the statesmen of the Soviet

Republic and the dictator in Rome, whatever their ethics and verbal flourishes, was mechanical comfort and prosperity for the masses. With the rapid erosion of the feudal orders in England and on the Continent by the extension of peasant proprietorship, the taxation of landed estates, or the destruction of monarchical houses, all European society was more nearly assimilated in substantial matters to that of the United States. The process of civilianizing, which had been transforming the world since the age of exploration and discovery, had broken down even the oldest feudo-clerical structures and promised, at the moment, to make all mankind akin in its economic machinery and corresponding tastes.

§

On intellectual pursuits in America the primitive manifestations of the World War and the forward sweep of the machine process sustained by natural science wielded influences both gross and subtle. In terms of religion and theological speculation they were manifest in forms ponderable and imponderable. Churches of every denomination were enriched in buildings and funds by gifts from the swelling patrimonies of the plutocracy and the middle classes. Social fear, the spirit of sacrifice, and reasoned belief conspired to enlarge the golden streams poured into the treasuries of the ecclesiastics. A Nordic Protestant, James J. Hill, and a Semitic skeptic, Max Pam, gave generous sums to Catholic institutions for the avowed purpose of helping to spread discipline over the restive working classes of the land. A school of journalism in a Catholic University, endowed by a Jew, showed how far the machine age had moved from the time of Thomas Aquinas, Abelard, and Saint Francis of Assisi. In the old home of Puritan dissent, Massachusetts, the estate of the Episcopal Church became so large that Bishop Lawrence, member of an old mercantile family, felt constrained to lay aside the purely spiritual functions of his holy office for the practical business of financial administration.

When the first quarter of the century had closed, all denominations reported a combined annual income of over half a billion dollars, the Methodists leading with at least a fourth of the total. In material equipment and capital investments, yearly gains were made that would have startled the bishops, trustees, and deacons of the middle period. Indeed, there were statisticians adventurous enough to estimate that in time the American clergy would enjoy a material power relatively as great as that which fell to the lot of the mediæval church before it was despoiled by the legislation and confiscation of the bourgeois. But such historical prophecies called for caution as well as rejoicing.

The age of machinery which gave wealth to the clergy, being also an age of democracy, intellectual strife, feminism, and associative enterprise among the laity, was marked by an increasing emphasis among all the sects on organizations and institutional arrangements for holding the rank and file in line. Among the Protestant denominations, societies of various kinds, such as the Young Men's Christian Association and its counterpart the Young Women's Christian Association, put aside insistence upon specific creeds, and sought to attract youth by providing social life, lodgings, gymnasiums, entertainment, travel, and instruction in such practical matters as bond selling, real-estate promotion, and elementary technology. Taking their suggestion from such undertakings, pastors in great cities often resorted to similar expedients in their attempts to retain within the fold a membership increasingly distracted by the clangor of industrial life and the flashing amusements offered by commercial agencies.

Even the Catholic Church, which deviated less from historic formulæ and surrendered fewer of the powers possessed by the hierarchy, could not wholly resist the pressure of the age. On no reckoning could the associative temper of its laymen, who in secular life flocked to trade unions and Rotary clubs, be ignored or schemes for attracting their interest be disdained. So the Knights of Columbus came to play in Catholic circles a rôle similar to that assumed by the Christian Associations in the Protestant sphere, offering assistance in obtaining employment and instruction in technical, business, and civic subjects. It was no accident that "the leading Catholic laymen's organization in the world" was founded in the chief business empire of the world and that it rose to power in the Church of the machine age. Nor did the Jews, professing a still more ancient faith keep aloof from the stream. Among them also lay organizations paralleled the associations of the Christian churches.

As the several denominations reached out for the laymen and sought to make religious applications fitted to their needs, social questions, already in evidence in the gilded age, assumed a larger place in clerical discussions. While Christian Socialism apparently gained little in numerical strength, the interest of the clergy in theories of that character varied directly with the intensity of the controversies in the realm of labor and capital. At the close of the World War when industrial unrest was sweeping through all western civilization, Catholics established a National Welfare Council devoted to scientific and humane inquiries into the pressing economic problems of the day. And Protestants, in addition to setting up a bewildering array of similar agencies, attempted federations looking toward unity and common community programs. As an evidence of a practical resolve, one of these agencies made a survey of the steel industry, producing findings which traversed the assertions of the proprietors and condemned the hours and working conditions in the mills. On certain aspects of the wages problem, the Young Women's Christian Association took such an advanced position that one of its heaviest financial supporters was definitely alienated. Though strong forces made for conservatism, the upward push of the laity into religious activities carried the discontents of secular life, such as there were, into that sphere.

Yet with all the efforts, clerical and lay, to hold the masses to some form of ecclesiastical connection, the fact remained that in 1926 more than one-half the Gentile population and nine-tenths of the Jews were outside the pale of organized religion. When it was pointed out that this estimate of nominal membership, based on statistical reports made by the clergy, included a large proportion of children, the width of the breach in the church universal became all the more striking.

Besides the drive of secular concerns competing for the attention of the masses more and more absorbed in the machine process, the clergy of every sect had to reckon with all kinds of intellectual currents running against orthodoxy in thought. Without interruption the skeptical Deism of the early republic, the growing Unitarianism of the middle period, and the higher criticism of the gilded age, though they resulted in no great congregations of the faithful, continued to make inroads upon established systems of theological opinion. All the while a great army of geologists, biologists, astronomers, physicists, and historians poured out into the streets through books, magazines, and newspapers sensational and disturbing ideas that did not square with the cosmogony and chronology of the Bible, raising a cloud of queries and doubts in the minds of laymen and suggesting to theologians that explanations, modifications, or counterblasts were in order.

Frankly accepting the stubborn facts of science and higher criticism, one school, calling themselves Modernists, tried to meet the situation by restating the substance of Christianity in terms compatible with modern knowledge. The thinker of this type, to use the language of Harry Emerson Fosdick, simply could not "take in earnest the man-sized representations of God on which, it may be, he was brought up—a god walking in a garden in the cool of the day, making woman from man's rib, confounding men's speech lest they build a tower too high, decreeing a flood to drown humanity, trying to slay a man at a wayside inn because his child was not circumcised, showing his back but not his face to a man upon a mountain top, or ordering the massacre of his chosen people's enemies, men, women, and children, without mercy. He is in revolt against all that." From such "old literalism" the Modernist demanded "intellectual liberation"—emancipation to expound "Christ's imperishable Gospel freed from its entanglements, the Shekinah distinguished from the shrine, to be preached with a liberty, a reasonableness, an immediate application to our own age such as no generation of preachers in the church's history ever had the privilege of knowing before."

Far from surrendering to the iconoclasm of modern science, theologians of an opposite tendency, known as "Fundamentalists," clung with unshaken loyalty to what they were pleased to call "the old faith"—their own selected essentials of Biblical theology. In a strict sense, of course, the Catholic Church, though occasionally disturbed by the writings of Modernists within its own fold, was pre-fundamentalist in doctrine, claiming, as it did, an unchanging and unchangeable creed of invariables which embraced contentions quite as difficult for natural science as Virgin Birth. But it was the conservatives of the Protestant persuasion who started the new vogue in dogmatism. Picking out a few tenets deemed necessary for salvation, they rejected the validity of scientific methods in theological criticism and declared war on freethinking of every type. In general they agreed on four or five points as tests for separating the sheep and the goats; such, for example, as the verbal inerrancy and inspiration of the Bible, a literal interpretation of its crucial passages, the fall of man, Virgin Birth, the scheme of atonement and salvation through the crucifixion, and the resurrection of Christ.

Lest there be uncertainty as to their position, Fundamentalists proclaimed their views in unmistakable language. The Baptist Bible Union, for instance, formulated its creed in the following terms: "that the Bible was written by men supernaturally inspired; that it has truth without any admixture of error for its matter; that as originally written it is both scientifically and historically true and correct; and therefore is and shall remain to the end of the ages the only complete and final revelation of the will of God to man; the true center of Christian union and the supreme standard by which all human conduct, creeds, and opinions should be tried." This broad and emphatic profession was followed by eight additional declarations pertaining to the Trinity, the acceptance of the Genesis account of creation "literally not allegorically or figuratively," Virgin Birth, atonement for sin, grace in the new creation, the mission of the Church, immersion, the resurrection and second coming of Christ, and the condemnation of evolutionary doctrines. Affirming its faith in dogmas similar in character, the Presbyterian Church at its general assembly in 1923 prefaced its bill of particulars with the assertion that "it is an essential doctrine of the Word of God and our standards that the Holy Spirit did so inspire, guide, and move the writers of the Holy Scriptures as to keep them from error." Whatever criticisms could be levelled against the Fundamentalists, it was admitted that they left no doubt as to the verbal forms of their beliefs.

By competent authorities the origins of the Fundamentalist movement have been traced to Bible institutes founded in various parts of the country for the purpose of training religious workers whose preliminary education did not, as a rule, qualify them for the theological schools tinctured by scientific and historical methods. It was in essence a popular movement, showing its greatest strength in rural districts where the machine process had as yet made little impression. Unquestionably, it was highly organized, well-financed, and resolute.

Not content with making war on the Modernists in theology, Fundamentalist leaders strove to get possession of state legislatures and force the enactment of statutes forbidding the teaching of evolution in schools supported either in whole or in part by public funds. With comparative ease, they accomplished this object in Tennessee, precipitating in the summer of 1925 a spectacular battle in the trial and conviction of a young teacher accused of imparting to his pupils the doctrine of evolution in violation of the law.

Among the freethinkers of two continents, especially among those who looked neither around nor back, the Tennessee case aroused amusement at the expense of the American hinterland, but undisturbed by scorn from such quarters, the Fundamentalists announced that they intended to carry on their campaign—preaching their gospel and forcing legislatures to pass bills against evolution until they had made their creed the faith of the American nation. And while the doubters scoffed, the straight sect of literalists, in their warfare on science, received hearty encouragement from theologians in England, Scotland, and Europe who were themselves put in similar jeopardy by the inroads which modern learning was making upon their own domain.

§

According to what seemed to be destiny American science in the machine age made its great contributions in the form of utilitarian applications rather than in pure speculation. At Menlo Park, Thomas Edison continued to work his witchery with a vitality undiminished by age. Until the close of his threescore and fifteen years in 1922, Alexander Graham Bell maintained his interest in the improvement of telephonic communications; and a number of other leaders from the older generation labored with unabated zeal through the opening decades of the twentieth century. To the long list of celebrated inventors who had given distinction to the previous period were added names full worthy of the forerunners—Michael Pupin in the extension of telephone and telegraph circuits, Charles P. Steinmetz in the field of general electricity, the Wright Brothers in aeronautics, Lee De Forest in radio transmission, and countless workers hardly less adroit in interpreting the ways and moods of nature.

Though the advance in technology had carried the

frontiers of inquiry far away from the dominion ruled by thumb and had pushed scientific problems deep into the mysteries of the new physics and chemistry, ingenuity seemed to keep pace with the most exacting requirements. No branch of applied mechanics was ignored; no demands of progressive industry went unheeded. As in the gilded age, every year brought forth its amazing achievements until a sated public could be scarcely moved by the most breathtaking revelation. In 1903 the first flight of more than five hundred feet was made by an airplane; in 1902 the first wireless message was carried across the Atlantic from Cornwall to Cape Cod; in 1915 the sound of the human voice sped from New York to San Francisco by telephone; in 1927 from New York to London by wireless.

When near the turn of the quarter a comparative study of the world's mechanical achievements was made, the United States led all the nations of the earth in the number of patents registered, having 1,397,000 against 645,000 for France; 594,000 for Great Britain; and 365,000 for Germany. With good reason could Secretary Hoover say in 1925: "We have in recent years developed our industrial research upon a scale hitherto unparalleled in history."

From the workshop the spirit of practical application radiated in every direction. If, as Spengler suggests, chiming clocks in church towers could give to renaissance Europe a fateful time sense unknown to the ancients, then it is not surprising to find that the clanging machinery of American civilization gave a utilitarian bent to the oldest sciences born of magic and necromancy. Having prefixed "industrial" to their title, chemists, whose forerunners once sought the philosopher's stone, now vied with one another in discovering new commercial substances or in turning old elements to novel uses in the manufacture of commodities, the increase of agricultural produce, or the destruction of diseases. From vexatious disputes with preachers over Mosaic cosmogony—from the long contest between the bourgeois and clerical estates which had opened in the sixteenth century—geologists swerved over to mundane affairs, taking pride in inquiries that yielded economic advantages.

In keeping with the spirit of the age, biology shifted its center of gravity. Once it had furnished the materials for the furious Darwinian battle, giving special attention to the theological implications of its researches. In the machine age, however, biology, besides branching out in all directions, assumed a more earthly guise, busying itself with improvements in the breeds of plants and animals, wars on disease, eugenics, population and the food supply, the relation of organic functions to mind and conduct, and theories of race, not overlooking the great conflict between the Nordics and their rivals. With a kindred indifference to theology, psychologists veered off from monastic introspection to the study of the human animal as a going concern in a world of physical and chemical reactions, venturing into the social bearings of their subject, deigning to serve employers in the search for efficient labor, merchants eager to sell more goods by alluring advertisements, and physicians concerned with healing.

By the predominance of practical considerations a decided stimulus was given to the popularization of science. New technical magazines designed for general and special publics packed the newsstalls. Books making clear the mysteries of advanced researches, such for example as Edwin D. Slosson's Creative Chemistry published in 1919, took their place with novels among the best sellers. In colleges and universities scientific courses multiplied; while societies for the promotion of scientific interests flourished. And Science Service, established in 1920, broke into the columns of the daily press. State and federal support for scientific work and endowments for research, notably the Carnegie Institution and the Rockefeller Institute, proved that science commanded the respect both of taxpaying masses and the possessors of great riches.

And the downward thrust of exact science into the commonalties of life continued unabated. Through a thousand channels its spirit poured into the nooks and crannies of American life, save in the remote hinterlands. With the expansion of machine processes, it covered an ever larger area of industry; with the growth of cities, municipal technology occupied spacious regions once dominated by political vagaries; owing to the agricultural revolution, work on the farm became as realistic as the moving parts of a steam engine. In the guise of labor saving devices, in the formula of balanced diets and domestic hygiene, science invaded the household, tilting at ancient practices based on rule of thumb and flouting old wives' prescriptions for the care and feeding of infants. If social opinion lagged behind the flow of scientific interests, the tendency of thought was as exigent as the kinematics of the sun.

In the higher realms of speculation and dialectics, similarly cumbered with the verbal patterns of former civilizations, the spirit and method of science also wrought transformations with respect to strategy and objectives. Whatever their practices, historians of the new century made solemn vows to truth, declaring that it was not their business to praise or condemn, pronounce ethical judgments, serve the cause of party, or play the rôle of chauvinist, but rather to ascertain the facts of particular situations, order them systematically, and draw from them only the deductions warranted by the evidence. Economists and sociologists in turn paid tribute to science; if they apologized for protective tariffs and ship subsidies, gave aid and comfort to organized labor, or forwarded the course of social legislation, they at least decorated their arguments with the gauds of the laboratory. In education, the quantitative measurements of physics and chemistry were paralleled by mechanical tests of intelligence, which gave pain to idealists of the old school who continued to imagine that there was something qualitative about character, capacity, and pedagogy. Though forty of the leading scientists of the country, including men as eminent as R. A. Millikan and Henry Fairfield Osborn, united in proclaiming that there was no real conflict between science and religion, Fundamentalists refused to be comforted, persisting in their distress over the conquest and subjugation of the mysterious by the critical method.

And yet, notwithstanding the swift advance of applied and popular science, in pure science—the disinterested search for truth—the United States lagged far behind the leading European nations. It is true that in the course of the machine age, the Nobel Prize was awarded four times to American scholars, to A. A. Michelson and R. A. Millikan in physics; to T. W. Richards in chemistry; and to Alexis Carrel in medicine. But there was no doubt that America on the whole held a subordinate position as a promoter of chivalric inquiries into the subtler mysteries of nature.

It was the recognition of this disconcerting fact that led a committee of distinguished citizens, headed by Secretary Hoover, to begin in 1926 the quest for a twenty million dollar endowment fund with a view to raising the United States in the scale of scientific accomplishment, evidently on the assumption that better material equipment and more leisure would automatically produce Darwins, Roentgens, Curies, Kelvins, and Einsteins. Though the project was greeted with a chorus of approval in academic circles as marking a turn in the history of American thought, all through the appeals for subscriptions ran the obtruding note that in the end even the most remote and abstract search for truth would pay dividends to business enterprise.

§

Bounded on the one side by machine industry and on the other by scientific research, humanistic studies took on the tone of the "temporal modalities." In philosophy the trend was unmistakable; the substitution of laymen trained in professional schools for seasoned clergymen had been practically completed by the opening of the period and had already commenced to bear fruit. Though no little cosmic anguish was transferred when speculative thought was separated from religious offices and emoluments, the provocations of hard, practical business in American culture could not be escaped. Attempts to offset native speculation by importing such restorers of historic vitalism as Henri Bergson merely made transitory flurries, confirming local authorities in their vernacular convictions.

In his later years, William James went entirely over to the devastating pragmatism of Charles Peirce—a curious combination of chance, love, and law, hospitable to all pertinent ideas, trusting somewhat naïvely in the general good and the general run; never was James more whimsically dangerous to "old absolutism" than at the close of his rich and versatile life in 1910. Nor was his colleague at Harvard, Josiah Royce, more consoling to intimates of Providence who thought that they could stand fast where they were. While Royce belonged essentially to the earlier period of American history, his attenuated Christian scheme left little room for special creation, the fall of man, and salvation by mere faith.

With complete frankness, the other outstanding thinker of the generation, John Dewey, broke with all fixed schemes and imagery, shifted the center of his speculation to naturalistic grounds, waited assiduously on the new revelations of science, listened to the changing voices of psychology, and gave to his thought the semblance of vitality and motion that accompanied the flow of all things. In his hands a branch of wisdom once deemed esoteric acquired a practical ring; in fact it conformed very closely to the requirements of an age committed to machine production, science, and progressive endeavor.

As a matter of course, this tendency in American opinion shocked æsthetes of a softer and thinner temper, especially those who found solace in the philosophies of less prosperous civilizations baffled in the quest for material abundance and content to find in speculation a comforting substitute.

After enriching American opinion with sparkling fancies and noble apologies for the mystic view, one of the most brilliant writers of this bent, George Santayana, fled from the scene to a haven in an older culture where the grime of economic subvention was not so evident or at least worked no such havoc in the pleasures of inward calm. Certainly it was difficult to reconcile what the Germans called Fordismus with anything that savored of Nirvana.

For dogmatic economics as for the philosophies of absolutism the veering weather of the machine age was not at all propitious. No one was strong enough, or at least no one attempted, to bend the bow which John Bates Clark had used with such effect at the close of the gilded age in defending a capitalistic system which distributed wealth according to deserts, particularly after Thorstein Veblen illuminated Clark's paradoxes in the most consummate piece of academic irony ever produced on this continent. It is true that many professors continued to write textbooks wearing the aspects of rotundity, but capitalism shifted its ground with such rapidity that it was no longer possible to reproduce the assurance of Adam Smith, Ricardo, and Nassau Senior. As far as they possessed unity of pattern, these texts at bottom were usually apologies for the prevailing modes of production and distribution; but even their unity was more specious than real.

Indeed the drive of technology was so remorseless that younger economists, like their brethren in physics and biology, turned from philosophy to research, pushing ever deeper into the currents of detail, historical and practical, thereby losing foothold on the banks of infallibility. Those with an inclination for profitable realism swung over to business schools or became advisers to banks; those with a temper for service gave thought to labor problems and humane legislation; others with a passion for exactness applied to such fragments of the economic world as were susceptible of measurement the methods of mathematics, with fruitful results in limited areas. By these and similar maneuvers, the spirit of science and inquiry harbored in the universities became mingled with the conduct of business, the direction of industry, and the conflicts of capital and labor.

Before the machine age had got into full swing, a new kind of approach called "institutional economics" was announced in the schools. According to this creed, the prime business of the economist was to "get the facts," observe the tendencies, examine the factors that conditioned particular situations, and possibly coöperate intelligently in realizing temporarily relevant policies. Perhaps the spirit of the age was voiced with fair accuracy by a distinguished professor of this direction when he declared in 1923 that his science could not be scientific if it served either capital or labor as mere apologetics and that a middle ground of mediation and interpretation was the only alternative to impossible dogmatizing. While to tough-minded men bent on higher profits or increased wages at all costs, the pronouncement seemed cold and unpromising, it was highly significant; the age of crude protective coloration was vanishing.

Caught in the same realistic tendencies, political science in its turn underwent a kindred transformation. In the hands of men trained in the verbalism of jurisprudence, it had long remained austere, aloof from use and wont. At the opening of the twentieth century nearly all the books dealing with government were tables of constitutional rules —rules that gave little or no clue to practice—or they were speculative treatises on the logic of an elusive abstraction called "the state," usually conceived more or less consciously in the interest of some party or faction. But that façade could not escape the scrutiny of curious minds.

In time doubts as to the value of this juristic formalism led to an inquiry into the nature and operations of political parties, those powerful organs of government as a going concern—an inquiry stimulated in 1902 by the publication in English of M. Ostrogorski's remarkable work on Democracy and the Organization of Political Parties, which carried into greater minutiæ the investigation made by James Bryce several years earlier. Once the juristic wall was breached, a search began for the springs of motive that induced individuals and groups to take part in the governing process and for efficient causes determining the functions of politics. As fitted the machine age in which the making and selling of material goods were the supreme activities of society, the search for such origins opened a way into the realm of economic enterprise. When that departure was made, no sanctum could elude intruders; no department of government, legislative, executive, or judicial, could avoid the light of scientific criticism.

While this invasion was taking place, political theory was subjected to pressure from another quarter, namely from the Taylorian practitioners of industrial efficiency. As national, state, and municipal budgets mounted and the functions of government expanded, nothing seemed more natural than to apply to the transaction of public business the modes of organization and the procedures found successful in corporate affairs. On one wing of political science, therefore, the quest for methods of economy in planning and executing public work became a dominant interest in research, resulting as in economics in the rise of an institutional school, concerned primarily with observing the state playing its historic rôle and with helping to perfect the technique of government in discharging the duties thrust upon it by the drive of parties and factions. Thus interpretation crowded dogma aside and practical studies, chiefly directed by bureaus of governmental research, took the place of hair-splitting analyses of political concepts.

Lagging somewhat in the rear came jurisprudence as a science, heavily handicapped by the load of professionalism carried on its back. Like theology, with which it was long associated in Western Europe, civil law, its vigilant guardians averred, was a mysterious substance discovered in the realm of abstract justice by adepts at the business. The mastery of the subject was to be attained mainly by a study of the words of lawgivers. On such verbal nutriment, generations of practising attorneys were brought to maturity and conviction, and, as long as they were able to keep their domain isolated from the inquiries of the profane, their authority was secure.

But under the all-penetrating searchlight of modern science it was impossible to maintain this cabalistic spell, especially as law now had to climb down to the market place. The action of legislatures in covering an ever larger area of legal rules with statutory enactments opened whole segments of jurisprudence to examination with reference to the nature and motives of legislative majorities. Contests over the political appointment of judges also made it manifest that there were human factors in judge-made law which could not be hidden from those concerned with the social sciences. Studies in the psychology of prejudice and rationalization shot damascus blades into the prestige of judicial logic. Battles among judges themselves, eventuating in dissenting opinions, revealed to an observant public the more esoteric magic of judicial determinations. "This case is decided upon an economic theory which a large part of the country does not entertain. . . . General propositions do not decide concrete cases. The decision will depend on a judgment or intuition more subtle than any articulate major premise," genially remarked Justice Holmes of the Supreme Court in 1907 when taking issue with his colleagues on the validity of a labor statute—as it were, anticipating the advent of Louis D. Brandeis.

To an ever-increasing audience it became apparent that the law was merely a form of social and economic expression, changing with the technology and processes of society and to be understood in connection with the living tissue of which it was a part. In these circumstances, to the consternation of jurists brought up on the common law and "the eternal principles of justice," there rose and flourished a new faith covered by the lugubrious phrase "sociological jurisprudence," and promulgated by an authority no less distinguished than Roscoe Pound, dean of the Harvard Law School. Under this dispensation, it became fitting for students to inquire into the economic and psychological motives of those who made and interpreted the law, into the "actual social effects of legal institutions and doctrines," and into the social forces that had produced the existing order and were bearing lawmakers, lawyers, and judges from timeless formalism into an endless development.

More remote from the transactions of the market place and court room, the historians of the machine age, primarily concerned with the past rather than the intimate nature of the world process, were not as deeply involved in the practical currents of the time as were the economists, political scientists, and lawyers. Though Henry Adams, as president of the Historical Association and an elder statesman, besought his colleagues to attempt a science of history, he excited no hearty response. "Historians," he lamented, "turned to the collection of facts as the geologist turned to the collection of fossils."

Perhaps an explanation for this nonchalance was to be found in a colloquy arranged by Adams himself. "What shape," he once asked, "can be given to any science of history that will not shake to its foundation some prodigious interest?" Then he answered the query by saying that anything more than a superficial chronicle or tale of a local episode was bound to run counter to at least one of the immense forces dominant in the modern world, namely, the church, government, property, or organized labor. To this suggestion the historians listened respectfully and then went on their way as usual collecting, annotating, editing, and framing well-documented surveys of significant events, either because they thought no science of history possible, or had come to the conclusion with Adams himself that after all "silence is best."

Hence there was written in the machine age no romantic history explaining the wonder-working providence of God in the United States after the fashion of Bancroft, no large philosophic view of America in a world setting after the style of Hegel, no interpretation of American intellect in terms of material circumstance according to the formula of Buckle. And yet it could not be doubted that immense gains were made in the period. The Doctors of Philosophy who acted as masters of ceremonies, if they felt unable to emulate Kant or Aristotle, at least cleared the ground of huge piles of naïve prejudices masquerading as "facts;" by the collection and analysis of genuine historical sources they prepared the way for a more accurate and more realistic description of the movement of social forces in the United States.

And they did more than that. Frederick Jackson Turner, followed by many disciples, made clear for the first time the deep influence of the western frontier on the course of American affairs. The drive of commercial interests in bringing the American Revolution to pass was fully revealed in the heavily documented writing of Charles M. Andrews, Allan Nevins, O. M. Dickerson, and Arthur Meier Schlesinger; while by William E. Dodd the curtain of mythology was raised on the Old South. At last in 1926 an artist's sketch was made for a synthetic view of American origins when J. Franklin Jameson published his lectures on the American Revolution considered as a social movement. The monopoly of the political chronicle was coming to a close. Moreover under the leadership of James Harvey Robinson the narrow confines of Clio's kingdom were widened to include the history of the intellectual classes and the rôle of intelligence in the drama of mankind. It could be truly said that the histories of the United States available for schools and general purposes were fully equal in scholarship, range, outlook, and fairness, to kindred works in any country of the world. If to lovers of romance their visibility seemed low, that fact had to be ascribed perhaps to the critical spirit, not to any lack of appreciation for creative powers.

§

If natural science gave a metallic ring to intellectual life in general, it did not entirely crush the fancies of those who labored at imaginative literature and criticism. It is true that for a time after the opening of the century, it seemed as if the culture of mercantilism was to swing in its orbit undisputed. Established journals transmitted by the gilded age, enriched by more extensive advertising, unfurled few sails to new breezes. After flourishing for a time on muckraking, the popular magazines returned rather contritely to the eternal triangle, current gossip, and the heroes of Samuel Smiles; while the historic monthlies of respectability, which had never strayed from the straight and narrow path, continued to follow traditional middle-class standards, though occasionally one or another shocked subscribers from the list by an aberrant article on sex or labor.

But in due course several significant departures were made. A number of metropolitan newspapers found it worth while to enlarge their book-review columns or to issue special sections devoted to literary comment; and an independent critical weekly, The Saturday Review of Literature, was founded by Henry Seidel Canby, an editor of catholic and discriminating taste. Evidently it paid—in appreciation, pride, or book advertising; in any case the fact was noteworthy. Still more impressive were novel adventures in the journalism of opinion. In 1914, Herbert Croly, whose Promise of American Life had won for him a distinct place in the history of American political thought, established the New Republic dedicated frankly to liberalism in politics and letters. Four years later The Nation, which had been sputtering around in a desert, started to wage battles for liberty under the direction of Oswald Garrison Villard. About the same time The Freeman, under the authority of Albert Jay Nock, began to scatter acid on many a sacred convention, keeping up the practice for three crowded years. Frightened by such obliquities, a few conservatives levied tribute on men of substance and launched The Review to check, as they said, "unthinking radicalism";

only to flounder soon in a devouring calm. Equally discontented with liberalism and the common run of ideas, Henry L. Mencken and George Jean Nathan, departing from the Smart Set, found hospitable shelter with the publisher, Alfred Knopf, from whose office they discharged the American Mercury, a monthly magazine of smashing, stinging audacity addressed to "the civilized minority," to which Henry Holt had earlier directed his short-lived Unpopular Review.

On the basis of their underlying assumptions, modes, and nuances the literary commodities that flowed haphazard from the pens of American writers admitted of some tabulation; for after all nothing essentially new appeared under the smoky industrial sky. Classification was possible even though it was true that one critic remarked: "Our distinctive note was to have no distinctive note, to be a conglomeration of sharply divergent entities, all on practically the same plane of importance."

Above the flood were highly visible those contented writers who saw or thought they saw in the American order —if turbulent change could be called an order—a tangible unity that was precious, praiseworthy, and deserving of linguistic approval. In its unrestrained exuberance this view of American culture took the form of an incorrigible romanticism, continuously represented in the stories published by magazines for women and in the novels of Harold Bell Wright and Gene Stratton Porter.

In its higher manipulation this creed appeared in a more learned and civilized garb, illustrated by the writings of Stuart P. Sherman. Finding in the United States "a national genius animated by an incomparably profound moral idealism," this eminent critic and essayist desired above all things to see "Americanism vital, devout, and affectionate"; he prayed that art and letters might be serviceable to democracy, energizing and giving permanency to national morals, making Puritanism beautiful—all to the glorious end that right reason and the will of God might prevail. For those who spoke contemptuously of the bourgeois, Sherman evinced a hearty dislike and he shrank from the grosser forms of sex display, except when, as in the case of Brigham Young, they were associated with industry, sobriety, thrift, and morality. Though Sherman used the language of Matthew Arnold, he appealed in fact to the sound heart of the great middle class—that class which his English mentor had harshly characterized by the phrase "Philistine."

On the other side of propriety but also above the flood flourished a school of writers who accepted Sherman's assumption that there was a cultural unity in America, essentially Puritan and middle class in its modes, but denounced its ethical pretensions as hypocrisies disguising the ideals of advertising agents. This school likewise ran true to historic form. Its ablest spokesmen, Jack London, Upton Sinclair, and W. E. Woodward, sardonically trouncing the culture of the bourgeoisie, threatened it with the unity of socialism, inspired, they alleged, by the ideals of science and the proletariat.

In a novel defiantly called Revolution, London described "the day" for American capitalism. With Biblical warmth, Sinclair damned the American order in gross and in detail. In The Jungle, he exposed conditions of life and labor in the Chicago stockyards, striking resounding blows that for the traditional nine days shocked the conscience of the nation, reverberated through the White House, and carried rumors of pork ethics all the way to the steppes of Siberia. In other studies, fiction, and essays, he assailed with the same energy what he called capitalist journalism, lock-step education from kindergarten through college, and the art of Mammon worship. More intimately acquainted with the practical aspects of money-making and the "jargon" of the market place than either London or Sinclair, Woodward, in his trenchant novel, called Lottery, pitched into the pieties and pretensions of business enterprise, declaring chance and vulgarity to be the great factors in the game of acquisition.

Revealing a similar skepticism with reference to the finality and virtues of mercantile culture, if showing less certainty about any possible or desirable substitute, were the works of Theodore Dreiser, Sinclair Lewis, and Sherwood Anderson, who led a school of writers that flayed with merciless portrayal the conventions of "the sound middle-class," the small town, the plutocracy, and the high priests at the American altar of success. In other words, by a perfect deluge of novels and poems, grave doubts were cast upon the authenticity of Stuart P. Sherman's national genius "animated by an incomparably moral idealism."

Scattered along the line between Harold Bell Wright and Upton Sinclair was an army of literary photographers, etchers, and artists who disavowed interest in cosmic schemes, whether naïve or sophisticated, and, oblivious to the metaphysical implications of their lightest words, wrote novels for the entertainment of those who would buy and read. But these writers who professed an air of detachment from the zeal of bard and critic were either drawn in their search for themes to the substance of American life in the machine age or were caught in the tragic sense of necessity that encompassed the production of commodities. By this time feudalism was so far gone in Europe that no Henry James or F. Marion Crawford seemed inclined to flee from the land of prosperity for the purpose of sketching the etiquette of dying ages. By this time the business man occupied the center of all western civilization and no effort of the imagination could cover him with the embroidered coat of King Arthur.

Certainly no one who dealt with America of the machine era could fail to see the pivot on which its civilization turned —neither Edith Wharton artistically analyzing seasoned generations trying to ward off climbers from the new gold coast and captains of industry expressing benevolence in welfare work; nor Frank Norris colorfully painting the successful iron man oppressed by the futility of a mere victory in dollars. With the same clank, the note of the counting house ran through the sectional fiction of "the new South." In James Branch Cabell's first novel the upstanding figure was a financial wizard who "had sent more men into bankruptcy and more missionaries into Africa than any other philanthropist in the country." The battle reflected in Ellen Glasgow's pages was between the decaying respectability of the old plantation and the dynamic aspirations of science and business enterprise. If it was not the business man who always occupied the center of the stage it was his wife or daughters—or the independent woman with a career created of the new economy and given a code of manners and morals appropriate to the order. Fainting heroines all died in the era of the full dinner pail.

If perchance the scene drawn was intensely local, the same atmosphere of fatality, adapted to the numerical epoch, hung over the characters and the play. Through the eyes of Edith Wharton, though thoroughly urban, could be seen the destiny of a New England farmer, Ethan Frome, chiseled out of cold, gray granite by a hand as remorseless as that which shaped the end of Agamemnon. On the canvas of Theodore Dreiser's American Tragedy, the sportive chance that by a trivial turn sent a luckless youth to the gallows instead of a respectable bank president's post, was as pitiless as Clytemnestra's furious revenge. Just as naturally the inevitable aspirations of the emancipated Negro, fed by popular education and economic opportunity, flamed up in Walter F. White's Fire in the Flint. In literature as in art irreverent science and feminine intransigence encouraged "the pursuit of the nude." The age of miracles, crusades, and knightly vigils seemed far removed from the epoch of business enterprise.

And yet it could not be maintained that machinery had completely destroyed sentiment, for not long after Marcus A. Hanna assumed the rôle of Warwick and the United States Steel Corporation was organized, a flock of poets began to sing. Like the novelists on the left, Edgar Lee Masters and Carl Sandburg, making no concealment of democratic sympathies, assailed the sublimated idealism of commonplace morality (often observed in the breach) and celebrated the heroes of the unusual. For Venice, "a dream of soft waters," Sandburg offered Chicago as "independent as a hog on ice."

Like all the skeptics on the right, Edwin Arlington Robinson, spoke more softly of respectable things, but betrayed an awful suspicion that

> It's all Nothing.
> It's all a world where bugs and emperors
> Go singularly back to the same dust.

Taking a lesson from men of science and efficiency experts, Amy Lowell and the imagists, casting off the cosmic longings of dreamers, drew little pictures of little things with a penetrating exactness that seemed to fit an age of interchangeable parts.

Whether it was nothing, as Robinson hinted, or composed of tiny fragments that could be accurately grasped, as Amy Lowell suggested, other poets did not care a fig. Edna St. Vincent Millay just "laughed and laughed into the sky," while Vachel Lindsay, beating his thunderous tom-tom, held a jubilee over General Booth, Abraham Lincoln, and cakewalk princes from the Congo.

Rich as the age was in fiction, poetry, and essays it produced only one or two humorists of power. In 1910, Mark Twain left on his long journey, full of honors and bitterness; and about the same time Mr. Dooley passed into the eclipse of silence. None seemed able to conjure up again the joyous specter of great laughter, although it had to be conceded that Will Rogers was a necromancer of no small merit. With the cultural nonchalance of a genial cowboy, Rogers threw his lariat over many a storied urn and animated bust and yanked it from its pedestal; occasionally he thrust a piercing rapier into the thick hide of the Philistine; sometimes he dissolved a pompous political show in a hearty uproar.

While the prevention of war was being bandied about by statesmen, Rogers suggested the drafting of money as well as men. "When the Wall Street Millionaire knows that you are not only going to come into his office and take his Secretary and Clerks but that you come in to take his Dough, say Boy, there wouldn't be any war. You will hear the question: 'Yes, but how could you do it?' . . . No, it will never get anywhere. The rich will say it ain't practical, and the poor will never get a chance to find out if it is or not." Calling Senator Lodge "the Confucius of Nahant," Rogers placed in that aristocratic scholar's mouth these words about President Coolidge: "I have known him ever since he got prominent enough for me to know. In the eight months that I have known him, I have found him to be patient, honest, and a Man who would not knowingly rob a single Filipino of his Liberty."

Reviewing the oil scandal, Rogers made one of the Senators ask, on hearing that President Coolidge would not give independence to the Philippines: "What's the matter? Have they struck oil, too?" In this spirit, Rogers surveyed the machine age, bringing within the range of his philosophic patter everything from chewing gum to foreign affairs—carefully avoiding the temptation to put too many plums into any single pudding. There was novelty and daring in his performance, if not genius—the spirit of the frontier revived.

Hovering around the circle of creative artists working at letters was a swarm of critics, more numerous perhaps than in any other country. The multiplication of book reviews and the clamor of printers for copy to fill space, while calling forth some essayists of penetrating power, gave employment to a motley assembly of writers who in less prosperous lands would have been relegated to the mechanical trades. In this general drift, much of the business of literary evaluation passed into the hands of professors trained in the forms of letters rather than learned in the substance of the civilization that produced them. No small part of the appraising that escaped the professors was done by amateurs recruited from journalism, who, if they had a college training at all, were unschooled in any discipline either classical or modern. So between those who brought academic arts to bear on beautiful letters and those who relied on nimble wits and clever newspaper tricks, literary criticism became mainly a craft of the higher verbalism.

When members of the reviewing gild stopped to examine the little logical rafts on which they cruised around in the chaos of the sensuous, they found their science in hopeless disorder—to which bore pathetic witness a little volume of collected confessions made public in 1924 under the title Criticism in America. Judging from that and kindred performances, critics who thought Europe had made the sibylline guess were evidently in a state no less parlous than the school of right reason. Certainly only a few of them betrayed any consciousness of the fact that there might be a vital relation between letters and the motive forces of social evolution.

Among those who worked at the literary craft the ancient dispute over the power of American civilization to bring forth and nourish artistic genius was continued with the same basic division of opinion. It was still maintained in some quarters that America was provincial in taste, thin in culture, unable to appreciate genuine talent, devoted to the commonplace, puritanical in temper, cold to creative art, engrossed in the collection of dollars. Sensitive souls that approved this indictment fled as before to retreats in older communities; while harder hearts of the same conviction, proposed reliefs and remedies—such as projects for raising a sanitary cordon between writers and the leveling masses, affording to genius the protection of a self-appointed intellectual aristocracy.

On the opposite side of the fence were critics and artists of equal merit who averred, certainly with more justification than their forerunners in the middle period, that America was in fact receptive to the arts, possessed more connoisseurs than any European country, offered themes to anybody possessing insight, interfered seriously with few books that were not æsthetically indecent, and on the whole provided materials and the opportunity to all who could imagine that letters were related to life. "In no country," defiantly answered one editor, George Jean Nathan, "are the first-rate author's lecture fees so high and do so many stockbrokers and automobile salesmen wish to take a look at him." Those who watched the battle of the bookmakers and commentators from the side lines found it hard to render any verdict; for there was no higher law to which the pleas were subject and the phraseology used by the contestants was as slippery as electricity.

In another respect the literary criticism of the machine age conformed to tradition. Through all the discussion of letters flickered the same plaintive eagerness for British approval on the one side and the same old contempt for that high court of judgment on the other. As in the days of Emerson and Whitman wistfulness was usually answered in familiar terms by genial patronage and contempt by flourishes in kind. One thing was certain: English novels sold in America by the million and American novels in England by the thousand. American magazines poured golden streams into the chests of English authors while English magazines returned the merest driblets to American writers. Since art, whether good or bad, then as always bore a vital relation to the culture that produced it and could be appreciated only in that relation, no one could tell in what proportions the literary judgments of England were to be ascribed to the weakness of the province or to the insularity of the metropolis. No formula could remove the dilemma. In any case, it was not certain whether the brusque and breezy style of American writers did not merely represent the transition from classical proprieties to a modern vernacular appropriate to the higher velocity of living.

Be that as it may, Americans of the machine age were certainly greedy to hear the latest word from Europe.

They brought over the seas for observation at first hand nearly all the literary and scientific lions; they rushed in mobs to hear Henri Bergson, the philosopher, Albert Einstein, the high priest of relativity, H. G. Wells, Chesterton, Coué, and a host of enlighteners, doctors, and entertainers great and small. Save Bernard Shaw, none of Europe's verbal heroes was apparently unwilling to exhibit himself to the American public for a consideration—and some of them, continuing the manners of the nineteenth century, after counting the gate receipts, betrayed their motives, by sneering at the United States as a "dollar democracy" and by belittling its natural curiosity.

§

However varied and excellent American letters in general might be, the influence of business enterprise upon the drama in particular betrayed a tendency to uniformity and banality. The conquest of the theater by commerce in the gilded age was followed by the mass production of plays in the machine age—all "made in the U. S. A." For the strings of theaters that now stretched from coast to coast under central management, a ceaseless flow of standardized entertainment was provided—all tuned to the simple tastes of a polyglot population that had money to spend on amusement and looked to business corporations to furnish it with the same facility with which they turned out bathtubs, shoes, hats, and underwear.

Owing to the financial considerations involved in this extensive trade, it was expedient to put forth play goods that could be sold to the largest public with the least possible friction. And apparently manufacturers were at no loss to find for their pattern-making departments heads capable of producing the required quantity and quality to order. Occasionally when genius could not create just the lines desired for the Great White Way, clever managers were able to cut and carve to suit the commonalty. Their course was made plainer by the competition of moving picture concerns which reached deeper still into social layers, almost driving traveling companies from the road and helping to spread uniformity of culture from sea to sea. Appropriately enough, the mechanics of gorgeous lighting, scenic displays, and whirlwind motion fitted to the age of the higher physics tended to thrust the human stars off the stage and the cold glow of ideas into the background, absorbing audience and players more and more in a kind of electronic storm.

With respect to subject-matter, the drama of the commercial theater conformed literally to the psychic requirements of the people who bought seats and paid for them—business men and their families in the overwhelming majority—just as the grand operas and heavy tragedies of the Old World fitted the tastes and ideals of their patrons. For the American males absorbed in the making and selling of goods, who spent their days in adventures as colorful as directors' meetings or as tuneful as the clack of adding machines could make them, varied only by an occasional flirtation with a stenographer, there were endless offerings precisely congruous. Served up to the ambitious, with a proper sauce of sentiment and profit-making ferocity, were the antics of Get-Rich-Quick Wallingfords giving practical examples of "lucky strikes" in acquiring fortunes overnight by robbing "boobs." For the fairly satisfied cog in the machine, "the little man," were the diversions offered by George M. Cohan; with the deliberation of a surgeon, that money-making entertainer analyzed the emotions of his ticket purchasers under three heads "(1) tears, (2) laughs, (3) thrills," and then frankly worked those primary emotions with the rhythmic thump of a hydraulic pump, reaching a masterful triumph in his interpretation of It Pays to Advertise.

For lighter and gayer hours there were the "vaudeville shows," unfailing sources of box-office receipts, repeating with the unbroken clatter of the rivetting hammer the same jokes, acrobatic acts, and dances to a race of people that could sit or stand with the same contentment in a factory watching the remorseless stamp of a box-making machine or in an office dictating letters, "Yours of the 3rd instant, received." Then to crown it all was the musical comedy. In the machine age the Paris can-can, which had delighted the lower orders of the gilded age, was refurbished and given the savors of modern spices assorted for the modern palates. To the ancient modes of the harem were now added still more gorgeous costuming, lighting, exotic dancing, and bizarre music—as one weird critic expressed it, new garnishings of parsley to the well-known meat. Action, like the production of goods, was speeded up; long waits for scenes were cut out so that in a whirr of tone and color the routine of turning out collars, shirts, candy, and tooth paste or selling stocks and bonds could be forgotten for an hour or two. In accordance with the machine principle of economy and efficiency, actresses approached as near to nudity as the statutes on public decency or the police conscience would permit and all classes of society were invited to witness spectacles which in puritanic days were not even offered in the slums to the lowest strata of society. Whether it was a temporary reaction such as swept over England in the age of the Stuart restoration or a triumph of nature over convention akin to that described by Juvenal could not be determined from the tangent of the thing.

To the feminine portion of the business community, given leisure by prosperity in the land of liberty, eager to be amused by matinée idols, were made special offerings graciously fitted to its spiritual needs. As women dominated taste in music, art, and letters, so they ruled with a rod of iron huge principalities in the dramatic realm—calling for precious things, mild emotions, nothing raucous with the broad laugh of the musical show or the hearty guffaw of the melodrama, risky but pure, dubious but fundamentally correct—themes of little men and little women faced with somewhat trying responsibilities and situations, novel but not revolutionary, all handled "with sympathy and understand-

ing," that is, the sympathy and understanding of comfortable people. Not without appeal to women as well as to
trade psychology were the many sentimental dramas dealing with Jews, Irish, Germans, and other racial stocks in the
American Babel and the numerous plots built on "social
climbing" in a volatile world.

Fairly on a level with the drama of the meglapolitan was
the moving picture business. When the industry reached a
high stage of perfection in the third decade of the century
the production of a single gorgeous spectacle sometimes
called for such an immense outlay of money that, according
to estimates, it required at least nine million purchasers of
tickets to meet the expenses of the undertaking and yield the
"legitimate profits." Inexorably the common denominator
of conceptions that attracted so many buyers set the tone
and taste for the trade. Any doubts about the matter could
be resolved by observing the periods of time allowed for
reading captions reduced to simplest terms—periods that
readily indicated the intelligence quotient of the multitudinous observers.

Given these conditions, it was inevitable that the supreme
artists in visual and verbal mass production should concentrate on simple themes, mechanics, and dramatic technique. It is true that some of the great plays which had
thrilled the cultured classes of all countries were adapted
with more or less success to the requirements of the Great
White Way; that science, exploration, and travel also received a respectful, if slight, consideration in the same
quarter. But one thing was unmistakable: "serious stuff"
that was not followed by a cowboy, melodramatic, or
custard-pie romance—the lowest common denominator—as
a reward for waiting brought scant returns to the management. What was to happen when inventors united the moving picture with the parlor radio remained among the mysteries of higher speculation.

If the uniformity of the machine smoothed out in a few set
designs the drama supported by business men and their

families and leveled the moving pictures provided for the lowest average box-office visitors, there were here and there signs of unrest and revolt—paralleling the course of economic discontent. During the years just preceding Roosevelt's charge at Armageddon, for example, the poignant fringe of the middle class that lent countenance to the progressive and liberal reforms of social democracy was accorded frequent recognition. In Charles Klein's Lion and the Mouse, presented in 1906, was portrayed the ruthless might of "big business," that monster of the little man, and in Edward Sheldon's The Boss, offered in 1911, was vividly illuminated the raw struggle of capital and labor. For the Christian Socialist, uneasy in his comfort, a pleasing emotional outlet was afforded by Charles Rann Kennedy's The Servant in the House, decorously received in 1908; while for the social workers who cheered the Progressives marching to the tune of "Onward Christian Soldiers," a doleful picture of the slums was drawn by Charles Kenyon, in Kindling, played during the year 1911. But the defeat of the Progressives and the decline of Socialism were followed by a relaxation of such moral overstrains and a general return to more conventional standards.

Only here and there on the side lines were there experiments in the unusual. Percy Mackaye, for instance, sought to revive in modern social form within the limits set by American democracy, the unity and ritual inherent in the Greek drama. A classical scholar, a child of the theater, a close student of his art, a profound believer in the high destiny of his country, and a tireless worker, Mackaye sought for a synthesis on which to found the structure of enduring plays. As sometimes hinted, he was too much of an ancient in spirit and too confused in his sense of direction to grasp the American process. Nevertheless he accomplished positive results: he broadened theatrical practices by the use of the allied arts of painting, sculpture, and music to enrich dramatic action—though he sometimes ran the risk of being conquered by his allies—and he carried the theater into the open community by the production of masques and pageants built on local themes drawn from fiction and history.

Reflecting a kindred revolt without discernible direction or vortical relation was the protest made by the "little theater movement" striving for variation, freshness, and freedom from the grind of making and selling. In some cases little theaters were operated by actor-guilds, in others by communities, sometimes by individuals wealthy enough to experiment or willing to take risks, now and then by a traveling playwright-producer with his own stage of portmanteau size. So promising were the tangible results of these efforts that many of the leading colleges began to aid the art by adding dramatics to their curricula. At Pittsburgh the Carnegie Institute of Technology early in its career established a special department of the drama and by 1925 almost a hundred institutions of higher learning were seeking to encourage the production of plays that did not fit exactly the machine mold of metropolitan managers. A prophecy of better work ahead was made in that year when Yale University called from Harvard, Professor George P. Baker, who had been successful in inspiring originality among his students, and gave him adequate facilities for the promotion of creative undertakings. In fact the little theater movement had then grown to such proportions that a national conference on the drama held at Pittsburgh, the first in a series, brought together the representatives of ninety universities and forty little theaters, besides numerous patrons of independent ventures. On the flanks the Drama League, founded in 1910, at Evanston, Illinois, strove to widen the horizon of theater-goers, stimulate the reading of plays, and enlarge the imagination of school children by providing material especially adapted to their years.

But most striking of all was the insurrection against complacent smugness and reasoned revolt represented in the emotional storms let loose by Eugene O'Neill, Maxwell Anderson, and Laurence Stallings. The first of these play, wrights, O'Neill, after a season at Princeton, a year at Harvard, and a varied career as gold hunter, sailor, actor, and reporter, startled hardened buyers of actors and plays by a series of explosions that could not be exactly located or classified. Casting aside old pleasantries and stereotyped forms, O'Neill went straight to the task of presenting agony, frustration, and defeat among the common people, without offering any explanation—theological, social, or moral—of the curse that befuddles the inhabitants of Moronia. After rich adventures in that mode, represented in The Hairy Ape, Emperor Jones, and Anna Christie, O'Neill did the same thing for business enterprise and its human fruitage—in Marco Millions, introducing, as it were, Marco Polo of Venice at a Tuesday luncheon of the Zenith Lions' Club. In a tumultuous uproar, O'Neill was greeted by intellectuals as the great American dramatic genius so long awaited. On other grounds and with good reason, a wider audience paid honor to Stallings and Anderson whose What Price Glory brought the filth and agony of imperialism and war under the microscope—to the eyes of civilians who had waved flags along the lines of marching heroes and fought battles over teacups and cocktails. Evidently the country was not completely and permanently conquered by the standardization of the Great White Way and there were omens of more significant things to come in the land of Fordismus.

§

A kindred protean spirit entered the realm of the plastic arts in the second decade of the new century. The Academy still flourished of course; and the great museums added more traditional favorites. Good work that passed the censorship of classical critics was done by a host of American artists—work so excellent in technique that one connoisseur confessed himself unable to tell any more whether a salon picture had been painted in Madrid, Paris, Berlin, or Indianapolis. Sargent, Whistler, La Farge, and Blashfield continued to labor in lines already set during the gilded age and younger artists of similar aspiration were hanging correct canvases in exhibitions beside the offerings of the masters. In 1925, it was estimated that more than twenty thousand men and women were making a living of some kind by brush, pencil, or chisel in New York City alone. Even sculpture so long neglected in America was beginning to come into its own.

But under the surface of things were rumblings of discontent. The protest begun in the gilded age against rigid canons of taste was now developing into a revolution under the direction of equally dogmatic leaders who declared that there could be no compromise between the art appropriate to an age of science and machinery and the art fit for an age of agriculture, mysticism, hand labor, and feudalism. Decrying the art of "truth and purity," the art of "photographic painting and sculpture, sentiment, charm, polish, and mere technique," the exponents of the new school tried to express by brush and chisel the dynamics, sciences, colors, forms, materials, motions, and mathematical abstractions of the era of mass production by machinery.

In Europe, where this revolt originated, it flourished under various names: Cubism in France owing to its extreme use of geometric forms, Futurism in Italy on account of its prophecy of development, Vorticism in England in response to the insistence that art must live near the center of things if it is to be creative once more. In its most reasoned form it was an effort to relate art to the vibrant life and the current ideas of the industrial epoch. "The world to-day," urged the modernist, Duchamp-Villon, "translates its thought in terms of the machine which with its power and speed, the dominant interests of the period, penetrates our whole conception of it." Or to put the matter in the language of an American exponent: "The life of our time has its more obvious expression in the size of buildings, the swiftness of vehicles, and the quantity of manufactures. But such things, by the very weight they lay on the imagination, make it seek more eagerly for an expression dealing with the essentials of our experience, not as they exist as expressed by typography, light, avoirdupois, and the yardstick, but as we know them in their assimilation into our thought and through the form and colors which so define them."

Art could no more escape the impact of such drives than religion and politics could refuse to deal with the fruits of technology, and in course of time all the vogues which had set Europe agog appeared in the United States. In 1913, American radicals of pencil, brush, and chisel made bold to exhibit their canvases and casts in New York City, supplementing their work by samples from the Old World. From that year onward, the circle of American art-heretics grew in numbers, in confidence, and in power. In 1920, a small but resolute band of rebels in New York organized the Société Anonyme for the purpose of proclaiming openly the revolution which America had begun to accept in the guise of "Modern Art"—a revolution that rejected the smooth, biologic, sensuous lines and surfaces of neo-classicism and accepted whole-heartedly the machine age with its hard, angular strokes and its metal planes all vibrant with dynamic force. How, they asked in effect, can the allegories of the Arthurian legend or ancient mythology find living expression in an age of electronic physics and mass production?

Fortunately for the thesis of modernism, few of its exponents did more than claim that a new era in art had dawned; the most cautious rested their case on the realities of the contemporary age and on the possibilities of the long future—on the changes wrought by science and machinery in the stuff of life and thought, changes which shook traditions and opened new avenues for the play of mind and imagination. Their argument moreover received support, more or less indirectly, from artists by no means identified with the rebellion, who grew increasingly interested in the essence of the machine society.

Joseph Pennell's urban and industrial etchings, wreathed

in steam and smudged with smoke, for example, blared forth a new emphasis on materials, making strange contrasts in galleries of Greek nudes and their imitations; while the commercial and industrial arts, forced into sharp competition with European manufacturers for a world market, showed marked tendencies away from historic elegance in the direction of adjustments to the exigencies of the machine age. If the upper crust remained intact, there were minor canvases and bronzes which revealed the thrust of American strength —pieces that made no great stir in the critical forum, but betrayed the coming of new energies and capacities, preparations for genius on another twist of the ever-turning spiral.

§

Stemming perhaps from the same emotional trunk was a synchronous foliation in American music. Just at the moment when, by diligent and devoted labors under the guidance of Europe's best musicians and teachers, American students of music began to perform and compose in a spirit somewhat akin to that of the masters, strange notes, up from the soil, began to strike American ears. As the gilded age drew to a close, a few radicals in composition, such as McDowell, had presented innovations superimposed on the classics, following the moods of the musical insurgents of Europe who had modified the traditions of tone just as artists had questioned the canons of form and color. There had also been earlier experiments with the chants of the Red Man and with Negro spirituals in efforts to create American operas and other musical forms.

But the new notes which the rising generation in America was beating out with hands and feet were akin to none of these variants. This music had the syncopated rhythm of the jungle in it—a rhythm which the young at first called "rag time," a slang name derived, it seems, from its Negro creators, who sang and shuffled to it as they "ragged" for funds to support their church or other racial enterprises. It gave vent to feelings allied to the passions that had edged their way up into European art from the primitive life of Gauguin's South Seas.

Yet expressed in pulsating groans, long wails, and fitful shrieks, the new music seemed a counterpart of the cacophonous uproar of manufacturing industries and urban life, so foreign to the smooth sophistication of a Liszt, a Haydn, or a Brahms. By giving supremacy to wind instruments, notably the saxophone with its opalescent notes, it stirred emotions ever near to the surface, emotions which classical music had overlaid with higher learning, and at the same time rode triumphantly on nerves clashing with the ceaseless din of the market place.

Though greeted at first by established musicians as a passing freak—the counterpart of the tom-tom—jazz music, as it was eventually called, showed both vitality and flexibility. It could run the whole gamut from purely primitive notes to mild modifications of ancient themes touched with the spirit of the new freedom. It could be divorced from the dance and made to give fresh tonal qualities to older musical forms, thus lending itself to creative composition and direction in the sphere of orchestration. Both simple and complex it made meteoric headway in popular favor in spite of increasing endowments for symphony orchestras.

Then came a triumphal march into Europe. Played by bands of Negro soldiers—the jazz bands of the World War —it made a similar appeal to the subcutaneous culture of old and mellow societies. According to press reports, even staid Queen Mary, at a ball given to her servants, forsook the waltz for the tango just as her forbears had forsaken the stately minuet for the waltz. From Europe jazz music passed round the world until it was heard in the hotels of Cairo, Singapore, Soerabaia, Shanghai, and Tokyo. The grave Japanese samurai, whose fierce fighting temper had long been subdued to the low and slow notes of the Noh, felt his sword leap once more from its scabbard as he heard the mournful cry of the saxophone calling across the deep but narrow chasm that separates all civilization from the dawn.

In such circumstances the moralists of the whole world were puzzled. Some saw in the new music nothing but a noisy shout for ears attuned to the riotous sounds of the forge and the market place; others looked upon it as only one of the passing manias induced by the shell shock of the World War or one more of the innumerable American inanities that were being distributed over the earth. But a few, as open and hospitable to the doings of the fates as Emerson and Whitman had been in their time, thought that jazz could be wedded to noble harmonies and made to invigorate the smooth and elegant texture of traditional symphonies. When in the winter of 1926, Walter Damrosch was reproached by some of the old families of New York for introducing the new muse into the sacred precincts of the Symphony Orchestra, he replied: "I would not encourage such efforts if I did not really believe in their truly great importance toward developing an American music in the higher sense of the word. After all, we are only following in the footsteps of Europe whose greatest masters have founded their art on the folk songs and dances of their country."

Whether jazz was a mere expression of a democracy engaged in mass production or not, there was no doubt that science and machines made a revolution in the distribution of music. The necessity of enlivening the silent moving picture with congruous notes gave to the pleasure-seeking multitudes that attended screen palaces more music, good and bad, than any generation had ever heard. Moreover the piano-player, the phonograph, and the radio carried into homes in town and country, far and wide, the noblest and best music of the past as well as the bars of the passing show, permitting buyers to choose according to their tastes. Millions who had never heard a good orchestra in their lives now discovered hidden deeps in their natures.

The creation like the distribution of music came under the

spell of the machine. Through the work of Russian and other experimenters, it was found that the piano-player could be used to produce types of composition unknown to past ages; the human player with but two hands and ten fingers was of necessity limited but the machine under his direction could multiply sounds and vary pressures, thus interposing unheard-of harmonies and dissonances at the pleasure of the composer.

§

As far as they were distinctive and not derivative, the achievements of American architects also sprang from a frank acceptance of exigent circumstances. Early designers, oppressed by the angular ugliness of business structures—men like Henry Hobson Richardson, Richard Morris Hunt, and Stanford White—had sought an escape by introducing alien decorations, chiefly façades, more appropriate to Florence and Ravenna than to Pittsburgh and Madison Square. If occasionally fitting, the result was often pathetic and sometimes absurd; at best it was exotic. Although the pressure of rising ground values, the congestion of population, the requirements of business economy, and the development of steel and concrete made imperative and practical giant business structures in the cities of the first rank, American architects long labored under the thraldom and disabilities of the schools, trying to deceive the eye in matters of height and form. Having confined their studies to temples, palaces, and political buildings, they were hampered by repressions that unfitted them to design for the money changers and mass producers of the machine age.

For good or evil, perhaps beyond both, in any case inexorably, the spirit of American business enterprise was not reverent, shrinking, or benign; it was the spirit of power, crude and ruthless, rash to the point of peril, defiant of all petty material limitations, given to action too swift for meters. When called upon to serve this spirit, architects for a long time came hobbling in the restraints of the acad-

emies; they deprecated it, scorned it, or if they took commissions tried to crush it. Many an artistic head was
shaken when, in 1880, Darius O. Mills, taking to New York
a fortune made on the Pacific coast, engaged Colonel
George B. Post to build him a "skyscraper" one hundred
and twenty feet high housing twelve hundred tenants. Despite the laments of the wiseacres the monument was built
and President Cleveland retiring from the White House at
the close of his first term was delighted to find an office in
it. By the opening of the twentieth century the perfection
of steel construction and the elevator made far more imperial designs feasible. In 1902, the Flatiron Building, the
first real skyscraper in the world since the days of Babylon,
rose on Twenty-third Street, to be followed in quick succession by other buildings, higher and higher, until in 1913
the nickels and dimes of the five and ten cent stores raised
to Woolworth, the mogul of retail business, not a pyramid but a tower of steel and stone sixty stories above the
sidewalks of New York.

As if by sheer accident, almost at that moment municipal
policy gave to business architecture a new and amazing direction. In the interest of light and air, the city of New
York, in 1916, forbade the erection of structures on narrow
streets in straight lines to indefinite heights, and required
builders to "step back" their skyscrapers after reaching a
certain altitude. On architecture the effect of this ordinance
was revolutionary. Huge citadels, sheathed in zoning en-
velopes and staggered with turrets, now shot upward in
anarchic and bewildering profusion above the dynamic energy and uproarious chatter of feverish business, symbols of
egotistic competition. Hotels, apartment houses, and civic
buildings, clothing cubist dreams in metal and concrete, overwhelmed beholders with the sense of power and Gargantuan
beauty made manifest in them.

Very soon the economy and the fervor that gave rise to
these new giants made an impress on ecclesiastical architecture. In the wilderness of business mountains, cathedrals

that once had dominated the landscape with their domes and spires were lost to view; but instead of giving up the battle for place the builders of churches climbed Alpine heights themselves. In New York and Chicago they erected vast temples of the monolithic style in which they tried to combine the grace of later Gothic with the economy of the factory and office structures—providing housing and business places as well as institutional facilities and meeting places for congregations. One of these new churches, begun in New York in 1925, included in its plans a large auditorium on the ground floor flanked by two apartment houses, topped by a towering hotel, and crowned by a flaming cross of Jesus Christ more than seven hundred feet above tidewater. Almost simultaneously the University of Pittsburgh published plans for a "cathedral of learning," a massive college building to rise fifty-two stories above the forges, markets, offices, and factories of that kingdom of steel.

At last the measureless energy of American life had been discovered and accepted, save by a few artists who hoped that time and tide might be turned back and that the spirit of Chicago might yet be bodied forth in the delicate refinements of Renaissance Gothic. In 1914, an English critic, Clive Bell, declared that American architecture seemed on the verge of a revival worthy of Florence but after the World War he began to think it was to be more like that of Augustan Rome. Naturally the future in 1927, as in every other time, was a closed book. Perhaps there was no more limit to architectural power than to the energy of the suns; perhaps it was subject to the same law of degradation. Possibly the steel frames and towering domes of business enterprise triumphant might grovel in the dust with the baths of Caracalla and the palaces of the Cæsars. Possibly the sweet agonies of saints might stand forth again in the austere loveliness of a new Sainte Chapelle. But that revolution if it was ever to come could only follow the ruin of the machine and its social processes. And one thing was certain; history does not exactly repeat itself.

Whatever their goal or limits the economic pressures and impulses of power which found an outlet in the architecture of mass were evidently anarchic in their manifestations. The new structures lunged forward and shot upward without reference to community symmetry, design, or convenience. They made all the more imperative, therefore, the rise of city planning, that art so sadly neglected in America since the days when L'Enfant laid the groundwork for the national capital. Slowly the deficiency was recognized by people of affairs as well as by artists.

At the opening of the century no general planning authority existed in any American city. Within twenty-five years more than two hundred cities had erected planning agencies, at least of an advisory character, while a number of municipalities had begun the execution of designs drawn by competent hands. In the meantime, the profession of city planning had become a recognized branch of community engineering; a national organization of that interest had come into being; an immense body of constructive legislation had been placed on the law books; an attack had been made on the skyscraper as a source of congestion; and the American literature of the new science had grown to respectable proportions.

No doubt the achievements seemed pitiable enough when viewed in the large but the surprising thing was the existence of the movement in a country still so individualistic in its life and work. In various ways it was hampered by difficulties peculiar to America. It was clearly one thing to plan for a fairly static community like Paris or London and quite another matter to plan for dynamic communities like New York and Chicago where permanent streets and civic buildings were likely to block imperative movements of business and population. In short, the flux of things made agreement upon fixed patterns very hard to reach. Nevertheless the art of municipal designing, humanistic and æsthetic, was high on the horizon of American thought before the machine age had grown very old.

§

Resting directly on technology, appealing to multitudes engaged in mass production, and driven by the profit-making impulses of capitalism, the press gathered swifter momentum in the machine age. Like the manufacturers of automobiles and hats, publishers of books with huge plants and selling agencies on their hands, had to print or perish—in last resort anything that "would pay its way." So between the egoism of aspiring authors and the zeal of publishers for business, the number of books and magazines rose like a flood, inexorable, inundating the market with mediocrities which in a less prosperous civilization would never have seen the light of day. With the steady growth in advertising it became possible for the proprietors of popular journals, such as The Saturday Evening Post, to sell their wares from coast to coast at a mere trifle, creating a uniform magazine audience of colossal magnitude. Responding to the mechanistic drive that carried standardized goods into every mountain hamlet and gave the same garb to flappers in Kennebunkport, Seattle, and Athens, American journalism, now aided by professional training, distributed the same models, tones, and verbal patter all over the land. By way of reënforcement, the economy of syndicated articles, comic strips, and editorials, the streams of "publicity matter" poured upon the desks of editors by "interests" of every kind, the "chain" newspaper system, the growing practice among dignitaries of handing out specially prepared "tabloid" interviews, the penalties imposed by the high priests of uniformity upon versatile and ingenious reporting likely "to rock the boat," the conquest of the news services by one or two great agencies, and a hundred other factors conspired to subdue journalism like everything else to the general régime of interchangeable parts.

Somewhat dazed by the universal tendency, critical writers, led by Upton Sinclair, declared that the newspaper business was now simply the rhetorical defense mechanism for the capitalist order, but they could not show that journalism would have been more accurate, varied, or piquant if the readers instead of the advertisers had stood on guard at the sanctum door. Perhaps the Chicago reporter who said that the editor like the merchant must put the right kind of goods in his window or perish sensed the situation with more penetration. At all events in the machine age, spectators of independent opinion were inclined to regard the metropolitan editor as a fixed planet rather than a vagrant comet and to classify the opinions of editorial columns with other products of multitudinous industry.

Harmonizing with the extension of the machine system throughout the publishing world was a downward thrust of quantity production in the search for more purchasers. To reach ever larger areas of the populace it was necessary to strike lower into the successive strata of general ignorance —and with the progressive development of cheap engraving, this delving process became easier and more profitable. In fact, the experiments of the illustrated magazines, the applause that greeted cartoonists, the effect of pictures and sketches on the circulation of the older newspapers hinted at an innovation that was bound to come—as inevitable as democracy itself. When at length, in 1918, the Illustrated Daily News appeared on the streets of New York, the new era was opened in journalism—one no less striking than that inaugurated by Hearst and Pulitzer in the gilded age. With paralyzing strokes the invader cut into the prosperity of the regular papers, not sparing the "yellow" sheets that had thriven on poster headlines, cartoons, comics, and other forms of picture-writing. However reluctantly, the gravest of traditional editors had to modify their strategy.

Equipped with the latest instruments, editorial manufacturers could now present to masses hitherto unreached at least that part of the day's news which called for no abstract thought or background of knowledge; at last, multitudes who could not vie with stable boys and kitchen maids in stumbling through giant headlines were permitted to join "the reading public." More than that; millions who spoke foreign tongues could grasp the illustrations, at least dimly, spell their way through picture captions, and gain some notion, true or false, of events taking place in the world about them. If they could not understand President Coolidge's political economy, they could at least see his face. What relation pictures could bear to the educative process or the educative process to national destiny, neither the psychologist nor the physicist could decide with any degree of satisfaction. In any case it could hardly be said that the patterns created by tabloid pictures were less authentic or more inimical to intelligent citizenship than the substance of the more reputable papers—the vast flood of political speeches and innumerable Associated Press dispatches masquerading as "news" on the authority of "some one near the President," or on the basis of "it is said," or on no foundation at all except the secret inspiration of some interested official or powerful individual, unnamed in the text, or of some partisan reporter.

§

Resting at bottom on the wide distribution of minute knowledge and producing large surpluses for social uses, machine industry strengthened all the tendencies of American education which had risen to the surface in the closing decades of the nineteenth century. The public schools, founded in the middle period and nourished in the gilded age were now given better houses, more magnificent equipment, more thoroughly disciplined teachers, more perfect furniture in general, and a crowning organization in the National Education Association—which took the place of the National Teachers Association in 1871. And the spirit of science so vital to industry crept steadily through the whole structure of learning, spreading its passion for measurements, standards, and precision.

Aptly enough in this age the mobilizing movement reached its acme in intelligence tests which, belligerent sponsors averred, permitted automatic and certain gradings of the huge mass of children annually ground into the educational system. If employees in factories from day laborers to expert technicians could be classified, why not the raw materials in the schools? To be sure, individuals who loved the faint aroma which still hung over from the days when Aristophanes and Vergil were read in the colleges made vehement protest and were not without support. But the iron law of circumstance was against them: on the military regimen imported earlier from Prussia was imposed the time-clock regimen of the machine era, making an inquiry whether mankind could be happier and more comfortable under a system of handicrafts and emotional liberty as irrelevant as an examination into the naval efficiency of wooden hulks.

However, in the wake of the standardizing process came its antithesis of criticism. It was said by way of objection that in their effort to raise levels through increased supervision, educational mechanicians had turned the schools over to administrators, show managers, who, besides being engrossed in red tape and report sheets, were ever engaged in the politics of promoting themselves to more lucrative positions. By the same operation, ran the lament, the teacher, though primarily concerned with the human material and the content of courses, was continually subjected to the rigors of administrative routine, thus transferring the control and art of education to a half-commercial bureaucracy. Moreover as the principals of the schools formed the bond of contact with the business men and the politicians on boards of education, another article was added to the bill of indictment, namely, that the school system, besides losing its humanity, had been made a cog in the mill of economic enterprise. In his customary style, Upton Sinclair tried to reduce the whole business of education to the caption, The Goose-Step.

To this arraignment the administrators replied that a complex of rules and regulations was necessary to the en-

forcement of higher standards, especially as long as the facilities for training teachers did not keep pace either with the growth of the population or the multiplying demands made upon the school system. On their part teachers, while alive to the perils of the machine routine, also offered a rejoinder in the form of a long list of novel experiments associated with such names as Dewey, Gary, Montessori, and Dalton—experiments in the segregation of the feeble-minded, in special opportunities for the brilliant, and in the breaking down of the rigidity of the lock step. Though conceding the dangers of the machine age, they claimed for it a freedom, range, and flexibility in education, even a humanity, never before enjoyed in America. And it was a blind critic who could see no truth in the paradox.

In the colleges and universities this dualism was even more apparent than in the lower schools. By the close of the first quarter of the century business men had elbowed aside nearly all the clergymen in the boards of trustees that governed the higher learning—whether patronized by democratic taxpayers or sustained by rich benefactors. Meanwhile with the growth of educational plants and budgets, the old gray-haired parson, wearing a white necktie and dressed in rusty black, disappeared from groves that now belonged to bond salesmen and corporation lawyers rather than to sacrificial preachers, missionaries, and teachers. In his place came the efficient high director who presided over push buttons, filing cases, telephones, and board meetings.

Learning itself, always subdued more or less to the major concerns of its age, bent like a reed before new demands as the curricula of colleges underwent changes adapted to an age of industry. With noteworthy fitness, business, law, medical, and other professional schools were given a hearty welcome by university corporations, and scientific laboratories overtopped halls dedicated to the liberal arts, making utility the watchword of the study and lecture room. Courses of instruction were divided and subdivided, dissolving earlier philosophies of life and practice and multiplying academic goods almost as rapidly as inventors multiplied material commodities. If the old titles, such as science, the arts, letters, economics, politics, still appeared in the announcements, the custom of listing subjects alphabetically, after the fashion of hardware catalogues, from art to zymotic diseases, followed by some institutions, more nearly expressed the inward spiritual state of which academic offerings were an outward symbol.

In one other significant respect the course of higher learning was true to form. As the major portion of the students attending collegiate institutions veered toward industrial, financial, and selling functions after graduation, it was both natural and appropriate that the great outdoor diversion of the business world, namely, sports, should be made one of the prime concerns of the colleges. In keeping with this development, directors of athletics were now paid salaries higher than the professors of literature and the fine arts; while the promotion of academic games became a form of business enterprise sometimes accompanied by professionalism, scandals, and corruption. When a popular film described a college as a small school attached to a vast stadium, it was greeted with rejoicing that was authoritative in its heartiness.

And yet they were right who claimed that learning in the American colleges of the machine age was more diverse, bolder, and more speculative, freer in spirit and more enlivened by the saving grace of humor than the same learning in earlier ages. It had to be conceded that schools of art, drama, and music flourished as never before. Certainly the whole process of education was subjected to a more searching analysis than in any previous period. Departing from all precedents, Thorstein Veblen raked the field of higher learning with the galling fire of his pungent irony while the popular magazines were packed with educational inquests.

Occasionally some of the students became alert enough to ask questions of their superiors, in this respect re-

sembling that caustic critic of distant days, Harrison
Gray Otis, who took his Alma Mater severely to task for
pedantry and for failing to educate him to his taste. At
Dartmouth College, the undergraduates were invited
by the administration to survey the offerings of their
elders — a thing that would have scandalized the wise
perfectionists of earlier days. At Indiana University, discontented occupants of benches took stenographic notes of
the worst lectures in the institution, and published them
to the world as illustrations of the futility against which
youth had a right to protest. On every hand doubts were
expressed about the entire academic routine, raising the
question whether it was not ruinous to creative intelligence
and damaging to productive genius. Nothing hitherto
deemed sacred was left intact. According to all calculators
more students drank deeply of the springs of wisdom than
in the gilded age; if the minority were submerged by the
flood of the new bourgeois who went to see and to cheer and
not to learn, that outcome was to be expected in a nation
dedicated to mass production and given to buying culture
in five-foot lengths.

As if in rebellion against the hard decrees of the machine
age and to insist upon the capacity of democracy to master
its own intellectual destiny, innumerable projects for the
continuous promotion of knowledge and taste among the
masses—projects generally covered by the blanket title of
adult education—were floated in the new century with bewildering profusion. Through such efforts, the appeal
made and the courses offered by the older lyceum, Chautauqua, and university-extension movements were widened—in
the end leaving no interest untouched in the diffusion and
"humanizing" of learning.

The passion for economic advancement supported hundreds of correspondence schools and institutions for technical training, which taught everything from salesmanship
and cartooning to cooking and bonnet-making. Wholly
apart from such utilitarian ends, a sheer quest for wisdom

evoked thousands of lectures, either free or at nominal cost, and whole libraries of easy guides and handbooks. Responding to the call of laymen, religious associations, Catholic and Protestant alike, organized courses of instruction, practical and cultural, for members desirous of prolonging the years of learning beyond the span of school and college. Finding educational centers springing up spontaneously under the auspices of local trade unions, the American Federation of Labor set the seal of its official approval upon this popular movement among the rank and file, by recommending in 1924 a levy on members to promote such experiments under the general direction of the Workers' Education Bureau. Alive to all these activities, public libraries and museums, once supposed to be the asylums of contented leisure, took on the character of community educational agencies, offering besides the most efficient facilities to be found anywhere in the world, regular guidance to the growing array of citizens in search of learning.

So striking were the vitality and promise of this movement that the Carnegie Corporation in 1925 announced its purpose to devote a material part of its great endowment to the encouragement of adult education. Without exaggeration it could be said that "the race between mind and matter" had become a major concern of those who took thought about the nature of American society and its future. Nothing was more evident in the midst of this intellectual ferment than the fact that the nation was turning fiercely upon itself, scrutinizing old values, inquiring whether under the clatter of the machine age there was a prophetic meaning not yet divined by idolators, critics, or singers.

§

In all the seasons of the modern epoch, especially since the rise of the concept of progress, thinkers have made attempts to force the iron gates of their own future. Of necessity statesmen have tried, with more or less success, to understand and direct the destiny in which they fain would work as dynamic factors. Though not so immediately concerned with the practical decisions of politics, theologians have likewise formed moral concepts with reference to the effect of faith and conduct on the mission of nations. With perhaps less sense of responsibility, speculative minds, reviewing the long trail of mankind away from barbarism, with its undulating curves, have sought to pierce the veil hiding the stretches beyond their living present. Only the most case-hardened scientist has been able to escape an inquiry as to whether the work of mankind was merely an aspect of physics and subject to the second law of thermodynamics, namely, the progressive degradation of force to the level of death.

It is true that the modern historian shrinks from the business of prophecy himself knowing, as he does, that often in the development of society, as in the case of the Protestant Revolt, what seem to be the invincible tendencies of centuries have been reversed by sharp antithetical processes. But bound by the duties of his office to notice intellectual currents as well as mass, number, velocity, and energy, he cannot ignore an expression of a life force or divine power which represents the striving of mind to get hold of the helm.

Now it happened that the machine age in America was particularly rich in criticisms, appraisals, and prophecies. Perhaps those who worked at polite letters were more given to the practice of these arts than any other special group. Certainly with constant repetition they asked whether American civilization had not reached its zenith, and made the downward turn toward an order hopelessly mechanical in spirit, devoid of intrinsic capacity for the appreciation of the fine arts, poverty-stricken in creative genius, rough in manner, and overbearing in conceit. In the mood of Matthew Arnold, they wondered whether it would not be better to have again peasant villages, manor houses, and Gothic churches, whether middle-class persons of moderate incomes were not crushed in aspirations by prosperous mechanics and dictatorial servants, whether the fairly good peaches and apples and autos available to working people atoned for the lack of the finest wines found on the best tables in Europe. Some of them thought they saw all American society sucked into the vortex of the machine process endlessly whirling to the tune of numbers. If these dire prophets despaired utterly of general improvement, they fell back with a kind of satisfied smile on the notion that, whatever was wrong with the mob, they could take comfort in associating with "the civilized minority"—a new kind of established church.

The economists, scientists, and publicists who made adventures in prophecies produced results as varied as their tempers. One of this school saw the nation settling down content under the servile régime of a "benevolent feudalism." A whole flock of geomancers cried out against what they called "the rising tide of color," auguring the destruction of civilization unless forsooth the white races could unite against Africa and Asia. Another horoscope represented the Anglo-Saxons—Nordics as the new term ran —in mortal peril of conquest by immigrant Latin and Semitic stocks and American civilization in danger of being carried down amid the wreck of matter and crash of worlds. A variant on that augury was a warning against the slow but resistless upward march of the mulatto.

With less evangelical fervor, scientists who felt dubious about the days ahead voiced the conviction that unless the American mind could be made over by fearless research and by a baptism of freedom, it could never catch up with the industrial machine and tame to ordered designs its huge organizations, its mass movements, its international belligerency; ruin being the alternative to a more desperate effort at thinking. After gazing long and intently into the crystal, that profound scholar, Henry Adams, saw on the scroll of destiny four frightful choices: the pessimism of Europe's dying civilization, the tyranny of labor or capital, a reaction to mysticism and clerical dominion, or the ceaseless reiteration of the old processes under new guises at a monotonous level, subject perhaps to the Law of Entropy.

If the generality of opinion, as distinguished from that of poignant specialists, was taken into account, there was no doubt about the nature of the future in America. The most common note of assurance was belief in unlimited progress —the continuous fulfillment of the historic idea which had slowly risen through the eighteenth and nineteenth centuries to a position of commanding authority. Concretely it meant an invulnerable faith in democracy, in the ability of the undistinguished masses, as contrasted with heroes and classes, to meet by reasonably competent methods the issues raised in the flow of time—a faith in the efficacy of that new and mysterious instrument of the modern mind, "the invention of invention," moving from one technological triumph to another, overcoming the exhaustion of crude natural resources and energies, effecting an ever wider distribution of the blessings of civilization—health, security, material goods, knowledge, leisure, and æsthetic appreciation, and through the cumulative forces of intellectual and artistic reactions, conjuring from the vasty deeps of the nameless and unknown creative imagination of the noblest order, subduing physical things to the empire of the spirit—doubting not the capacity of the Power that had summoned into being all patterns of the past and present, living and dead, to fulfill its endless destiny.

§

In the high noon of Coolidge prosperity, while prognosticators were trying to peer into the future—projecting their hopes, fears, and hatreds into the coming years—an economic crash, such as had overtaken the world periodically since the Napoleonic Wars, shook the cultural scene from Warsaw through Pittsburgh to Tokyo and Calcutta. In a few months the imagery of the heavens was altered, and the great body of opinion, absorbing the colors of the living present, took on the tones of darkness ranging from grey to black. The smugness of assurance which had characterized the preceding decennium retired from public places, to emerge again, perhaps, with the next upswing in the stock market, when, as, and if it came, to use the language of investment bankers.

Yet so far as outward signs were concerned, the social organization which had been evolving under the drive of acquisitive technology did not change radically in the early years of depression. The displacement of labor by automatic machinery and rationalization continued at a high tempo. Watchers of this ruthless process mercilessly recorded the downward trend of labor units in the commodities of production and prophesied a coming deadlock which could not be broken by fiscal expedients and social emollients. Still the collapse of economic hopes did not produce any violent disarrangement of classes. Individuals sank down by the thousands from the higher levels of earning into the lower regions but the grand divisions of financial, managerial, selling, and producing operations were not destroyed. Families were ruined by the thousands and the divorce rate of 1930 increased over the preceding year; but the family remained, such as it was. Women still strove for equality of opportunity and found it in strange places—in the breadline as well as in factories and offices. Only one marked social tendency of the previous decade was stayed: the drift to the city stopped and a tide of migration to rural regions set in. Although the membership of organizations, fraternal, benevolent, and social, declined, these associations continued to function, if in more subdued tones, and gave consideration to raising money for indigent comrades and neighbors.

On old forms of social coöperation, except charity, the depression naturally had a relaxing effect in so far as it reduced the money available for organization and propaganda. Machine discipline released its grip on millions of people,

turning them out to drift on their moods of hope and despair.   Social tension seemed to decline with the tempo of
industry.   With this disintegration of organized efforts, the
rigors of prohibition snapped.   The high mark of its dominion was reached in 1929, when Congress raised the penalties of the Volstead law to a fine not to exceed ten thousand
dollars or imprisonment not to exceed ten years or both.   As
had often happened in human affairs, vindictive triumph was
a sign of approaching defeat.   The opposition to prohibition now made such swift headway that in 1932, as we have
seen, the Democrats pledged themselves to repeal and the
Republicans to the submission of the question to the states
for review.   The prospect for repeal was also enlivened by
the possibility of raising huge revenues from the consumers
of beer, wine, and liquor, thus tendering relief to the payers
of income taxes.   Once it had been said that the saloon produced crime, insanity, and poverty; now it was said with
equal confidence that prohibition caused these things and
added wholesale racketeering.   Whatever might be the
logic of the situation, the outlook for continued prohibition
was bad as the year 1933 opened.

On those twin sisters of the spirit, religion and science,
economic vicissitudes had no visible effect, save perhaps to
draw them together in the presence of a menace which threatened their independence and prestige.   Never before had
efforts at reconciliation been more apparent to the naked eye.
The old order in which religion was sustained largely by
revenues from agriculture had almost disappeared except in
backward places.   Both religion and science now drew their
sustenance mainly from the same sources and were likely to
be disturbed by the same dislocation in the economic structure.   As time passed the physicists wrestled harder than
ever with the problem which had engaged theologians for
two thousand years: the nature and design of the universe;
and leaders among them announced the discovery of God in
the mysteries of the physical world, Sir James Jeans ascribing
to Him the characteristics of a Master Mathematician.   On

their part the theologians were grateful for these confirmations of their convictions and turned with renewed zeal to the Athanasian Creed and infant baptism. A few of the old-guard theologians and mechanists clung to their fundamentalism, but they seemed to be fighting a losing battle. One difference, however, emerged. Scientists made no concerted attack on the social problem of distress, while religious organizations, both Catholic and Protestant, issued warnings to complacent plutocracy, took note of economic planning, declared the prevailing disorder inimical to the Christian spirit, and hinted at possible transformations in capitalism.

Among those who made a business of thinking about society, the *paralysis agitans* of capitalism created an alarm. Quarrels broke out in the ranks of the economists. A few malcontents charged the whole army with intellectual bankruptcy in the presence of surpluses and starvation. Commissioned officers engrained with orthodoxy insisted that, in due course, after some tinkering with tariffs and debts, economic harmony would be restored, and defended their general helplessness on the ground that "social science" was still in a backward state. While academicians washed their linen or wrote treatises showing how difficult, if not impossible, it was to do anything about economic cycles, assuming their existence, outsiders, such as Stuart Chase, George Soule, and Adelbert Ames, as we have seen, proposed to attack this recurring disease by national planning and by control over the productive and distributive processes. Although these projects made a little excitement in the circles of politicians and editors, the academicians had no trouble in proving, to their complete satisfaction, that schemes for planning were wholly "impracticable." "We shall come out of it [the depression]," declared one of the most brilliant, "only through hard work and adjustments that are painful." If there was no Newton to give the mathematical formula or differential equation of economic optimism, there was certitude enough without him.

Yet when the learned editors of the *Encyclopædia of the Social Sciences* brought out in September, 1931, their volume containing the article on "Economics," lay readers were surprised to discover that there was no agreement on fundamentals. Instead of a summary of "principles" and "axioms" believed by the good and true, there was a kind of symposium. The chief editor opened with a historical introduction in which he declared that economics "has long been and will perhaps ever continue to be the battle ground of rationalizations for group and class interests." Then followed ten articles by specialists on ten different schools of economics; so that the plain citizen of the Republic, who knew little about any of them, was left to pass upon the merits of all and choose his own healing herbs.

Nor were the historians and political scientists in any better case. The former were supposed to know something about the "laws of historical development" and possess some insight into crises and revolutions, but if any among them felt an urge to illuminate the heavens by kindling some oil from Clio's lamp, he suppressed it before publication day. The political scientists had been dealing with the State, its structure, functions, and historic rôle, and now the State was rushing into new areas, was called upon to undertake heroic labors for the salvation of civilization. Yet from academic cloisters came principally works on direct primaries, county government, and township consolidation, rather than essays on statecraft in the grand manner of Machiavelli, Hobbes, Hamilton, Madison, Treitschke, and Marx. Whether this was merely the better part of wisdom could not be determined by any point of reference then available to observers.

To education in general, as well as to the social studies in particular, the noise produced by the grinding of the Ship of State on the rocks of depression gave tremors and qualms. While prosperity lasted, the huge system from the primary school to the university could turn endlessly, pouring out lawyers, doctors, engineers, bond salesmen, craftsmen, stenographers, and mistresses of domestic science and bonnet-making without making any fundamental queries respecting the course of things. But when starvation threatened its graduates and defaults menaced its endowments, disconcerting questions arose about the purpose of education and its relation to a society periodically sick from a mysterious economic malady. Just as the first blast of the storm began to blow, Abraham Flexner published a volume on universities which showed how near charlatanry some of them had fallen and presented a plea for a purification. Meanwhile the American Historical Association, over which Theodore Roosevelt and William Roscoe Thayer had once presided, put a commission to work on the social studies in the schools, seeking to find whether education was progressive chaos or, if not, by what sailing chart it was shaping its course. A little later, the National Education Association set up a committee to prepare the bold outlines of a plan for America to serve as the basis of the curriculum for civic education throughout the public school system. The day of entertaining children in the classroom was evidently passing and the quest for order and certainty in education had started, with inevitable conflicts in sight.

Even more than the world of education, the trade of letters was disturbed by the collapse of best-sellers and security. Less fettered by tradition, more responsive to the winds of opinion, artists of the written word were quick to feel the shock of panic. Like faithful newspaper reporters, they had already seen dark shadows even in the midday of prosperity and had made etchings for those not too heedless to look. At last these observers of reality had an audience —of middle-class persons sinking down into the proletarian under-kingdom of poverty and uncertainty and of upper-class persons sitting uneasily at their banquets. In such circumstances, young writers surged up on the left—John Dos Passos, Michael Gold, Charles Yale Harrison, Olive Dargan, Matthew Josephson, Edmund Wilson, Malcolm Conley, Grace Lumpkin, and Catherine Brody,—who often combined with biting portraiture of American miseries the quenchless optimism of Moscow. In his *Farewell to Reform,* John Chamberlain laid Theodore Roosevelt, Robert M. La Follette, and Woodrow Wilson away in their tombs with Charles I, Louis XVI, and Nicholas II.

§

So, Thought, weary Titan, continued to climb as for two thousand years the rugged crags between Ideology and Utopia.

INDEX